Betty Freidan (1921–2006)
The Feminine Mystique

Erving Goffman (1922–1982)
Presentation of Self in Everyday Life

Erving Goffman (1922–1982)
Gender Advertisements

Immanuel Wallerstein (1930–)
The Modern World System

Erving Goffman (1922–1982)
Forms of Talk

Margrit Eichler (1942–)
Non-Sexist Research Methods

Simone de Beauvoir (1908–1986)
The Second Sex

Wallace Clement
Canadian Corporate Elite and *Continental Corporate Power*

Jean Baudrillard (1929–2007)
Simulations

Dorothy Smith (1926–)

Robert Park (1864–1944)
Introduction to the Science of Sociology

C. Wright Mills (1916–1962)
The Power Elite

Roland Barthes (1915–1980)
The Pleasure of the Text

2000

John Porter (1921–1979)
The Vertical Mosaic

Hubert Guindon (1929–2002)
Social Class and Québec's Bureaucratic Revolution

Americans send Canadian Maher Arar to Syria for torture

Conscription begins Jan. 1, 1918

Newfoundland becomes a province

Auto Pact signed

The *Youth Criminal Justice Act* is passed

Asbestos Strike in Quebec

Canada adopts the maple leaf flag

Civil Marriage Act is passed, legalizing same-sex marriage

Women over 21 gain the right to vote federally

Canada Pension Plan (CPP) established

Capital punishment abolished

SARS epidemic hits China & Toronto; 44 people in Canada die

First female MP Agnes Macphail

CBC TV broadcasting begins

Montreal gets Olympics

NAFTA implemented between Canada, US, & Mexico

Colonel Russell Williams pleads guilty to 88 charges

"The Richard Riot" in Montreal

Montreal Expos' first MLB game

First Parti Québecois government elected

McGill founds the first Department of Sociology in English-Speaking Canada

St. Lawrence Seaway opens

Official Languages Act passed, making Canada officially bilingual

Terry Fox Marathon of Hope

September 11 terrorist attacks in New York City and Washington, DC

Facebook launches

Banting & Macleod become first Canadian Nobel Prize winners for discovery of insulin

CBC established

Jewish refugees on the ocean liner St. Louis were refused admittance to Canada

Diefenbaker extends the vote to "Registered Indians"

First referendum on Quebec sovereignty defeated

Massacre at l'École Polytechnique, Université de Montréal

Gulf Oil Spill releases millions of barrels of oil into the Gulf

Royal Commission on the Status of Women

Internment of Japanese Canadians as "enemy aliens"

Saskatchewan enacts medicare

Université du Québec founded

Canada Health Act passed

Oka Crisis

Nunavut becomes a territory

Robert Latimer released from jail

Dionne quintuplets born

Multiculturalism adopted as official policy

Bank of Canada established

Leduc oil fields in Alberta discovered

Team Canada beats Soviet Union

2010

1930

On-to-Ottawa trek of the Great Depression

1945

1960

1970

1980

1990

2000

2005 **2008** **2011**

Royal Air Force formed

Maurice "Rocket" Richard scores 50 goals in 50 games

First flight of delta-winged Avro Arrow

Trudeau becomes prime minister

Space shuttle Columbia launches with Canadarm

Second referendum in Quebec rejects sovereignty by less than 1%

First national postal strike

Montreal Expo

Abortion legislation (Section 251) passed

First female premier, Catherine Callbeck, PEI

Tsunami strikes Japan and kills thousands

Winnipeg General Strike

First NHL game outside Canada (Toronto vs Boston)

Stratford Festival opens

Charles de Gaulle's memorable "Vive le Québec Libre" speech

Toronto Blue Jays' first MLB game

First Constitution for Canada (including the Charter of Rights and Freedoms)

First female prime minister, Kim Campbell

Conservative's secure a majority government

Canadian National Railway incorporated

Women can vote in Quebec

John Diefenbaker appoints first female cabinet minister, Ellen Fairclough

Terrorists kidnap British Trade Commissioner James Cross, sparking the October Crisis

Quebec passes language legislation Bill 101

Canadian military joins operation enduring freedom in Afghanistan

third canadian edition

exploring sociology

bruce ravelli michelle webber   a canadian perspective

university of victoria   brock university

Toronto

Acquisitions Editor: Matthew Christian
Program Manager: Madhu Ranadive
Marketing Manager: Christine Cozens
Developmental Editor: Johanna Schlaepfer
Project Manager: Marissa Lok
Full Service Vendor Project Manager: Raghavi Khullar, Cenveo® Publisher Services
Copy Editor: Lila Campbell
Proofreader: Marg Bukta
Compositor: Cenveo Publisher Services
Permissions Project Manager: Kathryn O'Handley
Photo Researcher: Divya Narayanan, Lumina Datamatics Ltd
Permissions Researcher: Haydee Hidalgo, MPS North America LLC
Cover and Interior Designer: Anthony Leung
Cover Image: Galyna Andrushko/Veer.com (balloons in night); Fotolia.com (balloon in upper right corner)

---

10 9 8 7 6 5 4 3 2 1 [CKV]

Library and Archives Canada Cataloguing in Publication

Ravelli, Bruce, 1963–, author
    Exploring sociology: a Canadian perspective/Bruce Ravelli, Mount Royal University, Michelle Webber, Brock University.—Third Canadian edition.

Includes bibliographical references and index.
ISBN 978-0-13-339934-9 (pbk.)

    1. Sociology—Canada—Textbooks. 2. Sociology—Textbooks. I. Webber, Michelle, author II. Title.

HM586.R39 2014b   301.0971   C2014-904801-7

ISBN 978-0-13-339934-9

For John and Lisa

—BR

Brief Contents

> > >

Contents

Preface

Dear Colleagues:

Welcome to the third edition of *Exploring Sociology: A Canadian Perspective*. Over the past few years we worked very closely with Pearson to make sure that our review process included anonymous reviews from not only faculty, but also students from across the county. We have also engaged as many users of the text as possible to find out what was working for them and their students and what needed some attention. While the individual suggestions by reviewers are far too detailed to list here, the key recommendations we took away were that, while some felt there was still too much theory, we needed a deeper conversation about symbolic interactionism and some of the opening vignettes needed to be updated. Here is how we have responded to these comments.

First, we know that our text has too much theory for some; in fact, we know that we provide more theory than any other book on the market, but we do this intentionally. We believe that theory is the foundation for sociology and that students need to explore both classical and contemporary theory to fully grasp the sociological endeavour. In fact, the third edition actually provides a deeper analysis of symbolic interactionism and the work of Goffman than the second edition. While we appreciate that this may be too much material to cover in your lectures, we are convinced that the theoretical depth that this text provides gives students another vehicle to use to better understand theory.

Second, reviewers also suggested that some of the opening vignettes needed to be revised or updated. We agreed and have replaced or significantly revised almost half of them. We hope the changes make the chapters appear more engaging than they were before. Beyond these revisions to the vignettes, we made further changes based on our experience of teaching with the second edition. Some of the more notable changes for this edition include

- finding the most recent statistics available for all topics in all chapters
- reviewing the most recent sociological literature available
- updating/rewriting theme boxes to make sure they are timely and relevant and include questions to engage the sociological imagination

Writing the third edition, we listened to faculty, to students, and to ourselves as educators to make substantial improvements. We hope that *Exploring Sociology: A Canadian Perspective*, Third Edition, continues to help you inspire your students' sociological imaginations.

Dear Students:

Welcome! If you are new to your school or program, you are no doubt feeling overwhelmed. You have a number of classes to attend and dozens of assignments to complete, you probably work part-time, and you may also take care of a family. While we are older than the vast majority of you, we remember what it was like to be a student and to take a class in sociology. We did not have iPads, smartphones, or Facebook profiles, but we remember being broke, not wanting to study on the weekend, being bored in one class but inspired in another, and enduring all-nighters cramming for midterms and finals. We know the pressure you are under, and we tried to write this text in a way that will not only motivate you to take more sociology classes but also give you a wide range of resources to help you grasp important concepts and succeed in your classes.

You will see in other textbooks and hear in other classes the value of *thinking critically*, of challenging ideas and the social foundations upon which they are built. However, you will discover that the ability to think *sociologically* will be critical to your success in any sociology course and in life. What does that mean? To think sociologically is to put yourself within a larger social context and appreciate how individuals are influenced by the larger world around them. As sociologists, we are less concerned about whether you remember the definitions for specific terms (although this is certainly important) than we are about your ability to see the world as a sociologist. We wrote and revised this text with the intent of providing you with the tools to help you think *sociologically*, by asking you questions and presenting situations that inspire you to think like a sociologist.

Sociology explores the dynamic connections between individuals, groups, and the larger social world in which we all live. We are all connected to each other in diverse and fascinating ways. Through lectures and by reading this textbook, you will learn how social factors such as income level, gender, and minority status influence who we are and the people we become. You will discover that while it is easy and comfortable to be around people who share similar interests, there is tremendous value in engaging with those who are different from you. For a sociologist, human diversity is inspiring, humbling, fascinating, and challenging. We are diverse because we are female or male, of Asian or Aboriginal descent, from wealthy or poor families, young or old, gay, lesbian, heterosexual, or pansexual. We are in gangs or church choirs, we are mothers, and we are addicts—all our stories combine to create a rich social fabric that at times holds us together and at other times tears us apart. Every day we navigate our way through this tapestry that can make us feel lonely or loved, admired or despised. Sociology explores all of these realities, and our goal in writing this text is to encourage you to begin your own exploration of this exciting and important field.

We hope your education in sociology will inspire you to move beyond our society's fixation with competition and financial success and replace it with a desire to improve the world around you. Sociologists believe that while the world is becoming more economically interdependent and technologically integrated, it may also be becoming less caring and compassionate.

Here is our challenge to you, and here is the burden that you must now bear.

The challenge: Use the benefits of your education in sociology to improve yourself, your family, and those less fortunate than you.

The burden: You can no longer hide behind the cloak of ignorance to shirk your social responsibilities. From today forward, we hope you become more aware of the political and social world around you and that you take action where and when you see injustices occur.

Remember:

- Being a good sociologist means standing up for those who cannot stand up for themselves.
- Being a good sociologist means appreciating and supporting human diversity in all its rich and wonderful forms.
- Being a good sociologist means being humble—realizing that every person you meet has something to teach you if you are willing to learn.
- Being a good sociologist means living your life with equal parts passion and compassion.

We believe that the more people who share the sociological imagination, the more likely we are to leave this world in better condition than when we found it.

Text Features

Through its distinctive approach to the field, its readability, and its relevance to students' lives, *Exploring Sociology: A Canadian Perspective*, Third Edition, helps professors develop the sociological imagination in their students by encouraging them to see sociology through multiple lenses. Topics are presented in ways that allow students to engage with the material and to exercise their sociological imaginations.

The authors bring over 35 years of experience teaching introductory sociology to a variety of students, in large and small classes, at a variety of schools. This text, therefore, is the culmination of many years of teaching, and an expression of our passion for sociology and our commitment to our students. We created the following pedagogical features to inspire students to be as fascinated by sociology as we are.

THEME BOXES

Each chapter features a selection from four different theme boxes, all of which engage students with topical discussions to foster and to challenge their sociological imaginations.

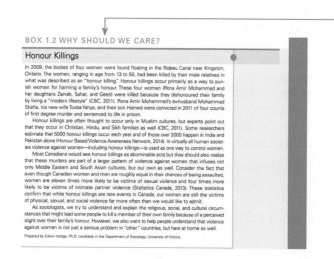

BOX 1.2 WHY SHOULD WE CARE?

Honour Killings

In 2009, the bodies of four women were found floating in the Rideau Canal near Kingston, Ontario. The women, ranging in age from 13 to 50, had been killed by their male relatives in what was described as an "honour killing." Honour killings occur primarily as a way to punish women for harming a family's honour. These four women (Rona Amir Mohammad and her daughters Zainab, Sahar, and Geeti) were killed because they dishonoured their family by living a "modern lifestyle" (CBC, 2011). Rona Amir Mohammad's ex-husband Mohammad Shafia, his new wife Tooba Yahya, and their son Hamed were convicted in 2011 of four counts of first degree murder and sentenced to life in prison.

Honour killings are often thought to occur only in Muslim cultures, but experts point out that they occur in Christian, Hindu, and Sikh families as well (CBC, 2011). Some researchers estimate that 5000 honour killings occur each year and of those over 2000 happen in India and Pakistan alone (Honour Based Violence Awareness Network, 2014). In virtually all human societies violence against women—including honour killings—is used as one way to control women.

Most Canadians would see honour killings as abominable acts but they should also realize that these murders are part of a larger pattern of violence against women that infuses not only Middle Eastern and South Asian cultures, but our own as well. Consider the fact that even though Canadian women and men are roughly equal in their chances of being assaulted, women are eleven times more likely to be victims of sexual violence and four times more likely to be victims of intimate partner violence (Statistics Canada, 2013). These statistics confirm that while honour killings are rare events in Canada, our women are still the victims of physical, sexual, and social violence far more often than we would like to admit.

As sociologists, we try to understand and explain the religious, social, and cultural circumstances that might lead some people to kill a member of their own family because of a perceived slight over their family's honour. However, we also want to help people understand that violence against women is not just a serious problem in "other" countries, but here at home as well.

Prepared by Edwin Hodge, Ph.D. candidate in the Department of Sociology, University of Victoria.

WHY SHOULD WE CARE?

These boxes explore many of today's pressing social issues, such as evolution and social Darwinism, Canada's commitment to First Nations peoples, African-centric schools, the 2010 Gulf oil spill, and more.

ISSUES IN GLOBAL CONTEXT

These boxes showcase and investigate issues around the world; for example, the Rwandan genocide, defining female beauty, child labour laws, sex trafficking, female circumcision, and religion and politics in the Middle East.

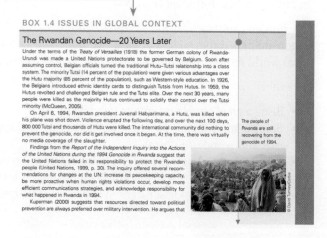

BOX 1.4 ISSUES IN GLOBAL CONTEXT

The Rwandan Genocide—20 Years Later

Under the terms of the *Treaty of Versailles* (1918) the former German colony of Rwanda-Urundi was made a United Nations protectorate to be governed by Belgium. Soon after assuming control, Belgian officials turned the traditional Hutu–Tutsi relationship into a class system. The minority Tutsi (14 percent of the population) were given various advantages over the Hutu majority (85 percent of the population), such as Western-style education. In 1926, the Belgians introduced ethnic identity cards to distinguish Tutsis from Hutus. In 1959, the Hutus revolted and challenged Belgian rule and the Tutsi elite. Over the next 30 years, many people were killed as the majority Hutu continued to solidify their control over the Tutsi minority (McQueen, 2005).

On April 6, 1994, Rwandan president Juvenal Habyarimana, a Hutu, was killed when his plane was shot down. Violence erupted the following day, and over the next 100 days, 800 000 Tutsi and thousands of Hutu were killed. The international community did nothing to prevent the genocide, nor did it get involved once it began. At the time, there was virtually no media coverage of the slaughter.

Findings from the *Report of the Independent Inquiry into the Actions of the United Nations during the 1994 Genocide in Rwanda* suggest that the United Nations failed in its responsibility to protect the Rwandan people (United Nations, 1999, p. 30). The inquiry offered several recommendations for changes at the UN: increase its peacekeeping capacity, be more proactive when human rights violations occur, develop more efficient communications strategies, and acknowledge responsibility for what happened in Rwanda in 1994.

Kuperman (2000) suggests that resources directed toward political prevention are always preferred over military intervention. He argues that

The people of Rwanda are still recovering from the genocide of 1994.

THAT WAS THEN, THIS IS NOW

These boxes capture how society changes over time—whether the Industrial Revolution can teach us about society today, the commercialization of academic research, Canada's residential school system, credential inflation, the coexistence of science and religion, and life after the Kyoto Protocol.

BOX 2.3 THAT WAS THEN, THIS IS NOW

Can the Industrial Revolution Teach Us Anything about the Cybernetic Revolution?

We often focus on the Industrial Revolution's technical developments: the mechanization it introduced and the invention of the steam engine and the printing press. Yet the Industrial Revolution was also "an intensely human experience" (Stearns, 1998, p. 57). We should not be surprised, then, that sociologists were and are interested in exploring its influence on society. In fact, during the period, "[n]o society managed to industrialize without massive social dislocation" (Stearns, 1998, p. 57).

The Industrial Revolution began in Western Europe and went on to change virtually every area of life. Massive transformations took place in people's jobs, their family life, and their government. People who had once lived in small, self-reliant farming communities were forced to work in factories, becoming dependent on wages and rarely consuming what they produced (Stearns, 1998, p. 5). As the population moved into cities, new social classes emerged: the ruling elite, who owned the factories, and the workers employed by them (Stearns, 1998, p. 7). Fathers and young children were obliged to leave the home and work in factories or mines to make enough money for their families to survive. However, even with these hardships, the family emerged as an invaluable source of spiritual life and support, a refuge from the stresses of paid labour (Stearns, 1998, p. 61). Government played a more central role in expanding railroads and creating new labour laws in the hope of diminishing child labour. It also provided funding for schools so that young people could be taught how to use the factory owners' equipment.

It is no wonder that some contemporary sociologists look to these insights to help them interpret today's changes. Given that we are experiencing a "cybernetic revolution" (Hansen, 2004, p. 16), the discipline of sociology "has a unique opportunity to provide critical analyses to make this next transition as informed as it can be" (Hansen, 2004, p. 18). Hopefully, some of the lessons learned from the Industrial Revolution will help us understand the immense social changes being inspired by information and communication technology (see Cheng, 2009).

Is it possible that the Internet and computer technology is (1) changing our economies from factories and the processing of raw materials to ones driven by information technology (e.g., the emergence of Google as a multi-billion dollar company), (2) altering the nature of our families and other personal relationships (e.g., increase in online dating services and online pornography), and (3) influencing political decision-making (e.g., impact of former NSA employee Edward Snowden)? What comparisons might we draw between the Industrial and cybernetic revolutions? Can any of the classical theories be applied to the changes brought about by communication technology?

This article is also a peerScholar assignment in MySocLab.

BOX 1.3 CANADIAN CONTRIBUTIONS TO SOCIOLOGY

Homelessness and Crime

John Hagan and Bill McCarthy's 1998 book *Mean Streets: Youth Crimes and Homelessness* was revolutionary; it has been considered the single most important study of crime in Canadian society in a generation (Brannigan, 2000, p. 385). The authors integrate positivist and anti-positivist methodologies to explore the rich and diverse realities of life on the street.

Among the forces that send young people to the streets, Hagan and McCarthy argue, are problems in parenting and conflicts at school (Hagan & McCarthy, 1998, p. 78). The authors' research began in 1987 when they interviewed 390 Toronto street youth living in shelters, drop-in centres, city parks, and on street corners. By 1992, they had completed 482 additional interviews with homeless youth living in Toronto and Vancouver.

Hagan and McCarthy suggest that the relationship between youth crime and homelessness is much more complex than initially believed. Youth who live on the streets are often overlooked as studies generally focus on youth who still live at home. They suggest that criminologists should look more closely at this group because the majority of street youth are also involved in criminal activity. They contend that contemporary society ignores the fact that lack of shelter, lack of proper nutrition, and joblessness make it virtually impossible for street youth to avoid living a life of crime (Hagan & McCarthy, 1998, pp. 18–21).

Hagan and McCarthy also found that homeless youth developed unique family structures that the authors refer to as *street families*. These interpersonal relationships help street youth to secure the necessities of life, such as food, clothing, and shelter. While the general population may tend to think of street families as gangs, the youth describe them in familial terms since they tend to form and exist based on survival. Some family members take on special roles, such as protection and safety or finding food, shelter, and money.

Hagan and McCarthy highlight that most Canadian youth do not become homeless and that the majority of youth crime is not committed by homeless youth. They do recognize, however, that a unique relationship exists between homelessness and criminal activity, and they argue that more research needs to be undertaken in this area. As a young sociologist, how might you explain a youth's desire to belong to a *street family*? Can street families be analyzed using Berger's *general in the particular* and *strange in the familiar*?

Sources: Brannigan, 2000; Hagan & McCarthy, 1992, 1998.

CANADIAN CONTRIBUTIONS TO SOCIOLOGY

Highlighting sociologists working in Canada and their contributions to sociology, these boxes showcase John Hagan and Bill McCarthy, Dorothy Smith, Michael Atkinson, William Carroll, Gary Kinsman, Himani Bannerji, Meg Luxton, Sandra Acker, Marshall McLuhan, Suzanne Staggenborg, and Ana Isla.

DEFINING FEATURES OF THE TEXT

We believe that theory is the foundation for sociology. *Exploring Sociology: A Canadian Perspective*, Third Edition, is the only Canadian textbook to devote an entire chapter each to classical and contemporary theories, respectively. Providing students and professors with a more complete discussion of theory will allow more opportunity for discussion, reflection, and debate about the strengths and weaknesses of various sociological insights. All chapters apply relevant sociological theories to the topics throughout each chapter. And *Exploring Sociology* remains the *only* textbook to incorporate post-structural theory throughout.

We also devote chapters to gender and sexualities, respectively, and integrate a complete discussion of racialization and post-colonialism into our analysis of minority populations. This approach is inspired by each of our complementary sociological backgrounds and training. By building upon our differences, we are able to present an even-handed yet challenging review of the sociological landscape.

Teaching Tools

CHAPTER AT A GLANCE

Each chapter begins with a brief overview of the key topics to be covered, allowing students to focus their reading and to integrate material from one chapter to the next.

To a sociologist, everything people do is fascinating. Have you ever waited in line for a movie and watched the people around you? One night, you notice two people, who are obviously smitten with each other, holding hands. A few minutes later, you see some young men push through the line in front of the couple and snarl "Fags!" as they walk by. You think to yourself, "Why are some people so offended by seeing two people show that they care for each other?" *Hurtful.*

Have you ever driven by homeless people and wondered how they got there and why no one seems to want to help them? *Depressing.*

Have you ever walked by an elementary school in the winter and seen a young boy chasing a girl with a handful of snow, yelling that she needs a "face wash"? You cannot help but chuckle as you notice the young girl screaming with a huge smile on her face. You remember that boys and girls at that age show who they like by acting as though they don't. *Interesting.*

Have you ever wondered whether new communications technology has changed the nature of our relationships? Today, virtually everyone has a cellphone, many have a Facebook profile, and perhaps a few even have a cottage in High Fidelity. What influence, if any, do these forms of communication have on today's relationships? *Intriguing.*

All of these scenarios, and your feelings and emotions about them, are of interest to sociology. These situations illustrate that our entire existence is defined by the reality that we are social beings who live and grow through our interactions with others. Therefore, we cannot hope to understand ourselves, or the world around us, without investigating the interplay between the individual and the social—this is what sociology is all about. Once you can master how sociologists can instantaneously switch their thinking from individual to social, from privileged to nonprivileged, and from Western to global, you are well on your way to appreciating the beauty and uniqueness of the sociological endeavour.

LEARNING OBJECTIVES

By the end of this chapter, students will be able to

❶ Explain what the sociological perspective is.

❷ Describe, and provide personal reflections about, C. W. Mills's concept of the sociological imagination.

❸ Explain Peter Berger's use of the terms *general, particular, strange,* and *familiar.*

❹ Understand the historical development of sociology.

❺ Define and explain the differences between positivism and anti-positivism.

❻ Explain microsociology and macrosociology, and identify the leading theorists of each.

❼ Describe the defining features of Canadian sociology.

❽ Review the importance of a global perspective.

LEARNING OBJECTIVES

By outlining the learning objectives for each chapter, students have a roadmap to use throughout to ensure that they stay on track and maximize their reading.

KEY TERMS

Boldfaced within the text, key terms are accompanied by brief definitions in the margins to provide a visual and efficient means of building and reinforcing sociological vocabulary. The end-of-chapter material includes key terms lists, organized alphabetically, which serve as a quick reference tool.

Key Terms

colonialism 79
desire 77
discipline 75
discourse 75
disembedding mechanism 87
expert systems 89
hegemony 68

identity 78
imperialism 79
normalization 76
Orientalism 80
patriarchy 71
ruling 71
symbolic token 87
time–space distanciation 87

REVIEWING THE CONCEPTS

Questions at the end of each chapter help students assess their understanding of the material and serve as good preparation for tests.

Reviewing the Concepts

1. How does Michel Foucault connect power with knowledge?

2. What is Dorothy Smith's critique of traditional approaches to sociology?

3. How does Anthony Giddens link time and space to globalization?

APPLYING YOUR SOCIOLOGICAL IMAGINATION

Found at the end of every chapter, these questions challenge students to flex their sociological imagination muscles through debate, discussion, and reflection.

Applying Your Sociological Imagination

1. What are some contemporary examples of hegemony (in addition to heterosexual hegemony and hegemonic masculinity)?

2. How might you use critical race theory to examine the aftermath of the tsunami that occurred in the Indian Ocean on December 26, 2004, or the earthquake in Haiti in January 2010?

3. What are some examples of a globalizing world (think culturally, economically, and politically)?

For the Instructor

INSTRUCTOR RESOURCES

The following instructor supplements are available for downloading from a password-protected section of Pearson Canada's online catalogue (www.pearsoned.ca/highered). Navigate to your book's catalogue page to view a list of supplements that are available. See your local sales representative for details and access.

Instructor's Resource Manual This useful teaching aid provides two complementary resources for each chapter: One offers an overview of the key terms and material within the chapter and the other features chapter and issue overviews, student assignments, and more.

PowerPoint® Presentations PowerPoint slides consist of graphics and text to provide pre-made lecture slides.

Image Library The image library showcases the figures and tables that appear in the text, allowing professors to incorporate the images easily into their lectures.

Test Item File The Test Item File provides more than 2000 multiple choice, true-false, short answer, and essay questions. This question bank is available in both Word® and MyTest formats.

MyTest With MyTest, a powerful assessment generation program, professors can easily create and print quizzes, tests, and exams online, allowing flexibility and the ability to manage assessments at any time and from anywhere.

ClassPrep ClassPrep is a dynamic database of all the instructor resources that accompany Pearson's leading Canadian introductory sociology textbooks. This powerful tool allows professors to search that database by topic, then view and select material from PowerPoint, image libraries, lecture outlines, classroom activities, and more. Professors can access MyClassPrep through the MySocLab that accompanies *Exploring Sociology: A Canadian Perspective*, Third Edition.

Multimedia Guide This teaching guide that can accompany any Pearson introductory sociology text helps professors bring sociological concepts to life in the classroom with material to which students relate. Featuring 20 scenes from Hollywood feature films, documentaries, and TV episodes, and over 30 songs, this guide provides

- a synopsis of the film, documentary, or TV episode and the relevant scene, the scene location on the DVD, and an explanation of how the selection relates to sociology

- the cultural context of the album and song as well as an explanation of how the song relates to sociological issues

- 5–10 discussion questions and one assignment follow each scene and song

NOTE: Pearson Canada does not provide the films, documentaries, television episodes, or songs.

Learning Solutions Managers Pearson's Learning Solutions Managers work with faculty and campus course designers to ensure that Pearson technology products, assessment tools, and online course materials are tailored to meet your specific needs. This highly qualified team is dedicated to helping schools take full advantage of a wide range of educational resources by assisting in the integration of a variety of instructional materials and media formats. Your local Pearson Canada sales representative can provide you with more details on this service program.

CourseSmart for Instructors CourseSmart goes beyond traditional expectations—providing instant, online access to the textbooks and course materials you need at a lower cost for students. And even as students save money, you can save time and hassle with a digital eTextbook that allows you to search for the most relevant content at the very moment you need it. Whether it's evaluating textbooks or creating lecture notes to help students with difficult concepts, CourseSmart can make life a little easier. See how when you visit www.coursesmart.com/instructors.

Pearson eText Pearson eText gives students access to the text whenever and wherever they have access to the Internet. eText pages look exactly like the printed text, offering powerful new functionality for students and instructors. Users can create notes, highlight text in different colours, create bookmarks, zoom, click hyperlinked words and phrases to view definitions, and view in single-page or two-page view. Pearson eText allows for quick navigation to key parts of the eText using a table of contents and provides full-text search. The eText may also offer links to associated media files, enabling users to access videos, animations, or other activities as they read the text.

Pearson Custom Library For enrolments of at least 25 students, you can create your own textbook by choosing the chapters that best suit your course needs. To begin building your custom text, visit www.pearsoncustomlibrary.com. You may also work with a dedicated Pearson Custom Editor to create your ideal text—publishing your own original content or mixing and matching Pearson content. Contact your local Pearson sales representative to get started.

STUDENT RESOURCES

MySocLab

The moment you know.

Educators know it. Students know it. It's that inspired moment when something that was difficult to understand suddenly makes perfect sense. Our MyLab products have been designed and refined with a single purpose in mind—to help educators create that moment of understanding with their students.

MySocLab delivers **proven results** in helping individual students succeed. It provides **engaging experiences** that personalize, stimulate, and measure learning for each student. And, it comes from a **trusted partner** with educational expertise and an eye on the future.

MySocLab can be used by itself or linked to any learning management system. To learn more about how MySocLab combines proven learning applications with powerful assessment, visit **www.mysoclab.com**.

CourseSmart for Students CourseSmart goes beyond traditional expectations—providing instant, online access to the textbooks and course materials you need at an average savings of 50 percent. With instant access from any computer and the ability to search your text, you'll find the content you need quickly, no matter where you are. And with online tools like highlighting and note-taking, you can save time and study efficiently. See all of the benefits at www.coursesmart.com/students.

peerScholar Firmly grounded in published research, peerScholar is a powerful online pedagogical tool that helps develop your students' critical and creative thinking skills. peerScholar facilitates this through the process of creation, evaluation, and reflection. Working in stages, students begin by submitting a written assignment. peerScholar then circulates their work for others to review, a process that can be anonymous or not depending on your preference. Students receive peer feedback and evaluations immediately, reinforcing their learning and driving the development of higher-order thinking skills. Students can then resubmit revised work, again depending on your preference. Contact your Pearson sales representative to learn more about peerScholar and the research behind it.

Acknowledgments

Because of the monumental effort by the editors and staff of Pearson Canada, *Exploring Sociology: A Canadian Perspective*, Third Edition, reflects the highest standards of textbook publishing in all its phases. Pearson provided us with the peer reviews, editorial comments, and suggestions for reorganizing and updating material that supported our desire to communicate our ideas to students and that nurtured our own creativity as authors. We would like to thank Johanna Schlaepfer for her enthusiasm and wonderful organizational skills, Matthew Christian for continuing to listen to our ideas and helping make them a reality, and Marissa Lok who pulled it all together. We were also fortunate to work with Madhu Ranadive, our Program Manager, and Lila Campbell, whose editorial guidance and support was second to none. We also appreciate the efforts of Edwin Hodge, our research assistant, for his ability to work within tight deadlines but also for his passion for teaching. Finally, we would like to thank our friends and families for their encouragement and support.

We would also like to recognize the following colleagues, who took the time and effort to provide thoughtful and meaningful reviews during the development of this third edition:

Francis Adu-Febiri, Camosun College
Seema Ahluwalia, Kwantlen Polytechnic University
Fiona Angus, Grant MacEwan University
Liora Barak, Fanshawe College
Adeesha Hack, George Brown College
Linda Henderson, St. Mary's University
Jana Lait, Mount Royal University
Yvonne LeBlanc, McMaster University
Josephine MacIntosh, University of Victoria
Barry McClinchey, University of Waterloo
Amir Mirfakhraie, Kwantlen Polytechnic University
Annette Reynolds, Kwantlen Polytechnic University
Sharon Roberts, University of Waterloo

We would also like to thank students from Mohawk College, Mount Royal University, and University of the Fraser Valley who participated in a survey for the first edition textbook in winter 2010. We are most grateful to the University of Waterloo students who reviewed chapters from our second edition manuscript:

Faryal Amjad
Justin Doyle
Devanshi Mehta
Donna Richard
Alexis Small

About the Authors

Bruce Ravelli is an award winning teacher who received his Ph.D. from the University of Victoria in 1997. He has taught introductory sociology for over 25 years, and receives strong teaching evaluations from his students because of his passion for sociology, his dedication to teaching, and his commitment to high academic standards. Bruce has published various textbooks, readers, articles, and book chapters on Canadian culture and cross-national value differences as well as students' evaluation of teaching. Bruce is the co-developer of award-winning free online software that allows teachers to anonymously assess their teaching/courses at any point during the term (**www.toofast.ca**). He offers workshops and presentations on the software and on anonymous student assessment across North America. Bruce teaches in the Department of Sociology at the University of Victoria. If any students or colleagues have questions or comments about the text, please feel free to contact him by email at bravelli@uvic.ca.

Michelle Webber received her Ph.D. from the University of Toronto. Her research interests lie in the sociology of education and sociology of gender. She has regularly taught introductory sociology over the last 10 years. Michelle has published articles and book chapters on feminist pedagogies, the regulation of academic work, the work of teaching assistants, the experiences of contingent faculty members, and feminist knowledges. She has co-edited *Rethinking Society in the 21st Century: Critical Readings in Sociology* (First, Second, and Third Editions) with Kate Bezanson. Her current research projects are both funded by SSHRC: 1. an investigation of accountability governance and its effects on the production of academic knowledge and subjectivities (with Sandra Acker, Co-Investigator, University of Toronto) and 2. faculty associations and the politics of accountability governance (Larry Savage, Principal Investigator, and Jonah Butovsky, Co-Investigator—both at Brock University). Michelle is an Associate Professor in the Department of Sociology at Brock University in Ontario. She can be contacted via email at mwebber@brocku.ca.

third canadian edition

exploring sociology

a canadian perspective

1 Understanding the Sociological Imagination

To a sociologist, everything people do is fascinating. Have you ever waited in line for a movie and watched the people around you? One night, you notice two people, who are obviously smitten with each other, holding hands. A few minutes later, you see some young men push through the line in front of the couple and snarl "Fags!" as they walk by. You think to yourself, "Why are some people so offended by seeing two people show that they care for each other?" *Hurtful*.

Have you ever driven by homeless people and wondered how they got there and why no one seems to want to help them? *Depressing*.

Have you ever walked by an elementary school in the winter and seen a young boy chasing a girl with a handful of snow, yelling that she needs a "face wash"? You cannot help but chuckle as you notice the young girl screaming with a huge smile on her face. You remember that boys and girls at that age show who they like by acting as though they don't. *Interesting*.

Have you ever wondered whether new communications technology has changed the nature of our relationships? Today, virtually everyone has a cellphone, many have a Facebook profile, and perhaps a few even have a cottage in High Fidelity. What influence, if any, do these forms of communication have on today's relationships? *Intriguing*.

All of these scenarios, and your feelings and emotions about them, are of interest to sociology. These situations illustrate that our entire existence is defined by the reality that we are social beings who live and grow through our interactions with others. Therefore, we cannot hope to understand ourselves, or the world around us, without investigating the interplay between the individual and the social—this is what sociology is all about. Once you can master how sociologists can instantaneously switch their thinking from individual to social, from privileged to nonprivileged, and from Western to global, you are well on your way to appreciating the beauty and uniqueness of the sociological endeavour.

LEARNING OBJECTIVES

By the end of this chapter, students will be able to

1 Explain what the sociological perspective is.

2 Describe, and provide personal reflections about, C. W. Mills's concept of the sociological imagination.

3 Explain Peter Berger's use of the terms *general*, *particular*, *strange*, and *familiar*.

4 Understand the historical development of sociology.

5 Define and explain the differences between positivism and anti-positivism.

6 Explain microsociology and macrosociology, and identify the leading theorists of each.

7 Describe the defining features of Canadian sociology.

8 Review the importance of a global perspective.

Look for the ✳ Explore, 👁 Watch, ✔• Practise, and ⟨⟨•• Listen icons throughout this text . . . these symbols lead you to online material on MySocLab (www.mysoclab.com) to enhance and to complement your textbook experience.

Look for the Learning Objective numbers next to some headings throughout the text. These numbers let you know where the objective is covered in the chapter.

Social Psychology vs. Sociology

Sociological Tour through Cyberspace

1 The Sociological Perspective

As an academic discipline, sociology is dedicated to exposing you to a new and unique way of seeing our social world. **Sociology** is the systematic study of human groups and their interactions. To understand the beauty of sociology is to appreciate its distinctive view of the social world, often referred to as the *sociological perspective*. In essence, the **sociological perspective** is the unique way in which sociologists see our world and can dissect the dynamic relationships between individuals and the larger social network in which we all live. Many people fail to realize how important social forces are in shaping our lives (Babbie, 1994; Bellah, Madsen, Sullivan, Swidler, & Tipton, 1996). As individuals, we make many decisions every day—for example, what you choose to wear to school or what you decide to eat when you meet your friends at the student centre. Even these seemingly mundane choices have rich social significance and reveal a great deal about what sociologists find so fascinating about human behaviour.

2 CHARLES WRIGHT MILLS AND THE SOCIOLOGICAL IMAGINATION

C. W. Mills was one of the most influential American sociologists of all time. Mills suggested that people who do not, or cannot, recognize the social origins and character of their problems may be unable to respond to them effectively. In effect, failing to appreciate how individual challenges are influenced by larger social forces diminishes a person's ability

sociology The systematic study of human groups and their interactions.

sociological perspective A view of society based on the dynamic relationships between individuals and the larger social network in which we all live.

Charles Wright Mills
Fritz Goro/Time & Life Pictures/Getty Images

to understand and resolve them. For Mills, the individual and the social are inextricably linked and we cannot fully understand one without the other.

To explore this connection, Mills highlighted the difference between what he called **personal troubles**, which result from individual challenges, and **social issues**, which are caused by larger social factors. For example, your sociology midterm can be considered a personal trouble because you have to write it. If you study, you should do well, but if you do not study, you might fail. If the exam is fair and other students did well on it, is anyone else responsible for your poor performance? Clearly, your grade would be considered a personal trouble. However, what if the entire class failed the exam? A low class average may occur because no one studied for the test, but this is unlikely. Instead, low scores would suggest that there is more going on—perhaps there was some confusion over what chapters and topics would be tested or perhaps the scores were tabulated incorrectly by the professor. In any event, a student who failed the exam might think that his or her score is a personal trouble, and to some extent it is, but once the class understands that everyone did poorly it may become a social issue—it involves a group of people, and collective action is required for the group's concerns to be acknowledged and potentially acted upon. So, once again, what appears to be a unique personal trouble (i.e., test score) can only be understood if the student takes into account the larger social environment as well (i.e., how other students did, pressure to achieve high grades, etc.).

According to Mills, many personal troubles never become social issues because people rarely equate what is happening to them with the larger social worlds in which they exist. For example, if you receive back a test that you have failed, chances are you will feel embarrassed and upset and will probably stuff it in your backpack—you assume that you are one of the only students who failed and do not want to draw attention to yourself. When people face situations of personal failure, such as on a midterm, very few ask for help. For Mills, not seeing such failure as partially, or entirely, the result of social forces is to lack what he called the **quality of mind**, which has nothing to do with a person's intelligence or level of education; instead, it is the ability to look beyond personal circumstance and into social context. For example, what would happen if none of the students in the class passed but no one said anything about it? No one would know that everyone else had failed; all of the students in that class would think that they had to deal with their failure on their own, and a possible social issue would never be addressed. Mills (1959/2000) reveals the importance of possessing the quality of mind when he writes that without thinking beyond one's own condition, "much private uneasiness goes unformulated; much public malaise and many decisions of enormous structural relevance never become public issues" (p. 12). Can this concept be applied to the feelings that many students have when they fail a test? Yes, it can.

When a student who has failed does not talk to classmates, family members, friends, or the professor about the test, there is little possibility for a social issue to emerge, even if everyone in the class failed. If no one talks about failing the test, then each student has a *trouble* and the class never realizes that there is an *issue*. Mills would say that these students lack the quality of mind because they did not try to understand their individual circumstance from within the larger social context: How did everyone else do? What could I have done better? How could I have studied more effectively? What have I learned from this experience? None of these questions defer from a student's responsibility to be prepared for all tests, but they recognize that the students are willing to think in social terms, even with regards to a specific situation.

To improve quality of mind, Mills (1959/2000) argued that sociologists need to expose individuals to what he called the **sociological imagination**, which is the ability to understand the dynamic relationship between individual lives and the larger society. It involves stepping outside of your own condition and looking at yourself from a new perspective—seeing yourself as the product of your family, income level, race, and gender. You employ the sociological imagination by asking yourself, *Who am I and why do I think the way I do?* This internal reflection requires us to think about ourselves differently and, by doing so, enables us to become more informed about the social forces that have come together to make us who we are. When people can see their own histories in a social context, they cannot help but improve their

personal troubles
Personal challenges that require individual solutions.

social issues
Challenges caused by larger social factors that require collective solutions.

 Watch

The Sociological Imagination and the Legacy of C. Wright Mills

quality of mind Mills's term for the ability to view personal circumstance within a social context.

sociological imagination C. W. Mills's term for the ability to perceive how dynamic social forces influence individual lives.

BOX 1.1 THE SOCIOLOGICAL IMAGINATION

Charles Wright Mills
by Kathryn Mills, daughter

C. Wright Mills was born in Waco, Texas, and graduated from a public high school in Dallas. He studied sociology and philosophy at the University of Texas, Austin, where he was awarded his B.A. and M.A. in 1939. Mills obtained his Ph.D. in sociology from the University of Wisconsin at Madison and began his teaching career at the University of Maryland, College Park, before moving to Columbia University, where he remained on the faculty until his death at the age of 45.

Mills's books are informed by his unique blend of progressive populism, classical social theory, intellectual and political muckraking, and advocacy of vigorous social responsibility combined with a strong respect for individual freedoms. He strove to create what he called sociological poetry in his empirically based works on American society, most notably *White Collar: The American Middle Classes* (1951) and *The Power Elite* (1956). President Eisenhower's famous speech in January 1961, which outlined the dangers of the military–industrial complex, echoed Mills's warnings in *The Power Elite*.

Many people who followed Mills into the social sciences were persuaded to do so by his description of the promise of the sociological imagination and intellectual craftsmanship in his book *The Sociological Imagination* (1959). His writings in periodicals and his widely read short books, which he referred to as pamphlets—*The Causes of World War Three* (1958) and *Listen Yankee: The Revolution in Cuba* (1960)—led many to refer to him as the father of the New Left in the United States.

Mills spent most of his adult life in New York, and periodically lived abroad as a visiting professor in Copenhagen, Mexico, and London, but he stayed connected to his Texan and rural roots. He discussed his grandfather's cattle ranch in Texas, his Irish immigrant heritage, and the impact of his international travels on his thinking in his autobiographical writings, published posthumously in *C. Wright Mills: Letters and Autobiographical Writings*, edited by Kathryn Mills with Pamela Mills (2000).

Mills's major works have been translated into more than a dozen languages and are now available in editions with new introductions or afterwords by Todd Gitlin, Russell Jacoby, Nelson Lichtenstein, and Alan Wolfe. Each year the Society for the Study of Social Problems chooses one book to recognize with the C. Wright Mills Award, so named to honor Mills's "search for a sophisticated understanding of the individual and society" (see: www.sssp1.org).

As Dan Wakefield wrote in his introduction to the collection of Mills's letters and autobiographical writings, C. Wright Mills "addressed the world through his books and ideas, which shook up and energized the gray flannel 1950's and gave grounding and voice to the radicals of the 1960's. His work continues to illuminate, inspire, and challenge those who hope to understand and even to ameliorate the circumstances in which we live."

quality of mind. Mills would suggest that people who judge others without understanding all of the issues involved may lack quality of mind and thus view the world in black-and-white terms. Mills referred to people who are unable or unwilling to see the social world as it truly exists as **cheerful robots**. However, when people understand themselves and others through the sociological imagination, they appreciate that very few things are black and white. The true beauty in the social world is visible only when one can see all shades of grey.

American sociologist Peter Berger builds on how sociologists see the world. In his 1963 book, *Invitation to Sociology: A Humanistic Perspective*, he defines the sociological perspective as the ability to view the world from two distinct yet complementary perspectives: seeing the general in the particular and seeing the strange in the familiar.

cheerful robots
People who are unwilling or unable to see the social world as it truly exists.

❸ PETER BERGER: SEEING THE GENERAL IN THE PARTICULAR

Peter Berger
The Canadian Press/STRRNS

According to Berger, seeing the *general* in the *particular* is the ability to look at seemingly unique events or circumstances and then recognize the larger (or general) features involved. For example, think about the last time you saw a street person asking people for spare change. Certainly, this is a specific and particular incident; it occurred at a specific time and place. But to see the general is also to recognize that while you may have seen only one street person, you know that there are many more you do not see. To appreciate an individual circumstance like this and broaden your perspective to the larger social patterns that create and perpetuate people's living on the streets in one of the richest nations in the world is to employ the sociological perspective. Indeed, the ability to move from the particular to the general and back again is one of the hallmarks of the sociological perspective. Our experience suggests that some students have difficulty switching from the general to the particular, but if you take your time and work through your own examples of both approaches, you will be able to do so more quickly and accurately over time.

SEEING THE STRANGE IN THE FAMILIAR

According to Berger, sociologists also need to tune their sociological perspective by thinking about what is *familiar* and seeing it as *strange*. For example, as you read this text, everything seems as it should be. Chances are that you are sitting at home, or perhaps at your school's library, doing your best to stay interested and take notes on the text so that you will do well on your exam. However, while all of this seems familiar and normal, if you really think about it, it is truly strange.

> > > Thinking Sociologically

Use Berger's two concepts to explore who should pay for dinner on a first date, binge drinking on campus, and why social media have become so popular.

Everyone, even those who have never attended university, understands that for students to do well they need to go to class, memorize material, and write tests. But, why? Granted, your professor needs you to learn material by memorizing some fundamental concepts and definitions and to demonstrate your command of the material on an exam; after all, he or she must receive something from you to justify your grade. But have you ever considered why students are graded in the first place?

> > >

Sociologists understand that seeing one homeless person means there are many more we do not see.

Masterfile

Is a student who gets an A in a course smarter than someone who receives a C? Do grades measure intelligence or command of course material, or do they simply acknowledge that someone is willing to work hard? (See Preckel, Holling, & Vock, 2006.) Asking these questions suggests that someone is looking at what appears normal and familiar and seeing it as peculiar and strange—evidence of the sociological perspective, of having quality of mind, and of beginning to develop the sociological imagination.

The ability to see the general in the particular and the strange in the familiar is the cornerstone of the sociological perspective. As you will learn, sociology is less about remembering details and specifics than about seeing the social world from a unique position—one that allows us to understand social context and to appreciate the position of others. Clearly, the work of both C. W. Mills and Peter Berger is complementary and speaks to the essence of the sociological perspective.

< < <

Students study their course materials as one way to learn content and improve their grades.

What Makes You, You? Engaging the Sociological Imagination

We all understand that we are individuals who think and feel independently of everyone else. Each of us, to some extent at least, has what some sociologists refer to as **agency**: the assumption that individuals have the ability to alter their socially constructed lives (Graham & Bruce, 2006). However, sociologists also stress the important role that structure plays in a person's life. Sociologists use the term **structure** to refer to opportunities and constraints that exist within a network of roles, relationships, and patterns that are relatively stable and persistent over time. For example, being employed as a receptionist in a large multinational corporation influences that person's life and the opportunities and challenges he or she faces. However, structure not only refers to large social parameters like occupation, minority status, or education level but also to small interactions between individuals (Alwin, 2008, p. 423). For example, interracial or gay couples' relationships are in part defined by the larger society's views on race and the heteronormative ideal (McClintock, 2010; Naugler, 2010). These contrasting perspectives highlight the classic structure-versus-agency debate in social theory (Connor, 2011), which revolves around whether or not individuals behave autonomously or are the expressive agents of the social structure (Brey, 2008, p. 71).

Using some of the ideas and concepts of Mills and Berger, how would you attempt to explain who you are and why you see the world the way you do? Working through this process will help you to understand that while we are all individuals, we are also the culmination of many social forces. Let's investigate *you* using five social factors and see which ones were the most influential in defining the person you have become.

agency The assumption that individuals have the ability to alter their socially constructed lives.

structure The network of relatively stable opportunities and constraints influencing individual behaviours.

MINORITY STATUS

Canadian sociological research suggests that people who are members of visible minority groups (Nakhaie, Lin, & Guan, 2009; O'Connell, 2010), who have a physical disability (DiGiorgio, 2009; Prince, 2010) or a mental disability (Corman, 2009; Leach Scully, 2010), or who are lesbian, gay, or bisexual (Dafnos, 2007; Ross, Epstein, Goldfinger, & Yager, 2009) face various forms of discrimination. As a budding sociologist, ask yourself whether being a member of any of these groups would influence a person's view of him- or herself or the world in general. If you personally identify with a minority group, how does this affect you? Does your minority status influence how you relate to others or how you view other minorities? If you are a Caucasian person who has never been diagnosed with a mental disability and who is able-bodied and heterosexual, you have experienced social advantage in Canadian society and are likely to have a positive and healthy self-image. However, can you appreciate how it might feel if you were a member of one of these disadvantaged groups? What it must feel like when people treat you as a second-class person, avoid eye contact, or, conversely, stare at you from across a room? Is it possible that these social experiences would influence the person you would become? By thinking about how you would react to these experiences, you are starting to apply your sociological imagination.

GENDER

patriarchy A system where men control the political and economic resources of society.

As we will explore in Chapters 8 and 9, society treats men and women differently. Canada, like virtually all human societies, remains a **patriarchy**—a system of rule that translates to "rule by the father" in which men control the political and economic resources of society. For example, Table 1.1 shows earning ratios between 2002 and 2011 and clearly demonstrates that full-time working women earn significantly less than men. Why do you think this is the case? If we think in terms of the general and the particular, you might argue that you know some women who make a lot more than some of the men you know. This may be true, but it does not diminish the importance of the overall trend, which is that men earn about 35 percent more than women. If you also consider that many students probably believe that they live in a more equitable society than these numbers suggest, you might think that this is somewhat *strange*. Why do people believe in something that so clearly is not the case?

SOCIOECONOMIC STATUS

socioeconomic status (SES) A combination of variables (income, education, occupation, etc.) used to rank people into a hierarchical structure.

As you consider the other students in your sociology class, are you aware of the different socioeconomic classes they represent? **Socioeconomic status (SES)** is a term used to describe a combination of variables to classify or rank people on criteria such as income level, level of education achieved, occupation, and area of residence. Would you agree that children from

TABLE 1.1 Average Earnings by Sex and Work Pattern

	All earners		
Year	Women	Men	Earnings Ratio
	$ constant 2011		%
2002	29 300	46 700	62.8
2003	29 000	46 000	62.9
2004	29 400	46 200	63.5
2005	30 000	46 900	64.0
2006	30 500	47 100	64.7
2007	31 300	47 800	65.5
2008	31 700	49 300	64.3
2009	32 600	47 400	68.6
2010	32 600	47 800	68.1
2011	32 100	48 100	66.1

Source: Statistics Canada. 2013. Average earnings by sex and work pattern (All earners) [online]. Last modified May 9, 2014, from http://www.statcan.gc.ca/tables-tableaux/sum-som/l01/cst01/labor01a-eng.htm

BOX 1.2 WHY SHOULD WE CARE?

Honour Killings

In 2009, the bodies of four women were found floating in the Rideau Canal near Kingston, Ontario. The women, ranging in age from 13 to 50, had been killed by their male relatives in what was described as an "honour killing." Honour killings occur primarily as a way to punish women for harming a family's honour. These four women (Rona Amir Mohammad and her daughters Zainab, Sahar, and Geeti) were killed because they dishonoured their family by living a "modern lifestyle" (CBC, 2011). Rona Amir Mohammad's ex-husband Mohammad Shafia, his new wife Tooba Yahya, and their son Hamed were convicted in 2011 of four counts of first degree murder and sentenced to life in prison.

Honour killings are often thought to occur only in Muslim cultures, but experts point out that they occur in Christian, Hindu, and Sikh families as well (CBC, 2011). Some researchers estimate that 5000 honour killings occur each year and of those over 2000 happen in India and Pakistan alone (Honour Based Violence Awareness Network, 2014). In virtually all human societies violence against women—including honour killings—is used as one way to control women.

Most Canadians would see honour killings as abominable acts but they should also realize that these murders are part of a larger pattern of violence against women that infuses not only Middle Eastern and South Asian cultures, but our own as well. Consider the fact that even though Canadian women and men are roughly equal in their chances of being assaulted, women are eleven times more likely to be victims of sexual violence and four times more likely to be victims of intimate partner violence (Statistics Canada, 2013). These statistics confirm that while honour killings are rare events in Canada, our women are still the victims of physical, sexual, and social violence far more often than we would like to admit.

As sociologists, we try to understand and explain the religious, social, and cultural circumstances that might lead some people to kill a member of their own family because of a perceived slight over their family's honour. However, we also want to help people understand that violence against women is not just a serious problem in "other" countries, but here at home as well.

Reprinted by permission from Edwin Hodge.

---

wealthier families whose parents are well educated, have good jobs, and live in a nice part of town have an advantage over children who do not share the same level of prosperity? While wealth and opportunity are certainly *familiar*, it is also *strange* when you consider how lucky these people were to be born into the families they were. Sociologists use the term **ascribed status** to define a situation in which a person is assigned advantage or disadvantage simply through birth. For example, being born to a wealthy family has nothing to do with an infant's individual qualities, and being born rich usually means a person will have opportunities for a postsecondary education and material pleasures. However, some people who are born to families with little money also achieve great wealth. For example, Guy Laliberté (creator of Cirque du Soleil), and Jim Balsillie and Mike Lazardis (creators of BlackBerry) all had humble beginnings and are now billionaires. Sociologists refer to this situation as **achieved status**, meaning the status a person has been able to gain through personal attributes and qualities. For example, while your parents "assigned" your sex (an ascribed attribute), your grades are the result of your effort and skill (an achieved attribute).

Thinking sociologically is to realize how people's beginnings influence what they can become. While many people can transcend their low socioeconomic status, they are the exception rather than the rule; sociology teaches us that the majority of those born poor remain poor (Keister, 2007).

ascribed status
Attributes (advantages and disadvantages) assigned at birth (e.g., sex).

achieved status
Attributes developed throughout life as a result of effort and skill (e.g., course grades).

TABLE 1.2 Persons in low income after tax (In percent, 2007–2011)

	1999	2000	2001	2002	2003	2004	2005	2006	2007	2008	2009	2010	2011
						%							
All persons	13.0	12.5	11.2	11.6	11.6	11.4	10.8	10.5	9.2	9.4	9.5	9.0	8.8
Persons under 18 years old	14.5	13.8	12.1	12.3	12.5	12.9	11.6	11.3	9.4	9.0	9.4	8.2	8.5
In two-parent families	9.4	9.5	8.3	7.4	7.9	8.4	7.8	7.7	6.6	6.5	7.5	5.7	5.9
In female lone-parent families*	41.9	40.1	37.4	43.0	41.4	40.4	32.9	31.7	26.6	23.4	21.5	21.8	23.0
Persons 18 to 64 years old	13.4	12.9	11.7	12.0	12.2	11.9	11.4	11.2	9.9	10.2	10.6	9.9	9.7
Persons 65 and over	7.9	7.6	6.7	7.6	6.8	5.6	6.2	5.4	4.9	5.8	6.6	6.8	6.4

*Data for male lone-parent families are somewhat erratic from year to year because of the relatively small number of families. The poverty rates for male lone-parent families are generally about half the rate for female lone-parent families. The highest poverty rate for male lone-parent families was 26.5% in 1994 but has been falling steadily to a record low of 7.2% in 2006 (National Council of Welfare, 2009).

Source: Statistics Canada, 2013. Persons in low income after tax (In percent, 2007–2011) [online]. Retrieved February 13, 2014, from http://www.statcan.gc.ca/tables-tableaux/sum-som/l01/cst01/famil19a-eng.htm

FAMILY STRUCTURE

Explore

Homelessness Could Spread to Middle Class, Crisis Study Warns

As we have seen, socioeconomic status does influence a person's opportunities. Children's well-being appears to be almost always associated with the household income of their families, according to a study by Statistics Canada (Phipps & Lethbridge, 2006). The study found that regardless of a child's age, higher income tends to be related to better physical, social/emotional, cognitive, and behavioural well-being.

Table 1.2 demonstrates that between 1999 and 2011 the percentage of people living in low income has declined However, the incidence of low income for female lone-parent families, while falling, remains more than three times higher than the incidence for two-parent families with children. As a sociologist, why do you think that higher family income levels are so closely associated with children's well-being? As you consider your answer, are you reflecting on the structure of your own family and how it may influence your views of yourself and those around you?

Therefore, family structure influences a child's development to the extent that female lone-parent families tend to have lower incomes than two-parent family structures. As we will discuss in Chapter 11, there are many new types of families today and the consistent theme in all of them suggests that loving parents with adequate incomes more often than not raise productive and well-adjusted children.

URBAN–RURAL DIFFERENCES

No doubt some of you reading this text were raised in small towns, while others grew up in cities. Do you think that where you grew up influences you? People who live in small towns report that they are distinct from urban dwellers and that their rural connections are an important defining feature (Mellow, 2005). Bonner (1998) suggests that sociologists have been trying to explain and understand urban–rural differences since the Industrial Revolution. While structural differences between small towns and large cities certainly exist (e.g., access to health care, diversity in entertainment and cultural events), the nature of growing up in either location is more subtle and contextual. For instance, if you grew up in a city, do you ever notice subtle differences when talking to friends who grew up in small towns? Conversely, if you grew up in a small town, do you notice any differences when talking to friends from a city? Is it possible that where you grow up also influences how you view the world?

As you can see from this brief analysis, our perceptions of ourselves and others are the product of many factors. As sociologists, our job is to try to view the world using the sociological perspective—to understand our own biases and investigate the social world by seeing the general, the particular, the strange, and the familiar. To help you determine the forces influencing your identity, locate yourself according to the criteria outlined in Table 1.3.

TABLE 1.3 Assessing Your Privilege

Group Membership	Associated Prejudice	Your Identity	Privileged/ Nonprivileged?	Scoring*
Gender (See Chapter 8)	Sexism (assertion that one gender is superior to another)	Man, woman		Man = 5 points Woman = 0 points
Class (See Chapter 7)	Classism (assigning more positive attributes to people of higher social classes)	Lower class, working class, lower-middle class, upper-middle class, upper class		Upper = 5 points Upper-middle = 4 points Lower-middle = 2 points Working = 1 point Lower = 0 points
Sexuality (See Chapter 9)	Homophobia (irrational fear and/or aversion to homosexuals), heterosexism (the pervasive assumption that the superior form of sexuality is heterosexual)	Heterosexual, gay, lesbian, bisexual, transsexual		Heterosexual = 5 points Gay, lesbian, bisexual, transsexual = 0 points
Ability (See Chapter 15)	Ableism (assigning an inferior value or worth to people who have developmental, emotional, physical, or psychiatric disabilities)	Able-bodied, physically and emotionally stable; physical, psychological, emotional disability		Able-bodied, physically and emotionally stable = 5 points Physical, psychological, emotional disability = 0 points
"Race"** (See Chapter 10)	Racism (assertion that one "race" is superior to another)	Traditionally, Caucasoid (white), Mongoloid (Chinese/Japanese), Negroid (black), Australoid (indigenous Australians/Southern Asians/Pacific Islanders)		White = 5 points Member of any visible minority group = 0 points
Religion (See Chapter 13)	Anti-Semitism/Islamophobia (irrational fear and/or aversion to Jews/Muslims)	Four largest global religions are Christianity, Islam, Hinduism, Buddhism		Christian = 5 points Other religion = 0 points
Age (See Chapter 15)	Ageism (assertion that one's age should determine his/her status and social position)	Child, adolescent, young adult, adult, senior		Adult = 5 points Young adult = 3 points Adolescent = 2 points Child = 1 point
			Privileged categories: ___ out of 7	Your score: ___ out of 35

* The scorings did not appear in the original resource and are not based on any scientific data. Instead, they are intended to reflect our perceived values on the various categories.
** The term *race* is used critically in sociology today because of its historical development and the fact that it is socially constructed and fraught with issues of power and inequality (see Chapter 10).

Adapted from "Your Social Identity and Social Location" in SOCW 2061 Study Guide—An Introduction to Social Work Practice. © 2005 Thompson Rivers University, Open Learning Division.

Once you have completed the exercise and calculated your score, you should start to see how privilege plays a role in everything that we do and, in part, defines the person we become.

If you have scored high, good for you: You are lucky. Realize, however, that with a high score comes social responsibility because you have gained privilege not by what you have accomplished but by being born into the family that you were. If you did not score very high, take heart. Even without the privilege of some of the other students in your class, you have begun your postsecondary education—a significant accomplishment in which to take pride. Also, realize that while everyone faces different opportunities and challenges, each of us has some control over what we do and how we respond to the world around us.

Now that we have considered the sociological perspective and the relationship between social forces and personal social identity, we will explore how the discipline of sociology began and evolved.

The Origins of Sociology

People have been pondering their place in the universe and their relationships with each other for thousands of years. The Chinese philosopher K'ung fu-tzu (known today as Confucius, 551–479 BCE[1]) and the ancient Greeks engaged in elaborate discussions and writings about society in general and the role of the individual citizen in particular. In ancient Greece (circa 400 BCE), a group of educators called the Sophists (who were the first paid teachers) travelled the country and catered to the rich, who wanted to learn how to live well and be happy (Jones, 1969). The Sophists were the first thinkers to focus their efforts on the human being, in contrast to the earlier tradition that concentrated on understanding the physical world.

Later philosophers, notably Socrates (469–399 BCE) and his student Plato (427–347 BCE), challenged the virtue of being paid for one's knowledge and advocated the necessity of deeper reflection on the human social condition. Plato's *The Republic* is one of the most important works in Western philosophy, as it asks what social justice is and what the characteristics of a just individual are. Plato writes, "[o]ur aim in founding the State is not the disproportionate happiness of any one class, but the greatest happiness of the whole; we thought that in a State which is ordered with a view to the good of the whole we should be most likely to find justice" (Jowett, 1892, as cited in Abelson, Friquegnon, & Lockwood, 1977, p. 575).

After the Greeks, Roman emperor Marcus Aurelius (121–180), Muslim philosopher and scientist Al Farabi (870–950), Italian theologian Saint Thomas Aquinas (1224–1274), British playwright William Shakespeare (1564–1616), and English philosopher John Locke (1632–1704) all explored the role of the individual in society.

The ideas that form the foundation of sociology, then, have been around for a long time. Although Ibn Khaldun (1332–1406) is recognized as the first social philosopher working from the sociological perspective (see Zahoor, 1996), it was not until 1838 that the term *sociology* was coined by Auguste Comte (Périer, 1998, p. 343). For his naming of the discipline, Comte is often referred to as the father of sociology.

---

1 BCE means "before common era" and has become the dating convention to recognize religious diversity. It replaces the previous notation of BC, "before Christ."

❹ Three Revolutions: The Rise of Sociology

In general terms, the emergence of sociology was a product of the time. So many striking changes were occurring in eighteenth- and nineteenth-century Europe that people realized that a new science was necessary in order to understand and manage social change. Three revolutionary events inspired the rise of sociology: the scientific revolution, the political revolution, and the Industrial Revolution.

THE SCIENTIFIC REVOLUTION

With the emergence of the Renaissance in the fourteenth to seventeenth centuries, the insights by thinkers such as Galileo, Newton, and Copernicus began to gain wider acceptance despite resistance from the Church. The development of the scientific method during the Enlightenment period that followed (circa 1650–1800) facilitated the pace of social change.

Auguste Comte (1798–1857) considered himself a scientist and believed that the techniques used in the hard sciences (physics, chemistry, etc.) to explain the physical world should be applied to the social world as well. He believed that to really understand the inner workings of society, one needed to understand how human thinking has changed through time. Comte is well known for his Law of Three Stages, which defines how advances of the mind created three different types of societies (Udefi, 2009).

Comte called the first stage the *Theological Stage*. It was the longest period of human thinking, beginning with our earliest human ancestors and ending during the Middle Ages (roughly 1300). This stage is characterized by a religious outlook that explains the world and human society as an expression of God's will and views science as a means to discover God's intentions (Zeitlin, 1994). During this stage, people would explain what they could see through the actions of spiritual or supernatural beings. For example, how might early humans have explained where the sun went every night? They would not have been able to comprehend the idea of a solar system or that they were travelling through space on a planet. Instead, they might have argued that there were two gods responsible for taking care of them: the Sun God and the Moon God. The Sun God was there to light their world and help keep them warm. When it was time to sleep, however, the Moon God took over and looked after them until it was time to wake up and start hunting for food. Perceptions like these helped early peoples to explain the world and their place in it.

The Theological Stage concluded with the emergence of the Renaissance and later the Enlightenment, when science, not religion, was used to explain the world. Comte called this next stage of intellectual development the *Metaphysical Stage*. The Metaphysical Stage (metaphysics, or "beyond physics," is a field of philosophy dedicated to an understanding of truth and the relationship between mind and matter) was a period during which people began to question everything and to challenge the power and teachings of the Church. It was characterized by the assumption that people could understand and explain their universe through their own insight and reflection.

Auguste Comte

Temple de la Religion
de l'Humanite, Paris, France/
The Bridgeman Art Library

Bettmann/Corbis

< < <

Many societies have used mythological beings to explain the world.

> > >

The scales of justice signify that everyone should be treated equally under the law. This view is entirely consistent with Enlightenment thinking.

Erick Jones/Shutterstock

To explore what it meant to be a conscious being, people tried to experience and understand their world through abstractions such as emotion and beauty. Artists, musicians, and poets all attempt to inspire or capture some insight into the human condition through images, sounds, and words, and these abstractions can be very powerful. For example, do certain smells remind you of your childhood? Do you remember how you felt when you saw the hijacked jets crash into the World Trade Center buildings? These smells and images are only abstractions, but they may inspire powerful emotional reactions—feelings, passions, and fears that were explored during the Metaphysical Stage as an attempt to understand ourselves better.

Comte referred to the final stage as the *Positive Stage* (Westby, 1991, p. 137). During this period, which began to emerge during Comte's lifetime, he believed that the world would be interpreted through a scientific lens—that society would be guided by the rules of observation, experimentation, and logic. Comte argued that sociologists would be ideal leaders for this emerging society because they would be trained in the science of society: sociology.

The Law of Three Stages is an interesting way of looking at history, but sociologists today do not grant much credibility to Comte's ideas for two main reasons. First, the idea of having only three stages is difficult, as it assumes that human thinking is currently as good as it will ever get. Second, the idea that the third (and final) stage was just emerging during Comte's lifetime is somewhat self-serving. However, even with these limitations, Comte's commitment to a positivistic approach to the social world is worth exploring in more detail.

⑤ Positivism **Positivism** is a theoretical approach that considers all understanding to be based on science (Hollinger, 1982). A positivist approaches the world through three primary assumptions (Bowie, 1990; Rhoads, 1991):

positivism **A theoretical approach that considers all understanding to be based on science.**

1. ***There exists an objective and knowable reality.*** Positivists assert that the physical and social worlds can be understood through observation, experimentation, and logic. This suggests that reality is objective and beyond individual interpretation or manipulation. For example, objective reality suggests that a chair is, in fact, a chair. While one could

argue that the chair can also have objects placed on it, and in this sense can be seen as having table-like properties, one could not argue that the chair is actually a puppy. That interpretation and observation is obviously wrong; therefore, objectivity is an absolute. Conversely, subjectivity is the attribution of emotional or subjective interpretations. While a chair is a chair, could a person not have a favourite chair? If so, that person is deciding that there is more to a chair than its function, thereby making subjective interpretations that go beyond what is logical or defensible.

<<<

Positivists assert that science allows us to shine a new light on any question of human interest.

The positivistic belief that we can understand our objective world is also grounded in the premise that we have the capacity to do so—that our physical and social existence is knowable. This sounds easier than it is. For example, theories try to explain the size of our universe (Alfonso-Faus, 2006). This seems fine, but can the universe actually end—and if so, what is just beyond it? Because of the overwhelming nature of the universe, we often say that it is infinite, but is that a valid answer or simply a reflection of the fact that we cannot explain how big the universe actually is? Positivists believe that we have the capacity to understand our universe and believe, thus, that it is knowable and that we can handle the answers that science will provide. Further, because these answers are objective and based on science, there is no room for subjective interpretation of the results.

2. *Since all sciences explore the same, singular reality, over time all sciences will become more alike.* Positivists assert that since there is only one correct explanation for the physical and social worlds, discipline and scientific boundaries will fall away as we progress in our studies and realize that all science is investigating the same reality. Thus, in the future there may only be one science instead of the divisions we see today (e.g., biology, chemistry, philosophy). As a student, have you ever noticed that some of the lecture materials in different courses overlap?

3. *There is no room in science for value judgments.* Since all science is exploring the same reality, only from different perspectives, there is no good or bad science. Searching for a vaccination to the AIDS virus certainly may seem more socially valuable than investigating how to shrink the size of the hydrogen bomb so that anyone can carry one around, but positivists would argue that the science for both is equally valuable for furthering our understanding of the world. This is not to say that positivists would promote potentially destructive behaviour, but they would argue that the decision to explode a new bomb is a social one and should not be used as an excuse to avoid scientific exploration on how to shrink the bomb.

Anti-Positivism In stark contrast to the positivistic tradition is **anti-positivism**, which is a theoretical approach that considers knowledge and understanding to be the result of human subjectivity. Anti-positivists would challenge each of the positivist assumptions.

1. *While hard science may be useful for exploring the physical world, the social world cannot be understood solely through numbers and formulas.* Anti-positivists assert that the formulas that positivists use to explain the universe have meaning only when we collectively assign social value to them—that is, numbers have only relative importance.

anti-positivism **A theoretical approach that considers knowledge and understanding to be the result of human subjectivity.**

For example, you would probably feel gratified by an 89 percent on your midterm sociology exam. However, what if the class average turns out to be 96 percent? Your score has not changed, but your feelings about it certainly have.

2. *All sciences will not merge over time and no single methodological approach (i.e., science) can reach a complete understanding of our world.* Science has been able to teach us a great deal about our physical world, but anti-positivists suggest that to truly understand the human condition we need to appreciate and validate emotions, values, and human subjectivity. In fact, as we begin to understand more about our world, scientists are finding entirely new areas to research, and in this sense our sciences are becoming more unique over time.

3. *Science cannot be separated from our values.* Sociologists define **values** as those cultural assessments that identify something as right, desirable, and moral. As we have seen, positivists argue that all sciences are equal and should not be tainted by value judgments; after all, science is science. However, anti-positivists suggest that what we choose to study is also a social expression. Would any society consider the shrinking of the hydrogen bomb as worthy as finding a vaccine for the AIDS virus?

values Cultural assessments that identify something as right, desirable, and moral.

Quantitative and Qualitative Sociology Reviewing the positivism–anti-positivism debate is an important grounding for an understanding of quantitative and qualitative sociology. The positivists' belief that science and experimentation will grant us the greatest insights into our world is in keeping with quantitative sociology. **Quantitative sociology** focuses on behaviours that can be measured—for example, the number of divorces per capita, crime rates over time, and the incidence of homelessness in Canadian cities. Conversely, anti-positivists' exploration of the world through human engagement, and their understanding that what is important is what we decide is important, is consistent with qualitative sociology. **Qualitative sociology** is the study of behaviours that cannot be counted so readily but still teach us a great deal about ourselves—for example, the emotional effects of going through a divorce, people's fears of living in what they think is an increasingly violent society (which is not the case and will be explored in Chapter 14), and the social factors that influence a person's likelihood of becoming homeless. As you can see, quantitative and qualitative sociology can explore the same things but they do so from different perspectives. Neither approach is better than the other; in fact, good sociology integrates components of both (to be discussed in Chapter 4).

quantitative sociology The study of behaviours that can be measured (e.g., income levels).

qualitative sociology The study of nonmeasurable, subjective behaviours (e.g., the effects of divorce).

THE POLITICAL REVOLUTION

The Renaissance and, later, the Enlightenment inspired a great deal of social and scientific change. With a new view of the world as separate from the teachings of the Church, society evolved to endorse democratic principles.

Renaissance thinkers such as Niccolò Machiavelli (1469–1527), René Descartes (1596–1650), and Thomas Hobbes (1588–1679) challenged social convention and inspired new ways of understanding the social world. For example, Machiavelli's famous work *The Prince* (1513) suggests that human behaviour is motivated by self-interest and an insatiable desire for material gain (Zeitlin, 1994, p. 224). This was a controversial position at the time because those who had ascended to power were considered to have done so by divine right, and thus should be followed. Machiavelli's assertion that anyone could become a prince—that nobility and power were not a birthright and that one could take power if and when the opportunity presented itself—challenged the establishment of the time. In fact, *The Prince* was considered so revolutionary that it was placed on a list of prohibited books (*Index Librorum Prohibitorum*) in 1564 by Pope Pius IV.

René Descartes is most famous for his commitment to the idea that we are thinking beings, as captured in his famous phrase *Cogito ergo sum*, or "I think, therefore I am." This assertion seems obvious to us today, but at the time it was a liberating position that that human beings were able to understand their world through rational reflection (a position that allowed for the emergence of Comte's positivism, discussed earlier). This idea that we are the masters of our own destiny was inherently revolutionary.

This position was also reflected in the works of Thomas Hobbes, who believed that people were driven by two primary passions: fear of death and the desire for power. This perspective led Hobbes to his infamous observation that our lives are "solitary, poor, nasty, brutish and short" (Piirimäe, 2006, p. 3). According to Hobbes, the true nature of humankind is therefore self-preservation, and he argued that long-term stability can be achieved only when citizens join together and agree to forgo their individual power to the gains achieved within a collective. We will elaborate on Hobbes' theories in Chapter 2.

Many of the philosophical and social trends that began during the Renaissance continued to develop through the Enlightenment. Two of the most influential Enlightenment thinkers in the development of sociology were John Locke (1632–1704) and Jean-Jacques Rousseau (1712–1778), whose ideas are also discussed further in Chapter 2.

John Locke is perhaps most famous for his assertion that ideas are not innate and that all knowledge is the result of experience (Zeitlin, 1994, pp. 4–5). The belief that people are born as *blank slates* is one of the defining features of the sociological perspective (see Chapter 6). Locke argued that the only way to increase our knowledge is to gather more information about the material world through science and experimentation. Once again, we can see how these ideas challenged the primacy of the Church and a belief system based on faith rather than on objective facts.

While not as supportive of objective science, Jean-Jacques Rousseau's writings also contributed to the emergence of sociology. His greatest contribution to social theory was his challenge to the true nature of social life. Rousseau suggested that, prior to organized society, human beings existed in a *natural state* whereby an individual's desire was solitary and self-centred. (In this sense, his approach is consistent with the earlier writings of Thomas Hobbes.) As society developed, these early beings began to see the benefits they could achieve when they agreed to work together (i.e., the social contract). At its essence, the social contract is the acknowledgment that we achieve more by working together than apart; while we lose some of our independence, the benefits we assume (e.g., government, libraries, hospitals) far outweigh the costs (e.g., loss of autonomy, privacy, independence) (Westby, 1991).

From Machiavelli to Rousseau, from the Renaissance to the Enlightenment, philosophers and social activists promoted novel ideals such as individual rights and social responsibility, equality of opportunity, and the political ideology of democracy. These ideas challenged tradition and nobility, inspired great debate and reflection, and ultimately led to the American and French revolutions. While we take these ideas for granted today, this transformation of how we saw ourselves, each other, and our entire society led to a restructuring of everything we knew, and it was into this period of tension and re-examination that sociology was born.

THE INDUSTRIAL REVOLUTION

Our human ancestors subsisted through gathering and hunting activities for millions of years, and then, 10 000 years ago, everything changed. Virtually overnight, people decided to settle in one area and raise crops and domesticate animals (O'Neil, 2006). This change must have had extraordinary ramifications for early humans. Only a few thousand years later, everything changed again. Around 1750, the Industrial Revolution replaced agriculture as our dominant means of supporting ourselves and our families (Hooker, 1996).

The Industrial Revolution changed virtually every aspect of life: family structures (Bengston, 2001), how people made a living (Delamotte & Walker, 1976), and even people's thoughts, dreams, and aspirations (Boxer, 2007). While many associate the Industrial Revolution with technological advancements (e.g., steam power, the cotton gin, electricity), what really inspired it were the profound social changes occurring at the time. Moving from an agricultural and rural economy to a capitalist and urban one has left a legacy that some would argue we are still trying to deal with today (Dawley & Faler, 1976; Rosenthal, 1992).

> > >

Many workers, including women and children, worked in deplorable conditions during the Industrial Revolution.

An agricultural economy is one based on local food production for local consumption. This means that farmers produce the food they require to survive without the need to compile vast surpluses for trade. Most nonagricultural goods (clothing, blacksmithing products, ceramics) were produced by individual families that specialized in manufacturing certain goods. Thus, most capitalist activity focused on mercantile activity rather than on production (Hooker, 1996). In these areas, then, the economy was local and people knew the makers of virtually all goods and services. Think of how this differs from life today. How many people today grow their own food or know the people who produce the things they consume? The movement from local production and consumption to regional and national distribution networks was largely the result of mechanization and industrialization. New production techniques created huge amounts of cheap goods that needed to be traded through larger and larger networks. Ultimately, the European economy became a global one. This expansion of trading networks for European goods drove the conversion from an agricultural to an industrial economy.

The emergence of the steam engine as a cheap means of power and locomotion was also instrumental in facilitating the rise of the Industrial Revolution. Millions of farmers abandoned traditional village life and moved into the rapidly growing cities in search of factory jobs (Hedley, 2002). The move from a rural to an urban environment led to a new series of social problems, including child labour in factories, crushing poverty, malnourishment, and exploding crime rates. Disturbed by these developments, early sociologists began to try to understand what was causing these conditions and what could be done to address them (Lindsey, Beach, & Ravelli, 2009).

Those of you who grew up in small towns and now live in cities have no doubt noticed many differences between the two environments. City dwellers tend not to feel as connected to their neighbours as do people in small towns (Brint, 2001). In a small town, you are far more likely to see people you know, but it goes beyond that—there is a different feeling of community. This is not to suggest that city dwellers do not have a sense of community—they do—or that everyone in a small town feels connected—they do not—but, rather, to reinforce that cities emerged as a result of the Industrial Revolution, and so mark a relatively recent change in how human beings live their lives.

>>> Thinking Sociologically

Given our brief review of these three important revolutions, do you think that any of them remain influential today? If so, how? If not, why?

❻ Macro- and Microsociology

Early sociologists wanted to understand the workings of the entire society so they could learn from our past and be able to head off future social, political, and military conflicts. Attempting to understand society as a whole is referred to as **macrosociology** (i.e., looking at the big picture first and at individuals second) and it defined early European sociology. **Microsociology**, in contrast, investigates individual or small-group dynamics (i.e., looking at individuals first and at society as a whole second) and it defined early American sociology.

macrosociology The study of society as a whole.

microsociology The study of individual or small-group dynamics within a larger society.

EARLY EUROPEAN MACROTHEORISTS: MARX, DURKHEIM, WEBER

As discussed, macrosociology focuses on groups and/or large social structures as the vehicle for understanding society. Macrotheorists are more interested in looking at system-wide phenomena (e.g., class structure, education system) than they are in exploring how individuals relate to the larger social system. In sociology, the most influential historical macrotheorists were Marx, Durkheim, and Weber.

Karl Marx (1818–1883) was a philosopher, an economist, a political scientist, a historian, and, to a much lesser extent, a sociologist. His greatest contribution to sociology was his insight into the nature of human relationships. Much like the earlier position of Hobbes, Marx believed that people were forced into competition with others because of the material changes brought about by the accumulation of wealth in early agricultural societies. This situation led to conflict because some people had more wealth than others.

According to Marx, all human relationships in capitalist economies have power imbalances. For example, in a university class, the professor has more power than do the students—all students want high grades, and it is the professor who assigns them. There is a power imbalance as well, not only between teacher and student, but also between students. Might a Caucasian male student in a class taught by another Caucasian male have some advantage over a visible minority female? This is not to suggest that the professor actively discriminates against minorities but that power imbalances exist everywhere. Do your parents have power over you? Do you have some power over your younger siblings? Do men have more power in Canadian society than women do? Power also influences how entire classes of people interact with each other—for example, majority groups with minority groups, or nuclear-armed countries with countries that are not similarly equipped. Marx's theory is discussed in more detail in Chapter 2, but in a nutshell, to understand Marx is to understand how power permeates the ways people interact, not only as individuals but also as entire classes.

In stark contrast to Marx's view of the world was that of French sociologist Émile Durkheim (1858–1917). One could argue that while Comte named the new discipline of sociology, Durkheim established it as a serious scientific endeavour. His view of human nature was less critical than either Comte's or Marx's; he believed that people wanted to work together for collective benefit. However, as we will discuss in Chapter 2, Durkheim believed that the new urban and industrial society presented many challenges to both the individual and the collective. He argued that low levels of social integration and regulation were a source of various social problems, including rising deviance and suicide rates. Most of his writings focus on the causes of this decline in moral society and on the institutions of religion and education, which he believed had the potential to lessen that decline (Lindsey, Beach, & Ravelli, 2009).

German sociologist Max Weber (pronounced VAY-ber) (1864–1920) ranks with Marx and Durkheim as a founding figure of sociology. Weber's contributions to sociology centre on his analysis of how the social world is becoming increasingly rationalized over time, by which he meant that people are becoming more focused on selecting the most efficient means to accomplish any particular end. For example, as a student, how motivated are you to do outside readings about sociology that will never help you achieve a higher grade? For many students, the thought of reading academic resources outside of class has no real appeal—how does it *help* them? Weber would see this as a perfect example of people becoming more focused on defining what they want and what they are willing to do to get it. However, while rationalization may make society more productive and efficient, it may also result in people who act like machines and do not appreciate the larger social world in which they exist. Weber's work, especially his analyses of bureaucracy and religion, continues to inform many areas of sociology today (see Gronow, 1988; Mulyadi, 2006).

While these macrosociological insights helped to define the young science of sociology, the American tradition, focusing on microsociological analyses, was just as important for establishing what contemporary sociology looks like today.

EARLY AMERICAN MICROTHEORISTS: MEAD, COOLEY, BLUMER

The work of George Herbert Mead (1863–1931), Charles Horton Cooley (1864–1929), and Herbert Blumer (1900–1987) was instrumental in establishing early American sociology as promoting a microsociological perspective of the world (Denzin, 1992; Lynch & McConatha, 2006). As discussed, microsociology focuses on individuals and/or small groups and how they behave in particular face-to-face social networks. Rather than consider system-wide processes and institutions (more characteristic of the work of Marx, Durkheim, and Weber), microsociologists look at individual lived realities and then generalize about their social relevance.

Mead viewed the individual mind and self as rising out of the social process of communication—in effect, we become ourselves through social interaction. Thus, instead of looking at the human experience as emerging from, say, one's social class, Mead looked at individual factors. This approach was a clear departure from the more structured, group-focused European tradition. Mead's approach, which became known as **symbolic interactionism**, was reflective of the American value system in its focus on the individual. After all, one of the defining features of the American Constitution is its commitment to preserving individual rights and freedoms (Berkowitz, 2005).

> **symbolic interactionism** A perspective asserting that people and societies are defined and created through the interactions of individuals.

Cooley, a like-minded scholar and a contemporary of Mead's, furthered the microsociological approach by suggesting that people define themselves, at least in part, by how others view them. Cooley theorized that by considering how others view us, we actually become the kind of person we believe others see us to be (see Chapter 2 for a discussion of the "looking-glass self") (Shaffer, 2005).

Besides actually naming symbolic interactionism in 1937 (Ritzer, 2000, p. 202), Herbert Blumer's contribution was to continue what Mead started through his long teaching career at the University of Chicago (which became known as the Chicago School, defined by its symbolic interactionist flavour). Blumer is also important because of his high profile in sociology (e.g., between 1941 and 1952, he was editor of the prominent *American Journal of Sociology*, and in 1956, he was elected president of the American Sociological Association) and his analysis of *meaning*, *language*, and *thought*. For Blumer, these core principles led him to conclude how people create their sense of self within the larger social world.

❼ Sociology in Canada

Sociology in Canada is not quite as old as it is in the United States (the first American department of sociology was established at the University of Chicago in 1892; the first Canadian one, at McGill University in 1924) and is obviously much smaller. The American dominance of North American sociology is largely due to that country's overwhelming size. For example, the American postsecondary system between 2006 and 2008 was estimated to have over 17 million undergraduate students while the Canadian system had just over 1 million in

BOX 1.3 CANADIAN CONTRIBUTIONS TO SOCIOLOGY

Homelessness and Crime

John Hagan and Bill McCarthy's 1998 book *Mean Streets: Youth Crimes and Homelessness* was revolutionary; it has been considered the single most important study of crime in Canadian society in a generation (Brannigan, 2000, p. 385). The authors integrate positivist and anti-positivist methodologies to explore the rich and diverse realities of life on the street.

Among the forces that send young people to the streets, Hagan and McCarthy argue, are problems in parenting and conflicts at school (Hagan & McCarthy, 1998, p. 78). The authors' research began in 1987 when they interviewed 390 Toronto street youth living in shelters, drop-in centres, city parks, and on street corners. By 1992, they had completed 482 additional interviews with homeless youth living in Toronto and Vancouver.

Hagan and McCarthy suggest that the relationship between youth crime and homelessness is much more complex than initially believed. Youth who live on the streets are often overlooked as studies generally focus on youth who still live at home. They suggest that criminologists should look more closely at this group because the majority of street youth are also involved in criminal activity. They contend that contemporary research ignores the fact that lack of shelter, lack of proper nutrition, and joblessness make it virtually impossible for street youth to avoid living a life of crime (Hagan & McCarthy, 1998, pp. 18–21).

Hagan and McCarthy also found that homeless youth developed unique family structures that the authors refer to as *street families*. These interpersonal relationships help street youth to secure the necessities of life, such as food, clothing, and shelter. While the general population may tend to think of street families as gangs, the youth describe them in familial terms since they tend to form and exist based on survival. Some family members take on special roles, such as protection and safety or finding food, shelter, and money.

Hagan and McCarthy highlight that most Canadian youth do not become homeless and that the majority of youth crime is not committed by homeless youth. They do recognize, however, that a unique relationship exists between homelessness and criminal activity, and they argue that more research needs to be undertaken in this area. As a young sociologist, how might you explain a youth's desire to belong to a *street family*? Can street families be analyzed using Berger's *general in the particular* and *strange in the familiar*?

Sources: Brannigan, 2000; Hagan & McCarthy, 1992, 1998.

2007/2008 (Statistics Canada, 2009d; U.S. Census Bureau, 2010). In 1999, there were more than 2400 departments of sociology in the United States (American Sociological Association, 2002), while Canada had around 45 universities and about 150 colleges offering at least introductory sociology (Association of Canadian Community Colleges, 2010; McMaster, 2007). Given the size of American sociology programs, it is not surprising that American sociology dominates. In fact, some Canadian sociologists suggest that Canadian sociology is a product of its experiences with, and at times resistance to, the larger and more dominant American sociological tradition (see Brym & Saint-Pierre, 1997; Hiller, 2001; Hiller & Di Luzio, 2001). This has resulted in Canadian sociology having four defining features that distinguish it from the American tradition (Lindsey, Beach, & Ravelli, 2009).

FOUR DEFINING FEATURES

Geography and Regionalism The particular nature of the American–Canadian relationship is seen in Brym and Saint-Pierre's (1997) discussion of how Canada's geography has influenced Canadian sociology. They suggest that one defining feature of Canadian sociology is its ability to survive over time (1997, p. 543), and they propose a core theme of the development and maintenance of a community in the face of hostile elements (e.g., cold winters) and outside forces (e.g., political and intellectual pressure from the United States).

Another internal force that helps define Canadian sociology is the role of regionalism in our country's development (e.g., west versus east) and, in particular, the role of Quebec, which offers a unique linguistic and cultural influence on Canadian society generally and on Canadian sociology specifically.

Canadian francophone sociology began in 1943, when the faculty of social sciences was established at Laval University in Quebec City. Although francophone sociology is comparatively young, it experienced rapid growth between the 1960s and the 1980s, as evidenced by rising student enrolment but also by the wealth of research produced by francophone sociologists (Brym & Saint-Pierre, 1997, p. 544). In addition, the significant social movement of the 1960s, called the "Quiet Revolution," saw the influence of the Catholic Church in Quebec fade, to be replaced by an expanded provincial bureaucracy. Ultimately, a resurgence in nationalistic sentiments fuelled the separatist movement, as seen in the growing influence of the Parti Québécois and its then leader, René Lévesque.

The Quiet Revolution not only inspired changes in Quebec society and politics, but also influenced sociologists to focus more on issues of social class and social policy (see Brym & Saint-Pierre, 1997; Hiller, 2001). In fact, some Quebec sociologists have played leadership roles in the transformation of francophone society as senior advisers and civil servants within the provincial government (Brym & Saint-Pierre, 1997, p. 544). This is consistent with Southcott's (1999, p. 459) position that francophone sociologists are more likely to see themselves as "agents of change" than are their anglophone colleagues.

Focus on Political Economy Wallace Clement, a leading figure in Canadian sociology, believes that a defining element of Canadian sociology is its interest in the political economy. **Political economy** is seen as the interactions of politics, government and governing, and the social and cultural constitution of markets, institutions, and actors (Clement, 2001, p. 406). According to Clement, this intellectual pursuit is characterized by the attempt to seek out tensions and contradictions within society in order to form the basis for social change.

---

political economy

The interactions of politics, government and governing, and the social and cultural constitution of markets, institutions, and actors.

> > >

At times, the Quiet Revolution in Quebec was anything but quiet.

Len Sidaway, The Gazette (Montreal)

Arguably, the first Canadian sociologist to investigate Canada's political economy was Harold A. Innis in *The Fur Trade in Canada* (1930/2001) and *The Cod Fisheries* (1940/1954). In these works, Innis developed what has been termed the *staples thesis*, which contends that Canadian development was based on the exploitation of raw materials that were sent to European countries to fuel their own industrial thirsts. Innis suggests that each staple had its own characteristics that imposed a particular logic on its development (Clement, 2001, p. 407). As Canada grew and these economic developments continued, Canadian raw materials were taken abroad, refined into more valuable commodities (e.g., furniture, automobiles), and then returned to Canada at vastly inflated prices. Innis suggests that being in a subordinate economic position to the British and American empires, Canadians took on the menial role of "hewers of wood, drawers of water." Canadian society seems to have been defined, at least in part, by the realization that Canada is not one of the world's major economic or social forces.

Canadianization Movement Canadian English-speaking sociology was influenced a great deal by American sociology as practised at the University of Chicago (see Brym & Saint-Pierre, 1997; Eichler, 2001; Hiller, 2001; Hiller & Di Luzio, 2001; Langlois, 2000; McKay, 1998).

Founded in 1892 by Albion Small, the department of sociology at the University of Chicago defined the American sociological tradition for much of the early twentieth century. As already introduced, the Chicago School of sociology was dominated by the symbolic-interactionist approach, focusing on social reform and collective social responsibility. Many early Canadian sociologists were trained at the University of Chicago: C. A. Dawson, Everett Hughes, Harold Innis, A. C. McCrimmon, and Roderick D. McKenzie, to name only a few. By the 1950s and 1960s, Canadian sociologists felt a pressing need to hire and train more Canadian sociologists in order to investigate and understand Canadian society from a Canadian perspective. In fact, Hedley and Warburton (1973, p. 305, as cited in Hiller & Di Luzio, 2001, p. 494) found that, in 1971, Canadian sociology departments with more than 20 faculty members had over 50 percent of their faculty from America, 20 percent from other countries, and only 28 percent from Canada.

Radical Nature Canadian sociology is more radical than the American tradition because of its greater focus on macrosociology as well as greater support for feminist ideas and social change (Brym & Saint-Pierre, 1997). As seen in earlier research on the political economy, Canadian sociology has never shied away from uncovering the hidden power structures that influence and guide society. For example, during the 1960s, Canadian sociology was influenced by the anti-war and civil rights movements and the emergence of Aboriginal peoples' political organizations. This radical tradition continues with many Canadian feminist who investigate how gender acts as a site of oppression and domination.

Margrit Eichler (2001) suggests that the simultaneous emergence of the Canadianization movement and the women's movement led to a politics of knowledge that proved helpful to both. The feminist movement found a new voice on expanding university campuses the 1960s and 1970s. Eichler attempts to reverse the "politics of erasure," which she argues has ignored the historical contributions made by female sociologists in Canada (to be explored more fully in Chapter 3). She conducted in-depth interviews with 10 leading female sociologists born before 1930. Their critical social presence within the expanding academic community was an important factor in advancing feminist issues not only on university campuses but also in the larger society.

In 1967, the Canadian government established the Royal Commission on the Status of Women to "inquire into and report upon the status of women in Canada and to recommend what steps might be taken by the federal government to ensure for women equal opportunities with men in all aspects of Canadian Society" (Royal Commission on the Status of Women, 2007). The final report was released in 1970 (with 167 recommendations) and became the blueprint for mainstream feminist activism. The women's movement inspired a new generation of women to reflect on their social surroundings and question social convention. The influence of the movement on early women pioneers was equally important, as it allowed them to critique their own intellectual foundations and their approach to sociology specifically and to society generally. As well-known sociologist Dorothy Smith notes, "Because we were free to take up issues for women, we didn't feel committed to reproducing the discipline, . . . it had the effect . . . of really liberating the discipline in general in Canada, so that you now have an orientation where people feel absolutely comfortable in raising current issues, in addressing what's going on in Canada" (as cited in Eichler, 2001, p. 394). The Royal Commission report opened the debate on women's position in Canadian society and also resulted in the formation of the Status of Women Subcommittee of the Canadian Sociology and Anthropology Association, which still exists today as the Canadian Sociological Association (see www.csaa.ca). The Canadian women's movement, and sociology's role within it, is just one example of how the critical foundations of Canadian sociology continue to influence the discipline today.

Canadian sociology remains more critical than the American tradition and continues to make significant contributions to our understanding of contemporary society.

EARLY CANADIAN SOCIOLOGISTS

Annie Marion MacLean

Reproduced by permission of the Adelphi University Archives and Special Collections (Garden City, NY)

Annie Marion MacLean (1870–1934) Born in Prince Edward Island, MacLean was the first Canadian woman to receive a Ph.D. in sociology (from the University of Chicago in 1900). MacLean was a forerunner on the subject of working women; her study entitled *Wage-Earning Women* (1910) was one of the first large-scale applications of survey research in Canada. In it, she surveyed 13 500 women labourers at 400 institutions in 20 different cities. The project was a massive undertaking and involved numerous staff, including 29 women (Eichler, 2001, p. 378).

Sir Herbert Brown Ames

House of Commons, Reproduced with permission, University of Toronto Archives (UTA) H. A. Innis, Associate Professor of Economic Geography, University of Toronto 2003–21–1MS (Acc#)

Sir Herbert Brown Ames (1863–1954) Born in Montreal, Ames was the son of American parents who owned a successful boot and shoe company. Ames is best known for his book *The City below the Hill: A Sociological Study of a Portion of the City of Montreal, Canada* (1897), one of the first Canadian examples of sociology that relied on various statistical analyses to document the slum conditions people experienced living just south of downtown Montreal. Ames was also a Member of Parliament and spent most of his life trying to help improve the plight of the poor.

Carl Dawson (1887–1964) Dawson was born in Prince Edward Island in 1887 and did his M.A. and Ph.D. work at the University of Chicago. He was the first sociologist to be hired at McGill University (in 1922) and served as chairperson of its department of sociology until 1952. He and colleague W. Gettys wrote an introductory sociology textbook that would become one of the most popular and widely used in North America for more than 20 years and contributed greatly to the establishment of the discipline. Dawson's other writings included *The Settlement of the Peace River Country: A Study of a Pioneer Area* (1934); *Group Settlement: Ethnic Communities in Western Canada* (1936); *Canadian Frontiers of Settlement* (1937); and *The New North West* (1947).

Harold Adams Innis

Reproduced by permission of the Adelphi University Archives and Special Collections (Garden City, NY)

Harold Adams Innis (1894–1952) Innis was born in Otterville, Ontario, and received his bachelor's and master's degrees from McMaster University and his Ph.D. from the University of Chicago. Innis is remembered for two primary contributions: his analysis of Canada's political economy through his staples thesis hypothesis and his studies of media theory. His investigation into Canada's experience as an exporter of raw materials and grains was instrumental in helping Canadian sociologists understand and explain the linkage between material goods, regionalism, and the political superstructure. His primary contribution to the field of communications was his division of different media *biases* and how they influenced society. For example, a time bias (e.g., ancient hieroglyphics) leads to a stable society over time but is fixed in geographic location, while a space bias (e.g., written communication on paper) creates a much more flexible and precise form of communication that is easy to transport over great distances.

Aileen D. Ross (1902–1995) Born in Montreal to a wealthy family, Ross became interested in sociology as she travelled through Europe and witnessed crushing poverty first-hand. She received her Ph.D. from the University of Chicago in 1951, but had been teaching for some time at the University of Toronto and at McGill University. Her work has strong ties to gender roles and includes *Control and Leadership in Women's Groups* (1958), *Becoming a Nurse* (1961), *Changing Aspirations and Roles: Middle and Upper Class Indian Women Enter the Business World* (1976), and *Businesswomen and Business Cliques in Three Cities: Delhi, Sydney, and Montreal* (1979).

S. D. (Samuel Delbert) Clark (1910–2003) Born in Lloydminster, Alberta, Clark was instrumental to the development of sociology in Canada. After completing his Ph.D. at the University of Toronto in 1938 he started teaching in the department of political economy there. Later, Clark became the first chair of the department of sociology at the University of Toronto in 1963. He remained in the department for his entire career and retired in 1976. Clark was influenced by his colleague Harold Innis, also at the University of Toronto, and wrote many books about the political and economic landscape of Canada, including *The Social Development of Canada* (1942), *The Developing Canadian Community* (1962), and *Canadian Society in Historical Perspective* (1976).

Helen Abell (1919–2003) Born in Medicine Hat, Alberta, Abell is generally regarded as the founder of rural sociology in Canada. After her family moved to Toronto, she attended the Macdonald Institute in Guelph and the University of Toronto and completed her master's (1947) and Ph.D. (1951) in rural sociology at Cornell University. After graduation, she returned to Canada and focused her work on farm families and the effects of modernization, contributions by farm women, and the decline of family farming. Her recognition of the efforts of farm wives was an invaluable contribution to both public consciousness and policymakers (Eichler, 2001).

Helen Abell
Courtesy of the Helen C. Abell Collection, Archival and Special Collections, University of Guelph Library, Archives and Research Collections, MacOdrum Library, Carleton University

Kathleen Herman (1920–) Born in Camrose, Alberta, Herman was one of seven in a desperately poor family. After hearing Aileen Ross speak, Herman decided to study sociology, and went on to teach at Queen's University for more than 20 years. She was chair of the Canadian Sociology and Anthropology Association's Canadianization movement and was an active supporter of women's rights through the Royal Commission on the Status of Women.

John Porter (1921–1979) Porter was born in Vancouver and completed his education at the London School of Economics in the United Kingdom. *The Vertical Mosaic: An Analysis of Social Class and Power in Canada* (1965) was his most important work. It was an investigation into equality in Canada and the use of power by Canada's bureaucratic, economic, and political elites. Porter challenged the impression that Canada was a classless society with no barriers to opportunity. He was the first full-time sociologist to be hired at Carleton University, where he spent almost 30 years teaching and writing.

John Porter
Courtesy of the Helen C. Abell Collection, Archival and Special Collections, University of Guelph Library, Archives and Research Collections, MacOdrum Library, Carleton University

Ruth Rittenhouse Morris (1933–2001) Born and raised in the United States, Morris moved to Canada in 1968. Her work focused on the attempt to abolish the penal system in favour of an alternative justice system. She founded several organizations, including Rittenhouse, Toronto Justice Council, St. Stephen's Conflict Resolution Service, and the Toronto Bail Program. She received many awards for her work, including a Governor General's Award, the YMCA Peace Medallion, the J. S. Woodsworth Award for the Elimination of Racial Discrimination, and the Order of Canada. Her books include *Stories of Transformative Justice* (2000) and *Transcending Trauma* (2005) (Lindsey, Beach & Ravelli, 2009, p. 13; York University Archives and Special Collections, 2007).

European and North American sociologists have made many contributions to the discipline, but we cannot assume that sociology is interested only in Western industrialized nations. Sociology today must take a broader look at the human experience and appreciate the importance of a global perspective.

⑧ Sociology in a Global Perspective

globalization

A worldwide process involving the production, distribution, and consumption of technological, political, economic, and sociocultural goods and services.

Understanding the historical footprint of sociology is important, as is an appreciation of the contributions of Canadian scholars. However, it is equally, if not more, important to look beyond our own Western boundaries and consider the dynamic forces of **globalization**, a process involving the production, distribution, and consumption of technological, political, economic, and sociocultural goods and services on a global basis (Hedley, 2002). Globalization is discussed in more detail in Chapter 19, but suffice it to say that our world today is increasingly interconnected and intermingled. As news events are presented in real time around the globe (e.g., terrorist attacks on the World Trade Center), we realize that the world feels as if it is becoming a much smaller place.

Canadian media scholar Marshall McLuhan is recognized for coining the term *global village* in his book *The Gutenberg Galaxy* (1962).[2] He used the phrase to describe how media collapse space and time and enable people everywhere to interact and experience life on a global scale. In effect, technology has shrunk the globe to the size of a village where we perceive a closeness that transcends the traditional boundaries of time and space. This discussion certainly relates to one of our questions at the beginning of the chapter, as it appears that communication technologies have in fact changed how we perceive and understand each other.

However, there is much more to a global perspective than simply an analysis of technology. Globalization also implies a realization of the primacy of capitalism as a defining feature of the global economy. Just as we investigated your identity as being defined by your socioeconomic class, gender, etc., as a sociologist you need to realize that Canadians have been taught to assume that capitalism is by default the only economic system possible. While it is hard to argue that another economic strategy can rival the dominance of capitalism, using your sociological imagination and seeing the strange in the familiar means asking whether capitalism is the right option or the only one available. Capitalism has enabled a great deal of wealth to be produced around the world; however, for many the concern is where that wealth has ended up.

As the map in Figure 1.1 demonstrates, much of the world's wealth is held in the Global North and the world's poverty in the Global South (Shah, 2009a). In fact, of the roughly 6 billion people alive today, only 1 billion live in developed countries. The remaining 5 billion live in developing countries, where many survive on less than a dollar a day. We must realize that poverty is not just lack of money but also lack of basic nutrition, health care, education, freedom, and personal autonomy. Poverty, then, is about being invisible, having no voice, and feeling powerless to improve your life or the lives of your loved ones (World Bank Group, 2010). To some extent, McLuhan was right in perceiving that everyone today is linked through such factors as international trade and migration, yet clearly our relationships are not equal. The world is out of balance: the 1 billion who live in developed countries control 80 percent of global resources. This leaves the other 5 billion people to try to survive on the remaining 20 percent. Is this fair? Is it justifiable?

Sociology studies how and why human beings interact and by doing so attempts to understand how to confront social issues such as poverty. Sociology is unique in that it can investigate human phenomena from local, individual realities to global, collective consciousness.

---

2 In fact, Wyndham Lewis was the first to use the term *global village* in his book *America and Cosmic Man* (1949), but McLuhan was the first to express the idea as it relates to media and is believed to have arrived at the concept independent of Lewis's work (McLuhan, n.d.).

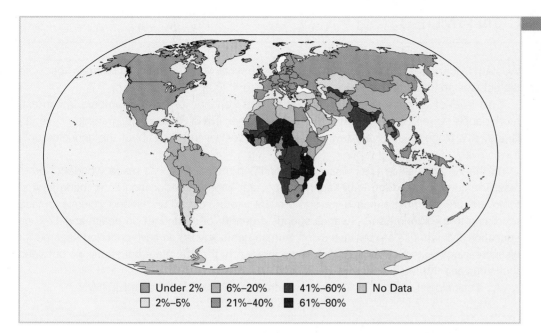

FIGURE 1.1

People Living on Less than $1 a Day

Based on Shah 2009b.

■ Under 2% ■ 6%–20% ■ 41%–60% □ No Data
□ 2%–5% ■ 21%–40% ■ 61%–80%

BOX 1.4 ISSUES IN GLOBAL CONTEXT

The Rwandan Genocide—20 Years Later

Under the terms of the *Treaty of Versailles* (1918) the former German colony of Rwanda-Urundi was made a League of Nations protectorate to be governed by Belgium. Soon after assuming control, Belgian officials turned the traditional Hutu–Tutsi relationship into a class system. The minority Tutsis (14 percent of the population) were given various advantages over the Hutu majority (85 percent of the population), such as Western-style education. In 1926, the Belgians introduced ethnic identity cards to distinguish Tutsis from Hutus. In 1959, the Hutus revolted and challenged Belgian rule and the Tutsi elite. Over the next 30 years, many people were killed as the majority Hutus continued to solidify their control over the Tutsi minority (McQueen, 2005).

On April 6, 1994, Rwandan president Juvenal Habyarimana, a Hutu, was killed when his plane was shot down. Violence erupted the following day, and over the next 100 days, 800 000 Tutsis and thousands of Hutus were killed. The international community did nothing to prevent the genocide, nor did it get involved once it began. At the time, there was virtually no media coverage of the slaughter.

Findings from the *Report of the Independent Inquiry into the Actions of the United Nations during the 1994 Genocide in Rwanda* suggest that the United Nations failed in its responsibility to protect the Rwandan people (United Nations, 1999, p. 30). The inquiry offered several recommendations for changes at the UN: increase its peacekeeping capacity, be more proactive when human rights violations occur, develop more efficient communications strategies, and acknowledge responsibility for what happened in Rwanda in 1994.

Kuperman (2000) suggests that resources directed toward political prevention are always preferred over military intervention. He argues that

The people of Rwanda are still recovering from the genocide of 1994.

David Turnley/Corbis

CONTINUED

Western leaders failed to appreciate and anticipate what was happening in Rwanda "because the act was so immoral that it was difficult to picture" (Kuperman, 2000, p. 117).

This level of violence is indeed difficult to comprehend. To put the numbers in context, more people were killed in the Rwandan genocide than live in Quebec City, Canada's seventh-largest city. Nonetheless, very few people in the West even heard about the genocide until it was over.

In the 20 years since the massacre, Rwanda, in many ways, has made wonderful progress. The current president, Paul Kagame, says that improving education and putting an end to poverty are the most effective ways to prevent a return of civil unrest and violence. In fact, according to the World Bank, Rwanda spends a quarter of its budget on health and 17% on education. While these are positive signs, human rights advocates have criticized Kagame for his increasingly authoritarian approach and some worry that the old ethnic tensions between the Hutus and the Tutsis may explode again (Dixon, 2014).

As a sociologist, do you believe a massacre like this could happen again? Why?

Summary

❶ The sociological perspective views the social world through the dynamic relationships between individuals and the larger social network in which they live.

❷ The sociological imagination, as defined by C. W. Mills, is the ability to view yourself as the product of social forces. In this way, you enrich your understanding of personal circumstances by seeing them within a wider social context.

❸ Peter Berger emphasized that the ability to recognize general social patterns in particular events is one of the hallmarks of the sociological perspective. Berger further encouraged the ability to perceive the strange in the familiar—that is, to question the assumptions behind seemingly rational, everyday social phenomena.

❹ Sociology emerged from the need to understand the striking social changes that occurred in Europe in the form of three revolutions: scientific, industrial, and political.

❺ A positivist approach views science as the rightful foundation of all understanding; it holds that there exists a single, objective reality that is knowable through observation, experimentation, and logic. Anti-positivists contend that we cannot understand our social world solely through science; we need to appreciate human subjectivity and judgments of moral value.

❻ Macrosociology, or the study of society as a whole, had its early influence in the theories of Karl Marx, Émile Durkheim, and Max Weber. The leading theorists of microsociology, the study of individual or small-group dynamics within a larger society, were George Herbert Mead, Charles Horton Cooley, and Herbert Blumer.

❼ Canadian sociology is influenced by four factors that differentiate it from the American tradition: the country's geography and regionalism, its focus on political economy, the Canadianization movement, and its radical nature.

❽ In today's interconnected world, it is vital to consider the dynamic forces of globalization and the inequities that result from the primacy of capitalism in the global economy.

Key Terms

achieved status *9*

agency *7*

anti-positivism *15*

ascribed status *9*

cheerful robots *5*

globalization *26*

macrosociology *19*

microsociology *19*

patriarchy *8*

personal troubles *4*

political economy *22*

positivism *14*

qualitative sociology *16*

quality of mind *4*

quantitative sociology *16*

social issues *4*

socioeconomic status (SES) *8*

sociological imagination *4*

sociological perspective *3*

sociology *3*

structure *7*

symbolic interactionism *20*

values *16*

Reviewing the Concepts

1. What is the sociological perspective? What examples would you use to help your room-mate understand the concept?

2. With reference to C. W. Mills's concept of the quality of mind, describe how someone with very little formal education can possess it while someone with a Ph.D. may not. What factors do you think influence a person's ability to gain the quality of mind?

3. Define *agency* and *structure* as they relate to sociology. How can these concepts be applied to your experience at college/university?

4. Review the similarities and differences between *micro-* and *macro*sociological theories.

Applying Your Sociological Imagination

1. How might you apply the sociological imagination to students' desire for high grades?

2. Using content from the chapter, how might a sociologist explain the popularity of Facebook?

3. As a sociologist, explore how privilege has or has not played a role in defining the person you have become.

4. Discuss how the sociological perspective helps one to better understand the individual and the collective.

MySocLab

Visit MySocLab to access a variety of online resources that will help you prepare for tests and apply your knowledge.

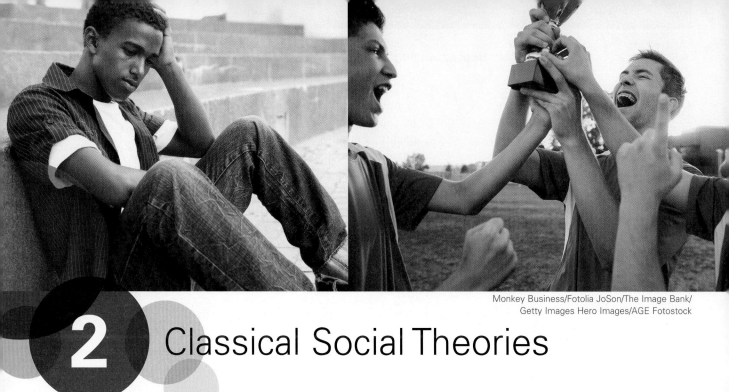

Monkey Business/Fotolia JoSon/The Image Bank/
Getty Images Hero Images/AGE Fotostock

2 Classical Social Theories

For us, these two images expose so much about what social theory can teach us. Why are so many young people lonely even though they have 500 Facebook friends? What it is about winning, competition, and being accepted by others that is so important to us? Theory helps us understand situations like these, as well as thousands more.

As social beings, we constantly assess ourselves in relation to those around us. If you have ever been around young children, you will know first-hand that one of their favourite words is *why*? "Why did you give that man a toonie for cleaning our windshield? Why do terrorists want to hurt us? Why is the sky blue?" All of these questions reflect a child's attempt to understand the world. As adults, we have the same desire for understanding, of course, and inevitably begin to think theoretically about the things we wonder about. For example, have you ever wondered why, on average, women make less than men for doing the same job? Sociological theory helps us explain how social forces influence our daily lives, whether we are business persons, skinheads, single mothers, or computer nerds.

A *theory* is a statement or analytical tool that tries to explain how certain facts or variables are related in order to predict future events. Social scientists use theories to help direct research and to inspire discussion and debate about how the world works; without theory we are often left floundering when we try to explain what we see. As a new sociologist, the thought of studying theory probably does not sound very interesting, and to a certain extent we understand this. However, as sociologists who have taught thousands of students over the years, we can assure you that your efforts to understand sociological theory now will serve you well later. Virtually all senior sociology courses require an understanding and application of theory on tests, papers, and assignments. Therefore, the more comfortable you are with theory, the better your chances are of understanding the social world and excelling in your sociology classes.

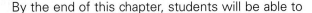

LEARNING OBJECTIVES

By the end of this chapter, students will be able to

❶ Describe the early contributions of social philosophers and their relevance to classical sociological theory.

❷ Review and critique functionalism and the contributions of its principal theorists.

❸ Review and critique conflict theory and the contributions of its founding theorists.

❹ Review and critique symbolic interactionism and the contributions of its founding theorists.

❺ Describe how marginalized voices contributed to sociological theory.

"Seeing" the World Theoretically

Watch

What Is the Importance of Sociological Theory to an Understanding of Society and Social Behaviour?

A **theory** is a statement that tries to explain how certain facts or variables are related in order to predict future events. The best way for new students of sociology to begin thinking about individual theories and theorists is to see the world as theorists do. Metaphorically speaking, imagine putting on a pair of sunglasses that are tinted with a different colour for each theorist. If you are able to view the world from the perspective of any given theorist, you are clearly demonstrating your sociological imagination—you are seeing the world from another person's perspective. Both authors of this text have their own theoretical preferences, but when they teach students, they are careful to present the ideas and perspectives of all theorists equally and to help students look at the world as the theorist would like them to. What is important is not that a certain theorist is "right" but, rather, that you develop the skills required to see the world from alternative perspectives. As you progress in your studies, you will no doubt find that each sociological theory has strengths and weaknesses and that each of the theorists we examine offers unique insights into our social world.

As you begin your reading of theory, consider whether each theorist's insights can be applied to society today. If a theory can help you explain a current issue or event, this strengthens its usefulness; if it cannot, be sure to consider why. By actively engaging with the theories in this way, you will be better able to both synthesize and compare different theoretical perspectives—a skill that all strong sociology students share.

theory A statement that tries to explain how certain facts or variables are related in order to predict future events.

❶ Philosophical Roots of Classical Sociological Theory

Our review of the philosophical roots of sociology begins with the writings of Thomas Hobbes (circa 1600) and concludes with the conservative reaction to the Enlightenment (circa 1700–1750). The striking developments in thought over this 150-year period provided the foundation for sociological theory. Though much of what you will read in this chapter is drawn from European history, it is important to appreciate that sociology emerged as a result of the work and ideas of many thinkers from around the world: from Thucydides, Plato, and the ancient Greek historians and philosophers, to the works of Ibn Khaldun, Sima Quian, and others. The insights of these thinkers helped to inform other, more recent thinkers, including those who have come to be known as the founders of modern sociology. Human history is a vast, interconnected web and as such, the modern fruits of all forms of inqury do not belong to any one intellectual tradition or person.

THOMAS HOBBES (1588–1679)

Thomas Hobbes, whose ideas were introduced in Chapter 1, suggested that people are responsible for creating the social world around them and that society could thus be changed through conscious reflection (Delaney, 2004, p. 2). This perspective conflicted with the earlier belief that human beings existed by virtue of God's will and possessed very little individual agency. This is an important point: Hobbes was one of the first theorists to view people as responsible and accountable for the society they created.

natural state Hobbes's conception of the human condition before the emergence of formal social structures.

Hobbes is also well known for his analysis of how humans existed before the emergence of formal social structures (e.g., government), a condition he referred to as the **natural state** (Westby, 1991, p. 24). Hobbes believed that people in the natural state existed just as all other animals did. However, humans were also naturally curious, which inspired them to learn about their social and physical environment (Nuri Yurdusev, 2006, p. 308). Hobbes also believed that, at their most basic, people are motivated by self-interest and the pursuit of power. Living in the natural state would have been a brutal existence; since everyone was in direct competition with each other, people would have lived in a constant state of fear (Delaney, 2004, p. 2). With their wants always seeming to exceed what was available, there would be constant potential for a "war of all against all" (Kavka, 1983). In his most famous work, *Leviathan* (1651), Hobbes argued that since people are naturally rational beings, in order to gain peace and protection they would be willing to enter into a collective agreement that would see them give up some of their individual freedom and autonomy to an absolute authority (e.g., democracy, monarchy) (Westby, 1991, p. 24). *Leviathan*, meaning "monster" or "ruler," refers to this authority apparatus.

> > >

The Arab Spring movement in 2010 was a clear indication that revolutionary movements are as evident today as they were in the past.

Benedicte Desrus/Alamy

This collective agreement represented an important transition in that it demonstrated the human capacity to forgo independence and autonomy in return for collective benefit. The role of government was to preserve peace but also to allow individuals to fulfill personal interests (e.g., acquiring wealth) that were consistent with their natural desire to gain personal power and influence, albeit within the confines of law (Delaney, 2004, p. 2; Nuri Yurdusev, 2006, p. 311). Further, Hobbes suggested that because the Leviathan is the result of collective will, the collective has the right to revolt against it should it fail to fulfill its obligations (Westby, 1991, p. 24). Hobbes's belief that the collective has the responsibility and power to overthrow a corrupt government was part of the justification behind the French and American Revolutions, and more recently, the protests in Egypt, Libya, and Syria.

Although no one can know for sure what the natural state was like (because it occurred before literacy and therefore no written records of it exist), a discussion of what people are really like, deep down, is a fascinating one. For example, do you believe that people are basically decent and want to help others or that they are basically corrupt and out for themselves? The answer to this question is one that defines how some theorists approach their understanding of the social world.

Hobbes's legacy with regards to the development of sociological theory is his assertion that individuals are the basic building blocks of society. Since human beings are "active, assertive and dynamic being[s]" (Nuri Yurdusev, 2006, p. 308), the appropriate role for government is to preserve the individual's ability to achieve self-interests (e.g., through the accumulation of wealth) while protecting everyone from others' natural, self-serving inclinations.

JOHN LOCKE (1632–1704)

John Locke continued much of Hobbes's work but approached his investigation of society from a very different perspective. While Hobbes believed that society was the result of human agency, Locke argued that God was responsible for the emergence of society and government. However, the key to understanding Locke's philosophy is his belief, set out in his *Essay Concerning Human Understanding* (1690), that people are born *tabula rasa* (a Latin term meaning "blank slate"), suggesting that there can be no knowledge independent of experience (see Arp, 2013; Gintis, 2006). Additionally, according to Locke, God granted certain rights to people—for example, the right to self-preservation and to private property. This approach helped Locke secure his belief in the sanctity of individual autonomy, a point of agreement with Hobbes. Using this foundation of individual rights, Locke was able to define the democratic principles that would become the foundation of the American Declaration of Independence (Delaney, 2004, p. 6).

Locke also disagreed with Hobbes's assertion that people in their natural state were so fearful of each other that they needed a government to protect them. Instead, Locke viewed the emergence of the state as being more about preserving an individual's right to maintain property than about protecting individuals from warring against each other. In this sense, the government itself has no rights but only obligations to the members of society. Locke ultimately agreed with Hobbes that if the state falters in its ability to provide what the collective needs, it should be overthrown.

Locke, as well as Hobbes, was committed to the ideals of democratic leadership and the rights of the masses to assert their power over corruption when it was necessary and warranted. Locke's contribution to social theory was his advocacy of individual freedom and autonomy, which ultimately built the foundation upon which democracy and the US Constitution were established.

CHARLES DE MONTESQUIEU (1689–1755)

Charles de Montesquieu's approach to the study of society was markedly different from that of earlier theorists. Turner, Beeghley, and Powers (2002, p. 310) suggest that early theorists were concerned with answering the question of where society originated, and that their philosophical answers were generally given in two parts. First, there was an original natural state that was either warlike (Hobbes) or peaceful (Locke). Second, people created society by agreeing to a social contract that subjugated them to a government. However, Montesquieu challenged these views by suggesting that people had never existed outside, or without, society. Instead of humans defining and creating society, he proposed that humans were defined and created *by* society.

Montesquieu's most famous works were *The Persian Letters* (1721) and *The Spirit of the Laws* (1748). *Persian Letters* may be the first clear example of the sociological perspective (Farganis, 2000, p. 1). The book is a fictional account of the letters exchanged between two Persian noblemen (Persia was where Iran is located today) while travelling through France. What makes the work so fascinating is that Montesquieu (who published the book anonymously) was able to write the letters from the perspective of someone outside his own culture. In effect, he practised the sociological imagination by forcing himself, and his readers, to look at themselves and see the *strange* in the *familiar*. The book was very popular reading at the time, both for its humour and for showing the French how to view themselves differently—in effect, sociologically.

The Spirit of the Laws was the result of more than 20 years of work by Montesquieu, who believed that analyzing the laws of a society enables one to see what that society deems to be important. In other words, the laws define the *spirit* of the people. Montesquieu employed **ideal types**—forms that are closest to the perfect form—to categorize three types of government from the infinite variations that existed. They were the *Republic* (which had two forms: democracy and aristocracy), the *Monarchy,* and *Despotism* (Turner, Beeghley, & Powers, 2002, p. 312; Zeitlin, 1994, pp. 8–9). Montesquieu believed that each form of government demonstrated different underlying social principles. The spirit behind the Republic was virtue, behind the Monarchy was honour, and behind Despotism was fear. According to Montesquieu, the variation in the forms of government did not happen by chance, and the variation provided the social scientist with a unique and rich view into the values of the people. Note that Montesquieu believed that the true nature or spirit of a society is not what it is (i.e., how it exists) but instead what it wants to become. Further, his interest in studying other countries and cultures demonstrated his comparative approach to research methods, and his application of ideal types was pioneering at the time (Zeitlin, 1994).

Montesquieu's contribution to sociological theory is his appreciation for cultural diversity (as evidenced in *The Persian Letters*) and his comparative methodology, which allowed social scientists to analyze various social phenomena cross-nationally.

JEAN-JACQUES ROUSSEAU (1712–1778)

Jean-Jacques Rousseau was one of the most famous philosophers of his time, and his insights into the *state of nature* and the *social contract* continue to inspire reflection and debate (Scott, 2012).

Rousseau agreed with Montesquieu that human beings did exist within a state of nature—a state in which people were presocial: "Natural man is simply man divested of what he has acquired in society" (Zeitlin, 1994, p. 19). Rousseau's most famous work, *The Social Contract* (1762), builds on his belief that the natural state was a primitive condition before laws or morality. However, in contrast to both Hobbes and Montesquieu, Rousseau did not believe that this natural state was an awful existence in which people were pitted against each other, but instead one in which people existed in a symbiotic and idyllic relationship based on equality (Westby, 1991, p. 40; Zeitlin, 1994, p. 21).

As noted earlier, the state of nature was purely a hypothetical construct; there is no way to reconstruct what it was really like. Nevertheless, Rousseau believed that we needed to understand the basic nature of the human condition so we could build a society that most closely resembled our natural tendencies and desires. A perfect society, in other words, would mirror our natural state. According to Rousseau, when our social arrangements

✳-[Explore

Jack Layton's Legacy and Our Yearning for Political Civility

ideal types **Classic or pure forms of a given social phenomenon (e.g., to some, the United States is an ideal form of democracy).**

> > > Thinking Sociologically

Do you believe Canadians have a defining *spirit*? Do Americans? Discuss.

were inconsistent with these natural rules, we suffered social problems (e.g., high crime and suicide rates).

Rousseau suggested that human beings are the only animal that is perfectible, and that people could achieve their potential only through society (Zeitlin, 1994). The inspiration for moving beyond the natural state and toward collective arrangements was increasing population pressures that forced people to work together to meet their material (e.g., food) needs. As humans progressed as a collective, certain individuals prospered because they were more gifted farmers, orators, or artisans, and for the first time society began to experience social and economic inequality. It was in this environment that Rousseau saw the greatest need for government; like Hobbes, he saw that people needed to be protected from each other and needed to secure their private property (Zeitlin, 1994, p. 23). The rise of government, then, was really the manifestation of the social contract.

Rousseau believed that people entered into the social contract as free and equal individuals, and not because they had to, as Hobbes would assert. While there is some submission of personal autonomy to the collective, there is also great potential for individual and social benefit. Zeitlin (1994) writes,

> The new society, or social contract, enables the individual to be absorbed into the common, general will without losing his own will, because in giving himself to the common will he gives himself to an impersonal force. When a man submits to it, no immoral dependency results. He loses little or nothing and gains in return the assurance that he will be protected by the full force of society against the encroachment of individuals and groups. He is now a member of a society of equals and has regained an equality not unlike the one he enjoyed in nature—but in a new form and on a higher level. (p. 26)

In Rousseau's view of the state, then, people can both aspire to their individual pursuits and be protected from others on the basis of socially defined rules (i.e., laws). However, Rousseau also cautioned that government is a corrupting element in society that will continually try to undermine the autonomy of the individual. Members of society therefore must be vigilant in keeping their governments accountable and representative of the collective will. Some have argued that Rousseau's belief in liberty, equality, and the accountability of government led ultimately to the French Revolution (Gitelson, Dudley, & Dubnick, 2012).

Rousseau's contribution to social theory was his analysis of the social contract and his belief in the autonomy of the individual—a clear demonstration of Enlightenment thinking.

THE ENLIGHTENMENT

The Enlightenment period represents an intellectual movement that began around 1650 and ended with the French Revolution (1789–1799). Enlightenment thinking challenged 400 years of Christian scholarship devoted to discovering God's intentions and the domination of knowledge practised by the Church (Zeitlin, 1994, pp. 2–3).

The main group of Enlightenment intellectuals were French, often referred to as the **Philosophes**—philosophers who advocated critical thinking and practical knowledge. They built on the natural sciences; in particular, Sir Isaac Newton confirmed that the universe was orderly and could be understood by science and human reason (Delaney, 2004, p. 11). The Philosophes also fought any attempt to limit free thinking and expression and believed that over time the human condition could be improved for all.

Before the Enlightenment, people's thinking was directed by God, the Church, and the aristocracy. Enlightenment thinking, however, promoted human agency and thus was a clear continuation of the writings of Hobbes, Locke, Montesquieu, and Rousseau. Today, seeing ourselves as engaged and autonomous beings seems obvious, but at the time this independence of thought created a great deal of turmoil, not only for the Church but also for society as a whole. The Enlightenment was nothing less than a reordering of how people saw the world and their role in it.

Philosophes French philosophers during the Enlightenment period who advocated critical thinking and practical knowledge.

> > >

The American and
French Revolutions
were arguably the
result of Enlightenment
thinking, the basis
for the conservative
reaction and, ultimately,
the birth of sociology.

Eugene Delacroix/The Gallery Collection/Corbis

Enlightenment thinking was the culmination of the inherently revolutionary views expressed in Machiavelli's *The Prince,* published more than 250 years earlier. As discussed in Chapter 1, Machiavelli suggested that anyone could become a prince given the right set of circumstances. Enlightenment philosophers continued this line of reasoning by challenging many beliefs that were grounded in tradition (e.g., inherited titles and wealth that were not based on demonstrated ability or skill) (Ritzer, 2000, p. 11).

The ability of the masses to take control of their lives and challenge their oppressors ultimately led to the American and French Revolutions. Some estimates suggest that over 25 000 people died during the American Revolution (Zinn, 2012) and that between 17 000 and 40 000 people were executed (mostly by guillotine) during the French Revolution (Research Machines, 2007). It is ironic that Enlightenment thinking, which advocated rational and practical inquiry, could result in so much death and destruction. However, both revolutions had a lasting influence: For the first time in history, entire societies were completely reorganized according to the secular ideals of social equality and liberty (Giddens, 1987, as cited in Delaney, 2004, p. 14). The long-term social and political ramifications of these revolutions cannot be underestimated. However, the significance of these events to sociology has less to do with the events themselves and how they fostered greater personal freedoms and equality and more to do with the commitment they engendered to ensure that such social turmoil and bloodshed never occurred again. In essence, then, sociology was born not from the revolutionary ideas of Enlightenment thinking but, rather, from the conservative reaction against them.

CONSERVATIVE REACTION TO ENLIGHTENMENT THINKING: THE BIRTH OF SOCIOLOGY

Enlightenment thinkers who advocated for individual autonomy, liberty, and the primacy of rationality and reason were challenged by conservatives who promoted a return to earlier times when society was more stable. In effect, conservatives challenged the very basis of Enlightenment thinking. After all, they would suggest, the culmination of that thinking led to revolution, something no one should want. As discussed, one of the guiding principles of the Enlightenment was the belief in individual autonomy and the absolute necessity of independent thought and reflection. To Enlightenment thinkers, the individual was the building block for the entire society. In contrast, conservatives believed that society is not the product of individuals but, rather, an entity in itself, independent and separate from the individuals who make it up (Delaney, 2004, p. 12).

In an invaluable synthesis, Zeitlin (1981, as cited in Ritzer, 2000, p. 12) provides 10 propositions of conservative reaction thinking. Note that they are counter to virtually every principle behind the Enlightenment:

1. Society exists on its own with its own laws and is independent of individuals.

2. Society, not the individual, is the most important unit of social analysis, and it produces the individual, not the other way around.

3. Individuals are not the basic unit of social interest; society consists of components such as roles, relationships, structures, and institutions, and individuals are simply those who fill these positions.

4. The smallest unit of social analysis is the family.

5. The parts of society are interrelated and interdependent.

6. Change is a threat both to individuals and to society as a whole.

7. Social institutions (e.g., education system, legal system) are beneficial both to individuals and to society as a whole.

8. Modern social changes (e.g., industrialization, urbanization) are disorganizing elements that create fear and anxiety and need to be diminished whenever possible.

9. Traditional elements of social life, such as ritual, ceremony, and worship, (considered irrational factors by Enlightenment thinkers) are important to society and tend to offer a stabilizing influence.

10. A return to social hierarchies would be good both for individuals and for the collective because they promote a system of differential status and reward. This reinforces the principle that healthy competition between individuals is a good thing.

The importance of the conservative reaction to classical theory cannot be overemphasized. Enlightenment thinking was inherently revolutionary as it confirmed the importance of self-reflection, and challenged tradition, the Church, and the rich and powerful. Conversely, conservative reaction thinking suggested that society was independent of human experience, that change threatened everyone, and that hierarchical arrangements were natural and necessary for a stable society. As you read about the various theories, you should be able to determine if they are more consistent with Enlightenment or conservative reaction thinking. The legacy of the conservative reaction to sociological theory is still evident today.

Legacy of the Conservative Reaction for Sociological Theory Traditionally, sociological theory is generally separated into the macro/micro perspectives introduced in Chapter 1. Recall that macrosociology investigates society-wide structures and phenomena (e.g., education system, political economy) and is more associated with conservative reaction theory, while microsociology tends to focus on individual and small-group behaviours (e.g., how people act during a first date) and is more consistent with Enlightenment thinking. Macro- and microsociology differ along other lines as well. Macrosociology tends to be deductive, sees behaviour as predictable, and is associated with European classical social theory. Microsociology tends to be

> > > Thinking Sociologically

Compare and contrast how Enlightenment thinkers and conservative reaction theorists might explain legalizing marijuana. Are there any areas where these two perspectives might agree?

inductive, sees behaviour as creative, and is characteristically North American and contemporary (Wallace & Wolf, 2006). While these classifications are not exact (as will be reinforced here and in Chapter 3), they offer an important template with which to compare classical and contemporary sociological theory.

So far, this overview has been very broad so that you could gain a general appreciation of classical sociological theory. Next, we build on this foundation and delve more deeply into individual theoretical perspectives.

❷ Functionalism

Watch
Functionalism

Functionalists view the social world as a dynamic system of interrelated and interdependent parts. Social structures (e.g., the postsecondary education system) exist to help people fulfill their wants and desires, as defined by social values. For example, a good education will make it easier to get a well-paying job, which is an expression of our value system that recognizes and promotes the accumulation of material wealth as an expression of success. Therefore, postsecondary education is functional in the sense that it makes this possible. Universities and colleges are certainly structural (i.e., they have buildings, employees, operating procedures, and enrolment policies) but they are also functional. The two-part system of structures and their associated functions has led some to call this theory *structural-functionalism*. However, consistent with the position of Wallace and Wolf (2006), we prefer to call the approach simply *functionalism* for two main reasons. First, this term recognizes the clear link to the classical sociological theorists (e.g., Comte, Durkheim). Second, the two most famous and influential American functionalists, Robert Merton and Talcott Parsons (discussed later in this chapter), preferred the narrower, more precise terminology (see Wallace & Wolf, 2006).

organic analogy The belief that society is like an organism with interdependent and interrelated parts.

Functionalists view human society as being similar to an organism—for example, a human being—a perspective often referred to as the **organic analogy**. Like the human body, society is made up of interrelated and interdependent parts that each has a structure and performs a function for the whole. For example, your skin helps to regulate body temperature, provides surface tension, and protects you from the sun's harmful ultraviolet rays. However, it is also just one part of a much larger system. Your skin is certainly important, but it, in turn, depends on your heart, your lungs, and every other organ in your body that must work together for you to

> > >

The Occupy movement in 2011 spread across the world, including this demonstration in Calgary. For a functionalist, the Occupy movement showed that the system was not working for the majority and therefore needed to be adjusted.

The Canadian Press, Jeff McIntosh/AP Photo

continue living. By suggesting that society is like an organism, functionalists also suggest that the system's natural state of affairs is one of equilibrium, a point at which the system is stable and homeostatic. For example, how does your body react when you sit outside in very hot weather or when you work out at the gym? It sweats. Perspiration helps the body to cool itself so that it can maintain a certain temperature—if you get too hot or too cold, you will die. Your body's response to temperature is one example of how it operates as a homeostatic system, one designed to maintain regularity. When it fails this task, the system—in this case, the human body—will suffer. According to functionalists, the same homeostatic properties are present within social systems.

Like the human body, society is made up of structures that work together for the good of the collective. For a social system to be considered healthy, all individuals who are part of that social system must feel valued and content. The society must meet the needs of the majority; when it does not, the system is *sick* and must make adjustments to return to a state of equilibrium and harmony. For example, a functionalist would argue that when farmers drove their tractors through the streets of Ottawa in 2006, this action was intended to draw attention to their "rural revolution," which pointed out that the system was not meeting farmers' needs. Much like a fever is a symptom of the flu, their demonstration was a symptom of the changing nature of farming in contemporary society and an indication that the system needed to respond (see Hughes & Roesler, 2004, for a review of the concerns that inspired the farmers' rally). Short-term periods of strife and conflict can occur, but over time these events will be addressed by the system and it will return to a state of homeostasis.

Arguably, functionalism can be linked to the work of Ibn Khaldun and Auguste Comte, and to the conservative reaction movement, as well as to Vilfredo Pareto. Ibn Khaldun is considered by some to be the true founder of sociology because he was the first to develop important sociological concepts such as social forces, social facts, and social laws. However, as described in Chapter 1, Comte is generally seen as the father of sociology; he believed that the techniques and principles used to study the physical world (i.e., the hard sciences) should be employed to study the social world, as well. Pareto (1848–1923) was another early thinker who helped to form the basic principles upon which functionalism was built. An Italian economist and sociologist, Pareto offered functionalist insights similar to Comte's, but he also argued that individuals within the system were like "molecules" that interacted because of their common interests, values, drives, and sentiments. He was one of the first to describe fully how social systems were achieved from the interrelations and mutual dependencies of all of their constituent parts. Pareto's ideas about how social systems adapt and change and at the same time maintain stability were adopted by American functionalist Talcott Parsons (Wallace & Wolf, 2006, p. 19). Another theorist, Herbert Spencer, also offered a biological model to explain human social development.

HERBERT SPENCER (1820–1903)

Herbert Spencer is best known for coining the term **survival of the fittest**—which implies that only the strong should survive—and for his application of the principles of biological evolution to human societies, referred to as *social Darwinism*. After reading Thomas Malthus's *Essay on the Principle of Population* (1998/1798), Spencer agreed that overpopulation would become more of a problem over time and believed that, as a result, people would be forced to compete over increasingly scarce resources. This led him to coin the term *survival of the fittest* 10 years before Charles Darwin developed the idea of **natural selection** (Delaney, 2004, p. 41), the biologically based principle that environmental pressures allow certain beneficial traits to be passed on to future generations. Spencer argued that growing competition would mean that those individuals and groups who were better able to compete would survive, and those who could not would perish. What is important here is that while Darwin's concept of **evolution** explains how biological organisms can be selected for by environmental pressures, Spencer moved beyond the biological application of evolution and argued that societies can be selected for as well.

This resulted in Spencer's concept of **social Darwinism**, which states that societies evolve just as biological organisms do. One can see that Spencer is employing a functionalist approach by suggesting that societies evolve because there is a *reason* for the changes (i.e., they need to

survival of the fittest Spencer's interpretation of biological principles to justify why only the strong should survive.

natural selection The biologically based principle that environmental pressures allow certain beneficial traits to be passed on to future generations.

evolution The biological process by which genetic mutations are selected for, and against, through environmental pressures.

social Darwinism Spencer's assertion that societies evolve according to the same principles as do biological organisms.

survive). Spencer's approach became very popular in the United States, as it helped to explain why some people in society were doing well and others were not: Some were simply more evolved or better adapted than others. And since this was a *natural* process, many believed that nature should be allowed to take its course and that to interfere would only make matters worse (Ritzer, 2000, p. 32). The belief that it is best to leave things alone and let them take care of themselves is called a **laissez-faire** approach, and it is often used by some economists to suggest that market forces should not be interfered with (e.g., the government should not provide subsidies to companies or industries that cannot survive on their own). Spencer's views on social welfare programs, or any initiatives intended to help those who were not doing well, were clear:

laissez-faire **A point of view that opposes regulation of or interference with natural processes.**

> Fostering the good-for-nothing at the expense of the good, is an extreme cruelty. It is a deliberate stirring-up of miseries for future generations. There is no greater curse to posterity than that of bequeathing to them an increasing population of imbeciles and idlers and criminals. . . . The whole effort of nature is to get rid of such, to clear the world of them, and make room for better. . . . If they are not sufficiently complete to live, they die, and it is best they should die. (Spencer, as noted in Ritzer, 2000, p. 34, citing Abrams, 1968, p. 74)

Clearly, this position is inconsistent with the sociological imagination since it denies an appreciation of inherited social disadvantage and outright discrimination (e.g., visible minority status; see Chapter 10).

Today, sociologists view Spencer's ideas with a critical eye for a number of reasons. First, these ideas provided justification for colonial expansion by rich and powerful countries to poor and weak ones simply because these countries were capable of it. However, to borrow a line from *Spider-Man* (2002), "With great power comes great responsibility"; to dominate the weak simply because you can is neither ethical nor moral. Second, how would Spencer explain the fact that some children of the rich maintain their advantage even though they do not possess any of their parents' positive attributes? Third, Spencer's argument equates evolution with progress and assumes that over time human society will inevitably improve (Delaney, 2004, p. 53). However, can we really argue that given climate change, international terrorism, and worldwide poverty and malnourishment, we as a species are better off today than we were 10 000 years ago? Are larger, more complex societies necessarily better than smaller, less complex ones?

While most contemporary sociologists are uncomfortable with many of Spencer's ideas, we recognize his role in helping to promote sociology (Carneiro & Perrin, 2002).

ÉMILE DURKHEIM (1858–1917)

Émile Durkheim is considered by many to be the founder of modern sociology; he committed tremendous energy to establish sociology as a legitimate and serious academic endeavour (Calhoun et al., 2012). Durkheim followed Comte's commitment to positivism, and his explanations of human behaviour were always based on his assumption that human actions originate in the collective rather than in the individual—one of the defining features of conservative reaction thinking.

At first glance, this assumption implies that the choices we make are not our own. For example, while we may believe that our decisions about what we had for breakfast this morning or what we wore to school today were not influenced by anyone but ourselves, Durkheim would argue that even these seemingly small personal choices have large social origins. Your decision to have cereal rather than a bowl of pasta for breakfast is influenced by what our society considers to be appropriate foods to eat in the morning. Further, even though it may get very hot in the summer, we doubt you will see many young men attending your sociology class wearing a skirt, even though skirts are much cooler and more comfortable than trousers. Again, the collective has defined what is appropriate for men to wear. For Durkheim, both of these examples would support his contention that individual behaviours are inspired by collective social forces (Garner, 2000, p. 64).

According to Durkheim, culture and society exist outside of the individual, are independent of the individual, and outlive the individual. He referred to this external collective force as the **collective conscience** that drives your behaviours without you even being aware of it. The collective conscience is the "totality of beliefs and sentiments common to average citizens of the same society [that] . . . has its own life" (Turner, Beeghley, & Powers, 2002, p. 332). Garner (2000, p. 64) offers an excellent example of how to conceptualize the way in which the collective influences all of us. Garner suggests that language has many of the same properties as the collective conscience. For example, all healthy human beings are able to learn language from a very early age. Language predates all of us, influences the manner in which we perceive our world, is resistant to change by any individual, and will be around after our death. In this sense, language exists outside of us but still influences us. To be able to consider the nature of the collective conscience is to understand that, for Durkheim, it is more a reflection of a shared experience by individuals than it is a "thing" that can be measured or directly studied. However, while Durkheim appreciated that studying the collective conscience directly was impossible, he believed that one could study what he called "social facts."

Social facts are general social features that exist on their own and are independent of individual manifestations—for example, laws, beliefs, customs, and morals (see Wallace & Wolf, 2006, p. 20). Social facts are the creation of human actions but are not the intended consequences of them—they are unintentional outcomes of collective behaviour and inter-action. Social facts, like the collective conscience, operate outside of anyone alive today but also can be seen as givens since they provide the context for our thinking; and by doing so, they constrain us and coerce us to behave in established, predictable ways (e.g., what you chose to have for breakfast and what you decided to wear to school today). According to Durkheim, the significance of social facts is that they are evidence of the collective con-science. Remember, since we cannot see the collective conscience directly, we are forced to study reflections of it; these reflections are the social facts.

Durkheim's analysis of suicide rates throughout Europe was a classic example of his positivistic methodology and his belief that individuals are directly influenced by the collec-tive. His book *Suicide* (1897) investigated his assertion that the degree of social integration (i.e., the extent to which individuals feel connected to each other in social networks) and the degree of social regulation (i.e., the extent to which individual desires, behaviours, and emotions are regulated by society) are important causes of a society's suicide rate (Tartaro & Lester, 2005). Figure 2.1 illustrates Durkheim's theory. He argued that societies with levels of integration or regulation that are too high or too low will suffer from higher suicide rates. For

collective conscience Durkheim's concept highlighting the totality of beliefs and sentiments that are common to the average person in a society.

social facts General social features that exist on their own and are independent of individual manifestations.

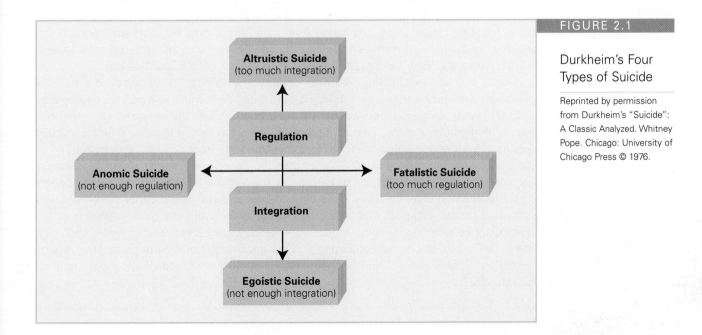

FIGURE 2.1

Durkheim's Four Types of Suicide

Reprinted by permission from Durkheim's "Suicide": A Classic Analyzed. Whitney Pope. Chicago: University of Chicago Press © 1976.

BOX 2.1 WHY SHOULD WE CARE?

Evolution and Social Darwinism

Charles Darwin was born in Shrewsbury, England, on February 12, 1809. He was educated in Edinburgh from 1825–1827, where he studied medicine but dropped out after his second year. From 1828 to 1831 Darwin attended Christ's College in Cambridge to study theology. It was there that he met Professor J. S. Henslow, who recommended Darwin for the position of naturalist on a survey voyage of the *HMS Beagle*. The voyage lasted five years from 1831 to 1836 (Kimble & Wertheimer, 1998, p.18).

Charles Darwin's writings include *The Origin of Species by Means of Natural Selection* (1859) and *The Descent of Man* (1871). His research pointed to a biological process he termed *natural selection*, which meant that organisms may experience genetic mutations that may help them adapt to changes in their physical environments (Park, 2004, pp. 40–42). A modern example of natural selection is demonstrated by rats, which have recently become immune to the drug Warfarin that was once a primary component of rat poisons (Pelz et al., 2005). Natural selection occurred when a single rat was born with a random genetic mutation that protected it from Warfarin and allowed it to pass this trait on to its offspring. Since this mutation was beneficial it is referred to as a *selective advantage*. What is important to realize about genetic evolution is that it is based on random mutations—evolution is not directed and may work against you just as often as for you. Darwin's work is grounded on biology principles and should be viewed in those terms.

Herbert Spencer, however, read the ideas of Darwin and adapted them to the study of society. Spencer applied Darwin's evolution to human *societies* and this approach was referred to as *social Darwinism* (McIntyre, 2006, p. 22). He believed that evolution occurs in the social environment as well as the biological—societies that are better suited to their environment flourish, while those that are not die out. This idea inspired Spencer to coin the phrase "survival of the fittest" in the mid-nineteenth century.

While Spencer opened the debate about who was *fit* and *unfit* in society, he was certainly not the only one to do so. The eugenics movement was seen in almost all modern societies during the first half of the twentieth century (Jackson & Weidman, 2006, p.109). Eugenics is a pseudo-scientific approach that argues that the best way to improve the human race is to improve the gene pool. In 1916, American lawyer Madison Grant published *The Passing of the Great Race*, in which he argued that the Nordic race was superior to all other racial types, including blacks, Jews, and Native Americans. At the time his ideas were popular and approved of by many, most notably perhaps by Adolf Hitler, who referred to Grant's work in his autobiography, *Mein Kampf* (1924) (Jackson & Weidman, 2006, pp. 110–112).

During the first part of the twentieth century, the United States launched a national campaign of ethnic cleansing by subjecting the "unfit" population to legislated segregation and sterilization programs. The victims included poor people, brown-haired white people, blacks, immigrants, Indians, Eastern European Jews, the sick, and anyone else classified outside the superior genetic lines drawn up by American "raceologists" (Black, 2003). The campaign sterilized around 60 000 Americans. In Canada, eugenicist Helen MacMurchy encouraged the National Council of Women to support the forced sterilization of "degenerate" mothers in order to prevent the birth of "degenerate" babies. This movement was supported by the group of Alberta women in the early twentieth century known as the "Famous Five." Among its most ardent supporters were Emily Murphy, Nellie McClung, and Irene Parlby. Support was so strong that the government of Alberta passed the *Alberta Sexual Sterilization Act* in 1928. Between 1929 and 1972, 2822 individuals were sterilized (Marsh, 2007).

CONTINUED

▶

As these issues make clear, the application of science is often difficult and imperfect. Sociologists must be vigilant that their findings and social insights remain focused and not be used by some members of society to dominate and control others. The sociological perspective is grounded on the belief in the value and preservation of human diversity. As a young sociologist, how might you explain the attraction some people have to the belief that different groups of people are more highly "evolved" than others?

example, when people do not feel connected to the group, they are more likely to commit *egoistic suicide*, while if they are too connected, rates of *altruistic suicide* increase. Along the same line of reasoning, if society fails to provide adequate direction and regulation of behaviour, *anomic suicides* occur; when overregulation exists and people feel that life is too harsh and strict, people commit *fatalistic suicide* (Garner, 2000, p. 67). According to Durkheim, then, any social organization that increases a person's healthy connection to others (e.g., marriage, family, organized religion) will decrease the likelihood of suicide and minimize the chances of people suffering from anomie.

Anomie is a state of normlessness that results from a lack of clear goals and creates feelings of confusion that may ultimately result in higher suicide rates. For example, some students suffer from anomie when they attend school but really do not know what they want to do as a career or when they have graduated from school but still cannot find jobs. The feeling of doing everything right but not getting the intended rewards often makes people feel restless and unfulfilled; that is, they are suffering from anomie.

Using various national statistics, Durkheim was able to link what we consider to be one of the most personal acts (suicide) to large-scale collective phenomena. Thus, the individual's decision to commit suicide is a function of his or her relationship, or lack thereof, to the group. By exploring the interaction of individual behaviours and collective forces, Durkheim furthered sociology's commitment to investigating the interaction between individuals and society.

Durkheim is also well-known for his analysis of how societies grow and change over time. In *The Division of Labor in Society* (1964/1893), he introduced the idea that the collective conscience increases over time and that early society was much more individually oriented, harsh, and strict than it is today. Individuals today may not feel as connected to each other, but they have much more freedom than they did before. Durkheim referred to early societies as having mechanical solidarity and to contemporary society as having organic solidarity. **Mechanical solidarity** was organized around people's similarities, but people were still independent of each other since they were largely self-sufficient. People are social beings, however, and enjoy being together, particularly when they share world views and value systems. In these early societies, the division of labour was very low (the few occupations that existed were largely defined by one's sex and/or age) and people came together out of choice, which resulted in low levels of interpersonal conflict. A good example of this type of society is people who exist through the hunter-gatherer subsistence pattern.[1]

This situation contrasts with contemporary **organic solidarity**, which is organized around interdependence and the increasing division of labour. Today, people are no longer self-sufficient but instead depend on the collective to meet their individual and social

anomie Durkheim's term for a state of normlessness that results from a lack of clear goals and may ultimately result in higher suicide rates.

mechanical solidarity Describes early societies based on similarities and independence.

organic solidarity Describes later societies organized around interdependence and the increasing division of labour.

---

1 There is controversy surrounding this terminology, as some believe that *gatherer-hunter* is a less sexist term in recognition of the greater contribution of women gatherers than male hunters (Bolender, 2003).

needs. For example, how many of us know how to grow our own food, fix our own cars, or set a broken leg? Further, specialization has segmented professions to the extent that farmers grow only certain crops, mechanics work on only particular types of cars, and doctors specialize in certain diseases or ailments. We are arguably freer but are also more likely to suffer from anomie. You may have many Facebook "friends", but how many would you really trust with your secrets and how many are you confident would be there for you if you needed them?

Durkheim suggested that while we are more collectively oriented and live in a less punitive society today than in the past, we no longer have the *choice* to coexist—instead, we *need* each other to survive. Losing the ability to choose to live with the collective takes away our independence and results in more social unrest and tension because we lack a basic sense of freedom and independence. Our increasing division of labour and the resulting specialization means that we have become completely interdependent. Durkheim argued that this increasing differentiation of our roles in society was the inevitable outcome of progress since all organisms develop from simple to complex through time (Turner, Beeghley, & Powers, 2002, pp. 334–335), an idea certainly informed by Spencer's writings on the subject.

> >> > Thinking Sociologically

Taking the position of a Durkheimian functionalist, is there any individual action or behaviour that cannot be argued as being the result of collective influences?

Durkheim's contribution to establishing sociology as a serious academic endeavour is beyond question. He, perhaps more than any other sociologist of his time, built a rigorous and informed theoretical foundation for sociology. Although there are weaknesses within classical functionalism, it was the first theoretical tradition within sociology to demonstrate a new way of looking at the social world.

While Durkheim's work established functionalism in Europe, two American theorists, Talcott Parsons and Robert K. Merton, are largely responsible for introducing it to North America.

TALCOTT PARSONS (1902–1979)

Talcott Parsons was an influential American functionalist who spent virtually his entire academic career teaching and writing at Harvard University. His first major work, *The Structure of Social Action* (1937), was America's introduction to the writings of Max Weber and began to establish Parsons's intellectual reputation (Weber is discussed more fully in Chapters 7 and 13). His later and more famous publication *The Social System* (1951) secured his position as a leader in American sociological theory.

social action theory Parsons's framework attempting to separate behaviours from actions to explain why people do what they do.

behaviours For Parsons, the almost mechanical responses to specific stimuli.

actions For Parsons, the results of an active and inventive process.

Throughout his career, Parsons was interested in explaining why people do what they do. His **social action theory** was an attempt to separate **behaviours**, which he saw as almost mechanical responses to specific stimuli, from **actions**, which he viewed as the results of an active and inventive process (Delaney, 2004, p. 241). Parsons viewed people as "actors" in that they played roles either as individuals or as collectives, and he outlined a four-step process to explain their motivations and goals. First, actors are *motivated* to achieve a goal or end as defined by the cultural system in which they live. For example, your decision to attend university or college and achieve good grades occurred because you are motivated to have a productive and satisfying career, which you believe requires a post-secondary education. Second, actors must find the *means* to achieve their goals. Students need to gather the financial resources necessary to cover the costs of going to school (e.g., tuition, books, living expenses). Third, actors need to face the challenging *conditions* that stand in the way of achieving their goals. Students may have to complete difficult required courses, take classes from teachers who are hard to understand, and write term papers on topics in which they are not interested. Finally, actors must work within the *social system* to achieve their goals. Students are required to pay all of their fees on time and comply with the rules of the institution (see Delaney, 2004, p. 241). Parsons's four-stage process enabled functionalists to begin to dissect and explain why and how people behave the way they do.

Parsons also expended a great deal of effort to outline four functional imperatives—referred to as AGIL for the first letter of each imperative—that are required for a social system to maintain homeostasis (a key feature of all functionalist systems):

1. **Adaptation**. The social system must be able to gather and distribute sufficient environmental resources. Further, the system must be able to adapt to changes in the environment or manipulate the environment to achieve system needs—for example, employing mechanized farm equipment to increase food production on limited arable land. The social institutions generally responsible for responding to adaptation problems are the economic, political, legal, religious, and educational systems, as well as the family (Wallace & Wolf, 2006, p. 38).

2. **Goal attainment**. The system needs to establish clear goals and priorities. As stated by Wallace and Wolf (2006, p. 39), the central question that goal attainment must answer for the social system is how to use legitimate power to implement social decisions. This may seem obvious, but the goals of different social systems often vary. For example, your goals and priorities may differ with regards to your part-time job and your volunteer efforts. At your job, you are interested in performing well so that you will be paid and perhaps even promoted; your volunteer efforts, however, are not about money but, rather, about a commitment to help others. The primary agency responsible for this function in society is the political system (Delaney, 2004).

3. **Integration**. The system needs to maintain solidarity within it as well as have the different units in society work together. The system must coordinate and adjust to the needs and aspirations of the various subgroups in society. It must find ways to motivate actors to play their roles and to regulate their actions when they do not. For example, a university's social system includes procedures and regulations on plagiarism that outline the expected standards with which all students must comply. If students contravene these regulations, they may face severe sanctions, including expulsion from the institution. For actors to support these regulations, the rules must be applied equally to every student regardless of class or minority status. Promoting appropriate social control begins early in one's life within the family but soon extends to schools, mass media, church organizations, and, ultimately, the legal system.

4. **Latency**. The system needs to motivate individuals to release their frustrations in socially appropriate ways, and to the imperatives of tension maintenance and pattern maintenance. **Tension maintenance** recognizes the internal tensions and strains that influence all actors, while **pattern maintenance** involves socially appropriate ways to display these tensions and strains. To maintain equilibrium, the social system must find ways to both motivate individual actors and provide them with opportunities to release their frustrations in socially sanctioned ways. For example, during midterm exams, all students tend to be anxious; some find that working out at a gym helps them to relax while others wait until the exams are over and then head to the student pub. Both of these behaviours are acceptable in this situation, but would the same be said if a student continually skipped classes to go to the gym or was inebriated all of the time? Regulating actors' tensions in appropriate ways is often managed by such social institutions as the family, religion, education, and sports (Delaney, 2004, p. 246).

Parsons's AGIL typology was an important contribution to functionalist theory as it outlined the mechanisms for maintaining social equilibrium. According to Parsons, what allows all four imperatives to operate harmoniously is the process of socialization and social control (discussed more fully in Chapters 6 and 14, respectively). If the process of socialization is successful, all members of society will be committed to the same values and will

adaptation The social system must be able to gather and distribute sufficient resources and adjust to changes in its environment.

goal attainment The system needs to establish clear goals and priorities.

integration The system needs to maintain solidarity while allowing the aspirations of subgroups.

latency The system needs to motivate individuals to release their frustrations in socially appropriate ways.

tension maintenance Recognizes the internal tensions and strains that influence all actors.

pattern maintenance Involves socially appropriate ways to display tensions and strains.

agree to work together to achieve common goals. When this does not occur, social control mechanisms are triggered to ensure that those who are contravening collectively-held values (e.g., laws) are sought out and punished (Wallace & Wolf, 2006, p. 42).

ROBERT K. MERTON (1910–2003)

Robert K. Merton, a former student of Parsons at Harvard University, furthered our understanding of functionalist theory by stressing that social structures have many functions, some more obvious than others. Arguably, his most lasting contribution to sociology was his analysis of manifest and latent functions (Crothers, 2004). According to Merton, **manifest functions** are the intended consequences of an action or social pattern, while **latent functions** are the unintended consequences of an action or social pattern. For example, your intent behind studying for your sociology midterm is to do well on the exam; studying, after all, should improve your grades (an intended consequence). However, what if while you were studying in the library you started up a conversation with someone at the next table and that person eventually became your future spouse? This was certainly not an intended consequence of your studying.

While Parsons's work implies that all social institutions are inherently good and functional for society, Merton's analysis suggests that sometimes this is not the case. Merton warned sociologists to reflect on what is functional, and for whom (see Wallace & Wolf, 2006). For example, many wealthy people would argue that lowering taxes is always a good thing because it encourages people to spend more money, which helps to create jobs and is therefore functional. However, what if you are on social assistance and the decrease in taxes means that the government cuts some programs for the poor? Clearly, decreasing taxes would not be a good thing for you and may lead to dire circumstances. Thus, to a greater extent than Parsons would acknowledge, the social system may have parts that are in fact not functional for everyone. Merton's contribution to sociological theory rests mainly in his analysis of manifest and latent functions and in his caution that functionalist theorists need to recognize that what is considered functional often varies by the person or the group (Holton, 2004).

Functionalism was the dominant theoretical paradigm between the late 1920s and the early 1960s, but has lost its prominence over the past 50 years. A refined theoretical application of functionalism, termed *neofunctionalism*, began in the mid 1980s and is discussed more fully in Chapter 3.

CRITIQUING FUNCTIONALISM

Functionalism correctly assumes that changes in one area of society may lead to changes in others; after all, society is an integrated and interrelated system. However, if one argues that society is similar to an organism, one must apply the characteristics of the organism when describing society. How, then, can functionalism account for social change when the organism's natural state is homeostasis?

To be fair, functionalists assert that change is possible when the system faces challenges or dysfunctions. For example, a civil rights demonstration may lead to legislative changes and invoke long periods of stability. However, some critics charge that the functionalist perspective overemphasizes the extent to which harmony and stability actually exist in society. By implying that order is more basic than change is (a point entirely consistent with conservative reaction thinking) and maintaining that change is frequently dysfunctional, functionalists seem to be saying that the status quo is almost always desirable. Yet we all understand that change is badly needed at times in order to create a new, more just, and ultimately more effective system. In short, although efforts are now being made to correct this failing (see Alexander, 1998), classic functionalism often overlooked the positive consequences that can result from conflict and struggle (Coser, 1956; Merton, 1968).

---

manifest functions
The intended consequences of an action or social pattern.

latent functions
The unintended consequences of an action or social pattern.

❸ Conflict Theory

Conflict theory is based on the assumption that society is grounded on inequality and competition over scarce resources that ultimately result in conflict, which often inspires social change. Two basic principles that all conflict theorists share are (1) power is the core of all social relationships and is scarce and unequally divided among members of society, and (2) social values and the dominant ideology are vehicles by which the powerful promote their own interests at the expense of the weak (see Wallace & Wolf, 2006, p. 69). The intellectual roots of conflict theory go back to Machiavelli, Hobbes, and Rousseau (see Chapter 1).

As discussed, Rousseau is well-known for his writings on the social contract, but his insights into the origins of inequality are most salient to the discussion of conflict theory. Rousseau (1754) argued that there are two kinds of inequality among people. First, **natural or physical inequality** is based on physical differences established by nature (e.g., age, physical health, strength, intelligence). Second, **moral or political inequality** is the result of human classification of valuable things (e.g., money, social status, power). Thus, Rousseau believed that society *imposes* some forms of inequality that are not based on natural differences but instead on elements that we decide are important—whether they are or not. For example, is there any justifiable reason why taller people are considered to be more successful and generally make more money than shorter people? (See Ingalls, 2006; Judge & Cable, 2004.)

According to Rousseau, inequality is the original evil and explains virtually all forms of conflict between individuals and/or entire societies. Types of inequality that are the result of social definitions and are, therefore, *artificial* demonstrate differences in power between individuals and groups in society. This perspective is one of the defining features of the work of the most famous conflict theorist: Karl Marx.

natural or physical inequality According to Rousseau, inequality based on physical differences established by nature (e.g., strength, intelligence).

moral or political inequality According to Rousseau, inequality based on human classification of valuable things (e.g., money, social status).

MARX AND ENGELS

Karl Marx (1818–1883) was a philosopher and economist. Though not a trained sociologist, he must be considered one given his tremendous contributions to the discipline (Ritzer, 2000, p. 41). Marx and his lifelong collaborator, Friedrich Engels (1820–1895), investigated the nature of the human condition and helped to define an influential sociological theory that offered a clear alternative to functionalism.

To conflict theorists, society is characterized by how power defines and influences virtually all human interactions. Society is not a homeostatic system operating for the benefit of the whole (as it is for functionalists) but, rather, a system based on tension and struggle. Consider the 10 principles of the conservative reaction to Enlightenment thinking listed on page 37. These principles advocated stability and tradition, while Enlightenment thinking valued self-realization, achieving human potential, and searching for rules by which to guide society so as to improve it for everyone (Delaney, 2004, p. 64). Functionalism endorses virtually all of these principles, while conflict theory challenges almost every one.

> ### >>> Thinking Sociologically
>
> Provide three examples of contemporary conflicts, either personal or society-wide, that *cannot* be explained as being the result of inequality.

Much of Marx's early thinking about society was defined by his analysis of Georg Wilhelm Friedrich Hegel's (1770–1831) philosophy. In fact, while studying at the University of Berlin, Marx joined a group called the Young Hegelians, which debated the finer points of Hegel's philosophy (Turner, Beeghley, & Powers, 2002, p. 103). The Young Hegelians challenged much in their society; for example, they asserted that organized religion limited the achievement of human potential and therefore must be eliminated. According to the Young Hegelians, "if you rid the world of religious illusions, you remove the misery from people's real condition" (Delaney, 2004, p. 66).

> > >

In late 2011, four women from Saskatchewan (Aboriginal and non-Aboriginal) were worried that a new piece of federal legislation—Bill C-45—would not only challenge indigenous land rights, but also diminish environmental standards that protected water, land, and air quality. Bill C-45, an omnibus budget bill, made changes to the *Indian Act*, the *Navigation Protection Act*, and the *Environmental Assessment Act*. The Idle No More movement drew attention to the belief that the government was trying to push through these changes without proper consultation or due process.

Mark Spowart/Alamy

dialectics Hegel's view of society as the result of oppositions, contradictions, and tensions from which new ideas and social change can emerge.

idealism The belief that the human mind and consciousness are more important in understanding the human condition than is the material world.

Marx agreed with Hegel that to understand social development and history one needs to understand dialectics and idealism. Hegel viewed **dialectics** as a way of seeing history and society as the result of oppositions, contradictions, and tensions from which new ideas and social change can emerge. For Hegel, every idea or position has within it the seeds of an opposing state of being and therefore forms yet another opposition or contradiction (Desfor Edles & Appelrouth, 2010, p. 31). This position counters early functionalist thinking that viewed social change or conflict as a negative and not the primary source of social progress. You can understand dialectics by considering your own life and experiences. Have you and a friend ever worked through a disagreement until you were both able to appreciate each other's position and to agree to do things differently in the future? This is just one example of how conflict can result in a positive change. Hegel and Marx argued that human history unfolds as a series of conflicts and results in continuous transformations. Dialectics assumes that social structures are dynamic and change over time.

For Hegel, **idealism** emphasized that the human mind and consciousness are more important in understanding the human condition than is the material world. Idealists argue that the material world does not reflect what we are, and that the only thing that is truly knowable is consciousness itself. In short, what matters to an idealist is what people think about instead of what they build. Hegel's position as an idealist put him at odds with positivists, who advocated for an objective and scientific view of the world (described in Chapter 1).

Ultimately, however, Marx rejected Hegel's idealistic philosophy as being impractical and dismissive of the importance of the interaction of the material and social worlds.

One of the people most influential in helping Marx investigate the inner workings of society and the economy was Friedrich Engels. Engels was born in Barmen, Germany, to a wealthy family of industrialists. In 1838, before he had finished high school, he was sent by his father to Bremen for business training and worked as an unsalaried clerk at an exporting

BOX 2.2 ISSUES IN GLOBAL CONTEXT

The Gap between the Rich and the Poor Continues to Grow

By 1:00 p.m. on January 2, 2014, Canada's wealthiest CEOs had already made more money than most Canadians make in the enire year (Mackenzie, 2014). A study by the Canadian Centre for Policy Alternatives (CCPA) reveals that the average salary for the CEOs of the largest 240 companies as listed on the Toronto Stock Exchange had annual compensation packages averaging $7.96 million. The report also shows that between 1998 and 2012 the average earnings of the top 100 CEOs in Canada rose by 73 percent, while the average weekly earnings for the rest of Canadians only rose 6 percent over the same period. In 2012, Canada's top paid 100 CEOs made 171 times more than what average Canadians made ($46,634) or 380 times more than a person working full-time (i.e., 40 hours per week) for minimum wage ($20,989) (Mackenzie, 2014). This trend of the rich getting richer is certainly not restricted to Canada.

In fact, the last 30 years has seen an unprecedented growth of the rich at the expense of the poor across the world. For example, when including capital gains, the wealth of the richest 1 percent of Americans has doubled since 1980, from 10 to 20 percent. Further, the share going to the top 0.01 percent (around 16 000 families with an average income of $24 million) has quadrupled over the same period, from just over 1 percent to almost 5 percent of all wealth (Beddoes, 2012). In China, the richest 10 percent take home almost 60 percent of all income. Globally, the wealth of the richest 11 percent has increased 60 percent over the last 20 years (Oxfam, 2013).

According to Oxfam, global economic inequality is a pressing issue and one that actually promotes economic inefficiency, is politically corrosive, socially divisive, environmentally destructive, as well as unethical. In a report, Oxfam cites Ghandi who said "Earth provides enough to satisy every man's need, but not every man's greed" (Oxfam, 2013). For Oxfam, addressing global inequality will require national governments to regulate corporations and increase taxes in order to provide more free public services and support for the world's poor. One estimate suggests that up to one quarter of the world's wealth (around $32 trillion) is held in offshore accounts and is not subject to any taxes. Oxfam reports that if this money was taxed it could generate at least $189 billion in additional tax revenues to help confront global inequality (Oxfam, 2013).

Global inequality is clearly a pressing issue for many. However, for a sociologist it is also an opportunity to explore how theory can be applied to a contemporary social issue. For example, a conflict theorist would see increasing inequality as the natural and inevitable outcome of capitalism; capitalists, in the pursuit of profits, will exploit workers and the environment as much as they can. For functionalists, inequality might be seen as a useful vehicle for inspiring people to work harder to gain economic security for themselves and their families.

Figure 2.2 shows the distribution of the world's wealth. Are you surprised by which countries were the richest? Poorest?

company (Delaney 2004, p. 68; Symonds, 1995). During this time, Engels became increasingly interested in the plight of the working class and in Hegelian philosophy. While completing his required military service, Engels attended lectures at the University of Berlin and ultimately joined the Young Hegelians. Although not a trained academic, he had tremendous insight into the day-to-day condition of the poor. He wrote articles for the radical newspaper *Rheinische Zeitung,* located in Cologne, and met Marx there for the first time in 1842 (Delaney, 2004, p. 69).

FIGURE 2.2

World Wealth
Levels 2013

Reprinted by permission
from Credit Suisse AG,
Source: Credit Suisse
Research Institute, Global
Wealth Databook 2013,
Page 19, Figure 2-2:
https://publications.credit-
suisse.com/tasks/render/
file/?fileID=BCDB1364-A105-
0560-1332EC9100FF5C83

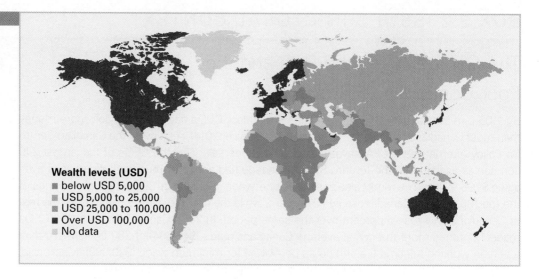

Wealth levels (USD)
- below USD 5,000
- USD 5,000 to 25,000
- USD 25,000 to 100,000
- Over USD 100,000
- No data

In 1845, Engels published *Condition of the Working Class in England*, a damning criticism of the oppression of the working class by the rich. Although many attribute to Marx the belief that the poor would ultimately rise up in revolution against the rich, it was actually Engels who initially argued that social revolution was the inevitable result of capitalism. Marx's partnership with Engels would inspire both men to view the world in new and unique ways. In his biography of Marx, Franz Mehring summed up the intellectual relationship between Marx and Engels as follows:

> Engels always recognized the superior genius in Marx, and he never aspired to play anything but the second fiddle to the other's lead. However, Engels was never merely Marx's interpreter or assistant, but always an independent collaborator, an intellectual force dissimilar to Marx, but his worthy partner. At the beginning of their friendship Engels gave more than he received on a very important field of their activities, and twenty years later Marx wrote to him: "You know that, first of all, I arrive at things slowly, and, secondly, I always follow in your footsteps." (Mehring, 1979, as cited in Symonds, 1995)

Marx and Engels believed that human consciousness and human interaction with the material world could change society, a perspective at odds with conservative reaction theorists, who believed that an external force defined and directed human activity. For Marx, then, people had the capacity to alter the human environment so that it could provide a supportive foundation for the achievement of human potential (Delaney, 2004, p. 64). However, Marx also realized that society could be manipulated by the rich and powerful so that it met their needs first and everyone else's second. While much of what follows focuses on Marx and Engels's insights into capitalism, it should be noted that their theory also applies to pre-capitalist economies (Bratton, Denham, & Deutschmann, 2009, p. 96; Hamilton, 2001, p. 91).

To appreciate how Marx saw the dynamic relationship between the material and social elements of society, refer to Figure 2.3. In Marx's base/superstructure model, the **base** is the material and economic foundation for society, made up of two separate elements: the forces of production and the relations of production. The **forces of production** are the physical and intellectual resources a society has with which to make a living; you can think of these resources as society's tool kit. The forces of production also include human labour power and the means of production (e.g., tools, machines, factories, buildings). For example, if you live in Saskatchewan, you know that your provincial economy is dependent on farming, mining, and oil and gas. These are the resources that your province uses to sustain itself. The nature

base The material and economic foundation for society, made up of the forces of production and the relations of production.

forces of production The physical and intellectual resources a society has with which to make a living.

FIGURE 2.3

Marx's Base/
Superstructure
Model

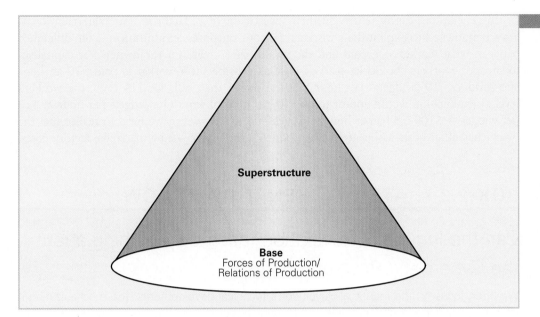

of these resources constrains what the province can do—obviously, it would be difficult to establish a viable commercial fishing economy in Saskatchewan.

Marx argued that the forces of production influence not only the type of society that develops but also the lives of individuals. For example, societies based on the exploitation of raw materials (e.g., Canada) have different histories and are noticeably different from countries that rely on manufacturing (e.g., Germany). Further, according to Marx, what people do for a living influences their perceptions of the world. Do you think that because you are in school you see a slightly different world than you would if you were working full-time? Marx would say yes. As a student, while you may have the luxury of not having to work full-time, you also may not have a lot of money to spend on nonessentials.

Marx also observed that in order to exploit the forces of production, even at a very basic level, workers and owners need to work together. Marx called the relationship between workers and owners the **relations of production**, a relationship based on power that defines a society's use of productive assets and the relationship between social classes. For Marx, a **social class** was a group of people who shared a similar relationship to labour and who were aware of their conflict with other classes (Katz, 1993, p. 382; Ritzer, 2008b, p. 62). **Class conflict** occurs when the interests of one class are in opposition to another. For example, in capitalist society, Marx explained, there are two main classes: the workers (which he called the **proletariat**), who do not own land, and the owners of the means of production (which he called the **bourgeoisie**). As discussed in Chapter 1, the Industrial Revolution changed how people made a living. In hunting and gathering societies or those based on agricultural/pastoral production, people were largely self-sufficient since they could feed themselves. The transition from self-sufficiency to having to work for someone else changed the very nature of the human condition. Over time, workers began to feel **alienated** from what they were producing; that is, they lacked connection to what they produced and became separated from themselves and other workers.

Marx's primary focus was the relationship between workers and owners. In a capitalist economy, the worker and owner are in diametrically opposed positions: the worker wants to make the most money for the least amount of effort and the owner wants to obtain the most labour for the least amount of money. The constant tension that exists between workers and owners is a classic example of a dialectical relationship (described earlier in the chapter). Workers feel that owners do not care about their well-being—they are interested only in profits. Conversely, owners know that workers do not care about the quality of the products they produce—they are interested only in how much they are paid for their work.

relations of production The relationship between workers and owners.

social class A group who share a similar relationship to labour and who are aware of their conflict with other classes.

class conflict When the interests of one class are in opposition to another.

proletariat The workers.

bourgeoisie The owners of the means of production.

alienation Marxist concept to describe the process by which workers lack connection to what they produce and become separated from themselves and other workers.

exploitation The difference between what workers are paid and the wealth they create for the owner.

To generate a healthy return on their investment (e.g., factories, raw materials), owners are motivated to exploit their workers. For our purposes, **exploitation** is the difference between what workers are paid and the wealth they create for the owner. For capitalism to prosper, workers should be paid as little as possible. If a worker is paid $10 an hour and produces 10 "widgets" per hour that the owner then sells for $10 each, the worker's level of exploitation would appear to be $90 per hour of work (10 widgets per hour × $10 per widget = $100 − $10 per hour in wages = $90). However, we need to realize that the owner has other costs associated with producing the widgets (raw materials, factory costs,

BOX 2.3 THAT WAS THEN, THIS IS NOW

Can the Industrial Revolution Teach Us Anything about the Cybernetic Revolution?

We often focus on the Industrial Revolution's technical developments: the mechanization it introduced and the invention of the steam engine and the printing press. Yet the Industrial Revolution was also "an intensely human experience" (Stearns, 1998, p. 57). We should not be surprised, then, that sociologists were and are interested in exploring its influence on society. In fact, during the period, "[n]o society managed to industrialize without massive social dislocation" (Stearns, 1998, p. 57).

The Industrial Revolution began in Western Europe and went on to change virtually every area of life. Massive transformations took place in people's jobs, their family life, and their government. People who had once lived in small, self-reliant farming communities were forced to work in factories, becoming dependent on wages and rarely consuming what they produced (Stearns, 1998, p. 5). As the population moved into cities, new social classes emerged: the ruling elite, who owned the factories, and the workers employed by them (Stearns, 1998, p. 7). Fathers and young children were obliged to leave the home and work in factories or mines to make enough money for their families to survive. However, even with these hardships, the family emerged as an invaluable source of spiritual life and support, a refuge from the stresses of paid labour (Stearns, 1998, p. 61). Government played a more central role in expanding railroads and creating new labour laws in the hope of diminishing child labour. It also provided funding for schools so that young people could be taught how to use the factory owners' equipment.

It is no wonder that some contemporary sociologists look to these insights to help them interpret today's changes. Given that we are experiencing a "cybernetic revolution" (Hansen, 2004, p. 16), the discipline of sociology "has a unique opportunity to provide critical analyses to make this next transition as informed as it can be" (Hansen, 2004, p. 18). Hopefully, some of the lessons learned from the Industrial Revolution will help us understand the immense social changes being inspired by information and communication technology (see Cheng, 2009).

Is it possible that the Internet and computer technology is (1) changing our economies from factories and the processing of raw materials to ones driven by information technology (e.g., the emergence of Google as a multi-billion dollar company), (2) altering the nature of our families and other personal relationships (e.g., increase in online dating services and online pornography), and (3) influencing political decision-making (e.g., impact of former NSA employee Edward Snowden)? What comparisons might we draw between the Industrial and cybernetic revolutions? Can any of the classical theories be applied to the changes brought about by communication technology?

This article is also a peerScholar assignment in MySocLab.

packaging, distribution, advertising), so the real level of exploitation depends on many factors. Nonetheless, the owner's natural inclination is to minimize all costs of production, including wages and employee benefits, and to maximize the prices charged for products, thus increasing profits. Within capitalism, the exploitative nature of labour is hidden within the wage system. For example, unless there is outright fraud, workers are hired and perform work for a specified period and receive wages in return. At first glance, it appears that an equal and open exchange has taken place—but this is simply not the case (Lapon, 2011).

The contrasting interests of workers and owners can be seen as the fuel that drives capitalism to evolve and change. For no extended time are workers or owners in complete control of the other. For example, when unemployment rates are low, workers can demand healthy raises and improvements to their benefits. However, when unemployment is high, owners have their choice of who to hire. Workers know that they can be replaced easily, which gives owners more power over them. The dialectical relationship between these two primary groups is one of the defining contrasts between conflict theory and functionalism—that is, conflict theory incorporates and advocates for social change while functionalism presents a much more conservative and stable view of society.

Returning to the base/superstructure model illustrated in Figure 2.3, Marx and Engels suggested that the superstructure was made possible upon the base of society. The **superstructure** can be understood as all of the things that society values and aspires to once its material needs are met (in this sense, it resembles Maslow's famous hierarchy of needs; see Brown & Cullen, 2006). The superstructure includes such things as religion, politics, and law. In essence, it is what Durkheim called the collective conscience (see page 41). According to Marx, however, these collective manifestations do not spring from some external force but instead are the inevitable result of our relationship with the physical world as experienced through the base of society. In this sense, then, our physical environment influences our collective thoughts and aspirations. Canadian society is built on our desire for equality and fairness (e.g., democracy, equal representation for all, protection of religious diversity), but where are these standards defined, and by whom? To understand how these social values develop, Marx investigated the role of ideology in society.

Ideology can be defined as a set of beliefs and values that support and justify the ruling class of a society. Ideologies are present in all societies where there are systematic and ingrained inequalities between groups. The concept of ideology connects closely with that of power, since ideological systems serve to legitimize the reasons why some groups in society have more power than others (Giddens, 1997, p. 582). Parkinson and Drislane (2007, p. 72) provide some excellent examples of ideological assumptions:

1. Capitalist ideologies assert the value of competition, morality, and achievement.
2. Socialist ideologies advocate against capitalist oppression and see the value of collective ownership and economic equality.
3. Patriarchal ideologies advocate the primacy of everything male and the social domination of the "weaker" sex (i.e., women).
4. Racist ideologies are used to justify slavery and/or colonial expansion.

What all of these ideologies have in common is the domination of one group by another; this allows those in power to define what is right and wrong and thus maintain their privileged position. What would you say the leaders in Canadian society have in common? With some exceptions, Canada's political, economic, and social elite are Caucasian men. As a society, we tend to believe that these people are where they are because they have earned it (i.e., an achieved status, as defined in Chapter 1). However, if you begin to look beyond these individuals' capacities, you will

superstructure All of the things that society values and aspires to once its material needs are met (e.g., religion, politics, law).

ideology A set of beliefs and values that support and justify the ruling class of a society.

> > > Thinking Sociologically

Make a list of occupations in Canadian society that are highly paid, socially respectable, and dominated by women. What does your list say about Canadian society?

find that as a society, we rarely challenge the ideological assumptions that support either the accumulation of wealth by individuals at the exclusion of the poor (i.e., capitalism) or the belief that what men do is more important than what women do.

The dominant ideology of a society, then, is one that maintains the position of the ruling elite. Marx and Engels were interested in exploring how the rich and powerful maintain their control over the majority of society—that is, how is it possible that the wealthy few maintain their wealth and the poor, who are in the majority, do nothing about it? To explain this situation, Marx used the concepts of false consciousness and class consciousness.

Marx believed that people differ from animals by virtue of their consciousness and their ability to link what they think with what they do (Delaney, 2004, p. 73). **False consciousness**[2] is present when people believe in and defend the very system that oppresses them. For example, have you ever seen a group of homeless people demonstrating in order to convey that they need more social support funding? Marx would argue that the people who need help in our highly competitive society are the very people who rarely ask for it because they suffer from false consciousness—they do not recognize or appreciate how the system exploits them.

However futile false consciousness may sound, Marx and Engels believed that people could liberate themselves from oppression through class consciousness. **Class consciousness** occurs when the proletariat realize their domination and oppression by the bourgeoisie and commit to doing something to change it. According to Marx, the proletariat become class conscious when they recognize their mutual interests and begin to create their own political organizations. Marx and Engels expected that, over time, the proletariat would develop a sense of common destiny with other workers because they worked and lived so close together. By talking to each other, workers would begin to understand their plight and the necessity of advocating for their collective needs. By taking such action, by seeing the world as it really is, the proletariat's false consciousness would be destroyed—no longer would workers be alienated from themselves or each other.

If you are thinking that seeing the world from this new perspective sounds like Mills's concept of the quality of mind, you would be right. Achieving class consciousness is effectively seeing the world in shades of grey, understanding the world as socially constructed, and appreciating your role in it. As a conflict theorist, Mills was well aware of macro-level Marxist terminology (class consciousness) but his terminology (quality of mind) accentuated the changes also occurring on the micro level.

CRITIQUING CONFLICT THEORY

Conflict theory is almost the mirror image of functionalism because of its focus on conflict and power imbalances to explain social life; issues such as child abuse, terrorism, sexism, and globalization seem well suited to a conflict analysis. However, the conflict approach tends to diminish the many areas of our lives where we experience an uncoerced consensus about things we feel are important—for example, public support for equal access to health care in Canada. Social conflict certainly occurs, but so does cooperation and harmony. Conflict theorists also sometimes fail to acknowledge that much struggle today is not about a personal desire for power but instead is institutionalized in such contentious events as political elections and collective bargaining between labour unions and corporate management. In these situations, people compete to win, which may inspire more conflict and tension than exists in everyday life.

In contrast to some functionalists, conflict theorists tend to believe more strongly that they should become actively involved in advocating for those people in society who lack social power (Fay, 1987). However, critics argue that this advocacy may violate scientific objectivity

false consciousness
Belief in and support for the system that oppresses you.

class consciousness
Recognition of domination and oppression and collective action to change it.

---

2 Some claim that Marx never used the term *false consciousness* in his writings (see McCarney, 2005) but others disagree (see Göçmen, 2006). In any event, false consciousness is entirely consistent with Marx's analysis of class consciousness and should be considered complementary to it.

and be interpreted by some as nothing more than social activism. Conflict theorists respond that when social scientists uncover unfair social conditions but do nothing to try to address them, they are no different than bystanders who turn a blind eye to the suffering of others.

Conflict theory is also criticized for its insistence on the primary and driving role of economics and materialist interpretations of social life (Wallace & Wolf, 2006, p. 99). Critics agree that the insights achieved through Marx's analysis of the forces of production and relations of production, while useful, are perhaps too narrow to allow for a complete understanding of social motivation and social organization.

The final criticism of classical conflict theory is that it focuses too much on macro-level issues and fails to investigate individual motivations and reactions to tensions and conflicts in people's lives. The criticism that conflict theory lacked tangible application to everyday lives inspired the emergence of the first microsociological theory: symbolic interactionism.

Symbolic Interactionism

Watch

Melissa Milkie:
Symbolic
Interactionism

The third major classical theoretical perspective, symbolic interactionism, originated in the United States and is largely based on the works of George Herbert Mead and Charles Horton Cooley, although it was named by Herbert Blumer (1900–1987).

Functionalists and conflict theorists view society as objectively real and, at times, as exerting a strong, even coercive influence over human behaviour. Symbolic interactionists, on the other hand, emphasize that society and all social structures are nothing more than the creations of interacting people and that they can, therefore, be changed. This point of view was eloquently summed up early in the last century by W. I. Thomas in what has come to be known as the **Thomas theorem**: "If men [sic] define situations as real, they are real in their consequences" (Thomas & Thomas, 1928). In other words, if, for example, we as a group define prisons as awful places where criminals are sent to pay for their deeds, and if we build them with that idea in mind, then that is what they will become. However, if we think of them as places where people can be rehabilitated and our prisons reflect that position, then that is what they will be (Lindsey, Beach, & Ravelli, 2009, p. 17).

Thomas theorem
Assertion that things
people define as
real are real in their
consequences.

According to Ritzer (2000, p. 357), symbolic interactionism maintains seven fundamental principles:

1. Unlike other animals, human beings have the capacity for thought.

2. Human thinking is shaped by social interaction.

3. In social settings, people learn meanings and symbols that allow them to exercise their distinctively human capacity for thought.

4. Meanings and symbols enable people to carry on uniquely human actions and interactions.

5. People are able to change meanings and symbols that they use given their interpretation of various social situations.

6. People are able to make these modifications in part because they have the unique ability to interact with themselves. By doing so, they examine different courses of action and select the one with the most advantages and the least disadvantages.

7. The culmination of patterns of action and interaction make up groups and societies.

These seven principles present a very different view of the individual and his or her relationship to society than functionalism or conflict theory do. Symbolic interactionism is distinct from the other two theories in part because of its microsociological orientation. Instead of focusing on groups, organizations, institutions, and societies, symbolic interactionists study specific cases of how individuals act in small groups and in face-to-face interactions (Brickell, 2006; Denzin, 1992).

> > >

Men and women use many interpersonal signals to show interest in each other.

Monkey Business Images/Shutterstock

Symbolic interactionists highlight the important ways in which meanings are created, constructed, mediated, and changed by members of a group or society (Brickell, 2006, p. 417). Meanings and understandings of our social world are the result of our interactions with others and of how we choose to construct the social world in which we live. What is important here is that our perceptions, values, and meanings are the result of mediated experiences with the people we meet each and every day. For example, as you mature, you are influenced by those around you, not because you depend on them (a functionalist view) or are coerced by them (a conflict view) but because we all look to those around us for insights into our world. These interactions and shifting definitions of the social world are influenced by commonly held rules and definitions that influence how, why, when, and where we interact.

The intellectual roots of symbolic interactionism can be traced to two early sociologists: Max Weber and Georg Simmel.

MAX WEBER (1864–1920)

verstehen **Weber's term for a deep understanding and interpretation of subjective social meanings.**

Max Weber made many contributions to sociological theory, and is generally associated with conflict theory, but for us his contribution to symbolic interactionism is also of note. For example, his emphasis on **verstehen**, a German term meaning to employ a deep understanding and interpretation of subjective social meanings in order to appreciate both the intention and the context of human action, is entirely consistent with symbolic interactionism (Wallace & Wolf, 2006, p. 199). *Verstehen*, then, refers to understanding the meaning of an action from the actor's point of view. Human actors are not seen as the product of external forces that direct their lives, but instead as active agents who engage with others to organize their world and give it meaning (Parkinson & Drislane, 2007, p. 165). This approach is also entirely consistent with the sociological imagination—to put yourself in another person's shoes and see the world from his or her position. Weber's emphasis on an individual's subjective analysis and interpretation of an action or situation challenged positivist social science and inspired the emergence of symbolic interactionism.

GEORG SIMMEL (1858–1918)

Georg Simmel is perhaps best known for his contributions to sociological theory from an independent scholar's perspective.[3] For example, he was one of the first sociologists to challenge, and reject, the organic theories of social development as proposed by Comte, Durkheim, and Spencer. According to Simmel, society was not a living thing, as some functionalists suggested, nor was it an abstract creation of the intellect, as the idealists argued (Delaney, 2004, p. 115). Instead, Simmel viewed society as the summation of human experience and its patterned interactions.

Simmel promoted what he referred to as the formal school of sociology (Littlewood, 2002). **Formal sociology** argues that society is the result of social processes and, therefore, forms of interactions can be isolated from their content so that seemingly different interactions can be shown to have similar form. For example, you might assume that you are very different from students who attended university 50 years ago. While there are no doubt demographic differences between the two groups, in one respect they are similar: the way that students write papers is surprisingly constant over time. Today's students rely on computer-based search engines when doing their research, while students in the past consulted printed indexes, but both techniques generate far more sources than you could possibly read for one paper. While you can now gather articles from the comfort of your home, you still have to write the paper, and the skill of gleaning quality information from an overwhelming pool of resources is the same today as it was in the past. Thus, social processes that seem very different (writing of term papers over a 50-year period) are actually comparable (ability to glean quality information from an overwhelming pool of resources).

Simmel's approach to sociology influenced later American theorists in their development of symbolic interactionism.

> **formal sociology**
> Simmel's theory that argues that different human interactions, once isolated from their content, can be similar in form.

GEORGE HERBERT MEAD (1863–1931)

Mead's most famous work, *Mind, Self and Society* (1934), consisted of a series of lecture notes compiled by a group of former students after Mead's death. Mead suggested that the "social organism" is not an organic individual but "a social group of individual organisms" (Mead, 1934, p. 130). The individual, therefore, exists as a member of a social organism, and his or her acts can be understood only in the context of social actions that involve other individuals. Society is not a collection of pre-existing autonomous individuals (as suggested by Hobbes, Locke, and Rousseau) but instead is the result of individuals defining themselves through participation in social acts (Cronk, 2005).

According to Mead, the human mind results from the individual's ability to respond to and engage with the environment. The mind emerges and develops once individuals demonstrate an ability to communicate their thoughts to others and to themselves (Strauss, 1956, as cited in Delaney, 2004, p. 179). The concept of *self* emerges once individual actors can reflect on themselves as objects and see their actions as the result of social processes. To help understand the social nature of the individual, Mead defined the differences between the *I* and the *Me*.

According to Mead, human behaviour is virtually always the product of interaction with others. As babies mature, they begin to interact with the world and, by doing so, begin to define themselves by their relationships to it. In Mead's classification, the **I** is the unsocialized self, the entity that is spontaneous, creative, and impulsive. The **Me** is the

> **I** The unsocialized part of the self.
>
> **Me** The socialized part of the self.

---

3 Simmel spent most of his academic career as a private lecturer; he did not achieve a full-time appointment until age 56 (at the University of Strasbourg). Some suggest that being outside the academic mainstream made him more creative and flexible in what he chose to research (e.g., sociology of the senses, philosophy of money) (Delaney, 2004, p. 111).

socialized self that monitors the actions of the I. That is, it is the judgmental, reflective, and controlling side of the self that reflects the values and attitudes of the society. It develops gradually as the individual engages with and internalizes the community. In short, the I represents the individual's response to the actions of others and the Me controls the response of the I (Delaney, 2004, p. 180). Mead writes, "The attitudes of the others constitute the organized 'me,' and then one reacts toward that as an 'I' " (cited in Wallace & Wolf, 2006, p. 206). The individual personality (i.e., the self) then emerges with the combination of the I and the Me.

Mead's contribution to symbolic interactionism is beyond question. He was one of the most important figures in establishing the Chicago School of Sociology, which would train Erving Goffman and Herbert Blumer, who both left the university to accept teaching positions at Berkeley. Along with Charles Cooley, these men were most clearly associated with defining symbolic interactionism.

CHARLES H. COOLEY (1864–1929)

sympathetic introspection Cooley's concept of the value of putting yourself into another person's shoes and seeing the world as he or she does.

Like Mead, Cooley held that sociology should be the study of social reality, including individual consciousness. Cooley suggested that the best way for a sociologist to examine the social world was through a method he called **sympathetic introspection**. This technique required sociologists to analyze an actor's consciousness by putting themselves in his or her shoes. This process allowed sociologists to appreciate the actor's reality and to experience the social reality as he or she would (University of Colorado, n.d.). Sympathetic introspection is similar to Mills's concept of the sociological imagination.

While Mead is considered to have had a stronger, more lasting impact on symbolic interactionism, Cooley's contributions remain relevant today (Shaffer, 2005). One of Cooley's most lasting contributions was his concept of the looking-glass self, which he outlined in *Human Nature and the Social Order* (1902).

looking-glass self Cooley's belief that we develop our self-image through the cues we receive from others.

The **looking-glass self** is an active, imaginative process by which we develop our self-image through the cues we receive from others (Shaffer, 2005). There are three basic components to the looking-glass self. First, we must imagine how we appear to others. Second, we need to imagine how others would judge that appearance. Third, we must reflect on that image and develop some self-feeling (e.g., pride, fear, embarrassment) as a result (Ritzer, 2000, p. 361). According to Cooley, the looking-glass self is in essence our reflection in the eyes and actions of others. The impressions you see in the eyes of people you meet help to define who you think you are. Cooley argued that at some level, we internalize these impressions and ultimately may become the kind of person we believe others see us as—a phenomenon he termed **self-fulfilling prophecy** (Kornblum, 1997, as cited in University of Colorado, n.d.).

self-fulfilling prophecy A prediction that, once made, causes the outcome to occur.

Cooley's efforts to situate symbolic interactionism in the personal and subjective realms of who we are and how we gain our sense of self were a clear departure from the macrosociological approaches of functionalism and conflict theory.

ERVING GOFFMAN (1922–1982)

Like other symbolic interactionists, Goffman (born in Manville, Alberta) was interested in interactions between small groups—or even simply pairs—of people. One of Goffman's most important contributions to symbolic interactionism was his concept of *dramaturgical analysis*. This approach sees the 'self' as emerging from the performances we play and how the other actors relate to us. In other words, the 'self' does not really exist but rather is a function of the social interactions we have with others and how they interpret the signs and signals we convey. Through deceptions and misrepresentations, or by enacting idealized notions of how a person ought to behave, we try to control how others see us and at times put on a mask to hide our true feelings or motivations. We are all actors who are protective of the characters that we play. According to Goffman, no interaction is as simple as it first appears.

Goffman argued that interactions are influenced by each person's personal history and experiences and that these ultimately define and flavour each and every interaction (Goffman, 1959). All interactions occur within spaces where actors send and receive signals to and from each other in order to understand and manage their individual roles and performances. For example, suppose you stop by your professor's office to discuss your midterm on which you did not do very well. You are upset by your score (afterall, you did study . . . really, you did) and you are also frustrated that you just can't seem to "get" conflict theory. As you sit across from your professor, your body language conveys your nervousness, your disappointment, your frustration and you do your best to avoid eye contact with her. You feel defensive and you feel judged. Your professor sits behind the desk, skims over your exam, and points out a number of key concepts you failed to mention on your exam. She is also frustrated. She is also upset. She believes that she covered all the required material in lectures and deep down feels that students today, like you, just don't work as hard as she did.

To fully understand Goffman, though, is to realize that in this scenario, both parties are not only trying to manage the signals they send to each other, but also how those signals are being perceived. For example, in the meeting you controlled your emotions as best you could but at one point you started to cry. On one level you are aware of losing control but on another you are actively assessing how your professor is reacting to you—is she leaning forward and signalling compassion and sympathy or is she sitting back and rolling her eyes? Goffman would want you to realize that your professor is undertaking the same reflective process as you are—what does she learn about herself by you starting to cry?

Can you see how you and your professor are both influenced by the signals you are sending and receiving and that you are both influenced by your histories, your experiences, and the role you are now playing? For Goffman, human interactions are always fluid and intricate but also a rich source of sociological insight.

CRITIQUING SYMBOLIC INTERACTIONISM

Symbolic interactionism is an excellent vehicle for directing sociologists to study the way in which people define the social situations they find themselves in. It reminds us that social reality is, in the final analysis, a human construct. This theory also adds an important microsociological perspective to classical sociological theory. However, macrosociologists, especially conflict theorists, argue that symbolic interactionists fail to acknowledge how difficult it is to change long-established social arrangements. Critics also point out that symbolic interactionism does not account for the importance of social structures and institutions in defining the world in which we live. The assertion that one can understand and respond to the social world is important, but so is the realization that economic class, education level, minority status, and other structural entities exist and define people's life opportunities. Although people of a lower economic class may understand the importance of a positive self-identity, it may not help them to succeed in the face of institutional prejudice (discussed more fully in Chapter 10).

⑤ Marginalized Voices and Social Theory

No doubt many of you have noticed that the discussion so far has been dominated by the ideas of white men from Western countries. This observation is accurate and speaks to many issues of interest to contemporary sociologists: sexism, racism, and ethnocentrism (discussed more thoroughly in Chapters 9, 10, and 5, respectively). The point is not that women, visible minorities, and non-Westerners had nothing to say but, rather, that no one wanted to listen. This theme of exclusion and oppression of the weak is as relevant to classical theory as it is for every topic area in sociology.

CONTRIBUTIONS BY WOMEN

Many women have made substantial contributions to classical theory and are finally being recognized (see Thomas & Kukulan, 2004). These writers include Mary Wollstonecraft (1759–1797), Harriet Martineau (1802–1876), Flora Tristan (1803–1844), Florence Nightingale (1820–1910), Beatrice Potter Webb (1853–1943), Anna Garlin Spencer (1851–1932), Anna Julia Cooper (1858–1964), Ida Wells-Barnett (1862–1931), Charlotte Perkins Gilman (1860–1935), Jane Addams (1860–1935), Annie Marion MacLean (1870–1934), Marianne Weber (1870–1954), and Rosa Luxemberg (1871–1919). Their writings often focused on promoting social equality and activism, and were significant in the development of Western society generally and of sociology specifically. However, only recently have their contributions been recognized and this fact should not be seen as a reflection of the quality of their insights or their popularity at the time, but instead as a function of the patriarchy that devalued virtually all contributions by women to academic endeavours (Kimmel, 2007; Finlay, 2007).

Mary Wollstonecraft's *A Vindication of the Rights of Women* (1792) challenged social convention by suggesting that marriage was a form of legal prostitution and confirmed her as one of the first feminists. She also argued that the only way to achieve true equality was to educate boys and girls together as one way of challenging the male-focused family and parental tyranny (Frazer, 2008, p. 251). As adults, women's oppression was confirmed when women accepted their powerlessness because they could rely on their sexual power to seduce men. This made it easier for women to deceive themselves into believing they had more power than they really did (Kimmel, 2007, pp. 89–90).

Another woman offering significant insight into classical sociology was Harriet Martineau. Martineau was a British author who is probably best known for having translated Comte's works into English. A strong supporter of feminism and a passionate opponent of slavery, Martineau toured the United States in 1834 and, three years later, published a perceptive book called *Society in America* that was based on fieldwork at a time when empirical sociological research was uncommon. One year later, she wrote *How to Observe Manners and Morals*, one of the first books to explore sociological methodology. Martineau helped define how sociologists studied the social world and was motivated by answering the question, "What constitutes a better life for people?" (Delaney, 2004, pp. 286–187).

Born on Prince Edward Island, Annie Marion MacLean was the first Canadian woman to receive a Ph.D. in sociology (University of Chicago in 1900). MacLean's work centred on women and their role as wage earners. In 1898–1899 MacLean investigated the lives of department store clerks in Chicago. During the holiday season MacLean found that many clerks worked from 8:00 a.m. to 10:00 p.m. and that compensation for overtime varied greatly. She also found that the stores employed *cash children*, who worked for cash and were often under 12 years old. Her book *Wage-Earning Women* (1910) continued her interest in the lives of working women and surveyed 13 500 women labourers at 400 companies in 20 Canadian cities. Her research was one of the first large-scale uses of survey research in Canada (see Bumb, n.d.). MacLean's work was instrumental in helping sociologists understand the plight of the working classes in North America.

CONTRIBUTIONS BY VISIBLE MINORITIES

Just as women's writings were marginalized, so too were the insights from minority authors. As new sociologists you can begin to appreciate that our criticisms of society, e.g., sexism and racism, can often be applied to our own discipline as well.

Anna Julia Cooper (1858–1964) was born a slave in Raleigh, North Carolina. In spite of this difficult beginning, her achievements demonstrated great personal fortitude as she continually confronted racism and exclusion throughout her life (Finlay, 2007, p. 63). Cooper felt that she was destined to try to enlighten people in the hopes of reshaping society (Delaney, 2004, p. 292). As a trained teacher, she was able to influence a great many of her students at M-Street High School in Washington, an all-black school, where she served briefly as its principal. In 1892 she published *A Voice from the South*, which was a collection of essays focusing on race, education, gender, and other topics of social significance. By the end of her career, she became an internationally known spokesperson for social and racial issues and ultimately achieved her Ph.D., at the age of 65, from the Sorbonne in Paris following the publication of her dissertation, *Slavery and the French Revolutionists (1788–1805)* in 1925.

Ida Wells-Barnett (1862–1931) was a civil rights leader, suffragist, journalist, and public speaker. Her parents were born slaves but gained their freedom after the American Civil War. In the 1880s she began writing articles about the atrocities of black lynchings that were all too common in the American South (Watkins, 2008). Her efforts to understand the particular experience of black women in America and how they confronted both racial and sexual discrimination became instrumental to the contemporary concept of intersectionality (Delaney, 2004, pp. 292–296) (see Chapter 8).

Perhaps the most influential black sociologist contributing to the emergence of sociology was the American W. E. B. (William Edward Burghardt) Du Bois (1868–1963). Du Bois was a popular civil rights leader, social scientist, political militant, and founder of the National Association for the Advancement of Colored People (NAACP). After completing his Ph.D. at Harvard University in 1895 (the first Ph.D. to be awarded to a black person by the university), he spent a year in Philadelphia doing research into the black community, which resulted in *The Philadelphia Negro* (1899). In 1903 he published *The Souls of Black Folk*, arguably his most famous work (Kimmel, 2007, p. 363).

In this work, Du Bois introduces his concept of **double-consciousness**—a way of seeing one's self through the eyes of someone else that for American blacks resulted in a sense of *two-ness*. Black Americans experienced a divided identity, where on the one hand they were members of the majority as Americans but on the other they were discriminated against because they were black (Griffin, 2003, p. xvi). For Du Bois, American racial inequality deflected attention away from the critiques of white racial dominance and toward other nonracial social concerns like immigration, class inequality, politics, and cultural nationalism (Twine & Gallagher, 2008, p. 9).

double-consciousness
Du Bois's concept of the divided identity experienced by American blacks.

Du Bois's contribution to sociological theory is secure given his rich account of minority experiences as well as the fact that we continue to reflect on his body of work, which includes over 100 articles and 20 books (Finlay, 2007, p. 132).

CONTRIBUTIONS BY NON-WESTERN SCHOLARS

As described earlier, classical theory is generally associated with European and, to a lesser extent, American social theorists. Students are rarely exposed to writings of sociologists from developing nations but this should not imply that they have not made significant contributions. Given the lived experiences of many of these writers, it should come as no surprise that many focus their attention on exploring colonial racism.

Writers such as Frantz Fanon (1925–1961), C. L. R. James (1901–1989), George Padmore (1903–1959), and Kwame Nkrumah (1909–1972) (former president of Ghana) were leaders in the anti-colonial, pan-Africanist movements whose writings became integral to the push for independence from colonial powers (Adi & Sherwood, 2003). These writers influenced later authors and activists from oppressed groups that had suffered under the history of colonial racism. African and Caribbean leaders drew on the work of these early writers that helped set the tone for their own resistance to colonialism and racism (Adi & Sherwood, 2003).

BOX 2.4 EXPLORING THEORY

Theory	Leading Theorists	Key Insights	Key Concepts
Functionalism	Herbert Spencer; Émile Durkheim; Talcott Parsons; Robert K. Merton	Society is an organic entity that naturally resists change and is homeostatic.	Social Darwinism, survival of the fittest; collective conscience, mechanical and organic solidarity; AGIL; manifest and latent functions
Conflict	Karl Marx; Friedrich Engels	Society is grounded on the competition over scarce and unequally distributed resources.	Dialectics, forces, and relations of production; bourgeoisie and proletariat; exploitation, alienation, ideology, false and class consciousness
Symbolic Interactionism	Max Weber*; Georg Simmel; G. H. Mead; C. H. Cooley	Society, including its structures, is the result of interacting and active individuals.	*Verstehen*; formal sociology; I and Me; sympathetic introspection, looking-glass self, self-fulfilling prophecy
Contributions by Women	Mary Wollstonecraft; Harriet Martineau; Anne Marion MacLean	Began questioning, and challenging, traditional views of women in society.	Oppression of women within patriarchy
Contributions by Visible Minorities	Anna Julia Cooper; Ida Well-Barnett; W. E. B. Du Bois	Added social insight into how race played a defining role in contemporary (largely American) society.	Double-consciousness
Contributions by Non-Western Scholars	Frantz Fanon; C. L. R. James; George Padmore; Kwame Nkrumah	Explored the legacy of colonial experiences of peoples around the world.	Colonialism, pan-Africanism

* While largely associated with conflict theorists, we believe his concept of *verstehen* is a notable contribution to symbolic interactionism.

Frantz Fanon established his position as a leading theorist on black identity, colonial rule, and decolonization. Fanon supported the resistance to French colonialism in Algeria through his works *The Wretched of the Earth* (1961) and *Studies in a Dying Colonialism* (1965[1959]). Fanon argued that racism generates harmful psychological constructs that blind the minority to their oppression and alienation (Gordon, Sharpley-Whiting, & White, 1996). Language also influences how people view themselves. For example, when traditional languages are replaced by the language of the colonizers, the colonized, over time, begin to accept and support the culture of the colonizer as represented through language.

C. L. R. James, author of *Beyond a Boundary* (1963), an autobiographical reflection on his experience with cricket and its links with British imperialism in Trinidad, also contributed to the growing anti-colonial struggle (Renton, 2007). James explored the damage and suffering caused by slavery as well as challenged the mythology surrounding racial inferiority (Renton, 2007). His work *The Black Jacobins* (1938) examined the Haitian (San Domingo) Revolution of 1791–1803 that demonstrated the revolutionary potential of the masses. The work offered a blueprint for other revolutionary leaders on how to challenge colonial rulers.

George Padmore is known for his works on pan-Africanism, communism, and colonialism. His writings *The Life and Struggles of Negro Toilers* (1931) and *How Britain Rules Africa* (1936) were particularly influential and gave a new voice to the exploited and oppressed working class. Padmore is given credit for radicalizing much of the Caribbean working class and was a leading advocate for colonial revolution (Adi & Sherwood, 2003; Baptiste & Lewis, 2008).

Because these writers' works focused on the oppression resulting from colonialism, their works received limited profile in Canada and the United States. This is not because they were not seen as colonial empires or that colonial relationships no longer existed (e.g., our experience with indigenous peoples). Rather, it is a reflection of who this material "spoke" to (i.e., the oppressed). Additionally, these works were ignored by the mainly white sociologists working at North American universities.

Writers from the developing world offer a unique perspective that has helped shape the course of African and Caribbean history as well as our Western views of the world. As you will learn in Chapter 3, contemporary social theory has embraced many of these insights and attempts to further explore our social world.

Summary

1. Early social philosophers contributed to classical sociological theory through these fundamental tenets: Thomas Hobbes's assertion that government's appropriate role lies in preserving peace while allowing individuals to pursue their self-interests; John Locke's belief in individual freedom and autonomy; Charles de Montesquieu's comparative methodology and his appreciation for cultural diversity; and Jean-Jacques Rousseau's analysis of the social contract and his belief in individual autonomy.

2. Functionalism encompasses a view of the social world as a dynamic system of interrelated parts. Its early thinkers include Auguste Comte and Vilfredo Pareto; later theorists include Herbert Spencer, Émile Durkheim, Talcott Parsons, and Robert Merton.

3. Conflict theory holds that power lies at the core of all social relationships and is unequally divided, and that the powerful maintain their control of society through the dominant ideology. The most influential conflict theorists are Karl Marx and his collaborator, Friedrich Engels.

4. Symbolic interactionism emphasizes that society and social structures are created by the interactions between people, and that therefore these structures can be changed. This theory, unlike the preceding two, has a microsociological orientation. Its early theorists are Max Weber and Georg Simmel; later American theorists include George Herbert Mead, Charles H. Cooley, and Erving Goffman.

5. The contributions by women, minorities, and scholars from the developing world, while historically marginalized, have influenced the development of sociology. These "voices from the margins" have taught us a great deal about the nature of human society as well as the history of our discipline.

Key Terms

actions *44*
adaptation *45*
alienation *51*
anomie *43*
base *50*
behaviours *44*
bourgeoisie *51*
class conflict *51*
class consciousness *54*
collective conscience *41*
dialectics *48*
double-consciousness *61*
evolution *39*
exploitation *52*
false consciousness *54*
forces of production *50*
formal sociology *57*
goal attainment *45*
I *57*
ideal types *34*
idealism *48*
ideology *53*
integration *45*
laissez-faire *40*
latency *45*

latent functions *46*
looking-glass self *58*
manifest functions *46*
Me *57*
mechanical solidarity *43*
moral or political inequality *47*
natural or physical inequality *47*
natural selection *39*
natural state *32*
organic analogy *38*
organic solidarity *43*
pattern maintenance *45*
Philosophes *35*
proletariat *51*
relations of production *51*
self-fulfilling prophecy *58*
social action theory *44*
social class *51*
social Darwinism *39*
social facts *41*
superstructure *53*
survival of the fittest *39*
sympathetic introspection *58*
tension maintenance *45*
theory *31*
Thomas theorem *55*
verstehen 56

Reviewing the Concepts

1. What were the defining features of Enlightenment thinking? Using contemporary examples, is there any evidence of these concepts today? If so, where? If not, why?

2. Why is the concept of the organic analogy so important to functionalism? Discuss.

3. What does the term *survival of the fittest* mean? Can this concept be applied to society today? How? If not, why not?

4. Compare and contrast mechanical solidarity with organic solidarity.

Applying Your Sociological Imagination

1. Review Montesquieu's work *The Spirit of the Laws*. Do you feel that Canadians and Americans have different defining spirits? Discuss.

2. Durkheim argued that the choices we make are often influenced by the social forces around us. What choices have you made today that confirmed you were thinking of the collective when you made them, and have you made any decisions today that were solely your own?

3. How could conflict theory be applied to your sociology class? An undergraduate education? A career as a sociologist teaching at a college or university?

4. Using your choice of functionalism or conflict theory or symbolic interactionism, how would the theory explain the marginalization of women, minorities, and scholars from the developing world? Discuss.

MySocLab

Visit MySocLab to access a variety of online resources that will help you prepare for tests and apply your knowledge.

3 Contemporary Social Theories

What are some contemporary questions or happenings that social theories can help to elucidate? For example, how do you experience the social world? Do you move through it with ease? When you get up in the morning, how do you adorn your body? Have you thought about why you dress the way that you do? Have you considered why you have the friends that you do? Who are you sexually attracted to? What kinds of social activities pique your interest? How much do your extracurricular activities cost? And what about your future, what are your aspirations after postsecondary schooling?

As we navigate the social world, contemporary social theories can help us to explain everyday happenings like the ones noted above. Even questions that seem to be personal—such as those about your future aspirations—can be analyzed through a social lens. As you will see as you progress through this course, so many of the things that happen to us, as well as the things that we do, can be linked to social relations.

By the end of this chapter, students will be able to

1 Describe Antonio Gramsci's Marxist concept of hegemony.

2 Outline second- and third-wave feminist thinking using the examples of Dorothy Smith and bell hooks.

3 Explain the major post-structural concepts of Michel Foucault.

4 Explain the three principal areas of queer theory.

5 Describe the approach of post-colonial theory in general, and Edward Said's Orientalism in particular.

6 Understand Canada's colonial past.

7 Define the principal tenets of critical race theory and the approach to "whiteness" as a racial identity.

8 Explain Anthony Giddens's theoretical approach to globalization.

What Are Contemporary Social Theories?

We should not think of contemporary social theories as being completely separate and different from the theories discussed in Chapter 2. Rather, the theorists we highlight in this chapter continue the conversation that began in the previous one. Indeed, social theorists draw on each other's work in their formulations; queer theorists, for example, draw heavily on the work of Michel Foucault.

One theme that runs through the theories addressed in this chapter is that of power. While there are certainly differences in how power is theorized, it is nevertheless a major focus in contemporary studies.

Western Marxism

In Chapter 2, we discussed Karl Marx's argument that the *forces of production* influence not only the organization of a society, but also people's experiences of that society. Marx further believed that over time, the proletariat would develop a common class consciousness and revolt against the bourgeoisie. Western Marxism takes a slightly different approach to this classic formulation.

Western Marxism refers to more independent and critical forms of Marxism than those practised by the more dogmatic Soviet and Chinese regimes (Kellner, 2005). In fact, the term was first derisively by the Soviet communist regime to refer to the varied forms of Marxism that emerged after the 1920s in a rapidly changing Western Europe (Kellner, 2005). Several theorists are associated with Western Marxism, namely György Lukács, Antonio Gramsci, Theodor Adorno, Max Horkheimer, Herbert Marcuse, and Louis Althusser.

Here, we focus on Antonio Gramsci and his influential concept of hegemony. We highlight hegemony because of its enduring significance in contemporary sociology (Garner, 2007).

❶ GRAMSCI'S CONCEPT OF HEGEMONY

Antonio Gramsci (1891–1937) helped found the Communist Party of Italy in 1921. He was imprisoned in 1926, sentenced to 20 years by Mussolini's regime because of his opposition to fascism. While imprisoned, Gramsci continued to think and write, and his sister-in-law smuggled his notebooks out of the prison. Parts of these notebooks were later published as the influential book *Selections from the Prison Notebooks*.

Gramsci accepted Marx's analysis of the struggle between the ruling class and the subordinate working class, but he diverged from Marx in his analysis of *how* the ruling class ruled (Burke, 2005). Marx had explained that the ruling class dominated through both force and coercion, using the strong arm of the state—that is, the police and the military (Burke, 2005). However, absent from this analysis, according to Gramsci, was a consideration of the ruling class's subtle yet insidious *ideological* control and manipulation (Burke, 2005; Thomson, 2010).

According to Gramsci, then, there are two different forms of political control: domination and hegemony (Burke, 2005). *Domination,* in this context, refers to the direct physical and violent coercion exerted by the police and the military to maintain social boundaries and enforce social rules (Burke, 2005; Kellner, 2005). **Hegemony** refers to ideological control and consent. According to Marx and Engels (1846, p. 64), "the ideas of the ruling class are in every epoch the ruling ideas." Ideological control, then, means that a society's dominant ideas reflect the interests of the ruling class and help to mask social inequalities. Note that hegemony also involves *consent*. Gramsci argued that regardless of how authoritarian a regime may be, no regime would be able to maintain its rule by relying principally on organized state power and armed force (Burke, 2005; Thomson, 2010). Rather, to enjoy longevity and stability of rule, a regime must have the allegiance of the masses (Sassoon, 1994). So, the hegemony of the dominant group's ideas and cultural forms works by bringing about the consent of the subordinate class (Burke, 2005; Kellner, 2005).

hegemony Domination through ideological control and consent.

Recall from Chapter 2 that Marx viewed the economic base of a society as a determining force for the shape of social relations (the superstructure). Gramsci separated the superstructure into the *state* (coercive institutions such as the police, military, government, and system of laws) and *civil society* (schools, media, religion, trade unions, and cultural associations). He focused on the role that civil society plays in establishing hegemony (Kellner, 2005; Thomson, 2010). These institutions are critical for the permeation of the philosophy, culture, and morality of the ruling class; through them, the population internalizes the ruling class's ideas and cultural forms, which then become accepted as common sense (Burke, 2005).

For example, if you have grown up in North America (and hence in a capitalist economic society), it is probably difficult for you to imagine that a political economic system such as socialism represents a viable alternative to capitalism. Capitalism, in its longevity, is considered to be common sense and thus enjoys hegemonic status. For example, think of some common-sense notions in capitalist societies about the need to work hard. Those who are unemployed are thought of as lazy, unproductive, and without motivation. A prevailing idea is that those who work hard and diligently will be rewarded with financial success. Such ingrained notions sustain the more or less smooth operation of capitalism as well as the hegemony of the bourgeoisie (Palamarek, 2008).

According to Gramsci, hegemony is a process that is constantly negotiated and renegotiated. In other words, hegemony is not static, and as such the ruling class cannot take it for granted. The consent secured by the ruling class is an *active* consent. In order to secure it, the ruling class constantly incorporates elements of the subordinate class's culture so that the subordinate class never feels wholly oppressed by the ruling class's culture (Sassoon, 1994).

< < <

This *New Yorker* cartoon depicts the hegemony of capitalism.

Edward Koren/The New Yorker Collection/ www.cartoonbank.com

"I totally agree with you about capitalism, neo-colonialism, and globalization, but you really come down too hard on shopping."

An example from popular culture demonstrates how Gramsci's concept of hegemony is also useful in exploring ideological control that is not reducible to social-class interests. The television show *Will & Grace* featured two gay men (Will and Jack) and two heterosexual women (Grace and Karen). Jack was stereotypically constructed as a flamboyant gay man (whom audiences could laugh at and dismiss), while Will was constructed as serious (and mainstream audiences could see him as being like heterosexuals, and thus not a threat). The fact that Will and Grace lived together further reduced the subversive potential of the show. The audience could easily forget that Will was a gay man since he lived with a woman and, for much of the show, did not have romantic partners. So, while we may imagine that some gay men might appreciate having their lives portrayed on television, gay life on *Will & Grace* was presented as being so palatable that the show did little to challenge the

The Canadian Press/STREVT

< < <

While we can assume that some gay men might appreciate being represented in popular culture, the show *Will & Grace* does little to challenge heterosexual hegemony. By having only limited scenes depicting Will with romantic male partners, and through his cohabitation with Grace, we can easily forget that Will's character is gay. In the end, the show does not live up to its subversive potential.

heterosexual hegemony of the ruling class. Ultimately, then, the show was not truly subversive in that it did not challenge balances of power. The fact that people laughed along with it shored up heterosexual hegemony.

As you will see in subsequent chapters, many theorists use Gramsci's concept of hegemony as a way to explain how particular features of social organization come to be taken for granted and treated as common sense, such that it becomes difficult to imagine another way of being. For example, as discussed in Chapters 8 and 9, theorists talk about *heterosexual hegemony* and *hegemonic masculinity*—terms that refer to dominant cultural forms of sexuality and masculinity that are considered to represent a "natural" state of affairs.

❷ Feminist Theories

＊ Explore

Why We Still Need Booster Shots of Feminism

👁 Watch

Feminism - The F Word

There is no single feminist theory; rather, feminist theorizing has many strands. These various approaches differ, for example, in their explanations of women's oppression and the nature of gender and in their ideas about women's emancipation. Yet all of the approaches have at their core a concern for gender oppression. Much of the focus of early feminist theorists was directed at the issue of equality, both social and political, between men and women. In virtually every society, men (and those things associated with men) are held in higher regard than women (Seidman, 2008). As a group with social power, men thus have an interest in maintaining their social privilege over women (Seidman, 2008). Accordingly, feminist theories offer a view of the world from the position of a socially disadvantaged group (Seidman, 2008).

We use the "wave" metaphor of feminism to distinguish between different approaches to feminism on a large scale. That said, using the wave metaphor to capture some theoretical commonality within a wave does not mean that each wave itself is fully homogenous, nor does it mean that the thinking in one wave supplants the thinking of the earlier waves (Karaian & Mitchell, 2010; Mills, 2008). Here, we introduce each of the three waves but focus on second-wave and third-wave feminism and put forward two feminist theorists as exemplars of each wave: Dorothy Smith and bell hooks. Both of these theorists have made exceptional contributions to feminist social theorizing.

SECOND-WAVE FEMINISM

First-wave feminism took shape in the mid-1800s, concluding just after World War I with the victory for (some) women of the right to vote (Calixte, Johnson, & Motapanyane, 2010; Le Gates, 2001). In Canada, "The Persons Case" (1929) is also an example of first-wave feminist activism which saw women being defined as "persons" under the law, thus paving the way for women to be able to occupy positions in public office (Calixte, Johnson, & Motapanyane, 2010).

Second-wave feminism finds its roots in the social movements of the 1960s in North America (Thornham, 2000; Zimmerman, McDermott, & Gould, 2009). At its core, second-wave feminism is characterized by understanding "women" as a coherent social group with a common experience *as women*. Women, as a category, are understood as "peaceful, nurturing, and cooperative . . . innocent victims of sexist oppression and patriarchy" (Adams, 2008). As a group, women also shared primary responsibility for domestic labour and social reproduction (Seidman, 2008).

Gender oppression, then, was conceived of as being experienced in the same way by all women. If women were united in their experience, then such a unified experience could form the basis for a political project of emancipation (Armstrong, 2006). Women could have a single, shared voice that would adequately represent all women in their struggle against

patriarchy—a pervasive and complex social and cultural system of male domination (Abbott, Wallace, & Tyler, 2005). This focus on homogeneity underlies much of the third-wave critique of second-wave feminism.

Second-wave feminism is also associated with consciousness-raising groups. The thinking is that if women share a common experience and if they get together to discuss those shared experiences, they would come to a realization about their mutual oppression—that is, they would understand that things that seem completely personal (such as primary responsibility for domestic labour and child rearing, and violence against women) are actually widely shared and part of the patriarchal structure (Snyder, 2008; Zimmerman, McDermott, & Gould, 2009). In this way, the personal is political (Snyder, 2008).

We move now to briefly consider the work of Dorothy Smith as an example of second-wave feminist theorizing.

Dorothy Smith Dorothy Smith's approach reflects a second-wave approach to feminist theorizing. While she recognizes that there are variations in the experiences of both men and women, what women share is domination by men (Seidman, 2008). Smith's project, then, is organized around the desire to produce a sociology for women (although in later writings she refers to this as a sociology for people) (Smith, 1987, 1990a, 1990b, 1999, 2000a). Of central concern for Smith is the gendered character of the social production of knowledge. Smith is critical of classical sociological approaches that produce what she calls objectified forms of knowledge and knowledge that is *androcentric* (meaning "male-centred"). Smith argues that women have been left out of knowledge production—as both knowers and actors (Seidman, 2008). Sociology, traditionally, has been organized around men—around their experiences and their positions (Seidman, 2008). Men have been the subjects and the authors while women have been ignored. Thus, sociology itself has contributed to the "erasing and devaluing" of women's experiences and perspectives (Seidman, 2008, p. 204). As it has been traditionally performed, sociology, according to Smith, has produced an androcentric intellectual world that presents itself as both universal and objective.

As an alternative, Smith is interested in a feminist sociology that can provide for women an account of the social relations that shape their lives—to explain that social relations that are both within our direct world and extend beyond it create the conditions of what is possible. As Smith (1999, p. 45) puts it, "we . . . seek from particular experience situated in the matrix of the everyday/everynight world to explore and display the relations, powers, and forces that organize and shape it."

Smith wants a sociology that retains the presence of an active subject: "the subject/knower of inquiry is not a transcendent subject but situated in the actualities of her own living, in relations with others as they are" (Smith, 1999, p. 75). Her approach stands in contrast to macrosociological accounts that produce what Smith calls objectified forms of knowledge. In other words, she is critical of knowledge that treats the world as being "out there" as an object to be discovered. Rather, Smith directs researchers to always look for the ways in which social processes happen through people's actions. As Smith (1999) states,

> Whatever exists socially is produced/accomplished by people "at work," that is, active, thinking, intending, feeling, in the actual local settings of their living and in relationships that are fundamentally among particular others—even though the categories of ruling produce particular others as expressions of its order.

Smith is interested in a sociology that helps women come to understand the broader conditions within which their experiences arise. After all, our experiences are not entirely shaped by daily interactions; rather, our experiences are often the result of ruling relations in everyday circumstances. Smith uses the concept of **ruling** to indicate the "socially-organized exercise of power that shapes people's actions and their lives" (Campbell & Gregor, 2002,

patriarchy A pervasive and complex social and cultural system of male domination.

ruling The exercise of power shaping people's actions.

BOX 3.1 CANADIAN CONTRIBUTIONS TO SOCIOLOGY

Dorothy Smith

Dorothy Smith is a pioneer in the development of Canadian women's studies programs and feminist courses. Born in England, she received her Ph.D. in sociology from the University of California at Berkeley in the early 1960s (Seidman, 2008). She taught at the University of British Columbia before moving to Toronto to work at the Ontario Institute for Studies in Education (OISE) at the University of Toronto in the late 1970s. She remained at OISE until her retirement, and today is a professor at the University of Victoria and a professor emerita at the University of Toronto.

In her essay "Whistling Women: Reflections on Rage and Rationality," Smith (1992) discusses the Montreal Massacre, during which Marc Lepine murdered 14 female engineering students at L'École Polytechnique on December 6, 1989. Rather than viewing the killings as an isolated act of a madman, Smith links them not only to wider social relations of men's violence against women but also to questions of rationality and knowledge.

As Lepine dismissed the men from the engineering classroom before murdering the female students, he yelled, "I hate feminists" (CBC, 1989). Were women pursuing engineering studies feminists in Lepine's mind? After all, women's presence in the academy, whether as students or as faculty members, challenges the patriarchal social order. Women's studies furthers this challenge by incorporating feminist-based, nontraditional approaches to knowledge. According to Smith (1992), academia's taken-for-granted regime of male rationality is made visible when challenged by women. Moreover, Smith argues that while feminism may be tolerated in women's studies programs (far away from "real" scholarly pursuits), it is met with anger when it crashes through the gate guarding "real" scholarly disciplines:

> Far from threatening the foundations of the university, critiques of racism and sexism are better understood as committed to removing deformations that have been historically sedimented in the everyday working life and the intellectual practises of universities in North America. Those who make the critique can be seen as measuring a university against an implicit ideal of fully reciprocal and symmetrical dialogue as foundational to universities' claims to universality and commitment to rational discourse. (Smith, 1999, p. 223)

Dorothy Smith
Photo by Sam Rowan

Drawing on a saying from her youth in northern England—"A whistling woman and a crowing hen, lets the devil out of his pen"—Smith (1992, p. 207) points to how gender reversals disrupt a supposedly natural social order. To many, women pursuing engineering studies represent just such a reversal. However, rather than shy away from altering social relations, Smith encourages women to continue to challenge the prevailing patriarchal social order. "After all," she writes, "we want a new kind of order in which hens may crow if they will and women can surely whistle" (Smith, 1992, p. 224).

p. 32). Ruling relations are the abstract, conceptual, and "extra-locally organized relations of state, professions, corporations, academic discourses, mass media and so on" (Smith, 2004, p. 31). These ruling relations exist in a generalized form and work to coordinate, from outside the local sites of our bodies, what people do (their actions) (Smith, 2004).

Part of Smith's task, then, is to "demystify ruling relations" (Salerno, 2013, p. 110). Smith's approach involves studying how these concepts and theories are implicated in the constituting of social relations (Smith, 2000a). As Campbell and Gregor (2002, p. 31) explain, "social relations are not done to people, nor do they just happen to people. Rather, people actively constitute social relations."

As students, how is your academic life shaped by your institution's course offerings? How is the size of your institution's classes dictated by your department? Who determines the hiring practices of your institution? Obviously, our experiences cannot be explained entirely on the basis of our typical or preferred activities. Smith's point is that we need to know and understand what is not visible from our individual locations. We need to make visible the social relations that frame the conditions of our experiences. The kind of sociology that Smith envisions can provide such an account of social relations that may transform women into active social agents (Seidman, 2008).

As mentioned, Smith's approach differs from that of *macro*sociology (discussed in Chapter 1), which tends to produce accounts of social processes as if they were external to the individual. Her approach also differs from *micro*sociology accounts, which remain firmly rooted in the microcosms of daily life. Rather, Smith wants to produce an account that tells people how things happen that go beyond the local sites of their experiences—and that they can possibly use to effect social change. In sum, Smith is interested in a sociology that can show people how the relations of ruling shape their lives.

THIRD-WAVE FEMINISM

One of the major critiques levied against second-wave theorizing is that the singular voice that supposedly represents all women is really the voice of white, middle-class, heterosexual, educated women (Zimmerman, McDermott, & Gould, 2009). While some second-wave theorists, like Dorothy Smith, did attempt to take social class into account, most theorizing was framed around a homogenous notion of "women"—difference was not recognized, let alone theorized.

Rather than a singular voice, third-wave feminists believe that what is needed is attention to the multiplicity of women's voices (Snyder, 2008). Third-wave feminists challenge second-wave thinking that women indeed shared a common experience; they challenged the coherence of the category of *woman*. Third-wave thinkers emphasize the "need for greater acceptance of complexities, ambiguities, and multiple locations" (Pinterics, 2001, p. 16). These feminists are interested in creating space for a feminism that takes up difference based on race, social class, sexuality, and so forth. Dichotomous positioning around gender and sexuality, for instance, is rejected and replaced with more fluid understandings (Mann & Huffman, 2005).

We now turn to a brief address of a pivotal theorist, bell hooks, who challenged second-wave thinking on the uniformity of women's experiences.

bell hooks bell hooks is in fact a pen name, borrowed from her maternal great-grandmother, for Gloria Jean Watkins. hooks uses lower-case letters to emphasize her ideas rather than herself as an author (Marriott, 1997). She is a critical figure in black feminist thought, also called anti-racist feminism and multicultural feminism.

She argues against second-wave feminist theorizing when she draws our attention to the fact that race is inextricable from gender:

> From the onset of my involvement with the women's movement I was disturbed by the white women's liberationists' insistence that race and sex were two separate issues. My life experience had shown me that the two issues were inseparable, that at the moment of my birth, two factors determined my destiny, my having been born black and my having been born female. (hooks, 1981, p. 12)

> > >

bell hooks, a prominent figure in black feminist thought, is critical of much feminist theorizing that automatically positions home life as patriarchal spaces of oppression for women. For many women, this is not the case! As is illustrated here, the household is often a refuge for women, especially from the institutionalized racism experienced in the labour force.

hooks argues that no one in the 1960s civil rights or women's movements seemed to pay attention to the realities of black women's lives: "We are rarely recognized as a group separate and distinct from black men, or as a present part of the larger group 'women' in this culture" (hooks, 1981, p. 7). hooks (1981) goes on to argue that when people talk about blacks, they focus on black *men;* and when people talk about women, they focus on *white* women. In such a framework, black women's identities are erased (hooks, 1981). Although hooks focuses her writings on black women, her goal is the liberation of all people (hooks, 1981).

hooks has also criticized feminist theorizing that automatically positions households as places of patriarchal oppression for women. Such positioning is based on the assumption that gender segregation exists in the labour market in capitalist societies (Adkins, 2005). According to these theories, because women and men are divided in the labour force (into "men's jobs" and "women's jobs") and women earn far less, their financial dependency leads in turn to their subjection and exploitation in households (Adkins, 2005). hooks argues against such universal assumptions about women's experiences. She points to the historical reality that for many, households have been spaces of refuge, resistance, and solidarity from racism, including the institutionalized racism of the labour force (Adkins, 2005; hooks, 1990).

❸ Post-Structuralist Theory

As discussed in Chapter 2, Enlightenment thinking views scientific knowledge as being the key to human freedom. Post-structuralists challenge this view, arguing that scientific knowledge, or ideas about absolute "truth," cannot stand outside power relations. This means that to study the underlying structures of a cultural object, such as a text or a film—as structuralists do—is to analyze it from the perspective of social relations that already exist. *Post*-structuralists, then, are concerned with how knowledge is socially *produced*. Post-structuralist thinking has influenced feminist theory, queer theory, post-colonial theory, and anti-racist theorizing.

MICHEL FOUCAULT

French philosopher Michel Foucault (1926–1984) was interested in the ways that power and knowledge work together. Foucault critiqued Marxism, for instance, for emphasizing class and the political economy as being the key principles in social organization. According to Foucault, this emphasis meant that struggles based on race, gender, and sexuality were marginalized (Seidman, 2008). After all, social movements are varied, and Foucault dismissed the idea that these uprisings could be explained on the basis of a totalizing theory such as Marxism (Seidman, 2008).

Here, we introduce some of Foucault's main ideas and concepts, many of which we draw on in subsequent chapters.

Power, Knowledge, and Discourse One of Foucault's greatest contributions to post-structural thought is his rethinking of power. His definition of power is different from the Marxist theory of power as oppression (Foucault, 1980), a position that Foucault refers to as the *repressive hypothesis*. This hypothesis holds that truth is opposed to power and can therefore play a liberating role. It views "truth" as something that can be produced outside of power relations and therefore as something that can be objective.

But, according to Foucault, power is not a thing possessed by one individual over another. Rather, he views power relations as being created within social relationships. As such, power relationships are multidirectional, can be found everywhere, and are always at work. Power relations, then, can produce particular forms of behaviour (Foucault, 1977). For example, we have the ability to *resist* power. That is, although Foucault understands that we are all subjected to particular forces, he also acknowledges that one group does not always dominate. In other words, Foucault understands individuals as, in a sense, having *agency*—meaning the capacity for self-directed action—since they have the ability to resist power relations and to alter power relations (Foucault, 1977).

Power is also linked with knowledge (Ritzer, 2008a; Salerno, 2013). According to Foucault, truths or facts are contextual, meaning that they can never be separated from the relations of power that they are produced within. To know something (particularly the "truth" about something or someone) is to exercise power. Think of medical doctors, who in our society are afforded a great degree of power because of the specialized knowledge they possess (McGrath, 2005). Doctors make pronouncements about our health, labelling us as "sick" or "healthy" (see Chapter 15). These kinds of pronouncements have the power to alter how we choose to live our lives (by eating certain foods, engaging in certain activities, and so forth) (McGrath, 2005). Despite the link that Foucault makes between power and knowledge, he does not envision a society that is run by a conspiracy among elites (Ritzer, 2008a).

Moreover, Foucault outlines how truths and facts come together in systems that he refers to as **discourses**, which guide how we think, act, and speak about a particular thing or issue, as well as determine *who* is authorized to speak. To return to the medical example, we can identify the medical discourse as being a system of "facts" that works to organize and produce how we think about medicine—that is, how we understand the human body, how we view doctors as the skilled and rightful people to practise medicine, and how we understand medicine to be grounded in good science (McGrath, 2005).

discourse A system of meaning that governs how we think, act, and speak about a particular thing or issue.

Discourses not only tell us what the world is, but also what the world *ought* to be like (Abbott, Wallace, & Tyler, 2005). Using the medical example again, discourses tell us about the need to be "healthy"—what a healthy body looks like, what healthy eating practices are, the importance of being healthy. This normalizing aspect of discourses leads us to another of Foucault's influential concepts: discipline.

Discipline Foucault (1977) uses the term **discipline** to mean how we come to be motivated to produce particular realities: "Disciplinary power works to produce bodies, practises and subjectivities that . . . bear the imprint of a given interest and logic. . ." (Green, 2010, p. 320). Using the discourse of health as an example, we are encouraged to exercise on a regular basis,

discipline The means by which we become motivated to produce particular realities.

> > >

Medical discourse is powerful. Doctors are positioned as the skilled and rightful people to practise medicine—the experts. Medical doctors are afforded a great deal of power because of the specialized knowledge they are seen to possess.

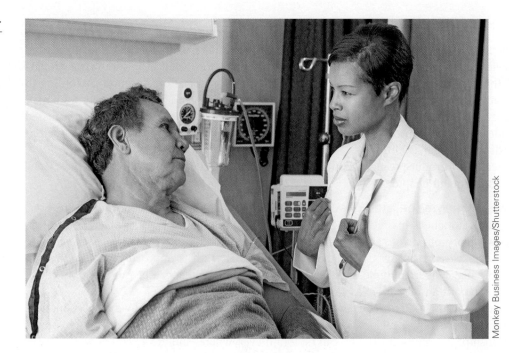

Monkey Business Images/Shutterstock

to eat nutritious foods, and to stay away from "bad" choices. Think of how often you see commercials and news items about trans fats! By paying attention to this thing called *health*, you are *disciplining* your body.

To use another example (discussed more fully in Chapter 8), we also engage in discipline to produce our bodies as "feminine" or "masculine." Think of all of the practices you engage in on a daily basis that contribute to your being understood by others as appropriately feminine or masculine. Examples of such practices include styling your hair; shaving; applying makeup; adorning your body with tattoos, piercings, and jewellery; and choosing your clothing. Such discipline also extends to your exercise regimen (or lack thereof) and your eating practices: do you conform to standards of thinness for women or of muscularity for men?

Think of the university, a setting in which both professors and students are embedded within the networks of power that operate there (Palamarek, 2008). Professors and students alike conform to specific and general expectations about their behaviour and performance. Students attend lectures, write essays and exams, behave appropriately in class, and so forth, while professors prepare their lectures, support their students, and so forth.

Foucault thought about how power operates by producing some behaviours while discouraging others. According to Foucault, discipline, as a form of modern power, can work through what he termed *surveillance*—acts of observing, recording, and training (Ritzer, 2008a; Seidman, 2008). These techniques function without relying on force or coercion (Hunt & Wickham, 1994). Think about your student record, and the accompanying threat of something being added to your "permanent record" in grade school or high school. If you were sent to the principal's office, a file about you may have been created in which your behaviour could be recorded. Your teachers observed your behaviour and admonished you for not sitting up straight, for failing to raise your hand before speaking, and so forth. All of these factors contribute to producing docile students.

normalization A social process by which some practices and ways of living are marked as "normal" and others are marked as "abnormal."

Such disciplinary power is exemplified by the normalizing judgment—a type of internalized (self-policing) coercion that divides, classifies, and controls through regulation (McGrath, 2005). This is what Foucault calls **normalization**—a social process by which some practices and ways of living are marked as "normal" and others are marked as "abnormal" (McGrath, 2005). An associated set of rewards and punishments encourages homogeneity (Foucault, 1977). Normalization, then, is a method of standardizing, of creating standards. As discussed in Chapter 9, in North American society heterosexuality is constructed as *normal* while any other sexuality is constructed as *abnormal*.

Finally, unlike classical Marxist theorists, Foucault contends that resistance to modern disciplinary power is not manifested in revolution but, rather, *within* power relations. As Foucault (1978, p. 96) writes, "there is no single locus of great Refusal, no soul of Revolt, source of all rebellions, or pure law of the revolutionary. Instead, there is a plurality of resistances, each of them a special case." These pluralities of resistances occur as ruptures or cracks that unsettle the smooth operation of disciplinary power. Consider those who try to construct "alternative femininities" by rejecting the dominant beauty ideal that is enshrined, for example, in slenderness. Resistance is both local and necessarily diverse (Seidman, 2008).

Queer Theory

Within the civil rights and women's movements of the 1960s, gays and lesbians felt that they were marginalized. In fact, a rather large rupture occurred within the women's movement between feminist heterosexual women and feminist lesbian women (Seidman, 2008). A key focus of all of these social movements was the belief that everyone should have equal treatment under the law, enjoying the rights and privileges afforded to all citizens (McGrath, 2005). Queer theory problematizes the assumption that we are all the same and deserve the same treatment (McGrath, 2005). Instead, as discussed further in Chapter 9, queer theorists foreground *difference* as the basis for political and intellectual endeavours (McGrath, 2005). Queer theory is also concerned with deconstructing sexual identities by exploring how these identities are historically and culturally situated (Ritzer, 2008a). These are the challenges of queer theory.

Three areas of queer theory that we will explore in turn are *desire, language,* and *identity.* These concepts overlap and are implicated in each other.

DESIRE

Queer theorists want to open up the concept and reality of **desire** as wide as possible. Theorists are not solely concerned with marginalized sexualities (McGrath, 2005), but, instead, aim to disrupt categories of normal sexuality and acceptable sexuality and allow instead for sexuality's diverse and numerous expressions. Sexual expression, after all, should not just be understood as the missionary position, engaged in solely for the purpose of procreation (McGrath, 2005). Ideas from Foucault (1978) come into play here as Foucault understood that our sexual identities are created, and that normalization is seen to create stratification (in this case, the division between "normal" and "abnormal") and self-policing (regulation). Although it is hard for us to think outside the categories of "normal" and "abnormal," these categories are, of course, not value-neutral (McGrath, 2005). Such binaries continue to shape sexualities (Ritzer, 2008a).

desire **Our sexual attractions and wants.**

LANGUAGE

Queer theorists are also concerned with how language is related to power. Unless confronted with a problem of miscommunication, few of us stop and consider our use of language—that is, many of us take language itself and our use of it for granted (McGrath, 2005; Turner, 2000). But language and language use is not so straightforward, so let us consider it in more detail.

Just as Foucault understands that knowledge is inseparable from power, it is impossible to disentangle language from knowledge since language is the vehicle of knowledge (Foucault, 1977; McGrath, 2005). Queer theorists ask us to consider the fact that language is not transparent. Rather, queer theorists argue that it is value-laden as opposed to being a neutral description of some reality (McGrath, 2005). Think about words such as *black* and *white*, *up* and *down*. They are not merely descriptions; like the normal/abnormal categories discussed above, they contain value judgments. *Up* conjures thoughts of heaven and "good," while *down* brings to mind images of hell and "bad" (McGrath, 2005). These terms are not simply designations of spatial locations (up and down), then, but have come to signify much more.

Similarly, the term *normal* is not always simply deployed to mean the statistical average; it has come to be associated with what is "good," or considered "right," and so forth, while *abnormal* means bad and wrong. The term *normal* has become the standard by which all else is measured. How we use language is connected to the concept of power, in that language produces reality. Sexualities that are produced under the category of *abnormal* are then governed, examined, and legislated by the "normals" (Ritzer, 2008a). Being *abnormal*, in the context of sexuality, is not necessarily a matter of being statistically different but, rather, becomes a matter worthy of intervention and alteration—legal and medical and so forth (McGrath, 2005). Such is the power of language to produce reality.

Language operates with a logic of binaries—these are either/or dualities wherein one element in a pair is defined by what it is not (West versus East, women versus men, skinny versus overweight, good versus evil). These binaries are not neutral definitions but, rather, are value-laden. One element of each is typically more highly valued, while the other is devalued; this valuation/devaluation is how power is implicated in language or discourse. These binaries, along with their implicit valuations, actually work to structure how we understand reality, ourselves, and how we move through the world (McGrath, 2005; Turner, 2000).

IDENTITY

identity Our sense of self, that is socially produced, is fluid, and is multiple.

> > >

Queer theorists are concerned with pursuing social justice and equity in an arena not of sameness, but of difference. Queer theorists aim to disrupt binary categories of "normal" and "acceptable" sexuality in favour of allowing for its multiple expressions.

This brings us to how queer theorists deal with **identity**, which again draws from Foucault's insights. Identity, in this perspective, is not some coherent entity that emerges from within

Image Source Plus/Alamy

our "souls," making us who we are (McGrath, 2005). Rather, identity is socially produced and is fluid and multiple (Foucault, 1978; Ritzer, 2008a; Turner, 2000). Our understanding of others and even of ourselves is always partial and contextual. This partiality connects to our discussion of language above—language is unable to convey the totality of objects or persons. Our identity is often tied to our connections with others (whether we are a mother, daughter, sister, student, friend), and as such our identity is situated within, and contextualized by, the multiple social relations within which we are embedded (McGrath, 2005). If we talk about ourselves as being skinny or overweight, blond or brunette, white or black, all of these categories carry an implicit social relation. You are skinny compared with whom? You are overweight compared with whom? This example illustrates how identity is implicated in the restrictions and limits of language as well as the relations of power and discourse.

Identity is constructed through social relations and through discourses around gender (man versus woman) and sexuality (straight versus gay) and thus there are no core identities (Seidman, 2008; Turner, 2000). Queer theorists use this idea as a way to reveal and renegotiate the social inequalities in society. That is, if everyone's identity is constructed, then no one person's identity (including one's sexuality) should be the standard by which another's identity is measured. One's identity is no more normal than, say, the painting of one artist in comparison to the painting of another artist—they are simply different (McGrath, 2005; Ritzer, 2008a).

Post-Colonial Theory

Post-colonial theory focuses on the political and cultural effects of colonialism. The colonial practices of imperial nations can include conquests of land, resources, and people's labour, as well as political rule and the imposition of language (Cook, 2001). The term **imperialism** refers to the ideas, practices, and attitudes of *colonizers* (that is, "what happens at home") (Cook, 2001). Former imperialist nations include Britain, Belgium, France, Germany, and Portugal. The term **colonialism** refers to the effects of imperialism within colonized spaces, including concrete and ideological effects ("what happens away from home") (Cook, 2001). Examples of former colonies include India, virtually all countries in Africa, the Bahamas, Grenada, and many others.

The *post* in post-colonial theory suggests a focus on events that happened after formal colonialism ended in the early 1960s. However, post-colonial studies are not only concerned with happenings after colonialism. Post-colonial theory (also called colonial discourse studies) addresses several kinds of questions: Why were certain nations able to become imperial powers and gain so much control over the non-Western world? How were imperialism and colonialism practised by the West? What were the relationships between the colonizers and the colonized? How did colonizers defend their domination over others? How did people resist colonialism? Although formal colonialism has ended, what kinds of imperial and colonial relations persist? What are the enduring effects of colonialism? Are countries truly *post-colonial*? (See Cook, 2001; Salerno, 2013; Seidman, 2008.)

imperialism The conquest of land, resources, and people's labour; the ideas, practices, and attitudes of colonizers.

colonialism The effects of imperialism, including concrete and ideological effects, within colonized territories.

SAID'S CONCEPT OF ORIENTALISM

Edward Said (1935–2003) is a pivotal figure in post-colonial theory. A Palestinian, Said was born in Jerusalem but lived in the United States for most of his adult life, earning his Ph.D. from Harvard University in 1964. Until his death, he was a professor of English at Columbia University (Seidman, 2008). In Said's most influential work, *Orientalism,* he critiques Western nations' colonial dominion, which remained in place even as they championed ideals of personal freedom, social progress, and national sovereignty (Seidman, 1998, 2008).

> > >

Gendered Orientalist scripts, long a feature of colonial discourse, position Asians as morally and culturally inferior to the West.

Blend Images - Hill Street Studios/Getty Images

While the study of empire most certainly concerns conquests of land and resources, it also concerns cultural meanings (Seidman, 1998). Said (1978) outlines **Orientalism** as a Western style of thought that creates a false opposition between the Orient (East) and the Occident (West). He views Orientalism as a discourse of power, one that works to naturalize the East as being inferior to the West (Cook, 2001; Salerno, 2013). In this way, Said's work draws on Michel Foucault's notion of discourse as being implicated in relations of power and knowledge.

Orientalism **Said's concept of a discourse of power that creates a false distinction between a superior West and an inferior East.**

Said speaks of three kinds of Orientalism; all three are interdependent:

1. *Academic Orientalism* refers to knowledge that is produced by academics, government experts, historians, sociologists, and anyone else who is producing information or writing about the Orient. Said perceives that this knowledge is not neutral but is embedded in power relations. He argues that people make a distinction between the East and the West as the starting point for their theories, political accounts, and so on (Said, 1978).

2. *Imaginative Orientalism* refers to any representation making a basic distinction between the Orient and the Occident. These representations may include art, novels, poems, images, and social descriptions (Said, 1978).

3. *Institutional Orientalism* refers to the institutions created by Europeans such that they could gain authority over, alter, and rule the Orient (Said, 1978).

Said recognized that the discourse of Orientalism guided the representation of the East and provided the conditions for Orientalism to succeed as a mode of imperial domination (Cook, 2001). The characterization of the East as inferior, childlike, and incapable of progress and development is in stark contrast to the characterization of the West as superior, rational, and developed (Cook, 2001; Said, 1978; Salerno, 2013). The East is to be feared (for example, the Yellow Peril—the fear of Asian immigration to Western countries in the late 1800s) and thus is in need of being controlled (by pacification, research, and complete occupation) (Said, 1978).

We can see lingering imperial notions in the United States as it continues to seek to control "over there." Consider the invasion of both Iraq and Afghanistan, countries that

<<<

The colonial practices of imperial nations can include conquests of land, resources, and labour, in addition to political rule and the imposition of language. Here we have a historical shot of colonial rule.

were (and are) positioned in Western media as backward, barbaric, and in need of Western order and control.

Even the Disney Corporation was criticized by the American-Arab Anti-Discrimination Committee (Wingfield & Karaman, 1995) for the Orientalist lyrics in the original version of the opening song "Arabian Nights" in the 1992 film *Aladdin*. The first version of the soundtrack contains the song's original wording, while all releases since July 1993 contain new wording. The DVD release also contains the revised lyrics. The original lyrics draw on Orientalist notions about the East as meting out arbitrary acts of violence—where you might have your ear cut off at someone else's whim. While this overt reference to savagery was removed and replaced with lyrics about a scorching wasteland, the revised lyrics nonetheless still position the East as inferior and barbaric.

Critics of Said's work point out that he fails to consider how non-Westerners view themselves and the West (Seidman, 2008). Many of those living in the East resist the imposition of Western culture and try to maintain their own cultures and/or fashion new hybrid cultures (Seidman, 2008). Homi Bhabha (1994) argues that the West has a more ambivalent relationship with the East than Said describes, in that Western discourses also reveal a longing or attraction to the East (Seidman, 2008). Bhabha points out that the West and the East are enmeshed in a relationship that is not completely oppositional, "but involves identification, a mix of repulsion and attraction, and a standpoint of dominance that is always in danger of reversal" (Seidman, 2008, p. 257). He reminds us that power does not flow only from colonizer to colonized but is multidirectional, even if the colonizers do occupy a more powerful position. After all, the colonizers must always rely on the colonized to uphold their rule (Seidman, 2008).

Said's work has been helpful for those sociologists who explore the social production of the "Other," whereby one group differentiates itself from another by a superior/inferior opposition (Seidman, 2008). Further, because Said draws from Foucault's work, we are reminded to always consider that the production of knowledge is never neutral and is always implicated in relations of power.

>>> Thinking Sociologically

Conduct a search of news photographs relating to Canada's presence in Afghanistan. Can you discern any instances of Orientalism in these representations?

6 CANADA AND COLONIALISM

Canada has its own colonial history—it was a British colony. Canada won its independence (both economic and political) such that it was able to develop as a rich and powerful nation in its own right (Cook, 2001).

However, when we consider Canada's Aboriginal population, perhaps the "post" in post-colonial has not yet been realized (Cook, 2001). Aboriginals are among the most marginalized people in Canada—economically, socially, and politically—with Aboriginal women being the hardest hit (Native Women's Association of Canada [NWAC], n.d.). There is a long history of internal colonial action in Canada with regard to the treatment of Aboriginals. Residential schools are often cited as horrific examples of colonial actions within Canada: Aboriginal children were taken from their families, made to live at these schools, and forced to learn English. Their histories were denied to them: they were not allowed to see their families or use their first language or practise their culture (de Leeuw, 2009). The goal of these schools was assimilation into the dominant culture—no matter the human cost. In 2008, Stephen Harper, as prime minister of Canada, formally apologized for the country's role in the residential schooling system. We explore the legacy of residential schooling in more detail in Chapter 12.

CANADA AND GENDERED ORIENTALISM

We can see that Orientalism is still an important theoretical concept today and is still at work in contemporary Canadian society. For example, Hijin Park's (2010) research explores mainstream media depictions of attacks on six Asian women and girls who were living in Vancouver while studying English in 2002. Park's critical discourse analysis of newspaper and magazine articles that covered the attacks is informed by feminism and post-colonialism. Park's research provides an excellent example of how social theories can explain what is happening in our social world. You will recall from our discussion of Edward Said's Orientalism that the West creates and perpetuates views of the East as backward, in need of help, and

> > >

Orientalism, as a mode of imperial domination, characterizes the East as inferior and barbaric, while the West is viewed as superior, rational, and developed. Such a characterization is captured in this image, which juxtaposes US military power with local Iraqi ways of being.

John Moore/AP Photo

inferior. Park (2010) traces how the media depictions of the attacks on these women and girls positioned them as being in need of Western protection.

Of course, this contemporary incident cannot be separated from Canada's past practices with respect to Asian immigration, which was largely blocked in Canada until the 1950s, as well as the internment of Japanese Canadians during World War II. Nor can these incidents be separated from the economics of the English-as-a-foreign-language industry in Vancouver. As Park (2010, p. 344) notes, "whether Asian students were afraid appeared to be of less concern than whether their fear would correspond to a loss of revenue for the EFL and tourism industries."

Park notes how the media included Orientalist interview quotes from police that situated "Asian" behaviour in contrast to "Canadian" behaviour. For example, "[Staff Sergeant] Worth believes that men target Asian women because of the perception they will not complain to authorities" (Park, 2010, p. 347). Such statements are positioned against statements about Canadian equality. These kinds of statements and positioning are not new but, rather, have long been a feature of colonial discourse. The West is positioned as "humane and democratic in relation to 'the rest'" (Park, 2010, p. 347).

Overall, Park argues that the media coverage of the Vancouver attacks against Asian girls and women is a reassertion of gendered Orientalist scripts that position Asians as morally and culturally inferior to the West.

❼ Anti-Racist Theories

CRITICAL RACE THEORY

Critical race theory (CRT) is said to have its origins in a 1981 student protest and student-organized course on Race, Racism, and American Law at Harvard Law School (Lawrence, Matsuda, Delgado, & Crenshaw, 1993). The protest was sparked by the departure of Harvard's first African-American professor, Derrick Bell, who had left to become dean of Law at the University of Oregon. With only two professors of colour remaining at Harvard Law School, students were attempting to convince the administration to hire additional faculty of colour. When the administration did not meet the students' demands, the students organized the course mentioned above such that leading academics of colour were invited to lecture to the students each week and to discuss Professor Bell's work. These events proved to be a vehicle for the creation of CRT as both a field and a movement (Lawrence, Matsuda, Delgado, & Crenshaw, 1993).

Watch

Questions and Debates in the Field of Race and Ethnicity

CRT is defined by the following tenets:

1. "CRT recognizes that racism is endemic to American life" (Lawrence, Matsuda, Delgado, & Crenshaw, 1993, p. 6). CRT is interested in exploring how the status quo of American life (characterized by federalism, privacy, property interests, etc.—a set of interests and values) actually operates as a vehicle of racial oppression and subordination (Lawrence, Matsuda, Delgado, & Crenshaw, 1993).

2. "CRT expresses skepticism toward dominant legal claims of neutrality, objectivity, color blindness, and meritocracy" (Lawrence, Matsuda, Delgado, & Crenshaw, 1993, p. 6). CRT does not understand acts of racism as individual, isolated, random acts. Rather, CRT argues that racism is institutionalized (Aylward, 1999; Lawrence, Matsuda, Delgado, & Crenshaw, 1993).

3. "CRT challenges ahistoricism and insists on a contextual/historical analysis of the law" (Lawrence, Matsuda, Delgado, & Crenshaw, 1993, p. 6). CRT argues that contemporary racial inequalities are linked to earlier historical periods. Contemporary situations of income disadvantage, disproportionate imprisonment of black men, and unequal levels

of education and political representation are all linked with historical practices (Lawrence, Matsuda, Delgado, & Crenshaw, 1993).

4. "CRT insists on recognition of the experiential knowledge of people of color and our communities of origin in analyzing law and society" (Lawrence, Matsuda, Delgado, & Crenshaw, 1993, p. 6). CRT sees value in drawing on the experiences of those who have experienced racism (Aylward, 1999).

5. "CRT is interdisciplinary and eclectic" (Lawrence, Matsuda, Delgado, & Crenshaw, 1993, p. 6). CRT draws from a number of traditions, including Marxism, feminism, post-structuralism, and liberalism. This interdisciplinary approach allows CRT to use a methodology or a theoretical insight strategically in order to advance the pursuit of racial justice (Lawrence, Matsuda, Delgado, & Crenshaw, 1993).

6. "CRT works toward the end of eliminating racial oppression as part of the broader goal of ending all forms of oppression" (Lawrence, Matsuda, Delgado, & Crenshaw, 1993, p. 6). CRT takes an intersectional approach in understanding that racism exists simultaneously in people's lives with sexism, classism, and heterosexism. To achieve racial justice, CRT understands that our entire social organization must be refashioned (Aylward, 1999; Lawrence, Matsuda, Delgado, & Crenshaw, 1993).

CRT allows us to view contemporary social situations through a lens of historical racism. In this way, we can connect historical inequities to contemporary practices and situations. For instance, consider Hurricane Katrina, which hit the Gulf Coast of the United States in August 2005. Many social scientists have focused on how the nexus of race and social class was implicated in the evacuation of citizens, rescue efforts, and governmental action and inaction (T. Allen, 2007; Campanella, 2007; Denzin, 2007; Hartman & Squires, 2006; Kaiser, Eccleston, & Hagiwara, 2008; Katz, 2008; Morris, 2008; Sharkey, 2007; Zottarelli, 2008). After the hurricane, there was a lack of an organized government rescue response for

> > >

This image of the National Guard patrolling the Lower 9th Ward in New Orleans one year after Hurricane Katrina depicts some of the social and economic effects on poor neighbourhoods in the aftermath of the storm. Abandoned homes are commonplace.

Ann Johansson/Corbis

citizens trapped in New Orleans because of flooding. Those who had made their way to the Superdome stadium lived in appalling conditions in terms of food and sanitation.

Consider the social landscape of New Orleans prior to Hurricane Katrina. Poverty was a major concern in New Orleans as 28 percent of residents were poor. In this large city, many (more than 105 000) individuals did not own a car and so did not have access to a vehicle for evacuation from the city when Katrina hit. This landscape is also raced. Almost 70 percent of those generally affected by Katrina were African American. Forty-four percent of those affected by the flooding were African American. Two-thirds of those without access to a vehicle to use for evacuation were African American (T. Allen, 2007).

Many of the scholars who wrote about Katrina argue that the "natural" disaster of Hurricane Katrina was so devastating precisely because of decades of institutionalized racial inequality, as evidenced in the statistical conditions mentioned above. Hurricane Katrina revealed for the world the enduring effects of racial segregation and racial inequalities in housing and occupation (Katz, 2008).

In Canada, the case of *R.D.S. v. The Queen* provides an example for critical race theorists to show that legal principles, such as "the reasonable person," are not colour-blind. A black youth in Nova Scotia was arrested and charged with assaulting a white police officer as the officer tried to arrest another youth (Aylward, 1999). The original judge in the case, Judge Corrine Sparks, was the only black woman judge in Nova Scotia (Graycar, 2008; Women's Legal Education and Action Fund [LEAF], 1997). Judge Sparks acquitted the youth and made reference to tensions between the police and nonwhite persons. Critical race theorists point out that white judges make decisions based on their experiences daily, but when a black woman judge made reference to racial tensions, the case was appealed to the Supreme Court. The Court upheld the original acquittal and accepted the argument that a reasonable person would use his or her knowledge of the social context of the community and race relations, as long as that knowledge was relevant, not based on stereotype, and did not prevent a fair decision (Graycar, 2008; LEAF, 1997). As critical race scholars argue, this case challenged notions of colour-blindness.

Critical race theorists and practitioners, then, are committed to ending racial oppression. Another important development in anti-racist theorizing is a focus on whiteness and the privileging of whiteness.

> > > > Thinking Sociologically

Conduct a search of newspaper stories or television news reports that appeared immediately following Hurricane Katrina. Did the media connect race and social class to the rescue efforts? How was racism and poverty addressed in the news coverage? Consider examining documentaries that have been produced since Hurricane Katrina. How have race and social class been portrayed since the immediate aftermath? Do you see a difference in the way the effects of Katrina were addressed immediately after the hurricane and years later?

THEORIZING WHITENESS

While a great deal has been written in the social sciences about race (especially race and racism in an American context), it was not until the 1980s and 1990s that social theorists began to consider whiteness as a racial identity (Seidman, 2008).

Richard Dyer's (1997) book *White* addresses whiteness as something that is both visible and invisible: "At the level of racial representation. . . . Whites are not of a certain race, they're just of the human race" (Dyer, 1997, p. 3). In countries such as the United States, Germany, England, and Denmark (among others), whites are plainly visible, often occupying front-line positions (managers, doctors, servers, concierge), while nonwhites are often out of sight (kitchen staff, janitors, housekeepers) (Seidman, 2008).

Race is often thought of as a colour—as being nonwhite (Seidman, 2008). The prevailing approach to whiteness is that it is colourless or, as Dyer (1997, p. 3) states

Watch

White Privilege in the US

> > >

Whiteness as a taken-for-granted category was highlighted during the 2008 American presidential campaign. News coverage consistently referred to Barack Obama as a "black" candidate, while there was never any mention of John McCain's whiteness. Such representation is an example of the *deracializing* of whiteness, whereby whiteness is constructed as the default position, to which everything else is marked.

The Canadian Press/Gerald Herbert/AP Photo

above, "just [members] of the human race." Within such an approach, disturbing dualisms emerge in which whites are thought of as simply people while nonwhites are understood as distinct races (Seidman, 2008). For example, during the 2008 American presidential race, news coverage of Barack Obama consistently referred to him as a black senator, while no mention was made of John McCain as a white senator; McCain was referred to simply as a senator. Such marking (or nonmarking) of race represents the *deracializing* of whiteness. In other words, whiteness is constructed as the default position, and only those who do not fit within this default category are marked (Seidman, 2008).

Steven Seidman is careful to point out that white and nonwhite is a binary construction, a relationship of contrast: whiteness is *real* simply because there are people who are not white (Seidman, 2008). Whiteness carries with it privilege; as Seidman (2008, p. 232) points out, "Whites rule the institutions of many Western nations." While visibility indicates privilege, so too does the invisibility of whiteness—the assumption that white represents *the* human race (Dyer, 1997). In the same way that Said (1978) argues that Orientalism is a discourse that normalizes the centrality and supremacy of the West, whiteness is the standard against which all others are measured (Seidman, 2008). As Dyer (1997, p. 9) argues, "White people have power and believe that they think, feel and act like and for all people. . . . White people set standards of humanity by which they are bound to succeed and others bound to fail. . . . White power none the less reproduces itself regardless of intention . . . because it is not seen as Whiteness, but as normal."

"All people are racialized" (Salerno, 2013, p. 200). We are all assigned a race and that assignment is linked to privilege (Salerno, 2013). As sociologists, we need to understand that whiteness affords structural advantage (Frankenberg, 1993). Those engaged in white studies endeavour to reveal the social underpinnings of whiteness with the goal of challenging its privileged status (Seidman, 2008).

❽ Globalization

Globalization, which is the subject of Chapter 19, is not solely an economic phenomenon, but also one that influences sociocultural and political processes. Today, the world is increasingly interconnected, owing not only to technological advances in communication but also to the global flow of money, capital, and commodities. However, for the most part, it is Westerners who have the privilege of experiencing the world in this global way (Clarke, 2006). So how do we theorize these changing aspects of contemporary global life?

According to British sociologist Anthony Giddens (1998, pp. 30–31), globalization "is not only, or even primarily, about economic interdependence, but about the transformation of time and space in our lives." In premodern societies, time was linked to the changing seasons and there was little concept of space beyond a collection of villages (Clarke, 2006). In these traditional societies, most people would interact with those who were geographically close, and would rely on people they knew for assistance. Distant others were precisely that—distant and unknown.

This sense of time and space changed dramatically with the invention of the clock and the Industrial Revolution (Clarke, 2006). As Giddens (1990) writes,

Shutterstock

<< <

Globalization is an economic, social, cultural, and political process. Today, we find the world to be increasingly interconnected in the face of advanced technological communication and the global flow of money, capital, and commodities.

✦[Explore

Job on the Line

> The invention of the mechanical clock and its diffusion to virtually all members of the population (a phenomenon which dates at its earliest from the late eighteenth century) were of key significance in the separation of time from space. The clock expressed a uniform dimension of "empty" time, quantified in such a way as to permit the precise designation of "zones" of the day e.g., the "working day." (p. 17)

((•—[Listen

Pew Study on Globalization

Moreover, with the 1884 adoption of Greenwich Mean Time (GMT)—in which GMT is the starting point for all of the world's time zones (GMT+1, GMT+2, GMT–1, GMT–2, etc.)—time was globally standardized.

Giddens refers to what he calls the **time–space distanciation**, which allows social relations to shift from a local to a global context. This separation of time and space marked a crucial distinction between traditional and modern institutions. Social relations could then exist across "infinite spans of time and space" (Clarke, 2006, p. 138). Giddens was interested in explaining just how this expanding out of time and space occurs (Allan, 2006). He focused on what he calls **disembedding mechanisms** that served to affect the shift in social relations from local to global contexts (Allan, 2006). According to Giddens, the two mechanisms that allow for this reconfiguration of social relations are *symbolic tokens* and *expert systems*.

Symbolic tokens are media of exchange that can be passed around without consideration of the specific person or group involved. Symbolic tokens—of which the primary example is money—make it possible for people to move from one local space to another, creating the illusion of a shrinking world (Clarke, 2006). As a common currency, "money permits the exchange of anything for anything, regardless of whether the goods involved share any substantive qualities in common with one another" (Giddens, 1990, p. 22). We

time–space distanciation The separation of time and space, which allows social relations to shift from a local to a global context.

disembedding mechanism A mechanism that aids in shifting social relations from local to global contexts.

symbolic token A medium of exchange (such as money).

BOX 3.2 EXPLORING THEORY

Theory	Leading Theorists	Key Insights	Key Concepts
Western Marxism	Antonio Gramsci	The rule of the dominant class involves ideological control and consent.	Hegemony
Second-wave feminism	Dorothy Smith	Women's common experiences could be used as the basis for a political project of emancipation.	Relations of ruling
Third-wave feminism	bell hooks	Challenges the coherence of the category of "woman"; recognizes diversity of women.	
Post-structuralist theory	Michel Foucault	Power is productive—it produces particular forms of behaviour. The production of knowledge cannot stand outside of power relations.	Power, knowledge, discourse, discipline
Queer theory	Draws on insights from Michel Foucault	Seeks to destabilize and deconstruct sexual identities. Sexuality is socially constructed.	Desire, identity
Post-colonial theory	Edward Said	Orientalism is a Western style of thought that creates a false difference between the Orient (East) and the Occident (West). Orientalism is a discourse of power that has the effect of naturalizing the East as being inferior to the West.	Orientalism
Critical race theory	Charles Lawrence; Mari Matsuda; Richard Delgado; Kimberle Crenshaw	Racism is widespread in North America. Challenges the supposed neutrality of law and principles such as objectivity and colour-blindness.	Historical racism
Globalization	Anthony Giddens	Explores transformations in our lives dealing with time and space. Globalization is an economic, social, cultural, and political process.	Time–space distanciation, disembedding mechanisms

can even use our credit cards to move around the world, with our banks doing the currency conversion for us (Clarke, 2006).

Expert systems of knowledge are also associated with modernity. Giddens understands these systems as disembedding because they shift the centre of our lives away from the local to the abstract expert systems of knowledge that may be distant (Allan, 2006). Think about how traditional societies operated: if you had questions about child rearing or how to grow healthy crops, you would rely on people in your local social network (Allan, 2006). Today, though, we rely on those trained in abstract knowledge. We do not even have to actually "go" to experts to be reliant on expert systems of knowledge (Allan, 2006). Western medicine, for example, is a system that dominates globally; polio vaccinations in North America are the same vaccinations used in the Sudan (Clarke, 2006). As a result, other forms of medicine are rendered "alternative" or even suspect (see Chapter 15).

Expert systems implicate us in relations of trust and risk. We trust that engineers and architects know something about construction, such that we do not fear that the roof will cave in as we enter a building. When boarding an airplane, we are both risking and trusting in an expert system that states that the aircraft is fit to fly: "In high modernity, trust and risk are inseparable" (Clarke, 2006, p. 139).

Expert systems of knowledge, then, are incorporated into both institutional and individual practices (Seidman, 2008), and institutional dimensions of modernity are clearly linked with globalization (Allan, 2006). Giddens identifies these institutional dimensions as capitalism, industrialism (international division of labour), monopoly of violence (world military order), and surveillance (nation-state) (Allan, 2006). These institutional dimensions are interlaced and support one another (Clarke, 2006).

Giddens (1990) argues that globalization is an inevitable feature of modernity, but one that is based on a Western worldview (Clarke, 2006). As time and space are stretched and/or removed from the actual, institutions can further remove the social from the local. This removal can then allow further abstract relations at the global level (Allan, 2006). Globalization, according to Giddens, then, is "the intensification of worldwide social relations which link distant localities in such a way that local happenings are shaped by events occurring many miles away and vice versa" (1990, p. 64). In other words, there is a dialectic relationship between the local and the distant. Importantly, Giddens go beyond understanding globalization as a purely economic phenomenon, viewing it as something that transforms the social (Clarke, 2006).

expert systems
Systems of knowledge on which we rely but with which we may never be directly in contact.

Summary

❶ Gramsci's concept of hegemony holds that the ruling class dominates through the permeation of its ideology. Its prevailing philosophy, culture, and morality become internalized by the population and appear as common sense. In this way, the subordinate classes never feel wholly oppressed by ruling-class culture.

❷ As an example of second-wave feminism, Dorothy Smith's feminist theory begins with the actualities of people's lives and addresses how they are influenced by social relations outside their particular worlds. bell hooks, our third-wave feminism example, critiques the erasure of black women's identities in the context of the women's movement, and focuses on the inseparability of race and gender.

❸ Michel Foucault understands power not as an entity, but as constituted within social relations. This approach thus perceives individuals as having the agency to resist and even change power relations. Foucault links power with knowledge through his concept of discourse, a system of "truths" that serve to structure how people think about certain subjects. Discipline, according to Foucault, is a form of modern power that works through normalizing judgment rather than force or coercion.

4 Queer theory's three principal areas of critique are desire, language, and identity. With regard to desire, queer theorists aim to disrupt categories of "normal" and acceptable sexuality and allow for its multiple expressions. Language is understood as having the power to create reality in that, far from being neutral, language is laced with implicit values. Identity is perceived not as inherent within us but rather as constructed: it is fluid, multiple, and emerges through our relationships with others.

5 Post-colonial theory is concerned with relations of power, whether past or present, between colonizing powers and those colonized. Edward Said's concept of Orientalism outlines the West's false opposition between it and the Orient (or the East), whereby the West is considered superior to the East. This Orientalism takes three forms: academic, imaginative, and institutional.

6 Canada has its own colonial past. Internal colonialism for Aboriginals in Canada has resulted in severe forms of marginalization—economic, social, and political.

7 Critical race theory holds that racism is endemic in American life, is institutionalized, and is linked to historical practices. It also recognizes the experiential knowledge of those who have experienced racism, is interdisciplinary, and works toward the elimination of racism. The understanding of "whiteness" as a racial identity implies an important recognition that whites are generally viewed as the default position, with only those who do not fit into this category being marked.

8 Giddens understands globalization as occurring through the separation of time and space, whereby social relations shifted from local to global contexts. Two mechanisms associated with the process are symbolic tokens (money) and expert systems of knowledge. Giddens also links globalization to such institutions as capitalism, industrialism, and world military order.

Key Terms

colonialism *79*

desire *77*

discipline *75*

discourse *75*

disembedding mechanism *87*

expert systems *89*

hegemony *68*

identity *78*

imperialism *79*

normalization *76*

Orientalism *80*

patriarchy *71*

ruling *71*

symbolic token *87*

time–space distanciation *87*

Reviewing the Concepts

1. How does Michel Foucault connect power with knowledge?

2. What is Dorothy Smith's critique of traditional approaches to sociology?

3. How does Anthony Giddens link time and space to globalization?

Applying Your Sociological Imagination

1. What are some contemporary examples of hegemony (in addition to heterosexual hegemony and hegemonic masculinity)?

2. How might you use critical race theory to examine the aftermath of the tsunami that occurred in the Indian Ocean on December 26, 2004, or the earthquake in Haiti in January 12, 2010?

3. What are some examples of a globalizing world (think culturally, economically, and politically)?

MySocLab

Visit MySocLab to access a variety of online resources that will help you prepare for tests and apply your knowledge.

4 Research, Methodology, and Ethics

If you are a fan of popular culture, you are certainly not alone. Let us say that you get excited about seeing a newly released movie every week and even adjust your social life so that you can watch it (or perhaps you *make* it your social life by getting friends together to go to the movies each week). Do you plan home screenings of films nominated for awards (such as an Oscar night)? Why are you so interested in *movies?* Does your interest lie in the films themselves, in the experience of watching a film in the theatre, of sharing that experience with others?

Think about how you could frame your interest sociologically: Might an interest in movies and the enjoyment of particular films be linked to social class, gender, race, or ethnicity? And how could you research this issue to find out? You could certainly construct a survey and have a wide variety of people answer it. Or, are you more interested in knowing in more detail, through one-on-one interviews, what people "see" when they watch movies? Or you might ask about how they experience movie-watching—is it that people like to get lost in a story? The questions are endless . . .

Research is not separate from everyday life; in fact, our everyday experiences often drive what we end up researching. While you read about each method, try to imagine how you could use it to answer intriguing queries you may have as you navigate daily life.

LEARNING OBJECTIVES

By the end of this chapter, students will be able to

① Understand the connection between sociological theory and research questions.

② Distinguish between quantitative and qualitative approaches, and between inductive and deductive reasoning.

③ Understand the overall research process.

④ Grasp the essential concepts involved in conducting research.

⑤ Distinguish between the main methods used in sociological research.

⑥ Link social theory and research questions to individual research methods.

⑦ Recognize the types of sexism that can occur in research.

⑧ Understand key principles in ethical research.

① Connecting Theory to Research Questions

We all use phrases such as "everybody knows that" or "it just makes sense" when we talk about various aspects of our world. But, really, how do we know these things to be "true"? "Everybody knows the earth is round." While this may seem to be common sense now, at one time prevailing wisdom stated that the earth was flat. "Smoking contributes to cancer." Again, this is the current wisdom, but at one point smoking was encouraged. Consider, for example, the popular image of the Marlboro man in the 1950s; at that time, smoking was considered sexy and macho. So how do we come to "know" particular "truths"? Research is conducted in both biomedical and social-science disciplines. While the topics will differ and some intricacies of procedure may vary, for the most part all researchers are pursuing the same outcome: creating knowledge through a process of discovery. **Research**, then, is a systematic approach to gathering data using an agreed-upon set of methods that social scientists have developed over the years. The data that we gather helps us as researchers to understand and describe the world (Bouma, Ling, & Wilkinson, 2009). This chapter explores these research methods.

The kinds of research questions you ask will always depend on the theoretical perspective from which you are working; different theoretical perspectives will lead you to ask different research questions. For example, consider the general topic of families. A researcher working from a functionalist perspective is interested in the smooth functioning of society—for example, how roles and shared values promote equilibrium. A functionalist, then, may be concerned with how families socialize children into their appropriate societal roles and may pose the following research question: What are the consequences of changing family forms for the smooth running of society?

 Watch

Experimental Methods Explained

research A systematic approach to gathering data using an agreed-upon set of methods.

> > >

A researcher working from a symbolic interactionist perspective might seek to understand how immigrant families negotiate their sense of identity in their new surroundings.

Blend Images - KidStock/Getty Images

Conflict theorists, on the other hand, are concerned with the struggle over scarce resources by different groups in society and how elites control the less powerful. Therefore, a conflict theorist may be interested in how families cope with current economic strains. Researchers working from this perspective may be interested in examining government and corporate policies that disadvantage families by privatizing or withdrawing particular social supports.

As discussed in Chapter 2, both functionalist and conflict perspectives are considered to be macrosociological theories and therefore ask "large" questions. Symbolic interactionism, on the other hand, is a microsociological perspective; researchers working from this approach would therefore ask different kinds of questions. Symbolic interactionists are interested in face-to-face encounters and the meanings that people use to facilitate social life. Working from this perspective, a researcher may be interested in how immigrant families negotiate their sense of identity in their new surroundings.

While no unified feminist theory exists, feminist researchers are generally interested in examining issues pertaining to gender and inequality. For example, a researcher may wish to examine Canadian child-rearing practices to determine whether they promote gender equality or inequality. A feminist researcher may also investigate the incidence of family violence as a gendered issue in Canadian families.

Queer theorists are interested in troubling—that is, problematizing—taken-for-granted concepts such as the term *normal*. They seek to expose these concepts as socially constructing and as regulatory. Researchers who approach their topics using queer theory may wish to question the idea of what constitutes a "normal" family by investigating a variety of family forms.

As you can see, the particular theoretical perspective you assume will allow you to pose research questions that make sense only within that theoretical paradigm. The same is true for the methods you use to obtain answers to your research questions. There is no best method for every project; rather, the method you use will depend on the research questions you ask (this relationship is discussed later in the chapter). We will now look at the more fundamental ways in which we arrive at knowledge.

Avenues to Knowledge and Reasoning

Research methods are not only related to theoretical orientation, but also depend on your understanding of what can constitute knowledge. Can knowledge be produced from talking with accredited "experts," or can everyone be considered an "expert" on his or her life? Is knowledge credible only if it can be reduced to a statistical relationship, something to be counted? Must you experience something directly to "know" it to be true?

❷ QUANTITATIVE AND QUALITATIVE APPROACHES

As discussed in Chapter 1, there are two main approaches to social research: quantitative and qualitative. On a basic level, *quantitative* refers to numerical data while *qualitative* refers to non-numerical data. Although some researchers might use a combination of both approaches within one study, many others are firmly located in one "camp" or the other. Yet both approaches are valuable. Again, the approach you take will depend on your theoretical orientation and on your research question or focus.

Quantitative Approaches Conducting and analyzing research quantitatively involves converting aspects of social life into numbers and determining whether a significant relationship exists between sets of numbers. For instance, each answer checked off on a questionnaire can be converted to a numerical form and analyzed. One person's answers can then be compared with another person's on a range of variables. The people whose answers can be compared will likely be numerous since quantitative studies tend to have larger samples so that researchers can generalize from their findings (Bouma, Ling, & Wilkinson, 2009).

Suppose that a survey is investigating first-year university students' study habits. You may be asked whether you live in residence or off-campus, whether you live alone or with others, whether you pull all-nighters before an exam or ensure that you get a full night's sleep, and whether you study with others or by yourself. All of your answers can then be assigned a value and compared on the basis of living arrangements, study habits, gender, age, and so forth. One conclusion the researchers might draw from the results is that first-year university students prefer to prepare for exams by studying in groups.

Qualitative Approaches Qualitative approaches do not involve the conversion of social life to numerical form; rather, the focus is on rich detail. Qualitative studies tend to have smaller samples than quantitative studies because they are, generally, more in-depth. Cost is a factor, too, as qualitative studies tend to be more expensive to carry out, especially on a large scale.

In qualitative studies, the researchers themselves are the research instruments. Qualitative approaches use interviewing and observation as the main techniques of data collection. For example, in interview-based studies, researchers conduct interviews with participants, but also make observations about feelings, moods, location, body language, and so forth of both the participants and

✳ Explore

Graphing Data

✳ Explore

Measures of Central Tendency: Mean, Median, and Mode

◉ Watch

Social Psychology Methods for Sociology

< < <

Quantitative approaches to social research involve converting aspects of social life into numbers and determining if relationships exist between sets of numbers. Researchers use surveys to gather information from respondents. Survey data are then converted to numerical values and can be analyzed for patterns within a larger group.

Alamy

> > >

Interviewing is one of the primary tools of data collection employed by qualitative researchers. Sometimes sociologists perform group interviews, known as focus groups.

Eric Audras/PhotoAlto Agency RF Collections/Getty Images

themselves. These observations are just as valuable as the interview transcripts in terms of being considered viable data.

For example, Elizabeth McDermott (2004) noticed that class differences surfaced when her participants talked about their lives as lesbians. The working-class women were uncomfortable and uncertain during the interviews while the middle-class women seemed to welcome the opportunity to discuss their lives openly. McDermott argues that researchers need to be aware of the subtle ways in which social class operates during interviews.

SYSTEMS OF REASONING

Researchers use two systems of reasoning: *inductive logic* and *deductive logic*. Those using **inductive logic** move from data to theory, while those using **deductive logic** move from theory to data (Heit & Rotello, 2010).

inductive logic A system of reasoning that moves from data to the formation of a theory.

deductive logic A system of reasoning that moves from theory to the formulation of hypotheses for testing.

Inductive Logic What does moving from data to theory actually mean? In this system, a researcher gathers information about a topic before developing theories about how to explain particular aspects of it. An example is Paul Willis's (1977) classic study of working-class white males. Willis was interested in learning how working-class youth end up with working-class jobs. Through his observations, he was able to theorize that despite the boys' attempts to create countercultural activities, most of these activities resulted in the reproduction of culture rather than its transformation (Gordon, 1984). While in school, the boys practised a counter-school culture that celebrated a version of masculinity that was violent, racist, and sexist. Their efforts to resist conforming to school expectations, however, ultimately led them to lives spent in working-class shop-floor jobs, thus reproducing existing capitalist relations. (Countercultures are discussed further in Chapter 5.)

> > > Thinking Sociologically

Would a qualitative or quantitative approach best suit the following research problems? Explain your choices. Are there instances when using a combination of approaches would work best?
1. How does the iPod (and other similar devices) influence youth culture?
2. Has the meaning of "going on a date" changed very much since the 1960s?

BOX 4.1 WHY SHOULD WE CARE?

Academic Freedom and Social Research

Academic freedom is a cornerstone of higher learning. As the Canadian Association of University Teachers (CAUT) puts it, "Universities are a community of scholars that depend on vigorous and open debate to advance knowledge and understanding" (CAUT, 2006). CAUT defines academic freedom as follows:

> Includes the right, without restriction by prescribed doctrine, to freedom of teaching and discussion; freedom in carrying out research and disseminating and publishing the results thereof; freedom in producing and performing creative works; freedom to engage in service to the institution and the community; freedom to express freely one's opinion about the institution, its administration, or the system in which one works; freedom from institutional censorship; freedom to acquire, preserve, and provide access to documentary material in all formats; and freedom to participate in professional and representative academic bodies. (CAUT, 2005)

Two recent Canadian examples point to the continued need for the protection of academic freedom.

Dr. David Healy

Dr. David Healy, a well-known scholar from the University of Wales, College of Medicine, was recruited in 1999 as clinical director of the mood and anxiety disorders program at the Centre for Addiction and Mental Health (CAMH) in Toronto and as professor of psychiatry at the University of Toronto. In 2000, Healy was invited to deliver a talk in which he raised concerns about the possibility of some patients committing suicide while on Prozac and other selective seratonin reuptake inhibitors (SSRIs). He noted that, even though a controversy surrounds this issue, no research had been undertaken to investigate the relationship (CAUT, 2001a). He also noted that pharmaceutical companies may be avoiding such investigation because it could reveal that their products are dangerous to patients (CAUT, 2007a).

Following Healy's talk, CAMH's physician-in-chief informed him that he no longer held a position there: "We believe that it is not a good fit between you and the role as leader of an academic program in mood and anxiety disorders at the Centre and in relation to the University" (CAUT, 2001a).

Was Healy dismissed because he voiced concerns about a drug produced by a major pharmaceutical company (Eli Lilly) that donates money to CAMH? The president of the University of Toronto denied that this was the case (CAUT, 2001a). Nonetheless, revoking Healy's position due to the content of his talk constituted a serious breach of academic freedom.

Dr. Nancy Olivieri

Dr. Nancy Olivieri, a hematologist at the Hospital for Sick Children in Toronto, was involved in clinical trials of a thalassemia drug sponsored by Apotex Inc. During these trials, she discovered that the drug carried an unexpected risk; however, when she attempted to inform her patients (and research subjects) about her findings, Apotex ended the clinical trials and threatened legal action if she contacted her patients about the matter. Nevertheless, Olivieri chose to inform both her patients and other scientists about the risks she had discovered (Thompson, Baird, & Downie, 2005).

CAUT's Academic Freedom and Tenure Committee insisted that an independent committee of inquiry be appointed to review the case because Olivieri was being subjected to workplace and other harassment (CAUT, 2007b).

 Explore

Carleton Asks Judge to Throw Out Discrimination Case

CONTINUED

This case proved to be the impetus for the University of Toronto and its affiliated teaching hospitals to alter their industry-sponsored research policy. The policy now ensures that researchers and scientists will not be prevented from informing patients of discovered risks in a timely manner (Thompson, Baird, & Downie, 2005). The case also highlights the importance of informed consent and researcher responsibility. Corporate-sponsored research (or any sponsored research) should never result in a situation in which researchers are unable to inform their participants fully of any harm and/or risk.

From a student's point of view, why is academic freedom an important aspect of university life worth protecting? Think about how professors approach teaching—if professors did not have the protection of academic freedom, how might it change how they teach and what they teach?

Deductive Logic Deductive logic begins at the level of theory. Researchers develop a theory or set of theories to explain or predict a pattern. They then test their theory to see if the expected pattern transpires. For example, Mallie Paschall, Kypros Kypri, and Robert Saltz (2006) were interested in class schedules and college students' alcohol use. They predicted that, based on the students' experiences during first semester, heavier-drinking students would be less likely to schedule a Friday class in the next semester. They surveyed 866 New Zealand college students to test this prediction. After analyzing the data, the researchers were able to confirm their prediction: heavier-drinking students were less likely to have a Friday class in the second semester. The researchers were also able to conclude that students who scheduled at least one class on Fridays reduced the probability of heavy alcohol consumption on Thursdays.

Researchers who use a qualitative approach often use inductive reasoning. Likewise, researchers who favour a quantitative approach typically use deductive reasoning (Bryman, Teevan, & Bell, 2009). This pairing of approaches is not an absolute rule but simply a general preference.

❸ Overall Research Process

Before we move to a discussion on the individual elements and methods involved in conducting research, it is necessary to provide a brief introduction to how those individual aspects fit into the overall picture of research—the research process. Before you can conduct an interview, for example, you must consider how that interview fits into the whole of a research project. Typically, you begin with an area of interest: What piques your curiosity? What do you want to learn more about? You then conduct a search of the scholarly literature to find out what others have written about your general area of interest. You ask yourself questions like the following: What is addressed? What theoretical perspectives have been used? What methods have people used to explore this topic? What seems to be left unaddressed? In other words, you are looking to ascertain how you might make a contribution to the literature—how might your research extend the literature or fill a gap in it?

As an example, you might find that you are interested in men's use of cosmetic surgery, but you are not sure what specifically you would like to know. You should first turn to the literature to find out what other scholars have researched on the general topic. Your review of the literature shows you that much has been written about women's use of cosmetic surgery in their efforts to live up to narrow societal prescriptions of appropriate feminine beauty standards. However, you discover that very little of this literature considers how particular constructions of masculinity might encourage men to surgically alter their bodies.

After your review of the literature, you will be in a more informed position such that you will be able to refine your general area of interest into a more specific research question (or questions) that can be addressed through your project. Using our example, you develop three related research questions: (1) What are men's reasons for seeking elective cosmetic surgery? (2) How do men experience the process of seeking elective cosmetic surgery? (3) What are men's experiences post-elective surgery?

With your research questions in hand you then move on to design your project. How will you go about answering your research questions? You must consider what information you need to gather in order to answer your questions. You then need to think through how you will be able to get that information (will you use an interview, a survey, etc.?). For our example, as an exploratory project, in-depth interviews seem an appropriate method. Next, appropriate interview questions need to be generated—questions that will elicit the kind of data needed to answer your overarching research questions.

Once you have your method, you need to figure out where, and with whom, you will be able to get your needed information. This means your sample—if you are doing a policy analysis, for instance, from what grouping of documents will you glean information? If you are sending out a survey and you have already figured out who the ideal population is, how will you select the sample from that population? Using our example of men seeking elective cosmetic surgery, you know that you want to conduct in-depth qualitative interviews. But whom do you contact? One of your research questions specifically addresses the post-surgery experience, so you know you need a strategy that will include those who have already completed the surgery. You decide to ask local plastic surgeons who advertise for elective surgery for their permission to leave flyers in their offices that describe the project. Individual patients can then contact you if they are interested in learning more about the project or in participating.

Depending on where you are conducting your research, and if it involves human subjects, you may need to submit an ethical review application for permission to proceed. You will need to think through some ethical safeguards (discussed more fully later in the chapter). In our example, you need to submit an ethical review application that describes how you will protect your participants' confidentiality and how you will ensure that informed consent is given to participate in the project. Once you have this permission (if necessary), you are ready to gather your data. You then contact the men who have responded to your flyers. You arrange a mutually convenient time and place for the actual interview. You must consider whether the space is quiet or noisy, whether the participant will feel comfortable speaking openly in such a space, and so forth.

Once the data are collected, it is time to analyze those data (the processes involved here will again vary depending on whether you are using a quantitative approach or a qualitative approach). In our cosmetic surgery example, we are using a qualitative approach. You transcribe the interview transcripts and thematically code the data. You might find that men's sense of self is improved after their surgical intervention but that this improved sense of self comes with a tension—that is, the men are uncomfortable with feeling like they "had no choice" because of social pressures to conform to rigid prescriptions of appropriate masculinity.

The last stage of the research process is dissemination. This means you will write up your research and share it with others. Faculty members typically do this in the form of writing scholarly articles and books, and they often present their results at scholarly conferences. You will also hear about the results of scholarly research on the news or read about it online or in newspapers.

So far, we have looked at broad, abstract approaches to research. Next, we turn to more specific concepts involved in the actual construction of research studies.

④ Essential Research Concepts

The following concepts will help you to think about the kinds of issues that arise for researchers as they begin to formulate any given study.

HYPOTHESES

When beginning a quantitative study, you usually have a theory that you want to test. For example, you may have noticed that, just like you, a lot of university students live in basement apartments in your neighbourhood. This may lead you to wonder who the landlords are. Do particular features of their lives lead them to rent out their basements to students? You also recognize that your neighbourhood could be described as working class. You wonder if there is an association between being a landlord of a university student and social class.

    To investigate this, you would develop a hypothesis to test. A **hypothesis** is a tentative statement about a particular relationship—whether between objects, people, or groups of people—that can be tested empirically. In our student housing example, a possible hypothesis would be this: "If renting out one's basement is related to social class, then working-class homeowners are more likely to rent out their basements to university students than are middle- or upper-class homeowners." You could then test this hypothesis.

hypothesis A tentative statement about a particular relationship (between objects, people, or groups of people) that can be tested empirically.

variables Characteristics of objects, people, or groups of people that can be measured.

INDEPENDENT AND DEPENDENT VARIABLES

In quantitative studies, **variables** are used to measure relationships between objects, people, or groups of people. *Independent variables* can be varied or manipulated by researchers. The *dependent variable* is the reaction (if one occurs) of the participants to this manipulation. So, in our example, social class (i.e., whether the neighbourhood is working, middle, or upper class) is the independent variable since you vary the neighbourhoods you study. Landlords of basement apartments is the dependent variable since through your research you discover that, indeed, whether people rent out their basements to university students *depends* on their social class. Your research results, then, have proven your hypothesis: that working-class homeowners are more likely to rent their basements to university students than are middle- or upper-class homeowners.

    Let us look at a couple examples of how variables have been used in published studies. The first is Browning and Erickson's (2012) research on neighbourhoods and violence among Canadian high school students. In their study, the number of violent acts committed in a 12-month period was the dependent variable. The variables "neighbourhood context" and alcohol use were the manipulated or independent variables. The researchers found that there is indeed a relationship between neighbourhood context, alcohol use, and violent offending. The strength of that relationship varied by social class and immigrant status of the neighbourhood (Browning & Erickson, 2012).

    In another example, researchers from the Netherlands were interested in the success of Internet sites in helping singles meet each other. They focused their study on an Internet marriage agency (IMA), which they claim is the online version of a mail-order bride service. Sahib, Koning, and van Witteloostuijn (2006) examined a sample of Russian women who wished to meet (or had successfully met using the IMA) partners from Western countries. In their study, marital status was the dependent variable (all women, single women, married or engaged women). The independent variables, including age, weight, height, "describes herself as attractive," "speaks English well," "asks for a provider figure," and "asks for an attractive partner," were used to determine what type of information mattered to prospective suitors. The researchers concluded that women who speak English and who are from major Russian cities are more likely to be successful in the Internet marriage market. They also noted with surprise that women's prior marital status and the existence of children from a previous relationship mattered little in terms of whether women found a mate using the IMA.

We can draw another example from a study that tested the relationship between gender equality and sexual assault rates (Martin, Vieraitis, & Britto, 2006). The sexual assault rate was the dependent variable and gender equality was the independent variable. Of course, measuring gender equality is conceptually difficult; therefore, the researchers needed to develop an **operational definition**—a description of something that allows it to be measured—of gender equality for their study. Various factors such as female earnings, education, employment status, the ratio of female to male earnings, and the ratio of female to male employment were used as measures of "gender equality." The researchers concluded that sexual assault rates varied according to what the researchers called "women's absolute status" (Martin, Vieraitis, & Britto, 2006, p. 333). That is, when women live in cities where they have higher incomes, labour force participation, levels of education, and occupation status, sexual assault rates are significantly lower.

operational definition **Description of something that allows it to be measured.**

VALIDITY AND RELIABILITY

The **validity** of a measurement is important to consider. If a measurement is valid, it means that it is accurately measuring the concept. In the study on gender equality and sexual assault rates, the researchers would have had to ask whether their measures of gender equality were valid. They needed to be confident that education, income, employment, and so on were accurate indicators of gender equality.

validity **The accuracy of a given measurement.**

Validity differs from reliability. **Reliability** refers to the consistency of a given result. Are your results reliable? That is, when you use the measurement for gender equality, do you consistently get the same results? Researchers want to be confident that their results are consistent over time (Frankfort-Nachmias & Leon-Guerrero, 2011).

reliability **The consistency of a given result.**

Howver, reliability and validity are *interconnected*. Researchers must have a reliable measurement before they can be confident that they have a valid measurement (Frankfort-Nachmias & Leon-Guerrero, 2011). What this means is that a researcher would be unable to measure or observe a phenomenon if the measure he or she is using yields results that are inconsistent. A measurement can be reliable (yield consistent results) yet not be valid (not accurately measure the concept).

 Explore

Correlations Do Not Show Causation
Cause, Effect, and Correlation

CORRELATION AND CAUSALITY

It is important to distinguish between correlation and causality. A **correlation** is a relationship between two variables; it can range from weak to strong. For example, a study was conducted to determine whether there is a correlation between women who apply condoms to their male sexual partners and their attitudes toward sexuality and the frequency of their sexual activity (Sanders et al., 2006). The researchers concluded that there is in fact a correlation (relationship) between condom-applying women and positive attitudes toward sexuality. They further concluded that condom-applying women are more likely than non-condom-applying women to have a higher rate of sexual activity (Sanders et al., 2006).

correlation **A measure of how strongly two variables are related to each other.**

Causality, on the other hand, means that one variable *causes* a change in the other variable. For years, medical researchers have argued that smoking causes cancer. In 1968, the US Surgeon General Advisory Committee issued a report that outlined how cigarette smoking causes bronchitis and chronic non-neoplastic bronchopulmonary disease and lung cancer (Public Health Service, 1969).

causality **Relationship in which one variable causes a change in another variable.**

A **spurious correlation** can also exist. This occurs when one variable seems to produce a change in another variable, but in reality the correlation is false. For example, one might try to insist that ice-cream sales cause sexual assaults because the data may show that when ice-cream sales are at their highest (say, from June to August), so too are reported sexual assaults. However, it is more likely that there is a relationship between warmer weather, which brings more people outdoors into public spaces, and the incidence of sexual assaults. In this example, ice-cream sales and sexual assaults represent a spurious correlation.

spurious correlation **A false correlation between two or more variables, even though it appears to be true.**

RESEARCH POPULATION

research population **A group of people that a researcher wishes to learn something about.**

When engaging in any research activity, one must think about what participants are needed to answer the research question. This is the **research population**, a group of people that a researcher wishes to learn something about. From a research population, a **sample** (a subset of the larger research population) is drawn. In large-scale quantitative studies, a random sample is often used. This means that every person in the targeted research population has an equal chance of being selected to participate in the study. For example, Reutter and colleagues (2006) selected eight neighbourhoods in Toronto and Edmonton to include in their study of public attitudes about poverty in Canada. Their research population included both higher-income and low-income neighbourhoods, the latter as defined by Statistics Canada's low income cut-offs. Within these neighbourhoods, they conducted telephone surveys of randomly selected English-speaking adults. Random samples enable the researcher to make generalizable claims. If the sample is representative of the larger population being studied, the results from the sample can be said to apply to the larger population.

sample **A subset of the larger research population.**

As we have seen, qualitative studies tend to be smaller than quantitative studies—but, again, this is not a hard-and-fast rule. Crouch and McKenzie (2006, p. 496) argue that small samples (i.e., fewer than 20) in qualitative research are actually the best way to conduct "analytic, inductive, exploratory" studies. Small and nonrandom samples do not allow the researcher to generalize to a larger population, but these studies yield in-depth, detailed data not typically seen in larger quantitative studies.

❺ Research Methods

research methods **Strategies used to collect data.**

Sociologists use a variety of research methods to answer their research questions. **Research methods** are the actual strategies used to collect data. We discuss seven methods: surveys, interviews, participant observation, content analysis, secondary analysis, participatory action research, and multiple research methods.

SURVEYS

survey **A research method in which respondents answer pre-set questions.**

Surveys, a research method in which respondents answer pre-set questions, are often used in large-scale research projects, although many small-scale projects also use them. In fact, surveys are the most extensively used method for data collection in the social sciences (Roberts, Kampen, & Peter, 2009). They are well suited to asking about *what* people do or think, but not as helpful in answering *why* people do particular things or think a certain way. As an example, surveys were used in the study of condom-applying women described earlier. Given that the researchers found a correlation between condom-applying women and positive attitudes toward sexuality, it is then the researchers' job to speculate as to why this correlation exists.

There are three main types of surveys: self-administered questionnaires, telephone surveys, and in-person surveys.

Research Methodology

When Can We Use Qualitative Methods?

Self-administered Questionnaires Self-administered questionnaires (surveys) can be mailed to prospective participants at relatively little cost. The researcher often includes a postage-paid envelope that the respondent can use to return the completed survey. These questionnaires tend to be used mainly in quantitative research. Questions often list several possible answers (closed-ended questions) and the respondent is asked to check off one answer per question. You have probably received these types of surveys at your home in the form of market research.

Perhaps the most well-known self-administered survey in Canada is the Census of Population (commonly known as the Census) performed by Statistics Canada every five

Marc Asnin/Corbis

<<<

Reutter and colleagues (2006) conducted a study on public attitudes about poverty in Canada. Random samples such as theirs enable the researchers to generalize their claims as representative of the larger population being studied.

 Watch

Discussion of
Methodology

years. Households are required by law to provide all sorts of information, including the number of people living in the dwelling, hours spent on unpaid domestic labour, occupation, education, income, and origin or ancestry. Answers to all of the Census questions help to form a statistical representation of Canada. The results help various levels of government (and other policy-makers) to develop and/or alter social policies (welfare, daycare, etc.) and to assess the needs of particular groups (new immigrants, the elderly, etc.).

Census data are presented in a variety of units, with the smallest at the level of neighbourhoods and the largest at the level of the country as a whole. Census questions remain relatively stable, enabling researchers and policy-makers to analyze data over time. However, the Census also responds to changing societal contexts and issues and introduces new question areas or modifies existing questions to account for these changes. For example, the definition of a Census family now includes partners of the same sex.

Telephone Surveys Telephone surveys work in much the same way as questionnaires—a researcher asks respondents questions over the telephone. The researcher then provides a list of possible answers if closed-ended questions are being used. If the questions are open-ended, the researcher notes the respondents' answers.

For example, in a study on whether pets act as a channel for social networks, closed-ended questions were used, such as "Do you talk to other pet owners when walking your dog, yes or no?" (Wood, Giles-Corti, & Bulsara, 2005, p. 1163). Other questions can be answered on a scale. In the pet study, respondents were asked, "In general, would you say that most of the time people are willing to help each other out?" Respondents then rated their answers on a five-point scale with 1 representing "strongly disagree" and 5 representing "strongly agree" (Wood, Giles-Corti, & Bulsara, 2005, p. 1163). The advantage of a telephone survey over a mailed survey is that respondents can talk with the researcher directly if they have any questions or require clarification before answering a particular question.

Courtesy Egale Canada www.egale.ca

The organization Egale (Equality for Gays and Lesbians Everywhere) actively lobbied for the Canadian Census to include a question on sexual orientation.

interviews Involve a researcher asking a series of questions of participants; they may be structured, semi-structured, or unstructured.

In-person Surveys In-person surveys are similar to telephone surveys. Again, the advantage is that the researcher can provide clarification or answer questions for the respondent. In-person surveys may be particularly useful with children, people whose first language is not English, people who lack strong literacy skills, or people with visual impairments, all of whom may have difficulty completing a mailed survey.

Kara Chan and James McNeal (2004) used an in-person survey when they explored Chinese children's attitudes toward television advertising. They surveyed 1758 children, ranging in age from 6 to 14, about whether they liked particular commercials and whether they perceived the information provided in the commercials to be true.

INTERVIEWS

Interviews can be unstructured, semi-structured, or structured. Again, the approach a researcher takes will depend on the kinds of information he or she is hoping to gather. Qualitative researchers typically use semi-structured or unstructured interviews, although quantitative researchers may use them as well. When researchers use semi-structured interviews, they approach the interview with a set of questions but are also open to the interviewees introducing topics that they think are important. There is a philosophy that the interview can unfold in the form of a dialogue between interviewer and interviewee. An unstructured interview begins without any predetermined questions being set by the interviewer. Rather, the idea is for the interview to proceed conversationally. When interviews are structured, they fall outside the qualitative range. Structured interviews are typically used in quantitative studies where it is crucial for analysis that each and every respondent is asked the same questions in the same order with no room for deviation.

Interviews in Qualitative Studies Deirdre Kelly, Shauna Pomerantz, and Dawn Currie's (2006) post-structuralist feminist study on "girl power" included a subset of "cyber girls." The first part of their study included girls who self-identified as "computer geeks" and "Internet girls" (Kelly, Pomerantz, & Currie, 2006, p. 8). The researchers decided to follow up on this theme of girls seeming to enact alternative femininities. They created a poster to recruit

> > >

Kelly, Pomerantz, and Currie (2006) conducted a post-structuralist feminist study on "girl power" including a subset of "cyber girls." Their study included girls who self-identified as "computer geeks" and "Internet girls." The researchers concluded that online interactions allowed the girls to "try out" various forms of femininity before enacting them offline.

Ammentorp/Fotolia

cyber girls in Vancouver and ended up with 16 research participants. The girls were asked open-ended questions (semi-structured interview) such as "Tell me about a time when you felt powerful online" (Kelly, Pomerantz, & Currie, 2006, p. 7). The study's conclusions draw on the girls' accounts of being gender rebellious and enacting femininities that counter the mainstream femininity discourse. Online interactions allowed the girls to "try out" particular forms of femininity (e.g., being rebellious, switching one's sexuality, pretending to be older) before attempting to enact them offline.

Research into the experiences of nursing home staff around the deaths of residents drew on unstructured interviews (Parker Oliver, Porock, & Oliver, 2006). The researchers argue that we deny death in North American culture. They chose unstructured interviews to explore the experiences of those who constantly work around death in their caring roles in nursing homes. The researchers speculated that the practices of the nursing home would mirror those of wider society and would thus deny the frequency of death. During unstructured interviews, registered nurses, licensed practical nurses, and social-service designees each shared their experiences of the hidden reality of death in these long-term-care facilities. Parker Oliver et al. connect Erving Goffman's (1959) dramaturgical perspective to reveal what is normally relegated to the backstage, the staff's private reality of dealing with death, while they attempt to maintain the frontstage performance of highlighting the rehabilitative elements of long-term-care facilities.

Interviews in Quantitative Studies Julie Christian and Dominic Abrams (2004) investigated various predictors for homeless people's likelihood of using a number of outreach programs in London and New York. This type of quantitative study requires consistent data collection (e.g., asking everyone the same questions through structured interviews) to ensure that the data can be compared. In an effort to make their sample representative of homeless people, the researchers recruited participants from shelters as well as the streets. The researchers noted that collecting data from homeless people is an expensive and time-consuming task; they had to develop relationships with outreach personnel who then accompanied them on "streetwalks" to introduce them to potential participants. Among other findings, Christian and Abrams discovered that differing cultural contexts play an important role in the intentions, behaviours, and attitudes of the homeless people they interviewed and in whether these people were likely to take advantage of outreach programs.

Interviews and Relations of Power Interviews are imbued with relations of power; in fact, no research method stands outside of power relations. At the outset of an interview, there is an unequal relationship between interviewer and interviewee. Those who conduct the interviews and subsequently analyze and report the data are in a position to select what is studied (setting the scene for what knowledge is produced), who is studied (who is given a voice, which persons or groups can be learned about), which data are reported (ultimately setting the direction of the public presentation of new knowledge), how the data are reported (another issue of "voice" concerning whether amalgamated data, summaries of people's experiences, or actual interview excerpts are presented), and so forth. All of these aspects of research involve the exercise of power and ultimately influence what is "knowable."

As Herzog (2005) points out, in the context of the interview relationship, the interviewer is the "taker" while the interviewee is the "giver." Many researchers are aware of this unequal power relation and attempt to work through the complexities of the interview process in as equitable a manner as possible. For example, you may consider the interview location to be merely a logistical decision—whether the participants can get to the interview site, whether nonparticipants will be able to hear the interview, and whether the tape recorder will pick up only the voices of the interviewer and interviewee in a public or semi-public location. However, as Herzog (2005) argued in her article about her interview-based project with Palestinian citizens of Israel, location can be a far more complex issue. Interview location is crucial to our understanding of what is knowable in that context. Who chooses a particular location and what location is chosen affect not only what is revealed in a study but also who is able to reveal.

PARTICIPANT OBSERVATION

participant observation **Active participation by a researcher in a research setting; combines observation and participation in daily-life activities of research subjects (also known as** *fieldwork***).**

Participant observation (also referred to as *fieldwork*) involves a researcher's active participation in the daily-life activities of those he or she is observing. The degree of involvement varies from study to study, with some researchers remaining distant observers and others trying to live as much like the research subjects as possible. Participant observation is a qualitative method that uses processes of induction as opposed to deduction. In other words, these researchers do not develop hypotheses; instead, they are interested in exploring a particular place and people in an in-depth way.

For example, consider Canadian researcher Jane Helleiner's (2000) fieldwork among a group of Travellers in Ireland. (*Travellers* are a group of people more commonly referred to as gypsies or itinerants.) Helleiner bought a trailer in a fairly settled Traveller "camp," and then lived in the camp for nine months. As a result, she was able to observe camp life over time and to interact with both the Travellers who lived in the camp and those who came to visit. These interactions and observations enabled her to understand the production of Traveller culture (see Chapter 3 for a discussion of how cultures are produced).

Participant observation is often meant to be informal. That is, researchers want the research to unfold before them rather than have a preconceived, rigid plan in place before "entering the field." An example of this unfolding is characterized in Fiona Angus's (2000) research on masculinity in a western Canadian carnival. Angus began her association with the carnival as a temporary worker (originally scheduled for five days); the possibility for a participant observation study developed and so she began her project. As she writes, " . . . the opportunity to study a carnival, quite simply, fell into my lap" (2000, p. 6).

Field Research

Participant observation can, however, be difficult to explain and justify to a university's research ethics board (REB). REBs approve, in advance, all research activities conducted by their members. REBs are uncomfortable not knowing ahead of time which people will be included in a study, what questions will be asked of which participants, and so forth. A cornerstone of modern ethics is informed consent, which usually requires the signature of a prospective research participant on a consent form. You can imagine how difficult this requirement may have been for Jane Helleiner; as soon as she met a Traveller, she would have had to produce a consent form and explain it to that person. What was intended as an informal conversation would instead be framed in a formalized, bureaucratic manner.

Participant observation can be covert, semi-covert, or open. *Covert research* means that the people in the research setting are not informed of the researcher's status; they do not know that they are being observed for the purposes of a research project. This kind of deception is uncommon, however, and REBs require extensive justification of the benefit of such an approach. *Semi-covert research* involves revealing the nature of your study to only some of the people involved. An excellent example is Danielle Egan's (2006) participant observation study of exotic dance clubs in New England. Egan described herself as transitioning from full observer to full participant (as an exotic dancer) during the study, in which she interviewed many of her fellow dancers. However, Egan noted that, for safety reasons, she did not inform the club owners that she was a researcher. Nor did she inform all of the customers she came into contact with since it was the dancers and not the customers who were the focus of her study.

CONTENT ANALYSIS

content analysis **A research method involving analysis of texts.**

Content analysis is the analysis of texts—which may include magazines, newspapers, television programs, movies, blogs, and so forth. In this framework, a text can be "printed, visual, aural, or virtual" (Bryman, Teevan, & Bell, 2009). Content analysis can be either quantitative, qualitative, or a combination of both. Let us first consider a quantitative approach to content analysis.

A quantitative approach means that you will be measuring your variables by counting in order to answer your research questions. For example, Kenneth Dowler (2006), a researcher at Wilfrid Laurier University, wanted to explore how sex crimes are presented in televised newscasts. Having assessed what past literature had to say on the topic—that the reporting of sex crimes is often sensationalized and inaccurate—Dowler set out to explore the similarities and/or differences between how sex crimes and how other crime news (homicide, robbery, assault) are reported. He recorded 400 episodes of news reporting from American and Canadian television (Detroit, Toronto, Toledo, Kitchener). He developed a coding sheet that included items such as city, date, time, whether the story was the lead story, whether there was live reporting, whether interviews were included in the broadcast, the stage of the crime (pre-arrest, arrest, court), whether a motive was presented, and so on. Dowler was then able to use his data sheets to provide an analysis of the reporting of sex crimes. Of the 108 reports involving sex crimes, Dowler (2006) found several statistically significant elements in the reporting of sex crimes. Specifically, he found that newscasts are meaningfully related to the presentation of fear, sensationalism, reporting of a firearm, and the reporting of motives.

A qualitative approach to content analysis, on the other hand, is interested in a thematic analysis (Bryman, Teevan, & Bell, 2009). A qualitative analysis will consider what themes underlie the material under study. Different from a quantitative approach, there will typically be fewer predefined categories directing the researcher's attention. More concern is focused on *how* a topic is presented rather than on how many times a topic is addressed. For example, Lehti et al. (2010) analyzed published scholarly medical articles for their representation of gender and ethnicity related to depression. The researchers analyzed 30 articles and identified three main analytic categories: "illness complaints," "illness meaning," and "depression diagnosis" (Lehti et al., 2010, p. 103). Overall, the researchers argue that a

< < <

Pictured here are children living in a Traveller camp, similar to the camp that researcher Jane Helleiner lived in as she conducted participant observation.

Photo by Derek Speirs

Document Research

Western gaze permeates the medical literature on depression such that variable cultural expressions of what we might term *depression* are not taken into account in the medical community. Lehti and her colleagues (2010) also argue that hegemonic constructions of masculinity are rarely problematized in the literature and can have consequences for the diagnosis of depression.

Lastly, content analysis can also be a combined effort of both qualitative and quantitative approaches. An example of a combined content analysis is McMullan and Miller's (2009) study of lottery ads in Atlantic Canada. A sample of 920 lottery ads was analyzed both quantitatively and qualitatively, coding such elements of the advertisements as intended audience, word count, advertiser, voiceover, number of frames, colour scheme, camera position, pace, appeal, vocabulary, sound, products, odds of winning, sexualized imagery, and theme. Overall, the researchers argue that the images, tone, pace, and so forth, of the ads all create a successful packaging of "lottery products as commodities" (McMullan & Miller, 2009, p. 289). The advertisements present an idyllic world replete with luxury, happiness, and never-ending freedom.

SECONDARY ANALYSIS

secondary analysis
A research method involving analysis of existing data.

Researchers often make use of existing data for **secondary analysis**. Archival research is well suited not only for studying past events but also for examining trends over time. For example, recall Durkheim's suicide study, described in Chapter 2, which could conceivably be replicated in different locations and different time periods.

Archives are found not only in university libraries but also in government bodies and churches. As well, particular social clubs may maintain information records, minutes of meetings, and so on. Newspapers, magazines, and other periodicals are also archived.

Interestingly, it was Jane Helleiner's previous archival research that led her to conduct her fieldwork on Travellers. She combed through hundreds of Irish newspaper accounts and parliamentary debates to find references to Travellers. Helleiner (1997) analyzed the articles and debates and was able to identify historical discourses of racism and gender that were used to justify Ireland's implementation of a program to settle Travellers in the mid 1960s.

StatsCan: Doing Secondary Analysis on Census Data

Criminologists often make use of court records in their research. One Canadian researcher, Kirsten Kramar (2005), used legislation, court records, coroners' reports, and various government documents to trace shifts in attitudes toward (and action concerning) maternal neonaticide (that is, a mother killing her baby). Kramar showed that maternal neonaticide was originally thought of as stemming from socioeconomic disadvantage. The thinking then shifted to understanding it as a psychiatric condition arising from giving birth and lactation and, finally, to having no legitimate justification whatsoever: the "infant-victim has a 'right-to-life' that the courts must protect by punishing fully responsibilized mothers" (Kramar, 2005, p. 16).

The advantage of secondary analysis is that the information already exists; the researcher simply has to access it. It is often a less expensive form of research than having to collect primary data. The disadvantage is that the researcher is restricted to whatever information has already been collected and recorded. Silences or gaps in the data are then important to note.

participatory action research (PAR)
Research that combines an action-oriented goal and the participation of research subjects.

PARTICIPATORY ACTION RESEARCH

Participatory action research (PAR) brings together two approaches: action research and participatory research. *Action research* is designed to effect change, which may come in the form of a new social policy, modifications to an existing policy, or other changes to the lives

Researchers engaged in participant observation research often take part in the practices of the setting under study.

of disadvantaged people. In action research, though, there is no commitment to involve members of the concerned group or population in the design and implementation of the research project. *Participatory research* does not necessarily have an action component, but it does invite concerned individuals to be part of a project's design and execution. Participatory action research (PAR) puts these two traditions together. In other words, PAR projects have both an action component and a collaborative component.

An example of participatory action research is found in the work that Michelle Fine and Maria Elena Torre (2006) have done on a college program within a women's maximum security prison. They formed a research collective comprising both academics and women prisoners and held regular sessions every two to four weeks over a four-year period. They also conducted archival research, focus groups, interviews, and surveys. The goal of their project was to persuade legislators to restore funding for college-in-prison programs. Fine and Torre concluded that there has been some movement toward education in prisons.

MULTIPLE RESEARCH METHODS

You will find that some researchers use more than one research method in a single project. There are two main classifications associated with multiple research methods: mixed methods and triangulation.

A **mixed methods** research project happens when researchers choose to design a single research project that uses elements of both qualitative and quantitative procedures (Creswell, 2003). People who advocate for the use of a mixed method approach argue that no one research method is the best and that all methods have limitations. By straddling both quantitative and qualitative approaches, the hope is that the biases inherent in particular methods are neutralized by the use of multiple approaches (Creswell, 2003).

mixed methods **An approach in which both quantitative and qualitative procedures are used.**

BOX 4.2 ISSUES IN GLOBAL CONTEXT

Using the Internet as a Research Tool

The Internet is now firmly a part of our lives, of course, and today scholars are making use of online technologies in novel ways. Some scholars discuss online data collection as a way to access people who are geographically diverse (Oringderff, 2004; Turney & Pocknee, 2005). Others point out how Web technologies are opening up spaces for methodological innovation (Bampton & Cowton, 2002; Hine, 2005). And still others write cautionary tales about the ethics of conducting online research (Bassett & O'Riordan, 2002; Berry, 2004; Varnhagen et al., 2005).

We focus here on one example of an actual research project conducted online. Jennifer Oringderff (2004) used online focus groups to investigate the experiences of international expatriates as they relocated to a different cultural space. She began by using Yahoo's free discussion group capability to form a group about international expatriates. She then posted invitations for people to join her group on relevant sites and discussion boards. She posted messages to her group, and then members of her research project responded to discussion threads when it suited them.

In other words, Oringderff created an asynchronous online focus group (OFG). This means that participants could access her questions and respond at their leisure. The benefits of such an approach include a flexible time period for data gathering since discussion groups can be monitored and maintained for as long as the researcher chooses. Assuming that the researcher already has access to the Web, this approach also represents an inexpensive method of data gathering. One can have a large or small research group, depending on the time the researcher has to monitor it. As well, using online vehicles for data gathering allows access to a wide population, potentially spread out across the globe. Oringderff (2004) also identifies the possibility of gathering rich detail from participants, as they respond to the discussion group on their own time and may be able to write more than they would be able to share verbally in an interview situation.

Oringderff (2004) does point out some limitations of this research method. Because people must have access to a computer, in some cases recruitment can be difficult. Further, creating and moderating a discussion group can prove to be time consuming. She also notes that group dynamics play out in distinct ways due to lack of vocal cues, body movement, and so on. Meanings can be misunderstood more easily without verbal and nonverbal cues.

Online research is still quite new to sociologists, but the Internet certainly opens up endless possibilities for new forms of research. What other kinds of projects might use the Internet as a research tool?

In her study of Canadian university students' use of both online and offline modes of communication, Anabel Quan-Haase (2007) employed both a quantitative survey and qualitative focus groups (group interviews) in her overall research design. Through both sources of data, Quan-Haase's study on the maintenance of social ties among students found that friends are students' most dominant communication partners and that instant messaging is the dominant form of communication (over email, cellphones, and texting).

Triangulation happens when researchers employ more than one research method in an attempt to more fully understand what they are researching. Like the justification above for using mixed methods, using more than one method often gives researchers a fuller picture. They are able to blend different ways of understanding or move from generalities to specifics. The difference between triangulation and mixed methods is that, in triangulation, all data from a particular project could be generated from more than one qualitative method or more

triangulation An approach in which more than one research method is used in an attempt to more fully understand an area of study.

than one quantitative method—there is no expectation that the data will necessarily include both quantitative and qualitative data.

Watch

Using Multiple Data Sets

For example, Brady Robards's (2012) Australian research examining transitions from the social network site MySpace to Facebook merged two qualitative projects that both used two methods of data collection. Robards first employed a discourse analysis of user profiles—paying particular attention to how profiles were constructed and displayed, the number of friends and contacts, as well as entries about status and the posting of links and videos. Then Robards interviewed a total of 40 participants, ranging in age from 15 to 24. Robards notes that the interviews served to "bring to life" the observations made during the discourse analysis. In all, Robards's research is an interesting look into the formation and performance of "self" online. There are two main forms of what Robards calls "narratives of transition" (2012, p. 394): positive and negative. A positive transition is, for example, using the site for locating roommates, thus enabling the transition from a parental home to an independent living space. An example of the documenting of a negative transition is that which gets shaped as "youthful hijinks" (2012, p. 394), such as photos of individuals in compromised situations (perhaps alcohol-induced) that youth hope prospective employers will not find. In combination the two methods used gave rise to a rich data set.

Another example of the triangulation of data is Nancy Cook's (2006) research in Gilgit, Pakistan. Cook was interested in how Western women in Gilgit negotiate their subjectivities in a post-colonial context. She demonstrated how these Western women draw on imperialist discourses (e.g., the benevolence of white women) and racialized discourses (e.g., that Pakistani men are sexually aggressive) in shaping their subjectivities. She used group interviews, unstructured interviews, and participant observation to understand facets of these expatriate women's lives. While all three methods yielded important information, Cook noted that the nine months of participant observation enabled her to form long-term and complex relationships with the women in her study.

Connecting Research Questions to Methods

We began this chapter by highlighting the relationship between one's theoretical perspective and the kinds of research questions one might ask. Now that we have outlined some of the basic research methods, we can expand on this relationship. As discussed in Chapters 2 and 3, there are microsociological theories, macrosociological theories, and theories that combine them or aim for a middle ground. Certain research methods are suited to these different levels of theory and problems.

We begin with a macro approach. Conflict theorists, for example, tend to use a macro approach in examining particular relationships and happenings in society. They would therefore devise a research project that asks a question with a wide-reaching scope. Let's return to the topic of families. Conflict theorists may be interested in current government policies on social support and the effects that these policies have on families. Researching this topic would require a macro method—and here, quantitative surveys would be useful. You could devise a survey that determined the social supports that people think are most essential to families in Canada.

Working from a micro approach—that is, one interested in face-to-face interactions and the meanings that people use to negotiate social life—also requires a suitable research method. Symbolic interactionists, for example, would choose a qualitative method, such as semi-structured or unstructured interviews or secondary analysis of journals or diaries. To continue with the topic of families and social supports, a symbolic interactionist may interview family members who are caregivers for elderly relatives. The researcher could explore how these family members negotiate their multiple identities (spouse, child and elder caregiver, parent, worker, etc.).

When researchers adopt a combined micro and macro approach, the method needs to be in line with the proposed project. Feminist researchers, for example, may want to study policy issues pertaining to women and children, and the effects of these policies. They could accomplish this using a combination of surveys and interviews. Interviewing would provide them with a day-to-day focus (micro) and surveys would provide them with a broad overview that would address economic implications (macro).

❼ Sexist Bias in Social Research

Feminist scholars maintain that some social research has been, and continues to be, characterized by a sexist bias. Sexism is the belief that one sex is innately superior to the other. Sexism can be particularly prevalent in research.

Canadian academic Margrit Eichler (1991) identified seven distinct problems of sexism in research:

1. *Androcentricity* is "a vision of the world in male terms, a reconstruction of the social universe through a male perspective" (Eichler, 1991, p. 19). Women are not seen as active subjects to the same extent as men but, rather, as passive objects to whom things happen.

2. *Overgeneralization* occurs when researchers include only one sex in their study but present their findings as being applicable to both men and women (Eichler, 1991). A study that interviews only women about parenting and then draws conclusions about "parents"

BOX 4.3 THAT WAS THEN, THIS IS NOW

The Emerging Commercialization of Academic Research

Today, university faculty members are expected to contribute to their university's budget by applying for (and being rewarded with) external research grants (Tudiver, 1999; Webber, 2009). These grants can be obtained from both the public and the private sectors. As a result, research is now promoted as being of service to business (Smith, 2004), and entrepreneurialism has seeped into the very language and organization of the academy (Tudiver, 1999). Should sociologists be cautious about such developments? The case of Dr. Nancy Olivieri (discussed in the Why Should We Care? box on p. 97) demonstrates the deleterious effects of corporate-sponsored research in the medical sciences.

The commercialization of academic research also affects gender equality. Several Canadian authors have pointed out how the corporatization of our universities has particularly problematic implications for women and the gains they have made (Acker, Webber, & Smyth, 2010; Gordon & Blum, 2004; Haley, 2004; Hornosty, 2004; Meaghan, 2004; Paul, 2004; Polster, 2004; Reimer, 2004). Hornosty argues that feminist paradigms have successfully challenged the male hegemony of the university, and she worries that the corporatization of the academy will undermine progress toward a "woman-friendly" institution (2004, p. 47). She points to the danger of corporate sponsorship beginning to drive research agendas, and argues that this will leave little space for feminist scholarship given that feminist projects have low marketability. Women academics are located mainly in the social sciences and humanities. Will they lose out in this push to tie research to the marketplace?

rather than "mothers" overgeneralizes, as does a study that samples male university students but then generalizes about "students." *Overspecificity* occurs when sex-specific terms are used in situations that are relevant to both sexes. Terms such as *mankind* and *man-made* are instances of overspecificity.

3. *Gender insensitivity* occurs when gender is ignored as a socially important variable (Eichler, 1991). If, at the end of reading a study, you are not sure whether men, women, or both were involved, that study is gender insensitive. A study that fails to take into account how a particular social policy may affect women and men differently would also be gender insensitive.

> >> Thinking Sociologically

Researchers wish to investigate how families are coping in difficult economic times. They decide to contact 100 families and interview the individuals who identify themselves as "head of the household." Those individuals then answer questions on how their families earn money, pay bills, take care of household chores, and so on. What are the potential problem areas of this study with respect to sexism?

4. A study uses a **double standard** when it employs different means to evaluate or measure the same actions, qualities, or circumstances.

5. **Sex appropriateness** is a specific instance of a double standard. Eichler specifies that sex appropriateness occurs "when *human* traits or attributes are assigned only to one sex or the other and are treated as more important for the sex to which they have been assigned" (1991, p. 8). Childbirth is a sex-specific attribute, as is ejaculation; child rearing is not.

6. **Familism** is a problem derived from gender insensitivity. It occurs when families are taken as the smallest unit of analysis in situations where specific individuals within those families are responsible for particular actions or experiences.

7. **Sexual dichotomism** is an extreme form of a double standard. It occurs when the two sexes are treated as completely separate and distinct social and biological groups rather than as two groups with overlapping or similar characteristics (Eichler, 1991).

Sexism, then, comes in many forms and is important to keep in mind when devising research projects and research instruments. As Eichler writes, "little is gained if we eliminate one type of sexism only to replace it with another one" (1991, p. 166).

The Ethics of Research

Ethical principles (essentially, statements about right and wrong) and policies are in place to guide researchers' actions during all phases of a research project. In the university setting, researchers are subject to the scrutiny of a research ethics board (REB) or committee that vets all research enterprises of faculty, staff, and students. Those wishing to conduct research must receive clearance from their institution's regulatory body.

In 1998, the *Tri-Council Policy on Ethics Involving Human Subjects* was adopted by the three government research funding bodies: the Canadian Institutes of Health Research, the Natural Sciences and Engineering Research Council of Canada, and the Social Sciences and Humanities Research Council of Canada. Any research that would be funded by one of these three bodies was meant to be approved under the guidelines of this policy. However, it has come to pass that *all* research at Canadian universities and colleges (whether funded or not and whether conducted by faculty or students) is now subject to this policy (van den Hoonaard, 2001).

One of the main principles of current research ethics is respect for others (Babbie & Benaquisto, 2010; Simmerling & Schwegler, 2005). This principle is upheld through current practices of informed consent. Every person who takes part in a research project must understand his or her obligations in the study (how much time is required, what is required—tasks, interview, etc.); the risks or harms that may be faced as a result of participation (emotional trauma, social embarrassment); the benefits that may be realized (a greater understanding of some aspect of his or her life); and his or her rights (freedom to end participation in the study at any time without penalty). In addition, every person must voluntarily agree to such participation.

Ethical guidelines intend to ensure that researchers will balance the risks people are subject to in the course of their involvement in a research study and the benefits of the study to the wider community. In other words, the risks to participants should not outweigh benefits to the scientific community and to wider society.

There are some concerns that current ethical guidelines are inflexible, monolithic, paternalistic, protectionist, and unsuitable to certain kinds of research (Dawson & Kass, 2005; Haggerty, 2004; Rhodes, 2005; Simmerling & Schwegler, 2005; Swauger, 2011; van den Hoonaard, 2001). Some researchers speculate that rigid REB protocols and expectations make research difficult for particular social groups, namely those that would be understood as vulnerable and/or marginalized, such as "psychiatric consumers, children, prisoners, homeless persons, and people involved in illegal activities" (Blee & Currier, 2011, p. 402).

Even when ethical clearance is granted, the approved protocols can have unintended effects. For example, take Melissa Swauger's (2011) research on adolescent girls. She sought to observe girls in their daily routines before conducting interviews. Her REB required that she secure parental consent prior to conducting her observations; this is a typical requirement for research projects involving minors. However, some of the girls in her potential pool of participants were in foster care. Swauger was informed that she needed to obtain the permission of a biological parent; the consent of a foster parent was considered inadequate. Swauger reports that she believed this requirement to be ethically questionable. Even worse, though, were the effects this requirement had on some of the girls themselves. Swauger was approached by one of the girls who was in foster care, and was asked why she was not invited to participate in the project. Swauger informed the girl that foster children were excluded

> > >

Stanley Milgram's Obedience Study (1961) epitomized unethical research. Current ethical principles state that research participants must provide informed consent—that is, they must fully understand what the study is about and what their role and obligations are to the study.

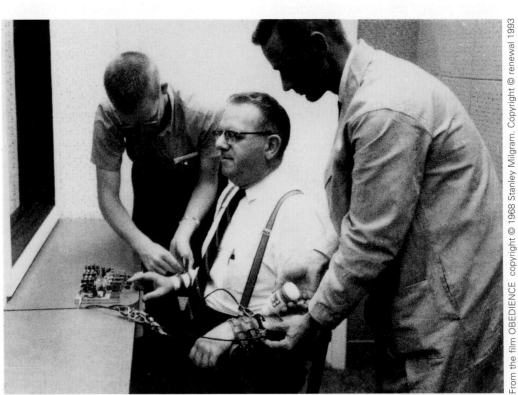

from her study. The effect of the REB's requirement for biological parental consent produced its own ethical consideration, namely the further marginalization of a girl living as a foster child (Swauger, 2011).

Ethical policies and practices originally developed as a result of atrocities that occurred during experiments conducted by Nazi doctors during World War II. As a result of military tribunals held after the war, the Nuremberg Code was established in 1949 to outline ethical standards for research involving human subjects. It details 10 principles for ethical research, covering such topics as voluntary consent, beneficial results for society, avoidance of unnecessary harm (both physical and mental), and so forth. The Nuremberg Code did not specifically address patient–physician relationships in the context of research. In an attempt to provide guidelines that take into account these relationships, the World Health Organization released the Declaration of Helsinki (also known as the Helsinki Accord) in 1964 (Carlson, Boyd, & Webb, 2004). The Declaration's primary purpose was to place the interests of individual patients before the interests of society (via research). However, current codes go beyond these original guidelines and now apply to both medical and social-science research.

ETHICAL DEBATES IN RESEARCH

There is no shortage of egregious examples of unethical research; they range from injecting cancer cells into people without informing them of it (Beecher, 1966) to not treating poor African-American men in Tuskegee, Alabama, for syphilis so that researchers could learn about the natural progression of the disease in the human body. However, ethical issues do not just arise in the form of "unethical" research—the ethics of research can be debated from many vantage points. To conclude this chapter we consider three examples: the first two are widely heralded as epitomes of unethical research, while the last example takes up the ethical dilemma a Canadian researcher faced when he was presented with a court order to breach the confidentiality he had promised his research participants.

Milgram's Obedience Study Stanley Milgram, a social psychologist at Yale University, was interested in the effects of authority on obedience. He was intrigued by the war crime trials, during which Nazi soldiers had denied responsibility for their actions on the basis that they were simply following orders. In 1961, Milgram devised an experiment in which he could witness whether people were willing to "harm" others simply because a researcher told them to do so.

Men were recruited as participants in what they thought was a study on learning and memory. The participants were told that the researchers were interested in the effects of punishment on learning. The "experimenter," who was dressed in a white lab coat, instructed participants to administer electric shocks to another "participant" in an adjoining room whenever a wrong answer to a question was given. The participants did not know that the person in the other room was part of the experiment, that his screams and pleas for the experiment to stop were staged, and that no electric shocks were actually administered. When participants questioned the experimenter about stopping or expressed concern about the other "participant," they were instructed to continue. Milgram discovered that two-thirds of the participants continued to "shock" another human being even as they heard sounds of pain and pleas to stop the experiment.

This experiment and its results stunned the research community. One ethical issue raised was whether the participants were harmed by their participation in the project. Can a debriefing by the researcher after the experiment be enough to mitigate a participant's reaction to discovering that he was willing to "harm" another person simply because someone in a position of authority told him to do so? Current ethical guidelines dictate that people must be fully informed about the nature of any study in which they are involved. Milgram's participants were certainly not fully informed. Deception in social research now

> > >

The "prisoners" line up in Philip Zimbardo's Stanford Prison Experiment— an exploration of how social settings and roles shape our behaviour.

Philip G. Zimbardo

needs to be justified; a convincing argument must be made that the knowledge that will result from such deception outweighs any harm that may come to people as a result of their participation in a study.

Students today often propose two criticisms of Milgram's study: (1) the results would not be replicated today because we are more aware of and more skeptical of authority, and (2) the study used only men, and women would not be as willing to harm others because they are more empathic than men.

Interestingly, recently, ABC's *Primetime* (2007) aired a modified version of the experiment in collaboration with the American Psychological Association and Dr. Burger of Santa Clara University. The experiment stopped "shocking" at 150 volts, a much lower level than what Milgram's participants were asked to deliver. Both men and women were included, as well as people from a range of ethnicities and educational levels. The pattern remained the same for the men in both studies, with 65 percent of the male participants fully complying with the experimenter's orders. Like the students we cited above, ABC expected that women would not be as compliant; in fact, 73 percent of the female participants complied with the experimenter's instructions. These women's readiness to obey orders comes as no surprise if we view our society as patriarchal—that is, women are used to being subordinates.

What rationales did the "shockers" and "nonshockers" provide for their actions? The common theme was responsibility. Those who were willing to "shock" established that the researcher and/or the person being shocked were responsible for the health of the "shockee."

With this rationale, the participants are able to avoid blame for their actions. Many stated during the debriefing that they did not feel good about what they had done, but knowing that it was someone else's responsibility allowed them to continue. In contrast, those who withdrew their participation before the completion of the experiment took responsibility for their actions. One participant even referred to the Nazi war crime trials and pointed out that while people may have been following orders, they were still charged with war crimes. ABC's replication tells us that the results of Milgram's initial study are still relevant today.

The Stanford Prison Experiment Another infamous research study that went horribly wrong is the Stanford Prison Experiment. In 1971, Philip Zimbardo asked the question "What happens when you put good people in an evil place?" (Zimbardo, 2008).

He and his colleagues devised a two-week experiment: a prison was constructed in the basement of Stanford University and male students were recruited as participants. The participants were randomly assigned roles as either a guard or a prisoner. The men then engaged in role play—guards ordered the prisoners to engage in particular actions, and the prisoners followed these orders. After only six days, the study was terminated because of the condition of the participants. As Zimbardo (2008) notes on his website detailing the experiment, "our guards became sadistic and our prisoners became depressed and showed signs of extreme stress."

Ethical troubles started early on in this project. The participants who were designated as prisoners were "arrested" by real police officers, handcuffed, and put in cruisers in front of their families and neighbours. These bystanders did not know that the men were simply participating in a research project. As well, "prisoners" were subjected to problematic conditions, including being denied food, made to eat food that had been on the floor, forced to urinate in buckets that were not emptied immediately, and psychologically harassed by the "guards."

Russell Ogden's Study on Assisted Suicide Russell Ogden was a graduate student at Simon Fraser University in the School of Criminology. He applied to SFU's Ethics Committee for approval to conduct his master of arts thesis on assisted suicide among persons living with HIV/AIDS. In his application, he indicated that he would offer his participants "absolute confidentiality" (Ogden, 1997). His study received ethics approval from SFU. Ogden's completed M.A. thesis came to the attention of the Vancouver regional coroner, who then issued a subpoena and ordered Ogden to reveal confidential data as the coroner was investigating some deaths that may have been assisted suicides (Ogden, 1997). Despite having approved Ogden's research, SFU refused to legally support Ogden in his fight to uphold his commitment to his research participants of absolute confidentiality; the research participants did not participate in the legal proceedings. Ogden did, however, find scholarly support from the University of British Columbia—Professor Richard Ericson and Mr. Andrew Johnson provided expert opinion on the unquestionable significance of protecting confidentiality in research. Ogden was successful in that the court accepted a common-law argument that there would be more societal harm committed by breaching confidentiality than there would be by upholding confidentiality.

A Quebec superior court recently upheld the right for researchers to protect confidential information gathered as part of their academic work (*Parent & Bruckert v Queen & Magnotta*, 2014). Montreal police sought access to a voice-recorded interview with an accused killer who had taken part in acaedemic research on sex workers, carried out by researchers at the University of Ottawa (Chris Bruckert and Colette Parent). The judge ruled that protecting the identity and information provided by research participants ensures that vital information can be gathered that otherwise would be impossible if such protections were not in place. In her decision, Judge Sophie Bourque emphasized that researcher–participant privilege is not an absolute and will continue to be assessed on a case-by-case basis—weighing the public interest that is gained by allowing academic research against the investigation of serious crimes (CAUT, 2014; *Parent & Bruckert v Queen & Magnotta*, 2014).

((•—Listen

Abu Ghraib and the
Dark Side of Humanity

Summary

1 Sociological theory and research questions are inextricably linked; the theoretical perspective a researcher uses will influence the type of research questions he or she asks.

2 Sociological research entails using either a quantitative (numerical) or qualitative (non-numerical, richly detailed) approach, or a combination of the two. Researchers employ either deductive reasoning (moving from theory to data) or inductive reasoning (moving from data to theory).

3 The overall research process begins with an area of interest. A literature search helps with the development of a research question. The question leads to the research design and conducting of the research. One then analyzes the data and disseminates the findings.

4 The essential concepts involved in formulating a research project are hypothesis, independent and dependent variables, validity and reliability, correlation and causality, and research population.

5 The seven main research methods used in sociological research are surveys, interviews, participant observation, content analysis, secondary analysis, participatory action, and a mix of two or more of these methods.

6 Just as the theoretical perspective informs the questions a researcher asks, the research questions in turn influence the choice of research methods.

7 Sexism has been prevalent in academic research. According to Margrit Eichler, the seven types of sexism found in research are androcentricity, overgeneralization/overspecificity, gender insensitivity, double standard, sex appropriateness, familism, and sexual dichotomism.

8 Key principles in ethical research include respect for others, upheld through informed consent, and balancing participant risk with benefits to the wider society.

Key Terms

causality 101
content analysis 106
correlation 101
deductive logic 96
hypothesis 100
inductive logic 96
interviews 104
mixed methods 109
operational definition 101
participant observation 106

participatory action research (PAR) 108
reliability 101
research 93
research methods 102
research population 102
sample 102
secondary analysis 108
spurious correlation 101
survey 102
triangulation 110
validity 101
variables 100

Reviewing the Concepts

1. Compare and contrast surveys and interviews. Think of a research project that might use a survey and another project that might use interviews. Explain your examples.

2. Distinguish between covert and semi-covert research. Under what circumstances might researchers use deception in their projects? Can using deception be ethical?

3. What is academic freedom and why is it worth protecting?

Applying Your Sociological Imagination

1. Think through how you might approach interviewing politicians versus prisoners. What would you do differently in each case? Why?

2. Using a general topic such as families or gender, develop potential research projects that would make sense with different theoretical perspectives. What methods would you choose? Why? Work through why the methods you chose makes sense for your theoretical perspectives.

3. What are the implications for our understanding of the social world if people dismiss sexism as unimportant?

4. Can you design an ethical research project that investigates obedience and people's response to authority (like Milgram's did)? What would it look like? Would it have the potential to yield results similar to Milgram's?

MySocLab

Visit MySocLab to access a variety of online resources that will help you prepare for tests and apply your knowledge.

5 Culture

North American society has grown up around the automobile. Our cities—especially those emerging in the second half of the twentieth century—were planned to include cars and the belief that virtually every family would own at least one. In many ways the car shaped Canadian and American culture, from our beliefs about car ownership and independence, to drive-through restaurants and bank machines, to our growing concerns over the environmental costs associated with burning fossil fuels. The impact of the automobile to our culture, and our environment, could not have been predicted when automobiles were first mass-produced in the early twentieth century.

W. F. Ogburn (1957) introduced the concept of "cultural lag" to describe how technology often outpaces society's ability to adjust to it. The car is a good example of how one technology transformed culture in ways that would have been impossible to predict. For example, might we have made different choices (e.g., investing more heavily in mass transit or renewable energy resources) if we could have forseen the environmental costs associated with fossil fuels?

culture lag Ogburn's concept describing how technology often outpaces society's ability to adjust to it.

Culture lag may also be relevant today when we consider whether or not social media are changing our culture in ways we cannot predict. The Internet was arguably one of the most important technological revolutions of the last century and perhaps today's social media are becoming the defining feature of this century. In 100 years from now, which technology, automobiles or social media, do you think will be seen as being more significant to defining the culture of the twenty-second century?

LEARNING OBJECTIVES

By the end of this chapter, students will be able to

1 Understand the meaning of *culture* and review its defining features.

2 Compare and contrast ethnocentrism and cultural relativism.

3 Understand the role that language plays in culture.

4 Distinguish between subcultures and countercultures.

5 Review the defining features of Canadian culture and values.

6 Describe how discovery, invention/innovation, and diffusion inspire cultural change.

7 Review and critique sociological theories and their application to culture.

1 What Is Culture?

Culture is generally regarded as a complex collection of values, beliefs, behaviours, and material objects shared by a group and passed on from one generation to the next. You may think of culture as the combination of spices that makes each society unique (Ravelli, 2000). There is nothing good or bad about culture—it just is what it is.

The tremendous diversity that human cultures display is fascinating. For example, think about what we eat. All cultures define what is appropriate to eat; our bodies do not care which foods provide nourishment. Many Canadians eat hamburgers and french fries, but some are known to crave prairie oysters, cod cheeks, or peanut butter and pickle sandwiches. Still, you might feel a little uncomfortable while visiting friends in France if they served you *tête de veau* (calf's head). How would you feel about eating haggis, the Scottish delicacy consisting of a sheep's stomach stuffed with oatmeal and then steamed? In Thailand, water bugs (large, black, hard-shelled insects) are a common cooking ingredient. The foods that each culture defines as appropriate to eat are simply a reflection of human cultural variation.

ORIGINS OF CULTURE

No one can really determine when culture began for three primary reasons. First, very little material evidence, the things cultures make, survives over a long period of time. Second, much of culture is non-material (e.g., a belief system) and, therefore, cannot be preserved for future generations to study. Third, many of the developments that enabled our ancestors to become cultural (e.g., increasing brain size, bipedalism, dietary changes, emergence of language, use of technology, etc.) were all interconnected and integral for the emergence of culture (Tattersall, 2008). Paleoanthropologists and archeologists have studied various aspects of the evolution of human culture to determine when in fact human culture may have begun. Consider the following findings

culture **A complex collection of values, beliefs, behaviours, and material objects shared by a group and passed on from one generation to the next.**

 Watch

Culture: Making Meanings

(for an excellent overview see the Smithsonian National Museum of Natural History, n.d.; Ravelli, Webber, & Patterson, 2011, p. 69):

1. *Social life.* There is evidence that our early **hominid ancestors** lived in groups as far back as 4.4 million years ago (Bower, 2010).

2. *Parental care.* Early hominids had smaller brain sizes than our more recent ancestors. As brain size increased, birthing needed to occur at an earlier stage of development because a large head would not fit through a female's birth canal. This resulted in the need for greater parental care as the offspring were born at a less advanced developmental stage. Scientists believe that this change probably occurred with *Homo erectus* around 1.9 million years ago.

3. *Pair-bonding.* The attachment of a male to a female is believed to have occurred between 2.4 and 1.9 million years ago (Fuchs, 2000, p. 11). As offspring became more dependent for longer periods of time, the need grew to secure food and to protect the young.

4. *Subsistence.* The stages in acquiring and distributing food took place over a number of periods. Evidence of tools used for hunting date as far back as 2.6 million years, while evidence of organized hunts dates back 500 000 years. Evidence of fishing dates back 100 000 years, and farming dates back approximately 10 000 years.

5. *Environmental adaptation.* The use of caves dates back 800 000 years. The use of fire dates back 450 000 years, and evidence of the sewing of hides for clothing dates back 30 000 years.

6. *Thought, language, art, and religion.* The oldest known piece of art dates back 250 000 years (the figure of a woman carved in stone). Pigments of black and red have been found in caves dating back 400 000 years, with cave paintings dating back over 30 000 years. There is also evidence of Neanderthals performing funerals over 100 000 years ago.

Can we pinpoint the beginning of culture based on these findings? No. But they do suggest that elements of "human" culture predate modern humans. You should realize that evidence of the existence of modern humans, *Homo sapiens*, dates back only 200 000 years. *Homo sapiens* emerged out of Africa and began to move through Asia between 80 000 and 60 000 years ago. The earliest civilizations, large and complex cities, can be traced back to Jericho, West Bank, around 11 000 years ago—a blip in the timeline of human evolution (Smithsonian National Museum of Natural History, n.d.).

From these early beginnings human interactions were being defined by culture.

DEFINING FEATURES OF CULTURE

Sociologists suggest that culture has five defining features:

1. *Culture is learned.* No one is born with culture. Rather, as we grow up we are constantly immersed in the cultural traditions of our parents, siblings, and peers. Everything from our language to our attitudes, values, and world views are learned. This does not mean that your culture defines everything about you, but it does suggest that your culture modifies and influences your perceptions, values, and perspectives. For example, as already discussed, what you define as suitable food is a reflection of what your culture deems appropriate.

2. *Culture is shared.* Culture develops as people interact and share experiences and meanings with each other. For example, by cheering for your home team, you are sharing cultural experience with others. Cheering for Team Canada when it plays the Russians is one manifestation of shared cultural values. Shared collective symbols (the Canadian flag, the maple leaf, the Royal Canadian Mounted Police) help to create and maintain group solidarity and cohesion.

3. *Culture is transmitted.* Cultural beliefs and traditions must be passed from generation to generation if they are to survive. Communicating cultural traditions and beliefs to the next generation is an important requirement for any culture. For example, many preliterate societies have rich oral traditions in which they tell long and detailed stories as a way

<<<

Musicians, like Canadian band Arcade Fire, often write songs that express the unique features of a society's culture.

of communicating the lessons and experiences of their ancestors. By hearing these stories, children learn about what is important to their culture and what separates them from others.

4. ***Culture is cumulative.*** As members of each generation refine and modify their cultural beliefs to meet their changing needs, they build on the cultural foundation of their ancestors. For example, Canadian students today are exposed to computers from a very early age and are therefore far more computer literate than students even 10 years ago. This experience with technology will continue and expand with each successive generation.

5. ***Culture is human.*** Animals are considered to be social (e.g., a pride of lions, an ant colony) but not cultural. Animals certainly communicate with each other, but the reasons that they communicate are defined by instinct. Natural hierarchies in the animal world are generally based on physical attributes. In contrast, culture defines how, when, and why humans communicate with each other, and with whom. For example, culture helps to define who is appropriate for you to date and guides how and when you ask these people out. Animals do not posses the capacity to plan and organize their behaviours in this way. Since culture is the product of human interaction, it is a distinctly human endeavour[1] (Ravelli, 2000).

These five defining features of culture are important in understanding both the complexity of culture and how groups maintain their uniqueness over time. Culture influences every area of our lives. From what we choose to wear in the morning to the person we decide to marry, culture is everywhere. If you stop reading for a moment and take a look around, you will notice that no matter where you are (your dorm room, the library, your favourite coffee shop), everything around you is a reflection of your culture. Even if you are sitting in the park or studying at the library, these environments are shaped by our culture. For example, many cities design park spaces in the urban core to help people feel more relaxed and comfortable, while the library is intended to be a quiet sanctuary where you can focus on your studies so that you can contribute to society after you graduate. These examples illustrate that culture

 Explore

Ultimate Ticket: How Extreme Fighting Captured a Generation—and Its Money

---

1 There is some debate as to the ability of animals to act according to cultural standards. The debate generally involves whether the ability of animals to use tools and to transmit skills from one generation to the next is evidence of culture (see Davidson & McGrew, 2005).

material culture The tangible artifacts and physical objects found in a given culture.

nonmaterial culture The intangible and abstract components of a society, including values and norms.

Research on Culture

values Beliefs about ideal goals and behaviours that serve as standards for social life.

norms Culturally defined rules that outline appropriate behaviours.

folkways Informal norms that suggest customary ways of behaving.

mores Norms that carry a strong sense of social importance and necessity.

taboo A prohibition on actions deemed immoral or disgusting.

law A type of norm that is formally defined and enacted in legislation.

sanction A penalty for norm violation or a reward for norm adherence.

can be divided into two major segments: **material culture**, which includes tangible artifacts, physical objects, and items found in a society; and **nonmaterial culture**, which includes a society's intangible and abstract components, such as values and norms. Both components of culture are inextricably bound with each other.

Material culture encompasses the physical output of human labour and expression. At the most basic level, our material culture helps us to adapt to, and prosper in, diverse and often challenging physical environments. For example, the Inuit of Canada's North must endure long, cold winters, and their material culture has responded by developing exceptionally warm clothing and shelters (Balikci, 1970). Conversely, the material culture of the Yanomamö of South America reflects their adaptation to a hot and humid climate through lack of heavy clothing and open-walled huts (Chagnon, 1997). Canadian material culture, like that of the Inuit or Yanomamö, is everything we build and create. A hockey stick and this textbook are examples of Canada's material culture, as are paintings, snowmobiles, and written music. Canada's material culture is evident in the university or college you attend, the clothes you wear, and the double-double you drink at hockey games.

Culture is, of course, more than the sum of its material elements. For sociologists, nonmaterial culture represents a wide variety of values and norms that are passed on from generation to generation.

VALUES, NORMS, FOLKWAYS, MORES, LAWS, AND SANCTIONS

For sociologists, values form the foundation of what is considered acceptable. **Values** are the standards by which people define what is desirable or undesirable, good or bad, beautiful or ugly; in other words, they are attitudes about the way the world ought to be. Values are general beliefs that define right and wrong or specify cultural preferences. The beliefs that racial discrimination is wrong and that democracy is right are both values. Values provide the members of a society with general guidelines on what their society deems to be important. For example, in 2007, Canadians viewed government-sponsored health care as one of the most important defining features of their society (Jedwab, 2007; see also Ravelli, 1994, p. 467).

Norms are culturally defined rules that outline appropriate behaviours for a society's members. Norms help people to know how to act in given social situations. One example of a Canadian norm is our belief that it is rude to speak while your mouth is full. Norms provide general guidelines on how we should act, and because we learn them from an early age, they offer some comfort that we will know how to act in situations we have never faced before (e.g., on your first dinner date, you already know not to speak with your mouth full).

American sociologist W. G. Sumner expanded our understanding of norms in his book *Folkways* (1906/1960). He suggests that there are two different types of norms: *folkways* and *mores*. **Folkways** are informal norms that do not inspire severe moral condemnation when violated—for example, walking on the left side of a busy sidewalk. **Mores**, on the other hand, do inspire strong moral condemnation—for example, extramarital affairs—while some actions are considered to be such a violation of social mores that they are absolutely forbidden. Actions such as necrophilia, bestiality, or cannibalism are considered **taboo** in many societies and are often dealt with harshly. The important distinction between folkways and mores is not necessarily the act itself but, rather, the social reaction that the act inspires. Values, norms, mores, taboos, and folkways all help society to control those behaviours it deems unacceptable.

A **law** is a particular kind of norm that is formally defined and enacted in legislation. In Canada, it is illegal to steal your neighbour's lawnmower or to cheat on your taxes because there are laws defining these as illegal behaviours. In both cases, the state reserves the right to charge you with a crime because you have broken the law (discussed more fully in Chapter 14).

A **sanction** is anything that rewards appropriate behaviours or penalizes inappropriate ones. An example of a reward for appropriate behaviour is getting an A on your sociology exam because you studied and answered all of the questions correctly; an example of a penalty for inappropriate behaviour is getting an F on the same test because you never studied and answered only 5 of the 25 questions.

These various forms of social control demonstrate the many informal and formal ways in which society responds to behaviours that are deemed to be unacceptable. Our discussion so far has concentrated on our own values and how we respond to members of our own culture when they contravene generally held assumptions about proper behaviour. However, what happens when we encounter actions by people from other cultures?

Fashion as a Folkway

Ethnocentrism and Cultural Relativism

Have you ever travelled to a different country? If so, you probably already know that some of the ways that Canadians think about the world are not shared by everyone. If, for example, you have travelled through Europe, you probably noticed that many more people use mass transit there than we do in Canada. While some Canadian cities have very good public transportation, mass transit in Canada pales in comparison to what exists in most European cities. Why are Canadians so resistant to taking public transit? The explanation is probably related to our love affair with our cars but is also perhaps a function of Canada's geography—we are a large country with few people, so the need to move many people efficiently is a relatively recent phenomenon. Only by comparing our own cultural beliefs and customs with those of others can we hope to learn more about ourselves.

Culture is such a powerful influence on our lives that most people exhibit **ethnocentrism**—a tendency to view one's own culture as superior to all others. Being a member of a particular culture instills a sense of group loyalty and pride that is important when unity is necessary—for example, during wars or natural disasters. But for sociologists, or anyone who wants to understand another culture, ethnocentrism is inconsistent with the sociological perspective because it restricts one's ability to appreciate cultural diversity. How boring would it be if everyone you met while travelling behaved in the same way as people at home? The best part of travelling is experiencing how other people live.

ethnocentrism The tendency to view one's own culture as superior to all others.

An alternative to ethnocentrism is **cultural relativism**—appreciating that all cultures have their own mores, norms, and customs and should be evaluated and understood on their own terms, rather than according to one's own cultural standards. To a certain extent, cultural relativism is an ethical position that assumes that no one should judge other people's customs and traditions before truly trying to understand them (Caduff, 2011). To view the world from a culturally relativist position is often easier said than done because other cultural traditions may seriously challenge our own. Canadians generally adore their pets, so how would you feel if you visited another culture where the dog you petted upon arrival was going to be prepared for dinner that night?

cultural relativism Appreciation that all cultures have their own mores, norms, and customs and should be evaluated and understood on their own terms, rather than according to one's own cultural standards.

Some critics of the philosophy of cultural relativism argue that by adopting the position, people give up the ability to determine if an action is right or wrong, moral or immoral. Critics argue that some things, like torture or sexual assault, are wrong *regardless* of cultural context. Therefore, to some, the claim that we should not judge the activities of other cultures is, at best, naive. Consider the case of universal human rights. If we cannot determine if an action is right or wrong without being a part of that culture, then the pursuit of universal human rights is doomed from the start. It is only by first accepting that human rights are in fact universal, that the pursuit can have any possibility of succeeding. On some level, universal human rights are contradicted by narrowly conceived ideas of cultural relativism.

In philosophical debates, this criticism carries a great deal of weight, and it is important to consider the extent to which one can adhere to a strong philosophy of cultural relativism, but as new sociologists, the important thing to consider is the value of engaging with unfamiliar cultures with an open mind—to refrain from condemning or judging a culture in its entirety, simply because it is different from our home culture.

> > >

Interacting with diverse and unfamiliar cultures makes some people feel uncomfortable and disoriented, an experience sociologists call *culture shock*.

Bob Krist/Corbis

culture shock
The feeling of disorientation, alienation, depression, and loneliness experienced when entering a culture very different from one's own.

At times, when people encounter cultures that are very different from their own, they experience **culture shock**—a feeling of disorientation, alienation, depression, and loneliness that subsides only once a person becomes acclimated to the new culture (Oberg, 1960). In his original definition and analysis of the term, Oberg listed a four-stage model to understand a person's progression through feelings of culture shock:

1. *Honeymoon*—a feeling of admiration and awe regarding the new host culture, and cordial interactions with locals.
2. *Crisis*—differences in values, signs, and symbols begin to inspire feelings of confusion and disorientation that lead to feelings of inadequacy, frustration, anger, and despair.
3. *Recovery*—crisis is gradually resolved with a growing understanding of the host culture and recognition that its values are consistent with its view of the world.
4. *Adjustment*—an increasing ability to function effectively and enjoy the host culture despite occasional feelings of anxiety or stress (Oberg, 1960, as cited in Austin, 2005, p. 135).

Oberg's research demonstrates that although people need time to adjust to new cultural standards, they *will* adjust. Many people who have experienced culture shock often feel that they have an enhanced appreciation of diversity they may not have experienced otherwise. Anthropologist Napoleon Chagnon described his own feelings of culture shock when he first met the Yanomamö:

I looked up and gasped when I saw a dozen burly, naked, sweaty, hideous men staring at us down the shafts of the drawn arrows! Immense wads of green tobacco were stuck between their lower teeth and lips making them look even more hideous, and strands of dark-green slime dripped or hung from their nostrils—strands so long that they clung to their pectoral muscles or drizzled down their chins . . . I just stood there holding my notebook, helpless and pathetic. Then the stench of decaying vegetation and filth hit me and I almost got sick. I was horrified. What kind of a welcome was this for the person who came here to live with you and learn your way of life, to become friends with you? (Chagnon, 1983, p. 10)

Chagnon eventually grew accustomed to Yanomamö life and became a full member of their society over his many visits, which spanned almost 25 years. He not only learned to accept Yanomamö culture but also grew to appreciate and admire it. While Chagnon's research has been widely criticized (see Beckerman et al., 2009; Conklin, 2008), his experiences clearly show how, over time, culture shock and ethnocentrism often give way to cultural relativism.

Being aware of ethnocentrism and cultural relativism helps you to become a more informed and critical thinker. Indeed, possessing the sociological imagination requires a conscious effort to appreciate the context of all social behaviour. Anything that makes you question your own values and beliefs, while often a difficult and challenging process, affords you with an opportunity to explore your own world—a key to being a good sociologist and citizen of the world.

Language and Culture

Another important aspect of understanding culture is to appreciate how language and culture are intricately intertwined, mutually dependent, and socially constructed. All human beings communicate through symbols—a **symbol** is something that stands for or represents something else. A **language** is a shared symbol system of rules and meanings that governs the production and interpretation of speech (Lindsey & Beach, 2003, p. 48). Language is a symbolic form of communication because there is no obvious relationship between the letters *H-U-N-G-R-Y* and the desire to eat, for example. These letters are symbols that English-speaking people have agreed mean that a person wants to eat. Thus, symbols must have established meanings or no one would understand the thoughts or emotions they are trying to convey. Agreed-upon meanings shared by a group of people are, in essence, what distinguishes one culture from another.

As discussed in Chapter 2, one of the main principles of symbolic interactionism is that society (and culture) is socially constructed. This principle suggests that every time we interact, we interpret the interaction according to the subjective meanings each of us brings to it. Although shared cultural symbols allow us to interact more smoothly, each of us may bring slightly different meanings to the symbols. For example, some students put much more pressure on themselves to get an A than do others; while the symbol *A* is the same for everyone, students' motivation to get an A varies because of their individual meanings and motivations.

Researchers use a variety of techniques to distinguish cultures, but most consider language to be the key identifier of cultural boundaries. Navajo artist Fred Bia states, "My language, to me, . . . that's what makes me unique, that's what makes me Navajo, that's what makes me who I am" (McCarty, 2002, p. 179, as cited in McCarty, Romero, & Zepeda, 2006, p. 28).

LANGUAGE EXTINCTION

When a language is lost, the culture to which it belonged loses one of its most important survival mechanisms (Harrison, 2010; 2007).

Languages die out when dominant language groups (as defined by political, economic, or sociocultural dominance) are adopted by young people whose parents speak a traditional language. When young children are encouraged to speak the dominant language, the traditional language of their parents can be lost in a very short time. In central Siberia, for example, the language of the Tofa people is spoken by only 30 individuals, and all of them are elderly. Traditionally, the Tofa were reindeer herders and hunter-gatherers, and their language was highly specialized as a result. For example, the term *döngür* means "male domesticated reindeer in its third year and first mating season, but not ready for mating." Today, most Tofa people are learning to speak Russian, which has no equivalent term for *döngür*.

According to K. David Harrison (2007, p. 1), approximately 7000 languages exist in the world today and fully half of these are in danger of extinction within the next 100 years. Harrison's research indicates that more than 3500 of the world's languages are spoken by only

symbol Something that stands for or represents something else.

language A shared symbol system of rules and meanings that governs the production and interpretation of speech.

0.2 percent of the world's population, and that some languages are spoken by only a single person. When these people die, so will their languages. Why should we care?

When a language dies, a little bit of culture dies with it, and this is a loss to all of us. Harrison suggests that there are at least three reasons why we should be concerned about losing languages. First, as a human collective, each time we lose a language we lose knowledge, because each language serves as a vast source of information about the past and about how we have adapted to our environments (e.g., the term *döngür* tells us something about what the world is like for a Tofa). Second, when a language dies, so do its related cultural myths, folk songs, legends, poetry, and belief systems. This loss results in what Harrison calls "cultural amnesia" and lessens our ability to live peacefully with diverse populations because our understanding of cultural diversity decreases. Third, the demise of the world's languages hinders our exploration of the mysteries of the human mind. Understanding how people process information from the world around them is only made possible through language—without the ability to convey ideas, we cannot hope to see the world from another's perspective. Harrison (2007) writes this:

> As languages fall out of use into forgetfulness, entire genres of oral tradition—stories, songs, and epics—rapidly approach extinction. Only a small fraction have ever been recorded or set down in books. And the tales captured in books, when no longer spoken, will exist as mere shadows of a once vibrant tradition. We stand to lose volumes: entire worldviews, religious beliefs, creation myths, observations about life, technologies for how to domesticate animals and cultivate plants, histories of migration and settlement, and collective wisdom. And we will lose insight into how humans fine-tune memory to preserve and transmit epic tales. (p. 159)

One important question to consider given the central role of language to culture is this: Does your language influence the way you think about and interpret your world?

DOES LANGUAGE DEFINE THOUGHT?

Two early researchers who investigated the potential for language to influence how we interpret our world were Edward Sapir (1884–1939) and Benjamin Lee Whorf (1897–1941). Their approach, commonly known as the **Sapir-Whorf hypothesis**, suggests that language influences how we perceive the world. For example, if we lived in an area where it does not snow, we would not have a term for this type of precipitation. Our perception of the world, then, is influenced by the limitations of our language; people who speak different languages comprehend the world differently (Koerner, 2000).

Salzmann (2007, p. 54) found that Whorf offered two principles for how language and perception interact. The first principle, called **linguistic determinism**, assumes that the way you think is determined by the language you speak (Grelland, 2006). The second principle, called **linguistic relativism**, suggests that differences between languages do not determine but reflect the different worldviews of their speakers. Kovecses (2006, p. 34) suggest that you can view the Sapir-Whorf hypothesis as having two forms, a strong version (linguistic determinism) and a weak version (linguistic relativism):

- *Strong version*—language *determines* how we see the world.
- *Weak version*—language *reflects* the way we think.

Recent research has shown, however, that while language and culture are intertwined, there is little evidence to suggest that language actually determines thought or that people who speak different languages cannot perceive the same social reality. Much research has been conducted to determine whether different linguistic groups, given their environmental conditions, have more or fewer terms for colour. For example, Davies et al. (1998) found that while English speakers have 11 basic colour terms, Setswana speakers in Botswana have only 5. This does not mean that they cannot see as many hues on the colour spectrum—colour perception is stable across populations—but, rather, that culture influences specific terminology.

Sapir-Whorf hypothesis The assertion that language influences how we perceive the world (also known as *linguistic determinism*).

linguistic determinism Language determines how we perceive the world.

linguistic relativism Language reflects how we perceive the world.

BOX 5.1 WHY SHOULD WE CARE?

When Languages Die

Estimates suggest that every 14 days a language dies (Disapearing Languages, 2014). Places in the world where native languages are in danger of becoming extinct are known as "language hotspots." A language hotspot is defined as an area that has high linguistic diversity and intercultural contact that has not been studied. The Living Tongues Institute has identified roughly 20 hotspots in the world today. The top five are Northern Australia, Central South America, Northwest Pacific Plateau, Eastern Siberia, and Oklahoma–Southwest United States (Living Tongues Institute, 2007).

As you can see in Figure 5.1, the Northwest Pacific Plateau (including much of British Columbia) ranks third in the world's language hotspots. As a result of colonization, three native languages in this area are already extinct. Of the 36 remaining languages, 13 are spoken by fewer than 50 people and one, the South Tsimshian language, is spoken by a single person (Poser, as cited in Woodward, 2007). In British Columbia, only 0.2 percent of the population can speak any of the indigenous languages with any fluency—a total of around 9200 people—and of those, less than 2000 speak an indigenous language as their primary language; that is so few that meaningful statistics cannot even be located (Statistics Canada, 2011b).

Much of the blame for this language extinction can be traced to the area's residential schools, where Aboriginal children were not allowed to speak their native languages and instead were forced to speak English (Woodward, 2007).

Sociologists appreciate that the loss of any language is a loss to all of us. Are there any languages around your own community that may be declining and at risk of becoming extinct?

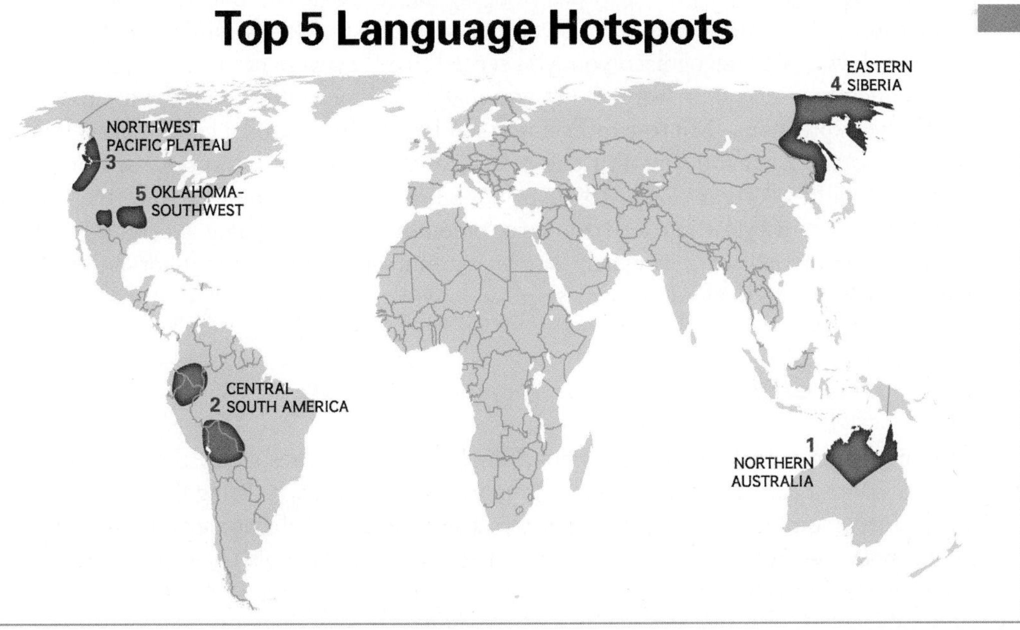

Top 5 Language Hotspots

FIGURE 5.1

Top Five Language Hotspots

Reprinted by permission from National Geographic Creative.

So, although the work by Sapir-Whorf was popular in the 1940s and 1950s, contemporary research shows very little support for the assertion that language defines how we interpret the world.

NONVERBAL COMMUNICATION

Nonverbal communication is a complex system of body language that conveys a great deal about what we feel is important. The adage "it's not what you say that is important; it's how you say it" is certainly true. For example, what cues do you use when trying to determine

((•—[Listen

A Town for Sign Language Users

whether a person is lying to you? Generally, you rely on a spectrum of cues (eye contact, nervous tics, body position) that help you to ascertain if you can believe this person. The main components of nonverbal communication include the following:

- *Body language,* which uses motions (shrugs, tapping of feet, drumming of fingers, eye movements such as winking, facial expressions, and gestures) to convey meaning
- *Proximity,* which uses personal space (sitting very close to or far away from someone) to convey meaning (privacy, attraction, or fear)
- *Haptics,* which uses personal contact (touching) to convey meaning
- *Oculesics,* which uses eye contact (staring, looking away when the person you are looking at returns eye contact) to convey meaning
- *Chronemics,* which uses time (not calling someone back when you said you would, taking long pauses while talking) to convey meaning
- *Olfactics,* which uses smell (freshly showered, wearing perfume or cologne) to convey meaning
- *Vocalics,* which uses voice (volume, tone, speed, accent) to convey meaning
- *Sound symbols,* which use audible cues (grunting, mumbling, sounds such as *mmm, er, ah, uh-huh*) to convey meaning
- *Adornment,* which uses accessories (types of clothing, jewellery, hairstyles, tattoos) to convey meaning
- *Locomotion,* which uses movement (walking, running, staggering, limping) to convey meaning (see Eryilmaz & Darn, 2005)

Of the different types of nonverbal communication listed above, body language (particularly facial expressions and gestures), eye contact, and proximity are the ones you are probably most familiar with. However, some of the messages we convey to others can be unconscious. For example, have you ever met someone you know while coming around a corner and when they recognized you, you sensed that they were not really happy to see you even though they said they were? What you might have picked up on are what researchers call micro-expressions. **Micro-expressions** are largely uncontrollable full-face emotional expressions that last about one-thirtieth of a second before they are suppressed or covered up with a smile (Bartlett et al., 1999, p. 9). Some researchers suggest that these micro-expressions are a window into a person's true emotions (Yan, Wu, Liang, Chen, & Fu, 2013).

Given the myriad ways in which people communicate with one another, an analysis of cultural diversity itself should prove useful.

micro-expressions
Largely
uncontrollable,
instantaneous full-
face emotional
reactions.

④ Cultural Diversity

Watch

Challenging Cultural
Traditions

Everyone understands that culture is not a single entity; nor does it stay the same over time. Cultural diversity is a global fact of life—from new immigrants who bring their traditions with them to new communication technologies that expose us to behaviours from other cultures we have never seen before. In the face of such change, some people try to promote their distinctiveness while others challenge the cultural traditions and value systems of the majority.

SUBCULTURES: MAINTAINING UNIQUENESS

subculture A group
within a population
whose values, norms,
folkways, or mores
set them apart from
the mainstream
culture.

A **subculture** is a group within a population whose values, norms, folkways, or mores set them apart from the mainstream culture. You can see this diversity in any one of Canada's many ethnic communities: Toronto's two Little Italy neighbourhoods, Vancouver's Chinatown, Montreal's Jewish community, and Halifax's black community are all examples of subcultures existing, and prospering, within the larger Canadian culture.

As these examples suggest, subcultures are often based on race, ethnicity, and religion. But they can also be based on age, sexuality, occupation, recreational activities, or any activity, belief system, or special interest that the participants value enough to want to associate with others like themselves (Lindsey & Beach, 2003, p. 56). Subcultures exist largely to promote their members' interests but not in a manner that is contrary to the larger culture that surrounds them. For example, the majority of student clubs or groups at your school no doubt focus on single activities or interests (ski club, student safewalk programs); their members welcome the association with each other, and society as a whole is not worried about students' membership in this group. Members of subcultures often promote their own rules of behaviour and provide support and guidance for their members, just as the larger society does.

COUNTERCULTURES: CHALLENGING CONFORMITY

When members of a subculture become increasingly distinct from the larger society around them, they may become a counterculture. A **counterculture** is a type of subculture that strongly opposes the widely held cultural patterns of the larger population.

counterculture **A type of subculture that strongly opposes the widely held cultural patterns of the larger population.**

The term was popularized by American history professor Theodore Roszak in his book *The Making of a Counterculture* (1969). When this book was published, it captured the imaginations of young American students who were protesting the Vietnam War, rebelling against traditional society, and experimenting with drugs (Dyck, 2005). Roszak's work investigated the frustrations of many student radicals and hippie dropouts who rejected the goals and aspirations of corporate America. This movement filtered into Canada as an estimated 50 000 young men from the United States fled the draft (Hagan & Hansford-Bowles, 2005). The anti-war movement became associated with rock music, sexual experimentation, and illegal drug use (particularly marijuana)—all of which parents and society as a whole viewed as subversive, dangerous, and immoral. Protesting against a war that many considered to be unjust also began to inspire young people to challenge what they wanted out of life: Was there not more to happiness than going to school, finding a job, getting married, and having 2.3 children? Members of the counterculture wanted to live differently from their parents, and they questioned traditional values such as nationalism and patriotism. They also wanted to live for the moment instead of for retirement, and to act as thinking and questioning individuals rather than as robots stuck on the conveyor belt of life. The anti-war movement is just one of a number of countercultures that have emerged at different times and in different places.

< < <

Hippies from the 1960s challenged the dominant definitions of sexuality, appearance, and the need to "sell out" to corporate ideals.

The Canadian Press

> > >

UFC Fighters like Georges St. Pierre are global superstars. As a sociologist, how might you explain the growing popularity of MMA?

Francis Specker/Landov

> > > Thinking Sociologically

Mixed martial arts (MMA), as seen in the Ultimate Fighting Championship (UFC), targets young male viewers and is big business with annual revenues of around $500 million (Santos, Tainsky, Schmidt, & Shim, 2013; Warnica, 2013). As a sociologist, why do you think this sport is so popular and, do you think it is influencing Canadian culture? If we were to look at MMA competitions through the lens of gender for example, what might the popularity of such a violent competition among young men tell us about societal expectations of men? Of women?

Other countercultures include religious minorities that find themselves in opposition to the broader society, such as the Puritans in seventeenth-century England. In twentieth-century Canada, the Sons of Freedom Doukhobors blew up property and paraded naked to express their opposition to sending their children to school and serving in the armed forces (Soukeroff, 1959). Criminal subcultures such as the Mafia or the Hells Angels Motorcycle Club are also examples of countercultures.

A wide variety of countercultures continue to exist today. As was the case in the 1960s anti-war movement, many members of countercultures, though certainly not all, are young. Teenagers and young adults are likely to use appearance to express opposition, with the flowing hair of the 1960s giving way to torn clothing, spiked hair, body piercings, and tattoos. Today's countercultures include people who gather at international conferences to fight what they perceive as the threat of globalization and corporate culture, people who seek a freer and more egalitarian society, or people who chain themselves to trees slated to be bulldozed so that highways can be built. Other groups, such as the Aryan Nation and the Heritage Front, have a racist, anti-Semitic agenda, and have been implicated in numerous violent activities. Still other countercultures, such as youth street gangs, have no interest in social reform; instead, they seek a sense of belonging, often expressed through special clothing, secret signs, and specialized language. What these diverse countercultures have in common is that, like other subcultures and the broader culture within which they exist, they provide feelings of belonging as well as support for their members.

Defining Features of Canadian Culture

According to many Canadian sociologists, Canadian culture has been shaped by an intricate and diverse set of geographic, historical, and social circumstances (Ravelli, 2000).

Geographically, Canada is the second largest country in the world and is blessed with rich and diverse natural resources (Hiller, 1996). Noted Canadian writer Margaret Atwood believes that Canada's adaptation to a harsh physical environment has defined its culture, and to some extent has defined what it means to be Canadian (Atwood, 1972, p. 33, as cited in Lipset, 1986, p. 124). Socially, Canadian culture has been defined by the coexistence of, and conflict between, the English and the French (Hiller, 1996). The fact that more than 80 percent of people living in Quebec identify French as their mother tongue suggests that, on this criterion at least, Quebec is certainly distinct from the rest of the country. However, the province's distinctiveness does not rest solely on language but also on Quebecers' shared history, symbols, ideas, and perceptions of reality (McGuigan, 1997). The influence of Quebec society on Canadian culture is beyond challenge.

The search for elements that define Canadian culture is necessarily a comparative exercise because we cannot try to understand ourselves in a vacuum. Indeed, Canadians, historically at least, have defined themselves by what they are not: Americans (Lipset, 1990, p. 53). Studying how Canadians are different from Americans fascinates Canadians and, particularly, Canadian sociologists. As well, one American sociologist, Seymour Martin Lipset (1922–2006), based a career on studying what makes Canadians and Americans different (Waller, 1990). Lipset's book *Continental Divide* (1990) summarizes and consolidates his almost 50 years of research on Canadian–American differences. He argues that Canadians are more elitist and ascriptive than Americans (that is, they are more inclined to accept that people are born with different statuses). They are also more community-oriented than Americans and more appreciative of racial and ethnic variation.

According to Lipset, the primordial event that generated the different founding ideologies of Canada and the United States was the American Revolution. The United States emerged from the Revolution as a manifestation of the classic liberal state, rejecting all ties to the British throne, the rights gained by royal birth, and communal responsibility. On the other hand, English Canada fought to maintain its imperial ties through the explicit rejection of liberal revolutions (Lipset, 1986). Canadian identity was not defined by a successful revolution but, instead, by a successful counterrevolution (Lipset, 1993). The United States, conversely, was defined by a rigid and stable ideology Lipset calls Americanism.

Lipset argues that evidence of Canadian and American founding ideologies is present in each country's literature. American literature concentrates on themes of winning, opportunism, and confidence, while Canadian writing focuses on defeat, difficult physical circumstances, and abandonment by Britain (Lipset, 1990). Lipset cites Atwood, who suggests that national symbols reveal a great deal about the cultural values a nation embraces. According to Atwood, the defining symbol for the United States is "the frontier," which inspires images of vitality and unrealized potential; for Canada, the defining symbol is "survival": "Canadians are forever taking the national pulse like doctors at a sickbed; the aim is not to see whether the patient will live well but simply whether he will live at all" (Atwood, 1972, p. 33, as cited in Lipset, 1986, p. 124). Lipset suggests that the symbols, attitudes, and values of a people do not exist in a vacuum but, rather, are embodied in and reinforced by social and political institutions (Baer, Grabb, & Johnston, 1990; Lipset, 1990).

Lipset's research has been the subject of much interest, debate, and pointed criticism. Sociologists generally agree that Canadian and American cultural values differ, but there is no clear consensus on what constitutes their specific differences.

CANADIAN VALUES IN GLOBAL PERSPECTIVE

Values manifest themselves in all social realms and structures. The Canadian Values Study, a joint project of the *National Post*, the Dominion Institute, and Innovative Research Group, found that while Canadian values are largely similar to those of other advanced democracies, there are some interesting differences (*National Post*, 2005).

According to the study, 89 percent of Canadians said that they believed in God; in contrast, the World Values Survey found comparable figures of 96 percent in the United States, 95 percent in India, 94 percent in Italy, 72 percent in Britain, and 62 percent in France (www .worldvaluessurvey.org). However, when asked whether religious leaders should try not to influence government decisions, 67 percent of Canadians agreed (with similar levels seen in India, Italy, and Britain), compared with only 51 percent of Americans. This is an especially interesting result given that the American Constitution requires a formal separation of church and state.

Another interesting finding was how values relating to welfare systems vary around the world. While Canadians are generally assumed to support a strong social safety net, 60 percent of the study's respondents agreed with the view that "People who don't get ahead should blame themselves, not the system" (*National Post*, 2005, p. 2). Further, when asked to select from a list of 10 qualities they would encourage their children to have, only 53 percent of Canadians selected "hard work" compared to 86 percent in China, 85 percent in India, 61 percent in the United States, 39 percent in Britain, 36 percent in Italy, and 23 percent in Germany. Clearly, working hard to achieve material comfort at the possible expense of other activities is more important in some areas of the world than in others. This trend continues when the value of competition is considered. Sixty-eight percent of Canadian respondents reported that competition was good. This compares quite closely to Americans at 71 percent, Chinese at 70 percent, and Germans at 64 percent, with British at 57 percent, Italians at 55 percent, Indians at 48 percent, and French at 45 percent.

The survey results indicate that while Canadian values are largely consistent with other industrialized nations, there are also some notable cultural differences.

❻ Cultural Change

As you can see, cultures are always changing to address new social and technological challenges. Consider how Canadian culture was changed by the implementation of the telephone, television, and affordable air travel, or by modifications to the laws allowing divorce and abortion. Social scientists generally consider three different sources for inspiring cultural change: discovery, invention/innovation, and diffusion (Grubler, 1996; see also Ravelli, 2000).

discovery Occurs when something previously unrecognized or understood is found to have social or cultural applications.

Discovery occurs when something previously unrecognized or understood is found to have social or cultural applications. Historically, discovery involved findings from the natural world—for example, fire and gravity. Today, discoveries can occur as a result of the scientific process—for example, the ability to split the atom allowed the production of weapons of mass destruction but also the generation of inexpensive electricity.

invention/innovation Occurs when existing cultural items are manipulated or modified to produce something new and socially valuable.

Invention/innovation occurs when existing cultural items are manipulated or modified to produce something new and socially valuable. The differences between invention and innovation may appear slight, but the distinction is important. *Invention* refers to creating something completely new that has not existed before—for example, Marconi's (1874–1937) device that received the first transatlantic wireless communication at Signal Hill in St. John's, Newfoundland, in 1901. *Innovation* refers to manipulating existing ideas or technologies to create something new, or to applying them to something for which they were not originally intended—for example, the carbon filament in light bulbs was replaced when the much more trustworthy and long-lasting tungsten filament was used (Dresselhaus, Dresselhaus, & Phaedon, 2001).

BOX 5.2 ISSUES IN GLOBAL CONTEXT

What Makes a Woman Beautiful?

Men have admired female beauty for as long as we can remember. The ancient Greeks believed that beauty could be studied objectively through mathematics; to them, beauty was a matter of symmetrical proportions. If symmetry determines beauty, then women's ideal body shape should remain the same over time since ideal mathematical proportions do not vary. This has not been the case, however.

Until the early twentieth century, women were considered to be physically attractive if they were "richly equipped" and had voluptuous feminine curves (see University of Regensburg, 2007). This body ideal is evident in the paintings of Flemish artist Peter Paul Rubens (1577–1640).

Today, the women depicted in Rubens's paintings would be considered overweight—if not "obese" by many contemporary viewers. The primary criterion for female attractiveness today is to be thin (Media Awareness Network, 2010). What has inspired such a rapid transformation in women's ideal body shape?

Some argue that mass media images are responsible for this change (Vandenbosch & Eggermont, 2012). Advertisers sell women the idea that they can be attractive and popular only if they are thin; after all, the multi-billion-dollar cosmetic and diet supplement industry is well served by creating negative body images in women (see Wolf, 1991). In effect, advertisers have "created" our fixation on the thin ideal and what we consider to be beautiful.

Even girls as young as six are influenced by the images they see on television (Dohnt & Tiggemann, 2006). Researchers found that girls who watch programs that emphasize attractive appearance (e.g., *America's Next Top Model, Jersey Shore, Trophy Wife*) are more likely to be dissatisfied with their own appearance. In a sample of the US population, 24 percent of women and 17 percent of men said that they would give up "three years of their lives to be thinner" (Alam & Dover, as cited in Dohnt & Tiggemann, 2006, p. 539). It is no wonder, then, that so many women suffer from low self-esteem, poor body image, and eating disorders.

Regardless of culture or ethnic background, the thin ideal is becoming one of the world's defining criteria for beauty (see Gangestad & Scheyd, 2005; Langlois & Kalakanis, 2000). As American mass media continue to expand their reach into every corner of the world, we as social scientists must continue to study the negative influences of the thin ideal and advocate healthier and more realistic media images.

Do you believe media images influence how you feel about yourself?

The Three Graces, c.1636-39 (oil on canvas) by Peter Paul Rubens (1577-1640) Prado, Madrid, Spain/Giraudon/Bridgeman Images

diffusion Occurs when cultural items or practices are transmitted from one group to another.

Diffusion occurs when cultural items or practices are transmitted from one group to another. Consider, for example, the influence that American media have on cultural practices throughout the world. Canadian sociologist Marshall McLuhan understood the power of media and their ability to transcend geopolitical borders when he used the phrase *global village* (McLuhan, 1964). While telecommunications have made the world feel like a smaller place, American mass media have also promoted a "culture of thinness" that has diffused throughout popular culture (Pidgeon & Harker, 2013).

⑦ Sociological Approaches to Culture and Culture Change

As you learned in Chapters 2 and 3, sociological theory attempts to explain all social phenomena—and culture is certainly of great theoretical interest.

 Watch

Lynette Spillman: Sociologists and Culture

FUNCTIONALISM

Functionalism approaches the value of culture from the premise that, since every society must meet basic needs (water, food, and shelter), culture can best be understood as playing a role in helping to meet those needs. What is fascinating is how differently human societies go about it: Thais eat water beetles and Scots eat haggis; the Inuit live in igloos and the Pueblo live in adobes. And, while North Americans dam rivers not only to quench their thirst but also to water their lawns, the situation in India is far more dire in that some predict that by 2020 India will no longer be able to meet its domestic water needs (The World Bank, n.d.).

cultural universals

Common cultural features found in all societies.

Yet within this diversity are common features that all known societies are believed to share, referred to as **cultural universals**. The first researcher to investigate these universals was George Peter Murdock (1897–1985), a functionalist anthropologist and sociologist. In *The Common Denominator of Culture* (1945), Murdock compiled a list of more than 70 cultural features common to virtually all known human societies (see Table 5.1).

Table 5.1 highlights that all known human societies treat people differently based on their age (age grading), have rules about who can be considered appropriate sexual partners (incest taboos), use personal names for individuals, and play games (to name only a few cultural universals). Although the particulars may vary (e.g., the specific ages that define age grades, the types of games played), functionalists assert that these universals reinforce the position that social life is best understood by considering what individual practices or beliefs do for the collective.

TABLE 5.1 Cultural Universals

Age grading	Body adornment
Division of labour	Courtship
Property rights	Music and dance
Family/kinship groups	Incest taboos
Status differences	Cleanliness training
Cooking	Magic/luck/superstitions
Personal names	Hospitality/greetings
Language	Games
Gestures	Jokes

Reprinted by permission of Sociology Central, 2007, Chris Livesey (www.sociology.org.uk) © 1995-2014.

Functionalists argue that unique cultural traditions and customs develop and persist because they are adaptive and improve a people's chances of survival (Lindsey, Beach, & Ravelli, 2009, p. 68). **Cultural adaptation** is the process by which environmental pressures are addressed through changes in practices, traditions, and behaviours as a way of maintaining stability and equilibrium. Because functionalists argue that every social practice leads to some collective benefit, any practice that diminishes a culture's ability to prosper will be unlikely to survive.

cultural adaptation
The process by which environmental pressures are addressed through changes in practices, traditions, and behaviours.

For example, Canadians have begun to realize the hazards of drinking and driving. The most recent statistics suggest that Canadian culture is changing as it relates to drinking and driving. In 2009, alcohol-related fatalities represented 27.7 percent of all vehicle deaths, almost 10 percent below the national high-water mark of 35.2 percent recorded in 1995 (Vanlaar, Robertson, Marcoux, Mayhew, Brown, & Boase, 2012). This same study indicates that while Canadians are concerned about a number of different safety issues, the problem of impaired driving remains one of the most prominent. Attitudes about drinking and driving are changing and are no doubt the result of various campaigns educating people about the terrible social and economic costs associated with the behaviour.

Critiquing the Functionalist Approach to Culture One of functionalism's greatest strengths is how it demonstrates that some elements of culture do operate to fulfill human needs. However, by focusing on how cultural elements work together to maintain stability, functionalism does not take into account tension from subcultures or countercultures. While a group of women getting together on the weekends to play recreational hockey (a subculture) may be of no threat to social stability, an outlaw biker gang that challenges the larger society's laws, value system, and beliefs (a counterculture) may warrant concern. Even though a countercultural movement may inspire progressive social change, the overriding assumption of functionalist theory is stability. To assume that cultural traditions are always useful for the system denies the real pain and suffering they sometimes cause. For example, before the US Civil War, many people accepted slavery because it was "just the way things have always been done." However, the advantages for the rich white slave owners do not excuse this morally reprehensible practice. Cultural traditions may help to bind people together, but it may be impossible to justify or defend how they benefit society as a whole (i.e., what were the "benefits" of slavery for the slaves?).

CONFLICT THEORY

As discussed in Chapter 2, conflict theory views society as based on tension and conflict over scarce resources. Conflict theorists assert that those who hold power define and perpetuate a culture's ideology, and create a value system that defines social inequality as just and proper (Lindsey, Beach, & Ravelli, 2009, p. 69). Conflict theorists would certainly approach the slavery example we used above from a very different perspective: that slavery was allowed to exist because it benefited rich white people. Consider our own contemporary views of wealth and success. The culture and the values that support the belief that success requires money are a demonstration of the power of ideology. After all, if people are working hard their whole lives trying to get ahead, how much time do they have to think about how the system exploits them? Conflict theorists view the link between money and success as an expression of the ruling elite's power and influence.

A clear Canadian example of how the elite can use their power to dominate the less powerful is the Canadian residential school system. Between the 1890s and 1970s, the Canadian government funded the residential school system for Aboriginal children. Almost everyone recognized that the government's motive was not only to educate the children but also to assimilate them into the dominant white society. In 1969, the government's White Paper recommended the elimination of all legal discrimination against Aboriginal peoples, the abolition of the Department of Indian Affairs, and the integration of First Nations peoples into

BOX 5.3 THAT WAS THEN, THIS IS NOW

Canada's Residential School System

The residential school system predates Confederation and was largely a result of the missionary efforts of numerous religious organizations. The Canadian government began to play a more focused role in 1874 when the *Indian Act* outlined the government's obligation to provide education for Aboriginal peoples and to assist them with their integration into Canadian society.

Over the years, residential schools were located in every province and territory, except New Brunswick and Prince Edward Island. Some estimates suggest that about 100 000 children attended the more than 130 residential schools across Canada.

The residential school system was jointly managed by the federal government and individual religious organizations until 1969, when the government assumed full responsibility. Many were closed by the mid 1970s, and only seven remained open through the 1980s. The last federally managed residential school was closed in Saskatchewan in 1996.

In 1998, the federal government announced a program called Gathering Strength: Canada's Aboriginal Action Plan. As part of this initiative, the government offered a Statement of Reconciliation that acknowledged its role in the development and administration of residential schools.

> Sadly, our history with respect to the treatment of Aboriginal people is not something in which we can take pride. Attitudes of racial and cultural superiority led to a suppression of Aboriginal culture and values. As a country, we are burdened by past actions that resulted in weakening the identity of Aboriginal peoples, suppressing their languages and cultures, and outlawing spiritual practises. We must recognize the impact of these actions on the once self-sustaining nations that were disaggregated, disrupted, limited or even destroyed by the dispossession of traditional territory, by the relocation of Aboriginal people, and by some provisions of the Indian Act. We must acknowledge that the result of these actions was the erosion of the political, economic and social systems of Aboriginal people and nations.
>
> One aspect of our relationship with Aboriginal people over this period that requires particular attention is the Residential School system. This system separated many children from their families and communities and prevented them from speaking their own languages and from learning about their heritage and cultures. In the worst cases, it left legacies of personal pain and distress that continue to reverberate in Aboriginal communities to this day. Tragically, some children were the victims of physical and sexual abuse.
>
> The Government of Canada acknowledges the role it played in the development and administration of these schools. Particularly to those individuals who experienced the tragedy of sexual and physical abuse at residential schools, and who have carried this burden believing that in some way they must be responsible, we wish to emphasize that what you experienced was not your fault and should never have happened. To those of you who suffered this tragedy at residential schools, we are deeply sorry. (Indian and Northern Affairs Canada, 2004a)

On June 11, 2008, Prime Minister Stephen Harper rose in the House of Commons and on behalf of the government of Canada, formally apologized to the victims of the residential school system. The government's compensation package to the victims is estimated at $1.9 billion and is intended to make restitution to all victims of Canada's residential schools (www.residentialschoolsettlement.ca).

How can both conflict theory and functionalism be applied to the residential school system? As a sociologist, do you believe the government's compensation package will lead to greater or lesser marginalization of Aboriginal peoples? Why?

< < <

The pain and suffering caused by the residential school system continues to affect tens of thousands of Aboriginal people across Canada.

the dominant society (see Murray, 2003). Any policy advocating the assimilation of a unique minority group is an abuse of power and a demonstration of the dominant culture's attempt to absorb a less powerful one.

According to Karl Marx, the dominant culture eventually becomes part of the oppressed group's value system. Ultimately, the oppressed group begins to view its own culture as inferior and tries to improve its position by adopting the ways of the dominant culture. Given what you know, do you understand why some Aboriginal peoples may feel like outsiders and want to become more like members of the dominant (i.e., white) culture? If this is the case, can the Canadian residential school system be seen as an example of ethnocentrism?

Critiquing the Conflict Approach to Culture The conflict approach suggests that cultural systems perpetuate social inequality. As discussed in Chapter 2, conflict theorists believe that society's elite use ideology to further their own interests and protect themselves from opposition. By defining what the dominant classes perceive as positive, cultural elements promote social inequality through the belief that to be successful you have to be like the elite and perpetuate their control and power.

On one hand, conflict theory would be supportive of Aboriginal peoples' efforts at cultural preservation, but, on the other hand, it would recognize that by maintaining their traditions Aboriginals are isolating and marginalizing themselves from the dominant culture. Overall, the conflict approach favours the notion that cultural change is more beneficial to oppressed people than is cultural continuity (Lindsey, Beach, & Ravelli, 2009, p. 70).

Functionalists view culture as a way of integrating and building on similarities and establishing a sense of community, while conflict theorists view culture as a vehicle for promoting and maintaining social inequality. Both perspectives would benefit from greater reflection on the other theory's insights. For example, functionalism would benefit by recognizing that culture can be used as a vehicle for oppression, and conflict theory would benefit by acknowledging the potential social benefits gained by uniting people into a common cultural group.

SYMBOLIC INTERACTIONISM

As discussed in Chapter 2, symbolic interactionists argue that social reality is the result of human interaction. One of the most famous symbolic interactionists, Herbert Blumer (1969), suggested that people do not respond directly to the world around them but, instead, to the meanings they collectively apply to it. As a microsociological perspective, symbolic interactionism investigates how culture is actively created and recreated through social interaction. Thus, as people go about their everyday lives, they create and modify culture as they engage in the negotiation of reality based on shared meanings grounded in cultural symbols.

The values and norms defining minority status, for example, are the result of mutual interaction and social definition. People interpret and actively engage with nonmaterial cultural artifacts (symbols) in every social situation they encounter. Therefore, minority status is a social category created by interacting individuals and manifests itself in society through negotiated social interaction. For example, each time a member of the dominant (i.e., white) culture encounters an Aboriginal person, he or she assigns that person to a category based on predefined cultural meanings, which influences how he or she interacts with that person. This serves to reinforce the dominant cultural norms of who minority people are and how they are supposed to act (e.g., be deferential). However, since these meanings are actively negotiated, there is also great potential for resisting and changing dominant cultural meanings as they are fluid and constantly open to reinterpretation and reflection. According to symbolic interactionists, then, culture is the set of symbols to which we collectively assign values and the result of our active engagement with those around us (Lindsey, Beach, & Ravelli, 2009, p. 72).

Critiquing the Symbolic Interactionist Approach to Culture Symbolic interactionists rightly point out that culture results from social interaction and collective engagement with our surroundings. However, suggesting that changing cultural definitions requires changing how we define and classify people diminishes the reality that some cultural definitions result from structural oppression and discrimination (e.g., residential school system, Japanese-Canadian internment camps during World War II). As a microsociological approach, symbolic interactionism, while tremendously insightful about interpersonal definitions of cultural meanings, is less able to explain large cultural manifestations than are functionalist or conflict theories.

Each theoretical approach, then, views culture quite differently; however, as we continue to stress, this diversity is not a sociological weakness but, rather, a strength.

Summary

1. Culture—a complex collection of values, beliefs, behaviours, and material objects shared by a group and passed on from one generation to the next—possesses five defining features: it is learned, shared, transmitted, cumulative, and human.

2. Ethnocentrism is the tendency to perceive one's own culture as superior to all others; cultural relativism, in contrast, appreciates that all cultures have intrinsic worth.

3. Language, comprising a system of symbols having agreed-upon meanings shared by a group of people, can distinguish one culture from another; with the death of its language, a culture loses one of its survival mechanisms.

4. A subculture is a group that shares common attributes that distinguish it from the larger population; a counterculture is a type of subculture that opposes the widely held cultural patterns of the larger population.

5. Canadian culture has been defined by its vast and, in places, harsh physical environment; by the coexistence of, and conflict between, French and English; and by its primary and enduring differences from the United States.

6. Cultural change occurs through (1) discovery, when something previously unrecognized or understood is found to have social or cultural applications; (2) invention/innovation, when existing cultural items are manipulated or modified to produce something new and

socially valuable; and (3) diffusion, when cultural items or practices are transmitted from one group to another.

7 Functionalists hold that cultural traditions develop and persist because they are adaptive and maintain stability. Conflict theorists, on the other hand, view cultural systems as a means of perpetuating social inequality, with the dominant culture assimilating less powerful cultures. Symbolic interactionists understand culture as being actively created and recreated through social interaction.

Key Terms

counterculture *131*
cultural adaptation *137*
cultural relativism *125*
cultural universals *136*
culture *121*
culture lag *120*
culture shock *126*
diffusion *136*
discovery *134*
ethnocentrism *125*
folkways *124*
hominid ancestors *122*
Homo sapiens *122*
invention/innovation *134*

language *127*
law *124*
linguistic determinism *128*
linguistic relativism *128*
material culture *124*
micro-expressions *130*
mores *124*
nonmaterial culture *124*
norms *124*
sanction *124*
Sapir-Whorf hypothesis *128*
subculture *130*
taboo *124*
symbol *127*
values *124*

Reviewing the Concepts

1. What is culture? What evidence exists about when it emerged?

2. What is culture lag?

3. What are the similarities between linguistic determinism and linguistic relativism?

4. In your everyday life, when do you find yourself relying on nonverbal communication most? Why?

Applying Your Sociological Imagination

1. Using your sociological imagination, how might you explain the impact the automobile has had in defining Canadian culture?

2. In your opinion, are there any situations when ethnocentrism is good and cultural relativism is bad? Discuss using your own examples.

3. As a sociologist, how might you explain why so many people believe that being thin is in?

4. With reference to the material in the chapter, what impact do you believe the residential school system has had on Aboriginal culture? Discuss.

MySocLab

Visit MySocLab to access a variety of online resources that will help you prepare for tests and apply your knowledge.

PM Images/Getty Images

6 Socialization and Social Interaction

What makes us who we are? Do you think we are born with inherent characteristics, or do we develop our personalities as we move through life? Consider the differences between the sexes. For example, although certainly an overgeneralization, many would argue that men are more likely to pursue multiple sexual relationships than are women. But why do men and women behave differently? Do these differences stem from biology, whereby genetics define each sex's responses to the social world, or do they arise from the social environment, whereby our perceptions and behaviours result from how we are raised and interact with the social world?

In the simplest terms, the biological argument suggests that because men are capable of impregnating multiple women at the same time, they have an evolved desire for multiple partners, preferably those who are young and physically attractive (Jæger, 2011; Price, Kang, Dunn, & Hopkins, 2011). Conversely, since women can reproduce through only one pregnancy at a time, they have an evolved desire for partners who can provide for them and their children (Barker, 2006). According to this view, then, genetically based instincts and physical capacities define men's and women's desires and behaviours.

However, sociologists challenge these biologically based assumptions. They perceive behavioural differences, to the extent that they actually exist, as the result of socialization and social interaction—the subject of this chapter.

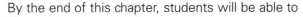

LEARNING OBJECTIVES

By the end of this chapter, students will be able to

1 Review and critique the nature versus nurture debate as it relates to socialization.

2 Explain the development of the self from the sociological and psychological perspectives.

3 Outline how the agents of socialization influence a person's sense of self.

4 Describe how socialization continues past childhood and throughout the life course.

5 Explore the concept of resocialization and the characteristics of total institutions.

1 Becoming "Human"

Can't Stand Putting Your Money at Risk? Blame DNA

To fully understand what it means to be human is to appreciate that, as far as we know, we are the only organisms that can *think about thinking*. How we think about ourselves and the world is an important and dynamic area of research for social scientists.

There are two basic approaches to understanding how we develop our **personalities**—broadly defined as an individual's relatively stable pattern of behaviours and feelings—and become members of the larger society. These are the biological approach and the environmental approach, traditionally referred to as the **nature versus nurture** debate. The *nature* side of the debate holds that our actions and feelings stem from our biological roots. Those on the *nurture* side of the debate argue that we are the product of our **socialization**—the lifelong process by which we learn our culture, develop our personalities, and become functioning members of society. Our sense of the world and of ourselves, then, is held to be the result of **social interaction**, which encompasses all of the ways that people interact in social settings while recognizing each person's subjective experiences and/or intentions.

THE NATURE ARGUMENT: BEING BORN YOU

The nature argument suggests that most of our behaviour is determined by our genetic makeup. Although sociologists assume that the nurture side is more important in determining the person you become, they also appreciate that biology plays a role in explaining some key aspects of your behaviour, such as athletic ability and intellectual capacity.

Recent medical research demonstrates that evolutionary forces have led to women and men having very different brain structures that influence how each sex responds to the world around it.

personality An individual's relatively stable pattern of behaviours and feelings.

nature versus nurture The debate between whether biological forces or environment define the person we become.

socialization The lifelong process by which we learn our culture, develop our personalities, and become functioning members of society.

social interaction The ways in which people interact in social settings, recognizing each person's subjective experiences and/or intentions.

In the brain centers for language and hearing . . . women have 11 percent more neurons than men. The principal hub of both emotion and memory formation—the hippocampus— is also larger in the female brain, as is the brain circuitry for language and observing emotion in others. This means that women are, on average, better at expressing emotions and remembering the details of emotional events. Men, by contrast, have two and a half times the brain space devoted to sexual drive as well as larger brain centers for action and aggression. Sexual thoughts float through a man's brain many times each day on average, and through a woman's only once a day. Perhaps three to four times on her hottest days. (Brizendine, 2006, p. 5)

sociobiology A science that uses evolutionary theory and genetic inheritance to examine the biological roots of social behaviour.

The science of **sociobiology** uses evolutionary theory and genetic inheritance to examine the biological roots of social behaviour. It began in the early 1960s and is associated with the animal behaviour studies of Nobel Prize–winner Konrad Lorenz (1903–1989) and the research into the social behaviour of ants by two-time Pulitzer Prize–winner Edward O. Wilson (1929–). Wilson's groundbreaking 1975 book *Sociobiology: The New Synthesis* applies the principles of Darwinian inheritance to show how human behaviours are selected for and passed on from one generation to the next.

The core assertion of sociobiology is that social behaviour among humans, as with all organisms, has evolved over time to secure the survival of the species (Buss, 2008, p. 17). In evolutionary terms, the most important achievement for an organism is to leave as many offspring as possible. Those attributes (physical or behavioural) that help an individual to produce offspring are selected for, and those attributes that diminish an individual's ability to produce offspring are selected against (Fetchenhauer & Buunk, 2005, p. 98). Sociobiology argues that, for example, the physical and behavioural differences we see in women and men today are the result of millions of years of natural selection.

evolutionary psychology A relabelled form of sociobiology that argues that Darwinian inheritance can explain contemporary human behaviour.

Sociobiology has gained popularity in recent years under its new name: *evolutionary psychology* (see Jæger, 2011; Hopcroft, 2009; Kinzler, Shutts, & Correll, 2010). Like sociobiology, **evolutionary psychology** argues that Darwinian inheritance can explain contemporary human behaviour (Brown & Richerson, 2013). For example, according to anthropologist John Patton, the fact that the Achuar Indians of Ecuador have one of the world's highest murder rates can be explained by the fact that killing is part of their culture and has been selected for over many generations (as cited in Roach, 1998). Among the Achuar, being a warrior is the highest status a man can achieve; the best warriors—those most likely to survive battle—were considered to be the most attractive and would therefore father the greatest number of children. Thus, according to Patton, evolution explains why the Achuar have such high murder rates: Murder has been selected for.

In a completely different application of the theory, Victor Nell suggests that evolutionary psychology can explain why young men are more likely to drive faster than women and older men. Nell (1998, p. 19) argues that when young men reach the "mating and fighting age" (16 to 20 years), their sense of invincibility is at an all-time high because of deep evolutionary urges that inspire them to take risks to gain social status and the most desireable mate.

Evolutionary psychologists, and sociobiologists before them, have had some success in applying evolutionary theory to explain human behaviours (Baker & Maner, 2008). However, empirical support for their overall assertion that human behaviour is determined by genetics remains contentious and has only limited support in the social sciences. Social scientists suggest that to extend biological theories of behaviour beyond the animal realm disregards the ability of humans to think before they act. Our capacity to reflect on our own behaviour is one that social scientists believe must be fully recognized and appreciated. In fact, some advocates for the evolutionary perspective also suggest that the structure of our brain, and the emotions and behaviours it inspires, does not mean that the mind cannot transcend biology.

If we acknowledge that our biology is influenced by other factors, including sex hormones and their flux, we can prevent it from creating a fixed reality by which we are ruled. The brain is nothing if not a talented learning machine. Nothing is completely fixed. Biology powerfully affects but does not lock in our reality. We can alter that reality and use our intelligence and determination both to celebrate and, when necessary, to change the effects of sex hormones on brain structure, behaviour, reality, creativity—and destiny. (Brizendine, 2006, pp. 6–7)

Sociologists generally acknowledge that some genetic linkages exist and influence human behaviour; however, they remain committed to the belief that the factors influencing the people we become are defined not by nature but, rather, by nurture.

THE NURTURE ARGUMENT: LEARNING TO BE YOU

Perhaps the most compelling argument to explain why sociologists believe that we become the people we are through social interaction is what happens when young children are isolated from human contact.

Effects of Social Isolation One of the most famous cases of isolation was that of a five-year-old girl, Anna, who was discovered in 1938 by a social worker visiting a Pennsylvania farmhouse. When she was discovered, Anna was tied to a chair and was so severely undernourished she could barely stand on her own. It was discovered that she had been born out of wedlock to a mentally handicapped mother and kept in the attic by her grandfather because he was embarrassed about her illegitimacy (Lindsey, Beach, & Ravelli, 2009, p. 83). Upon hearing about Anna, sociologist Kinsley Davis immediately travelled to see her and was overwhelmed by what he found. Deprived of normal human contact and receiving only a minimal amount of care to keep her alive, Anna could not talk, walk, or do anything that demonstrated even basic intellectual capacity.

< < <

Some evolutionary psychologists suggest that young men's risky behaviours demonstrate their vitality and invincibility—evolved attributes intended to attract women.

Vitalii Nesterchuk/Shutterstock

After working with Anna for two years, Davis had been able to teach her to walk, understand simple commands, and feed herself. After two more years, she had learned basic toilet habits, could use a spoon when eating, and could dress herself. However, at age nine she was less than 1.3 metres tall and weighed only 27 kilograms. When Anna died at age 10 from a blood disorder, she had only progressed to the intellectual capacity of a two-and-a-half-year-old. While she could talk in phrases, she never developed a true capacity for language. Her isolation from other people during virtually her entire early life prevented her from developing more than a small fraction of her intellectual potential (adapted from Davis, 1947; Lindsey, Beach, & Ravelli, 2009, p. 83).

Another disturbing example of human isolation is the case of five-year-old Jeffrey Baldwin, who was found dead when Toronto emergency workers arrived at his home in 2002. The subsequent investigation revealed that he had been confined to his room for years (*CBC news: The Fifth Estate,* 2007). At the time of his discovery, Jeffrey weighed only 9.5 kilograms and was less than 1 metre tall. It was obvious from the condition of his body that he had died from malnutrition and neglect—an especially horrible outcome in a home with six adults and five other healthy children. Both grandparents were sentenced to life imprisonment after being convicted of second-degree murder. Although Jeffrey's intellectual and social development at the time of his death is uncertain, research into human isolation suggests that he never would have recovered from such abuse if he had lived.

> > > Thinking Sociologically

As a sociologist, explain why people are attracted to biological explanations for human behaviour.

The importance of human interaction is obvious in light of such cases of children who have suffered from severe neglect. Sociologists argue that social reality is constructed by people every time they interact with others. In fact, contemporary research suggests that the nature/nurture debate may in fact be a false dichotomy (see Moore, 2013; Wagner, 2009). Human beings are the wonderful product of both genetics and social interactions. Our genetic makeup (nature) gives us the capacity to be social beings, but it is the process of social interaction (nurture) that enables us to develop that capacity.

The chapter began by looking at how men and women behave differently because of their genetic makeup. As we have now learned, while the nature argument is interesting, sociologists argue that nurture plays a far more central role in defining our behaviour than a genetic legacy from our past.

❷ Development of Self: Sociological Insights

self One's identity, comprising a set of learned values and attitudes that develops through social interaction and defines one's self-image.

self-image An introspective composition of various features and attributes that people see themselves as having.

Every person is unique; just like snowflakes, no two people are completely alike. The **self** may be defined as "a composite of thoughts and feelings" from which we derive our "conception of who and what" we are (Jersild, 1952, p. 9). The self, or one's identity, comprises a set of learned values and attitudes that develops through social interaction and defines one's self-image. Our **self-image** is an introspective composition of various features and attributes that we see ourselves as. The self is a key component of *personality*, defined on page 143 as an individual's relatively stable pattern of behaviours and feelings. In healthy individuals, the personality and self join to give an individual the sense that he or she is unique and special.

IMAGINING HOW OTHERS SEE US: C. H. COOLEY

In Chapter 2, we discussed Cooley's concept of the looking-glass self, whereby what we think of ourselves is influenced by how we imagine other people see us (Cooley, 1902). Indeed, as evidenced by isolated and feral children, consciousness cannot develop without social interaction. According to Cooley, to be aware of oneself, one must be aware of society.

Self-consciousness and social consciousness are inseparable because people cannot conceive of themselves without reference to others. Therefore, the self does not emerge independently in the mind but instead is the result of social interaction.

One of Cooley's most famous statements was that sociologists must "imagine imaginations" (as cited in Rossides, 1998, p. 225). According to Cooley (1902), sociologists could not hope to understand the social world until they could project themselves into the minds of others and see the world as those people did—the essence of the sociological imagination and the sociological perspective.

UNDERSTANDING OURSELVES AND OTHERS: G. H. MEAD

Building upon Cooley's investigation into the development of self, Mead argued that the self is composed of two complementary elements. He referred to the first element as the **I**, the part of self that is spontaneous, creative, impulsive, and often unpredictable (Lindsey & Beach, 2003, p. 94). The I is the part of consciousness that responds to things emotionally. For example, imagine how you might respond if you found out that you had won a free trip to Mexico. Chances are you would jump up and down and wave your arms in the air to express your excitement.

However, Mead suggested that while you are jumping up and down, you are also conscious of how others view you. Excitement is one thing, but we have all witnessed instances where someone does not recognize when "enough is enough." Mead termed this second level of consciousness the **Me**. According to Mead, the Me is the socialized element of the self, the part of consciousness that thinks about how to behave so that, for example, you don't embarrass yourself. The Me, in other words, helps us to control the spontaneous impulses of the I. The sense of conflict we feel when we are compelled to act one way but discipline ourselves to act in another demonstrates the dynamic relationship between the I and the Me, and their influence on our everyday behaviour.

Our understanding of ourselves and our social environment is also influenced by those around us. When we are with our friends, for example, we tend to behave differently than we do when we are with our family. To understand this influence more fully, Mead investigated how we attribute different levels of importance to those around us (Mead, 1934). People we want to impress or gain approval from he termed **significant others**. When we are children, our parents are the most important people in our lives and so are considered significant others. As we mature (around age 12), the importance of our family wanes somewhat and we become aware of those in the broader social world who influence our behaviours. Mead called these people the **generalized other**—not any one specific person but, rather, a compilation of attributes that we associate with the average member of society. This conception of a generalized other represents the recognition that other members of society behave within certain socially accepted guidelines and rules. Understanding the generalized other and how it would feel or behave in certain situations gives the individual a reference point for proper and expected behaviour.

Critical to explaining symbolic interactionists' analysis of how we interpret ourselves, other people, and the social world is the concept of **role-taking**—assuming the position of another to better understand that person's perspective. Role-taking is critical for empathizing with another person's situation. By imagining what it would be like to be homeless, for example, you inevitably become more empathetic to how homeless people must feel and more compassionate about their needs. Similarly, imagining how other people may respond to a given social situation enables you to better anticipate their actions and to respond to them in a manner you have considered in advance.

Mead also contributed to understanding how we develop our sense of self through social interaction by investigating how young children are socialized. He asserted that, as they grow up, children pass through a series of three distinct stages.

Watch

The Looking-Glass Self

I Mead's term for that element of the self that is spontaneous, creative, impulsive, and often unpredictable.

Me Mead's term for the socialized element of the self.

significant others People we want to impress or gain approval from.

generalized other A compilation of attributes associated with the average member of society; represents an individual's appreciation that other members of society behave within certain socially accepted guidelines and rules.

role-taking Assuming the position of another to better understand that person's perspective.

BOX 6.1 WHY SHOULD WE CARE?

Feral Children: What Can They Teach Us?

Feral (meaning "wild") children are those who have been isolated from human contact from a very young age. They have little or no experience with love or human interaction, nor do they have a grasp of language. They are often confined by a negligent human caregiver or raised by animals (Dellbrügge, 2010; *Gale Encyclopedia of Childhood and Adolescence,*1998; Saniotis, 2009). In the latter case, the children exhibit behaviours we commonly associate with the parenting species—for example, walking on four legs, eating raw meat, being nocturnal, fear of or indifference to humans. More than a hundred cases of feral children have been reported around the world (Ward, n.d.); they are of interest to sociologists because they offer a unique, albeit disturbing, insight into the necessity of human interaction to make an individual fully human.

In 2002, when Traian Caldarar was discovered in the Transylvanian countryside, he was naked, living in a cardboard box, and thought to have been raised by stray dogs. Though Traian was estimated to be seven, his body size was that of a three-year-old. When officials tried to get Traian to a hospital, his behaviour became like that of a wild dog—he became violent and excitable. At the hospital, he preferred to sleep under the bed. Traian now lives with his mother, Lina, who was severely abused by Traian's father and fled from the household when Traian was only three years old. Lina had assumed that Traian would do the same as soon as he was able.

When 13-year-old "Genie"(so named by the scientists who studied her) was discovered in Los Angeles in 1970, researchers estimated that she had been locked in her room, alone, for more than 10 years. Investigation revealed that during the day Genie was strapped to a potty chair and at night, if her caregivers remembered to put her to bed, she was tied into a sleeping bag. After Genie was hospitalized, it was discovered that she lacked even the most basic language skills, moved with a "bunny-like gait" (she was only rarely allowed to move from her seat or sleeping bag), and held her hands in front of her body like paws. She was not toilet trained, had difficulty focusing her eyes beyond 12 feet, weighed less than 27 kilograms, and was less than 1.5 metres tall.

Once she was safe and properly cared for, Genie exhibited a thirst for knowledge. Scientists from around the world descended on Los Angeles to investigate the process of human socialization and the effects of long-term isolation and neglect. Though Genie made much progress, she was never able to learn language. Scientists were unsure whether her lack of speech was due to her prolonged isolation or the result of the physical abuse she suffered whenever she made noise while confined in her room

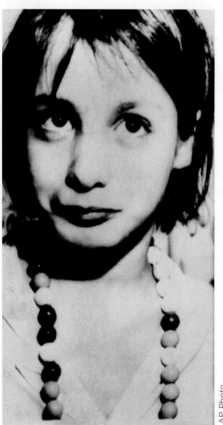

AP Photo

"Genie", above, is an example of how social interaction plays a crucial role in the development of healthy human beings.

CONTINUED

▶

(Ward, n.d.). Genie is still alive but has been moved from one adult care facility to another as scientific interest in and human compassion for her situation have steadily declined. In 2001, a movie entitled *Mockingbird Don't Sing* was made of Genie's life.

Studying feral children offers social scientists a unique glimpse into the crucial role of social interaction in the development of healthy human beings. For example, do you think children's development is hindered when their parents do not take an active interest in them? Could this be considered a form of social isolation?

Preparatory Stage (Birth to Age Three) Young children's first experiences when interacting with others are to imitate what they see others doing. Although children do not understand the meanings behind these early interactions, they want to please the significant others in their lives (usually their parents). Through positive and negative reinforcement, children begin to develop the *I*, but the *me* is also forming in the background.

Play Stage (Ages Three to Five) Children learn a great deal about themselves and the society around them through play. As children begin to assume the roles of others ("I'll be Batman and you be Robin"), they move beyond simple imitation and assume the imagined roles of the characters they are playing. During this stage, the *me* continues to grow because children want to receive positive reinforcement from their significant others. Because language skills are developing throughout this stage, children can more accurately communicate their thoughts and feelings—a skill that must be mastered before a stable sense of self can emerge.

Game Stage (Elementary-School Years) As children continue to develop, they become increasingly proficient at taking on multiple roles at once (student, son or daughter, friend) and by doing so begin to identify with the generalized other. Participating in complex games that require them to play a particular role (e.g., playing defence on a field hockey team) teaches them to understand their individual position as well as the needs of the group. The skills developed during the game stage are readily transferred to other real-life situations (Lindsey, Beach, & Ravelli, 2009, p. 90; Mead, 1934). According to Mead, the game stage marks the period during which **primary socialization** occurs; this is when people learn the attitudes, values, and appropriate behaviours for individuals in their culture. As language skills are refined throughout the game stage, children begin to gain their first sense of self as a unique individual.

Secondary socialization occurs later, in early adolescence and beyond, through participation in groups that are more specific than the broader society and that have defined roles and expectations. Part-time jobs, city-wide sports teams, and volunteer activities are all examples of secondary groups. Because these groups are more specialized than primary groups, they allow individuals to develop the skills needed to fit in with various other groups of people throughout their lives (Chaudhari, 2013).

Considered from a sociological perspective, socialization is a lifelong process: After all, we interact with others throughout our lives, and constantly change and grow as a result.

DOUBLE-CONSCIOUSNESS: W. E. B. DUBOIS

In 1903, American black sociologist, W. E. B. DuBois (1868–1963) published the groundbreaking work, *The Souls of Black Folk*. In the book, DuBois famously described

primary socialization Occurs when people learn the attitudes, values, and appropriate behaviours for individuals in their culture.

secondary socialization Follows primary socialization and occurs through participation in more specific groups with defined roles and expectations.

double-consciousness
double-consciousness
DuBois's term for
a sense of self that
is defined, in part,
through the eyes of
others.

W. E. B. DuBois

Library of Congress
Prints & Photographs
Division Washington,
DC [LC-USZ62-16767]

> > >

Playing in groups helps
young people perform
multiple roles at one
time.

black Americans as possessing a **double-consciousness**—being caught between a self-concept as an American but also as a black person of African descent. As DuBois put it, "The Negro ever feels his two-ness—an American, a Negro; two souls, two thoughts, two unreconciled strivings . . . two warring ideals in one dark body, whose dogged strength alone keeps it from being torn asunder" (as cited in McWhorter, 2003). For DuBois, double-consciousness was on one hand a deprivation (the inability to see oneself independently from the white majority) but on the other hand a gift (because it enabled a type of "second sight" that allowed a deeper reflective comprehension of the contemporary world) (Edwards, 2007, p. xiv). Black Americans had to see the world and themselves as whites did in order to survive and to prosper in dominant white society. But, at the same time, they maintained a separate consciousness, one fully aware of their oppression. So, double-consciousness is necessary and possible only through, and because of, their ongoing oppression.

For our purposes, double-consciousness is similar to Mills's sociological imagination in that it requires the person to transcend the taken-for-granted world. To be socialized as a member of any minority group (described more fully in Chapter 10) requires a perception of self that is at least partially defined through the eyes of others. Ultimately, the power of the dominant culture to stereotype minority groups is a form of cultural imperialism, where negative images are internalized by minorities, and results in oppression and subjugation (Allen, 2008, p. 162).

Not only do DuBois's insights continue to help sociologists explore the social realities of black Americans but also of any socially marginalized groups, including racial, ethnic, and sexual minorities.

Central to understanding socialization are what sociologists refer to as the *agents of socialization.*

68/Ocean/Creative/Corbis

BOX 6.2 ISSUES IN GLOBAL CONTEXT

Child Labour Around the World

In Western society, childhood is viewed as a time for play, growth, learning, and enjoyment. Parents educate themselves on how best to raise their children, make sure that their children are fed properly, and provide shelter, clothing, education, and medical attention to ensure that they flourish into happy and productive adults. Many parents in the West would see making children work as inconsistent with their responsibilities as parents.

A 2013 International Labour Organization (ILO) report estimates 168 million children worldwide are in child labour and 85 million of them are working in hazardous conditions. Though the numbers are daunting, significant progress has been made recently. Between 2000 and 2012 the estimated number fell from 171 million; the number of child labourers who were girls fell by 40% and for boys 25% (ILO, 2013). Clearly, this is a trend in the right direction, however, these numbers are relative: The worldwide number of children labourers is still almost five times the population of Canada, a shocking indication of the realities of survival for so many people around the world.

One organization committed to helping children is Free the Children, founded in 1995 by 12-year-old child rights activist Craig Kielburger. Today, the organization has more than 2.3 million youth involved in educational and development programs in 45 different countries (Free the Children, 2014). Its goal is to eradicate child labour through a series of steps that include compulsory education for all children, increased social awareness campaigns, resources to rehabilitate child labourers, and stricter legislation to protect children from becoming labourers.

Free the Children lists some things that we can do to help: learn more about child labour and the laws that affect children, speak with others about the problem, volunteer time at an agency that protects children, and observe World Day Against Child Labour (June 12). Through the efforts of groups such as UNICEF, ILO, and Free the Children, our global community can work together to help overcome the incidence of child labour.

With the help of organizations such as those listed above (and many others), do you believe that child labour will ever be eradicated? Why?

The Canadian Press/Mustafa Quraishi/AP Photo

❸ Agents of Socialization

agents of socialization
Individuals, groups, and social institutions that together help people to become functioning members of society.

The **agents of socialization** are the individuals, groups, and social institutions that together help people to become functioning members of society. Although we are defined by our biology as well as by our psychological development, according to sociologists we are defined most significantly by the society around us. Today, the four principal agents of socialization are families, peers, education, and mass media.

FAMILIES

Families are by far the most important agents of socialization because they are the centre of children's lives. During the important formative period, families provide children with nourishment, love, and protection and guide their first experiences with the social world (a topic we return to in Chapter 11). In the first years of life, families are largely responsible for children's emerging identities, self-esteem, and personalities. In fact, the first values and attitudes that a child embraces are generally simple reflections of his or her family's values and attitudes. Canadian researchers (Hastings, McShane, Parker, & Ladha, 2007) found that parents teach children how to behave prosocially (i.e., be nice) from a very early age. Families are also responsible for establishing acceptable gender roles, social classes, and ethnic identities for children.

gender stereotyping
The assignment of beliefs to men and women, respectively, that are not based on fact.

Much like symbolic interactionists, social learning theorists emphasize the importance of observing and imitating the behaviours, attitudes, and emotional reactions of others (Bandura, 1977). When parents model what they believe to be acceptable roles for men and women, their child tends to imitate and internalize those patterns. For example, some parents assign different chores to daughters and sons (e.g., the daughter may help in the kitchen while the son may mow the lawn), which reinforces **gender stereotyping** that influences what each child considers to be appropriate roles for men and women.

socioeconomic status (SES) Social status as determined by family income, parents' education level, parents' occupations, and the family's social standing within the community.

Families are also responsible for assigning the **socioeconomic status (SES)** position to its members (discussed more fully in Chapter 7). Socioeconomic status is determined by the family's income, parents' education level, parents' occupations, and the family's social standing within the community (e.g., member of local organizations, involved in recreational programs). Growing up rich or poor, knowing whether you are expected to attend university or college, and appreciating how your family is viewed within the local community become part of a person's identity. Affluent parents are better able to provide their children with diverse leisure activities (music/dance lessons, extracurricular sports, travel) that tend to contribute to children's **cultural capital**, a term coined by French philosopher and sociologist Pierre Bourdieu (1930–2002). He described how children's social assets (values, beliefs, attitudes, and competencies in language and culture), gained from their families, help them in school and prepare them for success, which in turn reproduces ruling class culture (Bourdieu, 1973).

cultural capital Social assets (values, beliefs, attitudes, competencies) that are gained from one's family and help one to succeed in life.

PEERS

Would you agree that the extent of your family's influence on your life changed when you became a teenager? As we saw in the discussion of developmental stages, the importance of one's friends, or peers, increases during adolescence. During this time, friends are very influential in defining what adolescents think about the world and how they feel about themselves. Part of growing up is leaving the support of your family and putting yourself in situations that can be as frightening as they are invigorating (think, for example, of your first school dance).

peer groups Consist of people who are closely related in age and share similar interests.

Peer groups consist of people who are closely related in age and share similar interests. We first formally meet other young children in school. There, children have to make their own friends for the first time, and they soon find out that not everyone likes them (unlike in

<<<

Peer groups are an important agent of socialization.

their families). This puts a great deal of pressure on them to find peers they can relate to and prefer to spend time with. Recent research by Abrams, Rutland, Pelletier, and Ferrell (2009) investigates how children exclude others from their peer groups as a way of asserting their membership with the "in" group. If you think back to junior high, we are confident you can come up with some examples of the negative effects suffered by kids who were excluded and ostracized from their peers.

 Watch

Youth, Sex, and Crime

As children mature, their friends become increasingly important to them. To a young person, belonging to a peer group is vital for establishing a sense of community as well as for achieving and maintaining social influence (Matthews, 2005, p. 42). When you think back to some of the regrettable things you have done, many of them likely occurred when you were with your friends. Research confirms that teenagers who have friends who are disruptive in school are more likely to become disruptive themselves (Berndt & Keefe, 1995). This finding supports the wealth of research suggesting that peer involvement is the key ingredient in adolescent drug use and other forms of delinquent behaviour (Donnelly, 2013; McCarthy, 2007; McCarthy & Casey, 2008).

In a related study of skater girls, Kelly, Pomerantz, and Currie (2005) found that some of these young women actively participated in an alternative girlhood in which they redefined themselves in ways that challenged the traditional discourse of what it meant to be feminine. By doing so, they were able to distance themselves from the sexism evident in skater culture and forge a positive identity for themselves. Post-structuralists (discussed in Chapter 3) would argue that by deconstructing their images, these young women were actively engaged in defining who they were and were not afraid to push social boundaries. Sara, a 14-year-old skater, commented on the freedom gained by breaking away from social expectations:

That's why I like being alternative, because you can break so many more rules. If you hang out with the cliques and the mainstreamers and the pop kids, there's so many more rules that you have to follow. And if you don't follow [them] . . . you're no longer cool, and they start rumors about you. (Kelly, Pomerantz, & Currie, 2005, p. 246)

EDUCATION

Consider how long you have been in school. From daycare to university, you were, and are, being socialized. In contrast to the family, school ideally evaluates children on what they do rather than who they are. Children not only acquire necessary knowledge and skills but also learn new social roles by interacting with teachers and peers. In Canadian culture, the socialization function of education emphasizes that children learn academic content, social skills, and important cultural values (Lindsey, Beach, & Ravelli, 2009, p. 84).

Another important consideration is the role of the **hidden curriculum** (also discussed in Chapter 12). The hidden curriculum asserts that beyond schools' conscious, formal obligations to teach course content are the unconscious, informal, and unwritten rules that reinforce and maintain social conventions. For example, while the conscious purpose of your English courses is to teach you how to interpret literary texts, the unconscious purpose of reading all of those books and writing all of those papers is to reinforce how to behave in society.

Some of you may have read S. E. Hinton's novel *The Outsiders* (1967), in which the main character, Ponyboy, believes that there are two kinds of people in the world: greasers and socs. Greasers (so named because of their greased-back hairstyle) live on the outside of society and forever need to defend themselves, whereas socs (short for *socials*) are wealthy and can get away with just about anything. Ponyboy, a proud greaser, is willing to rumble against a gang of socs for the sake of his fellow greasers, but the story takes a critical turn when one of Ponyboy's greaser friends is accused of killing a soc. *The Outsiders* is generally interpreted as a story of adolescent turmoil and conflict; at the same time, however, the novel reinforces the hidden curriculum by accentuating the divisions of class as well as underlining the need for moral behaviour.

The hidden curriculum also plays an important role in gender role socialization. Teachers, even those who care deeply about their students and believe that they are treating girls and boys equally, are often unaware that they perpetuate gender-based stereotypes (Myhill & Jones, 2006, p. 100). Teachers often perceive that girls work harder and that boys are more likely to be disruptive. While our memories of school may reinforce this perception, it is important to note that if a teacher enters the classroom thinking that girls are more diligent and boys are more difficult to handle, this may become a *self-fulfilling prophecy*—a prediction that, once made, makes the outcome occur (as described in Chapter 1).

Research shows that although schools can unintentionally socialize children to perpetuate stereotypes, they also genuinely strive to use their influence to benefit children and society. Sociologists recognize that today's schools are shouldering a bigger share of the socialization function in Canada than ever before (Lindsey, Beach, & Ravelli, 2009, p. 84).

MASS MEDIA

Mass media are also becoming a more influential socializing force. Mass media are forms of communication produced by a few people for consumption by the masses (discussed in more detail in Chapter 17). Unlike schools, the socialization function of mass media is more subtle, with much of it occurring unconsciously.

Historically, television was by far the most influential of the mass media. In 2013, 98 percent of all Canadian households had at least one colour television, and 94 percent of those had access to cable, satellite, or some other television service (Television Bureau of Canada, 2013, p. 13).

People over the age of 55 watch the most television in Canada, at just over 32 hours per week (Television Bureau of Canada, 2013, p. 26). Research also shows that children from poor homes watch television more than those from affluent homes, minority populations watch more than Caucasians, and working- and lower-class children watch more than those whose parents have higher education and income (Lampard, Jurkowski, & Davison, 2013).

hidden curriculum
The unconscious, informal, and unwritten norms and rules that reinforce and maintain social conventions.

mass media Forms of communication produced by a few people for consumption by the masses.

Although television provides some reinforcement for prosocial behaviour (e.g., situations in which people help someone else without the motivation being personal gain), the majority of its content reinforces competition and the desire for financial wealth (consider such reality programs as *Survivor*, *Big Brother*, and *The Bachelor*).

Television defines and reinforces standards of behaviour, provides role models, and communicates expectations about all aspects of social life. We rely more and more on the mass media, especially television, to filter the enormous amount of information that is available today. When television images (e.g., definitions of beauty) are reinforced by other mass media, the impact on socialization is substantial (Leong, 2006, p. 178). Research also reveals that the more physically attractive politicians are, the more television coverage they receive (Tsfato, Elfassi, & Waismel-Manor, 2010).

However, as most of you would predict, the dominance of television is being replaced by the Internet. In 2013, Canadians between the ages of 18 and 34 spent over 30 hours a week

BOX 6.3 CANADIAN CONTRIBUTIONS TO SOCIOLOGY

Michael Atkinson

What do tattoos represent to you? If you think they are something pretty to spruce up your shoulder blade, Dr. Michael Atkinson's research into tattoo culture might surprise you. His book *Tattooed: The Sociogenesis of a Body Art* (2003) is based on three years of participant observation within the tattoo culture. He points out that although academics have traditionally viewed people with tattoos as social misfits and/or deviants, the current tattoo revolution is inspiring great sociological interest. According to Atkinson, tattoos represent a new vehicle for social communication in that they can reflect not only one's position in a social network but also one's identity and sense of self.

Atkinson draws on the theory of Norbert Elias, who established the term *figurational sociology*, meaning that individuals are bound to one another by extended networks of interdependencies. Atkinson asserts that, within the tattoo culture, these networks are exhibited in the form of body art. For example, one participant's tattoo—of a cross—symbolized for him a rich combination of relationships: school completion (and his parents' faith in him that he would graduate), his Christian faith, and his masculinity (the latter communicated by the tattoo's location on his body).

Because people's tattoos are an expression of their individuality—their tattoos literally become a part of them—they can be powerful statements about how people see the world. Not surprisingly, then, many tattoos are intimately associated with strong emotions. Atkinson found that it is not uncommon for individuals to get a tattoo after the death of a loved one or some other significant loss. The tattoo acts as a coping mechanism for those who are in various stages of the grieving process.

Besides *Tattooed*, Atkinson has published numerous journal articles on tattoo culture, including "Tattooing and Civilizing Process: Body Modification as Self-Control" (2004), "Figuring out Body Modification Cultures: Interdependence and Radical Body Modification Process" (2004), "The Civilizing of Resistance: Straightedge Tattooing" (2003), and "Pretty in Ink: Conformity, Resistance, and Negotiation in Women's Tattooing" (2002). More recently, Atkinson's research investigates masculinity and male cosmetic surgery (2008), the new urban running phenomenon called *parkour* (2009), and boys' bullying behaviour (Atkinson & Kehler, 2012).

👁 **Watch**

Flesh Wounds:
Marked Bodies in the
Civilizing Process

Courtesy Michael Atkinson

Michael Atkinson

online, compared to 16.6 hours watching television (Television Bureau of Canada, 2013). Findings also confirm that men spend more time online than women, averaging 20 hours per week compared to 16 (*Broadcaster,* 2010). Research suggests that while Internet use for both men and women is seen as important, men are more likely to spend time viewing pornography and playing games than are women, who are more likely to spend time on health-related sites (Helsper, 2010).

Internet use at home is also becoming an important factor in our socialization. In 2012 estimates suggest that over 28 million Canadians surfed the Net from home, or around 83 percent of the population (Internet World Stats, 2013). Research also reveals some interesting class differences in who accesses the Internet: 95 percent of individuals in the highest income category used the Internet in 2012, while only 62 percent of those in the lowest income category did so (Statistics Canada, 2013a). In addition, 89 percent of adults with at least some post-secondary education used the Internet, compared to 66 percent of adults with less education (Statistics Canada, 2010b). In other words, those with higher income and education levels may be the first to benefit from using the information highway—perhaps not much of a surprise but certainly of sociological interest. The Internet today may be what the television was in the 1950s: a new and powerful influence on what we think about and how we define ourselves.

> > > Thinking Sociologically

American mass media are undoubtedly powerful socializing agents. Do you believe that their influence is increasing or decreasing? Why?

❹ Socialization across the Life Course

life course
Socialization that occurs throughout one's adult life.

birth cohort **All of the people who are born during a given period of time and therefore experience historical events at the same points in their lives.**

Sociologists tend to distinguish the socialization that occurs during childhood as *primary socialization* and socialization that occurs throughout one's adult life as the **life course** (Hetherington & Baltes, 1988; Kobali, 2004; Salari & Zhang, 2006). One way that sociologists track how events may influence people's lives is by analyzing a **birth cohort**, which encompasses all those who are born during a given period and therefore experience historical events at the same points in their lives. Investigating birth cohorts allows researchers to explain and predict how different groups respond to situations. For example, those who grew up during the Depression are often very concerned with accumulating wealth and "saving for a rainy day." Their cohort's experience of living in poverty became one of the defining features of who they would become as adults.

As we mature and develop, our experience guides us in making the many decisions we face every day. We understand that as we age, we change. Our personalities are not fixed; instead, they evolve as we experience more challenges and opportunities and learn from the decisions we have made in the past. The ability to change how we see both ourselves and the world around us is at the core of adult development (Atchley, 1999).

EARLY TO MIDDLE ADULTHOOD

In Canada, we generally identify people around the age of 20 as young adults. The exception to this rule occurs when young adults continue their education beyond high school; in those situations, the adult classification generally is not applied until these people have completed their education. Thus, young adults are generally defined as those who have completed school. They may be in a serious romantic relationship, raising young children, and working hard to establish their careers. Women who have children may choose to stay home while they raise them. This can lead to considerable tension if their career aspirations are compromised as a result.

To resolve this situation—or *crisis*, in Erikson's terminology—a woman may choose to end her career, put it on hold, or work only part-time (Tomlinson, 2006). Resolving this crisis depends on the woman's long-term self-esteem and the support of the family unit.

In 2009 there were 151 940 marriages in Canada (Statistics Canada, 2010f), but many people are marrying later or choosing not to marry at all (Kobali, 2004). According to the 2006 Canadian census, for the first time ever there were more unmarried people (aged 15 and over) than legally married people. In fact, 51.5 percent of the population was unmarried (never married, divorced, separated, or widowed), compared to 49.9 percent five years earlier. This is a significant change from 20 years ago when only 38.6 percent of the population aged 15 and over was unmarried (Statistics Canada, 2007b).

Even so, marriage is one of the most important decisions an adult can make since it is usually the longest lasting and most emotionally charged relationship in one's life. Today, many traditional expectations of marriage have changed (e.g., most mothers work outside the home, there is greater social acceptance of same-sex marriages) and both married and live-in partners have greater flexibility in how they live their lives than ever before.

>>> Thinking Sociologically

What social trends do you believe explain why more Canadians are choosing to marry later, or not at all?

LATER ADULTHOOD

Later adulthood, generally between the ages of 40 and 60, is a time of increased focus on career achievement, children leaving home, the birth of grandchildren, and preparation for retirement. This phase of life also includes increased recognition of one's declining health as the first signs of physical aging occur (loss of hair, need for reading glasses, increase in aches and pains).

During later adulthood, women are said to be more likely than men to become depressed as the last child leaves home, a situation often referred to as the **empty nest syndrome**. However, research suggests that this condition is largely a myth (Mitchell, 2010; Mitchell & Lovegreen, 2009). The majority of women in fact experience an *increase* in life satisfaction and psychological well-being when children leave the home (Harris, Ellicott, & Holmes, 1986). Further, more recent research suggests that retiring from work is a more difficult transition than having children leave home (Crowley, Hayslip, & Hobdy, 2003). Today, most women recognize that once their children leave home, they finally have the time to pursue interests and hobbies that were put off during child rearing. Reduced work and parental responsibilities help to explain increased marital satisfaction in later life for both men and women.

Men also face some significant challenges in later adulthood. During what is often referred to as a "mid-life crisis," men may experience both physical and emotional symptoms. Physical symptoms may include muscle stiffness and sore joints, night sweats, hair loss, and weight gain, while emotional symptoms may include irritability, loss of libido, erectile dysfunction, fatigue, and depression (Fielder, 2003). Often, the psychological and emotional turmoil associated with these symptoms

empty nest syndrome The depression that some mothers experience when their children have left home.

< < <

The proportion of Canadians aged 65 and older is expected to rise sharply over the next 50 years.

Supri Suharjoto/Shutterstock

is linked to hormonal changes, including a significant decline in testosterone levels (Brizendine, 2006). Because Western culture associates masculinity with sexual performance, the hormonal changes that may affect a middle-aged man's ability to achieve or maintain an erection can inspire a great deal of fear and anxiety. The popularity of drugs like Viagra and Cialis—whose combined sales are almost $4 billion annually (Phillips, 2013)—which promise to enhance men's sexual performance, may be linked to this fear. Estimates suggest that over 100 million men globally suffer from erectile dysfunction (Bradfield, Parker, & Goodwin, 2009, p. 347).

Still, adulthood is a period during which both men and women grow more confident in themselves and focus much of their attention on their family and careers. As middle adulthood transitions into later adulthood and then old age, many people begin to take stock of their lives and try to enjoy the fruits of their labours.

"OLD" AGE

The reason we have placed quotation marks around the word *old* is to highlight and challenge our culture's traditionally negative view of the elderly (discussed in much more detail in Chapter 15). There are many different functional and chronological definitions of *old age*. A functional definition could, for example, include declining health or mental faculties as a result of the aging process. In Western societies like Canada, the definition of *old* is largely based on age and not related to health status or physical abilities. This results in a fit, healthy 66-year-old who works full-time and a frail 90-year-old who lives in a nursing home both being called "old" (Thompson, 2006).

The Canadian Old Age Pension (OAP) plan, introduced in 1927 for people over 70, and the Old Age Assistance (OAA) program, implemented in 1952 for Canadians aged 65–69, were **means-tested programs** (i.e., based on financial need) while Old Age Security (OAS), introduced in 1952 for all Canadians over age 70, was a **universal plan**. (Herbert Emery & Matheson, 2008). For many years, mandatory retirement at age 65 was the standard across the country. However, this practise has recently been challenged as constituting age discrimination that can no longer be justified since we are living longer and remaining healthier than we did when retirement legislation was introduced. Today, the majority of provinces and territories do not have mandatory retirement.

Canada's population is getting older (see Table 6.1), as is the case for almost every other developed nation in the world. As of 2006, the median age for a Canadian was a record high of 38.8 years, compared to 38.5 a year before and 37.2 in 2001 (Statistics Canada, 2006i).

means-tested programs Social programs based on need.

universal plans Social programs provided to everyone.

TABLE 6.1   Population, Median Age, and Age Distribution, Canada, 1946 to 2056

Year	Population	Median Age	0 to 19 %	20 to 64 %	65 and Over %
1946	12 292 000	27.7	36.6	56.3	7.2
1966	20 014 880	25.4	42.1	50.2	7.7
1986	26 101 155	31.4	28.6	60.9	10.5
2006	32 623 490	38.8	24.0	62.8	13.2
2009	33 739 859	39.5	*	*	13.9
2031 (medium-growth scenarios)	39 029 400	44.3	19.9	56.7	23.4
2056 (medium-growth scenarios)	42 510 900	46.9	18.4	54.4	27.2

*Values were not indicated in the 2009 Statistics Canada resource.
Source: Statistics Canada (2009; 2006).

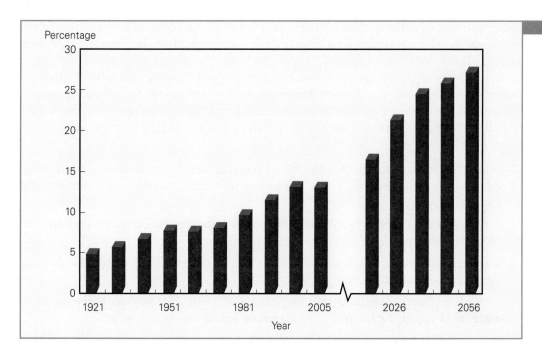

FIGURE 6.1

Percentage of
Canadian Population
Comprising Persons
Aged 65 or Older,
1921 to 2005, and
Projections to 2056

Source: Statistics Canada
(2007).

This increasing median age means that the number of seniors is projected to grow from 4.2 million to 9.8 million between 2005 and 2036. As illustrated in Figure 6.1, people aged 65 and over accounted for 13.9 percent of the Canadian population in 2009 and this figure is expected to rise to 27.2 percent by 2056 (Statistics Canada, 2009d; 2006i). Statistics Canada estimates that seniors will outnumber children by 2015 and that by 2031 there will be 100 seniors for every 54 to 71 children (depending on different population growth scenarios) (Statistics Canada, 2005c, p. 45).

As the proportion of seniors in the Canadian population increases, the common stereotype of seniors as feeble and vulnerable may well lose currency. Indeed, the Canadian economy needs these older people to continue working. Today, there are six workers for every retired person, but by 2020 this will decline to three workers for every retired person. To address the shortage of workers both now and in the future, some companies are introducing programs such as "retirees on call" and "phased retirement." These types of plans are attractive to employers who support mandatory retirement because they can maintain access to the retired workers' expertise but also unload workers who are at the peak of their earnings. Companies can often hire two young workers for the price of one older one.

The socialization that occurs during late adulthood and old age is somewhat different than that occurring during earlier stages. The preceding life stages are marked by acquiring new responsibilities and taking on new challenges, whereas retirement and old age can entail a *loss* of identity and satisfaction when people retire from their careers and have grown children who no longer need their day-to-day support. Yet these transitions can also be liberating for aging people, as they are now free to pursue travel and other personal interests they may have deferred in favour of their families and/or careers (Brizendine, 2006). In short, late adulthood and old age involves both the learning of new roles and the unlearning of others, as well as preparation for the final stage of life.

SOCIALIZATION INTO DYING AND DEATH

The final stage of one's life is associated with old age and the realization of approaching death. The scientific study of old age and aging is called **gerontology**. During late middle

gerontology **The
scientific study of old
age and aging.**

age, people usually confront their own declining health and the death of their parents, events that begin their own socialization into death. For the elderly, death becomes a fact of their everyday lives.

The process of dying has been studied through the pioneering research of Elisabeth Kübler-Ross (1926–2004). Through interviews with hundreds of terminally ill people, Kübler-Ross (1969) developed a series of stages that people go through as they deal with their own mortality. Just as there is a life course, there is a death course. The general sequence of stages is as follows:

1. *Denial.* People who are told that they have a terminal illness experience shock and disbelief. Aside from the personal horror of the news, in a death-denying society this is clearly a logical response.

2. *Anger.* Individuals express hostility and resentment, often toward others who will live on. "Why me?" they ask, with a strong sense of injustice.

3. *Bargaining.* Bargains are made, usually with God: "I will be a better person if only I can live, so please spare me."

4. *Depression.* With the realization that they cannot negotiate their way out of the situation, depression occurs. Sorrow, guilt, and shame are linked with this stage.

5. *Acceptance.* By discussing their feelings openly, people move into a final stage in which death is accepted. Kübler-Ross believed that only with acceptance can inner peace be reached.

dying trajectories The courses that dying takes in both social and psychological senses.

Kübler-Ross established the idea of **dying trajectories**, the courses that dying takes in both social and psychological senses. Her model has been used not only to describe the sequence of dying but also to suggest a set of overall therapeutic recommendations as to how dying "should" take place. Hospital staff are frequently taught to interpret terminally ill patients' behaviour according to the stage theory and to work with them so that they can accept their inevitable death. Symbolic interactionists suggest that such therapeutic recommendations socially construct the process of death; that is, the stage theory becomes a prescription for reality (Charmaz, 1980, as cited in Lindsey & Beach, 2003, p. 108; Valentine, 2006, p. 60). Yet, Kübler-Ross herself did not advocate such a position; in fact, she warned against the use of the model as a prescription for how we should die. Unfortunately, because the stages are so easy to learn and recognize, the biggest single mistake that many make is to use the model in a strict, linear, sequential way (e.g., "It's good that Mr. X is depressed today because now he's making progress.").

Moreover, recent research into Kübler-Ross's theory has raised concerns about her model (Cassem, 1988; Kastenbaum, 1998). Robert Kastenbaum (1998) challenges her work on a number of levels:

• No independent evidence exists to support the assertion that people move from stage one through to stage five.
• The fact that a person may experience emotions and reactions from different stages at the same time challenges the premise that there are definable stages in the grieving process.
• The totality of the person's life is neglected in favour of the supposed stages of dying.
• The tremendous diversity of resources, pressures, and characteristics of the dying individual are not taken into account.

euthanasia The deliberate ending of the life of a person who has an incurable or painful disease.

These criticisms notwithstanding, Kübler-Ross deserves great credit for bringing analysis of dying to the forefront of social science and to the popular arena.

For example, one contemporary social debate concerns euthanasia and assisted suicide (Ogden, Hamilton, & Witcher, 2010). **Euthanasia** is the deliberate act by one or more persons to bring about a gentle or easier death to another, such as do-not-resuscitate orders for terminally ill patients in palliative care facilities (Brink, Smith, & Kitson, 2008). **Assisted suicide** is the act of intentionally killing oneself with help from others who provide the knowledge or means of death (Dickens, Boyle, & Ganzini, 2008, p. 72). For example, it is assisted suicide if a person injects poison into a willing recipient but it is also considered assisted suicide when a person only supplies the poison (Dyer, 2009, pp. 30–31). The right to die issue will continue to challenge contemporary Canadian society because of our aging population and our ongoing debate about personal rights and social mores.

As you can see, socialization into death is similar to other socialization experiences throughout the life course. Sociologists recognize that our entire lives are the result and expression of socialization and social interaction.

While our analysis of the life course corresponds to the vast majority of people's lives, we turn now to a related but far more extreme and less common phenomenon in which people undergo a process known as *resocialization*.

assisted suicide
Intentionally killing oneself with help from others.

❺ Resocialization: The Total Institution

Resocialization is the profound change or complete transformation of a person's personality as a result of being placed in a situation or an environment dedicated to changing his or her previous identity (Parkinson & Drislane, 2007, p. 136). It generally occurs against one's will and in a location where the person has little or no control over the situation. Classic examples of this type of resocialization occur in prisons or mental institutions, where the desired outcome is to change the way a person behaves. As a rule, resocialization usually occurs within what are called **total institutions**, settings in which people are isolated from society and supervised by an administrative staff.

Erving Goffman was a pioneer in studying the resocialization that occurs in total institutions. In his groundbreaking book *Asylums* (1961), Goffman outlines five types of total institutions:

1. Institutions that help people who are incapable of taking care of themselves and can be considered harmless (homes for the blind, the aged, the orphaned, and the indigent)

2. Institutions that take care of people who are incapable of looking after themselves and pose a threat to the community, albeit an unintended one (mental hospitals or institutions for those with communicable diseases)

3. Institutions that protect the community from those who would do it harm (prisons or prisoner-of-war camps)

4. Institutions that perform instrumental tasks that require unique work arrangements (army/work camps or boarding schools)

5. Institutions that act as retreats from the rest of the world and serve as locations for religious training (monasteries and convents) (Roberts, n.d.)

According to Goffman, total institutions are defined by three important characteristics. First, an administrative staff supervises all aspects of the inmates' or residents' lives, using electronic surveillance to observe their every move and action. Second, every activity is controlled and standardized so that formal schedules define everything that occurs (e.g., people exercise at the same time each day; every Tuesday is meatloaf day). Third, formal rules and/or policies define everything about the inmates' or residents' daily lives (Goffman, 1961).

Resocialization usually occurs in two distinct stages. In the first stage, people's existing identities are stripped from them in what Goffman (1961) termed **mortifications of the self**. To accomplish this separation from their past, inmates have all of their personal possessions taken away, they lose all control over their daily schedule, they often have to wear

resocialization
The profound change or complete transformation of a person's personality as a result of being placed in a situation or an environment dedicated to changing his or her previous identity.

total institution A setting in which people are isolated from society and supervised by an administrative staff.

mortifications of the self The first stage of the resocialization process, in which a person's existing identity is stripped away.

> > >

Prisons are one type of total institution.

Greg Smith/Corbis

uniforms, they have their hair cut, and there is no real way to escape the organizational rules and procedures. In most of these settings, the institutional goal is to recreate the individual to fit the demands of the organization (Margolis & Rowe, n.d.). During this initial stage, inmates often feel anxious and worthless and have low self-esteem (Walsh, 2001). In the second stage of the resocialization process, the administrative staff members build up inmates through a system of rewards and punishments. By breaking people down in the first stage and then building them up in the second stage, the resocialization process allows for the formation of a new identity that is distinct from the one that entered the total institution. In the case of a prison or a mental institution, one can appreciate why such drastic changes are necessary, but it is less clear why such a process was required for educating Aboriginal peoples in the residential schools. As we learned in Chapters 3 and 5, and as we will explore in more detail in Chapter 10, Canadian residential schools were a systematic attempt to resocialize Aboriginal children (Chrisjohn & Young, 1997; Milloy, 1999). By relocating children away from their families and having them under the guidance of schoolmasters who followed rigid daily schedules, the residential schools were arguably a state-sponsored total institution (Canadian Lawyers for International Human Rights, n.d.). Their purpose was to resocialize the children by forcing them to assume new roles, skills, and values. To achieve this, teachers controlled nearly every aspect of their students' lives (Llewellyn, 2002a).

> As total institutions, Native residential schools imposed conditions of disconnection, degradation, and powerlessness on the student. The nature of these institutions permitted and even encouraged the abuse that commonly marked children's experiences. (Llewellyn, 2002b, p. 257)

Clearly, this form of socialization is extreme, but it does reinforce the point we have been making throughout this chapter—that the development of a sense of self is a dynamic process that influences us each and every day of our lives.

BOX 6.4 WHY SHOULD WE CARE?

Resocialization and the Canadian Forces

When MCpl David Billet[1] completed a six-month tour of duty in Kandahar Province, as part of Canada's contribution to the military mission in Afghanistan, he was a different person than when he had left his hometown of Edmonton, Alberta. During the time spent "on tour," MCpl Billet was shot at, shelled with mortars, and was involved in a four-hour gun battle with heavily armed Taliban insurgents. He saw close friends injured and killed and began to exhibit the symptoms of post-traumatic stress disorder. At the end of his tour, Mcpl Billet was sent, along with other soldiers whose tours were up, to the island of Cyprus in the Mediterranean for a four-day period known as "decompression." In Cyprus, Mcpl Billet began the process of resocialization where he was encouraged to shed his training in order to return to civilian life.

In particular, Mcpl Billet needed to learn to suppress the heightened state of alertness he had come to rely on while on tour. In combat, soldiers must instantly identify and prioritize potential threats, as well as spot suspicious behaviours, individuals, or objects within their field of vision. Back in civilian life however, this heightened awareness often leads to extreme overreactions to commonplace occurrences. A backfiring car could see Mcpl Billet dive for cover or drop into a fighting stance; a cardboard box laying beside the sidewalk could trigger his combat training that sees any unidentified container as a possible improvised explosive device (IED).

Soldiers are trained to see all strangers as potential threats, always have an escape route, and to never let their guard down. When they do, people die.

Soldiers around the world die for us every day. We train them to do things that no one should be asked to do. They never complain. They are always there when we need them. Then, when they come home, we hug them, tell them we love them, and that we are here to listen. But can we really understand what they need to tell us, and could we handle it if they did?

The armed forces is one example of a total institution and the skills that soldiers learn, while necessary on the battlefield, must be "unlearned" if they are to successfully return to civilian life. Some do but many do not.

---

[1] This is a real account from a current serving member of the military; however, his name has been changed.

Summary

❶ In the nature versus nurture debate, the "nature" argument, represented today by evolutionary psychologists, holds that our genetic makeup determines much of our behaviour. The "nurture" argument, while appreciating the role that biology plays in some aspects of our behaviour, holds that socialization is a more important force in determining who we are. Some suggest that this binary between nature and nurture may be overly simplistic.

❷ The sociological perspective holds that the self develops through social interaction in a series of stages.

❸ The four principal agents of socialization that influence people's sense of self and help them to become functioning members of society are families, peers, education, and mass media.

❹ Throughout the life course—from early and middle adulthood to late adulthood and old age to approaching death—adults face challenges that change how they see themselves and the world.

❺ Resocialization, and the profound change to the self that it brings, is experienced by those forced into total institutions, such as homes for the aged, mental hospitals, prisons, and, arguably, the residential school system.

Key Terms

agents of socialization 152
assisted suicide 161
birth cohort 156
cultural capital 152
double-consciousness 150
dying trajectories 160
empty nest syndrome 157
euthanasia 160
evolutionary psychology 144
gender stereotyping 152
generalized other 147
gerontology 159
hidden curriculum 154
I 147
life course 156
mass media 154
Me 147

means-tested programs 158
mortifications of the self 161
nature versus nurture 143
peer groups 152
personality 143
primary socialization 149
resocialization 161
role-taking 147
secondary socialization 149
self 146
self-image 146
significant others 147
social interaction 143
socialization 143
sociobiology 144
socioeconomic status (SES) 152
total institution 161
universal plans 158

Reviewing the Concepts

1. What is evolutionary psychology?

2. What does the research on feral children teach us about the importance of human interaction as children?

3. Review and discuss primary and secondary socialization. Be sure to use your own contemporary examples to demonstrate your command of the concepts.

4. What are the four agents of socialization? Which do you feel is the most important for explaining teenagers' behaviour? Defend your selection.

Applying Your Sociological Imagination

1. With reference to chapter material, critique the nature/nurture debate. From your informed opinion, do you see the binary nature of this "debate" as helpful when exploring socialization? Defend your position.

2. Using your sociological imagination, explore your own socialization. What were the most important factors that shaped the person you are today? Discuss.

3. Review Mead's concept of the *generalized other*. How might this concept apply to relationships between professors and students? The rich and the poor? The physically attractive and the less attractive?

4. Review the chapter's discussion of total institutions. Are there any organizations in your community that would fulfill Goffman's three characteristics of total institutions? Discuss.

MySocLab

Visit MySocLab to access a variety of online resources that will help you prepare for tests and apply your knowledge.

7 Social Inequality

In 2005, one of this text's authors, Bruce Ravelli, was approached by a student who wanted to discuss a video that had just been shown in class. The video, *In the Gutter and Other Good Places* (Richey, 1993), is an ethnographic study of bottle-pickers in Calgary (many of whom are homeless), and the student, Genevieve, said that she had met some of them when she herself had lived on the streets. Now in her late twenties, Genevieve has agreed to share her story.

Genevieve was homeless for a total of about four years during different periods in her life. Her first experience on the street was in Quebec City, after her parents kicked her out of the house; she was eight years old. After being informally "adopted" by a family acquaintance (a drug dealer), Genevieve grew up in a very unconventional family but was still able to finish high school and obtain a college diploma. However, from her late teens to her mid twenties, she lived on and off the streets of Montreal, Winnipeg, and, finally, Calgary.

Genevieve recounts that setting money aside to survive was a constant struggle, and more of a concern than street violence. Life on the streets, she says, can be violent if you look for trouble, but most street people join together at night for protection, friendship, and mutual support. Genevieve points out that becoming homeless can happen to anyone. Her advice to the "squares" is to appreciate what you have, to love and support your families and friends, and to help those who are less fortunate than we are.

Today, Genevieve and her boyfriend have bought their first house together and are looking forward to the rest of their lives.

Genevieve's ability to transcend horrible personal circumstances is truly inspirational. However, the fact that in any given year at least 200 000 Canadians make use of an emergency shelter or are forced to sleep outside (Gaetz, Donaldson, Richter, & Gulliver, 2013) suggests that we could be doing so much more to help the poor.

LEARNING OBJECTIVES

By the end of this chapter, students will be able to

❶ Define *social stratification* and *inequality* from the sociological perspective.

❷ Review and critique sociology's theoretical explanations for social stratification and social inequality.

❸ Review and analyze the Canadian class structure.

❹ Review and discuss the factors influencing the likelihood of becoming or staying poor in Canada.

❺ Discuss how global inequality and poverty rates are calculated and what they tell us about the world we live in.

❶ What Is Social Stratification?

Social stratification is a society's hierarchical ranking of people into social classes (see Nayebi & Abdollahyan, 2006). An individual's **social class** is based on both birth and achievements in life, while an individual's position within the class structure is called his or her **social status**.

While we may want to believe that everyone in Canada is equal, our look at what it is like to live on the streets suggests that some Canadians are more equal than others. The question to ask yourself is, Why are all complex human societies (those with specialized tasks and occupational separation) stratified (see Service, 1962)?

Social stratification is based on a few key principles. First, all societies redistribute materials and social rewards to individuals (food, money, social prestige). Because material resources are always in short supply, a stratified system ensures that those individuals who do more or are more capable receive more material wealth and social recognition (Nayebi & Abdollahyan, 2006, p. 250). By rewarding deserving individuals, society allocates its limited resources to those who offer the greatest benefit to the whole. For example, Canadians recognize the tremendous dedication and talent that physicians and surgeons possess and therefore grant them relatively high material rewards as well as social recognition and profile. In this sense, then, social stratification makes sense—it allows people who offer more to society to have more. For this system to work, people in the society must believe that they can achieve wealth and status through individual attributes, a system of rewards called a **meritocracy**. A meritocracy reinforces the ideological assumption that people achieve what they deserve (Knowles & Lowery, 2012). For example, the grades you obtain in college or university should be based on how well you do on your tests and assignments and not on your age, sex, or physical appearance. In a meritocratic system, your grades are based on your demonstrated achievements over the term.

The second principle is that since social stratification transcends any single generation (with social position largely granted by one's parents), the system is relatively stable over time. Although there is some movement between social classes—which sociologists refer to as

social stratification A society's hierarchical ranking of people into social classes.

social class A group of individuals sharing a position in a social hierarchy, based on both birth and achievement.

social status An individual's position within the class structure.

Class, Status, and Social Mobility

meritocracy A system of rewards based on personal attributes and demonstrated abilities.

As Wealthy Fill Top Colleges, Concerns Grow Over Fairness

social mobility
Movement between social classes.

intergenerational mobility The comparison of adult children's social class to that of their parents.

intragenerational mobility Status movement throughout one's lifetime.

social mobility—the reality is that very few people are able to move out of the social class into which they were born (Western & Wright, 1994). Social mobility is typically measured by comparing adult children's status to that of their parents (called **intergenerational mobility**), but it can also be measured by comparing an individual's status position over his or her lifetime (called **intragenerational mobility**). For example, a young woman who grows up in a poor family may achieve a scholarship to university and ultimately become a successful lawyer. Sociologists use social mobility to measure a society's equality of opportunity (Reay, 2013, p. 661). As a rule, social stratification has little relationship to skills or abilities. High-status people, even those who lack talent or intelligence, generally find it far easier to obtain property, prestige, and power than do those who are more capable but reside in the lower classes.

The third principle of social stratification is that although it is present in all known human societies, it varies in how it expresses itself. For example, in societies like our own, some status is granted by how much money one has, while in others status is granted by how much wealth one gives away (as in Northwest Coast potlatch ceremonies; see Godelier, 1999; Roth, 2002). Further, even in our own society, we are quick to judge when someone achieves material wealth in a manner we do not condone or respect. A drug dealer and a surgeon may make the same annual income, but we would certainly grant the drug dealer lower social status and prestige than the surgeon.

Fourth, while all societies recognize differences in wealth and prestige, the criteria by which they are granted are nonetheless considered fair and just by the majority of the population—even those in the lower classes. This acceptance of often unjust criteria is grounded in the dominant ideology—the set of beliefs and values that support and justify a society's ruling class.

What Is Social Inequality?

social inequality
Exists when certain attributes affect a person's access to socially valued resources.

Social inequality occurs when attributes such as gender, minority status, and class affect a person's access to socially valued resources (e.g., money, status, and power but also health care, education, political representation, etc.) (Price & Feinman, 2010, p. 2). Would you agree that some people in Canada today are better off than others? Social inequality is unfair because it treats some people better than others; however, social inequality is difficult to detect and challenge because it is hidden behind ideologies that name the processes associated with their perpetuation as "normal" and "just" and their harmful consequences as being the fault of the disadvantaged. People are often discouraged from talking meaningfully about the real affects of social inequality because it is easier to talk about the ideals of diversity and multiculturalism than it is to challenge social exclusion and discrimination (Williams & Keating, 2005).

 Watch

Social Inequality

Social inequality results from collective decisions about what is important in evaluating a person or a group. This inequality takes many forms: women may be paid less than men for the same job; members of visible minority groups may be less likely to be hired than members of the majority; those with more education tend to make more money than those with less education. Inequality, then, results from a system that ranks people from high (better) to low (worse) on such subjective criteria as gender and minority status. These criteria are considered *subjective* because they have no material influence on whether a person can actually perform a particular job. In other words, there is no inherent necessity for the majority of truck drivers or lawyers to be men, or for most elementary school teachers and social workers to be women. These subjective assessments of people's worth are supported not by individual capability but by the dominant ideology.

> > > Thinking Sociologically

What traits do you associate with high-status occupations? Low-status occupations? What characteristics do many Canadians associate with the people in each type of occupation? How might critical race theory explain this situation?

Classism

Most Canadians are aware of the biases inherent in the ideologies that have traditionally supported racial, gender, and age inequality (called racism, sexism, and ageism, respectively). Yet the same ideological support for discrimination also exists for social class. **Classism** is the belief that people's relative worth is at least partly determined by their social and economic status (Byrd, Martinez, & Scott, 2014, p. 182). Classism legitimates economic inequality and ". . . includes the ideology of competitive individualism through winning and losing that celebrates a few at the expense of the rest who are put down, disrespected, and wasted" (Henry, 2009, p. 1253).

Classism is grounded in the idea that everyone in society starts out with the same chances of success. This perception has often been referred to as the "American dream" and is, of course, one of the cornerstones of capitalistic ideology. However right or wrong, classism results in the belief that the wealthy deserve what they have and that the poor are responsible for their failure.

JP Laffont/Sygma/Corbis

< < <

Many women today are working in jobs traditionally associated with men.

classism An ideology that suggests that people's relative worth is at least partly determined by their social and economic status.

Watch

Debates about Social Class

micromonkey/Fotolia

< < <

Men, in turn, are pursuing careers usually dominated by women.

This belief constitutes one of two broad perspectives that explain why people are poor: one that blames the victim and one that blames the system (Napier, Mandisodza, Andersen, & Jost, 2006; van den Bos & Maas, 2009).

BLAMING THE VICTIM

blaming the victim
A perspective that holds individuals responsible for the negative conditions in which they live.

The **blaming the victim** perspective assumes that the poor need only to work harder in order to transcend their poverty (Weiner, Osborne, & Rudolph, 2011, p. 201). This view is widely accepted by the general population, which often criticizes the poor for not doing enough to help themselves. Sociologists have found little to no evidence to support the assertion that social inequality is the result of individual attributes (Lindsey & Beach, 2003, p. 218; Ryan, 1971). If it were, how could events like the Great Depression or the economic collapse of 2008 be explained? Surely no one could argue that these economic failures were the result of lazy workers. Certainly, some poor people are lazy and do not want to work, but this criticism holds for some rich people as well.

culture of poverty
A fatalistic belief system held by the poor as an adaptation to systemic discrimination.

In his investigation into the lives of the poor, American anthropologist Oscar Lewis (1914–1970) coined the phrase the "**culture of poverty**" (Lewis, 1966) to accentuate his belief that the poor have different subcultural value systems than the larger American society and that these systems limit their ability and desire to escape their poverty. He found that the poor feel marginalized, helpless, and inferior, and are fatalistic in their view of the future. Poor families are characterized by high divorce rates; children are generally raised in families headed by women. People who adopt the culture of poverty rarely participate in community life, politics, or school (Blacks Academy, n.d.).

deferred gratification
The ability to forgo immediate pleasures in the interest of achieving greater rewards in the future.

Lewis suggested that the poor are socialized to view the world in a certain way; in particular, they appear not to appreciate the value of **deferred gratification**—the ability to forgo immediate pleasures in the interest of achieving greater rewards in the future. Conversely, middle-class people learn to save money, study, and work hard now so that they may reap the rewards later. This seems to support the blame the victim approach. However, Lewis (1998, published posthumously) argued that the culture of poverty is not necessarily a bad thing; it could represent an important cultural adaptation to systemic discrimination. In fact, Harvey and Reed (1996) contend that Lewis's work is entirely consistent with a Marxist critique of the rich and powerful and their desire to keep the poor weak by promoting the capitalist ideology that blames the poor for their poverty.

Lewis's approach can be considered less biased than other beliefs that simply view the poor as lazy and thus responsible for their plight. Nonetheless, the traditional interpretation of Lewis's work holds that a portion of the poor do in fact have difficulty deferring gratification (Mayer, 1997). But is it even possible to test this assumption? One could argue that since the poor have a fatalistic view of the future, it makes sense that they learn from an early age to take what they can now rather than risk getting nothing later (Lindsey & Beach, 2003, p. 219).

We suggest that there is indeed a culture of poverty that can trap the chronically poor. But we need to emphasize that this is largely the result of, and a reaction to, the fact that those in society's lowest classes need to adapt as well as possible. As sociologists, we argue that changing the structural realities of being poor (e.g., better education and job training for the chronically unemployed) will result in a decline of poverty over time.

BLAMING THE SYSTEM

blaming the system
A perspective that holds that systemic discrimination exists within the social system.

The **blaming the system** perspective recognizes the systemic discrimination that exists within social systems and is more consistent with the sociological perspective than the blaming the victim approach. Systemic explanations for poverty argue that the larger socioeconomic system imposes certain restrictions on certain members of society (Bradshaw, 2007, p. 16). For example, one structural variable that influences unemployment, and by extension poverty levels, is the loss of well-paying factory jobs as a result of **deindustrialization**—the transformation of an economy from one based on manufacturing to one based on services (Domínguez & Arford, 2010; Kaya, 2010; Ornstein, 2011). The poor lack the skills needed to compete for the new, more highly skilled jobs that replace industrial jobs. This situation puts downward pressure on wages and increases the competition among workers for fewer and fewer jobs. Deindustrialization, then, creates poverty in a manner that is beyond the control of any individual.

deindustrialization
The transformation of an economy from one based on manufacturing to one based on services.

To address the negative impacts of deindustrialization, well-planned, community-based, comprehensive anti-poverty programs may be able to compensate for structural factors that cause poverty (Murphy, 2009; Elbers et al., 2004). Yet some continue to resist such programs (Torjman, 1997). These people believe that social welfare programs encourage laziness, dependency, and poverty, even though some American research suggests otherwise. One large study found that the proportion of the poor would have almost doubled, to some 27 percent of the American population, if social welfare programs had not been enhanced and reformed during the 1980s (Coder, Rainwater, & Smeedling, 1989, as cited in Lindsey & Beach, 2003, p. 220). This particular study suggests that anti-poverty programs make sound economic sense.

FROM PERCEPTION TO POLICY

In a classic work, sociologists Huber and Form (1973) found that wealthy and middle-class Americans saw themselves as deserving of their wealth and status. They believed that their success was the result of their own abilities, skills, and effort. The poor, on the other hand, were more likely to see their economic plight as being the result of structural factors such as high unemployment rates, lack of opportunity, and the failure of society to provide adequate schooling (Newman & Smith, 1999).

Newman and Smith (1999) argue that these perceptions of why people succeed or fail have important policy implications for government. If decision-makers believe that poor people lack motivation, then government should focus on reducing people's dependence on subsidy programs, such as welfare. However, if poverty is viewed as the result of structural barriers for the poor, then policy-makers should focus on increasing educational and occupational opportunities for everyone. Both perspectives lead to vastly different ways of trying to help the poor.

As we saw above, classist thinking can lead people to reject policies that would help the disadvantaged to overcome the structural factors that limit their opportunities to improve their chances of upward mobility. However, some suggest that classism is being challenged more frequently today, and that awareness of class discrimination is improving (Nakhaie, 1997; Simpson, Stark, & Jackson, 1988). Not only are educational levels rising in Canada, but communication technology is making it easier for marginalized groups to spread their message and join collective efforts to promote social change. Even with these developments, people around the world continue to rank each other because of their birth or their class.

Closed and Open Social Systems

Sociologists define two major ways in which social systems rank people: closed systems and open systems. **Closed systems** are those based on ascribed status—that is, the status associated with attributes that people are born with, such as race and sex. These systems are "closed" because innate attributes cannot be changed, and thus allow for very little social mobility. Conversely, **open systems** are based on achieved status, which is made possible by one's personal attributes. In other words, people can move up from a poor social background (or down from a wealthy one) through their own efforts and abilities. In theory, then, where you end up in an open system is where you deserve to be.

closed system A social system in which status is based on attributes ascribed at birth.

open system A social system in which status is based on achieved attributes.

CLOSED SYSTEMS: CASTE

Caste systems—ascribed systems of hereditary class designation—allow virtually no social mobility. Given the tremendous disparities in wealth, social status, and occupational prestige among castes, these systems usually emphasize a legitimating ideology, nearly always religious in character, to support and justify such differences. The very idea of social mobility is foreign within caste societies. A person's caste is a central component of who they are and determines virtually everything in their lives, including what they can wear, what jobs they can perform, and who they can marry.

caste system An ascribed system of hereditary class designation.

> > >

2008 Academy Award winner for Best Picture, *Slumdog Millionaire*, showed audiences the striking contrasts between the rich and the poor in India.

India One of the more infamous examples of a caste society is India's, which is thought to date from as early as 350 bce, when the *varna* system (a Sanskrit word meaning "colour") divided Indian society into four primary groups (Lahiri, 2005). While some challenge the overly simplistic fourfold typology (Gannon, 2002, p. 5), each caste was broadly associated with the types of work its members performed:

- *Brahmin*: teachers, doctors, and other scholars
- *Kshatriya*: warriors and politicians
- *Vaishya*: merchants and artists
- *Shudra*: workers in the service occupations (Howard, 2006)

Beneath these four primary castes are the *Dalits*, "untouchables," who literally have no caste and whose name translates as "oppressed" or "crushed" (Dhanda, 2009, p. 49). Many Dalits are landless labourers (Govinda, 2008, p. 428) who perform the most menial and despised tasks and are believed to pollute people of higher caste. In fact, if a higher-caste Hindu is touched by a Dalit or crosses into one's shadow, he or she is considered polluted and must go through a series of rigorous cleaning rituals. There are about 250 million Dalits living in India today (Dalit Freedom Network Canada, n.d.).

The Western perception of the Indian caste system is that it is hereditary and that thus one cannot change his/her caste. Therefore, even when a person of low caste becomes wealthy or a high-caste person loses all of his or her money, their castes can never change. However, this is not the case; Indian women can change their caste through marriage (Cooke, 1999). Unfortunately, the only way that Indian men can change their caste is through **reincarnation**, whereby they may move to a higher or lower caste in their next life.

reincarnation The belief, associated with Eastern religions, that one's essence does not die and instead is reborn in another form.

The Indian Constitution of 1950 abolished the caste system. In fact, the Indian government has instituted various affirmative action policies to provide the lower castes with access to government jobs, higher education, and politics (Dhanda, 2009). The aim of these policies is to improve the plight of historically stigmatized populations and promote them into positions that would strengthen their representation and preserve their rights (Raman, 1999).

However, although the caste system is changing in India's urban areas, it remains an important feature of everyday life in small towns and villages. What few people in the West realize is the role that European colonialism played in India's caste system (Dirks, 2001). Dirks (2001) argues that the caste system, as we perceive it today, is the specific product of

The Canadian Press/Gautam Singh/AP Photo

< < <

Although India's caste system was outlawed in 1950, caste continues to shape the lives of many Indians.

the historical encounter between India and Western colonial rule (see also Gannon, 2002). The fact that so few Westerners know this demonstrates the ability of the British to make caste the central symbol of Indian society and one that continues to hinder the perception of India as a modern state (Dirks, 2001, p. 5). As we learned in Chapter 3, post-colonial theory offers important insight into how contemporary scholars explore the historical legacy of colonialism and its effects on former colonies (Berg, Barry, & Chandler, 2010).

Japan An active caste system is also found in Japan. A group known as the *Burakumin*, which means "people of the village" (Nishimura, 2010, p. 119) is similar to the Dalit of India. The Burakumin are descendants of outcast communities of the Japanese feudal era. They held occupations that were considered impure (e.g., butchering animals or burying humans) or nonhuman (e.g., beggar or prostitute) and traditionally lived in isolated hamlets and ghettos (Gordon, 2006). In 1871, the Burakumin were legally liberated from outright discrimination when the Japanese government abolished the feudal caste system; however, this did not improve their social standing or decrease the level of discrimination they faced.

The Burakumin continue to be disadvantaged today (Gordon, 2006). Although some advances have been made, many Japanese still associate the Burakumin with the underclass and with unclean occupations. These stereotypes permeate workplaces, schools, and governmental offices and place the Burakumin in a disadvantaged position in society. In fact, some employers refuse to hire someone if he or she is Buraku (SAHRDC, 2001). Further, the Burakumin continue to be segregated in ghettos and, despite various government efforts to improve their situation, they continue to face various forms of discrimination (Nishimura, 2010).

The plight of the Burakumin and the Dalit highlights the fact that closed caste systems continue to exist even when governments try to abolish them. However, in general, societies become more open as they move from pre-industrial to industrial and finally to post-industrial economies. The main reason for this shift is that modern production techniques require a more highly educated workforce (Rahman, 2009; Treiman, 1970). As levels of education increase, so does recognition of the inequities of class-based systems. This recognition often inspires the disadvantaged to become more politically active as a means of achieving greater equality.

OPEN SYSTEMS: CLASS

class structure A society's economic hierarchy that categorizes groups of people based on their socioeconomic status.

In an open social system, status or social rank is the result of one's own merit within the **class structure**—the overall economic hierarchy that categorizes groups of people based on their socioeconomic status. As introduced in Chapter 1, socioeconomic status (SES) is largely comprised of three loosely related indicators (or measures) of social position: income, occupational prestige, and education (Veenstra, 2006). It is important to analyze each of these indicators in coordination with the other two because looking at only one can be misleading. For example, based solely on income, a drug dealer and a lawyer (both of whom live in nice houses and drive Porsches) are comparable. But the drug dealer, while financially successful, is involved in illegal activities, does not have what the larger society considers to be a prestigious career, and may not have completed high school. Conversely, the lawyer has a prestigious occupation and an extensive postsecondary education. As you can see, looking at one SES indicator in isolation may leave out a great deal.

intergenerational earnings A comparison between a father's and a son's earnings.

As we saw earlier, the closed caste system is not necessarily as closed as one might think (i.e., Indian women can change their caste through marriage) nor is the class system as open as we would hope: The reality is that social mobility does occur (Corak & Heisz, 1999, p. 505), but such mobility is relatively rare (Western & Wright, 1994). Social mobility is typically measured through **intergenerational earnings** and income elasticity (IGE). The IGE is calculated by comparing the son's and the father's earnings[1] (Contoyannis & Dooley, 2010, p. 327). IGE scores range from 0.0 (no relationship between father's and son's earnings) to 1.0 (fathers and sons make exactly the same). Lower IGE scores indicate a more open class system. The most recent estimates available calculate Canada's IGE score at 0.19 (Causa & Johansson, 2010, p. 8), which places Canada among high-mobility societies such as Finland and Sweden. Low-mobility societies include the US and the UK, with IGEs of 0.47 and 0.50, respectively (Contoyannis & Dooley, 2010, p. 327). This confirms that Canadians can move between classes, but we should not assume that one's social class is solely the result of individual effort.

Property and Occupational Prestige: Two Components of Inequality

PROPERTY

income Money received annually from all sources.

Property is an important indicator of where one resides in the class structure. Sociologists generally divide property into two categories: income and wealth. **Income** is defined as the money one receives annually from all sources, such as salaries, fees paid for services, rents, grants, support payments, government assistance, and interest and dividends paid from stocks and bond holdings. **Wealth** is defined as one's net accumulated assets, including homes, land, automobiles, jewellery, factories, and stocks and bonds. Income, then, is what you earn, and wealth is what you have.

wealth Net accumulated assets, including homes, land, and stocks.

How is Canadian income distributed? As illustrated in Figure 7.1, you can see that the top 20 percent of the population was the only group that saw their after-tax income rise substantially between 1976 and 2011. These data confirm that the richest 20 percent of Canadians have increased their income by around 40 percent since 1994, while the lower 80 percent have only seen negligible gains over the same period.

OCCUPATIONAL PRESTIGE

When we meet people for the first time, one of the most common questions we ask is "What do you do?" Their answer helps us to determine their class position, and, for many of us, this

---

1 Information on daughters' earnings is limited (Aydemir, Chen, & Corak, 2009, p. 379) and demonstrates both androcentricity and gender insensitivity (as described in Chapter 4).

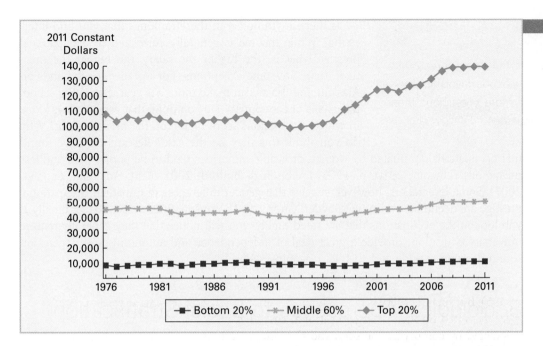

FIGURE 7.1

Average After-Tax Income, by Income Group, Canada, 1976–2011

influences how we interact with them. We do this, in part, because people generally agree on the prestige, and, therefore the social value, of various occupations (Goyder & Frank, 2007). Table 7.1 lists Canada's top 20 occupations, as measured by occupational prestige, as well as the bottom 20.

<<<

TABLE 7.1 Occupational Prestige Rankings

Rank Occupation

Rank	Occupation	Rank	Occupation
1.	Specialist (Physician)	500.	Chainsaw and skidder operators
2.	General practitioner	501.	Shoe repairers & shoemakers
3.	Dentist	502.	Ironing & pressing & finishing occupations
4.	Judge	503.	Sewing machine operator
5.	Lawyer	504.	Fishing vessel deckhands
6.	School principal	505.	Nursery & greenhouse workers
7.	University professor	506.	Tailors/dressmakers
8.	Optometrist	507.	Operators & attendants at amusement, recreation, and sport
9.	Meteorologist	508.	Silviculture & forestry workers
10.	Architecture/science manager	509.	Service station attendants
11.	Physicist/astronomer	510.	Light duty cleaners
12.	Geologist, geochemist, geophysicist	511.	Babysitters & nannies
13.	Chemical engineer	512.	Food counter attendants
14.	Aerospace engineer	513.	Aquaculture & marine harvest labourer
15.	Computer information system manager	514.	Fish plant worker
16.	Metallurgical & materials engineer	515.	Labourer in fish processing
17.	Software engineer	516.	Couriers & messengers
18.	Economist	517.	General farm worker
19.	Petroleum engineer	518.	Harvesting labourer
20.	Mining engineer	519.	Sports officials, referees
		520.	Trappers, hunters

Source: Monica Boyd, Occupational Prestige Rankings, Boyd, Monica. 2008. A Socioeconomic Scale for Canada: Measuring Occupational Status from the Census. Canadian Review of Sociology 45(1):51–91, Canadian Review of Sociology. Reprinted with permission.

Is there anything about these rankings that you find interesting? While income is generally correlated to occupational prestige (that is, the higher the salary, the higher the prestige), there are some exceptions. For instance, deck hands on Alaskan crab boats can make more per year than some school principals or economists. Do you think that gender plays a role in which occupations score highly on the prestige scale? Why do you think this may be the case? Researchers have found that occupations dominated by women or visible minorities tend to be poorly paid and less prestigious (Lincoln, 2010, p. 1973; Preibisch & Binford, 2007; Reid, Adelman, & Jaret, 2007). Some researchers, however, suggest that gender differences in Canadian occupational prestige are declining over time (Goyder, Guppy, & Thompson, 2003; Lips, 2013). Finally, if you look at the occupations that are rated highly, you will notice that they generally require university education, provide a great deal of independence and autonomy, and depend on sound decision-making and abstract reasoning skills.

❷ Sociological Approaches to Social Stratification

FUNCTIONALISM

One of the most influential functionalist theories of social stratification was developed by Kingsley Davis (1908–1997) and Wilbert Moore (1914–1987). Commonly referred to as the **Davis-Moore thesis**, it holds that social inequality serves two important social functions: It instills in the proper individuals the desire to fill certain social positions, and it instills in those who are assigned to those positions the desire to complete their duties and responsibilities (Davis & Moore, 1945, p. 242; Nayebi & Abdollahyan, 2006). In other words, surgeons are paid more than gardeners because of their higher level of skill and training. According to functionalists, in order to attract the most capable and skilled people into important and demanding occupations, the rewards (i.e., money and prestige) must be high enough to compensate them for their time and effort.

Davis-Moore thesis The theory that social stratification is functional for society because it ensures that key social positions are held by the most capable people.

The functionalist explanation for social stratification sounds reasonable—the system needs to attract the best people to fill important social roles and thus must provide sufficient rewards to justify their investment of time and effort to achieve the necessary training. Yet the application of the Davis-Moore thesis to social stratification has been widely criticized on a number of fronts (Tumin, 1953; Wrong, 1959). We will consider four of these criticisms here.

First, one of the rewards that social elites receive is the ability to help their children assume the same social benefits they have. There is no guarantee that these children are as capable or as skilled as their parents, and yet they maintain their upper-class status independent of their own strengths or weaknesses.

Second, even in modern, open, class-based societies, there is substantial discrimination in terms of who is eligible to assume elite positions. Canadian society still discriminates on the basis of gender and minority status (Creese & Wiebe, 2012; Preibisch & Binford, 2007), a fact that limits access to elite positions even for highly skilled and talented people. Further, the comparatively low salaries of such socially important (but female dominated) occupations as daycare workers, public school teachers, and social workers demonstrate the extent to which gender bias may influence salary levels.

Third, the capitalist economy determines the salary of a given occupation not on the basis of the work's value but, rather, through market forces. We may all agree that the care and education of children is one of our most important collective responsibilities, but daycare workers and elementary school teachers are nonetheless paid less than plumbers and welders, and much less than some professional athletes.

< < <

Some dynamic individuals can translate personal attributes into wealth and influence.

Barry Rosenthal/Taxi/Getty Images

Fourth, social inequality is extreme. Senior executives at large multinational corporations can earn hundreds of millions of dollars per year, and athletes and Hollywood actors can earn tens of millions per year. Yet around 9.8 percent of Canadian children live in poverty, a rate that is only slightly lower than in the late 1980s (United Way, 2011, p. 2). Although most would agree that providing financial compensation for the expertise of gifted people is necessary in order to attract the very best into demanding roles, how much inequality between the rich and the poor is acceptable? And can the present levels be justified in functionalist terms? That is, how much inequality is necessary to inspire people to work hard due to fear of failure and poverty?

In its recognition of the need to reward those willing to contribute to collective social benefit, the Davis-Moore thesis offers an important insight into the functional benefits of social stratification. However, the theory largely ignores the power of the social elite and the negative impacts on the poor and the lower classes (Porter, 1965).

CONFLICT THEORY

According to conflict theorists, a society that contains social classes is simply a manifestation of competition between those who have social power and those who do not. And while Marx and Weber would agree that competition exists between classes, they differ on why social stratification occurs and whether it is inevitable.

Karl Marx Marx believed that class struggle was the most important inspiration behind the historical transformation of societies. Further, he viewed social stratification as a mechanism that institutionalizes inequality and promotes social stability over time (Nayebi & Abdollahyan, 2006, p. 251). And, as you have learned, Marx believed that class inequality was neither desirable nor inevitable.

As discussed in Chapter 2, Marx believed that all of social life is influenced by how people interact during the process of economic production. As society began to accumulate more surplus wealth when production techniques moved from subsistence economies to industrialization, some groups were able to secure ownership of the new wealth while others had

> > >

According to Marx and Weber, conflicts between workers and owners are grounded in economic inequality.

QMI Agency/Sun Media Corporation

to sell their labour to survive. In this way, the class structure of owners (bourgeoisie) and workers (proletariat) emerged.

Marx argued that the interests of these two social classes are incompatible. The bourgeoisie are motivated to maintain their control over society so that they can accumulate as much profit as possible, while the proletariat try to get as much money for their labour as they can. The only way the proletariat can hope to improve their position is by overcoming their false perception of class consciousness and overthrowing the bourgeoisie. The bourgeoisie, in turn, try to control the proletariat through the state machinery (police, prisons, the military) to protect their class interests. Thus, according to Marx, social stratification is the embodiment of class conflict and is inevitable in capitalist economies that require the exploitation of the working classes.

Marx's analysis of social inequality continues to influence sociologists today. However, while much contemporary sociology is undertaken from a conflict perspective, Marx's focus on revolutionary ideas that advocate the overthrow of capitalism remains controversial and somewhat outdated. While capitalism continues to exploit many workers around the world, it has also led to a rising standard of living. Further, workers have created extensive labour organizations and in many areas of the world enjoy more protection under the law than ever before (Shalla, 2004).

Max Weber Weber agreed with Marx's conclusion that capitalism led to class conflict but also suggested that Marx's single-minded focus on economic production was overly simplistic and failed to appreciate the multidimensional nature of social class, inequality, and the role of cultural values (Inglehart & Baker, 2000, p. 19). Thus, according to Weber, the classless society is not inevitable and social stratification is, at some level at least, unavoidable and necessary.

Weber agreed with Marx that modern society is divided into economic classes and that the ownership of property is important for gaining influence. However, he also argued that there are other sources of influence: class, status groups, and party (Weber, 1946 [1906]).

Class According to Weber (and Marx), class differences are largely based on economic inequality, with rich landowners in the higher echelons of society and poor workers in the lower echelons. Yet Weber thought that economic class was relatively unimportant, given that most people lack class consciousness (Lindsey & Beach, 2003, p. 203) and are therefore unlikely to challenge the status quo.

Status Groups People rarely consider themselves as members of a particular status group. According to Weber, **status groups** are composed of people who share similar social status, lifestyles, world views, occupations, and standards of living (Nayebi & Abdollahyan, 2006, p. 252). Status groups based on ethnicity include, for example, First Nations, Asians, blacks, and Ukrainians. Status groups based on religious beliefs include Jews, Muslims, and Catholics. Other groupings are based on occupation: manual labourers, academics, dentists.

Cassano (2008, p. 177) argues that Weber saw classes as being stratified according to their relations to production and acquisition of goods while status groups are stratified according to their consumption of goods. This suggests that people are more likely to act collectively as part of a status group (e.g., as a member of a First Nations band) than they are as part of an economic class (see also Turner, 1986). This makes sense when we consider that beyond family and friends, we usually feel more connected to those we share experiences with than to those in the same economic class.

Party According to Weber, "parties" are organizations that attempt to achieve certain goals in a planned and logical manner. Parties are associations of people that have the power to influence social action and change. (Think of nongovernmental organizations [NGOs] such as the Canadian Red Cross or Mothers Against Drunk Driving.) For sociologists, **power** is defined as the ability to make others do something they would not otherwise do. According to Marx, power generally originates with the possession of wealth and privilege, but Weber went beyond this to investigate alternative types of power in developed societies.

Weber's analysis of bureaucracy (see Chapter 16) revealed that there are workers who, even though they lack economic power and status, can still exert a tremendous amount of power because they have the authority to make important decisions (Zeitlin, 1994, p. 217). For example, if your college or university application failed to include, say, your final grade in high school English, the admissions manager has the authority to withhold your registration until you have provided it—a delay that could affect your ability to register for courses.

Weber also suggested that because three distinct systems of stratification are at work (class, status, and power), there exists the possibility of status inconsistency. **Status inconsistency** occurs when an individual occupies several differently ranked statuses at the same time. For example, as we saw earlier, a drug dealer may have a great deal of money and live in a big house but have little social prestige.

Weber's contribution to the sociological analysis of stratification is his recognition that social stratification and inequality are not the same thing but are instead a combination of many factors.

SYMBOLIC INTERACTIONISM

Interactionists are less interested in trying to explain why stratification exists than they are in looking at how people interpret and construct their responses to class inequality. Instead of speculating about the function or inevitability of stratification, interactionists are principally interested in how class affects patterns of everyday social life. In particular, they consider how people use and respond to status symbols (Hartl, Novak, Rao, & Sethi, 2003).

Status symbols are material indicators that demonstrate a person's social and economic position. One of the pioneers in the study of status symbols was Thorstein Veblen (1857–1929), with his concept of conspicuous consumption. **Conspicuous consumption** is the purchase of expensive goods simply because they are valuable, not because there is any innate

status group A group of people who share similar social status, lifestyles, world views, occupations, and standards of living.

power The ability to make others do something they would not otherwise do.

status inconsistency Occurs when an individual occupies several differently ranked statuses at the same time.

status symbols Material indicators that demonstrate a person's social and economic position.

conspicuous consumption The purchase of expensive goods simply because they are valuable, not because there is any innate satisfaction in them.

> > >

Expensive homes and lavish lifestyles are public demonstrations of social class.

AbleStock/Jupiterimages/Getty Images

conspicuous leisure
The demonstration of one's high social status through forms of leisure.

conspicuous waste
The disposal of valuable goods to demonstrate wealth.

satisfaction in them—for example, paying $100 for a designer T-shirt. Veblen would argue that people are willing to pay $100 for the shirt because they want to be seen by others as being able to pay such an amount. The satisfaction is not in the product's functionality, then, but rather in the status it implies (Mukherjee, 2006).

In *The Theory of the Leisure Class* (1899/1979), Veblen developed two other key concepts to show how people communicate their social wealth to others: *conspicuous leisure* and *conspicuous waste*. According to Veblen, **conspicuous leisure** is the demonstration of one's high social status through forms of leisure that include taking long vacations in exotic locales. **Conspicuous waste** is the disposal of valuable goods to demonstrate wealth; for example, giving a $100 tip to a valet for parking your car.

Veblen suggested that people want to be seen as living one class stratum above where they actually live. Until recently, households were largely trapped in their class stratum because they had limited means by which to reach the next level. However, Scott (2007) argues that credit cards have changed people's ability to reach, or at least appear to reach, that next higher level. He suggests that conspicuous consumption is more prevalent today than at any other point in history since credit cards allow people to purchase things they may not be able to afford or justify if they had to pay cash for them (Scott, 2007, p. 570). Nevertheless, material objects such as houses and expensive clothes are still strong indicators of social class (Mazur, 1993). Owning a large home in a prestigious area of town is an effective indicator of social class, just as is renting a small apartment in a rough part of the city.

There are non-material indicators of social class as well. For example, in places like Great Britain, an individual's accent is a powerful indicator of social position. Even subtle social cues may indicate class differences; some research suggests that the lower a person's social status is compared to the status of someone that person is waiting to see, the longer the wait. There is truth in the adage that in the working class, your name goes on your shirt; in the middle class, on the door of your office; and in the upper class, on your company (Lindsey & Beach, 2003, p. 204).

Veblen's contribution to the study of stratification, then, was his analysis of how we seek to appear as belonging to a higher social class than our actual one. This approach is entirely consistent with symbolic interactionism and its belief that we constantly define and reconstruct impressions of ourselves and others. Veblen's insights, while over 100 years old, still help social scientists understand and explain contemporary society (Scott, 2010).

FEMINIST THEORY

Feminist theory considers how the dominant (that is, male) perspective permeates our society's evaluation of what is deemed valuable and important. Feminist insight into the workings of social inequality generally follows two lines of investigation: (1) recognizing the working lives of women within capitalism (Armstrong & Armstrong, 1994), and (2) investigating the role of class position in determining one's view of the world (Harding, 2006; Sangster, 2007).

The feminist investigation of the working lives of women focuses on how gender influences what Canadian sociologists Pat and Hugh Armstrong (1994) have termed "the double ghetto." The **double ghetto** (or *double shift*; see Chapter 11) is the situation in which women who have full-time jobs outside the home often work another "shift" when they get home. Regardless of class, men maintain a superior social position over the women in their lives because men, as a group, own most of the social wealth. This fact puts many women in a subordinate position both in the world of work and in their own homes.

Feminists also view social classes as one of the primary locations for struggle within society, and believe that this is where most people form important memories and life experiences that help to define who they are. In other words, the production of social reality (one's individual perspective of the world) is influenced by one's class (Ritzer, 2000, p. 479). For example, Lichterman's (1995) research into the environmental movement found that women's class position (and their resulting life experiences) leads low-income women to prefer more collective, egalitarian, and participatory approaches to life than women from higher classes, who tend to favour more hierarchical, bureaucratic organizations that support individual effort to achieve goals (as cited in Statham, 2000). Another example is Sandra Harding's (2005, 2006) critique of science and social inequality. Harding argues that Western science was developed specifically for the needs of European expansion and conquest. She emphasizes that it promotes social inequalities through discriminatory orientations, philosophies, technologies, and the social structure (Day, 2007).

Table 7.2 summarizes our discussion of stratification by outlining some of the key features of each of the sociological approaches.

double ghetto A situation in which women who have full-time jobs outside the home often work another "shift" when they get home.

TABLE 7.2 Theories of Social Stratification

Theory	Origin of Inequality	Is Inequality Justified?	Leading Theorists
Functionalism	Social position is determined by personal skills and abilities.	Yes, society needs to redistribute limited resources to those who can benefit society the most.	Émile Durkheim Talcott Parsons Kingsley Davis Wilbert Moore
Conflict	As wealth is accumulated in fewer and fewer hands, elites solidify their control of resources at the exclusion of the poor.	No, social wealth is accumulated by the elite, who continue to exploit the lower classes for personal gain; the rich get richer while the poor get poorer.	Karl Marx Max Weber Ralf Dahrendorf
Symbolic Interactionism	The origin of inequality is less important than how existing class positions influence everyday human interaction.	Depends on the individual; one person may view inequality as fair and justified while another will view it as the result of inheritance.	Thorstein Veblen
Feminist	The subordinate position of women is due to patriarchy and learned world view resulting from one's social class.	No, inequality is the result of capitalism and Western ideology that promotes colonial expansion and domination.	Pat and Hugh Armstrong Sandra Harding

❸ The Canadian Class System

Canadian researchers take several different approaches when describing the Canadian class system (Myles, 2003; Walks & Bourne, 2006; Russell, 2009, p. 132). Some follow the lead of Erik Olin Wright (1996), an American sociologist who focuses on three important forms of social control:

1. Economic ownership that entails real control over the economic surplus
2. Command of the physical means of economic production (e.g., owning/supervising the control of machines)
3. Supervisory control over other workers (Veenstra, 2006, p. 114)

According to Wright, the bourgeoisie have all three forms of control, while the proletariat have none; the petit bourgeoisie have some of the first two forms of control but no supervisory control over workers, while managers have supervisory control. These forms of control, then, correspond to four distinct classes: *bourgeoisie, petit bourgeoisie, managers,* and *proletariat.* Perhaps the most interesting element of Wright's model is his observation that two of these classes share characteristics with both capitalists and workers, and thus occupy what he calls "contradictory class locations." Figure 7.2 provides a graphical representation of Wright's model.

The first class is the petit bourgeoisie—small shop owners and other entrepreneurs (comparable to today's middle class). They own capital, but since they employ few if any workers, they exercise very little authority. Wright also understands that as capitalism matures, the petit bourgeoisie become more diverse, therefore altering the traditional class dynamics of rich versus poor.

The second class is the managers who work in firms owned by the capitalists but who have direct authority over large numbers of workers. Even though most managers identify with the bourgeoisie, they are ultimately just as expendable as any other employee—a fact that became a bitter reality to many middle managers during the era of corporate downsizing in the 1980s and 1990s (Lindsey & Beach, 2003; McLaren & Farahmandpur, 2000).

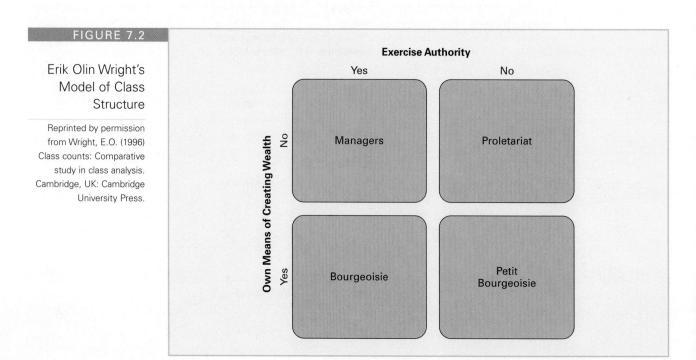

FIGURE 7.2

Erik Olin Wright's Model of Class Structure

Reprinted by permission from Wright, E.O. (1996) Class counts: Comparative study in class analysis. Cambridge, UK: Cambridge University Press.

Although Wright's model has much to offer, most sociologists prefer to analyze the class system in terms of a somewhat simpler scheme represented by the work of American sociologists Dennis Gilbert and Joseph Kahl (1993). The following discussion of the Canadian class system is based on their interpretation.

THE UPPER CLASS

Although relatively few Canadians reside in the upper class, the influence of this class is hard to overestimate. They earn at least several hundred thousand dollars a year, yet their chief economic resource is accumulated wealth rather than income. Most upper-class families inherited the bulk of their money (Cagetti & De Nardi, 2006; Morck, Stangeland, & Yeung, 1998).

While some Canadians may argue that the rich do not pay their fair share of taxes (Lee, M., 2007), recent Statistics Canada figures (2007) challenge that assertion. In 2004, the richest 5 percent of Canadians who filed tax returns received 25 percent of all income and paid 36 percent of all personal taxes. In contrast, the bottom 95 percent of the population received 75 percent of income and paid 64 percent of personal taxes. However, some also suggest that in recent decades, the elite benefited from their political influence to reshape the tax code and received beneficial tax cuts between 1990 and 2005 (Lee, M., 2007).

Members of the very rich are often viewed as comprising two different populations (Allen, 1989). At the extreme top are the "old rich," families like the Thomsons, Westons, and Irvings, who have been wealthy for generations. The "new rich" include people like Daryl Katz (owner of Rexall drugstores and the Edmonton Oilers), Chip Wilson (founder of Lululemon), and Jeffrey Skoll (eBay's first employee and president). This group also includes a few highly paid athletes and actors as well as some top professionals (e.g., plastic surgeons, defence lawyers).

Male members of the old rich may work, but many simply manage their investments. Many of the new rich, meanwhile, occupy top executive positions in the largest corporations. For this reason, the latter group is sometimes called the "corporate class." Women in both groups sometimes work but often focus on civic and charitable activities (Lindsey & Beach, 2003; Ostrander, 1984). In some cases, the new rich may be wealthier than the old rich, but members of both groups generally acknowledge the higher social status of the old rich.

Traditionally, members of the upper class were almost entirely white Protestants of British descent, but today the class appears to be opening up to people of other religions and ethnic backgrounds. Yet there are still comparatively few visible minority members in the upper class. Upper-class people tend to live in a small number of elite communities, marry within their class, send their children to the same schools, join the same clubs, and vacation in the same exclusive resorts (Newman, 1998). More than any other class, members of the elite form insulated social networks out of the public eye.

Professional athletes like Canadian NBA star Steve Nash can be paid millions of dollars per year and become members of the upper class.

THE UPPER-MIDDLE CLASS

Few people have much contact with the upper class because its members tend to use their wealth to maintain their privacy (Kingston & Köhler, 2006). Not so for the upper-middle class, whose members tend to be highly visible. Lacking significant power at the national level, these are often the movers and shakers within local communities (Trounstine & Christensen, 1982).

The upper-middle class is generally comprised of people working in professional careers (e.g., doctors and lawyers). Those in the upper-middle class are not enormously wealthy but are financially secure and tend to drive new cars, take international holidays, and live in very nice homes. Much of the success of this class results from having good educations; virtually

BOX 7.1 CANADIAN CONTRIBUTIONS TO SOCIOLOGY

William Carroll

Since receiving his Ph.D. from York University in 1981, William Carroll has been a leading voice in Canadian sociology. His work has spanned a wide range of subjects including social inequality, globalization, social movements, political sociology, and a unique approach to exploring corporate capitalism. He has published dozens of articles and a number of books, two of which were awarded the Canadian Sociology Association's John Porter Memorial Prize for making a distinguished sociological contribution to the understanding of Canadian society.

Carroll's most recent book, *The Making of a Transnational Capitalist Class: Corporate Power in the 21st Century*, uses network theory to trace the emergence and growth of a new type of corporate power that, unlike earlier forms, is not confined by national borders and whose members have become all-encompassing global entities that embed themselves within organizations like the World Trade Organization and the World Economic Forum to promote their own profit-motivated self-interests.

In addition to his long list of research contributions, Carroll also enjoys teaching undergraduate and graduate courses in social inequality, political sociology, globalization, and theory. He also helped develop the interdisciplinary program in Social Justice Studies at the University of Victoria and remains not only an active and engaged member of his department and university, but also his community.

William Carroll

everyone in the upper-middle class has a university degree, and a significant number have graduate degrees. Upper-middle-class families usually live in the suburbs, and are often active in municipal politics and volunteer organizations. Although mostly white, they are more ethnically diverse than the upper class (Marger, 1998).

THE LOWER-MIDDLE CLASS

The Canadian lower-middle class is made up of managers, small business operators, senior executive assistants, and some minor professionals, such as school teachers and social

workers. The majority of people in this class have at least some college or university education, but only a few have completed their degrees. In most lower-middle-class families, both
spouses work so that they can support a moderately comfortable lifestyle, albeit one more
tenuous than that of the higher economic levels, given that this class lacks substantial investment income or sizable cash savings. However, most people in this class take occasional vacations, eat out fairly regularly, drive later-model cars, and send their children to university or
community colleges. Historically, most families in the lower-middle class own their homes,
but they also have a sense of insecurity and vulnerability to market forces, particularly interest
rates on home mortgages (Lochhead & Shalla, 1996).

People in the lower-middle class typically encourage their children to continue their
education in the hopes that they can achieve a profession, more financial security, and
independence in their chosen careers. The majority of this class rarely participates in local,
provincial, or national politics because they feel powerless and do not believe that they could
make substantial change. In general, this class quietly follows the rules as defined by their
managers and superiors.

THE WORKING CLASS

Roughly 30 percent of the Canadian population can be considered working class.
However, as you have no doubt already noticed, the criteria separating these classes are
somewhat vague. Most members of the working class are skilled and semi-skilled manual
workers. The skilled working class includes such occupations as carpenters, plumbers,
and electricians. The semi-skilled working class includes low-level clerical workers, sales-
people, and many female pink-collar workers, such as waitresses and cooks. Most jobs in
this class are highly routine and closely supervised. Typically, both members of a couple
within this class must work outside the home to pay their bills (Lindsey & Beach, 2003,
p. 215; Rubin, 1976).

Working-class people usually complete high school, but few go on to college or university. While many own their own homes, the majority have no other significant assets and are
vulnerable to a financial crisis resulting from illness or unexpected and long-term unemployment (Rubin, 1994). Most working-class people drive used cars, take holidays that are close
to home, and live in modest neighbourhoods.

While upward mobility is encouraged in the working class, many people in this stratum
emphasize the importance of being respected by their community as a means of underscoring
their superiority over the lower classes.

THE "UNDERCLASS"

Some Canadians face long-term, chronic poverty in which they have little ability to realize
their potential since they are in a constant struggle to meet their immediate needs (Bradshaw,
2007). Sociologists disagree about what to call this group (Bagguley & Mann, 1992). Some
use the term *underclass* (Auletta, 1982), but others argue that this word is stigmatizing (Gans,
1995). Others have suggested *welfare class* or *lower-lower class*, but these are also harmful and
derogatory terms. Whatever term is used, the members of this class generally lack marketable skills and have little or no experience with full-time work (Welshman, 2006). Unless
given extensive training and educational upgrading, many are virtually unemployable. Their
annual household income is typically below $15,000, so for many the only legitimate source
of income is social assistance. Many survive only through an elaborate network of sharing
based largely on kinship ties (Stack, 1975).

In Canada, many anti-poverty activists refer to the poverty line as Statistics Canada's definition of the **low income cut-off (LICO)**, which represents the level of income at which a
household in a particular location must spend 20 percentage points more of its gross income
on food, shelter, and clothing than does the average Canadian household. This currently

Explore

Exploring Myths about
the Poor

**low income cut-off
(LICO)** The level of
income at which a
household spends
55 percent or more of
its gross income on
basic necessities.

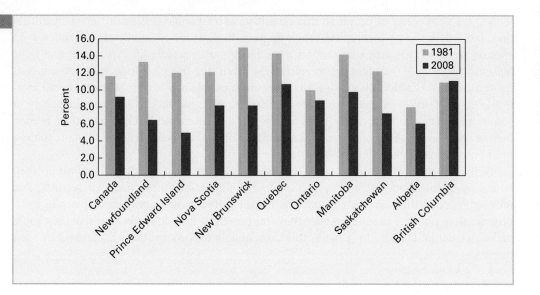

FIGURE 7.3

Poverty Rate Based on LICOs, Canada and the Provinces, Percent, 1981 and 2008

Osberg, L., & Sharpe, A. (2009). New estimates of the index of economic wellbeing for canada and the provinces, 1981-2008 No. 2009-10). Ottawa, ON: Centre for the Study of Living Standards.

means spending about 55 percent of gross income on these basic necessities. However, as Statistics Canada regularly points out, this is a measure of income inequality (Fellegi, 1997), and such relative definitions do not really tell us about poverty but, rather, about inequality. Figure 7.3 outlines LICO scores by Canadian province between 1981 and 2008 and reinforces that while poverty remains a concern, rates are falling over time.

❹ Factors Influencing Social Inequality in Canada

> > > Thinking Sociologically

Using first a functional and then a conflict perspective, speculate on why more is not being done to address poverty in Canada.

Geographic Location Figure 7.3 shows that different provinces have different poverty rates. The Canadian poverty rate was around 11.5 percent in 1981 and 9 percent in 2008. The highest poverty rates in 1981 were found in New Brunswick, Quebec, and Manitoba (all over 14 percent) and in 2011, in British Columbia and Quebec (around 11 percent each). The most striking changes over this 27-year period were the significant declines in poverty rates in New Brunswick, Prince Edward Island, and Newfoundland. These data suggest that where a person lives may influence his or her chances of being poor.

Gender As shown in Figure 7.4, Canadian women continue to earn less than men across occupations—a situation that exists in virtually all contemporary societies (Jurajda & Harmgart, 2007; United Nations, 2006, p. 54) and one that many Canadians perceive as "natural" (Gazso, 2004).

feminization of poverty **The universal phenomenon whereby women are more susceptible to poverty than are men.**

Sociologists, however, use the phrase **feminization of poverty** (coined by Diana Pearce in the 1970s) to recognize the universality of women's wage discrimination (Thibos, Lavin-Loucks, & Martin, 2007). In fact, even though the *Pay Equity Act* of 1987 makes it illegal to pay someone less, or more, for their work on the basis of gender, women continue to be paid less for the same work as men (Kovach, 1996; Phillips & Phillips, 2000). Additionally, women are outnumbered by men in the highest-paying jobs and dominate in the lowest-paying jobs. Clearly, then, being female is an important factor when we consider who is likely to be poor in Canada.

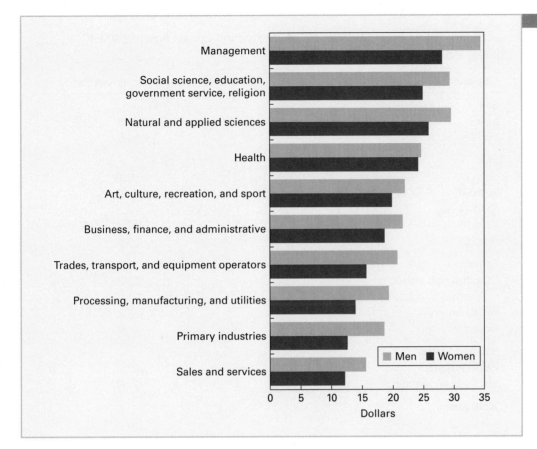

FIGURE 7.4

Hourly Wages, by
Occupation and
Sex, 2007

Source: Statistics Canada.
2008. Hourly wages,
by occupation and sex.
Retrieved February 15,
2014, from http://www
.statcan.gc.ca/pub/71-222-x/
2008001/c-g/c-g-j5-eng.jpg
(Actual report is at: http://
www.statcan.gc.ca/pub/71-
222-x/2008001/sectionj/j-
hourly-horaire-eng.htm)

Work Status One of the most obvious factors that determines whether people live in poverty is whether they have jobs. Table 7.3 demonstrates that only 20.7 percent of people who work live in poverty compared to 68.2 percent of people who do not have a job. You can predict that while periods of economic growth give rise to more jobs, when the economy suffers a downturn, those who lack savings and support networks can wind up living in poverty very quickly.

Age In 2011, 571 000 children under 17 lived in low-income families, virtually unchanged from 2010 but fewer than the 854 000 in 2003. The proportion of children in low-income families was 8.5 percent in 2011, close to half of the 1996 peak of 18 percent (Statistics Canada, 2011c). Research by Statistics Canada also suggests that the chance of a child living in a low-income family is almost five times higher in a female-headed lone-parent family than it is in a two-parent family (Statistics Canada, 2011c).

Further, Table 7.3 shows that people in their late teens and early twenties are most likely to live in poverty in Canada. This age group is just entering the labour market and beginning to develop their marketable skills. However, after age 34 there is a steady rise in the incidence of people living in poverty.

Visible Minority Status There are several Canadian studies of ethnic and racial discrimination in labour markets and hiring practices (Al-Waqfi & Jain, 2008; Richards, Vining, & Weimer, 2010; Walks & Bourne, 2006). One common finding is that a significant proportion of the existing wage gap between white and nonwhite workers is not directly attributable to the demographic, educational, or occupational characteristics of workers.

TABLE 7.3 Low-Income Rates of Unattached Individuals Aged 18 to 64, [2005] 2011

Characteristic	Low-Income Rate (%)
Sex	
Male	29.9
Female	36.0
Age	
18 to 24	[58.1]
25 to 34	21.8]
35 to 44	[26.9]
45 to 54	[31.6]
55 to 64	[39.9]
Education	
Less than high school	[55.0]
High school completed	[31.4]
Postsecondary	[33.3]
University	[17.6]
Minority Status	
Visible minority	[43.8]
Not a visible minority	[31.8]
Work Status	
Employed	[20.7]
Self-employed	[39.7]
Not employed	[68.2]

Sources: Statistics Canada, 2013. Percentage of persons in low income (1992 base after-tax income, low-income cutoff) [online]. http://www.statcan.gc.ca/tables-tableaux/sum-som/l01/cst01/famil19a-eng.htm (accessed February 12, 2014).

Statistics Canada, 2010. Percentage of persons in low income (1992 base after-tax income, low-income cutoff) [online]. http://www.statcan.gc.ca/daily-quotidien/100617/t100617c3-eng.htm (accessed May 16, 2011).

Instead, the wage gap appears to be the result of racial discrimination by employers in the hiring and promotion of visible minority workers (Canadian Heritage, 1998). Table 7.3 shows that 43.8 percent of visible minorities live in poverty, compared with only 31.8 percent of nonvisible minorities.

Education In 2007, two years after graduation, 90 percent of university graduates found employment. The median annual earnings for those working full-time varied by credential held: $35,000 for a college diploma, $45,000 for a bachelor's degree, $60,000 for a master's, and $65,000 for a doctorate. These numbers show that, on average, those with a bachelor's degree earned 29 percent more than those with a college diploma, and that those with a master's degree earned 33 percent more than those with a bachelor's. People with their doctorate on average earned 8 percent more than those with their master's (Statistics Canada, 2009d). Statistics consistently confirm that education increases earnings as well as employment rates (Statistics Canada, 2009d).

As shown in Figure 7.5, poverty rates in 2007 were lowest for people who had university degrees. In fact, fewer than 5 percent of families with the major income earner possessing a university degree lived in poverty. However, when a family's major income earner did not have a high school education, its poverty rate was 9 percent while the rate for individuals without high school was 34 percent. Staying in school, then, offers some protection against living in poverty.

FIGURE 7.5

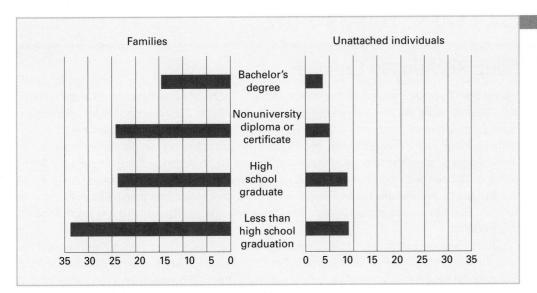

Poverty Rates and Education Levels

Source: National Council of Welfare, 2009

Family Structure As shown in Table 7.4, in 2011, two-parent families (5.9 percent) were much less likely to live below the LICO threshold than were female lone-parent families (23.0 percent), which accords with the pay inequality between men and women. However, since 1999, the trends for both types of families seem to have been moving in the right direction. Overall, virtually all family types in Canada are showing declining poverty rates.

Global Inequality

Analysis of global inequality is a relatively recent area of social research, having begun only in the early 1980s. Before that time, reliable per capita income levels from the former Soviet Union and its constituent republics, China, and large areas of Africa were simply not available

((••⊣Listen

Haiti's Dark Secret: The Restavecs

TABLE 7.4 Percentage of Persons in Low Income (1999–2011)

	1999	2000	2001	2002	2003	2004	2005	2006	2007	2008	2009	2010	2011
							%						
All persons	13.0	12.5	11.2	11.6	11.6	11.4	10.8	10.5	9.2	9.4	9.5	9.0	8.8
Persons under 18 years old	14.5	13.8	12.1	12.3	12.5	12.9	11.6	11.3	9.4	9.0	9.4	8.2	8.5
In two-parent families	9.4	9.5	8.3	7.4	7.9	8.4	7.8	7.7	6.6	6.5	7.5	5.7	5.9
In female lone-parent families*	41.9	40.1	37.4	43.0	41.4	40.4	32.9	31.7	26.6	23.4	21.5	21.8	23.0
Persons 18 to 64 years old	13.4	12.9	11.7	12.0	12.2	11.9	11.4	11.2	9.9	10.2	10.6	9.9	9.7
Persons 65 and over	7.9	7.6	6.7	7.6	6.8	5.6	6.2	5.4	4.9	5.8	6.6	6.8	6.4

Source: Statistics Canada, 2010. Percentage of persons in low income (1992 base after-tax income, low-income cutoff) [online]. Retrieved May 16, 2011, from http://www.statcan.gc.ca/daily-quotidien/100617/t100617c3-eng.htm

Statistics Canada, 2013. Persons in low income after tax (In percent, 2007-2011) [online]. Retrieved February 13, 2014, from http://www.statcan.gc.ca/tables-tableaux/sum-som/l01/cst01/famil19a-eng.htm

*Data for male lone-parent families are somewhat erratic from year to year because of the relatively small number of families. The poverty rates for male lone-parent families are generally about half the rate for female lone-parent families. The highest poverty rate for male lone-parent families was 26.5% in 1994 but has been falling steadily to a record low of 7.2% in 2006 (National Council of Welfare, 2009).

BOX 7.2 THAT WAS THEN, THIS IS NOW

Soup Kitchens in Canada

During the Great Depression of the 1930s, when millions of Canadians lived hand-to-mouth and missing meals was an everyday occurrence (Struthers, 2007), soup kitchens flourished. How did they begin? Strangely, Al Capone, the notorious gangster, established the first soup kitchens in the United States in the late 1920s in an effort to improve his public image.

Since then, soup kitchens have sprung up across North America. Today, most soup kitchens are affiliated with nonprofit or religious organizations. Some of the largest soup kitchens in Canada include the Union Gospel Mission in Vancouver, the Yonge Street Mission in Toronto, Romero House in Saint John, the Union Mission in Ottawa, and the Hope Mission in Edmonton.

During a downturn in the Canadian economy in the 1980s, food banks emerged to help feed the poor, and the Canadian Association of Food Banks (CAFB) was established in 1985 to advocate for food banks across the country. In 2013, the CAFB estimates there were almost 900 food banks in Canada, feeding around 830 000 people per month. Thirty-six percent of all meals served at Canadian food banks were for children (Food Banks Canada, 2013). Compared to 2008, the number of people assisted at food banks across Canada has increased in all provinces but Newfoundland and Labrador. However, the trend over the past year is promising in that all provinces (except Quebec, New Brunswick, and Prince Edward Island) saw a decline from the previous year.

The table below illustrates that poverty remains a significant concern in Canada. Even though we live in one of the richest countries in the world, some Canadians still fall through the cracks. As a sociologist, how would you explain the growing need for food banks? Do you think the need for them will increase or decrease in the next decade? Why?

Food Bank use in Canada, by Province/Territories

Province/Territory	Total Assisted, March 2013	Percent Children, March 2013	Total Assisted, March 2012	Total Assisted, March 2008	Change, 2008–2013	% Change, 2008–2013	Change, 2012–2013	% Change, 2012–2013
British Columbia	94,002	29.5%	94,966	78,101	15,901	20.4%	−964	−1.0%
Alberta	48,653	44.1%	53,512	33,580	15,073	44.9%	−4,859	−9.1%
Saskatchewan	22,465	43.8%	24,621	17,751	4,714	26.6%	−2,156	−8.8%
Manitoba	60,229	44.7%	63,482	40,464	19,765	48.8%	−3,253	−5.1%
Ontario	375,814	35.0%	404,373	314,258	61,556	19.6%	−28,559	−7.1%
Quebec	156,750	37.1%	155,574	127,536	29,214	22.9%	1,176	0.8%
New Brunswick	19,989	33.2%	19,524	15,638	4,351	27.8%	465	2.4%
Nova Scotia	21,760	32.0%	23,561	16,915	4,845	28.6%	−1,801	−7.6%
Prince Edward Island	3,502	35.8%	3,406	2,892	610	21.1%	96	2.8%
Newfoundland & Labrador	26,412	37.9%	27,044	27,260	−848	−3.1%	−632	−2.3%
Territories	3,522	37.5%	2,316	1,340	2,182	162.8%	1,206	52.1%
Canada	**833,098**	**36.4%**	**872,379**	**675,735**	**157,363**	**23.3%**	**−39,281**	**−4.5%**

Reprinted by permission from Food Banks Canada (2013), Hunger Count 2013 Toronto: Food Banks Canada

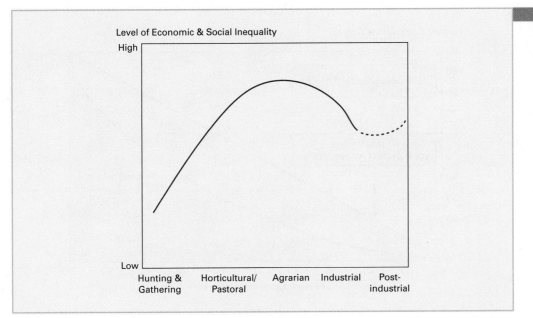

FIGURE 7.6

Kuznets Curve

Kuznets, S., 1955. Economic growth and income inequality. American Economic Review, 49: 1-28 http://www.aeaweb.org/aer/top20/45.1.1-28.pdf

(Milanovic, 2006). Now, however, we are in a much better position to investigate levels of inequality around the world.

One way to assess whether a society's class structure is open or closed is to examine the gap between the rich and the poor. Economist Simon Kuznets (1901–1985) developed an approach that predicts how social inequality changes as societies develop economically (Kuznets, 1955). Commonly referred to as the **Kuznets curve** (see Figure 7.6), the theory argues that as societies developed, they became more unequal until the early phases of the Industrial Revolution, after which inequality tended to decline.

While some question the assumption that development necessarily brings greater equality (Weeks, 2005), the overall trend appears to hold true in industrialized societies. One explanation of why economic development influences inequality is provided by the evolutionary theory of Gerhard and Jean Lenski with their colleague Patrick Nolan (Lenski, Lenski, & Nolan, 1970). Their theory suggests that while hunting and gathering societies are open and nearly classless, significant social stratification emerges in horticultural societies and then expands throughout agrarian and industrial economies (Lenski, 1996). Inequality, then, is viewed largely as resulting from the level of technology a society has to exploit its environment. In hunting and gathering societies, the technology is relatively simple, and redistribution among members of society is based on need and familial obligations. But as technology develops, wealth accumulates into fewer hands, resulting in greater social inequality.

Italian statistician Corrado Gini (1884–1965) developed a way to assess the relative distribution of wealth within a country. The **Gini Index** (also referred to as the Gini Coefficient) is a measure of inequality of wealth or income distribution. A single number is used to summarize any given society's level of economic equality (Gastwirth, Modarres, & Bura, 2005, p. 457). To calculate the number, a line is drawn by plotting the percentage of cumulative wages (A) against the percentage of cumulative workers (B) (see Figure 7.7). If a society has perfect wage equality (everyone has exactly the same proportion of wealth), the Gini Index score is 0 and the line is perfectly straight and sloped at a 45-degree angle. Gini scores vary between 0 (*perfect equality*, meaning that everyone has the same wealth) and 100 (*perfect inequality*, meaning that one person has all of the wealth).

Kuznets curve
A graphic representation of the relationship between a society's economic development and its social inequality.

Gini Index A measure of the inequality of wealth or income distribution within a country.

FIGURE 7.7

Lorenz Curve and Gini Coefficient

Reprinted by permission of Oregon Employment Department.

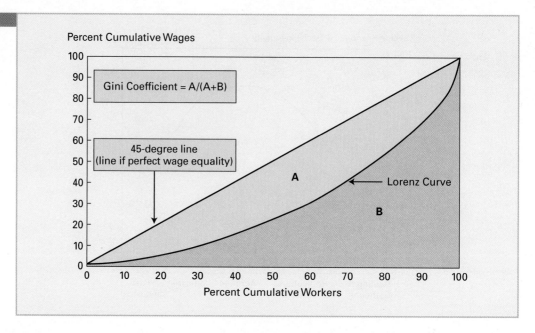

Lorenz curve A graphical line representing a society's deviation from equal wealth allocation.

Since it is impossible for human societies to be either perfectly equal or unequal, deviations from the 45-degree angle are referred to as the **Lorenz curve** (also shown in Figure 7.7). Named after Max O. Lorenz (1880–1962), the Lorenz curve exists when, for example, the bottom 20 percent of wage earners receives only 5 percent of the total earnings (Moore & Peniston, 2004).

To better understand these concepts, see Figure 7.8, which shows that in 2013 some of the world's most unequal nations were in Africa and South America while the least unequal were in Europe. Recent research suggests that the richest 10 percent of the global population earns 50 percent of the world's wealth. To put an even finer point on the distance between the world's rich and poor peoples, the ratio of the average income received by the richest 5 percent to that received by the poorest 5 percent is 165 to 1 (Milanovic, 2006, p. 16).

FIGURE 7.8

Global Gini Coefficient Scores, 2013

Data from Central Intelligence Agency.

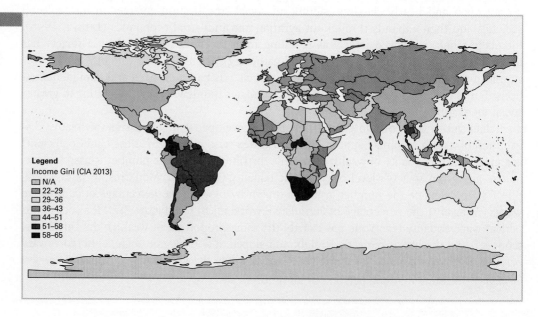

Many developing countries have Gini Index scores of 45 or higher, while most Western European countries have scores in the twenties or low thirties. Canada fares moderately well at 32.6 and compares favourably with the United States, whose 45 score suggests a less equal society than our own.

How might we interpret these Gini Index scores? Functionalists might contend that some economic inequality is a positive thing, in that it may inspire the poor to work harder to make a better life for themselves. Conflict theorists would suggest that global inequality is simply the natural progression of the world's wealth continuing to move into fewer and fewer hands; as the rich get richer, the poor will become poorer. Symbolic interactionists would investigate how people respond to their economic situations in both rich and poor countries; in the former, they might consider our growing infatuation with conspicuous consumption. Feminist theorists would target the role of patriarchy and class position in defining one's view of a world in which inequality is promoted and supported. Critical race and post-colonial theorists would target the role of minority status and the legacy of colonialism to explain why some countries are much more "equal" than others.

> > > Thinking Sociologically

How might a post-colonial theorist explain the relationship between Gini Index scores and colonialism?

BOX 7.3 WHY SHOULD WE CARE?

Canada's Commitment to First Nations Peoples

The vision of Aboriginal Affairs and Northern Development Canada (AANDC) states: "Canada's economic and social well-being benefits from strong, self-sufficient Aboriginal and northern people and communities." Aboriginal Affairs and Northern Development represents the Canadian government's obligations and commitments to Canadian Indigenous peoples, and is mandated to support the growth, independence, and sustainability of Indigenous communities.

As a department of the federal government, the AANDC draws its mandate from the *Indian Act*, some of whose tenets are expressions of Parliament's legislative jurisdiction found in section 91(24) of the *Constitution Act, 1867*. In short, AANDC is responsible for administering more than 50 federal statutes with an annual budget of almost $8 billion (Aboriginal Affairs and Northern Development Canada, 2013).

In light of this budget amount, how are Aboriginal peoples doing today? The Assembly of First Nations (AFN), which does not include Inuit or Métis, advocates for First Nations' rights and promotes Aboriginal dignity and pride (Assembly of First Nations, 2013). This is a daunting task, given the systemic racism against Aboriginals throughout Canada's history, and their constant struggles with the federal bureaucracy. The following statistics are provided by the AFN.

First Nations Children

- Forty percent of First Nations children live in poverty, compared to 12 percent of non-Indigenous Canadian children. They have double the rate of disability, and more than a third of their homes are overcrowded.
- Year-end 2003 data from DIAND indicated that 9031 First Nations children living on reserves were in child welfare care, representing a 70 percent increase from 1995.
- A recent report found that while Aboriginal children make up just 3 percent of the child population in Canada, they represent almost 15 percent of the children in the child welfare system.
- As many as 27 000 First Nations children are currently under care.

CONTINUED

First Nations Homes

- In addition to a higher rate of overcrowding, First Nations homes are about six times more likely to require major repairs compared with Canadian homes. As well, mould contaminates almost half of First Nations homes.

- A 2011 assessment of the water supplies in Aboriginal communities revealed that 73 percent of Aboriginal people are affected by water supplies that have been deemed "high risk" and "moderate risk." Water that falls into these categories needs to be boiled or treated before consumption.

- Six percent (more than 5000 homes) are without sewage services and 4 percent lack at least one of hot water, cold water, or flushing toilets.

First Nations Communities

- First Nations communities rank 68th out of 174 nations when using the United Nations Development Index (2001). This compares to other Canadian communities, which rank sixth.

- Unemployment is greater than 50 percent, and rises to more than 60 percent for those without high school completion.

- First Nations peoples are more likely to require health services than are other Canadians. For example, diabetes among Aboriginals is at least three times the national average, and tuberculosis is eight to ten times more prevalent among First Nations.

- Life expectancy for First Nations men is 7.4 years less, and for First Nations women is 5.2 years less, than other Canadian men and women, respectively.

- These statistics, along with the Residential School Settlement between the federal government and First Nations peoples (estimated at roughly $2 billion), suggest that mistakes of the past continue to hinder the future of Canada's original peoples.

One way in which these statistics could be interpreted would be to see them as evidence that in Canada, despite its commitments to concepts like equality, acceptance, and multiculturalism, there continues to exist two distinct levels of citizenship: the citizenship enjoyed by the cultural and ethnic majority, and a second-tier, second-class citizenship granted to Indigenous peoples. In one of the richest, most advanced nations on earth, people—Canadian citizens—continue to live in conditions better suited to impoverished nations in the developing world. Does this interpretation fit with any of the main theoretical models in sociology?

Sources: Assembly of First Nations. (n.d.). *Royal Commission on Aboriginal People at 10 Years: A Report Card.* Retrieved June 11, 2010, from www.afn.ca/cmslib/general/afn_rcap.pdf; The Residential Schools Settlement Has Been Approved: The Healing Continues. (2010). Retrieved February 13, 2014, from www.residentialschoolsettlement.ca

✦ ⊣Explore

Report Urges 100 Fixes to Stop Native Teen Suicides

As the world's poor continue their struggle for survival, one wonders if they are frustrated by the material excesses displayed in the American media. What must it be like to sit in a community centre in a small town in, say, Zimbabwe and watch an already lucky American win $1 million on *Survivor*? For many people around the world, everyday existence is a struggle to survive, and they are not likely to win anything for their trouble. Some suggest that the only thing holding us back from eradicating global inequality is the feeling that it may be too overwhelming a task to take on (Räikkä, 2004).

BOX 7.4 ISSUES IN GLOBAL CONTEXT

Sex Trafficking

Sex trafficking is a global criminal enterprise that victimizes primarily women and girls, who are forced, deceived, or coerced into what is, in effect, sexual slavery. It is defined as the recruitment, harbouring, transportation, provision, or obtaining of a person for the purpose of a commercial sex act (U.S. Department of State, 2007).

A 2006 United Nations Office on Drugs and Crime (UNODC) report describes human trafficking as a process rather than a single offence: Individuals are abducted or recruited in their country of origin, transported to another country, and then exploited. Human trafficking primarily focuses on the sexual exploitation of women, adolescent girls, and young girls. The UNODC report estimates that between 600 000 and 800 000 victims are acquired each year and delivered to about 137 different countries (UNODC, 2006, pp. 44–45). Tran (2007) estimates that human trafficking is a $13 billion industry worldwide.

The UNODC report notes that the destinations for trafficked victims are usually Western Europe, North America, Western Asia, and Turkey, and that the highest-ranked countries of origin are Belarus, Moldova, the Russian Federation, Ukraine, Armenia, Georgia, Kazakhstan, and Uzbekistan (UNODC, 2006, pp. 28, 102). The destination countries hold all of the power, as their demand drives an international economy to fill it (Desyllas, 2007, p. 58).

Included in the UNODC report are the results of a 2005 study entitled "Trafficking in Women from Romania into Germany (Phase I)." Following is an excerpt.

- Upon arrival in Germany, the victim would be taken to a bar or club and forced into prostitution using psychological or physical violence. She would be subjected to verbal assault, and forced to pay off a debt.

- The money earned would be, in most cases, taken by the trafficker. In a few cases, the victims were allowed to keep half the amount.

- The rotation of victims between cities, such as between Cologne and Dortmund, was quite common. The transfer of women between countries also occurred in order to avoid the risk of deportation if the victim was identified in a police raid.

- In brothels, women underwent constant surveillance through video cameras.

- In some cases, women tried to escape. They were then physically assaulted and threatened by traffickers with harm to their families so as to deter the other women.

- Women were forced to prostitute themselves with numerous clients a day, in some cases the whole week long. Seizure of documents, threats, and psychological and physical violence were used to control the victims. The level of psychological control held by the traffickers over the victims was generally so high that the victims were often not able to act on any opportunity to escape. (UNODC, 2006, p. 66)

It should come as no surprise that the women who fall victim to this treatment are often young, poor, and marginalized by their society; their status makes them susceptible to exploitation. As a sociologist, explore what social factors allow these women to be treated as commodities—to be bought and sold to the highest bidder.

Victims of sex trafficking are often the youngest and most marginalized in society.

Christopher Pillitz/Getty Images

Summary

1 Social stratification is the hierarchical ranking of groups of people according to such criteria as education and wealth. In closed societies, social inequality results when groups of people are ranked according to their ascribed status, such as race and gender. In open, or class, societies, on the other hand, inequities among people stem from achieved status—that is, differences in property and income, occupational prestige, and education.

2 Functionalists recognize that social inequality serves the purpose of attracting highly skilled people to important jobs by offering relatively high rewards. Conflict theorists view social classes as the embodiment of the inevitable struggle between the powerful and the less powerful. Symbolic interactionists look at how people interpret and construct their responses to class inequality, and feminist theorists consider how the patriarchal perspective influences what society deems to be important.

3 The Canadian class structure comprises an upper class, an upper-middle class, a lower-middle class, a working class, and what some refer to as an "underclass."

4 The factors influencing social inequality in Canada are gender, work status, family structure, age, education, visible minority status, and location (urban versus rural, province).

5 Social inequality can be measured for countries across the globe using the Gini Index, which compares a country's cumulative wages and workers to calculate the level of economic equality.

Key Terms

blaming the system *170*
blaming the victim *170*
caste system *171*
class structure *174*
classism *169*
closed system *171*
conspicuous consumption *179*
conspicuous leisure *180*
conspicuous waste *180*
culture of poverty *170*
Davis-Moore thesis *176*
deferred gratification *170*
deindustrialization *170*
double ghetto *181*
feminization of poverty *186*
Gini Index *191*
income *174*

intergenerational earnings *174*
intergenerational mobility *168*
intragenerational mobility *168*
Kuznets curve *191*
Lorenz curve *192*
low income cut-off (LICO) *185*
meritocracy *167*
open system *171*
power *179*
reincarnation *172*
social class *167*
social inequality *168*
social mobility *168*
social status *167*
social stratification *167*
status group *179*
status inconsistency *179*
status symbols *179*
wealth *174*

Reviewing the Concepts

1. What evidence in the chapter confirms that inequality remains a problem in Canada?

2. Review and critique the Davis-Moore thesis.

3. Review Veblen's concepts of conspicuous consumption, leisure, and waste. Do his observations about people's desire to demonstrate their social and economic position still exist today? What examples can you give for each of the three concepts?

4. What are the Gini Index and Lorenz curve and how do they help explore global inequality?

Applying Your Sociological Imagination

1. Thinking back to Genevieve's experiences at the beginning of the chapter, do you think the condition of Canada's homeless is improving or getting worse? What evidence can you provide to support your answer?

2. As a sociologist, what factors might influence a person's chances of moving up or down in the social hierarchy? Discuss.

3. Poverty rates in Canada have been declining over the past 20 years. Do you think this trend will continue? Why? Why not?

4. Compare any two sociological theories and how they explain social inequality. Which explanation do you prefer and why?

MySocLab

Visit MySocLab to access a variety of online resources that will help you prepare for tests and apply your knowledge.

8 Gender

The fact that you are reading this chapter means you are a student in an institution of higher education. What is your major? What are your education plans? What are your career aspirations? What are your plans for your future (or current) family life? While they may seem to be deeply personal pursuits and decisions, we hope that you can see, as a budding sociologist, how your answers to these questions are embedded within contemporary gender relations in Canadian society. For example, if you are a woman, your presence in an institution of higher education represents a hard-won victory by pioneering women who went before you.

If you are a man, perhaps you will challenge prevailing gender relations by entering a female-dominated occupation. If you are a woman, perhaps you will enter a male-dominated field or be voluntarily childless. You may choose to reproduce prevailing gender relations, or perhaps you will both challenge *and* reproduce normative constructions of gender.

Whatever your future pursuits, we hope that you will use your sociological imagination to understand how some of the decisions you make in your life, while feeling very personal, are indeed implicated in larger social relations.

LEARNING OBJECTIVES

By the end of this chapter, students will be able to

❶ Understand the complexity of defining, and distinguishing between, *sex* and *gender*.

❷ Outline the characteristics of the dominant forms of masculinity and femininity.

❸ Understand how gender divisions are produced and reproduced through families, education, and the media.

❹ Explain how our perceptions of our bodies as "gendered" are reinforced through such avenues as self-improvement shows, plastic surgery, and men's sports.

❺ Describe how the labour force is segregated by gender and the reasons underlying the wage gap between men and women.

❻ Understand how gender intersects with race and class to produce social inequality.

❼ Review the major theoretical approaches to understanding gender as socially constructed.

❶ Sex and Gender

People often use the terms *sex* and *gender* interchangeably. Yet each term has a significantly different connotation, so it is important to distinguish between them. We will consider each one in turn.

Those who make a distinction between *sex* and *gender* tend to refer to **sex** as being rooted in biology—that is, the term refers to our physical bodies, whereby we distinguish between female and male. This division of the human population into two categories is a *binary construction,* meaning that it is based on the idea that a given phenomenon can be located within one or the other of two mutually exclusive categories (Nelson, 2006). Categorizing based on binaries thus implies that these groups are diametrical opposites—as depicted by the oft-used phrase "opposite sex" (Nelson, 2006).

In the 1970s, feminist theorists argued that we needed a way to distinguish between biology and the social effects of biological differences. As a result, these theorists began using the term *gender* as a way of directing attention to the social realm. **Gender**, then, refers to the socially constructed characteristics associated with girls and boys, women and men—what we call *masculinity* and *femininity*.

Notice that this concept of gender also suggests only two possible categories. In other words, just as *sex* is understood as a binary opposition between male and female, *gender* is understood as a binary opposition between masculinity and femininity.

Contemporary theorizing, however, has problematized the sex/gender distinction as a false dichotomy. Feminist theorists are now more comfortable with accepting how our understanding of biology and biological "discoveries" is socially shaped. That is, our attempts to understand even our physical bodies—in terms of chromosomes or

sex A determination of male or female on the basis of a set of socially agreed-upon biological criteria.

gender Social distinctions between masculinity and femininity.

> > >

This *New Yorker* cartoon depicts the important distinction between "sex" and "gender"—two concepts often used interchangeably.

V
V
V

"Sex brought us together, but gender drove us apart."

Barbara Smaller/The New Yorker Collection/www.cartoonbank.com

The Duke of Burgundy demonstrates how gender is constructed over both space and time. In seventeenth-century France, being masculine meant wearing frilly shirts, wigs, and powdered makeup. Current Western notions of masculinity clearly differ from this model.
Gianni Dagli Orti/The Art Archive at Art Resource, NY

intersexed individuals
Individuals born with ambiguous genitalia.

hormones, and so on—are laden with ideas of gender; we are unable to dissociate one from the other. Further, any effort to do so denies the social nature of how we understand our biology.

For example, even though biologists are perceived as dealing solely with bodies, they may do so in a way that draws on discourses of gender. Anthropologist Emily Martin (2009) demonstrates how scientists draw on discourses of gender to explain conception—the story of the egg and the sperm. Despite new research that casts doubt on the "aggressiveness" of sperm and the "passivity" of an egg (instead demonstrating a more interactive relationship between egg and sperm), biologists draw on dominant constructions of masculinity (aggressive) and femininity (passive) in their accounts of the fertilization process. Martin (2009) details such gendered presentations of conception (the terms she cites in quotation marks are those used in science textbooks):

> It is remarkable how "femininely" the egg behaves and how "masculinely" the sperm. The egg is seen as large and passive. It does not *move* or journey, but passively "is transported," "is swept," or even "drifts" along the fallopian tube. In utter contrast, sperm are small, "streamlined," and invariably active. They "deliver" their genes to the egg, "activate the developmental program of the egg," and have a "velocity" that is often remarked upon. Their tails are "strong" and efficiently powered. Together with the forces of ejaculation, they can "propel the semen into the deepest recesses of the vagina." For this they need "energy," "fuel," so that with a "whiplashlike motion and strong lurches" they can "burrow through the egg coat" and "penetrate" it. (Martin, 2009, p. 250)

Part of contemporary feminist work, then, is to try to convince biologists that their social assumptions shape their scientific accounts of the natural world. Sex and gender are not distinct; rather, they are intertwined.

THE BIOLOGICAL FEMALE AND MALE?

Further problematizing the sex/gender distinction, and the category of sex itself, is the assertion that our bodies are distinctly female or male. **Intersexed individuals**—those born with ambiguous genitalia—do not fit into either of these categories. Also referred to as hermaphrodites, these people tend to have some combination of male and female genitalia and/or chromosomes (Kessler, 1990).

Consider the case of Maria Patiño, a top woman hurdler who was set to compete for Spain in the 1988 Olympics. The International Olympic Committee (IOC) requires proof of femininity in the form of a doctor's certificate. Patiño forgot her certificate and reported to what researchers refer to as the "femininity control head office" (Fausto-Sterling, 2009, p. 6) to have her cheek scraped for cells that were then tested to prove her female status. A few hours later, she was asked to submit to further examination. Later that day, officials told Patiño that she had failed the test; despite looking like a woman and living as a woman, Patiño was informed that she had a Y chromosome and internal testes and had neither ovaries nor a uterus (Fausto-Sterling, 2009). Patiño was not allowed to compete in the Olympics, as the IOC deemed that she was not a woman.

As a result of the IOC testing and subsequent media coverage, Patiño was banned from all future competition, stripped of her past athletic titles, and evicted from Spain's athletic housing (Fausto-Sterling, 2009). Doctors eventually explained to her that while she had a Y chromosome and testes (and her testes did produce testosterone), her cells did not respond to the testosterone in her body and thus she developed a female shape (breasts, narrow waist, wide hips) (Fausto-Sterling, 2009).

< < <

Stanislawa Walasiewicz (Stella Walsh), pictured here, was an athlete and Olympic gold medallist. Stella presents a challenge to the typical sex/gender dichotomy, as she is an intersexed individual—born with ambiguous genitalia.

Bettmann/Corbis

While not addressing the particularities of intersexed individuals, the IOC has addressed the instance of transsexual athletes and competition. The IOC, in 2004, developed a policy that would allow transsexuals to compete in the Olympics. Athletes must have undergone surgical reassignment, their assigned sex must be legally recognized, and they must have completed hormone therapy for at least two years prior to competition (CNN, 2004).

More recently, a similar controversy surrounded South African runner Caster Semenya's performance at the World Athletics Championships. After her performance, the International Association of Athletics Federations revealed that Semenya had been asked to submit to gender verification tests—to verify that indeed she is "female" (Greenemeier, 2009). In November 2009, South Africa's sports ministry revealed that the results of the gender verification will not be made public. Semenya was able to keep her gold medal for her victory at the World Championships. It was not revealed whether Caster Semenya will be able to compete in the future as a "female" (Longman, 2009). Semenya competed in the 2011 World Championships as well as the 2012 Olympic games (London 2012 Olympics, 2011).

These examples illustrate the social process involved in determining who is a man and who is a woman, and how our social categories of gender render particular bodies as "unintelligible" (Fausto-Sterling, 2009): "A body's sex is too complex. There is no either/or. Rather, there are shades of difference. . . . Our beliefs about gender affect what kinds of knowledge scientists produce about sex in the first place" (Fausto-Sterling, 2009, p. 7).

> > > Thinking Sociologically

From birth, we categorize people on the basis of gender—"Is it a boy or a girl?"—and hence expectations. Go to your local card store and look at the "new baby" section. Count the number of blue cards for boys and pink cards for girls. Now count the number of cards that do not reinforce the binary distinction between girls and boys. Any luck in finding some? How do these neutral cards compare in number to the pink and blue cards? What does this tell you about the social importance of gender?

GENDER AS SOCIALLY CONSTRUCTED

❋–[Explore

Women Not Good at Math? Blame Nurture, Not Nature

gender relations
Organizing principles that shape and order interactions between, as well as the relative social importance of, women and men.

To understand that gender is socially constructed means understanding that ideas about appropriate gender vary across cultures and across time. For example, in seventeenth-century France, to be masculine meant wearing frilly shirts, wigs, and powdered makeup—a view that obviously differs radically from current Western notions of masculinity.

Moreover, **gender relations** act as organizing principles in society—they shape and order interactions between women and men. They also shape the relative social importance and worth of women and men (Cook, 2007). Throughout most of the world, that which is associated with masculinity and men is more highly valued than that which is associated with femininity and women (Cook, 2007; Kimmel, 2004).

Gender also intersects with other organizing principles in society, such as race, class, and sexuality. Of course, women and men are not homogenous groups; our experiences are further shaped by our location within these various social hierarchies. As a result, while there may be *dominant constructions* of masculinity and femininity, in reality there are multiple masculinities and femininities.

❋–[Explore

Condemning Our Kids to Life on Mars or Venus

transgender An umbrella term for a range of people who do not fit into normative constructions of sex and gender.

TRANSGENDER AND TRANSSEXUAL

Transgender is often used as an umbrella term for a range of people who do not fit into normative constructions of sex and gender. The term refers to people who live as the gender they identify themselves as being, with or without sex reassignment procedures. Transgendered individuals include transsexuals, transvestites (including drag queens and drag kings), intersexed individuals, tombois (individuals with female bodies who socially present as men), and those who do not identify themselves as either male or female (Blackwood, 2009; Hines, 2004; Namaste, 2005; Nash, 2008). Some present themselves as deliberately gender incoherent, which, as Bobby Noble (2006) argues, is a form of resistance to dominant constructions (and expectations) of gender.

The 1970s and 1980s gave rise to *transsexualism,* which in the early 1970s became a diagnostic term—meaning that it appears in medical discourse as a pathology, or something in need of treatment (Devor, 2005). The term **transsexual** is often used as a more precise category to encompass those individuals who undergo sex reassignment (some use the term *sex realignment*), which can include facial reconstruction surgeries, genital reassignment surgery, and hormone treatments (Hines, 2004). The terms *preoperative*, *postoperative*, and *nonoperative* refer to whether an individual has undergone or is waiting to undergo sex reassignment surgery. Some people reject the transsexual label because of its connection to medical discourse; these people instead prefer the terms *transman* or *transwoman* (Hines, 2004). *Transvestites*, in contrast, engage in cross-dressing (publicly, privately, or both), but unlike transsexuals, they do not necessarily identify as another gender.

transsexual A person who undergoes sex reassignment, which may include surgeries.

Today there is a growing academic field called trans studies. Many disciplines, including sociology, geography, anthropology, history, law, philosophy, and psychology, are represented within the field (Browne & Nash, 2010; Weiss, 2004). Some of the work that academics are pursuing includes exploring the experiences of trans people (including their experiences on particular sites, such as university campuses); asking whether transgender is understood as being part of the LGBTQ (lesbian, gay, bisexual, trans, questioning) community; exploring the existence of a range of genders (asking whether there are genders beyond masculine and feminine); questioning whether people who do not undergo sex reassignment surgery can be called transgender; exploring the consequences for transpeople of social relations organized within a framework of a gender binary; and exploring the tensions between trans theorizing and queer theory (Ellis, 2009; Nash, 2008; Sanger, 2008; Weiss, 2004).

② Dominant Forms of Masculinity and Femininity

While there is no single form of masculinity or femininity in Western societies, there are, nonetheless, culturally dominant forms—and these are known, respectively, as hegemonic masculinity and emphasized femininity (Connell, 1987). Hegemonic masculinity and emphasized femininity are complementary. We turn now to look at how each is socially constructed.

HEGEMONIC MASCULINITY

Our views of masculinity are constructed through multiple social relationships—ourselves, others, and the social world (Kimmel, 2001). **Hegemonic masculinity** is the normative ideal of masculinity that men are supposed to strive to achieve. Although it is not necessarily the most prominent form of masculinity, it is the one that is most socially endorsed. The notion of *hegemony,* or dominance, derives from Italian theorist Antonio Gramsci, whose work we discussed in Chapter 3. Despite how it sounds, the term actually does not imply force but, rather, a large measure of *consent.* The maintenance of hegemony, then, requires men's and women's participation in sustaining images of the ideal masculinity (Connell, 2002).

In North American culture, hegemonic masculinity is associated with the traits of aggressiveness, control, strength, drive, ambition, and not valuing women; in other words, it is constructed as the opposite of everything that is feminine (Connell, 1987; Prohaska & Gailey, 2010). Hegemonic masculinity is also associated with whiteness, heterosexuality, and the middle class (Connell, 1987).

This prevailing notion of manhood requires men to be successful, capable, and reliable—"a man *in* power, *with* power, and *of* power" (Kimmel, 2001, p. 29). The very definition of such manhood, or masculinity, helps some men to maintain power over other men as well as over women (Kimmel, 2001).

Hegemonic masculinity is irrevocably tied to heterosexuality (Connell, 2002; Kimmel, 2001), which acts as a veritable precursor for defining masculinity in Western societies.

hegemonic masculinity **The normative ideal of dominant masculinity.**

Globe Photos/ZUMA Press, Inc./Alamy

< < <

The character of James Bond (played by Daniel Craig) is an example of hegemonic masculinity—the normative ideal of masculinity that men strive to achieve. In North American culture, hegemonic masculinity is associated with aggressiveness, strength, drive, and ambition.

> > >

Audrey Hepburn (being channelled here by Jennifer Love Hewitt in a photo shoot) is an example of emphasized femininity, which is based on women's compliance with their subordination to men's interests and desires. Like hegemonic masculinity, emphasized femininity is a normative ideal that women strive to achieve.

Archives du 7e Art/Photos 12/Alamy

Kimmel argues that *homophobia* is central to our definition of masculinity and is much "more than the irrational fear of gay men"; it is also the fear that "men will unmask other men," emasculate them, and reveal to the world that they do not measure up to the ideal construction of masculinity (Kimmel, 2001, p. 35).

This fear of being unmasked leads to shame and silence. In turn, men become complicit in the subordination of women and of other men (Kimmel, 2001). This occurs, for example, when men fail to intervene when other men make sexist or racist jokes, when they turn a blind eye when a woman is harassed on the street by other men, and when they join in the laughter that follows gay-bashing jokes. In these ways, men's fear of being revealed as frauds ("not man enough") results in the continued perpetuation of gendered behaviour and stereotypes (Kimmel, 2001).

EMPHASIZED FEMININITY

emphasized femininity **The normative ideal of femininity, based on women's compliance with their subordination to men.**

Connell (1987) uses the term *emphasized femininity* to contrast with hegemonic masculinity. **Emphasized femininity** is based on women's compliance with their subordination to men and is oriented to obliging men's interests and desires (Connell, 1987). Stiletto heels, for example, are an enduring signifier of emphasized femininity (Kelly, Pomerantz, & Currie, 2005). Defined at the level of social relations, emphasized femininity is the most culturally valued form of femininity. Like hegemonic masculinity, emphasized femininity need not be the most prevalent form of femininity; rather, it is understood as the ideal that women should try to achieve.

Characteristics associated with emphasized femininity include "supportiveness, enthusiasm and sexual attractiveness" (Grindstaff & West, 2006, p. 500). For example, in their research on cheerleading, Laura Grindstaff and Emily West demonstrate how femininity is "performed" in concert with athleticism. Female cheerleaders are expected to dress in ways that emphasize their femininity—they wear short skirts and form-fitting tops (often with stomachs bared) and tie up their long hair with ribbons, all of which suggests a blend of "youthfulness and sexual availability" (Grindstaff & West, 2006, p. 509). One cheerleader commented that the coaches police appearances: "We're told to be in full makeup, to do our hair. Because we're performing. If you're not wearing lipstick, that's the first thing [the coach] will say to you, 'why isn't your lipstick on?'" (Grindstaff & West, 2006, p. 509). Cheerleading is an excellent example of a "performative" emphasized femininity—one that is performed particularly for heterosexual men (Grindstaff & West, 2006).

Other research suggests that girls and women who are involved in athletics often practise apologetic behaviour (Davis-Delano, Pollock, & Vose, 2009). In North American culture, sport is often aligned with masculinity. Girls and women involved in sports will "apologize" for their participation in a masculine realm, therefore, by practising an emphasized femininity (Davis-Delano, Pollock, & Vose, 2009).

❸ Reproducing Gender: Families, Education, and Media

FAMILIES

Gendered expectations begin at birth, after the proclamation of whether a baby is a girl or a boy. Family, friends, and co-workers who flock to see a new baby girl are often loaded down with pink balloons, pink flowers, and teddy bears wearing pink ribbons and pink frilly dresses. Within hours of giving birth to a girl, a hospital room can be transformed to such an extent that one wonders if a can of pink paint has exploded. The same ritual by colour is found after the birth of boys, except that people bring blue balloons and blue clothes, with nary a dress in sight. Think about your forays into toy stores. Toys are organized into "toys for girls" and "toys for boys"—often with signage using pink and blue.

Such gendered interactions do not stop there. Parents' child-rearing practices are deeply gendered. For instance, research finds that mothers respond more quickly to the cries of their baby girls than they do to the cries of their baby boys (Kimmel, 2004). This speed of response is most likely connected to our ideas about gender and emotion—that girls are more emotional and so it is okay for them to cry, whereas boys should not cry (think of the phrase "big boys don't cry"). In the first six months of life, boys are more likely than girls to be held, rocked, and kissed, but this situation reverses after six months, when girls receive more physical touch (Kimmel, 2004). Further, research on mothers' interactions with their children illustrate that mothers encourage independent and self-initiating behaviour from their sons while encouraging more relational behaviour from their daughters (Lovas, 2005). From a sociological perspective, we can theorize that this practice has to do with normative constructions of gender—the idea that boys and men are to be more independent than girls and women.

Studies also show that parents tend to spend more time talking to little girls while leaving boys alone, and they punish their sons more often than they do their daughters (Armstrong, 2004). Girls often receive toys, and then choose to favour toys that reinforce the stereotypical role of care-taker (dolls to dress and care for, nursing kits, and so forth) (Francis, 2010). Barbie dolls and kitchen sets, complete with accessories, adorn girls' rooms, while boys are more likely to have toys that involve action, such as toy cars, video games, and sports equipment (Francis, 2010). Interestingly, research documents that at an early age (around 2 to 2.5 years), boys are just as interested in playing with dolls and dollhouses as are girls. Yet parents' negative reactions and redirections to more *masculine* toys communicate to boys that it is gender-inappropriate

> > > Thinking Sociologically

Have you ever stopped to consider why professional women's basketball is known as the WNBA (Women's National Basketball Association) while the men's league is known just as the NBA (as opposed to the MNBA)? Have you noticed that when women athletes are featured in sports magazines they are often presented as sex symbols as opposed to athletes? What does this tell you about gender relations?

Lawrence Manning/Spirit/Corbis

< < <

Gendered expectations begin at birth, where new baby girls are bombarded with all things pink and boys with all things blue. Such gendered interactions continue throughout child rearing.

for them to be interested in such toys (Kimmel, 2004). These very toys, and parents' practices, encourage the reproduction of hegemonic masculinity and emphasized femininity—boys as active and girls as passive.

Later, boys and girls take on gendered household tasks at the behest of their parents: Boys take out the garbage and shovel the snow while girls do dishes and wash floors (Armstrong, 2004). These child-rearing practices work to reinforce notions that there are gender-appropriate behaviours for girls and boys.

EDUCATION

((•—[Listen

Is There a Link between Gender Inequality in Education and the Gender Typing of Work?

As will be explored in more detail in Chapter 12, rather than acting as the great equalizer between boys and girls and men and women, schools remain a gendered space and experience (Webber, 2010b). The hierarchical organization of schools (wherein men tend to dominate), interactions between teachers and students, and curricular materials all contribute to normative constructions of masculinity and femininity. Through a hidden curriculum (see Chapter 12), girls continue to learn that they are not as important as boys. Such learning can affect their self-esteem and occupational aspirations.

Moreover, as will also be discussed in Chapter 12, the increasing number of Canadian women graduating with university degrees has yet to translate into wide occupational rewards. Women continue to earn less than their male counterparts with comparable levels of education, and remain poorly represented in the top positions of power hierarchies (Webber, 2010b).

Student–Teacher Interactions As also discussed in Chapter 12, both male and female teachers tend to interact more with the boys in their classes than they do with the girls (Abbott, Wallace, & Tyler, 2005; deMarrais & LeCompte, 1999; Renzetti & Curran, 1999; Skelton, 1997). For example, boys are praised more by their teachers when they successfully complete a task, whereas girls tend to be applauded for presenting an attractive appearance or for being quiet (Nelson, 2009). Teachers also tend to praise girls for being "congenial" and "neat," while they more often praise boys' work for its intellectual quality (Renzetti & Curran, 1999). These types of gendered interactions may contribute to the promotion of girls' dependence and boys' independence (Webber, 2010b).

This work of reproducing masculinity and femininity also affects teachers themselves. For example, research on male teachers

> > >

Girls often receive toys that reinforce caretaking actions, such as dolls or kitchen sets. Boys, on the other hand, tend to receive video games and sports equipment.

Manfred Baumann/IGG Digital Graphic Productions GmbH/Alamy

BOX 8.1 ISSUES IN GLOBAL CONTEXT

Female Genital Cutting or Female Genital Mutilation?

The surgical altering or injuring of female genitals—known as either female genital cutting (FGC) or female genital mutilation (FGM)—is a highly contested subject. In fact, which term you use more or less locates your position in the debate over this practice.

Those who use the term *female genital cutting* tend to approach the debate from a cultural standpoint (although some do use it as a general term that is not meant either to condone or to condemn the practice). They try to understand FGC from a viewpoint within the practicing culture. They ask questions: Why is FGC practised? What are its social and economic benefits? What are its health consequences? What are the consequences of not undergoing the procedure? Those who use the term *female genital mutilation,* on the other hand, hold the view that it is mutilation and represents a violation of a girl's or woman's human rights (World Health Organization [WHO], 2008, 2010a, 2013). The fact that those who take this approach tend to be from the West constitutes an example of Edward Said's concept of Orientalism (see Chapter 3). That is, a culture of non-Westerners is evaluated from a Western standpoint and characterized as barbaric; in this particular case, virtually all of Africa is demonized.

Today, approximately 140 million girls and women worldwide have undergone FGC, and the practice is most prevalent in African countries (where approximately 101 million girls over the age of 10 have undergone FGM (WHO, 2010a; 2013). The procedure typically takes place between infancy and age 15 (WHO, 2008). People who practice FGC have a range of cultural beliefs about it—for example, it may be seen as preserving a family's honour, a girl's virginity, and her marriageability (Women's Health Bureau, 2000). Anthropologist Harriet Lyons (2007) encourages us to take a polythetic approach to understanding genital surgeries rather than the more monothetic approach that has been characterized by white Western feminists who see these surgeries as solely about sex or control. Taking a polythetic approach means understanding that there are multiple meanings associated with FGC, both sexual and nonsexual (Lyons, 2007).

Those who practice FGC also believe that it protects girls and women against disease and improves feminine hygiene (Women's Health Bureau, 2000). The World Health Organization, however, adamantly declares that not only does FGM have no health benefits, it results in such harmful consequences as increased risk of recurring infections, cysts, infertility, and complications with future childbirth (WHO, 2008; 2013).

While FGC is illegal in Canada, as it is in most other Western countries, it is practised in at least 40 countries worldwide, 30 of which are in Africa (Scott, Schwartz, & VanderPlaat, 2000; Women's Health Bureau, 2000; WHO, 2013a). Other countries known to practice FGC are in the Islamic Mideast, India, Southeast Asia, Malaysia, Indonesia, and South America (Scott, Schwartz, & VanderPlaat, 2000, p. 161).

We encourage you to read the articles published in a special issue of the journal *Africa Today* (2007, Volume 53, Issue 4) that is dedicated to exploring FGC from a range of perspectives, including those that support these surgeries and those that seek their eradication. Search for a recent news item concerning female genital cutting or female genital mutilation. Identify from which perspective the article is written. What arguments are included in the article to either support or criticize the practice? Evaluate the strength of the arguments made.

in a boys-only school found that these teachers actively negotiate their masculinities (Martino & Frank, 2006). They speak of feeling the need to establish themselves as embodying a "normalized heterosexualized masculinity" (Martino & Frank, 2006, p. 22). For example, a male teacher of art (a subject area that goes against dominant assumptions about what is appropriate for men) drew on his position as a football coach in order to assure his students of his heterosexual masculine identity (Martino & Frank, 2006).

The "Chilly Climate" Gendered patterns of interaction do not happen only in elementary and secondary schools, but also persist in institutions of higher education. In the United States, Roberta Hall and Bernice Sandler (1982) wrote the first report that documented faculty members' often unintentional but differential treatment of men and women students. They coined the phrase "chilly climate" (also discussed in Chapter 12) to represent women's experiences on university campuses. There is a cumulative effect when people experience even small instances of inequity, so these micro processes of power really do matter. Faculty members call on male students more often (even when female students have their hands raised) and engage more with male students during classroom interactions (e.g., praising, criticizing, providing feedback). At the same time, women's issues, such as violence against women, are downplayed or trivialized. Recent studies continue to find that women experience a "chilly" climate in their college and university classes (Tatum, Schwartz, Schimmoeller, & Perry, 2013).

A group of faculty members from the University of Western Ontario, calling themselves the Chilly Collective, published an edited collection called *Breaking Anonymity: The Chilly Climate for Women Faculty* (1995). The impetus for this project was one woman's experiences during her first year as a member in the faculty of law at Queen's University, where she encountered overt harassment, exclusion, and devaluation of her worth and intellectual capabilities (Chilly Collective, 1995).

MEDIA

Gender divisions are reflected in and reinforced by all forms of media. From children's books and movies to programming directed at teens and adults, from advertisements for cars to those for the hottest new clothing trends, and from country ballads to rap and hip hop, we are continually bombarded with masculine and feminine imagery.

For many years, researchers have understood that depictions of gender in the media have the capacity to create and reinforce normative constructions of femininity and masculinity (Armstrong, 2004; Lauzen, Dozier, & Horan, 2008; Nelson, 2009; Smith, Pieper, Granados, & Choueiti, 2010). Historically, hegemonic masculinity and emphasized femininity have been embodied by portrayals of white men as aggressive, physically competent leading characters, and white women as beautiful, nurturing, and docile. Current depictions do little to alleviate such gender-typing (Smith, Kennard, & Granados, 2011). And these depictions are linked with age. Have you ever noticed that men's romantic interests in movies stay about the same age, even as the male actor ages (Wade, 2013)?

Television Shows Even though women are increasingly portrayed in leading roles on prime-time television, with shows focusing completely on their lives (e.g., *Army Wives, Pretty Little Liars, Desperate Housewives*), many female characters remain manipulative, using helplessness or seduction to get their way, and are shown as willing participants in their own objectification (Basow, 1992; Kim et al., 2007; Kramer, 2005). In fact, media critics have debated whether strong female characters (as seen in *Xena: Warrior Princess* or *Buffy the Vampire Slayer*) actually represent progressive roles (Kramer, 2005). Buffy is a vampire slayer—she is strong, has many skills, and relies on her friends when she needs help—yet is still a young, beautiful, heterosexual woman.

While there are many examples of current television shows in which women play strong leading characters (*Cougar Town, Rookie Blue, Criminal Minds, Private Practice,* and *Grey's Anatomy,* among others), the actors who star in these shows are beautiful, most of the characters are heterosexual, and, with a few exceptions, the leading women are white.

Gender and race intersect in media depictions of women and men. While white men tend to be portrayed as heroes, black men tend to be portrayed as frightening, scary characters (Kramer, 2005; Matthews & Beaman, 2007). White women are beautiful and docile, while black women are constructed as welfare queens or aggressive with bad attitudes (Kramer, 2005; Matthews & Beaman, 2007). Even on shows that are heralded as progressive, like *Buffy the Vampire Slayer*, the main characters remain steadfastly white. In Candra Gill's (2007) exploration of race in that series, she finds that despite its positive portrayal of a female heroine, the show was conventional in its treatment of race. However, in its seventh and final season, the writers finally took up the issue of race and racism. After one nonwhite woman is mock-killed in training, her character, responding to a question about why she died, replies ironically, "'Cuz the Black chick always gets it first" (Gill, 2007, p. 249).

The reality television trend, which has pervaded our airwaves for more than a decade, is but one example of the ways in which media shower us with normative images of men and women and masculinity and femininity. One need only watch one or two episodes of *America's Next Top Model, Big Brother, The Biggest Loser, The Bachelor* and/or *The Bachelorette, Survivor,* or *The Amazing Race* to see how reality television reinforces normative gendered constructions; glorifies competitive, cutthroat behaviour; promotes an ethic of individualism; and effectively deceives audiences into thinking that what they are watching is unfiltered, real, and unedited, while in reality these shows are heavily edited (Brancato, 2007; Waddle, 2006). The women in these shows tend to be depicted as whiny, emotional, and manipulative backstabbers, whereas the men tend to be portrayed as tough and interested in women, sex, and drinking.

Television Commercials Commercials also contribute to the reproduction of particular forms of masculinity and femininity. Research on toy commercials reveals that boys are more clearly associated with competitive play and playing outdoors while girls are shown playing inside a home in more cooperative play scenarios (Kahlenberg & Hein, 2010). At the adult level, consider the ads aired during the Super Bowl, one of television's most-watched events. Researchers studying these ads found four dominant gender themes:

1. Advertisements for alcohol primarily construct men as "losers" who hang out with their male buddies, self-mock, and are ironic about their loser status.

2. Male friendships are the centre of most of the ads.

3. Men in these ads are not in committed relationships and are always ready to engage in sexual activity with fantasy (and, hence, unattainable) women.

4. The women in these ads are dichotomously depicted either as "hotties" (sexualized fantasy objects who often humiliate the men) or as "bitches" (wives or girlfriends who undermine men's freedom to enjoy male bonding). (Messner & Montez de Oca, 2005)

Commercials such as these reinforce the notion that average men cannot pursue beautiful women, and that if they attempt such pursuits, the women will embarrass them (Messner & Montez de Oca, 2005). In contrast, the nonfantasy women (the wives or girlfriends) are depicted as wanting to capture men for a commitment and limit their freedom (Messner & Montez de Oca, 2005).

Talk Shows "Trashy" talk shows (think *Jerry Springer*) have come under much scrutiny for their portrayals of lower-class masculinities and femininities (that is, linked to being loud and crass and behaving badly according to middle-class standards). Yet, while we do not see many transgendered characters in mainstream television shows or movies, we may see real transgendered people on talk shows. Producers parade these gender nonconformists for high ratings, of course, but agreeing to be on such shows actually increases the visibility of trans people (Gamson, 2007). Their presence on television talk shows challenges the previous silence around what is and is not acceptable content. In this way, the boundaries of normality are challenged (Gamson, 2007).

Historically, girls and boys often used separate school entrances and playgrounds and were educated in separate classes, where they were taught different subjects.
Bailey-Cooper Photography/Alamy

Companies make millions of dollars a year selling beauty to individuals. Their media compaigns encourage women to strive for "fantasy woman" status by using their beauty products to remain attractive and youthful.

Blue Images/Ivy/Corbis

Despite some progressive movement in media characters (with strong heroines and such unlikely heroes as Homer Simpson), gender depictions in the media continue to reproduce normative constructions of gender (Armstrong, 2004; Nelson, 2009; Smith, Kennard, & Granados, 2011).

❹ Gendered Bodies

A good way to discern gender as a social practice is to examine gender and our bodies. How we present our bodies, our efforts to shape them, and how we interpret others' bodies—these acts are all accomplished socially (Bordo, 1993). How we feel about our bodies and how we adorn and display them are influenced by societal messages about how a feminine or masculine body should both look and feel (Bordo, 1993; Ricciardelli, Clow, & White, 2010). Companies make millions—or even billions—of dollars a year selling beauty through diet products, muscle-building supplements, cosmetics, surgeries, and fashion to both men and women, who in turn attempt to live up to quite unattainable representations of femininity and masculinity.

TELEVISION PROGRAMMING

Entire television networks are directed at helping individuals achieve unrealistic beauty ideals. While networks such as The Learning Channel (TLC) also focus on other capitalist pursuits, such as having the ideal home or becoming wealthier through real estate ventures (*Flip that House, Property Ladder*), a large portion of their programming is directed at achieving the normative feminine or masculine appearance. Programming such as *What Not to Wear, 10 Years Younger, Makeover Train,* and *Big Medicine* fill TLC's programming schedule, with the emphasis in each being on improving one's physical appearance (getting it as close to the normative ideal as possible). And one does not need to look far to

< < <

Researchers studying television advertisements for alcohol that air during the Super Bowl often construct men as losers who hang out with their male buddies and engage in self-mockery.

see other such shows being aired on competing networks: examples are *Queer Eye for the Straight Guy* and *The Biggest Loser*. These are programs that focus on self-improvement through style makeovers and body modification. These programs convey the message that moulding one's appearance to more closely resemble dominant constructions of femininity and masculinity will also lead to a better sense of self. In other words, these shows do not just make the participants look better, they make them feel better. The message is clear though: There is an "ideal"—take the outcome of the 15th season of *The Biggest Loser*. The winning contestant, Rachel, was praised throughout the season for continually dropping weight and winning weekly competitions up until the final "reveal." She began the season at 260 pounds and weighed in during the finale at 105 pounds. Immediately after the airing of the finale, the critiques of her and the show appeared in the news and on social media—did she go *too* far? To what degree is the show responsible for what some are labelling an "unsafe" weight? Is it fair to dangle a prize of $250,000 in people's faces as a motivation to lose weight?

PLASTIC SURGERY

Plastic surgery has become normalized as an individualized strategy to achieve a more culturally dominant feminine or masculine appearance in order to become more successful; thus, many people believe that having plastic surgery will lead to true happiness and self-fulfillment. Both men and women are submitting themselves to popular notions of what constitutes a perfect body based on narrow constructions of ideal bodies depicted in popular culture (Turner, 2004).

While feminists have long critiqued plastic surgery, arguing that people need to accept their gendered bodies rather than submit to narrow, rigid patriarchal constructs of femininity and masculinity, some individuals argue that this form of body modification can be understood as empowering (Heyes, 2007; Tait, 2007). Indeed, reality television shows actually draw on feminist notions of empowerment to portray cosmetic surgery as a way to remedy one's troubled psyche by aiding the unhappy to become happy and self-fulfilled: "Facial and bodily features which are culturally reviled become increasingly contingent: 'ugliness' becomes our choice and responsibility" (Tait, 2007, p. 127). In this way, women's liberation is achieved at an *individual* level of transformation, rather than by questioning and transforming larger societal notions of appropriate gendered bodies (Tait, 2007).

According to the International Society of Aesthetic Plastic Surgery (IASPS), as of January 2012 Canada ranked 15th of the top 25 countries for number of aesthetic surgeries performed (the United States is still number one) (ISAPS, 2012). Worldwide, breast augmentation surgeries are no longer the most frequent surgery performed (although breast augmentation surgeries are the most popular plastic surgery in Canada); rather, liposuction (surgical removal of excess body fat) has taken the lead. Breast augmentations, blepharoplasty (eyelid lift), rhinoplasty (nose reconstruction), and abdominoplasty (tummy tuck) round out the list of top surgeries performed. Botox, laser hair removal, and autologous fat injections (taking fat from one location and transferring it to another) topped the list for nonsurgical procedures. Women overwhelmingly remain the primary consumers of these cosmetic procedures worldwide (IASPS, 2012).

Whereas these procedures are generally aimed at conforming to the ideals of femininity and masculinity, female professional athletes and body builders, in contrast, are often viewed as *rejecting* notions of femininity by conditioning their bodies in ways that make them resemble men's bodies. Although one might argue that a hyper-muscular female body builder is actually an example of subversion, the practice of body building remains structured by traditional notions of femininity and masculinity. Breasts, for instance, are a gender marker. Body building transforms the fat of breast tissue into muscle, and thus women body builders lose this obvious feminine marker. As a result, many of the women get surgical breast implants so that they display an appropriate feminine appearance (Schippert, 2007). Despite the fact that body builders need to lose every ounce of body fat and excess water for competition day, breasts for women are viewed as a requirement (Schippert, 2007). Indeed, makeup and hairstyles are also required in order for a woman body builder to be considered appropriately feminine (Schippert, 2007).

MEN'S BODIES AND THE NFL DRAFT

Men's bodies are not immune to such normalization. After all, the muscular, athletic body is a Western cultural ideal—and the epitome of hegemonic masculinity (Oates & Durham, 2004; Ricciardelli, Clow, & White, 2010). The annual NFL draft is an interesting site for analysis, as it is "arguably the most prominent [event] in American male culture—male bodies are catalogued, classified, ranked and valued via an extensive and complex system of quantification" (Oates & Durham, 2004, p. 302). Doctors measure each player's height, weight, and hand size and estimate body fat percentage. Each player undergoes a series of questions and tests designed to determine his health, with one popular measure being the Cybrex score, a quantified measurement of the strength and power of each leg's muscles (Oates & Durham, 2004). Based on the results of these measurements, as well as a series of other tests, each player is assigned a numerical value that conveys his perceived worth to prospective teams (Oates & Durham, 2004).

An analysis of the NFL draft reveals an interesting relationship between athletic men's bodies and race. Oates and Durham (2004) argue that the draft's statistics on "useful bodies" is profoundly implicated in the exercise of power, in that the physical tests to which the potential draftees submit produce an overall measurement of each player's worth. This process of measurement transforms the athletes' bodies into commodities (Oates & Durham, 2004). In the case of the NFL draft, it is mainly black men's bodies that are turned into commodities for overwhelmingly white male owners and coaches (Oates & Durham, 2004).

Masculinity is afforded a privileged position over feminin-ity in our society. If we simply consider body ideals, we can see this process at work, in that men are encouraged to take up more physical space than women (muscles for men versus slender ideal for women). Yet in the case of the NFL draft, other axes of power are involved. Oates and Durham (2004, p. 319) remind us of the classic post-structuralist formulation of a gaze: "Men look at women. Women watch themselves being looked at." In other words, whoever gazes has power over the object of this gaze. In the NFL draft, both gazer and gazee are men; however, the relations of power hold (Oates & Durham, 2004). The gazers (owners and coaches) are privileged in terms of both race and class. Thus, the NFL draft reinscribes both racial and class hierarchies (Oates & Durham, 2004).

In summary, then, our bodies do not sit outside social relations. Rather, our daily practices with regard to how we present our bodies, how we wish our bodies looked, and how we evaluate others' bodies are embedded in social constructions of masculinity and femininity and thus embedded in relations of power.

>>> Thinking Sociologically

What are some of the bodily practices that you engage in to communicate your gender identity to others? Do you diet and exercise to achieve the ideal image of masculinity or femininity? How much time do you spend each day on your appearance in terms of making it feminine or masculine (shaving, doing your hair, choosing an outfit, and so forth)?

Gender and Work

The greatest change in Canada's labour force since the 1960s has been the dramatic increase in the number of employed women, in particular married women with children (Nelson, 2009). Whereas in 1901, only 14 percent of women were employed in the formal labour market (Luxton & Corman, 2005), by 2009 that number had soared to 58 percent of women aged 15 and older (compared with 72 percent of men)—represent-ing 48 percent of the total labour market (Ferrao, 2010). According to Statistics Canada, the first six months of 2009 marked the first time ever that more women than men were employed in the paid labour force (Monsebraaten, 2009). By 2009, 76 percent of women 25 and older were employed in the for-mal labour market. This enormous growth in women's labour force par-ticipation resulted from inflationary pressures that require higher family incomes, the decline of the manu-facturing sector, the growth of the service sector, and changing gender expectations.

Yet despite these changes, the labour force is characterized not only by gender segregation but also by a gender-based wage gap. Let us look at each of these in turn.

< < <

During World War II, women filled job positions in sectors that would otherwise be male dominated.

Fred Ramage/Hulton Archive/Getty Images

THE GENDERED LABOUR FORCE

While the legal framework is in place to enable women to succeed on equal terms with men, we have not yet seen drastic changes in employment stratification. Studies consistently find that gender interacts with social class in two important senses: It provides the ground for segregating occupations into men's and women's jobs, and women hold more lower-paying positions than men in the labour force (Li, 1992).

For men, industrialization brought movement out of agriculture but relative stability in the manufacturing sector (which has since become much more unstable). For a large percentage of women, however, industrialization has meant a shift from unpaid domestic labour to combining this labour with paid employment in the service industries (Boyd & Myles, 1991). However, although women dominate numerically in the service sector, they are rarely supervisors and managers of men (Boyd & Myles, 1991; Robertson, 2002).

The changes in the structure of the labour market have also resulted in a greater proportion of part-time workers. The Canadian labour force saw an increase of more than 100 percent in part-time workers between 1976 and 2000 (Nelson, 2009), and women are consistently overrepresented in nonstandard, precarious employment, both in Canada and globally (Nelson, 2006; Monsebraaten, 2009; Young, 2010). While many women *choose* to work part-time (wanting flexible hours), 23 percent of working women state that they work part-time because they are unable to locate full-time work (Almey, 2009). While nonstandard work is helpful for women who want to combine paid work with child-rearing responsibilities, it is also detrimental for women because remuneration for part-time work is often lower than full-time wages (Stier & Mandel, 2009). In a 2003 labour force survey, 39 percent of women reported that they work part-time due to family obligations, compared with fewer than 5 percent of men (Nelson, 2006). In 2006, one in five women reported working part-time due to personal or familial responsibilities (Almey, 2009). Women tend to work part-time throughout the life cycle, whereas for men, part-time work is associated with their youth and initial entry into the labour market (Comfort, Johnson, & Wallace, 2003).

Child-rearing and other family responsibilities are most often cited as reasons for women's part-time work (Almey, 2009; Comfort, Johnson, & Wallace, 2003). Generally, women leave work for at least short periods of time to bear children, and often for longer periods to rear their children full-time. This discontinuity in employment is one of the greatest barriers faced by professional and nonprofessional women alike. Impressions about one's commitment to work, current earnings, lifetime earnings, opportunities for advancement, and future employability are all greatly influenced by interruptions in one's career (Nelson, 2009). Women who work in male-dominated industries (e.g., manufacturing, construction, engineering, finance) are more likely than women in other occupations to never marry or to remain childless (Marshall, 1984; Mason & Goulden, 2004). These women find that their co-workers and bosses are quite intolerant of the difficulties women face in trying to combine full-time paid work and child-rearing responsibilities (Wolf-Wendel & Ward, 2003).

THE GENDERED WAGE GAP

✸ Explore

Male vs. Female Salaries by Occupation

Paid work influences gender relations and is implicated in many tensions associated with them (Nelson, 2009). The employment conditions that most women face, as well as the structural barriers to obtaining and sustaining careers, have the potential to make workplace participation less appealing and less rewarding for them than for men.

The gendered wage gap has been found to exist in all occupational categories (Nelson, 2009). Women have, however, made some gains in nontraditional occupations. For example, McMullen, Gilmore, and Le Petit (2010) report that in 2006 women experienced some gains in architecture, marketing and advertising, and physical sciences. Women also accounted for 15 percent of all police and fire fighters in 2006; while this is not a substantial portion, the number is up 10 percent in just one decade (McMullen, Gilmore, & Le Petit,

BOX 8.2 WHY SHOULD WE CARE?

The Feminization of Poverty

Statistics Canada uses a measure called the low income cut-off (LICO) to determine poverty levels. Falling below this cut-off point means that a family is spending a larger proportion of its income on the basic necessities of life (food, shelter, and clothing) than an average family spends (see Chapter 7). When calculating the LICO, Statistics Canada takes into account both family size and geographic location (community size). For example, in 2009, the LICO for a family of four living in an urban setting (population between 30 000 and 99 999) was $29,089 (Statistics Canada, 2010e).

Sociologists note that poverty is a gendered phenomenon. More women than men live in poverty in Canada (Collin and Jensen, 2009). Because women disproportionately live in poverty, sociologists call this the feminization of poverty (also discussed in Chapter 7). Women continue to have much higher poverty rates than men, although this gap has lessened in recent years (CFAIA/CLC, 2010).

Women are consistently the poorest of the poor. Unattached senior women and female-headed lone-parent families have high rates of poverty (Hay, 2009). Many Canadian children also live in poverty. Poverty, then, is not just a women's issue: It is a social issue. In 2010, 550 000 Canadian children (under the age of 18) lived in poverty (Statistics Canada, 2010d). Some of the consequences of living in poverty are poor-quality food and health (less expensive foods tend to be lower in nutritional value), reliance on social assistance (welfare), and homelessness (Harman, 2005).

Select one theoretical perspective and explain through that lens how it is that poverty is gendered.

2010). But, despite substantial gains in earnings during the past two decades, women still earn much less than men. In 2002, women working in full-time, full-year positions earned an average of $36 000, while employed men working the same schedule earned $50 500 (Statistics Canada, 2003b). According to Statistics Canada, in 2009, women working full-time in full-year employment earned on average 75 percent of what men earned (Statistics Canada, 2011d). This gendered wage gap is even larger for university-educated women, who earned only 63 percent of what university-educated men earned in 2007. This represents a slight increase from 61 percent in 1998 (CMEC, 2010). Additionally, Aboriginal women and minority women earn less money than white women (Luxton & Corman, 2005; Collin & Jensen, 2009).

The wage gap can be explained by such factors as occupational segregation (women and men being employed in different employment sectors), the undervaluing of women's work (paying women less than men for working in the same positions), the restructuring of women's work by privatization and outsourcing, and the lack of affordable, quality childcare (limiting women's choices for employment) (Fleras, 2009).

> **>>> Thinking Sociologically**
>
> How is gender implicated in your career goals? For example, do you want a career in a traditionally female-dominated or male-dominated profession?

FAMILIES AND UNPAID WORK

Our families represent one of the key environments in which gender relations are produced and sustained. In Canada, by the age of 45, 97 percent of women and 96 percent of men have

Explore

Men and Women's Participation in Housework

lived in a union or raised children (Beaujot, 2000). Although the majority of marriages in the 2000s include two income earners rather than a lone male breadwinner, domestic labour is still overwhelmingly performed primarily by women while men remain the primary decision-makers (Nelson, 2009). Gender, then, remains an organizing principle in heterosexual marriages and unions. While little research exists on same-sex families and domestic labour, Patterson, Sutfin, and Fulcher (2004) found that the lesbian couples in their study were more likely to share both paid and unpaid labour. Rather than using structural issues (hours in paid labour force) as the predictor for how labour was divided (as it was for the heterosexual couples in the study), the lesbian couples approached the division of labour on a more ideological basis that encompassed their ideals of what a division of labour ought to look like.

Given that, on average, women make about 70 percent of what men make, one argument as to why housework remains primarily women's work concerns the imbalance in their economic contribution to the household. This argument is the basis for the **exchange theory**, which suggests that power in a relationship is influenced by the resources that a partner brings to a relationship (Bittman et al., 2003). Thus, economically-based relationship power influences who does what chores around the house. Researchers, using data from Australia and the United States, tested this theory and found that women do indeed decrease their housework as their earnings increase, right "up to the point where both spouses contribute equally to income" (Bittman et al., 2003, p. 186).

After this "equal" point, women earning *more* money than their male partners may compensate by performing more of the domestic labour and child-rearing responsibilities than their partners. Indeed, as women provide more income than their male partners, researchers found that the women's unpaid domestic labour actually increases per week by about five to six hours (Bittman et al., 2003). So, earnings do not seem to translate necessarily into reduced domestic labour responsibilities for women who contribute between half of a family's earnings to all of the family's earnings (Bittman et al., 2003); gendered expectations are present regardless of paid employment.

Men who remain at home performing the majority of child rearing or who actively participate in unpaid domestic labour risk having their masculinity judged and questioned—by themselves and by others. Fathers who raise their children are scrutinized for their decision to be, and action as, primary caregivers as opposed to the more normative role of primary wage earners (Doucet, 2004, 2007). In a qualitative study of 70 stay-at-home fathers in Canada, Andrea Doucet (2004) reveals that each father interviewed felt negatively judged by his peers for taking on caring work rather than being the family's earning partner. As a strategy to protect their masculinity, the majority of the men in Doucet's study engaged in some form of part-time work such that they would have something that was understood as meaningful to talk about with other men. The men in this study felt a loss of masculinity as a result of taking on the caring work for their children. Even in situations where normative categories of gender are disrupted, then, men and women still work hard to live up to hegemonic masculinity and emphasized femininity.

In sum, women who earn more money than their male partners attempt to address this disruption in gender relations by increasing their contribution to their household's domestic duties, while men who stay at home to parent proactively take on part-time work and home renovations to assert their masculinity (Bittman et al., 2003; Doucet, 2004, 2007).

exchange theory The assertion that power in relationships is influenced by the resources that a member brings to the relationship.

Racialized women are one of the most disadvantaged groups in Western society. The sex worker pictured here undoubtedly experiences disadvantages based on the intersectionality of her gender, race, and social class position.
Per-Anders Pettersson/Getty Images

intersectionality ❻
The simultaneous influence of multiple social relations, including race, gender, ethnicity, and class.

Intersectionality: Gender, Race, and Social Class

Gender, class, and race all function as mechanisms for the production of social inequality (Acker, 2006; West & Fenstermaker, 2002). One cannot experience gender without simultaneously experiencing race and class. Thus, an **intersectional** analysis of inequality

< < <

Gender relations are produced and sustained within families where women remain primarily responsible for domestic labour. A man taking active responsibility for the day-to-day care of children is not common in heterosexual families.

incorporates the complex relationship between race, gender, ethnicity, and class (and other social axes) in shaping social outcomes (Fleras, 2009).

As was outlined in the section on bell hooks in Chapter 3, the principles of gender equality can, at times, run up against the claims of racialized groups. That is, although women as a group may share some common experiences because of male dominance—for example, disadvantage in terms of power or privilege—all women are not equally and similarly disadvantaged. Some assert that racialized women are one of the most disadvantaged groups in Western societies, owing to their location within a predominantly "pale-male" world (Fleras, 2009). As one psychologist put it, while white women are increasingly present on the floors of powerful corporations, racialized women are still seen mopping those same floors (Hurtado, 1996).

Women of colour, immigrant and refugee women, and Aboriginal women not only face many of the same problems as racialized men but are variously disadvantaged because of gender (Fleras, 2009). An intersectional approach, then, is key to understanding the complex experiences of how relations of gender, race, and social class work together to position some individuals as privileged and others as disadvantaged (Fleras, 2009).

 Watch

Race, Class, and Gender

Racialized women are subordinated due to their position in relation to white women; in their own minority group communities, they are subordinated due to their position in relation to minority men (Jiwani & Young, 2006). Racialized women are thus exposed to greater dangers in the workforce as a result of their marginalization in low-paying, insecure jobs, which can include prostitution and the sex trade, and they are at increased risk of being victims of violence (Fleras, 2009; Jiwani & Young, 2006).

Taking an intersectional approach, then, means acknowledging the complexity and messiness of reality. This approach allows us to see that our experiences of masculinity and femininity are not homogenous but, rather, are fractured along other axes of power (Cook, 2007).

BOX 8.3 ISSUES IN GLOBAL CONTEXT

● Gender Equality

According to the World Economic Forum's 2012 report on global gender equality, Canada ranked 21st out of 135 countries (more than 90 percent of the global population), down from 20th in 2010 and 18th in 2011. Iceland (first), Finland (second), Norway (third), and Sweden (fourth) were the highest-ranking countries, with Syria (132nd), Chad (133rd), Pakistan (134th), and Yemen (135th) comprising the lowest-ranked countries (WEF, 2009). The World Economic Forum (WEF) argues that women's position vis-à-vis men's within a nation influences the growth or development of that nation. The WEF report examined the gap between women and men in the following areas: educational attainment, economic participation and opportunity, political empowerment, and health and survival.

Canada ranked 12th in terms of economic participation and opportunity. This category examines the labour force participation rates of men and women; women's incomes as a ratio of men's earnings; the proportion of women who are legislators, senior officials, and managers; and the proportion of women who are either professionals or technical workers (WEF, 2012).

Canada ranked 70th in terms of educational attainment, scoring 0.9909 out of a possible 1.0 (indicating that there is very little meaningful separation among the highest-ranking countries on this measure). This category measures the literacy of women compared to men, as well as women's access to all levels of education (WEF, 2012).

Canada ranked 38th in terms of political empowerment. Important here is the fact that Canada's score, out of a possible 1.0, was only 0.1959. So, while Canada did rank 38th, this is actually our country's poorest score on all of the measures. This category examines the gap between women and men in political decision-making positions. The length of time that women have served as prime minister over the past 50 years is also factored in (WEF, 2012).

Canada ranked 52nd in terms of health and survival, but it is important to note that the score was 0.9780 out of a possible 1.0, so again there is very little meaningful separation between many countries. Men's and women's life expectancies and years of expected good health, as well as the sex ratio at birth, are captured in this category (WEF, 2012).

Among these global rankings, gender equality is positively correlated with economic development. That is, richer countries are more gender equitable than are poorer countries. As a result of these types of rankings, countries are encouraged to be aware of the continuing challenges posed by gender inequality and to enact social change to eradicate gender disparities (WEF, 2007).

The 2012 Gender Gap Report (WEF, 2009) can be accessed at http://www3.weforum.org/docs/WEF_GenderGap_Report_2012.pdf

Using your sociological insight, why might Iceland, Finland, Norway, and Sweden be at the top of this list?

❼ Sociological Approaches to Gender

Watch

Sociological Perspectives on Gender

In this section, we discuss some of the major theoretical approaches to the study of gender. You will notice differences in the approaches as some perspectives focus on the roles that women and men play in society, while others focus on inequalities that arise from our practice of differentiating between women and men.

FUNCTIONALISM

Most sociologists criticize approaches that view gendered behaviour as inevitable or as somehow natural, arguing that these behaviours are socially produced. As you will recall from earlier chapters, functionalists maintain that human societies are composed of interrelated parts, with each part serving a function that helps to maintain equilibrium in the whole. Consequently, as will be discussed in Chapter 11, functionalists argue that women and men perform separate, distinct, specialized, and complementary roles to maintain cohesiveness within families and in wider society.

According to functionalists, men fulfill an instrumental role: Through their paid labour in the public sphere, they provide the money for food, shelter, and other necessities as well as make decisions for the family unit. Women are positioned as fulfilling the expressive role, in that they provide emotional support and nurturance for all members of the family unit (Parsons & Bales, 1955). According to this perspective, such well-defined roles reduce confusion and conflict in the family unit regarding gender expectations and also ensure that societal tasks are fulfilled (Nelson, 2009).

Women, who are primarily responsible for rearing society's next generation, are understood as being key in reproducing the moral fabric of society. Such a conservative approach also holds women directly responsible for changes in gender relations (such as women entering the paid labour force or fighting for social equality with men) that may disrupt the smooth functioning of family life. According to the functionalist perspective, upsetting the supposed natural order in this way may result in higher crime rates, illicit drug use, and incidents of violence—all because women are not at home to provide care (Gilder, 1986).

CONFLICT THEORY

As you will recall from earlier chapters, conflict theorists assume that societies are characterized by struggles between various social groups for scarce resources, including power, wealth, and prestige. For many theorists, using conflict theory to examine gender means redefining Marx's concept of class to refer to groups identified by sex and/or gender (Nelson, 2009). Conflict theorists who take up gender tend to focus their attention on how gender affects one's control of, and access to, scarce resources.

For example, Engels argued that in capitalist societies, private property produced gender stratification (Kimmel, 2004). He asserted that a capitalist economy gave rise to private property, and as such, lines of inheritance became important. If a man was going to be able to bequeath his wealth to his heir (that is, his son), he required a way to ensure that his heir was actually *his* (Kimmel, 2004). As such, the nuclear family, monogamous marriage, and men's control of women's sexuality emerged from this need, in capitalist societies, to ensure paternity. The nuclear family also works to sustain men's dominance over women (Kimmel, 2004). Monogamous marriage, as an institution, developed out of a need to ensure paternity in order to determine inheritance rights, thus having little to do with notions of romantic love.

SYMBOLIC INTERACTIONISM

Symbolic interactionists are interested in the *meanings* of male and female and of masculinity and femininity. They argue that gender is created through social interaction, mainly through the mechanism of role-taking. In this way, people learn contrasting expectations about gender on the basis of their perceived sex.

According to this perspective, children learn gender-related behaviours through social institutions, such as families, schools, peers, and mass media. The process is based on *operant conditioning*, whereby positive reinforcements increase socially gender-appropriate behaviours while negative reinforcements decrease behaviours deemed to be socially inappropriate.

This approach has been criticized for not theorizing social change and for presenting individuals as empty and passive recipients of socialization rather than as active beings (Francis, 2006). Responding to these critics, Candace West and Don Zimmerman (1991) introduced the idea of gender as an accomplishment—something that we "do." "Doing gender," as they put it, means that we actively create the differences between girls and boys—and that any differences we see are not natural, nor are they essential, or biological. We "do" gender through social interaction—when we display ourselves as a member of a gender. As West and Zimmerman (1991, p. 16) state, "gender is not a set of traits, nor a variable, nor a role, but the product of social doings of some sort." We can each "do" gender somewhat differently while still adhering to normative expectations of femininity and masculinity.

Once gender differences are socially constructed, they can actually be used to fortify what gets understood or labelled as "the essentialness of gender" (West & Zimmerman, 1991, p. 13). That is, we end up taking these constructions for granted—so much so that we no longer see them as an outcome of social interaction or social relations; rather, we assume that gender differences are firmly based in biology (West & Zimmerman, 2002). These gender constructions can then become institutionalized in ways that make them appear normal and natural. We see, for example, that women's washrooms have different fixtures and different trimmings (think more mirrors in the women's bathroom), which works to reinforce the notion of differences between genders. Yet when we look to the privacy of most homes, there is no difference in fixtures—men and women both use a toilet (as opposed to a urinal for men) (West & Zimmerman, 2002). Using different kinds of equipment to accomplish the task of relieving oneself is offered as a "natural" outcome of sex differences, but instead the variation in equipment actually *produces* differences between women and men (Goffman, 1977).

FEMINIST THEORY

Although there are many different strands of feminism, they tend to share a basic premise: that men and women in all societies are valued and treated differently and inequitably. Many women experience conditions of subordination and oppression, conditions that are neither

> > >

Skater girls demonstrate the performativity of gender as well as the possibility of enacting alternative femininities.

Shutterstock

natural nor inevitable (Nelson, 2009). Thus, gender is viewed as a socially constructed concept that has significant and at times negative consequences in the lives of both men and women. Feminists, then, endeavour to identify the ways in which institutionalized and internalized gendered norms can limit women's behaviours and opportunities. Feminist theorizing is typified by the statement "Biology is not destiny." Since women's oppression is socially produced, it follows that there is hope for social change.

More contemporary feminist work takes an intersectional approach in its analysis of how gender, race, class, and so forth simultaneously produce relations of privilege and relations of subordination. It also seeks to explore the multiplicity of femininities and masculinities.

For example, skater girls studied by Kelly, Pomerantz, and Currie (2005) saw themselves as enacting an alternative femininity. Engaging in skateboarding includes taking physical risks and persevering through injuries, while engaging in skateboarding culture includes wearing clothes associated with skater culture as well as shunning "girly" practices. One skater girl related how she responded to her mother's distaste over her baggy clothing and androgynous look: "She'll go out and buy me shoes, but they'll have the heels on them. I cannot stand the heels" (Kelly, Pomerantz, & Currie, 2005, p. 230). Another participant also mentioned high heels (an iconic image of emphasized femininity): "I can skate in a heel. I have done it, and it hurts. You can't land an ollie [a skateboarding move] properly in heels, but I have done it" (Kelly, Pomerantz, & Currie, 2005, p. 230).

POST-STRUCTURALIST THEORY

Drawing on the work of Michel Foucault, post-structuralists understand people as positioned within, and produced by, *discourse* (as discussed in Chapter 3) (Francis, 2006). Gender discourses position all people as either men or women—and these categories are relational (Francis, 2006). Using such an approach, masculinity and femininity and even sex itself are understood as being socially and discursively constructed.

Judith Butler (1997) is the key theorist associated with this approach. She argues that although feminists rejected the idea that biology is destiny, many developed an understanding of patriarchal culture that positioned masculine and feminine genders as inevitable. Butler argues instead that there is no essential basis to gender, nor is there some authentic femininity or masculinity that is rooted in female or male bodies. Butler asserts that gender can be viewed as a performance: "there is no gender identity behind the expressions of gender. . . . [I]dentity is performatively constituted by the very 'expressions' that are said to be its results" (Butler, 1990, p. 25). In other words, gender is your performance of gender at particular times and in particular spaces rather than some universal, coherent notion of "who you are."

You may be asking yourself what the difference is between West and Zimmerman's symbolic interactionist approach of "doing gender" and Butler's approach of gender as performance. The major difference between them is their treatment of the self (also called the *subject* in post-structuralist theorizing). While symbolic interactionists argue that a relatively coherent, stable self (your sense of who you are, the *real* you) underlies social interactions, post-structuralists argue that there is no coherent or essential self behind our performances—our identities are fragmented, contradictory, and always in flux. According to post-structuralists, our "performances" are driven by discourses of power that shape the limits and possibilities for the construction of our identities. Gender is but one of these performances.

Gender Equality and Social Change

Was Hillary Clinton's run for the Democratic presidential candidacy a sign that times are changing in North America? Is gender equality now an attainable vision? While Canada has made some important progress toward gender equality, the journey is not complete. As we have seen throughout this chapter, persistent inequalities remain in relation to the wage gap between men and women, responsibility for housework and childcare, and the normalization of particular bodies.

We have laws that prohibit discrimination on the basis of gender. Yet normative gender constructions remain powerful in Western society, where girls and women are still encouraged to reproduce socially defined perceptions of femininity and boys and men are still encouraged to be aggressive and live up to the ideals of hegemonic masculinity. Overcoming such normative constructions of gender is easier said than done, since gendered ways of being have been institutionalized and continue to be reproduced through our social interactions.

Summary

1 Whereas the term *sex* is often used to refer to our physical bodies, either male or female, *gender* refers to the socially constructed characteristics of masculinity and femininity. Yet both divisions rely on binary, either/or constructions. The male/female opposition is complicated by the existence of intersexed individuals, and even our attempts to understand our physical bodies are laden with ideas of gender. The masculinity/femininity opposition is also complicated by the multiplicity of gendered behaviours.

2 The dominant forms of masculinity and femininity are called, respectively, *hegemonic masculinity* and *emphasized femininity*. In Western society, both are normative ideals, in that they are held up as something to which men and women should aspire. The former is associated with aggressiveness, strength, drive, and ambition, while the latter is associated with obliging men's interests and desires.

3 Gender divisions are reproduced through families from birth, and are sustained through child-rearing practices that differ according to the sex of the child. In schools, curricular materials and student–teacher interactions tend to underline traditional gendered expectations of girls and boys. All forms of media further reinforce normative constructions of femininity and masculinity.

4 How we present our bodies is influenced by societal messages about how a feminine or masculine body should look. These messages are conveyed through, for example, self-improvement television shows as well as the normalization of plastic surgeries, such as liposuction and facelifts. And men's bodies are not immune to societal expectations, either: Professional sports, for example, commodify male athletes' bodies according to masculine ideals.

5 Gender segregation in the labour force is evident in the large percentage of women who work in low-paying jobs in the service industries and in the prevalence of women in part-time work. Reasons for the continuing wage gap between men and women include the undervaluing of women's work and the lack of affordable childcare. The fact that domestic labour is still performed primarily by women in heterosexual relationships is attributable partly to women's lower economic contribution to the household and partly to gendered expectations.

6 Gender, race, and class often work simultaneously to produce social inequality. For example, while women may be similarly disadvantaged as a result of masculine privilege, minority women are variously disadvantaged in a white-dominated, classist society. An intersectional approach takes into account how these different axes of power can combine to heighten societal disadvantage.

7 Functionalists tend to hold women responsible for any change in traditional gendered roles that would disrupt family and societal cohesiveness; conflict theorists examine gender stratification in light of men's need to subordinate women to ensure paternity and hence the line of inheritance; symbolic interactionists view gender-related behaviours as learned through socialization; feminist theorists view gender as a socially constructed concept that has detrimental consequences for women; post-structuralists view gender as a performance, not by a stable self but by identities that are continually in flux.

Key Terms

emphasized femininity *204*
exchange theory *216*
gender *199*
gender relations *202*

hegemonic masculinity *203*
intersectionality *216*
intersexed individuals *200*
sex *199*
transgender *202*
transsexual *202*

Reviewing the Concepts

1. How do intersexed individuals (such as Maria Patiño and Caster Semenya) complicate common understandings of sex?

2. How do proponents of cosmetic surgery draw on feminist notions of empowerment? Would feminists be comfortable with this kind of empowerment argument?

3. How might functionalist theorists respond to women's strides toward equity with men?

4. How is gender portrayed on television in contemporary shows? Does the gender presentation vary by the show's genre?

Applying Your Sociological Imagination

1. In what ways has your family been influential in the development of your femininity or masculinity?

2. How can bodily practices associated with femininity and masculinity be understood as constraining?

3. Do you think that the government should financially compensate people for domestic labour? How might such a plan be organized? What are some of the challenges of implementing such a system (standards of cleanliness, for instance)?

4. Review and discuss how gender is socially constructed. Be sure to use your own examples to supplement your answer. How are hegemonic masculinity and emphasized femininity part of the social construction of gender?

MySocLab

Visit MySocLab to access a variety of online resources that will help you prepare for tests and apply your knowledge.

9 Sexualities

If you engage in a particular sex act, does this dictate your sexual identity? How is your sexual identity determined? Is there a connection between sexual acts and sexual identities? To what degree is there a connection? Are you open to considering that social norms constrain your sexual behaviours and identities?

In this chapter, we address the social construction of sexualities. We argue that sexualities are fluid—they are not fixed. One's sexual identity can change over time. Further, this chapter explores the close connection of gender with sexuality. Consider the gendered consequences around those who have many sexual relations: Men are often applauded as "studs" while women are often cast as "sluts".

By the end of this chapter, students will be able to

❶ Understand how sexuality is socially constructed.

❷ Review a range of sexual identities: homosexuality, heterosexuality, bisexuality, pansexuality, and asexuality.

❸ Outline a variety of sexual relationships: monogamy, serial monogamy, non-monogamy, and polyamory.

❹ Analyze the complex relationship between gender and sexuality through an examination of the sexual double standard.

❺ Describe theoretical approaches to sexuality.

❻ Outline sexual health issues—sexually transmitted infections, safe sex practices, and sex education—as socially shaped and as having social implications.

❶ The Social Construction of Sexualities

Did you think about why this chapter is entitled "Sexualities" as opposed to "Sexuality"? We are beginning from the premise that there are multiple sexualities and that we need to recognize such multiplicity. But what is sexuality? And why are sociologists interested in this private matter? We challenge you to consider whether your sexuality is really all that private. We also challenge you to think about why, despite there being a wide range of possible sexualities, heterosexuality is the dominant form of sexuality in North American culture.

Sexuality includes your sexual orientation (who you are attracted to sexually), your sexual identity (butch, femme, heteroflexible, queer, straight, genderqueer), and sex acts (masturbation, bondage, kissing, oral sex, barebacking, penetration). Sexuality also includes our sex lives (polyamory, monogamy, infidelity, age of consent) and the commodification of sex (prostitution, pornography). Sexual politics (activism, family values, homophobia, heteronormativity) are also a part of sexuality, as are reproductive politics (abortion, adoption), and sexual violence. Our bodies are also part of sexuality (orgasm, erection, circumcision, sexually transmitted infections, Viagra).

◉⊸Watch

What is "Social" about Sexuality?

As sociologists, we are interested in all of the above, particularly in examining how our understanding of these aspects of sexuality is socially constructed (Steele, 2005a). These meanings are embedded in our language, laws, popular culture, social rituals, and even medical definitions (Weeks, 2009). We learn what is deemed socially appropriate and inappropriate through our interactions with others and our culture. Understanding sexuality as a social construction, then, means understanding that the meanings of sexual desires and sexual acts, as well as which sexual expressions

> > >

Sex acts, such as kissing, are included in an understanding of sexuality.

Alamy

have social approval and which are disavowed, are all socially organized (Seidman, 2010). Moreover, these meanings are fluid; they change over time and from culture to culture.

Consider the kiss. Do you think that kissing is a natural act? In North American society, we associate kissing with romance and sex, as well as with affection. We also use the kiss for nonsexual purposes, including "greeting and farewell, affection, religious or ceremonial symbolism, deference to a person of high status" (Tieffer, 2005, p. 25). We grow up watching a range of kissing practices in television shows and movies (the peck, the French kiss). So would it surprise you to learn that anthropological researchers have found several societies in which sexual kissing is unknown? These societies include several from Oceania (Balinese, Chamorro, Manus, Tinguian), Africa (Chewa, Thonga), South America (Siriono), and Eurasia (Lepcha) (Tieffer, 2005). In these cultures, mouth-to-mouth kissing is deemed disgusting, unsafe, and unhealthy (Tieffer, 2005). According to anthropologists, Thonga individuals in Africa laughed when they first witnessed Europeans kissing, and said, "Look at them—they eat each other's saliva and dirt" (Tieffer, 2005, p. 24). Therefore, while kissing involves parts of our bodies, its meaning and practice are shaped by our culture.

❷ Sexual Identities

sexual identity A broad term that can include our masculinity or femininity, our knowledge of our bodies, our sexual histories, and our sexual preferences.

Sexuality is basic to our identity and, hence, to our way of life. **Sexual identity** is a broad term that can include our sense of self as masculine or feminine (our society recognizes only these two alternatives), our knowledge of our bodies (function, pleasure, pain), our sexual histories, and our sexual preferences (or orientation). We convey our sexual identity through, for example, how we speak about our sexual attractions and how we interact with others. Identities, then, are what Michel Foucault called *disciplinary*: They are not biological realities but, rather, are produced socially and maintained through continuous performance. Only some identities are socially recognized, yet many exist nonetheless, which demonstrates that some people actively resist disciplinary power.

Part of our identity is, of course, our **sexual orientation**, which refers to an individual's sexual and emotional attraction to a person of a particular sex. We now look at five sexual identities: homosexuality, heterosexuality, bisexuality, pansexuality, and asexuality.

HOMOSEXUALITY

People with a **homosexual** identity are sexually attracted to, and engage in sexual activities with, members of the same sex. Historically, homosexuals have been closeted and subjected to systemic oppression. Such oppression was legitimated through medical and legal practices (McAndrew & Warne, 2010; Weststrate & McLean, 2010). Despite significant shifts in both social attitudes and legal status, heterosexism and homophobia still exist in our society. **Heterosexism** is the practice of holding up heterosexuality as the ideal and normal sexuality, rendering all other sexualities as abnormal and deviant.

Homophobia is an irrational fear or hatred of homosexuals; homosexuality is considered deviant, abnormal, and thereby punishable. Homophobia can lead to discrimination, harassment, and violence against homosexuals. Homophobic discourses are often expressed through language that constructs gay men as promiscuous, oversexed, and effeminate, and lesbians as manly or butch. Homophobia also has the effect of asserting heterosexuality in public spaces. For example, in research on homophobic harassment in American schools, the words *faggot* and *dyke* are found to be used routinely against lesbian, gay, bisexual, transgendered, and questioning (LGBTQ) students as well as against heterosexual students (Pettett, 2007). Such harassment can lead to anxiety, depression, isolation, and even suicide (Doolin, 2010; McAndrew & Warne, 2010; Pettett, 2007).

The Emergence of Homosexual Identities As discussed earlier, lesbian and gay identities are, like any other sexual identity, socially produced. In countering what he sees as the myth of the "eternal homosexual," social historian John D'Emilio (2005) emphasizes the distinction between homosexual *behaviour* and the development of homosexual

sexual orientation
An individual's sexual and emotional attraction to a person of a particular sex.

homosexual **An individual who is sexually attracted to members of the same sex.**

heterosexism **The holding up of heterosexuality as the ideal and normal sexuality, rendering all other sexualities as abnormal and deviant.**

homophobia
An irrational fear or hatred of homosexuals that can lead to discrimination, harassment, and violence against them.

< < <

The emergence of homosexual identities can be attributed to the creation of social spaces where individuals could express their desires following the Industrial Revolution. Pictured here are young gay men at La Caverne, a Soho bar and nightclub, in 1955.

Joseph McKeown/Stringer/Getty Images

identities. He argues that lesbian and gay identities are a product of the social changes that came about first during the Industrial Revolution and later in the early part of the twentieth century.

Prior to industrialization, the family was a unit of both production and consumption—men, women, and children all farmed, and women used the materials produced by the farm for the family's consumption. Everyone worked interdependently to ensure the family's survival (D'Emilio, 2005). However, with the advent of the Industrial Revolution—and the wage labour to which it gave rise—the family was no longer needed as a self-sufficient household economy and instead became primarily responsible for the emotional satisfaction of its members separate from the "public world of work and production" (D'Emilio, 2005, p. 217). Moreover, as rates of wage labour increased, children were no longer required to work on family lands.

Taken together, these changes in the family (which are discussed in greater detail in Chapter 11) paved the way for sexuality to become dissociated from a procreative imperative (D'Emilio, 2005). By helping to separate sexuality from procreation, capitalism helped to create conditions that allowed some women and men to arrange private lives around their erotic and emotional attractions to members of their own sex (D'Emilio, 2005). As a result of these changes, it became possible for lesbians and gay men to establish gay communities (mainly in urban spaces) and, later, to establish a sexual identity–based politic through the gay liberation movement (D'Emilio, 2005).

However, initially, there were no public social spaces in which to take such attractions and preferences and carve out a way of life for one's self—in other words, to create an identity (D'Emilio, 2005). It was only in the early part of the twentieth century that this sexual identity truly began to emerge.

The Gay Liberation Movement In North America, gay men and lesbians began to congregate in social spaces in the 1920s and 1930s as gay and lesbian bars opened in large cities. A gay subculture concretized during the 1950s and 1960s, allowing increasing numbers of gay men and women to find other homosexuals more readily than had previously been possible (D'Emilio, 2005). The publishing world took notice of the emergent gay and lesbian world and produced newspaper and magazine articles and novels depicting lesbian and gay male life (D'Emilio, 2005).

Gays and lesbians were nonetheless subjected to oppression, much of it state sanctioned—including the criminalization of homosexual acts, a ban in the United States against employing lesbians and gay men in the federal government (implemented by President Eisenhower), and increased police surveillance in the name of morality (D'Emilio, 2005). This oppression led to the gay liberation movement of the 1960s (D'Emilio, 2005).

The 1969 Stonewall Riots in New York City are considered to be the pivotal point marking the start of the gay liberation movement (Weststrate & McLean, 2010). On June 27 of that year, New York City detectives raided the Stonewall Inn, a gay bar in Greenwich Village. They required patrons to produce proof of age and then escorted those who appeared to be cross-dressers to police vans waiting outside.

During other raids, once at the vans, the men would be examined to verify their sex, as well as to determine whether they would be charged with any criminal offences. On this night, though, displaced patrons did not leave the scene immediately, as was typical during other raids. Instead, a crowd gathered on the street. As some of the cross-dressers struggled with the police who were taking them to the vans, members of the crowd shouted their support (Marotta, 2006). When an individual was able to break free from one of the police vans, the crowd shouted its support again. Soon, the crowd began to taunt the police officers and eventually threw rocks, bottles, and bricks at them. As the detectives retreated inside the Stonewall Inn, the crowd gained momentum, broke the bar's windows and doors, and experienced a "surging sense of power at having challenged and intimidated long-feared authority

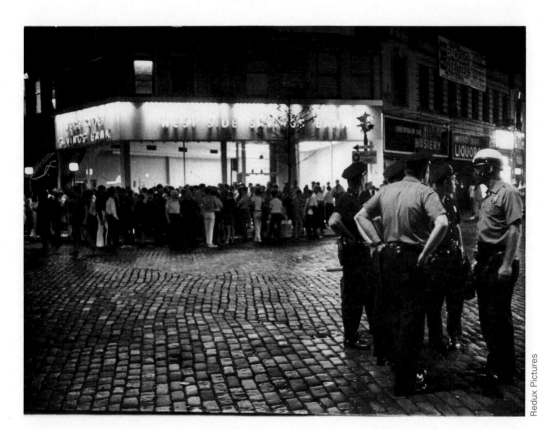

<<<

The 1969 Stonewall Riots are heralded as the pivotal point marking the start of the gay liberation movement. Here, we see a disturbance in Sheridan Square, NYC, with police standing vigilant as crowds gather.

Redux Pictures

figures" (Marotta, 2006, p. 35). The street demonstration continued for three nights and was dubbed the Stonewall Riots.

This demonstration was indeed epochal. It sparked "a chain reaction of community-building and political organizing that was emulated across the country and publicized throughout the world. Overnight this unprecedented surge of organizing transformed what had been a largely underground vanguard movement into a highly public mass movement for gay pride, power, and community" (Marotta, 2006, p. 35).

In Canada, the first gay rights demonstration took place in Ottawa in August 1971, when demonstrators from across the country demanded civil rights from Parliament (Smith, 1998). Until only two years earlier, homosexual sex acts had been included in the Criminal Code (D'Emilio, 2005, p. 216), and the demonstration was part of an organized attempt to further legitimize gay and lesbian identities. While the achievement of equality rights was of prime importance, the gay social movement also helped to create both gay communities and gay political identities (Smith, 1998).

Today, gays and lesbians can claim many victories; for example, as will be discussed in Chapter 11, gay marriages are now legal in Canada as well as in several other countries, such as the Netherlands, Belgium, South Africa, Portugal, Iceland, and Spain.

HETEROSEXUALITY

Heterosexuals are individuals who are attracted to and/or engage in sexual activities with members of the opposite sex. As the dominant (accepted) sexuality in Canadian society, heterosexuality is more than an individual identity—it also represents a norm and a socially approved role (Katz, 2005). As a social construct, heterosexuality is reinforced coercively through what Michel Foucault termed *surveillance*; that is, we police

heterosexual An individual who is attracted to members of the opposite sex.

our own and others' sexualities, granting approval to some while disparaging others. For example, how many times have you heard homophobic remarks like "you fag" or "you queer"? Heterosexuality is also reinforced through the organization of society and through propaganda, which can include media images, religious teaching, and school curricula (Renold, 2006).

As with any other identity, heterosexuality comes in multiple forms and means different things to different people. You can practise heterosexual monogamy or heterosexual non-monogamy. You may be very "girlie" in your heterosexuality or may be a "manly man." The meaning and social organization of heterosexuality vary across time and location, although the term first appeared only in the late 1800s (Katz, 2005). Dr. James Kieman of Chicago is said to be the first North American to have used the word *heterosexual*, in a medical journal article in 1892 (Katz, 2005). Kieman, however, defined heterosexuals by their mental condition—one of "hermaphroditism," which included the symptom of "inclinations to both sexes" (Katz, 2005, p. 53). He also understood these people to have inclinations to "abnormal methods of gratification," meaning that they were interested in experiencing pleasure from sexual activity rather than engaging in it solely for procreation (Katz, 2005, pp. 53–54). As you can see, the meaning of a word can certainly change over time. Kieman's use of *heterosexual* is quite different from our contemporary understanding of the word.

In Western societies, heterosexual desires tend to be organized around marriage or other long-term relationships and monogamy. Heterosexuals enjoy social privilege because heterosexuality is constructed as *the* normal sexuality (L. Allen, 2007). It is privileged as both normal and natural, and is simultaneously prevalent and invisible. Social interactions, language, and social institutions are all organized according to heterosexual norms (Renold, 2006). Heterosexuality also acts as the dominant standard against which all other sexualities are measured and compared.

Many feminist sociologists argue that sexuality and gender are inextricably linked. That is, those who assume a heterosexual identity are often understood as having simultaneously established a so-called normal gender identity (Seidman, 2010). Gender deviance or variance is thus assumed to be a sign of homosexuality. Such an assumption leads people to cultivate identities of *masculine* men and *feminine* women to avoid being mislabelled as homosexual (Seidman, 2010).

BISEXUALITY

bisexuality Being attracted to both women and men.

As a sexual identity, **bisexuality** includes individuals who are romantically and/or sexually attracted to both men and women; it also tends to be linked with non-monogamy (Klesse, 2005; Rodríquez Rust, 2000). Bisexuals tend not to be equally attracted to both sexes simultaneously, and those identifying as bisexual may shift between heterosexual and homosexual relationships over their lives. Bisexuality challenges the notion that heterosexuality and homosexuality are mutually exclusive and oppositional categories (Klesse, 2005). As such, bisexual individuals tend to be constructed as individuals in perpetual conflict.

When a bisexual individual is in a monogamous relationship, his or her sexual identity as bisexual is perceived by some to be destabilized (Klesse, 2005). This is because powerful discourses limit what can be understood as bisexuality and who can be considered bisexual—that is, those who "maintain relationships to people of both male and female genders at the same time" (Klesse, 2005, p. 448). Therefore, "authentic bisexuality" is understood as always happening within a non-monogamous context (Klesse, 2005, p. 448). While participants in Klesse's UK research on bisexual-identified women reject such a narrow definition of bisexuality, they nevertheless experience the effects of such a powerful discourse. They find it difficult to sustain a bisexual identity when they are not (or imagine that they may not be) engaged in relationships with both women and men. These findings demonstrate mono-gramy's destabilizing effect on bisexual identities.

BOX 9.1 WHY SHOULD WE CARE?

Transgender Day of Remembrance

Transphobia refers to discrimination directed toward transsexuals or transgendered individuals (McKenzie, 2004). (See Chapter 8 for a discussion of trans people.) It includes verbal harassment and/or physical violence (stemming from fear and/or hatred) as well as more subtle discrimination, such as lack of access to resources like medical and legal services (Bauer et al., 2009; McKenzie, 2004). The 1993 murder of Brandon Teena (a female-to-male transsexual) in Humboldt, Nebraska, is perhaps the most widely known instance of transphobia in North America. The film *Boys Don't Cry* (1999) and the documentary *The Brandon Teena Story* (1998) both document Teena's life and murder (McKenzie, 2004). While violence directed toward trans people is the most publicized and researched form of transphobia, other forms of discrimination occur—such as being fired from one's employment or being denied housing (Lombardi, 2009; Stotzer, 2009).

Karen Struthers/Shutterstock

Transgender is an umbrella term used to describe a range of people who do not fit into normative constructions of sex and gender; this category includes transsexuals, transvestites, intersexed, and those who do not identify themselves as either male or female.

The Transgender Day of Remembrance commemorates the lives of all those killed due to transphobia. Originating in San Francisco in 1999, the Transgender Day of Remembrance now takes place annually in cities across North America. In addition to memorializing lives lost, it advocates for a change to societal attitudes.

The Remembering Our Dead website (a web-based project aimed at chronicling transphobic violence and discrimination ending in death) reports that between 2000 and 2010, there were 413 deaths worldwide attributable to anti-trans violence (St. Pierre, 2011). Of these deaths, four occurred in Canada (St. Pierre, 2011). The site is able to include only those deaths that are known to the transgender community or reported in the media; hence, while there may be many more anti-trans murders, those deaths may not have been recorded as such (St. Pierre, 2011).

Transphobia draws our attention to the discrimination, violence, and even murder that all trans people "are forced to anticipate simply because they exist" (Green, 2007, p. 36).

Do you see similarities between transphobia and homophobia? If so, what are they? How might discrimination vary for transsexuals?

transphobia
Discrimination directed toward transsexuals or transgendered individuals.

Biphobia, like homophobia, is the irrational fear or hatred of bisexuals. Biphobia can result in discrimination, marginalization, and even violence (Klesse, 2005). Biphobic stereotypes include assuming that bisexuals have heightened levels of sexuality and are promiscuous. Discrimination is experienced in both heterosexual and homosexual contexts. Bisexual women, in particular, are constructed as highly sexualized, and are perceived as risky and untrustworthy partners. To use Foucault's terminology again, we can understand such discourses of promiscuity as being *disciplinary*; that is, they work to regulate our sexualities. They also can have the effect of associating bisexual women with being unchaste and dishonourable (Klesse, 2005).

biphobia The irrational fear or hatred of bisexuals.

Within lesbian circles in particular, bisexuality is marked as especially problematic (Klesse, 2005; Matheson & Endicott, 1998; Rust, 1995). In this context, bisexuality is constructed as an act of disloyalty to lesbian and gay politics (Matheson & Endicott, 1998; Rust, 1995). Women who identify as bisexual are perceived as giving in to compulsory (normative) heterosexuality; in short, they are considered to be "sleeping with the enemy" (Rodríguez Rust, 2000). Such marginalization can contribute to the erasure of bisexuality as an identity, especially within lesbian cultural and political spaces (Klesse, 2005). The gendered view of bisexuality also extends to men as there is a long-standing assumption that bisexual men "are actually homosexual but also homophobic" (Goldie, 2008, p. 96).

pansexuality

Romantic and sexual desire for people regardless of their gender identity or biological sex.

PANSEXUALITY

The term **pansexuality** refers to romantic and sexual desire for people regardless of their gender identity or biological sex (*pan* is a Greek word meaning "all" or "every"). In other words, it means sexual attraction to all genders. Pansexuality is distinct from bisexuality in that it includes attraction to transsexuals and transgendered individuals (Hird, 2004).

BOX 9.2 CANADIAN CONTRIBUTIONS TO SOCIOLOGY

Gary Kinsman

Gary Kinsman is a prominent sociologist who studies the social organization of sexuality. Through his research, he is able to demonstrate how the state is powerfully implicated in people's daily lives, even with something as personal as sexuality.

In his work, Kinsman traces the moral regulation of lesbian and gay male sexualities. For example, in the Canadian national security campaigns of the 1950s and 1960s, heterosexuality was normalized while gay and lesbian sexualities were constructed as deviant, risky, and immoral. These historical anti-queer constructions continue to shape social practices of discrimination against people whose sexualities challenge heterosexual hegemony (or dominance), including lesbians, gay men, bisexuals, and transgendered persons.

In his book *The Regulation of Desire: Homo and Hetero Sexualities* (1996), Kinsman writes about how he challenges his sociology students to appreciate the pervasiveness of heterosexual hegemony and privilege, and how this privilege is enacted through social practices on a daily basis. He challenges his heterosexual students to think about what it would be like to live as queers for one week, having them consider what it would be like to declare themselves as gay or lesbian to their families, friends, co-workers, and anyone else they encounter.

His most recent book, with Patrizia Gentile, is *The Canadian War on Queers: National Security as Sexual Regulation* (2010).

Consider Kinsman's challenge to his students. Some of you may have already made this declaration to your families. For those of you who have not, can you imagine how your family and friends would react to such a declaration? Might such an announcement create discomfort, pain, derision, fear, and even violence? By thinking about how this announcement might be met, are you able to see social power and oppression at work?

Courtesy Gary Kinsman

Gary Kinsman

However, it does not entail sexual attraction to all people or acceptance of all sexual practices. While virtually no sociological research has been conducted on pansexuality, what is fascinating is that pansexualism problematizes such categories as bisexual, heterosexual, and homosexual, favouring instead more fluid notions of sexual pleasure without categorization (Hird, 2004).

ASEXUALITY

The term **asexuality** refers to an absence of sexual desire (Brain, 2004). Asexuality is different from abstinence (wherein someone refuses to engage in sexual activity for a particular period of time). Asexuality can be understood as "a (conscious) cultural rejection of sexual identities" (Brain, 2004, p. 9). For example, Fahs (2010) situates the deliberate choice of asexuality as a political statement. In this sense, asexuality can be understood as a statement that is meant to unsettle prevailing gender hierarchies (Fahs, 2010). For some, asexuality represents a "logical, even empowering, response to oppression" (Fahs, 2010, p. 456). Joined with our theoretical discussion later in this chapter, asexuality challenges essentialist assumptions about the naturalness of heterosexuality.

asexuality An absence of sexual desire.

Sexual Relationships

All sexual relationships, whether they are monogamous or take one of the several forms of non-monogamy, are socially shaped. Of interest to sociologists is how monogamous relationships have come to be privileged in society while non-monogamous relationships have been rendered problematic. We explore this question by looking at each form of relationship in turn.

"And do you, Rebecca, promise to make love only to Richard, month after month, year after year, and decade after decade, until one of you is dead?"

Tom Cheney/The New Yorker Collection/www.cartoonbank.com

MONOGAMY

monogamy The coupling of two people, excluding the intimate involvement of others.

Monogamy refers to the coupling of two people, excluding the intimate involvement of others. It is commonly contrasted with *polygyny*, which refers to the coupling of one man and more than one woman (Loue, 2006). Notice the spelling of *polygyny*. You are probably more familiar with the term *polygamy*, which actually refers to either a man *or a woman* being married to more than one partner of the opposite sex (although it tends not to be used that way). *Polyandry*, on the other hand, is the practice of one woman being linked to more than one man.

Monogamy currently has a variety of different meanings and reference points: marital relationships, sexual relationships, and male–female sexual relationships. For example, *monogamy* can refer to marriage to one person at one time, or to a single sexual relationship during one's lifetime. At one level, monogamy means never engaging in a sexual relationship with more than one person at a given time. At another level, it is the creation of a long-term and lifelong project with another person. Other social meanings associated with the term *monogamy* include sexual exclusivity, dependency, and possession. For the purposes of this chapter, monogamy suggests a relationship, most often a sexual relationship, with only one person at a time (Loue, 2006).

According to discourses of monogamy, individuals who have sex with other people without the knowledge or consent of their primary partner are adulterous or disloyal. However, there are some variations to this theme among monogamous couples. Monogamy can mean different things to different people at different times, so our held assumptions about monogamous sexual relationships can be problematic (Loue, 2006). Monogamous people tend to assume that their long-term relationships, cohabitating, and "steady" relationships are monogamous when such a situation may not be the case.

There are several dominant assumptions about monogamy: It builds trust and respect between partners, it is a display of love, and it signifies mutual sexual satisfaction and a loss of sexual opportunities with other people (Loue, 2006). For some people, monogamy implies lifelong coupling. For others, there is no guarantee that either partner will remain sexually or emotionally faithful. For example, popular culture and media exposés (*The Oprah Winfrey Show* in 2004, *The New York Times Magazine* in 2003) have exposed the practice of men in heterosexual, monogamous relationships who, unbeknownst to their wives,

> > >

Infidelity, a painting by Paolo Veronese, depicts non-monogamy.

SuperStock/Maxx Images

also have sex with men on the side (Gerald, 2007; Ward, 2008). This practice is commonly referred to as being on the "down low," which connotes the secrecy surrounding this behaviour (Gerald, 2007). Although these men engage in sexual activity with both men and women, they do not self-identify as bisexual.

In a society that privileges heterosexual, monogamous coupledom, dominant sexuality discourses shape our thinking so that we come to believe that each individual should have only one sexual relationship at a time, while our friendships can be open and nonexclusive. Any relationships other than monogamous sexual ones are to be categorized as "friendship." Moreover, dominant discourses constrain the acceptable and appropriate ways in which we should interact with our friends (Ritchie & Barker, 2006). Even the category of "friend" becomes complicated when we consider polyamorous relationships (discussed below). According to dominant sexuality discourses, one sexual relationship should take precedence over all other relationships. Socially, then, our friendships are to be understood as less valuable than our sexual relationships. The common phrase "just friends" is an example of this hierarchy of relationships (Ritchie & Barker, 2006).

Serial Monogamy Sexuality scholars such as Anapol (1997) and Loue (2006) refer to successions of monogamous partnerships as **serial monogamy**. This refers to a relationship pattern that has one monogamous relationship (whether long-term or short-term) following another (Loue, 2006).

Of course, when the intervals between these exclusive relationships are short, the distinction between serial monogamy and monogamy is not always clear-cut (Loue, 2006). In fact, serial monogamists tend to have a series of short-term relationships, one after the other. Serial monogamy usually occurs when individuals do not have any overriding economic, legal, or moral reasons (including child dependents) to stay together in a single lifelong monogamous relationship (Anapol, 1997).

Many sexuality scholars therefore identify serial monogamy as a form of, or replacement for, multiple-partner sexuality. In this sense, it could be considered a form of non-monogamy (Loue, 2006). If the serial monogamist has multiple sexual partners, with each partner separated merely by linear time, we may even understand serial monogamy to be a kind of fictional monogamy (Anapol, 1997).

NON-MONOGAMY

Non-monogamy refers to sexual interactions with more than one person during a given period, or to any sexual relationship involving more than two people (Anapol, 1997). Although popular discourses situate those engaging in non-monogamy as having deviant sexualities—and even as engaging in frequent public sex environments such as parks, parking lots, clubs, parties, and other subcultural contexts—their social activities in fact differ little from those who practise monogamy (Anapol, 1997). Non-monogamous relationships vary according to the number of partners, arrangements, legal status, genders, and sexualities. They also vary according to degrees of intimacy, closeness, and commitment (Klesse, 2005).

Polyamory **Polyamory** is a distinct form of non-monogamous relationship that involves mutually acknowledged emotional, sexual, or romantic connections with multiple partners. The term *polyamory*, deriving from the Latin word for "love" and the Greek word for "many," translates to "many loves" or "more than one love" (Klesse, 2006, p. 568). American science fiction writer Robert Heinlein is credited with coining the term in his novel *Stranger in a Strange Land* (1961). It gained ground in the 1990s and has now been in use for the past few decades (Barker, 2005).

Polyamory emphasizes long-term, emotionally intimate relationships that transcend sexual intimacy. As one participant in Klesse's (2006) UK research on polyamory remarked, "People who identify as polyamorous believe in the idea of more than one relationship, meaning more than one love relationship. And they don't even have to be sexual" (p. 567). Respondents in this study revealed the difficulties many people have in understanding these often nonsexual partnerships. As one woman noted, she finds it hard to explain polyamory to her friends as they wrongly interpret these relationships as close friendships. Klesse (2006) quotes this participant as stating, "they're closer than a close friendship—they're people that I love" (p. 568).

This same participant goes on to stress that while sexual relations are important in her life, the point of polyamory is not about having many sexual relationships. Indeed, people

---

serial monogamy
A relationship pattern that has one monogamous relationship following another.

((•—**Listen**

Defending and Attacking Polygamy in Saudi Arabia

non-monogamy
Sexual interactions with more than one person during a given period, or any sexual relationship involving more than two people.

polyamory Mutually acknowledged emotional, sexual, or romantic connections with multiple partners.

✳—Explore

Making Their Bed: Some 16 Groups Take Sides on Polygamy in a Landmark Case

in polyamorous relationships often invoke a moral distinction between their relationships and those involving casual sex or "swinging" (associated with couples who have casual sex with others or who "swap" partners) (Klesse, 2006). Polyamory, then, is understood as "responsible non-monogamy" that excludes sexual experiences that do not involve love (Klesse, 2006).

Polyamory is also characterized by both honesty and consensus (Bloomquist, 2000; Klesse, 2006; Lano & Parry, 1995). A man in Klesse's study emphasized just such a focus when he stated in his interview that the mantra in the polyamory community is "honesty, honesty, honesty!" (2006, p. 571).

Interviews with those engaged in polyamorous relationships reveal the importance of communication, responsibility, and negotiation (Klesse, 2006; Ritchie & Barker, 2006). When primary partners engage in polyamory, they make honesty central to their relationship and desire full disclosure by all members of the network and anyone affected by that network (Sheff, 2005).

Polyamorous relationships come in many forms. Typically, a polyamorous individual will have one or two primary partners and any number of secondary or tertiary partners. These varying degrees of intimacy and commitment are marked by, for example, the amount of time spent with a partner, the energy devoted to a particular partner, and the expectations of a partner (Klesse, 2006). In some instances, groups of three partners (called "triads") or groups of four partners (called "quads") may form (Anapol, 1997). The language of *primary, secondary,* and *tertiary* partners is not very radical; given that it establishes a hierarchy of affective and sexual connections, it does not differ much from the discourse of coupledom found in monogamy or even swinging.

Many polyamorous people build families of sexual partners that may remain consistent for decades. Some pursue "group marriage," sometimes referred to as "multilateral marriage" (Barker, 2005). Usually, Western legal systems and mainstream religions do not socially sanction group marriages (Rubin, 2001). They tend to be long-term, committed, primary relationships that involve three or more adult partners. Some group marriages limit sex to the primary partners, while others are open to sexual activity outside the group.

> > >

Polyamory involves mutually acknowledged connections with multiple partners. Polyamory enables people to develop sexual relationships without adhering to strict cultural patterns based on dominant discourses of monogamy.

AAGAMIA/Iconica/Getty Images

Additional partners sometimes join the group, as long as everyone agrees to these additions (Anapol, 1997).

American research reveals that polyamorous people in the United States tend to be educated, middle-aged, white, middle- to upper-class individuals who work in professional occupations (Sheff, 2005). No particular sexual identity best represents participants in the polyamory movement, although Christian Klesse's (2006, p. 566) research notes that a significant portion of the UK polyamory landscape tends to be bisexual—or, as one participant called them, "heteroflexibles."

Polyamory, then, enables people to develop sexual relationships without adhering to strict cultural patterns based on dominant discourses of heterosexual monogamy (Anapol, 1997). The growth of polyamorous discourse is an example of the increasing visibility of non-monogamous relationships. Nonetheless, as discussed above, many individuals who practise polyamory still draw on dominant discourses of morality and responsibility to distance themselves from being labelled as promiscuous.

In summary, just as we demonstrated that sexual identities are socially organized, so too are sexual relationships. As we have seen, morality discourses figure centrally in the judgment of acceptable and nonacceptable sexual relationships. Despite many people's assumption that monogamy is natural, the privilege accorded to monogamous relationships in Western societies is a social process.

Sexuality and Gender: The Sexual Double Standard

As discussed in Chapter 8, sexuality is socially embedded within a matrix of power relations that are shaped by our gender as well as by our social class, race, ethnicity, age, ability, and so forth (Abbott, Wallace, & Tyler, 2005). We "perform" our gender every day, through what we choose to wear, how we style (or do not style) our hair, how we speak, and how we interact with others. All of these acts contribute to our presentation of ourselves as feminine or masculine (or other) beings. Yet, contrary to dominant discourse, a natural (biological) or fixed (stable) gender is in fact an illusion (Renold, 2006). That is, our gendered selves are fluid; they are socially produced and can change over time. Consider how your own presentation of masculinity or femininity has changed from one year ago, five years ago, and so forth.

Still, Western culture demands that we choose which gender to identify with, masculine or feminine. These normative gender identities tie into heterosexuality as the dominant presumption; in other words, a "correct" gender includes heterosexuality. "Abnormal" gender performances are subject to policing and shaming, which helps to reproduce gender inequality (Renold, 2006).

You are probably very familiar with the sexual double standard, whereby those who have many sexual relations experience gendered consequences: Men are heralded as "studs," while women are marked as "sluts." In this way, the double standard divides men and women into two opposing groups: active and passive. It further classifies women according to the binary (either/or) construction of Madonna/whore. Let us look at how masculine and feminine identities are constructed.

THE CONSTRUCTION OF "MASCULINITY"

Hegemonic masculinity (meaning the dominant cultural form of masculinity) depicts *real* men as always being interested in sex (with women); being in physical and emotional control; being strong, aggressive, and physically dominant; and not needing help from others

BOX 9.3 THAT WAS THEN, THIS IS NOW

● Viagra and Masculinity

Today, more and more aspects of human life are being medicalized, with pill-popping touted as a means of treating all of our ills. In fact, pharmaceuticals currently represent the most profitable global industry; as such, it influences the creation of government health and business policies (Tiefer, 2006).

The 1998 approval of the drug Viagra marked a new era in the pharmaceutical treatment of sexual "problems" (Tiefer, 2006). Designed to treat impotence in men, Viagra quickly became a household name. Even popular television series—*Sex and the City, The Sopranos, Law and Order, ER*—and movies—*That Awkward Moment*—have referred to the drug (Vares & Braun, 2006). Viagra is now a "cultural metaphor for sexual potency" (Holt, 2009, p. 746).

Sociologically, we understand that sexuality is a central site for the enactment of masculinities. So we can ask: How does Viagra contribute to or disrupt dominant constructions of masculinity? The promotional materials and television and print advertisements for Viagra demonstrate these dominant constructions of masculinity: heterosexual, mainly white, age 40 and above (Vares & Braun, 2006). The "penetrating (ever-ready, ever-hard) male body" is privileged in Viagra ads (Vares & Braun, 2006, p. 319). If men are unable to perform sexually, their masculinity is at risk (Gray, 2009; Holt, 2009). Rather than work to disrupt dominant constructions, then, such advertisements reproduce the emphasis on a performing penis as an integral aspect of contemporary masculinity (Holt, 2009; Vares & Braun, 2006).

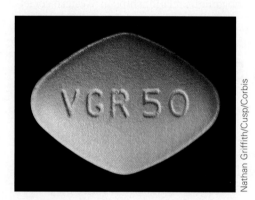

Viagra, made by Pfizer, perpetuates the cultural notion that a man's penis needs to be ever-performing.

Think about all of the contexts in which you hear references to Viagra. How are these references connected to masculinity? What kind of masculinity is implicated?

(Courtenay, 2000; Kumar, Larkin, & Mitchell, 2002; Ringrose & Renold, 2012). Dominant discourses of masculinity also position men as being somewhat sexually irresponsible, which can undermine their sexual health (Larkin, Andrews, & Mitchell, 2006). Masculine sexuality is constructed as uncontrolled and uncontrollable, with women often positioned as the gatekeepers of sex (Larkin, Andrews, & Mitchell, 2006). The concrete effects of these ideals manifest in many ways, such as when men pressure women for sex, commit sexual assaults against both women and men, and ignore the risks of sexually transmitted infections/diseases (Duck, 2009; Kumar, Larkin, & Mitchell, 2002).

Sexual competency also defines masculinity (Tieffer, 2005). Since they are always interested in sex, masculine men are encouraged to deny emotional and interpersonal factors, which they consider to be the domain of femininity (Tieffer, 2005). In North America, having sex with multiple women is a cultural ideal that men are pressured to achieve (Kumar, Larkin, & Mitchell, 2002). By exchanging sexual stories (bragging about their conquests), men use sex as a means of bonding and achieving social status with other men (Tieffer, 2005). Indeed, men are congratulated for engaging in sex (Tanenbaum, 2005).

THE CONSTRUCTION OF "FEMININITY"

In dominant constructions of femininity, women are largely positioned as being subordinate to men's sexual desire. They are constructed as the passive objects of men's sexual desire, with limited sexual agency (Beres & Farvid, 2010; Cram & Jackson, 2003). Yet, at the same time, women are often positioned as responsible for controlling or reining in men's sexuality. For example, in a study of Canadian and New Zealand 19- to 25-year-olds, Beres and Farvid (2010) found that women are the ones who ensure that "safe" sex happens (condoms are used) in casual sex encounters. When young women do talk about sex, they tend to frame their discussions in terms of men's needs, desires, and bodies (Holland et al., 1996; Cram & Jackson, 2003). Given that the dominant construction of sex is understood as vaginal penetration, with women as passive recipients of men's sexual action, young women may find it difficult to talk about sex in terms of their own sexual agency (Kumar, Larkin, & Mitchell, 2002, p. 37).

Moreover, women are divided into one of two categories: "good" girls and "bad" girls, Madonnas and whores. Within this construction, bad girls are disposable and good girls are to be treated well (Tanenbaum, 2005). The sexual double standard is enforced through the social power of reputation; as noted above, men who engage in sexual relations with more than one woman are *studs*, whereas women who behave in similar ways are *sluts* (Cram & Jackson, 2003). Women experience tension between feeling pressure to have sex and needing to preserve their reputations as good girls for fear of being labelled promiscuous. As a result, women are often less comfortable with sexual interaction than men are (Tanenbaum, 2005). Women's fear of damaged reputations as a result of their sexual behaviour works to constrain their behaviour, since men (and sometimes women) may use labels such as "slut" and "whore" to describe women they perceive as promiscuous (Cram & Jackson, 2003). Further, these negative sexual labels that are levied at girls and women are a form of sexual harassment that often goes unrecognized as harassment (Rahimi & Liston, 2009).

Use of the Term *Slut* Throughout history, the term *slut* has had many meanings. Originating in the fourteenth century, *sluttish* was used to describe dirty and untidy men and women (Attwood, 2007). In the fifteenth century, *slut* came to have two distinct meanings, one neutral (kitchen girl) and one pejorative (bold or saucy women). By the twentieth century, *slut* was exclusively used as an abusive term marking promiscuity and was directed only at women (Attwood, 2007).

Today, people continue to use the term *slut* to define sexual women negatively (Attwood, 2007). *Slut* is clearly located within the sexual double standard that positions women in the Madonna/whore binary cited above (Attwood, 2007). The term marks and shames women who are perceived as promiscuous or who have a casual attitude toward sex (Tanenbaum, 2005). These types of negative labels denigrate and censure active and desiring female sexualities.

Contemporary uses and meanings of *slut* continue to reinforce the idea that men can express their sexuality but women cannot and that women bear the responsibility for morality (Rahimi & Liston, 2009; Ringrose & Renold, 2012; Tanenbaum, 2005). The threat of being labelled a slut ensures that many young women come to believe that sex is bad and will lead to a bad reputation (Tanenbaum, 2005). In fact, Tanenbaum's research with women who had been labelled sluts in either middle school or high school found that the threat of being cast as a slut actually decreased the likelihood of using contraceptives or carrying condoms. Being called a slut can also follow a girl into adulthood. It may cause her to shut down her sexuality or become a target for further forms of harassment (Tanenbaum, 2005).

Slut-bashing affects not only girls. The culture that is created through this practice also teaches boys that there are two kinds of girls—good girls and bad girls—and hence that there are two ways to treat girls, depending on which category a girl is located in. Good girls are treated well; bad girls are expendable (Tanenbaum, 2005).

There have been attempts to reclaim *slut* as a "positive identity marker"; consider, for example, the development of the term *ethical slut* (Easton & Liszt, 1997, p. 4). Trying to reclaim this term means trying to reshape social thinking about women's sexuality—"to be an ethical slut is to be a force for good" (Attwood, 2007, p. 235). Easton and Liszt (1997, p. 4) proclaim that an ethical slut is "a person of any gender who has the courage to lead life according to the radical proposition that sex is nice and pleasure is good for you." Reclaiming the term is a strategy of resistance, but whether this strategy is successful is highly contentious. Another form of resistance around rape culture and violence against women are the *SlutWalks* that take place annually in several countries. The first walk grew out of reaction to the comments that a Toronto police officer made about women's responsibility for their own sexual victimization as a result of dressing like sluts (Leach, 2013).

Use of the Term *Promiscuous* Promiscuity discourses work in the same way as slut-bashing. *Promiscuous* is a derogatory term used to describe anyone who is assumed to have had sex with an "unreasonable" number of sexual partners (Klesse, 2006). Of course, as sociologists, we should ask: Who gets to decide what constitutes unreasonable numbers? Promiscuity discourses are a means of subjecting people, particularly women, to a disciplinary regime of morality (Klesse, 2006). As discussed, such discourses can be damaging for women because, by rendering their actions as offensive and immoral, they constrain women's sexuality (Beres & Farvid, 2010; Klesse, 2006). The very fact of "promiscuous" women challenges dominant discourses of female sexuality that position women as naturally passive and submissive. Calling a woman promiscuous, then, is a means of regulating her sexuality and encouraging her to remain firmly located within the boundaries of the sexual double standard.

> ### >>> Thinking Sociologically
>
> We learn a lot about sexuality from our parents. Can you remember any ways in which your parents restricted or monitored your sexuality (through, say, curfews or warnings)? Can you link any of these to gender? For example, was your gender-opposite sibling treated differently in relation to dating?

THE RACIALIZED SEXUAL DOUBLE STANDARD

The sexual double standard is also differentiated by race. For example, we can still feel the effects of European and American slavery and colonialism that took place between 1870 and 1914. During this time, the sexual exploitation of black women was institutionalized (Hall, 2005). White women were constructed as asexual, beautiful, and chaste, while black women were positioned as sexually available and largely unable to protest (Hill Collins, 2005). Black women were perceived as biologically inferior to white women and likened to promiscuous wild animals. Enslaved black women were beaten and killed if they did not submit to white men's advances (Hill Collins, 2005). To justify their enslavement, black people were constructed as primitive people with animal natures and insatiable sexual appetites (Lewis, 2007). Dominant sexuality discourses continue to construct black men as degenerate, hypersexual, and carnal (Coad, 2008; Hill Collins, 2005; Rahimi & Liston, 2009). This system of oppression represents black men as rapists, black women as whores, and both as chronically promiscuous (Hill Collins, 2005; McGruder, 2009).

We also see a racialized double standard today with the construction of black and Asian women as sexually exotic (Abbott, Wallace, & Tyler, 2005). Consider Kim and Chung's (2005) research on images of Asian-American women in advertising. Their analysis of contemporary advertisements reveals the construction of these women as "Lotus Blossoms" (Kim & Chung, 2005, p. 80). Historical Lotus Blossom images constructed these women as exotic, inviting, subservient, and enticing. Contemporary ads are no different; these women have "suggestive smiles and gazes but hesitate to speak" (Kim & Chung, 2005, p. 80).

We have seen, then, that the sexual double standard creates a situation in which it is ideal for women to be ever faithful to their male partners, while men are encouraged to seek out multiple sexual partners. Today, the double standard is eroding, yet it continues to constrain women's sexual autonomy while it enables men's (Klesse, 2005).

⑤ Theoretical Approaches to Sexuality

The key questions in sociological approaches to sexuality concern the role of biology, the function of sexuality, the influence of the social world, the commodification of sexuality, the learning of sexual scripts, and the degree to which identity is understood as something that is fixed and relatively stable or as fluid and always in flux. We begin with a look at biology.

ESSENTIALIST THEORIES

Essentialists argue that sex is pre-social, meaning that sex is understood as a product of biological forces or as predetermined by biology (Seidman, 2010). Essentialists argue that sexuality is part of an individual's core self or essence, and that an objective reality exists outside social relations.

Four basic assumptions ground an essentialist approach to sexuality:

1. Sexuality is a basic human drive or force that exists prior to social life.
2. Sexuality is determined by the biological or psychological makeup of human beings.
3. Sexuality resides or exists within the human body.
4. Sexuality functions throughout our lives essentially as a "property" of the individual (Abbott, Wallace, & Tyler, 2005, p. 199).

The essentialist perspective implies, then, that our sexual identities are fixed, stable, and coherent. The four basic assumptions lead to further assumptions about what constitutes a sexual identity and about sexual intercourse in the Western world:

1. Sex is natural.
2. What is natural is heterosexual.
3. Genital sex is primary and determining.
4. "True" sexual intercourse is *phallocentric* (that is, centred on the phallus, meaning penis).
5. Sex is something that ideally takes place within marriage, or at least in a long-term relationship (Abbott, Wallace, & Tyler, 2005, p. 199).

This approach takes for granted the social process of classifying particular behaviours as sexual (Abbott, Wallace, & Tyler, 2005). Also taken for granted is the categorization of some behaviours as *normal* and *natural* and other behaviours as *abnormal* and *unnatural*. In contradistinction to social constructionist approaches to understanding sexuality, essentialist theorists attempt to make links between human sexuality and nature and biology (Steele, 2005a). Such an approach, in North America, treats heterosexuality, for example, as a natural instinct, whereby women and men are naturally attracted to each other (Seidman, 2010).

Essentialist theorists also assume that the primary purpose of sex is procreation (Seidman, 2010). While this assumption has fallen out of favour, essentialists continue to conceive of heterosexuality as *the* normal and natural sexuality (Seidman, 2010). This approach is also criticized for being gendered—constructing men as having high sex drives and being naturally sexually active and constructing women as sexually passive (Abbott, Wallace, & Tyler, 2005). Such theorizing, of course, fuelled the sexual double standard discussed earlier.

FUNCTIONALISM

Functionalists may be interested in analyzing how sexuality is functional to the smooth running of society. As an example, can you think through how prostitution might be functional for society? Kingsley Davis (1937), an American sociologist who was the key person writing about sexuality at the time, argued that prostitution actually helps to keep families together (at the time Davis was writing, he would have assumed families to be heterosexual and nuclear) (Plummer, 2010). According to Davis, if the husband is not having his sexual needs and wants fulfilled, prostitution provides an avenue to meet those needs. The women prostitutes were labelled as deviant, but not the men who used their services (Heidensohn, 2010). Therefore, according to Davis, prostitution serves a function. (Notice the sexist assumption that it is always the husband whose needs are unfulfilled.)

CONFLICT THEORY

commodification The process whereby goods and services become available for purchase in the market.

Conflict theorists, as you know, tend to explore how various social groups compete over scarce resources; they study the exercise of power and relations of inequality. They are also interested in the **commodification** of goods and services and in exploring how various aspects linked to our sexualities become commodified (that is, available for purchase in the market). Services such as prostitution and pornography are good examples of such commodification.

Capitalist consumerism has the ability to shape contemporary sexualities as new sexual products and services emerge to meet an ever-expanding range of sexual desires (Seidman, 2010). Diversification of sexual practices and subcultures expands the market and helps to produce new consumer markets (Seidman, 2010). However, some Marxists are concerned about the narrowing of the range of sexual possibilities since commodification may halt the expansion of desire by offering fixed, repetitive, identical images, activities, and services for purchase (Evans, 1993).

SYMBOLIC INTERACTIONISM

sexual scripts Cultural expectations about appropriate sexuality that are learned through social interaction.

> > >

Adam and Eve in the garden of Eden—the origin of sin according to Christianity.

Since symbolic interactionists study the meanings attributed to aspects of social life, they are interested in the social meanings that a society attributes to sexuality, including sexual behaviour. Of course, symbolic interactionists are also concerned with the everyday micro interactions people have with other members of a society.

William Simon and John Gagnon (1986) are credited with developing the important concept of **sexual scripts**—the cultural expectations we hold about what constitutes appropriate sexuality, as manifested in language, practices, and social rules. Through social interaction, then, we learn the sexual scripts of our culture. Shelly Ronen (2010) explores these scripts in her research on sexualized dancing at US college student parties. Ronen found that the scripts enacted at these parties reflect and reproduce wider relations of the sexual double standard—men enjoy agency while women are constricted by the Madonna/whore dichotomy.

Hulton Archive/Getty Images

< < <

The couple pictured here is acting out a sexual script—accepted forms of sexual behaviour.

Image Source Plus/Alamy

These scripts are flexible, in that different situations and contexts require different behaviours and attitudes. Consider the practice of masturbation—while a common practice, it is not one that is socially acceptable in public places. We learn, then, that sexuality depends on context.

POST-STRUCTURALIST THEORY

Unlike an essentialist approach that views sexuality as a pre-social, biologically-based drive, post-structuralists argue that sexual behaviour and sexual identity are products of *discourses* (that is, ways of speaking, thinking, and writing about the world). Recall from Chapter 3 that dominant discourses in society shape behaviours, attitudes, and identities—and thereby regulate what is considered normal. We see this process at work in the taken-for-granted acceptance of heterosexuality as "normal" sexuality. As instruments of power, discourses regulate sexuality. They define and sanction what is "true" and "normal," as manifested in language, concepts, institutions, practices, behaviours, and objects. Discourses describe how the world is and, importantly, shape our views about how the world *should* be (Abbott, Wallace, & Tyler, 2005).

Michel Foucault is one of the most prominent sexuality scholars (his work was introduced in Chapter 3). He studied the ways in which discourses constitute our understandings of social life, our relationships with others, and our sense of self (Abbott, Wallace, & Tyler, 2005). Foucault argued that what we understand today as sex is a product of the *discourse of sexuality*. Challenging the idea that sex is natural and biological, he contended that we are not born sexual beings; instead, we *learn* to be sexual. This process of becoming sexual can occur only in a society that has created the idea of "sexuality" (Seidman, 2010). Of course, Foucault was not arguing that erotic feelings, pleasures, and behaviours were *created* by discourses but, rather, that these feelings, pleasures, and behaviours came to be *categorized* as expressions of human sexuality (Green, 2010; Seidman, 2010). In turn, discourses of sexuality constitute individuals as particular sexual subjects—as having either a normal sexuality or a pathological sexuality (Green, 2007).

Foucault argued that sexuality discourses emerged in the late eighteenth century from the Christian practice of confession. That is, as Christians confessed their sins and sinful desires, they were forced to understand the erotic as something having moral significance (Seidman, 2010). Foucault viewed this traditional religious thought, and the scientific explorations of sexuality that developed in the nineteenth century, as being equally implicated in relations of power.

FEMINIST POST-STRUCTURALISM

Feminist post-structuralists, influenced by Foucault's work, argue that sexuality is fashioned and refashioned through discourse (Abbott, Wallace, & Tyler, 2005). They appreciate the politically liberating possibilities of such an understanding of sexuality and power relations. That is, since sexuality is neither fixed nor grounded in biology, its traditional shaping through patriarchal discourses can be renegotiated in feminist ways (Abbott, Wallace, & Tyler, 2005).

Judith Butler's work is of particular importance to this perspective. She dismisses essentialist theorizing in favour of an analysis that positions sexualities as "created and lived through their performance" (Abbott, Wallace, & Tyler, 2005, p. 207). According to Butler, there is no true, coherent self under the multiple identities we perform, just as there is no one true sexuality (Abbott, Wallace, & Tyler, 2005). Our sexual identity is merely one performance among many possible performances.

According to Butler, gender is constituted through what she calls a *heterosexual matrix*. This matrix is established through the linked avenues of discourse and *epistemology* (a term that refers to the nature and production of knowledge). Butler argues that for people to be "intelligible" (that is, understandable) to others, they must align their bodies (female and male) with their gender (feminine and masculine) within a heterosexual context. She understands this matrix as operating "oppositionally," meaning that male/female, masculinity/femininity, and heterosexuality/homosexuality are (problematically) understood as binaries.

Butler also sees this matrix as a hierarchical one, in that masculinity is ranked above femininity, and heterosexuality above homosexuality. In sum, then, heterosexuality operates as the norm through which our genders, our bodies, and our desires are defined. Here is how Butler expresses her conception of the matrix:

> I use the term heterosexual matrix . . . to designate that grid of cultural intelligibility through which bodies, genders, and desires are naturalized . . . a hegemonic discursive/ epistemological model of gender intelligibility that assumes that for bodies to cohere and make sense there must be a stable sex expressed through a stable gender (masculine expresses male, feminine expresses female) that is oppositionally and hierarchically defined through the compulsory practice of heterosexuality. (Butler, 1990, p. 151)

Emma Renold's (2006) UK research in primary schools shows that this heterosexual matrix is at play at a young age. For example, girls and boys often draw on discourses of romance to legitimate spending time with those of the opposite sex. During conversation, girls would designate whether they were someone's "girlfriend" or whether they were "single." This discussion of status in relation to boys and romantic relationships was not replicated among the boys (that is, the boys did not make the same kinds of references). Girls who did not participate in the boyfriend/girlfriend culture were disparagingly referred to as "square-girls." Among the boys, though, being a "boyfriend" confirmed their masculinity. Renold (2006) found that the romance culture of the school was feminized; in other words, the girls were key to maintaining this heterosexual gendered culture.

As we saw earlier, if one's gender practices stray from normative femininities or masculinities (and therefore become what Butler calls "unintelligible genders"), one's heterosexuality can be seen as being in doubt. Heterosexual performances are regulated through disciplinary techniques, such as shaming and/or monitoring others' sexual/gender practices as abnormal and deviant—for example, calling effeminate boys "sissies" (Renold, 2006). When people's gender practices deviate from what their "natural" (a social construct) gender should be, individuals themselves rather than the regulatory gender frame are blamed for the "problem."

QUEER THEORY

Queer theory emerged in the late 1980s. The name itself signifies the re-appropriation of the term *queer*—historically a derogatory term directed at gays and lesbians (Green, 2007). Queer theory has its foundations in the work of Michel Foucault, Eve Sedgwick, and Judith Butler. Sedgwick and Butler developed their approaches after finding themselves frustrated with feminist theorizing that was supposedly emancipating but, nevertheless, assumed an implied heterosexuality (Reynolds, 2004).

Queer theory challenges *heterosexism*, which is the belief that heterosexuality is naturally superior to all other sexual identities. Queer theorists seek to deconstruct and dissolve normalizing sexuality discourses that are used to control and constrain people (Green, 2007). By exposing how identity is constructed through discourses, queer theorists dismiss binary (either/or) constructions of gender and sexual identities—male/female, masculine/feminine, and heterosexual/homosexual (Reynolds, 2004). Instead, queer theorists propose an ever-changing range of possibilities (Reynolds, 2004).

The "Heterosexual Questionnaire" Rochlin (2009) developed a questionnaire that is meant to invert the many questions typically asked of gay men and lesbians about their sexuality. It is directed at heterosexuals as a means of exposing *heteronormativity*—the assumption that heterosexuality is *the* natural and normal sexuality. Rochlin asks about the causes of heterosexuality and the realization that one is heterosexual. She asks the heterosexuals reading the questionnaire to consider that their sexuality might be a phase that one outgrows. She troubles other assumptions about gayness by reversing them to ask the same of heterosexuals, such as suggesting that having sex with someone of the same sex might snap them out of their heterosexuality. She also troubles connections that people make between child molestation and homosexuality, asking whether it is okay that children are exposed to heterosexual teachers.

What are your reactions to such a questionnaire? Why is it that some people feel so free to ask lesbians and gays but not heterosexuals about these issues? How does such an exercise challenge your assumptions about heterosexuality and homosexuality?

Sexual Health

Sexual health means not only avoiding sexually transmitted infections and unplanned pregnancies but also fostering healthy relationships (McKay, 2004a). As a result, sexual health is not just a biological reality but also part of the social world. That is, individuals' behaviour and practices are not isolated happenings but, rather, the result of decisions and practices that are firmly rooted in the social realm.

SEXUALLY TRANSMITTED INFECTIONS

Sexually transmitted infections (STIs) are transmitted from one person to another during unprotected sex, including oral, anal, and vaginal sex. Canada requires that health practitioners report incidences of three STIs: chlamydia, gonorrhoea, and infectious syphilis (Public Health Agency of Canada [PHAC], 2008). Public Health Agency of Canada reports that despite public campaigns around safer sex, the rates of these three infections have risen steadily since 1997 (PHAC, 2009b). Recent Canadian data (a study of 20- to 34-year-olds) reveal that condom use declines with age, meaning that people may perceive their risk for an STI to lower as they age (Rotermann & McKay, 2009).

In Canada today, STIs are most common among youth and young adults (McKay, 2004a; Sex Information and Education Council of Canada [SIECCAN], 2009; PHAC, 2012). Chlamydia is the most highly reported STI in Canada; it affects both women and men and, when untreated, can cause ectopic pregnancies, pelvic inflammatory disease, increased

sexual health The avoidance of sexually transmitted infections and unwanted pregnancies and the fostering of healthy relationships.

sexually transmitted infections (STIs) Infections transmitted during unprotected sex (oral, anal, vaginal).

> > >

The rainbow flag is a symbol of diversity and inclusivity.

Oleksiy Maksymenko/Alamy

vulnerability to HIV, chronic pelvic pain, and infertility (McKay, 2004a; PHAC, 2009b, SIECCAN, 2009; PHAC, 2012).

Racism, economic inequality, sexism, homophobia, and transphobia all intersect to shape individual risk for STIs. Risk factors such as poverty (which affects the affordability of condoms, dental dams, and so forth, and even fear of sexual violence) and lack of sex education can affect sexual decision-making (Herdt & Howe, 2007; Larkin, Andrews, & Mitchell, 2006). In Western countries, minority men and women with limited economic resources tend to be most vulnerable to STIs (Kumar, Larkin, & Mitchell, 2002). Because of racism and subtle methods of exclusion, minority women are likely to encounter difficulties when trying to access social services.

When individuals are diagnosed with STIs, it tends to alter the way they understand themselves as sexual beings. Many people deny that they have an STI, even to themselves. As a result of grappling with the social stigma of having an STI, people fear that their family, friends, and/or potential partners will reject them. They fear that they will repulse other people.

For example, in Nack's (2005) research on women with herpes and the human papilloma virus (HPV), several participants tried to dissociate themselves from their STIs and to pass as being disease-free. For example, when a participant's friend commented about another woman, "That girl, she's such a slut. She's a walking STI," the participant talked about how she remained silent, pained at the thought that her friends could just as easily make that comment about her (Nack, 2005, p. 404). Other participants blamed past and current sexual partners to deflect the stigma associated with having an STI. However, this practice also led these women to assume that their future partners would also be infected.

HIV/AIDS The overwhelming majority of those living with HIV/AIDS (97 percent) are found in low- and middle-income countries, with a high concentration found in Sub-Saharan Africa (69 percent of all cases) (AIDS.gov, 2012; WHO, 2013b). In today's global HIV/AIDS pandemic, young women are emerging as the most vulnerable cohort (Larkin, Andrews, & Mitchell, 2006). Worldwide, girls and young women represent 62 percent of those aged 15 to 24 who are infected with HIV/AIDS (Germain & Kidwell, 2007). In Uganda, for example, for every one boy/man (aged 15–24), there are four girls/women infected with HIV (Tigawalana, 2010). HIV rates among young African women are three to five times higher than the rates for young African men

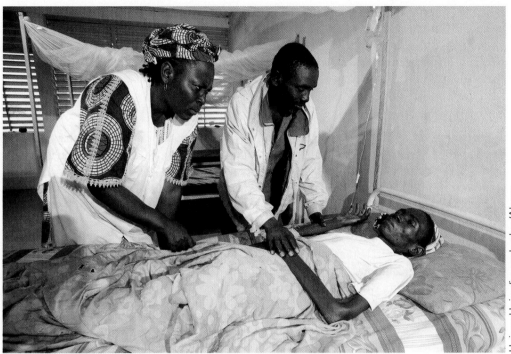

< < <

Undergoing treatment for HIV/AIDS—a global pandemic.

(UNAIDS, 2000). In South Africa, one in four young women between ages 20 and 29 is infected (Larkin, Andrews, & Mitchell, 2006).

While Canadian rates of HIV infection are far from the numbers found in South Africa, they are increasing, with teenagers being infected in numbers higher than ever before (Kumar, Larkin, & Mitchell, 2002; Larkin, Andrews, & Mitchell, 2006). In 2011, 23.8 percent of all new HIV cases in Canada were women, compared with 8.5 percent of new cases in 1995 (PHAC, 2009a; 2011). Young women aged 15 to 19 represented 58.3 percent of new HIV cases reported for this age group in 2008 (PHAC, 2009a).

How can we link this disease to social patterns and social relations? HIV/AIDS is a gendered disease, given that gender is a risk factor for contracting HIV/AIDS. Women are both socially and biologically more susceptible to HIV infection than men (Kumar, Larkin, & Mitchell, 2002; Tigawalana, 2010). Biologically,

> the risk of HIV infection during unprotected vaginal intercourse is as much as two to four times higher for women. During heterosexual sex, the exposed surface area of the vagina and labia is larger in women than the vulnerable surfaces are in men . . . semen infected with HIV contains a higher concentration of the virus than female sexual secretions. (Kumar, Larkin, & Mitchell, 2002, p. 36)

Researchers have also found that male-to-female transmission of HIV is more likely than female-to-male transmission (Kumar, Larkin, & Mitchell, 2002). Worldwide, 80 percent of women who contract the virus do so through heterosexual contact (Kumar, Larkin, & Mitchell, 2002). Socially, young women's infection can be linked to dominant constructions of active masculinity and passive femininity (Larkin, Andrews, & Mitchell, 2006). Because dominant constructions position young women as sexually passive, they may fear repercussions to their reputations if they act assertively about their sexual health (e.g., insisting that their partner use a condom and/or providing their partner with a condom) (Kumar, Larkin, & Mitchell, 2002).

Melendez's (2007) research on American transgendered women and HIV documents how discrimination heightens these women's vulnerability to contracting HIV (participants included women who were born male and had sex reassignment surgery, individuals who were taking female hormones and living as women without sex reassignment surgery, and individuals who were living as women but not taking hormones or undergoing sex reassignment surgery). Experiencing tremendous discrimination in the paid labour force, many of Melendez's participants exchanged sex for money—with many clients willing to pay extra to engage in unprotected sex. Once diagnosed with HIV, transgendered women continue to experience discrimination since there are not enough specialized health services available to serve their particular needs (Melendez, 2007).

SAFER SEX

The term *safe sex* tends to be associated with the use of condoms and thus with penetrative sex (Larkin, Andrews, & Mitchell, 2006). In other words, safe sex is narrowly understood as penile–vaginal penetration using a condom. Because many youth consider penile–vaginal penetrative sex as the only form of real sex, other sexual activities are reduced to foreplay and considered "less than sex." This narrow definition of sex limits the possibility that youth will choose to engage in less risky sexual activities in place of coitus (Larkin, Andrews, & Mitchell, 2006).

A broader definition of sex opens up possibilities for various sexual activities that carry less risk of spreading STIs (Larkin, Andrews, & Mitchell, 2006). The term **safer sex** refers not only to using condoms or other barriers but also to engaging in various types of nongenital contact and to avoiding behaviours that are considered high risk (such as oral sex). However, it is still important to consider the ways in which sexuality discourses both enable and constrain safer sex practices.

safer sex Avoiding sexual behaviours that are considered high risk as well as engaging in various types of nongenital contact.

Safer Sex and Monogamy
Practising safer sex has been found to be more difficult in longer-term relationships than in casual relationships (Loue, 2006). Discourses of monogamy lead people to think that long-term monogamous relationships are inherently safe, regardless of whether there has been honest communication about sexual histories, health, and current behaviour. Practising safer sex is understood to be a barrier to intimacy and particularly inappropriate for monogamous relationships. Many people in these relationships do not initiate condom use, fearing that it implies a lack of trust or commitment. Even when individuals find out that their partners have had sex with other people without their consent, many find it difficult to start using condoms after having had a prolonged sexual relationship without them (Loue, 2006).

Some people think that they are not at risk of contracting STIs because they are having sex with only one person. As a consequence, many people are not tested regularly for STIs and therefore do not know their sexual health status. People in monogamous relationships often do not consider themselves to be at risk, and further trust that their commitment to their partner will protect them from STIs.

Racist and homophobic assumptions also lead some people to think that they are safe from STIs by virtue of being white and heterosexual and only having sex with other white heterosexuals. As a result, many people believe that having only one partner obviates the necessity for safer sex practices (Loue, 2006). However, a first partner, a long-term partner, or a spouse can also transmit infections in the context of relationships considered monogamous. This reality challenges the dominant assumption that monogamous relationships are inherently safer than non-monogamous ones. Monogamous sexual relationships may be riskier in some ways precisely because of these common assumptions.

Safer Sex and Power Imbalances
Also affecting safer sex are gendered power imbalances in heterosexual relationships that constrain sexual negotiation (Larkin, Andrews, & Mitchell, 2006). Many women find it difficult to negotiate safer sex because they are expected to be sexually passive. When women suggest using condoms, it implies that they are sexually experienced, assertive, and promiscuous. To avoid being perceived as a "slut," many women leave the decision to use or not use condoms to men (Kumar, Larkin, & Mitchell, 2002). Some women are reluctant to raise the topic of condoms for fear of offending their partner or implying a lack of trust (Schneider & Jenness, 2005). The social pressure to present the image of a "good girl," then, actually puts women at risk (Kumar, Larkin, & Mitchell, 2002). And this pressure does not just affect adult women: In a study of Canadian youth (ages 12 to 16), girls were more likely than boys to report feeling pressured for sex and condom non-use (Gallupe, Boyce, & Fergus, 2009). This gendered imbalance of power

within many heterosexual relationships makes it difficult for women to insist that their need for safety trumps men's desire for penetrative sex without condoms.

Further, masculinity is implicated in condom use. Research shows that young men resist using condoms for a variety of reasons, such as lessened physical sensation during intercourse, bad smell, expense, and so forth (MacPhail & Campbell, 2001; Measor, 2006). Measor's research in the UK with sexually active young women (ages 18 to 22) draws a careful link between young men's resistance to condoms and dominant notions of masculinity. For example, one woman reported that her partner declared, "Speak to any self-respecting bloke and they'll tell you that condoms are just no sensation and they make you lose your stiffy just like that" (Measor, 2006, p. 396). These sorts of statements are mirrored in a Canadian study of heterosexual male youth (14 to 18 years old) (Manseau, Blais, Engler, & Bossé, 2007). As one participant stated, "It doesn't give me as much pleasure as without one. . . . Not having it feels better. . . . It's not as warm so it's not the same. . . . It's not as good" (Manseau et al., 2007, p. 54). Statements like this were common and demonstrate a link between young men's resistance to condoms and a fear of male impotence—that they will not be "man enough" to sustain an erection. Rather than risk dealing with the potential loss of an erection, young men are willing to sacrifice safer sex practices to sustain their masculine sexual identities (Measor, 2006).

SEX EDUCATION

Canadian youth may look to their families for information about sex, but most of the information they glean actually comes from school-based sex education programs (McKay, 2004a). Sex education is intended to equip students with adequate information so that they can make informed decisions about their sexual and reproductive health (McKay, 2004a; SIECCAN, 2009). Yet in most sex education curricula, understandings of sex are reduced to anatomy and biology and rarely focus on human relationships (Schneider & Jenness, 2005). Sex education tends to exclude discourses of pleasure and desire and also ignores myriad emotional aspects of sexual relations, such as the pain of ending a relationship (L. Allen, 2007). Further, research reveals that popular "abstinence-only" programs do not in fact lead to a reduction in adolescent and youth sexual behaviour (SIECCAN, 2009).

Sex education also tends to encourage heterosexism, as it promotes, normalizes, and naturalizes heterosexuality (Renold, 2006; Schneider & Jenness, 2005). Sex education programs do not inform students of the wide range of sexual options available, in that they tend to ignore

Marmaduke St. John/Alamy

< < <

Most of the information young adolescents learn about sex is gained from school-based sexual education programs.

homosexuality, bisexuality, and transsexualism (Schneider & Jenness, 2005). Recent Canadian guidelines by the Public Health Agency of Canada recommend including sexual diversity in school-based sexual education classes (SIECCAN, 2009).

Sex educators should expose students to alternative discourses of masculinity and femininity to promote a broader range of sexual possibilities, meanings, and relationships and to promote safer sex (Connell & Elliott, 2009; Larkin, Andrews, & Mitchell, 2006). Sex education should challenge gender relations, teach positive values about sex, and teach women and men that they can construct their own sexual identities—that they have agency in their sexualities (Connell & Elliott, 2009; Schneider & Jenness, 2005). Sex education, then, can be particularly effective when it enables students to examine their sexual assumptions, attitudes, behaviours, and values (McKay, 2004a).

> > > Thinking Sociologically

Do you remember your school-based sex education? What were the main topics covered? Were you presented with a range of information about a variety of sexualities? Did the curriculum focus at all on the social and political aspects of sexuality, or did it remain firmly rooted in biology?

Summary

❶ The meanings that people attach to sex are socially constructed; they differ from culture to culture and change over time as a result of economic, social, and cultural shifts.

❷ As an integral part of personal identities, sexual identities are likewise socially produced. Given that heterosexuality is held to be the norm in Western societies, it is privileged as being normal and natural. The homosexual identity (as opposed to homosexual behaviour) began to emerge in North America only in the early part of the twentieth century. Bisexuality challenges the idea that heterosexuality and homosexuality are mutually exclusive; as a result of prevailing discourses that limit the definition of *bisexual*, those having this identity tend to be perceived as non-monogamous. Pansexuality, or the romantic and sexual desire for people regardless of gender or biological sex, disrupts the categories of sexual orientation by favouring more fluid notions of sexual pleasure. Asexuality, the absence of sexual desire, can be understood as a conscious political act.

❸ The meaning of monogamy ranges from having a sexual relationship with only one person at a given time to having a single, lifelong relationship. Serial monogamy involves having one short-term or long-term monogamous relationship after another. Non-monogamy is defined as either sexual interactions with more than one person at a given time or any sexual relationship involving more than two people. Polyamory involves emotional or romantic connections with multiple partners.

❹ The normative gender identities of masculine and feminine, intertwined with the norm of heterosexuality, produce the sexual double standard: Men are perceived as physically dominant and sexually aggressive, while women are perceived as passive objects of men's sexual desire and as having limited sexual agency. Women thus tend to be divided into the categories of "good" girls and "bad" girls.

❺ The essentialist approach to sexuality holds that sex is determined by people's biological makeup and that our sexual identities are fixed and stable; it perceives heterosexuality as the natural state. Functionalists analyze how sexuality contributes to the smooth running of society; conflict theorists may look at the commodification of sex; and symbolic interactionists consider our sexual scripts, or the expectations we have about what is appropriate in a given context. Post-structuralists understand sexual behaviour as a product of the discourse of sexuality; feminist post-structuralists hold that sexuality, having been shaped through patriarchal discourse, can be reshaped in feminist ways. Queer theorists challenge heterosexism—the view that heterosexuality is naturally superior—as well as binary constructions of both gender and sexual identities.

❻ Sexual health issues are linked to social patterns and social relations: Individual risk for sexually transmitted infections is shaped by a variety of social factors; discourses of sexuality both enable and constrain safer sex practices; and sex education in schools tends to normalize heterosexuality and, in its focus on anatomy and biology, rarely provides information on human relationships.

Key Terms

asexuality *233*
biphobia *231*
bisexuality *230*
commodification *242*
heterosexism *227*
heterosexual *229*
homophobia *227*
homosexual *227*
monogamy *234*
non-monogamy *235*

pansexuality *232*
polyamory *235*
safer sex *248*
serial monogamy *235*
sexual health *245*
sexual identity *226*
sexual orientation *227*
sexual scripts *242*
sexually transmitted
    infections (STIs) *245*
transphobia *231*

Reviewing the Concepts

1. What are sexual scripts? Which theoretical perspective are they associated with? Can you think of an example of a sexual script?

2. Why might Foucault argue that sexuality is a modern invention?

3. In what ways is heterosexuality normalized? Does the legalization of gay marriages challenge that normalization?

Applying Your Sociological Imagination

1. Explore how transgenderism is dealt with in popular culture. In what ways are these individuals portrayed: Are they main characters or peripheral characters? Are they strong characters or victimized ones? Are they taken seriously? Does the portrayal harm or hurt transgenderism?

2. Explore whether your college or university has any programs in place that promote diverse sexualities on campus. If so, what programs are available? Who is included in these programs? If not, should your school develop such programs? For whom?

3. Does your college or university guard against discrimination on the basis of sexuality for students, faculty, and staff? Should it?

4. Why do you think the government is not interested in sanctioning group marriages? What are the political, economic, and moral issues at stake?

MySocLab

Visit MySocLab to access a variety of online resources that will help you prepare for tests and apply your knowledge.

10 Race and Racialization

The first thing you probably notice about the four young women in these photographs is that they are from different racial groups. However, as a sociologist, your task is to go beyond this obvious conclusion and employ your sociological imagination to understand the social forces influencing these women.

These women likely experience life quite differently simply because of the way they look. The white woman, as a member of the dominant majority in Canada, may never feel different or out of place while living in Canada (although, as a woman, she no doubt understands that Canadian society is largely patriarchal). The black woman, the Aboriginal woman, and the Pakistani woman, in contrast, understand that they are not members of the dominant majority, which influences their sense of self and how they experience the social world. You would all agree that being a member of a visible minority group influences a person, but as sociologists we realize that white people are also the product of social forces because skin colour defines everyone.

Traditionally, the so-called black/white binary is an approach that puts people into one of two separate and unequal categories: white (superior, defined in opposition to blackness) or black (for some, literally of black African ancestry; for others, all nonwhite or marginalized minorities). The black/white binary is both powerful—it influences the laws we make (Bond, 2010), the books we write, the movies we watch—and problematic, in that it helps maintain artificial social barriers between people. Contemporary researchers, particularly critical race theorists, continue to struggle with the dangers, possibilities, and limitations of the traditional black/white binary (Deliovsky & Kitossa, 2013).

Contemporary sociologists examine the intersections of how individual experiences emerge from larger social forces and, in turn, how they influence one's life.

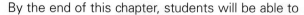

LEARNING OBJECTIVES

By the end of this chapter, students will be able to

❶ Define the term *minority* and explain its two components.

❷ Explain the social construction of race.

❸ Review and describe the psychological and sociocultural theories of prejudice, racism, and discrimination.

❹ Describe the five general categories of intergroup minority relations.

❺ Review the changing demographic picture of immigrants to Canada.

❻ Discuss Canada's two special status groups as well as Chinese and black minority groups.

❼ Explain the role of the Canadian Charter of Rights and Freedoms in preserving minority rights.

❶ What Is a Minority?

For sociologists, a **minority** is any definable category of people who are socially disadvantaged. Membership in a minority group has two components: the group lacks social power, and it is definable as being distinct from the majority. The **majority** is not defined by any inherent characteristics but, rather, by those characteristics that define the dominant group. For sociologists, the defining feature of the majority is that it uses its dominance to control the social system. In Canadian society, the dominant group is generally considered to be white males of European descent.

The first component of minority group membership accentuates the sociological principle that, despite what the term implies, it is not the number of individuals in a given group but, rather, its lack of power that makes it a minority. A classic example of this principle was the South African system of *apartheid* (from the Afrikaans word for "apartness"), wherein the numerically inferior white population dominated the numerically superior blacks. Apartheid, as a legally entrenched system, lasted from 1948 until the early 1990s (Kallaway, 2002, p. 13).

Because of their powerlessness, minorities often experience both prejudice and discrimination. Members of minority groups are often stigmatized by members of the dominant group and assigned attributes that do not exist; in other words, stigmatization is based on perceived attributes (Nelson, 2004, pp. 317–318). For example, actively or passively avoiding a Sikh man can be the result of his wearing a turban, based on a person's or group's perceived associations with turbans. To be stigmatized, then, is to be socially excluded and diminished because

minority **A definable category of people who are socially disadvantaged.**

majority **A definable category of people who are socially advantaged.**

The KKK

> > >

Canadian Aboriginal peoples are considered a minority because they often lack social power and are visually unique.

The Canadian Press/Hamilton Spectator - Sheryl Nadler

of one's minority status. For this reason, most minorities develop a strong sense of ingroup solidarity (Bernd & Brown, 2000, p. 328).

The second component of minority groups is that they are definable—that is, they are recognizably different from the majority. Race is often considered to be the key differentiating feature of a given minority group; however, as discussed in the next section, race is a socially constructed concept.

 Watch

Perceptions of Race Rooted in Life Experience

Around the world, minority groups are defined by various cultural and physical characteristics. Canadians may think first of language (French or English); Americans, of skin colour (black or white); and the Northern Irish, of religion (Catholic or Protestant). As a general rule, the more obvious the defining characteristic (language, skin colour, religious belief) is, the more severe the stigma, or negative social labels, assigned to the minority (Lindsey, Beach, & Ravelli, 2009, p. 175). The situation becomes even more challenging for people who happen to be members of more than one minority group; think of Aboriginal people who speak only their native languages and adhere to traditional spiritual practices. The cumulative effect of visible difference, language, and religion heightens these individuals' exclusion and increases their chances of experiencing prejudice and discrimination.

❷ Race: The Social Construction of Difference

race Historically, a group of people that was physically and genetically distinguished from other groups.

Race and race relations have been central concerns for sociologists for many years. The assignment of individuals to racial categories can determine people's quality of life and even how long they live (Nkansah-Amankra, Agbanu, & Miller, 2013). Historically, a **race** was defined as a group of people who were physically and genetically distinguished from other groups. These differences were largely evident in skin colour, hair texture, and facial features. For European and American researchers, the differences resulted from various groups of people becoming isolated and having to adapt to their unique environments. The fact that European populations were generally white (Caucasoid), people from Africa were generally black (Negroid), and people from Asia were generally "yellow" (Mongoloid) confirmed researchers' beliefs that people developed differently and could therefore be compared on various criteria (including intelligence).

However, since we now know that genetic differences do not determine significant behavioural or substantive biological differences, early researchers can be understood to have invented the "myth" of race (Fish, 2011, p. 6). The assignment of people to racial categories is, therefore, a function of social construction. Indeed, social scientists today assert that what most people call *race* is little more than a historical legacy of Western colonialism and ethnocentrism. While there are certainly variations around the world in how people look, these differences are simply cosmetic. Today, such concepts as biracial, multiracial, and racially hybrid further challenge the historical legacy of racial purity because such a thing does not exist in contemporary society (Korgen, 2010; Townsend, Markus, & Bergsieker, 2009); given worldwide travel and interracial unions, whatever genetic differences may have existed have certainly been diminished over time (Gravlee, 2009; Smedley, 2007).

Some estimates suggest that about 75 percent of all genes in a human being are identical to those in every other human being. With regards to the 25 percent of genes that do vary between people, about 85 percent of that variation occurs even if those people are related to each other. Another 9 percent of the variation results from membership in a particular nation or from membership in a tribe within a race—for example, both Swedes and Germans are part of the traditional Caucasoid classification. Only the final 6 percent of genetic variation results from what has been called "race." Researchers suggest that a person's race accounts for a tiny 0.24 percent of his or her genetic makeup. One might think of it this way: It is entirely possible that Avril Lavigne shares more genetic material with Rhianna than she does with Scarlett Johansson (see Gardner, 2000; see also Gross, 2009).

Moreover, there does not appear to be any credible evidence to substantiate the claim that people of different "races" are innately superior or inferior in temperament or in mental or physical abilities (Kenny, 2004, p. 410; Shanklin, 1994, 2000; Stubblefield, 2007, p. 163).

Yet the fact that the term *race* is biologically meaningless (Berthold, 2010) does not mean it is unimportant—especially to sociologists. Race remains a crucial area of study for sociologists because it is real as a social category and thus affects the lives of all people, whether through the invisible privileges that whiteness carries or the blatant or subtle discrimination that minorities face regularly (Nielsen, 2008). As the Thomas theorem tells us (see Chapter 2), what people believe to be real is real in its consequences. Since members of minority groups are perceived as different, over time they may *feel* different and begin to assume the attributes that others credit them with—in effect, a self-fulfilling prophecy. In other words, if the majority constantly views minority group members as failures, then some will indeed become failures.

Sometimes sociologists use the term **racialization** to describe the process of attributing complex characteristics (e.g., athletic abilities, intelligence) to racial categories (Dalal, 2013; Paul, 2011). For example, racialization occurs when people infer that black athletes are better than white ones, and that white coaches are better than black ones. A related concept, **internalized racism**, occurs when members of a racial group assume the attributes associated with that racial classification and internalize them as part of their identities (Ogden, 2008, p. 157; Rajiva, 2006). This can result in identity confusion, whereby people are torn between wanting to belong on one hand and wanting to embrace their differences from the majority on the other (Masko, 2005).

Today's sociologists prefer not to use the term *race*, then, (1) because it is socially constructed, (2) because there is a lack of evidence that meaningful genetic differences exist between groups, and, (3) perhaps most importantly, because the term has colonial and ethnocentric biases (Ash, 2010, p. 9; Omi & Winant, 2008). Wherever possible, the term *race* should be replaced with either *minority group* or *racialized population*, since the latter terms de-emphasize biology and accentuate the importance of a group's socially constructed status and lack of social power.

✱—[Explore

The Nation; and There Was Light, and It Was Good?

racialization
The process of attributing complex characteristics (e.g., intelligence) to racial categories.

internalized racism
The internalization of racial categorizations into a person's identity.

> > >

Many Canadian cities offer vibrant and diverse ethnic communities.

◉ Watch

Multiracial Identity

Dick Hemingway

Race, then, is an important concept for sociologists to understand by appreciating not only its colonial history, but also how it continues to influence visible minorities and their integration into contemporary society:

> The legacies of imperial domination and colonialism continue to influence our under-standing of difference, identity and belonging. The denial of Canada's history of racial violence has contributed to the production of an atmosphere that serves both to silence current experiences of racial injustice as well as to trivialize the differential effects of racism on both the perpetrator and the survivor. In short, the symbols and structures of our everyday life reproduce an atmosphere and a sensibility which communicate hostility towards those perceived as the racial other and, by extension, functions to reproduce notions of the superiority of Whites and whiteness. (Douglas, 2008, p. 44)

How does race differ from ethnicity? While genetic makeup is, of course, fixed at conception (an ascribed attribute, as defined in Chapter 1), one's ethnicity is largely a function of voluntary group membership and identity (an achieved status).

Ethnicity: The Social Construction of Group Identity

ethnicity A multidimensional concept that includes one's minority or majority status, ancestry, language, and often religious affiliation.

ethnic group A collection of people who identify with each other and share a common culture.

Sociologists suggest that like race, one's ethnic identity is socially constructed (Doane, 1997, p. 376) and significant in defining one's perception of self. **Ethnicity** is a multidimensional concept that includes one's minority or majority status, ancestry, language, and often religious affiliation. For example, identifying with your family's Greek, Chinese, or German heritage and customs is part of your ethnicity and helps to define your self-concept. An **ethnic group** is a collection of people who identify with each other and share a common culture, art forms, language, music, traditions, and beliefs (Breton, 2005; Fischer, 2007).

Canada is home to many different ethnic minorities, which we often associate with their country of origin or ancestry (e.g., Irish Canadians, Italian Canadians, Chinese Canadians, Vietnamese Canadians). As these terms suggest, ethnicity is closely linked to migration (Bathum & Bauman, 2007). This makes sense, because people naturally gravitate to others like themselves when they relocate to a new country. This is especially true when the new immigrants are quite different culturally or physically from the dominant group and may face open prejudice and discrimination (Sharma, 2005, p. 105). However, the longer that immigrants live in Canada, the more they look like members of the dominant group, the more friends they have, and the more likely they are to associate themselves with being Canadian (Walters, Phythian, & Anisef, 2007, pp. 59–60). Research confirms that with each subsequent generation, the immigrant population becomes more like the dominant culture (Rumbaut, 2004, p. 1162). This does not mean, however, that ties with the country of origin do not remain important for individuals, families, or ethnic communities.

To fully appreciate how minority groups in Canada and around the world are treated, we turn now to the concepts of *prejudice*, *racism*, and *discrimination*.

((•—[Listen

Hispanics Now
Largest Minority

BOX 10.1 WHY SHOULD WE CARE?

The Dark Enlightenment

Not all social movements focusing on issues of discrimination or minority rights are concerned with reducing social inequality. In recent years, several online communities have emerged that aim to halt—or even reverse—many of the gains made by women, racial minorities, and sexual minorities in Western societies. Members of such groups see the elimination of decades of racial and gender privilege that have favoured white, heterosexual men as a serious threat to their way of life and, they claim, against the "natural order" of the world.

These online communities (and some real-world groups as well) have embraced a set of beliefs that together are referred to as the "Dark Enlightenment." This perspective sees women as naturally inferior to men, nonwhite people as less intellectually evolved than whites, and that racial categories are objective and based on sound biological principles (e.g., see various posts appearing on the website www.thedarkenlightenment.com). This last set of beliefs is often labelled "race realism" or "human biodiversity" and runs against everything sociologists, anthropologists, and biologists have learned about human populations over the past century. The Dark Enlightenment also argues that Western, multicultural democracies are doomed to fail and that the very best governments are those that are either strictly authoritarian or are so limited in their scope that they do little more than defend their borders.

Caught up in the web of these beliefs are groups targeting "Men's Rights" and "White Rights," along with a host of Christian traditionalist, anti-Semitic, anti-secular, and anti-feminist groups, most of which argue that attempting to reduce social inequality has resulted in the persecution of traditionally dominant groups, like white, heterosexual men.

At the heart of the evil that Dark Enlightenment adherents see all around them is the "Cathedral," a vast, overarching set of ideologies built upon the belief that the modern university system is dedicated to churning out brainwashed liberal progressives who, in turn, will enact policies designed to undermine Western civilization and its white founders (Sigl, 2013).

Like many other conspiratorial movements, the Dark Enlightenment can be difficult to counter effectively. Anyone who disagrees with Dark Enlightenment "truths" is brainwashed; any counterarguments are propaganda. Those who embrace it often come to feel that they know some deep truth about what society is really like.

CONTINUED

> As a sociologist, discuss how the proliferation of sites like these can be seen as: (1) a valuable demonstration of freedom of speech; or, (2) further evidence that the anonymity provided online often inspires more racist/sexist views to proliferate than would normally be the case.

❸ Prejudice, Racism, and Discrimination

PREJUDICE

prejudice A negative prejudgment about a person or group that is irrational, long-lasting, and not based on fact.

ecological fallacy
Drawing conclusions about individual attributes from data gathered from an entire group.

exception fallacy
Drawing conclusions about an entire group based on observations of individuals.

stereotype A stable and sweeping generalization about a category of people.

racism An ideology that maintains that one "race" is inherently superior to another.

Important Questions and Debates

Media Race Relations

Recalling an Ugly Time

Prejudice is a prejudgment—a negative assessment about what a person or group is like before you actually meet them. Prejudice is irrational, long-lasting, and not based on fact.

When people draw conclusions about individuals based on generalized perceptions about an entire group, they make a mistake researchers call an **ecological fallacy**. For example, to assert that all white people are hard-working is just as absurd as suggesting that all Chinese students are good at math. Thus, ecological fallacies occur when you attribute generalized characteristics to individuals. Conversely, when people draw conclusions about an entire group based on observations of individuals, they make a mistake called an **exception fallacy** (Trochim, 2006). If a black student in your class is highly intelligent, you cannot correctly conclude that all black people are just as intelligent. Thus, exception fallacies occur when you attribute individual attributes to an entire group.

Sociologists generally view prejudiced attitudes as being the result of dominant group members' classifications because these are the people who have the power to impose their views on others. These views often result in the most harm. While minority group members may themselves hold prejudiced views of the dominant group or other minorities, they are generally not in a position to systematically impose their views on others. One particular type of a prejudice (again, a prejudgment about a person or group) is called a stereotype.

Stereotypes are stable and sweeping generalizations about a category of people that are applied to all members of that category (e.g., all blond-haired people are slow-witted) (Millard & Grant, 2006, p. 659). Stereotypes may be accurate for some members of a group, but assuming that all members of a group adhere to that generalization is inaccurate. Nevertheless, stereotypes may influence some people's interactions with members of that group. Even when stereotypes appear favourable (e.g., the common belief that Chinese Canadians are good at math), they still cause some people to pigeonhole others, thus distorting their perceptions of them.

RACISM

Another type of prejudice is, of course, racism. As we have seen, people are often treated differently because of the belief that there is such a thing as "race" and that biological differences are directly related to ability or character. Sociologists view racism as an ideology that justifies treating people differently because of their racial category. More formally, **racism** is an ideology that maintains that one race is inherently superior to another (Miles & Brown, 2003).

Today, some sociologists suggest that a racist ideology is an invaluable tool in helping a group to feel better about itself (Tredoux & Finchilescu, 2007, p. 675). By defining others as inferior, the majority group reinforces its own collective identity and sense of superiority. Further, other sociologists point out that recent initiatives to produce equality for all, termed

<<<

The American Civil Rights Movement inspired many confrontations during the 1960s.

by some as **democratic racism** (the belief that "we're all just people" and should treat everyone equally), in fact perpetuate minority differentiation and oppression. This occurs because, without real change, dominant groups will simply continue to maintain their positions of privilege (Henry & Tator, 1994; Walker, 2006).

Stereotypes and racism are the result of social processes, and to some extent everyone has some stereotypical views of other people and groups. When a person or group does something to another person or group based on those views, however, it is a cause for more serious concern.

democratic racism A system that advocates equality but in fact perpetuates minority differentiation and oppression.

DISCRIMINATION

Discrimination occurs when a person or group either denies or grants advantages to members of a particular group (Bonilla-Silva, 2013, p.124). If you decide not to hire particular people (or decide *to* hire them) based on your preconceived ideas about what you can expect from the group to which they belong, you are guilty of discrimination. In most modern societies, it is illegal to discriminate. Teachers and employers, for example, cannot let factors such as minority status, ethnicity, and gender influence how they treat their students or employees. Anyone who violates these norms is guilty of discrimination as defined by the Charter of Rights and Freedoms. Sociologists also understand that discrimination exists on various levels, and can be classified as *individual* (Booker, 2007), *direct institutional* (Owens, 2000), or *indirect institutional* (Hemphill & Haines, 1997).

Individual discrimination is just what the term implies—individuals advantage or disadvantage others because of their group membership. For example, deciding not to hire a tutor for your sociology class because she is Italian would constitute individual discrimination—no one told you to not hire the person; you made this decision on your own. In contemporary Canadian society, few people would try to justify such actions, even though they happen each and every day. **Direct institutional discrimination** occurs when an institution employs policies or practices that are discriminatory against a person or group in that they deny that person or group a right or a freedom (Helly, 2004). Canada's residential school system is

discrimination Actions that deny or grant advantages to members of a particular group.

individual discrimination Occurs when an individual advantages or disadvantages another because of that person's group membership.

direct institutional discrimination Occurs when an institution employs policies or practices that are discriminatory against a person or group.

FIGURE 10.1

Percentage of People Reporting Discrimination or Unfair Treatment "Sometimes" or "Often" in the Past Five Years, by Visible Minority Status, 2002

ᴱ Use with caution.

Note: Refers to Canada's non-Aboriginal population aged 15 and older reporting discrimination or unfair treatment in Canada because of ethnocultural characteristics.

Source: Statistics Canada (2003).

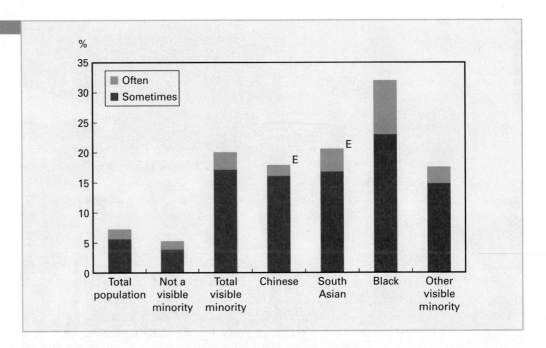

indirect institutional discrimination **When individuals are treated differently based on unlawful criteria (physical disability, cultural origin, age, gender, religion), even though this action was never intended to be discriminatory.**

 Listen

Brown v. Board: Integration as Racism

Explore

The UN Upbraids Canada for Its Use of the Term "Visible Minority"

an example of direct institutional discrimination. With many people today becoming more informed about their rights, the instances of direct institutional discrimination are declining, although they do continue to exist (Feagin & Feagin, 2008).

Indirect institutional discrimination occurs when an action results in individuals being treated differently based on unlawful criteria (physical disability, cultural origin, age, gender, religion), even though this action was never intended to be discriminatory. One of the most common examples of this form of discrimination is the weight or size requirement to become a police officer or a firefighter. While not intended to exclude certain individuals (e.g., women are, on average, physically smaller than men), this requirement effectively limits some people's ability to pursue these careers (Helly, 2004). Additionally, while Canadian law requires that people performing the same work receive the same pay, a study by Hou and Coulombe (2010) shows that people from non-European origins experience a clear disadvantage in the Canadian job market even after age and education levels are controlled for. This finding reinforces the fact that Canadian minority populations continue to face discrimination.

In contemporary Canadian society, visible minorities continue to face discrimination, both in the workplace and elsewhere (see Figure 10.1). For landed immigrants in Canada (the majority of whom are visible minorities), the most common form of discrimination faced is due to race, culture, or ethnicity (Nangia, 2013). The most frequently reported types of discrimination include being passed over for jobs and missing out on promotions, while travelling through airports or bus depots, and while trying to access medical care through provincial health systems (Nangia, 2013).

Sociologists continue to explore how the various forms of discrimination continue to influence people's lives (see Hilsdon, 2007; Walker, 2010); however, we must acknowledge that whatever the reasons given to support discrimination (e.g., deciding not to hire someone in a wheelchair because that person may be ostracized by co-workers) do not matter: All forms of discrimination should be challenged. To fully explore discrimination one should always consider how any actions or policies may negatively impact particular individuals or groups. Whenever an action and/or policy excludes or marginalizes someone, then regardless of the intention behind the action and/or policy, it is still discriminatory (Shankar, 2010).

IS PREJUDICE THE SAME AS DISCRIMINATION?

This is a good question—what do you think? Most people assume that how people act reflects how they feel, but this is not necessarily the case. Consider an unprejudiced white man living in Toronto in the nineteenth century. If he was a university engineering professor, do you think he would have advocated for the right of women to attend his classes? Probably not. During this time, very few women attended university, and he may not have wished to challenge the status quo (Miller-Bernal & Poulson, 2007). Consider the same male teacher today, who believes strongly that his female students are not as good at engineering as his male students. (Female engineering students appear to be as good as, if not better than, male engineering students; see Chen et al., 2003.) Is he likely to try to restrict women's access to his courses? Again, probably not. He may not even believe that he is discriminating against women.

Even when we do not intend to discriminate, it is sometimes hard not to; we are social beings who are often influenced by the world around us. As a rule, we generally spend time around people who are like us; the adage "Like attracts like" does have some merit (Mazzarella, 2004). However, by interacting with people from our own racial, ethnic, or professional organizations, we may be discriminating against others and not even know it. If you hire someone who went to the same university as you (but whom you don't know), are you guilty of discrimination? Are you discriminating against graduates from other schools?

The point is that we cannot always predict what people are thinking or what motivates their actions. Sociologists have known for a long time that what people think, say, and do isn't always consistent (LaPierre, 1934).[1] As Robert Merton (1938) illustrated more than 75 years ago, the relationship between being prejudiced, or not, and discriminating, or not, is a complex one. He pointed out that people can be prejudiced discriminators and nonprejudiced nondiscriminators, but also prejudiced nondiscriminators and nonprejudiced discriminators. Figure 10.2 will help you to visualize Merton's typology.

> >> Thinking Sociologically

Develop examples of situations that illustrate each of the four quadrants in Merton's typology. How do prejudice and discrimination intersect in your examples?

FIGURE 10.2

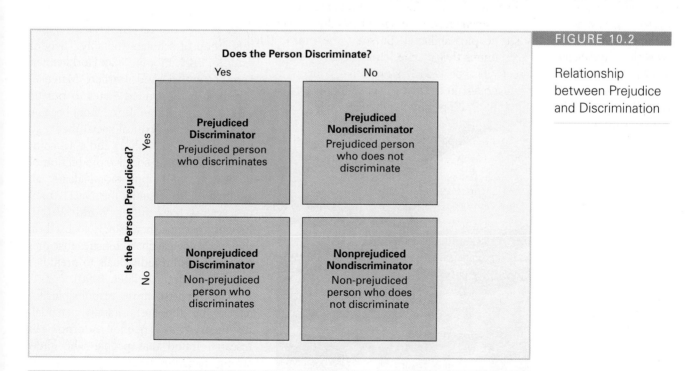

Does the Person Discriminate?

	Yes	No
Is the Person Prejudiced? — Yes	**Prejudiced Discriminator** Prejudiced person who discriminates	**Prejudiced Nondiscriminator** Prejudiced person who does not discriminate
Is the Person Prejudiced? — No	**Nonprejudiced Discriminator** Non-prejudiced person who discriminates	**Nonprejudiced Nondiscriminator** Non-prejudiced person who does not discriminate

Relationship between Prejudice and Discrimination

1 For a critique of LaPierre's classic study, see Dockery and Bedeian (1989).

Explaining Prejudice and Discrimination

scapegoat theory
The assertion that prejudice and discrimination originate in the frustrations of people who want to blame someone else for their problems.

authoritarian personality theory
Asserts that extreme prejudice is a personality trait of people who strongly believe in following cultural norms, traditions, and values.

Frankfurt School A group of German social philosophers dedicated to understanding the role of culture and mass communication in the Nazi regime.

> > >

Adolf Hitler salutes the ranks of German youth from his car during the Reich Party Day parade in 1935.

Both social psychologists and sociologists have offered several theories to explain prejudice and discrimination.

PSYCHOLOGICAL THEORIES

Scapegoat Theory If you sat back and considered why prejudice exists and why some people discriminate against others, how would you explain it? To many, **scapegoat theory** makes a lot of sense. Scapegoat theory asserts that prejudice and discrimination grow out of the frustrations of people who want to blame someone else for their problems. The theory originated with the work of American psychologist John Dollard (Dollard et al., 1939), who suggested that people displace their frustrations about virtually anything onto other identifiable people whom they can target as being responsible for their problems (Weatherley, 1988, p. 88). As stated by Babad, Birnbaum, and Benne (1983, p. 83), "when there is tension and social problems seem insurmountable, find an innocent, weak and distinctive group to blame and victimize" (as cited in Gibson & Howard, 2007, p. 193). Let's say that a Canadian factory closes because cheaper products are available from China, and a laid-off worker directs his anger at his Chinese-Canadian neighbour. As you can see, victims of scapegoating rarely have anything to do with the situation at hand (Chinese Canadians have nothing to do with China's more economical production techniques), but they suffer discrimination anyway.

Authoritarian Personality Theory According to the **authoritarian personality theory**, extreme prejudice is a personality trait linked to people who believe strongly in following cultural norms, traditions, and values. People with an authoritarian personality are generally conformists, faithfully follow instructions from their superiors, and reject those they consider to be inferior to them.

The theory is largely the result of work by researchers from what is called the **Frankfurt School**—a group of German social philosophers who worked from the conflict perspective as employed by Karl Marx and Max Weber. Fleeing the rise of the Nazi regime, this group of scholars (notably Theodor Adorno, Erich Fromm, Max Horkheimer, Leo Löwenthal, and Herbert Marcuse) travelled to the United States to pursue their work. The Frankfurt School became famous for using critical social theory to explore the role of culture and mass communication in the social reproduction of domination and oppression—clearly an attempt to understand the Nazi atrocities against Jews during World War II. Its work became increasingly focused on the psychological characteristics that predisposed certain individuals to prejudice and racial hatred (Kellner, 1990).

The theorist most responsible for developing the authoritarian personality theory was Theodor Adorno. His research found that people who show strong negative reactions toward one minority group generally feel negatively

United States Holocaust Memorial Museum

about all minorities. People with these traits see a black-and-white world in which there are clearly right and wrong solutions to all social problems. Adorno and his colleagues (1950) speculated that these characteristics may develop early in a child's life and that authoritarian personalities seem to be linked to having demanding parents who failed to provide adequate emotional support. One of Adorno's lasting contributions was his development of the *f*-test (with *f* standing for *fascist*), which assessed a person's personality and his or her likelihood of holding prejudicial attitudes (you can take an online version of the *f*-test at www.anesi.com/fscale.htm). For example, would you agree with the following statements?

f-test Adorno's assessment tool to determine a person's personality and likelihood of holding prejudicial attitudes.

- People can be divided into two distinct classes: the weak and the strong.
- Some people are born with the urge to jump from high places.
- No weakness or difficulty can hold us back if we have enough willpower.
- Most of our social problems would be solved if we could somehow get rid of the immoral, crooked, and feeble-minded people. (Authoritarian Personality, n.d.)

According to Adorno, the answers to these questions offered a glimpse into a person's likelihood of holding prejudicial views. Although widely criticized (Altemeyer, 1981; McKinney, 1973), the *f*-test is still popular, and to some it is a sound predictor of a person's racist tendencies (Ray, 1988).

SOCIOCULTURAL THEORIES

Culture Theory **Culture theory** suggests that some prejudice is found in people all over the world; it is a part of culture. As discussed in Chapter 1, some belief in the benefits of one's own culture over others (called *ethnocentrism* as described in Chapter 5) is healthy since it unifies the group. However, as also discussed, to think sociologically is to look for the beauty in all forms of cultural diversity.

culture theory **The assertion that some prejudice is healthy and part of all cultures.**

In one of the earliest attempts to understand intercultural diversity, Emory Bogardus (1925) examined the opinions of 110 businessmen and school teachers regarding 39 different ethnic and racial groups. Bogardus developed the social distance scale to investigate how people feel toward members of numerous ethnic groups in the United States (Parrillo & Donoghue, 2005). The scale was based on a person's willingness to participate in social situations with different types of people. Bogardus found that people were able to rank different ethnic groups based on how close or distant they felt to them, a concept he referred to as **social distance** (Bogardus, 1925, 1967).

In 1993, Kleg and Yamamato replicated Bogardus's research by studying the views of 135 school teachers. Their findings were remarkably consistent with Bogardus's, almost 70 years later. The most welcome groups were Western and Northern Europeans and the least tolerated were Middle Easterners, Asians, and African Americans. After all these years, it appears that American society continues to maintain relatively stable stereotypical attitudes toward different ethno-racial groups (Kleg & Yamamoto, 1998, p. 183). Canadian research in the 1970s (Mackie, 1973) found similar results, suggesting that there is consistency not only within cultures but across them as well (as cited in Macionis & Gerber, 2011).

social distance **Bogardus's concept of the relative distance people feel between themselves and other racial/ethnic groups.**

Bogardus's research challenges the assumption of authoritarian personality theorists by demonstrating that prejudice is not simply the result of an individual's personality but rather part of a culture's social fabric. It may be the case that there really is a **culture of prejudice**:

culture of prejudice **A value system that promotes prejudice, discrimination, and oppression.**

> The culture of prejudice is the antithesis of human freedom and the mortal enemy of human self-realization. It is a system of ideas and values that is rooted in the impulse of some segments of humanity to improve their condition at the expense of other humans, non-human life forms, and the health of the planet. As such, the culture of prejudice is a mainstay of social oppression and exploitation—a fount of selfish and ill-founded judgments and attitudes that are disseminated by the socially privileged

> > >

Workers in poor countries often work long hours to produce goods for wealthy consumers in rich countries.

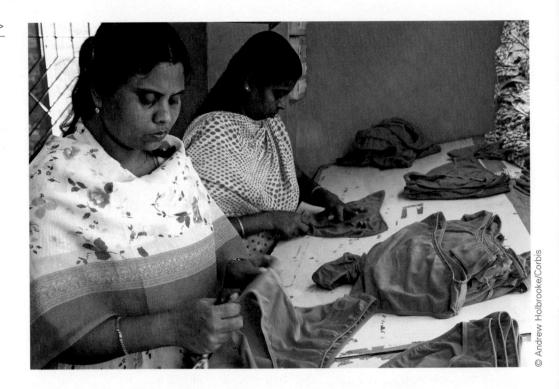

and often uncritically accepted by those who are its victims. Its chief function is to discourage the kind of critical, rational thought that might inspire collective action to achieve social justice, human equality, and genuine social progress. (Blackwell, Smith, & Sorenson, 2003, p. 13)

Functionalist Theory According to the functionalist perspective, what may be the social benefit of prejudice and discrimination? If you think about it, one positive outcome of targeting people who are different from you is that it draws your own group closer together. By identifying an individual, group, race, or nation as "other," the dominant groups in society are able to come together and confront the common enemy. Racist ideologies and the prejudice and discrimination that they breed often promote social stability. Racist ideologies allow the dominant groups to benefit from a system that they control while the minority groups face restricted opportunities and social exclusion from the rewards and opportunities available to the majority. Moreover, some suggest that minority groups have been socialized to accept racist belief systems, and that this makes them less likely to challenge existing social convention (Levin & Levin, 1982).

Contemporary functionalists also recognize, of course, that discrimination has some costs (Farron, 2000). Economically, it does not make sense to discriminate—not hiring people because of their minority status hinders a business's ability to compete with businesses that do not discriminate (Farron, 2000, p. 181). Thus, discrimination prevents a society from maximizing the benefits of diversity and the abilities of all of its citizens, while at the same time discrimination runs the risk of increasing social problems such as poverty and crime. Discrimination also requires substantial social-control expenditures to suppress those discontented minorities that do not accept the dominant ideology (Lindsey, Beach, & Ravelli, 2009, p. 180).

Conflict Theory You will remember that conflict theory assumes that people naturally compete for limited resources; of course, prejudice and discrimination are logical outcomes of that competition. Because a group's minority status is primarily defined by its lack of social power, contemporary conflict theory offers several different avenues of thought.

The first approach is called the **dual labour market theory** (also called the split labour theory), which argues that modern societies have two distinct types of labour markets. The *primary labour market* includes secure positions that pay people a healthy salary (instead of an hourly wage), offer attractive fringe benefits (such as vacation time and bonus structures), and have the potential for upward mobility within an organization. The *secondary labour market* includes jobs that offer none of these advantages; they are often insecure and temporary, pay workers hourly wages, provide only legally required benefits, and rarely offer any training to advance a worker's position. Members of minority groups are disproportionately found in the secondary labour market (Salaff, Greve, & Ping, 2002; Schaefer, 2008). Cheap, transitory labour benefits the entire dominant class because people in this labour pool do the jobs that members of the majority would find demeaning and/or distasteful. Members of the dominant group defend their advantage by keeping visible minorities out of their unions and opposing equal rights initiatives (Lindsey, Beach, & Ravelli, 2009, p. 180).

The second approach is commonly referred to as the **Marxist exploitation theory**, which views the powerful economic elite, rather than the entire dominant group, as benefiting the most from discrimination (Cox, 1948). Exploitation theory maintains that the ruling class deliberately promotes prejudice and discrimination in order to divide workers so that they cannot present the rich with a united front of opposition. Minority groups are taught to view each other, instead of the ruling class, as the enemy. As a result, workers around the world are unlikely to join together to demand fair treatment and better wages (Olzak, 2006). Due to this lack of coordinated opposition, the economic elites continue to oppress the workers and maintain control over the society that clearly benefits them.

The third approach, termed **critical race theory**, emerged in the United States as part of an initiative to examine legal rulings that appeared to preserve the interests of the rich and powerful rather than upholding the legal principle of equality under the law (Delgado & Stefanic, 2001). Critical race theory aims to redress social inequalities of the past, which makes it uniquely critical. It is typically interdisciplinary, and relies on multiple research methods to investigate the intersections of race, class, ethnicity, gender, and sexuality (Arai & Kivel, 2009; Levine-Rasky, 2011). As we reviewed in Chapter 3, critical race theory has many propositions, three of which are as follows:

1. Race remains a significant factor in determining inequity in modern society.

2. Status in modern society is largely based on property rights.

3. The intersection of race and property creates an analytical tool by which scholars can begin to understand social inequality. (Ladson-Billings & Tate, 1995, p. 323)

Although critical race theory began within the legal profession, it quickly spread into many other areas. For example, teachers may find critical race theory important to their understanding of classroom dynamics, testing, and potential curriculum biases; and politicians may find critical race theory useful in gaining a better understanding of voter characteristics and determining which issues are most salient for different groups.

All of these conflict-based approaches view prejudice and discrimination as the logical outcome of groups trying to control limited resources. Conflict theorists would argue that without restructuring modern class systems and global capitalism, substantive changes to the position of minority groups is unlikely.

Symbolic Interactionist Theory Symbolic interactionists are keenly aware of the social environment when constructing their insights into prejudice and discrimination. They believe that a person's attitudes and perceptions about minority groups are not innate but, rather, are learned as a required component of culture or an expression of class conflict. It follows that because prejudice is learned, it can be unlearned.

dual labour market theory Asserts that modern societies have two distinct labour markets (called the primary and secondary labour markets).

Marxist exploitation theory The assertion that the powerful economic elite promotes, and benefits from, prejudice and discrimination.

critical race theory An interdisciplinary approach used to investigate the intersections of race, class, ethnicity, gender, and sexuality to explain prejudice and discrimination.

> > > Thinking Sociologically

Using critical race theory, explore how discrimination, while illegal, continues to exist in Canada.

> > >

The contact hypothesis suggests that in most situations, the more time a person spends with members of a minority group, the less likely that person is to be prejudiced.

selective perception
The process whereby people see only those things that reinforce their preconceived perceptions.

contact hypothesis
The proposal that prejudiced attitudes can decline with intergroup contact.

multiracial feminism
An approach that investigates race, class, and gender and gives a voice to women of colour who may feel alienated from traditional white feminism.

© Corbis Super RF/Alamy

Research shows that negative racial and ethnic attitudes are developed between the ages of four and seven and are often greatly influenced by media images portrayed on television (Al-Shehab, 2008, p. 49; Dawkins, 2010; Aboud, 2008, p. 57). As we grow older, if prejudiced attitudes and discriminatory behaviour are consistently reinforced, we learn to limit our perception of the positive attributes of minority groups and accentuate our perceptions of the negative attributes—a process commonly referred to as **selective perception** (Fendler & Tuckey, 2006, p. 591). For example, selective perception is at work when you complain every time you witness a woman or a member of a visible minority group being a bad driver; do you also make a mental note every time you see them driving well? Prejudiced people focus on the negative, and this reinforces—to them, at least—the accuracy of their judgment of the person or group.

Symbolic interactionists also point out the powerful role that language plays in covertly reinforcing prejudiced attitudes and values. As just one example, consider the use of the word *boy* by slave owners in the American South when referring to their adult male slave labourers.

These theorists further stress the effects of living as a minority, and how minorities develop strategies to protect their self-image (Cutler, 2006; Rosenberg, 1999). For example, according to the **contact hypothesis**, intergroup contact can reduce prejudice (Tredoux & Finchilescu, 2007, p. 669; Wessel, 2009, p. 5). Three conditions must be met for this to occur:

1. Contact must be between individuals of equal status (the contact between an Aboriginal woman and the rich white family she works for would tend to reinforce and perpetuate existing stereotypical views).

2. The contact between equals must be sustained and regular (ad hoc, short-term contact does not give either party enough time to appreciate the other fully).

3. Social norms favouring equality must be agreed to by both parties (having members of the black community meet with white skinheads would probably not be productive, given that skinheads have little interest in equality). (Andersen & Francis, 2006, p. 282)

Multiracial Feminist Theory One avenue of feminist thinking that relates directly to prejudice and discrimination is **multiracial feminism**, which incorporates multiple understandings of what it means to be a woman or a man in today's society. This approach provides a framework for examining the historical, cultural, racial, and economic differences among racial groups and offers a new perspective for women of colour who may feel alienated from traditional white feminism (Harnois, 2005; Marbley, 2005, p. 610; Taylor, Rupp, & Whittier, 2006). These theorists argue that domination and oppression are not simply the result of one's race, gender, or class, but the outcome of an entire system of inequality that diminishes both women and men. Because there are multiple sites of oppression, multiracial feminists believe that to dismantle this system of domination requires an equally robust and multifaceted approach.

Post-colonial theory Post-colonial theory, as introduced in Chapter 3, investigates countries around the world that have achieved political independence from a colonial empire; examples include India, Jamaica, and Nigeria (to name only a few). **Post-colonial theory** examines the ways in which the colonial past has shaped the social, political, and economic experiences of a colonized country (Bhambra, 2007; Jones, 2010, p. 274). The theory integrates an analysis of both the past and the present to help to understand the effects of the historical legacy of the colonial experience and its impact on social institutions and structures as well as the formation of people's identities.

A country's colonial experience has a tremendous impact on the social fabric of its society. The long-term effects of imperialism and dependence on the colonial empire often translate into feelings of exclusion, and at times result in people rejecting the ideas and attitudes of the dominant culture—for example, challenging perceptions of race and ethnicity and promoting a desire for autonomy and independence. In the post-colonial atmosphere, social scientists investigate how the emerging society expresses and defines itself. By investigating the cultural products of these societies (e.g., literature, politics, and popular culture), researchers gain a glimpse into the aspirations and dreams of their people.

In September 2009, Prime Minister Stephen Harper announced to dignitaries at the G20 Summit in Pittsburgh that Canada has no history of colonialism (Reuters, 2009). While this is true in that Canada has never had a formal colonial relationship with another country, it does have a colonial history (O'Malley, 2010; Morgensen, 2011). In discussing Harper's comments, O'Malley (2010) suggests three truths about Canada's colonial past:

1. Canada was created by controlling and acquiring lands occupied by other nations (i.e., Aboriginal peoples).

2. Canada was built as a settler society and grew according to the needs and interests of the colonizers.

3. Canada's economy was built, and continues to depend on, the exploitation of natural resources for the use and benefit of its settlers.

Harper's comments offended many people who saw Canada's treatment of Aboriginal people as clear evidence of colonialism. Harper's position was particularly troublesome in that only a year earlier, on behalf of the Government of Canada, he apologized for the treatment of Aboriginal children in residential schools (Fitzpatrick & Nguyen, 2008). As we explored in previous chapters, the residential school system inflicted two related, but distinct, injustices on Aboriginal people. The first was the many incidences of physical and sexual abuse and neglect suffered by students. The second was the policy of assimilation that permeated the intent behind these schools—the desire to "kill the Indian in the child" (O'Malley, 2010). Today, post-colonial theory helps sociologists to interpret not only the historical patterns of prejudice and discrimination, but also how we need to challenge the dominant Western (Eurocentric) view of the world—not just in former colonial areas, but everywhere.

Table 10.1 summarizes the key points of each of the major schools of thought concerning prejudice and discrimination.

post-colonial theory
An approach that examines the ways in which the colonial past has shaped the social, political, and economic experiences of a colonized country.

The Five Categories of Minority Relations

All nations need to integrate diverse minority populations, which include indigenous peoples (Canada's Aboriginals, Australia's Aborigines), linguistic groups (Canada's French-speaking people, Estonia's Russian-speaking people), groups arranged by sexual orientation (heterosexual, homosexual, bisexual), and ethnic communities (Ukrainians living in Winnipeg, New York's Chinatown), to name only a few. Since no nation today can completely control who enters or moves outside of its borders, a national strategy is usually developed to manage

TABLE 10.1 Theoretical Explanations for Prejudice and Discrimination

	Key Ideas	Examples/Reflections
Psychological Theories		
Scapegoat Theory	People displace their anger and direct it toward an identifiable minority as the cause of their problems.	After a factory is moved to Southeast Asia to take advantage of lower labour costs, a displaced worker blames "those people" for taking his job.
Authoritarian Personality Theory	Extreme prejudice is a personality trait and may result from demanding parents who provided inadequate emotional support.	Those who seem to be angry at everyone and often act as if they're superior to everyone else.
Sociocultural Theories		
Culture Theory	A limited amount of prejudice acts to unify groups, and is a characteristic of all cultures.	Many Canadians are passionate about hockey and feel that this "national sport" is superior to others, a shared enthusiasm that, by contributing to a national self-definition, serves to help unify a culture.
Functionalist Theory	Limited prejudice is functional for a society, as it promotes social cohesion and stability.	By focusing on our collective similarities, we are better able to come together when faced with such broad challenges as wars and natural disasters.
Conflict Theory		
Dual Labour Market Theory	Two labour markets exist: 1. the primary labour market that includes secure, long-term jobs with good benefits 2. the secondary labour market that includes low-paying, insecure jobs with no benefits Separation of markets allows the dominant group to maintain control.	A university student begins a lucrative career after graduation, while old high school friends are still working for an hourly wage and have little prospect of promotion. Over time, the differences between them escalate until they have little in common.
Marxist Exploitation Theory	The small economic elite promote prejudice to divide workers and maintain their rule; this results in oppression and domination of all workers.	Professionals and hourly wage earners fail to realize that, in effect, they are both workers; the differences that they feel exist between them allow the truly rich and powerful to control and oppress both groups without their knowing it.
Critical Race Theory	Race remains a significant factor in determining inequity in modern society. Status in modern society is largely based on property rights, and the intersection of race and property creates an analytical tool by which scholars can begin to understand social inequality.	Prejudice and discrimination are not the result of any single thing, but rather the culmination of myriad interacting social factors. Minority status, gender, sex, property, and class come together in a unique manner to define people and how they see others.
Symbolic Interactionist Theory	Prejudice is learned and therefore can be unlearned, perhaps through more contact between different groups.	How people see the world is the result of what they've been taught; if their parents were racists, they may have lingering beliefs about what certain minority groups are like, but they can choose to "unlearn" these views.
Multiracial Feminist Theory	Domination and oppression are not simply the result of one's race, gender, or class, but the outcome of an entire system of inequality that diminishes both women and men.	By understanding how inequality is grounded in the very fabric of how we view the world, we are able to deconstruct received assumptions—for example, the global costs of the Western ideal of "success."
Post-colonial Theory	A country's colonial experience has a tremendous impact on its social fabric.	After gaining political independence, a new country can begin to throw off the colonial chains of oppression, racism, and dependence and to encourage indigenous languages, traditions, and world views.

intergroup relations, whether between minority groups or between the dominant group and minority groups. These relations can be either positive and mutually beneficial or fraught with conflict and struggle.

Sociologists put forth five general categories to help define how dominant groups interact with minority groups, from the most exclusionary to the most inclusive: genocide, expulsion or population transfer, segregation and separatism, assimilation, and cultural pluralism or multiculturalism.

GENOCIDE

Genocide is the intentional extermination of all members of a minority group. Genocide is most likely to occur when three conditions are met: (1) the dominant group is much larger than the minority, (2) the minority is of little or no economic value to the dominant group, and (3) the dominant group needs a scapegoat to blame for economic or military setbacks (duPreez, 1994).

genocide The intentional extermination of all members of a minority group.

There have been a number of horrific examples of genocide in the past 100 years. Perhaps the most infamous is the Holocaust. Hitler and his Nazi regime exterminated 6 million Jewish men, women, and children as well as hundreds of thousands of Roma (Gypsies), homosexuals, Jehovah's Witnesses, physically and mentally disabled people, communists, political opponents, prisoners of war, and others (Bauman, 1989; Chirot & McCauley, 2006; Gerlach, 2006). During the late 1970s, the Khmer Rouge in Cambodia killed at least 2 million of its own people in an effort to wipe out all Western influence—even going so far as to attempt to kill everyone who could read and write (Shawcross, 1979, as cited in Lindsey, Beach, & Ravelli, 2009, p. 182). In the 1995 Srebrenica massacre, Bosnian Serbs executed and bulldozed into mass graves 7000 Muslim men and boys in an act of "ethnic cleansing" (Evans, 2006, p. 388). And, as discussed in Chapter 1, the Hutu massacred the Tutsi in 1994 (Jones, 2006, p. 232). As of 2014, reports that have emerged from the civil war in Syria indicate that the Syrian government has engaged in the "industrialized" killing of over 11 000 prisoners and detainees (Black, 2014).

In Canada, genocide was perpetrated against the indigenous Beothuk, who lived in what is now Newfoundland. Their population at the time of European contact is thought to have been between 500 and 1000, but shortly after the Europeans settled, the Beothuk (and many other Aboriginal groups) faced disease, malnutrition, and armed conflict with settlers and other Aboriginal groups that ultimately resulted in their extinction in 1829 (Pastore, 1997). Many other Aboriginal populations in Canada were also decimated by disease and malnutrition, resulting from contact with explorers and settlers.

EXPULSION OR POPULATION TRANSFER

Sometimes, under the same circumstances that can lead to genocide, the dominant group forces a minority to leave the country or confines them to a particular location. The decision to expel or transfer the minority rather than exterminate them is partly due to a mix of morality and political practicality, but the goal is essentially the same: to remove the minority group from society (Lindsey, Beach, & Ravelli, 2009, p. 183).

There are several instances of expulsion or population transfer in Canada's history. An early example of population transfer occurred between 1755 and 1763, when French-speaking Acadians were exiled by the British from what is now Nova Scotia. More than 12 000 people were exiled and many died from illness, drowning, misery, and starvation (Canadiana, 2010; Doucet, 2000). In addition, in the nineteenth century, the Canadian and American governments forced many Aboriginal people onto reserves. Two other examples from Canadian history clearly demonstrate the challenges faced by minorities during times of war: the internments of Ukrainians during World War I and of Japanese during World War II. (Germans and Italians suspected of spying were also placed in internment camps during World War II.)

> > >

During World War II,
22 000 Japanese
Canadians were sent to
forced-labour camps.

With the outbreak of World War I, the Canadian government implemented the *War Measures Act* in 1914. Under this legislation, 8579 "enemy aliens" were interned, more than 5000 of whom were Ukrainians who had emigrated to Canada from areas under the control of the Austro-Hungarian Empire. An additional 80 000 people (mostly Ukrainians) were obliged to register as enemy aliens and to report regularly to local authorities (Breti, 1998). These internees were used as forced labourers at Banff National Park; in the logging industry in northern Ontario and Quebec; in the steel mills of Ontario and Nova Scotia; and in the mines of British Columbia, Ontario, and Nova Scotia. This policy was intended to protect Canadians but also to help Canada build its industrial infrastructure. The forced labour program was so successful in helping businesses prosper that the internment of these immigrants lasted for two years after the end of World War I (Breti, 1998).

After the Japanese attack on the American naval base at Pearl Harbor on December 7, 1941, many Canadians worried that Japanese Canadians might be sympathetic to, or even work on behalf of, the Japanese Empire. The federal government once again invoked the *War Measures Act* to allow the largest mass expulsion in Canadian history. Japanese-Canadian men, and later their families, were sent to cramped, under-heated internment camps in the British Columbia interior and to farms in Alberta, where they were used as forced labour. Their businesses, property, and most of their personal possessions were sold by the government at a fraction of their value. In all, roughly 22 000 Japanese Canadians were forced to move to these camps (Granatstein & Johnson, 2008, p. 222).

A United Nations report suggests that today more than 43 million people around the world are forcibly displaced as a result of conflict and persecution. Of these, 15 million people have fled their home countries while 27 million are displaced within their own homelands. As of 2014, the major refugee populations include Palestinians (4.8 million), Afghans (2.9 million), Iraqis (1.8 million), Somalis (700 000), Congolese (456 000), Myanmarese (407 000), Colombians (390 000), and Sudanese (370 000) (United Nations, 2014).

SEGREGATION AND SEPARATISM

Segregation is the formal physical or social separation of dominant and minority groups. It often allows the dominant group to benefit from the exploited labour of minority groups while maintaining its superior social position.

The Canadian Aboriginal reserve system is one example of segregation. Today, there are 2675 land reserves for First Nations peoples in Canada covering about 13 percent of the country (BC Ministry of Aboriginal Affairs, 2007). In most cases, these reserves are isolated from urban centres and lack many of the social services and municipal infrastructures common in Canadian cities and towns. Registered Indians living on reserves remain some of the poorest people in Canada.

There are several examples of segregation in other countries. One was the segregation of blacks in the United States, where slave labour was essential to the plantations of the American South and where, prior to 1865, African Americans were subjected to the ultimate degradation of being "owned." In addition, in South Africa, under apartheid, although blacks were technically free, their rights to live, work, and travel where they wished were restricted (Sparks, 1990). In these two cases, blacks were regarded as less than fully human, denied most or all civil rights, and frequently treated with great brutality (Lindsey, Beach, & Ravelli, 2009, p. 184).

A concept related to segregation is separatism. **Separatism**, also called ethnic nationalism, occurs when minority groups believe that the dominant group will never allow them to assimilate or to exist within a truly pluralistic society. While segregation is imposed by the majority to separate it from minority groups, separatism is pursued by minority groups as a means of preserving their cultural integrity. Separatism may take the form of seeking to form an independent state, as in the Quebec sovereignty movement and among the Kurds in central Asia. It may also take the form of seeking to live a largely separate life within a country dominated by a different group—for example, those living in Vancouver's Chinatown, who preserve their traditions and choose to live in close proximity to other Chinese Canadians. Another classic Canadian example of separatism is, of course, the French in Quebec. (See the discussion of Québécois later in this chapter.)

ASSIMILATION

Over time, some dominant group–minority group relationships reach the point where assimilation occurs. **Assimilation** is a one-way process that occurs when a minority group sheds its differences and assumes the traits of the dominant group. This transition is made easier when five conditions are met:

1. Members of the minority group migrate to the area voluntarily.

2. Members of the minority group arrive during a period of economic prosperity.

3. Members of the minority group are physically similar to the dominant group.

4. The minority group is culturally similar to the dominant group.

5. The number of members in the minority group is relatively small. (Blauner, 1972; Brown & Bean, 2006; Simpson & Yinger, 1985)

Not one of these conditions applies to Canada's Aboriginal peoples. Nonetheless, the federal government's 1969 White Paper advocated total assimilation of First Nations peoples. All legislation pertaining to them was to be repealed, thereby denying their unique and special status in Canada. The report also rejected existing treaties and land claims and was an obvious attempt to sever all ties between the First Nations peoples and the federal government (Lazar, 2003).

In the face of strong opposition, the federal government never enacted any of the contentious policies proposed in the 1969 White Paper. Yet the legacy of the residential

segregation The formal physical or social separation of dominant and minority groups.

separatism Voluntary structural and cultural isolation by minority groups from the dominant group.

assimilation A one-way process that occurs when a minority group sheds its differences and assumes the traits of the dominant group.

school system, along with the poor living conditions on reserves and Aboriginals' ongoing economic plight, demonstrates that new strategies for helping Aboriginal peoples to prosper must be pursued.

While complete assimilation holds the promise of full acceptance of the minority group, it comes at a significant cost (Snipp & Hirschman, 2004; Viruell-Fuentes, 2006, p. 338). The minority group loses its unique identity and risks never being fully accepted. Is it possible

BOX 10.2 ISSUES IN GLOBAL CONTEXT

UN Decades of the World's Indigenous Peoples

The United Nations estimates that 370 million indigenous people are living in more than 70 countries around the world. These populations include the Aborigines in Australia, the Masai in Kenya, the Anka Hill tribe in Thailand, the Mapuche in Chile, Native Americans in the United States, and Aboriginal peoples in Canada (United Nations, 2009).

Some characteristics of indigenous populations are universal. They all suffer from discrimination and are often the poorest individuals in their society. According to the World Health Organization, indigenous populations have a higher rate of infant mortality, a shorter life expectancy, and a greater likelihood of suffering from such chronic illnesses as diabetes and heart disease. Industrial development of ancestral lands often displaces indigenous peoples from their traditional ways of life (Indian and Northern Affairs Canada, 1998). Land disputes between indigenous populations and the colonizers of a particular area are not uncommon.

Western Australia's native Aborigines, particularly the young, suffer from respiratory, gastrointestinal, infectious, and parasitic diseases. Contributing factors to these diseases include inadequate housing, poor personal hygiene, lack of clean water, poor sanitation, obesity, substance abuse, and exposure to violence.

The Mapuche (meaning "people of the land") of Chile, who traditionally subsisted as farmers, have been pushed off their native lands since as long ago as 1530. In 1986, they were again displaced as logging companies moved into their area to try to meet the growing demand for wood chips by industrialized countries, putting a great deal of pressure not only on the Mapuche, but also on their environment (Diaz & Nuñez, 1993).

Native Americans and Canadian Aboriginals contend with similar issues, including outstanding land claims, lack of political representation, forced assimilation programs, abuse, chronic unemployment, poverty, and an overrepresentation in the criminal justice system. As a result of these conditions, the indigenous populations in both Canada and the United States have been forced to take part in many protests and demonstrations to raise awareness about issues affecting them and to bring political pressure to bear on elected officials. According to Wilkes (2006, pp. 511–512), indigenous peoples of the United States have been more politically active on a national scale than have their Canadian counterparts. For example, Wilkes argues that strong leadership, well-developed political networks, and a strong collective national identity exist in the United States more than they do in Canada.

In 1994, and then again in 2004, the United Nations launched the International Decade of the World's Indigenous Peoples in order to draw attention to the plight of these peoples. The UN's goal was the "strengthening of international cooperation for the solution of problems faced by indigenous people in such areas as culture, education, health, human rights, the environment and social and economic development, by means of action-oriented programs and specific projects, increased technical assistance, and relevant standard-setting activities" (United Nations Permanent Forum on Indigenous Issues, 2007).

In your opinion, do global initiatives like this one make any difference to the world's indigenous peoples? Why?

that some members of the dominant group will never consider visible minorities to be equals (Zweigenhaft & Domhoff, 1998)? Some minority group members assume that assimilation is little more than abandoning one's cultural identity in the pursuit of material gain (Nagel, 1994).

Some see the American approach to integrating minority populations as a form of assimilation; this approach is commonly referred to as a **melting pot**, a metaphor for minority integration whereby new immigrants willingly blend their traditions and cultural identity into the dominant American culture (Leidman & Wiggins, 2010; Newman, 2006). In fact, during the nineteenth century, many influential Americans believed that the "American race" could effectively absorb and permanently improve the less desirable traits of all immigrant groups (Mason, 2007, p. 102).

melting pot The blending of new immigrants' traditions and cultural identity into the dominant American culture.

CULTURAL PLURALISM OR MULTICULTURALISM

The final pattern of minority group–dominant group relations is **cultural pluralism**, commonly referred to as **multiculturalism**. This situation exists when minority groups retain their cultural identities and the larger society promotes cultural, ethnic, and racial diversity— arguably, the Canadian approach to minority integration. In 1971, Canada became the first country in the world to adopt multiculturalism as official policy—an interesting turnaround just two years after the notorious White Paper discussed above (Canadian Heritage, 2007a). The policy also confirmed the rights of Aboriginal peoples and the status of Canada's two

cultural pluralism or multiculturalism The retention of minority groups' cultural identities and the promotion of cultural, ethnic, and racial diversity by the larger society.

BOX 10.3 CANADIAN CONTRIBUTIONS TO SOCIOLOGY

Himani Bannerji

Himani Bannerji is a professor of sociology at York University. Born in what is now Bangladesh, she is well known not only for her analyses of race, gender, and multiculturalism, but also for her studies in Canadian literature (Kain, 2000, p. 8).

Bannerji's critiques of the inner workings of class, gender, and race have contributed a great deal to our understanding of contemporary society. Her analysis of the "intersectionality" of racism, sexism, and heteronormativity, when combined with other forms of exclusion and oppression, illustrates how complex and dynamic the forces of domination really are. Her theoretical approach is greatly influenced by Karl Marx, whose writings, like Bannerji's today, challenged conventional political and academic debate. In Bannerji's introduction to *The Writing on the Wall*, a 1993 volume of essays, she notes that she "remain[s] very suspicious, not about naïveté, or revolutionary romanticism, but about the pragmatism of our 'postindustrial, postmodern, postsocialist, posthuman' world" and the "issues spinning out of colonialism, imperialism, class and gender" (Bannerji, 1993, as cited in Kain, 2000, p. 9).

Bannerji's novels for young people similarly focus on race. For example, *Coloured Pictures* (1991) involves a 13-year-old South Asian girl, Sujata, who stands up to a racist bully in her class (Kain, 2000, p. 10).

Dr. Bannerji has edited many collections of sociological theory, including *Of Property and Propriety: The Role of Gender and Class in Imperialism and Nationalism* (2001), *The Dark Side of the Nation: Essays on Multiculturalism, Nationalism and Gender* (2000), *Thinking Through: Essays on Feminism, Marxism and Anti-Racism* (1995), and *The Writing on the Wall: Essays on Culture and Politics* (1993).

Himani Bannerji

Courtesy Himani Bannerji

official languages. Later, in 1985, Canada's *Multiculturalism Act* confirmed the federal government's intention of preserving and enhancing the spectrum of human diversity in Canada, be it racial, cultural, or linguistic. By so doing, Canada affirmed the value and dignity of all Canadian citizens regardless of their racial or ethnic origins, language, and religious affiliation.

Canadian multiculturalism is grounded on the belief that, while all citizens must be treated equally, we should not overlook how our differences enrich our society. Multiculturalism confirms that all citizens can retain their unique cultural and ethnic identities and be proud of their ancestry, yet still feel a sense of belonging as Canadians. However, sceptics may question whether the dominant white majority follows through on its commitment to multiculturalism in light of how many react during times of economic hardship or during international conflicts. Some critics perceive multiculturalism as merely the superficial encouragement of ethnic dancing and traditional foods; while, immigrants are still expected to adopt the values and attitudes of the dominant society. Others complain that multiculturalism tends to freeze cultures in a fixed state and does not allow them to evolve (Lindsey, Beach, & Ravelli, 2009, p. 186).

❺ The Changing Demographic Picture of Immigration

✳⟦Explore

Immigration

Many minority groups gain their inferior social status only once they migrate to other countries. Others, such as Aboriginals in Canada or Catholics in Northern Ireland, became minorities when more dominant outsiders came to their land and settled.

Immigration levels are the result of many forces: displacement of people caused by war and political upheaval, economic growth or collapse, changes in immigration policies and procedures, and changes in global communication and transportation networks. Figure 10.3 shows that immigration levels spiked during the late 1880s, the 1910s, and the 1950s, and they have remained comparatively high and stable since the 1990s.

During the beginning of the twentieth century, new immigrants to Canada were instrumental not only in developing the West, but also in setting up various industrial plants throughout the country. Not surprisingly, World War I and the Great Depression led to lower immigration levels. The 1950s saw vast postwar economic growth, as well as global recognition that Canada was a safe and stable place in which to settle and raise a family. In 1967, Canada implemented a points system as a way to encourage skilled workers to immigrate to

FIGURE 10.3	
Number of Immigrants to Canada (Permanent Residents), 1860 to 2010	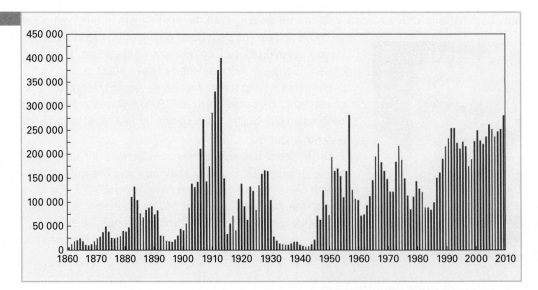

Reprinted by permission from Citizenship and Immigration Canada, 2012 [online]. [Permanent Residents] Retrieved May 5, 2014 from http://www .cic.gc.ca/english/resources/ statistics/facts2010/images/ perm_res_1860_2010.gif

FIGURE 10.4

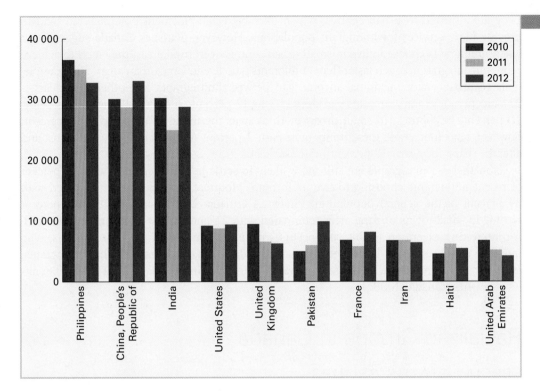

Canada: Permanent
Residents by Top 10
Source Countries,
2010–2012

Reprinted by permission
from Canada – Permanent
residents by top source
countries, 2010-2012 [online].
Retrieved March 6, 2014,
from http://www.cic.gc.ca/
english/resources/statistics/
facts2012/images/figure8.jpg

Canada. Under this system, there were no quotas on the number of people who could immigrate to Canada but prospective immigrants were assigned points if they possessed a number of desired qualities. These qualities included whether they knew English or French (Canada's two official languages); had arranged for employment in Canada; had a relative or family member in Canada; had university education or special training; and were immigrating to an area of Canada with high employment (Makarenko, 2010). The economic problems experienced through the 1970s and 1980s saw immigration rates fall once again, only to recover somewhat with the economic prosperity of the mid-1990s.

More recently, changes to federal immigration policy have made it easier to relocate to Canada, a situation that many believe is in the best long-term interests of the country since immigration promotes diversity and facilitates population growth. Indeed, without immigration, Canada's population growth would slow—an unhealthy condition for any country (Wayland, 1997).

In 2011, more than 6.7 million foreign-born people were living in Canada, representing 20.6 percent of the total population—the highest proportion in the past 75 years (in comparison, the United States has 13 percent foreign-born people, and Australia has 26.8 percent). The largest group of recent immigrants is from Asia (including the Middle East) at 56.9 percent, followed by Europe at 19.7 percent, and Central and South America and the Caribbean at 12.3 percent (Statistics Canada, 2012b). Figure 10.4 shows the top 10 countries of origin between 2010 and 2012. Between 2006 and 2011, over 1.1 million foreign-born people immigrated to Canada (Statistics Canada, 2012b). The figure also shows that the Philippines has become the largest country of origin for Canadian immigrants (up from tenth place in 1981), while China, India, the United States, and the United Kingdom remain important sources of immigrants (Statistics Canada, 2012b).

Immigrants tend to settle in the most populous provinces—Ontario, Quebec, and British Columbia—and are least likely to settle in the northern regions (Chui, Tran, & Maheux, 2007).

>>> Thinking Sociologically

What social and economic factors might influence immigrants' decisions about where to live when they move to Canada?

They are attracted to urban centres, which offer better employment potential and tend to provide more services for immigrant populations. However, Statistics Canada suggests that when immigrants choose to live in small urban centres or in rural areas, they tend to achieve economic integration much faster than immigrants who live in large urban areas. For example, in large urban areas, the initial income gap between immigrants and other Canadians is 37 percent; after four years, this gap decreases to 22 percent; and after 12 years, falls below 10 percent. In contrast, in small urban or rural areas the initial income gap is 14 percent; however, after four years, these immigrants earn 2 percent more than other Canadians, and after 11 years, they earn 18 percent more (see Chui, Tran, & Maheux, 2007).

Nonetheless, immigrants are still more likely to settle in urban centres, with 63 percent of recent immigrants choosing to live in Toronto, Montreal, or Vancouver (compared with 34 percent of the general population) (Statistics Canada, 2011b) and less than 3 percent settling in small towns or rural areas (compared with 22 percent of the general population). An interesting exception to this rule occurs with immigrants from the United States, who integrate more quickly in larger centres than they do in smaller ones. All other immigrants, especially those from Asia, integrate more rapidly (in economic terms, at least) in smaller cities (Statistics Canada, 2008q).

⑥ Racialized Groups in Canada

SPECIAL STATUS GROUPS

Aboriginal Peoples In 2011, Aboriginal peoples accounted for 4.3 percent of Canada's total population, an increase from 3.3 percent in 2001 and 2.8 percent in 1996 (Statistics Canada, 2011a). The Canadian Aboriginal population has grown much faster than the non-Aboriginal population; in fact, it has been classified as a "population explosion." For example, between 2006 and 2011, the Aboriginal population's rate of growth was 20.1 percent, while the rest of the Canadian population grew at a rate of around 5.2 percent during the same period (Aboriginal Affairs and Northern Development, 2011). Table 10.2 shows the Aboriginal population in Canada by number, province, and percentage of total population.

Many Aboriginal communities have made impressive strides to increase education levels, decrease infant mortality rates, and address substance abuse issues. Despite these successes, Aboriginal people remain at higher risk for illness and die younger than the Canadian population as a whole. They also suffer from more chronic diseases such as diabetes and heart disease than the general population, and there is evidence that these illnesses are getting worse (Health Canada, 2005; Jardine, Boyd, & Furgal, 2009).

Inadequate housing and crowded living conditions are factors in the higher rates of respiratory problems and other infectious diseases among Aboriginal children. Children within Aboriginal families also have higher rates of unintentional injuries and accidental deaths. Young men, particularly in Inuit communities, are far more likely to commit suicide than their peers in Canada as a whole (Health Canada, 2005). Aboriginal children in some communities are more likely than children in the general population to smoke, drink, and use illegal drugs.

Québécois From the earliest contact between European explorers and Aboriginal peoples, it became clear that Canada would develop according to the needs and practices of the French and English, which sociologist John Porter (1965) termed Canada's **charter groups**. Porter argued that French and English settlers quickly became the social, economic, and political elite of Canada, a situation that remains largely unchanged today. While the dominance of the English-speaking group in Canada is unquestioned, the unique influence of French-speaking Canadians cannot be overestimated. The French have always seen themselves as a distinct

charter groups The French and the English in Canada; Porter recognized the important role these groups played in Canadian history and contemporary social and political development.

TABLE 10.2 Number and Distribution of Population Reporting Aboriginal Identity, 2011

Provinces and Territories	Aboriginal Identity Population	Percent Distribution	Aboriginal Identity Population as a Percentage of the Total Population
Canada	1 400 685	100.0	4.3
Newfoundland and Labrador	35 800	2.6	7.1
Prince Edward Island	2 230	0.2	1.6
Nova Scotia	33 845	2.4	3.7
New Brunswick	22 615	1.6	3.1
Quebec	141 915	10.1	1.8
Ontario	301 425	21.5	2.4
Manitoba	195 900	14.0	16.7
Saskatchewan	157 740	11.3	15.6
Alberta	220 695	15.8	6.2
British Columbia	232 290	16.6	5.4
Yukon	7 705	0.6	23.1
Northwest Territories	21 160	1.5	51.9
Nunavut	27 360	2.0	86.3

Source: Number and distribution of the population reporting an Aboriginal identity and percentage of Aboriginal people in the population, Canada, provinces and territories, 2011[online]. Retrieved March 6, 2014, from http://www12.statcan.gc.ca/nhs-enm/2011/as-sa/99-011-x/2011001/tbl/tbl02-eng.cfm

society within Canada; when Prime Minister Stephen Harper suggested in 2006 that the "Québécois form a nation within a united Canada" (Sheppard, 2006), it was the latest demonstration of the central role that the tension between French and English Canada continues to play in setting the national political agenda.

Quebec separatism has been a contentious issue throughout much of Canadian history. Since the eighteenth century, when England defeated France in the battle for control of North America, the relationship between English Canadians and French Canadians has been strained. The English–French relationship has been defined as "one country, two histories" and as "two solitudes" (MacLennan, 1945). Even before Canada's birth in 1867, there were French Canadians who believed that their province must become an independent state or the French would face the loss of their language and culture. Throughout much of the nation's history, the Québécois have felt that they are an oppressed minority. Even in Quebec, where the French are the majority, political and economic life was often dominated by the English.

This situation began to change during the 1960s, when Quebec underwent the **Quiet Revolution**, when the province moved into a more modern phase of its development and challenged the traditional power of the Catholic Church while advocating for greater economic, political, and cultural equality with the rest of Canada (Juteau, 2002, p. 450).

In 1976, the first separatist government came to power in the province. The Parti Québécois (PQ) held a referendum on separatism in 1980, but 60 percent of Quebecers voted against the idea. In 1995, a second referendum on "sovereignty association" also resulted in a "no" vote, but the narrow margin of votes (50.6 percent "no" versus 49.4 "yes") emphasized the strength of separatist feelings. While the movement has since retreated, many Québécois

Quiet Revolution A movement in Quebec during the 1960s, when political and religious traditions were challenged and the French struggled for greater economic, political, and cultural equality with the rest of Canada.

> > >

Rene Levesque led the separatist Parti Québécois to victory on November 15, 1976.

still feel strongly about the need to protect their distinct culture and their language (Guibernau, 2006).

Language laws have also been a point of tension on the national stage for well over 400 years. In 1974, Quebec Liberals passed Bill 22, which made French the province's official language and restricted enrolment in English schools. Three years later, the newly elected Parti Québécois, under the leadership of René Lévesque, introduced the Charter of the French Language, or Bill 101, as it became known (Conrick, 2006). Within that bill was the declaration that, with few exceptions, French was to be the only language allowed on commercial signs in the province. In 1988, the Supreme Court of Canada ruled that English could not be prohibited altogether but that requiring the predominance of French on commercial signs was a reasonable limit on freedom of expression. In response, Premier Robert Bourassa invoked the "notwithstanding" clause that overrode the Charter of Rights and Freedoms, and later introduced Bill 178, which decreed that only French could be used on exterior signs while English would be allowed inside commercial establishments. In October 2009, the Supreme Court of Canada once again weighed into the language debate declaring a Quebec law barring certain students from going to public English-language schools unconstitutional (Bishku-Aykul, 2009).

After nearly 100 years of fiery debate and highly controversial language legislation—and despite the massive English presence surrounding Quebec, the pervasive influence of English television, and the burgeoning borderless use of the Internet—82.5 percent of Quebecers still speak French at home (Statistics Canada, 2014).

OTHER RACIALIZED GROUPS

Chinese Canadians Chinese Canadians are currently the second-largest visible minority group in Canada. Unfortunately, their history in this country has been fraught with hardship.

The Chinese first began settling in the United States after slavery was abolished. Wealthy American farmers and businessmen found that poor, landless Chinese men from Guangdong and Fujian provinces were willing to perform the back-breaking work formerly carried out by African slave labourers. Some of these Chinese men ultimately immigrated to Canada when gold was found in British Columbia's Fraser River Valley in 1858 (Willmott, 1970, p. 43). Once here, the Chinese found that they were allowed access to the mines only after white prospectors had extracted virtually all of the gold. By 1860, other Chinese had begun arriving in British Columbia directly from China. Between 1881 and 1884, more than 15 000 Chinese travelled to Canada to work.

About 17 000 Chinese immigrants became labourers on the Canadian Pacific Railway, performing very difficult and dangerous work. In all, more than 700 Chinese men lost their lives helping Canadians to build their national railway. Chinese workers were paid half as much as white workers who did the same job. The only other work the Chinese were able to get was as cooks and launderers—two occupations that did not threaten white male workers since these jobs were considered to be "women's work" (CBC News in Review, 1999).

Although the Chinese were tolerated when their labour was needed, once the railway was completed in 1885, they were no longer welcome. Thousands of labourers were laid off from the railway, and the Canadian government imposed a "head tax" on any Chinese person wanting to enter Canada. The head tax was initially set at $50, but in 1900 it was increased to $100, and in 1903 was increased again—this time to $500, the equivalent of two years' salary for Chinese labourers at that time. The Chinese were the only ethnic group that had to pay such a tax. On July 1, 1923, the Canadian government passed the *Chinese Immigration Act* (also known as the *Chinese Exclusion Act*), which prevented any further Chinese immigration to Canada (Lee, 2002, p. 78).

The act meant that Chinese men already living in Canada could not bring their wives and children from China, and therefore had to face their hardships alone. The women and children left behind experienced starvation and extreme economic hardships as well. Many families were separated for long periods, and some never reunited. For many years, Chinese Canadians protested against the *Chinese Exclusion Act* by closing their businesses on July 1 and boycotting celebrations on Dominion Day (now known as Canada Day), which they referred to as "Humiliation Day" (Chinese Canadian National Council, 2006).

It was not until 1947 that Canada finally granted Chinese Canadians full status rights as Canadian citizens and the right to vote in federal elections (Holland, 2007, p. 153; CBC News in Review, 1999). However, as a highly visible minority group with cultural traditions very different from those of the European majority, they continued to face prejudice and discrimination.

In 2006, Stephen Harper apologized in the House of Commons for the Canadian government's implementation of the head tax and subsequent exclusion of Chinese immigrants. The government also announced that it would make symbolic payments of $20,000 to living head taxpayers and to persons who had been in a conjugal relationship with a now-deceased head taxpayer.

The Canadian government is undertaking further historical recognition initiatives. In 2006, it launched the $24 million Community Historical Recognition Program and the

< < <

As Canada's second largest visible minority group, Chinese Canadians often express their unique culture through events like this one in Vancouver's Chinatown.

Reuters/Andy Clark

$10 million National Historical Recognition Program. The purpose of these programs is to "commemorate and educate Canadians about the historical experiences and contributions of ethnocultural communities impacted by wartime measures and immigration restrictions" (Government of Canada, 2007b).

From a sociological perspective, Chinese Canadians are remarkable for how resilient they are, how successful they are, and the tremendous contributions they have made to Canadian society.

Black Canadians Black Canadians, the third-largest visible minority group in Canada, have also had a long and troubled history.

The history of black Canadians really began in the United States with the slave trade. In the seventeenth and eighteenth centuries, tens of millions of Africans were shipped in deplorable conditions to the United States to work on sugar plantations. Some estimate that only 15 million survived the journey. In their new homeland, harsh living conditions and cruelty led to many more deaths from disease and exhaustion. Thus began their quest for freedom: the international clandestine uprising that has come to be known as the underground railroad (Owen Sound's Black History, 2004), a loosely constructed network of escape routes that began in the Deep South, continued through the northern free states, and eventually led to Canada. In Canada, as in Mexico and the Caribbean, blacks could live as free citizens.

The network was so secretive that very little is known about its actual operation. However, historians estimate that between 40 000 and 100 000 freedom seekers made it to Canada. As a result, a substantial black population established itself in Upper Canada (now known as Ontario). When peace and civil rights returned to the United States, many former slaves travelled south to reconnect with family and friends (Owen Sound's Black History, 2004).

Although slavery was never a significant part of Canada's social structure, we should not believe that slavery never happened here. It was not until 1793 that Lieutenant-Governor John Graves Simcoe banned the importation of slaves to Upper Canada. However, because a number of United Empire Loyalists had brought enslaved people with them, those already in the colony would remain enslaved under the law; the children of enslaved women would

> > >

Halifax's poor but vibrant Africville community, established in the 1840s and made up of about 400 black residents, was bulldozed in the 1960s in the name of urban renewal—an act considered by many to be based on racial discrimination.

Nova Scotia Archives and Records Management, Two young women walking by a house, Africville, Bob Brooks, photographer, ca. 1965; NSARM, Bob Brooks fonds, 1989-468, box 16 (neg. sheet 7, image 15)

be freed at age 25. In 1834, the *Emancipation Act* abolished slavery in all British holdings, including Canada (O'Connell, 2005).

Today, many black Canadians enjoy educational and economic prosperity and have become an integral part of Canada's social landscape. There are currently more than 1 million blacks in Canada. This number represents a steady increase over the past few decades, owing in part to increasing overall immigration levels and to the elimination of immigration policies that were preferential to European immigrants.

Immigration decisions are now largely based on a point system (discussed earlier in this chapter) that rewards immigrants with high employability potential. Black immigrants have competed very successfully under these new immigration procedures. The majority of black immigrants come not from the United States, but from the Caribbean and, more recently, from Africa, including refugees from Ethiopia and Somalia.

Canada's black population is growing quickly, and while black children are more likely to live in lone-parent families than are nonblack children, they are just as likely as other Canadians to attend university. However, they are more likely to earn less and be unemployed more often than other Canadians (Statistics Canada, 2004a).

> >> > Thinking Sociologically
>
> Briefly review and reflect on the historical treatment of Aboriginal peoples, as well Japanese, Chinese, and black immigrants to Canada. Which sociological theory do you feel best explains these minority groups' experiences? Why?

The Charter and Minority Rights

The Canadian Charter of Rights and Freedoms is one component of the Canadian Constitution, a series of laws containing the basic rules about how our country should operate. The Charter, which came into law in 1982, sets out the rights and freedoms that Canadians believe are required in an open and democratic society. These include the following:

- Freedom of expression
- The right to a democratic government
- Freedom to live and to seek employment anywhere in Canada
- Legal rights for people accused of crimes
- The right to equality, including the equality of men and women
- The right of French and English linguistic minorities to an education in their own language
- The rights of Canada's Aboriginal peoples
- The protection of Canada's multicultural heritage (Canadian Heritage, 2007c)

Section 15 of the Charter, Equality Rights, came into effect three years after the Charter, on April 17, 1985, a delay that allowed various levels of government enough time to ensure that their laws were adjusted to be consistent with the new section.

The Charter has had a major impact on the promotion and protection of human rights in Canada. For more than 30 years, it has been the driving force of change and progress and the affirmation of our society's values. Canadian courts have rendered more than 300 decisions in which they invoked the Charter to bring Canadian laws into accordance with the principles and values of Canadian society.

Any individuals or groups who believe that their rights or freedoms have been violated can go to court and seek a remedy. Until recently, financial support was provided for people who did not have the resources to proceed with a court challenge. The Court Challenges Program of Canada was a national nonprofit organization set up in 1994 to provide financial assistance for important court cases that advance language and equality rights guaranteed under Canada's Constitution, including challenges to federal laws, policies, and practices. Prime Minister Stephen Harper's Conservative government cancelled the program in 2006 (Alliance for Equality of Blind Canadians, 2008).

Summary

❶ A minority group is any definable category of people who are socially disadvantaged; minority groups lack power and are recognizably different from the majority group.

❷ Race is considered to be a socially constructed concept because actual genetic differences between "races" are tiny and determine neither behavioural nor biological differences. Ethnicity is socially constructed to the extent that it encompasses minority or majority status, language, customs, and religion.

❸ Psychological approaches to prejudice and discrimination include the scapegoat and authoritarian personality theories. Sociocultural approaches include culture, functionalist, conflict, symbolic interactionist, multiracial feminist, and post-colonial theories.

❹ The five general categories of intergroup minority relations, from most exclusionary to most inclusive, are genocide, expulsion or population transfer, segregation and separatism, assimilation, and cultural pluralism or multiculturalism.

❺ Today, the percentage of foreign-born people living in Canada is at an all-time high, with the largest group of recent immigrants coming from the Philippines. The largest number of immigrants live in Ontario, Quebec, and British Columbia, and in urban centres more so than in rural areas.

❻ Canada's two special status groups are Aboriginals and the Québécois. Today, Chinese Canadians are the second-largest visible minority group, and black Canadians are the third-largest.

❼ The Canadian Charter of Rights and Freedoms upholds the right to equality for all peoples, and includes Aboriginal rights and protection of the country's multicultural heritage.

Key Terms

assimilation *271*
authoritarian personality theory *262*
charter groups *276*
contact hypothesis *266*
critical race theory *265*
cultural pluralism *273*
culture of prejudice *263*
culture theory *263*
democratic racism *259*
direct institutional discrimination *259*
discrimination *259*
dual labour market theory *265*
ecological fallacy *258*
ethnic group *256*
ethnicity *256*
exception fallacy *258*
Frankfurt School *262*
f-test *263*
genocide *269*

indirect institutional discrimination *260*
individual discrimination *259*
internalized racism *255*
majority *253*
Marxist exploitation theory *265*
melting pot *273*
minority *253*
multiculturalism *273*
multiracial feminism *266*
post-colonial theory *267*
prejudice *258*
Quiet Revolution *277*
race *254*
racialization *255*
racism *258*
scapegoat theory *262*
segregation *271*
selective perception *266*
separatism *271*
social distance *263*
stereotype *258*

Reviewing the Concepts

1. Review the key characteristics of prejudice and discrimination. Given the discussion in the text, explain how a person who is not prejudiced can still discriminate.

2. As a sociologist, review and critique the scapegoat theory of prejudice and discrimination.

3. Compare and contrast the melting pot with cultural pluralism. What do you see as the main advantages and disadvantages to both approaches? Defend your answer.

4. What was the Quiet Revolution?

Applying Your Sociological Imagination

1. As a sociologist, why do you believe racism continues to exist in contemporary society?

2. In your informed opinion, can post-colonial theory be applied to Canada's Aboriginal peoples? Why or why not?

3. Do you believe that Aboriginal peoples and the Québécois make Canadian culture stronger or weaker? Defend your answer using your sociological imagination.

4. Explore how the concept of "binary" can be applied to "race" and racialization.

MySocLab

Visit MySocLab to access a variety of online resources that will help you prepare for tests and apply your knowledge.

11 Families

We tend to think of our families as deeply personal, unique, and often quirky groupings, and inevitably, they are. Yet at the same time, every family constitutes a thread in a broader social fabric—a fabric that has its failings and that can sometimes, disastrously, tear.

Consider the highly publicized 1990 case of common-law partners Angelique Lavallee and Kevin Rust, who had an abusive relationship. This case, although from over 20 years ago, remains a pivotal ruling in Canadian justice. One night, after Kevin had physically assaulted Angelique and threatened, "Either kill me or I'll get you," she shot and killed him. In a landmark ruling, the Supreme Court of Canada acquitted Angelique based on the battered woman syndrome and the argument that, fearing for her life, she had acted in self-defence.

The following excerpt from the Court's majority decision illustrates that domestic violence is not an isolated, private trouble but, rather, a pervasive social issue:

> Laws do not spring out of a social vacuum. The notion that a man has a right to "discipline" his wife is deeply rooted in the history of our society. The woman's duty was to serve her husband and to stay in the marriage at all costs "till death do us part" and to accept as her due, any "punishment" that was meted out for failing to please her husband. One consequence of this attitude was that "wife battering" was rarely spoken of, rarely reported, rarely prosecuted, and even more rarely punished. Long after society abandoned its formal approval of spousal abuse, tolerance of it continued and continues in some circles to this day. (*R. v. Lavallee*, 1990, S.C.R. 852)

As you will learn from this opening and the broader chapter, sadly, our families are not always safe havens away from the happenings in the broader social system; rather, they are microcosms of the larger social system.

LEARNING OBJECTIVES

By the end of this chapter, students will be able to

1 Understand the factors involved in developing a definition of *family*.

2 Review the significant legislative changes and overall trends in marriage and divorce in Canada.

3 Grasp the major theoretical approaches to understanding families: functionalist, conflict, symbolic interactionist, feminist, post-structuralist, and queer.

4 Understand the issues involved in balancing income generation and household management.

5 Analyze family violence and intimate femicide as social issues.

1 Developing a Definition of *Family*

How do we define *family* today? The term is said to be "one of the most misused concepts in the English language" (Peters, 1999, p. 55); at the same time, some say it "carries a sense of the best in relationships" (Peters, 1999, p. 56). As sociologists, why do we care about pinning down a definition of *family*? And do sociological approaches take into consideration "the best" in relationships?

Sociologists have held several long-standing definitions of *family*. Here is one of the most widely cited and influential: "a social group characterized by common residence, economic co-operation, and reproduction. It includes adults of both sexes, at least two of whom maintain a socially approved sexual relationship, and one or more children, own or adopted, of the sexually cohabiting adults" (Murdoch, 1949, p. 1). Can you think of any groups who are not included here?

⊙ Watch

Recent Research

Courtesy Frances Hughes

< < <

What constitutes a "typical" family changes over time. In contemporary Canada, a large family characteristic of the early 1800s, like the Parrott family of Chatham, Ontario, is just one type of family that exists alongside many other family forms.

> > >

Today's families come in many forms.

Photos.com/Jupiter Images

◉ Watch

How a Family Is Defined

nuclear family **An adult male, an adult female, and their offspring.**

extended family **Multiple generations of adults living with their spouses and children.**

family of orientation **The family into which one is born.**

family of procreation **The family one creates by having children or adopting children.**

Another prominent definition holds that family is "a social arrangement based on marriage and the marriage contract, including recognition of the rights and duties of parenthood, common residence for husband, wife and children, and reciprocal obligations between husband and wife" (Stephens, 1963, p. 5). Again, ask yourself who is included and who is excluded from such a definition. Also, consider whether there is a cultural bias to this definition.

A modern recasting of the classic functionalist definition of *family* aims for more precision:

a group manifesting the following organizational attributes: It finds its origin in marriage; it consists of husband, wife, and children born in their wedlock, though other relatives may find their place close to this nuclear group, and the group is united by moral, legal, economic, religious and social rights and obligations (including sexual rights and prohibitions as well as such socially patterned feelings as love, attraction, piety, and awe). (Coser, 1964, p. xvi)

Who is excluded in this instance?

Common approaches to family often refer to two dominant family forms: *nuclear family* and *extended family*. A **nuclear family** includes an adult male, adult female, and their offspring. An **extended family** includes multiple generations of adults living with their spouses and children. In Canada, recent immigrants from both the Middle East and South Asia rely on the extended family as an important living arrangement (Mandell & Duffy, 2005b). As children become adults, they may start to distinguish between their **family of orientation** (the family into which they were born) and their **family of procreation** (the family they create by having children or adopting children). As you can see, these kinds of concepts make it possible to find yourself a member of multiple families simultaneously.

< < <

Same-sex marriages were legalized in Canada in 2005 with the passing of Bill C-38, the *Civil Marriage Act*.

Notice, however, that the definitions of family we have outlined above all involve an economic relationship, heterosexuality, children, and a common residence (Peters, 1999). None of them includes either same-sex couples or common-law couples (that is, couples who live together without being married, and who account for 16.7 percent of all Canadian families). Nor do they include lone-parent families (16.3 percent of Canadian families) or couples without children. Today, in Canada, these forms *are* considered families—especially by the people within them. In fact, if we used the narrow definition of family as comprising Mom and Dad (legally married) and their children (who reside with them), less than half (34 percent) of Canadian families would fit it (HRSDC, 2010).

THE CHANGING FACE OF FAMILIES

Our understanding of what constitutes *family* changes over time. We need only consider the definitions that Statistics Canada uses from one census to the next to see the changing nature of family relationships in Canada.

In the 2006 Census, Statistics Canada used two definitions of family. As illustrated in Figure 11.1, the first definition is the "census family," defined as "A married couple (with or without children of either or both spouses), a couple living common-law (with or without children of either or both partners), or a lone parent of any marital status, with at least one child living in the same dwelling. A couple may be of opposite or same sex. 'Children' in a census family include grandchildren living with their grandparent(s) but with no parents present."

The second type of Statistics Canada family is the "economic family," which is defined as "A group of two or more persons

Watch

Newest Debate in Family Studies

> > > Thinking Sociologically

Is there such a thing as an ideal family structure? Which persons (or groups of people) may be interested in categorizing one family form as the ideal family? What would this family ideal look like? What purpose would it serve?

Distribution of Census Families, Canada, 2012

Source: Based on Figure 1, Distribution (in percentage) of census families by family structure, Canada, 1961 to 2011. Statistics Canada.

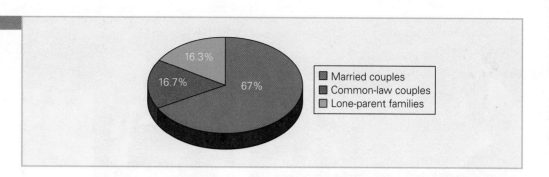

Watch

Idealized Family Family Images

Explore

Young People Are Not Leaving Home

Watch

Deconstructing Ideal Understandings of Family

who live in the same dwelling and are related to each other by blood, marriage, common-law or adoption. A couple may be of opposite or same-sex. For 2006, foster children are included." The economic family definition encompasses a wider range of people than does the census family definition. For example, two or more census families (related by blood, marriage, common law, or adoption) living together in the same dwelling constitute one economic family. Implicit in this definition is the sharing of economic resources.

These census definitions represent two significant changes from the 2001 Census, conducted only five years earlier. The 2006 Census represented the first time that same-sex married couples were counted, a development that reflects the legalization of same-sex marriage in Canada with the passing of Bill C-38 (the *Civil Marriage Act*) in 2005. The 2001 Census did include same-sex common-law couples as family, but not, of course, as "married."

The other significant change concerns the status of children. Prior to the 2001 Census, children living with their parents had to be "never married" to be considered members of the census family. With the change in definition, there is recognition that previously married children may live with their parents and should be included as members of that family.

THE EXPANDING BOUNDARIES OF *FAMILY*

Margrit Eichler (1988) argues that we operate with a monolithic bias when we think in terms of "*the* family." The concept itself signals that we consider one ideal type of family to be "normal." For example, as students, how do you define your family? If you're living with roommates, are they "family"? If you're renting a room in a family's home, are you part of their family? While you're away from home, are you still considered part of your parents'/parent's family? If you're living alone, who is your family?

To overcome the narrowness of holding up the nuclear family as the ideal to which all should aspire, Eichler (1988) suggests that we expand our understanding of what a family is. She argues that important aspects of families are socialization, emotional relationships, residence, economics, sexuality, and reproduction. Not all of these dimensions need to be present simultaneously, though, for a social arrangement to be understood as a "family" (Peters, 1999). The contemporary focus on human rights and equality, the role of law, and the feminist movement all contribute to the need to re-examine the boundaries of what we consider families to be (Peters, 1999).

Defining *family*, both socially and legally, has important consequences, not only for our individual lives but also for how we are situated in relation to social institutions (Mandell & Duffy, 2005b; McDaniel & Tepperman, 2011). For example, the legalization of same-sex marriages has made certain rights and benefits available to married same-sex couples that were at one time available only to married heterosexual couples. Recognized partners can have access to each other's employment benefits, and they are able to apply to adopt or to foster children. In the event of a medical emergency, partners are the first persons contacted and are able to make decisions on their partner's behalf. Legalization also affords partners rights and benefits in terms of inheritance in the event of the death of their partner (Mandell & Duffy, 2005b).

Our challenge as sociologists is to research effectively the wide variety of family forms both in Canada and globally. Providing a *universal* definition of family that is relevant in Canada and elsewhere, however, is both highly problematic and undesirable. The term *family* is a "minefield of contested values and power relationships" (Mandell & Duffy, 2005b, p. 4), with some groups lobbying for more inclusive definitions of families and others for tighter restrictions on who can be included in a family. Moreover, different definitions of *family* are invoked in particular circumstances—in law, in government policy, in religious doctrine, and so forth. The reality, then, is that the boundaries of the concept of *family* must be understood as fluid.

Marriage and Divorce Trends in Canada

MARRIAGE

One of the most significant shifts we have seen in marriages in Canada came with the 2005 passing of Bill C-38, the *Civil Marriage Act*, which legalized same-sex marriages. At the time, this legislation placed Canada among only a small group of progressive countries— the Netherlands, Belgium, and Spain—that had legalized same-sex unions. We now see even more countries that have legalized same-sex marriages—including Argentina, Iceland, Norway, Portugal, South Africa, and Sweden. Prior to this act, several provinces had enacted a range of legislative measures enabling a variety of same-sex entitlements. The legalization of same-sex marriages, however, brings both social legitimacy and legal rights and benefits to these partners. It also demonstrates the fluidity of our social categories.

Marriage as a Legal
Relationship

Marriage and Status

Ironically, over the past quarter-century, the overall proportion of married couples in Canada has declined. Couples are increasingly choosing to live in common-law relationships, with regional rates highest in Quebec (McDaniel & Tepperman, 2011; Statistics Canada, 2007b). This trend is repeated in the United States, Australia, New Zealand, and throughout most of Europe (McDaniel & Tepperman, 2002). In 2011, 67 percent of Canadian families were married couples (with or without children), down from 83 percent in 1981 (see Figure 11.2). In the same year, common-law relationships (with or without children) represented 16.7 percent of Canadian families, up from only 5.6 percent in 1981. In the past, common-law unions tended to be associated with the working class; today, however, these unions are prevalent among all social classes (McDaniel & Tepperman, 2011). Women's increased labour force participation and education levels are two factors associated with the rise in cohabitation (McDaniel & Tepperman, 2002).

Despite what appear to be dramatic declines in marriage rates, the majority of Canadian women and men will get married at some point in their lives (McDaniel & Tepperman, 2002). The ideals of marriage are still attractive; common-law union, after all, mimics marriage in its ideals of a monogamous, committed relationship. That is, couples are living together but are just not "tying the knot" (Mandell & Duffy, 2005b, p. 15).

Common-law unions may be viewed by some people as a less binding, flexible relationship than legal marriage; however, governments are increasingly treating long-term (two years or more) cohabitation as legally binding. If these unions dissolve, the parties are expected to support each other financially although the degree to which this is required varies from province to province (McDaniel & Tepperman, 2011). One thing is certain, though: The line between legal marriage and cohabitation is no longer clear (McDaniel & Tepperman, 2011).

DIVORCE

The most significant changes surrounding divorce in Canada came in 1968 and 1985. Prior to the 1968 *Divorce Act*, divorces were granted only on the basis of adultery, desertion, or imprisonment, or when the spouses had lived separately for three years (Gorlick, 2005). The liberalization of divorce laws in 1968 led, unsurprisingly, to an increase in Canadian divorce

Kids of Divorce Face
Challenges at School

FIGURE 11.2

Marriages and
Common-Law
Unions as a
Percentage of
Canadian Families,
1981–2011

Source: Based on Figure 1,
Distribution (in percentage)
of census families by family
structure, Canada, 1961 to
2011. Statistics Canada.

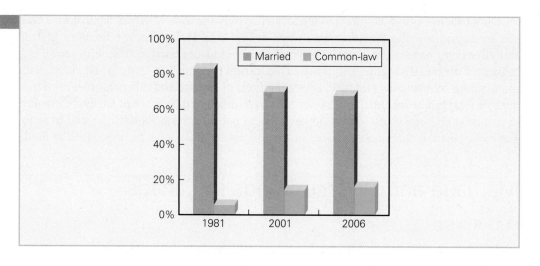

FIGURE 11.2

Marriages and
Common-Law
Unions as a
Percentage of
Canadian Families,
1981–2011

Source: Based on Figure 1,
Distribution (in percentage)
of census families by family
structure, Canada, 1961 to
2011. Statistics Canada.

rates. In 1968, there were 54.8 divorces per 100 000 population; in just one year, that number soared to 124.2 divorces per 100 000 (Eichler, 2008). This number continued to climb until levelling off in the early 2000s, when total divorces per year were in the low 70 000s, or 223.6 divorces per 100 000 population (Kelly, 2012; Statistics Canada, 2006d).

In 1985, "no-fault" divorce laws took effect—and in the subsequent two-year period, the numbers and rates of divorces rose significantly. In the peak year of 1987, 96 200 divorces were granted, which represents a rate of 362.3 divorces per 100 000 population (Gentleman & Park, 1997). No-fault divorce reduced the waiting time prior to being able to file for divorce to one year, and uncontested divorces were granted after a separation of three years (Gorlick, 2005).

((•—Listen

Being a Child of
Divorce

Other significant changes occurred in 1997 with regard to issues of child support. Changes to the *Divorce Act* mean that child support is now calculated based on the income of the noncustodial parent and takes into account the cost of living in each province. Judicial discretion in the setting of child support was removed, creating uniformity in the way support payments are calculated across Canada. This standardization is meant to ensure that adequate supports are provided for children within the financial means of the supporting parent. The Child Support Guidelines also take into account split custody and shared custody arrangements.

>>> Thinking Sociologically

The state takes an interest in the enforcement of child and adult support payments. Alberta, for example, has a Maintenance Enforcement Program: http://justice.alberta.ca/programs_services/mep/Pages/default.aspx

Visit the above site and explore the role of this program in the maintenance of families.

Additionally, changes in the federal *Income Tax Act* finally halted the practice of noncustodial parents being allowed to deduct monies paid for child support and custodial parents having to pay income tax on child support payments received (Gorlick, 2005; Philipps, 2004).

❸ Sociological Approaches to Families

Sociologists are interested in exploring questions about how families are organized and what their relations are to the wider society and social policies. Sociologists are also concerned with how families work, what challenges they face, and what meanings people hold about them. It is to these questions that we turn now.

FUNCTIONALISM

As we have seen in earlier chapters, functionalist approaches are concerned with order, consensus, equilibrium, and harmony. Societal institutions are understood to be interdependent

< < <

A nuclear family includes an adult male, an adult female, and their offspring.

and to exist in harmony with one another. When change occurs in one institution (such as the economy or the education system), change will inevitably take place in other institutions as well. In the functionalist perspective, family is understood to be a major societal institution.

Certain social functions are accomplished within families. Individuals are provided with love, emotional and economic support, and sexual expression. Children in families are socialized to learn the values and norms of the larger society. Families are also responsible for disciplining children. Social status is established and reproduced by families through the parents' wealth as well as through inheritance from other family members.

American functionalist Talcott Parsons (1955) argued that with industrialization (1780–1840), families no longer functioned as economic units of production; that is, they no longer produced only the food and goods needed. As a result, the functions associated with families became more specialized, with specific roles developed for men, women, and children.

Parsons differentiated between **instrumental roles** and **expressive roles** of adults. For groups to run smoothly, both a task leader and an emotional leader are necessary. Parsons argued that women should take on the expressive role while men should fill the instrumental role. The expressive role was understood as being responsible for the emotional well-being of family members and the socialization of children, while the instrumental role involved men leaving their families to engage in paid labour and deal with the world "out there." A definite split, then, developed between men and women, and public and private worlds.

Functionalists have been widely criticized for their conservative approach to gender and for expecting roles in families to be played out on the basis of biology. Functionalists have also been criticized for not adequately dealing with social conflict and social change. While Meg Luxton (2001, p. 38) discredits Parsons's approach to the family as "benign in intent," she does assert that his elevation of the nuclear family as "functional" and "natural" allowed for

instrumental role
Responsible for engaging in paid labour outside the home.

expressive role
Responsible for the emotional well-being of family members and the socialization of children.

other family forms to be cast as "deviant" or "dysfunctional." As social historians have shown us, the idyllic family, as presented by functionalists, was just that—a normative construction as opposed to a real engagement with the reality of multiple family forms (Coontz, 1992).

CONFLICT THEORY

Conflict theorists argue that how people are situated in relation to the means of production, wealth, and power fundamentally shapes the ways in which they both experience and see the world. It follows, then, that when these theorists look at the family, they consider its relationship to the state. They might ask, for example, how a given nation's economy influences the lives of its families.

These theorists perceive that the inequalities inherent in the larger society are perpetuated inside families. So, whereas functionalist theorists argue that the family meets the needs of the larger *society*, conflict theorists assert that the family is organized to meet the needs of *capitalism* and, more specifically, to serve ruling class interests (Abbott, Wallace, & Tyler, 2005). People working within this theoretical approach assert that conflict is built into social structures and is, thus, a part of social life. Conflict, though, is not always understood as negative; rather, conflict is what drives social change. Through reform or revolution, social conflict can be minimized or even resolved altogether.

Industrialization and the Family Historically, you will recall, conflict theory has its roots in the work of Karl Marx and Friedrich Engels. In his groundbreaking book *The Origin of the Family, Private Property and the State*, Engels argued that along with the other vast changes generated by the Industrial Revolution, family forms were radically altered.

With the rise of industrialism, workplaces shifted from homes to factories. Men became workers in these factories, forced to earn a wage for their labour and thus made dependent on business owners for their material survival. Families likewise shifted from being sites of production to sites of consumption. That is, families were no longer organized around producing at home mainly for their own consumption; instead, they purchased goods and services in the marketplace. Essentials such as clothing and food became commodities—articles available for sale or trade in the marketplace.

As a conflict theorist, Engels argued that material conditions determine family life. He pointed out that as societies industrialized, those who were able to provide the necessities of life (i.e., men) amassed social power. Women and children commanded the lowest wages on the earnings ladder, and were thus dependent on male wage earners (Mandell & Duffy, 2005b). Engels demonstrated that with the development of class-based societies, women's social position, relative to men's, declined (Luxton, 2001).

Contrary to popular nostalgia, married women often engaged in waged work. Nonetheless, they were "defined by their domestic roles as private, subservient domestic labourers subject to male control and authority within the home" (Mandell & Duffy, 2005b, p. 10). Not only women but the family itself was now viewed differently—as a private affair, separate from the public sphere of business and politics.

social reproduction
The necessary activities that guarantee the day-to-day reproduction and survival of the population.

domestic labour The activities required to maintain a home and care for the people who live in it.

Social Reproduction and the Family Marxist-feminist theorists also call attention to the essential work of **social reproduction** that families performed. Social reproduction refers to the day-to-day activities that ensure the reproduction (and survival) of the population (Luxton & Corman, 2011). Capitalism requires that after a day of work, workers be rejuvenated—and this is where families come in. At home, workers are fed, their clothes are laundered, and they are able to rest. In short, their immediate needs are taken care of, thus enabling them to return to work the next day. This is not simply a daily cycle; families are also needed to produce the next generation of workers.

Yet Marxist work in the area of families has been criticized for largely taking for granted the division of **domestic labour**—the full range of activities required to maintain a home

<<<

With industrialization came new conceptualizations of family. While women often participated in waged labour, they were still defined through their domestic labour. Here, Mrs. Arthur Beales performs domestic work in the early twentieth century.

and care for the people who live in it, including housework, managing money, and caregiving (mainly of children) (Mandell & Duffy, 2005a).

Both functionalist and conflict approaches to families examine the complex relationships that connect families to larger society rather than explore intra-familial relations (Abbott, Wallace, & Tyler, 2005). We will now examine the family itself.

SYMBOLIC INTERACTIONISM

Symbolic interactionists take a micro approach to studying family life; that is, they investigate how family members' behaviours are shaped by their definitions and interpretations of particular situations. Context, then, is crucial to symbolic interactionists; they perceive that symbolic meanings vary from one family to the next, and may even vary among members of the same family unit. Researchers working in this area may examine how families contribute to their children's development of self. Overall, symbolic interactionists tend to explore families as cooperative groups with shared interests (Luxton, 2001).

One contemporary example of family research drawing on symbolic interactionism is Suter, Daas, and Bergen's (2008) project on how lesbian mothers negotiate their family identities through symbols and family rituals. The researchers explored how the symbolic use of a child's last name, for instance, concretizes for some lesbian mothers the legitimacy of their family as a family. Some of the mothers in this study gave their child a hyphenated surname made up of both partners' last names. These mothers reported that this practice tends to provide them with ease of access on occasions such as emergency-room visits. In addition, given that people will often ask which woman is the child's mother, such questions provide an opportunity for the women to proclaim that both of them are the child's mother, again symbolically asserting their family as legitimate.

The lesbian mothers studied also draw on rituals to establish family identities (Suter, Daas, & Bergen, 2008). For example, many of them attended a same-sex parenting support group. Participating in such a group was positive not only for the mothers themselves and for their sense of family but also for their children, who are able to interact with other children of two-mother families.

BOX 11.1 ISSUES IN GLOBAL CONTEXT

Anti- and Pro-Natalist Policies around the World

Governmental policies can fundamentally affect what is often thought of as a natural phenomenon: the birth rate of a country. These policies, as we will see, often intersect with economic interests. *Anti-natalist* (that is, anti-birth) policies attempt to limit the population by opposing or limiting child-bearing. Consider China's anti-natalist "one-child" policy, implemented in the late 1970s.

China's attempt to curb population growth in order to encourage modernization and improve the living standards of the average citizen has resulted in efforts to limit families to one child (although rural families are permitted two children if the first child is a girl). The one-child policy is organized through a system of rewards and penalties (e.g., having to pay for services that are provided free of charge to the first child or receiving preferential housing for those who comply), as well as through social stigmatization (Ding & Hesketh, 2006; Shaou-Whea Dodge & Suter, 2008). The penalties escalate when families have more than two children. Both contraceptives and abortions are provided to the citizenry free of charge. China's aggressive policy has dramatically curtailed its fertility rate, which has fallen sharply from 6 children per woman in the 1970s to the current rate of 1.6 children per woman (Goldstein, 2004; Yuan, 2004).

Chinese citizens have long had a preference for male children. Following patriarchal tradition, sons carry on family lines while daughters marry and most often move in with their husband's family (Shaou-Whea Dodge & Suter, 2008; Sullum, 2007). Sons, especially in rural areas, can help to work the land as well as provide support to their families (particularly as their parents age). This preference for sons has resulted in sex-selective abortions (Beech, 2002; Trovato, 2004), and there are even reports of Chinese peasants killing their newborn daughters so that they can try again to have a son (Goldstein, 2004; Potts, 2006; Sen, 2003). Another consequence of China's anti-natalist policy is the immense number of Chinese girls adopted by members of Western countries. China's policy, then, does not just affect those living in China but extends beyond the country's borders to other parts of the world.

The World Health Organization calculates that as a result of its one-child policy, China is missing 50 million females (Beech, 2002). Amartya Sen calculates a similar figure by comparing the average ratio of births of girls to boys in Western countries (typically 95 girls to 100 boys) and China (only 86 girls to 100 boys) (2003). When Chinese children become adults,

Anti-natalist policies attempt to limit the population by opposing or limiting child-bearing. Pictured here is a poster promoting the one-child policy implemented in China in the 1970s.

© Owen Franken/Corbis

CONTINUED

▶

the lower number of available brides means that some Chinese men now marry relatives, such as first cousins (Beech, 2002).

At the other end of the spectrum are those countries that encourage childbirth by enacting *pro-natalist* policies and/or practices. These include disallowing abortions, not providing access to birth control, and offering monetary awards for childbirth. For example, the Soviet government offered annual cash rewards based on how many children a woman had beyond her first six, and an even higher amount for women with more than ten children (Hoffman, 2000). After the staggering loss of life encountered during World War I, many European countries offered awards to mothers with each subsequent birth. These governments understood the connection between a country's population size and both military and labour power (Goldstein, 2004; Hoffman, 2000). Among these countries, France's policies were further fuelled by racialized discourses about the "yellow peril"—the idea that the climbing population in Asian countries might pose an economic threat to a white Europe (Camiscioli, 2001). France banned abortions as well as the advertising of contraceptives (Höhn, 1987). These laws were amended only in the recent past, with the law prohibiting the advertising and sale of contraceptives being abolished in 1967 and abortion being liberalized in 1975 (Höhn, 1987).

Should the state play a role in regulating births and family size? Are there any conditions or circumstances under which state intervention would be tolerable (acceptable) and/or necessary?

Research demonstrates that some lesbian mothers negotiate their family identities through the use of symbols and family rituals.

Roles in Families Symbolic interactionists have used "roles" as one of the basic concepts in their work. Canadian sociologist Erving Goffman argued that like actors in the theatre, people play roles in daily life (Goffman, 1959). Symbolic interactionists examine the multiple roles we play on a daily basis and over the course of our lives. You may be a student when you are at school, a roommate when you are eating your breakfast in residence, an employee when you are working, a daughter or son when you go home for a visit, and so forth. In other words, your interactions (and actions) will fluctuate depending on the situation, the setting, and the expectations of those with whom you interact.

Some researchers use this concept to show how our competing roles in families often result in **role strain**—the stress that results when someone does not have sufficient resources to play a role or roles. Some researchers, for example, have studied the strain that mothers experience when they enter the paid labour force—that is, the strain between their responsibilities as mothers and as employees. Since mothers still bear most responsibility for childcare, they are most satisfied with the balance between home and work when they are able to reduce their time commitments to paid work while their children are still living at home (White, 1999). Role strain, however, is not the exclusive domain of working mothers, as fathers also experience strain as a result of trying to balance their employment and home lives (White & Klein, 2008).

role strain **Stress that results when someone does not have sufficient resources to play a role or roles.**

A further example of role strain germane to contemporary Canada happens among those who are "sandwiched" between caring for dependent children and elder relatives. Three generations of one family living in the same household is not necessarily a new phenomenon. However, what is different is that the majority of working-age Canadian women are now employed in the labour force, leaving little time to provide care to both children and dependent elders (Luxton & Corman, 2011; Williams, 2005).

Symbolic interactionists have been criticized for largely accepting the idea of families as sites of harmonious relationships (Luxton, 2001). For instance, some of these theorists view family violence as resulting from the peculiarities of individuals rather than as connected to the larger social issue of the subordination of both women and children (Luxton, 2001). This latter issue is taken up by feminist theory, which we turn to next.

FEMINIST THEORY

Overall, feminist theory holds that families remain primary sites for the continued subordination of women (Abbott, Wallace, & Tyler, 2005). Feminist theorists argue that no one family form is inherently natural or functional, not even the oft-heralded heterosexual nuclear family (Luxton, 2001). Rather, feminist theorists argue that family forms are specific to both time and place and that even processes of conception and childbirth are socially mediated (Luxton, 2001).

One of the most significant contributions of feminist theorizing to the sociology of families is its analysis of familial ideology (Luxton, 2001). For example, sociologists Margrit Eichler (1988) and Janet Finch (1989) demonstrate both the political and the ideological nature of holding up the nuclear family as the ideal, and the harmful consequences for women of such an ideal (Luxton, 2001). They argue that imposing one family model that privileges men and subordinates women through its very structure is indeed a political and ideological exercise.

Feminist work that uses a structural approach focuses on how inequality for women is enabled and sustained through laws, social policies, and labour market practises. Marxist feminists, in particular, have argued that the exploitation of women in families fundamentally serves capitalist interests (Abbott, Wallace, & Tyler, 2005). For example, the majority of workplaces are organized around the assumption that employees have no obligations that conflict with their work lives. This is unrealistic for the majority of women, who have domestic and childcare responsibilities in addition to their paid work responsibilities (Luxton, 2001; Luxton & Corman, 2011). Since women primarily take responsibility for domestic labour, childcare, and other forms of caregiving (e.g., care of elder relatives), many remain economically dependent on men in addition to the many disadvantages that they face accessing paid employment and income (Baker, 2001; Luxton, 2001; Luxton & Corman, 2011).

Feminist work also challenges the assumption that family life is private and separate from public spheres of life (Thorne, 1982). Social and economic policies can (and do) affect family life: marriage and divorce laws; laws concerning adoption, custody, and child support; as well as tax benefits concerning children and childcare all affect family life (Baker, 2001, Beaujot, 2000). For example, in Canada, our taxes are assessed on an individual level, except when determining child tax benefits and GST/HST credits, which are calculated on the basis of family income. Such calculations are meant to aid poorer families (Beaujot, 2000).

Through a feminist lens, we are also able to understand the history of imperialism in Canada and its devastating effects on Aboriginal peoples and their established family relationships. Aboriginal familial practices were quite different from European practices. According to accounts written by white settlers, Aboriginals enjoyed spousal relationships without hierarchy, divorces happened with consent, children were clearly loved, anti-corporal punishment attitudes were in place, and adults enjoyed sexual freedom following marriage (Mandell & Momirov, 2005). However, as the Europeans settled, their marriage practices (in which men's

BOX 11.2 CANADIAN CONTRIBUTIONS TO SOCIOLOGY

Meg Luxton

Meg Luxton is a professor of sociology, social and political thought, and women's studies at York University in Toronto. Her research interests are women's work (paid and unpaid), gendered divisions of labour, feminist political economy, feminist theory, and social policy.

Luxton, with Kate Bezanson, is currently conducting a longitudinal study of Ontario households to explore the effects of "family-friendly" or "work–life" policies on the daily lives of those people the policies are designed to help. That is, they are examining how maternity and parental leaves, and provisions for childcare and homecare (support for family members who are providing care in their own homes), help people to combine their caregiving responsibilities with their jobs.

Luxton is also interested in discovering which factors best help people to combine caregiving with employment. These factors include family-friendly legislation, provisions garnered through collective bargaining (although this would apply only to unionized workers, who make up roughly a third of Canada's workforce), and other arrangements (most likely organized on an individual level).

Luxton's acclaimed book *More Than a Labour of Love: Three Generations of Women's Work in the Home* (1980) situates women's domestic labour within a capitalist context. She is also the author of *Getting by in Hard Times: Gendered Labour at Home and on the Job* (with June Corman) (2001), *Minds of Our Own: Inventing Feminist Scholarship in Canada and Quebec, 1966–1976* (with Wendy Robbins, Margrit Eichler, and Francine Descarriers) (2008), co-editor of *Social Reproduction: Feminist Political Economy Challenges Neoliberalism* (with Kate Bezanson) (2006), and *Neoliberalism and Everyday Life* (with Susan Braedley) (2010).

authority was protected through law) were instituted, to women's disadvantage (Luxton, 2001). As a result of colonization, communal modes of production and nonhierarchical forms of family were destabilized, resulting in reconstituted gender and family relations (Anderson, 1991; Bourgeault, 1983; Luxton, 2001).

Other feminist work focuses on interpersonal relations, examining everyday interactions as gendered and as perpetuating gender hierarchies. Barrie Thorne (1982) argues that feminist work challenges conventional sociological approaches to studying families, since it accepts as a basic premise that family members experience family life differently.

Proulx and Helms (2008) explored parent–adult child relationships in a US-based study. The researchers argued that it is problematic simply to use categories such as "parent" and "adult child" to discuss familial relationships because gender fundamentally shapes such relations. Therefore, it is more appropriate to explore mother–son, mother–daughter, father–son, and father–daughter relationships since this specificity recognizes that mothers and fathers may have different kinds of relationships with their children (Proulx & Helm, 2008). Ignoring the possibilities of nuance in familial relationships simplifies them as being gender neutral. The researchers also argued that familial relationships are fluid and, thus, change over time. This specificity and fluidity is illustrated by a mother who reported a relationship with her son that was increasingly conflict-ridden, whereas the father was not experiencing similar conflict with the son (Proulx & Helm, 2008).

Most contemporary feminist work rejects any assertion that men's and women's roles within families are a natural outcome of biological differences. Women are not born knowing how to do laundry, iron clothes, vacuum, or bake, just as men are not born knowing how to work a lawn mower or to shovel snow. All of these activities are social practices.

Watch

Family Relationships Change over Time

> > >

Women are not born knowing how to do laundry or cook, nor are men born with knowledge of how to shovel snow or mow the lawn. Activities such as cooking and mowing the lawn are social practices, not biological ones.

© PhotoAlto Agency RF/Jupiter Images

((•—Listen

Fathers Taking a More Active Role in Raising Children

One contemporary example of research in this area is Belinda Leach's (2005) work on transformations in steelworker families in Hamilton, Ontario. Leach investigated how shifts in global capitalism play out in the gender politics of family life. That is, she was interested in what happened to working-class family life when good jobs in the steel industry became increasingly insecure and employment security existed only on a week-to-week basis. Leach documented how these working-class families struggled with the unravelling of the local historical norm of breadwinner-model families. In the face of economic uncertainty, women entered the paid labour force in unprecedented numbers. While many steelworkers' wives had worked for pay previously during strikes and layoffs, historically they had contributed a low level of income to these families (Leach, 2005). Having to enter the paid labour force challenged taken-for-granted constructions of masculinity and femininity predicated on a heterosexual family unit—that is, that men work for income and women contribute their labour in the domestic realm (by cleaning, cooking, and caring for children).

POST-STRUCTURALIST THEORY

Post-structuralists are likely to seek to dismantle prevailing discourses about families—for example, the adage that the family serves as "a haven in a heartless world." Post-structuralists may also question the concept of the "good mother" (one who is married, heterosexual, cares about children, and so forth) or the notion that "good fathers are good breadwinners" (Park, 2006). Post-structuralists argue that such categories are saturated in power relations. That is, notions of good mothers and good fathers operate as *normalizing discourses*—they set the boundaries of what is acceptable and appropriate, and work to govern people's behaviour. To demonstrate how such discourses gain currency, post-structuralists examine relations of power.

Benjamin Baez and Susan Talburt (2008) conducted research on the regulation of family life through a series of pamphlets, directed at parents, released by the United States Department of Education. Baez and Talburt (2008) argue that these pamphlets are laden with normalizing discourses that aim to teach parents how to "make their children better students, better citizens, and ultimately well-rounded, self-reliant adults" (p. 26).

In this study, we see that the family is targeted as a site for state intervention. Families are being socially managed and governed through these pamphlets—albeit subtly. The pamphlets lay out for parents what the "payoffs" of good parenting are and also warn of the risks for children's futures when parents are not teaching "appropriate" values and behaviours. The pamphlets list such risks as "dropping out of school, drug use, teenage pregnancy, violent crime," etc. (Baez & Talburt, 2008, p. 30).

Baez and Talburt point out that what is evident in this series of pamphlets is that the home and family is meant to be the "moral training" ground for children. The pamphlets are couched in progressive and seemingly benign language with terms such as "freedom" and "progress," such that the power of such discourses and governing remains hidden.

Similarly, Canadian sociologist Glenda Wall (2013) examined issues of *Today's Parent* magazine for discourses of motherhood and childhood in relation to mothers' employment and childcare. Wall examined articles during two time periods—the mid to late-1980s and the mid to late-2000s. She documents an increased emphasis on "children's vulnerability, innocence, dependence, and cognitive development" (Wall, 2013, p. 164). Motherhood was portrayed as *the* primary source for women's life satisfaction. Discursively, women's/mother's employment is understood as time away from children; motherhood should come before career.

QUEER THEORY

Queer theorists are often influenced by post-structuralist theory. As discussed in Chapter 3, queer theorists are interested in questioning normative categories, especially *heteronormativity* (that is, heterosexuality as the norm). In relation to family life, those using a queer theory

< < <

Queer communities today may experience tension between a kind of conservatism that aims for cultural acceptance or assimilation ("We're just like the monogamous heterosexual family, only queer") and an effort to create and practice alternative family forms.

Alamy

lens may question the assumption that all families are formed through heterosexual unions, and further question expectations of "heterorelationality—of co-residence, romantic love, monogamy and the primacy of the conjugal couple" (Budgeon & Roseneil, 2004, p. 129).

Andrew Gorman-Murray's (2007) Australia-based research illustrates a queer approach to exploring family life and domestic spaces. He demonstrated that the detached suburban house—with its "master bedroom" and smaller bedrooms, presumably for children—is inextricably bound to the heterosexual nuclear family form (Gorman-Murray, 2007, p. 195). He also showed how gay men's and lesbians' use of domestic space provides a challenge to the heteronormative assumptions about "home." For example, one respondent, Anthony, used to live with his cousin: "When you're living with someone, they're constantly censoring what you'd hang on the walls. . . . But now she's gone this is the one place where I feel like I don't have to cover anything up" (Gorman-Murray, 2007, p. 208). One important domestic practice that Anthony engages in is flying a rainbow flag outside his home to indicate that his is a gay household: "I'm telling you who I am. This is my community too; even though I'm a gay person I don't have to be hidden" (Gorman-Murray, 2007, p. 208). Gorman-Murray argues that such a practice is a deliberate challenge to the construction of suburban neighbourhoods as the exclusive domain of heterosexual families.

Another way in which lesbians and gays challenge heteronormative domestic spaces is in their frequent use of houses for social gatherings. Using domestic spaces to develop and maintain queer relationships, friendships, and communities—especially where gay/lesbian commercial venues are hard to find—subverts the heterosexual norm of homes as the site of private family relationships (Gorman-Murray, 2007).

❹ Competing Demands: Income Generation and Household Management

The question "Who makes up a family?" is perhaps not the most useful one we can ask. What happens when we shift the question to "What does a family do?" Further, we could ask, "How do you recognize and support the people who do what families do?" These questions enable us to investigate the relationship between larger social relations (including economic and political ones) and what families "do."

Typically, families are units that cooperate economically. Families depend on two kinds of labour: (1) income-generating work, and (2) unpaid domestic labour. In capitalist societies such as Canada's, the demands of domestic labour and income-generating work are organized to be in conflict with one another. The state negotiates the conflicts between these two spheres only partially, through schools and health care (Luxton & Corman, 2011).

◉ Watch

Women and Work

> > >

Families depend on both income-generating work and unpaid domestic labour to survive. Some women attempt to combine income-generating work with their domestic responsibilities (i.e., childcare).

Orange Line Media/Shutterstock

Two big changes in recent decades have affected how families negotiate the competing demands of income generation and managing households. The first is a change in the number of hours of income-generating work required to support a household. Today, the standard of living for an average family of two adults and two children requires more paid hours than it did 30 years ago. In the 1970s, only 44 hours of income-generating work per week were required to sustain such a household, whereas by the 1990s, 65 to 80 hours per week were required (Wolff, 1994).

The need for more paid labour hours to maintain the average standard of living has translated into a higher proportion of women working in the paid labour force, and families with two income earners are now the statistical norm among Canadian families. Seventy-two percent of two-parent families with children under 12 years of age have both parents engaged in the paid labour force (Lapierre-Adamcyk, Marcil-Gratton, & Le Bourdais, 2006). In 45 percent of these families, both parents are working full-time (30 hours or more per week) (Lapierre-Adamcyk, Marcil-Gratton, & Le Bourdais, 2006).

Of course, women have entered the paid labour force increasingly since the 1950s. Participating in paid labour began mainly with single women and childless women; mothers of school-aged children followed soon after, and then mothers of small children (Lapierre-Adamcyk, Marcil-Gratton, & Le Bourdais, 2006). In 2012, 74.2 percent of women aged 15 to 65 were in the formal labour force, compared with 14 percent in 1901 (Luxton & Corman, 2005; Statistics Canada, 2013b). Labour force participation of men aged 15 to 65 stands at 81.5 percent (Statistics Canada, 2013b).

When Both Parents Work

The second big change affecting Canadian contemporary families is the major cutbacks in government support to schools, health care, and social service agencies over the past 20 years (Luxton & Corman, 2011). These spending cuts have resulted in caregiving responsibilities falling increasingly to families, and most often to women. In other words, the cutbacks mean that more unpaid work is required in order for households to survive. For example, cuts in health care lead to people being sent home from hospital while they still require care.

How are people negotiating the competing demands of more hours required in the paid labour force and more hours required for domestic labour? One strategy is to increase their hours of paid labour in order to be able to purchase more services. For example, individual family members may find themselves working more than one paid job in order to pay for a housecleaning service. Another strategy is to decrease the hours engaged in paid labour in order to have more time available for domestic labour, including childcare (Luxton & Corman, 2011).

Yet even when all family members (including men and children) participate in domestic labour and childcare, there is still not enough time in a day or week to get everything done to a satisfactory level (Luxton & Corman, 2011). In heterosexual families, as we have seen, mothers more often than fathers are the ones who adjust their work lives to take care of home responsibilities, with women frequently taking on part-time rather than full-time employment (Baker, 2004; Cheal, 2002; Ravanera & McQuillan, 2006). Some couples find "off-shifting" a viable strategy for meeting their work and family goals (Pagnan, Lero, & MacDermid Wadsworth, 2011). Off-shifting is where one partner will work nonstandard work hours. Increased father involvement in domestic labour and childcare is the most common benefit reported in Canadian dual-earner couples who off-shift.

This problem of the competing demands of paid labour and domestic labour is not easily solved at the level of individual families and households. Critical sociologists point to the need for broader state supports for families. These may include a national, state-funded childcare program, increased state-legislated provisions for family leaves, sufficient levels of education funding such that parents are not relied on for school fundraising, and quality, affordable elder care (Luxton & Corman, 2011).

DOMESTIC LABOUR

One achievement made by feminists in the area of families is the recognition of the importance and value of domestic labour. Society as a whole, not just individual family members, benefits from the enormous contribution of unpaid domestic labour (Luxton, 2001). In her book *If Women Counted*, Marilyn Waring (1990) argues that unpaid domestic labour should be calculated and valued such that women could be compensated and have their work socially recognized. Statistics Canada has valued unpaid domestic labour at $297 billion a year, which represents 33 percent of the country's gross domestic product (Hamdad, 2003).

The pattern of women's dual responsibility holds regardless of race, class, and culture (Canadian Council on Social Development, 2006). Sociologist Arlie Hochschild (1989, 2003) coined the term **second shift** to refer to the domestic labour performed by employed women at home after finishing their paid workdays.

Couples who attempt to divide household responsibilities more equitably nonetheless exhibit persistent gendered patterns. Repetitive, regular indoor household tasks, such as cleaning the house and bathing children, are more likely to be performed by women. Men, on the other hand, are more likely to engage in outdoor tasks and tasks for which completion times are not as rigid, such as mowing the lawn and repair jobs around the home (Baker, 2001; Daly, 2000; Hochschild, 2001).

Signalling a change in attitudes, we do see attempts to share household tasks more equitably among young, well-educated couples who have a small number of children or no children (Baker, 2001).

second shift The domestic labour performed by employed women at home after finishing their paid workdays.

BOX 11.3 WHY SHOULD WE CARE?

Childcare Expenses as a Tax Deduction?

From 1982 to 1985, Beth Symes, a full-time practising lawyer, employed a nanny to care for her children. In her personal tax returns for those years, Symes claimed the wages she paid to the nanny as a business expense. Revenue Canada initially allowed the deductions in 1982 and 1983. However, through notices of reassessment, Revenue Canada subsequently disallowed the deductions for the entire period of 1982 to 1985. Revenue Canada's position was that "the expenses were not outlays or expenses incurred for the purpose of gaining or producing income from business, as required under s. 18(1)(a) of the *Income Tax Act*, but were personal or living expenses, deduction of which was prohibited by s. 18(1)(h)" (*Symes v. Canada*, 1993). Symes took her case to trial, and the Federal Court "held that the appellant could deduct the payments to the nanny as business expenses." However, the Federal Court of Appeal reversed the lower court's decision. The case was then appealed to the Supreme Court of Canada.

In 1993, the Supreme Court ruled against Symes in a majority decision. The Court split along gender lines, with seven male justices ruling against Symes and the two female justices providing dissenting judgments. Neither the Federal Court of Appeal nor the Supreme Court of Canada "was prepared to see the costs associated with child care as ones incurred in the public domain—that is, the public market (or business) in contrast to the private family" (Young, 2003, p. 1926).

This decision communicates that the responsibility (and cost) of children remains with our families. Also, Young (2003) argues that the discourse of "choice" runs through the majority decision of the Supreme Court. That is, an underlying perception on the part of the court is that it is women's personal choice to have children.

It is interesting to note that the dissenting judgment in *Symes v. Canada* showed promise of understanding the gendered nature of the case—that since women overwhelmingly bear the primary responsibility for childcare in Canada, they are disproportionately affected in terms of possible or actual labour force participation. The dissent drew on feminist research and gender equity principles:

Child care expenses should not be disallowed as a business expense under s. 18(1) (h) as being personal in nature. While for most men the responsibility of children does not impact on the number of hours they work or affect their ability to work, a woman's

CONTINUED

▶

ability even to participate in the work force may be completely contingent on her ability to acquire child care. Many business deductions have been permitted in the past even though these expenditures have a personal element. The real costs incurred by businesswomen with children are no less real, no less worthy of consideration and no less incurred in order to gain or produce income from business. (*Symes v. Canada*, 1993, 4 S.C.R. 695)

Even though Symes "lost" the argument that childcare costs are a legitimate business expense, legislative changes that expanded allowable childcare deductions following *Symes v. Canada* can be considered a small victory.

What do you think? What factors would you take into account if asked to determine whether childcare costs should be an allowable business expense? Would there be any scenario in which you would be inclined to accept an argument that a parent should be able to deduct childcare costs as part of business costs?

Family Violence: A Social Issue

Family violence as a concept brings up a paradox. On the surface of things, "family" and "violence" are often taken up as opposites. Family is construed as a "haven in a heartless world" (Lasch, 1977). Many of us understand that our families are (or should be) sites of intimacy, love, caring, and safety.

Those who are uncomfortable recognizing families as sites of violence often say that it occurs only in exceptional cases, perpetrated by sick individuals. However, this approach is not a useful one for understanding family violence from a sociological perspective.

We tend to internalize messages that state that violence lurks out in the world rather than at home, and yet women are in fact at greater risk of violence in and near their homes than in the public arena (Canadian Centre for Justice Statistics, 2003). Women are more than twice as likely to be assaulted by someone known to them than by a stranger. In 2010, 25 percent of all reported violent crimes in Canada involved instances of family violence, and 49 percent of these were committed by a spouse or ex-spouse (Sinha, 2012). Women account for 85 percent of victims of family violence (Brzozowski, 2004). In Canada, women are about three times more likely than men to be the victims of serious forms of spousal violence (Statistics Canada, 2011e). Young adults are more likely than older adults to be victims of violence by their intimate partners (Fortin, Guay, Lavoie, Boisvert, & Beaudry, 2012); according to 2009 and 2010 statistics, women aged 25 to 34 continue to be victimized by their spouses more often than older women (Sinha, 2012; Statistics Canada, 2011e).

Sadly, these numbers tell us that violence is pervasive in Canadian families. When we take into account the amount of money spent in Canada in connection with family violence through social services, the criminal justice system, absenteeism from work, and health care costs (estimated to be more than $4 billion per year) (Alberta Learning Information Service, 2006), we can see that family violence is not an issue that affects merely a few, unfortunate people. It is a social issue, not a private trouble. Sociologists investigate family violence from this premise.

Feminist analyses that foreground gender have contributed greatly to our understanding of family violence. Such analyses demonstrate that mainstream approaches, which simply total individual episodes of violence (hitting, slapping, shouting, throwing objects, and so forth) and lead people to conclude that family violence is gender neutral, do little to convey the enormous gendered effects of family violence (Duffy & Momirov, 2005). For example,

Domestic Violence

Intimate Partner Violence in Same-Sex Relationships

Measuring Intimate Partner Violence

> > >

Violence is pervasive in Canadian families, with women representing 85 percent of victims.

AbleStock/Jupiterimages/Getty Images

intimate femicide The killing of women by their intimate male partners.

while women are more likely than men to use weapons, their weapons of choice are household objects that are immediately at hand: scissors, wooden spoons, hairbrushes, and television remotes. When men use weapons, they use objects like firearms, baseball bats, hammers, and metal pipes (Glasbeek, 2005). The point is that the quantity of violence does not tell us as much as the quality of violence experienced by both women and men. Women are more likely than men to be severely assaulted, to suffer injury and require medical attention, and to live in fear for their lives (Glasbeek, 2005). Feminist analyses foreground patriarchal social arrangements and men's social power over women (Duffy & Momirov, 2005).

INTIMATE FEMICIDE

Intimate femicide—the killing of women by their intimate male partners—accounted for the majority of women killed in Ontario (between 63 and 76 percent) during the period between 1974 and 1994 (Gartner, Dawson, & Crawford, 1998). Gartner, Dawson, and Crawford's 1998 research is the only recent work that includes "killings of women by their estranged common-law partners and current and former boyfriends" in the calculation of intimate femicides; most research includes only current common-law partners and current and ex-spouses. Recent research on spousal homicide includes legally married and common-law relationships, both intact and estranged, but dating relationships are not included (Dawson, Bunge, & Balde, 2009). A separation or an estrangement, or its imminent possibility, is the most prevalent motive for intimate femicide (Dawson, Bunge, & Balde, 2009). In Canada, victims of spousal homicide are more likely be women than men (Statistics Canada, 2011e).

Who are the victims of intimate femicide? The answer may surprise you: women from all social classes, age groups, and cultural and ethnic origins. The average age at death is 37. Half of the women were employed (51 percent), most had children (80 percent), and most were born in Canada (76 percent) (Gartner, Dawson, & Crawford, 1998). The motives for intimate partner homicides are gendered. Women who kill their intimate partners are more likely to do so out of fear for their safety (as in the Lavallee case cited at the beginning of the chapter). Whereas men who kill their partners are more likely to be motivated by "sexual jealousy and male proprietariness" (Diem & Pizarro, 2010, p. 522).

However, the researchers point to some "risk markers" that identify certain women as having a higher risk of victimization. Statistics from Canada, the United States, Australia, and Great Britain demonstrate that estrangement from the intimate partner and common-law status are both linked to a greater possibility of spousal killings of women. Canadian data demonstrate that women's risk of femicide increases sixfold when they are estranged from their male partners (DeKeseredy, 2001; Wilson & Daly, 1994).

Another risk marker is ethnicity. For instance, whereas in the United States, African-American women face a disproportionate risk of intimate femicide, in Canada, Aboriginal women are at increased risk. During the 21-year period under study, Gartner, Dawson, and Crawford (1998) discovered that at least 6 percent of all victims of intimate femicide in Ontario were Aboriginal women. Given that only 1 percent of women in Ontario during this time frame identified as Aboriginal, Aboriginal women were overrepresented as intimate femicide victims (Gartner, Dawson, & Crawford, 1998). This risk marker is problematic in that it categorizes all Aboriginals into one group, which ignores important differences between Aborignal groups. Further, what is not clear when citing quantitative research is why this category of ethnicity is a risk—is the risk a feature of the effects of poverty and other social factors or does it have more to do with particular values about the role of women in certain cultures?

A further risk marker is the partner's violent history. Much research demonstrates that men who murder their spouses (or estranged spouses) have a long history of violent behaviour—one that is not restricted to marital relationships (Brownridge, 2006; Gartner, Dawson, & Crawford, 1998; Johnson, 1996).

Further undermining the notion that our homes are our refuge, 75 percent of intimate femicides take place in the victim's home, with almost half of these killings occurring in the bedroom (Gartner, Dawson, & Crawford, 1998). Firearms are the most common weapons used by men who kill their wives (Dawson, Bunge, & Balde, 2009; Statistics Canada, 2011e). Offenders use firearms in a third of these killings, and in the remaining two-thirds "stabbed, bludgeoned, beat, strangled, or slashed the throats of their victims" (Gartner, Dawson, & Crawford, 1998, p. 151).

How can we understand intimate femicide? Gartner, Dawson, and Crawford (and many others) argue that it is best understood as a "manifestation of extreme (if ultimately self-defeating) controlling and proprietary attitudes and behaviours by men toward their female partners" (1998, p. 151). That women are the victims of spousal homicides is not incidental. Intimate femicide "is violence that occurs and takes particular forms because its target is a woman, a woman who has been intimately involved with her killer" (Gartner, Dawson, & Crawford, 1998, p. 151). As feminists argue, we can understand this violence as an extension of men's proprietary attitudes toward the intimate women in their lives.

As demonstrated, women are more likely than men to be killed by their intimate partners. Researchers argue that such gendered patterns are reflective of larger social relations of masculinity and femininity, in which men occupy more dominant positions in our social hierarchy (Brownridge, 2006; Dawson, Bunge, & Balde, 2009; Duffy & Momirov, 2005).

BOX 11.4 THAT WAS THEN, THIS IS NOW

Corporal Punishment of Children

Have you ever heard the phrase "the rule of thumb"? This phrase has been associated with an English judge, Sir Francis Buller, who in 1782 is said to have ruled that a man could beat his wife with a stick so long as it was "no thicker than his thumb" (Quinion, 1999). Although the historical truth of this ruling has been contested (see Hoff Sommers, 1994), the use of physical force to control someone remains a significant issue. While we have come a long way in protecting women (and men) from physical assault—but have much further to go—we seem to be moving more slowly on the use of force against children.

Corporal punishment of children is defined as any physical force with the intent of causing a child to experience pain in the hope of changing that child's behaviour (Gagné, Tourigny, Joly, & Pouliot-Lapointe, 2007). Its use "breaches their fundamental human rights to respect for human dignity and physical integrity. Its legality in almost every state worldwide—in contrast to other forms of inter-personal violence—challenges the universal right to equal protection under the law" (Global Initiative to End All Corporal Punishment of Children, 2007).

According to the Global Initiative, 29 countries have made corporal punishment of children illegal: Austria, Bulgaria, Costa Rica, Croatia, Cyprus, Denmark, Finland, Germany, Greece, Hungary, Iceland, Israel, Kenya, Latvia, Liechtenstein, Luxembourg, the Netherlands,

CONTINUED

New Zealand, Norway, Poland, Portugal, Republic of Moldova, Romania, Spain, Sweden, Tunisia, Ukraine, Uruguay, and Venezuela. You will notice that Canada is not listed; in this country, corporal punishment is, to some extent, considered legal. Section 43 of the Canadian Criminal Code stipulates that parents, teachers, and others who act in the place of a parent can use force to correct a child's behaviour.

The Canadian Foundation for Children, Youth and the Law brought a case on the legality of corporal punishment to the Supreme Court of Canada (Watkinson, 2006, p. 531). The Foundation argued that Section 43 of the Criminal Code discriminates against children on the basis of their age, which is contrary to Section 15 of the Canadian Charter of Rights and Freedoms. In 2004, however, the Court ruled, in a 6–3 decision, that Section 43 does not violate children's rights. Yet the Court did set limits on the conditions under which Section 43 can be used as a defence. For example, the Court stated that it is not reasonable to use corporal punishment on children who are under the age of two, since they do not have the capacity to understand why they are being punished. Similarly, children who are disabled are not able to understand the application of force. In these instances, the measures taken are not considered corrective and immunity will not be provided under Section 43. In addition, corporal punishment is not to be used on teenagers, since they can exhibit aggressive or anti-social behaviour in response to such force. Weapons such as rulers and belts are not tolerated in administering corrective behaviour, nor are slaps or blows to the head (Watkinson, 2006, p. 533).

In North America, corporal punishment of children remains a controversial issue. For example, in a survey of 1000 adults from Quebec, spanking was found to be the most common form of corporal punishment. Those participants who were spanked during their childhood, and who believe that spanking rarely results in physical harm, were in favour of spanking, while those who were physically abused as children tended to be opposed to spanking (Gagné et al., 2007, pp. 1294–1297).

What are your thoughts on this issue? What broader social factors are involved? Choose two theoretical perspectives (such as conflict theory, symbolic interactionism, or feminist theory) and think through how a theorist using that lens might view corporal punishment.

Several interventions have been made to help stem violence against women: There are many shelters that provide a safe space for women who need to escape the violence of their own homes; numerous treatment programs for violent men; police practices, which include mandatory arrests; and specialized domestic violence courts in several Canadian jurisdictions (Dawson, Bunge, & Balde, 2009).

Summary

1. Traditional definitions of *family* as comprised of husband, wife, and children have been expanded to include same-sex and common-law couples, lone-parents, and childless couples in order to encompass the many forms that families take today.

2. One of the most significant legislative changes in Canada regarding marriage is the legalization of same-sex marriages, while the most significant trend is the overall decline in marriage rates and corresponding increase in common-law relationships. Changes to divorce laws since 1968 have resulted in an increase in the divorce rate and improvements in child-support calculations.

3. The functionalist perspective views family life as supporting not only its members but also wider societal structures; conflict theory perceives how family forms change in response

to large-scale economic changes; symbolic interactionism takes a micro approach to understanding familial relations; feminist perspectives point to families as continued sites for the perpetuation of women's subordination to men; post-structuralist theory deconstructs normative constructions of the family; and queer theories question normative assumptions about heterosexual family life.

4. With higher levels of income required to sustain today's average standard of living, and the greater number of work hours that this entails, managing households requires either more work hours to buy more services or fewer work hours to allow time for domestic labour—a situation not easily resolved at the level of individual families.

5. Family violence and intimate femicide are not considered to be private, personal problems but, rather, symptomatic of the broader social issue of women's continuing subordination to men.

Key Terms

domestic labour *292*
expressive role *291*
extended family *286*
family of orientation *286*
family of procreation *286*

instrumental role *291*
intimate femicide *304*
nuclear family *286*
role strain *295*
second shift *302*
social reproduction *292*

Reviewing the Concepts

1. What is social reproduction and why might feminists argue that it is an important concept and vital to our society?

2. What is the importance of power when using a post-structural framework?

3. How is family violence a social issue?

Applying Your Sociological Imagination

1. Why is developing a universal definition of *family* so problematic? Are you able to generate a definition that is universal, yet still meaningful for social policies?

2. How was domestic labour organized in your household when you were growing up? Has your study of sociology led you to think differently about this aspect of family life?

3. Who should be responsible for care of the elderly—families, the state, or a combination of the two? Or is there another option? Explain.

4. What types of initiatives might be effective in ending domestic violence against women?

MySocLab

Visit MySocLab to access a variety of online resources that will help you prepare for tests and apply your knowledge.

12 Education

If you are reading this chapter then you are most likely a Canadian university or college student. Have you developed your sociological imagination about how you came to be such a student, or a student in a particular school, or a student in a particular program, or a student in a particular country? How might you connect social relations to your choice to take your program, in your school? How did your familial situation affect your choice? Our decisions about postsecondary education are not individual decisions devoid of a connection to social relations. Sociologists identify enduring patterns of education in relation to social class, gender, race, ability, and other socially organizing principles. For example, men continue to be overrepresented in the maths and sciences while women are overrepresented in the education and health fields.

How did you decide to attend your current school? What factors affected your decision? Your decision was likely affected by social class. Being able to attend a school away from home, without going into serious student debt, is connected to you and your family's ability to pay for your education and your costs associated with being away from home. Also consider the particular program you chose. Whether you are able to afford a professional program is associated with your social class; professional programs are the most costly programs in Canadian universities. In addition, the opportunities that education can provide are also constrained by wider social relations. We hope that this chapter will help you develop your sociological imagination in connection with education.

LEARNING OBJECTIVES

By the end of this chapter, students will be able to

❶ Review the history of public schooling in Canada, and the levels of educational attainment today both in Canada and worldwide.

❷ Understand how functionalist, conflict, symbolic interactionist, feminist, anti-racist, cultural, and post-structuralist theorists approach the study of education.

❸ Outline the impact of rising tuition rates in colleges and universities.

❹ Review gendered enrolment rates in postsecondary institutions.

❺ Describe some of the key issues facing institutes of higher education today, including research funding, accountability, and academic integrity.

❶ Education in Canada

Education, as an institution, is responsible for the transmission of particular knowledge, skills, values, and attitudes deemed desirable in a given society. Generally speaking, we can look at education as a means of producing good citizens (Bromley, 2011; Osborne, 2000). Education happens in both formal and informal ways. Most formal education—that which occurs in institutional settings—tends to be regulated and organized by the state (Wotherspoon, 2004). Informal education involves learning activities that people seek outside of formally structured educational spaces (Wotherspoon, 2004). Both formal and informal education contribute to *social reproduction*; that is, by stressing societal norms and values, education works to socialize the next generation.

ORIGINS OF PUBLIC SCHOOLING IN CANADA

Most Canadians take for granted that, until the age of 16, formal public schooling is compulsory. Few of us even question the need for formal education; we understand that it is an integral part of childhood in Canada and in most other industrialized nations. Yet this contemporary situation stands in stark contrast to the picture of education in Canada just a century ago.

Residential Schools The earliest forms of formal education in Canada were established in the nineteenth century by missionaries and religious orders (Wotherspoon, 2004). Before this time, Aboriginal peoples practised an organic education—one that was tailored to the practical needs of families, clans, and communities and that took place in communities amid the natural environment. There were no formal teachers; instead, individual community members were responsible for ensuring that each child in their community learned key knowledge, skills, traditions, and values. Education, then, was a means of ensuring cultural survival (Wotherspoon, 2004).

European missionaries and religious orders sought to replace Aboriginal knowledge and lifestyles in the belief that these practices were inferior to European morality and consciousness (Wotherspoon, 2004). Such colonizing attitudes paved the way for the great tragedy that marked one of Canada's earliest forays into formal education: residential schooling (introduced in Chapter 5).

In the last half of the nineteenth century, an overtly racist, government-supported, church-operated residential school program was created in part to solve "the Indian problem" (Dyck, 1997, p. 340). The prevailing wisdom was that Aboriginal children were in need of help; as a result, the decision was made to separate them from their families and teach them the ways of "civilized" folk. The intent was to assimilate Aboriginal children into the dominant economic and cultural system since "Canada's First Nations peoples were in the way of the relentless onrush of capitalist and industrial expansion" (Schissel & Wotherspoon, 2003, p. 36).

In residential schools, akin to total institutions (see Chapter 6), Aboriginal children were not permitted to speak in their own languages, were prevented from seeing their families except for short periods during the year, and were subjected to harsh disciplinary measures. Recent research is revealing the full extent of the abuses suffered by Aboriginal children in these schools. Further, we are only now learning about the connections between these abuses, the state policy of assimilation, and contemporary dilemmas faced by Aboriginal communities (Schissel & Wotherspoon, 2003).

In June 2008, Prime Minister Stephen Harper offered a formal apology to the approximately 80 000 living former students of the residential school system. During his lengthy speech in the House of Commons, he said, "We now recognize that, in separating children from their families, we undermined the ability of many to adequately parent their own children and sowed the seeds for generations to follow" (Legacy of Hope, 2013). He went on to ask for "the forgiveness of Aboriginal peoples for failing them so badly" (Legacy of Hope, 2013).

Mass Education Both industrialization and immigration created the need for an education system that would educate the masses. School reformers in Canada in the late 1800s

> > >

Pictured here are Mi'kmaq girls in sewing class at the Roman Catholic–run Shubenacadie Indian Residential School in 1929. Residential schools were an attempt at the forced assimilation of Aboriginal children into the white/European settler culture.

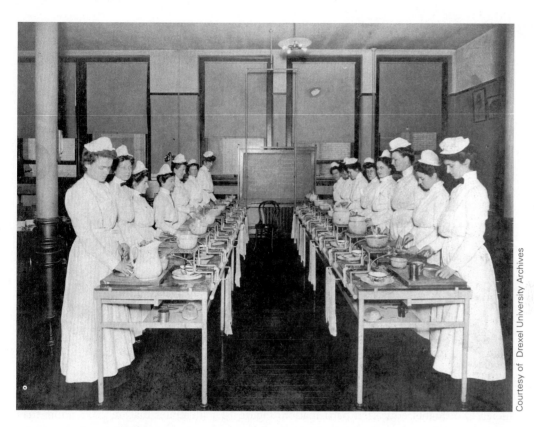

< < <

Education, as overtly
gendered, schooled
girls and young women
for preparation as
wives and mothers.

argued that education was essential to Canada's economic development (Kendall, Lothian
Murray, & Linden, 2007). Further, supporters argued that mass education would serve the
public good by providing a common moral education (Davies & Guppy, 2006). Citizens
were thus encouraged to commit new tax monies for compulsory schooling for girls and
boys. Ontario was the first province to offer free, compulsory education; the other provinces
followed suit, and by the early 1900s children were able to attend tax-supported elementary
schools in all Canadian provinces. The compulsory exit age was raised from 12 to 16 in
1919 (Hale, 1990).

A "common" education was not to be understood as the "same" education, however
(Davies & Guppy, 2006). Schooling in the early years was similar, but by age 10 boys
were directed to vocational training and higher education in preparation for the labour
market and girls were streamed into domestic science courses (Davies & Guppy, 2006).
While boys and girls attended the same schools, they were often segregated within those
schools—with separate entrances, separate playgrounds, and separate seating in classrooms (Gaskell, McLaren, & Novogrodsky, 1989; Prentice, 1977). Gendered expectations
reinforced teachers', and presumably parents', notions that girls and boys should be prepared for different occupational and social roles: Girls were prepared to be housewives or
to work in a limited set of nurturing occupations (e.g., nursing, teaching in elementary
schools), while boys were prepared for vocational trades or advanced studies (Davies &
Guppy, 2006). Overt gender streaming remained firmly in place until at least the 1950s
(Davies & Guppy, 2006).

RISING POSTSECONDARY PARTICIPATION RATES

Today, Canadians are spending more years in school. It used to be that having a university
degree allowed one to claim membership in a privileged, elite group. Over the past several
decades, however, we have seen a significant rise in postsecondary educational attainment. In
1961, only 2.9 percent of those aged 15 and older had completed a postsecondary certificate,

FIGURE 12.1

Educational
Attainment in
Canada among
Those over
Age 25, 2013

Source: Based on CAUT
Almanac of Post-Secondary
Education, 2013.

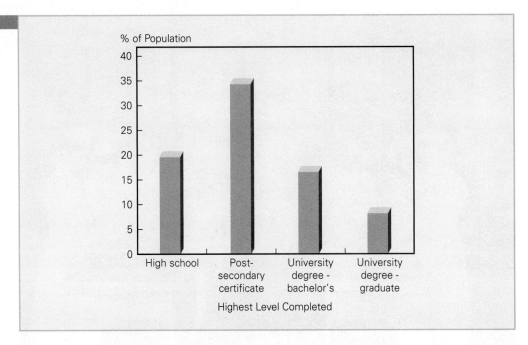

diploma, or degree. This number jumped to 21.9 percent in 1986 and to 59 percent in 2013 (ages 25 and older) (CAUT, 2013; Wotherspoon, 2008), constituting a **massification** (a mass increase) of higher education participation. Figure 12.1 illustrates that, in 2013, more than 59 percent of Canada's population over age 25 had had some form of postsecondary education (CAUT, 2013).

As a result of this massification, a high school diploma today can no longer garner the same kind of paid job that it could even just a few decades ago (see Box 12.1). Also striking is the fact that, as of 2010–2011, women account for 57 percent of full-time undergraduate students in Canadian universities (CAUT, 2013). In the past, men outnumbered women as undergraduate students. However, by 1988, women's and men's enrolment was equal, and 1999 marked the first time that the women's undergraduate enrolment rate exceeded that of men's (Drakich & Stewart, 2007).

How do Canada's levels of education compare with those of other countries? Worldwide enrolments in "tertiary education" (which in Canada is college and university) increased 2000 percent between 1900 and 2000 (Davies & Guppy, 2006). When we look at the rate of high school completion among those aged 25 to 64 in OECD[1] countries, Canada fares very well, with 62 percent of the population having more than a high school education (CAUT, 2013). Poorer-faring OECD countries in this respect include the Czech Republic (17 percent), Italy (15 percent), and France (30 percent) (CAUT, 2013).

Canada also ranks high in postsecondary attainment, with 26 percent of those aged 25 to 64 having earned a university degree. Other high-ranking OECD countries in this category include the United States (32 percent), Norway (35 percent), the Netherlands (30 percent), and New Zealand (24 percent). The two lowest-ranked OECD countries are Austria (12 percent) and Italy (14 percent) (CAUT, 2013).

Why do international comparisons matter? Formal and continual training are emphasized in globalized and globalizing societies. A key indicator of a country's development is the education levels of its citizenry. Education leads to jobs, greater income, improved health

massification The
mass increase in
postsecondary
enrolment, in contrast
to the smaller
numbers that once
constituted an elite
group.

((•—[Listen

School Funding Laws

---

1 OECD is the acronym for Organisation for Economic Co-operation and Development, which comprises 30 countries that are "committed to democracy and the market economy" (www.oecd.org).

BOX 12.1 THAT WAS THEN, THIS IS NOW

Credential Inflation

University degrees, college certificates, high school diplomas, and the like are all *credentials*—items of academic capital that can potentially be parlayed into economic capital. Will the credential that you are working toward now prove as valuable as it was, say, even 30 years ago?

Credential inflation, the ever-increasing cache of educational credentials required for a particular job, occurs in the same way as monetary inflation. Just as today's dollar does not have the same purchasing power it had three decades ago, today's high school graduates are unable to acquire the same jobs that they could then (Davies & Guppy, 2006). Credential inflation, then, has allowed schooling to act as a means of exclusion (Collins, 1979). Particular jobs have required an increasing number of credentials in the form of certificates, diplomas, and degrees. Take, for example, your professor—he or she most likely has a Ph.D., as do the overwhelming majority of university professors today. In fact, the proportion of university professors with a Ph.D. is now a measure of the "quality" of a university in the annual survey by *Maclean's* magazine (discussed later in the chapter). Fifty years ago, however, professors were not required to have a Ph.D.

Credential inflation occurs partly as a result of the increased technical knowledge required for particular positions. Because incredible developments have taken place in such fields as mechanics, computers, and engineering, it makes sense that people working in these fields need to be certified as having the most up-to-date knowledge possible. Yet we can point to many occupations whose credential requirements have changed over the past 40 years, but whose actual practices have arguably not changed to the same degree (Davies & Guppy, 2006). For example, to advance in the field of social work, one now requires a Master of Social Work (M.S.W.). Nurses in most Canadian provinces and territories now require a Bachelor of Nursing (B.N.) or a Bachelor of Science, Nursing (B.Sc.N.) in order to be eligible for a registered nurse (R.N.) designation (CNA, 2011). Finally, those seeking positions in today's business world should probably earn not only a Bachelor of Commerce (B.Com.), but also a Master of Business Administration (M.B.A.) (Davies & Guppy, 2006).

Employers can demand an ever-increasing set of credentials simply because there are so many applicants for various positions. This unfortunately limits the possibility of capable lower-class individuals being considered for particular positions simply because they do not have the required education credentials. We are seeing an increase in those pursuing graduate degrees as they find that their undergraduate degrees are not "enough" in today's labour market (Zarifa, 2012).

What credentials are required for your future career? Research what credentials are required for the position today. Compare these requirements with past ones (10 years ago, 20 years ago). What are the differences, if any?

> **credential inflation**
> The ever-increasing cache of educational credentials required for a particular job.

status, and other indicators of a good (or increasing) standard of living. Nations interested in economic development (and other noneconomic benefits, such as improved well-being) encourage educational expansion beyond mandatory levels (OECD, 2001).

Sociological Approaches to Education

Sociologists theorize about education by considering how educational institutions work. They may approach this study at the macro level (e.g., considering how globalizing processes are shifting priorities in education) or at the micro level (e.g., considering the daily work of teachers in schools). Theorists not only explain educational processes but also investigate changes in education over time. They may be interested in asking the following sorts of questions: Under what conditions do we see certain changes in education? How do these changes happen? Who is involved in these changes? In whose interests are these changes made?

FUNCTIONALISM

A classical functionalist approach to understanding the social role of education and schooling is illustrated in Talcott Parsons's "The School Class as a Social System: Some of Its Functions in American Society" (1959). Because schools function as social systems, Parsons argued that they need both to serve and reflect the values and interests of the society in which they operate. Schools help children to make the transition from being immersed in their individual homes and families to being future citizens able to function as workers in competitive spaces and as participants in public life.

Schools help to maintain the equilibrium of the social system through two functions: allocation and socialization (Wotherspoon, 2004). Through *allocation*—assigning grades and handing out certificates, diplomas, and degrees—schools act as a sorting mechanism for future roles in society. That is, whether one has completed grade school, has a high school diploma, or has earned an undergraduate degree fundamentally affects the kind of paid position one can expect to obtain in our capitalist society. Education credentials matter as an indication of where people may find themselves in the social hierarchy. You will recall from Chapter 2 that functionalists view this social hierarchy, or structural inequality, as a necessary feature of societies, as it helps maintain equilibrium in the system. Schools contribute to maintaining this equilibrium by training and sorting people to fulfill roles at all levels of the hierarchy.

As an agent of *socialization*, schools teach students how to function in the larger society—how to assimilate into that larger society. Children learn to respond to authority (teachers and principals) and to respect punctuality (by responding to bell rings and buzzer sounds). Ultimately, schools teach children to be "good" future citizens. As discussed in Chapter 6, this function is not limited to instruction through the formal curriculum. Rather, learning also happens by way of a hidden curriculum. This term is taken up differently by various

> > >

Kindergarten acts as an initial foray into the world of structured expectations— behaviour, punctuality, respect for authority, and so forth.

Comstock/Stockbyte/Getty Images

<<<

Some sociologists argue that schools constrain creativity by requiring conformity to narrow expectations.

theorists, but to functionalists, *hidden curriculum* refers to the informal or less overt aspects of schooling that nonetheless influence and shape students by teaching them to be obedient, to value competitiveness, and so forth.

Harry Gracey's (1977) classic essay, in which he describes kindergarten as academic boot camp, explores these informal processes. Kindergarten is a space for children to learn the "student role." The crux of this student role is obedience of classroom routines. Class time, for the most part, is structured: students are told what to do, how to do it, and where it should be done—hence the likening of this early school experience to military boot camp. Kindergarten prepares students not only for the rest of their schooling careers, but also for successful participation in the work world.

Functionalist analyses of education are rarely used in contemporary Canadian research. This approach to understanding education and schooling has come under heavy criticism for clinging to the idea of society as a **meritocracy**, wherein resources are distributed fairly on the basis of merit (Wotherspoon, 2004). Within this perspective lies a failure to understand how one's social location (gender, race, class, ability, sexuality, etc.) and other larger sociopolitical relations and conditions affect one's achievements.

meritocracy A society in which resources are distributed fairly on the basis of merit.

CONFLICT THEORY

Conflict theorists understand schooling as serving the capitalist aims of profit and compliant workers (Wotherspoon, 2004). Schools are perceived as instrumental in preparing future conformers and thus as relinquishing their revolutionary possibilities for human development and progress.

Samuel Bowles and Herbert Gintis's *Schooling in Capitalist America* (1976) is a classic Marxist study of education. In this work, Bowles and Gintis criticize liberal education reforms, arguing that they were unsuccessful because they were based on the liberal assumption that one's success is tied to innate ability. Inequality is instead embedded in the very design of our capitalist society, and until these inequalities are remedied, educational reforms alone cannot work.

correspondence principle The principle whereby the structures of workplaces are reflected in the structures of schools.

Bowles and Gintis argue that a **correspondence principle** prevails between schools and the workplace—in other words, that schools are structured to reflect workplaces. Both use similar methods—grades and wages—to motivate behaviour through external rewards. We see the alienation of workers from the products they produce and the corresponding alienation of students from the curriculum. Finally, there are similar authority structures, with managers corresponding to teachers, principals, and school administrators, and workers corresponding to students.

Bowles and Gintis (1976) also demonstrated that students from privileged class backgrounds are more likely to continue to higher levels of schooling than are students from lower social class backgrounds. They argue that schools in a capitalist society are structured in such a way as to prevent social class mobility. In short, they understand class inequality as inevitable. A look at current Canadian tuition rates supports this view.

3 **Tuition Rates and Class Inequality** Tuition costs at Canadian universities have skyrocketed over the past decades. For example, as Figure 12.2 shows, over the past 27 years these costs have increased by a staggering 280 percent for general arts programs (Bouchard & Zhao, 2000; CAUT, 2007c; 2013). In 2012–2013, the average annual cost of tuition for Canadian students in the arts was $5,581.

This figure is considerably higher in the professional disciplines. Two of the most expensive undergraduate university programs in Canada in 2012–2013 were dentristy and law programs. The dentristy program at the University of Saskatchewan was the most expensive with tuition set at $32,960 (CAUT, 2013). Graduate programs also cost considerably more than undergraduate programs (Zarifa, 2012).

The realities of social class are particularly highlighted in Canadian medical schools. Most students come from families with high household incomes, high-status parental occupations, and high levels of parental education (Beagan, 2005). Beagan is concerned not only about the absence of students from lower-class backgrounds, but also that, as a result, patients do not have access to doctors who are from a range of social classes and thus more likely to understand certain realities of patients' lives (Beagan, 2005).

FIGURE 12.2

Average Arts Tuition Costs in Canada

Source: Based on CAUT (2010; 2013) and Bouchard and Zhao (2000).

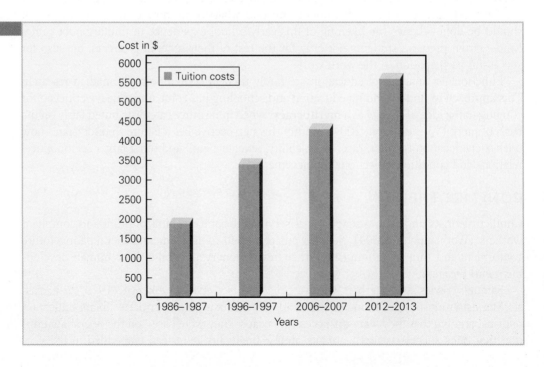

Of course, tuition is not the only cost associated with higher education; students also need money for books, materials, rent, food, clothing, and so forth. More so than in the past, students are forced to combine paid work with their studies in colleges and universities. Of students registered full-time, 48 percent are engaged in paid work while 85 percent of part-time students are combining paid work with education (CAUT, 2013).

Few students are able to receive fully funded scholarships, leaving the financial burden of higher education on the students themselves and on their families. High tuition rates mean that only the wealthiest students can afford to pursue professional degrees. The contemporary costs associated with pursuing higher education, then, create structural barriers that limit the participation of those located in lower social classes.

BOX 12.2 WHY SHOULD WE CARE?

Black-Focused Schools

Are black-focused schools an example of segregation or a progressive attempt to educate marginalized youth? How should educators approach teaching in such a setting? Will their teaching methods be different in such a setting?

In early 2008, following a proposal spearheaded by parents, the Toronto District School Board (TDSB) voted in favour of piloting an Africentric alternative school. This school was proposed partly to address the poor education performance and disengagement of black students in Toronto. Supporters of the proposal argued that the education system itself needed to bear some responsibility for its high dropout rate of black students. There have also been calls for similar schools in Halifax and Montreal (Hampton, 2010).

At the time of the proposal, critics argued that this approach is reminiscent of the days of racial segregation. However, supporters were quick to dismiss this criticism by pointing out that students and their families would choose whether to attend the black-focused school. Unlike the days of segregation, when racialized groups were effectively barred from meaningful societal participation, the Africentric school is meant to enable the educational success of a marginalized youth population.

Supporters of the school also pointed out that it is in line with the 36 other alternative schools (at both elementary and secondary levels) in the TDSB. Currently, there are schools without homework, grades, and competition; schools that have multi-age, multiple-grade classrooms; schools for youth labelled as at risk; and a school for lesbian, gay, bisexual, transsexual, and queer (LGBTQ) youth.

The pilot school follows the Ontario Ministry of Education's approved curriculum. According to TDSB documents, the school will integrate an intersectional analysis to address how race, class, and gender shape students' lives, broaden the European-dominated historical focus of curricular materials to include the histories of people of African descent (as well as other groups in Canada who are often marginalized), and weave positive African-centred resources throughout (TDSB, 2008).

The school opened in September 2009 with 115 students, ranging in levels between kindergarten and Grade 5 (Robertson, 2009). Scholar George Dei, who has long argued for an alternative way of schooling for black youth in Toronto, insists that any lessons learned from this pilot initiative are not isolated to the alternative school but could be used to assist all students, regardless of schooling format (Dei, 2008).

Black-focused schools seek, among other things, to address how race, class, and gender intersect to shape students' lives.

Jim West/Alamy

CONTINUED

What do you think? Should black-focused schools exist alongside other schools? Why might such schools be important? How might educators in this school address concerns about student disengagement? Is there a way for educators in mainstream schools to address student disengagement? Should there be a limit on the range (and number) of alternative schools that a school board provides? How would you decide which alternative schools should be allowed? How would you assess the success of an alternative school?

SYMBOLIC INTERACTIONISM

As you will recall, symbolic interactionists argue that society and social arrangements are fluid—that is, they are constantly negotiated and renegotiated. People act toward things based on the meanings they have for those things. These meanings are constructed through social interaction and vary depending on social context. Symbolic interactionist theorists' approaches to education and schooling, then, tend to examine the meanings attached to school practices—not only for students but also for teachers, administrators, and parents. Symbolic interactionists also explore the symbolic aspects of education—for example, curriculum materials, language, and knowledge (Wotherspoon, 2004).

In his interview-based research on teachers and classrooms, Howard Becker (1952, 1953) explored how teachers' categorization of students affected students' experiences of education as well as their opportunities of achieving success in school (Wotherspoon, 2004). As discussed in Chapter 6, teacher-imposed labels can lead to a *self-fulfilling prophecy* among students (Wotherspoon, 2004). That is, if you are labelled a troublemaker, you're more likely to become one. Conversely, if a teacher identifies you as, say, a hard worker, you're more likely to work hard. Through this interactive process, you come to embody the label.

The Self-Fulfilling Prophecy: A Classic Study The classic research on the self-fulfilling prophecy is Ray Rist's (1970) participant-observation study. While observing a kindergarten class, Rist noticed that the teacher, after only eight days with the students, felt convinced that she could divide the class into three groups according to educational performance: fast, average, and slow learners. Each group sat and worked together at its particular table. Those labelled "fast learners" were located at the table closest to the teacher's desk, the "average" students were in the middle of the classroom, and the "slow learners" were at the back of the room. Rist noted that there was no formal assessment to back up the teacher's perception of the students. There was, however, one variable that explained the groupings: social class. The majority of the "fast learners" were from middle-class households while those labelled "average" and "slow learners" were mostly from lower-class households.

As the school year progressed, the "fast learners," being closest to the teacher, received the most and best attention, and began to perceive their "superiority" over the other students. Not surprisingly, the "slow learners" did not perform well. As these students moved into Grade 1, their new teacher examined their progress during kindergarten, and once again the "fast learners" were spatially located in a way that delineated them as "superior students" to both themselves and the rest of the class.

What does this research tell us? Despite best intentions on the part of teachers to value students equally, they nonetheless may treat certain students as inferior. There appears to be an association between social class and perception of ability. We can extrapolate from these data to argue that students who are labelled as "different" may find themselves treated in a similar fashion to the way the lower-class students were in Rist's 1970 study.

The Self-Fulfilling Prophecy: Contemporary Studies Recent work in this area demonstrates that the self-fulfilling prophecy remains a relevant concern, especially when the intersections of race, class, and gender in schools are considered (McKown & Weinstein, 2002, 2003). In other words, teachers' expectations of their students are moderated by students' gender, race, and class. For example, African-American children are found to be more likely than white children to confirm teachers' low expectations (McKown & Weinstein, 2002). Similarly, Aboriginal students report that teachers, administrators, and school guidance counsellors all have lower expectations of their Aboriginal students compared to other students (Neegan, 2005). Such low expectations may lead to student disengagement and potentially to limited opportunities for them as adults (Neegan, 2005). On the other hand, recent Canadian research demonstrates that schools where positive student-teacher relationships are fostered have increased levels of students pursuing university-level studies (Frempong, Ma, & Mensah, 2012).

Another study demonstrated a positive aspect of the self-fulfilling prophecy. It used a mixed-method design of questionnaires and interviews to explore identity formation as students transitioned to their first year of university (Scanlon, Rowling, & Weber, 2007). The researchers found that since students were expected to learn more independently in university, they had to take greater personal responsibility for their learning. Students also often felt a loss of continuity since they now needed to develop identities as university students, characterized, for example, by different forms of social interaction with their professors than they were used to with their high school teachers. As well, the number and diversity of students at first contributed to feelings of anonymity. However, such feelings soon subsided, and interaction with this new network of people became critical to the students' identity formation (Scanlon, Rowling, & Weber, 2007). Students began to rely on each other, rather than on their professors, to navigate their way through their first year of university.

FEMINIST THEORY

Early Feminist Studies In the 1970s, feminist work in the field of education concerned the sexism embedded in both school texts and classroom practices. For example, girls and women were represented in curricular materials as passive objects, or were absent altogether. Women and girls were constructed traditionally and narrowly as mothers baking cakes and cookies or as girls playing with dolls. Boys were subjected to equally sexist treatment, depicted as active and powerful people, playing sports with fathers who work outside of the home, preferably as educated professionals (Gaskell, McLaren, & Novogrodsky, 1989). Moreover, observations of classroom practices demonstrated teachers' tendencies to engage more with boys than with girls, and to stream boys and girls into "gender-appropriate" subjects.

Until the past half-century, gendered expectations reinforced teachers' notions that girls and boys were to be prepared for different occupational and social roles, as discussed earlier in this chapter. To address these concerns, the Royal Commission on the Status of Women in Canada (1970) recommended that textbooks portray both men and women in diverse roles and careers and that, for example, sports programs be made available to both girls and boys.

Contemporary Studies Contemporary studies continue to document gendered patterns of interaction. For example, regardless of whether their teachers are women or men, boys have more classroom interaction with teachers than girls do (Abbott, Wallace, & Tyler, 2005; deMarrais & LeCompte, 1999; Osborne, 2000; Skelton, 1997). Boys are also more likely to call out answers in class without raising their hands, and teachers typically accept this behaviour. Yet when girls engage in the same practice, teachers tend to correct them and tell them that their behaviour is inappropriate (Renzetti & Curran, 1999).

Curricular materials, however, are no longer unashamedly sexist. But these materials do subtly communicate the legitimacy of the status quo—that is, middle-class masculinity (Arnot, 2002). Boys and men continue to be depicted as active subjects while women and girls are still depicted as passive objects (Abbott, Wallace, & Tyler, 2005). In some subjects, such as history, women's contributions are ignored altogether (Abbott, Wallace, & Tyler, 2005).

While textbook creators have attempted to create gender-neutral characters, these characters are often interpreted as being male and masculine (Abbott, Wallace, & Tyler, 2005).

The forms of masculinity and femininity portrayed in curricular materials, then, tend to be ideologically driven. Many forms of masculinity and femininity exist, of course, yet these materials generally show two dominant constructions: hegemonic masculinity and emphasized femininity (Connell, 2002). As discussed in Chapter 8, Connell uses the term *hegemonic masculinity* to express the dominant cultural form of masculinity that changes both over time and from place to place, and that in Canada is currently associated with white, middle-class, heterosexual men. *Emphasized femininity,* according to Connell, is the dominant cultural form of femininity that is constructed in relation to hegemonic masculinity and that is currently associated with white, middle-class, heterosexual women. When curricular materials draw only on these two dominant forms, they render alternative masculinities and femininities both inferior and invisible.

4   **Gendered Postsecondary Enrolment Trends** As discussed earlier, women now account for almost 60 percent of full-time students in Canadian undergraduate programs. How do we account for this increase?

First, these higher participation rates can be linked to the success of the 1960s women's movement in arguing that education facilitates the achievement of life goals by acting as an equalizing agent between men and women (Davies & Guppy, 2006). In response, colleges and universities established programs to promote gender equity and to encourage admissions applications from women (Davies & Guppy, 2006). Second, the professionalization of a variety of occupations dominated by women (nursing, social work, teaching) required the acquisition of educational credentials, and thus increased women's postsecondary participation rates (Davies & Guppy, 2006).

Contemporary patterns of enrolment by discipline reveal that gender remains a salient feature of our schools and of wider society. As illustrated in Figure 12.3, female undergraduate students are still concentrated in education, humanities, and social sciences, while male undergraduates dominate in mathematics.

Gendered enrolment trends lead to differences in career options and salaries for women and men. That is, despite the fact that Canadian women now outnumber men in

> > > Thinking Sociologically

In what way was your own schooling gendered at the elementary and high school levels, and now in college or university? Consider your teachers' practices, for example. Were you ever divided into groups of boys and girls for activities or for seating? Did your curricular materials include both women and men, and how was each gender presented? What is the gender ratio in your university courses, and does it change from discipline to discipline? Do you notice gendered interactions with professors and/or teaching assistants?

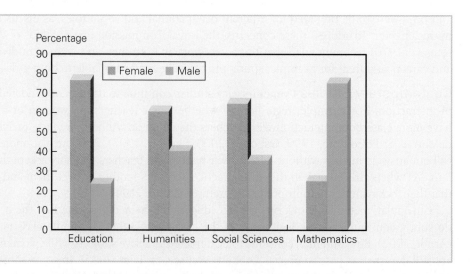

FIGURE 12.3

Undergraduate Enrolment by Discipline and Sex, Canada, 2010–2011

Source: Based on CAUT Almanac of Post-Secondary Education, 2013

< < <

Students entering their first year of university often feel a sense of anonymity among a more diverse student body.

undergraduate studies, they remain concentrated in disciplines that do not lead to the highest-paying jobs (Webber, 2010b). Men continue to earn higher annual salaries than women with comparable levels of education do (Hogan, Perrucci, & Behringer, 2005).

Educational Institutions as Gendered Workplaces When we look at educational institutions as workplaces, we also find gender distinctions. At the elementary school level, women account for 83 percent of teachers while high school levels differ, with women accounting for 57 percent of teachers (Statistics Canada, 2006e). Yet despite this over-representation of women as teachers, women account for 53 percent of elementary school principals, and only 32 percent of high school principals (Statistics Canada, 2006e). Women represent only 36 percent of all university professorial positions (CAUT, 2013). In addition, women professors in Canadian universities are congregated in the lowest ranks. Figure 12.4 summarizes women's and men's positioning across all academic ranks. Assistant professor represents the lowest rank in Canadian universities (people typically spend four to six years at this rank before applying for promotion), associate professor represents the middle rank, and full professor represents the highest rank.

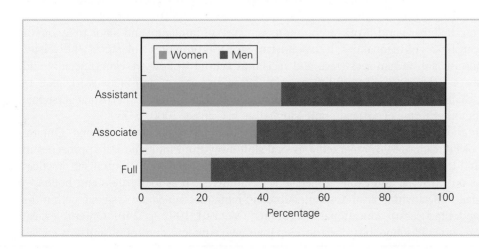

FIGURE 12.4

Canadian Professoriate by Rank, 2010–2011

Source: Based on data from: Full-time teaching staff at Canadian universities, by rank and sex. Statistics Canada, CANSIM, table 477-0017.

chilly climate **The lack of warmth or encouragement that girls and women feel in school as a result of sexism.**

As introduced in Chapter 8, pioneering work that explored women's experiences in academia documents a **chilly climate** (i.e., a lack of warmth or encouragement) for female students and faculty (Sandler & Hall, 1986). Female students and professors have claimed to feel like outsiders in the halls of academe. Sandler and Hall (1986) demonstrate that sexism in educational institutions goes beyond overt and direct harassment or discrimination—it operates in subtle and ubiquitous ways.

This chilly climate still exists today. For example, it affects the way in which work is distributed among faculty, how students evaluate their professors (women perceive that they are evaluated more harshly than their male colleagues), and how certain kinds of knowledge are valued—for example, the valuing of quantitatively derived knowledge over qualitative research, and the dismissing of feminist knowledge as biased or as merely personal opinion (Webber, 2005; Webber, 2010a). Women faculty's encouragement and mentoring of female students is documented as a taken-for-granted assumption and expectation (Acker & Feuerverger, 1996; Acker & Webber, 2006; Barnes-Powell & Letherby, 1998). "Institutional housekeeping"—service and committee work—also appears to be unduly allocated to women (Bird, Litt, & Wang, 2004; Park, 1996).

A contemporary activist project, started by two students at the University of Western Ontario (Sarah Ghabrial and Sheetal Rawal), has been engaged in lobbying efforts to the Ontario Ministry of Education to get women's and gender studies curriculum into high schools. Reflecting on their own experiences in an introductory women's studies course, they realized that their high schools had not introduced them to the idea of gender and its intersections with other social organizing principles (Miss G. Project, 2011). Their efforts connect with the academic feminist work that has been ongoing for many years.

In sum, rather than acting as the great equalizer for girls and boys, women and men, schools (through their organization, interactions, and curricular materials) reproduce and regulate particular normative constructions of masculinity and femininity.

ANTI-RACIST APPROACHES

Anti-racist approaches to education comprise "an action-oriented, educational and political strategy for institutional and systemic change that addresses the issue of racism and the interlocking systems of social oppression (sexism, classism, heterosexism, ableism)" (Dei & Calliste, 2000, p. 13). As discussed in Chapter 10, there is no scientific validity to the category of "race," yet it persists as a social category owing to the power that lies behind its construction and deployment as a social reality.

Anti-Racism versus Multiculturalism In a Canadian context, it is important to explain how anti-racism differs conceptually from multiculturalism. Multiculturalism, as a *political doctrine*, promotes Canada as a culturally diverse space—not just its population but its social, political, and moral fabric (Bromley, 2011; Dei & Calliste, 2000). Multiculturalism as an *ideology*, on the other hand, works to promote sameness of humanity and tends to ignore or minimize instances of inequalities. It depoliticizes race and promotes "tolerance" of diversity.

In contrast, anti-racism sees "race and racism as central to how we claim, occupy and defend spaces" (Dei & Calliste, 2000, p. 21). Those engaged in anti-racist work seek to "identify, challenge and change the values, structures and behaviours that perpetuate systemic racism and other forms of societal oppression" (Dei & Calliste, 2000, p. 21).

In Ontario, a report by the Provincial Advisory Committee on Race Relations (Ontario Ministry of Education, 1987) marked a pivotal shift away from multicultural approaches in schools and toward an anti-racist approach. The report criticized multiculturalism practices that focus on "material and exotic dimensions of culture such as food, dress and holidays" and that fail to deal with "racial discrimination and inequities which are systemic within the policies and 'practices' of educational institutions" (McLeod, 1992, p. 240). Ontario legislation now requires all school boards to develop their own ethnocultural equity and anti-racism

BOX 12.3 CANADIAN CONTRIBUTIONS TO SOCIOLOGY

Sandra Acker

Sandra Acker is a professor in the Department of Sociology and Equity Studies at the University of Toronto's Ontario Institute for Studies in Education (OISE). She is a sociologist of education, with interests in gender and education, higher education, and teachers' work.

Acker conducted an ethnographic study that explores the myriad facets of a teacher's job beyond classroom teaching: "Teachers ran assemblies, kept records, put up displays, led singing, taught the recorder, organized dancing, took children to sing in a home for the elderly, collected money, conferred with parents, met together, consulted educational psychologists or other specialists, purchased or collected supplies, presented curriculum evenings for parents, attended PTA activities, ran sports matches, reorganized the school library, took charge of the school fair and went on courses" (Acker, 1999, p. 83).

We tend to take for granted that somehow all of the above will get done without considering who is responsible for that work or whether it will even be considered work. Teaching is hard work, yet social discourses frame it as easy and natural—especially for female teachers working with young children. The teaching of young children is often framed as an extension of women's maternal abilities. Acker, while demonstrating that gender indeed shapes people's perceptions of teaching, challenges the notion that teaching is simply an extension of the caring work that women routinely provide to their children.

Sandra Acker

Acker also draws our attention to the importance of considering schools as workplaces. So much attention is paid to schools as spaces for children that we often fail to consider what they mean to the work lives of adults.

Sandra Acker's books include *Gendered Education* (1994) and *The Realities of Teachers' Work: Never a Dull Moment* (1999).

policies within parameters set by the Ministry of Education and Training (Dei, 2003). As of 2009, Ontario established an Inclusive Education Branch in order to help identify structural barriers in place that impact student achievement (CRRF, 2010).

Anti-racism challenges white privilege, but also allows space for white persons to be part of the production of an anti-racist identity (Bedard, 2000). Given that the majority of teachers in Canadian schools are white, it is imperative that everyone be committed to an anti-racist framework. White teachers need to reflect on the ways in which they reproduce colonialist, imperialist, and capitalist histories in their classrooms (Bedard, 2000).

Racism, Curriculum, Perception, and Pedagogy Canadian, American, and British studies document the racialized treatment of students across all levels of schooling (Codjoe, 2001; Dei, 2008; Sadker & Sadker, 2009; Skelton, 1997). In American primary schools, white boys have been found to be the most likely recipients of teacher attention, followed by boys of colour, followed by white girls. Girls of colour are the least likely to receive attention from their teachers (Sadker & Sadker, 2009).

Morris's (2007) American research on working-class black girls and their middle-school classroom experiences demonstrates how teachers encourage the girls to conform to a normative model of a docile femininity. Teachers hold racialized perceptions about black girls' femininity, perceiving the girls as "coarse and overly assertive" (Morris, 2007, p. 491). Rather than focusing on the girls' academic development, teachers focused more on their social

> > >

Anti-racism and
multiculturalism
are conceptually
distinct, but both
have implications for
education in a Canadian
context.

Gareth Boden/Pearson

etiquette (Morris, 2007). The girls' actions were seen as "challenging to authority, loud and not ladylike" and thus drew the teachers' attention (Morris, 2007, p. 501). Black Canadian high school students report similar experiences of being ignored in their classes and being treated as unimportant by teachers, administrators, and fellow students (Codjoe, 2001).

An anti-racist pedagogy challenges educators to be mindful of their own practices as well as attentive to the problems within official curricular materials. Aboriginal peoples, for example, have been "romanticized or stereotyped" in curricular materials, in which they are represented either as peacefully living off the land or as savages (Archibald, 1995, p. 349). Curricular materials should incorporate positive contributions of Aboriginal peoples, such as their history, "languages, food and medicine" (Neegan, 2005, p. 11). Research on race, schooling, and black Canadian students reveals that these students desire a more inclusive curriculum than currently offered in the predominantly white, male, Eurocentric materials used in their classrooms (Codjoe, 2001; Dei, 1997, 2008). For example, one participant remarked:

> I really didn't feel as though I got any education from school as far as Black education was concerned . . . I didn't learn anything about Black history in high school. There was no subject [in Black studies] for you to take, and in regular social studies classes they didn't discuss anything Black or African. They might have said something about slavery once or twice but they really didn't say anything in depth and they didn't say anything positive. (Codjoe, 2001, p. 355)

Research on the presence of racism in our classrooms is not limited to elementary and secondary schools. Frances Henry and Carol Tator (2009) argue that a "culture of whiteness" (p. 8) pervades Canadian universities. This whiteness is found in curricular materials, in who is authorized to teach, in who leads our universities, and so forth.

Teachers need to be aware not only of the differences in their classrooms, but also of how these differences are vested in relations of power and result in silencing and marginalizing those marked as different. Further, teachers should aim to create classroom spaces—both materially, in curriculum materials, and socially, through interactions and activities—that enable students to think through and question their assumptions about the world, and thereby deconstruct the social relations around them.

CULTURAL THEORY

Cultures tend to reproduce themselves, meaning that cultural values and norms are transmitted from generation to generation. French sociologist Pierre Bourdieu was interested in how inequality was reproduced in this way, and how aspects of culture contribute to its reproduction. He explored, for instance, how privilege is transferred generationally through social symbols that are associated with high status.

Bourdieu uses the term *cultural capital* to explore how people can use particular cultural resources for economic and social success. As discussed in Chapter 6, cultural capital encompasses things like interpersonal skills, habits, manners, education credentials, tastes, and so forth. Possessing an expansive vocabulary, understanding how to approach social situations with elegance and grace, feeling at ease in an expensive restaurant, and wearing designer clothing are just a few examples of cultural capital. Note that these qualities tend to be associated with high status. Cultural capital, then, "like trumps in a game of cards, are powers which define the chances of profit in a given field" (Bourdieu, 1991, p. 230). This capital is made up of resources, and not all resources are valued equally. In our class-based society, for example, attending the opera carries more cultural capital than going to a country music concert, just as playing golf garners more cultural capital than being a wrestler.

With regard to education, Bourdieu argued that schools reproduce existing power relations; they are not value neutral. He argued that the culture of the dominant class is successfully reproduced through schooling because schools endorse a particular way of speaking, writing, and behaving. Teachers will reward students who most closely emulate the standards of the dominant culture—even for seemingly small things like saying *please* and *thank you*, raising one's hand and waiting to be called upon before speaking, writing neatly, and obeying authority.

Children from higher social backgrounds come to school with greater cultural capital (behaviour: calm, polite; habits: clean clothes, good hygiene; attitudes: obedient, willing to

< < <

Access to education varies globally—this access is further mediated by one's gender. Educating girls remains a key factor for developing countries to move toward economic sustainability.

Michael Jenner/Robert Harding Picture Library Ltd/Alamy

v
v
v

Pierre Bourdieu argues that schools reproduce existing power relations through their endorsement of particular ways of speaking, writing, and behaving. As depicted here, our school systems value obedient and well-mannered students.

Comstock/Stockbyte/Getty Images

learn) that they are able to parlay into educational success. Children who come from lower social backgrounds are disadvantaged in a school system that is implicitly based on middle-class conventions and is thus not familiar to them.

An example of cultural capital at work can be seen in Annette Lareau's 1989 study of teachers' understandings of home–school relationships and parental involvement. Indicators of cultural capital in this study included such things as parents' interactions with other parents, their understanding of school processes, their interactions with school personnel, and their communication skills (Lareau, 1989). These indicators were used to explore the level of parental involvement of both upper-middle-class and working-class parents (Lareau, 1989).

In keeping with Bourdieu's framework, Lareau found that the upper-middle-class children's home lives more closely mirrored the language, structure, and organization of schooling than those of their working-class counterparts. The upper-middle-class parents, having had comparable schooling experiences, were aware of what would be considered appropriate relations between school and home, and hence what their parental involvement ought to look like (Lareau, 1989).

Parents who understood school processes were able to meet (or exceed) teachers' and administrators' expectations regarding parental involvement, and thus these parents were viewed as competent in supporting their children's education (Lareau, 1989). Lower levels of home–school involvement by working-class parents, who were not as aware of these expectations, were misinterpreted by teachers and administrators; these parents were perceived as not being concerned with or caring about their children's education (Lareau, 1989).

The teachers in Lareau's (1989) study believed that a strong positive relationship exists between levels of parental involvement and children's academic achievements. Lareau's findings remind us that while class may provide certain social and cultural resources, these resources nevertheless must "be invested or activated in order to become a form of cultural capital" (Lareau, 1987, p. 84).

POST-STRUCTURALIST THEORY

A number of post-structural researchers take up the theoretical work of Michel Foucault and apply it to the setting of education. Recall from Chapter 3 that Foucault talks about *power/ knowledge* as a nexus—that is, power is always implicated in the production of knowledge; we cannot separate knowledge from the context in which it is produced. Further, Foucault uses the term *discourse* to describe systems of thought that govern how we might think, speak, or act about a particular topic.

Racism in History Textbooks: A Post-Structural Study

An interesting study links knowledge production—and how such production is embedded in power relations—with Ontario high school history textbooks. The study examines the discourses of racism in government-approved history textbooks published in the 1960s and in 2000 (still currently in use). Tracing how racism is discursively constituted (that is, how the subject of racism is framed and discussed) in these textbooks tells us something about how Canada is actively constructed as a just nation—one that is antithetical to racism (Montgomery, 2005).

While there is no one agreed-upon definition of *racism*, many sociologists understand it as being multidimensional and complex. Racism is understood as intersecting with other social relations (gender, class, sexuality, ability, and so forth) and has material consequences for the oppressed (those who are harmed by exclusionary forms of power) as well as the oppressors (those who benefit from such forms of power) (Montgomery, 2005). "Racism is not just a singular and extraordinary problem 'in them' (i.e. racists), but a complex set of relations constituting 'normal' everyday life in and around 'us'" (Montgomery, 2005, p. 430). It is from this understanding of racism that Montgomery (2005) carries out his analysis of history textbooks.

One marked shift between the textbooks of the 1960s and the ones currently in use is the prominence afforded to discussions of racism (Montgomery, 2005). Such discussions are

BOX 12.4 ISSUES IN GLOBAL CONTEXT

Women's Literacy

Despite increasing enrolment rates worldwide at all levels of education for both girls and boys, a gender gap in educational opportunities persists (Abbott, Wallace, & Tyler, 2005). A United Nations (2003) report documents that in 22 African and 9 Asian nations, girls' school enrolment is less than 80 percent of boys' enrolment. The gender gap in participation rates is greatest in Southeast Asia and sub-Saharan Africa, where girls represent less than 40 percent of high school enrolments (United Nations, 2003).

While global literacy rates are increasing, women nevertheless make up the majority of the world's illiterate population (Abbott, Wallace, & Tyler, 2005). The United Nations Educational, Scientific and Cultural Organization (UNESCO) documents that there are 860 million illiterate adults worldwide and at least 100 million children who have no access to education. Of these adults and children, 60 percent are female (www.esrc.ac.uk).

Access to education varies globally. In areas where access to basic schooling is high (countries in southern Africa, Latin America, and East Asia), girls tend to outnumber boys (Abbott, Wallace, & Tyler, 2005). However, in regions with lower levels of educational participation, we see a gender gap, with boys accessing schooling at higher rates than girls. This trend is particularly stark in rural areas. For example, "in Niger . . . there are 80 girls for every 100 boys in schools in cities, but in rural areas the corresponding ratio is only 41 to 100" (Abbott, Wallace, & Tyler, 2005, p. 108).

The United Nations (2003) reports that these participation rates reflect parents' ideas about the potential benefits of their children's educations. Some parents choose to invest in educating only their sons, who have greater access to better-paying employment opportunities (Abbott, Wallace, & Tyler, 2005). Further, some parents are reluctant to invest in a daughter's education because they believe that this investment will be realized by her future husband's family rather than themselves. Gendered ideas about the relevance of paid work for women also keeps parents from investing in their daughters' educations; some see household work as more relevant for women and thus remove their daughters from schooling or prevent them from attending school altogether (Abbott, Wallace, & Tyler, 2005). This disadvantage combines with other existing gender inequalities, and thus has the potential to further support women's subordinate place in many societies (www.esrc.ac.uk).

Researchers have also demonstrated a link between literacy rates and birth rates. Literate women have an average of two children while illiterate women have six to eight children (http://www-01.sil.org/literacy/wom_lit.htm). A woman's literacy is further linked to her overall health and to the health of her children. Literate women tend to have better housing conditions, income, and access to water and sanitation measures (http://www-01.sil.org/literacy/wom_lit.htm).

Educating girls, then, remains a key factor for those developing countries moving toward economic sustainability (Abbott, Wallace, & Tyler, 2005).

What role should the state play in the education of its citizens?

now included throughout history textbooks. However, these books normalize racism as an act of individuals, deriving from individual attitudes and beliefs (Montgomery, 2005). It is presented as devoid of power relations and as disconnected from institutional relations of power. Such constructions fail to account for the assorted privileges, power, and wealth accumulated by some (that is, white individuals) as a consequence of racism (Montgomery, 2005). In other words, while the textbooks acknowledge that various people have been harmed in Canada as a result of specific, time-bound instances of racism (e.g., Aboriginals in residential schools, internment of Japanese Canadians), there is no acknowledgment that this harm may have benefited others (Montgomery, 2005).

Today's textbooks also situate racism in Canada as an element of the past and not part of the country's current social fabric (Montgomery, 2005). Contemporary instances of racism are discursively framed as human rights violations and as restricted to individuals. They are presented as contained events whose wrongs are righted through the Canadian legal system (e.g., Ernst Zundel denying the Holocaust and expressing racist ideas, Baltej Singh Dhillon seeking the right to wear a turban as an RCMP officer, the wrongful murder conviction of Donald Marshall, Jr.) (Montgomery, 2005).

Such individualized discussions of racism perpetuate a "grand redemptive narrative of Canadian nationalism" (Montgomery, 2005, p. 438). Canada is thus configured as a "good and tolerant space in which racism is imagined to be the exception" (Montgomery, 2005, p. 438). The presentation of Canada as a just state perpetuates "mythologies of white settler benevolence" and directs attention away from the ordinary racisms upon which Canada is constructed and reconstructed (Montgomery, 2005, p. 439).

A post-structural analysis of educational materials, such as high school history textbooks, allows us to uncover the discursive structures of dominance that are presented to Canadian students as truth (Montgomery, 2005). Such an analysis further exposes that knowledge is socially produced and is always implicated in power relations.

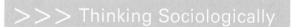

> > > Thinking Sociologically

How do you think school practices might inhibit student engagement and/or participation? How might a student's cultural background shape his or her educational engagement?

❺ Higher Education: Contemporary Issues

Today's postsecondary institutions are facing a number of challenges. Over the past few decades, government funding of these institutions has declined dramatically. And while the number of Canadian faculty members has decreased as a result, student enrolment, as we have seen, has increased (Grant, 2002).

Decreased funding has resulted in a greater reliance on private dollars, mainly in the form of higher student tuition fees (Drakich, Grant, & Stewart, 2002). Additionally, faculty increasingly must rely on private research monies (Drakich, Grant, & Stewart, 2002). Startlingly, corporate sources now account for the majority (greater than 52 percent) of clinical medical research dollars (Westheimer, 2010). University buildings are also in disrepair; according to a report by the Canadian Association of University Business Officers, our universities are in desperate need of at least $3.6 billion to refurbish classrooms, laboratories, and research space (Drakich, Grant, & Stewart, 2002).

Added to these consequences of decreased funding is the current restructuring of Canadian universities on a more corporate model—a development that may be considered a result of a market ideology and business practices associated with globalization (Currie & Newson, 1998; Peters, 2013; Westheimer, 2010).

RESEARCH FUNDING

Over the past decade, Canadian universities have become more involved with industry and the private sector as a means of generating revenue (Shanahan & Jones, 2007, p. 41; Westheimer, 2010).

As discussed in Chapter 4, one avenue for generating this revenue is research. In 2002, the federal government identified the challenges facing Canadian universities over the coming decade; these include (1) "more than doubling basic and applied university research activities," (2) "contributing to a rapid expansion in the amount of R&D [research and

v
v
v

Research is one way universities can generate revenue in a time when postsecondary institutions are facing numerous challenges due to decreasing levels of government funding.

Creatas Images/Jupiterimages

development] conducted in Canada both by performing research for industry and government and by supplying the economy with far more master's and PhD graduates," and (3) "tripling the revenues generated from commercialisation of university based R&D" (Gauthier, 2004, p. 98).

Faculty members are now, more than ever, encouraged to seek external research funding as a way to contribute to their university's cost-recovery program (Tudiver, 1999). In this way, research itself becomes a market commodity, promoted as a potential service to business (Smith, 2004). Peters (2013) refers to universities operating in this mode as the "entrepreneurial university" and the "enterprise university" (p.13). Yet as James Turk, executive director of the Canadian Association of University Teachers, cautions, "Universities exist to serve the public interest, not just corporate interests" (Grant, 2002, p. 269).

QUALITY AND ACCOUNTABILITY

Associated with the rise of neo-liberal universities, which include an emphasis on increased efficiency and business practices, are calls to evaluate the quality of our universities and establish their accountability.

However, what is quality education? Should quality be based on students' experiences of their educational careers (which are difficult to quantify), or should it be measured by students' future successes? How can we measure quality instruction, research, administration, and student services? Quality education is difficult to measure through quantitative considerations since these fail to capture the human and social elements of schooling. And, of course, one's notion of what constitutes quality will reflect one's attitudes about the purpose of education—that is, whose interests it should serve. For example, should education produce well-rounded citizens, or should it focus on transmitting skills geared to market trends? The seeming shift away from explicit citizenship training has some critics worried as skills-training for the marketplace is being afforded primacy over teaching values; likewise, training is being prioritized over education (Osborne, 2000; Westheimer, 2010). Universities are being turned into what Joel Westheimer calls "certification factories" (2010, p. 10).

Even though governments are currently providing dwindling resources, accountability requirements are increasing (Drakich, Grant, & Stewart, 2002), and these requirements are being based on quantitative measures.

At the level of individual faculty members, evaluations based on academic considerations are being replaced with quantitative measures that prioritize particular forms of scholarly work (for example, publishing refereed journal articles is highly valued, yet writing textbooks is not) (Drakich, Grant, & Stewart, 2002). Rather than considering the quality and potential impact of an academic's work, publications are now counted, external research grant monies are tallied, and journals in which the academic's work appears are ranked against other journals; even the number of times a particular publication is cited may be used as a measure of the quality of an academic's work.

> > > Thinking Sociologically

Did you consult the *Maclean's* rankings (or other rankings) when considering which postsecondary institution to attend? If so, were these measures useful? If not, why not? Now that you are attending a postsecondary institution, what sort of measures would you have found useful? What elements would you include in a definition of quality education?

At the level of individual institutions, the Ontario Ministry of Training, Colleges and Universities, for example, now requires colleges and universities to report on (and make public) four performance indicators: graduation rates, employment rates (at six months and two years after graduation), and defaults on government student loans. Government funding is then tied to each institution's performance on these indicators. While linking students' graduation rates to specific institutions makes sense, it is more difficult to understand how defaulting on loans and employment rates reflect the performance of the

> > >

Class sizes at Canadian
universities are on the
rise in addition to a
shrinking professoriate.

Zucchi Uwe/dpa/Corbis

BOX 12.5 WHY SHOULD WE CARE?

Pepsi–Coke Wars

Does your university have an exclusive soft drink contract? That is, are you able to buy only Pepsi products or only Coke products on campus? And, does your school have an ethical purchasing policy?

There has been much debate in recent years about the lucrative exclusivity contracts that schools, colleges, and universities have signed with soft-drink manufacturers. Two kinds of arguments address why we should be concerned about these agreements: that they allow corporate cultural values to infiltrate our campuses, and that schools should not do business with vendors who engage in unethical labour practises.

In Canada, Coca-Cola has garnered much press regarding allegations of "widespread labour, human rights and environmental abuses worldwide" (Johnson, 2007)—and several universities have seen student-led protests as a result. In October 2007, students at Guelph University voted in a binding referendum to remove Coca-Cola from campus (Johnson, 2007). In 2005, York University students spoke out through their student society when they passed a resolution that advocated a complete boycott of Coca-Cola (Markle, 2007).

Student activist groups argue that our campuses should not support unethical corporations that pursue profit at any cost. Rather, as "global citizens [we need] to work toward the proliferation of worker-controlled, co-operative structures for businesses. ... it is crucial that our governance structures introduce ethics into the process of exchange by implementing Ethical Purchasing Policy" (Markle, 2007, p. 24).

As we asked you at the beginning of this section—does your campus have exclusive contracts? What are the pros and cons of such an approach for students on your campus? How are these exclusivity contracts a feature of the neo-liberal university?

This article is also a peerScholar assignment in MySocLab.

institution. Indeed, we could argue that the government has failed to exercise its sociological imagination in this instance, given that many social factors are involved in employment and loan repayment.

Accountability based on these performance indicators is increasing; Ontario, for example, is beginning to require "multi-year, institution-specific, enrolment and accountability agreements with government" (Shanahan & Jones, 2007, p. 40). The looming threat behind such agreements is that if institutions fail to meet their enrolment and accountability targets, they will lose government funding. As a result, some institutions will become the "haves" while others may become the "have-nots." The Higher Education Quality Council of Ontario (HEQCO), established in 2006, is responsible for studying quality issues in Ontario higher education and formulating recommendations for the provincial government on potential quality standards, measures, and targets.

Maclean's magazine entered the accountability game almost 20 years ago with its annual ranking of Canadian universities. *Maclean's* does not send questionnaires to Canadian universities with a student population of less than 1000 or to institutions with a "strictly religious or specialized mission" (Dowsett Johnston & Dwyer, 2004, p. 38). The aim of its questionnaire is to "offer students and parents a rare view into the ivory tower—a unique opportunity to make informed decisions on the comparative strengths of public universities across Canada" (Dowsett Johnston & Dwyer, 2004, p. 38). Institutions are ranked on criteria such as entering students' high school averages, graduation rates, size of classes by year of study, proportion of faculty members with Ph.D.s, faculty awards, proportion of budget spent on student services, library holdings, and so forth.

Critics argue that the *Maclean's* criteria are "simplified and arbitrary," perceiving that such quantified indicators do not translate easily into quality (Eisenkraft & Berkowitz, 2007, p. 29). Indeed, students often rely on factors other than the ones used by *Maclean's* when deciding which postsecondary institutions to attend. Students say that they are primarily interested in institutional reputation, program reputation, campus location, campus safety, and financial costs (Eisenkraft & Berkowitz, 2007).

UNIVERSITY OF McDONALD'S?

We can link all of the contemporary changes discussed above to George Ritzer's notion of **McDonaldization** and apply it to universities, meaning that these institutions are expected to function in ever more efficient ways, with a high degree of predictability and standardization (Ritzer, 1998, 2002). Students (and their parents) are understood as customers who consume education just as they would any other commodity available in the marketplace. Universities, like businesses, must compete for and retain students. McDonaldized universities come to resemble each other just as McDonald's restaurants do. Ritzer (2002) argues that "the problem is not McDonaldization per se, but excessive McDonaldization and the inappropriate extension of McDonaldization to domains that ought not to be McDonaldized to any great extent" (p. 31). Neal Curtis is highly critical of a consumer model of education. He worries that setting up the professor–student relationship as a salesperson–customer relationship will produce students who lack the capacity for independent thought, are hesitant to take risks, and will not pursue (or see the merit of) self-directed learning (Curtis, 2010, p. A2).

Increased class sizes, fewer faculty members, less direct government funding, and increased tuition costs—all of these factors combine to diminish the possibility of Canadian institutions offering high-quality, accessible education (Drakich, Grant, & Stewart, 2002).

ACADEMIC INTEGRITY

Another salient topic in higher education is that of academic integrity—more commonly referred to as cheating. Academic misconduct is, of course, anathema to the key values of learning, so why are people cheating?

McDonaldization **The notion that insitutions are expected to function in ever more efficient ways, with a high degree of predictability and standardization.**

The McDonaldization of Society

Why Many International Students Get a Failing Grade in Academic Integrity

A 2006 study revealed that "53% of nearly '15,000' Canadian undergraduates admitted to cheating on written work at least once in the 12 months before the survey" (Gillis, 2007, p. 12). The authors of this landmark study point out that although data have long been available on academic misconduct in the United States, little research exists on the topic in Canada (Christensen Hughes & McCabe, 2006).

All constituents of the academic population—faculty, teaching assistants, undergraduate and graduate students—participated in the study, which explored both perceptions (what various parties understand to be academic misconduct) and behaviours (activities parties have actually engaged in). Among undergraduate students, the five most frequently reported academic misconduct behaviours were "working with others when asked for individual work, getting questions and answers from someone who has already taken a test, copying a few sentences of material from a written source without footnoting, copying a few sentences from the Internet without footnoting, and fabricating or falsifying lab data" (Christensen Hughes & McCabe, 2006, p. 10).

Alarmingly, the study found that 46 percent of faculty and 38 percent of teaching assistants ignored cases of suspected academic misconduct (Christensen Hughes & McCabe, 2006). While lack of evidence dominated the reasons for ignoring such cases, it is disturbing how many faculty and teaching assistants cited a perceived lack of support from administration and the amount of time required to pursue these cases. The study also found, unsurprisingly, that students perceived little risk of being caught and/or penalized.

The study recommends that "institutions should recommit themselves to academic integrity and that considerable effort needs to be put into understanding where existing policies are failing" (Christensen Hughes & McCabe, 2006, p. 17).

Summary

1 Mass education was established in Canada in the early 1900s as a means of serving the public good by providing a common moral education. Postsecondary participation rates have risen over the past several decades.

2 Functionalists view schools as institutions that reflect the larger social system; conflict theorists argue that schools sort students on the basis of social class, gender, and race; symbolic interactionists recognize that teachers' labelling of students influences their success in school; feminist theorists examine the sexism embedded in both school texts and classroom practices; anti-racists challenge teachers to be mindful of racialized texts and treatment of students; cultural theorists perceive education's ability to reproduce particular class cultures; and post-structuralists focus on schools as sites of the power/knowledge nexus.

3 Rising tuition rates in both arts and professional disciplines create structural barriers that limit participation of those in the lower social classes.

4 Although women's postsecondary enrolment rates are now higher than men's, women remain concentrated in disciplines that do not lead to the highest-paying jobs.

5 Due to decreased government funding, colleges and universities currently must seek more research funding through external sources; they are also facing more quantifiable accountability requirements and issues of academic integrity.

Key Terms

chilly climate *322*
correspondence principle *316*
credential inflation *313*
massification *312*
McDonaldization *331*
meritocracy *315*

Reviewing the Concepts

1. What are some examples of cultural capital from your upbringing? Were these helpful in your schooling?

2. What is an honour code? Does your university or college require students to sign an honour code regarding academic integrity? If not, would you be willing to sign one? Why or why not?

3. What is the distinction between multiculturalism as a political doctrine and as an ideology?

Applying Your Sociological Imagination

1. Do you think that education should be a private responsibility or a public responsibility? Why?

2. Should schools be organized around the interests of a particular community? Or should they be shaped by provincial (or even national) interests?

3. The next time you walk around your campus, take note of whether there is a corporate presence there. What are some of the implications of such a presence?

4. Whose responsibility is it to ensure that anyone who is qualified and wants to attend a postsecondary institution has the ability to do so: the individual, the individual's family, the state, or a combination of these? Provide a rationale for your answer.

MySocLab

Visit MySocLab to access a variety of online resources that will help you prepare for tests and apply your knowledge.

13 Religion

Despite the growing numbers of people who profess to hold no religious beliefs, North Americans have focused on religion and religious beliefs for generations. The terrorist attacks of September 11, 2001, accentuated, once again, how religion can bring out the very best and the very worst in people. Since the attacks, the relationship between religion and extremist beliefs has fuelled countless debates not only in popular media, but among academics as well.

Religion has inspired some of the most beautiful works of art, literature, music, and architecture the world has ever seen. Religion has also inspired the birth of universities and scientific insights. In fact, a number of the world's scientists today are also religious (Ruth, 2014).

In this chapter, we are going to explore the complicated and often contentious relationship between religion and secular society. We are going to examine what it means to be religious, the structure of religious institutions, and how they influence the larger society around them. We will see that the role of religion in society is certainly changing, but in ways that do not diminish its importance to the contemporary social landscape.

By the end of this chapter, students will be able to

1 Review the different types of religious belief systems: animism, polytheism, and monotheism.

2 Define and provide examples of the different types of religious groups, including new religious movements, sects, and churches.

3 Explain the belief systems of the world's largest religions.

4 Review the key trends in church attendance as well as the influence of immigration on the Canadian religious landscape.

5 Discuss how various sociological theories explain religion.

6 Assess some of the challenges facing religious organizations today.

1 Religious Belief Systems

Religion is defined as a set of organized beliefs about the supernatural or spiritual worlds and their associated ceremonies that guides people's behaviour (see Parkinson & Drislane, 2007, p. 135) and joins them into communities of believers. While some offer alternative definitions of religion (see Swenson, 1999, pp. 65–69, for a thorough review), one of the key components of religion is the concept of faith. **Faith** is a belief system based on conviction that does not require objective evidence to substantiate its claims (e.g., a person can have faith that God exists without first-hand evidence to support the claim). By investigating religion as an important social institution, sociologists continue their tradition of looking at the individual's relationship to the social—the central focus of the sociological endeavour.

One of the earliest anthropologists to study religious diversity around the world was E. B. Tylor (1832–1917). Tylor saw that just as cultures naturally evolve from simple, primitive communities to modern, complex states over time, so, too, do religions. He argued that religion evolved through distinct stages. The first stage he referred to as **animism**, in which supernatural beings or spirits are believed to inhabit both living things (plants, animals, people) and inanimate objects (mountains, rivers); in other words, within every substance there is a separate entity or being (Joshi, 1996, p. 28). According to Tylor (1883), this attribution of conscious life to natural objects or phenomena ultimately results in the notion of a soul. The next stage, **polytheism**, occurs when a society begins to recognize a series of independent supernatural beings or gods (Rea, 2006, p. 133). In *diffuse polytheism*, all gods are considered equals; in *hierarchal polytheism*, gods are ranked in importance or power. The final stage, **monotheism**, occurs when a religion identifies with a single, all-powerful, all-knowing god (Lindsey, Beach, & Ravelli, 2009, p. 155; Tylor, 1883).

Tylor's classification of religious development is certainly interesting in a historical sense; however, his universal evolutionary theme is

religion A set of organized beliefs about the supernatural or spiritual worlds that guides behaviour and joins people into communities of believers.

faith A belief system based on conviction that does not require objective evidence to substantiate its claims.

animism Belief that all things possess a spirit.

polytheism Belief in many gods; can be diffuse, with all gods considered equal, or hierarchal, with gods ranked in importance or power.

monotheism Belief in a single, all-powerful, all-knowing god.

> > >

The Judeo-Christian roots of American society are evident in many cultural symbols, not the least of which is the inscription of "In God We Trust" on their currency.

Rsooll/Fotolia

no longer reputable. Neither societies nor religions progress along a simple and universal line of development. Contemporary anthropology and sociology could not support the idea that contemporary animistic and polytheistic religions are somehow less evolved or substandard than monotheistic ones. For social scientists, all religions are equal and no single belief system is more worthy or truthful than any other.

civil religion (secular religion) Exists when sacred symbols are integrated into the broader society regardless of their individual religious affiliations.

Sociologists often use the term **civil religion** or **secular religion** to describe a system in which sacred symbols are integrated into the broader society regardless of their individual religious affiliations (Cristi, 2001; Fujiwara, 2007). For example, Judeo-Christian symbols permeate American society (e.g., "In God We Trust" is inscribed on US currency) and promote the belief that democracy is a divinely sanctioned political system (Bellah, 1975). Like other religions, civil religion involves intense emotions that come with patriotism, nationalism, and reverence for national symbols such as the flag, the Charter of Rights and Freedoms, and the Christian-based holidays of Christmas, Thanksgiving, and Easter. If Tylor were alive today, he would no doubt consider civil religion as the most highly evolved, since patriotism does not rely on the concept of a god or the supernatural.

❷ Types of Religious Groups

((•—Listen

Freethinkers

Every human society must organize its religious beliefs in some way. Sociologists are interested in understanding the rich diversity of human belief systems, from the very small to the state-sponsored. By understanding the different ways in which religious groups organize themselves, we are better able to appreciate how they begin, grow, change, or die out.

NEW RELIGIOUS MOVEMENT

new religious movement An informal group without defined structure; generally emerges around authoritarian and charismatic leaders who suppress rational thought to isolate members from the larger society.

Most of today's large organized religions began as what sociologists used to call a *cult* but now refer to as a *new religious movement*. The change in terminology stems from the fact that most sociologists recognize that the term *cult* has a strong pejorative connotation in most Anglo-Saxon societies (Possamaï & Lee, 2004, p. 337). While *cult* is still used in the literature (e.g., Dawson, 2006), we believe that the change in terminology is justified and reflects the direction of most contemporary sociologists studying religion (see Swenson, 2008, p. 29). A **new religious movement** is usually defined as an informal group without defined structure; it generally emerges around authoritarian and charismatic leaders who suppress rational thought to isolate members from the larger society and sever former relationships (Healy, 2011; Joosse, 2012; Possamaï & Lee, 2004, p. 337).

Max Weber used the term *charisma* to describe a personality attribute that sets some people apart because they are believed to possess exceptional powers or qualities that in some instances can be viewed as supernatural or superhuman (Parsons, 1947). Charismatic leaders often develop a special bond of trust and love with followers that reinforces loyalty and obedience. A new religious movement is the only type of religious organization that relies solely on charismatic authority to maintain and legitimize its mission. Because new religious movements are so closely associated with a charismatic leader, they usually disband once the original leader dies. However, at times, some new religious movements are able to make the transition to the next type of religious organization: the sect.

SECT

A **sect** is a small religious body, with exclusive or voluntary membership, that is somewhat separate from or hostile to the larger society. A sect usually emerges after the death of the founding member of a new religious movement. Weber described this process as the "routinization of charisma," in that the leadership becomes routine and part of the belief system that transcends the lives of any of the leaders (Eisenstadt, 1968; Swenson, 1999, p. 34). Joining a sect is voluntary and usually follows some form of conversion experience. Sects are often formed after a group breaks away from a larger religious group (a church) because the dissidents believe that the parent organization does not practise or believe in the true religion as it was originally conceived (Stark & Bainbridge, 1985).

CHURCH

A **church** is an institution that brings together a moral community of believers in formal worship and integrates itself within the larger secular world. The church is a long-standing and well-integrated part of society and is organized in the same way as many other large bureaucratic organizations. For example, churches employ professionally trained clergy, who are usually ordained in seminaries representing a specific theology (Bruce & Voas, 2007, p. 1; Greeley, 1972). We should point out that our use of the term *church* does present a somewhat Western and nineteenth-century bias in that this definition may not apply to other belief systems. For example, some local religious belief systems may not have professionally trained leaders and as such would not qualify for the designation of a "church" even though all other criteria may apply. Traditionally, churches are most prevalent in societies with a high degree of **religious pluralism**. The close integration of churches with other social institutions helps to minimize any tensions that might exist as they all try to compete for people's time, commitment, and money.

When a church enters into a formal relationship with the state, whereby all citizens are considered members, it is called an **ecclesia**, or state religion. The ecclesia is the largest, most formal, and most powerful of all religious organizations. Membership is generally ascribed at birth and nearly universal within the society. Ecclesias have highly bureaucratized structures and rituals that are often highly abstract and rarely include demonstrations of emotion (Johnson, 2000, p. 98). Contemporary examples of ecclesias are the Catholic Church in Italy, Islam in Iran, the Lutheran Church of Sweden, and the Anglican Church of England.

In a religiously pluralistic society, the term *denomination* refers to a socially accepted religious body that has bureaucratic characteristics similar to those of a church. A denomination is self-governing but has an official and recognized relationship with a larger church; examples include Anglicanism and Orthodox Judaism. While the distinction between denomination and church is a blurry one, denominations represent subdivisions within the church and therefore more accurately reflect the diversity encompassed by any world religion. In relation to other major social institutions (e.g., the state), a denomination neither promotes nor opposes the status quo but, rather, simply coexists within the larger society (Johnson, 2000, p. 82).

((•─ Listen

New Religion in America

sect A small religious body, with exclusive or voluntary membership, that is somewhat separate from or hostile to the larger society.

church An institution that brings together a moral community of believers in formal worship and integrates itself within the larger secular world.

religious pluralism A system in which many religions coexist and often compete with one another for members.

ecclesia A system in which a church and the state have a formalized relationship.

>>> Thinking Sociologically

The movement of religions from new religious movements to sects to churches is a fascinating one for sociologists. Can you think of other examples in contemporary society where new practices began as slightly outside mainstream society but have since become commonplace (e.g., online dating sites, tattoos, botox injections, etc.)?

Denominations of one religion share a common fundamental theology but vary in their specific interpretations of religious text. They are also divided according to how strongly they embrace traditionalism and how much they accommodate the demands of a modernizing society. A denomination can also be seen as the midpoint between church and sect. Christianity, for example, moved from a new religious movement to a sect to a church to numerous denominations. On the other hand, denominations can split into sects or even into new religious movements if members feel that there is too much accommodation to secular society.

However, research by Bruce and Voas (2007) suggests that the traditional distinctions between new religious movements/sects and churches/denominations are largely disappearing. They argue that societal hostility toward new religious movements and sects is increasingly rare, and when it does occur, the criticisms levelled can just as often be applied to churches and denominations. In other words, anyone who is deemed to be overly dogmatic is viewed negatively, regardless of their particular beliefs. Instead of traditional classifications that rely on the external perceptions of outsiders, Bruce and Voas (2007, p. 1) suggest focusing on what members of a group expect from the outside world and from its own members.

❸ World Religions

To begin our discussion of religious diversity, we draw on the classification system of Max Weber, who argued that the world's major cultures and their religions could be classified according to how they view the world and people's place in it. Weber proposed three main orientations:

1. World of nature: animals, fish, plants, rivers

2. Other people: some of whom may be seen as subhumans, inferiors, slightly different, or equals

3. The body: the human body is not seen as just another part of nature, but instead as something "special" (Hall, Held, Hubert, & Thompson, 1996, p. 167)

Weber contrasted "Oriental" (Eastern) religions (e.g., Confucianism, Hinduism, Taoism, and Buddhism) with Occidental (Western) religions (e.g., Judaism, Christianity, and Islam). He found that those emerging from Eastern cultures sought *harmony* with the natural world, other people, and the human body. In contrast, "Middle Eastern" cultures (located in Persia, Arabia, and North America) focused on *mastery* over the natural world, other people, and the human body. Weber called the first orientation **mysticism** (based on harmony) and the second orientation **asceticism** (based on mastery) (Hall, Held, Hubert, & Thompson, 1996, pp. 167–168).

Weber also suggested that a religion's orientation could be either *inner-worldly* or *other-worldly*. **Inner-worldly** orientations are those that focus on the tangible world in which we live and on our own creature comforts and aspirations; they promote the accumulation of wealth and support a system of social recognition for positions such as merchants, politicians, lawyers, and soldiers. **Other-worldly** orientations focus on separation from the everyday world; they promote engagement with the abstract and finding spiritual enlightenment. They support a system of social recognition for positions such as monks, priests, scholars, intellectuals, and artists.

Table 13.1 outlines Weber's four types of religious belief systems according to their orientation to the world and their means of social recognition.

As we move through the following descriptions of the world's major religions, keep Weber's insights in mind and see whether they hold true in each instance.

mysticism Weber's term for religions that seek harmony with the natural world, other people, and the human body.

asceticism Weber's term for religions that seek mastery over the natural world, other people, and the human body.

inner-worldly An orientation that focuses on the tangible world and our own creature comforts and aspirations.

other-worldly An orientation that focuses on separation from the everyday world and finding spiritual enlightenment.

TABLE 13.1 Weber's Classification of World Religions

Orientation to the World	Focus of Social Recognition	
	Inner-Worldly	Other-Worldly
Mysticism (harmony)	Hinduism, Taoism, Confucianism	Buddhism, Sufism
Asceticism (mastery)	Calvinism	Catholicism, Islam, Orthodox Judaism

Source: Compiled from Hall, Held, Hubert, and Thompson (1996, p. 168).

CHRISTIANITY

Christianity began approximately 2000 years ago, when Jesus was born in Bethlehem to the Virgin Mary and her husband, Joseph. In its early years, Christianity constituted a new religious movement with beliefs deeply rooted in Judaism. From these humble beginnings, Christianity became the world's largest religion, with more than 2 billion adherents today (see Table 13.2).

TABLE 13.2 Comparison of the World's Religions

Religion	Date Founded	Sacred Texts	Title of Local Leader	Membership	Percentage of World
Christianity	30 CE	The Bible	Pastor, priest, minister	2039 million	32% (dropping)
Islam	622 CE	Quran, Hadith	Imam	1570 million	22% (growing)
Hinduism	1500 BCE	Bhagavad-Gita, Upanishads, Rig Veda	Priest, pandit	950 million	13% (stable)
No religion[1]	NA	None	None	775 million	12% (dropping)
Buddhism	523 BCE	The Tripitaka, Sutras	Monk	364 million	6% (stable)
Tribal religions, Shamanism, Animism	Prehistory	Oral tradition	Shaman	232 million	4%
Atheists	No date	None	None	150 million	2%
Sikhism	1500 CE	Guru Granth Sahib	Granthi (professional reader)	23.8 million	<1%
Judaism	See note 2	Torah, Tanach, Talmud	Rabbi	14.5 million	<1%
Baha'i Faith	1863 CE	Alkitab Alaqdas	Usually a lay leader	7.4 million	<1%
Jehovah's Witnesses	1879 CE	The Bible, New World Translation of the Scriptures	No professional clergy, but elders usually lead local communities	6.5 million	<1%
Confucianism	520 BCE	Lun Yu	Unknown	6.3 million	<1%
Jainism	570 BCE	Siddhanta, Pakrit	Priest, pandit	4.3 million	<1%
Zoroastrianism	6000 to 600 BCE	Avesta	Mobed, dastur	2.7 million	<1%
Shinto	500 CE	Kojiki, Nohon Shoki	Priest	2.7 million	<1%
Taoism	550 BCE	Tao-teh-Ching	Priest	2.7 million	<1%
Other	Various	Various	Various	1.1 million	<1%

[1] Persons with no formal, organized religion include agnostics, freethinkers, humanists, and secularists.

[2] There is controversy over the founding of Judaism. Some claim that Adam and Eve were the first Jews and lived circa 4000 BCE; others that Adam and Eve never existed. Some place the date at the time of Abraham, circa 1900 BCE; others consider Abraham to be a character.

Source: Constructed from Number of adherents of world religions [online]. www.religioustolerance.org/worldrel.htm (accessed May 6, 2014); and The Big Religion Comparison Chart [online]. http://religionfacts.com/big_religion_chart.htm (accessed May 6, 2014). Reprinted with permission. For more information on the world's religions, see www.religionfacts.com and www.adherents.com.

Followers believe that Jesus's virgin birth and his resurrection after being crucified confirm his divine origin and his status as God's only son. While relatively little is known of Jesus's early life, many believe that by age 30 he was a dynamic teacher and healer who was a challenging presence to the political structure of the Roman Empire, which ultimately crucified him on a cross. Jesus's 12 closest followers, called the apostles, were present on the day he died; Jesus's crucifixion is the primary reason why the cross is such an important religious symbol for Christians around the world.

Today, Christianity exists in an amazing variety of churches, denominations, and sects. However, all Christian groups believe that Jesus is the son of God, the messiah, who was crucified and resurrected from the dead and who will return as the salvation for the world. These stories are recorded in the New Testament of the Bible, the holy book of Christianity. After Christianity was established as an institutionalized religion, missionary work and military conquest bolstered its expansion to the Western world.

ISLAM

Today, Islam is the world's second-largest and fastest-growing religion, with over 1.5 billion adherents. Like Christianity, Islam is based on prophecy, prophethood, and a sacred text. Islam, whose followers are called Muslims, is based on the teachings of the Prophet Muhammad (570–632). Muslims believe that Muhammad was the most important of God's prophets; these prophets include the divinely inspired (but not divine) Jesus, as well as Abraham and Moses. Muhammad is not considered divine but, rather, as the greatest of all of God's messengers. His revelations are recorded in the Quran (Koran), the holy book of Islam. In 622, Muhammad founded the first Islamic state, a **theocracy**, in Medina, a city in western Saudi Arabia. A theocracy is a form of government in which a god or other supernatural being is seen as the supreme civil ruler. Earthbound religious leaders in Islam are called *imams*.

Following Muhammad's death, a power struggle emerged between two primary groups—the Sunni and the Shiite—over control of the empire, a division that remains to this day. The Sunni branch believes that the first four caliphs—Muhammad's successors—rightfully took his place as the leaders of Muslims. Therefore, they view the heirs of the four caliphs as the legitimate religious leaders. These heirs ruled continuously in the Arab world until the breakup of the Ottoman Empire following the end of World War I (History News Network, 2006). Shiites, in contrast, believe that only the heirs of the fourth caliph, Ali,

theocracy **A form of government in which a god or other supernatural being is seen as the supreme civil ruler.**

> > >

Followers of Islam, called Muslims, follow the teachings of the Prophet Muhammad. Islam is the fastest-growing religion in the world.

Jon Spaull/Dorling Kindersley

are the legitimate successors of Muhammad. Shiite Muslims, who are concentrated in Iran, Iraq, and Lebanon, believe that they suffered the loss of divinely guided political leadership when the twelfth Imam disappeared in 931, a seminal event in their history. Not until 1978, when the Ayatollah Ruhollah Khomeini ascended to power in Iran, did the Shiites believe that they had once again begun to live under the authority of a legitimate religious figure (Appleby, as cited in History News Network, 2006).

The Sunni and Shiite groups generally fit the definition associated with a denomination. Muslims are not organized into a formal church structure; instead, the focus is on the believer and God. While each group has slightly different prayer rituals (called *salat*), all Muslims pray five times each day: at dawn (*al-fajr*), at midday (*al-zuhr*), in the afternoon (*al-'asr*), at sunset (*al-maghrib*), and in the evening (*al-'isha*). Muslims always direct their prayers toward the Kaaba shrine at Mecca in Saudi Arabia.

Central to an understanding of Islam are the five pillars of Islam: (1) Shahadah—the statement of faith in one Allah (God) and the Prophet Muhammad, who is his messenger; (2) Salat—attending to prayer five times a day; (3) Sawm—fasting during Ramadan (the holy month of fast); (4) Zakat—giving to the poor; and (5) Hajj—performing a pilgrimage to the holy place of Mecca (AlMarri, Oei, & Al-Adawi, 2009, pp. 415–416; Devadoss & Ismail, 2013).

JUDAISM

Judaism is one of the oldest religions in the world, and also one of the smallest. Although Judaism numbers about 14.5 million adherents worldwide, nearly 3.5 billion others follow belief systems directly influenced by Judaism (including Christianity and Islam), and they all trace their spiritual lineage to the biblical figure of Abraham. Judaism was formed as part of a divine revelation at Mount Sinai more than 3200 years ago under the guidance of Moses. Jewish people today view their moral guidelines and ritual obligations as a contract (or covenant) with God as defined at Mount Sinai (Segal, 2002, p. 33).

Jewish beliefs are recorded in the first five books of the Hebrew Bible, which Jews call the Torah (meaning "learning"). The Torah tells that a Messiah will eventually bring Jews to a promised land—a state of paradise. The Torah also contains 613 commandments, including the Ten Commandments that God gave to Moses on Mount Sinai, that are viewed as rabbinic law. These and other Jewish scriptures set down important beliefs and rituals, such as the promotion of community among all Jews, dedication to a synagogue or temple, doing mitzvah or good deeds, religious observances in families, and the belief that the human condition can be improved (Lindsey, Beach, & Ravelli, 2009, p. 160).

Today, divisions within Judaism are known as "movements," and have emerged in response to the forces of modernity. Orthodox Judaism is the most conservative group, retaining virtually all traditional rituals and practises. Conversely, Reform Jews maintain their Jewish identity and some of the traditions but take a much more liberal approach to many Jewish beliefs and practices. Conservative Judaism lies in between the two extremes, and takes a moderate approach in its application of Judaism to the modern world (ReligionFacts, 2008c). The Jewish world view is greatly influenced by 2000 years of

> > >

Orthodox Jews are often identifiable by their dress and hairstyles. Orthodox Jews are the most traditional expression of modern Judaism.

Antoine Gyori/Sygma/Corbis

BOX 13.1 ISSUES IN GLOBAL CONTEXT

Religion and Politics in the Middle East

Since 1000 BCE, when Moses led the Hebrews out of Egypt and into the Promised Land (known as Canaan), Christians, Muslims, and Jews have fought over what each group considers to be its sacred land. The area commonly referred to as Palestine (today broadly defined as Israel and Jordan) has been claimed by several empires, including Persians, Babylonians, Assyrians, Greeks, and Romans.

When the Roman Emperor Constantine converted to Christianity, he laid claim to the Holy Land and Christians controlled the region for roughly 300 years. Then, in 640, Arabs captured Palestine and built the Dome of the Rock, a holy Islamic shrine, in Jerusalem. The shrine was built on the place where it was believed the prophet Muhammad had ended his Farewell Pilgrimage and died. Jews refer to the site as Temple Mount, and the Muslims call it Haram al-Sharif (or the Noble Sanctuary).

The area became part of the Ottoman Turkish Empire for approximately 400 years until 1918, when Arab leaders joined the Allies in World War I. After the war, France and England shared the region's administration, with Britain controlling the area known as Palestine, first by military rule and later through the mandate of the League of Nations.

During World War I, the British played on Arabs' desire for independence from colonial rule while making secret agreements with the French to divide the region between them after the war. Zionism, a Jewish political movement intended to establish a homeland for Jews, was also active in Britain, and resulted in the famous 1917 Balfour Declaration that supported the idea of a homeland for Jews in Palestine. (The Declaration also confirmed the civil rights of Arabs in the area, but that clause was largely ignored.) The Balfour Declaration allowed increased immigration of Jews into Arab areas. This policy, instituted without consulting the Arabs, led to many skirmishes between Arabs and Jews.

The persecution of millions of Jews by Nazi Germany during World War II led Britain to increase immigration levels of Jews moving into Palestine. In 1945, Arabs reacted to the flood of Jewish refugees by forming the Arab League, a coalition of nations dedicated to promoting Arab interests to compensate for growing Zionist support in Palestine. Then, in 1947, the United Nations voted to divide Palestine into Arab and Jewish states, with the Jews occupying 55 percent of the land west of the Jordan River. A year later, Zionist leader David Ben-Gurion declared Israel to be an independent state—one that was immediately invaded by Arab military forces.

Over the next 35 years, military strikes were launched by both sides, but the Six-Day War, from June 5 to June 10, 1967, had the most dramatic political implications for the Middle East conflict. It began when Egypt, Syria, and Jordan closed the shipping channel in the Gulf of Aqaba. Israel retaliated and crushed the Arab military forces both in the sky and on the ground. The Arab territories seized by Israel after this war remain a major point of conflict between Jews and Arabs.

Over the years, the United States has sent billions of dollars to Israel in the form of direct aid and military armaments, which has led to increasingly tense relations between the US and Arab states. Although the 1978 Camp David Peace Accord between the US, Egypt, and Israel provided some short-term stability, military conflict continues.

Using your choice of sociological theories, explore why religion may inspire conflict between people of different faiths. As a sociologist, can you apply your sociological imagination to the conflict in the Middle East? How?

persecution, from slavery in Egypt to the Roman conquest to the mass extermination of 6 million Jews by the Nazis during World War II. While all Jews rejoiced at the formation of their own state of Israel in 1948, the country's strategic location and its profound importance as a religious site for Christians, Muslims, and Jews make it a prime target for world conflict. Today, Judaism is facing political and military pressure as well as trying to cope with assimilation, young people marrying outside of the faith, and an overall decline in people's interest in religion (de Vries, 2006, p. 69; Kaplan, 2001; McKinney, 2004, p. 32). Nonetheless, the unique history of Judaism suggests that it will remain a dynamic and vital religion.

HINDUISM

Hinduism is the oldest (established around 3500 bce) and third-largest of the world's major religions, with more than 900 million followers, most of whom live in India. Hinduism differs from Christianity and Islam in that it does not have a single founder, a specific theological system, a single system of morality, or a centralized bureaucratic structure. The Hindu tradition encourages believers to seek spiritual and moral truth wherever it may be found; each individual must find truth through his or her own effort. Our individual experiences, our ability to reason, and our engaged discussion with others are the vehicles for testing our understanding of spiritual and moral truths.

Hinduism is a polytheistic religion that has no single sacred text nor one autonomous and rigid belief system. A number of sources are used for guidance on morality in accordance with **dharma**, the moral responsibilities and guidelines that define an entire way of life (McIntire, 2006, p. 88). Gods and goddesses are not usually ranked in a strict hierarchy, nor does a supreme being sit in judgment of people and their actions while on earth.

In orthodox practice, Hinduism cannot really be separated from the caste system in which it originated (see Chapter 7). This system is congruent with the Hindu belief in **samsara** or what we refer to commonly as reincarnation: the cycle of birth, death, and rebirth in which people are reborn into higher or lower states depending on how well they acted out the ideal life dictated by dharma (Reddy, 2009, p. 178). In each cycle of rebirth the assumption is that the person largely gets what he or she deserves in the next life. For those who reach **moksha**, the state of spiritual perfection, the soul has been liberated and no longer needs to be reborn (Jain & Kripal, 2009, p. 203).

BUDDHISM

Buddhism, which grew out of Hinduism, has about 500 million proponents around the world. It was founded around 500 bce by Siddhartha Gautama, a wealthy upper-caste Hindu whose father, Suddhodana, ruled over a district near the Himalayas that is today located in Nepal. In an attempt to shelter his son from the poverty and turmoil of the outside world, Suddhodana confined Gautama to the palace, where he had all of the creature comforts that come with wealth. However, despite his father's efforts, Gautama left the palace one day and experienced the darker side of life that existed outside the palace walls. During this trip, he saw four things that forever changed his life: an old man, a sick man, a dead man, and a beggar. Deeply disturbed by what he had seen, Gautama decided to leave his luxurious palace life and begin a quest to discover how to stop human suffering and pain (Zukeran, 2002). Gautama left his family, travelled, and sought wisdom.

Although a Hindu, he became disillusioned with the teachings of Hinduism and began a period of self-discovery, reflection, and deep meditation. Legend has it that while deep in meditation under a fig tree known as the Bohdi tree (meaning "tree of wisdom"), Gautama experienced nirvana. From that point on, Gautama became known as Buddha, the enlightened one (Zukeran, 2002).

Buddhists, like Hindus, believe that every person experiences a process of birth and rebirth until he or she has reached the state of nirvana in which this cycle can be broken.

dharma **The moral responsibilities and guidelines that define an entire way of life.**

samsara **Reincarnation where the soul undergoes a series of births and deaths.**

moksha **A state of spiritual perfection.**

Sheldan Collins/Encyclopedia/Corbis

The Dalai Lama, His Holiness Tenzin Gyatso, is the spiritual and political leader of Tibetan Buddhists.

karma The belief in cause and effect in a person's life; you reap what you sow.

According to the law of **karma** (the belief in cause and effect in a person's life; you reap what you sow), "You are what you are and do what you do, as a result of what you were and did in a previous incarnation, which in turn was the inevitable outcome of what you were and did in still earlier incarnations" (Taylor & Offner, 1975, p. 175, as cited in Zukeran, 2002). For a Buddhist, what one will become in the next life depends on one's actions in this life. Unlike Hindus, Buddhists believe that a person can break the cycle of rebirth no matter what class he or she is born into. By following a strict path of righteous living and focusing on meditation and proper conduct, an individual can achieve enlightenment, the highest level of human consciousness. In each incarnation, the soul continues its journey toward **nirvana**, the point at which spiritual perfection is achieved, the soul is absorbed into the universal spirit, and the reincarnation cycle ends.

nirvana The state of spiritual perfection.

CONFUCIANISM

Today, Confucianism has more than 6 million followers. It originated with the writings of the Chinese philosopher Confucius (551–479 bce). Like Buddhism (Gautama and Confucius lived around the same time), Confucianism is based on a code of self-discipline and meditation designed to maintain proper relationships that enhance loyalty, respect, and morality. Two important virtues are **jen**, a benevolent and humanitarian attitude, and **li**, maintaining proper relationships and rituals that enhance the life of the individual, the family, and the state.

jen Confucian virtue of possessing a benevolent and humanitarian attitude.

li Confucian desire to maintain proper relationships and rituals that enhance the life of the individual, the family, and the state.

Confucians hold that the individual is a socially embedded being and does not stand apart from, over, or against the larger community (Nuyen, 2003, p. 78). As the foundation for a life of perfect goodness, Confucius insisted on following the four virtues of sincerity, benevolence, filial piety, and propriety. Sincerity, for Confucius, was a cardinal virtue, and he believed it was important to be truthful and straightforward, faithful to one's promises, and conscientious in one's works. To be benevolent was to be kind to others and help people in times of need. For Confucius, filial piety was at the root of all virtue, and meant that one should respect and admire one's parents and bring happiness and honour to their name. Reverence for one's ancestors is probably the closest Confucianism comes to the idea of worship. For a virtuous person, propriety embraces the entire spectrum of human behaviour and directs a person to always do the right thing according to the rules of moral conduct (Aiken, 1908).

Confucianism thrives in collectivistic societies, such as China, which emphasize meritocracy, hierarchy, harmony, and respect for authority and tradition (Nuyen, 2003).

We should note that the three religions from the East (Buddhism, Confucianism, and Taoism) are often referred to as ethicalist religions because they are not interested in divine beings or supernatural forces, but instead in strict adherence to moral codes of behaviour as the path to achieving happiness.

JEHOVAH'S WITNESSES

Jehovah's Witnesses adhere to a restorationist belief system founded in 1879 by Charles Taze Russell, a Pennsylvania businessman. **Restorationist belief systems** assert that contemporary Christianity has moved so far away from the original Christian principles that it no longer reflects its foundational ideas; Jehovah's Witnesses view themselves as the restoration of true Christianity. Russell's Protestant Adventist background and study of the Bible led him to believe, among other things, that the second coming of Christ would occur in 1914 and that God's name is Jehovah. Jehovah's Witnesses challenge the Christian belief in the Holy Trinity (the Father, Son, and Holy Spirit) in that they believe that God (Jehovah) is the creator and Jesus is His first creation and His son, separate and not equal. They also believe that the Bible is the word of God and is more important than tradition, and that 144 000 people will eventually dwell in heaven, but the rest of the saved will live eternally on earth (Watchtower, 2006).

> **restorationist belief systems** Assert that contemporary Christianity no longer reflects its foundational ideas.

Today, there are more than 6 million practising Jehovah's Witnesses worldwide. They are very active in outreach programs and missionary work, and are perhaps best known for their door-to-door witnessing campaigns, in which they offer literature and answer questions in the hope of recruiting and converting people. Jehovah's Witnesses continue to adhere to Russell's teachings and emphasize that we are in the "time of the end," clean and moral living, the equality of all races, and adherence to the teachings of the Bible. They also continue to reject blood transfusions because of the New Testament's command to "abstain from blood," and they neither vote nor serve in the military (ReligionFacts, 2008b; Watchtower, 2006).

SIKHISM

Sikhism was founded more than 500 years ago by Guru Nanak Dev (1469–1539) in Punjab, India, and today claims approximately 24 million proponents worldwide. Followers of Sikhism, called Sikhs (meaning "disciple" or "learner"), follow a single, all-powerful God who has no gender or defined physical form (Chilana & Zabel, 2005, pp. 108–109). The perception of God is not a physical one but instead a manifestation of oneness with the universe. To find God, then, is not to search in remote places but instead to eliminate one's ego, thereby achieving a deeper, more accurate understanding of the world.

According to Sikh tradition, baptized Sikhs should carry five symbolic articles (popularly known as the five Ks) to demonstrate and confirm their faith:

1. *Kesh*—uncut hair
2. *Kanga*—a comb
3. *Kara*—a steel bracelet

Five baptized Sikhs lead a religious procession at the Golden Temple in Amritsar, India. Sikhs do not believe in imposing their beliefs on others or in converting members of other faiths to their own.

4. *Kachera*—an undergarment

5. *Kirpan*—a ceremonial sword

Sikhs also believe that they should not impose their beliefs on others or entice members of other religions to convert. In fact, Sikhs are required to defend the freedom to worship other religions just as they would their own. Finally, Sikhs do not believe that followers of other religions are doomed in the eyes of God, regardless of their personal character and behaviour, nor does being born into a Sikh family guarantee salvation. Sikhs believe that when a person dies, he or she is absorbed into the universal nature from which he or she came. At death, all individuality is lost and the joining into the larger whole is complete. Sikhs do not believe in heaven or hell as separate places that one attains only in the afterlife. Instead, heaven can be found when one is in tune with God while still alive. It follows, then, that the suffering and pain caused by failing to control one's ego can be considered hell on earth. Sikhs view spiritual pursuits as positive and rewarding events in themselves and not as something an individual should do only to reap rewards upon death (Sikhism. com, 2007). Sikhism is more concerned with how one lives today than with what one will attain in death.

FUNDAMENTALISM

fundamentalism A movement designed to revitalize faith by returning to traditional religious practices.

We are currently experiencing a worldwide rise in fundamentalism, the view that a previous golden age existed that must be recovered. **Fundamentalism** is not a belief system or religion per se but, instead, a movement suggesting that a return to past practices is necessary to confront the challenges that contemporary society faces. In this sense, fundamentalism is an anti-modern sociocultural movement that is more reactionary (wanting to return to the past) than conservative (wanting to maintain and preserve what already exists) (Herriot, 2009; Swift, 1991). For example, fundamentalists might advocate that wives stay home with the children, while conservatives might try to open a daycare as a way of helping families to cope.

Fundamentalists are particularly focused on upholding traditions and maintaining the "true faith" as a defensive reaction to a perceived threat—for example, the moral breakdown of contemporary society (Lechner, 1989, p. 51). As a rule, fundamentalists do not accept the functionalist view that adaptation is necessary in order to maintain religious integrity; instead, they suggest that accepting change is a compromise that ultimately leads to the surrender of their religious integrity.

Fundamentalism is often linked to religious intolerance but not necessarily to using violence to achieve goals. Fundamentalists, particularly Islamic groups, are depicted as reactionaries and extremists by the media and by other religious organizations that see them as threats. In the case of Islamic groups, this can inspire feelings of Islamophobia in the general population (Hopkins, Greenwood, & Birchall, 2007, p. 681).

Like liberation theology, fundamentalism is complex and diverse. For example, many fundamentalist groups (e.g., Jehovah's Witnesses) do not participate in political activism because they prefer to pursue their religious vision in settings that are under their control. Sects of ultra-orthodox Jews in Israel and Canada also reflect this pattern, even as they struggle with the need for religious commitment and the economic realities of modern capitalist society (Heilman, 2000). Christian fundamentalists, also known as evangelicals (Waldrep, 2007, p. 817), especially in the United States, may also see a strong role for faith in government and may be likely to see threats to their way of life in the actions and beliefs of people in other countries.

AGNOSTICISM AND ATHEISM

agnostic Someone who thinks it is impossible to know whether gods exist, but does not deny the possibility.

Some estimates suggest that roughly 1 billion people have no formal religion, meaning that they are either agnostics or atheists (see Table 13.2). An **agnostic** is someone who thinks it

BOX 13.2 THAT WAS THEN, THIS IS NOW

Can Science and Religion Coexist?

In the first episode of the 2014 television series *Cosmos*, hosted by astronomer Neil deGrasse Tyson, the audience is introduced to Giordano Bruno, a controversial seventeenth century Italian monk, who was one of the first to consider an infinite universe. The episode documents how Bruno was hounded by the Church for his beliefs; and was chased out of every major kingdom in Europe, excommunicated from the Church, and finally burned at the stake for heresy. The writers of *Cosmos* imply that Bruno was executed for his beliefs about the universe; the presentation reinforces the position that religion and science are fundamentally opposed, as one is built on reason, and the other on faith. But, as Corey Powell (2014) points out, it is far too simplistic to present science and religion as diametrically opposed perspectives (see also, Ruth, 2014).

As Emile Durkheim argued, religion is more than just a group of people who believe in a higher power. Religion gives believers an integrated system of morals, membership in a community, and access to cultural traditions that help to reinforce the shared values of a society. None of these requires a belief in God or the supernatural, nor do they preclude believers from also pursuing scientific interests. Some modern scholars of religion, including anthropologist Scott Atran, argue that it was through religious institutions that human beings first conceived of the notions of free will and universal humanity—two ideas that underwrite much of our legal, philosophical, and historical traditions (Atran 2010).

Many of the earliest scientists were also religious. For example, Georges Lemaitre, one of the scientists credited with developing the Big Bang theory, was also a Catholic priest, as was the Augustinian monk Johann Mendel who conducted some of the very first genetic experiments. Some people might argue that since most people were connected to the Church during the medieval and early modern periods, it was inevitable that most early scientists would also be religious, but that may be a somewhat weak argument. If religion and science were truly incompatible, these pioneers could not have been both priest and scientist, monk and geneticist.

Cosmos is just another example of how presenting science and religion as opposites diminishes the complexity and richness of the discussion. As sociologists, however, we understand why binaries (e.g., us/them, right/wrong, good/evil) are so effective in dividing people.

If you were asked to speculate, would you say that the debate between creationism and evolutionism will increase or decrease with time? Why?

---

is impossible to know whether gods exist, but who does not deny the possibility. An **atheist** is someone who denies the existence of any supernatural beings or forces.

There appears to have been a recent upsurge in questioning the existence of a god and the role of religion in contemporary society. The success of such books as Sam Harris's *The End of Faith* and *Letter to a Christian Nation*, Richard Dawkins's *The God Delusion*, Christopher Hitchens's *God Is Not Great: How Religion Poisons Everything*, and Daniel Dennett's *Breaking the Spell* provide some evidence of this upsurge.

This movement challenges religious beliefs as a misguided attempt to find purpose and meaning in our lives; its proponents believe that the world and our position within it can be understood without looking to supernatural forces or beings.

Now that we have studied the world's largest religions, a review of the religious landscape in Canada seems in order.

atheist Someone who denies the existence of any supernatural beings or forces.

④ Religion in Canada

Canada is one of the most religiously pluralistic societies in the world. Indeed, appreciation of religious diversity and the separation of church and state are important attributes of Canadian democracy. While religious pluralism is certainly more inclusive than the alternative (i.e., a theocracy), such pluralism also means that different religious groups compete with each other to attract new members and hold on to the ones they already have.

> > > Thinking Sociologically

How many different religions are evident in your own community? Where are they located? Can the geographic location of where they worship be linked to how "mainstream" their beliefs might be? Discuss.

Despite some recent changes, Canada is still largely a Christian nation, with roughly 7 of every 10 Canadians identifying themselves as either Roman Catholic or Protestant (see Table 13.3). In fact, for more than 100 years, Protestants were the dominant group in Canada. In 1901, Protestant faiths accounted for well over half (56 percent) of the total population, compared with 42 percent for Roman Catholics. This distribution was largely the result of Canada's immigration policies, which favoured immigrants from the United Kingdom and the United States (Statistics Canada, n.d.).

Over time, however, the sources of immigrants to Canada began to change. Groups such as Italians, Portuguese, and Latin Americans swelled the Catholic ranks, and their numbers continued to grow with each generation. In 1971, for the first time since Confederation, Roman Catholics (at 46 percent of the population) outnumbered Protestants (at 44 percent); by 2001, Protestants made up less than a third (29 percent) of Canada's population.

One reason for the relative decline of both Protestantism and Catholicism continues to be immigration. Much of Canada's population growth results from immigration (as discussed in Chapters 7 and 10), and more immigrants now come from Asia than from Europe. Of the 1.8 million new immigrants who arrived in Canada during the 1990s, Muslims accounted for 15 percent; Hindus, almost 7 percent; and Buddhists and Sikhs, about 5 percent each. As a result, the Muslim population more than doubled over 10 years, with Buddhist, Hindu, and Sikh populations growing rapidly as well (see Table 13.3).

> > >

Roman Catholicism continues to be Canada's largest denomination; however, many other religions are growing much more quickly.

The Canadian Press/John I. White

TABLE 13.3 Canada's Major Religious Denominations, 1991 and 2001

	1991		2001		Percentage Change 1991–2001
	Number	%	Number	%	
Roman Catholic	12 203 625	45.2	12 793 125	43.2	4.8
Protestant	9 427 675	34.9	8 654 845	29.2	–8.2
Christian Orthodox	387 395	1.4	479 620	1.6	23.8
Christian, not included elsewhere*	353 040	1.3	780 450	2.6	121.1
Muslim	253 265	0.9	579 640	2.0	128.9
Jewish	318 185	1.2	329 995	1.1	3.7
Buddhist	163 415	0.6	300 345	1.0	83.8
Hindu	157 015	0.6	297 200	1.0	89.3
Sikh	147 440	0.5	278 415	0.9	88.8
No religion	3 333 245	12.3	4 796 325	16.2	43.9

*Includes persons who report "Christian," as well as those who report "Apostolic," "Born-again Christian," and "Evangelical."

Source: Statistics Canada. (2004). Religion in Canada: 2001 Census [online]. http://www12 .statcan.ca/english/census01/Products/Analytic/companion/rel/charts/cdachartmedian.cfm (accessed May 24, 2011).

Catholics declined slightly as a proportion of the population during the 1990s, but their actual numbers increased slightly. In contrast, the actual number of Protestants decreased as did their proportion of believers (see Table 13.3). The largest decline occurred in the Presbyterian Church, where membership declined by almost 36 percent. Other declines occurred among Pentecostals (15 percent), United Church (8 percent), Anglicans (7 percent), and Lutherans (5 percent). A major factor is that congregations are aging (see Figure 13.1), and these churches are not attracting as many young people as they previously did (Statistics Canada, n.d.).

In contrast, fundamentalist churches grew: the Evangelical Missionary Church expanded its membership by 48 percent, the Adventists grew by 20 percent, and the Christian and Missionary Alliance grew by 12 percent. And, as shown in Table 13.3, the number of "other" Christians—including "born-again" and "evangelical" Christians— nearly doubled.

At the same time, the population reporting no religion grew. This represents the continuation of a more dramatic long-term trend. Before 1971, less than 1 percent of the Canadian population reported having no religion. By 2001, that percentage had risen to 16 percent, and largely represented a young population (see Figure 13.1). Some of that increase was due to immigration. One-fifth of the 1.8 million immigrants who arrived in Canada between 1991 and 2001, especially those from China and Taiwan, reported they had no religion (Statistics Canada, n.d.). However, these numbers are not enough to account for the growth in this category. Foreign-born teens are also more likely to be religious when they arrive, but whether that faith will persist over the coming generations remains to be seen (Lunau, 2009).

These results suggest that the older, larger Protestant denominations are losing adherents, who appear to be heading in two different directions: Some drift away from religion

Explore

What Canadians Think of Sikhs, Jews, Christians, Muslims . . .

FIGURE 13.1

Major Religions
by Median Age,
Canada, 2001
Census

Source: Statistics Canada.
(2004). Religion in Canada:
2001 Census [online]. http://
www12.statcan.ca/english/
census01/Products/Analytic/
companion/rel/charts/cdacha-
rtmedian.cfm (accessed May
24, 2011).

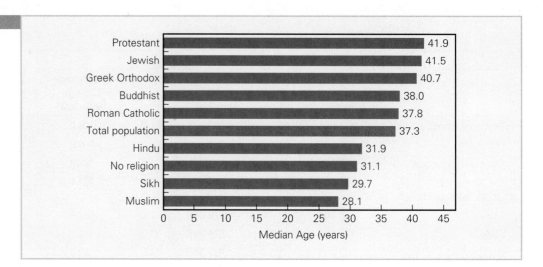

altogether, while others join the more fundamentalist churches. What could account for these two opposing trends?

One explanation for the drifting away could be the North American cultural values of individualism and personal autonomy, sentiments that may reduce religious commitment (Lindsey, Beach, & Ravelli, 2009, p. 165; Martin, 2005, p. 154). Modernization contributes to this effect by reinforcing faith in science rather than in religion for problem solving. This trend also may be responsible for the overall drop in church attendance. In 1946, about two-thirds of the adult population attended religious services weekly. However, by 2008, monthly attendance had dropped to around 25 percent (Statistics Canada, 2010j). Seniors have the highest attendance, while those aged 25 to 34 have the lowest (Clark, 2003, pp. 2–3).

One explanation for the second trend, toward fundamentalist churches, could be an attraction to churches that offer a more intensive and personal experience. Research supports the argument that the stricter the church, the stronger the church, and fundamentalist churches often require deep commitment, participation, and energy (Bermanis, Canetti-Nisim, & Pedahzur, 2004, pp. 162–163).

⑤ Theoretical Insights into Religion

Approaches to
Religion

Sociologists studying religion investigate its relationship with social forces, and how these forces influence individuals and their lives. As we have seen in earlier chapters, sociological theory enables sociologists to explore and explain religion within the broader social context.

FUNCTIONALISM

profane Elements of
the everyday world
that do not inspire or
motivate.

sacred Things or
activities that are
set apart, ritualized,
and at times inspire
emotional reactions.

Émile Durkheim's classic work *The Elementary Forms of Religious Life* (1912/1954) is considered the defining analysis of religion from a functionalist perspective. Central to Durkheim's analysis is his assertion that all religions originate in society, which creates religion by separating the world into the profane and the sacred (Ritzer, 2000, p. 91). According to Durkheim, the **profane** encompasses the secular aspects of life: the objects, practices, and behaviours that we experience every day. In contrast, the **sacred** encompasses those things that we set apart, ritualize, and at times have deep emotional connections to. For example, during Communion, Catholics consume wine (or grape juice, in some churches) and unleavened bread to symbolize their ongoing connection to Jesus Christ, who they believe

< < <

For Hindus, water is considered sacred; it is believed to have spiritual cleansing powers.

sacrificed his own life for humanity's sins. The wine and bread are not in themselves sacred but become so when they are associated with a ritual that constitutes a deeply personal and spiritual experience for many practising Catholics. Anything can become sacred—from the small ceremonial knife for male Sikhs (called a kirpan) to the cross for Christians—when it is set apart from the profane world and ritualized. At times, these sacred objects can become what Durkheim called a **totem**, an object that has special significance and meaning for a group of believers.

According to Durkheim, the sacred originates within members of society, who collectively assign special meanings to certain objects or rituals. Religion is an extension of society and functions to join members of the group according to shared meanings and world views, or what Durkheim called the *collective conscience*. In early societies, the collective conscience created religion as the expression of an all-encompassing representation of collective morality (Ritzer, 2000, p. 90).

Durkheim also believed that religion was a strong source of social power that could inspire collective action. When people feel caught up in a heightened sense of this collective action and join together for a common purpose, Durkheim believed this to be a manifestation of the *collective effervescence*. The collective effervescence is expressed when a social group achieves a new and dynamic expression of the group's will and can motivate rapid changes in the social structure (e.g., the Reformation or the Renaissance) (see Richman, 2002, p. 39; Ritzer, 2000, p. 92).

Functionalists perceive that a group of people gathered together around a common belief system serves an important purpose, particularly in the face of a common enemy. According to functionalists, religion answers the problems of meaning—that is, what life is all about (O'Dea, 1966, p. 6).

Functionalists perceive many other functions of religion within society:

1. *Religion joins people into communities of believers that promote social stability and a sense of belonging.* Religion allows a balanced and cohesive moral community to form. It protects individuals from the forces of anomie and alienation and helps them to resist disruptive social movements that may be attractive to those without such connections to the

totem An object that has special significance and meaning for a group of believers.

Studying Religion

larger collective. Shared religious experiences provide the social glue that binds people together and fosters unity and consensus (Selfe & Starbuck, 1998).

2. *Religion provides people with a social identity.* This is often achieved through special ceremonies as part of a person's acceptance into a religious tradition (e.g., christening and baptism in the Christian faith or the bar mitzvah in Judaism). Durkheim suggested that group solidarity is affirmed and enhanced through public rituals and ceremonies.

3. *Religion provides social control through the establishment of moral standards of behaviour.* Durkheim viewed society as a moral community in which members were socialized to accept certain behaviours and reject others. This process continues throughout our lives, as we continually adjust our values and morals to suit our changing social environments (e.g., your view of the world may change somewhat as you age, or if you move to a different country). According to Durkheim, an orderly social existence is possible only when people share common moral values; when they do, these values are an expression of society itself.

4. *Religion provides people with a sense of purpose and brings meaning to their lives.* When confronting death, disaster, disease, and even the trials of everyday life, people often search for some purpose to their lives. Religious belief offers people comfort in times of crisis, since it explains where they came from and where they are going. Religion often gives people the strength to go on, and by doing so promotes the long-term stability of society.

5. *Religion provides a social service function.* In many societies, religious groups offer a great deal of support to people in need and provide enormous amounts of voluntary services that are beneficial to the community (Ammerman, 1997, pp. 211–212; Lindsey, Beach, & Ravelli, 2009, p. 153).

While Durkheim's analysis of religion continues to inform our contemporary understanding (Smith & Alexander, 1996; Whitney, 2007, p. 54), his functional interpretation does have some limitations.

First, to assume that religion is purely functional completely dismisses instances in which it is clearly dysfunctional. For example, while religion may be an important source of social cohesion for a group, it is also the reason for much conflict, tension, and bloodshed between groups. Religious groups have been in conflict with each other for thousands of years (think of the Crusades, the witch hunts in medieval Europe, and the ongoing conflict in the Middle East), and this often leads to a great deal of social upheaval and human suffering.

> > >

In Judaism, the bar mitzvah is a coming-of-age ceremony for young boys and girls that symbolizes their commitment to follow their faith.

Nathan Benn/Corbis

Second, while some level of social control is necessary for society to function, some religious traditions are very strict and often deny people the ability to think for themselves (Stark & Bainbridge, 1996). For example, a 2006 documentary film entitled *Jesus Camp* (Dubuc & Thompson, 2006) depicts Pastor Becky Fischer's "Kids on Fire" summer camp, where children as young as six are taught to become Christian soldiers in "God's Army." This level of intense group identification was seen by some as a form of child abuse and ultimately led to the camp being closed shortly after the film was released (Curtis, 2006).

Some suggest that a third limitation of Durkheim's functional interpretation of religion is his analysis of the sacred and profane, which is overly rigid and does not fit the anthropological record. In fact, Evans-Pritchard (1966, pp. 64–65) argued that the two were so closely intermingled as to be inseparable.

Fourth, religions today must compete with other social institutions and categories that are sources of personal identity—for example, race, social class, and nationality. These may become increasingly important as formerly insulated societies (e.g., member states of the former Soviet Union) become more interconnected as a result of globalization.

Fifth, the functional analysis of religion fails to recognize the roles that social class, power, and gender play in the development and maintenance of religion—an important component of how conflict theorists explain religion.

Finally, because religion is considered to be the expression of a collective conscience, it suggests very little opportunity for individual agency—that is, the ability of people to define and experience their own sense of spirituality and morality, an important aspect of how symbolic interactionists explore the social significance of religion.

CONFLICT THEORY

The conflict theory of religion is grounded on three primary assumptions:

1. Religion is socially constructed and built upon economic relationships.
2. Religion diminishes feelings of frustration resulting from the forces of alienation.
3. Religion is used by the social, political, and economic elite to control the workers (Swenson, 1999, p. 329).

Marx viewed religion as a form of social control that dulls the pain of oppression for the proletariat and prevents members from seeing the world as it truly exists (Marx & Engels, 1964). He considered religion to be one of the primary ways that the bourgeoisie ensures that the proletariat maintains a state of false consciousness, a misunderstanding of one's true social condition and true social self. According to Marx, then, religion is an illusion that not only makes the proletariats' pain of oppression bearable but also keeps them submissive. That is, even though workers' lives may be fraught with hard work and relative poverty, if they believe in God and follow his teachings (as defined by the church), they can expect to be rewarded with entry into heaven and to receive everlasting salvation (Heclo, 2007, p. 70). They remain malleable out of their fear of going to hell if they challenge the rich, or the church, which for Marx were one and the same. Two famous quotations encapsulate Marx's position:

> The first requisite for the happiness of the people is the abolition of religion. (Marx, as cited in Smith, 2003, p. 44)

> Religion is the sigh of the oppressed creature, the heart of a heartless world, just as it is the spirit of a spiritless condition. It is the opium of the people. (Marx, as cited in Swatos, 1998, p. 287)

Marx perceived that religion is an ideological expression of the contradictions and tensions present in human relations, and that by studying and critiquing religion one is able to uncover the problems at the root of social relations (Turner, 1998, p. 179).

Since Marx considered the capitalist economic system to be the cause of human misery, the solution he envisioned was its forcible removal by and replacement with a

> > >

Going to church continues to be an important part of many Canadians' lives.

Brand X/Jupiter Images/Alamy

nonexploitative economic system, namely communism. Thus, Marx argued that before people could be truly happy, they had to throw off the blinders that prevented them from seeing (and doing something about) their true, exploited position. In this respect, the role of intellectuals such as Marx was to explain to the working class the nature of their ideological oppression.

At the same time, Marx understood that exposing the oppressive role of religion was not in itself sufficient to alert people to their true ideological interests. After all, religious beliefs, like any other form of ideology, are not simply imposed upon the weak-minded. Quite the contrary: Such beliefs grow out of the conditions under which people interact with their social and physical worlds. Ideologies are deeply rooted in the very conditions in which people live. When people are oppressed and exploited in the real world, the illusory happiness of religion may be a necessary sub-stitute for real happiness. By focusing on the future, religion helps to distract people from the inequities and difficulties that exist today. Therefore, to understand religion, one must understand the social, economic, and political landscape of the people.

Although Marx's insights are an important contribution to our understanding of religion, they have some limitations.

First, Marx's assumption that religion supports and maintains the status quo in society is challenged by the work of Max Weber, who argued that religion can be the inspiration behind great social change. For example, in *The Protestant Ethic and the Spirit of Capitalism* (2005/1904), Weber argues that **predestination**—the doctrine that God alone chooses (or elects) who is saved—inspired such angst among believers who were looking for any sign that they were in God's favour, and thus going to heaven, that it formed the basis of capitalism. That is, by working hard and accumulating material wealth, Protestants saw their resulting economic success as evidence that they were following their **calling** and doing God's will (Sukidi, 2006, p. 197; Swatos, 1998, p. 69).

Second, some contemporary religious movements actually challenge the rich and powerful by advocating income redistribution in society. For example, **liberation theology** is a movement by religious fundamentalists who advocate a literal interpretation of the Bible to promote greater social equality. Although liberation theology originated in Latin America, it is gaining a following in Canada and the United States (Lindsey, Beach, & Ravelli, 2009, p. 155). Marx would not have predicted that leaders of organized religions would advocate for such significant changes to income redistribution.

Third, the sense of community that some people find in religion is a positive force, inspiring many to help the less fortunate and to participate in political movements.

predestination The doctrine that God alone chooses (or elects) who is saved.

calling One's work, believed to be an expression of God's will, particularly if that work brings financial success.

liberation theology A movement by religious fundamentalists who advocate a literal interpretation of the Bible to promote greater social equality.

SYMBOLIC INTERACTIONISM

Symbolic interactionists view religion as an important source of rituals and symbols that help to define people's perceptions of their social world.

Swenson (1999, p. 185) defines *ritual* as

repeated consecrated (sacred) behaviour that is a symbolic expression of the moods and motivations of religious participants and unseen powers. Ritual forms a bond of friendship, community, and unity with the believer and her/his god. . . .

Because religious rituals bond a group of believers into a moral community, by logical extension such rituals influence how these believers behave and identify themselves. Rituals (e.g., confession for Catholics; the salat, or five daily prayers, for Muslims) help to reinforce group membership in a number of ways:

1. *Ritual as remembering*—rituals confirm the common historical connection between believers and remind them of their group's myths and beliefs.

2. *Ritual as social bonding*—rituals promote social cohesion through shared experiences and world views.

3. *Ritual as regulating moral behaviour*—rituals allow a public demonstration of moral standards and confirm the expectation that they are followed.

4. *Ritual as empowerment*—rituals facilitate a connection to the supernatural, which creates feelings of inspiration and motivation (adapted from Swenson, 1999, pp. 187–196).

While these four features of ritual can certainly be seen as "functional" according to the functionalist perspective, the important element for symbolic interactionists is how they combine to influence how people see themselves.

To appreciate how religion influences one's identity, a brief analysis of what happens when a person converts to a new belief system will accentuate how different social environments change a person's self-perception.

Religious Indoctrination and Identity Andersen and Francis (2006) outline a three-phase process that people undergo when converting to a new religion. The first phase occurs when potential converts experience events or episodes that make them question themselves and wonder whether there is more to life than what they have experienced so far. These emotions and thoughts make people open to significant changes in their lives. For some, the attraction of starting a new life and forgetting one's past is very tempting; people are more susceptible to radical religious movements that promise a new life when they are unhappy than when they are happy and content. The first phase of conversion concludes when initiates actually enter the new religious organization.

The second phase occurs when initiates begin to incorporate the ideas of the new group into their own world views. At this stage, it is critical that initiates sever all ties to their previous lives and become increasingly reliant on the new group for social and emotional support. The new group will often foster this dependence by conducting week-long workshops or seminars that further separate initiates from their friends and family, thereby forging closer connections to the new group. Also characteristic during this phase of conversion is the showering of new recruits with constant attention and affection, which may culminate in what the Unification Church refers to as "love-bombing" (Long & Hadden, 1983, as cited in Andersen & Francis, 2006, p. 467).

The final phase occurs during a period of intense interaction with the new group, wherein the initiates' time is completely dominated by duties and obligations; they have very little time to reflect and consider the often drastic changes to their lives and how they see themselves. The conversion is often solidified when the new members sacrifice their material wealth, which is usually donated to the operation and maintenance of the new group (Andersen & Francis, 2006, p. 467).

Symbolic interactionists view religion from a microsociological perspective that attempts to understand individuals' thoughts, feelings, and motivations that reflect the role religion plays in their everyday lives. For some people, participation in religious activities may be relatively light, but for others it can become the defining feature of who they are.

FEMINIST THEORY

In 1895, Elizabeth Cady Stanton (1815–1902), on behalf of a committee of women, published *The Woman's Bible* to correct biblical interpretations that she believed were biased against women (Mace, 2009). This work was one of the first examples of a woman challenging the traditional Christian interpretation of gender roles. Cady Stanton's analysis concluded that the Bible and organized religion had hindered women's emancipation (Hill Lindley, 2003, p. 275). In her introduction, Cady Stanton (1895) states:

> The Bible teaches that woman brought sin and death into the world, that she precipitated the fall of the race, that she was arraigned before the judgment seat of Heaven, tried, condemned and sentenced. Marriage for her was to be a condition of bondage, maternity a period of suffering and anguish, and in silence and subjection, she was to play the role of a dependent on man's bounty for all her material wants, and for all the information she might desire on the vital questions of the hour, she was commanded to ask her husband at home. Here is the Bible position of woman briefly summed up. (As cited in Hill Lindley, 2003)

> > >

The Hindu goddess Sarasvati is commonly depicted as the wife or consort of Brahma, the creator god. She is the Hindu muse: the inspiration for all music, poetry, drama, and science.

Louise Batalla Duran/Alamy

Cady Stanton and her colleagues emphasized that the Bible was a literary work. They repudiated its divine authority, pointing out that it was written by men and constitutes a clear expression of the patriarchal culture. Cady Stanton argued that women needed a different belief system, given that Christianity is based fundamentally on the oppression of women and cannot adequately represent the "ideals of liberty, justice and equality" (Marsman, 2003, p. 10).

While Cady Stanton's analysis specifically targeted Christianity as being patriarchal, feminist scholars argue that the same criticism holds for virtually all organized religions (Gross, 1996, p. 1). Both women and men need support and compassion as they try to answer life's questions, and belonging to a religious community often provides that. However, as Dhruvarajan and Vickers (2002, p. 274) assert, the kinds of answers women receive from the world's dominant religions are different from those given to men. They argue that these religions present a picture of women as being both biologically and spiritually inferior to men.

For example, religions have variously portrayed women as being unclean because of menstruation and childbirth, impulsive, morally deficient, and unable to control their sexual urges. Religious teachings over generations have reinforced the position that these attributes legitimate treating women differently and justify their subordinate social position. Further, rituals and symbols of patriarchal religions reinforce the assumption that a gender hierarchy is natural and normal. As a result of growing up in environments that advocate these religious positions, women are socialized to believe in and accept their lower status (Dhruvarajan & Vickers, 2002, p. 274).

Dhruvarajan and Vickers also point out that all three of the world's monotheistic (meaning "one god") religions—Christianity, Judaism, and Islam—view the divine presence as male. Although a polytheistic (meaning "more than one god") religion, in Hinduism the goddesses have lower status than the primarily male godheads. Buddhism, which has no gods and instead focuses on moral and ethical behaviour, privileges the perception of teachers and leaders as being men, not women. Similarly, Confucianism, based on the teachings and insights of Confucius, presents a clear patriarchal bias (Dhruvarajan & Vickers, 2002, p. 274). Finally, while Sihkism advocates that women can achieve all positions of influence within the religion, few do (see Jakobsh, 2006, p. 188).

Dhruvarajan and Vickers point out that while there is a great deal of diversity in how different groups within a major religion interpret equality (e.g., Islam as practised in Iran is far more conservative and male-focused than it is in Malaysia; Dhruvarajan & Vickers, 2002, p. 274), many women struggle with the need to find comfort and meaning in their lives within patriarchal organizations.

There is no single feminist approach to religion. Some argue that our entire patriarchal society (and therefore religion, as well) needs to be fundamentally restructured, while others believe that they can inspire change from within religions by being active and vocal members of religious groups and working with them to facilitate progressive social change that seeks equality for everyone.

> > > Thinking Sociologically

Sociological theories of religion span a wide range of perspectives and it is relatively easy to contrast them (e.g., religion plays a positive social role for Durkheim and a negative one for Marx), but perhaps a more interesting question might be to consider how the perspectives are similar. What are the common attributes among all the sociological theories of religion?

POST-STRUCTURALIST THEORY

As explored in Chapter 3, post-structuralists are less interested in seeking scientific "truths" than they are in exploring how power defines our socially produced reality. One leading post-structuralist theorist, Michel Foucault, offers a unique analysis of institutional norms and how they situate the individual's experience within them.

Foucault suggests that social institutions, including organized religions, are best understood as networks of power that dominate their subjects through tradition and institutional authority (Wolosky, 2009, p. 13). For Foucault, this institutional existence influences a person's physical self, creating what he refers to as "docile bodies" in his book entitled *Discipline and Punish* (1975). In this way, religious life can act as a vehicle for directing and restricting the body. According to Foucault, dominating the body in this way can demonstrate institutional power (Wolosky, 2009). For example, consider the way that many Christians view sin and salvation (Besley, 2005).

Some Christians believe that suffering is the result of our sinfulness. But, to Christianity, there is the possibility for salvation thanks to Jesus Christ's death on the cross, where he paid for our sins (Thiem, 2007). This belief system creates an elaborate interplay of salvation, sanctification, and thanksgiving to God and is based on the belief that one's

> > >

According to many Christian faiths, baptism marks the beginning of a child's journey of faith and connects that child to the worldwide Christian family.

J. McPhail/Shutterstock

sinfulness exists at birth and is never fully shed in this life. Sin is based on the needs of the desirous body. Within Christianity, the only way to avoid eternal damnation is through faith in Jesus Christ, which can liberate a person from his/her sinful body and allow that person to achieve a new, eternal, pure body. Achieving and maintaining this new body requires constant vigilance and prayer because of the basic depravity of human nature (Thiem, 2007, pp. 332–333). In this way, Foucault would argue, organized religion and its beliefs and practices demonstrate how power can influence virtually everything followers do, including how they relate to their own bodies.

Today, many people are trying to move beyond these rigid rules governing their lives to explore their own spirituality outside of organized religion. This relatively recent trend toward personal responsibility and empowerment can be seen in the popularity of television programs like *Dr. Phil*, which commonly advocates taking control of one's life.

In today's society, it is easy for people to move between religious groups or to neglect them altogether. What fascinates many sociologists today is wondering what the future holds for religion (Borowik, 2011; Cipriani, 2011; Smith, 2008).

❻ The Future of Religion

As we have seen, religion remains an important element in many people's lives. The support it brings, and the sense of meaning and purpose that having religious beliefs and being a member of a close-knit community provide, are important sources of strength during difficult times, especially in a world that seems to be more cold and impersonal than it was in the past. There is no doubt that people will continue to be drawn to the emotional and spiritual comforts that religion provides; however, there are certainly winds of change that suggest that the religions and church organizations of the future will be different than they are today.

Notwithstanding fanatical and fundamentalist movements, many believe that the power of religion to define people's lives is currently in decline. Sociologists refer to this as **secularization**—the process by which developed societies move away from explanations based on religion to ones based on science, rationality, and logic. According to Sommerville (1998), secularization is associated, in part, with the following:

1. An increasing differentiation between economic, political, and legal systems in contemporary society

2. An increase in the number of secular institutions taking on activities traditionally associated with religious institutions (e.g., preschool programs, soup kitchens)

secularization The process by which developed societies move away from explanations based on religion to ones based on science, rationality, and logic.

3. A shift in individuals' focus from spirituality to day-to-day experiences (e.g., people become less interested in seeking out the "meaning of life" than in what their university major should be)

4. An overall decline in the importance of religion in contemporary society

◉ Watch

Decline in the Number of Roman Catholic Priests

Some sociologists suggest that the centrality of religion in people's lives will continue to decline. Generally, sociologists point to three reasons for this.

First is the belief that the forces of secularization will continue into the future. As various levels of government continue to administer more and more social services that were previously the responsibility of religious organizations (e.g., education, social welfare), the more separated religion will become from people's daily lives. Further, advances in science mean that our world is becoming increasingly guided by the secular rather than the spiritual. The shift to understanding our world through science and our own intellect will continue to challenge the traditional role of religion to help us explain ourselves and our place in the universe.

Second, as discussed, the world's major religions are to some degree patriarchal (Moore, 2010). As feminists rightly point out, for religion to fully engage and resonate with today's women it will have to promote equality meaningfully.

Third, as the baby boomers retire (marking a major demographic shift, discussed in Chapter 18), churches must attract younger people in order to survive. Yet traditional religions are finding this difficult; as we have seen, younger people today seek a more vital and personal connection with their spirituality than perhaps their parents' generation required or wanted. Figure 13.2 shows that the percentage of teens that identify as Christian is falling (except for the broad category of "other faiths"), and the percentage having no faith at all is rising (Lunau, 2009).

The percentage of teens who identify as Christian is shrinking

	1984	1992	2000	2008
Roman Catholic	50%	41%	39%	32%
Protestant	35%	28%	22%	13%
Other faiths*	3%	10%	14%	16%
No faith at all	12%	21%	25%	32%

*Includes: Islam, Buddhism, Judaism, Hinduism, Sikhism, Aboriginal; source: Project Teen Canada

FIGURE 13.2

The Percentage of Teens Who Identify as Christian Is Shrinking

Source: Reprinted by permission from Lunau, K. (2009). Youth survey: Teens lose faith in droves. Retrieved 28/07/2010, 2010, from http://www2.macleans .ca/2009/04/07/teens-lose-faith-in-droves/ © Maclean's Magazine

Even with these trends in mind, many people have found comfort in the belief that their lives have purpose and that they are somehow connected to something larger than themselves. There is no doubt that people will continue to be drawn to organizations that provide them with such support and meaning.

Summary

① Animism is the belief that spirits inhabit living forms, polytheism is the belief in multiple gods, and monotheism is the belief in a single, all-powerful god.

② A new religious movement is an informal grouping of people around authoritarian and charismatic leaders; a sect is a small religious body that is either somewhat separate from or hostile to the larger society; and a church is an institution that brings believers into formalized worship and is an integrated part of society.

❸ The world's largest religions are Christianity, Judaism, Islam, Hinduism, Buddhism, Confucianism, and Sikhism.

❹ Although Canada is still largely a Christian nation, both Protestantism and Catholicism have declined as percentages of the Canadian population over the past century, due in part to increasing numbers of immigrants from non-Christian countries and to a general, long-term decline in church attendance.

❺ Functionalists perceive religion as providing an important means of social cohesion and stability; conflict theorists view it as a tool of capitalist oppression; and symbolic interactionists consider it a source of rituals and symbols that influence how we see ourselves. Feminists understand religion as a patriarchal institution, and post-structuralists' emphasis on power points to a personal spirituality that challenges the absolutes of religious belief.

❻ Today, the role of religion in people's lives is challenged by three factors: secularization and the resulting separation of religion and daily life; the continuing patriarchal nature of religion; and the need to attract young people, who tend to look for a more personal spirituality.

Key Terms

agnostic 346
animism 335
asceticism 338
atheist 347
calling 354
church 337
civil religion or secular religion 336
dharma 343
ecclesia 337
faith 335
fundamentalism 346
inner-worldly 339
jen 344
karma 344
li 344
liberation theology 354

moksha 343
monotheism 335
mysticism 338
new religious movement 337
nirvana 344
other-worldly 339
polytheism 335
predestination 354
profane 350
religion 335
religious pluralism 337
restorationist belief systems 345
sacred 350
samsara 343
sect 337
secularization 358
theocracy 340
totem 351

Reviewing the Concepts

1. Compare and contrast any two theoretical explanations for religion. Which theory do you prefer and why? Be sure to defend your answer using text material and contemporary examples.

2. Review and critique Weber's classification of religions into *inner-worldly* and *other-worldly* orientations. What do you consider the key strengths and weaknesses of his argument?

3. Define and review the concept of secularization. What evidence can you give to both support and challenge the assertion that society is becoming more secular?

4. Define and discuss the terms *agnostic* and *atheist*.

Applying Your Sociological Imagination

1. In your educated opinion, is organized religion a positive or negative force in contemporary society? Is it possible that your answer might be influenced by what country you live in? Discuss.

2. Can a religious fundamentalist possess the sociological imagination? If so, how? If not, why?

3. Do you believe that the number of young people participating in religion will continue to fall? As a sociologist, what evidence do you have to defend your position?

4. Given your own experiences, how are religions portrayed by the mass media? Do you think some are presented more positively than others? Discuss.

MySocLab

Visit MySocLab to access a variety of online resources that will help you prepare for tests and apply your knowledge.

14 Crime, Law, and Regulation

When we watch the news in Canada, we are often informed of high profile cases that then dominate news cycles for months or years.

In May 2013, Tim Bosma was murdered after leaving his home with two men who had arranged a test drive of the truck that Bosma was selling and had recently advertised online. Two individuals stand accused of first-degree murder in the case; under Canadian law, they are presumed innocent until proven guilty (Hayes, 2013).

In October 2010, Colonel Russell Williams pleaded guilty to 88 charges—two of these charges were for first-degree murder, two for sexual assault, and two for forcible confinement. His murder victims were Jessica Lloyd and Corporal Marie-France Comeau. Dating back to 2007, Williams had broken into many homes and stolen women's undergarments and family photographs. He had also taken photos of himself at the crime scenes (CBC, 2010). The first-degree murder charges bring with them an automatic life sentence (with no possibility of parole for a minimum of 25 years).

In December 2007, Robert Pickton, a farmer from British Columbia, was convicted of the second-degree murders of six women and sentenced to life in prison with no chance of parole for 25 years. Rebecca Guno, a sex-trade worker, was the first of 61 women who would eventually be placed on a list of women (mostly sex-trade workers) who disappeared mysteriously from the area over many years. Sociologists are interested in the answers to questions such as 'Why did the police not pursue the missing women cases earlier?' and 'Why might the police not have taken the concerns of the missing women's families seriously?'

Why are we so well informed about high-profile murders and yet tend to know very little about the effects of corporate crime? Why do some victims garner more sympathy than others? These are just two of the questions that people interested in the study of crime grapple with. And, of course, many more behaviours fall outside of society's norms. Crime knows no boundaries—and, as we will see in this chapter, it is often not about "sick" or "deviant" individuals but rather is connected to wider social relations.

By the end of this chapter, students will be able to

1. Understand the distinction between crime and deviance.
2. Describe the beliefs that underlie classical criminology.
3. Explain biological approaches to understanding crime.
4. Distinguish among the major sociological approaches to understanding crime.
5. Distinguish among major approaches to theorizing law.
6. Understand the media's influence on our perceptions of risk and the beliefs that inform moral regulation.

What Is Criminology?

Criminology is a multidisciplinary field that draws on sociology, law, psychology, political science, anthropology, history, and geography. It is devoted to the development of information about the causes, patterns, and trends of crime. Criminologists who adopt a sociological approach have a tendency to focus on the social context within which criminal law is both created and applied. Taking a sociological approach also means focusing on explanations of crime that consider structural factors, such as poverty and discrimination.

Criminology can be defined as a scientific approach to the study of crime causation, crime prevention, and the punishment and (potential) rehabilitation of offenders. According to the influential definition proposed by Sutherland and Cressey (1960, p. 3), criminology is "the body of knowledge regarding crime as a social phenomenon. It includes within its scope the process of making laws, breaking laws, and reacting towards the breaking of laws." Such a definition highlights important areas of interest to criminologists: the development of criminal law and its use in defining crime, the causes of law-breaking behaviour, and societal responses to crime and criminal behaviour (Sacco & Kennedy, 2008).

criminology The study of crime causation, crime prevention, and the punishment and rehabilitation of offenders.

1 The Relationship between Crime and Deviance

Although the terms *crime* and *deviance* are often used interchangeably, they are two distinct phenomena that at times overlap. **Crime** is a concept used to designate particular behaviours or actions (including acts of negligence) that require a formal response through social control and that warrant some form of social intervention (Winterdyk, 2006). **Deviance**, on the other hand, involves actions or behaviours that violate certain social norms, which may or may not be against the law (Winterdyk, 2006). **Social norms** are understood here as a given society's shared and accepted standards and social expectations.

crime Behaviours or actions that require social control and social intervention, codified in law.

deviance Actions or behaviours that violate social norms, and that may or may not be against the law.

social norms Shared and accepted standards and social expectations.

The difficulty with this definition of deviance is how these social norms are defined, and by whom. For example, to what degree do your own notions of proper conduct match those of others? Is it possible that some of your behaviours are unacceptable to some people? Are you somehow "deviant"? Behaviours as diverse as committing a violent crime, joining a nudist colony, and acquiring an abundance of body piercings are all seen as deviant acts by a large portion of Canadian society.

Most, but not all, crimes are understood as deviant, but not all deviant acts are considered criminal. For example, assisted suicide is against the law, yet many people do not view it as deviant. In Western cultures, a woman in her 50s dating an 18-year-old man is seen as deviant by some (and lucky by others), but the relationship is certainly not criminal. We also need to ask why some acts are criminalized while others are not. Drinking alcohol is legal (once one reaches the age of majority) while other forms of ingesting drugs are illegal.

Over time, some deviant acts come to be deemed criminal and some criminalized acts become legalized. Consider the use and distribution of marijuana. Despite being criminalized in 1923, marijuana still enjoys widespread popularity; in fact, between 1994 and 2004 the number of Canadians using marijuana doubled (CBC News, 2004a). The Canadian Addiction Survey found that 45 percent of Canadians report having used marijuana at least once in their lives (CBC News, 2004a). Marijuana use is four times higher in Canada than the world average. According to the 2010 World Drug Report, Canada leads the industrial world in cannabis consumption with 16.8 percent of Canadians between the ages of 15 and 64 having smoked marijuana or used a cannabis product in the preceding year (UNODC, 2010). The world cannabis consumption average ranges between 2.9 percent to 4.3 percent (for persons between the ages of 15 and 64) (UNODC, 2010). There is currently much debate over whether marijuana use should be decriminalized.

Perceptions of deviance can also change: Acts that were once considered deviant can become an accepted element of society, while acts that were once considered "normal" can actually shift to be understood as "deviant" over time. In Canada, women's body modifications, whether in the form of plastic surgeries, piercings, or small tattoos, are not nearly as deviant as they were just 20 years ago. And, back then, smoking was a widespread activity that occurred in university lecture halls, at movie theatres, in bank lineups, and even at your doctor's office; today, however, smoking is rapidly becoming understood as a deviant act, thanks in part to government regulations prohibiting smoking in most public settings.

So the distinction between what is or ought to be considered deviant and what is or ought to be considered criminal is not as clear-cut as one might think. Two cases in point are pornography and prostitution. When does sexually expressive material cross the line into pornography? What acts make pornography illegal? Does any person have the "right" to sell her or his body for sex? Can prostitution be understood simply as work?

DEVIANCE

What Is Deviant to Some Is not Deviant to Others

Sociologists use the term *deviance* to refer to any acts that involve the violation of accepted social norms. As Howard Becker (1963) argued, the act itself is not inherently deviant but rather people's reactions to the specific act make it deviant. In other words, a particular act or behaviour needs to be viewed from the standpoint of the culture within which it takes place, since what is socially acceptable in one culture may actually be seen as deviant in another. We can see an example of diverging social norms in the widespread media coverage of the May 2008 raids on a polygamous Mormon sect in Texas. Within this sect, polygyny, arranged marriages, and young brides are considered socially acceptable. However, in the wider societal context of North America, these acts are viewed as problematic and immoral, and thus resulted in an intervention that saw the removal of more than 150 of the sect's children from the community for a period of time. In Canada, the British Columbia government is testing the legality of Canada's 1890 polygamy law (Section 293 of the Criminal Code) (MacQueen,

2010). The constitutional case is before the courts as a result of failed prosecutions against two men practising polygamy in Bountiful, British Columbia.

Who gets to define deviance? In Canada, some of the most powerful groups involved in this process of defining what is deviant are politicians and governments, scientists, religious leaders, and the media (Bereska, 2008). Each of these individuals may act as **moral entrepreneurs**—those who influence or change the creation or enforcement of a society's moral codes (Becker, 1963; Linden, 2009). People who act in ways that stray from what is deemed to be socially acceptable behaviour are then subject to social controls, both informally and formally.

moral entrepreneur
A person who influences or changes the creation or enforcement of a society's moral codes.

Informal social control occurs through our social interactions and includes the ways we attempt to both communicate and enforce standards of appropriate behaviour. How we respond to behaviours can make people stop and question whether their behaviour is socially appropriate or inappropriate (consider a friend's reaction: "You did what?!?"). When informal social controls are not effective, the state can exert formal social controls through mechanisms such as the criminal justice system, social workers, and psychiatrists. Gossiping about someone for being sexually promiscuous is an example of an informal social control, while being imprisoned for having sex with a minor is an example of formal social control.

Criminologists, then, are concerned with the ever-shifting definitions of deviant behaviour and their links to our conceptions of crime. Both deviance and crime are fluid definitions that change over time. Crime, as an instance of deviance that has been made formal via criminal law, is often referred to as "hard" deviance—that is, particular acts or behaviours that are likely to result in arrest and imprisonment (Goode, 2010). We turn now to the theories concerning *why* people commit crimes.

> >> **Thinking Sociologically**

Over one evening, count how many crime-based shows (e.g., *CSI, Law & Order, COPS*) are broadcast on the major television networks. Then think of recent Hollywood films. How many of those have some sort of law enforcement focus? Why do you think we are so interested in watching shows about crime? What does this tell us about our society?

Classical Criminology: Rational Choice Theory

Taking a scientific approach to the study of crime is actually a relatively recent event (Siegel & McCormick, 2010). Although written criminal codes have existed for thousands of years, attempts to understand *why* people commit crimes came much later (Siegel & McCormick, 2010). Throughout the Middle Ages, people believed that those who committed crimes or violated social norms were possessed—and as a response by the community, they were burned at the stake. Estimates from the sixteenth and seventeenth centuries in Europe are that 10 000 people were accused of witchcraft (Siegel & McCormick, 2010).

By the mid-eighteenth century, a movement had emerged to overhaul approaches to law making and punishment to balance crime fairly with its accompanying punishment (Siegel & McCormick, 2010). This approach took as its base the philosophy of *utilitarianism*, which held that behaviour was not the result of supernatural or other-worldly forces but rather was purposeful (Siegel & McCormick, 2010). The key reformers were Cesare Beccaria (1764), an Italian aristocrat, and Jeremy Bentham (1838), an English philosopher. Both Beccaria and Bentham argued that if crime produces some form of pleasure for a criminal, then pain is necessary to prevent a crime. In addition, they argued that sentences must be proportionate to the seriousness of the crime (Siegel & McCormick, 2010).

Classical criminology was thus developed on the basis of four basic beliefs:

1. Crime is a rational choice as people enjoy free will—they are able to choose to engage in criminal acts or in lawful acts.

2. Criminal solutions requiring less work yet yielding greater payoffs are understood as being more attractive than lawful solutions.

BOX 14.1 WHY SHOULD WE CARE?

Discrimination in the Criminal Justice System?

Today, many criminologists argue that discrimination is embedded in our criminal justice system. Although statistics on race and crime are not normally released in Canada, available information indicates that particular racial minorities are overrepresented in the correctional system (Wortley, 1999; COP, 2008). While Aboriginals represent approximately 3 percent of the total Canadian population, they account for nearly 2 out of every 10 federal prison inmates (17 percent) (CBC News, 2008c). Similarly, while blacks account for only 2.5 percent of the total Canadian population, they represent more than 9 percent of those housed in federal correctional institutions, which is up from 6 percent in 2008 (Crawford, 2011; COP, 2008). Much debate exists, however, as to whether these overrepresentations are a result of discrimination within the criminal justice system or of social conditions (i.e., poverty or powerlessness) that position particular groups at greater risk (Fitzgerald & Carrington, 2011; Fleras & Elliot, 2006).

Denney, Ellis, and Barn (2006) note that "on one hand, Canada represents an example of an advanced society noted for its fairness and equity, while on the other, it appears as subject to the same racially biased disparities within its criminal justice system as many other comparable developed western countries" (p. 2). Indeed, studies of pretrial releases consistently reveal that black youth are significantly more likely to be denied pretrial release on bail and to be incarcerated for particular offences than are whites (Roberts & Doob, 1997; COP, 2008).

According to Canada's Department of Justice, Aboriginal youth across Canada are incarcerated at a rate eight times higher than that of non-Aboriginal youth (Latimer & Foss, 2004). Aboriginal people accounted for 71 percent of incarcerated individuals in Manitoba and 79 percent in Saskatchewan in 2006 (Juristat, 2008). Some researchers suggest that these rates do not appear to result from racial discriminatory practices in sentencing but rather from Aboriginal peoples' low socioeconomic status, lack of education, and high rates of victimization, substance abuse, and gang participation (La Prairie, 1990, 2002; Latimer & Foss 2004; Martel, Brassard, & Jaccoud, 2011). Researchers also argue that this overrepresentation is in part due to demographics (Latimer & Foss, 2005): Since Canada's Aboriginal population is significantly younger than its non-Aboriginal population, there is a higher probability of the former being in the age group most associated with being at the highest risk of offending (Boe, 2002).

Aboriginal women are also overrepresented in the federal prison population. Their rates of incarceration have increased progressively since 1997 when only 15 percent of all incarcerated women were Aboriginal. The Elizabeth Fry Society reports that, worldwide, women represent the fastest-growing group within the prison population and young women actually represent a greater proportion of youth sentenced to custodial care than young men (CAEFS, 2004). Although women offenders are of relatively low risk to the community in comparison with men, federally sentenced women are subject to poorer treatment and more limiting confinement conditions than men (CAEFS, 2008). The Canadian Centre for Justice Statistics has not released a gender-specific report since 1990, a fact that has led some criminologists to question whether the continued lack of interest in women offenders reflects an ideological disposition in Canadian criminological thought (Winterdyk, 2006).

Calling the overrepresentation of Aboriginal peoples in Canadian prisons a "national disgrace," the Supreme Court, the Royal Commission on Aboriginal Peoples, and the Auditor General have all joined the appeal to halt the overrepresentation of Aboriginal peoples in Canadian prisons (G. Wilson, 2009).

Do you agree with the sociological argument that the disparities noted above are the result of bias? This was certainly the finding of the Commission on Systemic Racism in the Ontario Criminal Justice System in 1995. What other factors might explain these disparities? How would you go about investigating whether disparities in Canadian sentencing practices exist?

3. A fear of punishment can control a person's choices.

4. When criminality is met with measured severity, certainty of punishment, and swiftness of justice, a society enhances its ability to control crime and criminal behaviour. (Siegel & McCormick, 2010)

Classical criminological approaches thus argued that before a person commits an offence, he or she engages in a rational evaluation of the pros and cons, costs and benefits of the situation. Thus, the person first evaluates the risk of apprehension, then evaluates the seriousness of the potential punishment, and finally judges the value to herself or himself of the criminal activity. A person's decision to commit a crime is thus based on the aggregate outcome of this rational weighing of gains and risks. Such a classical approach is now widely critiqued (as discussed below), yet many of its principles remain influential in our current criminal justice system. For example, punishment is still based on the principles of proportionality and deterrence.

Randy Faris/CORBIS/Glow Images

< < <

Proponents of rational choice theory argue that before committing a crime, an individual engages in rational calculation of the pros and cons of the situation.

Biological Perspectives in Understanding Crime

The strongest critique of the classical conception of crime came in the nineteenth century from an emerging school of thought that was later identified as positivism (Jackson, 1995) and involved applying the scientific method to the social world. Positivists focused on the level of the individual. Positivists assumed that once we were able to identify specific physical features distinguishing criminals from noncriminals, it would then be possible (and desirable) to figure out how to prevent and control criminal behaviour, with the eventual goal of eliminating criminal behaviour (Jackson, 1995). Such a view came to be known as **biological determinism**: Drawing influence from Charles Darwin's evolutionary theory, it marked a distinct shift from "rational evil" to "fated evil" (Jackson, 1995). By the late nineteenth century, positivists had attacked the classical school of thought, arguing that increased crime rates were the result of the failure to identify the causes of crime.

Cesare Lombroso (1835–1909), an Italian physician, was the major proponent of this new approach. While a physician in the army, Lombroso examined the cadaver of a notorious criminal and discovered that this man shared physical characteristics commonly associated with animals (Siegel & McCormick, 2010). Lombroso attempted to apply the scientific method to his investigation of criminals. Lombroso argued that some individuals were born criminals—that they were lower on the evolutionary ladder as a result of a particular anatomy (Jackson, 1995; Linden, 2009; Siegel & McCormick, 2010). The criminal man, according to Lombroso, could be distinguished by his anatomy: an asymmetrical face, large ears, particular eye defects, and so forth (see Figure 14.1).

Biological theories fail to consider the wider influence of environment, and are mostly disregarded by contemporary criminologists. However, some biological criminology research

biological determinism The hypothesis that biological factors completely determine a person's behaviour.

FIGURE 14.1

Cesare Lombroso's
Criminal Man

Source: Duke University
Press, 2006

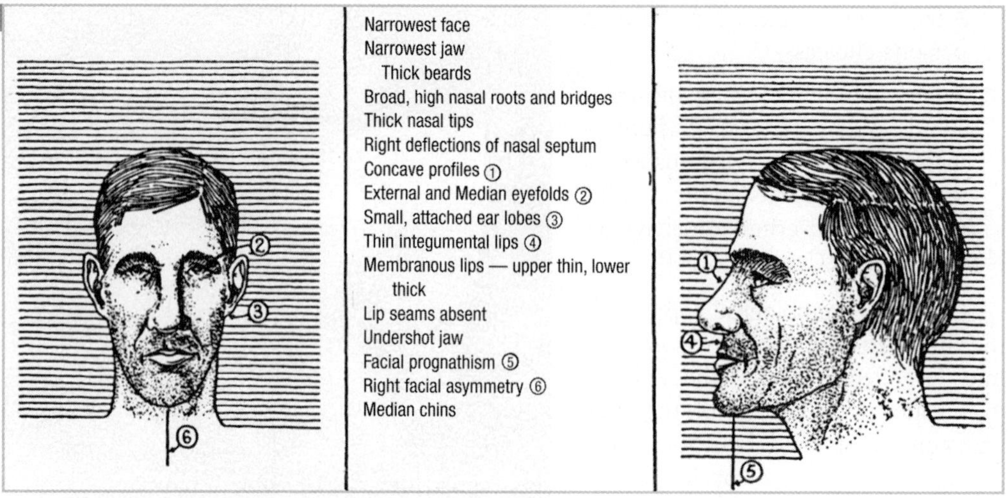

Narrowest face
Narrowest jaw
    Thick beards
Broad, high nasal roots and bridges
Thick nasal tips
Right deflections of nasal septum
Concave profiles ①
External and Median eyefolds ②
Small, attached ear lobes ③
Thin integumental lips ④
Membranous lips — upper thin, lower
    thick
Lip seams absent
Undershot jaw
Facial prognathism ⑤
Right facial asymmetry ⑥
Median chins

is still used today in court, such as work connecting nutritional deficiencies with anti-social behaviour (Schoenthaler, 2000) or other research that draws a connection between high carbohydrate and sugar diets and reasoning processes (Ferguson, 1986; Knox, 1988).

❹ Sociological Approaches to Crime

Studying Crime and
Deviance

Sociologists argue that crime is not simply the result of genetic disposition, nutritional choices, personal failure, or an individual's free will. Since the beginning of the twentieth century, sociologists have been working to shift the focus of criminology toward a consideration of the social environments in which people are located (Messner & Rosenfeld, 2007). After all, explanations of crime at the level of the individual fail to explain persistent crime patterns. We see variations of crime rates based on geographic location, which would not happen if punishment was handed out uniformly across Canada. Sociologists emphasize the *ecological* distribution of crime (such an approach encompasses all of the social, geographical, and temporal inequalities connected with the access to and use of environmental resources and services). Sociologists also emphasize the effect of social change and the interactive nature of crime itself. Together, these emphases form the basis of modern criminology (Siegel & McCormick, 2006, p. 190). We turn now to the major theoretical approaches to crime from a sociological perspective.

FUNCTIONALISM

We often associate deviance and crime with notions of dysfunction. Yet the functions of crime and deviance are in fact important for societies. As you will recall, functionalists stress the ways in which the many groups in society coexist. Although there are bound to be tensions between and among these groups, functionalists argue that the balancing of these tensions produces society. When a particular group or individual threatens this balance, efforts are made to ensure that everything returns to a state of homeostasis (meaning "balance," or "the status quo").

The functionalist approach to criminality has its roots in Émile Durkheim's notion of anomie (first discussed in Chapter 2). Durkheim believed that as societies evolved from the preindustrial model to the industrial model, rules governing behaviour broke down; as a result, people no longer knew what to expect from one another. Anomie, then, is a state of normlessness in which norms are confused, unclear, or absent. Durkheim felt that such normlessness leads to deviant behaviour.

Strain Theory Robert Merton (1938) developed **strain theory** by drawing on Durkheim's assertion that societal structure can produce particular social pressures that may result in deviant or criminal behaviour. According to this approach, anomic conditions are produced through a relationship between two cultural elements. When culturally defined goals cannot be met through socially approved means, anomic conditions result (Winterdyk, 2006). Those of low socioeconomic status may feel strain since legitimate avenues for success (means to acquire wealth and power) are less open to them than they may be to more affluent persons. For example, individuals with little or no formal education may find it more difficult than those with higher levels of education to acquire material wealth through legitimate means, such as a successful career (Siegel & McCormick, 2010). It is important to understand that this perspective is not suggesting that individual people are simply incapable of controlling their individual desires, but rather that unattainable goals and desires are being produced at the level of a society (Siegel & McCormick, 2010).

Strain theorists argue that most people within the same society share similar goals and values, and that when legitimate avenues to achieving those goals are not readily accessible, some will resort to deviant methods (e.g., theft, drug trafficking) to achieve them. Alternatively, some people will reject socially accepted goals altogether and will instead substitute them with more deviant or criminal goals. Merton's theory remains influential as he provides an explanation for the continued existence of high-crime areas as well as the prevalence of criminal behaviour among the lower class (Siegel & McCormick, 2010).

Merton's typology of social adaptations included five social goals along with the means of achieving the goals:

1. *Conformity* happens when individuals both accept social goals and have the means to achieve those goals.

2. *Innovation* takes place when an individual accepts society's goals but she or he is incapable of achieving those goals through socially approved means. Of all of Merton's adaptations, innovation is most strongly linked with criminal behaviour (think of a bank robber or a drug dealer).

3. *Ritualism* as an adaptation happens when social goals are reduced in importance. An example of a ritualist would be someone belonging to a religious order; the societal goal of material success, for example, does not drive such a person's activities.

4. *Retreatists* reject societal goals and the legitimate means of achieving such goals. Retreatists are often found on the margins of society as their lack of success leads to social withdrawal.

5. *Rebellion* involves the creation of an alternative set of goals and means, thus supplanting conventional ones. Rebellion happens when people call for and engage in radical change and alternative lifestyles. (Siegel & McCormick, 2010)

Illegitimate Opportunity Theory Richard Cloward and Lloyd Ohlin (1960) sought to extend Merton's strain theory by considering specific environments. Cloward and Ohlin agreed with Merton that the lower classes are more likely to feel goal strain and find themselves frustrated enough about their inability to achieve approved social goals such that they are willing to engage in deviant behaviour. Where they differ from Merton is in their contention that illegitimate opportunities are not necessarily equally accessible to all lower- and working-class individuals; people are constrained by available opportunities. Their **illegitimate opportunity theory** asserts that individuals must be located in deviant "learning environments" that provide them with the opportunities to both learn and develop the expertise needed to engage in criminal behaviour (Akers & Sellers, 2008).

In their study of adolescent boys, Cloward and Ohlin (1960), while recognizing that gangs engage in a range of illegal activities, found that gangs develop specialized delinquent subcultures according to the illegitimate opportunities available to them in their neighbourhoods (Akers & Sellers, 2008). Cloward and Ohlin (1960) identified three types of youth

strain theory The assertion that people experience strain when culturally defined goals cannot be met through socially approved means.

illegitimate opportunity theory The assertion that individuals commit crime as a result of deviant learning environments.

> > >

Illegitimate opportunity theorists argue that individuals must be located in a deviant learning environment that provides individuals with the skills and ability to commit crime.

Patrick Batchelder/Alamy

gangs: criminal, conflict, and retreatist (Siegel & McCormick, 2010). Criminal gangs are categorized as existing in "stable but poor areas" within which youth are able to establish close connections with adult offenders, thus creating an environment in which crime can be successfully committed (Siegel & McCormick, 2010, p. 245). Conflict gangs are characterized by neighbourhoods that are much less stable than ones associated with criminal gangs. These neighbourhoods often have a high rate of temporary residents, are in physical disrepair, and are incapable of providing either legitimate or illegitimate opportunities to their youth. Crime in these neighbourhoods is without organization and operates on an individual and petty level (Siegel & McCormick, 2010). Last are retreatist gangs. Retreatist gang members are ones who have been unable to achieve success through socially approved means and are also not inclined to gain success through illegal means. Members here often sell drugs or commit petty crimes to have enough money to supply themselves with drugs and alcohol (Siegel & McCormick, 2010).

The illegitimate opportunity theory has its critics, however. Goode (2010) argues that Cloward and Ohlin's typology of young gangs is "largely a fantasy," and he maintains that although this "specialization" of youth gangs may have been evident in the early 1950s and 1960s, it is not an enduring trend. Rather, Goode argues that most contemporary gangs, regardless of neighbourhood, are engaged in the use and distribution of drugs, theft, and acts of violence.

CONFLICT THEORY

As you might expect, conflict theorists primarily view crime as the product of class struggle. Their goal, then, is to situate and explain crime within economic and social contexts. In contrast to the functionalist emphasis on the strain that individuals may experience as a result of their socioeconomic status, conflict theorists instead focus on, for example, the role that a government plays in producing **criminogenic environments** (environments in which laws privileging certain groups are in part responsible for breeding criminal behaviour) and on the relationship between social power and criminal law. Conflict theorists challenge the commonly held belief that law is neutral and reflects the interests of society as a whole.

criminogenic environment An environment that, as a result of laws that privilege certain groups, produces crime or criminality.

< < <

Members of conflict gangs earn status through being tough and violent.

Conflict theorists are also interested in examining how bias plays out in the criminal justice system. They argue that crimes committed by the wealthy, such as corporate crimes, are punished far more leniently than are crimes committed by those of the lower classes. Mosher and Hagan's (1994) historical research, focusing on the relationship between class and crime in the sentencing of narcotics offences, provides evidence of just such an approach—and within their research, the criminal act is constant (i.e., the charges were the same). They examined patterns of sentencing in Canada between 1908 and 1953. They argue that members of the upper class disproportionately received lenient treatment while members of the working class received harsher scrutiny and treatment (Mosher & Hagan, 1994).

Conflict theorists take as their base the work of Karl Marx. Marx argued that economic relations (forces of production and one's position relative to the means of production) structures social relations—including the legal system (Kramar, 2011a). Within a capitalist economic society, the legal system is designed to protect the interests of the ruling class. Further, this protection of the ruling class, and thus exploitation of the working class, is obscured from view by ideological constructs such as "fairness" and "equity" for all under the law. Positioning criminal acts as the result of individuals' poor choices rather than as an outcome of an economic system serves to protect and sustain the capitalist class (Kramar, 2011a).

Researchers demonstrate that class interests are at play when we examine who is the subject of frequent police attention (Siegel & McCormick, 2010), the overrepresentation of Aboriginal peoples in our criminal justice system (Latimer & Foss, 2004), and how quickly the justice system responds to particular kinds of victims (white, wealthy men) (Siegel & McCormick, 2010).

SYMBOLIC INTERACTIONISM

Interactionists who are interested in deviance and crime argue that criminal behaviour is learned in the same way as any other type of behaviour: through social interactions with others. We consider two symbolic interactionist approaches: differential association theory and labelling theory.

Differential Association Theory

differential association theory **Criminal behaviour occurs when our association with definitions favourable to crime outweighs our definitions favourable to law-abiding behaviour.**

Differential Association Theory One of the most prominent and lasting approaches to explaining how criminal behaviour is learned behaviour is Edwin Sutherland's (1939) **differential association theory**. Here he sought to explain how people come to engage in criminal activity. He took as his starting point that crime, like all other behaviours, is a learned behaviour and could therefore affect anyone.

The main principles of differential association theory assert that we learn how to behave in criminal ways in the same manner that we learn how to engage in any behaviour and that this learning takes place within social interactions with close associations (friends, family, peers). Further, we come into contact with people who believe in varying definitions of crime—both for and against. And these differential associations affect our decision to engage in criminal acts or not—we are influenced by the intensity, frequency, and duration of our interactions with people. When our interactions are dominated or influenced more by people with favourable dispositions to crime, criminal behaviour will then occur (Siegel & McCormick, 2010).

Differential association remains influential in studying the friendship patterns of delinquent youth. For example, examining data from self-reporting surveys with students in Grades 9 through 12 from six schools in Texas, Holly Miller (2010) explored the relationship between measures of differential association and severity of criminal activity. She found that peer delinquency (having a network of friends that includes people who break the law) is a significant and strong correlate for committing serious acts of delinquency.

Differential association positions criminal activity as grounded in rationality and thus ignores crimes that we might categorize as crimes of passion or ones that happen in the heat of the moment (Siegel & McCormick, 2010). Sutherland's work has also been criticized for using vague terms such as someone having "an excess of definition toward criminality" (Siegel & McCormick, 2010, p. 263). It is virtually impossible to test the ratio of definitions toward criminality against definitions toward law-abiding behaviour (Siegel & McCormick, 2010). Further, feminists criticize Sutherland's failure to explain why more men than women become criminals (Abbott, Wallace, & Tyler, 2005).

Watch

The Influence of Romantic Relationships and Family on Criminal Behaviour

Listen

Crime Study Challenges Past Assumptions

labelling theory **The assertion that once labelled as deviant, people come to accept the label as part of their identity.**

Labelling Theory Howard S. Becker, an early interactionist theorist, first discussed his approach to **labelling theory** in his book *Outsiders: Studies in the Sociology of Deviance* (1963). Influenced by Cooley's looking-glass self, Mead's understanding of the internalization of the self, and Lemert's social constructionism, Becker was interested in the effects of people's reactions and their effects on individuals when particular acts, and those committing the acts, were labelled as deviant (Kramar, 2011a). As Becker (1963) argued, "social groups create deviance by making the rules whose infraction constitutes deviance and by applying those rules to particular people and labeling them as outsiders" (p. 9). In this framework, one becomes deviant when the label of "deviant" is applied.

Labelling theorists are interested in the consequences for people once they have been singled out and defined as deviant—they ask "what are the effects of such labels?" For example, to be labelled a criminal in our society, one need only commit a single criminal offence. Once labelled, it is difficult for an individual to shed this label. Because the label stigmatizes individuals and leads to self-concept modification, labelling can act as a self-fulfilling prophecy.

A research study based in Rochester, New York, tested the accuracy of labelling theory. Would youth who came into contact with the juvenile justice system become more likely to increase their criminal behaviour and associate with others labelled as "criminals"? Bernburg, Krohn, and Rivera (2006) interviewed 1000 Grade 7 and 8 students in Rochester, NY, and followed them longitudinally. The researchers also drew on data from the police, the courts, their schools, and various social service agencies. Based on Rochester's diverse population and relatively high crime rate, the researchers were able to generalize their findings to the larger American population. Their results show that, indeed, one's involvement with the juvenile justice system does lead to an increased likelihood of future involvement with "delinquent" peer networks. Further, they found that youth who had at least one involvement with the justice system significantly increased their likelihood of gang membership.

Consider, as Ricciardelli and Moir (2013) did, the potential effects of bearing the criminal label with the additional stigma of the label of sexual offender. Their research on Canadian convicted sex offenders revealed the effects of this additional stigma on incarcerated men. These individuals faced both physical and verbal abuse, social isolation, and further victimization (Ricciardelli & Moir, 2013).

Critics of labelling theory argue that it is unable to articulate why some people are labelled and carry that stigma through life while others remain "secret deviants" (deviant but not labelled as such) (Siegel & McCormick, 2010). Labelling theory also fails to explain variances in crime rates across time and place.

FEMINIST THEORY

If we think back to our address of feminist theories in Chapter 3, relating to criminology, "first-wave" feminists (1800s through to early 1900s) were largely concerned with the reformation of property rights for women. Those of the "second wave" (1960s through the 1970s) identified widespread social norms (including the criminal law) as problematic for women. These feminists attempted to expose men's violence against and sexual control over women and argued that such violence needed to be addressed on a societal level rather than viewed as being the result of individual men's poor behaviour—that is, men's violence over women needed to be understood as a social issue (Kramar, 2011b). Second-wave feminists campaigned to "decriminalize abortion, reform rape law, police wife-battering and censor violent, degrading and dehumanizing pornography" (Kramar, 2011b, p. 117). In the 1990s, those of the third wave (uneasy with the second wave's treatment of the category of "woman" as a monolith) built upon the political action of feminists who preceded them. For example, they sought to understand how women of colour, being differentially positioned from white women, might then have different requirements or needs within a legal system than those that were currently being addressed.

Perceptions of Female Criminals
Otto Pollak (in his *The Criminality of Women*, 1961) argued that women criminals were actually worse criminals than men because their violations were harder to determine due to being primarily located in the domestic sphere, hidden from public view (Kramar, 2011b). Based on sexist assumptions, he also asserted that this masked nature of women's crime was linked to women's manipulative and devious natures. While Pollak did concede, to some extent, that women were oppressed by men, he used this assertion as a basis to argue that women's criminality was thus women's retribution against men (Kramar, 2011b). Pollak advanced the **chivalry hypothesis**, which asserted that agents of the criminal justice system (police, courts) afforded women and girls leniency when compared with the treatment of men and boys, based on chivalrous attitudes. This differential treatment, Pollak argued, is what accounted for women's lower crime rate.

Current research by Elizabeth Comack and Salena Brickey (2007, p. 1) contends that people often label women who commit violent acts as one of three distinct but interconnected constructs—"'victim,' 'mad,' and 'bad'"—but label these women without fully capturing their complex lives. Comack and Brickey (2007) detail how recent media attention, including Hollywood films, characterize violent women as "monsters" (p. 2). In Canada, specifically, Comack and Brickey (2007) trace the portrayal of Karla Homolka as "Canada's most notorious female offender" as being both "bad" and "mad" (p. 2). The effect, according to Comack and Brickey, is that women's violence is positioned as individual pathology. Taking a post-structural approach, they argue that such rigid categories are inadequate to explain the complexity of women's identities. Further, they argue that researchers need to understand women's violence within its social context—as such violence may be a consequence of living on the streets or engaging in sex work, for example. Neither of these instances is used to excuse particular behaviour but to enable us to see how choices are constrained by social conditions (Comack & Brickey, 2007).

chivalry hypothesis
The argument that women and girls accused of criminal activity are treated more leniently by law enforcement officials as a result of the latter's traditional, chivalrous attitude toward women.

 Watch

Women and Criminal Behaviour

❺ The Sociology of Law

The sociology of law is a subdiscipline of sociology as well as an approach within the field of legal studies. Sociologists who study law attempt to position laws, regulations, particular legal decisions, and the administration of criminal justice more generally into a social context. They might examine how law is socially constructed and the social development of legal institutions, as well as how law responds to social change. Sociologists study both the underpinnings and the influences of the legal process. Further, they analyze how the criminal justice system shapes our social values and behaviour (Burtch, 2003).

Interest in examining law from a sociological perspective increased after World War II. Sociologists looked at the inequalities that racialized groups faced and began to understand the law to be a relevant factor (Vago & Nelson, 2010). Although laws are meant to protect all citizens, sociologists recognized that racialized groups were not afforded the same protection as nonracialized individuals.

During the social unrest of the late 1960s, many sociologists working from a critical perspective began to study social conflict and societal inequities. Critical sociologists examined the gap between the ideals and the realities of the legal system, arguing that the law was not applied uniformly. At the same time, however, conservative sociologists defended the law, arguing that the legal system handled social conflicts appropriately (Vago & Nelson, 2010). The field of "law and society" developed from these debates (Vago & Nelson, 2010).

CANADIAN LAW

rule of law **The requirement that no person is above the law and state power should not be applied arbitrarily.**

Canada's legal institutions have been shaped by a number of principles adopted from Britain. One principle is that of the **rule of law**, meaning that no person, including monarchs, government officials, and police officers, is above the law, and that state power should not be arbitrarily applied (Yates, Yates, & Bain, 2000). The rule of law is meant to ensure that laws are shaped, managed, and implemented on the basis of acceptable procedures that promote fairness and equality (Goff, 2011).

> > >

Mohamed Junaid Babar testifies at the trial of Momin Khawaja in an Ottawa courtroom in June 2008 in this artist's sketch.

The Canadian Press/Tammy Hoy

The application of another adopted principle that critical theorists strongly criticize is that everyone is entitled to equal justice under the law. Our laws are meant to set out clear legal rules to be applied uniformly across society. But is this the case? Sociologists question whether the law is indeed fair and just or whether it is based on serving the interests of specific groups (as discussed next).

THEORIZING THE LAW

Just as there is no single theory that explains the causes of crime, there is no unified or comprehensive theory of the law. Historically, sociologists used three approaches to law: the *consensus view*, the *conflict view*, and the *interactionist view*.

The consensus view dominated criminological thought until the late 1960s. Proponents of the consensus perspective argue that the law is a neutral framework for sustaining social stability. From this perspective, formal mechanisms are viewed as necessary in order to create and preserve cooperation leading to the maintenance of order and stability (Vago & Nelson, 2010). Within this perspective, the defining of crime is actually a function or outcome of norms and morality and is both uniformly and fairly applied to all persons (Siegel & McCormick, 2010).

In contrast, the conflict view perceives society as a diverse collection of groups that are continuously in conflict (Siegel & McCormick, 2010; Vago & Nelson, 2010). Within this perspective, the law is understood as a tool that protects the "haves" (those "with") from the "have-nots" (those "without"). As a tool of the ruling class, the law protects the property interests of the powerful and also serves to suppress potential political threats to those in power (Vago & Nelson, 2010).

Finally, the interactionist view holds that crime and the law reflect the beliefs of people who force their definitions of right and wrong on the members of society (Siegel & McCormick, 2010). Moral crusaders attempt to influence the shaping of the legal process in ways that match their norms and values. Interactionists argue that only when acts viewed and marked as deviant are sanctioned do they become significant and potentially life-changing events (Siegel & McCormick, 2010).

While some sociologists studying law still adhere to the consensus, conflict, or interactionist perspectives, exciting contemporary theoretical approaches to law are now taking precedence. Most notably, the critical legal studies movement, feminist legal theory, and critical race theory have added to the ongoing debate.

Critical Legal Studies The critical legal studies movement focuses on the ambiguities and contradictions embedded in law. Law is contradictory and ambiguous in that it permits the context of a given case to control its outcome. Because the law is unable to cover all situations (a situation known as *indeterminacy*), judicial decisions are not isolated and "self-contained" decisions (Vago & Nelson, 2010, p. 48). Scholars working from this perspective contend that legal reasoning does not operate independently of the personal biases of police officers, lawyers, and judges. Critical scholars reject the notion that law can ever be value-free and stand outside political, economic, and social considerations (Vago & Nelson, 2010).

Critical legal studies has its roots in a Marxist tradition. These theorists argue that laws are not neutral (Vago & Nelson, 2010). Rather, laws exist as a legitimized and formal way to support and maintain the interests of specific classes and groups of people; laws are a constellation of beliefs and prejudices that help legitimize the status quo, including societal injustices (Vago & Nelson, 2010). To date, the most significant contribution of critical legal studies is its focus on the pervasive and insidious influence of politics on the legal system (Goodrich, 1993). Critical legal scholars argue that law does not stand outside of the system of power in society; rather, law is implicated in power.

An excellent example of critical legal scholarship is Anna Pratt and Sara Thompson's (2008) work on how race and racialized risk knowledge shape the front-line work of border control officers at a major Canadian land port of entry. Pratt and Thompson (2008) demonstrate how

Statues of Lady Justice can be found in many courtrooms. The scales she holds in one hand represent the weighing of a case between support and opposition. The double-sided sword in her other hand represents reason and justice, which can be wielded at any time. The blindfold represents the ideal of justice—that justice is blind and will be served regardless of a person's identity or position in society.

Jorgen Priewe/Alamy

the Canadian nation gets constructed as a "damsel in distress" that is in need of "constant vigilance against risky foreigners" (p. 622). Border officials draw on particular kinds of knowledge about race, ethnicity, social class, religion, and gender along with other signifiers, such as one's city of origin, the kind of car that one is driving, and the route one is travelling, in order to make assessments about the risk to Canada and its citizens when making decisions about who to allow entry into the country. While the practice of racial profiling is decried at a formal policy level, the front-line border officials do acknowledge that race absolutely enters into their decision making about who is a "risky" subject (Pratt & Thompson, 2008). As we can see from their research, though, just focusing on race obscures the multiple ways that "racialized risk" knowledge shapes the protectionist work of these border officers.

Feminist Legal Theory Feminist legal theory (also known as *feminist jurisprudence*) emerged out of the mass political and social movements that were organized in the late 1960s around equality issues. Feminist legal theory holds that the law is a key instrument in women's historical subordination. Feminists interested in the law look at how it plays a role in maintaining women's inferior status; such feminists are committed to altering women's status by reworking how law approaches gender.

Feminist legal scholars argue that despite significant gains (such as access to abortion, recognition of marital sexual assault, and the elimination of legislation that overtly differentiates on the basis of gender), women in Western societies continue to be disadvantaged by masculinist laws (Vago, 2009). For example, feminist legal scholars argue that a masculinist legal culture contributes to trivializing or dismissing women's claims about sexual harassment and sexual assault (Vago & Nelson, 2010). Some feminists are concerned that a conventional approach to law reform—in which women are simply being added into existing legal consideration (also known as the "add women and stir approach")—is not a strong enough approach to law reform (Burchard, 2009; Smart, 1989). Rather, some feminist scholars would like to see a much more fundamental reconsideration and reorganization of legal values and principles to rid the criminal justice system of its deeply embedded sexism (White & Haines, 2009). For example, in research on judicial decision-making in the English and Welsh legal system, Elvin (2010) documents that appellate judges continued to use sexual stereotypes and also failed to address the problematic use of such stereotypes on the part of trial judges.

Critical Race Theory Critical race theory focuses on issues of oppression and discrimination and questions the absence of diversity in the legal profession (Johnson, 1997). Sociologists have long held that race profoundly affects the lives of individuals as well as the development and organization of social institutions. Critical race theorists argue that racism is an embedded feature of modern society and one that is impossible to eliminate; the goal, then, is to "struggle to countervail racism" (Vago, 2009, p. 67). Critical race theorists explore the links between race and law, particularly the ways in which race and law are *mutually constitutive* (that is, because racism is embedded in society, the development of laws will reflect such racism).

One topic of interest for critical race theorists is the practice of racial profiling by police in both Canada and the United States. For example, in her book *Racial Profiling: Research, Racism and Resistance*, Karen Glover (2009) examines such racial profiling in the United States. Glover argues that racialized stops and searches are ongoing processes that render particular groups of people as second-class citizens with inferior rights. Glover (2009) further argues that these traffic stops and the connection often made between racialized minorities and criminality challenge the idea that the law is fair and just. Canadian research demonstrates that blacks in Canada view racial profiling as a significant problem, while whites and Asians in Canada understand racial profiling as an effective tool for law enforcement (Wortley & Owusu-Bempah, 2011).

A Toronto-based study found that African-Canadian students are four times more likely to be pulled over by the police than white students in the same location (COP, 2008). Further, more than 50 percent of blacks without any type of police record reported being searched by police in the previous two years (COP, 2008). A study of more than 10 000 arrest records found that once arrested, "Blacks were twice as likely as Whites to be held over night for a bail hearing [and were] much more likely to be charged for offences that could only be detected *after* being pulled over in traffic by police" (COP, 2008).

While consensus approaches embrace the view that laws are used in society for the purpose of maintaining social cohesion, and conflict approaches focus on the use of the law to uphold the power of the elite, critical legal studies, feminist legal theory, and critical race theory all claim that the law heavily privileges the wealthy and powerful (Vago & Nelson, 2010). Such theoretical approaches understand that the law is not class-, gender-, or race-neutral. Although these approaches differ substantially from one another, all attempt to expose how laws, regulations, specific legal cases, and the administration of criminal justice are embedded in a complex web of social relations.

Crime, Risk, and Regulation in Canada

So far, we have discussed how criminologists have theorized criminality and the law. We now consider the current criminal climate in Canada. Where does our knowledge of crime come from? Is crime really as pervasive as we assume it to be? Canada, like most developed countries, has created an elaborate system to ensure that we live in a safe society. In addition to the criminal justice system, discursive practices are used to control the population and to prevent deviant or criminal behaviour. This section discusses how victims of crime have been constructed through the media and other agents of socialization, as well as how certain groups or individuals are morally regulated.

"AT RISK" FOR CRIME?

Media are governed by a code of conduct that requires them to report the news accurately. Many people assume that this requirement means that media constitute reliable sources of information (Winterdyk, 2006). This code of conduct affects our knowledge of crime since much of what we know about crime comes from media portrayals, whether through the Internet, television, radio, newspapers, or magazines.

The media actively construct our sense of who is "at risk" of victimization as well as of who is at risk of becoming a criminal. People consistently rely on media outlets for crime statistics, making them influential in people's perceptions of potential victimization. Media are able to create **moral panic**—a group's reaction based on the false, distorted, or exaggerated perception that some group or some individual or collective behaviour threatens the well-being of society—when they sensationalize images of crime (White & Haines, 2009). In Canada we saw a moral panic emerge around the "nasty girl" and the supposed trend of rampant "girl violence" after the well-publicized murder of Reena Virk by a group of mainly female teenagers in Victoria, British Columbia, in 1997 (Barron & Lacombe, 2005). However, the reality is that the most common types of crime, such as property crimes, receive little to no media attention, whereas violent crimes, which are relatively uncommon, receive greater coverage (White & Haines, 2009).

Indeed, media convey horrific images and stories that instill fear for our own safety and the safety of those dear to us. If you speak with your Canadian-born parents or grandparents about crime and safety, you will surely hear a version of the same story: "It wasn't like this in the old days; it was safe to keep your doors unlocked. Kids could play outside without a parent having to worry that someone was going to abduct them." Yet despite the widespread public belief that crime is "out of control," the Canadian Centre for Justice Statistics (2006) reports that the national crime rate, defined as the total number of Criminal Code incidents (excluding traffic and drug offences) divided by the population, dropped by 3 percent in 2006 and by another 5 percent by 2008 (Statistics Canada, 2010h).

moral panic The reaction of a group based on the false, distorted, or exaggerated perception that some group or behaviour threatens the well-being of society.

FIGURE 14.2

Police-Reported Crime Severity Indexes, 2001–2011

Source: Chart 2, Police-reported crime severity indexes, 2001 to 2011. Police-reported crime statistics in Canada, 2011 By Shannon Brennan. Statistics Canada catalogue 85-002-x.

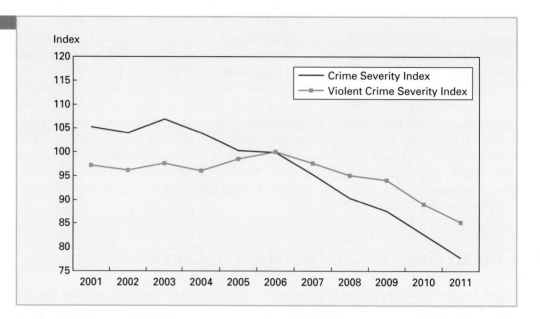

In fact, since 1991 the crime rate has significantly decreased, putting the 2011 crime rate at its lowest level in more than 25 years. We have also seen a slight decline in violent crime in Canada; however, this decline is at a slower rate than the overall drop in crime. Canada's Crime Severity Index (CSI), which measures the seriousness of crimes reported to police, dropped 6 percent in 2011, down 26 percent from its measure in 2001 (see Figure 14.2) (Brennan, 2012). The areas in Canada with the highest CSI values are the Northwest Territories and Nunavut, and provinces with the highest values are Saskatchewan and Manitoba. The provinces with the lowest CSI values are Ontario, New Brunswick, and Prince Edward Island (see Figure 14.3) (Brennan, 2012). The homicide rate in Canada experienced a slight increase in 2011, with 598 homicides reported in 2011—an increase of 44 over the previous year (Brennan, 2012). Youth crime also appears to be declining in terms of level of seriousness in Canada (Carrington, 2013). We should note that these statistics are based only on reported crimes entered into the Uniform Crime Reporting System. As such, these statistics are limited as they do not account for never-reported offences.

FIGURE 14.3

Police-Reported Crime Severity Indexes, by Province and Territory, 2011

Source: Chart 3, Police-reported Crime Severity Index, by province and territory, 2011. Police-reported crime statistics in Canada, 2011 By Shannon Brennan. Statistics Canada catalogue 85-002.

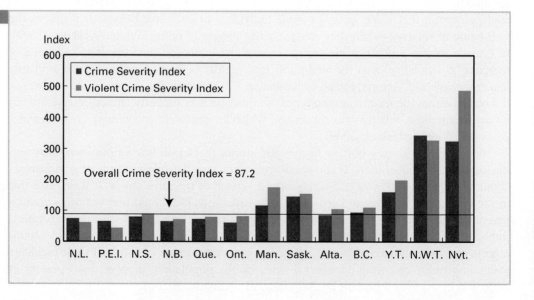

Masterfile

< < <

There is a greater fear of victimization of crime among women than men—despite the statistical reality that men are more often victims of crime than women.

Women's Fear of Crime Government-sponsored national victimization studies in several countries consistently continue to demonstrate that fear of violent crimes is significantly higher than the chance of actually becoming the victim of a violent crime, especially among women (Fitzgerald, 2008; Keane, 1998; Smith, 1988). Fear of crime is measured by one's generalized feeling of vulnerability or a perception of safety in one's neighbourhood (how one might feel walking alone at night in her/his neighbourhood), as well as a more specific fear of actually becoming a victim (Keane, 1998). Regardless of whether the fear is warranted, being fearful of becoming a victim can lead some people to avoid outings and interactions with the potential of negatively affecting one's life satisfaction (Kohm et al., 2012). In 2009, Statistics Canada conducted its fifth General Social Survey (GSS) on victimization, asking Canadians aged 15 years and older about their experiences as victims of crime, about their fear and perceptions of crime, and about the criminal justice system. Not surprisingly, feelings of anxiety about being victimized while waiting for or taking public transportation at night were more prevalent among women than men. Further, women expressed higher levels of fear compared with men when home alone at night (Statistics Canada, 2010h). However, men are more likely than women to be the victims of violent crime perpetrated by strangers. As discussed in Chapter 11, women continue to be more likely to be victimized by the intimate men in their lives than by a stranger lurking in the bushes.

Public Safety Canada reports that people's fear of criminal victimization remains relatively steady. In urban spaces, 18 percent of Canadians aged 15 and older report that they are fearful of crime when they are walking by themselves after dark (Fitzgerald, 2008). However, women are more likely than men to report being fearful (3.6 times higher than men) (Fitzgerald, 2008). Fear of crime also varies with geographical location, with the lowest levels of fear occurring in the Atlantic provinces (14 percent) and the highest levels in British Columbia (39 percent) (Roberts, 2001).

Women's increased fear of victimization represents a **fear-gender paradox** (Keane, 1998). Despite men's significantly higher risk of victimization, women consistently report higher levels of fear of victimization. Fear of victimization is also higher among those with the lowest income levels and educational attainment, and those in the eldest age groups (Fitzgerald, 2008).

fear-gender paradox
The phenomenon whereby women experience higher rates of fear of being victimized even though men are more likely to be victims of crime.

> > >

Gender often plays a role in the enactment of laws. Take, for example, efforts to exclude street people such as "squeegee kids" from public spaces in Toronto. Gendered notions of fear and victimization, particularly women's supposed need to be protected, were used as justification by politicians during the legislative debates about the *Safe Streets Act*.

Courtesy of Eye Steel Film

Many scholars have documented the processes that underlie our popular conceptions of who is "at risk." Feminist scholars in particular have challenged the idea that "risk" is a neutral category (Chan & Rigakos, 2002). Dominant images of criminals as poor, racialized men and images of victims as white, middle-class women serve to perpetuate our notions of who ought to be legitimately concerned about becoming a victim of crime and by whom (Chan & Rigakos, 2002).

There are significant consequences of women's fear of crime (Scott, 2003). Several policies have been enacted in the name of addressing women's safety. For example, consider the legislative debates that took place in relation to the *Safe Streets Act* in 2000. Gender was a salient feature of those debates, as women's fears of victimization, coupled with concerns for women's safety, were deployed as part of a law-and-order agenda aimed at addressing "visible poverty in urban spaces"—that is, "squeegee kids" in Toronto (Glasbeek, 2006a, p. 55). Homeless people were constructed as "dangerous or disorderly" via a public safety discourse (Chesnay, Bellot, & Sylvestre, 2013). Analyzing media articles and legislative debates, Glasbeek (2006a) demonstrates the ways in which fear for women's safety was used to justify the enactment of a "coercive and punitive piece of legislation that aimed to exclude street people from the public" (p. 75).

Many feminists argue that these representations of women as being in need of protection (as damsels in distress) are used to increase both women's fear of public spaces and their dependency on "protective" men (Chan & Rigakos, 2002; Glasbeek, 2006a). Further, by focusing on risk, responsibility shifts from the state protecting the citizenry to individuals being responsible for avoiding risk and risky situations. Whether fear stems from actual crime or from perceptions of risk, such a neoliberal approach to crime encourages individuals to avoid risk-taking behaviours and to be individually proactive in crime prevention (Garland, 1996). The threat of becoming a victim shifts responsibility to individuals, and encourages women especially to engage in "safe-keeping" acts that include monitoring how they dress and avoiding certain public spaces (Campbell, 2005). This focus on risk aversion "overemphasizes women's risks in the public sphere, and dangerously underestimates women's risks in the private sphere" (Glasbeek, 2006a, p. 61).

Contemporary risk discourses also act as a form of moral regulation (Glasbeek 2006a; Hunt, 2003). "Risk is not just a condition to be encountered, avoided or managed but is itself, also, productive of moralized subjectivities—that is, the 'good' citizen who avoids 'risky' behaviours" (Glasbeek, 2006a, p. 60). It is to moral regulation that we now turn.

> > > Thinking Sociologically

As a woman, do you think about where you are willing to go at night, and how you are willing to get there? As a man, do you think about this? Does fear of victimization affect how you see the world and how you act in it?

public order crimes (victimless crimes)
Crimes such as prostitution, gambling, and pornography that are believed to run contrary to moral principles.

MORAL REGULATION

Within the field of criminology, certain acts are often referred to as **public order crimes,** or **victimless crimes**. They are understood as victimless since the harm is incurred by the perpetrators themselves (Vago & Nelson, 2010). These acts are considered to be crimes on the basis of societal moral principles, and include such things as prostitution, gambling, pornography, euthanasia, and substance abuse (Vago & Nelson, 2010). The primary goal of the law in this context is to protect society by legislating behaviours that are considered immoral, not in the public's interest, and socially harmful; yet, in relation to these crimes, there is much debate about who gets to decide what is considered morally acceptable.

The concept of **moral regulation** is used to describe how some behaviours become constituted as immoral and are thereby regulated (Glasbeek, 2006b). Moral regulation scholars ask why particular groups of people and their behaviours deserve public scrutiny, interference, and action (Glasbeek, 2006b). Let us begin with a look at history.

moral regulation
The constitution of certain behaviours as immoral and thereby requiring public regulation.

The Social Purity Movement Beginning in the late nineteenth century, the social purity movement, "along with temperance and Sunday observance, helped to constitute a powerful if informal collation for the moral regeneration of the state, civil society, the family, and the individual" (Valverde, 2006, p. 119). This movement included various actors who were interested in raising "the moral tone" of Canada—included were such people as religious devotees, doctors, and teachers (Valverde, 2006, p. 119). Sexual morality (sexual purity) was the movement's primary aim and those in the movement created pamphlets and books on the topic of the need for sexual morality, including abstinence (Sethna, 2010; Valverde, 2006). Social purists also focused on issues of poverty, criminality, and vices such as alcohol and drugs, even calling for prohibition of alcohol (Sethna, 2010; Valverde, 2006).

While there was certainly a focus on criminals and those living in poverty, others also found themselves to be under scrutiny and in need of "character building," especially youth: "an individual without character . . . was a miniature mob: disorganized, immoral and unhealthy, as well as an inefficient member of the collectivity" (Valverde, 2006, p. 128). Instead of solely supplying charity to those who had fallen, the social purity movement focused on "training the poor in habits of thrift, punctuality and hygiene" (Valverde, 2006, p. 121).

Welfare Recipients The welfare recipient represents one of the most poignant examples of moral regulatory practices. While attempting to meet the economic needs of lone parents, for example, social assistance regulations historically attempted to also meet the moral needs of society. In *"No Car, No Radio, No Liquor Permit": The Moral Regulation of*

< < <

From the 1800s to early 1900s, Canada experienced a social purity movement against vices such as sex, crime, and drugs.

Glenbow Archives/NA-1639-1

Single Mothers in Ontario, 1920–1997, Margaret Little (1998) demonstrated how social assistance policies are premised on and promote traditional (and conservative) notions of masculinity, femininity, and morality. Through constant surveillance, lone mothers' lives are scrutinized to ensure they are deserving (both morally and economically) of publicly funded financial aid.

In the early years of social assistance, eligibility was based primarily on the premature death of a woman's husband. However, over time, other categories of eligibility surfaced: unwed and deserted mothers. The forms of moral regulation also shifted with time. In the early years, surprise home visits were a tool that caseworkers used to ensure that the women were keeping clean homes that were free of alcohol and that their children were also clean (Little, 1998; Valverde, 2006). Over time, though, the terrain of moral scrutiny shifted to investigations about sex, sexuality, welfare fraud, and employment (Little, 1998).

The 1990s witnessed a distinct shift whereby a nexus was formed, joining poverty, welfare, and crime. In 1995, the Canadian Assistance Plan was replaced with the Canadian Health and Social Transfer program. Many researchers document the ways in which rhetoric constructing welfare recipients as "lazy" and "criminals" was used to implement coercive state policies (Chunn & Gavigan, 2006; Evans & Swift, 2000; Little, 2003; Mosher, 2000; Swift & Birmingham, 2000). The state, primarily concerned with "welfare cheats," aimed attacks at the poor, at women, and at racialized minorities. In Ontario, there were significant funding cuts to social assistance benefits, a broader definition of a spouse, legislated changes producing a particular focus on "work," compulsory drug testing, anonymous "snitch" telephone lines, and "zero tolerance" for those found guilty of welfare fraud (Chunn & Gavigan, 2006; Little & Morrison, 2001; Morrison, 1998). "Welfare fraud became welfare *as* fraud" (Chunn & Gavigan, 2006, p. 329).

With slashed government budgets in the 1990s, lone mothers living on welfare experienced an incredible amount of increased state scrutiny of their lives (Little, 1998). While the state maintains that such scrutiny is necessary for fiduciary financial reasons, it nonetheless has moral implications.

The state is reluctant to financially support lone mothers when fathers are theoretically available to provide such support—the state would rather individual families take care of their own financial needs. As a result, numerous strategies were created to identify and track down potential breadwinning men. All lone mothers must complete a questionnaire, introduced in 1992, before they are determined eligible for social assistance payments. While the intent of the questionnaire is not explicitly stated, its purpose is to ascertain whether the prospective social assistance recipient is involved in a sexual relationship with anyone who is living under the same roof as her or who occasionally stays with her (Little, 2001). Caseworkers have actually checked the snow for tire tracks, read notes left on fridges, and searched toiletries for razors and shaving cream, all in their effort to determine whether a man is present in the home (Little, 2001). Such scrutiny of women's lives constructs all sexual relationships as ones that ought to be breadwinning relationships—if a woman is on social assistance, any man in her life must financially support her and her children.

Moral investigation of single mothers on welfare has intensified in the past decade.

✱─⌐Explore

We Need to Pay for
Social Services

> > >

The Elizabeth Fry society actively works to reduce the number of women being criminalized and incarcerated in Canada.

women
don't
belong
in cages

80% of imprisoned women are inside for poverty related offences.

90% of Aboriginal and 82% of all women in prison are survivors of incest, rape or physical assault.

The number of women in prison increased 200% in the past 15 years.

prisons are the real crime

Courtesy of Canadian Association of Elizabeth Fry Societies www.elizabethfry.ca

This scrutiny is carried out not only by the state and its agents but also by citizens who are encouraged as "paid workers" (and, hence, responsible citizens) to actively scrutinize welfare recipients and report any and all suspected cases of welfare "fraud" (Little & Morrison, 2001). Such a constant fear of scrutiny with the potential to lead to losing one's assistance leads women to "self-censor" their activities (Chunn & Gavigan, 2006, p. 345). This breed of moral scrutinizer is widespread in low-income housing projects and small communities (Little, 2006). Social assistance policies, and the practices that flow from these policies, are intrusive and morally based (Little, 2006). Individual caseworkers enjoy a good degree of freedom in the way that they assess who is "deserving" or "undeserving" of assistance: "These regulations and the relationship between the regulator and the regulated help to reinforce dominant race, class, and gender interests in society at large" (Little, 2006, p. 230).

Sex and Sexual Relationships Another pervasive area of moral regulation in our society is sex and sexual relationships. Prostitution and homosexuality are two areas in which sexual morality and crime are linked. While we live in a society in which sexual norms have changed quite drastically since the 1950s, sexual behaviour between consenting adults is still criminalized at times, as in the case of prostitution. In a 2012 Canadian study, women were more likely than men to support the criminalization of prostitution (Morton, Klein, & Gorzalka, 2012).

Focusing on the moral regulation of homosexuals through Canada's anti-homosexual national security campaign in the 1950s and 1960s, Gary Kinsman (2004) argues that homosexuals were constructed as having "immoral," "risky," and "deviant" sexualities. During this period, thousands of homosexuals and suspected homosexuals lost their jobs in the public service and military as a result of their sexuality or suspected sexuality (Kinsman, 2004). "Sexual deviance" was viewed as a threat to the stability of family life and was thus constructed as a threat to national security. As a result, social policing of sexuality focused on the regulation of sexualities through the Criminal Code. Since homosexuality was considered immoral, those who engaged in homosexual acts were constructed as "untrustworthy" and as "security risks" (Kinsman, 2004). This rhetoric was then used to legally eliminate the jobs of any known or suspected homosexuals.

Kinsman (2004) argues that the construction of homosexuality as both a moral and political problem has been made possible by the construction of homosexuals as "different," "other," and "abnormal." Drawing on the work of Foucault, Kinsman asserts that a key strategy of disciplinary power is normalization. As discussed in Chapter 3, Foucault used the term *normalization* to represent how certain behaviours, for example, get constructed as normal. These idealized norms are then reinforced by truth claims of doctors, psychiatrists, and other "experts" (Kinsman, 2004). Based on such norms of behaviour, people are either rewarded or punished for conforming to or deviating from the ideal. In North American society, heterosexuality is normalized.

Crime Victims Moral regulation also pervades our perceptions of crime victims. For female victims of crime, entrenched notions of proper or respectable femininity contribute to our understanding of who is a "worthy" victim, deserving of sympathy. Take, for example, the case of Paul Bernardo and Karla Homolka in St. Catharines, Ontario. When Bernardo and Homolka's murder victims, Kristen French and Leslie Mahaffy, went missing, there were search parties, intensive police activity, national media attention, and appeals for the safe return of these two young white girls. School photographs of the girls accompanied the media coverage. In contrast to this sense of urgency, the women missing from Vancouver's Downtown Eastside remained faceless and silent, some for as long as two decades. One must question how it is possible that 61 women were missing from one geographic location, yet the story received no media coverage for such a long time. Why are there such differences in the levels of attention given to these victims?

Focusing on five years (2001 to 2006) of newspaper coverage of the missing Vancouver women, Jiwani and Young (2006) demonstrate how hegemonic discourses of Aboriginality,

∨
∨
∨

Robert Pickton has been convicted of killing several Canadian sex-trade-workers. The media's treatment of this case made it easy for the general public to view his crimes as ones committed by a "pathological" individual rather than looking at his actions from a much wider social framework of men's violence against women.

Global BC

drug addiction, and prostitution combined with tropes of geographic morality (that is, particular areas associated with degeneracy) to frame the media coverage of the case. While some stories appeared sympathetic, most underscored stereotypical portrayals of drug-addicted Aboriginal prostitutes. Police described the women as itinerant workers, constantly moving from one location to the next, thus making them responsible for their own disappearances or murders (Jiwani & Young, 2006). When the missing women did receive media attention, police mug shots were used, thus reinforcing the women's association with criminality.

Additionally, when news first broke about the arrest of Paul Bernardo and followed with details of Karla Homolka's role in the heinous crimes, the couple was portrayed as "Ken and Barbie," a seemingly perfect pairing that appeared to fit neatly dominant constructions of masculinity and femininity. In contrast, Robert Pickton's arrest brought forward a photograph of him with "wild, stringy hair and a blank stare" (Jiwani & Young 2006, p. 905). The photo suggested an "aberrant masculinity," making it easy for the public to believe that "only deviant males commit such heinous sexual acts" (Jiwani & Young, 2006, p. 905). In this way, Pickton's crimes were viewed as the acts of a "sick" or "pathological" individual rather than seen within a larger framework of the prevalence of men's violence against women (Jiwani & Young, 2006, p. 911).

Portraying some women as unfortunate victims deserving of much sympathy and other women as somehow culpable in their own victimization, next to depictions of women offenders as "pathological," reinforces dominant hegemonic values. In light of these glaring discrepancies, Jiwani and Young (2006) call for the recognition that women are first and foremost "human beings whose material conditions are determined by interlocking legacies of colonialism and a racialized and sexualized economy of representations that privileges some women over others" (p. 912).

Summary

❶ Whereas *crime* is defined as those behaviours that require legal control and social intervention, *deviance* involves actions that depart from social norms and may or may not be illegal.

❷ Classical criminology's basic tenets are as follows: (1) crime is a rational choice; (2) if criminal solutions entail less work for greater payoff than legal ones, they are seen as more attractive; (3) fear of punishment can control people's choices; and (4) society can better control criminal behaviour if it is met with measured severity, certainty of punishment, and swiftness of justice.

❸ Historically, biological approaches posited that some individuals were born to crime as a result of congenital factors, including body type.

❹ Functionalists hold that the structure of society can produce social pressures that result in criminal behaviour; conflict theorists view crime as the outcome of class struggle and focus on how power relationships shape criminal law; symbolic interactionists view criminal behaviour as arising through shared experiences and perceptions; and feminist theorists are concerned with issues of power and view patriarchy as the underlying condition behind certain crimes.

❺ The three traditional sociological approaches to theorizing law are the consensus view, the conflict view, and the interactionist view. Contemporary theoretical approaches include critical legal studies, feminist legal theory, and critical race theory.

6 Today's media contribute to the phenomenon whereby fear of violent crime is greater than the chance of actually becoming a victim. Public order crimes are those considered by the state as immoral. Moral regulation through the law focuses on, for example, social assistance recipients and, in the past, sexuality laws. Moral regulation also affects the perception of crime victims.

Key Terms

biological determinism 367
chivalry hypothesis 373
crime 363
criminogenic environment 370
criminology 363
deviance 363
differential association theory 372
fear-gender paradox 379

illegitimate opportunity theory 369
labelling theory 372
moral entrepreneur 365
moral panic 377
moral regulation 381
public order crimes (victimless crimes) 380
rule of law 374
social norms 363
strain theory 369

Reviewing the Concepts

1. Review the theoretical perspectives outlined in the chapter. Which perspective best explains crime to you? Why?

2. How is the state (and other social organizations) implicated in processes that create and perpetuate moral regulation?

3. What is the fear-gender paradox? How might this negatively affect women's lives?

Applying Your Sociological Imagination

1. What are the main images of crime and criminals in popular television shows? What are the effects of such constructions of crime and criminals? Does popular culture contribute to crime and deviance? If so, how?

2. How does critical race theory challenge the neutrality of law?

3. Can you think of something you have done that was considered deviant in the past but no longer would be? Or something that you did that was a conforming behaviour in the past but would now be considered deviant? Can you account for the societal change in attitude?

MySocLab

Visit MySocLab to access a variety of online resources that will help you prepare for tests and apply your knowledge.

Saeed Khan/AFP/Getty Images

15 Health, Aging, and Disabilities

Do you remember what you wanted for your high school graduation gift? A car? A new suit? Well, today, more and more young women are not thinking about getting a new car for graduation, but rather, new breasts—and, their parents are paying for them (Fowler & Moore, 2012, p. 109). In the United States, close to 307 000 breast augmentation surgeries are performed every year, a 45 percent increase between 2000 and 2011 (ASPS, 2012). In Canada, some estimate there are around 30 000 breast augmentation surgeries per year (Wagner, 2010) and the numbers are increasing. Make no mistake, while breast augmentation surgeries are relatively commonplace, they are still surgical procedures that involve risk. Inserting breast implants can lead to complications associated with general anesthesia, infection, haematoma, hemorrhage, thrombosis, skin necrosis, delayed wound healing, and the need for additional surgeries (US Food and Drug Administration, 2013). Further, after the implants are in place, they may need to be repaired or replaced, grow hard to the touch, rupture or leak, become painful and/or cause the loss of sensation around the nipple and breast (US Food and Drug Administration, 2013).

Plastic surgery in general, and breast augmentation surgery in particular, is a fascinating and dynamic area of research (see Adams, 2010; Elliott, 2009; Heyes, 2009). Plastic surgery is becoming a global phenomenon where people are altering their bodies to gain social acceptance (Elliott, 2009; Mackie & Stevens, 2009, Pitts-Taylor, 2009; 2007). The desire to change a perfectly healthy body is the result of many social dynamics. For example, should we be surprised that women make up 91 percent of all cosmetic surgeries? (ASPS, 2010). However, men are also increasingly drawn to cosmetic surgery, and recently their participation rates are rising sharply (Atkinson, 2011, p. 112). As a sociologist, what social forces do you feel help explain why so many people are attracted to cosmetic surgery?

LEARNING OBJECTIVES

By the end of this chapter, students will be able to

① Discuss how health is defined and review how it is influenced by income level, minority status, and gender.

② Outline the defining features of Canada's health care system and review some of the challenges it faces today.

③ Discuss issues facing seniors today, including financial support, victimization, the need for long-term care, and global policies relating to euthanasia.

④ Outline the nature and extent of disabilities in Canada, including mental illness and mood disorders.

⑤ Review the discrimination faced by people with disabilities, particularly as it relates to the workplace.

⑥ Explain the principal sociological approaches to health, aging, and disabilities, respectively.

① What Is Health?

The World Health Organization (WHO) defines **health** as a "state of complete physical, mental and social well-being and not merely the absence of disease or infirmity" (World Health Organization, 2014). This definition suggests that health is the result of a complex interaction between physical, mental, and social factors (Creatore et al., 2010; Dahrouge et al., 2010).

Sociologists use various measures to determine a population's health. The most common measure is to assess how long the average citizen will live in a given society. **Life expectancy** represents the average lifespan of a newborn, and is an indicator of the overall health of a country. Life expectancy rates can fall because of famine, war, disease, and overall poor health, and can rise when health and welfare programs are initiated. As a rule, the higher the life expectancy, the healthier is a given population. Life expectancy rates for Canadians are generally high, with women, on average, outliving men. Between 1920 and 2009, average life expectancy at birth rose substantially in Canada, from 58.8 to 78.8 years for males and from 60.6 to 83.3 years for females (Statistics Canada, 2012c). In 1979, women were expected to live 7.4 years longer than men. This difference has narrowed over time and was 4.5 years in 2009 (Employment and Social Development Canada, 2014). Figure 15.1 shows that the gap in life expectancy at birth between males and females has changed over time. The gap between the sexes is partly related to differences in lifestyle, such as men's greater propensity to risk-taking behaviours that could result in injury or death.

health A state of complete physical, mental, and social well-being.

life expectancy The average lifespan of a newborn.

Life Expectancy at
Birth, by Gender,
1979–2009

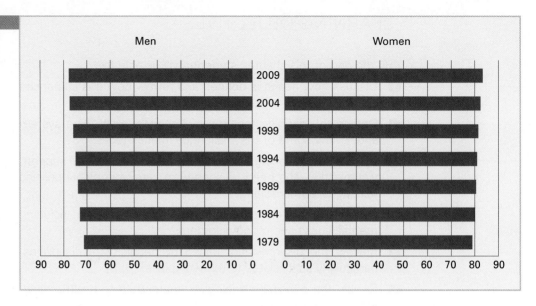

SOCIAL DETERMINANTS OF HEALTH

social determinants of
health **The conditions
in which people are
born, grow, and live.**

Sociologists refer to the diverse interactions between health and social factors (e.g., income, minority status, gender) as the **social determinants of health** (Johnson et al., 2008).

The social determinants of health are the conditions in which people are born, grow, live, work, and age, including the health care system. These conditions are influenced by a society's distribution of wealth, power, and social resources (Wanless, Mitchell, & Wister, 2010). The social determinants of health are largely responsible for health inequities—the unfair and avoidable differences in health status seen within and between countries (WHO, 2010b). The conditions we will focus on are income inequality, minority status, and gender.

INCOME INEQUALITY AND HEALTH

Income and social position have long been known to influence an individual's health (Babones, 2008; Gupta & Ross, 2010; Vafaei, Rosenberg, & Pickett, 2010). Data demonstrate that the higher one's social standing, economic status, and income are, the better overall one's health is. Therefore, all other factors being equal, the wealthier one is the healthier they will be (Public Health Agency of Canada, 2013). This is good news if you are lucky enough to be born into a family with money, but what if you are not so lucky?

Of Canadians who live in the lowest income bracket, only 47 percent rate their health as very good or excellent, while more than 70 percent of Canadians in the highest income bracket rate their health as very good or excellent (Public Health Agency of Canada, 2013). In spite of this, in a 25-year review (1978–2003) of health care utilization in Canada, Curtis and MacMinn (2008) found that people in Canada with lower socioeconomic status (SES) were less likely to visit a physician compared to others, and that this trend was stable over time (Public Health Agency of Canada, 2013).

Other research has found that people on social assistance were far more likely to be ill than people who were not. Canada's poor have significantly higher rates of poor health and chronic conditions on 38 of 39 health measures, with rates as much as 7.2 times more than those of the nonpoor group (Wilson, 2009). Wilson (2009) found that people on social assistance have higher rates of diabetes, heart disease, chronic bronchitis, arthritis and rheumatism, mood disorders and anxiety disorders. Additionally, Canadians living in low-income neighbourhoods have higher rates of hypertension, diabetes, smoking, and other cardiac risk factors (CIHI, 2010a); while children in low-income areas are more likely to be obese (Statistics Canada, 2008p). So perhaps it follows that Canadians living in the least-affluent neighbourhoods are more likely to have a heart attack than those in more-affluent areas, according to the Canadian Institute for Health Information (CIHI, 2010a). People who are poor are also more likely to hospitalized for injuries (CIHI, 2010b).

In Canada, individuals who live in households with combined incomes of less than $20 000 are almost three times more likely to experience self-reported poor health than are people with the highest incomes. A study published in the *International Journal of Behavioral Medicine* (2007) investigated the relationship between income and self-rated health over a two-year period and what role, if any, stressors (e.g., problems at work, financial pressures) have in helping to explain the relationship. The report found that, compared with those in the highest income group, people in the lowest and second-lowest income groups had significantly higher odds of experiencing a decline in health. The study concluded that a small but important portion of the relationship between lower income and the decline in self-rated health was associated with these stressors (Statistics Canada, 2007f).

MINORITY STATUS AND HEALTH

Life expectancy is also related to minority status. For example, a gap of six years has been found to exist between the life expectancies of Aboriginal people and the rest of the Canadian population (Frideres, 2002, p. 155; King, 2010). Figure 15.2 shows that men and women in all three Aboriginal groups (Indian, Métis, and Inuit) have lower life expectancy at birth than the total Canadian population (Statistics Canada, 2010i).

The social factors that help to explain these differences include Aboriginal people's level of poverty (Garner, Carrière, & Sanmartin, 2010), access to health care facilities, and diet. Cultural factors also play a role; according to Frideres (2002), while many Aboriginal people use the health care system, some prefer traditional healing techniques and others report that they experience negative stereotyping when dealing with some

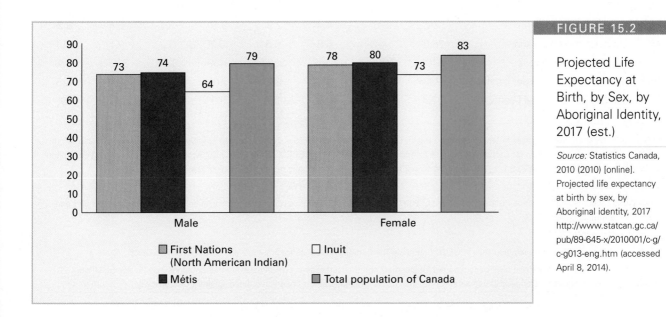

FIGURE 15.2

Projected Life Expectancy at Birth, by Sex, by Aboriginal Identity, 2017 (est.)

Source: Statistics Canada, 2010 (2010) [online]. Projected life expectancy at birth by sex, by Aboriginal identity, 2017 http://www.statcan.gc.ca/pub/89-645-x/2010001/c-g/c-g013-eng.htm (accessed April 8, 2014).

health care professionals. However, Frideres (2002, p. 162) also notes that over time, Aboriginal peoples have been experiencing a better quality of life, particularly in the area of health.

While the health trends for Aboriginal peoples show some signs of improvement, the same cannot be said for some other members of Canadian society. In particular, immigrant Canadians—especially those who have lived in Canada for less than 10 years—often report health disadvantages compared to nonimmigrant Canadians, and these disadvantages are magnified by age, poverty, and social isolation (Kobayashi & Prus, 2010). While some researchers point to the so-called "healthy immigrant" effect, in which new immigrants to Canada report higher levels of health than their Canadian-born counterparts, the effect all but disappears when researchers controlled for other factors (Kobayashi & Prus, 2010).

Table 15.1 compares key health care statistics for a number of countries. As you can see, Canada compares fairly well on a number of criteria (e.g., life expectancy, number of adults who smoke, per capita health spending) but falls behind on some others (e.g., obesity rate, number of MRI machines per million persons). Note how much the United States spends

TABLE 15.1 International Comparisons of Key Health Care Statistics*

Variable	United States	Australia	Belgium	Canada	Denmark	France	Germany	Japan
Infant mortality per 1000 births (2004)	6.8[†]	5	3.7	5.3[†]	4.4	3.6	3.9	2.8
Life expectancy at birth (2004)	77.8[†]	80.9	79.4[†]	80.2[†]	77.9	80.3	79	82
Population age >65 y (2007), %‡	12.5	13.1	17.4	13.3	15.2	16.4	19.4	20.0
Obesity rate	32.2[†]	20.4[†]	12.7[†]	18	11.4	9.5[†]	13.6	3[†]
Adult smoking rate	16.9	17.7[†]	20	17.3	26[†]	23[†]	24.3§	26.3 (2006)
Practicing physicians per 1000 persons	2.4	2.7[†]	4	2.2[†]	3.6	3.4	3.4[†]	2
Generalists of practicing physicians (2000), %¶	43.6	51.9	NA	47.5	19.1**	48.8	32.7	NA
Inpatient beds per 1000 persons	2.7	3.6[†]	4.4	2.9[†]	3.1[†]	3.7	6.4	8.2
MRI units per 1 million persons	26.6[†]	4.2	6.8	5.5	10.2[†]	3.2	7.1	40.1
Per capita, health spending, $	6401	3128[†]	3389	3326	3108	3374	3287	2358[†]
Prescription drug spending per capita, $	792	383	344	559	270	NA	438	425
Drug spending as % of total health, $	12.4	13.3	11.3	17.8 (2006)	8.9	16.4	15.2	19[†]

*Data are for 2005 (unless otherwise noted) from: World Health Organization. World Statistics 2007. Accessed at www.who.int/whosis/whostat2007.pdf on 22 May 2007 and Organization for Economic Co-operation and Development (OECD). OECD Health Data 2007. Accessed at www.oecd.org/document/ 30/0,3343,en_2649_37407_12968734_1_1_1_37407,00.html on 23 July 2007. MRI = magnetic resonance imaging; NA = not available.

† Latest available data: 2004.

‡ CIA World Facebook. Age Structure 65 Years and Over (%) 2007. Accessed at www.photius.com/rankings/population/age_structure_65_years_old_and_over_2007_0.html on 10 May 2007.

§ Latest available data: 2003.

¶ Colombo F, Tapay N. Private Health Insurance in OECD Countries: The Benefits and Costs for Individual and Health Systems. OECD, 2006.

** The low percentages of generalist physicians reported for Denmark and the Netherlands compared with other countries may be due to different methods for collecting and reporting workforce data. Further research is needed to better understand these apparent discrepancies.

Source: Ginsburg, Doherty, Ralston Jr., & Senkeeto (2008, p. 56).

per capita on health care ($6401 compared with Canada's $3326); despite this relatively high rate, almost 44 million Americans (or 14.8 percent of the population) have no insurance coverage (Ginsburg, Doherty, Ralston Jr., & Senkeeto, 2008, p. 55). For proportionately less, Canada provides health care coverage for all of its citizens.

GENDER AND HEALTH

Researchers today understand that sex and gender play critical roles in defining one's health. **Gender and Sex-based Analysis (GSBA)** is used to describe an approach to research that systematically explores biological (sex-based) and sociocultural (gender-based) differences between women and men, boys and girls, without starting from the position that any differences exist. The purpose of GSBA is to promote sex/gender-sensitive health research that expands understanding of health determinants for everyone regardless of biological or sociological categorizations. GSBA is a development beyond research that either fails to account for sex and gender differences or presumes that they exist without evidence (Canadian Institutes of Health Research, 2010).

GSBA (Gender and Sex-based Analysis) **An approach that explores sex and gender differences without assuming differences exist.**

In 2008, the WHO Commission on the Social Determinants of Health concluded that differences in power, privilege, and opportunity affect people's health, and that men and women frequently have different access to health resources. Thus, clearly, health is a sex and gender issue. Gender, sex, age, ethnicity, religion, and other social factors influence who is most likely to become ill and what resources are available to cope with the illness once it occurs (Clow, Pederson, Haworth-Brockman, & Bernier, 2009). For example, according to Public Health Agency of Canada (2013), Canadian men are more likely to die prematurely than women, largely because of higher rates of heart disease, fatal unintentional injuries, various forms of cancer, and suicide. While women live longer than men, they are more likely to suffer from illness and diseases including strokes, pneumonia, alzheimer's disease, and kidney disease. Additionally, women are at double the risk of being injured as a result of family violence, and have an increased risk of death as a result of family violence (Sinha, 2012).

PRINCIPLES OF THE CANADIAN HEALTH CARE SYSTEM

Canadians have a health care system that is often, though mistakenly, referred to as *socialized medicine*. In socialized medicine, the government owns and operates most medical facilities and employs most physicians; Sweden is one example of this type of system. Canada, in contrast, has *socialized insurance*, whereby the government pays doctors and hospitals for the services they provide according to a schedule of fees set annually by governments in consultation with professional medical associations. While the federal government provides some funding to the provinces to manage health care, the provinces are responsible for its administration.

Market Principles in Health Care

Through the *Hospital Insurance and Diagnostic Services Act* of 1957, the *Medical Care Act* of 1966, and the *Canada Health Act* of 1984, five universal principles of health care have been enshrined in Canadian law:

- *Universal:* the system must cover all Canadians
- *Accessible:* the system must provide reasonable access for everyone and must be unimpeded by financial or other barriers so that no one can be discriminated against on the basis of age, income, or health status
- *Comprehensive:* the system must cover all medically necessary services
- *Portable:* the system must provide coverage between provinces should a person move
- *Publicly Administered:* the system must be operated by a public body on a not-for-profit basis (Government of Canada, 2003)

Providing Health Care for the Poor in the US

In 2003, the federal and provincial governments developed a 10-year plan to strengthen health care in Canada. One of the outcomes was the creation of a Health Care Council that would monitor progress toward reducing wait times, enhancing primary care (including more support for homecare and catastrophic drug coverage), improving diagnostic and medical equipment, and investigating electronic medical file technologies (www.health-councilcanada.ca) (Health Canada, 2006a).

HEALTH CARE ISSUES

In this section, we discuss three salient issues related to health care in Canada today: access, costs, and the expansion of alternative health care.

Access Many Canadians are concerned with unequal access to health care. For some, this means that they do not have a regular family doctor, they live in rural areas without health care facilities, or they have to wait in a long queue for particular non–life threatening services (e.g., hip replacement surgeries).

Although wait times are a barrier for some procedures in some provinces, there are signs that they are improving (Health Council of Canada, 2008) but remain a significant cost to the Canadian economy (The Centre for Spatial Economics, 2008). For example, in Ontario, wait times have dropped substantially over the past four years for cataract surgery (from 311 to 118 days), knee replacements (from 440 to 253 days), hip replacements (from 351 to 198 days), and cancer surgeries (from 81 to 57 days) (Ontario Health Quality Council, 2008). As one way to improve access and efficiency, Ontario has instituted a Web service (www.ontariowaittimes.ca) that allows patients to view wait times at specific hospitals for specific procedures.

> > >

Many Canadians face long waiting lines when attempting to access the public health care system in Canada.

Masterfile

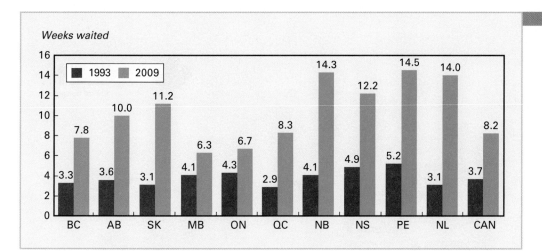

FIGURE 15.3

Canadian Hospital Waiting Lists

Reprinted by permission from Bacchus Barua, Mark Rovere, and Brett J. Skinner, Waiting Your Turn: Hospital Waiting Lists in Canada, 2010 report (20th ed). The Fraser Institute, p. 10 www .fraserinstitute.org

Yet "access" means more than just wait times; it also means that everyone is treated equally when they need health care, which is not always the case. For example, the rich can choose to skip the line in Canada and pay for medical services in another country, an option not available to the poor. As well, members of the military, members of the RCMP, prisoners, and workers' compensation claimants all receive more timely health services because they are not covered by the *Canada Health Act* (Jacobs, 2005).

A significant challenge to Canada's public health care system came in 2005 with the Supreme Court of Canada's decision in the Chaoulli case (Carpay, 2006). The case was brought to the Court by a physician, Jacques Chaoulli, and his patient, George Zeliotis. Over a number of years, Zeliotis experienced various health problems for which he received treatment, including heart surgery and a number of operations on his hip, within the public health care system. However, he had experienced significant waits before obtaining treatment. Dr. Chaoulli, a long-time advocate of greater private sector involvement in Canadian health care, challenged the prohibition against private insurance because, he argued, it effectively violates the rights to "life, liberty, personal security" as defined in the Quebec Charter of Human Rights and Freedoms and the Canadian Charter of Rights and Freedoms. In its decision, the Supreme Court concluded that when the government fails to deliver health care in a reasonable manner and increases the risk of complications and death, it interferes with life and security of the person as defined in the Charter (Lundell, 2005).

These concerns notwithstanding, according to Health Canada, most people are satisfied with their access to health care. For example, of the 2.8 million people aged 15 or older who visited a medical specialist in 2005, only 19 percent reported that they faced difficulties accessing care. Of the 1.6 million people who reported that they had nonemergency surgery, only 13 percent had difficulty accessing care (Statistics Canada, 2006a). However, even though wait times for specific surgical procedures may be falling in some provinces, Figure 15.3 demonstrates that wait times to see a specialist were much longer in 2009 than they were in 1993.

Costs In 2012, per capita spending on health care in Canada averaged $5,988, from a high in Nunavut of $13,152 to a low of $5,531 in Quebec (see Figure 15.4). In 2011, over 11 percent of Canada's GDP was spent on health care (see Figure 15.5), a level of spending that is similar to that of most high-income countries. The exception is the United States, which allocates almost 18 percent of its GDP to health care. The high proportional costs

FIGURE 15.4

Health Spending:
How do the
Provinces and
Territories
Compare? (per
capita, 2012)

Reprinted by permission
from Canadian Institute for
Health Information (2013).

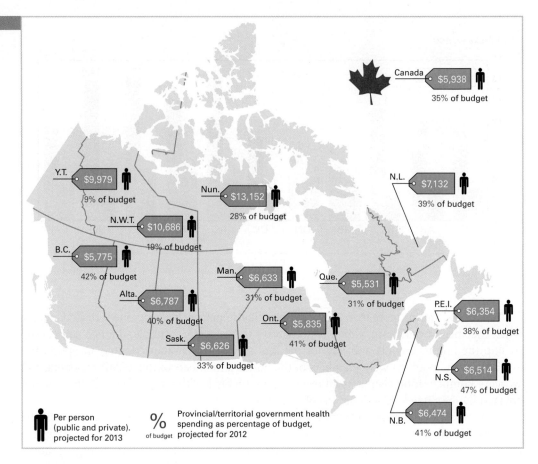

in the United States are largely the result of administrative costs: Some estimates suggest that 24 percent of all health care spending in the United States is for administration, which includes the paperwork associated with hundreds of private health care companies (Le Goff, 2005).

While Canada's numbers seem reasonable at first glance, health care is the single largest expense in many provincial budgets. For example, in 2012, health care accounted for 41 percent of Ontario's, 42 percent of British Columbia's, 31 percent of Quebec's, and 40 percent of Alberta's budgets, respectively. As the population ages, these numbers are expected to rise. Ontario and New Brunswick are in the worst financial position, as health spending in those provinces was predicted to exceed 50 percent of total available revenue in 2014 (Rovere, 2010, p. 30).

alternative medicine
Those treatments not normally taught in medical schools, used in hospitals, or included in health care plans (e.g., acupuncture).

Alternative Health Care In Canada, **alternative medicine** (also known as complementary medicine) is defined as "those treatments and health care practices not widely taught in medical schools, nor routinely used in hospitals, and not typically reimbursed by health benefit plans" (Millar, 2001, p. 9; see also Fries, 2008a, p. 1571). In 2006, nearly three-quarters of Canadians had used at least one form of alternative therapy at least once in their life. The most popular forms of alternative medicine are chiropractics (40 percent of Canadians have tried it), massage therapy (35 percent), relaxation techniques (20 percent), prayer (18 percent), and acupuncture (17 percent) (Esmail, 2007, p. 4). Fries (2008a) studied Canadian doctors' responses to alternative therapies and found generally high support for chiropractic care, acupuncture, massage therapy, relaxation therapy, and biofeedback, as well as spiritual or religious healing, when used to supplement more traditional biomedical treatments.

FIGURE 15.5

Health Expenditure as Share of GDP (2011) for OECD Countries

Reprinted by permission from Canadian Institute for Health Information (2013).

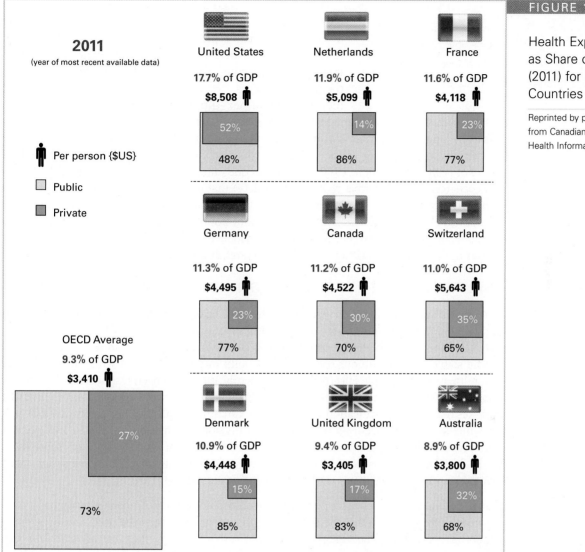

2011
(year of most recent available data)

Per person {$US}

☐ Public

☐ Private

United States
17.7% of GDP
$8,508
52%
48%

Netherlands
11.9% of GDP
$5,099
14%
86%

France
11.6% of GDP
$4,118
23%
77%

Germany
11.3% of GDP
$4,495
23%
77%

Canada
11.2% of GDP
$4,522
30%
70%

Switzerland
11.0% of GDP
$5,643
35%
65%

OECD Average
9.3% of GDP
$3,410
27%
73%

Denmark
10.9% of GDP
$4,448
15%
85%

United Kingdom
9.4% of GDP
$3,405
17%
83%

Australia
8.9% of GDP
$3,800
32%
68%

Esmail (2007, p. 5) estimates that Canadians spend about $8 billion annually on alternative health care; yet, despite this significant outlay, fully 60 percent of Canadians believe that these procedures should not be covered under provincial health plans. Alternative health care is used by

- women more than men
- middle-aged people more than the young or elderly
- people with higher educational levels more than those with lower educational levels
- people with higher incomes more than those with lower incomes
- people with a diagnosed chronic condition more than others (Statistics Canada, 2005f)

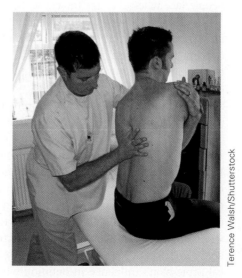

Terence Walsh/Shutterstock

< < <

Alternative health care (e.g., chiropractics, massage therapy, acupuncture, etc.) are becoming increasingly popular in Canada.

>>> Thinking Sociologically

What factors might explain why people with higher incomes and education levels are more likely to use alternative health care?

In addition, an earlier study found that those who were more proactive about their own health care were more likely to consult alternative providers (Millar, 2001, p. 17). Millar (2001) concluded that these people were generally "supplementing, not rejecting, conventional health care," and that as the population ages, "the demand for alternate therapies could increase even further" (pp. 19–20).

However, the fact that Canadians are increasingly turning to alternative health care presents a challenge on a number of fronts. First, alternative health care workers may not undergo the same type of training as the university-educated practitioners in our existing medical model of health care (Haigh, 1999, p. 146). Second, alternative health care systems have hidden costs (e.g., testing herbal remedies for safety) that could overwhelm the system's ability to pay (Danzon, 1992). Third, many alternative medical treatments lack scientific evidence to establish their effectiveness. Perhaps even more troubling is that some forms of alternative medicine, like homeopathy, not only lack any evidence of efficacy but have been scientifically proven not to work at all (Brien, Lewith, & Bryant, 2003; see also Ernst, 2002).

THEORETICAL PERSPECTIVES ON HEALTH CARE

Functionalism The functionalist approach views health care as an important mechanism through which society administers the care and treatment of its citizens. By providing hospitals and trained staff, the health care system is able to treat the ill and, in doing so, maintain a more stable and harmonious society. Critics point out, however, that while the health care system treats many people effectively and efficiently, it has also been responsible for harming some people's health. For example, a study of hospital records from 2000 to 2001 found that mistakes (e.g., wrong medication or dose given, catching an infection) or accidents (e.g., falling while in hospital) occurred in 7.5 percent of hospital admissions; of these, 36.9 percent were preventable and 20.8 percent resulted in death (Baker et al., 2004). In this sense then, the health care system is not functional for every individual involved, and the system itself may make people ill (Williams, Deber, Branek, & Gildiner, 2001, p. 11).

Conflict Theory The conflict perspective would point out that Canada already has a two-tier health care system in that the rich can get treatment faster than the poor simply by going to another country. Conflict theorists would assert that the poor must instead wait their turn in an overburdened health care system, at times dying before they can be treated (Peat, 2008). Further evidence of inequality in Canadian health care is seen in the problems that Aboriginal people face when they try to access the system from remote locations.

Conflict theorists would also argue that the medical profession legitimates and sanctions its control over people's health in a process known as **medicalization**. Medicalization is a concept popularized by Ivan Illich (1926–2002). One of Illich's central insights was how health care professionals, drug companies, medical equipment companies, and indeed the entire medical establishment have a vested interest in sponsoring sickness to promote unrealistic health expectations that require more treatments and resources (Hammond, 2005, p. 13). For example, nervousness, attention deficit disorder, and shyness can all be classified as medical problems worthy of medications, treatment, and therapy. Illich also used the term **iatrogenesis** to describe the sickness and injury that are caused by the health care system. Illich suggests that the health care system transforms pain, illness, and death from a personal challenge into a technical problem: Medical practice removes the potential for people to deal with their health on their own and by doing so, promotes a new kind of "un-health" (Illich, 2003, p. 919). The point is not that these conditions may not be helped by medical treatments, but that we need to recognize that the boundaries of what is considered acceptable have narrowed over time. Similarly, Michel Foucault described the spread of the medical profession's influence in defining what is normal and abnormal (Reznick, 2006, p. 85). According to conflict theorists, these definitions reflect the needs of the rich and powerful.

medicalization The increasing influence of the medical profession in defining what is normal/healthy and abnormal/ill.

iatrogenisis Term used to describe the sickness and injury caused by the health care system.

Symbolic Interactionism The symbolic interactionist perspective on health rests on two central insights. The first is the influence of labelling. People use the labels *health* and *illness* as fixed, binary opposites, whereas in reality what can be considered healthy falls within a wide spectrum. Once labelled as being ill, people often assume a set of expectations that are based on both the diagnosis and the individual. Symbolic interactionists would point out that these labels (e.g., sick, healthy, cancer survivor) are social constructions that can be changed (Lindsey & Beach, 2003, p. 342).

The second symbolic interactionist insight is the influence of the self-fulfilling prophecy (Buunk, Zurriaga, & González, 2006, p. 793). For example, the growth of alternative medicine suggests that it works for many people and cannot be dismissed simply as a medical fluke. The power of the mind to influence one's health or illness is in part explained by the self-fulfilling prophecy—if a person thinks a remedy might work, it may have a greater chance of doing so. On the other hand, patients who believe that they are beyond healing and thus do not seek help are more likely to suffer the most negative effects of their illness.

Feminist Theory Feminist theorists are critical of how the medical profession treats women. For example, medical research is often androcentric, in that findings from research conducted on men are inferred as also applying to women. Feminists also point out that combining *medical* and *science* into *medical science* confirms a strong male-centred bias in that it seeks to find universal truths. This approach suggests that when knowledge is gained through impersonal, objective methods, it can have the effect of diminishing the value of the individual human experience. Thus, the attributes that define women's reality—intuition, subjectivity, and emotions—are generally dismissed by the medical establishment (Williams & Mackey, 1999, p. 31). This system therefore attributes childbirth, for example, as a purely biological process and not the culmination of emotional and subjective realities. Thus, our dominant cultural categories that influence science and medicine (e.g., male, white, upper-middle class) make it difficult for anyone (patients or medical professionals) to re-evaluate and alter the dominant patriarchal categories that typify traditional health care (Kinser & Lewis, 2005, p. 423).

BOX 15.1 WHY SHOULD WE CARE?

Brian Sinclair: Victim of Racialization, Medicalization, or Both?

On September 21, 2008, an Aboriginal man named Brain Sinclair was found dead. Though he was mentally and physically disabled, an addict, and socially excluded, his body was not found in some anonymous back alley, but rather, in the emergency room iat Winnipeg's Health Sciences Centre.

According to a chief medical examiner's inquest, Sinclair died from a treatable bladder infection, after spending 34 hours in the hospital's waiting room and being repeatedly overlooked by the doctors, nurses, and medical aids. Indeed, even though Sinclair went to the hospital for medical help, he was never triaged despite being seen by 17 different hospital staff and having several bystanders attempt to get him help. After his death, Sinclair's cousin told the media that Brian was "ignored to death."

Sociologists use the term *racialization* (see Chapter 10) to describe how perceived racial differences often lead to systemic discrimination. In this case, Sinclair was seen as just another mentally ill and addicted Indian. Many people use visible differences to explain the behaviours of different groups—this is the essence of racialization. As Dr. Alika Lafontaine, vice president of the Indigenous Physicians Association of Canada, points out, physicians and other health care professionals are not immune to stereotyping (Lafontaine, 2014). Because of racialization, health care professionals may see racial differences instead of medical issues.

CONTINUED

Racialization is so embedded in the Canadian health care system that hospitals are trying to manage it through special Aboriginal health programs, cultural sensitivity training, and hiring Aboriginal staff to treat Aboriginal patients. Like so many, Brian Sinclair was categorized according to his "race." Recognizing the racially divided character of Canadian society, health care policies are being implemented to try and ensure that people aren't discriminated against because of how they look.

While racialization was a factor in Sinclair's death, so was the process of medicalization. Medicalization is a term used by sociologists to explore how social factors intersect with medicine. For example, addictions are increasingly defined as medical issues requiring formal medical care intervention rather than the product of social alienation. When someone does not fit in or behaves in ways that are not "normal" we see them as being "broken" and in need of "fixing" through medical intervention.

Brian Sinclair's death is a terrible example of how racism, racialization, and medicalization came together to allow someone to die in a hospital filled with doctors and nurses.

This is a revised version of an earlier opinion editorial first appearing in the *Winnipeg Free Press*, May 22, 2010.

Reprinted by permission from Christopher J. Fries, a health sociologist in the Department of Sociology at the University of Manitoba and co-author of 'Pursuing Health and Wellness: Healthy Society, Healthy People' (Oxford University Press, Canada).

Post-Structuralist Theory Modernists believe that an underlying, unified truth can be found through objectivity, causality, and the pursuit of impartial observation. In contrast, post-structuralists attempt to suspend all preconceived judgments and to deconstruct conventional wisdom (Newbold, 2005, p. 440). According to post-structuralists, then, health care must become more responsive to the needs of the individual patient and become less about the need of health professionals to "fix" the problem. For example, people today are more likely to take ownership of their own health (as seen in the rise of alternative medicine) and to actively critique their own clinical treatment to determine if it is what they believe they need. If it isn't, they are more likely to terminate the treatment independent of what doctors may recommend. In this way, empowerment flows to the patient and turns the traditional modernist hospital on its head. Foucault's concept of **biopower** occurs when actors become self-regulating subjects through "technologies of the self" (Foucault, 1988 as cited in Fries, 2008b, p. 354).

biopower Foucault's term to explain people taking ownership of their bodies and their health.

Biopower is a form of social power that flows from medical knowledge. The idea is that medicine defines the reality of the human body and because the body is closely bound up with identity, biopower controls how we understand ourselves. This in turn influences how we behave (e.g., going on a diet, choosing organic foods, going to the gym). This suggests that people see themselves as works-in-progress and work hard to manage their own health. In a post-structural sense, the emergence of alternative medical techniques is completely reasonable. "When patients enter the 'postmodern hospital,' they come neither to be disciplined into a morally improved state, nor to be 'operated upon' by the medicine machine: they come to comparison shop. In this world of consumer medicine, the very categories of disease and health alter, along with the shifting, ever reconstructed identity of patients who purchase and doctors who provide" (Galison, 1999, as cited in Newbold, 2005, p. 445).

Aging

((•─[Listen

Naturally Occurring Retirement Communities

As Canada's proportion of elderly persons grows, we need to appreciate that a new kind of older adult is emerging—one who is healthier, better educated, and more financially secure than ever before (Arsenault, Anderson, & Swedburg, 1998, p. 101).

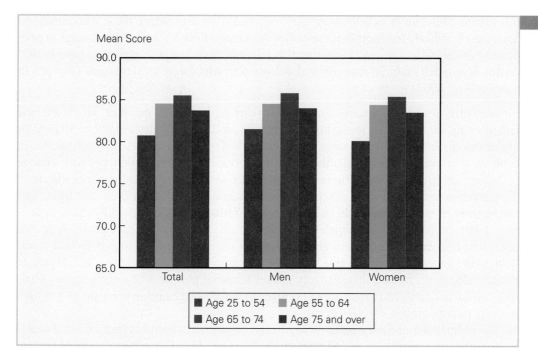

FIGURE 15.6

Canadians' Scores on the Well-Being Scale, by Age Group and Sex, 2002

The well-being scale is a measure of individuals' feelings about various aspects of their lives, such as the frequency with which they feel self-confident, satisfied with their accomplishments, and loved and appreciated. The scale ranges from a minimum of 3 to a maximum of 100.

Statistics Canada, A Portrait of Seniors in Canada, 89-519-XIE2006001, February 2007; http://www.statcan .gc.ca/bsolc/olc-cel/ olc-cel?chropg=1&lang= eng&catno=89-519-X

Table 6.1 and Figure 6.1 (see pages 158 and 159) showed that the proportion of seniors (65 years and older) in the Canadian population increased from just over 5 percent in 1921 to more than 13 percent in 2006, and is projected to exceed 27 percent by 2056. If this prediction is correct, the importance of the elderly in society will continue to grow. And the elderly population will become more diverse; according to Statistics Canada, the proportion of seniors who are visible minorities and of Aboriginal descent will also continue to rise (Turcotte & Schellenberg, 2007).

SENIORS' WELL-BEING AND HEALTH STATUS

Most Canadian seniors today are happy and healthy. Figure 15.6 shows that men and women between the ages of 65 and 74 report the highest scores on measures of well-being. We can infer from these results that people between the ages of 25 and 54 (most of whom are hard at work building careers and starting families) are not yet experiencing the freedom one enjoys upon retirement—nor, it must be added, the life-experience that often comes with age.

ISSUES FACING SENIORS

Despite the good news discussed above, six issues stand out for seniors as areas of concern: transition to retirement, financial pressures, age discrimination, vulnerability to crime, chronic pain and the need for long-term care, and preparing to die.

> > > Thinking Sociologically

What social factors do you think might explain why people aged 65 to 74 are higher on the well-being scale than those 25 to 54?

Transition to Retirement In Canada, labour laws do not specify a retirement age for employees. However, some laws or government policies governing specific occupations set an age limit for persons employed in those occupations (Human Resources and Social Development Canada, 2007). Forcing employees to retire due to their age is considered by many to be a human rights issue, since it discriminates against people on the basis of age. For this reason, virtually all Canadian provinces have done away with mandatory retirement legislation.

For many, leaving a career is difficult; after all, so much of *who we are* is defined by *what we do*. While most people retire voluntarily, others are forced to do so as a result of corporate downsizing (Turcotte & Schellenberg, 2007, p. 123). Unsurprisingly, those who choose to retire are more likely to report that they enjoy life more. However, a small percentage of people who are enjoying life less after retirement remains; these people have fair to poor health, do not have much financial support, and did not plan adequately for retirement (Turcotte & Schellenberg, 2007).

((•—Listen

French Workers Asked to Sacrifice a Day for Elderly

Financial Pressures Among Canadian workers with average incomes, family income falls after age 60, continues to decline until age 68, and then stabilizes at about 80 percent of the income level they had at age 55 (LaRochelle-Côté, Myles, & Picot, 2008, p. 4). In contrast, low-income individuals (those in the poorest 20 percent) experience little change in income throughout their retirement, largely due to the income-maintenance effects of the Canadian pension system. After periods of income instability in their late fifties and early sixties, their income tends to stabilize after retirement. Wealthy individuals experience a substantial loss of income; however, they often have significant personal wealth upon which to draw. More recent groups of retirees are experiencing higher income levels than earlier cohorts, largely because of higher private pensions (LaRochelle-Côté, Myles, & Picot, 2008, p. 4). In fact, the relatively greater financial resources of today's seniors challenge an earlier concern that an aging population would place undue pressure on younger workers to support it.

elderly dependency ratio The ratio of seniors to workers.

The **elderly dependency ratio** measures the proportion of seniors (aged 65 and older) to workers (aged about 20 to 64) (Wu & Li, 2003, p. 24). As the proportion of seniors in the population increases, the number of workers supporting them falls. According to some, given our aging society, the number of seniors being supported will ultimately outweigh society's ability to provide for them (Huber & Hennessy, 2005, p. 100). We should note that the term *elderly dependency ratio* is challenged by some as an ageist assumption in that it implies all elderly people are dependent (Chappell, McDonald, & Stones, 2008, p. 29). Some believe that the basis upon which the ratio is calculated is fundamentally flawed. For example, the calculation might make sense if people actually retired at 65. Today, however, mandatory retirement has largely been eliminated; so more people over the age of 65 will work because they want to or, in some cases, because they have to (Pesce, 2011).

healthy aging Perspective that reinforces the inherent value of older people to society.

Conversely, the concept of **healthy aging** "presumes that older people are of intrinsic value to society rather than a burden and that their autonomy and sense of personal control are essential for maintaining human dignity and integrity" (Oxley, 2009, p. 9).

Seniors are supported through the Canadian public pension system, which is made up of the federal government's transfer payments through Old Age Security (OAS), Guaranteed Income Supplements (GIS) from income taxes, and mandatory employment deductions from the Canada/Quebec Pension Plan (CPP/QPP). The elderly dependency ratio in Canada was 14.7 seniors per 100 workers in 1960, 20.3 in 2000, and is projected to increase to 43.7 in 2040. This puts Canada in the middle of the pack compared with other member countries of the Organisation for Economic Co-operation and Development (OECD). For example, OECD averages for the same years were 15.9, 22.9, and 46.3. The lowest projected ratio for 2040 was Turkey at 23.9; the highest were Italy and Switzerland, both at 63.9 (Huber & Hennessy, 2005, p. 104).

Watch

Seniors

Although Canada's rising elderly dependency ratio is reason for some concern, the federal transfer payment system appears stable and well prepared for the future. OAS costs will grow as the population ages in the coming decades and are intended to remain affordable. As well, legislative changes to the CPP in 1998 increased payments from workers to ensure that the fund would meet future obligations (Chappell, McDonald, & Stones, 2008, p. 376). Further, Canadians are using the tax benefits of Registered Retirement Savings Plans (RRSPs) as well as employer-sponsored retirement plans to save money for their retirement. The growth of retirement plans across all sectors suggests a certain level of financial security for the vast majority of Canadian seniors. This is further confirmed by the fact that compared with other age groups, seniors have had the most substantial decline in those living with low incomes over the past 30 years.

As you can see, in the mid 1970s more than 30 percent of seniors were living under the low income cut-off (as described in Chapter 7; see page 191), but by 2004 this had declined to around 5 percent, where it remains. The decline was largely due to government transfer programs, employer plans, and RRSP savings (Human Resources and Social Development Canada, 2006b; Statistics Canada, 2007i). Over the past 25 years, retirement income has grown faster than any other income source for seniors. In 1980, retirement income made up less than 15 percent of total income for senior couples, but by 2005 it had increased to more than 30 percent. Over the past 25 years, in constant 2005 dollars, average retirement income more than tripled (Statistics Canada, 2008f). In fact, some seniors continue to support their children and grandchildren financially (Galt, 2008, p. B5). Of course, some seniors do live with low incomes and, as might be predicted from our earlier discussions (notably in Chapters 7 and 10), they tend to be women and recent immigrants.

Age Discrimination While seniors may face many forms of discrimination, the most obvious is ageism. **Ageism** is a system of inequality based on age that privileges the young at the expense of the old (Calasanti, Slevin, & King, 2006, p. 13). In contrast to other serious "isms" such as racism (Chapter 10) and sexism (Chapter 9), ageism may touch everyone if they live long enough. After all, as we learned in Chapter 6, much of our society is grounded in our social infatuation with youth. Consider how media portray the young in contrast to how they present the elderly—for example, how often are senior citizens the stars of television shows? Yet in many societies around the world, the elderly are not diminished and dismissed as ours are, but instead are considered to be knowledgeable and deserving of honour and respect (Palmore, 2004, p. 41).

Seniors in our society are routinely subjected to negative stereotypes regarding their physical and mental abilities. The power and prevalence of these cultural stereotypes affects not only how seniors are treated, but also how they see themselves (Horton, Baker, & Deakin, 2007, p. 1021; Slevin, 2010, p. 1003).

ageism A system of inequality based on age that privileges the young at the expense of the old.

> > > Thinking Sociologically

In your experience, how are elderly people portrayed in media? What do these portrayals say about growing old in our society?

< < <

Many elderly people are healthy and happy and play a significant role in their children's lives and society as a whole.

Monkey Business Images/Shutterstock

FIGURE 15.7

Seniors Have
Lowest Rates of
Police-reported
Violence, 2009

Source: Statistics Canada
(2011). Victims of violent
crime, by age group,
Canada, 2009 [online]. http://
www.statcan.gc.ca/pub/85-
224-x/2010000/ct009-eng.
htm (accessed May 24,
2011).

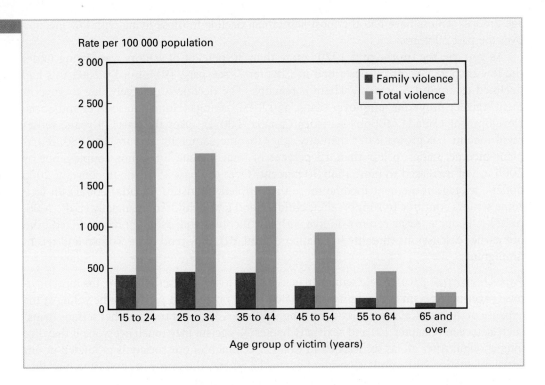

Vulnerability to Crime Although older people are far less likely than younger people to be victims of violent incidents (see Figure 15.7), they experience more fear of it and feel vulnerable when they leave their homes (Department of Justice Canada, 2013; Smolej & Kivivuori, 2006).

However, older people are more likely than younger people to be the targets of other types of crime. For example, seniors make up 60 percent of victims who lose money in telemarketing scams. Some estimates suggest that investment schemes and home improvement and telemarketing scams cost Canadians $3 billion—and that people over age 60 lose 84 percent of this total dollar amount, or about $2.5 billion (CARP, 2005). In 1998, the Canadian Association of Retired People (www.carp.ca) created a National Forum on Scams and Frauds, whose recommendations included providing more information to seniors, instituting cooling-off periods for contracts, and freezing the assets of scam artists (CARP, 2005).

elder abuse Any
form of mistreatment
that results in harm
or loss to an older
person.

Another form of victimization particular to seniors is **elder abuse**, defined as any form of mistreatment that results in harm or loss to an older person. Forms of elder abuse include psychological, physical, sexual, and economic abuse, but also neglect (Sev'er, 2009, pp. 279–281). E. K. Podnieks and her colleagues found that in the late 1980s, 4 percent of Canadian seniors (about 98 000) suffered from some form of abuse (as cited in Novak & Campbell, 2006, p. 310). In 2005, close to half (44 percent) of the homicides of seniors were committed by a family member. Of seniors killed by a family member, 37 percent of female victims were killed by a spouse and 37 percent were killed by an adult son or stepson. Among male victims, 57 percent were killed by an adult son or stepson. More than half of family violence incidents against seniors do not cause physical injury, and where injuries are sustained, they are generally minor (Statistics Canada, 2007c).

Victims of elder abuse may be vulnerable to complications resulting from physical violence, since physical injuries may worsen pre-existing health problems or inhibit an older person's ability to function independently. Many analysts believe that elder abuse is under-reported because victims, due to fear or shame, are often unwilling to report it to the police. Although some analysts initially believed that younger people were likely to exploit older

Rob Marmion/123RF

<<<

Health care workers can play a key role in helping elderly people meet their health care needs.

people who were psychologically and economically dependent on them, just the opposite has often proven true: Younger people are more likely to exploit elders upon whom they themselves are dependent (Novak & Campbell, 2006, p. 311).

Long-Term Care and Chronic Pain According to the 2001 Census, 93 percent of seniors live in private households while the remaining 7 percent reside in collective dwellings (primarily health care institutions such as nursing homes and hospitals). Institutional residency is related to age, increasing from 2 percent among young seniors (aged 65 to 74) to 32 percent among old seniors (aged 85 and older) (Turcotte & Schellenberg, 2007). When seniors can no longer take care of themselves, they often make use of long-term-care resources either in their home or in an institutional setting.

Long-term care is defined as the provision of any services required by persons who are dependent on others to meet their basic daily needs (e.g., bathing, dressing, eating, using the toilet, and moving around the home). Long-term care is often provided in combination with such basic medical services as changing wound dressings, pain management, provision of medications, rehabilitation, and palliative care (Huber & Hennessy, 2005, p. 17).

In Canada, health care, including long-term care, is under the jurisdiction of the provinces and territories (Health Canada, 2004). Although health care plans vary across the country, all jurisdictions provide some support for long-term-care institutions, palliative care, respite care, homecare nursing, rehabilitation services like physiotherapy and occupational therapy, and personal care services (Huber & Hennessy, 2005, p. 116).

According to the OECD, Canada spends 1.5 percent of its GDP on long-term care (of which around 1.25 percent is public funding and 0.25 percent is private) (OECD, 2010b). This compares favourably with the average 1.25 percent of GDP for the 19 OECD countries that have similar public/private health care systems. Among these countries, Sweden spent the highest percentage of GDP on long-term care (2.89 percent) and Mexico spent the lowest (less than 0.20 percent) (Huber & Hennessy, 2005, p. 26).

One of the primary objectives of long-term-care providers is to help their patients deal with chronic pain, a debilitating condition that affects many aspects of people's lives.

long-term care The provision of any services required by persons who are dependent on others to meet their daily needs.

👁️ Watch

Seniors and Daycare

chronic pain **Ongoing pain that lasts longer than three months after the usual recovery period for an injury or ailment.**

Chronic pain is generally defined as ongoing pain that lasts longer than three months after the usual recovery period for an injury or ailment (Geertzen, Van Wilgen, Schrier, & Dijkstra, 2006, p. 364). Constant pain is a significant concern for seniors who already may be coping with various changes as they age, including disease, cognitive impairment, and side effects from various medications.

Chronic pain is common among Canadian seniors, affecting 27 percent who live at home and 38 percent who live in health care institutions. Its incidence is likely to grow as Canada's population ages. Many seniors no doubt understand that some of the diseases they face cannot be cured, but they certainly experience a better quality of life if their pain can be adequately assessed and controlled (Ramage-Morin, 2008).

 Explore

Chinese Community Pushes for 500 New Nursing Home Beds

Preparing to Die As discussed in Chapter 6, as people age they inevitably begin to ponder their own death. Some go to great lengths to ensure that they are well prepared (e.g., by putting their wills and estates in order), while others deny their own mortality. No matter how a person prepares or fails to prepare for death, many worry about *how* and *when* they are going to die. So, for many, the idea of planning for their own death, on their own terms, is both comforting and empowering.

euthanasia **The deliberate ending of the life of a person who has an incurable or painful disease.**

In Canada, euthanasia and physician-assisted suicide are both illegal (Pereira, 2003, p. 167). **Euthanasia** (a word whose Greek roots mean "good death") is generally defined as the deliberate ending of the life of a person who has an incurable or painful disease (see Keown, 2000, p. 390). It occurs in several different ways. *Voluntary euthanasia* means that someone requests to be allowed to die. *Involuntary euthanasia* occurs when the person's wish to live is disregarded or not elicited (Cornock, 2005, p. 34). *Passive euthanasia* involves withholding or ceasing treatment of someone not likely to recover from a disease or injury. *Active euthanasia* means intervening to hasten someone's death from terminal illness—for example, with a lethal dose of sedatives. *Assisted suicide* means helping someone to end his or her life, for example, with drugs (Keown, 2000, p. 390). Because advances in medical technology have made it possible to keep people alive longer than in the past, questions are arising about the best time and method of dying.

 Explore

Hospice Care

In January 2014, the Supreme Court of Canada announced that it had agreed to hear a case on assisted suicide that opened a debate that had been raised over 20 year before in two high profile cases (Fine, 2014). In the first case, Sue Rodriguez, a 42-year-old woman who was suffering from amyotrophic lateral sclerosis (ALS), commonly known as Lou Gehrig's disease, appealed to the Supreme Court for the legal right to have someone help her commit suicide. In 1993, the Court ruled against her petition, upholding the law prohibiting assisted suicide (Smith, 1993). Rodriguez actually did die with the assistance of an unidentified doctor and Svend Robinson, an MP from British Columbia. In the second case, Robert Latimer asphyxiated his daughter, Tracy, who suffered from severe cerebral palsy. Despite Latimer's declaration that he wanted only to relieve her constant pain and suffering, he was charged with second-degree murder. He was found guilty and the judge imposed a two-year sentence that was appealed, resulting in a subsequent sentence of life imprisonment with no chance of parole for 10 years. In 2001, the Supreme Court of Canada refused to review that sentence. On December 6, 2010, Latimer was granted full parole (Ogrodnik, 2010).

An Angus Reid poll asked Canadians about the Latimer case specifically and mercy killing and euthanasia generally. It indicated that Canadians were very supportive of Latimer; almost three-quarters of those polled said that he had acted out of compassion and should have received a more lenient sentence (Sallot, 1999, p. A5). The poll also found that Canadians are quite supportive of legalizing euthanasia: 41 percent said that mercy killing should not be against the law under appropriate circumstances, 38 percent said it should be illegal but that perpetrators should be treated with leniency, and 18 percent said that it should be treated as any other murder would be (2 percent had no opinion). Notably, the young (18 to 34 years of age) were slightly less lenient than older Canadians. Recent opinion polls suggest that these perceptions have remained relatively stable since the early 1990s (Morrow, 2013).

< < <

Svend Robinson and
Sue Rodriguez

Some countries around the world have decided to make euthanasia legal. In April 2001, the Netherlands became the first country in the world to legalize euthanasia; a year later, Belgium did the same, and most recently, in 2011, the Supreme Court of India made it legal to remove life support for patients who were in a permanent vegetative state (NewHealthGuide, 2013). Whether Canadians will follow the lead of these countries is impossible to say. However, as our population ages, political pressure to legalize euthanasia is certainly increasing.

THEORETICAL APPROACHES TO AGING

Functionalism Functionalists stress harmony between society's institutions and the need for smooth transitions from one generation to the next. One functionalist approach concerned with aging is **disengagement theory**, which proposes that successful aging requires the gradual withdrawal from social activity (Cumming & Henry, 1961; Duay & Bryan, 2006, p. 423). This theory suggests that older people want to be released from roles that require hard work and responsibility; consider, for example, the London Life Insurance Company's ad campaigns touting "Freedom 55." According to functionalists, the transition to retirement is a welcome one, and not only for those who relinquish the pressure of stressful roles. Retirement also ensures that jobs are made available to younger people just starting their working careers.

One criticism of disengagement theory is that many older people enjoy becoming *more* involved with friends and family, as well as with social and political issues (Carstensen, 1995, p. 152). Additionally, given the declining birth rate and rising elderly dependency ratio, as well as the increased number of jobs that depend on brain power rather than muscle power, it is likely and perhaps necessary that people will continue to work after age 65. Accordingly, as discussed, most provincial governments have eliminated mandatory retirement.

Conflict Theory The conflict perspective highlights the roots of institutional ageism in that it focuses on the constant tension between the old and the young. For example, as workers

disengagement theory The assertion that successful aging requires the gradual withdrawal from social activity.

age, they are slowly removed from positions of power and influence to make way for younger "up and comers," creating economic competition between different age categories (Moody, 2006, p. 249). Conflict theory also suggests that the pressure either to exclude or to embrace the elderly is a direct consequence of labour market conditions. That is, during times of economic prosperity, older workers are enticed to stay on, but during a downturn, when fewer jobs are available, these workers become much less attractive (Morrow-Howell, Hinterlong, & Sherraden, 2001, p. 55).

Symbolic Interactionism

Symbolic interactionists stress that one's identity is constructed by performing many interacting roles. In contrast to disengagement theory, **activity theory** holds that people should remain engaged and active for as long as possible (Wicks, 2006, p. 263). Indeed, this theory, which rests on the assumption that remaining active and engaged has important positive benefits and leads to happier lives, has been influential in designing programs and services for older people (Duay & Bryan, 2006, p. 423; Neugarten, Havighurst, & Tobin, 1968).

activity theory The belief that people should remain engaged and active for as long as possible.

Activity theory asserts that people construct perceptions about themselves through the activities they do and the roles they play. As we remarked at the beginning of this chapter, since so much of who we are is defined by what we do, the transition from a full-time job to retirement challenges many people's perceptions of themselves. The retiree is no longer a manager, doctor, or engineer, but instead a *retired* manager, doctor, or engineer. Thus, it is very important for aging people to maintain activities, and to take on new ones, that reinforce their sense of self as valuable and important. Of course, all activities are not considered equal; joining a lawn bowling club, for example, may not be as rewarding as volunteering as chair of a community association.

An obvious limitation of this theory, and one that it cannot be expected to address, is that over time everyone becomes less able to remain active as a result of the inevitable physical degeneration that occurs in very old age.

Feminist Theory

The feminist perspective on aging explores, for example, how women respond to an aging body in a society fixated on appearance and youth. While much feminist literature accentuates the cultural preference granted to the masculine, we should appreciate that young, attractive women also possess social power. As women age, they lose this power; as well, as they reach menopause, they are devalued because they can no longer bear children. Contemporary feminist scholars explore what this transition means to women's perceptions of self as they age (Winterich, 2007, p. 54). Many feminists assert the value of "agelessness," in that all perceptions of age are socially constructed and therefore open to change (Calasanti, Slevin, & King, 2006, p. 16).

Post-Structuralist Theory

Post-structuralist thinkers approach the concept of aging as embedded in a framework of truth and knowledge that develops through circulating power relations within society. One of these "truths" about aging is that older people consume more of society's health care resources, which to some suggests that older people should remain in the labour force longer to help pay their way (Carroll, 2007, p. 73). Since so many seniors remain healthy well into their eighties and beyond, post-structural theorists question how social transitions like growing old are defined and how they change over time. Some contemporary researchers (Carroll, 2007) challenge negative stereotypes about the elderly; indeed, the fact that they are a dynamic and engaged population may represent a deconstruction of the entire category of what it means to be old (Holstein, 2005, p. 38; Morris, 1998, p. 236).

❹ Disabilities

As sociologists, we understand better than most how the society around us influences how we see ourselves. So far, we have reviewed how people are influenced by their culture (Chapter 5), socioeconomic status (Chapter 7), gender (Chapter 8), sexuality (Chapter 9), family (Chapter 11), education (Chapter 12), and religion (Chapter 13). However, we cannot

< < <

This cellphone ad challenges the negative view of the elderly and promotes an image of health and vitality.

neglect to appreciate how some in society react to people with disabilities, nor how this interaction must in part define how people with disabilities see themselves. In approaching disability studies, we introduce the concept of the **people first philosophy**. To operate from a people first perspective is to place the individual before the disability, to focus on a person's abilities rather than limitations, and to use the phrase "people with disabilities" rather than refer to people as "disabled" (Russell, 2008, p. 40).

people first philosophy **An approach that focuses on the individual and his or her abilities rather than limitations.**

WHAT IS A DISABILITY?

While aging affects everyone, disabilities are commonly thought to affect relatively few people. Only a small percentage of those with a disability were born with it; accidents, disease, and violence account for most disabilities in Canada. What is a disability, and how many Canadians have one?

A **disability** is defined as a mental or physical condition that limits people's everyday activities and restricts what they can do (Statistics Canada, 2008m). *Developmental disability* is the term used to describe lifelong impairments that are attributable to mental and/or physical disabilities (e.g., autism, cerebral palsy, and Down's syndrome being the most common) (Developmental Disabilities Association, 2010). In 2012, the Canadian Survey on Disability found that among Canadians aged 15 and older there were 3.8 million people reporting that their daily activities were limited because of a disability (or about 13.7 percent of the population over 15 years of age) (Statistics Canada, 2013a).

disability **A mental or physical condition that limits people's everyday activities and restricts what they can do.**

Research has also found that virtually all disability rates are increasing. Between 2001 and 2006, the overall disability rate for Canadian adults (aged 15 and older) rose from 14.6 percent to 16.5 percent (Statistics Canada, 2007g). This increase is no doubt a result of two main factors. First, with advances in medical technology today, many children born with a serious disability or many people injured in accidents are more likely to survive than they were in the past. Second, as the population ages, a higher percentage of people are more likely to experience chronic diseases (such as arthritis) that may have disabling consequences (see Figure 15.8) (Albrecht, 1992).

FIGURE 15.8

Disability Rates in Canada, by Age and Sex, 2006

Source: Statistics Canada (2007).

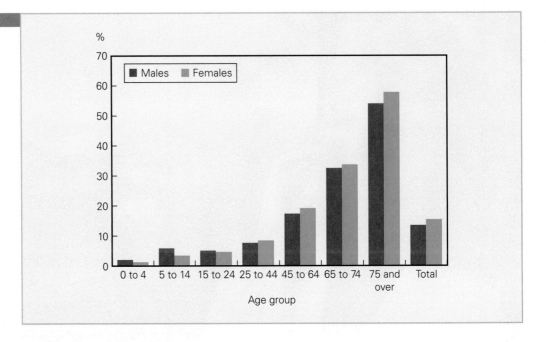

> > > Thinking Sociologically

With reference to the social construction of gender, what role might hegemonic masculinity and emphasized femininity (refer back to Chapter 9), play in how likely people are to report experiencing mood disorders?

downward drift hypothesis The assertion that those with mental illnesses, unable to finish their education or secure a job, tend to drift into low-income groups.

> > >

Over 1 million people, or about 5 percent of all Canadians, report suffering from depression.

For people between ages 15 and 64, the most common disability that limited daily living was pain, affecting about three-quarters of all respondents. Among those 65 and older, the most common disability was limited mobility (e.g., cannot walk without pain, difficulty standing for long periods or going up or down stairs) (Statistics Canada, 2007g).

About 60 percent of those with disabilities used or needed technical aids or specialized equipment to assist them with daily living. Of those needing assistive aids, about 30 percent did not have all of the aids they needed. The most frequently cited reason (about 56 percent of respondents) was cost, since these aids are not covered by health care insurance (Statistics Canada, 2008m).

Mental Illness & Mood Disorders According to the Canadian Community Health Survey (CCHS), 4.5 percent of people interviewed reported having experienced symptoms or feelings associated with major depression; almost 5 percent had experienced anxiety; and, when substance dependence was included, 1 in 10 Canadians aged 15 and older had experienced mental problems at some time within 12 months of the interview (Statistics Canada, 2003a). (See Figure 15.9.)

Figure 15.9 indicates that women have higher rates of mood disorders than men across all ages. As well, people in low-income groups are found to have higher rates of mental disorders than those in high-income groups. However, this relationship could be explained by the **downward drift hypothesis**, which asserts that because some people with mental illnesses and mood disorders are unable to function within the larger society, neither getting an education nor keeping a job, they tend to drift into the low-income groups (Warren, 2009).

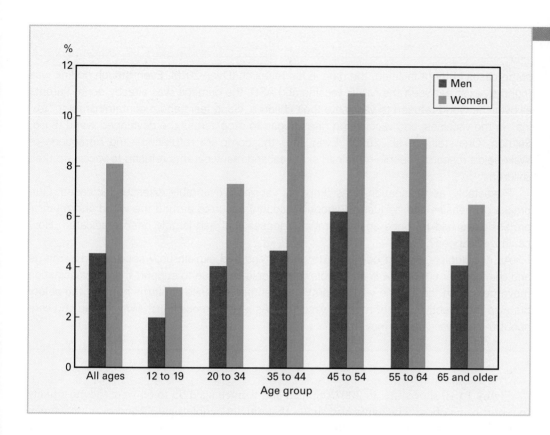

FIGURE 15.9

Percentage Reporting Mood Disorders, by Age Group and Sex, Household Population Aged 12 and Older, Canada, 2009

Source: Statistics Canada (2009) Mood disorders, 2009 [online]. http://www.statcan.gc.ca/pub/82-625-x/2010002/article/11265-01-eng.gif (accessed May 25, 2011).

Obesity A relatively new disability is affecting almost half of the Canadian population, and is considered by some to be a worldwide epidemic (see Huneault, Mathieu, & Tremblay, 2011; Dumme, 2008, p. 1177): obesity. **Obesity** is defined as a state characterized by a body mass index (BMI) of 30 percent or more in an adult (Barness, 2007, p. 78). **BMI** is calculated by dividing an individual's weight in kilograms (kg) by his or her height in metres squared (m²). A person with a BMI of 18.5 or less is considered to be underweight; someone with a BMI of 18.6 to 24.9 is considered to be of normal weight; someone with a BMI of 25.0 to 29.9 is considered to be overweight; and someone with a BMI of 30.0 or more is considered to be obese. Being overweight has been linked to heart disease, Type 2 diabetes, certain forms of cancer, and stroke (Agarwal, 2007, p. 65; Zohrabian, 2005, p. 104).

obesity A state characterized by a BMI of 30 percent or more in an adult.

BMI (body mass index) Calculated by dividing an individual's weight (kg) by height (m²).

BOX 15.2 WHY SHOULD WE CARE?

The Anti-Vaccine Movement

In 1998, *The Lancet*, one of the most prestigious medical journals in the world, reported on a remarkable medical discovery—Dr. Andrew Wakefield claimed he had discovered a link between the measles, mumps, and r (MMR) vaccine and autism spectrum disorder (ASD). The news made headlines around the world: Vaccines, a medical marvel of the twentieth century, were shown to be harming our children!

Parents of children with autism spectrum disorder (ASD) now had an explanation for the mysterious origins of their child's illness. All over the world, movements of parents, doctors, and activists began to emerge, all calling for the end of mandatory vaccination programs.

But there was a problem—other researchers could not replicate any of Wakefield's findings, and even more damning, it was soon discovered that Wakefield had distorted, and in

((•—[Listen

Parent Fears Keep Children from Vaccines

CONTINUED

some cases outright falsified, the data in his research (Dyer, 2010). Even though no link was found to exist between the MMR vaccine and ASD, the damage was already done. Parents all over the world refused to vaccinate their children, citing fears about contaminants or "toxins" in the vaccines, and vaccination rates began to drop across the developed world (Saad, Salmon, Orenstein, et al., 2009). Even after the complete refutation—and retraction—of Wakefield's research, people remained skeptical and many parents refused to vaccinate their children.

Predictably, as vaccination rates dropped, vaccine-preventable diseases increased. Outbreaks of measles and pertussis (whooping cough) occurred around the world and medical professionals had to, once again, combat diseases that had largely been eradicated. How could this happen?

As sociologists, part of our job is to understand and explain how social trends emerge and change over time. How is it possible that people continue to support the anti-vaccination movement even though the vast majority of scientific evidence confirms not only the safety but also the effectiveness of modern vaccines? As a young sociologist, why should you care about the anti-vaccination movement?

Figure 15.10 shows that in 2007/08, men and women aged 55 to 64 were the most likely to report being obese. The figure also shows that only in people aged 75 and over are women more likely to report being obese than men.

Obesity is not just a concern in Canada; it is found in all high-income countries. This creates a major economic burden and consumes 2 to 8 percent of overall health care budgets (World Health Organization, 2006). Figure 15.11 compares obesity rates across various countries.

Even with these statistics in mind, some social scientists are asking that we interrogate obesity more deeply and from a broader perspective than simply looking at tables and graphs (see Boero, 2007; Holmes, 2009; Oliver, 2006). For example, Holmes (2009) suggests that while obesity was once considered an individual's lifestyle choice, obesity today

FIGURE 15.10 Prevalence of Self-Reported Obesity by Age and Sex, Canada, 2007/08

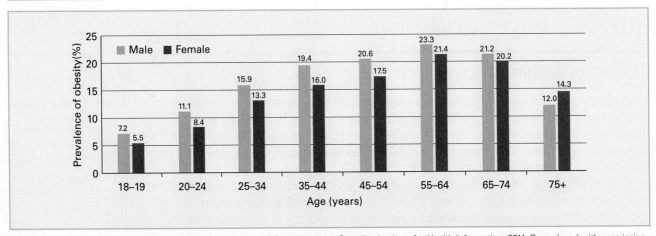

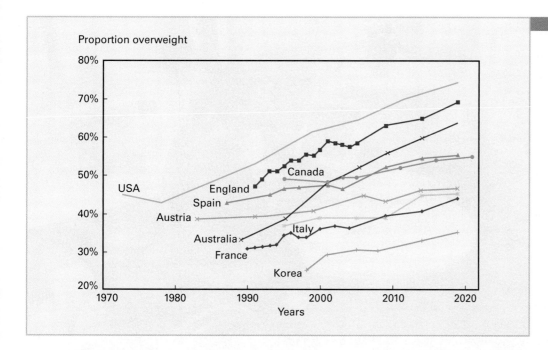

FIGURE 15.11

Past and Projected
Future Overweight
Rates in Selected
OECD Countries
(2010)

Reprinted by permission
from OECD (2010), Obesity
and the Economics of
Prevention: Fit not Fat,
OECD Publishing. http://
dx.doi.org/10.1787/
9789264084865-en

is seen as an epidemic requiring an international response. Holmes investigated media portrayals of obesity in Canadian newspapers in 1996, 2000, and 2005/06. Her analysis found that by 2005, the presentation of obesity as an epidemic was unquestioned. To see obesity simply as the result of people being lazy challenges the very foundation of capitalism that is built upon production and consumption; by constructing obesity as an epidemic, media provides the inspiration to effectively "prod" overweight individuals to get into shape through an entire industry focused on weight reduction (Holmes, 2009, p. 230). As Holmes's analysis shows, presenting obesity as an epidemic helps strengthen national pride and enhance an increasingly significant Canadian health research enterprise, and by doing so, stimulate the economy (Holmes, 2009). In terms of capitalism, seeing obesity as an epidemic that must be fought on all fronts is very good for business (see Oliver, 2006).

DISCRIMINATION AGAINST PEOPLE WITH DISABILITIES

As discussed in Chapter 10, discrimination occurs when a person or group either denies or grants advantages to members of a particular group (Feagin & Feagin, 2008; Giddens, 1997, p. 582). Section 15 of the Canadian Charter of Rights and Freedoms protects anyone who has a physical or mental disability from being discriminated against (Canadian Heritage, 2007c). Although federal and provincial laws have been enacted to protect the rights of people with disabilities, they are extremely difficult to enforce. Often, victims of discrimination are too embarrassed to report it (Woodcock, Rohan, & Campbell, 2007, p. 372). In Canada, 36 percent of people without disabilities reported witnessing discrimination against those with disabilities, and 52 percent of Canadians with disabilities reported that they have personally experienced regular or occasional forms of discrimination (Canadian Council on Learning, 2007).

The term **ableism** refers to discrimination against those who have a mental or physical disability on the basis of preconceived, stereotypical notions about their limitations (Castañeto & Willemsen, 2006; Morgan, 2011). People with a disability may indeed have certain limitations, but the belief that one form of disability means that a person is therefore incapable of other tasks is often unfounded (e.g., in addition to many other occupations, blind people can

ableism **Discrimination against those who have disabilities on the basis of preconceived notions about their limitations.**

> > >

People with a disability continue to face discrimination. However, there are some positive signs that employers are beginning to realize the tremendous contributions they can, and do, make to their organizations.

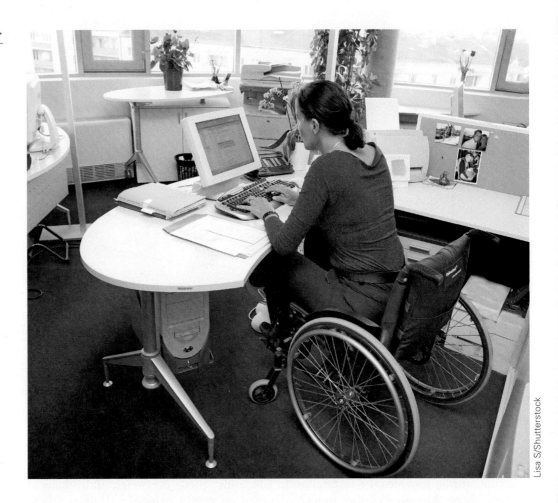

Lisa S/Shutterstock

become medical doctors,[1] psychologists,[2] and sociologists[3] in addition to many other occupations). The emotional impact of being discriminated against helps to explain why people with physical disabilities are more likely to report feeling lonely than are those from the general population (Rokach, Lechcier-Kimel, & Safarov, 2006, p. 681). Research shows that while some progress has been made, there is still some way to go before people with disabilities are treated equally within society (Prince, 2010).

6 THEORETICAL PERSPECTIVES ON DISABILITIES

Functionalism The functionalist perspective on disabilities is typified by Talcott Parsons's concept of the sick role. The **sick role** is a patterned social role that defines the behaviour that is appropriate for and expected of those who are sick. In this way, it is similar to all other social roles (e.g., student, mother) that include certain rights and responsibilities (Parsons, 1951). Those who are sick are temporarily exempt from usual role expectations (e.g., they can miss shifts at work) and generally are not seen as being responsible for being ill. Conversely, those who are sick are expected to want to get better, to seek out competent experts to help

sick role A patterned social role that defines the behaviour that is appropriate for and expected of those who are sick.

---

1 Tim Cordes graduated with a medical degree from the University of Wisconsin-Madison in 2005.
2 Paul Gabias holds a Ph.D. in psychology as well as an LL.D. and teaches at the University of British Columbia, Okanagan.
3 Rod Michalko holds a Ph.D. in sociology and teaches at Ontario Institute of Studies in Education, University of Toronto.

them recover, and to comply with these experts' recommendations (Parsons, 1951, p. 436). Functionalists would assert, then, that the sick role reinforces society's desire to give people time to recover while accentuating the need to seek professional help and to return to the roles they possessed before they became ill.

Critics of this perspective suggest that this concept is not adequate for people with disabilities, since it does not apply very well to those with lifelong physical or mental conditions (Wade, 2007, p. 295).

Conflict Theory

Conflict Theory As discussed, people with disabilities have higher rates of unemployment and low income than do people without disabilities. Moreover, many people with disabilities need specialized equipment (e.g., wheelchairs, hearing aids) that they may not be able to afford (Statistics Canada, 2008m). For conflict theorists, these facts underscore the fact that economic inequality affects people with disabilities differently.

The conflict perspective also stresses the work of disability advocacy groups. For example, many spokespersons for people living with disabilities objected to Richard Latimer's so-called mercy killing of his daughter (discussed earlier) by emphasizing that having cerebral palsy does not mean that a person cannot enjoy life and certainly does not justify taking the life of that person (see Council of Canadians with Disabilities, 1998).

Symbolic Interactionism Symbolic interactionists often focus on how labelling can have consequences for how people with disabilities are viewed and for how they view themselves (Charmaz & Rosenfeld, 2006). Consider the use of disabilities in a metaphorical, and usually disparaging, way. For example, to say that someone is "deaf or blind to the facts," or that "a strike has crippled production," is to use a disability as a negative stereotype. As you may have thought, this approach has been criticized as constructing a problem; after all, people generally do not intend to be offensive when they use physical metaphors such as "spineless," "stiff-necked," and "weak-kneed."

Feminist Theory The feminist perspective on disability emphasizes that our perceptions of what constitutes a disability are socially constructed in the same way that gender is. Feminists believe that by looking beyond a narrow definition of disability, one can begin to undertake a broad sociopolitical critique of systematic and binary opposition of abled/disabled and healthy/ill in the same manner as feminists have studied the binary oppositions of masculine/feminine and powerful/weak. "Feminism's often conflicting and always complex dual aims of politicizing the materiality of bodies while rewriting the category of woman are exactly the kinds of interrogations that should be brought to bear upon disability" (Garland-Thomson, 1997, p. 281). Feminist theorists would also assert that definitions of disability are a form of oppression that results from society's being ill-equipped to deal with anyone who is different, in whatever form that difference may take (McHugh, 2007, p. 28). In Canada, the Disabled Women's Network Ontario (http://dawn.thot.net) provides a wealth of information on contemporary feminist theory and disability studies. DAWN Ontario states, "As feminists, we are concerned with exclusion and inequality based on gender, as well as other factors such as class, race, education, or *ability* that limit women's full participation in the legal, social, political, economic and cultural benefits of society" (DAWN, 2003; emphasis added).

One criticism of the feminist approach to people with disabilities is that it may overlook the ways in which male health is as socially constructed as is female health (Fries, 2010). Feminist research may also seem overly theoretical and as such may not lead to the kinds of practical changes that would improve the lives of those living with disabilities.

Post-Structuralist Theory Post-structuralist theory has been instrumental in critiquing the notion of disability in that it challenges normative definitions of social order and individual identity (Prendergast, 2008, p. 55). Post-structuralists investigate how the concept of the body is constructed and deconstructed through individual and social interactions (O'Brien, 2005, p. 54). By reinforcing what is considered "normal," society develops a more narrow definition of what is acceptable. People with physical or mental disabilities are seen as even further from the ideal and therefore as less worthy of attention or concern.

One criticism of the post-structuralist approach is similar to that levelled at feminist theory—that theorizing issues of disability within the context of the postmodern economy, while potentially accurate, has little concrete application.

Summary

1 Health is defined as a state of complete physical, mental, and social well-being. While Canadians have a relatively high life expectancy, overall health is affected by income level, minority status, and gender.

2 The five universal principles of Canada's health care system are universality, accessibility, comprehensiveness, portability, and public administration. Health care issues in Canada include unequal access, the high percentage of provincial budgets devoted to health care, and the growth of alternative medicine.

3 Although those between ages 65 and 74 report the highest scores on measures of well-being, Canadian seniors face challenges in six areas: transition to retirement, financial pressures, age discrimination, vulnerability to crime, chronic pain and the need for long-term care, and preparing to die.

4 Disability affects many Canadians; pain is the most common disability for those between ages 15 and 64, whereas those age 65 and older most commonly suffer from limited mobility. Factors that influence rates of particular mental illnesses include gender, income, and age.

5 People with disabilities are often discriminated against. Ableism's effects are found particularly in the labour market: Although the percentage of people with disabilities in the workplace is increasing, it remains lower than that of people without disabilities.

6 With regard to health care, functionalists view the health care system as contributing to a stable society; conflict theorists highlight the economic inequality in Canada's (virtual) two-tier health care system and how increasing medicalization has served the interests of the rich and powerful; symbolic interactionists look at how labelling and the self-fulfilling prophecy affect the conception of one's own health; feminist theorists point out the androcentric nature of health care and the devaluation of subjective information; and post-structuralists highlight the changing nature of health care, whereby patients assume more responsibility and control over their health and so diminish the control traditionally exercised by doctors and the health care system.

With regard to aging, functionalists stress the disengagement of seniors from positions of power to allow younger people to assume these roles; conflict theorists point to economic competition between the old and the young; symbolic interactionists stress the importance of seniors' continuing engagement and activity; feminist theorists stress the extended disadvantage for senior women in a culture of youth; and post-structuralists critique the prevailing definitions associated with aging.

With regard to disabilities, functionalists hold that the sick role defines the expected behaviour of those who are sick; conflict theorists focus on the types of inequality experienced by people with disabilities; symbolic interactionists stress the importance of self-management for those with disabilities, as well as the negative consequences of labelling; feminist theorists critique the narrowly defined, binary opposition of abled/disabled as contributing to the oppression of people with disabilities; and post-structuralists likewise challenge normative definitions of the body and instead investigate it as socially constructed.

Key Terms

ableism *411*
activity theory *406*
ageism *401*
alternative medicine *394*
biopower *398*
BMI (body mass index) *409*
chronic pain *404*
disability *407*
disengagement theory *405*
downward drift hypothesis *408*
elder abuse *402*

elderly dependency ratio *400*
euthanasia *404*
Gender and Sex-based Analysis (GSBA) *391*
health *387*
healthy aging *400*
iatrogenesis *396*
life expectancy *387*
long-term care *403*
medicalization *396*
obesity *409*
people first philosophy *407*
sick role *412*
social determinants of health *388*

Reviewing the Concepts

1. Define and discuss what makes a person "healthy."

2. Review the five universal principles of Canadian health care.

3. What does the medicalization of health mean and why is it important for sociologists?

4. Discuss some of the key social challenges facing individuals as they age.

Applying Your Sociological Imagination

1. Review and discuss how health can be considered a social construction.

2. Using the sociological perspective, explore obesity in contemporary society.

3. As a sociologist, what concepts would you use to explain why the elderly and people with disabilities are discriminated against?

4. Explore people's attraction to plastic surgery through any of the sociological perspectives discussed in the chapter.

MySocLab

Visit MySocLab to access a variety of online resources that will help you prepare for tests and apply your knowledge.

Ryan McVay/Photodisc/Getty Images

16 Work and the Political Economy

Imagine that you are a single mother with a three-year-old son; you are taking three undergraduate classes and you have two part-time jobs. Your time is spent taking care of your son, keeping up with your school assignments, and getting as many shifts as you can at the coffee shop and the convenience store where you work. At times, you feel overwhelmed and that you are living separate lives: as a mother, as a student, and as an employee. Renowned sociologist Dorothy Smith felt the same way when she was working as an academic while raising two small children, an experience that led her to define a concept she calls *bifurcated consciousness*. Smith (1987) writes:

> I learned these relations . . . in thinking about my own experience when I combined work as an academic at the University of California at Berkeley with the single mothering of two small children. When I went into the university or did my academic work at home, I entered a world organized textually (though I would not have seen it that way at the time) and organized to create a world of activity independent of the local and particular. . . . But I went home or put down my books and papers to enter a different mode of being. I cleaned up after, fed, bedded down, played with, enjoyed, and got mad at two small children. I inhabited a local and particular world. . . . It was an absorbing world. (p. 6)

You may have experienced in your own life that *what we do* is not the same as *who we are*. As we will explore in this chapter, people often suffer from the stresses of having to make a living in ways that separate them from what they feel is truly important.

LEARNING OBJECTIVES

By the end of this chapter, students will be able to

① Appreciate the changing nature of work through time and its influence on a person's sense of self.

② Understand contemporary aspects of work: the three sectors of the economy, the primary and secondary labour markets, labour unions, self-employment, and education levels.

③ Discuss how sociological theory applies to an understanding of work.

④ Explore the different global economic systems.

⑤ Review and discuss aspects of the political economy, including bureaucracies, corporations, and global political systems.

⑥ Provide an overview of the Canadian political structure and the issue of Aboriginal self-government.

① Economies through Time

When we speak of social arrangements that organize the production, distribution, and consumption of goods, we are generally referring to the **economy**. From the earliest hunting and gathering subsistence pattern through to today's post-industrial society, we have always needed to secure food and shelter from the environment. How a group of people chooses to exploit its environment has a tremendous influence on both society as a whole and personal relationships. Our review of changing human economies relies on Gerhard Lenski's (1966) classification system of subsistence patterns through time (as cited in Llobera, 2003, pp. 108–109). Lenski's work reveals how different subsistence patterns can result in the emergence of very different social arrangements.

economy Social arrangements that organize the production, distribution, and consumption of goods.

HUNTING AND GATHERING

Some suggest that 99 percent of human history has been spent using a subsistence pattern known as **hunting and gathering** (Lee & DeVore, 1968, p. 3). The strategy behind hunting and gathering is to lightly exploit as many food resources as possible. By ensuring a diverse food supply, our ancestors were able to protect themselves from overexploiting any single animal or plant resource and secure a stable diet for everyone. Hunters and gatherers had few possessions and lived in small, mobile groups that followed whatever food resources were available in a given territory (Llobera, 2003, p. 108; Nolan & Lenski, 2006). Because this subsistence economy is based on the immediate fulfillment of need, the size of these groups was generally limited to 25 to 50 people.

In these societies, all healthy people participated in acquiring food for the group. Because of this daily obligation, there was little opportunity to develop specializations such as tool making, and this meant that hunting and gathering economies were not technologically

hunting and gathering An economic system based on small nomadic groups lightly exploiting animal and plant foods for immediate consumption.

advanced. However, because there was very little accumulation of wealth, social inequality was virtually nonexistent (Leacock, 1992). Everyone knew what was expected of them, and what people did was closely connected to how they lived. This close connection between individuals who worked together was precisely what Durkheim envisioned when he described *mechanical solidarity:* that which is based on people's similarities and yet grants them relative independence (see our discussion in Chapter 2).

HORTICULTURALISM

Between 10 000 and 12 000 years ago, hunter-gatherers in the Near East (and later in other areas around the world) began domesticating various species of animals and plants through an economic system known as **horticulturalism**.

horticulturalism
An economic system based on domesticating animals and plants.

Lenski outlined two types of horticulturalist societies: simple and complex. Simple societies relied on digging sticks and were relatively small, while complex societies employed metal hoes that generated more food and thus allowed a more advanced and complex social hierarchy to emerge (Llobera, 2003, p. 109). While these people were generally sedentary, many early horticulturalists practised shifting cultivation (also known as *slash-and-burn, milpa,* or *swidden cultivation*) (Clifton, 1968). This subsistence pattern saw people staying in one area for several years until the soil became exhausted, after which they would move to another area where the soil was more fertile. Groups would often cycle through a given area and return to regions they had cultivated previously. At times, some groups also practised the slash-and-burn technique, whereby they cut down and burned the ground cover in order to increase the soil's fertility, with the burnt vegetation acting as a fertilizer (Sodikoff, 2004, p. 368).

Although a comparatively simple technology, horticulturalism led to many dramatic changes in people's working lives. For example, because horticultural societies were able to produce substantially more food than hunter-gatherers, small bands could expand into tribes of several thousand people. The surplus of food also enabled some workers to remove themselves from daily subsistence work and spend time making more sophisticated tools. As well, full-time religious specialists and formal leadership structures (e.g., chiefs) emerged (Lindsey & Beach, 2003, p. 78).

The food surplus secured through horticulturalism allowed people to begin to specialize and develop different duties and obligations. Although people still had to "work" to meet their material and subsistence needs, opportunities existed to pursue tasks that allowed them to demonstrate their individual skills and abilities.

PASTORALISM

pastoralism An economic system based on tending herds of large animals.

Emerging around the same time as horticulturalism, **pastoralism** is a subsistence pattern wherein people make their living by tending herds of large animals. While the species of animal varies depending on the region (horses in Central Asia, cattle in East Africa, sheep and goats in Southwest Asia, camels in North and East Africa, and reindeer in Scandinavia), they all live in herds and eat grasses or other abundant plant foods (O'Neil, 2007). Pastoralists are usually nomadic, following their herds as they migrate from one area to another according to the season. Specialization in pastoral societies is similar to that in horticultural ones. They, too, generate a regular surplus and can support some full-time specialists. Social inequality increases as wealthy families begin to accumulate larger herds than others (Salzman, 2004; see also Mulder, 1999).

One could speculate that with the emergence of the idea that people could "own" their animals, we see evidence of inequality linked to the concept of wealth. Since social profile and influence are generally associated with wealthy individuals, people began to focus attention on accumulating resources to gain social stature.

David C Poole/Robert Harding World Imagery/Passage/Corbis

<<<

Pastoralists survive by tending herds of large animals. Many pastoralists are also nomadic and stay with their herds as they move from one area to another, following seasonal food sources.

AGRICULTURE

About 6000 years ago, in the valleys of the Tigris and Euphrates rivers (in what is now Iraq), innovations in metallurgy and the invention of the plow led to the practice of **agriculture**. V. G. Childe (1892–1957) viewed agriculture as a quantum leap in human history that led to dramatically increased population densities because it produced so much caloric wealth for a comparatively small investment of time and energy (Childe, 1951). Indeed, by using animals to pull plows, food production increased exponentially and allowed society to change in ways that were previously incomprehensible. To recognize the tremendous impact agriculture had on human history, this period is generally referred to as the *Agricultural Revolution*.

agriculture An economic system that employs plow technology.

Perhaps the most obvious change brought about by agriculture was the unprecedented population growth; large cities (some containing several million people) could now be supported by agricultural surpluses. As new cities emerged and even more people were liberated from food production, workers became specialists in virtually every possible endeavour—metallurgy, art, crafts, woodworking, and pottery, to name only a few. During this time, people were also able to study and learn more about the world around them; literacy increased, as did mathematics and scientific studies. Freeing some people from working in the fields, then, allowed society to benefit from these individuals' talents and passions. Yet, because agriculture was so productive, it also allowed social inequality to accelerate: The agricultural surpluses were controlled by a few wealthy families, with many others remaining poor even though there was more food than ever before (Bird & O'Connell, 2006).

For the first time in human history, then, people were able to make a living by trading their specialized skills for food. As the need for these goods and services increased, a universal medium of exchange (that is, money) was established to facilitate efficient trade.

INDUSTRIALIZATION

As discussed in Chapter 1, **industrialization** is based on using nonanimate sources of energy (e.g., steam, fossil fuels) to produce goods. Emerging in Europe about 200 years ago,

industrialization An economic system based on using nonanimate sources of energy.

industrial production, much like the agricultural revolution 6000 years earlier, again transformed the very nature of human society. Macionis and Gerber (2011, p. 376) outline five important changes that resulted from the Industrial Revolution:

1. *New sources of power*. For the first time, people were able to use energy sources beyond those of human or animal muscle. The invention of the steam engine by James Watt allowed factories to use energy sources that were far more powerful than human or animal labour.

2. *Centralization of work*. People moved from farms in the countryside to live in cities and become labourers in factories. Factory work was generally impersonal and unfulfilling.

3. *Mass production*. The economy moved from the production of goods locally by individual craftspeople to an economy based on turning raw materials into a wide range of finished products that were distributed far beyond the local area.

4. *Specialization*. Workers did not need to be artisans who understood how to craft a final product but instead were required to perform small, menial tasks that collectively resulted in the finished product. While workers would become very efficient at performing these specific tasks, their overall skill level declined.

5. *Wage labour*. Workers exchanged their sweat and toil for wages from factory owners, who often cared less about workers than they did about the machines that workers were paid to operate.

Together, these five factors changed everything about working lives. Workers were no longer producing something with their own hands and something in which they took pride; instead, the vast majority now exchanged their labour for money.

> > >

Industrialization often requires large factories where the raw materials are transformed into consumer goods, as, for example, at the Knight Sugar Factory in Raymond, Alberta (photo from 1904).

Glenbow Archives/PD-310-83

POST-INDUSTRIALIZATION

The term **post-industrialization** recognizes that social institutions and social life have been fundamentally reorganized since the late 1960s. The term refers to the reorganization of society, resulting from the growth of information technology, global communications media, the service sector, global consumerism, integrated financial markets, and cultural pluralism (Dodd, 1999, p. 3). Today, advanced industrial societies are no longer primarily focused on manufacturing products but instead on providing services (e.g., online banking) and knowledge-based activities (e.g., computer programming). In this respect, then, our economy has moved from an industrial model of exploiting raw materials and human physical labour to one based on supplying services or information. Traditional factories that produced physical goods are becoming obsolete as new industries based on ideas are becoming increasingly powerful. For example, Microsoft, one of the world's largest corporations, is more interested in helping businesses to manage people's creative ideas than it is in producing cheaper widgets:

> We believe that organizations which put people at the center of processes and information are better positioned to meet the challenges of a fast-changing, globally integrated and interconnected world because they have invested in the most agile, resilient and creative asset available to them. (Microsoft, 2008)

Today, large factories in the Western world, full of well-paid, unionized labourers, are being challenged by smaller, more flexible companies spread around the globe that are focused on the creation, analysis, and distribution of information with the click of a mouse. Much of this new work is performed by part-time employees and this results in a decline in traditional working-class jobs (Bornschier, 2009, p. 4).

This shift to part-time work is the result of (1) rising educational requirements for jobs and the consequent need for people to stay in school longer (discussed in Chapter 12), (2) increasing numbers of women joining the workforce and thus heightening the competition for jobs, and (3) the shift toward jobs in the service industries.

Table 16.1 shows that in March 2014, part-time workers represented roughly 19 percent of all jobs in the Canadian economy. Figure 16.1 illustrates the increase in part-time employment rates between 1976 and 2012. Over this 36-year period, part-time employment rates

post-industrialization
An economic system based on knowledge-based activities and the service sector rather than on manufacturing goods.

> > > Thinking Sociologically

Using the sociological perspective, speculate on how technology has changed part-time employment over the past 10 years. In your opinion, has technology made part-time work more or less fulfilling? Why?

TABLE 16.1 Employment by Age, Sex, and Class of Worker (Canada)

	March 2014
Canadian labour force (both sexes, ages 15+)	17 833 200
15 to 24 years	2 453 200
Men	9 379 600
Women	8 453 600
Full-time	14 456 400
Part-time	3 376 800
Self-employed	2 704 600

Source: Statistics Canada (2014). Employment by age, sex, type of work, class of worker and province [Online]. Retrieved April 19, 2014, from http://www.statcan.gc.ca/tables-tableaux/sum-som/l01/cst01/labr66a-eng.htm

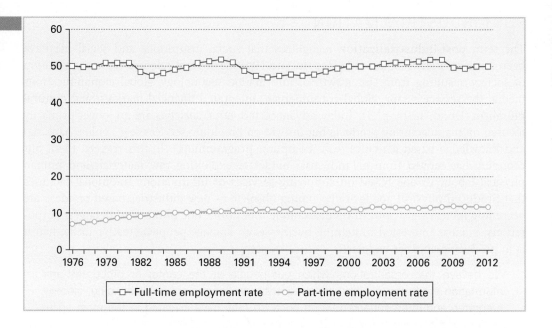

FIGURE 16.1

Part-time and Full-time Employment Rates, 1976 and 2012

Source: Statistics Canada (2014). Part-time and full-time employment Rates, 1976 and 2012 [online].

increased from 7.1 percent in 1976 to 11.6 percent in 2012, while full-time employment rates remained relatively stable at 50.0 percent in 1976 and 50.2 percent in 2012.

But some (see Dixon & Quirke, 2014) suggest that the changing nature of wage labour in industrialized economies has failed to even mention—until recently—the increasing number of people who find themselves underemployed, or those who engage in unpaid labour of all kinds. For example, what role does unpaid labour in the home play in maintaining the economy? How many stay-at-home parents or caregivers are paid nothing for their work—work that allows their partners or spouses to commit themselves to their careers or to maximizing their earning potentials?

There is also the challenge of balancing one's personal life with the demands of work, and this becomes ever more challenging in the face of wage depreciation and increased educational requirements for even entry-level jobs. How do individuals manage the increased emotional and psychological strain involved in working more hours, for less pay, while struggling to improve their level of education in order to do it?

The pace of change in our working lives appears to be accelerating. To understand how these changes influence society, we now turn to an analysis of today's world of work.

primary sector
Jobs dedicated to exploiting raw materials (e.g., logging, mining).

secondary sector
Jobs that transform raw materials into consumer goods (e.g., cars, furniture).

tertiary sector Jobs that provide services (e.g., teaching, nursing) rather than goods.

❷ The World of Work

THE THREE SECTORS OF THE ECONOMY

The federal government estimates that more than 30 000 different occupational specialties now exist in Canada (Service Canada, 2008). Contemporary sociologists divide these various jobs into three unique sectors of the modern economy. The **primary sector** includes those jobs dedicated to exploiting raw materials from the natural environment—for example, logging, farming, mining, and fishing. The **secondary sector** is made up of endeavours that transform raw materials into consumer goods—for example, cars and furniture. The **tertiary sector** comprises a broad spectrum of activities that provide not goods but services, which can include occupations ranging from waiters and store clerks to teachers, police officers, and physiotherapists.

In the nineteenth century, about 80 percent of all workers worked in the primary sector, mostly as farmers. With the level of mechanization at that time, a typical farmer could produce enough of a surplus to feed about five people. By 1900, about 50 percent of the labour force was still working in the primary sector. Today, that number has dropped dramatically, with farmers making up less than 2 percent of the Canadian workforce (see Table 16.2); however, each farmer can now produce enough to feed well over 100 people (Gourmetspot. com, n.d.).

Secondary-sector manufacturing jobs peaked around midcentury at approximately 40 percent of the labour force, but since then have steadily declined. Today, manufacturing jobs make up only about 11 percent of all Canadian jobs.

The tertiary sector has expanded rapidly over the past 100 years and continues to grow. Table 16.2 shows that the services-producing sector accounts for more than 75 percent of all jobs. If post-industrialist predictions are correct, we should see a continuing decline in both

TABLE 16.2 Employment by Industry (Canada)

Employment by Industry	2006	2010	2013	Percent Change
	thousands			
All industries	16 410.20	17 041.00	17 731.20	0.04
Goods-producing sector	3 975.90	3 740.00	3 883.40	−0.06
Agriculture	346.90	300.70	314.20	−0.13
Forestry, fishing, mining, oil, and gas[1]	334.10	329.40	367.40	−0.01
Utilities	121.30	148.30	143.50	0.22
Construction	1 066.40	1 217.20	1 323.70	0.14
Manufacturing	2 107.20	1 744.30	1 374.20	−0.17
Services-producing sector	12 434.30	13 301.00	13 847.70	0.07
Trade	2 616.40	2 677.80	2 705.20	0.02
Transportation and warehousing	794.80	805.70	863.20	0.01
Finance, insurance, real estate, and leasing	1 032.90	1 095.70	1 122.30	0.06
Professional, scientific, and technical services	1 082.10	1 266.70	1 347.70	0.17
Business, building, and other support services[2]	683.30	672.20	713.90	−0.02
Educational services	1 154.70	1 217.80	1 289.00	0.05
Health care and social assistance	1 779.00	2 030.70	2 176.50	0.14
Information, culture, and recreation	742.30	766.00	782.80	0.03
Accommodation and food services	1 013.90	1 058.40	1 131.80	0.04
Other services	701.10	753.50	769.50	0.07
Public administration	834.00	956.40	945.80	0.15

1. Also referred to as natural resources.

2. Formerly management of companies, administrative, and other support services.

Source: Statistics Canada (2014). Employment by Industry [online]. Retrieved May 05, 2014, from http://www .statcan.gc.ca/tables-tableaux/sum-som/l01/cst01/econ40-eng.htm

BOX 16.1 THAT WAS THEN, THIS IS NOW

Canadians' Standard of Living in Historical Perspective

According to the United Nations, in 2013 Canada ranked 11th in a list of the world's best places to live based on per capita income, education levels, health care, and life expectancy (United Nations, 2013).

During the early part of the twentieth century, much of the Canadian economy was rural-based. It was fuelled by a strong global demand for wheat until 1913 when wheat prices fell. At that point, many working farmers found it difficult to provide food and shelter for their families (Williams, 2000).

The 1920s began with a recession and an unemployment rate of 14 percent. However, the average salary increased to $960 annually, and as the economy grew throughout the decade, disposable income increased by more than 9 percent. During this time, the *Old Age Pensions Act* came into effect to help fund the living costs of the elderly (Williams, 2000, p. 8). Near the end of the 1920s, the stock market crashed and average salaries fell by almost 11 percent. As well, between 1928 and 1933, personal disposable income fell by 44 percent and the personal savings rate declined as people were forced to spend their savings to survive (Williams, 2000, pp. 8–9).

However, shortly after World War II, Canada ranked as the second-wealthiest industrialized country in the world (Shaw, 2002). By the end of the twentieth century, unemployment rates were lower than they had been in 10 years, the federal government was running a surplus for the first time since 1972, income tax rates had dropped, and disposable income had begun to rise at rates higher than inflation (Williams, 2000, p. 12). These factors contributed to a standard of living not previously seen in Canadian history. Some researchers point out, however, that it has been the rising incomes of the wealthy that are driving up both average income and income inequality and that one should be cautious of research that suggests that over time all Canadians are doing better (Osberg, 2008).

Figure 16.2 illustrates the continual rise in Canada's standard of living and labour. The figure reveals that two economic variables—standard of living and labour productivity—are closely related. Both variables moved in the same direction and fairly uniformly throughout the 1961–2008 period. These data demonstrate that as productivity increases, so does the standard of living. We tend to assume that people who earn more money are happier (see Stevenson & Wolfers, 2008), but is that in fact the case? Today, this question constitutes a very active area of scholarly debate (see Lucas & Schimmack, 2009; Morgan-Knapp, 2010). In your opinion, do you think people are happier today than they were, say, 50 years ago? What evidence is there to support your position?

FIGURE 16.2

Standard of Living and Labour Productivity in Canada, 1961–2008 (constant 2002)

Statistics Canada, GDP Data, CANSIM, 2009; Centre for the Study of Living Standards, Income and Productivity Data, Personal Income and Productivity Trends: Canada vs. United States, 2009.

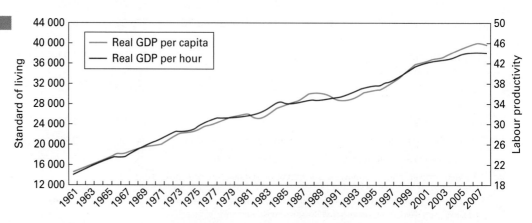

<<<

While farming remains an important component of the Canadian economy, many farm labourers have little long-term security or employee benefits.

resource exploitation and manufacturing as our economy becomes increasingly driven by the service and knowledge sectors.

PROFESSIONS AND "McJOBS"

When sociologists compare the types of occupations in the economy (beyond the broad economic classifications of primary, secondary, and tertiary sectors), they investigate specific types of jobs that individuals do and what these jobs mean to them. As discussed in Chapter 10, jobs that become careers and pay well are referred to as being in the primary labour market (not to be confused with the primary sector), while those that are transient and do not pay well are considered to be in the secondary labour market.

Jobs in the **primary labour market**, while often requiring postsecondary training or education, provide a stable and comfortable salary, future growth and promotion potential, and attractive fringe benefits (such as vacation time and bonus structures). These professions include medical doctors, lawyers, engineers, academics, and members of the clergy (to name just a few). **Professions** are defined as prestigious, usually white-collar, autonomous occupations that require a specialized body of knowledge, are community focused, and are regulated by a governing body (Cohen, 2006). To qualify as a profession, at least six characteristics must be present:

1. A common body of specialized knowledge
2. A set of regulated performance standards
3. A representative professional organization
4. An external perception by the public as a profession
5. A code of ethics
6. A formal program of training as well as ongoing professional development (Canadian Council of Human Resources Associations, n.d.)

primary labour market **Jobs that provide stable and comfortable salaries, potential for growth and promotion, and fringe benefits, but also require postsecondary training or education.**

professions **Prestigious occupations that require specialized knowledge and are regulated by a governing body.**

secondary labour market Jobs that are insecure and temporary, offer minimal pay, and provide few opportunities to advance.

Jobs in the **secondary labour market**, in contrast, are often insecure and temporary, are paid hourly wages, and only rarely offer any training to advance one's position. As explored in Chapter 10, we should not be surprised to learn that members of minority groups are disproportionately found in the secondary labour markets (Salaff, Greve, & Ping, 2002; Schaefer, 2008). Jobs in the secondary labour market are commonly referred to as "McJobs." In his book *The McDonaldization of Society*, sociologist George Ritzer (2004, p. 1) defines McDonaldization as "the process by which the principles of the fast-food restaurant are coming to dominate more and more sectors of American society as well as the rest of the world."

These principles, which Ritzer believes define the contemporary world of work, are efficiency, predictability, calculability (the ability to quantify virtually everything), and control (especially through the use of automation). Ritzer argues that, taken together, these principles culminate in jobs that devalue, demean, and oppress the worker. Maintaining a cheap, transitory labour force benefits the rich because people in this labour pool do the jobs that members of the majority would find demeaning and/or distasteful.

> ### >>> Thinking Sociologically
>
> According to our discussion of what defines a profession, do you think that plumbers, electricians, and house painters can be considered professionals? As a sociologist, how would you explain the desire of some workers to view themselves as professionals?

LABOUR UNIONS

labour unions Organizations that represent workers to improve wages and working conditions through collective bargaining and strikes.

Labour unions, much like professional associations, are organizations that represent workers to improve wages and working conditions through such means as collective bargaining and, at times, strikes. The union movement began in the eighteenth century, primarily in Britain, when people began to appreciate the tremendous transformations that were occurring as a result of the move from an agrarian economy to an industrial one. The introduction of machines resulted in downward pressure on workers' salaries; labour was no longer a form of craftsmanship needed to produce a final good but instead became a series of monotonous chores to maintain the machines. The fall of wages and the deterioration of the working environment led some workers to realize that they needed to join together for their collective good.

The earliest unions in Canada were established in the shipping ports of Halifax, Saint John, and Quebec City during the War of 1812. These early unions were intended not to provide services and support to their members but rather to gain profit from a labour shortage. Later, from the 1820s to the 1840s, other unions, such as the Montreal shoemakers and the Toronto printers, began to express their concern that skilled workers were losing their craft and status due to increasing automation (Canadian Labour Congress, n.d.). Labour unions have continued to play an important role ever since.

During the past three decades, unionization rates have diverged markedly across groups of workers. In 2011, about 29.7 percent of Canadian workers belonged to a union, down from 38 percent in 1981. Most of this decline occurred between 1989 and 1998, after which the rate has remained relatively stable.

Unionization in Canada has become far more polarized by age, with younger workers (particularly those under 35) experiencing sharper declines in union membership than older workers. Higher educated workers are also more likely to work in unionized workplaces. There are gender differences as well. Unionization rates for men are around 28.2 percent, marking a decrease since 1981; while 31.1 percent of working women are unionized, an increase over the same period. The decline in younger men's unionization is largely the result of a growing concentration of jobs in areas that have low union coverage (e.g., some construction, service industries), while women's increase is due to greater participation in public sector jobs (Statistics Canada, 2011d). In the private sector, unionization rates remain low for both men and women, with women's unionization rate hovering around 12.5 percent (compared to 19 percent of men), reflecting the fact that more women than men tend to work in service and sales—both of which are sectors of the economy that are often hostile to unionization (Statistics Canada, 2011d).

SELF-EMPLOYMENT

While union membership declined in all provinces between 1981 and 2011, the number of people who chose to become self-employed or work from home increased steadily (Statistics Canada, 2007e). In 2011, there were roughly 2.7 million self-employed workers in Canada, making up 16 percent of the employed labour force. Even during the economic collapse of 2008, self-employment rates rose by 3.9 percent while paid employment fell by 1.6 percent in the public sector and by 4.1 percent in the private sector (LaRochelle-Côté, 2010). This trend demonstrates a shift in our economy from the production of *things* to the creation, management, and distribution of *ideas* and *services*.

The increase in affordable and effective communication technologies (email, file-sharing software, and social networking sites) has enabled people to work from home much more easily and efficiently. Those who are self-employed and working from home are better able to set short-term and long-term goals, save the time and expense of commuting to and from the office, and have greater flexibility to work when they like (e.g., some people may be more productive in the evenings rather than in the mornings) (Finger & Flanagan, 2006, p. 104). As well, substantial tax advantages may accrue to those who own their own business and work from home (Carter, 2003).

LABOUR FORCE PARTICIPATION AND EDUCATION LEVEL

The education level of Canadian workers has steadily increased over the past few decades, as discussed in Chapter 12. The Canadian labour market has become increasingly knowledge-intensive, with the fastest growth occurring in jobs requiring more postsecondary education. Figure 16.3 shows that university-educated workers enjoyed the greatest employment growth between 1992 and 2011. However, research also confirms that those with less than a high school education have suffered the greatest employment decline over the past 20 years (HRSDC, 2007).

In fact, the proportion of the Canadian labour force with a postsecondary education has increased by more than 4 percent every year since 1990. Further, the number of individuals

✳ Explore

Where Have Georgia's Immigrant Workers Gone?

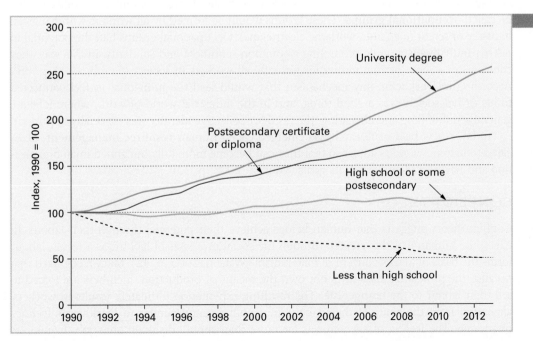

FIGURE 16.3

Employment Growth by Level of Education, Canada

Reprinted with the permission of the Minister of Finance Canada from "Employment Growth by Level of Education, Canada", in Source: Department of Finance (2014). Jobs Report: The State of the Canadian Labour Market Found at: http://www.budget.gc.ca/ 2014/docs/jobs-emplois/pdf/ jobs-emplois-eng.pdf.

with a university degree has risen by 4.4 percent a year. Whereas in 1990, university-educated workers accounted for 13.8 percent of all workers, in 2011 they constituted 30.8 percent of the working population. In contrast, the number of workers with a high school education has grown by an average of only 0.7 percent per year over the past 15 years, and those with less than a high school education has actually declined. Education levels are also related to employment levels. In 2011, the Canadian unemployment rate was 7.2 percent; however, the rate for people without a high school diploma was 14.8 percent; with a high school diploma, 8.2 percent; with a college diploma or trade certificate, 5.8 percent; and with a university degree, 5.0 percent (Statistics Canada, 2013e). Clearly, all else being equal, the more education one has, the lower one's chances are of being unemployed.

❸ Sociological Approaches to Work

Few things in life are as important as what we choose to do for a living, especially considering how much time we spend at work throughout our lives. In this section, we introduce how sociological theorists have attempted to understand work and its influence, not only on individual workers but also on the social fabric of society as a whole.

✸─[Explore

The Division of Labour in Society

FUNCTIONALISM

Functionalists view work as an integral part of the social structure, and look to the pattern of relationships that link people to their working lives. Central to Émile Durkheim's insights into work was his investigation of the dynamic relationship between individual agency and social structure. Because Durkheim believed so strongly in *organic solidarity* (based on interdependence and the division of labour, as described in Chapter 2), he was concerned with the trend, in his time, toward greater individualism. According to Durkheim, a type of healthy individualism could occur with industrial work that differed from the type that focused solely on the individual (Watson, 2003). As we have seen, Durkheim believed that when people do not feel connected to the social whole, they suffer from anomie—a feeling of normlessness.

For functionalists, the system is primary. Given their focus on the integration of individual parts, functionalists believe that workers need to feel a connection with their work. Durkheim believed that worker integration could be achieved in developed economies by building what he called **occupational groups**. These groups would be formed by all workers within a given industry or sector (e.g., auto workers, electricians). Occupational groups had the potential to restrict individualism while promoting a common sentiment and solidarity. In this way, they could foster a sense of community for virtually all workers in society (Grabb, 1990, p. 88). According to Durkheim, any mechanism that would lead the individual to feel connected to his or her society was a good thing, and in the industrial world of work, where jobs are generally unfulfilling and alienating, the need for collective identity was especially important.

Today, a new field of research has emerged called **human resource management**, dedicated to helping workers adjust so that they can become more fully integrated in an organization and begin to identify with its goals (Watson, 2003, p. 30).

occupational groups Durkheim's mechanism to promote the integration of workers.

human resource management An area of research dedicated to helping workers integrate into an organization and identify with its goals.

CONFLICT THEORY

Conflict theory suggests that human beings achieve their potential through their labour. In effect, the human world is created through the social processes of labour; as a result, labour forms the basis of Marx's concept of materialism (Watson, 2003, p. 42). Marx recognized that because the proletariat class does not own the means of production, members are forced to sell their labour to the bourgeoisie. The resulting exploitation ultimately results in workers' alienation from the fruits of their labour in a phenomenon similar to Durkheim's feelings of anomie. The feeling of alienation is far more than simply disliking one's job: It involves the feeling of being controlled by social institutions and lacking the agency to influence or change them (Lindsey & Beach, 2003, p. 380; Watson, 2003, p. 42). Alienated workers feel no connection to what they produce, to other workers, or to themselves; they feel powerless.

Marx's analyses of work continue to inform our understanding of contemporary labour processes. For example, modern industrial sociology uses the concept of the labour process to combine an analysis of worker behaviour, employee–employer relations, and how employees and employers interact within an organization (Watson, 2003, p. 44). The overall trend in industrial production is to " de-skill" workers so that their labour becomes increasingly efficient (think of factory jobs where workers perform the very same function over and over again, becoming very efficient over time but increasingly dehumanized in the process). Yet, recent trends in labour management suggest that some companies are actually focused on *expanding* worker skills (called *up-skilling*) as one way to inspire a connection between workers' labour and the company (Grimshaw, Beynon, Rubery, & Ward, 2002). Since Marx believed that people express themselves through their work, to be happy at their jobs, then, means that individuals need to see their work, and by extension themselves, as valuable and fulfilling.

> > > Thinking Sociologically

Use the concept of social drama to explore some of your own experiences in a work environment. What did these experiences teach you about yourself?

SYMBOLIC INTERACTIONISM

We have seen that symbolic interactionism views our sense of self as resulting from human interaction, from our interpretation of symbols, and from our engagement with the world around us. Our responses to people may influence their view of themselves, just as it may influence our own self-concept. From this perspective, then, one can see how important work is in defining a sense of self-worth and acceptance.

Perhaps the best-known symbolic interactionist analysis of work is that of Everett Hughes (1863–1931), who followed in the footsteps of Mead (1863–1931), Cooley (1864–1929), Park (1864–1944), and most sociologists at the Chicago School (Watson, 2003, p. 35). Hughes investigated the *social drama* of work; that is, he viewed work as a series of episodes that the worker navigates through each day and that define, influence, and alter his or her identity. In this sense, the workplace is just another, albeit significant, location in which we interact with others; by doing so, we learn more about ourselves. For example, Hughes was interested in how individuals adjust or adapt to the challenges of the work environment while maintaining their personal identity (Watson, 2008, p. 49).

FEMINIST THEORY

Dorothy Smith's analysis of the working lives of women, introduced at the beginning of this chapter, is a profound critique of the separate lives women are often asked to live. From worker to partner to mother, women today are being asked to move from one role to another. Feminist theory also challenges the functionalist model of work in that the patriarchal system often discriminates against women and marginalizes them into the periphery of the working world.

Feminist scholars look beyond economics and market relationships to consider the limitations imposed by capitalist ideology. For example, women's unpaid work (as homemakers, self-employed domestics, farmers, and mothers) does not fit into the traditional industrial class models. Instead, feminists argue that a broader definition of labour needs to be created that recognizes the lived realities of people today (Prügl, 2002, p. 33; see also Dixon & Quirke, 2014).

In 2003, feminist author and political theorist V. Spike Peterson published a book called *A Critical Rewriting of Global Political Economy*, in which she argued that traditional methods of gauging the success or strength of national and international economies ignore the

> > >

Many social theorists have investigated the relationship between a person's occupation and his or her sense of self.

John A. Rizzo/Photodisc/Getty Images

innumerable hours of unpaid labour worked by women around the world. Peterson argued that there are two distinct economic systems at work in the world: the productive economy, which is the one studied by economists and others, and the reproductive economy, which is composed of all of the types of labour that go in to reproducing the mechanisms required for the productive economy to operate—labour largely done by women. The reproductive economy, which includes things like childcare and child rearing, unpaid domestic labour (cooking, cleaning, etc.), and unpaid health care, is largely ignored by economists; but, Peterson argues, it is also largely responsible for maintaining cultural, social, and economic systems, many of which reinforce womens' unequal and marginalized positions (Peterson, 2003, p. 79). Put simply, Peterson argued that current economic systems privilege the economic power of men, while ignoring the work engaged in by women. Or, put another way, by not seeing this labour as valuable and worthy of being counted in national balance sheets, the work that women do is devalued and dismissed as not being important (see Postner, 1992).

POST-STRUCTURALIST THEORY

Post-structuralists reject the Enlightenment ideals and grand narratives of macrosociological theories, such as functionalism and conflict theory. Instead, post-structuralists challenge us to see how we produce society through our communicative behaviour. That is, the human notion of who and what we are is shaped by the dominant discourses that surround us. Foucault showed how power was exerted when, through the dominant discourse, people were categorized as homosexuals, criminals, or mentally ill (Foucault, 1980, as cited in Watson, 2003, p. 48). We can extend this analysis to the world of work by looking at how someone might be classified as a problem employee, for example. How does this change how others view that person and how that person views him- or herself? In effect, framing someone as a "bad employee" helps to perpetuate what it means to be a "good" employee and a part of the team. The post-structuralist contribution to our understanding of work, then, is to critically dissect the organization and its workers to see how the social environment has shaped both the individual and the collective labour process.

Sociological theory has provided a wealth of perspectives on how to interpret the tremendous changes in economic structures that have occurred over time, and what these changes mean to both individual workers and society as a whole. With this analysis fresh in our minds, we turn now to a review of global economic systems.

❹ Global Economic Systems

There are two broad economic systems at work in the world today: capitalism and socialism.

CAPITALISM

Capitalism is an economic system grounded on the private ownership of the means of production (Marshall, Rose, Vogler, & Newby, 1985, p. 260). There are three broad defining features of capitalism: (1) private ownership of property (e.g., factories, land); (2) the ability to pursue personal gain and profits (i.e., individuals are inspired to work hard and reap the material rewards of their efforts); and (3) competition among businesses in an open marketplace to attract consumers to their goods and services. Perhaps the best example of a capitalist economy is the United States (Klein, 2007); however, even there, market competition is constrained by the government (e.g., subsidized health care for the very poor is not consistent with pure capitalism). Today, pure capitalism does not exist; instead, there are state-managed economies that incorporate both free-market and socialist principles.

Capitalism is an undoubtedly productive economic system; by inspiring and valuing the individual accumulation of wealth, many people work very hard and have satisfying and productive lives. The drawback to this system of open competition is, of course, what happens to those who, for whatever reason (physical, mental, cultural, etc.), are not as able to compete.

State/Welfare Capitalism Many countries in North America, Western Europe, Latin America, and, indeed, most of the developing world offer a combination of free-market and socialist programs. **State or welfare capitalism** is a political and economic system that combines free-market principles (private ownership of property and the ability to accumulate private wealth through individual success) with varying degrees of social welfare programs (including state-funded health care plans, old-age security systems, and subsidized housing for the poor). Canada's largely capitalist economy contains elements of socialist principles, as evidenced by, for example, government ownership of Crown corporations (Canada Post, the CBC, Canadian National Railway, to name only a few) and government regulation of the banking, transportation, and telecommunication industries. Such government involvement in the economy is justified by the principle that society should use collective resources gained through taxes to assist all citizens (through such means as health care, education, and employment insurance).

Because state/welfare capitalism combines elements of capitalism and socialism, it is viewed by some as an ideal compromise between individual aspirations and the collective responsibility to help and support each other. One of the limitations of this system, however, is that relatively high wages and taxation levels make it more difficult to compete with countries that are better able to exploit their human and natural resources (China and Taiwan are two examples).

SOCIALISM

Socialism is an economic system in which raw materials and the means of production are collectively owned (Van Der Veen & Van Parijs, 1986, p. 636). As with capitalism, socialism has three defining features: (1) collective ownership of property and the means

capitalism An economic system grounded on the private ownership of the means of production.

state/welfare capitalism A political and economic system that combines free-market principles with varying degrees of social welfare programs.

 Watch

Global Financial Systems

socialism An economic system in which raw materials and the means of production are collectively owned.

of production (e.g., raw materials, factories); (2) a centralized, state-administered planning agency that defines, manages, and directs the economy; and (3) the production and distribution of goods with a view to the collective welfare without the profit motive that fuels capitalism.

In socialist economies, the state provides workers with all necessities (including health care, education, food, and housing). For example, in Cuba, people's living expenses are heavily subsidized by the state. State-owned homes cost only a few dollars a month, and state salaries are heavily regulated—even medical doctors earn only about $25 a month (see Cabezas, 2006). Other socialist economies include China, North Korea, and countries throughout Asia, Africa, and Latin America.

communism
Marx's hypothetical economic system in which ownership of the means of production is collective and workers' labour is not exploited.

It is important here to distinguish between communism and socialism. **Communism** was a hypothetical construct of Karl Marx based on his belief that after the fall of capitalism there would emerge a society in which everyone was equal. Marx believed that socialism was a transitory stage after capitalism and before communism. Yet communism (as envisioned by Marx, at least) has never existed at the state level of organization. Although some still define China as a communist country, sociologists who understand what Marx meant by the term appreciate that China's powerful—and, some suggest, oppressive—political structure would not exist in Marx's communism.

By definition, socialism is a system that attempts to address the needs of the majority. Historically, however, it has had limited success with human rights and equality of citizens. For example, although a very powerful military and economic force, China has a spotted record in terms of how it responds to challenges by its citizenry (consider the Tiananmen Square uprising in 1989 and, more recently, the suppression of Tibetan political demonstrations before and during the 2008 Olympic Games).

❺ The Political Economy

politics The endeavour to gain and maintain control of the state apparatus.

state An institution that maintains a monopoly over the legitimate use of force in a given territory.

Politics is generally defined as the endeavour to gain and maintain control of the state apparatus. Sociologists define the **state** as the institution that maintains a monopoly over the legitimate use of force within a given territory. In contrast, as discussed, the economy is the system that organizes the production, distribution, and consumption of goods and services. However, the state and the economy are so closely integrated that one cannot really be understood without the other. Adding to the complex relationship between the state and the economy is the pursuit and use of power by politicians and bureaucrats.

Wallace Clement (2001), a leading figure in Canadian sociology, believes that a defining element of Canadian sociology is its interest in the political economy. Political economy is generally viewed as the interactions of politics, government and governing, and the social and cultural constitution of markets, institutions, and actors (Clement, 2001, p. 406). According to Clement, political economists attempt to seek out tensions and contradictions within society to inspire progressive social change.

Arguably, the first Canadian sociologist to investigate Canada's political economy was Harold A. Innis in *The Fur Trade in Canada* (1930/2001) and *The Cod Fisheries* (1940/1954). In these works, Innis developed what has been termed the *staples thesis*, which contends that Canadian development was based on the exploitation of raw materials that were sent back to European countries to fuel their own industrial thirsts. Innis suggests that each staple had its own characteristics that imposed a particular logic on related development (Clement, 2001, p. 407). As the country grew and these economic developments continued, Canadian raw materials were taken abroad, refined into more valuable commodities (e.g., furniture, automobiles), and returned to Canada at vastly inflated prices. Innis suggests that being in a subordinate economic position to the British and American empires, Canadians took on the menial role of "hewers of wood, drawers of water."

A nation's society, then, is largely defined by how its politicians choose to shape its economy. To appreciate how politicians make these decisions, we look now at their use of influence and power.

WEBER'S POWER, DOMINATION, AND AUTHORITY

Max Weber's (1946) analysis of authority and power continues to inform our understanding of the political economy. Weber viewed power as the ability to achieve one's desires in the face of resistance or objection from others. In this sense, power is a demonstration of a social relationship and always involves the interactions of at least two parties (Lindsey & Beach, 2003, p. 357). Weber used the more particular concept of **domination** to refer to situations in which an entire group of people could be directed to comply with specific commands (Bartels, 2009, p. 457; Weber, 1968, p. 212). For example, both teachers and parents have a form of dominance that, at some level, requires an acceptance of compliance: Students and children invariably see teachers and parents as dominant. Dominance is always an expression of a hierarchy in that one group is stronger or can control the actions of another.

domination The exercise of power over a group of people to direct them to comply with specific commands.

Most, if not all, power relies on the threat of the use of force, be it physical (e.g., violence against self or others), psychological (e.g., coercion, guilt), or economic (e.g., being fired, having to pay fines). However, no society can exist solely on the use of force to control its citizens; oppressed people, at some point, will always try to subvert the rules and overthrow their oppressors. Consequently, those in power attempt to institutionalize their power. They try to convince their subordinates that their leadership and use of force is legitimate, justified, and—usually—supported through ideology.

Weber used the term **authority** to describe the situation in which subordinates consider the domination by leaders to be legitimate. In this context, *legitimate* does not necessarily imply that the domination is rational or fair. Instead, legitimacy exists when subordinates accept, obey, and support their domination and view it as preferable to any alternatives they might consider. Authority rests less on the actions of the dominant than it does on the willingness of the subordinates to believe in and support the claims of legitimacy by the dominant.

authority Exists where subordinates consider domination by leaders to be legitimate.

The relationship between power, domination, and authority is not fixed and absolute; rather, it is dynamic and, at times, somewhat subjective (Khan, 2009, p. 17). For example, in the work environment, bosses have the ability to direct what their employees do because these employees readily grant their bosses authority and recognize their dominant position. However, this does not mean that bosses can rely on physical power to force employees to do their bidding. Nor do bosses have the right to treat their employees unfairly or to subject them to sexual innuendos.

Weber's Three Types of Authority
Max Weber (1946) defined three separate types of authority: traditional, rational-legal, and charismatic. We will present these as ideal types, yet all three are fluid and influenced by individual leadership personalities and unique scenarios and situations.

Traditional authority is present when power is legitimated by respecting long-established cultural patterns and traditions. It is generally grounded in people's belief that the leadership is legitimate because it has always been that way. For example, cultures that have hereditary leaders recognize the leader's offspring as the rightful leaders for the next generation. The authority of leadership is granted through an ascribed status; that is, leadership is gained through birth, not through personal attributes.

traditional authority The exercise of power as legitimated by long-established cultural patterns and traditions.

> > >

Mahatma Gandhi was a charismatic leader who used nonviolent civil disobedience to gain India's independence from the British Empire in 1947.

Bettmann/Corbis

Traditional authority tends to decline as societies become more complex. As a society begins to incorporate a rational and scientific understanding of the world, people begin to challenge leadership structures that were based on tradition rather than reason. While some offspring are born and raised to take on the mantle of leadership, many others are ill-suited to lead others.

rational-legal authority The exercise of power as legitimated through laws, rules, and regulations.

Rational-legal authority is present when power is legitimated through laws, rules, and regulations. This type of authority is usually associated with achieved status: People work their way up through the system to attain positions of authority, as in the leadership structures of business and governmental bureaucracies. The important characteristic of rational-legal authority is that the legitimacy for the use of power or dominance resides not in the individual but instead in the office or position that the person holds. For example, professors have legitimate authority as a result of their academic training and the position they hold within their college or university. Outside the classroom, they have very little ability to wield any authority over students. Rational-legal authority must be applied universally (all professors have the same authority) and be clear and understood (the professor employed to teach your class is assumed to have met all of the hiring criteria necessary to teach the course). Because this form of authority is so rational and objective, it is a perfect fit for bureaucracy. In fact, Weber argued that the power of the bureaucracy could become so overwhelming that it had the potential to dehumanize people in modern societies (Cooke & Philpin, 2008, p. 43).

charismatic authority The exercise of power as legitimated through personal magnetism of individuals who compel people to believe in them and grant them their support.

Finally, **charismatic authority** is based on the personal magnetism of individuals who compel people to believe in them and grant them their support (Hopen, 2010, p. 5). Charismatic leaders do not need formal positions or offices; in fact, their charisma can enable them to transcend political leaders. The foundation for charismatic authority is people's belief in the leader's edicts. While this sounds irrational, the charismatic leader's stance can be revolutionary in its challenge of existing political structures and leaders. Even in highly developed societies, individuals can inspire a great deal of collective evil

BOX 16.2 ISSUES IN GLOBAL CONTEXT

The Silk Road: International, Digital Black Markets

In the fall of 2013, federal law enforcement agencies in the United States arrested 29-year-old Ross Ulbricht on charges of drug trafficking and facilitating murder-for-hire contracts. Ulbricht, also known as "Dread Pirate Roberts" was not some street-corner drug dealer or gangbanger; instead, Ulbricht was the owner and operator of the Silk Road, a shadowy network of drug dealers, contract killers, identity thieves, pornographers, and other less than savory characters. But what made Ulbricht's arrest so interesting was that the entire Silk Road network existed online, in a corner of the Internet that few people know anything about. Sometimes called the "deep Web," this digital frontier is concealed from the daily searches and transactions of most users because, unlike most other websites, Silk Road and other spaces like it are invisible to most standard search engines like Google or Bing. It is this anonymity that allowed Silk Road to operate and process thousands of transactions without anyone knowing. How big is the deep Web? According to some researchers, it is several orders of magnitude larger than the "surface Web" that we interact with daily (Bergman, 2001).

What also makes Silk Road so intriguing is that it is a modern-day, international version of more traditional black markets; anything and everything, from drugs to child pornography to hit men, can be advertised for—and acquired—by anyone with the right connections and some money. These sorts of networks have existed for almost as long as there have been formalized systems of commerce, but in the 21st century, buyers and sellers can exchange goods and services for money from across the world, without ever seeing each other.

But it wasn't just the anonymity of the users and the sites that made Silk Road so difficult for law enforcement to penetrate because, in addition to existing somewhere in the deep Web, most Silk Road buyers and sellers also made use of an entirely digital, online currency known as Bitcoin. This form of "cryptocurrency" (currency organized around principles of digital encryption and information transfer) is not backed by any government and so is not counted as part of any national economy (Brito & Castillo, 2013). Unlike traditional currencies, such as the Canadian dollar or the Euro, Bitcoin exists only as digital information, an online currency that some users will trade for traditional currencies.

Silk Road—and Bitcoin—represent an intriguing example of new systems of economic exchange that ignore national borders and cultural boundaries, and they present a new challenge to law enforcement agencies who no longer know who is buying what, from whom, and from where.

(Adolf Hitler, Idi Amin, Joseph Stalin) or collective good (Martin Luther King, Jr., Mahatma Gandhi, Nelson Mandela).

BUREAUCRACIES

A **bureaucracy** is a rational organization designed to complete many routine tasks as efficiently as possible. While some may argue that bureaucracies are more likely to inspire thoughts of unnecessary red tape, bureaucracies nevertheless process a great deal of information, for the most part very efficiently (Stephens, 1998, p. 233). In fact, some argue that the bureaucracy has become the dominant organizational form in contemporary society (Volti, 2005).

bureaucracy A rational organization designed to complete many routine tasks as efficiently as possible.

According to Max Weber (1946), bureaucracies exhibit the following defining characteristics:

- *An extensive division of labour.* Every employee in a nightclub (bouncer, bartender, server, manager, janitor), for example, has a set of specialized tasks to perform in order for the business to run smoothly (Lewis, 2006).
- *Written policies and procedures for workers and customers/clients.* In the ideal world, by making the rules clear, everyone benefits from understanding what he or she is supposed to do in virtually every situation.
- *Ongoing written records.* Printed documents make it possible to establish that rules do exist and are expected to be followed.
- *A hierarchy of authority.* Bureaucratic positions are ranked so that everyone knows who reports to whom. Organizational power and its legitimate use are invested in the position, not in the individual.
- *Performance-based hiring and promotion.* Bureaucracies are supposed to be based on meritocratic principles (i.e., the best person will get the job) (Beetham, 1996, p. 9; Lindsey & Beach, 2003, pp. 81–82).

Weber was concerned that as bureaucracies grow into larger and larger enterprises, they become so rule-bound and uncontrollable that they are essentially irrational in their operation.

For example, in 1995, the federal government instituted the *Firearms Act* (Bill 68) to help protect Canadians from illegal gun use. To manage the process, the government created a gun registry program that would cost roughly $2 million per year to run (Public Safety Canada, 2007). However, by 2005, the Auditor General confirmed that the program had cost $946 million over the previous 10 years (Ottawa Citizen, 2008). Although the logic behind the program made some sense (CMAJ, 2003), the bureaucracy that was created to manage what should have been a simple registration process ballooned into a nightmare—both for people trying to register their guns and the government trying to manage the process.

Watch

Where Did the Corporation Come From?

CORPORATIONS

The primary organizational structure in capitalist economies is the corporation. A **corporation** is a legal entity that has rights and liabilities that go beyond those of its individual members (usually referred to as shareholders). For example, like individuals, corporations can own property and enter into contracts. The corporation is legally separate from its owners and effectively shields them from any personal liability on behalf of the company. As well, because corporations continue beyond the lives of their owners, they can reap the benefits of long-term economic development.

corporation A legal entity that can own property and enter into contracts for the benefit of its shareholders.

Listen

Independent Boards

As legal entities, corporations are required to pay taxes, although at significantly lower rates than individuals do (see Table 16.3). To take advantage of these lower rates, shareholders often reinvest profits in the company to make it even more efficient and profitable—all the while paying lower taxes than individuals. As wealth accumulates within a company, shareholders have the flexibility to sell their interests in it when it best suits their individual tax situation (i.e., when people retire or when they invest their profits in a new business venture with even greater growth potential). Individuals do not have this flexibility in that personal taxes are payable annually.

The richest Canadians not only control the country's largest corporations but also possess a disproportionate share of the country's wealth. For sociologists, the main concern about corporations within advanced capitalism is that they are not beholden to any particular country; neither are they beholden to any moral or ethical standard. Their primary motivation is making profits, arguably by whatever means necessary. Yet despite corporations' enormous

TABLE 16.3 Federal Personal and Corporate Tax Rates in Canada, 2014

Personal Tax Rates[1]

15% on the first $43 953 of taxable income, plus

22% on the next $43 954 of taxable income (i.e., the portion of taxable income between $43 953 and $87 907), plus

26% on the next $48 363 of taxable income (i.e., the portion of taxable income between $87 907 and $136 270), plus

29% on taxable income over $136 270.

Corporate Tax Rates[2]

16.5% effective January 1, 2011

15% effective January 1, 2012

1. Each province collects taxes beyond these amounts.

2. Not including Canadian-controlled private corporations claiming the small business deduction. Also note that each province collects corporate taxes beyond these amounts.

Sources: Canada Revenue Agency (2014). Canadian income tax rates for individuals – current and previous years. [online]. Retrieved May 5, 2014 from http://www.cra-arc.gc.ca/tx/ndvdls/fq/txrts-eng.html

Canada Revenue Agency (2014). Corporation tax rates [online]. Retrieved May 5, 2014, from http://www.cra-arc.gc.ca/tx/bsnss/tpcs/crprtns/rts-eng.html (accessed May 5, 2014)

power, they are not the mechanism by which society manages its affairs and provides support for its citizens. That is the domain of politics.

GLOBAL POLITICAL SYSTEMS

There are around 200 nation-states around the world today, and most fall into four broad political systems: monarchies, authoritarian regimes, totalitarian systems, and democracies.

Monarchies In a **monarchy**, power and legitimacy reside in a single person or within a family that transfers its power from generation to generation. Historically, the power and influence of the monarch has varied a great deal. In an **absolute monarchy**, the leadership claim is based on either family membership or a divine connection with God or another supernatural being that legitimates and confirms the righteousness of the monarch's rule (Winichakul, 2008, p. 33). In a **constitutional monarchy**, the leadership is largely symbolic in that the true legitimate leadership is held by an elected body. The constitutional monarchy best known to Canadians is the British monarchy, currently led by Queen Elizabeth II. While Queen Elizabeth has a great deal of wealth and influence, she has no authority to make or pass legislation, a right that resides with the elected members of the British Parliament. While many monarchies still exist around the world (in Belgium, Jordan, Japan, Luxembourg, and Monaco, to name a few), their duties and responsibilities are largely ceremonial.

Authoritarian Regimes In **authoritarian regimes** political power is controlled by rulers who reject the rights of citizens to participate directly in the actions of government. The earliest forms of authoritarian regimes were monarchies where hereditary rulers relied on tradition as the basis for their use of force. A contemporary example of an authoritarian regime is Saudi Arabia.

Under a **dictatorship**, a "strongman" relies on personal loyalties and threats of force to maintain rule. Dictators generally emerge in poor areas where literacy rates are low,

monarchy A political system grounded on the rule of an individual or family that is passed from generation to generation.

absolute monarchy Monarchs are defined through family membership or a divine connection that confirms the righteousness of their rule.

constitutional monarchy Monarchs are largely symbolic in that true leadership is held by an elected body.

authoritarian regimes Political systems controlled by rulers who reject the rights of citizens to participate directly in the actions of government.

dictatorship A system in which a leader relies on personal loyalties and threats of force to maintain rule.

military juntas
Military leaders who seize political power.

democracy A political system in which individual adult citizens select their representative leaders through an electoral process.

participatory democracy A system that requires citizens to be involved personally in decision-making through open and engaged debate and discussion.

communication technologies are limited, and freedom of the press is restricted, all of which hamper the ability of the citizenry to mobilize (Gans, 2004; Ringen, 2005). **Military juntas** (military leaders who seize political power) are also a form of an authoritarian regime that continue to exist today—for example, in Niger.

Totalitarian Systems A totalitarian state is one in which there are no limits on leaders' use of force, and the state apparatus attempts to regulate virtually every area of people's lives. For example, during Nazi rule in Germany, it was common for party officials to enter private homes, search people's belongings, and confiscate them at will, all without the use of legal warrants. Some estimate that over 100 000 works of art stolen by the Nazis are still missing (Graefe, 2010, p. 474). Similarly, at the height of the Cultural Revolution in the late 1960s, the Chinese military often crushed anyone criticizing the government or its leaders. More recently, the oppressive rule by the Taliban in Afghanistan or the Ayatollahs in Iran (Azadi, 1987) are examples of governments that have unlimited control over their people and are often vicious and restrictive with regards to human rights and free access to information. Totalitarian regimes are ideologically diverse, from the ultra-right of the Nazi regime to the ultra-left of China and the former Soviet bloc.

Democracies A **democracy** is a political system in which individual adult citizens select their representative leaders through an electoral process. Historically, there have been two forms of democracy: participatory democracy and representative democracy.

A **participatory democracy**—as practised in ancient Athens (see Behrouzi, 2005, p. 138)—requires citizens to be involved personally in decision-making through open and engaged debate and discussion. Think of it as a "town hall" where individuals air their opinions before the group ultimately renders a decision on the issue at hand. This form of democracy requires a great deal of time and effort on the part

> > > Thinking Sociologically

Given our review of various political systems, can you foresee any situation in which a totalitarian state would be appropriate?

> > >

The Taliban in Afghanistan are an example of a totalitarian political system.

of citizens, which, combined with the difficult task of gathering everyone at the same time and place, makes it virtually nonexistent today.

In a **representative democracy**, citizens elect representatives to act on their behalf and to convey their concerns and issues to the broader collective (Klingemann, 2009, p. 9). The officials then join together to form a government that is representative of, and accountable to, those who elected them. This is the political form practised in Canada, the United States, Western Europe, and much of the developed world. As we will see shortly, however, while a representative democracy is preferred to many of the alternatives, the question to ask as a sociologist is this: In whose interests do the elected officials operate?

> representative democracy **A system in which citizens elect representatives to act on their behalf and to convey their concerns and issues to the broader collective.**

The Political System in Canada

Canada's system of government is referred to as a *parliamentary democracy*, meaning that Parliament is Canada's supreme authority and has sole responsibility for lawmaking, immigration, and other federal initiatives. Canada is also a federation in that the governance of the country is shared between federal and provincial or territorial governments. The federalist model allows the government of a country as large and diverse as Canada to meet the needs of its citizens as well as address regional or cultural interests (Canadian Heritage, 2004a).

THE DIVISION OF POWERS

The *Constitution Act* of 1867 gives the federal government responsibility for national matters, such as maintaining international borders, military operations, foreign affairs, regulating interprovincial and international trade and commerce, and establishing criminal laws, criteria for citizenship, and banking and monetary policy. Provincial governments have jurisdiction over matters that are of more local interest—for example, education, health and social services, property laws, and provincial and local courts.

< < <

Re-elected on May 2, 2011, Prime Minister Stephen Harper receives a standing ovation from members of his majority government.

The Canadian Press/Tom Hanson

The powers and responsibilities of the territorial governments (Yukon, Northwest Territories, and Nunavut) are similar to those of the provinces. Unlike provinces, however, territories do not have jurisdiction over land and natural resources. Further, territorial powers are not guaranteed by the Constitution but, rather, by the federal government, which can change them whenever it deems it necessary.

Municipalities manage the local affairs of cities and towns, and are established through the provincial legislatures. Municipalities are largely responsible for collecting property taxes and providing to their citizens services such as water and sewer systems, garbage disposal, road maintenance, building code inspections, parks, and libraries.

MANAGING THE GOVERNMENT

Prime Minister The head of the federal government in Canada.

In Canada, the **Prime Minister** is the head of the federal government and is generally designated as the leader of the political party that holds the most seats in Parliament. The Prime Minister is responsible for representing Canada in international affairs as well as selecting his or her Cabinet.

Cabinet A committee made up of ministers in charge of government departments.

The **Cabinet** is a committee made up of ministers in charge of government departments (e.g., Aboriginal Affairs and Northern Development, National Defence, Finance, Health, Justice). Cabinet ministers are members of the governing party and elected members of the House of Commons; by tradition, each province has at least one member in Cabinet. The Cabinet is a powerful vehicle for moving the government's agenda forward, as the ministers discuss legislation, prepare policies, and respond to specific matters of the day.

senators Nonelected officials appointed by the federal government to represent their constituencies as well as the interests of all Canadians.

Senators, much like members of Parliament, are intended to represent the people of their home region. While members of the House of Commons are elected and represent their constituencies, senators are appointed by the government in power and are intended to act in the interests of all Canadians. Currently, there are 105 seats in the Senate.

backbenchers Elected members of Parliament who do not hold a Cabinet position.

Members of the House of Commons who are not ministers are called **backbenchers**. Backbenchers are elected and responsible for representing their constituents as well as supporting the leader of their respective party (e.g., Conservative, New Democratic, or Liberal). Currently, there are 308 members in the House of Commons (Government of Canada, 2014).

Governor General The Crown's representative at the federal level in Canada.

lieutenant-governor The Crown's representative in each of Canada's 10 provinces.

territorial commissioner The federal government's representative in each of Canada's three territories.

The **Governor General** is appointed by the Queen on the recommendation of the Prime Minister and is the Crown's representative at the federal level. On the advice of the Prime Minister, he or she is responsible for calling Parliament into session and for dissolving it prior to elections. The Governor General appoints the Prime Minister and, by tradition, chooses the leader of the party with the most seats in the House of Commons. The Governor General (currently, the Right Honourable David L. Johnston) reads the Speech from the Throne that opens Parliament and establishes the government's priorities and objectives for the session. The Crown's representatives in the 10 provinces are called **lieutenant-governors** and have similar, albeit provincial, responsibilities to the Governor General.

Each of Canada's three territories has a **territorial commissioner**, whose duties are similar to those of lieutenant-governors but who represents the federal government instead of the Crown. Territorial commissioners are appointed by the federal government and act under instructions from the Minister of Aboriginal Affairs and Northern Development. More recently, however, territorial premiers and cabinets have held greater executive power, and the territorial commissioner's role has become more ceremonial and advisory (Canadian Heritage, 2004c).

ELECTIONS IN CANADA

The election of representatives to the House of Commons is based on geographical divisions known as *electoral districts*, commonly referred to as *ridings*. Since 1964, various independent commissions have adjusted riding boundaries, mainly because of population growth in some areas. Once every 10 years, a new commission is established to make any necessary changes

FIGURE 16.4   Voter Turnout, 1867–2011

Reprinted by permission from Elections Canada, Voter Turnout. 1867–2008; voter turnout 2011, Elections Canada; population estimate for Jan 1, 2011, Statistics Canada. Accessed June 30, 2011, from http://www.sfu.ca/~aheard/elections/historical-turnout.html

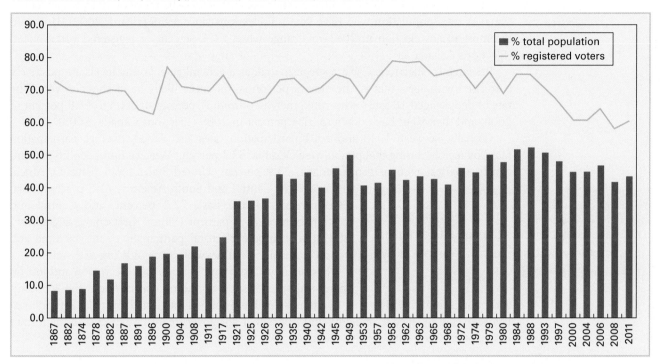

in each of the 10 provinces. The three territorial areas each constitute a single electoral district and therefore do not require any adjustments to their boundaries (Elections Canada, 2008d).

In Canada's *first past the post* system, the candidate with the most votes wins a seat in the House of Commons and represents that electoral district as its Member of Parliament. To win the seat, the candidate is not required to win more than 50 percent of the votes but simply must win more than any other candidate. The *popular vote* is the percentage of all voters who voted for a particular candidate. There may be times when a candidate wins an election with only 35 percent of the popular vote, but as long as no one else exceeds that number, that candidate still wins the seat.

Electing candidates to Canada's 308 electoral seats is an enormous task, and electoral participation rates vary greatly. The highest electoral participation rate in Canadian history occurred in 1958, when 79.4 percent of registered voters voted, while the lowest (nonreferendum) rate occurred

< < <

Jack Layton (1950–2011) led his New Democratic Party to become the Official Opposition in May 2011. Less than four months later he passed away from cancer.

Heinz Ruckemann/UPI/Landov

in 2008, when only 59.1 percent of Canadians voted in the general election (Elections Canada, 2010c). However, if you look at the percentage of votes cast as a percentage of the entire Canadian population, then the decline is not nearly so dramatic (see Figure 16.4). In fact, the 45-percent level registered in the 2000 and 2004 elections is well within the range of 40 to 50 percent of Canada's total population who have voted in elections since 1935 (Heard, 2008). However, the most recent election in 2011 this range when 61.4 percent of registered voters voted (Elections Canada, 2011).

Research by Elections Canada suggests that, as a general rule, voting levels are positively correlated with age—that is, the older a person is, the more likely he or she is to vote. The rate of people aged 18 to 24 who voted increased from 37 percent in 2004 to 43.8 percent in 2006, and then went back down to 37.4 percent in 2008 (Elections Canada, 2008).

Globally, between 1945 and 2001 participation rates also varied. Average participation rates, by region, during that period were Oceania, 83.1 percent; Western Europe, 82.6 percent; North America, 69.6 percent (Canada, 73.9 percent; United States, 66.5 percent); Africa, 64.5 percent; Central and South America, 71.5 percent; Asia, 74.0 percent; Middle East, 72.2 percent; and Central and Eastern Europe 71.9 percent (Pintor, Gratschew, & Sullivan, 2002). To compare electoral participation rates by time and country, take a look at www.electionguide.org.

> > > Thinking Sociologically

As a sociologist, discuss the social factors that may explain why older people are more likely than younger people to vote.

Historically, Canadian elections have been won and lost on many important issues, including conscription, the economy, and political scandal. However, two issues that have defined the Canadian social and political landscape are Quebec sovereignty and Aboriginal self-government. We discussed the former in Chapter 10; we turn now to the latter.

ABORIGINAL SELF-GOVERNMENT

Canada's Aboriginal peoples lived in the area we know as Canada for thousands of years before European explorers arrived. The contact between Aboriginals and Europeans has ranged from supportive and compassionate to hostile and cruel. Early European explorers were interested in exploiting Canada's rich natural resources and in claiming the new land in the name of their countries of origin.

King George III's Royal Proclamation of 1763 stated that Aboriginal land rights required the signing of treaties before settlement could occur. It confirmed that government has a fiduciary, or trust-like, responsibility over First Nations. This tradition continued through Canadian Confederation in 1867 (Indian Claims Commission, 2005).

Section 91(24) of the 1867 *Constitution Act* assigned the federal government jurisdiction over indigenous peoples and land reserved for the indigenous peoples; almost 10 years later, the *Indian Act* of 1876 consolidated all existing legislation regarding indigenous peoples (Wherrett, 1999). Much later, in 1939, a Supreme Court decision brought the Inuit under federal responsibility; the Métis (offspring of Aboriginal women and European men) were incorporated after constitutional changes made in 1982.

Until the early 1950s, government policy was largely directed toward assimilating Aboriginal peoples into Canadian society (Frideres, 1996; Wherrett, 1999). Even though indigenous band councils exercised some limited decision-making over local issues on reserves, ultimate authority rested with the federal minister in charge of Aborignial Affairs. However, over the next 20 years, the federal government began transferring control of various programs to bands themselves, to the provinces, and to other federal agencies.

As discussed in Chapter 10, in 1969 the federal government released its White Paper on Indian policy, which advocated terminating Aboriginals' special status in Canada and devolving, over time, all responsibility for services and programs for Aboriginal peoples to the provinces (Wherrett, 1999). The resulting widespread opposition from Aboriginals not only led to the withdrawal of the policy but also inspired a national movement among

Aboriginal peoples. While Aboriginals have asserted their rights to self-government since European contact, it was not until the 1970s that the movement gained traction and public recognition (Wherrett, 1999). Aboriginal self-government continues to be a high-profile issue.

Aboriginal issues were a major point of discussion during talks on constitutional reform held in the 1980s and 1990s. In fact, Section 35(1) of Canada's Charter of Rights and Freedoms (enacted in 1982) recognizes and confirms Aboriginal rights. However, during the 1987 Meech Lake Accord negotiations (inspired by the federal government's desire for Quebec to become a Charter signatory), Aboriginal leaders were largely dismissed when they sought recognition of their right to self-government. In response, Elijah Harper, a Cree member of the Manitoba legislature, voted against the Accord and effectively scuttled it. The federal government revisited constitutional issues during the Charlottetown Accord, which proposed formal recognition of the inherent right of self-government for Canada's Aboriginal peoples. On October 26, 1992, Canadians voted in a referendum to defeat the Accord, and since then the federal government has not reopened discussions on constitutional issues. However, there have been developments on other fronts.

In 1996, the government released the results of the Royal Commission on Aboriginal Peoples (RCAP), which found that Aboriginal peoples in Canada have the inherent right to govern themselves. The report stated that since Aboriginals were independent and sovereign nations before European contact, their right to self-government should be preserved in Canada's Constitution (Aboriginal Affairs and Northern Development, 2006). While this finding has not resulted in entrenching these rights in the Constitution, dozens of agreements that provide various forms of self-government (e.g., the Nisga'a agreement in August 1998) have been negotiated between Aboriginals and federal and provincial governments. Further, the establishment of Nunavut in April 1999 is a clear indication that the federal government is continuing to seek greater autonomy for Aboriginal peoples (Wherrett, 1999). Aboriginal issues in general, and self-government in particular, will undoubtedly remain important areas of political debate for many years to come.

< < <

Former politician and honorary Cree Chief Elijah Harper holds up one of two eagle feathers he held during the negotiations around the Meech Lake Accord.

The Canadian Press/Tom Hanson

Summary

❶ Human economies, and the types of work they entail, have changed over time in the following sequence: hunting and gathering, horticulturalism, pastoralism, agriculture, industrialization, and post-industrialization.

❷ Contemporary jobs are divided into three broad sectors (primary, secondary, and tertiary) as well as the primary (professional) and secondary (hourly wage) labour markets. Three trends in Canada's world of work are the decline in labour unionization rates, the increase in the number of self-employed, and workers' rising educational levels.

❸ Functionalists perceive that people need to feel a connection with their work; conflict theorists recognize that exploitation of the proletariat results in their alienation from the fruits of their labour; symbolic interactionists understand work as a means of defining one's sense of self; feminist theorists argue that the patriarchal system discriminates against women and the capitalist ideology fails to recognize women's unpaid work; post-structuralists analyze how dominant discourses shape both the individual and the collective labour process.

④ Capitalism is grounded on the private ownership of the means of production; state/welfare capitalism combines a free market with social programs; socialism involves the collective ownership of raw materials and the means of production.

⑤ The political economy encompasses the interaction of politics, government, and markets and institutions, and entails relationships of power, domination, and authority. Global political systems include monarchies, authoritarian regimes, totalitarian systems, and democracies.

⑥ Canada is both a parliamentary democracy and a federation, in that the federal and provincial/territorial governments share the country's governance. Two issues that have defined Canada's political landscape are Quebec sovereignty and Aboriginal self-government.

Key Terms

absolute monarchy *437*
agriculture *419*
authoritarian regimes *437*
authority *433*
backbenchers *440*
bureaucracy *434*
Cabinet *440*
capitalism *431*
charismatic authority *434*
communism *432*
constitutional monarchy *437*
corporation *436*
democracy *438*
dictatorship *437*
domination *433*
economy *417*
Governor General *440*
horticulturalism *418*
human resource management *428*
hunting and gathering *417*
industrialization *419*
labour unions *426*

lieutenant-governor *440*
military juntas *438*
monarchy *437*
occupational groups *428*
participatory democracy *438*
pastoralism *418*
politics *432*
post-industrialization *421*
primary labour market *425*
primary sector *422*
Prime Minister *440*
professions *425*
rational-legal authority *433*
representative democracy *439*
secondary labour market *426*
secondary sector *422*
senators *440*
socialism *431*
state *432*
state/welfare capitalism *431*
territorial commissioner *440*
tertiary sector *422*
traditional authority *433*

Reviewing the Concepts

1. Review Smith's concept of bifurcated consciousness and then list two situations in your own life where you seem to be operating in separate worlds (e.g., work, family, school, relationships).

2. Compare and contrast the types of work within two different economic systems through time (i.e., hunting and gathering, horticulturalism, pastoralism, agriculture, industrialization, post-industrialization). How might the jobs in these economies influence how people feel about themselves and their relationships with the larger society?

3. In your opinion, are there any social costs associated with the increasing proportion of part-time jobs versus full-time jobs? Discuss.

4. Review and describe which characteristics of the bureaucracy are evident at your university or college.

Applying Your Sociological Imagination

1. Even though much of university education (e.g., social sciences, humanities) is not targeted at training workers, how would you explain the association between higher education levels and low unemployment rates? In your opinion, what is it about education that seems to be so attractive to employers?

2. Compare and contrast any two sociological theories and their analyses of work. Which do you believe most accurately explains your own work experience? Be sure to use examples to support your position.

3. With reference to the chapter and to your own experiences, what are the primary advantages and disadvantages associated with capitalism? Discuss.

4. As a sociologist, speculate on why Aboriginal self-government is such a contentious political issue in Canada. Do you believe that it will be resolved in, say, the next 20 years? Why or why not?

MySocLab

Visit MySocLab to access a variety of online resources that will help you prepare for tests and apply your knowledge.

17 Mass Media

You know that our generation is more "connected" than any generation in history. We can text our friends in Spain from the comfort of our sociology class and at the same time, watch the student in front of us check out their Facebook page. These technologies were unimaginable even 20 years ago. Today, we can have real-time conversations with friends in Vancouver, Brazil, Portugal, and Iceland. Social media let us virtually "hang out" wherever we are, with whomever we want to.

And yet, Sherry Turkle argues that while we are more connected than ever, we are also more alone. In a *TED Talk* from 2012, Turkle talks about a man who would rather communicate with his co-workers through email and texting than by walking across the office and speaking to them in person. A student Turkle interviewed (via text), told her, "Someday, someday certainly but not now, I would like to learn how to have a conversation . . ." (Turkle, 2012). For Turkle, the student's confession speaks to a fundamental shift in how we interact with one another today: We do so on our own time, in our own way, and from a position of control that is not possible in most face-to-face conversations. Sending a text to a friend is cool, calculated, and impersonal, while meeting your best friend for a cup of tea can be heated, hilarious, spontaneous, and, at all times, absolutely personal. Online communication allows us to view only those texts and tweets and status updates that we want to, it also allows us to ignore, erase, unfriend, and otherwise dismiss any position or perspective we do not agree with.

This level of control and anonymity may sound appealing, but consider the bigger picture: How well do you really *know* the people you interact with online and how many of them really *know* you? How many of your Facebook friends have you actually met? How many would you want to go to dinner with? At first glance, our social networks appear broad and deep, but upon reflection, are usually narrow and shallow. Yes, we have lots of online friends, but how many of them would we really go for coffee with?

LEARNING OBJECTIVES

By the end of this chapter, students will be able to

1 Outline the progression of communication technologies through time and discuss their social impact.

2 Discuss contemporary forms of mass media and how they have altered societal relations.

3 Explain the key insights of Harold Innis and Marshall McLuhan as they relate to mass media.

4 Outline key legislation governing the broadcasting of Canadian content, the provision of federal funding, and the debate surrounding CanCon.

5 Review the key sociological theories that explain the role of mass media in contemporary society.

6 Discuss various aspects of the future of mass media.

1 Mass Media through Time

Everyone realizes how important media are for people today. From radio and television to text messaging and Internet searches, these technologies are influencing how individuals interact with the world around them. To begin our discussion, we distinguish between the terms **mass communication** and mass media. Mass communication is the transmission of messages by a person or group through a device to a large audience. Printing flyers about an upcoming political protest and posting them around campus constitutes mass communication; that is, printed flyers (the device) are used to communicate about the protest (the message) to everyone on campus (the audience). **Mass media**, on the other hand, include any medium (device) designed to communicate messages to a mass audience (e.g., newspapers, radio, film, billboards, the Internet, etc.).

We believe that to truly appreciate contemporary mass media and the role they play in society, we need to step back and see them from a historical perspective.

mass communication
The transmission of messages by a person or group through a device to a large audience.

mass media
Devices designed to communicate messages to a mass audience.

PREHISTORIC CAVE ART

Our human ancestors first began using paintings and engravings on cave walls to communicate their ideas and emotions during the Upper Paleolithic era (40 000 to 10 000 before present). The subjects of these images were usually animals and people (Ambrose, 2006). While we cannot know for certain, we assume that the artists understood that people would see these images long after they were created. Because we can still see the images today, after tens of thousands of years, we must appreciate the power they have to transcend time and to connect with a mass audience. These images are relatively easy to interpret because they are direct representations of objects or events.

> > >

Prehistoric cave art from the Caves of Lascaux, France.

Glasshouse Images/Alamy

CUNEIFORM, HIEROGLYPHICS, AND THE ALPHABET

The Sumerians of Mesopotamia (what is now Iraq) were the first to invent a form of writing called cuneiform around 3500 BCE; the Egyptians developed hieroglyphic writing around 3200 BCE (Greist, 2010; Lawler, 2001). **Cuneiform**, or "wedge-shaped" writing, was created by scribes who etched inscriptions on wet clay tablets using a reed stylus. While some believe that Mesopotamian cuneiform was a precursor (through diffusion) of Egyptian writing, most researchers today agree that writing was less about single inventions and more the result of a complex series of inventions going back long before the first evidence of writing (Lawler, 2001).

Researchers believe that somewhere between 4000 and 3000 BCE, the Egyptians developed hieroglyphic writing, which enabled them to communicate much more elaborate and abstract ideas to a mass audience (Aaron & Joshi, 2006). **Hieroglyphics** are made up of individual characters (called *hieroglyphs*). Some hieroglyphs are simple graphical representations (e.g., the image of a bird), while others are abstract representations that require translation.

Researchers were unable to translate Egyptian hieroglyphics until the discovery of the Rosetta Stone in 1799. The inscription on the Rosetta Stone (a message that announced the first anniversary of the coronation of 13-year-old Ptolemy V) presented the same passage in three different languages (Egyptian hieroglyphics, considered the appropriate form for important decrees; demotic, for everyday communication; and Greek, the language of the administration) (British Museum, n.d.). Since the ancient Greek language was already understood, researchers were able to use it to translate the Egyptian hieroglyphics. Discovery of the Rosetta Stone made it possible to begin translating the thousands of examples of Egyptian hieroglyphics that archaeologists had uncovered over the years, allowing contemporary archaeologists and historians a unique and immensely valuable look into the past.

The Egyptians were also responsible for introducing a form of writing paper, called **papyrus**, around 4000 BCE. The development of papyrus, along with the hieroglyphic writing system, contributed to the development of Egypt as one of ancient world's superpowers

cuneiform An early form of wedge-shaped writing developed by the ancient Sumerians.

hieroglyphics An early form of visual communication developed by the Egyptians.

papyrus An early form of writing paper developed by the Egyptians.

(Parks, 2005). Because it was lightweight, papyrus enabled written messages to be transported across great distances—a real development for the Egyptian and, later, the Roman Empires, which needed a means of accurate communication over great distances to manage their various military and economic campaigns.

More than 2000 years later, around 1500 BCE, the Greeks had developed a **phonetic alphabet**, which was written from left to right and represented the sounds of the spoken language (Couch, 1996, p. 103). Phonetic writing, of course, by being infinitely expandable, can efficiently transmit complex messages; indeed, the 26 letters in the English alphabet have created more than 170 000 words and our vocabulary is expanding all the time.

An example of cuneiform writing.

Egmont Strigl/imageBROKER/MaXx Images

phonetic alphabet
A system of writing developed by early Greeks that uses letters to represent spoken sounds, enabling the expression of complex ideas.

FROM BLOCK PRINTING TO MOVABLE TYPE

With the diffusion of written language throughout the world, people began to appreciate the potential uses of making exact copies of written text to allow more than one person access to the materials at one time. The earliest printing process, called **block printing**, was developed in China, during the T'ang dynasty (618–907 BCE) (Yao, 2002). This process involved engraving text and illustrations onto wooden blocks that were then inked and pressed onto paper (Avery, 2003). The process was used to print cards, calendars, and notices by merchants to promote their wares—an early form of advertisements. While this process allowed the production of virtually identical copies, it was a relatively labour-intensive process. The blocks had to be engraved (and if a mistake was made, one would have to start over), and if any changes were required, a new block would have to be produced. Around 1450, however, all of this changed.

Johannes Gutenberg's printing press had a tremendous influence on human social development. The revolutionary element of his invention was the implementation of movable type. In contrast to block printing, **movable type** used small metal shafts whose ends took the form of letters or images, which could be moved into sentences and patterns and then transferred to paper. If a mistake was made or a revision to the text was desired, only that which needed to be corrected had to be changed, and not the entire printing surface. Further, because the metal letters and images could be reused, the process was very economical.

Gutenberg's printing press would go on to transform human society. Not only was it one of the first major applications of mass production, but its interchangeable parts constituted one of the earliest instances of a technique that would become instrumental to the Industrial Revolution three centuries later. Moreover, by making affordable copies of the Bible and other documents, people outside the upper class were motivated to learn to read. In fact, because Gutenberg's printing press allowed inexpensive copies to be made available to the masses, it inspired a rapid increase in literacy levels across Europe (Eisenstein, 1979, p. xii).

block printing A process in which wooden blocks are engraved with images and text, inked, and then pressed onto paper.

movable type
Gutenberg's invention that allowed individual letters or images to be moved without influencing the surrounding text.

NEWSPAPERS

After the printing press made books (beginning with the Bible) and pamphlets accessible to the masses, newspapers also began to emerge across Europe. The oldest newspaper still in publication is Sweden's *Post-och Inrikes Tidningar*, which began printing in 1645. In 2007, after more than 350 years in existence, and perhaps a signal of change for all newspapers, its publisher announced that it would stop producing a paper copy and instead move completely online (Associated Press, 2007). The first Canadian newspaper was the *Halifax Gazette*, which began printing in 1752 (Province of Nova Scotia, 2003).

THE TELEGRAPH

After the newspaper, the next important medium of mass communication was Samuel Morse's telegraph, patented in 1843. The Morse telegraph used a keypad to send short and long electrical pulses—called Morse code—through telegraph lines to be received and translated at the other end (The Alberta Pioneer Railway Association, 2007).

As railroad companies built railway lines throughout the world, they would run telegraph lines along the tracks that allowed messages to be sent from one place to another with the tap of a telegraph key. Telegraph messages were far more efficient and timely than sending printed documents across the country by train. In fact, the telegraph became Canada's primary means of sending messages over long distances until the widespread use of the telephone almost 100 years later. Even after the telephone became popular, the railways continued to use the telegraph to transmit train orders and other communications. The last official telegraph transmitted in Canada was sent by Canadian Pacific Operator Rene Chevalier on May 30, 1972. It read: "This is the last telegram via Morse Code in Canada. What hath God wrought?" (The Alberta Pioneer Railway Association, 2007).[1]

THE PHONOGRAPH

Until the middle of the nineteenth century, mass communication was largely limited to printed text and fixed images. Then, in 1877, Thomas Edison's invention of the phonograph ushered in sound. Edison's phonograph used a spinning cylinder (made from paper, wax, and, ultimately, metal) and a needle that would scratch the surface (making grooves) as vibrations of sound were passed through a mouthpiece. Once the grooves were made on the cylinder, another needle was used to replay the recording (Library of Congress, n.d.).

While Edison is generally credited with inventing the first machine to capture and replay sound, recent research suggests that Parisian typesetter Édouard-Léon Scott de Martinville developed a similar device in 1860—17 years before Edison's. His machine, which he called

Thomas Edison and his phonograph.

Bettmann/Corbis

a *phonautograph*, was intended to record sounds visually, not to play them back. Scott's device had a barrel-shaped horn attached to a stylus (similar to Edison's), which etched sound waves onto sheets of paper blackened by smoke from an oil lamp.

These recordings were never intended for listening but, rather, as a visual representation of sound waves. However, American researchers at Stanford University discovered that they could use a "virtual stylus" to scan the images and then play them back. This finding challenges Edison's historical claim of being the first to invent a machine that captured and replayed sound (Rosen, 2008).

---

1 Although Alexander Graham Bell's invention of the telephone in 1876 was a technological marvel, the telephone does not qualify as a medium of mass communication. By definition, mass communication is sending a message from an individual or group to a mass audience; telephones (at least until recently) were unable to send a single message to large groups of people at one time.

MOVING PICTURES

It seems almost inevitable that if mass media were able to transmit text, static images, and sound (through the printing press, telegraph, and phonograph), the next development would be moving pictures. The first scientist to successfully provide the impression of visual movement was a Belgian named Joseph Antoine Ferdinand Plateau. In 1832, Plateau developed what he called the *phenakistoscope*, which consisted of two spinning disks that gave the impression of movement (the same process used when flipping through individual scenes in a flip book—the technique tricks the mind to infer movement where none exists, and "animate" the scene).

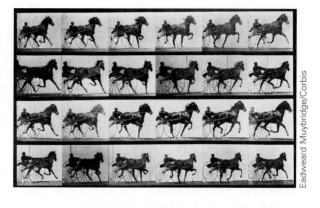

Eadweard Muybridge/Corbis

In 1877, Eadweard Muybridge used a process that linked 24 still cameras alongside a racetrack so that as a horse and rider went by, a string tripped each camera's shutter and made consecutive still photographs of the running horse. These images were then strung together and similarly tricked the mind to infer movement. The first invention to truly capture full-motion imagery was made by the prolific American inventor Thomas Edison.

Beginning in 1888, Edison developed a technique whereby photographic film could be run rapidly across a camera's shutter, which would expose the film in frames. Since the exposures were shown very quickly, one after the other, when they were played back, the impression of fluid movement was finally achieved. In the following decade, motion pictures would become a successful entertainment industry. Projector systems were used to play short films for large audiences, who were amazed by the moving pictures (Library of Congress, n.d.).

The first movie theatre in the United States, the Nickelodeon, opened on June 19, 1905, in Pittsburgh (Mondello, 2005); less than six months later, on January 1, 1906, the Ouimetoscope opened in Montreal. The Ouimetoscope offered two screenings a day with as many as 20 short films per show, each with accompanying live musical performances. Tickets cost between 10 and 35 cents (Stastna, 2006). Most of the early shows were about famous people, current events, and scenic tours of exotic destinations and other leisure activities. Over time, these documentaries declined in popularity and production companies began to cater to the public's growing desire for comedies and dramas.

< < <

Muybridge's photo-series was one of the first attempts to capture motion through still photography.

< < <

Charlie Chaplin was one of the first stars of moving pictures.

The Canadian Press/STREVT

RADIO

The development of radio technology began in the 1860s when Scottish physicist James Clerk Maxwell predicted the existence of radio waves. In 1886, German physicist Heinrich Rudolph Hertz showed that fluctuations of electric current could be projected into space as radio waves, and that they operated in a fashion similar to light and heat waves. However, the real breakthrough came when Guglielmo Marconi sent and received his first radio signal in Italy in 1895 (Bellis, 2008). Later, in December 1901, he transmitted the first transatlantic message (which was simply the letter *S* in Morse code) between Poldhu, England, and Signal Hill, Newfoundland, located just outside St. John's. A few weeks later Marconi received another transmission, this one from a colleague in England, 1700 miles away, saying the words "pip, pip, pip" (Webb, 2001).

Over the next decade, the technology improved to such an extent that commercial broadcasters became interested in radio's ability to reach a mass audience. The key development of radio over earlier technology was that it did not require wires and allowed a single signal to be transmitted to anyone with a receiver. Radio was capable of providing millions of people with news, public service announcements, and entertainment. Canada's first radio station—XWA, now CFCF—began broadcasting in 1919 (Nolan, 2001, p. 72), and one year later, KDKA in Pittsburgh became the first radio station in the United States (Winston, 1998, p. 77). In 1936, the *Canadian Broadcasting Act* established the Canadian Broadcasting Corporation (CBC Radio Canada, n.d.).

Radio's prominence as a mass medium has lessened over time. In fact, since 1999, the number of hours people listen to the radio has steadily declined, particularly among young people aged 12 to 24, who appear to be switching to digital music players and online music services (Statistics Canada, 2007n).

TELEVISION

[Explore

Number of Televisions Worldwide

∨
∨
∨

Televisions have come a long way in the last 50 years.

Hywit Dimyadi/iStock/ Thinkstock and IuriiSokolov/ iStock/Thinkstock

Television has become an integral part of the world's social, political, and economic landscape; indeed, few technological developments have had such a profound influence on the social fabric of our lives.

The first person to build a working mechanical television was German student Paul Gottlieb Nipkow. In the late 1880s, Nipkow was able to send images through wires and a rotating metal disk. The technology was called the "electric telescope" and had 18 lines of resolution (compare that to today's high-definition televisions, which have 1080) (Jezek, 2006; Metzger, 2007). Then, in the early 1900s, two inventors—A. A. Campbell-Swinton from England and Boris Rosing from Russia—were experimenting with two different approaches to television: mechanical scanner systems and cathode ray electronic systems. Although the former had some early success, today's televisions are based on electronic technologies. The first working model of an electronic television was invented by Philo Taylor Farnsworth in 1927 (Jezek, 2006; McGee, 1977).

Television really began in 1927, when General Electric inventor Ernst Alexanderson demonstrated that he could broadcast pictures and sound through the air and receive them on a television. Shortly thereafter, television broadcasting was born when station WRGB in Schenectady, New York, began offering short programs on January 13, 1928. A few months later, on May 10, the station began regular programming (twice a day, three days per week) that included local weather and farm reports (CBS, n.d.). Although Canadians received television signals from the United States as early as the 1940s, the country's first television station was Montreal's CBFT, which began broadcasting on September 6, 1952. By the mid 1950s, virtually all Canadian cities had television stations, and by 1958, the CBC network had stations from Victoria to Halifax (Vivian & Maurin, 2009, p. 114).

What are our television viewing habits today? In 2004, Statistics Canada found that Canadians preferred to watch dramas and comedies (35 percent of viewing hours), more

BOX 17.1 ISSUES IN GLOBAL CONTEXT

Global Media Ownership

Today's multinational media corporations are becoming more integrated and powerful all the time. As such, they present a significant challenge to the world community (Giddens, 1999, as cited in Meier, 2002, p. 299).

One of the ways that large corporations protect each other's interests is through *interlocking directorates*, a system whereby members of a corporation's board of directors are shared with other corporations. In the case of media corporations, linked directors may influence editorial content. Research conducted by FAIR (an American media watchdog association that follows media bias and censorship closely; see www.fair.org) has revealed a number of interlocking directorates involving media companies: ABC and Disney Corporation share board members with Boeing, FedEx, Staples, and City National Bank; NBC/GE shares directors with Avon, Coca-Cola, Kellogg, the New York Stock Exchange, and Sun Microsystems; CBS/Viacom shares board members with Amazon.com, American Express, MovieTickets.com, Pfizer, and Prudential Insurance (Fairness & Accuracy in Reporting, 2014).

Media takeovers also pose some risk to editorial freedom. The numerous mergers and buyouts of media and entertainment companies since the 1980s have translated into mainstream media concentrated in fewer hands (Shah, 2007), which in turn leads to uniform content and the presentation of a consistent worldview (Meier, 2002, p. 298).

While media still have the potential to compete fairly and openly and to provide an important mechanism to hold governments accountable, Shah (2007) remains concerned that corporate interests may dictate editorial content if there is a chance that advertising revenue will dry up if a story challenges corporate interests.

This growing media concentration is not restricted to the United States; it is a global phenomenon:

> Global conglomerates can at times have a progressive impact on culture, especially when they enter nations that had been tightly controlled by corrupt crony media systems (as in much of Latin America) or nations that had significant state censorship over media (as in parts of Asia). The global commercial-media system is radical in that it will respect no tradition or custom, on balance, if it stands in the way of profits. But ultimately it is politically conservative, because the media giants are significant beneficiaries of the current social structure around the world, and any upheaval in property or social relations—particularly to the extent that it reduces power of business—is not in their interest. (McChesney, 1999, pp. 13–14)

As a sociologist, do you believe we should be concerned with having a few large multinational corporations controlling media?

than 80 percent of which were foreign programs (mainly from the US). The second most popular programming was news and public affairs (24 percent), of which 75 percent was of Canadian origin.

THE INTERNET

The Internet had its beginnings in 1967 as a $19,000 American Department of Defense contract to design a computer network to act as a vehicle for communication that would be impervious to a nuclear strike (Federal Communications Commission, 2005). As the

TABLE 17.1   Individuals Using the Internet from any Location, 2012

	Internet use %
Canada	83
Newfoundland and Labrador	77
Prince Edward Island	80
Nova Scotia	79
New Brunswick	77
Quebec	81
Ontario	84
Manitoba	83
Saskatchewan	82
Alberta	85
British Columbia	87

Source: Statistics Canada (2013). Individuals using the Internet from any location, 2012[online]. Retrieved April 20, 2014, from http://www.statcan.gc.ca/daily-quotidien/131028/t131028a002-eng.htm

technology developed, its early adopters included not only military personnel but also researchers and academics, who quickly grasped how the technology could facilitate a new and virtually instantaneous form of communication. Table 17.1 shows that in 2012 British Columbia and Alberta reported the highest rate of individual Internet use, at 87 and 85 percent respectively, followed by Ontario at 84 percent. These relatively high levels of Internet use in these provinces was driven by high use rates in Victoria and Calgary.

What began as a military need, then, led to a technological revolution that has transformed how, and how quickly, we communicate with one another. We turn now to a discussion of the myriad forms this revolution takes today.

❷ Mass Media Today

In recent years, people have been making use of technologies that give them greater control over their own entertainment and their ways of staying in touch with each other. While traditional mass communication technologies (radio, newspapers, television) *push* content to their audiences, new technologies enable consumers to *pull* content that reflects their particular and unique interests whenever they want. People are no longer confined to the narrow media streams that existed only a few short years ago.

Web 2.0 Interactive online tools dedicated to promoting a greater sense of community.

The enabling technology for many new online media forms is often referred to as Web 2.0. **Web 2.0** represents a significant evolution over earlier technologies in that it encourages more interactivity among users and, as some argue, results in both a deeper learning and a better potential to build online communities (Kamel Boulos & Wheeler, 2007, pp. 3–4; Pinch, 2010).

In 2013, 87 percent of Canadian households had Internet access (up from 80 percent in 2010) (Canadian Internet Registration Authority, 2014). In 2012, 93 percent of Canadians aged 16 and older used the Internet for personal reasons, up from 73 percent in 2007 (Statistics Canada, 2012a.

Today's media landscape is marked by a number of communication avenues, ranging from advances in satellite television stations to the burgeoning use of cellphones, text messaging, Twitter, blogs, wikis, YouTube, and social networking sites. Let's look at each of these technologies in turn.

SATELLITE TELEVISION

Canadian satellite television programming—through Bell's ExpressVu and Shaw's StarChoice, for example—is an expanding and flourishing industry (Doyle, 2008). Satellite stations target a broad audience and offer hundreds of channels, an increasing number of which are in high-definition formats. With channels dedicated to such diverse pursuits as golf, cooking, and NASCAR, it seems that everyone can find something that appeals to them. Further, the advent of personal video recorders (PVRs) means that viewers can "pause" live programming, automatically record shows for later viewing, and even remove commercials. Television has come a long way since traditional networks "pushed" a limited selection of programs into homes. Today, people can watch what they want, when they want.

CELLPHONES

In 2002, the number of people with cellphones worldwide surpassed the number with fixed phone lines, confirming that cellphones had become the dominant form of voice technology (Srivastava, 2005). Estimates suggested that in 2014, there were 4.55 billion cellphones in use worldwide (eMarketer, 2014). Indeed, "the mobile phone has now moved beyond being a mere technical device to becoming a key 'social object' present in every aspect of a user's life" (Srivastava, 2005, p. 111). Users are increasingly attached to their cellphones, often using them as a calendar, an alarm clock, a camera, and even a calorie counter. In this way, the mobile phone has become part of a user's "personal sphere of objects," much like a wallet and

✱⊣Explore

Poor Arctic Communications Threaten Development, Canadian Sovereignty

Alamy

< < <

Today, cellphones are changing the way people communicate.

keys. Srivastava (2005) suggests that "it gives users the impression that they are constantly connected to the world outside, and therefore less alone" (p. 113). In fact, a study by Harkin (2003) revealed that 46 percent of mobile phone users interviewed in the UK described the feeling of losing their cellphones as a "form of bereavement" (as cited in Srivastava, 2005, p. 113). Devices such as the iPhone or BlackBerry, running on 4G networks, in addition to being a phone, allow users to cruise the Web and take a few quick "bites" of information or entertainment as part of their "mobile snacking" as they walk to work or wait for a bus (Marlow, 2011; Persaud, 2008, p. 45). At the beginning of this chapter, we introduced the notion that smartphones and other forms of handheld social media allow users to remain connected, yet physically separated from the people around them. Some people use their devices as an intermediary between themselves and those they communicate with. How has your smartphone influenced your social activities?

Cellphones have been criticized for contributing to poor spelling and grammar (due to text messaging), for being a distraction from tasks that require concentration, for promoting the demise of intimate face-to-face relationships, and even for causing brain cancer. Nonetheless, their use is becoming ubiquitous within a social landscape that Thompson and Cupples (2008) refer to as **digital sociality**. They argue that this sociality in fact promotes human interaction and contact. For example, as a result of cellphones' mobility and efficiency, young people are now more likely to call friends throughout the day than were their parents' generation. Even when you miss a call, you are still "connected"—you can always send a text message later.

digital sociality **A social landscape in which new communication technologies are promoting human interaction and contact.**

TEXT MESSAGING

Text messaging is becoming the most common form of mobile communication among young people. Estimates suggest that more than 50 billion instant messages will be sent worldwide each day in 2014 (BusinessETC.com, 2014). That works out to around 18 *trillion* texts per year. Figure 17.1 shows the rapid increase in text messaging in Canada from 2006 to 2012.

While some question the negative influence that text messaging has on writing ability (see Gray, n.d.; Jones, 2008), others see it as an opportunity for artistic expression. For example, Miyake's (2007) research into text messaging among Japanese youth found that they often expressed their individuality by creating new and artistic forms of written language that deviated from the largely conservative Japanese culture and its distaste for individuality. Japanese youth appear to enjoy the intimacy and creativity of sending visual messages to each other.

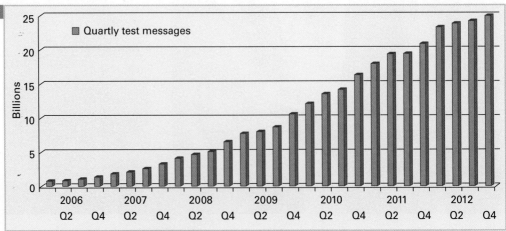

FIGURE 17.1

Mobile Originated Text Messages in Canada, 2006–2012

Reprinted by permission from the Canadian Wireless Telecommunications Association.

They also appreciate that text messaging maintains some distance, which they feel helps to alleviate social anxiety (e.g., the embarrassment that comes with "losing face"; see Malley-Morrison & Hines, 2004, p. 202).

How does text messaging qualify as a medium of mass communication? Certainly, the majority of text messaging occurs between two people; however, recent software developments make it possible for an individual or business to convey a message through virtually any text messaging device. For example, TXTLaunchPad (www.txtlaunchpad.com) urges potential buyers of its software to "Reach Your Audience Anytime, Any Place, Anywhere," while Omnilert (www.omnilert.com) says that its service allows "content providers to quickly offer their own private-branded mass communications system."

TWITTER

Twitter is a real-time information network connecting people to the latest information they find interesting. The information messages you receive, called "tweets," are small bursts of information that are up to 140 characters long. Tweets also contain links to additional information or to other embedded media (Twitter, 2011). Estimates suggest that in 2011 there were, on average, 1 billion tweets per week (Twitter Blog, 2014). Individually, each of these tweets can vary from the ridiculous to the arresting. But some argue that when you take them together they offer a unique glimpse into the moods, thoughts, and activities of society at large (Savage, 2011). For example, recent political events in China, Tunisia, Egypt, and other countries around the world demonstrated clearly Twitter's potential to galvanize public resistance to political issues (see Diamond, 2010; Frei, 2011; Bruns, Highfield, & Burgess, 2013).

BLOGS

Estimates suggest that the number of blogs on the Internet grew from 70 million in 2007 to 160 million in 2010, with approximately 172 000 new blogs appearing every day (Gaille, 2014). A **blog** (a shortened form of *web log*) is essentially an online diary in which an individual regularly reflects on events, specific topics, and/or personal experiences. Bloggers post their insights in a manner that may, for example, inform others or act as an opportunity to voice dissenting opinions or perspectives.

Many blogs go unnoticed and are little more than a series of thoughts that few people see; however, some become very popular and may even win a Bloggie (an annual award for the best blog in various categories; see www.bloggies.com). Regular readers of particular blogs can be informed by the web feed format known as **RSS (Really Simple Syndication)**, which provides either a summary of a new entry or its entire text, thus eliminating the need to continually revisit sites to check for updates.

The blog's principal attraction—the ability to present one's ideas to a global audience and invite a dialogue—means that, over time, these dialogues may take on the characteristics of an online global community (Vandegriend, 2006). Indeed, some of the web's best-known blogs (e.g., Yahoo!, Tumblr, Kotaku, Daily Kos) can have tens of thousands of visitors per day and hundreds of posts. In fact, the world's most popular blog, the Huffington Post, started by Arianna Huffington (purchased in 2011 by AOL) receives more than 74 million unique visitors every month (BusinessWire, 2013). Figure 17.2 shows the rapid growth of Yahoo! blog sites' traffic from 2008 to 2011.

As blogging has become more popular, several blogs—including the Huffington Post and the Daily Kos, both of which began as relatively small blogging sites—are taking on the role that was once dominated by more traditional forms of journalism. This trend also works in the other direction, as most of the major media outlets, such as the *New York Times*, have incorporated blogging into their daily media offerings. This trend was very visible during the 2012 election in the United States, where blog sites like the *New York Times*' FiveThirtyEight

blog An online diary in which an individual posts personal reflections on events, specific topics, and/or experiences.

RSS (Really Simple Syndication) A web feed format that informs subscribers of new information posted on online services.

FIGURE 17.2

Growth of Yahoo!
Blog Traffic,
2008–2011

The growth of Yahoo!
blogs over time dem-
onstrates that people
are becoming more
attracted to sources
of information beyond
those of the traditional
mass media.

Reproduced with permission
of Yahoo. ©2014 Yahoo
.YAHOO! and the YAHOO!
logo are registered trade-
marks of Yahoo.

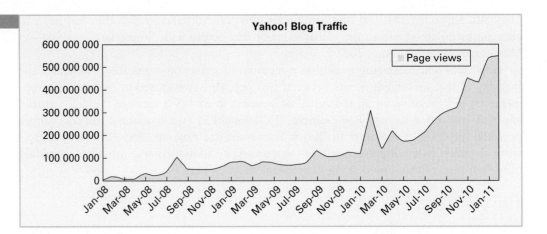

blog, run by statistician Nate Silver, dominated the news cycles with its election night predictions—predictions that turned out to be remarkably accurate (O'Hara, 2012).

Critics of online communications have argued that those who read blogs generally only
read those that confirm their already held beliefs—a practice referred to as the "echo chamber
effect." This concept asserts that some people insulate themselves from dissenting viewpoints
to such an extent that they are no longer able to understand or accept the beliefs or opinions
of those with whom they disagree (Colleoni, Alessandro, & Adam, 2014). How might the
echo chamber effect impact the way we see the world around us?

The mass media's targeting of a smaller segment of the audience is a process known as
demassification, which occurs when an audience is fragmented into small groups or niches
that mass media use as a basis to develop specific content. This is not to say, however, that
mass media are not still motivated by commercial interests to maximize profits (Wimmer &
Dominick, 2006, p. 9). Subscribing to any number of magazines (or satellite channels, or
websites) may give an individual the impression of being outside mainstream mass media,
and while some certainly are, big business is still responsible for most media content in all
of its forms. For example, even YouTube, an apparent alternative to mainstream media, is a
vehicle for corporate interests.

demassification A
process by which
the mass audience is
fragmented into small
groups or niches to
appeal to unique
interests.

WIKIS

wiki An online body
of information to
which anyone can
add or modify
content.

A **wiki** is an online body of information that is designed to allow anyone access to add
or modify its content. Arguably, the best-known wiki today is the online encyclopedia
Wikipedia. The greatest advantage of wikis over blogs is that wikis allow everyone to participate as a community that is nonhierarchical and nonregulated. Information posted on a
wiki is available right away and is open for review and discussion (Cernohous, 2007, p. 2).
The majority of wikis, then, provide an important resource for people who want to work
openly and collaboratively but they can also provide users with anonymity, for example,
with WikiLeaks.

WikiLeaks was launched in 2006 by the Sunshine Press as an international nonprofit
organization to post private, secret, and classified information from anonymous sources on
the Web (WikiLeaks, 2011). The high-profile face of the site, Julian Assange, an Australian
Internet activist, was runner-up for *Time* magazine's 2010 Person of the Year (won by
Mark Zuckerberg, the creator of Facebook) (Gellman, 2010). Although WikiLeaks was
originally launched as a traditional wiki where users could edit the contents of the site, it
now offers a more traditional model where submissions are reviewed by staff before being
posted to the site.

WikiLeaks has published a number of top-secret reports, including US government classified data about the wars in Iraq and Afghanistan, the Church of Scientology's "Operating Thetan" (previously unavailable for public review), and secret files relating to prisoners detained at Guantanamo Bay detention camp, to name only a few (WikiLeaks, 2011).

The influence of WikiLeaks on the public consciousness is yet to be determined, but one noted social commentator, Germaine Greer, recently stated that ". . . the construction of stateless, secure and indestructible Internet drop boxes cannot be undone. Secrets will never be safe again" (Greer, 2011). On October 24, 2011, WikiLeaks said they were suspending operations to focus on fundraising, but as of 2014, WikiLeaks continues to release information on a wide array of topics, from military information to environmental treaties and government declarations of all kinds (Wikileaks.org, 2014).

YOUTUBE

YouTube was created in February 2005 by Steve Chen, Chad Hurley, and Jawed Karim, who perceived a need for an easy-to-use website that would allow users to share personal videos. Within the year, registered users were downloading 2 million videos per day, and by July 2006, that number had increased to 100 million. In October 2006, YouTube was purchased by Google for $1.65 billion (Hinderliter, 2007). Today, YouTube is the third-most-visited website in the world (after Google and Facebook) (see www.alexa.com/topsites), with over 1 billion unique users each month (YouTube, 2014). YouTube has also played an important role in challenging oppressive political regimes by making available video clips that show abusive or repressive actions by government representatives (Bentley, 2008, p. 41), military soldiers, or police officers. The political uprisings in Africa and the Middle East in early 2011 confirmed YouTube's ability to disseminate images of political corruption and military atrocities around the world in minutes and was a game-changer for the revolutionary movements (Trussell, 2011). The days of conventional mass media controlling all of the information that the world sees may be over.

YouTube's tremendous growth and popularity provide an excellent example of how young people are attracted to new media forms that allow them to control their media experience. YouTube's tag line—Broadcast Yourself—encapsulates users' desire to present themselves to a global audience. It constitutes a fascinating example of how technology is transforming the individual's relationship to the social—which is, after all, the defining interest of sociology.

👁—Watch

Heavy Metal

SOCIAL NETWORKING SITES

Perhaps the best examples of how Web 2.0 technology can link people are the social networking sites MySpace and Facebook. Both sites are designed to provide users with a series of tools to help them connect with friends or to join groups with common interests (e.g., fringe music, sports teams, etc.).

MySpace was launched on August 15, 2003, by Brad Greenspan, who believed that social networking was the future of the Internet. Less than two years later, MySpace was purchased for $580 million by News Corporation, part of Rupert Murdoch's media empire, which also owns Fox Network (Scott-Joynt, 2005). In 2008, MySpace was the Web's largest social

< < <

Mark Zuckerberg, the creator of Facebook.

Norbert Von Der Groeben/Reuters/Landov

networking site, with more than 117 million users worldwide (Nakashima, 2008); however, since then its popularity has declined and MySpace currently serves around 63 million users (Mishra, 2011), far fewer than the new social networking goliath, Facebook.

Facebook was founded by Harvard University psychology student Mark Zuckerberg (then aged 23) in February 2004 (Phillips, 2007). Today, Facebook is a publicly traded company and claims to have more than 1.3 billion active monthly users (Statistic Brain, 2014) and has made Zuckerberg one of the richest men in the world with a personal worth of over $27.2 billion in 2014 (Forbes.com, 2014).

MySpace was the first site to make it easy for the common computer user to create a webpage, write a blog, or post photos online. Yet MySpace's appeal to both tech savvy users and novices is why some prefer Facebook. Until late 2006, Facebook targeted only university and college students, meaning that it had a relatively well educated and affluent audience. Facebook is both less customizable and more orderly than MySpace, and the graphics look more technical, less commercial, and more "high brow" (Falls, 2008). The class divisions between users on MySpace and Facebook have been demonstrated by other researchers as well (Boyd, 2007).

Our look at the evolution of mass media has covered the key technological changes and how they have influenced social development. To help you better understand these developments in context, we turn to the writings of two noted Canadian scholars: Harold Innis and Marshall McLuhan.

❸ Canadian Insights into Mass Media: Innis and McLuhan

HAROLD INNIS

Harold Innis (1894–1952), a political economist, is widely viewed as inspiring a uniquely Canadian perspective on media that would directly influence his more famous colleague Marshall McLuhan. According to Innis, every society needs to transcend what he called the problems of space and time; all societies that are able to solve these problems do so through communication (Innis, 1951, as cited in Smith, 2007, p. 108). Let's consider each of these problems separately.

Time Bias Innis believed that civilizations are shaped by whatever media are most pervasive in their cultures. According to Innis (1951), **time-biased media** transcend time because they are often very durable. (Consider the cave drawings and hieroglyphics we discussed at the beginning of this chapter.) These media have tremendous longevity, but they do not allow the message or image to exceed the view of people in the immediate vicinity. Thus, they neither facilitate nor encourage the distribution of a common message across large areas. While these media cannot readily transcend geographic distance, they can transcend time by linking one generation to the next (Smith, 2007, p. 109). As a result, Innis associated these time-biased media with traditional hierarchies that were based on age-old practices.

Space Bias According to Innis, media like papyrus and printed books are **space-biased**, in that their lightness means that they can convey messages as far as an individual wants to carry them (Comor, 2003, p. 91). These technologies, beginning with papyrus, allowed empires to emerge because military orders, laws, directions, and information bulletins could be sent over great distances. Today, of course, people can communicate instantaneously with anyone, anywhere in the world. New communications technologies are so light that you can carry them wherever you go and remain connected to everyone else. Indeed, we are the first generation to be able to truly transcend space. Of course, the messages we send tend to have

time-biased media
Media that have longevity but whose form prevents their transmission over physical distance (e.g., cave art, hieroglyphics).

space-biased media
Media that can convey messages readily over physical distance.

a limited lifespan; since people delete most messages, one can only wonder how many will remain extant 50 years into the future, let alone 5000.

Innis's analysis of the role of communication and communications technologies through time and their influence on the rise and fall of empires led him to recognize that societies were influenced by their dominant forms of communication. Further, our understanding of earlier civilizations, as well as our own, is confined by our own culture's bias toward specific forms of media. From cave art to paper, from radio to television, and from email to text messaging, we see a shifting progression in how each medium influences the society in which it exists. Each medium has a bias, one that changes in relation to other media and how our culture reacts to them (Soules, 2007).

Innis also believed that stable societies were able to achieve a balance between time and space biases—a point that influenced his Canadian colleague Marshall McLuhan.

MARSHALL McLUHAN

Marshall McLuhan (1911–1980), much like Innis, believed that media influence the ways in which individuals, societies, and cultures perceive and understand their environments (Skinner, 2000, p. 56). According to McLuhan (1964), the reason for studying media was to make visible what was invisible—to go beyond the actual material transmitted by media and uncover the underlying message. Indeed, McLuhan thought that to study media content was to miss the point, since the medium itself was most important. This belief, of course, is encapsulated in McLuhan's famous phrase: "The medium is the message."

The Medium Is the Message According to McLuhan, each medium influences the mind in largely unconscious ways. Thus, it is not the simple message (which appeals to the conscious mind) that is important but, rather, the manner in which it is conveyed (which appeals to the unconscious mind) (Soules, 2007). McLuhan never suggested that the content message was unimportant per se, just that to truly understand the social significance of media, one needed to understand the primary importance of the medium over the message.

McLuhan was concerned that we often focus on the obvious and that when we do we miss important and subtle changes that occur over time. For example, individual messages about murders contained in newscasts are not as significant as the resulting change in the public attitude toward crime or the creation of a climate of fear (Federman, 2004). McLuhan writes of how a medium's message influences human change:

> The message of any medium or technology is the change of scale or pace or pattern that it introduces into human affairs. The railway did not introduce movement or trans-portation or wheel or road into human society, but it accelerated and enlarged the scale of previous human functions, creating totally new kinds of cities and new kinds of work and leisure. (McLuhan, 1964, p. 8)

McLuhan's insight into the need to look beyond the simple message to the social influence of the medium itself has important sociological ramifications. The manner in which people communicate shapes not only the society in which they live but how they interact within it. Today, our ability to communicate instantaneously both locally and globally has changed how we perceive our world.

Hot and Cool Media McLuhan proposed that media could be classified as either "hot" or "cool" based on the nature of their content as well as the degree of attention required by their audience. **Hot media** are those of "high definition," in that they contain a great deal of information but usually involve only a single sensory organ (e.g., sight or sound) in such a way that they demand very little from their audience.

Examples of hot media include a newspaper and your sociology lecture. The newspaper presents all of the text right before your eyes, and you can read it at your leisure.

hot media Media that contain a great deal of information but involve only a single sensory organ and demand very little from their audience (e.g., newspapers).

BOX 17.2 CANADIAN CONTRIBUTIONS TO SOCIOLOGY

Marshall McLuhan

Marshall McLuhan was born in Edmonton on July 21, 1911. He received a B.A. in 1932 and an M.A. in 1934, both from the University of Manitoba, in English literature. He received another B.A. in 1936, a second M.A. in 1939, and his Ph.D. in 1942 from Cambridge University (Quiet PC, 2008).

McLuhan became interested in media analysis when he began his first teaching job at the University of Wisconsin. Though his first students were only slightly younger than he was, McLuhan felt a generation older. He wanted to investigate why he felt this way—and hypothesized that it might have something to do with mass media.

McLuhan's publications include The Mechanical Bride (1951), Explorations in Communication (1960), The Gutenberg Galaxy: The Making of Typographic Man (1962), Understanding Media: The Extensions of Man (1964), The Medium Is the Message(1967), War and Peace in the Global Village (1968), and City as Classroom: Understanding Language as Media (1977).

Marshall McLuhan
The Canadian Press/Robert Fleming

In 2003, Primitive Entertainment and the National Film Board of Canada produced a video entitled McLuhan's Wake about the life and work of Marshall McLuhan. In his discussion of the video, Denis Hlynka, a professor of institutional technology at the University of Manitoba, remarks that "[w]hat is most important is that McLuhan is being re-evaluated in the age of the internet. There is no doubt that he is coming up a winner. His work, it turns out, is neither dated nor 'far out.' It is amazingly accurate" (Hlynka, 2004). Hlynka also discusses the irony of what McLuhan would have likely found to be the most intriguing aspect of the film—that the medium of the DVD, with its ability to store vast amounts of data, would be more important to understand than the actual content of the film (Hlynka, 2004).

The sociology lecture also provides a great deal of information, which you take in as a passive listener. Neither form of communication requires a high degree of engagement or interaction on your part—you can be distracted by other things while reading the paper or daydream while sitting in class (the latter is not recommended). Generally speaking, hot media are visual spaces that are sequential, linear, and logical (Library and Archives Canada, 2007).

cool media Media that convey less information and require more participation from their audience (e.g., seminars).

Conversely, **cool media** are low in definition (that is, they involve less information; e.g., a cartoon) and demand more participation from the audience. For example, talking on the phone and participating in a sociology seminar both require active engagement with the discussion at hand. After all, the best phone conversations and seminars occur when everyone participates. In contrast to hot media, which favour precision and sequential ordering (e.g., pages in a book), cool media require the audience to engage with abstract concepts and to integrate knowledge from diverse areas; for example, skilled musicians move beyond thinking about "playing" someone else's sheet music and begin "feeling" it and making it their own.

While McLuhan's concepts of hot and cool media are well known, they are poorly defined and often contradictory. For example, McLuhan classified television as a cool medium, and while there are times when viewers may actively engage with television programs (e.g., political debates, a compelling documentary), the vast majority of what appears on television is more likely to lull the audience to sleep than it is to challenge their intellect.

McLuhan's ideas about media have been widely criticized, yet his legacy as a Canadian scholar who made us view media from a new perspective is secure (see Carey, 1967; Holmes, 2005, p. 38; Mielo, 2004).

> > > Thinking Sociologically

Do you think McLuhan would see Facebook as a hot or cool medium? Why?

Canadian Content Legislation

As discussed in Chapter 6, media are one of the principal agents of socialization and are, therefore, of critical importance to sociologists. Canadian media are greatly influenced by their close proximity to the United States; as a result, the federal government has implemented policies and programs to protect media companies and promote Canadian artists in the hope of preserving Canadian culture.

To this end, the Canadian Radio-television and Telecommunications Commission (CRTC) licenses, regulates, and administers the broadcasting industry in Canada. It has put forward strict Canadian content guidelines (popularly known as **CanCon**) that require Canadian radio and television stations to broadcast content written and performed by Canadian artists (CRTC, 2007). These regulations are contained in the *Canadian Broadcasting Act*, which aims to promote Canadian culture by

1. providing a wide range of programming that reflects Canadian attitudes, opinions, ideas, values, and artistic creativity;
2. displaying Canadian talent in entertainment programming;
3. offering information and analysis concerning Canada and other countries from a Canadian point of view (CRTC, 2007).

For a piece of music to qualify as Canadian content, it must fulfill at least two of the four criteria of the **MAPL system**:

1. The music (M) is composed by a Canadian.
2. The artist (A) who performs the music is Canadian.
3. The production (P) of the music occurred in Canada (that is, the music was recorded in Canada) or the music is performed in Canada and broadcast in Canada.
4. The lyrics (L) are written by a Canadian. (CRTC, 2001)

According to the CRTC guidelines, commercial radio stations must ensure that at least 35 percent of the popular music they play is Canadian, as defined by the MAPL system. French radio stations have a higher threshold in that they must play 55 percent Canadian content; if the music includes French-language vocals, the required percentage is 65 percent. Both English and French stations must meet these requirements over the broadcast week and between 6:00 a.m. and 6:00 p.m., Monday through Friday (this ensures that Canadian content is not broadcast only late at night). The regulations also stipulate that qualifying musical selections be played in their entirety (CRTC, 2009).

CanCon (Canadian content) Federal regulations that stipulate the required percentage of Canadian content in television and radio broadcasts.

MAPL system CRTC requirements used to determine whether a piece of music qualifies as Canadian content.

CanCon regulations attempt to promote Canadian artists and our cultural identity.

Graphic work prepared by the Canadian Radio-Television and Telecommunications Commission. Reproduced with the permission of the Canadian Radio-Television and Telecommunications Commission on behalf of Her Majesty in Right of Canada, 2014.

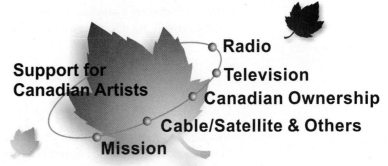

Support for Canadian Artists

Radio
Television
Canadian Ownership
Cable/Satellite & Others
Mission

Television content is treated in much the same way. For the CRTC to certify a television program as Canadian, the program must meet all three of the following criteria:

1. The producer is Canadian.
2. Key creative personnel are Canadian.
3. Seventy-five percent of service costs and postproduction lab costs are paid to Canadians.

Television stations and networks (e.g., CTV, Global, TVA) and ethnic television stations (e.g., CFMT) must achieve an annual Canadian content level of

1. 60 percent overall, measured during the day (between 6:00 a.m. and midnight); and
2. 50 percent, measured during the evening broadcast period (between 6:00 p.m. and midnight) (CRTC, 2004).

As a government-owned broadcaster, the CBC must ensure that at least 60 percent of its programming, including the evening broadcast period, is Canadian. If broadcasters present Canadian dramas during peak viewing hours (7:00 p.m. to 11:00 p.m.), they are eligible for a 125 to 150 percent time credit (CRTC, 2004). These credits are intended not only to promote Canadian dramas but also to encourage that they be shown during prime time. Consistent with the intent of the *Canadian Broadcasting Act*, the CRTC licensed the Aboriginal Peoples Television Network (APTN) in 1999 to promote Aboriginal issues on the national stage; the channel is available to all Canadians.

THE CANCON DEBATE

Many Canadians (including some artists) believe that the CanCon regulations are unreasonable and intrusive with respect to consumers, who should be able to make their own entertainment choices without government intervention or support. Critics also claim that requiring a defined level of Canadian content ensures mediocrity, given that Canadian performers and artists are protected from having to compete with the world's best. There is also concern that radio and television stations will overplay popular Canadian songs or programs in an attempt to meet their quotas (DePalma, 1999).

The CanCon debate was recently reignited as a result of new satellite radio technology that challenged the CRTC's ability to regulate content effectively. In June 2005, the CRTC approved two satellite radio licenses—Canadian Satellite Radio (CSR) and Sirius Canada—on the basis of new regulations that were intended to protect Canadian programming but that, given the unique nature of the technology, were somewhat relaxed. The Friends of Canadian Broadcasting (who had previously supported CanCon regulations) argued to quash the CRTC's decision, contending that satellite radio should have to meet the same requirements as conventional radio. Conversely, Indie Pool, the voice of independent recording artists (who had previously argued against CanCon regulations), supported the CRTC's decision, claiming that it would help new artists to showcase their talent to a wider audience (Friends of Canadian Broadcasting, 2005).

> > > Thinking Sociologically

In your opinion, what are the strongest arguments for and against Canadian content regulations?

CanCon will, no doubt, continue to be a heated topic of debate in the years to come.

❺ Sociological Approaches to Mass Media

FUNCTIONALISM

Functionalists view mass media as providing a unique and powerful ability to promote common values and beliefs. Generally, functionalists see four primary areas in which mass media contribute to society: socialization, surveillance, correlation, and entertainment (Perse, 2001, p. 54).

Mass media achieve the **socialization function** as they transmit values, beliefs, and traditions from one generation to the next. By reinforcing certain messages (e.g., the benefits of democracy and a free-market economy), mass media effectively promote social integration and the formation of a common cultural identity (Perse, 2001, p. 56). However, targeting messages to a mass audience often oversimplifies issues. As well, since mass media messages reflect the views of the dominant groups in society, these messages fail to promote alternative perspectives and largely ignore the voice of minority groups.

We can understand the **surveillance function** as the need for society to have a mechanism in place that gathers information for the population (e.g., weather reports, news items) and that allows members of society to focus on their own activities and interests. Traditionally, this function was fulfilled by mass media (e.g., newspapers, radio, and television), but, as discussed earlier, research suggests that more and more people are turning to alternative media (amateur podcasts, blogs, and other online resources) to get news and information (World Association of Newspapers, 2007).

Mass media carry out the **correlation function** when they present difficult and complex issues in a way that most people can understand. This filtering is necessary, given not only the sheer number of newsworthy events that occur every day but also the need to present stories as concisely as possible to maintain audience interest. In some respects, the correlation function is a check on the surveillance function in that there must be some filter through which vast amounts of information pass before reaching us—otherwise, the populace would be overwhelmed by such volume (Perse, 2001, p. 55). Over time, however, the audience may lose its ability to evaluate critically what mass media present and simply assume such information to be true—which, of course, is not always the case (Bronfen, 2006, p. 22).

The **entertainment function** allows people to rest, relax, and escape the pressures of everyday life (Dyer, 2002, p. 178). The popularity of comedy shows such as *The Big Bang Theory* and *South Park* is a testament to the fact that people enjoy losing themselves in a program. However, the entertainment function may distract people from important events that require action (Perse, 2001, p. 56). For example, spending an entire evening watching television or surfing the Web when you have a term paper to write is probably not the most effective use of your time.

Functionalists, then, view mass media as filling some important needs in society. While some find merit in using functionalist theories to understand the media landscape in contemporary society, others argue that these theories of media are outdated (see Couldry, 2004, p. 124).

socialization function Media's role in transmitting beliefs, values, and traditions from one generation to the next.

surveillance function Media's role in gathering and disseminating information to the population.

correlation function Media's role in filtering and making comprehensible the huge daily volume of news stories and issues.

entertainment function Media's role in helping people rest, relax, and escape the pressures of everyday life.

> > > Thinking Sociologically

With all of the new communication technologies available today, do you feel that you are better informed about the social and political world around you than your parents' generation was? Which generation do you believe was more politically active? Do you think a link can be made between advances in communication technologies and political activism?

CONFLICT THEORY

According to conflict theorists, mass media are vehicles used by the rich and powerful to control the masses and to reinforce their false consciousness.

Consider, for example, daily news broadcasts. Media scholar Michael Parenti argues that in capitalist societies, the corporate news media faithfully reflect the dominant classes' ideology in what they choose to cover and in the words they use to describe it—while at the same time giving the impression that they are being fair and objective (Parenti, 1993, 2001, 2007). That is, it is not so much that mainstream media define how we think; rather, it is that they grant legitimacy and exposure to certain views over others. The media also influence our perceptions of events through their use of negative and positive labelling. For example, words and phrases like *stability*, *the prime minister's firm leadership*, and *the healthy economy* all attribute positive slants to the story at hand, while terms like *terrorist*, *gang*, and *civil disturbance* provide a negative spin (Parenti, 2001).

Advertising similarly moulds our opinions through the images it presents. For example, marketing certain products to children in a school setting (Molnar, 2006, p. 623) and casting thin actors on television shows (Venturini, Castelli, & Tomelleri, 2006, p. 391) reinforce, respectively, the positive cultural value of consumerism and the negative perception of people, particularly women who are overweight (Rasberry, 2008, p. 423).

Conflict theorists argue that, taken collectively, media messages influence our perception of our social environment to promote corporate interests and perpetuate class differences. In their book *Manufacturing Consent* (1988), Edward Herman and Noam Chomsky assert that the media intentionally create a social environment favourable to the dominant classes. Indeed, since most mainstream media are owned by large corporations, information presented to the public may be slanted to protect the interests of those corporations.

For example, if Walt Disney Corporation was charged with tax evasion, ABC (which is owned by Disney) may choose to not cover the story or to cover it differently than another network would. According to this reasoning, news stories that endanger the financial interests of the parent company would present the greatest bias and potential for censorship. By manipulating the stories that they cover and the manner in which they present those stories, media effectively "manufacture" consent through their filtering (Herman & Chomsky, 1988, pp. xi, 2). This filtering generally takes two forms: (1) deciding not to cover a story, or (2) presenting a story in such a way as to diffuse or bias its content. As you can imagine, such filtering influences how people see and interpret the social world; it helps to define their reality.

Herman and Chomsky (1988, p. 298) suggest, then, that the primary role of mainstream media is to ensure popular support for the economic, social, and political agenda of the privileged classes. This perspective is commonly referred to as the **propaganda model** (Herman, 2003), which asserts that, since the dominant media are commercial enterprises, their content will reflect the interests of the rich and powerful. *Propaganda* can be defined as the large-scale use of messages or images designed to influence the opinions and/or behaviours of the majority of the population. Propaganda isn't simply providing information but, rather, actively creating content that appears to be truthful and accurate but is instead an intentional manipulation of the facts to promote a particular position or worldview.

propaganda model
The assertion that media companies, as businesses, will transmit content that reflects their commercial interests.

Let us take the American tobacco industry as one example. In 1979, it created the Social Costs/Social Values Project to construct an alternative cultural repertoire of smoking by using social scientists to create and disseminate nonhealth-related, pro-tobacco opinions without disclosing their financial relationship with the tobacco industry (Landman, Cortese, & Glantz, 2008). After the Surgeon General reported, in 1988, that nicotine was in fact an addictive substance, the tobacco industry formed Associates for Research in the Science of Enjoyment, whose members travelled the world speaking about the health benefits of using legal substances such as tobacco to relieve stress, without ever revealing that the group was formed and funded by the tobacco industry. Landman, Cortese, and Glantz's work (2008) documents how the tobacco industry employed social scientists (including sociologists) to create and disseminate research that presented tobacco in a positive light through reputable scholarly channels (including scholarly articles, books, conference presentations, and interviews in newspapers). This research influenced both public opinion and academic research on the social acceptability of smoking (Landman, Cortese, & Glantz, 2008). Even with this effort, however, the US government, in 1998, forced the American tobacco industry to pay $206 billion over 25 years to fight the enormous public health problems created by tobacco use in the United States (Sloan & Chepke, 2011).

Although the propaganda model is an important contribution to our understanding of media, some contemporary researchers (see Britt, 2003) challenge the assumption that audiences are passive, credulous recipients of media content. These researchers assert that audiences are critical of what they see and hear through the media; they understand that some media bias is inevitable, and thus control for it.

SYMBOLIC INTERACTIONISM

Symbolic interactionists view mass media as an important part of contemporary life but one that is no more important than any other. This approach rejects all forms of determinism and therefore views media as part of a complex and multifaceted process in which meaning is defined and granted by those involved in the interaction (Hodson & Vannini, 2007, p. 263; Saettler, 2004, p. 264).

Symbolic interactionists are interested in exploring how media influence our perceptions of our social world. Our engagement with mass media is no different from any other form of human communication in which meaning is actively constructed. Indeed, symbolic interactionists believe that people do not internalize media images passively but, rather, are actively involved in a dynamic process that views media images and messages, reshapes them, and stores them when they reinforce cultural beliefs (Baran & Davis, 2009; Pascali, 2006, p. 685). In this way, media help to form identities by presenting images and situations that reinforce our cultural ideals of what makes people happy or successful.

One of the clearest examples of how media messages influence our views is seen in our definition of ideal body types. A great deal of sociological and psychological research has found a relationship between media depictions of the thin ideal, body dissatisfaction (Bessenoff, 2006, p. 239; Jung & Peterson, 2007, p. 40), and eating disorders (Derenne & Beresin, 2006, p. 258). In short, people compare their bodies to those they see in the media, a comparison that often leads them to be overly critical of how they look (Bessenoff, 2006, p. 239). With constant exposure to media images of what one is "supposed" to look like, many begin to define themselves by their perceived shortfalls rather than appreciating their own beauty and vitality (for a very good overview of the effects of media advertising, see www.media-awareness.ca and www.jeankilbourne.com).

Altheide (2003) investigates the effect of electronic communication technologies on what he calls the **e-audience**, which comprises all those who spend time in cyberspace answering email and surfing or talking on their cellphones (which is to say, most of us). According to Altheide (2003, p. 664), the defining feature of this audience is the perception of control and sense of entitlement that comes from being able to communicate whenever they want.

e-audience Those who use electronic communication technologies.

FEMINIST THEORY

The feminist critique of mass media investigates their patriarchal nature by highlighting the use of images of women in advertising, the exploitation of women in the pornography industry, and the tendency to present a solely masculine view of the world. For example, Gaye Tuchman (1978) refers to the "symbolic annihilation of women" in her discussion of the way in which media ignore, exclude, and marginalize women and their interests (as cited in Strinati, 2004, p. 162).

Feminist researchers also critique media portrayals of women as they relate to the reality of women's lived experiences. Television shows such as *The Bachelor* and *America's Next Top Model*, for example, not only have little to do with women's actual lives but also reinforce the view that women need to compete with each other to "catch" a man or must be so beautiful that they could have their pick of men. Such portrayals devalue both women and men. Sexist imagery permeates television shows, Hollywood movies, the Internet, magazines, and, of course, advertising, which includes the multi-billion-dollar cosmetic industry.

One issue, but by no means the only one that feminists are concerned with, is pornography (Paasonen, 2010). Today, online pornography provides an accessible and efficient means for even greater exploitation of women. Feminists argue that pornography is a tool men use to control, objectify, and suppress women (Lubey, 2006). As a result, feminists have proposed two strategies to diminish the effects of pornography on society.

First, in the 1980s, early anti-pornography feminists rejected the idea of state censorship in favour of adopting a human rights approach that would allow those negatively affected

> > >

Media advertising often portrays women as sex objects in order to sell their products.

Bill Aron/PhotoEdit

by pornography access to the courts to seek damages (Jensen, 2007). In fact, two noted feminists, Catherine MacKinnon and Andrea Dworkin, helped to draft a Minnesota law that allowed victims of sexual assault and other sex crimes to sue pornographers for damages, reasoning that the culture created by pornography supported sexual violence against women (Brest & Vandenberg, 1987). Feminists appreciate the importance of preserving the right of free expression but argue that the harm resulting from the exploitation of women requires some legal remedy (Martinson, 2005).

Second, contemporary feminists point to the importance of educating the public about the effects of pornography—not just its effect on those involved in its production but on society as a whole. The intent of these education programs is to inspire a discussion about how mainstream pornography (the vast majority of which targets heterosexual men) is becoming increasingly cruel and degrading to women and is more openly racist than ever (Jensen, 2007). Confronting the pornography industry challenges us to acknowledge the deep **misogyny** and white supremacy that continue to exist in our society.

misogyny The hatred or deep dislike of women.

POST-STRUCTURALISM

One of the most important post-structuralist writers on mass media was French philosopher Jean Baudrillard (1929–2007). Baudrillard perceived that while modern societies focus on the production and consumption of commodities, postmodern societies focus on simulation and the creation and interplay of images and signs. In a world of simulation, identities are constructed by internalizing images that ultimately determine how people see themselves and others (Kellner, 2007). Baudrillard's analysis of media, then, centred on his concepts of simulation and hyperreality.

simulation
Baudrillard's assertion that media create a "simulated" world through the reinforcement of certain images and signs.

Simulation is Baudrillard's term for how media create what we see as real by reinforcing certain images and signs. Media convey to us the fashions we should like, the music we should listen to, and the art we should find appealing. According to Baudrillard, the **hyperreal** is the phenomenon that results when people define their experiences based on a perception of the world that has been simulated and constructed by the media (Redhead, 2007, p. 102). Media do not represent social life as it truly exists but, rather, as it is manufactured. The news media in particular present stories as theatre, whereby glorified, manipulated, and censored events are packaged and displayed.

hyperreal
Baudrillard's belief that people's perceptions, as defined by media, lead to the sense of a simulated reality.

Baudrillard argued that, dominated as we are by simulated experience and feelings, we have lost the ability to comprehend reality as it truly exists. What we see as "real" on television, for example, is the result of editing and simplification for distribution to the masses. Media content is produced with the lowest common denominator in mind and, as such, softens our intellect rather than challenging it. According to Dominic Strinati (1993), for example, the postmodern view of contemporary television reveals how the medium has

BOX 17.3 WHY SHOULD WE CARE?

No Logo and You

Estimates suggest that people receive between 3000 and 5000 product impressions per day (IPC Media, 2006; Johnson, 2009). Naomi Klein, Canadian author of the bestselling book *No Logo* (2000), reveals a great deal about the inner workings of the advertising industry and our increasingly branded society (Marshall, 2008).

Klein demonstrates that brands are much more than just symbols used to market products; they invoke associations with products but also, by extension, provide information about what the people who purchase them are like. Do you have preconceived ideas about how Tim Hortons customers differ from Starbucks habitués? Do you associate different attributes with each (e.g., working class versus middle class)? If so, you have internalized the brands' images. As Klein argues, brands today represent a lifestyle, a look, and a culture. For example, what does it mean to be a "Tommy Boy" or a "GAP Kid"?

Moreover, corporate sponsorship is changing our perception of public spaces. Klein cites as an example the banning of York University students from campus after they were "caught" distributing no-smoking pamphlets during the du Maurier Open tennis tournament being hosted by the university. In effect, a public university had been branded by a cigarette company. People are even agreeing to become walking billboards for products—for example, in 2002, a young man sold advertising space on his forehead through eBay (Paulson, 2007, p. 361).

Klein also points out the power of Walmart in determining what North American consumers get to see, read, and listen to. As the world's largest retailer, Walmart exerts tremendous influence on magazine, book, movie, and music companies that need their products to be sold in Walmart stores. The chain has been known to refuse media content if it does not comply with the retailer's family-oriented standards (Marshall, 2008). As a sociologist, why should we care when corporations try to influence public perception?

Are there any examples from your own community (e.g., billboards, newspaper ads, event sponsorship, etc.) that illustrate how different retailers want to be perceived by the public? Would these images influence your decision to shop there? Why?

become preoccupied with elementary, juvenile themes in place of a deeper understanding of the realities of the human condition.

Baudrillard did not suggest that what we perceive as reality is simply an illusion; instead, he argued that the illusion has *become* the reality. The line between what is real and what is simulated is blurred, and it becomes increasingly difficult to distinguish between the two (Baudrillard, 1983; Fox & Miller, 2005, pp. 650–654).

The Future of Mass Media

As sociologists, we see the future of mass media as challenging society in a number of ways.

HOMOGENIZATION OF CULTURE

As the forces of globalization continue to entrench Western media as the global default, cultural diversity will decline (a subject to which we will return in Chapter 19; see Leidner, 2010). "Like sand castles on a beach, local cultures are being eroded and flattened by the gradual impact of the endless tide of U.S. and other Western media products" (Croteau & Hoynes, 2003, p. 358). This homogenization is also making our cultures less complex and more alike—for example, shopping malls around the world contain the same megastores catering to increasingly similar consumers.

Moreover, attempts at cultural nationalism (e.g., CanCon legislation to promote national values in the face of the American media onslaught) are devoid of any real consequence in our electronic world because global media content is controlled by a handful of multinational corporations (Fotopoulos, 1999, p. 43).

> Every TV viewer in Nigeria, India, China or Russia now dreams of the American way of life, as seen on TV serials (which being relatively inexpensive and glamorous, fill the TV programs of most TV channels all over the world) and thinks in terms of the competitive values imbued by them. (Fotopoulos, 1999, p. 44)

INTERNET ADDICTION

People are becoming addicted to the Internet (Block, 2008; Stieger & Burger, 2010). Heavy Internet users (the majority of whom send text messages, surf pornography, or play online games) can suffer from withdrawal symptoms when they do not have Internet access; they lie to friends, family, and partners about their use; and they suffer from poor achievement, depression, fatigue, and social isolation (Block, 2008; Wallace, 2014, p.12).

Massively Multiplayer Online Role-Playing Games (MMORPGs) have been found to be particularly addictive. MMORPGs allow players to create virtual identities and become immersed in an online fantasy world. Estimates suggest that there are 400 million MMORPG players worldwide with over 7.8 million who play the most popular game, *World of Warcraft* (Makuch, 2014). The games are designed to require increasing playing time in order to achieve higher levels and obtain more money, weapons, skills, and power in the virtual worlds. At the highest levels, players must band together to go on raids that can require 10 or more hours of continuous play; some players have reported playing for more than 100 hours per week (Collins, Freeman, & Charnarro-Premuzic, 2012).

While the Internet can provide a wonderful opportunity to share with others, there is concern that with this openness comes risk (Whitlock, Lader, & Conterio, 2007). For example, recent research found that the more time adolescents spend on the Internet, the less satisfied they are with their lives (Wang, Chen, Lin, & Wang, 2008) and the more likely they are to be overweight (Fontaine & Allison, 2002, p. 611).

> > >

These ads in Bolivia suggest to some that Western capitalism is leading to the global homogenization of culture.

Road Trippin'/Alamy

INTERNET PORNOGRAPHY

> The way you know if your technology is good and solid is if it's doing well in the porn world. (Susan Struble, Sun Microsystems spokesperson, as cited in Bedell, 2001)

Tony Tremblay (1999) would agree with Struble in that all new media forms are initially pushed to their limits in their ability to convey sexual imagery and to titillate a new audience. He points out, for example, that some of the earliest movies produced were peep shows: *Serpentine Dance* (1895) and *Pull Down the Curtains, Suzie* (1904) (Tremblay, 1999, p. 168). Consistent with our approach to mass media in this chapter, Tremblay's investigation teaches us that we should understand Internet pornography in a historical context.

Tremblay argues that all new media begin by pushing the social boundaries of morality because they offer new avenues for people to explore their sexuality. Through his concept of **cybriety** (a neologism that combines *cyber* and *sobriety*), he captures the social response to these challenges of morality, which generally involve attempts to censor new media content (Tremblay, 1999, p. 168). Tremblay's historical analysis shows that as a new technology matures and becomes more commonplace, society adjusts and moral boundaries are broadened accordingly. Each medium is doomed to fail when the next new technology that promises more erotic potential emerges; that is, from written letters and stories to still pictures, movies, videos, cable, and the Internet, each new technology surpassed its predecessor. Yet Tremblay argues that despite the pervasiveness of online pornography, all technology ultimately fails because it cannot fulfill the human need for companionship and physical contact: "Internet censorship, or cybriety, is not new; it is a re-run of our favorite drama, the psychoanalytic morality play that teeters between our desires and our fears of their fulfillment" (1999, p. 181).

cybriety **Tremblay's term describing attempts to censor new media content that pushes the boundaries of morality.**

INCREASED MOBILITY AND ACCESS TO INFORMATION

The technology of the future will provide people with even greater ability to move wherever they like and remain connected to their friends, family, work, and school in ways that will continue to break down geographic barriers. Further, barriers to information will continue to fall as more and more people seek to find out what they want, when they want it. For example, research has found that more than two-thirds (71 percent) of Canadians who say they visit social networking sites use them to keep up with the news (Vision Critical, 2011).

Patrick Chapuis/Gamma-Rapho/Getty Images

< < <

Media technologies are enabling people to capture and post images to the Internet that could challenge existing power structures and lead to progressive social change.

Further, as cellphone technology continues to expand, the separation between the information people can gather from their computers and their phones will decline.

DEMOCRATIC POTENTIAL AND POTENTIAL TO BUILD ONLINE COMMUNITIES

The power of media to transform society and to challenge repressive regimes was first demonstrated in the 1950s with the civil rights movement; then in the 1960s when the American public rallied against its own government to oppose the war in Vietnam; and most recently, in Tunisia, Egypt, Lybia, and other African and Middle-Eastern countries. Television ushered in an age in which people could watch the world's events unfold in their living rooms, and what they saw often inspired them to rise up and seek change. From the young man in Tiananmen Square who stood in front of Chinese tanks to amateur videos of the aftermath of Hurricane Katrina and the occupation of Tahrir Square in Egypt, new media technologies are enabling people to capture and post images to the Internet that could challenge existing power structures and lead to progressive social change.

Web 2.0 technologies and social software also have tremendous potential to bring people together and provide, at some level at least, a sense of community. Facebook, blogs, and Twitter are just the tip of the social-software iceberg that could emerge in the coming months and years (Kamel Boulos & Wheeler, 2007).

◉ᐩ**Watch**

Facebook Etiquette

Summary

1 The earliest communication technology took the form of prehistoric cave art, followed much later by the Sumerians' cuneiform, Egyptian hieroglyphics, and later still by the phonetic alphabet. Block printing gave way to movable type, which resulted in the dissemination of books and newspapers. The inventions of the telegraph, phonograph, radio, moving pictures, television, and the Internet have resulted in today's instantaneous communication.

2 Today's communication technologies include satellite television, cellphones, text messaging, Twitter, blogs, wikis, YouTube, and social networking sites—all of which are changing the way people interact online.

3 Harold Innis distinguished between time-biased media (whose immovability and longevity are associated with traditional hierarchies) and space-biased media (whose ability to convey messages across distances is associated with the emergence of empires). Marshall McLuhan built on Innis's work with his insights into the primacy of the medium in understanding content ("The medium is the message") as well as his concepts of "hot" and "cool" media.

4 The CRTC's CanCon regulations are intended to promote Canadian culture by ensuring that radio and television broadcasts include certain minimum percentages of Canadian content. These requirements have been criticized, however, as ensuring mediocrity and as obliging media outlets to overplay popular Canadian content as a means of fulfilling quotas.

5 Functionalists view mass media as contributing to society in four areas: socialization, surveillance, correlation, and entertainment. Conflict theorists, in contrast, view mass media as a mechanism by which to uphold the ideology of the dominant class. Symbolic interactionists are primarily interested in how mass media influence our definitions of ourselves and others. Feminist theory targets mass media as an expression of patriarchy in its dissemination of sexualized imagery of women. Post-structuralists focus on how media create an imaginary world in which simulated experiences are perceived as real.

6 The future of mass media is likely to entail a continuation of current trends, negative and positive, in the following areas: erosion of global cultural diversity by Western mass media, Internet addiction, online pornography, increased mobility and access to information, the building of online communities, and the potential to challenge repressive regimes.

Key Terms

block printing *449*
blog *457*
CanCon (Canadian content) *463*
cool media *462*
correlation function *465*
cuneiform *448*
cybriety *471*
demassification *458*
digital sociality *456*
e-audience *467*
entertainment function *465*
hieroglyphics *448*
hot media *461*
hyperreal *468*

MAPL system *463*
mass communication *447*
mass media *447*
misogyny *468*
movable type *449*
papyrus *448*
phonetic alphabet *449*
propaganda model *466*
RSS (Really Simple Syndication) *457*
simulation *468*
socialization function *465*
space-biased media *460*
surveillance function *465*
time-biased media *460*
Web 2.0 *454*
wiki *458*

Reviewing the Concepts

1. Which of the four functions of media (socialization, surveillance, correlation, and entertainment) do you feel is most important when considering new online communication technologies?

2. What do you see as the strengths and weaknesses of Herman and Chomsky's propaganda model?

3. Do you feel that the decline in the number of people watching television will continue? What factors do you think make some young people more likely to watch a movie on their iPad than on their television?

4. Do you feel that mass media are becoming more or less exploitive of women over time? Give at least three examples to support your answer.

Applying Your Sociological Imagination

1. In your opinion and given your experiences, do social media promote feelings of connection or alienation? Discuss.

2. Review the concept of demassification. Can this concept be applied to your use of technology today? How, or why not?

3. Explore how McLuhan's assertion that the "medium is the message" can be applied to your sociology class.

4. As a sociologist, review and discuss YouTube's tagline, Broadcast Yourself. In your informed opinion, what is it about YouTube that makes it such a popular site?

MySocLab

Visit MySocLab to access a variety of online resources that will help you prepare for tests and apply your knowledge.

18 Social Change, Collective Behaviour, and Social Movements

In early 2011, Tahrir Square in Cairo, Egypt, became the focal point for a social and political revolution that ultimately forced President Hosni Mubarak from office. Motivated by a pressing need for political and social reform, and inspired by the recent success of the Tunisian revolution, Egyptians took to the streets on January 25, 2011, to protest Mubarak's oppressive political regime. As the world watched, over a million Egyptians gathered in the square to draw attention to their plight (*Anthropology Today*, 2011). For 18 days the protesters occupied the square, which became both the symbolic and physical centre of the revolution. The speed with which the square was transformed, literally within a few days, into both a symbol of the Egyptian people's aspirations and a functioning social universe was truly remarkable. As the tide of revolution swept across the Arab world, many protestors from diverse political and religious backgrounds united under the fundamental demands of freedom, equality, justice, and dignity (*Anthropology Today*, 2011). Mohammed Abouelleil Rashed, an Egyptian graduate student studying in London, went to Tahrir Square, and his account below demonstrates the profound influence social movements can have on both individuals and entire nations.

> I arrive in the square early on 30 January. The atmosphere is overwhelming. As an Egyptian who grew up criticizing a hyper-corrupt regime I, like my contemporaries, have never had the opportunity to openly express my political views in my own country. To find myself in the middle of Cairo chanting for an end to an oppressive and brutal 30-year rule is exhilarating. . . . Protesters of all ages, social classes, education levels and ideologies are talking politics and sharing their grievances, united by a simple goal: the status quo must end. (Rashed & El Azzazi, 2011, p. 25)

LEARNING OBJECTIVES

By the end of this chapter, students will be able to

❶ Define the terms *social change*, *collective behaviour*, and *social movement* and provide contemporary examples of each.

❷ Explain the inspirations behind social change.

❸ Review and critique the sociological theories that explain social change.

❹ Define *collectivity* and compare and contrast localized and dispersed collectivities.

❺ Review and critique the sociological theories that explain collective behaviour.

❻ Review the four different types of social movements: revolutionary, reformist, reactionary, and religious.

❼ Review and critique the sociological theories that explain social movements.

❶ What Is Social Change?

For sociologists, **social change** can be defined as changes in the typical features of a society (e.g., norms and values) over time (Tomasik & Silbereisen, 2009, p. 14). We can see evidence of social change everywhere in society, from what is considered deviant over time to the clothes we wear; social change is ongoing and inevitable. It occurs when there are modifications or adjustments to public policy, cultural traditions, or social institutions that at times are inspired by collective behaviours. **Collective behaviours** occur when people come together to achieve a single and meaningful short-term goal that may result in social change (Kurzman, 2008). Social scientists typically suggest that collective behaviours are not regulated by the everyday rules and expectations that normally shape people's actions—for example, the demonstrations at Tahrir Square.

Social movements are one particular type of collective behaviour. They are made up of groups and individuals that provide largely continuous and organized efforts to bring about—or resist—social change (see Carroll & Ratner, 2007). These movements generally emerge from grassroots organizations that operate outside existing social power structures, including established political parties and the legal system (Johnston & Almeida, 2006, p. 62; Sawchuk, 2009, p. 173; Jasper, 2011, p. 286).

Social change is a broad concept used to explore the changes that take place in interpersonal relations as well as in society's social organization (e.g., the influence of computers on communication between friends as well as on the education system). Sometimes, social change is predictable, as when a society is defeated in a war, but usually it is not (consider the unintended consequences of computers). However, the one unmistakable global trend today is the accelerating pace at which

social change
Changes in the typical features of a society (e.g., norms and values) over time.

collective behaviours
Behaviours that occur when people come together to achieve a meaningful short-term goal.

social movements
Collections of people who are organized to bring about or resist social change.

(((•—**Listen**

China's Communists Chart a New Course

social change occurs (Ginsberg & Gekonge, 2004, p. 354; Rudel & Hooper, 2005, p. 275). As a rule, social change is most likely to occur when

1. the change originates within what are seen as cutting-edge sources (e.g., fashion shows, academic research findings);

2. the change addresses a strongly felt need among the public (e.g., legislation to restrict access to questionable content on the Internet);

3. the change is material rather than nonmaterial (e.g., subsidizing the costs of alternative fuels versus brochures promoting the benefits of mass transit); and

4. the change is broadly compatible with people's existing values (e.g., recycling programs succeed because people's environmental awareness is rising) (Etzkowitz, 1992, as cited in Lindsey, Beach, & Ravelli, 2009, p. 286).

DIGITAL NATIVES AND DIGITAL IMMIGRANTS

digital natives Prensky's term for people who grew up with digital technologies.

One example of how technology can lead to social change is found in the work of Marc Prensky (2001) and his concepts of digital natives and digital immigrants. Prenksy argues that the education system is ill-suited to the needs and aspirations of today's students. He uses the term **digital natives** to describe students who have spent their entire lives using computers, accessing the Internet, using cellphones, and playing video games—and, as such, are "native speakers" of the digital language (Prensky, 2001, p. 1). **Digital immigrants**, in contrast, are those who did not grow up with digital technology and are often intimidated by it. Because digital immigrants are not native speakers of the digital language, they have an "accent" that they will never get rid of. Prensky's specific concern is that since the school system is designed, managed, and staffed by digital immigrants who are trying to teach digital natives, there are times when students and teachers cannot understand each other. Table 18.1 outlines the differences between the defining features of digital natives and digital immigrants; as you can see, digital natives and digital immigrants respond to technology in very different ways.

digital immigrants Prensky's term for people who grew up before digital technologies became commonplace.

> > > Thinking Sociologically

Reflect on the ages/approaches of all your professors this term. Is it possible to apply the concepts of *digital natives* and *digital immigrants* to how they organize their courses?

THE LIFE CYCLE OF SOCIAL CHANGE

innovation Something new that inspires social change (e.g., cellphones).

Social change can be seen to move through a type of life cycle. In the first stage of **innovation**—something new that inspires a change—a few "early adopters" adapt to the change. During this stage, change is very slow, but when it is adopted by 10 to 25 percent of the population, the rate of change accelerates very quickly—an idea consistent with Malcolm Gladwell's (2000) concept of the "tipping point." Most of the people who become early adopters are young, tend to live in cities, and are middle class (or higher) with good educations. Generally, early adopters enjoy distinguishing themselves from the crowd by setting trends, not following them.

exponential growth The adoption of a new technology or behaviour by the majority of the population.

The second stage of change is a time of **exponential growth**, when the majority of the population adopts the technology or behaviour. The final stage is referred to as **saturation**, whereby the change enters a society's traditions and normal daily practices (Orum, Johnstone, & Riger, 1999, p. 87).

saturation The point at which a new technology or behaviour becomes a part of everyday living.

OPPOSITION TO SOCIAL CHANGE

Of course, not everyone supports change—for example, the rich and powerful generally resist social change, given that it often occurs at their expense. In his book *Vested Interests and the Common Man* (2004 [1919]), sociologist Thorstein Veblen (whose concept of conspicuous

TABLE 18.1 Digital Natives and Digital Immigrants

Digital Native	Digital Immigrant
Studies or reads with music and/or television on	Studies or reads in silence
Frustrated when email is not replied to immediately	Calls to see if you have received email
Ignores email forwards	Replies to and sends email forwards
Uses text messaging	Does not see the point of text messaging or is confused by it
Reads text and emails from computer screen	Prints out texts and emails to read from paper
Embraces new technology	Is nervous of new technology
Buys music online	Buys music from a store
Reads online newspapers	Reads paper newspapers
Engages in instant chats	Communicates through phone calls
Keeps cellphone turned on at all times	Turns off cellphone
Has latest video games	Prefers older video games
Programs television so as not to miss an episode	Alters schedule around a television show or misses the episode
Uses Google maps	Uses paper maps
Multitasks	Does one thing at a time

Source: Adapted from www.theramartens.com/thesis_website/appendix.html (accessed July 16, 2010). Used with permission of the author.

consumption was discussed in Chapter 7) coined the term **vested interests** to describe why privileged members of society resist change. Veblen argued that since many in the leisure class gain their wealth and social position not by personal actions or attributes but through inheritance, these people would resist any change as it might cost them their lives of privilege (O'Hara, 2002, p. 87). This was certainly true when owners in the music industry went to court against those who were sharing music files over the Internet for free. However, perhaps the most famous example of people resisting social change is the case of the Luddites in the early nineteenth century.

The **Luddites** were a loosely bound group of displaced textile workers who destroyed the new machines that put them out of work (Kivisto, 2004, p. 12). The Luddite movement was well organized but lasted just over a year before the British army quashed it. It is important to understand that the Luddites were not against all technology—just those technologies that presented a direct threat to their way of life. (Today, the term *Luddite* is used to refer to someone who is resistant to new technology.) The lesson to take away from the Luddite uprising is their belief that technological advancement is neither inevitable nor uncontrollable—ideally, technology makes our lives better, not worse (Petch, 2002).

❷ INSPIRATIONS FOR SOCIAL CHANGE

Sociologists understand that social changes do not happen in a vacuum; instead, they are often inspired by the world around us. In this section, we review some of the inspirations for social change.

Technology **Technology** is broadly defined as the application of knowledge to achieve practical purposes; in effect, it is anything that provides an artificial means to achieve a given end or result. For example, technology is the tractor that allows one farmer to seed hundreds

vested interests Veblen's term to describe why privileged members of society resist change.

Luddites A loosely bound group of displaced textile workers who destroyed the new machines that put them out of work in the early nineteenth century.

technology Anything that provides an artificial means to achieve a given end or result.

> > >

The Luddites were displaced textile workers from the early nineteenth century who destroyed the machines that put them out of work.

Pictorial Press Ltd/Alamy

> > >

Members of unofficial militia groups in the United States believe that they have a duty to protect the American people from what they see as a corrupt and tyrannical federal government. There are currently several hundred such militia groups operating in the United States.

REUTERS/Rick Wilking

of hectares in a single day, or the microwave oven that can heat up a bowl of soup in less than a minute.

Both tractors and microwave ovens have become more powerful and efficient through the years; technology, then, builds on past discoveries. Also, technological developments can inspire a great deal of social change that similarly accumulates over time. The farmer's ability to seed, spray, fertilize, and harvest many more hectares than in the past has been one factor that has contributed to the decline in the number of small family farms. Microwaveable foods have contributed to our contemporary "drive-through" lifestyle, wherein we rarely sit down with our families to talk about what is going on in our lives.

Physical Environment Living through a cold Canadian winter is proof that people are able to adapt to a harsh physical environment. In order to survive, our Aboriginal ancestors needed to alter their material culture (e.g., the development of warm winter clothing) as well as their social behaviour (e.g., the sharing of food among families to protect against starvation) (Moran, 1981). Living in hot climates requires similar novel adaptations, as does living on the prairie. In short, diverse environments often provide the inspiration for social change. For example, in many tropical countries, homes are elevated above the ground to maximize the cooling effects of airflow, and many Canadian homesteads used underground ice cellars to keep food cool throughout the year.

Demographic Shifts As discussed in Chapter 15, the proportion of Canadians over age 65 is increasing—from just over 5 percent in 1921 to almost 15 percent in 2011—and is projected to exceed 27 percent by 2056. The growing population of healthy seniors who are well into their eighties has resulted in changes to mandatory retirement legislation as well as greater public awareness of such issues as long-term-care requirements. Other important inspirations for social change are immigration and migration patterns. When people move to a different country, or move from a rural area to an urban one, society needs to adjust to these people's preferences and expectations. Such adjustments may include the provision of more spaces in schools for ESL students and urban planning to provide a sense of community within large cities (Bradford, 2007; Dagenais, 2013).

Economic Competition The emergence of China and India as industrial powerhouses has led to a reordering of global capitalism. While the world's dominant national economy continues to be the United States (see Table 19.4 on page 520), the fact that China holds about 21.9 percent of all American foreign debt concerns many economists, in that the United States' primary political, military, and economic adversary holding that much debt weakens its ability to compete (Barrera, 2008, p. 295; Cella III, 2010; Labonte & Nagel, 2013; Morrison & Labonte, 2008). Competition can inspire innovation and progressive social change, but it can also create very clear winners and losers (see Chapter 19).

War Warfare has always been a prime inspiration for technological development—from gunpowder to nuclear weapons. At times, the technologies developed for military application (consider nuclear fission and the Internet) find their way into the larger society and can result in social change. After the terrorist attacks of September 11, 2001, the Bush administration slowly and methodically diminished Americans' civil rights on the premise that it required greater access to people's private information in order to protect everyone from terrorism (Pitt, 2011). In more recent years, warfare has again changed shape in response to the availability of new technologies. The Obama administration has made heavy use of drone warfare (using unmanned aerial vehicles [UAVs] to deliver missile strikes against ground targets in Afghanistan, Pakistan, Yemen, Syria, and elsewhere.

Ideas While we can readily perceive how technology, competition, and war can lead to social change, we cannot underestimate the power of ideas to inspire change as well. Think back to Chapter 2, where we reviewed the importance of Enlightenment ideals to human social development. Or consider how such ideas as free will, evolution, democracy, and freedom each played an important role in social change.

Governments Governments with strong political leadership can mobilize large-scale efforts to alter the character of a society. In Canada, for example, the federal government has contributed to significant changes in human rights legislation, health care reform, and environmental protection. In the United States, President Obama's health care reform legislation certainly altered the American political and social landscape.

Individuals From time to time, certain people inspire social change through their personality, charisma, and conviction. While there are many examples of leaders who diminish the value of human life—Adolf Hitler, Saddam Hussein, and, more recently, Robert Mugabe—there are others—Mahatma Gandhi, Martin Luther King, Jr., and Nelson Mandela, to name only three—whose actions have helped to make the world a better place.

One Canadian who is making a difference is Craig Kielburger. In 1995, when he was 12, Kielburger established Free the Children, an organization that has become one of the world's largest youth-driven charities. Working with a number of international organizations, Free the Children operates in over 45 countries, provides 55 000 children with daily education, and supplies more than a million people with clean drinking water (www.freethechildren.com).

Social Movements The emergence of grassroots movements, such as Greenpeace, proves that when ordinary people come together to fight for or against something, tremendous social changes can occur (Anheier, 2005, p. 286). Characteristics common to all successful social movements include a strong organizational capacity, a clear position on their grievances and goals, and active engagement with existing political power structures to facilitate the achievement of these goals (Pellow, 2007, p. 54).

③ Sociological Approaches to Social Change

Sociologists provide four theoretical perspectives on social change: functionalist, conflict, evolutionary, and cyclical.

FUNCTIONALISM

As a rule, functionalists are more interested in the forces that keep a society stable than in those that change it (recall from Chapter 2, for example, that the discipline of sociology grew out of the conservative reaction to Enlightenment thinking). Yet Talcott Parsons, while perceiving society in its natural state as stable and balanced, saw that change did occur through a process of differentiation (Gerhardt, 2001, p. 192). According to Parsons (1951), the emergence of a social problem indicates that the social system needs to make adjustments in order to regain a state of equilibrium. For example, the civil rights demonstrations in the 1960s were an expression of the need for American society to become more accepting of racial diversity. The demonstrations motivated politicians and lawmakers to begin changing the laws of segregation to reflect the new social values of the time.

equilibrium theory
The assertion that a system's natural state is one of balance and harmony.

This functionalist approach to change is guided by **equilibrium theory**, which holds that changes in one part of society require changes in other parts in order for society to return to its natural state of balance and harmony (Trevino & Smelser, 2001, p. xxxv). These adjustments, then, actually help to maintain social stability. So although Parsons's use of equilibrium theory incorporated the evolutionary belief of ongoing progress, its predominant focus was stability and balance (Tominaga, 1993, p. 205).

Critics of functionalist theory point out that, at times, social changes amount to far more than a simple adjustment. The two World Wars, for example, fundamentally changed international relations, and the eradication of apartheid in South Africa represented nothing less than a complete reordering of that country's entire society. To argue that societies can be understood as organic entities that maintain equilibrium is also problematic in that it confers intent and conscious action to the conceptual notion of society.

CONFLICT THEORY

Conflict theorists argue that since the rich and powerful maintain their control over society to benefit their interests, anything that challenges the status quo will be resisted. While Marx accepted a broad evolutionary path along which societies develop—from Asiatic to ancient to feudal to modern modes of production (Bottomore, Harris, & Miliband, 1991, p. 23)—he did not believe that each was necessarily an improvement over the earlier form. According to Marx, history is full of examples of societies that moved through stages defined by the exploitation of the poor. True equality is possible only in the final stage of social development: communism (Slattery, 2003, p. 43). To achieve this, Marx viewed social change as coming about through active revolt against oppression and exploitation. Unlike the functionalists' focus on stability, then, conflict theorists consider conflict as inevitable and necessary to inspire social changes that will ultimately rid the world of inequality.

Although conflict theory is well suited to explain changes that occur as a result of tension and confrontation (including union strikes and government overthrows), it is less able to explain long-term stability and change that can occur without conflict (see Mayer, 1960).

> > > Thinking Sociologically

Select any two sociological approaches to social change and compare how they might explain the relationship between labour unions and employers.

EVOLUTIONARY THEORY

As described in Chapter 2, some early sociologists in the nineteenth century began using Charles Darwin's theory of genetic evolution to explain how societies change over time. Sociologists as far back as Auguste Comte have used evolutionary principles to explain social change. Comte saw societies evolving from the theological and metaphysical stages to ultimately arrive at the scientific or positive stage (see Chapter 1). Émile Durkheim similarly proposed that, over time, societies inevitably become more complex, which many at that time interpreted as meaning that since European societies were the most complex, they were the most highly evolved. Herbert Spencer later argued that society was similar to a living organism with interrelated and interdependent parts that work together to achieve a common end. In short, Comte, Durkheim, and Spencer all proposed what are referred to as unilinear and universal evolutionary theories.

Unilinear evolutionary theories hold that there is only one path through which an organism or society can evolve (e.g., Comte's Law of Three Stages contended that no society could "skip" the metaphysical stage on its way to the positive stage). **Universal evolutionary theories** argue that all societies must progress in the same manner (e.g., in Comte's Law, no society can stay at the theological stage or evolve into any form other than the three stages). While these views of social development have been discounted, a new form of evolutionary theory has been proposed by Gerhard Lenski (Barnett, 2004).

Neoevolutionary theory highlights the role of technology in assisting human beings with their subsistence needs. Gerhard Lenski (1966, 1996) also addresses one of the key weaknesses of social Darwinism: unilinear and universal evolution. He argues that social change is instead multilinear, continuous, and fluid (Kennedy, 2004, p. 316). Despite their differences, all evolutionists would agree that all societies have some internal drive that inspires them to adapt to the environment better so that they can compete more effectively for survival—this applies not just to individuals but to entire societies as well (Sulkowski, 2012).

unilinear evolutionary theory The assertion that there is only one path through which an organism or society can evolve.

universal evolutionary theory The assertion that all societies must progress in the same manner.

neoevolutionary theory Lenski's analysis of the role that technology plays in people's adjustment to the physical world.

Evolutionary theory has been influential in the past, but continues to face criticism. First, there is no evidence to suggest that all traditional societies were alike, and when societies do change, there does not appear to be a fixed set of stages through which they pass. Another criticism of evolutionary theory is the underlying assumption that societies progress over time. After all, in terms of social development, defining *progress* is difficult. For example, while the standard of living in wealthy countries has been rising over the past 50 years (see Chapter 19), environmental degradation, warfare, global terrorism, poverty, and human rights abuses around the world challenge the assumption that societies inevitably make positive social "progress" (Becker, 2007).

CYCLICAL THEORY

The idea behind cyclical theory is that social change occurs in a way similar to the changing seasons throughout the year. Cyclical theory does not argue that social change occurs in a defined direction but, instead, that there is an ebb and flow through time according to a series of endless cycles.

The earliest sociologist to apply cyclical theory to social change was Pitirim Sorokin (1889–1968). According to Sorokin, the most influential elements of culture are those that relate to people's inner experiences—their ideas, passions, and emotions (Bainbridge, 2007, p. 207). He believed that the essence of a culture was evident in what people aspired to become and how they planned to get there. According to Sorokin, each civilization emerges from a state of chaos with a coherent set of spiritual beliefs that give it strength and purpose. He called this type of society **ideational**, in that it is defined by spirituality and is driven to seek and achieve spiritual goals. Ideational cultures are religious (Bainbridge, 2007, p. 207), yet, over time, people's faith begins to falter and they transition into what Sorokin defined as a sensate culture. A **sensate culture** is scientific in that it interprets the social and physical world through the senses.

Sorokin held that social change occurred over time by moving back and forth between these two opposites; in other words, as a society moves in one direction, the attraction of the opposing force becomes stronger until the society reverses course. And, according to Sorokin, contemporary society was in an "overripe" sensate phase in which science was so powerful that people were beginning to become attracted to all of the things that science cannot address. Sorokin (1937, vol. III, p. 537, as cited in Bainbridge, 2007, pp. 207–208) wrote,

> Neither the decay of the Western society and culture, nor their death, is predicted by my thesis. What it does assert . . . is simply that one of the most important phases of their life history, the Sensate, is now ending and that we are turning towards its opposite through a period of transition. Such a period is always disquieting, grim, cruel, bloody, and painful.

Cyclical theory is certainly compelling, given that some things really do appear to change in cycles (consider economic boom and bust cycles; see Broadway, 2007, p. 565). However, other changes, such as technological innovations, appear to grow upon each other, and thus imply a direction of increasing complexity. Furthermore, cyclical theory is far more descriptive than analytic. It is possible that it was more applicable in the past than it is today.

❹ Collective Behaviour

Collective behaviour occurs when people come together to achieve a single and meaningful short-term goal that may inspire social change (Kurzman, 2008). Some sociologists prefer to use the term *collectivity* rather than *group* to highlight the strength of the bonds between the people involved. A **collectivity**, then, is a substantial number of people who join together on the basis of loosely defined norms. Collectivities generate little solidarity or loyalty, usually last

ideational culture
Sorokin's term for a society driven to seek and achieve spiritual goals.

sensate culture
Sorokin's term for a society that interprets the social and physical world through the senses.

collectivity A substantial number of people who join together on the basis of loosely defined norms.

The Canadian Press

< < <

The 1919 Winnipeg General Strike lasted six weeks and demonstrated labour solidarity when local union and nonunion workers walked off their jobs.

only a short while, have no defined boundaries, recognize few leaders, and display only a basic division of labour between members. In **localized collectivities** the members are located in each other's immediate physical presence (think of crowds, demonstrations, and riots), while in **dispersed collectivities** they are in different places at the same time (through rumours, gossip, and fads) (Turner & Killian, 1993, as cited in Lindsey & Beach, 2003, p. 413).

LOCALIZED COLLECTIVITIES

Crowds are unorganized collections of people who gather temporarily for a particular cause and are united by a common mood (e.g., people attending a parade) (Budilova, 2003). Since individuals are able to blend into a crowd, some members feel a level of anonymity that at times may increase their willingness to violate conventional norms. Some suggest that crowds can enable people to lose themselves and get caught up in the moment (Best, 2006, p. 9; Schweingruber & Wohlstein, 2005). For example, young women "flashed" their breasts along Calgary's "Red Mile" during the 2004 Stanley Cup playoffs (see Danielewicz, 2005). Herbert Blumer (1969) identified four basic types of crowds: casual, conventional, expressive, and acting.

A **casual crowd** is a collection of people who just happen to be in the same place at the same time—for example, people shopping at a mall. The casual crowd lacks any formal leadership or structure and is the simplest and most rudimentary form of collective behaviour (Hooper, 2001, p. 160).

A **conventional crowd** emerges from structured social events, such as weddings, ethnic festivals, and hockey games. People who attend these events generally behave in ways that are appropriate to the given activity (e.g., it is more acceptable to paint your face with team colours to attend a hockey game than it is to wear jeans to a wedding). Conventional crowds may gather for emotional events, but they generally disperse without incident. As Blumer noted, there are times when individuals intentionally seek out specific types of experiences because they are enjoyable—for example, attending a rave (Boeri, Sterk, & Elifson, 2004).

Expressive crowds are intended to provide participants with the opportunity to express their emotions. For example, participants in Gay Pride parades want to express their joy and pride in who they are, while people attending a funeral want to deal with their own grief as well as provide support for the family of the deceased.

localized collectivities
Collectivities in which the members are located in each other's immediate physical presence.

dispersed collectivities
Collectivities in which the members are in different places at the same time.

crowds An unorganized collection of people who gather temporarily for a particular cause.

casual crowd A chance collection of individuals in the same location at the same time.

conventional crowd A collection of people who gather for a structured social event.

expressive crowd A collection of people who gather intentionally to express their emotions.

Stoyan Nenov/Reuters/Landov

> > >

Flash mobs, like this pillow fight, demonstrate the unique potential of technology to enable collective action.

acting crowd A collection of people who gather to express anger and direct it outwardly at a specific person, category of people, or event.

mob A crowd that gathers to achieve an emotionally driven goal.

flash mob A planned gathering of large numbers of people for a brief and predetermined period of time.

riot A type of acting crowd that directs its anger toward multiple targets, moving from one to another in unpredictable ways.

When a crowd gathers with the intention to express anger and direct it outwardly at a specific person, category of people, or event, Blumer called it an **acting crowd**. A **mob** is a crowd that gathers to achieve an emotionally driven goal, confronts it, and then fades away—for example, the various demonstrations held around the world to challenge China's treatment of Tibetan monks. A relatively recent phenomenon is referred to as a **flash mob** (Srivastava, 2005; p. 98; Traxler, 2009, p. 17), a planned gathering of large numbers of people who converge in a public or semi-public place for a brief and predetermined period of time and then disperse immediately after the event. Most of these flash mobs are coordinated through social media sites or text messaging. One unique example is a worldwide organization that arranges pillow fights: Participants show up, bash each other with pillows, and then leave (www.pillowfightday.com). On April 5, 2014 (World Pillow Fight Day), pillow fights were organized in well over 100 cities around the world. Rules for pillow fights are as follows:

1. Don't talk about Pillow Fight Club!
2. Don't gather at the location before the event.
3. Hide your pillows.
4. Rush in screaming, "PILLOW FIIIIIGHT!!!!!"
5. After exactly 15 minutes, leave.
6. Do NOT hit anyone without a pillow! (Facebook, 2008)

A **riot** is also an acting crowd, but unlike a mob that focuses on a single person or event, a riot involves public disorder and directs its hostility toward multiple targets, moving from one to another in unpredictable ways. Riots can last for days, with participants dispersing and regrouping in response to the actions of the agents of social change. A famous riot occurred in Los Angeles in April 1992; after police were acquitted in the beating of Rodney King, a young African American, many people became outraged and took to the streets. The riot lasted for six days and resulted in 53 deaths, 10 000 arrests, 2300 injuries, and 1000 buildings lost to fire. The cost to the city was estimated at more than $1 billion (Davis, 2007; Matheson &

< < <

The 1992 Rodney King riots erupted after the four police officers charged in the beating were acquitted.

Baade, 2004, p. 2691). Three examples of Canadian riots are the Maurice "Rocket" Richard riot of 1955, the G20 Summit in Toronto in 2010, and the 2011 Vancouver Riot following the defeat of the Canucks by the Bruins in Game 7 of the Stanley Cup Finals.

A fifth type of crowd, the protest crowd, was recently added to the four types originally identified by Blumer (Lindsey, Beach, & Ravelli, 2009, p. 278). **Protest crowds** are deliberately assembled by the leaders of social movements to demonstrate public support for these movements. Examples of protest crowds include the 1963 Civil Rights Rally in Washington, DC—at which more than 250 000 people heard Martin Luther King, Jr. give his famous "I have a dream" speech—and the 250 000 Americans who joined television personalities Jon Stewart and Stephen Colbert in The Rally to Restore Sanity in October 2010. One recent Canadian example of a protest crowd is the public demonstrations orchestrated by former BC premier Bill Vander Zalm to resist the Harmonized Sales Tax (HST) in 2010.

protest crowd
A deliberately assembled crowd to rally support for a social movement.

 Explore

Forget Freud, Forget Marx. Rioting, Above All, Is Fun

(((•—Listen

How Rumours Start

DISPERSED COLLECTIVITIES

Because people in a dispersed collectivity are not in physical proximity to each other, they are more likely to react in emotional and relatively unconventional ways to situations or messages (Lofland, 2004/1981). Sociologists define five types of collective behaviours: rumours; mass hysteria; disaster behaviour; fashion, fads, and crazes; and publics.

Rumours A **rumour** is a specific or topical proposition passed from person to person that lacks reliable evidence to substantiate its claim or claims (Houmanfar & Johnson, 2003, p. 119). Rumours are most likely to occur when people face ambiguous situations and desperately want accurate information even though none is available (Donovan, 2007). For example, when a company is losing money, the rumour mill works overtime as workers worry about layoffs or factory closures. Rumours play an important role in the emergence and development of the other forms of dispersed collectivities (e.g., fads and mass hysteria) because they can spread rapidly through a circle of friends, a community, or even the world via the Internet.

rumour **Specific information passed from person to person that lacks reliable evidence.**

> > >

Orson Welles at the 1938 broadcast of "The War of the Worlds."

Bettmann/Corbis

gossip **Intimate and personal communication meant to be entertaining.**

urban legend **A short, persistent, nonverifiable tale with an ironic or supernatural twist.**

Two types of rumours are gossip and urban legends. **Gossip** is intimate and personal communication meant to be entertaining and enjoyable, while rumours generally deal with more important matters. Simply put, rumours help to justify, explain, and provide meaning to ambiguous situations, while gossip is intended to be an enjoyable sharing of everyday information (Houmanfar & Johnson, 2003, p. 119). **Urban legends** are short, persistent, usually nonverifiable tales with an ironic or supernatural twist that are spread by word of mouth, either personally or through alternative means such as email. For example, according to one urban legend, spider eggs are an ingredient for a type of chewing gum (Noymer, 2001, p. 300; Weldon, 2001, p. 282).

There are times when media report urban legends and disseminate them to the larger public. Examples include the false claims that large numbers of children are abducted by Satanists and sacrificed in their rituals (Richardson, Best, & Bromley, 1991) and that deranged people are putting razor blades in the apples they pass out at Halloween. When rumours like these are reported in the media, they can inspire mass hysteria.

mass hysteria **Occurs when people react to a real or imagined event with irrational or frantic fear.**

Mass Hysteria **Mass hysteria** occurs when people react to a real or imagined event with irrational or frantic fear. One of the most famous cases of mass hysteria was Orson Welles's "The War of the Worlds" radio broadcast on October 30, 1938. The play, presented in the form of a newscast, was broadcast across the United States and depicted a Martian invasion. Princeton University psychologist Hadley Cantril (1940) estimated that more than 1 million listeners were frightened or disturbed by what they thought was a real broadcast. However, subsequent research by sociologists David Miller (1985) and William Sims Bainbridge (1987) concluded that there was scant evidence of substantial or widespread panic. The fact that the fictional program led some people to fear for their lives nonetheless demonstrates that people are influenced by the emotions and behaviours of others.

Disaster Behaviour **Disasters** are usually unexpected events that cause extensive damage to people, animals, and property, and include floods, earthquakes, hurricanes, and other natural or human disasters. Some researchers estimate that since 2000, disasters have affected more than 3 billion people, killed more than 950 000 (an estimated 200 000 people were killed in natural disasters in 2013 alone), and caused more than US$2.5 trillion in damages (United Nations, 2013b). The National Oceanographic and Atmospheric Administration (NOAA) has estimated that weather- and climate-related disasters since 1980 have cost the United States alone over 1 trillion dollars (National Climatic Data Center, 2013). When added to the costs of man-made disasters, that figure climbs even higher. On April 20, 2010, for example, the Deepwater Horizon, contracted to British Petroleum, exploded and sent around 200 million gallons of oil into the Gulf of Mexico (Couric, 2010).

After a disaster, people are often left to manage their everyday needs under extraordinary circumstances. As was made evident after the tsunami in Southeast Asia in December 2004, Hurricane Katrina in August 2005, the Burmese cyclone in May 2008, the Haiti earthquake in January 2010, the Japanese tsunami in March 2011, and Hurricane Sandy in 2012, drinking water, food, and shelter can be difficult to obtain during disasters.

At times, large disasters can result in a breakdown of traditional sociopolitical guidelines that can leave people feeling overwhelmed, demoralized, and depressed (Boin & McConnell, 2007, p. 51; Freudenburg, Gramling, Laska, & Erikson, 2009). According to Kai Erikson (1998), who has studied many disasters, victims often feel numb, experience feelings of guilt for having survived when others died, lose their faith and confidence in the natural and social order of things, and may feel disconnected from their previous lives. However, people are also very resilient, and most survivors return to normal lives (Vineburgh, Ursano, & Fullerton, 2005, p. 213; also see Haney, James, & Fussell, 2007).

Fashion, Fads, and Crazes **Fashion** refers to a social pattern that appeals to a large number of people—for example, what people wear, the music they listen to, and the colour and style of their cellphones. To be considered fashionable is to pursue items that partly establish a personal identity as an outward expression of confidence and being "with it." Some sociologists (see Glasser, 1976; Simmel, 1978) believe that contemporary society is becoming increasingly addicted to consumerism, which, although it provides a brief feeling of satisfaction, has no lasting influence on people's worth to themselves or to others (Foley, Holzman, & Wearing, 2007, p. 186).

A **fad** is a short-lived but enthusiastically embraced new cultural element. While many consider the contemporary attraction to tattoos to be a fad, the fact that they are largely permanent led Kosut (2006) to refer to them as "ironic fads," in that they cannot be discarded as easily as a pair of leg warmers once they go out of style. According to Lofland (1973), there are four distinct types of fads: *object fads* (cellphones, pet rocks, pogs), *idea fads* (astrology, UFOs, the occult), *activity fads* (Botox injections, tongue piercing, bungee jumping), and *personality fads* (Elvis, Oprah, Paris Hilton) (Lindsey, Beach, & Ravelli, 2009, p. 280).

A **craze** is similar to a fad but usually represents a more intense emotional connection to the phenomenon at hand. For example, fans of the band the Grateful Dead are referred to as Deadheads (see www.dead.net), some of whom spend a lot of time and energy following anything to do with the band. Other examples of ongoing crazes are fans of *Star Trek* (called "trekkies," see www.startrek.com) or those of Canadian pop singer Justin Beiber (who call themselves "Beliebers"). Even the latest fitness routines or diets, such as crossfit or the "paleo diet," can qualify as crazes.

Publics A **public** is defined as an accumulation of people who have a defined political interest for meeting and who are organized by a common mood but are not necessarily in direct contact with other members (Budilova, 2003, p. 18).

disaster An unexpected event that causes extensive damage to people, animals, and property.

fashion A social pattern that outwardly expresses an individual's identity as being "with it."

fad A short-lived but enthusiastically embraced new cultural element.

craze A widespread emotional connection to a cultural phenomenon.

public An accumulation of people who have a defined political interest for meeting and who are organized by a common mood.

>>> Thinking Sociologically

List one contemporary example of a fashion, a fad, and a craze. Then do the same for your parents' generation. Are there any similarities between the two lists?

This collective experience is intended to establish a new norm, law, policy, or practice that would guide people's behaviour and actions (e.g., public hearings on changes to legislation on dangerous offenders) (Attallah, 2002, pp. 103–104). Collective behaviour researchers view a public as an enduring collectivity that maintains an interest in a particular issue for an extended period of time. When a public becomes organized enough to convey its point of view actively to decision-makers, it becomes either an interest group or a social movement (Greenberg & Page, 2007).

❺ Sociological Approaches to Collective Behaviour

Our review of localized and dispersed collectivities highlighted several examples of collective behaviours—things that people do when they are in groups that they generally do not do on their own. Sociologists have developed three primary theories that attempt to explain the influence of a group on an individual: contagion, convergence, and emergent norm theories.

CONTAGION THEORY

French sociologist Gustave Le Bon (1841–1931) was the first to apply social psychology principles to understand why people behave differently when they are in groups than when they are alone. The theory's basic assumption is that the group exerts a powerful influence on the individual (Sampson, 2012, p. 80). Le Bon argued that when people gather in crowds, an individual loses his or her conscious personality and has it replaced by an uncivilized and potentially barbaric "collective mind" (Waddington & King, 2005, p. 491). Le Bon (1895) believed that the irrationality of the crowd was contagious and created a type of excitement that was similar to a hypnotic effect (Lothane, 2006, p. 185). For the collective mind to emerge, three complementary factors are required: *anonymity* (people have to feel that they are lost within the group), *suggestibility* (anonymity makes people more suggestible to the collective will), and *contagion* (with the other two factors present, it becomes increasingly likely that "mindless" emotional activity will spread through the group) (Waddington & King, 2005, p. 491).

Le Bon's ideas influenced a great many writers at the time, including Durkheim (Terrier, 2006, p. 290) and Sigmund Freud (Lothane, 2006, p. 185). However, these ideas have been largely discounted by contemporary researchers, who have found little evidence to suggest that people do in fact "lose themselves" to the group (Kimmel, 1990, p. 68; McPhail, 1991).

CONVERGENCE THEORY

Convergence theory argues that the group is not the source of negative, irrational behaviour but instead that such behaviour appeals to a particular type of person. When like-minded people converge, they are more likely to manifest the type of behaviour they were looking for in the first place. For example, football matches in Europe have been marred for decades by hooligans who intentionally go to games to get into fights and participate in violent behaviour (Frosdick & Newton, 2006, p. 410; Stott & Pearson, 2006, p. 242). Convergence theorists would suggest that a rally on Parliament Hill to oppose the war in Afghanistan is unlikely to change many people's attitudes toward the war. On the contrary, people who attend the rally are there because it already reflects their views. Convergence theory therefore does not view people as passive beings who cannot control themselves, as contagion theory suggests, but rather asserts that the actions of the group are an expression of its members' own desires for types of behaviours they are willing to seek out.

Convergence theory certainly helps to explain why some people take part in actions while in a group that they would not do on their own (e.g., rarely do people go to football matches

< < <

European football shows how people may behave very differently in groups than they do alone.

on their own and look to start a fight). However, the theory fails to explain why some people are drawn to those activities while others are not.

EMERGENT NORM THEORY

Emergent norm theory is a symbolic interactionist approach in which aggressive or anti-social behaviours are viewed as resulting from an adjustment to new norms that emerge within a given group and in certain situations (Mancini, Fruggeri, & Panari, 2006, p. 211). In most situations, these changing social norms arise in ambiguous situations wherein individuals turn to others for cues on how to behave or what course of action to take (Uhl-Bien & Pillai, 2007, p. 201). For example, many reality television shows involve challenging situations in which one contestant offers a plan of action that others can accept or reject. In these ambiguous situations, such early decisions often become the new norms of behaviour (Aguirre, Wenger, & Vigo, 1998, p. 302). In a classic symbolic-interactionist interpretation, the new norms are the result of ongoing interaction between members of the group. Those who choose to follow the new norms stay with the group while those who do not choose to do so generally leave the group, which acts to reinforce the display of unity among group members (McPhail & Wohlstein, 1983).

Emergent norm theory, as proposed by its pioneers, Ralph Turner and Lewis Killian (1993), views crowd behaviour as neither irrational (as contagion theory asserts) nor deliberate (as convergence theory argues) but rather as the result of dynamic exchanges between participants. In other words, the group's actions are influenced by existing norms and values but are open to new norms should the group believe they are necessary. Emergent norm theory, then, offers an attractive middle-of-the road perspective. However, critics point out that the theory has limited ability to predict how groups will behave because there are so many variables at work (e.g., time of day, weather, backgrounds of people involved, preceding events that may inspire tension or fear in the group) (Ward, 1980, p. 19).

❻ Social Movements

Social movements are the most highly structured, rational, and enduring form of collective behaviour. Most social movements are established to stimulate change. They usually begin as small groups of people who possess little social power and who seek legitimacy, recognition, and change from such existing social institutions as government, political parties, and civic leaders. Social movements are perhaps the most important variety of collective behaviour as they can lead to profound social change (Carroll & Ratner, 2007, p. 43; also Hallgrimsdottir & Benoit, 2007). Doherty (2002, p. 7, as cited in Fagan, 2004, p. 20) defines four characteristics of those who participate in social movements:

1. They have a shared common identity.
2. They act at least partly outside of traditional political institutions and use protest as one of their primary forms of action.
3. They rely on noninstitutionalized networks of interaction.
4. They reject or challenge dominant forms of power.

Corbett (2006) proposes that social movements generally fall into two forms: informal, grassroots groups and formal or institutional groups.

Informal social movements generally emerge in opposition to a specific local issue, be it a *direct hazard* (e.g., changes to a community's drinking water infrastructure), a *plan* (e.g., a proposal to construct a nearby dam or nuclear power plant), or a broader *concern or threat* (e.g., a petition to ban the domestic use of pesticides). The most common form of informal social movements is environmental groups that promote more responsible and sustainable lifestyle choices. These grassroots movements generally originate with one or more charismatic leaders, who can range from ordinary citizens to members of the intellectual or social elite (Corbett, 2006, p. 286). What these informal groups lack in resources (money, paid staff, office space) they make up for in passion and commitment. Members of informal social groups usually have a personal stake in the issues at hand, whereas members of larger, more formal social movement organizations may not.

informal social movement A social movement that emerges to challenge a specific local issue.

> > >

The revolutionary movement in Tunisia in 2011.

Zoubeir Souissi/Reuters/Landov

Formal social movements are large organizations that have existed for a long time, and as such have elaborate structures and procedures (Corbett, 2006, p. 287). Formal social movements exercise bureaucratic procedures, but they do not operate within a society's existing power structures (e.g., government or business) (Laverack, 2004, p. 8)—although they may lobby these structures to further their own interests. These groups—for example, Greenpeace or pro-choice organizations—are well integrated within society, well known to the public, and a mainstay of regular media coverage. Recent research also suggests that the growth of information technology has inspired a resurgence of interest in contemporary social issues and may promote greater democratic participation (Carty, 2010).

Sociologists refer to well-established social movements as social movement organizations (SMOs). Each has its own way of achieving its goals but also shares the methods of many other organizations. In fact, SMOs often influence, inspire, and complement each other's activities (Van Dyke, Dixon, & Carlon, 2007, p. 194).

formal social movement A large, well-integrated, and established organization with bureaucratic procedures.

BOX 18.1 CANADIAN CONTRIBUTIONS TO SOCIOLOGY

Suzanne Staggenborg

Dr. Suzanne Staggenborg is a sociologist whose wide-ranging research interests are all grounded in a keen interest in contemporary social movements and social change. Early in her career, Staggenborg became interested in how social movements operate within the larger society—for example, how social movements succeed or fail and how they sometimes inspire counter-movements that work against them (McCabe, 1998). According to Staggenborg, social movements must operate both locally and globally to survive. She states, "You can't be so centralized that there aren't opportunities for people to participate—you have to find ways for individuals to get involved and have their say. On the other hand, you have to have some kind of organized focus keeping things together" (Staggenborg, as cited in McCabe, 1998).

At the American Sociological Association's 2005 Annual General Meeting in Philadelphia, Staggenborg presented a paper on the growth of feminism at McGill from the 1960s to today. She argued that feminist activism was enhanced by the creation of a women's studies program and a women's research centre that promoted greater equality for women faculty, staff, and students. She notes that some of this progress was made possible by changes in the larger Canadian society (Staggenborg, 2005, p. 1). As her work confirms, to be successful, social movements need to be aware of the larger social landscape in which they exist.

Staggenborg earned her Ph.D. from Northwestern University in 1985 and taught for many years at McGill. She is a former chair of the Collective Behavior and Social Movements section of the American Sociological Association (McGill University, 2008) and is now teaching at the University of Pittsburgh.

Her publications include *The Pro-Choice Movement: Organization and Activism in the Abortion Conflict* (1991); *Gender, Family, and Social Movements* (1998); *Methods of Social Movement Research* (2002); and *Social Movements* (2010). She has also written a number of articles on the Montreal women's movement, grassroots social movements, abortion politics, and women's music festivals (McGill University, 2008).

Suzanne Staggenborg

TYPES OF SOCIAL MOVEMENTS

Social movements are classified according to a number of criteria:

- *Level of change* (e.g., a local movement targeting domestic pesticide use versus a national organization fighting the proliferation of genetically modified foods) (Turner & Killian, 1993)
- *Direction of change*, whereby some movements are seen as progressive and in line with public opinion (e.g., groups advocating the use of alternative fuels) while others wish to resist or reverse current trends (e.g., groups who oppose recent legislation allowing same-sex marriages) (Turner & Killian, 1993)
- *Speed of change*, whereby some movements seek immediate change (e.g., seal hunt protesters) and others work for gradual change (e.g., women's suffrage movement) (Ng, 2007, p. 107)
- *Target of change*, whereby some movements focus on individual behaviours (e.g., local recycling programs) while others are interested in society-wide change (e.g., legislative changes to the legal drinking age) (E. W. Johnson, 2008; Lindsey & Beach, 2003, p. 421).

Combining these various features results in four different types of social movements: revolutionary, reformist, reactionary, and religious.

revolutionary movement A social movement that seeks a complete reorganization of society.

Revolutionary Movements **Revolutionary movements** are the most extreme form of social change because they seek a complete reorganization of society (Goodwin & Jasper, 2009, p. 4). These movements typically emerge when previous efforts to bring about change have failed or proven inadequate. Revolutionary movements can be both peaceful (the recent struggles by the Québécois for greater sovereignty) and violent (the regime changes in Tunisia and Egypt initiated in early 2011). Some revolutionary movements transition from a more radical position to one that is more mainstream, as in the case of the Zapatista movement in Southern Mexico, which began as a violent movement in opposition to the Mexican government and has recently begun to focus on civil resistance (de la Luz Inclan, 2008). Such movements can be perceived by authoritarian regimes as attempts to undermine their rule and be deemed subversive and something to be crushed.

reformist movement A social movement that works within the existing social structure to improve society.

Reformist Movements **Reformist movements**, in contrast, work within the existing social structure to improve society by addressing specific issues. The American civil rights movement did not propose to reorder society but instead to confirm the rights of every American. In Canada, Mothers Against Drunk Driving (MADD) does not lobby to abolish alcohol but rather to educate the public on the effects of drinking and driving and to promote responsible drinking.

reactionary movement A social movement that emerges when groups resist an event or decision they feel they cannot tolerate.

Reactionary Movements **Reactionary movements** are often inspired when people feel that society is moving in a direction they cannot tolerate or when there is an event or decision that they feel must be challenged. For example, when Dr. Henry Morgentaler (1923–2013) was awarded the Order of Canada in July 2008 for his efforts to legalize abortion in Canada, many questioned the decision on moral and religious grounds, and some former recipients of the Order even returned their awards in protest (Pedwell, 2008). Often, the intent of these movements is to reverse the direction they feel society is travelling in and return to an earlier time. These movements appeal to people who are uncomfortable with the way things currently are and fear what the future might hold. For example, protests in Wisconsin by labour leaders who opposed Republican Governor Scott Walker's state budget that stripped away collective bargaining rights was an attempt to return to a time of more secure and better-paying jobs (MacAskill, 2011). Some Canadian examples of reactionary movements are the Aryan Nations, the Heritage Front, Canadian Liberty Net, and some pro-life groups.

In 2014, a reactionary movement with a long history in the United States, the "patriot" movement, resurfaced in defense of a Nevada rancher named Cliven Bundy, whose cattle were seized by federal agents after being caught illegally grazing on federally-owned land. Bundy, and the patriot groups who supported him, argued that the American government had become too powerful—even tyrannical—and needed to be stopped, violently if necessary. This reactionary movement has been a feature of extreme right-wing politics in the United States since at least the early twentieth century (George & Wilcox, 1996). In Canada, such armed groups are exceptionally rare; while militia or patriot groups occupy a legal grey area in the United States (one that is at least partially protected by the First and Second Amendments of the US Constitution), such groups would be considered illegal in Canada.

Religious Movements Some argue that successful social movements, whether celebrated (e.g., civil rights) or denounced (e.g., Nazism), all begin with driven individuals who have deeply held convictions (Shields, 2007, p. 112). **Religious movements** (also referred to as *expressive movements*) are grounded in spiritual or supernatural belief systems that are thought to inspire some form of inner change. Some researchers argue that these movements are most likely to emerge as a reaction to the effects of modernization. In essence, then, they are similar to reactionary movements but based on religious views of contemporary and future social change (Coreno, 2002, p. 336). Contemporary examples of religious movements that have emerged partially in protest of social change are the Westboro Baptist Church, Falun Gong, the Raelians, the Moonies, and Hare Krishnas (Barone, 2007, p. 118; Chan, 2013, p. 2; Britt, 2010, p. 648).

LIFE CYCLE OF SOCIAL MOVEMENTS

While there are many varieties of social movements, a number of sociologists point out that virtually all of them progress through a number of stages, from their emergence to their decline (Blumer, 1969; Mauss, 1975; Spector & Kitsuse, 1977). While theorists use somewhat different terminology, most suggest that the life cycle of a social movement involves four stages: emergence/incipience, coalescence, bureaucratization/institutionalization, and decline.

Emergence/Incipience During this initial stage of development, the movement is unorganized and does not have clear leadership or direction. Rather than having a defined set of issues or remedies, a segment of society feels dissatisfied or disillusioned with the current state of affairs. As outlined earlier, social movements are most likely to emerge during times of societal disruption caused by oppressive political regimes, economic collapse, controversial public policies, environmental change, or other events that inspire people to join with others to attempt to alter the direction of social change.

Coalescence As the movement matures, it begins to define itself and develop a strategy to achieve its goals. During this stage, the movement starts to gain some momentum and to attract new members. To manage its growth, the group begins to establish a formal organization in order to develop strategy and coordinate public demonstrations with an eye to attracting media attention so that group members can communicate their concerns to the larger society. The movement also may form alliances with other groups that share similar perspectives in the hope of expanding the reach and influence of both organizations.

Bureaucratization/Institutionalization For a movement to have an influence on social change, it must incorporate some bureaucratic organization to manage its affairs. Usually, this involves hiring a paid staff (a change from earlier stages, when much of the work is completed by volunteers), establishing a formal hierarchy of paid leaders, and moving to a full-time office space. As the organization grows, there is increasing pressure to attract donations and grants to ensure that employees and operating expenses are paid. As the movement grows

⊙ **Watch**

Choose Life

religious movement
A social movement grounded in a spiritual or supernatural belief system.

and gains stature, it becomes increasingly respectable, which usually means that its tactics become less confrontational over time.

Decline Although some social movements can last for a very long time, most are temporary. At times, movements are successful and actually lead to social change; otherwise, the movement collapses from internal or external pressures (Gamson, 1990).

To qualify as a success, a social movement must have its recommendations implemented by those in positions of authority (E. W. Johnson, 2008). When this happens, the movement largely becomes part of the system, and is referred to as an **interest group** that advocates for change from within the establishment (Piven & Cloward, 1977). Conversely, when the movement maintains its conflict with the establishment (Della Porta, 1995), there is potential for it to be infiltrated and destroyed from within. However, the most common reasons for a social movement's decline are the fragmentation of ideas, power struggles among its leaders (Frey, Dietz, & Kalof, 1992), or the loss of the original charismatic leader.

interest group An established lobby group that works within the system to promote change.

❼ Sociological Approaches to Social Movements

Sociologists offer a number of theories to explain when social movements are most likely to emerge and why people are attracted to join them.

RELATIVE DEPRIVATION THEORY

Relative deprivation theory suggests that the origin of many social movements resides in the discontent of those who are dissatisfied with their present condition. Sociologists appreciate that people's reactions to their objective circumstances, such as how well they are doing financially, often depend on their subjective comparison to those around them (Walker & Smith, 2002, p. 1). For example, some people would never think of getting a large-screen television until their neighbours begin to buy them. Feelings of deprivation can also arise when groups (based on racial, ethnic, sexual, or physical differences) perceive that they are not being treated fairly by the society around them (Leach, Iyer, & Pedersen, 2007; Morrison, 1971).

Yet critics of relative deprivation theory point out that some of the poorest and most deprived in society rarely complain or participate in any social movement (Johnson & Klandermans, 1995). While some deprivation is certainly relative, absolute deprivation, of course, also exists. Moreover, relative definitions of deprivation are difficult to measure (Ringen, 2006, pp. 125–126). For these reasons, relative deprivation theory is no longer as popular as it was in the 1960s.

MASS SOCIETY THEORY

The foundation for mass society theory can be traced back to Émile Durkheim and his belief that people need to feel connected to the society around them in order for the individual and the society to be healthy. Mass society theory suggests that the forces of industrialization and urbanization, as well as the sheer size and pace of our contemporary world, are diminishing our ties to those around us. Without these ties, people are left feeling alienated, vulnerable to manipulation by elites, and prone to extremist social movements (Thomson, 2005, p. 422).

Beginning with the work of William Kornhauser (1959), mass society theory has argued that people who feel socially isolated are attracted to social movements as a way of connecting with others and gaining a sense of importance and belonging. According to Kornhauser, then,

BOX 18.2 WHY SHOULD WE CARE?

Marijuana Legalization

A recurring debate in Canadian politics is the question of legalizing marijuana (a.k.a., "pot"). This debate has picked up steam in recent years; so much so that the question of legalizing pot was even discussed at the federal Liberal Party's leadership convention in 2013 and adopted as one of the planks in their party platform (Liberal Party of Canada, 2014). While some believe this controversy is new, others point out that the prohibition movement (i.e., prohibition of alcohol) from the last century was surprisingly similar.

Prohibition, to a large extent, was an example of the Canadian government trying to regulate morality and many modern-day marijuana activists argue that the criminalization of pot amounts to a similar practice (e.g., the popular perception that marijuana is a "gateway drug"). Pro-pot activists argue that since alcohol is legal to purchase, and it is demonstrably more harmful than pot, it makes little sense to criminalize pot while alcohol remains legal.

The debate around legalizing marijuana is an important one because it defines, at least in legal terms, whether or not a pot smoker is a criminal. As of 2014, it is legal for doctors to prescribe marijuana to patients for medical purposes. How might this affect how society views pot? Is it a dangerous drug? A recreational narcotic? Is it like any other medication?

It remains to be seen how future federal governments will deal with this issue, but while the federal Conservative Party remains steadfastly opposed to the prospect of legalization, both the federal Liberals and the NDP have adopted pro-decriminalization or pro-legalization positions.

Jorge Uzon/Corbis

Pot legalization rallies have taken place in front of provincial legislatures across Canada, and have even occurred on the lawn of Parliament.

the people who are most likely to participate in social movements are those who lack ties to the community. However, recent research challenges this assumption. For example, Thomson (2005) found no evidence to suggest that modern society has diminished people's kinship ties or connections to their local community. Additionally, those who feel most connected are most likely to join with others to achieve collective benefit (McAdam & Paulsen, 1994).

VALUE-ADDED THEORY

In 1963, functionalist Neil Smelser defined a new, and very influential, theory of collective behaviour, value-added theory (Moser, 2007, p. 126). This theory holds that six conditions must be met before a social movement can begin (Waddington & King, 2005, p. 494).

Condition 1: Structural Conduciveness Smelser suggests that social movements emerge when people can identify who or what is responsible for social problems (Anker, 2008). By having a clear target for their action, social movements are more likely able to focus their efforts. For example, in March 1990, the Mohawks at Kanesatake, west of Montreal, set up a roadblock to bring attention to their land dispute with the municipality of Oka, which was preparing to build a golf course on an Aboriginal burial site (Pertusati, 1997). For the Mohawks, it was clear that the target of their roadblock was all levels of government, which they believed were both responsible for their situation and necessary to help resolve it.

Condition 2: Structural Strain Structural strain exists when society can no longer meet people's expectations and little appears to have been done to fix the problem. Structural strain disturbs the smooth, predictable functioning of the social system. In this sense, the Oka blockade was merely another expression of anger over the way that Aboriginal peoples have been treated in this country (Lindsey, Beach, & Ravelli, 2009, p. 274).

Condition 3: Growth and Spread of a Generalized Belief Smelser's third condition is a clear statement of the causes of and solutions to a given problem. For people to rally around a cause, they must be confident that they understand how the movement plans to solve the problem. The generalized belief that developed in Oka after the blockade held that police brutality, poverty, and the general lack of opportunities available to members of the community were the inevitable consequences of white racism.

Condition 4: Precipitating Incident Frustration may simmer for years until a specific incident occurs that galvanizes the need for immediate and collective action. The spark that ignited the Oka conflict was the pending construction of the golf course.

Condition 5: Mobilization for Action Smelser's fifth condition is the readiness to take action, which can involve demonstrations and rallies. In the case of the Oka conflict, the mobilization for action occurred when the Mohawks began to set up road blockades.

Condition 6: Social Control The final condition for a social movement to occur is the involvement of a society's formal social control agents, which can include police officers, the military, elected officials, and civic leaders. Their response to the situation can either incite greater conflict, as seen at Oka, or bring everyone together to develop strategies to address the concern.

Smelser's value-added theory provides a valuable explanation of the conditions necessary for social movements to occur, but it fails to explore the roots of the tensions. While it is easy to explain the Oka conflict as the expression of discontent with land claims and the treatment of Aboriginal peoples, the value-added theory provides little insight into what role mass media play, for example, in the emergence or maintenance of social movements.

RESOURCE MOBILIZATION THEORY

Over the past 20 years, the two dominant schools of thought regarding the development of social movements have been the resource mobilization theory and the political process theory (Bevington & Dixon, 2005; Johnson, 2008; Klandermans, 1994). Resource mobilization theory investigates how members of social movements gather and use resources to meet their needs. To be successful, all social movements must secure money (for salaries, promotional materials, and so forth), time (for both paid staff and volunteers), and assistance from outside

< < <

The Oka crisis in 1990 was the culmination of a long-standing dispute over land rights between Aboriginal peoples and government.

agencies, politicians, and media (Johnson, 2008, p. 986; McCarthy & Zald, 1977). Resource mobilization theorists suggest that successful movements are those that can effectively acquire and manage these key resources (Gamson, 1990).

While rudimentary resources (such as office space, computers, and photocopiers) may be fairly easy to secure, the greater challenge lies in finding people with the right balance of passion, skills, and abilities to assume leadership roles within the organization. A social movement may be led by a charismatic leader early on, but as the movement matures and grows it requires more bureaucratic organization. (This is effectively the *routinization of charisma* we introduced when examining new religious groups in Chapter 13.)

The primary criticism of the resource mobilization theory is that by placing so much emphasis on resources, it diminishes the importance of the movement's actual focus. The resources of contemporary environmental groups, for example, while certainly benefiting their cause, do not detract from the great strides achieved by average people who believe in the cause (Buechler, 1993; Donnelly & Kimble, 2006).

POLITICAL PROCESS THEORY

Overlapping somewhat with resource mobilization theory, the political process theory emphasizes the dynamic relationships between social movement organizations and the larger economic and political reality in which they operate (Snow, Soule, & Cress, 2005, p. 1188). Doug McAdam (1999), one of the first to develop this theory, examines systemic factors that either encourage or discourage movement activism, success, and failure. Political systems, be they local, provincial, or federal, all have varying appetites for social movement initiatives and thus engender different levels of political opportunity. Some governments are comparatively open to change, while others seem to resist it at all costs.

Political process theorists are also interested in assessing how much, or how little, social movements influence the larger society. Two of the clearest findings related to this theory are that movements emerge more readily in democratic societies (Jenkins & Perrow, 1977) and

> > >

Environmentalists
use whatever means
possible, including
humour, to draw
attention to their cause.

The Canadian Press/Tom Hanson

that weak governments are especially vulnerable to pressure from activists (Lindsey & Beach, 2003, p. 420).

While the political process theory has been one of the dominant paradigms of the past 20 years, it has come under fire because it does not seem to provide social movement activists with much practical information that can be used to further their efforts (Bevington & Dixon, 2005, p. 186).

NEW SOCIAL MOVEMENT THEORY

New social movement theory originated during the social uprisings of the 1960s. New social movements, including environmental, peace, feminist, gay, and civil rights initiatives, were seen as distinct from old social movements, such as trade union and labour movements, and as representing a distinctly North American approach (Walter, 2007, p. 250). Whereas resource mobilization theory and political process theory view social activists as exercising variations of rational choice (by using funds wisely or by engaging political parties with whom the movement has the greatest likelihood of success), new social movement theory holds that forms of action are motivated by collective identity found in the culture, ideology, and politics of postindustrial society (Holford, 1995; Mayo, 2005, as cited in Walter, 2007, p. 250).

A defining feature of new social movements is that they are more globally focused than were earlier movements. Today, climate change, environmental destruction, and the loss of biodiversity are challenges that resonate with people around the world. In contrast to earlier movements inspired by the working class, new social movements are increasingly inspired by middle-class interests (Hilton, 2007, p. 123).

Critics of new social movement theory, however, point out that while this approach adds an important cultural context to social movements, it does not adequately account for the very real power and influence exerted by the political economy (Walter, 2007).

As we have seen, social movements may be important sources of social change. By promoting or resisting certain ideas, they are able to inspire debate and discussion about the future and about the kind of society we want to live in. As you will learn in Chapters 19 and 20, social movements have played an important role in pointing out some of the challenges associated with globalization and the environment.

Summary

1 *Social change* refers to changes over time in the typical features of society, including its norms and values. *Collective behaviours* occur when people come together to achieve a single, meaningful, short-term goal that may result in social change. *Social movements* involve groups and individuals whose organized efforts bring about or resist social change.

2 The inspirations behind social change include technology, physical environment, demographic shifts, economic competition, war, ideas, governments, individuals, and social movements.

3 Functionalists explain social change through equilibrium theory, which holds that changes in one part of society require changes in others in order to restore balance and harmony; conflict theorists view social change as coming about necessarily through active revolt against oppression and exploitation; evolutionary theorists hold that all societies have an internal drive that inspires them to adapt to their environment in order to better compete for survival; cyclical theorists argue that social change occurs not in a defined direction but, rather, through ebbs and flows in a series of endless cycles.

4 A *collectivity* is a substantial number of people who join together on the basis of loosely defined norms; members of localized collectivities, or *crowds,* are bonded through their immediate physical presence, whereas dispersed collectivities do not share physical proximity and are instead bonded to situations and messages through their emotional responses—including rumours; mass hysteria; disaster behaviour; fashion, fads, and crazes; and publics.

5 Contagion theorists argue that the irrationality of crowds is contagious and results in a "collective mind"; convergence theorists contend that the source of crowd behaviour lies not in the group but in the individuals who compose it; emergent norm theorists view crowd behaviour as neither irrational nor deliberate but rather as the result of dynamic exchanges between participants.

6 Revolutionary movements, whether peaceful or violent, seek a complete reorganization of society; reformist movements address specific issues by working within existing social structures; reactionary movements form in response to a movement, event, or decision that is deemed intolerable; religious movements are grounded in a spiritual or supernatural belief system thought to inspire a form of inner change.

7 Relative deprivation theory asserts that many social movements arise from people discontented with their present condition, a discontent that is relative to those around them; mass society theory has its basis in the view that people need to feel connected to their society, and hence contemporary alienation leaves many prone to extremist social movements; value-added theory holds that six societal conditions must be met for a social movement to begin; resource mobilization theory contends that successful social movements must be able to acquire and manage key resources; political process theory emphasizes the dynamic social relationships between social movement organizations and the larger economic and political reality in which they operate; new social movement theory holds that forms of action are motivated by collective identity found in the culture, ideology, and politics of post-industrial society.

Key Terms

Reviewing the Concepts

1. Review and critique Prensky's concepts of *digital natives* and *digital immigrants*. In your experience, what are the differences between how younger and older people use technology?

2. Review the life cycle of social change and whether or not it can be applied to the widespread adoption of smartphones.

3. Compare and contrast relative deprivation theory with mass society theory.

4. What is a flash mob? As a sociologist, what is it about them that makes them so appealing to some people?

Applying Your Sociological Imagination

1. Who were the Luddites? Do you have any friends or know of any groups who are trying to decrease their dependence on technology? Why do you think they are critical of technology? Discuss.

2. Can you apply the life cycle of social movements to explain a social movement from your own community and/or province/territory?

3. Briefly apply (one paragraph each) contagion theory, convergence theory, and emergent norm theory to explain hooligan violence at European football matches. Which do you feel offers the best explanation? Why?

4. How might a natural disaster like climate change or a tsunami result in widespread social change? Can you think of an example of this occurring during your lifetime?

MySocLab

Visit MySocLab to access a variety of online resources that will help you prepare for tests and apply your knowledge.

Betty Johnson/dbimages/Alamy

19 Globalization

Whether you walk the streets of Toronto, New York, Nairobi, Beijing, or Buenos Aires, the signs may be in different languages but they all tend to say the same thing: buy Pepsi, drive a BMW, and be sure to wear the latest summer fashions from Hollister. When you leave the sidewalk and enter a shopping mall, it does not get much better. Malls around the world are practically interchangeable; fast-food restaurants sell the same fare with only minor variations to accommodate local tastes. People everywhere drink the same soft drinks, smoke the same cigarettes, wear the same clothes, play the same computer games, watch the same Hollywood movies, and listen to the same music (Ellwood, 2003). For many, then, globalization has inspired the emergence of a worldwide homogeneous culture that is focused on the accumulation of wealth.

Is there really nothing more to globalization than the world's cultures becoming more alike over time? What about people in those areas of the world that do not have—and are far from having—the standard of living we enjoy in the West? How has worldwide economic and political integration influenced their lives?

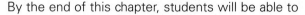

LEARNING OBJECTIVES

By the end of this chapter, students will be able to

1 Define *globalization* and describe how it has emerged through capitalism.

2 Define *global stratification* and explain the significance of the change in terminology from *First World*, *Second World*, and *Third World* to *Global North* and *Global South* and of the terminologies associated with "development."

3 Review the role of technological, political, and economic changes in the emergence of globalization.

4 Distinguish between absolute and relative definitions of poverty.

5 Discuss the relationship between globalization and inequality.

6 Review the theoretical approaches to globalization.

7 Explore the challenges that globalization poses in the area of cultural homogenization and the opportunity of cosmopolitanism to resist it.

1 What Is Globalization?

The term *globalization*, as previously defined in Chapter 1, is used to describe the worldwide exchange of money, goods, and services as well as the sociocultural changes that occur with increasing trade and human contact (Levine, 2005, p. 145). Globalization has been described as the entanglement of diverse cultures and economies (Ellwood, 2003; Martell, 2010, p. 5). Looked at another way, globalization is responsible for severing social arrangements based on geographic location as a result of accelerating transnational flows of people, images, and information (Beerkens & Derwende, 2007, p. 62). However, today's globalization is not a new development but, rather, the continuation of an international economic integration that began with European colonial expansion more than 500 years ago (Ellwood, 2003; Wang, 2010).

THE ORIGINS OF GLOBALIZATION

Hundreds of years before the advent of capitalism in the West, Arabs and Indians traded goods and spices across great distances (Feffer, 2002). In addition, according to Abu-Lughod (1989), an international trading economy existed between Western Europe and China more than 700 years ago. History is full of examples of people from different geographic areas coming together (at times, through military conquest) and forming large, integrated empires that shared common political and economic systems (Carruthers & Babb, 2000; Martinelli, 2005). However, Wallerstein (1976) argues that because these early empires spent most of their resources on supporting a large military, they simply could not afford to become *global* empires. Even though these early empires were politically integrated, true economic integration became possible only with the emergence of capitalism.

> > >

Early trading networks were one of the original factors leading to globalization.

Leandro da Ponte Bassano/The Bridgeman Art Library/Getty Images

colonizing The political, economic, and cultural domination of countries in Asia, Africa, and the Americas by European countries starting in the sixteenth century.

Beginning in the sixteenth century, Western European nations developed economic systems that were based on market principles, whereby goods and services were produced and exchanged for profit (Carruthers & Babb, 2000). In England, the feudal system of agricultural production was replaced by commercial enterprises. Access to property changed as common lands, a form of public property, were enclosed and privatized. This displaced many farmers, as the lands they had once farmed were now privately owned (Moore, 1966). The shift in land ownership during this time was one of the primary inspirations behind the emergence of capitalism.

As the merchant class continued to expand and grow wealthier, demand for more exotic goods from other areas around the world increased. To feed this growing desire for foreign goods, many European nations began **colonizing** the Americas, Africa, and Asia (Frank, 1998). The gold and silver of the New World, enslaved peoples from Africa, and the spices of Asia all contributed to the expanding capitalist economy in Europe. With increasing trade and investment, along with technological innovations in transportation (e.g., container ships) and navigation (e.g., radar), globalization continued to accelerate through to the second half of the twentieth century. However, for sociologists like Giddens, globalization as we conceptualize it today is a relatively recent phenomenon.

Giddens (2003) points out that globalization in the last 50 years is much different from globalization in previous times. Before the 1970s, national economies were defined by the exchange of goods—and, as we learned in Chapter 16, much of the economic activity today is in the service sector and the knowledge economy. Giddens argues that there is more to living in a globalized world than the proliferation of cellphones and satellite televisions. Instead, he argues that "we live in a world of transformation, affecting almost every aspect of what we do" (Giddens, 2003, p. 4).

GLOBALIZATION TODAY

Today's economies are more interdependent and integrated than ever before (Giddens, 2003). Consider how many fruits and vegetables at your local grocery store are grown in California or Mexico, or the fact that your jeans were probably made in China, or even that tutors at some Canadian universities are located not across campus or down the street but, rather, in

< < <

The fact that someone can buy a Coke or a Pepsi just about any-where, demonstrates the global reach of globalization

India (Tibbetts, 2008). These are only a few examples of a new level of economic and cultural integration that would have been unheard of only a few decades ago.

One result of this integration is that the power of individual nation-states to determine their own economic, political, and cultural destinies is declining. For example, the Asian financial crisis of 1998 (commonly referred to as the Asian flu) resulted from the actions of North American bankers and stock traders (Stiglitz, 2003). Similarly, the recent subprime mortgage disaster in the United States negatively affected the entire world's banking system (Dam, 2009; Lim, 2007). Events like these illustrate how decisions made in one part of the world can have drastic ramifications in others.

Advances in communication technologies have made the world an increasingly smaller place. Infectious diseases such as severe acute respiratory syndrome (SARS) and influenza are spread through international travel and trade. Columnist Ellen Goodman (2003) writes, "The world has shrunk to the size of an airplane ticket. And germs don't need a visa. You can have breakfast in Beijing, dinner in London, and end up hospitalized in Toronto."

Global development has created vast chasms between the rich and the poor around the world (Steger, 2002). It is to these gaps that we now turn.

Defining Global Stratification

As discussed in Chapter 7, stratification occurs when a society organizes people into a hier-archical system according to their social class (see Nayebi & Abdollahyan, 2006). Just as individuals are classified within a stratified society, so too are countries positioned within a global ranking system. The new global order is increasingly defined according to countries' wealth or poverty.

You may be familiar with the terms *First World*, *Second World*, and *Third World* to describe a nation's relative economic, political, and social development. While these terms were the standard for many years, scholars today are troubled by their obvious Western bias. For example, to refer to a country as being "First World" is to buy into the assumption that it is

((•─[Listen

Pew Study on Globalization

BOX 19.1 THAT WAS THEN, THIS IS NOW

● Global Citizenship

Historically, one's citizenship was defined by physical geography. This meant that the country in which you were born determined your citizenship. In most cases, citizenship was a necessary condition of being able to reap the benefits of the society in which you lived, such as voting rights or access to state services. But citizenship is a very fluid concept and it has changed dramatically over the years. At the turn of the twentieth century in Canada, for example, the only people who were capable of voting were white men; women and ethnic minorities were not allowed to vote (Canadian Human Rights Commission, n.d.). The right to vote was not extended to women in Canada until 1918 and Canada's indigenous peoples only gained the right in 1960.

As many researchers have pointed out, the concept of citizenship in Canada is an uneven one, with some Canadians reaping greater benefits from citizenship than others (Hallgrims-dottir, Benoit, & Phillips, 2013). The discussion of what it means to be a citizen is becoming even more complex in the twenty-first century as more and more people are constantly travelling between different countries for work. For example, consider migrant workers, who may spend years working in one country while "officially" residing in another. What nation are they citizens of: the nation in which they were born or the nation where they work and live?

What about people who live in a country like Canada, but who spend virtually all their time online accessing networks and services from around the globe? What does citizenship mean to a woman who rents an apartment in Vancouver, uses a German online service to design and produce goods, and then sells them to anyone in the world through an American online store? Is she a global citizen or merely a Canadian citizen engaging in online activities? Or, what about those retired Canadians who spend their winters in Florida, and who would prefer to live there year-round but do not want to lose their access to Canadian health care? In this context, what does "citizenship" really mean?

The concept of citizenship is changing and, as sociologists, it is our job to try and explain these changes and what they might mean to society.

---

the best, it has finished first, and it is the gold standard. While these nations are certainly strong economic forces in the world today, contemporary scholars are uncomfortable with the designation of some countries as "first" since this implies that all other countries are lagging behind. A similar argument can be made with reference to the "Second World."

The term *Second World* was used to describe the countries of the former Soviet Union. These socialist countries existed within a command economy as originally forged by Vladimir Lenin and Joseph Stalin. A **command economy** is one in which the state manages the production and distribution of goods (Brown, 2007, p. 5; Cech & Marks, 2007, p. 5). These countries, numbering around 30 and mostly in Eastern Europe, were largely cut off from the rest of the world until the fall of the Berlin Wall in 1989 (Sachs, 2005). Since the collapse of state socialism, the term *Second World* has been used only rarely (Bernstein, 2006, p. 46). However, some argue that the term should be revived because it allows greater flexibility than the dichotomy of *First World* and *Third World* (Marciniak, 2006, p. 36) or, by extension, *Global North* and *Global South* (discussed next). In any event, the majority of these former socialist countries are poorer and less industrialized than many countries in the Global North.

In his book *The Second World: Empires and Influence in the New Global Order*, Parag Khanna (2008) suggests that the role of these countries will become increasingly important in the coming years. Khanna argues that the natural resources found in countries like Azerbaijan,

command economy

An economy in which the state, rather than market forces, manages the production and distribution of goods.

Colombia, and Malaysia (to name only a few) will ultimately determine the fate of today's global superpowers: China, the European Union, and the United States. Khanna outlines how these countries are constantly stymied by the self-serving interests of the Global North as they continually struggle to improve their economic positions. He suggests, then, that globalization is becoming a battlefield of geopolitics, and that the United States may face descending into Second World status unless it can renew its leadership role in international politics (Khanna, 2008).

The terminology associated with "development" has also come under criticism. Rich, industrialized countries traditionally have been referred to as being **developed**, while poor countries have been called **undeveloped**, **underdeveloped**, or **developing**. These terms are being questioned in the contemporary literature because, again, they imply a Western bias. The term *undeveloped* suggests the lack of any economic talent or exposure, *underdeveloped* implies that some countries are "lesser" than others, and *developing* indicates that they are on the right path but have not yet arrived. These discussions are important; they demonstrate not only that Western researchers are beginning to reflect more closely on their own biases but also that non-Western academics are challenging existing beliefs and practices from a new and uniquely informed perspective.

For these reasons, most sociologists generally prefer to use the terms *Global North* rather than *First World*, and *Global South* rather than *Third World*. The term *Second World*, as well as vague descriptors of a country's level of "development," is now used only rarely. The over-riding principle here is the recognition that most economic prosperity has occurred in the northern hemisphere and most economic hardship has occurred in the southern hemisphere (Ford-Jones, 2009, p. 6; Kegley & Wittkopf, 2006, p. 135).

GLOBAL NORTH

The **Global North** includes the wealthy industrialized countries of Western Europe, Canada, the United States, Australia, and Japan. While most of the industrialized countries are located in the North, there are exceptions; for example, both Australia and New Zealand are wealthy countries located in the South. As a rule, states in the Global North are democratic and technologically advanced, have a high standard of living, and experience very low population growth. While some states in the Global South share some of these characteristics (e.g., Saudi Arabia is rich but not democratic), no single country in the Global South shares them all (Kegley & Wittkopf, 2006, p. 135). Citizens in the Global North are well educated, have access to health care and clean water, and exist within stable political structures. Given their economic, political, and social clout, it should come as no surprise that people who live in the Global North generally enjoy long, happy, and productive lives.

Notice that some of these countries were former colonial empires that colonized Global South countries in Asia, Africa, and Latin America. Colonization allowed countries in the Global North to dominate and alter the existing economic, political, and cultural structures in their colonies for their own gain (Frank, 1972).

GLOBAL SOUTH

The **Global South** includes the poor countries of the world that are largely located in Asia, South America, and Africa. Many of the countries in the Global South emerged after the end of colonial rule and decided not to follow the path of Western capitalism or of socialism as practised in the former Soviet Union. These countries attempted to achieve development and prosperity through a third method—that is, one between capitalism and socialism (Odd, 2005, p. 52; Sachs, 2005). However, the crushing inequalities left behind as a result of colonization made a realistic alternative impossible. Former colonies lacked the financial, industrial, and technological infrastructure necessary to develop their own vibrant and competitive economies.

developed countries Wealthy, industrialized countries.

undeveloped countries Countries with poor economies; problematically implies a lack of economic talent or exposure.

underdeveloped countries Countries that have yet to industrialize, or that have been intentionally restricted in their development by developed nations.

developing countries Countries considered to be on the road to industrialization.

Global North Wealthy, industrialized countries in the northern hemisphere (previously referred to as the First World).

Global South Poor countries in the southern hemisphere (previously referred to as the Third World).

> > >

The early promise of globalization to address poverty has yet to be realized by many countries in the Global South.

Vibrant Pictures/Alamy

We should note that the indigenous economies were neither backward nor handicapped in their ability to improve their situations. Rather, colonialism and globalization *constructed* dependence as a way of achieving the Global North's own ends (which include cheap labour, raw materials, and low environmental protection regulations). Today, virtually all Global South countries have turned away from their earlier idealism and are trying to improve their standards of living through international trade and foreign investment from the Global North's governments and corporations. Some suggest, however, that the only possible outcome of unrestricted economic globalization is a group of winners and a group of losers (Baran, 1957; Frank, 1972).

All Global South countries are less powerful, both economically and politically, than those in the Global North. This does not imply, however, that countries in the Global South are all the same; certainly, they are not. For example, India is faring better than Burma or Cambodia, and Mexico and Brazil fare better than Peru or Bolivia (World Bank, 2007a). Moreover, some countries in Asia and Latin America have begun to industrialize and are being referred to as **newly industrialized countries (NICs)** (Heo & Hahm, 2007, p. 119). Brazil and Mexico are considered NICs, as are the "Four Little Asian Tigers" of Hong Kong, Singapore, South Korea, and Taiwan, which have experienced phenomenal economic growth over the past 25 years (Heo & Hahm, 2007).

newly industrialized countries (NICs)
Poor countries that are beginning to industrialize.

While we may define these examples of economic growth as *success stories*, we should appreciate that this evaluation is based on our Western, Global North perspective. As sociologists, we should be concerned about the fact that the only way for countries to flourish today is to embrace Western capitalist economic structures and values.

The process of globalization has rewarded those countries best able to implement capitalist ideals, not only internally but by establishing colonies around the world to supply the raw materials necessary to fuel their own industrial growth. To further explore globalization, we must appreciate how technological innovations and political and economic changes combined to create an environment so conducive for its growth.

❸ Factors Contributing to Globalization

TECHNOLOGICAL CHANGE

As already suggested, today's globalization is a continuation of processes already at work for hundreds of years. What *is* new is the pace at which globalization is occurring, and this acceleration is largely due to technological innovations that have enabled worldwide trade.

Historically, one of the most important innovations that promoted worldwide trade was the development of container shipping (Hedley, 2002). Shipping lines had the economic clout to require producers to package their goods so they could fit into standardized containers; these containers allowed for a more efficient use of space on ships, and once the ships had docked, the containers could be loaded immediately onto trucks for further distribution. While shipping was important for transporting goods, the emergence of cost-effective worldwide air travel was instrumental in promoting social and cultural exchange (Hedley, 2002, p. 9).

POLITICAL CHANGE

Another factor that influenced the rapid pace of globalization was the collapse of the Soviet Union. After this collapse, most countries around the world saw that capitalism and democracy were the only viable economic and political options for participating on the world stage. In fact, Giddens (2003) believes that the demise of the Soviet Union came about as a result of globalization. He argues that the Soviet Union, "with its emphasis upon state-run enterprise and heavy industry, could not compete in the global electronic economy" (Giddens, 2003, p. 4). Further, Griswold (2006) claims that globalization not only enhances the spread of capitalism, but also spreads the Western ideal of democracy. For example, even though China remains a socialist country, it has adopted many free-market policies that inspire international trade and investment.

Indeed, today's flow of foreign capital into China, especially from Japan and the United States, is remarkable. In 2003, China became the world's largest net recipient of foreign direct investment, with US$53 billion (OECD Observer, 2003). This amount rose to US$117.6 billion in 2013 (Kujundzic, 2014). While China receives a great deal of capital investment from around the world, it is also the world's largest holder of US Treasury securities—totalling $1.2 trillion in 2013 or 21.9 percent of total foreign ownership of American securities (Labonte & Nagel, 2013). Of course, while China's economic success has been extraordinary, its human rights record is questionable. The protests during the 2008 Summer Olympics against China's oppression of Tibetan interests demonstrated that human rights is a global issue—and one increasingly influenced by advances in communication technologies. The Chinese government has attempted to circumvent such innovations in part through the banning of many Western social media sites, including Twitter. In 2009, a Chinese company launched *Sina Weibo*, a Chinese-language only Twitter-like social networking service that, as of 2014, remained heavily censored and monitored by Chinese authorities (Luckerson, 2014).

ECONOMIC CHANGE

The economic factors most commonly associated with the rise of globalization are expanding trade and the emergence of international banking (Acemoglu & Yared, 2010). While some suggest that international trade reached significant levels only in the 1950s (Reich, as cited in Curtis, Grabb, & Guppy, 2004), others contend that globalization was attained as early as 1914 (Laxer, 2004). While it is difficult to pinpoint exactly when international trade became global, its growth continues to expand every year. For example, whereas in 1980 international expenditures for goods and services between countries accounted for 44 percent of total global output, by 2005 it had increased to 58 percent (or about $26 trillion) (World Bank, 2007a, p. 185). However, the 2008 economic collapse reversed this trend with the value of world merchandise exports falling 23 percent to $12.15 trillion in 2009, while world commercial services exports declined 13 percent to $3.31 trillion. This was the first time since 1983 that trade in commercial services declined year on year (World Trade Organization, 2010). In recent years, this downward trend has reversed itself and, as of 2013, international trade for goods and services had risen again; merchandise exports rose again to $18.3 trillion, while services rose to $4.3 trillion (World Trade Organization, 2013).

In July 1944, delegates from all 44 Allied nations met in Bretton Woods, New Hampshire, to establish a framework for the postwar global economy. To facilitate this new economy, a

> > >

The Bretton Woods conference of 1944 led to the creation of the International Monetary Fund, the World Bank, and the World Trade Organization.

Alfred Eisenstaedt/Time & Life Pictures/Getty Images

cooperative international monetary system was developed to both promote trade and help to protect the global economy from future financial crises (Ellwood, 2003, p. 24). The Bretton Woods conference created three institutions: the International Monetary Fund, the World Bank, and the World Trade Organization.

International Monetary Fund

The International Monetary Fund (IMF), with a current membership of 187 countries, was established to promote international monetary stability, to foster economic growth, and to provide temporary financial assistance to poor countries (IMF, 2010). Its framers believed that international cooperation was necessary to avoid repeating the disastrous economic policies that led to the Great Depression of the 1930s (IMF, n.d.). The IMF's mandate was to create a global economy in which countries would participate in common economic exchange through trade and investment. The IMF was built on the premise that for economies to prosper, barriers to trade must be removed through privatization, deregulation, lowered tariffs, and economic liberalization. However, these objectives were not without controversy.

Some suggest that the IMF was never intended to act as a vehicle to promote global economic integration but instead as a tool for the West to maintain its economic and political dominance over the rest of the world (Ellwood, 2003). Others further point out that the actions of the IMF toward poor countries have been anything but supportive. For example, some loan repayment policies require recipient nations to cut spending on public services such as health care, education, and food subsidies, cuts that actually increase infant mortality rates and malnutrition levels, in the name of repaying IMF loans. In some cases, then, IMF involvement has made the living conditions in these countries worse.

Although IMF funding has provided hundreds of billions of dollars to projects around the world, some still see it as a mechanism through which the rich economies can control the poor economies (Ellwood, 2003). The IMF has vast financial resources: In April 2009, leaders of the world's largest economies (the Group of Twenty, or G20) agreed to triple the IMF's regular lending capacity to US$750 billion (IMF, 2009). Because of such vast resources, the IMF can exert tremendous pressure on recipient countries to adopt its formula for economic reform. For example, in 2004, the Zambian government announced that it could not hire an additional 9000 teachers because the IMF and the World Bank had capped the percentage of Zambia's **gross domestic product (GDP)** that could be spent on wages. If the government exceeded the limit, it would lose its debt-relief benefits. Thus, while schools had been renovated, desks purchased, and teachers trained, the schools never opened (Global Campaign for Education, 2004). This example demonstrates how the IMF can control the spending decisions of poor countries, and in doing so promote its own ideals and values (Stiglitz, 2003).

However, the IMF's influence reaches into developed nations as well, and some of the changes they insist upon are nearly as restrictive. In 2010, Greece's economy was suffering as a result of the global financial crisis. As it had in many developing nations, the IMF reached an agreement with the Greek government where the IMF would provide a loan in exchange

gross domestic product (GDP) The total market value of all final goods and services produced in a country in a given year.

for deep cuts to Greece's public spending (e.g., social security, pensions, etc.), as well as deregulating Greece's publicly-owned services and industries. The agreement, however, failed to help Greece's economic recovery and may have in fact hampered its long-term financial recovery (Janssen, 2010, p. 5)

World Bank The World Bank is also made up of 187 member states, and was created to help rebuild Europe after World War II (World Bank, 2010). By the late 1950s, however, Europe's reconstruction had been completed, and so the World Bank began to pay attention to the needs of the newly liberated colonized countries in the Global South.

The World Bank operates under the assumption that building infrastructure is the best way to help poor countries achieve economic growth and prosperity. From its perspective, poverty in poor countries is the result of improperly applied free-market rules, both locally and nationally (Frediani, 2007, p. 134). Accordingly, it provides loans to poor countries to build roads, bridges, and hydroelectric dams to support the creation of the infrastructure necessary for further economic development. However, the World Bank's behaviour in the development of poor countries is just as controversial as that of the IMF; it too has been accused of interfering with local decision making, and often in a direction not in the best interests of the local people (Randeria, 2007, pp. 18–22).

Checks and Balances at the World Bank

Some argue that by charging interest on loans, the World Bank is restricting the freedom of recipient nations to determine how best to spend their funds, since these nations are by necessity focused on making interest payments at the expense of local needs. World Bank loans, much like the quota system for the IMF, have often negatively affected people in the Global South. For example, the World Bank has financed more than 500 hydroelectric dams in poor countries over the past 60 years (valued at around $86 billion), yet these dams have forced approximately 10 million people from their homes and at times have resulted in significant environmental damage (Global Campaign for Education, 2004). The independent World Commission on Dams found that the World Bank–financed Par Mun Dam in Thailand resulted in a severe decline in the fish catch upstream of the dam. At least 50 fish species were eliminated, and the loss of farming income, completely unforeseen by project designers, forced thousands of villagers to seek work in urban areas (Buch-Hansen, Oksen, & Prabudhanitisarn, 2006, p. 49). In 2010, in defiance of sharp criticisms by environmental groups, the World Bank approved a $3.75 billion loan to South Africa for the construction of one of the largest coal-fired power plants in the world (Goldenberg, 2010). While the World Bank argued that the construction of the plant would ease energy shortages and help provide work for impoverished South Africans, critics noted that the plant would also inject over 25 tonnes of CO_2 into the atmosphere each year and by doing so cripple South Africa's ability to curb its greenhouse gas emissions.

World Trade Organization The third pillar of the Bretton Woods economic program was the General Agreement on Tariffs and Trade (GATT), formed in 1948; it was renamed the World Trade Organization (WTO) in 1995 (World Trade Organization, n.d.). The intent of the WTO was to promote fair trading practices between nations. Primarily, the WTO manages trade disputes between countries when one party feels that it has been the victim of unfair trading practices.

One of the continuing challenges facing the WTO is how to manage subsidized farming around the world. Many rich, industrial countries provide their farmers with agricultural subsidies so that these farmers can make a decent living and keep food prices low for the nations' consumers (a long-standing practice in the United States, Canada, and France, to name only a few countries). The problem is that this creates an unfair advantage, in that the farmers can sell their products on the world market for less than what they cost to produce. Some estimates suggest that farmers in high-income countries received roughly $236 billion in support in 2011 (Elliott, 2013, p. 4). Moreover, the United Nations states that a system of unfair subsidies, tariffs, and quotas has contributed to chronic poverty and reduced opportunities in developing nations (Shelton, 2013). The fact that the WTO has been unable to address such practices has led some to argue that it is more interested in maintaining commercial interests for the rich than in promoting humanitarian needs for the poor (Ellwood, 2003; Sinclair, 2003, p. 348). The latest indication of the WTO's failure to promote economic development came in July 2008, when rich and poor countries could not agree on various international

BOX 19.2 WHY SHOULD WE CARE?

Global versus Local Strategies to Help the Poor

GLOBAL STRATEGIES: NATIONAL ECONOMIC DEVELOPMENT PROGRAMS

Our discussion of the IMF, World Bank, and WTO raised serious concerns about whether global economic development initiatives have helped the world's poor. Research by Karger, Iyiani, and Shannon (2007) concludes that after 60 years, these programs have failed to lift a significant number of poor people out of poverty. They suggest that despite the billions of dollars spent on social and economic programs, there is little evidence that "top-down" approaches to poverty work (Karger, Iyiani, & Shannon, 2007, p. 83). As discussed, often the funding that is provided comes with a number of strings attached that diminish the recipient's ability to use the resources in a way that best suits its particular needs.

LOCAL STRATEGIES: MICROCREDIT

In contrast to these macro programs are those that have a local, "bottom-up" approach. One such program involves the provision of what is known as "microcredit."

The principle is simple: Microcredit programs provide small loans to the very poor so that they can start a small business or any other initiative that will help them to generate income through their own efforts (see www.microcreditsummit.org; www.kiva.org). By gaining access to small loans with low interest rates and flexible repayment terms, poor people are able to transition from perhaps tiny income-generating activities (e.g., selling newspapers on the street) to small microenterprises (e.g., opening a newspaper stand). Some microcredit programs offer other services to assist their clients, such as help in setting up a bank account, and training, advice, and peer support. In this way, the poor are able to take ownership of their lives and end their own poverty with dignity (Hietalahti & Linden, 2006). The following example of how this works illustrates the tremendous potential of these programs:

La Maman Mole Motuke lived in a wrecked car in a suburb of Kinshasa, Zaire with her four children. If she could find something to eat, she would feed two of her children; the next time she found something to eat, her other two children would eat. When organizers from a microcredit lending institution interviewed her, she said that she knew how to make chikwangue (manioc paste), and she only needed a few dollars to start production. After six months of training in marketing and production techniques, Maman Motuke got her first loan of US$100 and bought production materials.

Today, Maman Motuke and her family no longer live in a broken-down car; they rent a house with two bedrooms and a living room. Her four children go to school consistently, eat regularly, and dress well. She currently is saving to buy some land in a suburb farther outside of the city and hopes to build a house. (Microcredit Summit, n.d.)

As a sociologist, what theoretical linkages can you make between global and local strategies to help the poor? In your opinion, should people in the Global North be concerned with poverty in the Global South? Why?

FIGURE 19.1

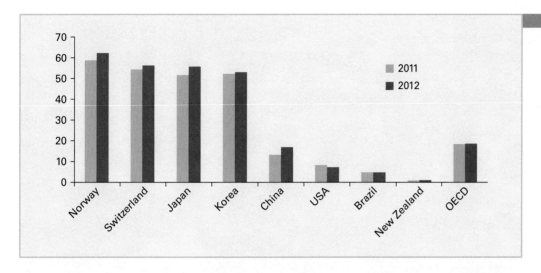

Producer Support Estimates as a Percentage of Gross Farm Receipts, by Country, 2011 and 2012

Reprinted by permission from OECD (2013), Agricultural Policy Monitoring and Evaluation 2013: OECD Countries and Emerging Economies, OECD Publishing. http://dx.doi.org/10.1787/agr_pol-2013-en

trade agreements—specifically, on the issue of agricultural subsidies (Klapper, 2008). As of 2014, the negotiations remain stalled.

Government subsidies for producers in the world's leading farming nations has increased over the last few years and reverses a long-term downward trend according to the OECD (OECD, 2013). In 2012, governments in OECD countries spent US$258.6 billion supporting producers; within this group, however, there are sharp differences between countries offering the most support (e.g., Norway, Switzerland, Japan, Korea, and Iceland) and the least (New Zealand, Ukraine, Australia, and South Africa). Figure 19.1 illustrates that while artificial support for producers has increased recently (in all countries except Canada, Russia, Mexico, Israel, and the United States), it remains a significant barrier to fair international trade between rich and poor countries.

There are many who criticize the IMF, World Bank, and WTO, suggesting that these organizations actually make nations poorer and redistribute wealth from the Global South to the North (Head, 2005; Perkins, 2004; Villaroman, 2009). Between 2000 and 2005, for example, 29 of the poorest countries of the world paid around $15.3 billion to service their combined external debts. By the end of 2010, the World Bank estimated that the combined amount of foreign debt owed by developing nations surpassed $4 trillion (World Bank, 2012, p.1). As some international monitoring agencies have pointed out, this means that in many of the poorest nations on Earth—and those with the highest rates of poverty, disease, and other health-related issues—more money is spent servicing external debt than is spent on national health care (Health, Poverty, Action, 2014). This money represents wealth that is transferred from these poor countries to the Global North. These huge debt financing costs seriously undermine these countries' ability to provide for their people. For example, children have been forced to quit going to school because of government-imposed school fees they could not afford; families have had to live in makeshift shelters because their government could not provide affordable housing; infants have died because their government could not supply adequate nutrition and protection from disease (Villaroman, 2009). Repaying these loans costs countries in the Global South a lot more than just money.

Transnational Corporations

Transnational corporations (TNCs), also known as *multinational corporations*, are large companies based in one country with overseas operations in two or more other countries. The defining feature of a TNC, then, is that its strategic decision-making is based entirely on economic goals, with little or no regard for national

transnational corporation (TNC) A large company based in one country with overseas operations in two or more other countries.

> > >

Protestors clash with police officers during the 2010 G20 Summit in Toronto.

The Canadian Press/Chris Young

boundaries (Gershon, 2005, p. 17). As researchers Jerome Klassen and William Carroll (2011) have pointed out, transnational corporations are increasingly operated by an emerging "transnational capitalist class"; members of this class see themselves as involved in—and concerned with—the international economy above anything else (p. 380). Such a class is less interested in the good of an individual state or nation, and more interested in developing the international economy.

Among all of the economic factors driving globalization, the role of TNCs cannot be over-emphasized. With different parts of their operations scattered across the world, these companies uncouple management, production, labour, and consumption from any single national economy (Tonkiss, 2006). Because of their sheer size and influence, TNCs have become some of the most powerful economic and political entities in the world today (Birch, 2007, p. 156; Brecher & Costello, 2006).

Table 19.1 lists the world's largest TNCs and confirms their economic importance to the global economy. For example, in 2013, these 10 firms alone had a combined market value of almost $2.8 trillion.

In 2002, there were 64 592 TNCs operating, along with a network of 851 167 foreign affiliates (Ietto-Gilles, 2003). While they are global in their reach, 90 percent of these companies are based in Global North countries, and more than half are from just five nations: France, Germany, Netherlands, Japan, and the United States (Karliner, 1997, p. 6).

In fact, many corporations are richer and more powerful than the countries in which they operate. For example, as shown in Table 19.1, Apple Inc. had a market value of $416 billion in 2013, and it employs more than 80 000 workers globally. To put this in perspective, Apple's market value is greater than the GDP of Denmark or Austria, and it is larger than the combined GDPs of over 100 of the world's poorest nations. In order to maximize its earnings, Apple—which, as of 2014, had more cash on hand than the United States government (Worstall, 2014)—has moved much of its production infrastructure out of the United States and into developing countries like China, where it is able to hire workers for lower wages and spend less money on health and safety measures in its factories. This practice was made apparent in 2011 when a fire at a Foxconn factory (Foxconn is one of Apple's top suppliers

TABLE 19.1 World's 10 Largest Transnationals in 2013 (By Market Value)*

Company	Country	Industry	Market Value ($Billions)
APPLE	United States	Technology	416
EXXONMOBIL	United States	Oil & Gas	404
GOOGLE	United States	Technology	263
BERKSHIRE HATHAWAY	United States	Financial Services	257
PETROCHINA	China	Oil & Gas	255
WALMART STORES	United States	Consumer Goods	246
GENERAL ELECTRIC	United States	Industrials	240
MICROSOFT	United States	Technology	240
IBM	United States	Technology	238
NESTLE	Switzerland	Consumer Goods	233

* Market value is calculated by multiplying the number of shares available on the market by the share price.

Reprinted by permission from PricewaterhouseCoopers LLP (2013). Global Top 100 [Onine]. Retrieved May 30, 2014 from: Companies http://www.pwc.com/gx/en/audit-services/capital-market/publications/top100-market-capitalisation.jhtml

of iPhone components) in China revealed appalling working conditions and numerous labour and health violations (Gupta & Chan, 2012).

Also consider the Nike Corporation. Nike began manufacturing in 1967, with some production in both Japan and the United States. However, when Japanese wages increased in 1972, Nike moved its plants to South Korea and Taiwan. When labour conditions improved there, Nike once again moved its factories, this time to Thailand and China, where wages were lower and labour laws more repressive. Today, Nike produces 38 percent of its shoes in China but also has factories in Vietnam, Thailand, and Indonesia (Brecher & Costello, 2006).

Nike's history illustrates a few important points about TNCs and globalization:

1. *As TNCs negotiate with different countries about where they will locate their factories, the countries compete with each other to gain whatever industrial development they can.* The consequence of this competition is a race to the bottom, and wages and social conditions tend to fall to the level of the most desperate (Brecher & Costello, 2006).

2. *One could argue that TNCs benefit the economies of these poor countries because they provide jobs, albeit low-paying ones, that increase the standard of living in the area.* To some extent, this is true, but since TNCs maintain no moral or social ties either to the communities they work in or to their employees, there is little to prevent a TNC from relocating its plant whenever it finds cheaper labour or a better deal with another government. Moreover, some argue that TNCs have too much control over their workers and that they actively restrict their ability to organize and to bargain for better working conditions (Brecher & Costello, 2006; George, 2008). The only concern for TNCs is profit.

3. *Since TNCs are driven solely by the desire for profit, they are less likely to be concerned about the environmental damage they may cause as a result of their activities* (as will be discussed more fully in Chapter 20).

No one can deny that globalization has resulted in a higher standard of living for many people. The question to ask, however, is this: Why have the benefits of globalization not been extended equally?

> > >

In April 2008, more than 20 000 workers at a Nike factory in Vietnam went on strike, demanding higher pay to cope with rising inflation.

Steve Raymer/Corbis

❹ Globalization and Poverty

Many scholars who study social change argue that globalization has facilitated the expansion of global poverty (Juhasz, 2006; Peron, 2006; Sachs, 2005). To investigate this relationship, we consider how global poverty is defined.

DEFINING POVERTY

 Watch

Slum Futures

Defining *poverty* would seem to be an easy task; however, it is not as simple as it appears. One might think that being poor may be simply defined as not having enough money, but would everyone agree on what constitutes "enough"? To explore what really constitutes poverty, sociologists compare it across national and cultural boundaries by measuring both *absolute* poverty and *relative* poverty.

absolute poverty The failure to meet the basic needs of life, including adequate food, clean water, and shelter.

Absolute Poverty **Absolute poverty** is defined as the failure to meet the basic needs of life. This includes not having enough food, clean water, or shelter (Iyenda, 2007, p. 28). Absolute poverty, then, is not concerned with social or cultural definitions of what it means to be rich or poor but, rather, with the minimum required for a human being to survive. Determining the level of absolute poverty is usually achieved by calculating the cost of buying a minimum diet of essential foods and the fuel needed to prepare it (Streeten, 1995, p. 37, as cited in Iyenda, 2007, p. 29). If people cannot afford this minimum diet, they are said to exist in absolute poverty.

The World Bank uses the absolute definition of poverty to demonstrate the needs of the poor. According to the World Bank's 1995 definition, anyone living on less than $1 a day is poor. However, while the overall number of people in this situation has been declining since 1990, there is much more work to do (Ferreira & Ravallion, 2008, p. 8). Table 19.2 illustrates that well over 1 billion people, and over 50 percent of the population in sub-Saharan Africa, live on less than $1 per day. Researchers at the World Bank have recently proposed raising the threshold of absolute poverty to $1.25 a day (Ravallion, Chen, & Sangraula, 2008).

TABLE 19.2 Selected Populations Living on Less than $1 a Day

Region	Total Population (millions)	Population living on $1 a day (millions)	Percent of population
East Asia and Pacific	1884	316	16.7
Latin America and the Caribbean	550	45	8.1
South Asia	1476	596	40.3
Sub-Saharan Africa	763	388	50.8
Total developing countries	4673	1345	28.8
Europe and Central Asia	473	17	3.5
Middle East and North Africa	305	11	3.6
Total	5451	1372	25.2

Source: Adapted from 2011 World Hunger and Poverty Facts and Statistics (World Hunger Education Service) at: http://www.worldhunger.org/articles/Learn/world%20hunger%20facts%202002.htm (accessed September 12, 2010).

Relative Poverty **Relative poverty** is defined as the inability to secure goods and services required to live a life equal to working-class standards (Iyenda, 2007, p. 28). Thus, those who cannot maintain a standard of living equal to their working-class neighbours are considered poor. The relative definition of poverty is essentially a measurement of social inequality.

Using the relative definition of poverty is much more threatening to the status quo than using the absolute definition. After all, even the poorest countries have some ability to alter their income distribution so that more of the wealth from the rich is reallocated to the poor. Yet this scenario is unlikely since those who could effect this redistribution (i.e., politicians and civic leaders) are the same people who would be hurt by it. Conversely, the absolute definition of poverty, at least in theory, allows for a reduction of poverty without changing the income distribution if the poor can earn money for themselves. That is, if everyone who wanted to work could find a job with an adequate wage, then even those on the bottom of the socioeconomic scale could live what is regarded as a decent life, without having to redistribute wealth from the rich. This idea is known as the **trickle-down theory** of poverty reduction (Blank, Card, Levy, & Medoff, 1993, p. 327). This theory asserts that society should spend less time focusing on the poor and concentrate on stimulating economic growth that will ultimately benefit everyone.

Table 19.3 demonstrates that a country's economic wealth translates to longer lifespans.

relative poverty The inability to secure goods and services required to live a life equal to working-class standards.

trickle-down theory The assertion that stimulating overall economic growth will ultimately help the poor.

THE GLOBAL POVERTY DEBATE

The issue of global poverty has generated a lot of debate among researchers and scholars of globalization. Articles published by the World Bank and the IMF make the argument that global poverty has been declining, while other researchers and scholars highlight the fact that the decline is not occurring fast enough and that the promise of globalization to promote greater equality has failed (Herman, 1999).

Some suggest that changes to foreign aid policies and debt repayment programs have made it particularly difficult for poor countries to raise their standards of living. Juhasz (2006) suggests that globalization—as seen through free trade arrangements, international deregulation, and more flexible financial policies—has failed to alleviate global economic inequality and poverty. In fact, he argues that globalization actually concentrates wealth into fewer and fewer hands.

> > > Thinking Sociologically

How might a functionalist, a conflict theorist, and a post-colonial theorist explain the existence of the Global North and the Global South?

TABLE 19.3 Top 10 and Bottom 10 Life Expectancies by Country, 2014 (est.)

	Country	Life Expectancy in Years
Top 10		
1	Monaco	89.57
2	Macau	84.48
3	Japan	84.46
4	Singapore	84.38
5	San Marino	83.18
6	Hong Kong	82.78
7	Andorra	82.65
8	Switzerland	82.39
9	Guernsey	82.39
10	Australia	82.07
(14	Canada	81.67)
Bottom 10		
214	Gabon	52.06
215	Namibia	51.85
216	Zambia	51.83
217	Somalia	51.58
218	Central African Republic	51.35
219	Swaziland	50.54
220	Afghanistan	50.49
221	Guinea-Bissau	49.87
222	South Africa	49.56
223	Chad	49.44

Source: Central Intelligence Agency (2014). Retrieved April 30, 2014, from https://www.cia.gov/library/publications/the-world-factbook/rankorder/2102rank.html

Sachs (2005), on the other hand, points out that China and India have been able to decrease the poverty in their countries because of the economic opportunities resulting from globalization. Certain cities and sectors in both China and India have benefited from foreign investment and have become economically competitive and successful.

❺ Globalization and Inequality

Globalization has created massive wealth in some parts of the world and crushing poverty in others. According to the World Institute for Development and Economics Research, almost 90 percent of the world's wealth is found in North America, Europe, and high-income Asia-Pacific countries (Research Institute, 2012). It has been calculated that if the 400 richest people in the world were charged a 4 percent tax on their wealth, that tax would generate enough money to provide food, clean water, basic sanitation, and health care for 1.2 billion of the world's poorest people (Ferrante, 2006). Further, according to Oxfam (2013) the incomes of the world's richest 85 individuals combined are greater than the incomes of the poorest 3.4 billion people combined. The net worth of Bill Gates (founder of Microsoft) alone is over $75 billion.

The International Labour Organization (ILO) reports that in 2013, there were 375 million workers worldwide who earned less than $1.25 a day, and 839 million workers (26.7 percent of all workers) who earned less than $2 a day (International Labour Organization, 2014, p. 11). The fact that 5 out of 10 people in the world are in vulnerable employment situations (e.g., part-time, seasonal, and/or in situations where plant closings are possible), and that 5 out of

<<<

Many Chinese enjoy the benefits of economic growth while many others still live in marginal conditions.

10 workers live in poverty, points to significant challenges facing the global economy. The ILO argues that even when countries improve their labour markets through investment and development, they must do so in a manner that includes all of their citizens. Only in this way can such labour market growth be sustainable (International Labour Organization, 2014, p. 12).

Some argue that corporate-led, finance-driven globalization has successfully transferred wealth from workers to corporations (George, 2008). Indeed, while globalization has had questionable results for the poor, it has been a boon for most TNCs. These TNCs use their economic and political influence to exploit market opportunities in order to maximize their profits (Isaak, 2005).

For the fiscal year ending on March 31, 2013, ExxonMobil, one of the world's largest oil companies, made a profit of $44.9 billion, while Apple made $41.7 billion (Huffington Post, 2013). If ExxonMobil were a country, its profits would exceed the gross domestic product of almost two-thirds of the member nations of the World Bank (Levelle, 2008). In 2012, the 10 most profitable companies in the world had profits of $318 billion and revenues of $2.1 trillion (CNN Money, 2014).

GDP PER PERSON

One measure of economic inequality is a country's gross domestic product (GDP) divided by its population—in other words, each person's share of the country's economic activity. Table 19.4 shows that while some national economies are immense (e.g., United States and China), the per person distribution is far lower in the Global South than it is in the Global North. For example, in 2012, the GDP per person in the United States was $51 749 and in Canada was $41 298. However, in the economically powerful countries of China ($9083) and Brazil ($11 716) it was far lower, and in the poorest countries, like Comoros ($1210) and São Tomé and Principe ($1822), it falls even further.

These data support the assertion that while there may be extensive economic activity in a country (consider the GDPs of China and India), this does not necessarily mean that everyone shares equally in its prosperity.

FOREIGN AID

Wealthy countries in the Global North provide a great deal of financial support to poor countries in the Global South. Commonly referred to as *foreign aid*, this support is generally seen as a deliberate effort to promote economic development in countries that are struggling. Bernstein (2006, pp. 46–47) refers to this form of development as providing the "material foundation of modernity" to address the negative influence of global capitalism through the reconstruction of social order.

In 1970, the United Nations resolved that development aid should account for 0.70 percent of gross national income (GNI) and by 2012 only five countries met the target (Luxembourg,

TABLE 19.4 Eleven Highest/Lowest GDP[1] Rankings, 2012

		National GDP (US$, millions)	Per Person GDP[2]
World		72 489 728	
Low income countries		505 676	
High income countries		49 768 446	
Highest 11			
1	United States	16 244 600	51 749
2	China	8 227 103	9083
3	Japan	5 961 066	35 618
4	Germany	3 428 131	42 700
5	France	2 612 878	36 785
6	United Kingdom	2 475 782	35 722
7	Brazil	2 252 664	11 716
8	Russian Federation	2 014 775	23 589
9	Italy	2 014 670	34 926
10	India	1 858 740	3870
11	Canada	1 779 635	41 298
Lowest 11			
179	St. Vincent and the Grenadines	713	11 047
180	Samoa	684	4493
181	Comoros	596	1210
182	Dominica	480	12 426
183	Tonga	472	4881
184	Micronesia, Fed. Sts.	326	3726
185	São Tomé and Principe	263	1822
186	Palau	228	18 722
187	Marshall Islands	182	*
188	Kiribati	175	2618
189	Tuvalu	40	*

[1] Gross domestic product is the total market value of all final goods and services produced in a country in a given year.

[2] GDP per person is calculated by dividing a country's GDP by the number of its citizens.

* no data available

Sources: Data from World Development Indicators Database, World Bank 2014 [online]. Retrieved April 30, 2014, from http://data.worldbank.org/data-catalog/GDP-ranking-table and http://data.worldbank.org/indicator/NY.GDP.PCAP .PP.CD?order=wbapi_data_value_2012+wbapi_data_value+wbapi_data_value-last&sort=asc

>>> Thinking Sociologically

Why do you think some European Union countries are willing to spend more of their national resources (e.g., GDP) on foreign aid than are Canada and the United States?

Sweden, Norway, Denmark, and the Netherlands). For most countries, the aid parameter set out by the United Nations remains a distant goal (Statistics Norway, 2013). In 2012, even with less than 0.20 percent of GNI, the United States remains, by far, the largest contributor to development aid at $30.58 billion, while in 2012, Canada contributed $5.5 billion (Foreign Affairs, Trade and Development Canada, 2013).

International development projects are generally targeted at building dams, roads, and industrial infrastructure without addressing the underlying systemic issue: the displacement of traditional economies by Western capitalism, whereby great wealth flows into fewer and fewer hands.

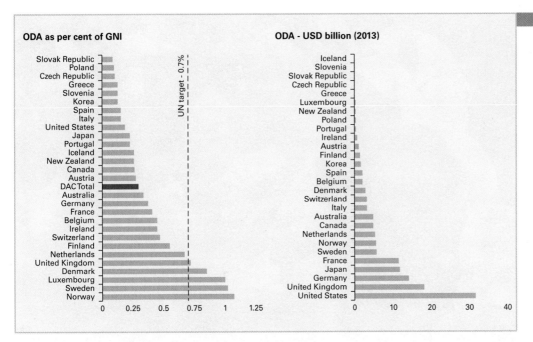

FIGURE 19.2

Official Development Assistance (ODA) by the 25 members of the OECD Development Assistance Committee (DAC).

Source: Compare your country - Official Development Assistance 2013, OECD http://www .oecd.org/statistics/datalab/ oda2012.htm

⑥ Theoretical Approaches to Globalization

As is evident from our discussion so far, although there is no causal link between globalization and poverty, they do appear to be correlated. During industrialization and colonial expansion, some wealthy countries were able to dominate others and exploit the colonized countries' raw materials for their own economic gain. Countries in the industrialized Global North were successful in exploiting the resources and labour of the Global South, and by doing so, they became increasingly powerful over time. As discussed next, some argue that globalization has been the vehicle through which the Global North has solidified its control of the global economy. Social scientists have proposed a number of theories to explain globalization and its influence on the world. The most prominent of these are modernization theory, dependency theory, and world system theory.

A note on terminology: Early theories of globalization were largely developed by economists and political scientists, who used different terminology than sociologists would. Therefore, while modernization theory is not called *functionalist* as such, you will see that it is entirely consistent with functionalism, just as dependency theory is consistent with conflict theory. As you continue to develop your sociological imagination and your command of sociological theory, you will likely begin to discern further parallels between sociological theory and the theories presented in other disciplines.

MODERNIZATION THEORY

Modernization theory was developed in the United States in the postwar period as a way of approaching the problems of the newly decolonized nations of Asia, Africa, and Latin America. One of its goals was to propose strategies for economic growth and political stability (Martinelli, 2005). Modernization theory arose in the historical context of the end of European **hegemony** and the beginning of the Cold War. It was an attempt by Global North scholars to explain what was happening, and what should happen, to nations in the Global South.

The foundation for modernization theory is the assertion that since industrialized nations are doing so well, poor countries should naturally want to be like them (Watson, 2007,

hegemony
Political and social domination of the bourgeois class in capitalist society, expressed not only in ideologies but in all realms of culture and social organization.

> > >

Poverty in the Global
South continues to
challenge the idea that
globalization benefits
everyone.

Andy Chadwick/Alamy

p. 176). These theorists argue that modernization is an inevitable, irreversible, and linear
process from traditional to modern society (Knöbl, 2003, pp. 96–97).

Modern societies are more focused on achievement, universalism, and individualism than
are traditional societies (Parsons, Bales, & Shils, 1962). The intent of modernization theory,
then, is to explain and promote the transition from traditional to modern society (Dube,
1988). Its proponents believe that the best way to achieve "modernity" is through economic
growth, especially through industrialization (Kiely, 1995). However, as Sachs argues, this idea
is overly simplistic and overlooks the complexity of poverty. He points out that, in effect, "the
rich countries told the poor countries *poverty is your own fault*. Be like us (or what we imagine
ourselves to be—free market oriented, entrepreneurial, fiscally responsible) and you too can
enjoy the riches of private-sector-led economic development" (Sachs, as cited in Snider, 2007,
emphasis added).

In general terms, modernization theorists (Eisenstadt, 1966; Rostow, 1960) believe that
the lack of capital in the Global South precluded its economies from growing and prospering.
Thus, modernization theory promotes the use of foreign capital to jump-start the process of
industrialization, and by doing so set a country on the road to modernity.

The ramifications of modernization theory are not limited to Western economics;
they extend into social and cultural areas as well. For example, the theory advocates the
diffusion of Western values as another mechanism to help poor countries adjust to the
new world and its new realities (Jaffee, 1998). Modernization theorists believe that the
success of the Global North is partly the result of a value system that admires the accumulation of wealth and that in turn supports sound economic decision-making (Jaffee,
1998; Martinelli, 2005, p. 33). This implies, of course, that the values of the poor are
outdated, backward, and contrary to those that are required for success in the modern
world (Frediani, 2007, p. 134). According to modernization theory, the problems of poverty and underdevelopment are largely the result of the internal inadequacies of the poor
countries themselves.

As you may have predicted, modernization theory came under heavy attack for being
too Eurocentric and too ethnocentric, for not appreciating the tremendous power imbalance

BOX 19.3 WHY SHOULD WE CARE?

Canadian Foreign Aid

In 1968, the federal government founded the Canadian International Development Agency (CIDA) to help poor countries. CIDA was an umbrella agency that managed Canada's official development assistance. CIDA's aim was to "manage Canada's support and resources effectively and accountably to achieve meaningful, sustainable results and engage in policy development in Canada and internationally, enabling Canada's effort to realize its development objectives, reduce poverty, promote human rights, and support sustainable development" (CIDA, 2009).

In fiscal 2008–2009, CIDA's budget for development aid was $3.575 billion (CIDA, 2009). One CIDA project provided funding for an agricultural union in Rwanda—Union des co-opératives agricoles de Gikongoro (UNICOOPAGI)—to promote greater equality for women. Although more than 50 percent of the union's members were women, they represented only 10 percent of the decision-makers and rarely benefited from the union's activities.

In Rwandan culture, women should not speak in the presence of men, and when they do, they should try to be as brief as possible. This situation is starting to change with CIDA's funding to help promote gender equality in UNICOOPAGI's member associations. Program funds were used for educational sessions to raise awareness of women's challenges and capabilities and the importance of gender equality to rural development. Today, women are much more active in the union and its associations. For example, 47-year-old Daphrose M. said, "After being trained and going on a field trip, we women have become more self-confident. We are now sure of ourselves when we speak at meetings" (CIDA, 2007).

In March 2013, the Conservative government announced that CIDA would no longer operate as an autonomous government agency but instead be folded into the Department of Foreign Affairs, which was renamed the Department of Foreign Affairs, Trade and Development. While still in principle committed to foreign aid, the Conservative government argued that aid projects needed to include some sort of benefit to Canada (Mackrael, 2013). How might this reorganization of Canadian foreign aid programs alter the kinds of aid that are offered to struggling nations?

CIDA projects often targeted educational programs.

MAECD-DFATO/Roger Lemogne

(economically and politically) between the Global North and the Global South, and for not acknowledging the negative results of colonialism. In addition, modernization theory conceptualizes the relationship between modernity and the world system in a naive way. To the extent that the theory examines relationships between different regions of the world, it assumes that they are based on consensus and shared values rather than on unequal power relations or conflict (Kiely, 1995). Obstacles to modernity, then, were thought to exist primarily within nations, not between them.

While modernization theory was an important theoretical position from the 1950s to the 1970s, today most of its assertions have been dismissed (Jaffee, 1998; Knöbl, 2003).

DEPENDENCY THEORY

The most pointed criticism of modernization theory came from dependency theorists, who were largely from Latin America (Sachsenmaier, 2006, p. 456). After World War II, when new nations were emerging as a result of the breakdown of the colonial system, it became necessary for wealthy countries to support their reintegration into the global economy (Foster, 2007). However, some dependency theorists began to argue that underdevelopment was the inevitable outcome of long-term inequality between advanced and less developed nations (Cardoso & Faletto, 1979; Frank, 1969).

Dependency theorists assert that globalization maintained and enhanced the wealth of some nations while creating poverty in others. The origins of this theory are mostly associated with Andre Gunder Frank (1969), but the significance of Paul Baran's earlier work (1957) should not be overlooked.

Baran (1957), using a neo-Marxist approach, argued that the economic relationships that existed between Western Europe and the rest of the world were grounded on exploitation. His views on the nature of global relations would inspire both dependency and world system theories (Foster, 2007; Jarvis, 2005, p. 210). Baran argued that European colonial expansion promoted the "outright plunder or . . . plunder thinly veiled as trade, seizing and removing tremendous wealth from the place of their penetration" (Baran, 1957, pp. 141–142). The result was a transfer of raw materials from the poor countries to the wealthy, where they were used to fuel their own economic growth. This relationship resulted in the poor country actually becoming *under*developed because of its exploitation. In this sense, then, the Global North created economic hardships for the Global South as a means of ensuring its own access to cheap materials and labour.

Paul Baran's *Political Economy of Growth* (1957) challenged the dominant views of the time and argued that the manner in which colonialism had penetrated underdeveloped countries had destroyed existing social structures and created the perfect conditions for lasting dependency on the colonial powers (Foster, 2007). This allowed the colonial powers to exploit these other countries' raw materials for their own gain but under the premise that they were trying to help develop these other economies (Bradshaw, 1988). Baran's work influenced the best-known dependency theorist, A. G. Frank.

Frank (1972) contends that Western capitalist development perpetuates underdevelopment in the Global South. According to Frank, development and underdevelopment are coexisting processes that cannot occur without each other. Although Frank borrows extensively from Marx, his theory of underdevelopment marks a radical departure from orthodox Marxism. While classical Marxists would view the lack of development as resulting from lack of capital, Frank contends that underdevelopment is a result of foreign capital (Frank, 1972). The solution for dependency theorists is for underdeveloped countries to take control of their own resources and pursue economic development only if and when the benefits flow directly back to them.

However, the economic success of such countries as South Korea, Taiwan, and Singapore leads some dependency theorists to advocate controlled participation in global markets. In Evans's (1995) study of South Korea, Brazil, and India, he argues that globalization can be beneficial for developing countries if governments are able to secure foreign capital on their own terms.

WORLD SYSTEM THEORY

Immanuel Wallerstein (1976, 2004) shifts the focus away from dependent relationships toward an investigation of the economic and political hierarchy that links all economies into a global system (Sachsenmaier, 2006, p. 457; Wells, 2006, p. 274). According to Wallerstein, the world's capitalist economies can be understood as a system linked by an international division of labour and a dispersal of raw materials necessary for industrial growth. He referred to wealthy, developed countries as the **core**; they extract resources from poor countries on the **periphery** (Wells, 2006, p. 274). Countries on the periphery lack strong central governments or are controlled by other states, they export raw materials to the core, and they rely on coercive labour practices. The core expropriates much of the capital surplus generated by the periphery through unequal trade relations. Between the two extremes are countries on the **semi-periphery**; these are generally core regions in decline or peripheries trying to improve their positions (Wallerstein identified Greece and Portugal as two countries on the

core Wealthy countries with developed economies.

periphery Poor countries that are exploited for their raw materials by core countries.

semi-periphery Peripheral countries moving toward becoming core, or core countries in decline.

semi-periphery) (Wallerstein, 1976). Today, Global North countries are considered to be core states that can exercise considerable economic power over nations on the periphery and semi-periphery (Wallerstein, 1976, 2004; Martinelli, 2005).

Driven by the exploitative logic of capital accumulation, the capitalist world system creates global inequalities based on the domination of Global South countries by Global North countries (Steger, 2002). Modernization theorists, and the more recent neo-liberal theorists, contend that only through foreign trade and investment will peripheral economies improve their situation; in other words, a better quality of life will be gained through trickle-down economics. In contrast, dependency theorists argue that foreign capital investment is not so benign; because it results in unequal relationships, poor countries must take matters into their own hands and develop their economies in ways that benefit them. World system theorists look beyond analyses of individual countries or economies to the vast web of interconnecting economic and political interests that characterize global capitalism.

Our theoretical analysis of globalization has highlighted the integrated nature of the global economy and demonstrated the power dynamics that exist between rich and poor countries. With this understanding in hand, we turn to one of the principal issues related to the future of globalization.

❼ Homogenization of Cultures?

So far, our analysis of globalization has focused on its economic impact, but globalization also influences culture. Indeed, as Steger (2002, p. 34) argues, just as globalization lies at the heart of modern culture, cultural practices lie at the heart of globalization. In a world dominated by Western mass media (as reviewed in Chapter 17), we run the risk of losing cultural diversity as people around the world strive for the American dream. Some have referred to the homogenization of culture as the "trend to blend" (Nederveen Pieterse, 2009, p. viii). This raises important questions for us as sociologists: Is the inevitable result of globalization the homogenization of culture? Do we run the risk of losing our cultural uniqueness as we become more and more interconnected and interdependent?

With today's technology, we can send words, images, and ideas around the world instantaneously. As we see more and more of the world and how others live, this will have a profound influence on how people experience their everyday lives (Steger, 2002). Culture is no longer tied to towns, cities, or nations. Rather, Steger (2002) suggests that our identities are becoming part of an emerging global context—one that is increasingly American. For instance, Barlow (2006) suggests that globalization promotes the cultural values of America, whose mass media transcend national boundaries and convey messages that reinforce the idea that in order to be happy and successful one must become rich, no matter the cost.

A number of scholars argue that globalization has facilitated the rise of an increasingly homogenized global culture dominated by the Anglo-American value system (Hedley, 2002; Ritzer, 2004; Steger, 2002). From theme parks to music, books, and videos, American capitalism is taking over local cultures and meanings (Steger, 2002). However, other scholars suggest that as American values diffuse throughout the world, many cultures tend to become **indigenized** in one way or another (Appadurai, 1996). This is true of, say, music and housing styles just as it is true of science and terrorism (Appadurai, 1996). Koropov (2006) similarly argues that it would be wrong to assume that people in poorer countries will blindly adopt and accept American or European cultures and values. Instead, cultures react and create hybrid cultures that maintain some traditions and incorporate new ones as well, but do so within their own cultural context (Koropov, 2006). These cultural fusions are reflected in many ways, including music, movies, language, and food. From this perspective, instead of creating a homogeneous culture, globalization will give rise to unique mixtures of different cultures. Thus, some argue that globalization may in fact lead to greater cultural diversity, not less—the concept of cosmopolitanism (Spisak, 2009).

indigenize **To incorporate new cultural values and messages into the local culture.**

cosmopolitanism

Seeing culture as fluid, which helps individuals resist cultural homogenization.

Waldron (2000, p. 1) defines **cosmopolitanism** as "a way of being in the world, a way of constructing an identity for oneself that is different from, and arguably opposed to, the idea of belonging to or devotion to or immersion in a particular culture" (as cited in Spisak, 2009, p. 86). Cosmopolitanism is a way of seeing the world that views individual identity and collective cultural ideals as fluid and open to change over time. Such fluidity transforms the relationship between the self and society and leads to the potential for the individual and the collective to change (Spisak, 2009, p. 86). No individual or society exists within a vacuum. As people begin to learn more about each other through communication technologies, they are arguably more likely to empathize with different cultures and by doing so develop their own sociological imaginations. In this way, cosmopolitanism may challenge the traditional view that globalization will inevitably lead to cultural homogenization (Jackson, 2011).

Summary

1 Globalization is the worldwide exchange of money, goods, and services as well as socio-cultural influences. It emerged in Europe when developing industrial economies began to establish colonies around the world in order to secure cheap raw materials to fuel their own development.

2 As a means of indicating countries' relative economic status, the terms *Global North* and *Global South* are now preferred over the use of *First World, Second World,* and *Third World*, since the latter terms connote value judgments. The terms associated with "development" (*developed, developing, underdeveloped*) have been similarly critiqued as stemming from a Western bias.

3 Technological changes (notably in transportation and communications) have served to accelerate global economic integration. Political changes after the fall of the Soviet Union reinforced the belief that capitalism and democracy were the world's dominant, and most successful, economic and political models. Economic factors contributing to globalization are expanding trade and the emergence of international banking. The International Monetary Fund, the World Bank, the World Trade Organization, and transnational corporations have promoted Western capitalist ideals, at times at the expense of the poor.

4 *Absolute poverty* is defined as the failure to meet the basic needs of life; *relative poverty* is defined as the inability to secure goods and services required to live a life equal to working-class standards.

5 Corporate-led, finance-driven globalization has created wealth in Global North countries and crushing poverty in Global South countries. Transnational companies in particular have benefited from their ability to exploit market opportunities and low-wage labour in Global South countries.

6 Modernization theorists promote the transition from traditional to modern society through industrialization (and the foreign capital it requires), arguing that poor countries need to emulate industrialized nations in order to join the modern world. Dependency theorists assert that advanced countries, by exploiting the resources of poor countries for their own industrial growth, created the dependency of the Global South. World system theorists investigate the economic and political hierarchy that links all economies into a global system, whereby wealthy (core) nations exploit poor (peripheral) countries through unequal trade relations.

7 Globalization has resulted in an increasing homogenization of culture, although some see poorer countries not as blindly adopting Western culture and values but instead as creating hybrid cultures. Cosmopolitanism may also help people appreciate the value of what makes us different, not the same.

Key Terms

absolute poverty *516*
colonizing *504*
command economy *506*
core *524*
cosmopolitanism *526*
developed countries *507*
developing countries *507*
Global North *507*
Global South *507*

gross domestic product (GDP) *510*
hegemony *521*
indigenize *525*
newly industrialized countries (NICs) *508*
periphery *524*
relative poverty *517*
semi-periphery *524*
transnational corporation (TNC) *513*
trickle-down theory *517*
underdeveloped countries *507*
undeveloped countries *507*

Reviewing the Concepts

1. Review the role of capitalism in the emergence of globalization.

2. Compare and contrast absolute poverty and relative poverty. Provide an example of each from your own community.

3. What do you see as the key advantages and disadvantages of globalization for countries in the Global North and the Global South?

4. What is the difference between undeveloped and underdeveloped? Why do sociologists believe this distinction is significant?

Applying Your Sociological Imagination

1. If it is true that the three pillars of the Bretton Woods conference (the IMF, the World Bank, and the WTO) promote Western ideals and values, what other international strategies do you think should be pursued to decrease global poverty and increase global equality?

2. What are the pros and cons of Canada devoting a larger proportion of its GDP to foreign aid? If you look forward five years, do you see our contribution increasing or decreasing? Why?

3. Using your sociological imagination, explore how post-colonial theory might critique modernization, dependency, and world system theories.

4. Do you think that globalization is leading inevitably to a worldwide homogenized culture? Do you believe that your views are more "cosmopolitan" than your parents' views? Discuss.

MySocLab

Visit MySocLab to access a variety of online resources that will help you to prepare for tests and to apply your knowledge.

20 Challenges to the Global Environment

On April 20, 2010, the explosion of the *Deepwater Horizon* oil platform in the Gulf of Mexico killed 11 men and resulted in the worst environmental disaster in US history. The explosion damaged the underwater wellhead, which then spewed millions of barrels of oil per day until it was capped on July 15.

The spill resulted in extensive damage to marine and wildlife habitats as well as to the Gulf's fishing and tourism industries. In late November 2010, 11 000 km² of the Gulf was re-closed to shrimping after tar balls were found in shrimpers' nets. The spill was a tragic event and while billions have been spent trying to clean it up, no amount of money can undo the damage that has already been caused to the sensitive ecosystem.

This disaster—like the environmental contamination at Love Canal in upstate New York (1970s); the nuclear catastrophes at Three Mile Island (1979), Chernobyl (1986), and Fukushima (2011); the gas leak poisoning at Bhopal, India (1984); the Exxon Valdez spill (1989); the Kuwaiti Oil Fires (1991); and, to some, the environmental damage of the Alberta Oil Sands and global climate change—was the result of human activity and entirely preventable. As human consumption continues to rise we will no doubt face future environmental disasters in our pursuit of the planet's resources. But how long can we continue damaging the environment before it is too late for it, and us, to recover?

Also, what role, if any, should sociologists or other academics, play in this? Should academics, who know about these issues better than most, become social activists or should they remain dispassionate and separate from the issues they study? Some Canadian researchers (Foote, Krogman, & Spence, 2009, p. 584) argue that not only should academics become more active, but such public engagement should also become an integral part of what good academic practice is. What do you think?

By the end of this chapter, students will be able to

1 Define *environmental sociology* and explain how it presents a different, contemporary view of the relationship between human beings and the environment.

2 Review key environmental challenges facing the global community.

3 Define and discuss the significance of the greenhouse effect and greenhouse gases and their role in global climate change.

4 Explain how biodiversity is being jeopardized by global climate change.

5 Define and provide examples of environmental racism.

6 Review and critique sociological theories that explain how humans relate to the environment.

1 What Is Environmental Sociology?

Environmental sociology is the study of the interaction between human society and the physical environment (Dunlap, 2002, p. 331). Modern environmental sociology is a recent addition to the discipline, emerging after the 1970 Earth Day demonstrations that inspired a new social consciousness about the environment (Hannigan, 2006, p. 1). The 1970s saw widespread public interest in the environmental issues of the day, which included nuclear safety and radioactive waste, air pollution, and the growth of urban landfills. Early environmental sociologists began to look beyond specific environmental issues to explore the underlying relationships between modern industrialized society and the physical environment (Dunlap, 2000, p. 22).

Environmental sociologists also began to connect with ecologists and the field of **ecology**—the study of how living organisms interact with the environment. Central to understanding our physical environment is appreciating that an **ecosystem** is a community of plants, animals, and smaller organisms that live, feed, reproduce, and interact in the same area. An ecosystem can be as large as the Canadian prairies or as small as the pond at the end of your street. Within any ecosystem, all organisms are interdependent and exist in an elaborate network of interactions (Environmental Protection Agency, 2007). Environmental sociologists apply these biological insights to enhance their own understanding of the relationship between human society and the physical environment. Emphasis is given to exploring how social factors affect the environment and the way in which society tries, or fails to try, to solve the problem of environmental degradation (Lueck, 2007, p. 250).

environmental sociology The study of the interaction between human society and the physical environment.

ecology The study of how living organisms interact with the environment.

ecosystem A community of organisms living, feeding, reproducing, and interacting in the same area.

In general terms, the relationship between humans and their physical environment can be seen in three broad orientations:

1. The physical environment is viewed as a warehouse of raw materials to be exploited; nature by itself has no intrinsic value (this is consistent with a scientific or economic approach to the environment).

2. The physical environment has an almost sacred and spiritual value, and humans have a unique obligation to act as its stewards and protectors (this is consistent with the mystical approach and deep ecology).

3. The physical environment and human beings exist in a harmonious relationship wherein human needs can be achieved without damaging the physical environment; the pursuit of human material wealth does not necessarily require the domination of the physical environment (this is consistent with sustainable development or more radical, utopian thinking). (See Hannigan, 2006; Harper, 2008.)

These three orientations not only illustrate how complex the human–nature relationship is, but also help us to explore people's changing attitudes toward nature throughout history.

Sociology has been deeply influenced by its Western cultural heritage, which viewed human beings as separate from, and above, the rest of nature—a perspective called **anthropocentrism** (Catton & Dunlap, 1978, p. 42; Wolloch, 2011). That the environment exists for the pleasure and exploitation of human beings was a perspective reinforced by hundreds of years of scientific and technological advances, which gave people the impression that they were superior to all other living things as well as to the physical environment (Dunlap, 2002, p. 331; Hannigan, 2006, pp. 3–4). Early sociologists, then, shared the view that the exceptional characteristics of our species (culture, technology, language, complex social organization) excluded humans from the forces of nature. As technology and science developed, humans were increasingly able to dominate the natural world for their own gain.

In 1978, Catton and Dunlap challenged this view with the **human exemptionalism paradigm**, which is based on the following assumptions:

1. Humans are unique among all creatures in that they possess culture.

2. Culture is highly variable, and is able to change far more quickly than biological traits.

anthropocentrism The view that human beings are separate from, and above, the rest of nature.

human exemptionalism paradigm The view that humans are exceptional but not exempt from the natural world.

> > >

The impact of human activities on the environment makes pristine ecosystems increasingly rare.

Jose Angel Astor Rocha/Shutterstock

3. Human differences are not innately biological; they result from social variation and are therefore able to change.

4. Cultural accumulation over time suggests that progress is unlimited and therefore that all social problems are solvable. (Catton & Dunlap, 1978, pp. 42–43)

Dunlap and Catton argued that while humans were certainly exceptional, they were not exempt from the natural world (Dunlap, 2002, p. 334). This position is also known as the *new environmental paradigm* (Bell & Carolan, 2004, p. 196; Stoddart, 2008, p. 1) or, most recently, the *new ecological paradigm* (Manoli, Johnson, & Dunlap, 2007, p. 4).

The **new environmental paradigm** emphasizes that human social actions occur within an ecosystem that has its own processes and limits. Contrary to anthropocentrism, which considered humans to be above nature, this approach recognizes that human societies and the natural environment interact with each other and that human actions do affect nature. The **new ecological paradigm** extends this thinking by emphasizing that modern industrial society is beginning to exceed the limits of the environment (Dunlap, 2002, p. 334; Manoli, Johnson, & Dunlap, 2007, p. 4). This paradigm was intended to cut across established boundaries within sociology and present a less anthropocentric (human-oriented) and more **ecocentric** view, wherein humans are only one part of the global ecosystem (Hannigan, 2006, p. 13). In sum, then, environmental sociology can be thought of as a conscious endeavour to overcome the anthropocentrism of our past (Stoddart, 2008). This way of thinking has forced some to rethink how capitalism interacts with the natural environment—an approach called the triple bottom line.

THE TRIPLE BOTTOM LINE

The concept of the **triple bottom line** was coined in 1994 by John Elkington (Elkington, 1997). Elkington argues that companies should rethink their business models as having three distinct bottom lines. The first bottom line would be the usual approach of measuring a company's expenses versus revenues—the traditional "bottom line." The second is the bottom line of a company's "people account"—a measure of how socially responsible an organization has been throughout its operations. The third is the bottom line of the company's "planet account"—a measure of how environmentally responsible the company is in the production of its goods and/or services. The triple bottom line therefore consists of three Ps: *profit*, *people*, and *planet* (The Economist, 2009). By measuring the total financial, social, and environmental performance of a company over a period of time, we are better able to assess and compare the true costs associated with the product.

While this concept has made many think beyond the traditional bottom line, others critique the idea as being impossible to truly calculate because of the complexity of all the factors involved (e.g., imagine the complexity of calculating the true cost of producing an automobile with its thousands of parts that are designed, produced, and assembled in factories all around the world) (Harmes, 2011; Tullberg, 2012). The triple bottom line is a useful as a concept that forces us to work harder at considering the environmental costs associated with producing the products and services that we consume.

SOCIOLOGY OF FOOD

Another relatively recent area of sociology investigating human interaction with the environment is the sociology of food. From the emergence of agribusiness and genetically modified foods (also known as GMOs—genetically modified organisms), to human health and obesity, to the special place food holds in so many of our social gatherings (e.g., weddings, holiday dinners, etc.), food fascinates sociologists. Food is not only a necessity for life but is also an expression of human diversity. There are a number of reasons why the sociology of food is becoming such a popular area of scholarship.

new environmental paradigm **The view that human social actions occur within an ecosystem that has its own processes and limits.**

new ecological paradigm **Emphasizes that modern industrial society is beginning to exceed the limits of the environment.**

ecocentric **The opposite of anthropocentrism; the view that humans are only one part of the global ecosystem.**

triple bottom line **A company's balance sheet according to** *profit, people,* **and the** *planet.*

>>> Thinking Sociologically

How might you apply your sociological imagination to what you had for breakfast this morning? Is eating a cold slice of pizza perceived differently than fried eggs and toast? Why?

First, there is a growing interest by many in the West to know where the food in their supermarkets actually comes from. As people become more informed about large mechanized farming operations and genetically modified foods, they often become more concerned about the large multinationals that provide food (Pechlaner, 2010). Second, there is a growing recognition that our diets are slowly killing us. For example, health researchers argue that there is an obesity epidemic in North America (Godley & McLaren, 2010). The reality that so many people in Canada are struggling with their weight shows that our bodies are changing because of the highly processed nature of many people's diets.

A third reason is that people are beginning to question how the food supply is regulated and governed (McMillan & Coveney, 2010). Food policy, once seemingly only directed at food labelling and packaging, is now starting to focus on many of the issues around the safety and quality of the entire food chain (Lang & Heasman, 2004; Lang, Barling & Caraher, 2009). For example, on May 20, 2003, Canada's beef industry was rocked after a single breeder cow in northern Alberta tested positive for bovine spongiform encephalopathy (BSE), commonly referred to as mad cow disease. Prior to the worldwide ban on Canadian beef products as a result of mad cow disease, Canada was the third largest exporter of beef in the world. In 2002, this export market was worth more than $4 billion annually. After the ban, the value of these Canadian exports dropped to virtually zero (Poulin & Boame, 2009). Food and food security is of interest to sociologists for a number of reasons and within many different perspectives. For example, some researchers have explored how access to nutritious food affects people of different genders and how industrialized food production is itself gendered (McMahon, 2011; McMahon & Johra, 2012).

❷ Environmental Challenges: Today and Tomorrow

As sociologists, we understand how the sociological imagination enables us to look beyond our own socialization at the larger world around us. Historically, this meant reflecting on our own lives, our society, and the cultural diversity around the world—all in an attempt to learn more about ourselves. Today, environmental sociologists challenge us to extend this anthropocentric thinking to better understand the biological and physical worlds as well.

NATURAL VS. TECHNOLOGICAL DISASTERS

In 1992, sociologist Ulrich Beck wrote a book entitled *Risk Society* that promoted the concept of risk and risk research in contemporary sociology (Jarvis, 2010). Indeed, his work on risk in contemporary society has become widely popular, capturing current concerns about the consequences of industrialization and technological development. Beck investigates how technology is creating global challenges that we could have never predicted. He notes that it has only been within the last few generations that human beings have created forms of technology that can have global consequences. For example, regarding the Japan earthquake, while the tsunami was the result of a "natural" event (i.e., an earthquake), the lasting danger is the result of technology (i.e., the escape of radioactive materials from the Fukushima nuclear facility). For Beck, the contemporary risk to society is less about natural disasters (volcanoes, earthquakes, floods, etc.) than it is about unrestricted technological development. Though natural disasters still occur, we do understand what to do to be better prepared for them and to recover more quickly when they do occur. However, we have less experience dealing with disasters resulting from technology (oil spills, climate change, plane crashes, etc.). For example, Japan has a long history of preparing for and cleaning up after earthquakes and tsunamis but no experience dealing with the catastrophic failure of a nuclear plant. Beck teaches us that technology adds yet another layer of risk to an already risky world (Beck, 2008; Haney, 2011).

❸ CLIMATE CHANGE

Perhaps the most well-known current environmental challenge is global climate change. While many use the phrase *global warming*, *global climate change* is more accurate because even though the planet is warming up, the more pressing concern is the effect that this is having on global weather patterns (Bell & Carolan, 2004, p. 5) and water supplies (Sivakumar, 2011).

The Earth's temperature is regulated by the **greenhouse effect** (Schneider, 2008, p. 31). Earth is similar to a greenhouse in that the atmosphere absorbs and traps heat over the Earth just as the glass panes in a greenhouse do. As shortwave radiation from the sun passes through Earth's atmosphere, it is absorbed by land and water and warms the planet. Part of the absorbed energy is then re-radiated to the atmosphere in the form of long-wave infrared radiation. Very little of this radiation escapes into space because it is trapped by gases in the atmosphere called **greenhouse gases** (notably carbon dioxide, methane, nitrous oxide, and water vapour). These gases act as a blanket and, over time, have increased Earth's temperature.

Estimates suggest that without greenhouse gases trapping this heat, the average temperature on Earth would be –18°C instead of the current average of 15°C (Lang, 2010). While these gases are necessary for life on our planet, we now realize that human activities have contributed to an accumulation of greenhouse gases in the atmosphere—a position supported by the world's leading scientists (Baer, 2008, p. 59; Campbell, 2008, p. 42; Hilton, 2008, p. 4; Schneider, 2008). However, even with the consensus of the scientific community, there still exists some resistance to the idea that human activity has resulted in climate change (Shalizi & Lecocq, 2010), a position that may be exacerbated by the diminishing media coverage of the issue (Young & Dugas, 2011).

Over the past 200 years, emissions of greenhouse gases from human activities have accumulated in the atmosphere because they take decades or centuries to break down. As a result, since the Industrial Revolution, concentrations of carbon dioxide have increased by 30 percent; methane, by 145 percent; and nitrous oxide, by 15 percent (Environment Canada, 2007a). In fact, research shows that greenhouse gas levels are higher today than they have been at any point in the past 800 000 years (CNRS, 2008).

While greenhouse gases naturally vary over time, the latest increase is assumed to be the result of industrialization and population growth (i.e., burning fossil fuels like coal, oil, and natural gas to generate electricity, power factories, and fuel cars). In addition, urbanization and agricultural development have resulted in the deforestation of vast tracts of land

G P Bowater/Alamy

greenhouse effect
The process by which Earth's temperature is maintained (Earth absorbs and retains heat much like a greenhouse).

greenhouse gases
Gases that trap long-wave infrared radiation and are responsible for rising global temperatures and climate change.

⊙—Watch

World Climate Change

< < <

Deforestation is one of the primary contributors to global warming.

((•—Listen

Soot Plays Big Role in Climate Warming

(particularly rainforests in Brazil and Indonesia), which decreases Earth's ability to absorb and store greenhouse gases and naturally regulate the atmosphere. Note that when natural matter, such as vegetation, soils, and oceans, absorbs more carbon than it emits, it is referred to as a **carbon sink**; when natural matter, such as burning fossil fuels, emits more carbon than it absorbs, it is referred to as a **carbon source**.

By increasing the amount of greenhouse gases, humans have altered global weather patterns. Higher temperatures threaten the world's boreal forests as well as increase the risk of fire; decrease the availability of fresh water (discussed below); increase the frequency of severe weather systems, including hurricanes; and enable tropical diseases to move northward, where populations have little or no immunity to them (Environment Canada, 2007b).

In Canada, climate change will affect the foods and crops we currently grow as higher temperatures and droughts will become more common. Higher temperatures will also remove insulating vegetative ground cover and melt the **permafrost**—ground that has been frozen for longer than two successive years—allowing vegetation to thaw and decompose, a process that also releases greenhouse gases. Some researchers estimate that 90 percent of the northern permafrost will disappear by 2100 (Walker, 2007, p. 719). Thawing permafrost also presents many difficulties in terms of constructing and maintaining pipelines, roads, and bridges that rely on a frozen foundation.

While many Canadians are seeking to use less energy, few people understand how much energy we consume and how much Canada contributes to rising levels of greenhouse gases. To put our consumption in perspective, consider that 33 million Canadians use more energy than all of the 760 million inhabitants of Africa, and that each Canadian burns the equivalent of 7700 litres of oil annually, which is about 50 times more than the average person living in Bangladesh burns (David Suzuki Foundation, 2007).

Figure 20.1 shows that Australia had the highest per capita emissions of carbon dioxide in 2012 at 18.8 tonnes. Emissions from the US were 16.4 tonnes and were just behind oil-rich Saudi Arabia with per capita emissions of 16.2 tonnes (Roberts, 2013). In 2005, the energy sector (i.e., fossil fuel production and consumption) accounted for 81.5 percent of greenhouse gas emissions in Canada (Mourougane, 2008, p. 9). As confirmed by Figure 20.2, Alberta remains Canada's largest emitter of greenhouses gases by far, and that increased by 47 percent between 1990 and 2012. However, perhaps more troubling to some is Saskatchewan's

carbon sink Natural matter that absorbs more carbon than it emits.

carbon source Natural matter that emits more carbon than it absorbs.

permafrost Ground that has been frozen for more than two successive years.

Explore

Meager Harvests in Africa Leave Millions at the Edge of Starvation

---

FIGURE 20.1

World Per Capita CO$_2$-Equivalent Emissions

Source: The Carbon Brief, 2013. Retrieved May 1, 2014, from http://www .carbonbrief.org/media/ 244186/graph3_550x303.jpg. Material is licensed under a Creative Commons Attribution No-Derivs 3.0 License.

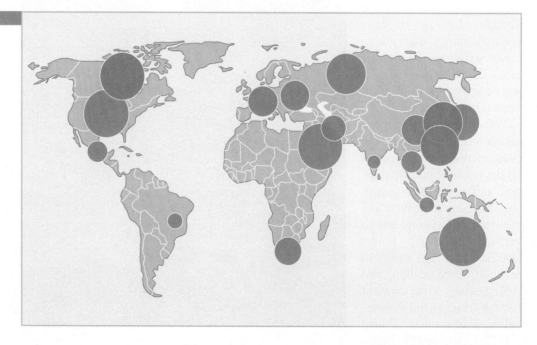

FIGURE 20.2

Province/Territory	1990	2005	2012	% change
Newfoundland and Labrador	9.20	9.90	8.70	−5.43
Prince Edward Island	2.00	2.20	1.90	−5.00
Nova Scotia	19.10	23.10	19.00	−0.52
New Brunswick	16.00	20.10	16.40	2.50
Quebec	84.00	85.60	78.30	−6.79
Ontario	177.20	206.50	166.90	−5.81
Manitoba	18.70	20.90	21.10	12.83
Saskatchewan	43.50	71.10	74.80	71.95
Alberta	169.60	231.80	249.30	46.99
British Columbia	49.40	62.30	60.10	21.66
Yukon	0.50	0.50	0.40	−20.00
Northwest Territories and Nunavut	1.50	2.00	1.70	13.33

Greenhouse Gas Emissions by Province and Territory, Canada, 1990, 2005, and 2012

Source: Data from Environment Canada (2014). [Greenhouse Gas Emissions Data]

increase of almost 72 percent over the same period. This increase is largely the result of high energy consumption during cold winters, dispersed populations that must travel long distances in their vehicles, and energy-intensive industries like potash mining and agriculture (Saskatchewan Environmental Society, 2011). There were five provinces and one territory that actually saw their emissions decrease: Newfoundland and Labrador, Prince Edward Island, Nova Scotia, Quebec, Ontario, and the Yukon.

Because natural resource industries are so important to the Canadian economy, Canadian policies to address greenhouse gas emissions are politically volatile and complex. Natural resources fall under the authority of the provinces, but international agreements and treaties are the responsibility of the federal government. While most provinces have some form of restrictions on greenhouse gas emissions, there are no provincial standards.

In December 2013, the federal government submitted a report to the United Nations stating that Canada was delaying the release of long-promised regulations to reduce emissions from the booming oil-sands sector for as long as two years. The report provided no details on how Canada would fulfill the commitment Prime Minister Harper made at the 2009 Copenhagen summit to reduce Canada's emissions by 17 percent from 2005 levels by 2020 (McCarthy, 2014). Whether or not the Canadian government can meet, or wants to meet, any emissions targets remains to be seen (Drexhage & Murphy, 2010).

Explore

World Energy Consumption

>>> Thinking Sociologically

In your opinion, what role, if any, should the federal government play in protecting the environment?

Listen

Senate Rejects Global Warming Bill

BIODIVERSITY

As we have seen, climate change is altering what farmers can grow, melting the ice caps, and thawing the permafrost. However, German zoologist Josef Reichholf argues that rising temperatures are not an entirely negative phenomenon, given that warmer climates promote species diversity (Stampf, 2007). Even so, the risk of extinction for many species, especially those that are already endangered, is increasing (Environmental Protection Agency, 2007). Nobel laureate Paul Crutzen coined the term **Anthropocene** to recognize the fact that the impact of human activities on the Earth is so significant that it constitutes a new geological era (Hilton, 2008, p. 4; Rose, 2008, p. 81; Steffen, Crutzen, & McNeill, 2007).

Biologists identify three different levels of biodiversity: ecosystem diversity, species diversity, and genetic diversity (Centre for Marine Biodiversity, n.d.; Hannigan, 2006, p. 122). **Ecosystem diversity** refers to the number and variety of habitats for organisms within a geographic area. As human activity continues to expand into previously pristine areas, more and more habitats are destroyed and fewer ecosystems remain. **Species diversity** is the number of species that exist in a given ecosystem (discussed more fully below). **Genetic diversity** refers to the amount of genetic information within a single population species (Hannigan, 2006, p. 122). As discussed in previous chapters, genetic evolution takes time and is a natural process of cumulative adaptations to environmental stressors. As you will see shortly, the rate of environmental change resulting from human activity may be outpacing many species' ability to adapt.

Biologists identify three central impacts of climate change on biodiversity: (1) individual species may become extinct; (2) ecosystems may be destroyed; and (3) species will be forced to move from one area to another (Verheyen, 2005, p. 209). While species are constantly evolving due to changing environmental pressures, the concern today is that human activities have increased the pace of change. For example, more than 1700 species-related studies found that climate change is already influencing virtually all plant and animal species (Verheyen, 2005, p. 209). Warming temperatures are an environmental stressor that may push some species over the edge (Gaston, 2008, p. 73). Today, the rate of extinction is 1000 times higher than the natural rate, which is estimated at 9 percent of all organisms becoming extinct every 1 million years (Verheyen, 2005, p. 209). The Intergovernmental Panel on Climate Change suggests that within 100 years, 20 to 30 percent of species may be at risk of extinction if global mean temperatures rise more than 2 to 3 degrees Celsius above preindustrial levels (Environmental Protection Agency, 2007).

Some argue, however, that the single greatest cause of mass extinction is not global climate change but rather the deforestation of tropical rainforests. Although estimates vary greatly, most scientists believe that there are between 10 and 30 million species on Earth, and that between 50 and 90 percent of them are located in tropical forests. With about 17 million hectares of tropical forests (roughly four times the size of Switzerland) being cleared every year, scientists estimate that between 5 and 10 percent of tropical forest species will become extinct within the next 30 years (World Resources Institute, n.d.). Figure 20.3 highlights the **human footprint**—the impact of human activities around the world. As the figure demonstrates, the highest human influence occurs in Western Europe, India, Southeast Asia, and eastern North America.

Anthropocene A new geological era resulting from the consequences of human activities on the Earth.

ecosystem diversity The number and variety of habitats for organisms within a geographic area.

species diversity The number of species that exist in an ecosystem.

genetic diversity The amount of genetic information within a single population species.

> > >

The consequences of human activity influence all organisms on the planet.

human footprint The impact of human activities around the world.

((•—Listen

Deforestation of the Amazon

Erwin and Peggy-Bauer/Animals Animals

WATER

Nearly three-quarters of Earth's surface is covered with water, the vast majority of which is salt water (around 97.5 percent). The remaining 2.5 percent of the world's water is fresh and suitable for drinking and irrigation. Considering that about 99.6 percent of all fresh water is frozen in glaciers and ice fields or in underground aquifers, it is easy to understand why preserving water is so important (Environment Canada, 2007c).

The OECD suggests that while virtually everyone in the Global North has access to safe water, more than 783 million people in the Global South do not have fresh water and more than 2.5 billion people lack adequate sanitation. This is a major concern because 80 percent of all diseases in the Global South are water related (United Nations, 2013a). The World Health Organization estimates that 1.4 million children per year die from diarrhea alone, the vast majority as a result of bacterial, viral, and parasitic organisms in contaminated water (Prüss-Üstün, Bos, Gore, & Bartram, 2008).

Clean water is necessary for all healthy ecosystems; when water is contaminated, it presents a risk to all aquatic and terrestrial life. For example, high concentrations of nitrogen and phosphorus in water can promote rapid aquatic plant growth, such as algae, that reduces the oxygen available to fish and other aquatic animals, and in some cases can be toxic to livestock and humans. Poor water quality can also affect economic activities such as fishing, tourism, agriculture, and recreational uses of water, such as swimming. Although Canadians by and large enjoy a safe and plentiful water supply (Government of Canada, 2007a), water pollution is a growing problem.

niderlander/Shutterstock

< < <

The melting ice pack presents a serious challenge to the polar bear's long-term survival.

✻ Explore

On Her Centenary, Some Critics Blame Her for All the Lives Lost to Malaria

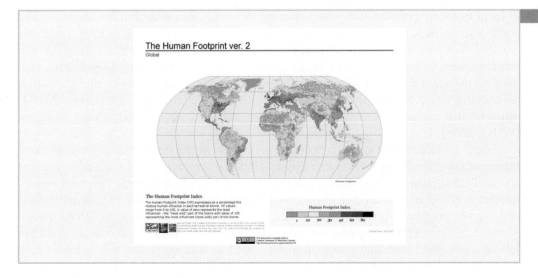

FIGURE 20.3

Human Footprint Index

Reprinted by permission from Center for International Earth Science Information Network (CIESIN), Columbia University. 2008. The Human Footprint Version 2: Global [Map]. Palisades, NY: NASA Socioeconomic Data and Applications Center (SEDAC). http://sedac.ciesin .columbia.edu/data/ collection/wildareas-v2

FIGURE 20.4

Global Physical and Economic Water Scarcity, 2012

Reprinted by permission from UN Water for Life 2005-2015. Accessed May 2, 2014, from http://www .un.org/waterforlifedecade/ images/scarcity/2013_ scarcity_graph_2.png

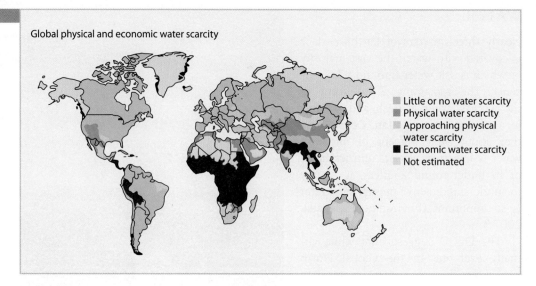

Global physical and economic water scarcity

Little or no water scarcity
Physical water scarcity
Approaching physical water scarcity
Economic water scarcity
Not estimated

Households and industries discharge hundreds of different substances, either directly or indirectly, into rivers, lakes, and treatment facilities. Government estimates suggest that in 2012, at least 674 180 tonnes of pollutants were discharged into Canada's air, water, and land (Environment Canada, 2012). However, the most common way that pollutants enter the fresh water supply is through runoff water from agricultural lands. Rainwater carries pesticides and herbicides from farms into rivers and aquifers that may end up as drinking water. Natural occurrences like seasonal snowmelts or heavy rainfalls can also diminish water quality, as they can introduce suspended sediments (such as metals and other contaminants) into the water supply (Environment Canada, 2007c). Figure 20.4 shows that while most of North America, South America, and Europe have little or no water scarcities (except for the American Southwest and parts of Mexico), much of Africa and some areas of Central Asia suffer from limited water resources.

AIR POLLUTION

Air pollution is a major health threat and a key risk factor for both acute and chronic respiratory diseases. Outdoor air pollution is largely, and increasingly, related to the use of fossil fuels for transportation, the generation of energy, and other human activities. The combustion of fossil fuels produces a variety of pollutants, including primary emissions (such as soot particles from diesel engines) and secondary pollutants (such as ozone and sulphate particles formed from the burning of sulphur-containing fuel). As in Beijing, outdoor air pollution remains a serious health concern in many large cities around the world, particularly those located in poor countries. The World Health Organization (WHO) estimates that a quarter of the world's population lives in areas with harmful air pollution (WHO, 2008).

Indoor air pollution is also a concern in poor areas as the fuels used to cook and heat homes release harmful pollutants into the air. Children are particularly vulnerable to these air conditions; research shows that indoor air pollution can lead to acute lower respiratory infections in children under age five, as well as to chronic obstructive pulmonary disease and lung cancer in adults (when coal is used as a cooking and heating fuel) (WHO, 2008). Research from the OECD suggests that every year respiratory failure caused by air pollution kills an estimated 1.8 million people, primarily in China and India, and this number could double if new policies are not put in place (OECD, 2012).

BOX 20.1 ISSUES IN GLOBAL CONTEXT

Fresh Water as a Commodity

Should fresh water be viewed as just another commodity to be bought and sold on the world market, or should we protect our water from exploitation by commercial interests?

Among many who think that Canada should consider selling its fresh water is former US ambassador to Canada Paul Cellucci. In 2007, Cellucci stated that "Canada has probably one of the largest resources of fresh water in the world. Water is going to be—already is—a very valuable commodity and I've always found it odd that Canada is so willing to sell oil and natural gas and uranium and coal, which are by their nature finite. But talking about water is off the table, yet water is renewable" (Bauch, 2007). Others, like Canadian social activist Maude Barlow, point out that global water consumption is doubling every 20 years—twice as fast as the human population is growing. Barlow (2002) suggests that within 20 years, the demand for fresh water will increase by more than 50 percent and as many as two-thirds of the world's population will be facing severe water shortages or absolute water scarcity.

Governments used to believe that water, health care, and education were such basic human services that they would not be included in international trade agreements. However, the 1994 North American Free Trade Agreement (NAFTA) between Canada, the United States, and Mexico opened up the discussion of selling water. In 1999, reacting to public concern over commercializing water, the Canadian government confirmed its desire to prohibit bulk water exports. According to the government, this was merely a formality because NAFTA did not provide for fresh water exports unless the water had already been altered into a commercial product (e.g., bottled water). The government felt that this protected water in its natural state as an environmental issue, not a trade issue (Johansen, 2007).

However, inspired by growing water shortages in the United States, the Security and Prosperity Partnership (SPP), a forum with representatives from the three NAFTA partners, met in 2005 to discuss water exports (Leahy, 2007). Yet a 2008 report by the Polaris Institute entitled *Turning on Canada's Tap* cautions the federal government about the costs of such exports and recommends that governments around the world put more effort into supporting conservation measures than exploiting natural resources.

Clarke (2008, p. 2) suggests that 24 percent of the United States' medium-sized cities and 17.3 percent of its large cities are expected to face serious water shortages by 2015. Indeed, Barlow (2002) predicts that pressure will increase from countries and businesses around the world that want to sell water just as they would grain, cars, or oil. In fact, fresh water is becoming such an important commodity that according to *Fortune* magazine, "water will be to the 21st century what oil was to the 20th" (*Fortune*, as cited in Barlow, 2002). Indeed, Leahy (2007) states that it takes three barrels of fresh water to produce one barrel of oil from Alberta's tar sands. It is possible, says the Global Water Corporation, that water is moving from being considered an unlimited, taken-for-granted resource to one that will be rationed and, when necessary, taken by force (Global Water Corporation, as cited in Barlow, 2002). In Canada, there is concern that American demand for fresh water will soon outstrip their domestic capacity and that there appears to be little legislative protection to ensure Canadian fresh water supplies remain sustainable (CTV News, 2008).

With another student in the class, take opposing sides on whether or not water should be treated like any other commodity.

Extracting oil from the oil sands is a costly process, both financially and environmentally.

Greenpeace

Annually, in Canada, smog is linked to more than 21 000 premature deaths, 620 000 visits to a doctor's office, and 92 000 emergency-room visits; the costs to the Canadian economy are over $8 billion each year (David Suzuki Foundation, 2009). In a report entitled *No Breathing Room: National Illness Costs of Air Pollution* (available at www.cma.ca), the Canadian Medical Association predicts that between 2008 and 2031 approximately 710 000 Canadians will die from the effects of long-term exposure to air pollution. The report also suggests that during the same period the costs of air pollution to Canada's economy (e.g., from increased health care costs and missed work due to air pollution) will increase from $8 billion in 2008 to more than $250 billion by 2031 (Sullivan, 2008).

SOLID WASTE

The amount of solid waste generated by a country is related to its level of urbanization, personal incomes, and lifestyle. Municipal waste is an important part of the total waste generated, and dealing with garbage collection, storage, and treatment usually absorbs more than one-third of the public sector's financial efforts to minimize and control all forms of pollution (OECD, 2008).

From 2008 to 2010, Canadians produced approximately 25.8 million tonnes of waste. The waste from Canadian households generally ends up in landfills. In 2008, about one-third of all waste was generated by households—8.5 million tonnes of waste or about 418 kilograms per person (up 19 percent from 2000)—with the remainder coming from industrial, commercial, institutional, and construction sites (Statistics Canada, 2010l).

residential recycling rate The amount of waste diverted from landfills as a proportion of total waste generated.

Figure 20.5 illustrates that Canada is still disposing of the majority of its waste in landfills, rather than by recycling or composting. Compared with other OECD nations, Canada is not doing so well. However, Canadians are recycling more today than in the past. The **residential recycling rate**—the amount of waste diverted from landfills as a proportion of total waste generated—increased between 2000 and 2004 from 19 to 27 percent (Babooram & Wang, 2008) (see Figure 20.6).

FIGURE 20.5 Municipal Waste Disposal and Recovery Shares, 2011

The OECD defines municipal waste as waste collected and treated by or for municipalities. It includes waste from households, businesses, and institutions, and excludes waste from municipal sewage networks and treatment as well as municipal construction and demolition waste.

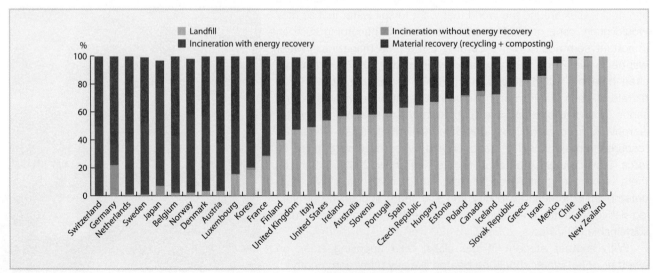

Reprinted by permission from OECD (2013), Environment at a Glance 2013: OECD Indicators, OECD Publishing. http://dx.doi.org/10.1787/9789264185715-en

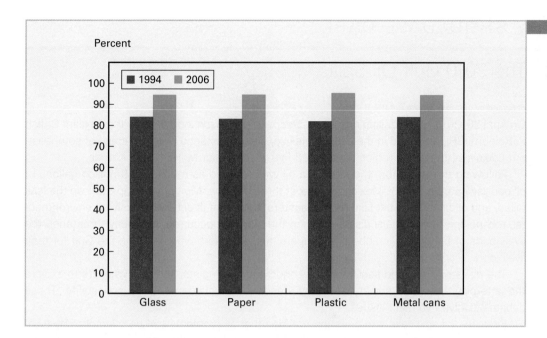

FIGURE 20.6

Percentage of Canadian Households with Access to Recycling Programs that Use Them, 1994–2006

Source: Statistics Canada, EnviroStats, 16-002-XIE2007001, vol. 1 no. 1, March 2008; http://www.statcan.gc.ca/bsolc/olc-cel/olc-cel?catno=16-002-XWE&lang=eng (accessed July 24, 2008).

While 93 percent of Canadians in 2007 recycled at least some waste (up from 73 percent in 1994) (Statistics Canada, 2010i), Canadians seem particularly receptive to composting. Between 2000 and 2004, composting at centralized facilities increased by 70 percent to 1.7 million tonnes; the average Canadian sent 51 kilograms of organic waste for composting in 2004, compared with just 32 kilograms in 2000 (Statistics Canada, 2008e).

These trends are promising, but many factors continue to impede further progress. For example, we live in a world where some people follow the social norm that *what we buy* is part of *who we are* (particularly relevant here is Veblen's concept of conspicuous consumption, discussed in Chapter 7). There are also some systemic barriers to recycling, such as distance to the nearest recycling depot and mandatory sorting of materials that some people find too onerous or time-consuming (Babooram & Wang, 2008).

POPULATION GROWTH/URBANIZATION

Some researchers argue that we cannot fully appreciate future challenges to sustainable development until we address the influence of population growth and urbanization (Sassen, 2011).

Between 2009 and 2050, the world population is expected to increase by 2.3 billion, growing from 6.8 billion to 9.1 billion. At the same time, the population living in urban areas is projected to increase by 2.9 billion, growing from 3.4 billion in 2009 to 6.3 billion in 2050. Thus, the urban areas of the world are expected to absorb virtually all of the population growth expected over the next 40 years. As a result, the world's rural populations are projected to start decreasing by 2020 and result in 440 million fewer rural inhabitants in 2050 than there are today (United Nations, 2012). This increasing urbanization is largely the result of capitalism.

Scott (2007) suggests that wherever capitalism emerges so, too, does urbanization. Capitalism requires the concentration of physical capital and human labour. Capitalists require that factories and supply systems be located as closely together as possible, and workers are drawn to these areas because of employment opportunities. The impact of this population growth and urbanization on the environment cannot be underestimated.

BOX 20.2 WHY SHOULD WE CARE?

The 2010 Gulf Oil Spill

Reprinted by permission from Timothy J. Haney.*

On April 20, 2010, an oil drilling rig named *Deepwater Horizon*, operated by the oil giant British Petroleum (BP), exploded in the Gulf of Mexico, a short distance from the coast of southeastern Louisiana, the same region devastated five years earlier by Hurricane Katrina.

Following the explosion, the deep-sea oil well spewed as much as 2.5 million gallons of oil per day into the Gulf of Mexico for almost three months. Multiple attempts to cap the leak failed, and oil filled the Gulf. Like most disasters, the event is simultaneously an environmental, technological, and social disaster. When the blow-out occurred, it directly threatened the livelihoods of fishermen, crabbers, shrimpers, and all others who relied on the Gulf for their livelihood.

The disaster prompted sociologists, economists, geologists, and policymakers to explore the interplay between society's energy needs and environmental sustainability. These debates involve five main issues.

First, the oil spill calls into question the idea that all problems can be overcome by technology and human ingenuity. The inability of the world's leading experts (in industry and government) to stop the spill confirms that we may not be as smart as we think.

Second, the oil spill has led some experts to question whether North America will be able to satisfy its growing energy needs without triggering other environmental catastrophes. For example, geologists in the 1970s pointed out that at some point easily accessible oil will run out. According to this theory, as oil becomes harder to get, oil companies will take more risks to reach it (Deffeyes, 2008), including deep-sea drilling (e.g., the Gulf of Mexico, off the coast of Newfoundland, or Europe's North Sea), from oil sands (like the ones in Northern Alberta), and from oil reserves located underneath vulnerable ecosystems (like Alaska's Arctic National Wildlife Refuge [ANWR]).

Third, many have questioned the role of government in regulating the energy industry. In this case, BP did not drill a relief well because American law did not require it to. Having a relief well would have prevented the tragedy but such wells are expensive to drill. As a result, many governments, concerned about oil companies taking their business elsewhere (thereby taking jobs and tax dollars with them), soften regulations to promote more drilling but at higher risk.

Fourth, the oil spill will hopefully promote efforts to find an efficient and sustainable replacement for oil. Currently, petroleum is used not only to fuel our cars but to make fertilizers and pesticides for crops, to transport our food, to pave our roads, and to make plastic products. Finding another product as energy-efficient and as versatile as oil has puzzled scientists for decades. Current proposals involve solar, nuclear, wind, hydroelectric, and hydrogen power. However, each technology has its own environmental risks. For example, solar panels require more energy to produce than the energy they return (Kuntsler, 2006).

Finally, the Gulf oil spill has made sociologists question whether the health and economic consequences borne by the citizens of the Gulf Coast are worth the jobs and tax dollars that the oil industry provides in the region. For nearly two generations, Gulf Coast communities have suffered from the environmental pollution and related health complications caused by the oil refineries that dominate the region, giving south Louisiana the nickname "Cancer Alley" (Lerner, 2005). Many in the region are now questioning whether the jobs and tax revenue are worth the costs.

After the oil spill, experts from a number of fields, including sociology, began debating many of the difficult issues mentioned above. In doing so, a sociological perspective can help

CONTINUED

▶

us see how the lives and problems of individual Gulf Coast residents (personal troubles) are intimately linked with the economy, politics, and the ecology of the region (public issues). Hopefully, using the sociological perspective will help you consider how your life is shaped by historical, geographic, economic, environmental, and social forces outside of yourself. As a sociology student, no matter your intended career path, this perspective should also prompt you to consider how you can prevent such a disaster from happening where you live and how you can contribute to a more equitable, just, and sustainable world.

As a sociologist, why do you think so few people prepare for disasters?

*Dr. Haney is an associate professor of sociology at Mount Royal University and the Founding Director of the Centre for Community-Based Disaster Research in Calgary, Alberta.

US Coast Guard Photo/Alamy

Offshore oil exploration may present environmental risks but some suggest it is worth the costs in order to feed our expanding energy needs.

Human beings have always had an impact on their natural environment; however, it was not until the twentieth century that this impact reached every corner of the world (Luke, 2003). Today, the inhabitants of hundreds of large cities all over the world are relentlessly reshaping the traditional and modern economies of every continent as they exert global and local demands for energy, food, information, labour, and goods exchanged on the world's markets (Luke, 2003). There is also a new concern on the horizon: the increasing populations of the world's "megacities." These are cities that have at least 10 million people; in 1970, there were only two such cities (Tokyo and New York), but today there are more than 20, most of which are found in Asia (United Nations, 2012). What sorts of issues might exist in cities this large?

⑤ ENVIRONMENTAL RACISM

Environmental racism is a form of discrimination against minority groups and people from poor countries who are subjected to a disproportionate share of environmental hazards (e.g., toxic wastes) and polluting industries (e.g., chemical plants) (Dodds & Hopwood,

environmental racism A form of discrimination against minority groups and people from poor countries who are subjected to a disproportionate share of environmental hazards and polluting industries.

> > >

Warning signs on the Aamjiwnaang First Nation, part of the region known as "Chemical Valley."

The Canadian Press/Carlos Osorio/AP Photo

2006, p. 269; Westra, 1999, p. 103). One of the earliest researchers to study environmental racism was American sociologist Robert Bullard (Hannigan, 2006, p. 49), considered to be the "father of environmental justice" (Dicum, 2006b).

In 1979, just two years out of graduate school, Bullard was asked by his wife, a lawyer who was contesting the location of a landfill site, to conduct a study on the locations of municipal landfills in Houston, Texas. Bullard found that in Houston, and across the United States, toxic waste facilities were more likely to be located in areas with large black and Hispanic populations (Dicum, 2006b; Hannigan, 2006, p. 49). In fact, he found that all city-owned landfills in Houston were in black neighbourhoods, even though blacks made up only 25 percent of the city's population. Further, three out of four privately owned landfills were also in predominantly black neighbourhoods, as were six out of eight city-owned incinerators (Dicum, 2006a). Houston had no formal zoning regulations at the time, which allowed local government officials to put the waste sites wherever they wanted. According to Bullard, this presented a classic case of environmental racism. In his book *Dumping in Dixie* (1990), Bullard uncovers numerous examples of environmental racism across the United States. The book became a bestseller and was instrumental in changing environmental policies in the United States. In 1994, President Bill Clinton signed an executive order to make environmental justice for minorities a specific concern for the Environmental Protection Agency (Westra, 1999, p. 103).

Some suggest that many instances of environmental racism exist in Canada as well (Schlosberg & Carruthers, 2010; Westra, 1999). For example, landfill sites are often located near Aboriginal communities (Bain Lindsay, 2006); logging is carried out in Aboriginal peoples' traditional-use areas; hydroelectric projects flood vast areas of land used by Aboriginal peoples (e.g., the James Bay Cree in Quebec); and 62 industrial facilities are located in "Chemical Valley" just outside the Aamjiwnaang First Nation near Sarnia, Ontario (MacDonald & Rang, 2007). In fact, the effects of industrial expansion on Aboriginal peoples have

> > > Thinking Sociologically

Are there any examples of environmental racism in your own community/province/territory? Discuss whether the local, provincial, and/or federal governments have met any of Bullard's five principles of environmental justice.

BOX 20.3 THAT WAS THEN, THIS IS NOW

First There Was Kyoto, and Now There Is . . .?

Climate change took centre stage in 1997 when countries gathered in Kyoto, Japan, to sign the Kyoto Protocol. The protocol's objective was (and still is) to cut greenhouse gas emissions in an effort to prevent climate change. It sought to have countries reduce their emissions of carbon dioxide (and other greenhouse gases) by around 5 percent from 1990 levels between 2008 and 2012. Countries that committed to these terms were expected to comply and to measure their emissions regularly. If a country found that it could not meet its targets, the protocol allowed it to engage in emissions trading with other countries. Under this system, developed countries could "buy" emission units from poorer countries that had not yet exceeded their emissions target (United Nations Framework Convention on Climate Change, 2008a).

Although the protocol was negotiated in 1997, only 84 countries had signed on by the end of the signatory period. Canada was one of the original signatories (signing on April 29, 1998), but it did not ratify the treaty until December 17, 2002. The Kyoto Protocol officially came into force on February 16, 2005 (United Nations Framework Convention on Climate Change, 2008b).

The United States has not ratified the Kyoto Protocol, and does not intend to. The Bush administration felt that the protocol's targets were unrealistic, not based on sound scientific principles, and would hurt the US economy (The White House, 2001). In Canada, the Kyoto Protocol was ratified by a Liberal government, and since taking office the Conservative government has all but forgotten Canada's Kyoto commitments (Stoett, 2006, p. 2), instead targeting a "made in Canada" solution to greenhouse gases. In April 2007, the federal government laid out its plan to reach Kyoto targets by 2020 or 2025—years after the original date set by the protocol.

In June 2008, Canada became the world's first country to be brought to court for failing to meet its obligations under the Kyoto Protocol. The lawsuit, filed by the environmental group Friends of the Earth Canada, is the first to attempt to enforce the terms of the protocol. The group claims that the Canadian government has not fulfilled its legal obligations to address greenhouse gas emissions as defined by the protocol (Cowan, 2008). In March 2010, the Supreme Court decided not to hear the case, effectively stopping any further proceedings.

In 2011, in what appeared to be a move designed to prevent Canada from paying fines for failing to meet its international obligations under Kyoto, the Conservative government under Prime Minister Stephen Harper officially withdrew Canada from the Kyoto Protocol—a decision sharply criticized within Canada and around the world (CBC News, 2011a). In the place of the emission targets set by Kyoto, the Canadian government has opted to aim for far lower targets that allow Canada to continue to develop its interests in the Alberta oil sands.

Do you believe that governments should be held accountable for the international agreements that they sign or should they be given the flexibility to manage the affairs of their citizens as they see fit? Discuss.

been referred to as a "treadmill of destruction" (Hooks & Smith, 2004, p. 562). The fact that few Aboriginal communities have safe drinking water is further evidence of environmental racism (Indian and Northern Affairs Canada, 2006).

To fight environmental racism, Bullard proposed five principles of environmental justice:

1. To guarantee the right of environmental protection
2. To prevent harm before it occurs

3. To shift the burden of proof to polluters

4. To not make it necessary to prove intent by those who discriminate

5. To redress existing inequities (Westra & Lawson, 2001)

Bullard's five principles provide a sound foundation for protecting minority groups from further harm and repairing the damage that has already occurred.

⑥ Sociological Approaches to the Environment

ENVIRONMENTAL PARADIGMS

In 1976, British sociologist Stephen Cotgrove (1976, p. 26) began to explore how society's utopian aspirations conflicted with the emerging environmental movement that was uncovering the effects of human activities on the natural environment (see also Cotgrove & Duff, 1981, p. 92). He argued that traditional views of the future were grounded on the belief that industrial, technological, and scientific development would continue to provide people's material needs forever. However, he also saw that early environmentalists were starting to propose an alternative perspective of the future that challenged the belief that continuous growth and development was possible or wise. Instead of the belief that larger, stratified societies were a sign of progress, environmentalists offered a more environmentally responsible, anti-industrial alternative to growth that advocated smaller, decentralized communities (Cotgrove, 1976, pp. 27–30). Cotgrove's 1976 analysis laid the foundation for his later work with Andrew Duff (Cotgrove & Duff, 1980, 1981), in which they contrasted the dominant social paradigm with the alternative environmental paradigm.

dominant social paradigm The capitalist view supported by an ideology that legitimates the domination of nature for the material benefit of humans.

The **dominant social paradigm** is based on capitalism, which views economic growth and large hierarchical societies as positive—a position supported by an ideology that legitimates the domination of nature for the material benefit of humans. The **alternative environmental paradigm** challenges this position and advocates smaller, nonhierarchical, decentralized societies that do not use science and technology to dominate the environment but instead to achieve harmony with it. Table 20.1 shows that the two paradigms propose very different views of human society and its relationship to the natural environment.

alternative environmental paradigm Advocates living in harmony with the environment, not dominating it.

One important outcome that emerged from these competing views was the idea that economic development could occur without damaging the environment, a position known today as **sustainable development**. Sustainable development means many things to many people, but the most common definition comes from a United Nations report entitled *Our Common Future* (1987) (commonly referred to as the Brundtland Report, after Norwegian prime minister Gro Harlem Brundtland, who was chair of the commission). The report states that

sustainable development The belief that economic development can occur without damaging the environment.

sustainable development is development that meets the needs of the present without compromising the ability of future generations to meet their own needs. It contains within it two key concepts:

- the concept of needs, in particular the essential needs of the world's poor, to which overriding priority should be given; and

- the idea of limitations imposed by the state of technology and social organization on the environment's ability to meet present and future needs (World Commission on Environment and Development, 1987, p. 43).

Like virtually all definitions of sustainable development, this one views the world as operating within an integrated system wherein actions in one area affect all other areas. However, some environmentalists point out how difficult and perhaps naive the concept of sustainable development is. For example, is it possible in the global capitalist economy for all areas to

TABLE 20.1 Competing Social Paradigms

	Dominant Social Paradigm	Alternative Environmental Paradigm
Core Values	Material (economic growth)	Nonmaterial (self-actualization)
	Natural environment valued as resource	Natural environment intrinsically valued
	Domination over nature	Harmony with nature
Economy	Market forces	Public interest
	Risk and reward	Safety
	Reward for achievement	Incomes related to need
	Differentials	Egalitarian
	Individual self-help	Collective/social provisions
Polity	Authoritative structures (experts influential)	Participative structures (citizen/ worker involvement)
	Hierarchical	Nonhierarchical
	Law and order	Liberation
Society	Centralized	Decentralized
	Large-scale	Small-scale
	Associational	Communal
	Ordered	Flexible
Nature	Ample reserves	Earth's limited resources
	Nature hostile/neutral	Nature benign
	Environment controllable	Nature delicately balanced
Knowledge	Confidence in science and technology	Limits to knowledge
	Rationality of means	Rationality of ends
	Separation of fact/value, thought/ feeling	Integration of fact/value, thought/ feeling

Source: Cotgrove & Duff (1980, p. 341). Reprinted with permission.

prosper at the same time? Is it possible that all areas of the world could develop at the same pace and reap the same rewards? Sustainable development is certainly a noble goal, but many argue that there are significant economic and ideological barriers to achieving it (Forero & Reclift, 2007, p. 205; Gantsho & Karani, 2007, p. 340).

TREADMILL OF PRODUCTION THEORY

The *treadmill of production theory* asserts that capitalism's insatiable quest for profits and economic expansion is at odds with protecting the environment (Freudenburg, 2006; Schnaiberg & Gould, 1994, p. 53). Capitalism is driven by profits and economic expansion, and little care or attention is given to how these factors affect the environment (Hooks & Smith, 2004, pp. 559–560; Obach, 2007, p. 230). Producing goods as cheaply as possible and selling them for the highest price possible are the only real considerations in pure capitalism. This approach reinforces the fact that capitalism's appetite for growth is insatiable while the earth's ability to provide raw materials is finite.

Allan Schnaiberg's influential book *The Environment: from Surplus to Scarcity* (1980) argues that a deep contradiction exists between industrial and economic growth and the well-being of the environment. In essence, the treadmill of production is a self-reinforcing process whereby capitalists strive for growth and profits and politicians respond to pressure from environmental groups by providing incentives to capitalists to expand their operations rather than promoting initiatives to decrease consumption (Hannigan, 2006, p. 20).

For example, in July 2008, President George W. Bush lifted an executive order banning offshore oil drilling that his father, President George H.W. Bush, had initiated in 1990. The decision to allow offshore drilling drew significant criticism because the United States has proven land-based oil reserves that are far less expensive to access; as well, a land-based spill would be less damaging to the environment than an ocean-based spill would be (Feinstein, 2008). According to the treadmill of production theory, President George W. Bush's actions expanded the exploitation of the environment rather than promoting conservation efforts. Treadmill of production theorists would suggest that he was more interested in helping the oil companies make money than in protecting the environment.

As Hannigan (2006, p. 20) points out, as environmental issues become more important to the public, governments are placed in a seemingly contradictory position of trying to facilitate economic growth and prosperity while fulfilling their role as regulator and champion of the environment:

> If the treadmill is to be slowed and reversed, the central social agency that will have to bring this about is the state, acting to rechannel production surplus in non-treadmill directions. But the state can only do so when there is both a sufficient crisis of faith in the treadmill, and sufficient political support for production apart from the treadmill. (Schnaiberg, 1980, p. 249)

Tellingly, by 2002, Schnaiberg had admitted that the treadmill of production theory was not popular in environmental sociological literature because it was considered too radical (as cited in Hannigan, 2006, p. 21).

ECOLOGICAL MODERNIZATION THEORY

Ecological modernization theory emerged in the 1980s from the work of German social scientist Joseph Huber, who presents an optimistic view of the future. Huber suggests that technology and scientific discoveries will keep pace with human and environmental pressures and allow economic expansion without destroying the environment. Ecological modernization theory suggests that under the proper political, economic, and technological conditions, capitalists are naturally drawn to environmentally responsible techniques as soon as there is a market for them (Carolan, 2004, p. 250). According to ecological modernization theorists, this makes sense because as the demand for environmentally friendly products increases, capitalists will rush to fill this need as an inevitable result of the free market (Obach, 2007, p. 229). According to Mol and Spaargaren (2004, p. 262), ecological modernization focuses on changing the nature of the traditional model of production and consumption through technological development as well as through modern market forces and democratic principles.

Obach (2007, p. 232) suggests that the growth of organic food sales over the past decade (growth of about 20 percent per year in the United States) demonstrates how private enterprise, expanding state regulation (e.g., through government-sponsored certification requirements for organic farmers), and expanding consumer demand for organic foods are achieving more responsible economic growth within a more sustainable environmental model. However, Obach (2007, p. 238) also suggests that there are troubling signs that production models, as defined in treadmill theory, may be beginning to emerge in the area of organic food as large multinationals enter production and displace small independent farmers.

H. Roger Segelken/Cornell University

< < <

Bioprospecting occurs when Western companies exploit indigenous peoples' knowledge and traditional practices in search of new consumer products.

ECOFEMINISM

Ecofeminism combines feminist and ecological insights into the exploitive domination of women and nature by men (Harper, 2008, p. 289; Stoddart & Tindall, 2011). As discussed in previous chapters, the system of domination by men is called *patriarchy*. Ecofeminists point out that oppression of women and destruction of the environment are both products of a masculine orientation to the social and physical worlds. The attempt to control nature is a confirmation of the anthropocentrism and human exemptionalism we reviewed earlier. Ecofeminists argue that modern patriarchal society devalues both women and the environment, and that this must change in order to save the environment.

Ecofeminists face an interesting struggle with other feminists over how best to promote environmental issues. On one hand is the long-standing connection between women, emotion, and nature, which feminists have tried to sever for well over a century (Banerjee & Bell, 2007). On the other hand, some ecofeminists argue that women do in fact have a deeper connection with the social and physical worlds around them and are therefore ideal advocates for environmental change (Harper, 2008, p. 290; Sutton, 2007, p. 51). One form of ecofeminism, called cultural ecofeminism, suggests a way out of this apparent dilemma.

Cultural ecofeminists argue that women's historical connection with emotions and nature, and men's with reason and culture, are simply the result of social construction and therefore open to change if there is the collective will to do so. Rather than adhering to dichotomous masculine and feminine roles, we should try to foster a set of "human ideals" for all people, ideals that diminish the cultural value of dominating nature and thus expose the stereotypical masculine orientations it entails (Sutton, 2007, p. 51; see also McMahon, 2011, p. 401).

A recent area of particular interest to ecofeminists is the Western corporate exploitation of indigenous peoples' resources and knowledge. The term **bioprospecting** refers to these companies' search for new sources of chemical compounds, genes, enzymes, proteins, and/or microorganisms in order to exploit

ecofeminism An approach that investigates the domination of women and nature by men.

cultural ecofeminists Challenge patriarchal assumptions, argue that gender roles are learned and therefore open to change, and promote human ideals for all people.

bioprospecting Occurs when companies search in poor or indigenous areas for new biological entities that they can exploit.

> > > Thinking Sociologically

Is colonialism the inevitable outcome of Western corporations doing business with indigenous peoples? Discuss.

BOX 20.4 CANADIAN CONTRIBUTIONS TO SOCIOLOGY

Ana Isla

Sociologist Ana Isla is a faculty member of Brock University's department of sociology. She has two B.A.s—one in education and one in sociology; an M.A. from Universidad Nacional Autonoma de Mexico; and a Ph.D. from OISE–University of Toronto. Her primary research interests include feminism, ecofeminism, women in development, women in developing countries, political ecology, and social justice, as well as indigenous knowledge, biopiracy, and ecotourism.

Isla's doctoral research examined the structure and functioning of the complex Canada–Costa Rica debt-for-nature agreement and the role of nongovernmental organizations. Debt-for-nature is a "new program of contemporary enclosure" of the industrial world (or creditors), set up within the neoliberal agenda, under the command of environmental nongovernment organizations (ENGOs). ENGOs have emerged as the new ideology of modernization and environmental protection; their discourse of "protecting" land, air, and water through private property has been paid by debt-for-nature swaps. Isla's dissertation received an international award sponsored by the American Rockefeller Foundation. Her research on ecofeminism is widely published and has inspired many to become involved in environmental issues (Brock University, 2008).

In a recent article, Isla (2007) applies an ecofeminist subsistence analysis to biopiracy in Latin America. Her research shows that biopiracy is just another instrument of domination by wealthy multinationals that continue to appropriate local knowledge for commercial gain. She states, "Western science transforms nature's bounty into commodities of global economic value. Biopiracy/bioprospecting is labeled sustainable development and justified by global financial institutions like the World Trade Organization, the World Bank, the Global Environment Facility, the World Intellectual Property Organization, and large environmental nongovernment organizations" (Isla, 2007, p. 324). Her research has laid bare many of the claims by Western corporations that they are interested in preserving vulnerable local ecosystems rather than exploiting local resources for financial reward.

Courtesy Ana Isla

Isla's most recent research focused on two primary areas: exploring subsistence economies in the Peruvian rainforest, and reviewing mining practices and their social impacts in Latin America.

their economic potential (e.g., pharmaceutical companies using the knowledge to create new medications). Bioprospecting also occurs when indigenous peoples' knowledge and traditional practices are exploited and commodified (Hayden, 2005, p. 186; Tauli-Corpuz, 2007, p. 333). This is often an expression of a dominant–submissive relationship between a Western corporation and a local people, a situation referred to as **biocolonialism** (Hawthorne, 2007, p. 318; Huggan & Tiffin, 2007, p. 1; Whitt, 1998, p. 34).

According to Shiva (2007), although the term *prospecting* implies the search for minerals and therefore does not do justice to everything that bioprospecting involves, it nonetheless highlights the negative consequences of commercial exploitation of indigenous resources and knowledge. When bioprospecting occurs without free, prior, and open consent by the people

biocolonialism

Occurs when Western companies exploit indigenous areas and express a dominant–submissive relationship.

involved, it is commonly referred to as biopiracy. **Biopiracy** is defined as the unauthorized appropriation of traditional biological and genetic knowledge, resources, and practices of indigenous peoples (Beattie et al., 2011; Hawthorne, 2007, p. 318; Isla, 2007, p. 326; Shiva, 2000, 2007). Indigenous peoples around the world have begun to assert that they have permanent sovereign rights over their natural resources and traditional knowledge.

DEEP ECOLOGY

Deep ecology originated in the work of Norwegian philosopher Arne Naess in the 1970s. Naess argued that a simple focus on conservation risked a "shallow" approach to environmental degradation; instead, he offered a "deep" approach that advocated a personal self-realization that connected the individual with all living things around him or her (Dolezal, 2008, p. 7). To achieve self-realization, Naess believed that people had to identify with nature and connect with the larger "other-than-human" global community (Diehm, 2007, p. 3). Deep ecology is the belief that unless we develop a profound connection to environmental issues they will never become "our" issues (Naess, 1988, p. 128). Deep ecologists contend that the only way to achieve lasting change is for people to feel a profound intuitive connection with all living things.

According to Harper (2008, pp. 286–287), deep ecologists emphasize four fundamental principles for the move from an anthropocentric view of the world to a biocentric or ecocentric one:

1. All life forms on Earth have intrinsic value and are being threatened by human activity.

2. Human life is privileged to the extent of satisfying immediate and vital needs in order to survive.

3. Maintaining and promoting biodiversity requires decreasing human contact in wilderness areas and increasing wilderness areas around the world.

4. Economic, technological, and cultural change is necessary in order to diminish the size of the human population and, by doing so, to increase the likelihood of preserving the natural environment.

Fulfilling these principles requires practical and realistic changes to people's world views and the ways in which they live their lives. Although deep ecologists value diverse lifestyles and social policies, Sutton (2007, p. 287) suggests that much of the literature promotes the value of small-scale, decentralized human communities as the best model for building a connection with nature and achieving self-realization.

Recently, an emerging field of research has been investigating *ecological* or *environmental citizenship* as one way to connect people's feelings of citizenry within a larger community with their responsibility to act as stewards of the environment (see Latta, 2007). According to deep ecologists, the time for moral arguments and debate is over; what is needed now are "beautiful actions" (Sutton, 2007, p. 48).

Margin notes:

biopiracy
Unauthorized appropriation of traditional biological and genetic knowledge, resources, and practices of indigenous peoples.

deep ecology
Belief that unless we believe environmental issues become "our" issues, very little can be accomplished.

Summary

❶ Environmental sociology is the study of the interaction between human society and the physical environment. In keeping with the new ecological paradigm, it seeks to overcome anthropocentrism by considering humans as only one part of the global ecosystem. The triple bottom line and courses on the sociology of food highlight the growing interest in human–environment interactions.

❷ The key environmental challenges facing the global community are climate change, threats to biodiversity (comprising ecosystem, species, and genetic diversity), water preservation, air pollution, waste, population growth, and urbanization.

3 Industrialization, population growth, urbanization, and agricultural development have resulted in an increase of greenhouse gases in Earth's atmosphere. This in turn has led to higher temperatures, which affect crops and contribute to a thawing of the permafrost and melting of the ice caps.

4 Global climate change is jeopardizing biodiversity in three ways: causing the extinction of individual species, destroying ecosystems, and causing the movement of species from one area to another.

5 Environmental racism is a form of discrimination against minority groups and people from poor countries who are subjected to a disproportionate share of environmental hazards and polluting industries; for example, in Canada, landfill sites are often located near Aboriginal communities.

6 Challenging the dominant social paradigm (which legitimates the dominance of nature for material benefit), the alternative environmental paradigm advocates societies' use of science and technology to achieve harmony with nature. The treadmill of production theory asserts that capitalism's insatiable quest for profits and economic expansion is at odds with protecting the environment. Ecological modernization theory holds that scientific and technological developments will allow for economic expansion without destroying the environment. Ecofeminism combines feminist and ecological insights into the exploitive domination of women and nature by men. Deep ecology advocates a personal self-realization that connects the individual with all living things.

Key Terms

alternative environmental paradigm 546
Anthropocene 536
anthropocentrism 530
biocolonialism 550
biopiracy 551
bioprospecting 549
carbon sink 534
carbon source 534
cultural ecofeminists 549
deep ecology 551
dominant social paradigm 546
ecocentric 531
ecofeminism 549
ecology 529

ecosystem 529
ecosystem diversity 536
environmental racism 543
environmental sociology 529
genetic diversity 536
greenhouse effect 533
greenhouse gases 533
human exemptionalism paradigm 530
human footprint 536
new ecological paradigm 531
new environmental paradigm 531
permafrost 534
residential recycling rate 540
species diversity 536
sustainable development 546
triple bottom line 531

Reviewing the Concepts

1. How does environmental sociology differ from earlier sociological perspectives? Discuss.

2. Review and discuss the similarities and differences between biocolonialism and environmental racism.

3. What is biocolonialism? Are there any examples of this occurring in Canada?

4. Review and discuss the key insights of ecofeminism and biopiracy.

Applying Your Sociological Imagination

1. As a sociologist, speculate on what might happen to countries in the Global North and the Global South should water become a commodity traded internationally just like oil.

2. When considering the Gulf of Mexico oil spill and the catastrophe at the Fukushima nuclear plant in Japan, are there any completely safe sources of energy?

3. In your opinion, what will it take for people to begin living in environmentally sustainable ways?

4. Deep ecologists suggest that the only way to make lasting changes in human behaviour that benefits the environment is to have people feel a personal connection with the larger physical world around them. Discuss this position from the sociological perspective.

MySocLab

Visit MySocLab to access a variety of online resources that will help you prepare for tests and apply your knowledge.

Glossary

ableism Discrimination against those who have disabilities on the basis of preconceived notions about their limitations.

absolute monarchy Monarchs are defined through family membership or a divine connection that confirms the righteousness of their rule.

absolute poverty The failure to meet the basic needs of life, including adequate food, clean water, and shelter.

achieved status Attributes developed throughout life as a result of effort and skill (e.g., course grades).

acting crowd A collection of people who gather to express anger and direct it outwardly at a specific person, category of people, or event.

actions For Parsons, the results of an active and inventive process.

activity theory The belief that people should remain engaged and active for as long as possible.

adaptation The social system must be able to gather and distribute sufficient resources and adjust to changes in its environment.

ageism A system of inequality based on age that privileges the young at the expense of the old.

agency The assumption that individuals have the ability to alter their socially constructed lives.

agents of socialization Individuals, groups, and social institutions that together help people to become functioning members of society.

agnostic Someone who thinks it is impossible to know whether gods exist, but does not deny the possibility.

agriculture An economic system that employs plow technology.

alienation Marxist concept to describe the process by which workers lack connection to what they produce and become separated from themselves and other workers.

alternative environmental paradigm Advocates living in harmony with the environment, not dominating it.

alternative medicine Those treatments not normally taught in medical schools, used in hospitals, or included in health care plans (e.g., acupuncture).

animism Belief that all things possess a spirit.

anomie Durkheim's term for a state of normlessness that results from a lack of clear goals and may ultimately result in higher suicide rates.

Anthropocene A new geological era resulting from the consequences of human activities on Earth.

anthropocentrism The view that human beings are separate from, and above, the rest of nature.

anti-positivism A theoretical approach that considers knowledge and understanding to be the result of human subjectivity.

asceticism Weber's term for religions that seek mastery over the natural world, other people, and the human body.

ascribed status Attributes (advantages and disadvantages) assigned at birth (e.g., sex).

asexuality An absence of sexual desire.

assimilation A one-way process that occurs when a minority group sheds its differences and assumes the traits of the dominant group.

assisted suicide Intentionally killing oneself with help from others.

atheist Someone who denies the existence of any supernatural beings or forces.

authoritarian personality theory Asserts that extreme prejudice is a personality trait of people who strongly believe in following cultural norms, traditions, and values.

authoritarian regimes Political systems controlled by rulers who reject the rights of citizens to participate directly in the actions of government.

authority Exists where subordinates consider domination by leaders to be legitimate.

backbenchers Elected members of Parliament who do not hold a Cabinet position.

base The material and economic foundation for society, made up of the forces of production and the relations of production.

behaviours For Parsons, the almost mechanical responses to specific stimuli.

biocolonialism Occurs when Western companies exploit indigenous areas and express a dominant–submissive relationship.

biological determinism The hypothesis that biological factors completely determine a person's behaviour.

biopiracy Unauthorized appropriation of traditional biological and genetic knowledge, resources, and practices of indigenous peoples.

biopower Foucault's term to explain people taking ownership of their bodies and their health.

bioprospecting Occurs when companies search in poor or indigenous areas for new biological entities that they can exploit.

biphobia The irrational fear or hatred of bisexuals.

birth cohort All of the people who are born during a given period of time and therefore experience historical events at the same points in their lives.

bisexuality Being attracted to both women and men.

blaming the system A perspective that holds that systemic discrimination exists within the social system.

blaming the victim A perspective that holds individuals responsible for the negative conditions in which they live.

block printing A process in which wooden blocks are engraved with images and text, inked, and then pressed onto paper.

blog An online diary in which an individual posts personal reflections on events, specific topics, and/or experiences.

BMI (body mass index) Calculated by dividing an individual's weight (kg) by height (m^2).

bourgeoisie The owners of the means of production.

bureaucracy A rational organization designed to complete many routine tasks as efficiently as possible.

Cabinet A committee made up of ministers in charge of government departments.

calling One's work, believed to be an expression of God's will, particularly if that work brings financial success.

CanCon (Canadian content) Federal regulations that stipulate the required percentage of Canadian content in television and radio broadcasts.

capitalism An economic system grounded on the private ownership of the means of production.

carbon sink Natural matter that absorbs more carbon than it emits.

carbon source Natural matter that emits more carbon than it absorbs.

caste system An ascribed system of hereditary class designation.

casual crowd A chance collection of individuals in the same location at the same time.

causality A relationship in which one variable causes a change in another variable.

charismatic authority The exercise of power as legitimated through personal magnetism of individuals who compel people to believe in them and grant them their support.

charter groups The French and the English in Canada; Porter recognized the important role these groups played in Canadian history and contemporary social and political development.

cheerful robots People who are unwilling or unable to see the social world as it truly exists.

chilly climate The lack of warmth or encouragement that girls and women feel in school as a result of sexism.

chivalry hypothesis The argument that women and girls accused of criminal activity are treated more leniently by law enforcement officials as a result of the latter's traditional, chivalrous attitude toward women.

chronic pain Ongoing pain that lasts longer than three months after the usual recovery period for an injury or ailment.

church An institution that brings together a moral community of believers in formal worship and integrates itself within the larger secular world.

civil religion (secular religion) Exists when sacred symbols are integrated into the broader society regardless of their individual religious affiliations.

class conflict When the interests of one class are in opposition to those of another.

class consciousness Recognition of domination and oppression and collective action to change it.

class structure A society's economic hierarchy that categorizes groups of people based on their socioeconomic status.

classism An ideology that suggests that people's relative worth is at least partly determined by their social and economic status.

closed system A social system in which status is based on attributes ascribed at birth.

collective behaviours Behaviours that occur when people come together to achieve a meaningful short-term goal.

collective conscience Durkheim's concept highlighting the totality of beliefs and sentiments that are common to the average person in a society.

collectivity A substantial number of people who join together on the basis of loosely defined norms.

colonialism The effects of imperialism, including concrete and ideological effects, within colonized territories.

colonizing The political, economic, and cultural domination of countries in Asia, Africa, and the Americas by European countries starting in the sixteenth century.

command economy An economy in which the state, rather than market forces, manages the production and distribution of goods.

commodification The process whereby goods and services become available for purchase in the market.

communism Marx's hypothetical economic system in which ownership of the means of production is collective and workers' labour is not exploited.

conspicuous consumption The purchase of expensive goods simply because they are valuable, not because there is any innate satisfaction in them.

conspicuous leisure The demonstration of one's high social status through forms of leisure.

conspicuous waste The disposal of valuable goods to demonstrate wealth.

constitutional monarchy Monarchs are largely symbolic in that true leadership is held by an elected body.

contact hypothesis The proposal that prejudiced attitudes can decline with intergroup contact.

content analysis A research method involving analysis of texts.

conventional crowd A collection of people who gather for a structured social event.

cool media Media that convey less information and require more participation from their audience (e.g., seminars).

core Wealthy countries with developed economies.

corporation A legal entity that can own property and enter into contracts for the benefit of its shareholders.

correlation A measure of how strongly two variables are related to each other.

correlation function Media's role in filtering and making comprehensible the huge daily volume of news stories and issues.

correspondence principle The principle whereby the structures of workplaces are reflected in the structures of schools.

cosmopolitanism Seeing culture as fluid, which helps individuals resist cultural homogenization.

counterculture A type of subculture that strongly opposes the widely held cultural patterns of the larger population.

craze A widespread emotional connection to a cultural phenomenon.

credential inflation The ever-increasing cache of educational credentials required for a particular job.

crime Behaviours or actions that require social control and social intervention, codified in law.

criminogenic environment An environment that, as a result of laws that privilege certain groups, produces crime or criminality.

criminology The study of crime causation, crime prevention, and the punishment and rehabilitation of offenders.

critical race theory An interdisciplinary approach used to investigate the intersections of race, class, ethnicity, gender, and sexuality to explain prejudice and discrimination.

crowds An unorganized collection of people who gather temporarily for a particular cause.

cultural adaptation The process by which environmental pressures are addressed through changes in practices, traditions, and behaviours.

cultural capital Social assets (values, beliefs, attitudes, competencies) that are gained from one's family and help one to succeed in life.

cultural ecofeminists Challenge patriarchal assumptions, argue that gender roles are learned and therefore open to change, and promote human ideals for all people.

cultural pluralism or multiculturalism The retention of minority groups' cultural identities and the promotion of cultural, ethnic, and racial diversity by the larger society.

cultural relativism Appreciation that all cultures have their own mores, norms, and customs and should be evaluated and understood on their own terms, rather than according to one's own cultural standards.

cultural universals Common cultural features found in all societies.

culture lag Ogburn's concept describing how technology often outpaces society's ability to adjust to it.

culture of poverty A fatalistic belief system held by the poor as an adaptation to systemic discrimination.

culture of prejudice A value system that promotes prejudice, discrimination, and oppression.

culture shock The feeling of disorientation, alienation, depression, and loneliness experienced when entering a culture very different from one's own.

culture theory The assertion that some prejudice is healthy and part of all cultures.

culture A complex collection of values, beliefs, behaviours, and material objects shared by a group and passed on from one generation to the next.

cuneiform An early form of wedge-shaped writing developed by the ancient Sumerians.

cybriety Tremblay's term describing attempts to censor new media content that pushes the boundaries of morality.

Davis-Moore thesis The theory that social stratification is functional for society because it ensures that key social positions are held by the most capable people.

deductive logic A system of reasoning that moves from theory to the formulation of hypotheses for testing.

deep ecology Belief that unless we believe environmental issues become "our" issues, very little can be accomplished.

deferred gratification The ability to forgo immediate pleasures in the interest of achieving greater rewards in the future.

deindustrialization The transformation of an economy from one based on manufacturing to one based on services.

demassification A process by which the mass audience is fragmented into small groups or niches to appeal to unique interests.

democracy A political system in which individual adult citizens select their representative leaders through an electoral process.

democratic racism A system that advocates equality but in fact perpetuates minority differentiation and oppression.

desire Our sexual attractions and wants.

developed countries Wealthy, industrialized countries.

developing countries Countries considered to be on the road to industrialization.

deviance Actions or behaviours that violate social norms, and that may or may not be against the law.

dharma The moral responsibilities and guidelines that define an entire way of life.

dialectics Hegel's view of society as the result of oppositions, contradictions, and tensions from which new ideas and social change can emerge.

dictatorship A system in which a leader relies on personal loyalties and threats of force to maintain rule.

differential association theory Criminal behaviour occurs when our association with definitions favourable to crime outweighs our definitions favourable to law-abiding behaviour.

diffusion Occurs when cultural items or practices are transmitted from one group to another.

digital immigrants Prensky's term for people who grew up before digital technologies became commonplace.

digital natives Prensky's term for people who grew up with digital technologies.

digital sociality A social landscape in which new communication technologies are promoting human interaction and contact.

direct institutional discrimination Occurs when an institution employs policies or practices that are discriminatory against a person or group.

disability A mental or physical condition that limits people's everyday activities and restricts what they can do.

disaster An unexpected event that causes extensive damage to people, animals, and property.

discipline The means by which we become motivated to produce particular realities.

discourse A system of meaning that governs how we think, act, and speak about a particular thing or issue.

discovery Occurs when something previously unrecognized or understood is found to have social or cultural applications.

discrimination Actions that deny or grant advantages to members of a particular group.

disembedding mechanism A mechanism that aids in shifting social relations from local to global contexts.

disengagement theory The assertion that successful aging requires the gradual withdrawal from social activity.

dispersed collectivities Collectivities in which the members are in different places at the same time.

domestic labour The activities required to maintain a home and care for the people who live in it.

dominant social paradigm The capitalist view supported by an ideology that legitimates the domination of nature for the material benefit of humans.

domination The exercise of power over a group of people to direct them to comply with specific commands.

double ghetto A situation in which women who have full-time jobs outside the home often work another "shift" when they get home.

double-consciousness Du Bois's concept of the divided identity experienced by American blacks.

double-consciousness DuBois's term for a sense of self that is defined, in part, through the eyes of others.

downward drift hypothesis The assertion that those with mental illnesses, unable to finish their education or secure a job, tend to drift into low-income groups.

dual labour market theory Asserts that modern societies have two distinct labour markets (called the primary and secondary labour markets).

dying trajectories The courses that dying takes in both social and psychological senses.

e-audience Those who use electronic communication technologies.

ecclesia A system in which a church and the state have a formalized relationship.

ecocentric The opposite of anthropocentrism; the view that humans are only one part of the global ecosystem.

ecofeminism An approach that investigates the domination of women and nature by men.

ecological fallacy Drawing conclusions about individual attributes from data gathered from an entire group.

ecology The study of how living organisms interact with the environment.

economy Social arrangements that organize the production, distribution, and consumption of goods.

ecosystem diversity The number and variety of habitats for organisms within a geographic area.

ecosystem A community of organisms living, feeding, reproducing, and interacting in the same area.

elder abuse Any form of mistreatment that results in harm or loss to an older person.

elderly dependency ratio The ratio of seniors to workers.

emphasized femininity The normative ideal of femininity, based on women's compliance with their subordination to men.

empty nest syndrome The depression that some mothers experience when their children have left home.

entertainment function Media's role in helping people rest, relax, and escape the pressures of everyday life.

environmental racism A form of discrimination against minority groups and people from poor countries who are subjected to a disproportionate share of environmental hazards and polluting industries.

environmental sociology The study of the interaction between human society and the physical environment.

equilibrium theory The assertion that a system's natural state is one of balance and harmony.

ethnic group A collection of people who identify with each other and share a common culture.

ethnicity A multidimensional concept that includes one's minority or majority status, ancestry, language, and often religious affiliation.

ethnocentrism The tendency to view one's own culture as superior to all others.

euthanasia The deliberate ending of the life of a person who has an incurable or painful disease.

evolution The biological process by which genetic mutations are selected for, and against, through environmental pressures.

evolutionary psychology A relabelled form of sociobiology that argues that Darwinian inheritance can explain contemporary human behaviour.

exception fallacy Drawing conclusions about an entire group based on observations of individuals.

exchange theory The assertion that power in relationships is influenced by the resources that a member brings to the relationship.

expert systems Systems of knowledge on which we rely but with which we may never be directly in contact.

exploitation The difference between what workers are paid and the wealth they create for the owner.

exponential growth The adoption of a new technology or behaviour by the majority of the population.

expressive crowd A collection of people who gather intentionally to express their emotions.

expressive role Responsible for the emotional well-being of family members and the socialization of children.

extended family Multiple generations of adults living with their spouses and children.

fad A short-lived but enthusiastically embraced new cultural element.

faith A belief system based on conviction that does not require objective evidence to substantiate its claims.

false consciousness Belief in and support for the system that oppresses you.

family of orientation The family into which one is born.

family of procreation The family one creates by having children or adopting children.

fashion A social pattern that outwardly expresses an individual's identity as being "with it."

fear-gender paradox The phenomenon whereby women experience higher rates of fear of being victimized even though men are more likely to be victims of crime.

feminization of poverty The universal phenomenon whereby women are more susceptible to poverty than are men.

flash mob A planned gathering of large numbers of people for a brief and predetermined period of time.

folkways Informal norms that suggest customary ways of behaving.

forces of production The physical and intellectual resources a society has with which to make a living.

formal social movement A large, well-integrated, and established organization with bureaucratic procedures.

formal sociology Simmel's theory that argues that different human interactions, once isolated from their content, can be similar in form.

f-test Adorno's assessment tool to determine a person's personality and likelihood of holding prejudicial attitudes.

Frankfurt School A group of German social philosophers dedicated to understanding the role of culture and mass communication in the Nazi regime.

fundamentalism A movement designed to revitalize faith by returning to traditional religious practices.

gender relations Organizing principles that shape and order interactions between, as well as the relative social importance of, women and men.

gender stereotyping The assignment of beliefs to men and women, respectively, that are not based on fact.

gender Social distinctions between masculinity and femininity.

generalized other A compilation of attributes associated with the average member of society; represents an individual's appreciation that other members of society behave within certain socially accepted guidelines and rules.

genetic diversity The amount of genetic information within a single population species.

genocide The intentional extermination of all members of a minority group.

gerontology The scientific study of old age and aging.

Gini Index A measure of the inequality of wealth or income distribution within a country.

Global North Wealthy, industrialized countries in the northern hemisphere (previously referred to as the First World).

Global South Poor countries in the southern hemisphere (previously referred to as the Third World).

globalization A worldwide process involving the production, distribution, and consumption of technological, political, economic, and sociocultural goods and services.

goal attainment The system needs to establish clear goals and priorities.

gossip Intimate and personal communication meant to be entertaining.

Governor General The Crown's representative at the federal level in Canada.

greenhouse effect The process by which Earth's temperature is maintained (Earth absorbs and retains heat much like a greenhouse).

greenhouse gases Gases that trap long-wave infrared radiation and are responsible for rising global temperatures and climate change.

gross domestic product (GDP) The total market value of all final goods and services produced in a country in a given year.

GSBA (Gender and Sex-based Analysis) An approach that explores sex and gender differences without assuming differences exist.

health A state of complete physical, mental, and social well-being.

healthy aging Perspective that reinforces the inherent value of older people to society.

hegemonic masculinity The normative ideal of dominant masculinity.

hegemony Domination through ideological control and consent.

hegemony Political and social domination of the bourgeois class in capitalist society, expressed not only in ideologies but in all realms of culture and social organization.

heterosexism The holding up of heterosexuality as the ideal and normal sexuality, rendering all other sexualities as abnormal and deviant.

heterosexual An individual who is attracted to members of the opposite sex.

hidden curriculum The unconscious, informal, and unwritten norms and rules that reinforce and maintain social conventions.

hieroglyphics An early form of visual communication developed by the Egyptians.

hominid ancestors Our human ancestors.

Homo sapiens Modern human beings.

homophobia An irrational fear or hatred of homosexuals that can lead to discrimination, harassment, and violence against them.

homosexual An individual who is sexually attracted to members of the same sex.

horticulturalism An economic system based on domesticating animals and plants.

hot media Media that contain a great deal of information but involve only a single sensory organ and demand very little from their audience (e.g., newspapers).

human exemptionalism paradigm The view that humans are exceptional but not exempt from the natural world.

human footprint The impact of human activities around the world.

human resource management An area of research dedicated to helping workers integrate into an organization and identify with its goals.

hunting and gathering An economic system based on small nomadic groups lightly exploiting animal and plant foods for immediate consumption.

hyperreal Baudrillard's belief that people's perceptions, as defined by media, lead to the sense of a simulated reality.

hypothesis A tentative statement about a particular relationship (between objects, people, or groups of people) that can be tested empirically.

I The unsocialized part of the self.

I Mead's term for that element of the self that is spontaneous, creative, impulsive, and often unpredictable.

iatrogenisis Term used to describe the sickness and injury caused by the health care system.

ideal types Classic or pure forms of a given social phenomenon (e.g., to some, the United States is an ideal form of democracy).

idealism The belief that the human mind and consciousness are more important in understanding the human condition than is the material world.

ideational culture Sorokin's term for a society driven to seek and achieve spiritual goals.

identity Our sense of self, that is socially produced, is fluid, and is multiple.

ideology A set of beliefs and values that support and justify the ruling class of a society.

illegitimate opportunity theory The assertion that individuals commit crime as a result of deviant learning environments.

imperialism The conquest of land, resources, and people's labour; the ideas, practices, and attitudes of colonizers.

income Money received annually from all sources.

indigenize To incorporate new cultural values and messages into the local culture.

indirect institutional discrimination When individuals are treated differently based on an unlawful criterion (physical disability, cultural origin, age, gender, religion), even though these actions were never intended to be discriminatory.

individual discrimination Occurs when an individual advantages or disadvantages another because of that person's group membership.

inductive logic A system of reasoning that moves from data to the formation of a theory.

industrialization An economic system based on using nonanimate sources of energy.

informal social movement A social movement that emerges to challenge a specific local issue.

inner-worldly An orientation that focuses on the tangible world and our own creature comforts and aspirations.

innovation Something new that inspires social change (e.g., cellphones).

instrumental role Responsible for engaging in paid labour outside the home.

integration The system needs to maintain solidarity while allowing the aspirations of subgroups.

interest group An established lobby group that works within the system to promote change.

intergenerational earnings A comparison between a father's and a son's earnings.

intergenerational mobility The comparison of adult children's social class to that of their parents.

internalized racism The internalization of racial categorizations into a person's identity.

intersectionality The simultaneous influence of multiple social relations, including race, gender, ethnicity, and class.

intersexed individuals Individuals born with ambiguous genitalia.

interviews Involve a researcher asking a series of questions of participants; they may be structured, semi-structured, or unstructured.

intimate femicide The killing of women by their intimate male partners.

intragenerational mobility Status movement throughout one's lifetime.

invention/innovation Occurs when existing cultural items are manipulated or modified to produce something new and socially valuable.

jen Confucian virtue of possessing a benevolent and humanitarian attitude.

karma The belief in cause and effect in a person's life; you reap what you sow.

Kuznets curve A graphic representation of the relationship between a society's economic development and its social inequality.

labelling theory The assertion that once labelled as deviant, people come to accept the label as part of their identity.

labour unions Organizations that represent workers to improve wages and working conditions through collective bargaining and strikes.

laissez-faire A point of view that opposes regulation of or interference with natural processes.

language A shared symbol system of rules and meanings that governs the production and interpretation of speech.

latency The system needs to motivate individuals to release their frustrations in socially appropriate ways.

latent functions The unintended consequences of an action or social pattern.

law A type of norm that is formally defined and enacted in legislation.

li Confucian desire to maintain proper relationships and rituals that enhance the life of the individual, the family, and the state.

liberation theology A movement by religious fundamentalists who advocate a literal interpretation of the Bible to promote greater social equality.

lieutenant-governor The Crown's representative in each of Canada's 10 provinces.

life course Socialization that occurs throughout one's adult life.

life expectancy The average lifespan of a newborn.

linguistic determinism Language determines how we perceive the world.

linguistic relativism Language reflects how we perceive the world.

localized collectivities Collectivities in which the members are located in each other's immediate physical presence.

long-term care The provision of any services required by persons who are dependent on others to meet their daily needs.

looking-glass self Cooley's belief that we develop our self-image through the cues we receive from others.

Lorenz curve A graphical line representing a society's deviation from equal wealth allocation.

low income cut-off (LICO) The level of income at which a household spends 55 percent or more of its gross income on basic necessities.

Luddites A loosely bound group of displaced textile workers who destroyed the new machines that put them out of work in the early nineteenth century.

macrosociology The study of society as a whole.

majority A definable category of people who are socially advantaged.

manifest functions The intended consequences of an action or social pattern.

MAPL system CRTC requirements used to determine whether a piece of music qualifies as Canadian content.

Marxist exploitation theory The assertion that the powerful economic elite promotes, and benefits from, prejudice and discrimination.

mass communication The transmission of messages by a person or group through a device to a large audience.

mass hysteria Occurs when people react to a real or imagined event with irrational or frantic fear.

mass media Forms of communication produced by a few people for consumption by the masses.

mass media Devices designed to communicate messages to a mass audience.

massification The mass increase in postsecondary enrolment, in contrast to the smaller numbers that once constituted an elite group.

material culture The tangible artifacts and physical objects found in a given culture.

McDonaldization The notion that insitutions are expected to function in ever more efficient ways, with a high degree of predictability and standardization.

Me The socialized part of the self.

Me Mead's term for the socialized element of the self.

means-tested programs Social programs based on need.

mechanical solidarity Describes early societies based on similarities and independence.

medicalization The increasing influence of the medical profession in defining what is normal/healthy and abnormal/ill.

melting pot The blending of new immigrants' traditions and cultural identity into the dominant American culture.

meritocracy A system of rewards based on personal attributes and demonstrated abilities.

meritocracy A society in which resources are distributed fairly on the basis of merit.

micro-expressions Largely uncontrollable, instantaneous full-face emotional reactions.

microsociology The study of individual or small-group dynamics within a larger society.

military juntas Military leaders who seize political power.

minority A definable category of people who are socially disadvantaged.

misogyny The hatred or deep dislike of women.

mixed methods An approach in which both quantitative and qualitative procedures are used.

mob A crowd that gathers to achieve an emotionally driven goal.

moksha A state of spiritual perfection.

monarchy A political system grounded on the rule of an individual or family that is passed from generation to generation.

monogamy The coupling of two people, excluding the intimate involvement of others.

monotheism Belief in a single, all-powerful, all-knowing god.

moral entrepreneur A person who influences or changes the creation or enforcement of a society's moral codes.

moral or political inequality According to Rousseau, inequality based on human classification of valuable things (e.g., money, social status).

moral panic The reaction of a group based on the false, distorted, or exaggerated perception that some group or behaviour threatens the well-being of society.

moral regulation The constitution of certain behaviours as immoral and thereby requiring public regulation.

mores Norms that carry a strong sense of social importance and necessity.

mortifications of the self The first stage of the resocialization process, in which a person's existing identity is stripped away.

movable type Gutenberg's invention that allowed individual letters or images to be moved without influencing the surrounding text.

multiracial feminism An approach that investigates race, class, and gender and gives a voice to women of colour who may feel alienated from traditional white feminism.

mysticism Weber's term for religions that seek harmony with the natural world, other people, and the human body.

natural or physical inequality According to Rousseau, inequality based on physical differences established by nature (e.g., strength, intelligence).

natural selection The biologically based principle that environmental pressures allow certain beneficial traits to be passed on to future generations.

natural state Hobbes's conception of the human condition before the emergence of formal social structures.

nature versus nurture The debate between whether biological forces or environment define the person we become.

neoevolutionary theory Lenski's analysis of the role that technology plays in people's adjustment to the physical world.

new ecological paradigm Emphasizes that modern industrial society is beginning to exceed the limits of the environment.

new environmental paradigm The view that human social actions occur within an ecosystem that has its own processes and limits.

new religious movement An informal group without defined structure; generally emerges around authoritarian and charismatic leaders who suppress rational thought to isolate members from the larger society.

newly industrialized countries (NICs) Poor countries that are beginning to industrialize.

nirvana The state of spiritual perfection.

non-monogamy Sexual interactions with more than one person during a given period, or any sexual relationship involving more than two people.

nonmaterial culture The intangible and abstract components of a society, including values and norms.

normalization A social process by which some practices and ways of living are marked as "normal" and others are marked as "abnormal."

norms Culturally defined rules that outline appropriate behaviours.

nuclear family An adult male, an adult female, and their offspring.

obesity A state characterized by a BMI of 30 percent or more in an adult.

occupational groups Durkheim's mechanism to promote the integration of workers.

open system A social system in which status is based on achieved attributes.

operational definition Description of something that allows it to be measured.

organic analogy The belief that society is like an organism with interdependent and interrelated parts.

organic solidarity Describes later societies organized around interdependence and the increasing division of labour.

Orientalism Said's concept of a discourse of power that creates a false distinction between a superior West and an inferior East.

other-worldly An orientation that focuses on separation from the everyday world and finding spiritual enlightenment.

pansexuality Romantic and sexual desire for people regardless of their gender identity or biological sex.

papyrus An early form of writing paper developed by the Egyptians.

participant observation Active participation by a researcher in a research setting; combines observation and participation in daily-life activities of research subjects (also known as *fieldwork*).

participatory action research (PAR) Research that combines an action-oriented goal and the participation of research subjects.

participatory democracy A system that requires citizens to be involved personally in decision-making through open and engaged debate and discussion.

pastoralism An economic system based on tending herds of large animals.

patriarchy A system where men control the political and economic resources of society.

patriarchy A pervasive and complex social and cultural system of male domination.

pattern maintenance Involves socially appropriate ways to display tensions and strains.

peer groups Consist of people who are closely related in age and share similar interests.

people first philosophy An approach that focuses on the individual and his or her abilities rather than limitations.

periphery Poor countries that are exploited for their raw materials by core countries.

permafrost Ground that has been frozen for more than two successive years.

personal troubles Personal challenges that require individual solutions.

personality An individual's relatively stable pattern of behaviours and feelings.

Philosophes French philosophers during the Enlightenment period who advocated critical thinking and practical knowledge.

phonetic alphabet A system of writing developed by early Greeks that uses letters to represent spoken sounds, enabling the expression of complex ideas.

political economy The interactions of politics, government and governing, and the social and cultural constitution of markets, institutions, and actors.

politics The endeavour to gain and maintain control of the state apparatus.

polyamory Mutually acknowledged emotional, sexual, or romantic connections with multiple partners.

polytheism Belief in many gods; can be diffuse, with all gods considered equal, or hierarchal, with gods ranked in importance or power.

positivism A theoretical approach that considers all understanding to be based on science.

post-colonial theory An approach that examines the ways in which the colonial past has shaped the social, political, and economic experiences of a colonized country.

post-industrialization An economic system based on knowledge-based activities and the service sector rather than on manufacturing goods.

power The ability to make others do something they would not otherwise do.

predestination The doctrine that God alone chooses (or elects) who is saved.

prejudice A negative prejudgment about a person or group that is irrational, long-lasting, and not based on fact.

primary labour market Jobs that provide stable and comfortable salaries, potential for growth and promotion, and fringe benefits, but also require postsecondary training or education.

primary sector Jobs dedicated to exploiting raw materials (e.g., logging, mining).

primary socialization Occurs when people learn the attitudes, values, and appropriate behaviours for individuals in their culture.

Prime Minister The head of the federal government in Canada.

profane Elements of the everyday world that do not inspire or motivate.

professions Prestigious occupations that require specialized knowledge and are regulated by a governing body.

proletariat The workers.

propaganda model The assertion that media companies, as businesses, will transmit content that reflects their commercial interests.

protest crowd A deliberately assembled crowd to rally support for a social movement.

public order crimes (victimless crimes) Crimes such as prostitution, gambling, and pornography that are believed to run contrary to moral principles.

public An accumulation of people who have a defined political interest for meeting and who are organized by a common mood.

qualitative sociology The study of nonmeasurable, subjective behaviours (e.g., the effects of divorce).

quality of mind Mills's term for the ability to view personal circumstance within a social context.

quantitative sociology The study of behaviours that can be measured (e.g., income levels).

Quiet Revolution A movement in Quebec during the 1960s, when political and religious traditions were challenged and the French struggled for greater economic, political, and cultural equality with the rest of Canada.

race Historically, a group of people that was physically and genetically distinguished from other groups.

racialization The process of attributing complex characteristics (e.g., intelligence) to racial categories.

racism An ideology that maintains that one "race" is inherently superior to another.

rational-legal authority The exercise of power as legitimated through laws, rules, and regulations.

reactionary movement A social movement that emerges when groups resist an event or decision they feel they cannot tolerate.

reformist movement A social movement that works within the existing social structure to improve society.

reincarnation The belief, associated with Eastern religions, that one's essence does not die and instead is reborn in another form.

relations of production The relationship between workers and owners.

relative poverty The inability to secure goods and services required to live a life equal to working-class standards.

reliability The consistency of a given result.

religion A set of organized beliefs about the supernatural or spiritual worlds that guides behaviour and joins people into communities of believers.

religious movement A social movement grounded in a spiritual or supernatural belief system.

religious pluralism A system in which many religions coexist and often compete with one another for members.

representative democracy A system in which citizens elect representatives to act on their behalf and to convey their concerns and issues to the broader collective.

research methods Strategies used to collect data.

research population A group of people that a researcher wishes to learn something about.

research A systematic approach of gathering data using an agreed-upon set of methods.

residential recycling rate The amount of waste diverted from landfills as a proportion of total waste generated.

resocialization The profound change or complete transformation of a person's personality as a result of being placed in a situation or an environment dedicated to changing his or her previous identity.

restorationist belief systems Assert that contemporary Christianity no longer reflects its foundational ideas.

revolutionary movement A social movement that seeks a complete reorganization of society.

riot A type of acting crowd that directs its anger toward multiple targets, moving from one to another in unpredictable ways.

role strain Stress that results when someone does not have sufficient resources to play a role or roles.

role-taking Assuming the position of another to better understand that person's perspective.

RSS (Really Simple Syndication) A web feed format that informs subscribers of new information posted on online services.

rule of law The requirement that no person is above the law and state power should not be applied arbitrarily.

ruling The exercise of power shaping people's actions.

rumour Specific information passed from person to person that lacks reliable evidence.

sacred Things or activities that are set apart, ritualized, and at times inspire emotional reactions.

safer sex Avoiding sexual behaviours that are considered high risk as well as engaging in various types of nongenital contact.

sample A subset of the larger research population.

samsara Reincarnation where the soul undergoes a series of births and deaths.

sanction A penalty for norm violation or a reward for norm adherence.

Sapir-Whorf hypothesis The assertion that language influences how we perceive the world (also known as *linguistic determinism*).

saturation The point at which a new technology or behaviour becomes a part of everyday living.

scapegoat theory The assertion that prejudice and discrimination originate in the frustrations of people who want to blame someone else for their problems.

second shift The domestic labour performed by employed women at home after finishing their paid workdays.

secondary analysis A research method involving analysis of existing data.

secondary labour market Jobs that are insecure and temporary, offer minimal pay, and provide few opportunities to advance.

secondary sector Jobs that transform raw materials into consumer goods (e.g., cars, furniture).

secondary socialization Follows primary socialization and occurs through participation in more specific groups with defined roles and expectations.

sect A small religious body, with exclusive or voluntary membership, that is somewhat separate from or hostile to the larger society.

secularization The process by which developed societies move away from explanations based on religion to ones based on science, rationality, and logic.

segregation The formal physical or social separation of dominant and minority groups.

selective perception The process whereby people see only those things that reinforce their preconceived perceptions.

self-fulfilling prophecy A prediction that, once made, causes the outcome to occur.

self-image An introspective composition of various features and attributes that people see themselves as having.

self One's identity, comprising a set of learned values and attitudes that develops through social interaction and defines one's self-image.

semi-periphery Peripheral countries moving toward becoming core, or core countries in decline.

senators Nonelected officials appointed by the federal government to represent their constituencies as well as the interests of all Canadians.

sensate culture Sorokin's term for a society that interprets the social and physical world through the senses.

separatism Voluntary structural and cultural isolation by minority groups from the dominant group.

serial monogamy A relationship pattern that has one monogamous relationship following another.

sex A determination of male or female on the basis of a set of socially agreed-upon biological criteria.

sexual health The avoidance of sexually transmitted infections and unwanted pregnancies and the fostering of healthy relationships.

sexual identity A broad term that can include our masculinity or femininity, our knowledge of our bodies, our sexual histories, and our sexual preferences.

sexual orientation An individual's sexual and emotional attraction to a person of a particular sex.

sexual scripts Cultural expectations about appropriate sexuality that are learned through social interaction.

sexually transmitted infections (STIs) Infections transmitted during unprotected sex (oral, anal, vaginal).

sick role A patterned social role that defines the behaviour that is appropriate for and expected of those who are sick.

significant others People we want to impress or gain approval from.

simulation Baudrillard's assertion that media create a "simulated" world through the reinforcement of certain images and signs.

social action theory Parsons's framework attempting to separate behaviours from actions to explain why people do what they do.

social change Changes in the typical features of a society (e.g., norms and values) over time.

social class A group who share a similar relationship to labour and who are aware of their conflict with other classes.

social class A group of individuals sharing a position in a social hierarchy, based on both birth and achievement.

social Darwinism Spencer's assertion that societies evolve according to the same principles as do biological organisms.

social determinants of health The conditions in which people are born, grow, and live.

social distance Bogardus's concept of the relative distance people feel between themselves and other racial/ethnic groups.

social facts General social features that exist on their own and are independent of individual manifestations.

social inequality Exists when certain attributes affect a person's access to socially valued resources.

social interaction The ways in which people interact in social settings, recognizing each person's subjective experiences and/or intentions.

social issues Challenges caused by larger social factors that require collective solutions.

social mobility Movement between social classes.

social movements Collections of people who are organized to bring about or resist social change.

social norms Shared and accepted standards and social expectations.

social reproduction The necessary activities that guarantee the day-to-day reproduction and survival of the population.

social status An individual's position within the class structure.

social stratification A society's hierarchical ranking of people into social classes.

socialism An economic system in which raw materials and the means of production are collectively owned.

socialization function Media's role in transmitting beliefs, values, and traditions from one generation to the next.

socialization The lifelong process by which we learn our culture, develop our personalities, and become functioning members of society.

sociobiology A science that uses evolutionary theory and genetic inheritance to examine the biological roots of social behaviour.

socioeconomic status (SES) A combination of variables (income, education, occupation, etc.) used to rank people into a hierarchical structure.

socioeconomic status (SES) Social status as determined by family income, parents' education level, parents' occupations, and the family's social standing within the community.

sociological imagination C. W. Mills's term for the ability to perceive how dynamic social forces influence individual lives.

sociological perspective A view of society based on the dynamic relationships between individuals and the larger social network in which we all live.

sociology The systematic study of human groups and their interactions.

space-biased media Media that can convey messages readily over physical distance.

species diversity The number of species that exist in an ecosystem.

spurious correlation A false correlation between two or more variables, even though it appears to be true.

state/welfare capitalism A political and economic system that combines free-market principles with varying degrees of social welfare programs.

state An institution that maintains a monopoly over the legitimate use of force in a given territory.

status group A group of people who share similar social status, lifestyles, world views, occupations, and standards of living.

status inconsistency Occurs when an individual occupies several differently ranked statuses at the same time.

status symbols Material indicators that demonstrate a person's social and economic position.

stereotype A stable and sweeping generalization about a category of people.

strain theory The assertion that people experience strain when culturally defined goals cannot be met through socially approved means.

structure The network of relatively stable opportunities and constraints influencing individual behaviours.

subculture A group within a population whose values, norms, folkways, or mores set them apart from the mainstream culture.

superstructure All of the things that society values and aspires to once its material needs are met (e.g., religion, politics, law).

surveillance function Media's role in gathering and disseminating information to the population.

survey A research method in which respondents answer pre-set questions.

survival of the fittest Spencer's interpretation of biological principles to justify why only the strong should survive.

sustainable development The belief that economic development can occur without damaging the environment.

symbol Something that stands for or represents something else.

symbolic interactionism A perspective asserting that people and societies are defined and created through the interactions of individuals.

symbolic token A medium of exchange (such as money).

sympathetic introspection Cooley's concept of the value of putting yourself into another person's shoes and seeing the world as he or she does.

taboo A prohibition on actions deemed immoral or disgusting.

technology Anything that provides an artificial means to achieve a given end or result.

tension maintenance Recognizes the internal tensions and strains that influence all actors.

territorial commissioner The federal government's representative in each of Canada's three territories.

tertiary sector Jobs that provide services (e.g., teaching, nursing) rather than goods.

theocracy A form of government in which a god or other supernatural being is seen as the supreme civil ruler.

theory A statement that tries to explain how certain facts or variables are related in order to predict future events.

Thomas theorem Assertion that things people define as real are real in their consequences.

time–space distanciation The separation of time and space, which allows social relations to shift from a local to a global context.

time-biased media Media that have longevity but whose form prevents their transmission over physical distance (e.g., cave art, hieroglyphics).

total institution A setting in which people are isolated from society and supervised by an administrative staff.

totem An object that has special significance and meaning for a group of believers.

traditional authority The exercise of power as legitimated by long-established cultural patterns and traditions.

transgender An umbrella term for a range of people who do not fit into normative constructions of sex and gender.

transnational corporation (TNC) A large company based in one country with overseas operations in two or more other countries.

transphobia Discrimination directed toward transsexuals or transgendered individuals.

transsexual A person who undergoes sex reassignment, which may include surgeries.

triangulation An approach in which more than one research method is used in an attempt to more fully understand an area of study

trickle-down theory The assertion that stimulating overall economic growth will ultimately help the poor.

triple bottom line A company's balance sheet according to *profit*, *people*, and the *planet*.

underdeveloped countries Countries that have yet to industrialize, or that have been intentionally restricted in their development by developed nations.

undeveloped countries Countries with poor economies; problematically implies a lack of economic talent or exposure.

unilinear evolutionary theory The assertion that there is only one path through which an organism or society can evolve.

universal evolutionary theory The assertion that all societies must progress in the same manner.

universal plans Social programs provided to everyone.

urban legend A short, persistent, nonverifiable tale with an ironic or supernatural twist.

validity The accuracy of a given measurement.

values Cultural assessments that identify something as right, desirable, and moral.

values Beliefs about ideal goals and behaviours that serve as standards for social life.

variables Characteristics of objects, people, or groups of people that can be measured.

verstehen Weber's term for a deep understanding and interpretation of subjective social meanings.

vested interests Veblen's term to describe why privileged members of society resist change.

wealth Net accumulated assets, including homes, land, and stocks.

Web 2.0 Interactive online tools dedicated to promoting a greater sense of community.

wiki An online body of information to which anyone can add or modify content.

References

Aaron, P. G., & Joshi, R. M. (2006). Written language is as natural as spoken language: A biolinguistic perspective. *Reading Psychology, 27*(4), 263–311. doi:10.1080/02702710600846803

Abbott, P., Wallace, C., & Tyler, M. (2005). *An introduction to sociology: Feminist perspectives* (3rd ed.). London: Routledge.

Abelson, R., Friquegnon, M., & Lockwood, M. (Eds.). (1977). *The philosophical imagination: An introduction to philosophy.* New York: St. Martin's Press.

Aboriginal Affairs and Northern Development. (2006). *Royal commission on Aboriginal peoples.* Retrieved 22/04/2008, from http://www.ainc-inac. gc.ca/ch/rcap/sg/sgmm_e.html

Aboriginal Affairs and Northern Development Canada. (2011). Aboriginal demographics from the 2011 national household survey. Accessed 03/06/2014, from http://www.aadnc-aandc.gc.ca/eng/1370438978311/1370439050610#chp2

Aboriginal Affairs and Northern Development Canada. (2013). Backgrounder – Aboriginal affairs and northern development Canada's financial picture (2013–2014). Accessed 02/13/2014, from http://www.aadnc-aandc.gc.ca/eng/1363029324938/1363029382616

Abrams, D., Rutland, A., Pelletier, J., & Ferrell, J. M. (2009). Children's group nous: Understanding and applying peer exclusion within and between groups. *Child Development, 80*(1), 224–243. doi:10.1111/j.1467-8624.2008.01256.x

Abrams, P. (1968). *The origins of British sociology: 1834–1914.* Chicago: University of Chicago Press.

Aboud, F. E. (2008). A social-cognitive developmental theory of prejudice. In *Handbook of race, racism, and the developing child* (pp. 55–71). Hoboken, NJ: John Wiley & Sons.

Abu-Lughod, J. L. (1989). *Before European hegemony: The world system A.D. 1250–1350.* New York: Oxford University Press.

Acemoglu, D., & Yared, P. (2010). Political limits to globalization. *American Economic Review, 100* (2, PAPERS AND PROCEEDINGS OF THE One Hundred Twenty Second Annual Meeting OF THE AMERICAN ECONOMIC ASSOCIATION), 83–88. Retrieved from http://www.jstor.org/stable/27804968

Acker, J. (2006). Inequality regimes: Gender, class and race in organizations. *Gender and Society, 20,* 441–464.

Acker, S. (1999). *The realities of teachers' work: Never a dull moment.* London: Cassell.

Acker, S., & Feuerverger, G. (1996). Doing good and feeling bad: The work of women university teachers. *Cambridge Journal of Education, 26*(3), 401–422.

Acker, S., & Webber, M. (2006). Women working in academe: Approach with care. In C. Skelton, B. Francis & L. Smulyan (Eds.), *The SAGE handbook of gender and education* (pp. 483–496). London; Thousand Oaks; New Delhi: SAGE Publications.

Acker, S., Webber, M., & Smyth, E. (2010). *Discipline and publish? Early career faculty meet accountability governance, new managerialism, and (maybe) gender equity.* Keele University, Staffordshire England: Gender, Work and Organization 6th Biennial International Interdisciplinary Conference.

Adams, J. (2010). Motivational narratives and assessments of the body after cosmetic surgery. *Qualitative Health Research, 20*(6), 755–767.

Adams, L. (2008). *The shifting terrain of feminist theory and activism: University-based women's centres and third wave feminism.* Unpublished MA, Brock University, St. Catharines.

Adi, H., & Sherwood, M. (2003). *Pan-African history: Political figures from Africa and the diaspora since 1787.* New York: Routledge.

Adkins, L. (2005). Feminist social theory. In A. Harrington (Ed.), *Modern social theory: An introduction* (pp. 233–251). Oxford: Oxford University Press.

Adorno, T. W., Frenkel-Brunswik, E., Levinson, D. J., & Sanford, R. N. (1950). *The authoritarian personality.* New York: Harper & Row.

Agarwal, G. (2007). Obesity registers. *CMAJ: Canadian Medical Association Journal Supplement, 176*(1), 65–65. doi:10.1503/cmaj.1060166

Aguirre, B. E., Wenger, D., & Vigo, G. (1998). A test of the emergent norm theory of collective behavior. *Sociological Forum, 13*(2), 301–320. Retrieved from http://library.mtroyal.ca:2048/login?url=http://search. ebscohost.com/login.aspx?direct=true&AuthType=ip,url,cookie,uid&db=a9h&AN=847808&site=ehost-live

AIDS.gov. (2012). Global statistics. Accessed 27/02/ 2014, from aids.gov/hiv-aids-basics/hiv-aids-101/global-statistics/

Aiken, C. F. (1908). *The Catholic encyclopedia: Confucianism* (Volume IV ed.). New York: Robert Appleton Company. Retrieved from http://www.newadvent.org/cathen/04223b.htm

Akers, R., & Sellers, C. (2008). *Criminological theories: Introduction, evaluation and application* (5th ed.). Los Angeles: Roxbury.

Al-Shehab, A. J. (2008). Gender and racial representation in children's television programming in Kuwait: Implications for education. *Social Behavior & Personality: An International Journal, 36*(1), 49–63. Retrieved from http://library.mtroyal.ca:2048/login?url=http://library.mtroyal.ca:2924/login.aspx?direct=true&AuthType=ip,url,cookie,uid&db=a9h&AN=30104108&site=ehost-live

Al-Waqfi, M., & Jain, H. C. (2008). Racial inequality in employment in Canada: Empirical analysis and emerging trends. *Canadian Public Administration, 51*(3), 429–453.

Alberta Learning Information Service. (2006). *Prevent family violence,* from http://www.alis.gov.ab.ca/tips/archive.asp?EK=7759

Albrecht, G. L. (1992). *The disability business: Rehabilitation in America.* Newbury Park, CA: Sage Publications, Ltd.

Alexander, J. C. (1998). *Neofunctionalism and after.* Malden, MA: Blackwell.

Alfonso-Faus, A. (2006). Mass-boom versus big-bang: An alternative model. *AIP Conference Proceedings, 822*(1), 107–109.

Allan, K. (2006). *Contemporary social and sociological theory: Visualizing social worlds.* Thousand Oaks: Pine Forge Press.

Allen, A. (2008). Power and the politics of difference: Oppression, empowerment, and transnational justice. *Hypatia, 23*(3), 157–172. Retrieved from http://library.mtroyal.ca:2057/login.aspx?direct=true&AuthType=ip,url,cookie,uid&db=a9h&AN=33024936&site=ehost-live

Allen, L. (2007). Denying the sexual subject: Schools' regulation of student sexuality. *British Educational Research Journal, 33*(2), 221–234.

Allen, M. P. (1989). *The founding fortunes: A new anatomy of the super-rich families in America.* New York: E.P. Dutton.

Allen, T. (2007). Katrina: Race, class and poverty: Reflections and analysis. *Journal of Black Studies, 37*(4), 466–468.

Alliance for Equality of Blind Canadians. (2008). *AEBC supports reinstatement of court challenges Program.* Retrieved 28/01/2008, from http://www.blindcanadians.ca/reports/index.php?ReportID=39

AlMarri, T. S. K., Oei, T. P. S., & Al-Adawi, S. (2009). The development of the short Muslim practice and belief scale. *Mental Health, Religion & Culture, 12*(5), 415–426. doi:10.1080/13674670802637643

Almey, M. (2009). *Women in Canada: Work chapter updates.* Retrieved 18/09/2010, from http://www.statcan.gc.ca/pub/89f0133x/89f0133x2006000-eng.htm

Altemeyer, R. (1981). *Right-wing authoritarianism.* Winnipeg: University of Manitoba Press.

Altheide, D. L. (2003). The mass media. (pp. 657–684). Walnut Creek, CA: Altamira Press.

Alwin, D. F. (2008). Handbook of cognitive aging: Interdisciplinary perspectives. In S. M. Hofer, & D. F. Alwin (Eds.), (pp. 418–444). Thousand Oaks, CA: Sage.

Ambrose, D. (2006). 30,000 BC: Painting animality. *Angelaki: Journal of the Theoretical Humanities, 11*(2), 137–152. doi:10.1080/09697250601029309

American Society of Plastic Surgeons (ASPS). (2012). 2011 plastic surgery statistics report. Accessed 01/04/2014, from http://www.plasticsurgery.org/Documents/news-resources/statistics/2011-statistics/2011-cosmetic-procedures-trends-statistics.pdf

American Sociological Association. (2002). *Departmental listings for 1999.* Retrieved 10/02/2002, from www.asanet.org/pubs/dod.html

Anapol, D. (1997). *Polyamory: The new love without limits secrets of sustainable intimate relationships.* San Rafael: Internet Resource Center.

Andersen, M. L., & Francis, H. T. (2006). *Sociology: Understanding a diverse society* (4th ed.). Belmont, CA: Thomson Wadsworth.

Anderson, K. (1991). *Chain her by one foot. The subjugation of women in 17th century New France.* New York: Routledge.

Angus, F. (2000). *Key to the midway: Masculinity at work in a western Canadian carnival.* Unpublished Ph.D., University of British Columbia, Vancouver.

Anheier, H. K. (2005). *Nonprofit organizations: Theory, management, policy.* New York: Routledge, Inc.

Anker, J. (2008). Organizing homeless people: Exploring the emergence of a user organization in Denmark. *Critical Social Policy, 28*(1), 27–50. Retrieved from http://library.mtroyal.ca:2048/login?url=http://search.ebscohost.com/login.aspx?direct=true&AuthType=ip,url,cookie,uid&db=a9h&AN=28842183&site=ehost-live

Anthropology Today. (2011). Front and back covers. *Anthropology Today, 27*(2), i–ii. doi:10.1111/j.1467-8322.2011.027c2.x

Arai, S., & Kivel, B. D. (2009). Critical race theory and social justice perspectives on whiteness, difference(s) and (anti)racism: A fourth wave of race research in leisure studies. *Journal of Leisure Research, 41*(4), 459–470. Retrieved from http://library.mtroyal.ca:2057/login.aspx?direct=true&AuthType=ip,url,cookie,uid&db=a9h&AN=47685961&site=ehost-live

Archibald, J. (1995). To keep the fire going: The challenge of First Nations education in the year 2000. In R. Ghosh, & D. Ray (Eds.), *Social change and education in Canada* (3rd ed., pp. 342–357). Toronto: Harcourt Brace.

Armstrong, E. A. (2006). Negotiating feminist identities and theatre of the oppressed. In J. Cohen-Cruz, & M. Schutzams (Eds.), *A boal companion: Dialogues on theatre and cultural politics* (pp. 173–184). New York: Routledge.

Armstrong, P. (2004). Gender relations. In L. Tepperman, & J. Curtis (Eds.), *Sociology* (pp. 380–401). Toronto: Oxford University Press.

Armstrong, P., & Armstrong, H. (1994). *The double ghetto: Canadian women and their segregated work.* Toronto, ON: McClelland and Stewart.

Arnot, M. (2002). *Reproducing gender: Essays on educational theory and feminist politics.* London: Routledge/Falmer.

Arp, R. (Ed.). (2013). *1001 ideas that changed the way we think.* New York: Simon and Shuster.

Arsenault, N., Anderson, G., & Swedburg, R. (1998). Understanding older adults in education: Decision-making. *Educational Gerontology, 24*(2), 101. Retrieved from http://library.mtroyal.ca:2048/login?url=http://search.ebscohost.com/login.aspx?direct=true&AuthType=ip,url,cookie,uid&db=a9h&AN=443551&site=ehost-live

Ash, A. (2010). The remainders of race. *Theory, Culture & Society, 27*(1), 1–23.

Assembly of First Nations. (2013). Charter of the assembly of First Nations. Accessed 02/13/2014, from http://www.afn.ca/index.php/en/about-afn/charter-of-the-assembly-of-first-nations

Association of Canadian Community Colleges. (2010). *About colleges and institutes: Members of the ACCC.* Retrieved 11/01/2010, from http://www.accc.ca/english/colleges/membership_list.htm

Atchley, R. C. (1999). *Continuity and adaptation in aging: Creating positive experiences.* Baltimore, MD: Johns Hopkins University.

Atkinson, A. B., Rainwater, L., & Smeedling, T. M. (1995). *Income distribution in OECD countries: Evidence from the Luxembourg income study (LIS)* (Social Policies Study No. 18). Paris: Organization for Economic Cooperation & Development.

Atkinson, M. (2011). *Deconstructing men & masculinities.* Don Mills, ON: Oxford University Presss.

Atkinson, M., & Kehler, M. (2012). Boys, bullying and biopedagogies in physical education. *Thymos, 6*(2), 166–187.

Atran, S. (2010). *Talking to the enemy: Faith, brotherhood, and the (un)making of terrorists.* New York, NY: Harper-Collins.

Attallah, P. (2002). The audience. In P. Attallah, & L. R. Shade (Eds.), *Mediascapes: New patterns in Canadian communication* (pp. 90–106). Scarborough, ON: Thomson/Nelson.

Attwood, F. (2007). Sluts and riot grrrls: Female identity and sexual agency. *Journal of Gender Studies, 16*(3), 233–247.

Auletta, K. (1982). *The underclass.* New York: Random House.

Austin, Z. (2005). Mentorship and mitigation of culture shock: Foreign-trained pharmacists in Canada. *Mentoring & Tutoring: Partnership in Learning, 13*(1), 133–149.

Authoritarian Personality. (n.d.). *Authoritarian personality (hypnotic world psychology).* Retrieved 16/01/2008, from http://psychology.hypnoticworld.com/influence_personality/authoritarian_personality.php

Avery, J. (2003). *Information theory and evolution.* New Jersey, NJ: World Scientific.

Aydemir, A., Chen, W., & Corak, M. (2009). Intergenerational earnings mobility among the children of Canadian immigrants. *Review of Economics and Statistics, 91*(2), 377–397. doi:http://library.mtroyal.ca:2325/loi/rest

Aylward, C. (1999). *Canadian critical race theory: Racism and the law.* Halifax: Fernwood.

Azadi, S. [with Angela Ferrante]. (1987). *Out of Iran: A woman's escape from the Ayatollahs.* Toronto, ON: McCelland-Bantam, Inc.

Babad, E. Y., Birnbaum, M., & Benne, K. D. (1983). *The social self: Group influences on personal identity.* Beverly Hills, CA: Sage Publications, Ltd.

Babbie, E. (1994). *What is society?.* Thousand Oaks, CA: Pine Forge Press.

Babbie, E., & Benaquisto, L. (2010). *Fundamentals of social research* (2nd Canadian ed.). Toronto: Nelson.

Babones, S. J. (2008). Income inequality and population health: Correlation and causality. *Social Science & Medicine, 66*(7), 1614–1626.

Babooram, A., & Wang, J. (2008). *Recycling in Canada.* Retrieved 24/07/2008, from http://www.statcan.ca/english/freepub/16-002-XIE/2007001/article/10174-en.htm

Baer, D., Grabb, E., & Johnston, W. A. (1990). The values of Canadians and Americans: A critical analysis and reassessment. *Social Forces, 68*(3), 693–713.

Baer, H. (2008). Global warming as a by-product of the capitalist treadmill of production and consumption—the need for an alternative global system. *Australian Journal of Anthropology, 19*(1), 58–62. Retrieved from http://library.mtroyal.ca:2048/login?url=http://search.ebscohost.com/login.aspx?direct=true&AuthType=ip,url,cookie,uid&db=a9h&AN=31341365&site=ehost-live

Baez, B., & Talburt, S. (2008). Governing for responsibility and with love: Parents and children between home and school. *Educational Theory, 58*(1), 25–43.

Bagguley, P., & Mann, K. (1992). Idle thieving bastards? scholarly representation of the 'underclass.' *Work, Employment and Society, 6*, 113–126.

Bain Lindsay, H. (2006). *Race and waste in Nova Scotia*. Retrieved 27/07/2008, from http://www.dominionpaper.ca/environment/2006/12/07/race_and_w.html

Bainbridge, W. S. (1987). Collective behavior and social movements. In R. Stark (Ed.), *Sociology* (2nd ed., pp. 544–576). Belmont, CA: Wadsworth.

Bainbridge, W. S. (2007). Converging technologies and human destiny. *Journal of Medicine & Philosophy, 32*(3), 197–216. doi:10.1080/03605310701396968

Baker, M. (2001). Paid and unpaid work: How do families divide their labour? In M. Baker (Ed.), *Families: Changing trends in Canada* (4th ed., pp. 96–115). Toronto: McGraw-Hill Ryerson.

Baker, M. (2004). *Families: Changing trends in Canada*. Toronto: McGraw-Hill Ryerson.

Baker Jr, M. D., & Maner, J. K. (2008). Risk-taking as a situationally sensitive male mating strategy. *Evolution and Human Behavior, 29*(6), 391–395.

Balikci, A. (1970). *The Netsilik Eskimo*. Garden City, New York: The American Museum of Natural History.

Bampton, R., & Cowton, C. (2002). The e-interview. *Forum Qualitative Sozialforschung/ Forum: Qualitative Social Research, 3*(2). Retrieved from http://www.qualitative-research.net/fqs/fws-eng.htm

Bandura, A. (1977). *Social learning theory*. New York: General Learning Press.

Banerjee, D., & Bell, M. M. (2007). Ecogender: Locating gender in environmental social science. *Society & Natural Resources, 20*(1), 3–19. doi:10.1080/08941920600981272

Baptiste, F., & Lewis, R. (Eds.). (2008). *Caribbean reasonings: George Padmore, pan-African revolutionary*. Kingston, Jamaica: Ian Randle Publishers.

Baran, P. (1957). *The political economy of growth*. New York: Monthly Review Press.

Baran, S. J., & Davis, D. K. (2009). *Mass communication theory: Foundations, ferment, and future* (5th ed.). Belmont, CA: Thomson Wadsworth.

Barker, L. (2006). Teaching evolutionary psychology: An interview with David M. Buss. *Teaching of Psychology, 33*(1), 69–76.

Barker, M. (2005). This is my partner, and this is my. . .partner's partner: Constructing a polyamorous identity in a monogamous world. *Journal of Constructivist Psychology, 18*(1), 75–88.

Barlow, M. (2002). *Water incorporated; the commodification of the world's water-globalization-global policy forum*. Retrieved 8/5/2008, from http://www.globalpolicy.org/globaliz/special/2002/0305water.htm

Barlow, M. (2006). Globalization harms the World's cultures. In L. I. Gerdes (Ed.), *Globalization opposing viewpoints* (pp. 42–48). New York: Thompson/Gale.

Barnes-Powell, T., & Letherby, G. (1998). All in a day's work: Gendered care work in higher education. In D. Malina, & S. Maslin-Prothero (Eds.), *Suviving the academy: Feminist perspectives* (pp. 69–77). London: The Falmer Press.

Barness, L. A. (2007). Obesity in children. *Fetal & Pediatric Pathology, 26*(2), 75–85. doi:10.1080/15513810701448755

Barnett, B. M. (2004). Introduction: The life, career, and social thought of Gerhard Lenski—Scholar, teacher, mentor, leader. *Sociological Theory, 22*(2), 163–193. doi:10.1111/j.0735-2751.2004.00210.x

Barone, C. (2007). A neo-Durkheimian analysis of a new religious movement: The case of Soka Gakkai in Italy. *Theory & Society, 36*(2), 117–140. doi:10.1007/s11186-007-9023-3

Barrera, A. (2008). Globalization's shifting economic and moral terrain: Contesting marketplace mores. *Theological Studies, 69*(2), 290–308. Retrieved from http://library.mtroyal.ca:2048/login?url=http://search.ebscohost.com/login.aspx?direct=true&AuthType=ip,url,cookie,uid&db=a9h&AN=32140358&site=ehost-live

Barron, C., & Lacombe, D. (2005). Moral panic and the nasty girl. *Canadian Review of Sociology and Anthropology, 42*(1), 51–69.

Bartels, K. P. R. (2009). The disregard for Weber's herrschaft. *Administrative Theory & Praxis (M.E.Sharpe), 31*(4), 447–478. doi:10.2753/ATP1084-1806310401

Bartlett, M. S., Donato, G., Movellan, J. R., Hager, J. C., Ekman, P., & Sejnowski, T. J. (1999). Face image analysis for expression measurement and detection of deceit. 6th Joint Symposium on Neural Computation Proceedings, 8–15.

Basow, S. (1992). *Gender stereotypes and roles* (3rd ed.). Pacific Grove, California: Brooks/Cole Publishing.

Bassett, E., & O'Riordan, K. (2002). Ethics of internet research: Contesting the human subjects research model. *Ethics and Information Technology, 4*(3), 233–247.

Bathum, M. E., & Bauman, L. C. (2007). A sense of community among immigrant Latinas. *Family & Community Health, 30*(3), 167–177.

Bauch, H. (2007). *Should we sell our water to the U.S.?* Retrieved 07/08/2008, from http://www.canada.com/montrealgazette/features/waterunlimited/story.html?id=24ca3d1d-fb73-4233-903b-ccd07dc00827

Baudrillard, J. (1983). *Simulations*. New York: Semiotext(e).

Bauer, G., Hammond, R., Travers, R., Kaay, M., Hohenadel, K., & Boyce, M. (2009). "I don't think this is theoretical; this is our lives": How erasure impacts health care for transgender people. *Journal of the Assioaction of Nurses in AIDS Care, 20*(5), 348–361.

Bauman, Z. (1989). *Modernity and the holocaust*. Cambridge, UK: Polity Press.

BBC News. (2010). *Over 5 billion mobile phone connections worldwide*. Retrieved 29/04/2011, from http://www.bbc.co.uk/news/10569081

BC Ministry of Aboriginal Affairs. (2007). *General B.C. and Canada First Nations statistics - Aboriginal relations and reconciliation*. Retrieved 21/06/2010, from http://www.gov.bc.ca/arr/reports/facts/overview.html

Beagan, B. L. (2005). Everyday classism in medical school: Experiencing marginality and resistane. *Medical Education, 39*, 777–784.

Beattie, A. J., Hay, M., Magnusson, B., de Nys, R., Smeathers, J., & Vincent, J. F. V. (2011). Ecology and bioprospecting. *Austral Ecology, 36*(3), 341–356. doi:10.1111/j.1442-9993.2010.02170.x

Beaujot, R. (2000). *Earning and caring in Canadian families*. Peterborough: Broadview Press.

Beccaria, C. (1764 (reprint 1963). *On crimes and punishments*. Indianapolis: Bobbs-Merrill.

Beck, U. (2008). *Risk society's 'cosmopolitan moment'*. Unpublished manuscript.

Becker, H. (1952). Social class variations in the teacher-pupil relationship. *Journal of Educational Sociology, 25*, 451–465.

Becker, H. (1953). The teacher in the authority system of the public school, *Journal of Educational Sociology, 27*(November, 1953), 128–141.

Becker, H. (1963). *Outsiders: Studies in the sociology of deviance*. London: Free Press of Glencoe.

Becker, M. (2007). World social forum. *Peace & Change, 32*(2), 203–220. doi:10.1111/j.1468-0130.2007.00427.x

Beckerman, S., Erickson, P., Yost, J., Regalado, J., Jaramillo, L., Sparks, C., Iromenga, M., & Long, K. (2009). Life Histories, Blood Revenge, and Reproductive Success among the Waorani of Ecuador. *Proceedings of the National Academy of Sciences, 106*(20), 8134–8139.

Bedard, G. (2000). Deconstructing whiteness: Pedagogical implications for anti-racism education. In G. J. S. Dei, & A. Calliste (Eds.), *Power, knowledge and anti-racism education: A critical reader* (pp. 41–56). Halifax: Fernwood Publishing.

Beddoes, Z. M. (2012). For richer, for poorer. *The Economist*, Oct 13, 2012 (print edition). Accessed online 01/03/2014, from http://www.economist.com/node/21564414

Bedell, D. (2001). *Unlikely innovators: Many online technologies were first perfected by the adult industry*. Retrieved 30/08/2008, from http://www.adultwebmasterschool.com/news/adulttech.htm

Beech, H. (2002, July 1). With women so scarce, what can men do? *Time*, 8.

Beecher, H. (1966). Ethics and clinical research. *New England Journal of Medicine, 274*(24), 1354–1360.

Beerkens, E., & Derwende, M. (2007). The paradox in international cooperation: Institutionally embedded universities in a global environment. *Higher Education, 53*(1), 61–79. doi:10.1007/s10734-005-7695-z

Beetham, D. (1996). *Bureaucracy* (2nd ed.). Minneapolis, MN: University of Minnesota Press.

Behrouzi, M. (2005). *Democracy as the political empowerment of the people: The betrayal of an Ideal.* Lanham, MD: Lexington Books.

Bell, M. M., & Carolan, M. S. (2004). *An invitation to environmental sociology* (2nd ed.). Thousand Oaks, CA: Pine Forge Press.

Bellah, R. N. (1975). *The broken covenant: American civil religion in time of trial.* Chicago: University of Chicago Press.

Bellah, R., Madsen, R., Sullivan, W. M., Swidler, A., & Tipton, S. M. (1996). *Habits of the heart: Individualism and commitment in American life.* (2nd ed.). Berkeley, CA: University of California Press.

Bellis, M. (2008). *The invention of radio.* Retrieved 04/05/2008, from http://inventors.about.com/od/rstartinventions/a/radio.htm

Bengston, V. L. (2001). Beyond the nuclear family: The increasing importance of multigenerational bonds. *Journal of Marriage & Family, 63*(1), 1.

Bentham, J. (1838 (reprint 1962)). In John Bowring (Ed.), *The works of Jeremy Bentham.* Russell and Russell: New York.

Bentley, C. S. (2008). The great information equalizer. *New American (08856540), 24*(8), 41–42. Retrieved from http://library.mtroyal.ca:2048/login?url=http://search.ebscohost.com/login.aspx?direct=true&AuthType=ip,url,cookie,uid&db=a9h&AN=31686042&site=ehost-live

Beres, M., & Farvid, P. (2010). Sexual ethics and young women's accounts of heterosexual casual sex. *Sexualities, 13,* 377–393.

Bereska, T. (2008). *Deviance, conformity, and social control* (4th ed.). Toronto: Pearson.

Berg, E., Barry, J., & Chandler, J. (2010). Essentially political: Gender and the politics of care in Mumbai. *International Feminist Journal of Politics, 12*(1), 25–44.

Bergman, M. K. (2001). White paper: The deep web: Surfacing hidden value. *Journal of Electronic Publishing, 7*(1). doi:10.3998/3336451.0007.104

Berkowitz, P. (2005). The court, the constitution, and the culture of freedom. *Policy Review, 132,* 3–25.

Bermanis, S., Canetti-Nisim, D., & Pedahzur, A. (2004). Religious fundamentalism and the extreme right-wing camp in israel. *Patterns of Prejudice, 38*(2), 159–176. Retrieved from http://library.mtroyal.ca:2048/login?url=http://search.ebscohost.com/login.aspx?direct=true&AuthType=ip,url,cookie,uid&db=a9h&AN=13133229&site=ehost-live

Bernburg, J., Kohn, M., & Rivera, C. (2006). Official labeling, criminal embeddedness and subsequent delinquency: A longitudinal test of labelling theory. *Journal of Research in Crime and Delinquency, 43*(1), 67–88.

Bernd, S., & Brown, R. (2000). Perceived intragroup homogeneity in minority-majority contexts. In C. Stangor (Ed.), *Stereotypes and prejudice: Key readings* (pp. 326–337). New York: Psychology Press.

Berndt, T. J., & Keefe, K. (1995). Friends' influence on adolescents' adjustment to school. *Child Development, 66*(5), 1312–1329.

Bernstein, H. (2006). Studying development/development studies. *African Studies, 65*(1), 45–62. doi:10.1080/00020180600771733

Berry, D. (2004). Internet research: Privacy, ethics and alienation: An open source approach. *Internet Research, 14*(4), 323–332.

Berthold, D. (2010). Tidy whiteness: A genealogy of race, purity, and hygiene. *Ethics & the Environment, 15*(1), 1–26. Retrieved from http://search.ebscohost.com/login.aspx?direct=true&AuthType=ip,url,cookie,uid&db=a9h&AN=50739222&site=ehost-live

Besley, A. C. (2005). Self-denial or self-mastery? Foucault's genealogy of the confessional self. *British Journal of Guidance & Counselling, 33*(3), 365–382.

Bessenoff, G. R. (2006). Can the media affect us? Social comparison, self-discrepancy, and the thin ideal. *Psychology of Women Quarterly, 30*(3), 239–251. doi:10.1111/j.1471-6402.2006.00292.x

Best, J. (2006). Blumer's dilemma: The critic as a tragic figure. *American Sociologist, 37*(3), 5–14. Retrieved from http://library.mtroyal.ca:2048/login?url=http://search.ebscohost.com/login.aspx?direct=true&AuthType=ip,url,cookie,uid&db=a9h&AN=23815021&site=ehost-live

Bevington, D., & Dixon, C. (2005). Movement-relevant theory: Rethinking social movement scholarship and activism. *Social Movement Studies, 4*(3), 185–208. doi:10.1080/14742830500329838

Bhabha, H. (1994). *The location of culture.* New York: Routledge.

Bhambra, G. K. (2007). Sociology and postcolonialism: Another 'missing' revolution? *Sociology, 41*(5), 871–884.

Birch, K. (2007). The totalitarian corporation? *Totalitarian Movements & Political Religions, 8*(1), 153–161. doi:10.1080/14690760601121739

Bird, D., & O'Connell, J. (2006). Behavioral ecology and archaeology. *Journal of Archaeological Research, 14*(2), 143–188. Retrieved from http://library.mtroyal.ca:2048/login?url=http://library.mtroyal.ca:2924/login.aspx?direct=true&AuthType=ip,url,cookie,uid&db=a9h&AN=21844837&site=ehost-live

Bird, S., Litt, J., & Wang, Y. (2004). Creating status of women reports: Institutional housekeeping as "women's work." *National Women's Studies Association Journal, 16*(1), 194–206.

Bishku-Aykul, J. (2009). *Supreme court rejects bill 104 - the McGill daily.* Retrieved 22/06/2010, from http://www.mcgilldaily.com/articles/22204

Bittman, M., England, P., Sayer, L., Fohlbre, N., & Matheson, G. (2003). When does gender trump money? *American Journal of Sociology, 190*(1), 186–214.

Black, E. (2003). *War against the weak.* New York, New York: Four Walls Eight Windows/ Turnaround.

Black, I. (2014). Syrian regime document trove shows evidence of 'industrial scale' killing of detainees. Accessed 02/10/2014, from http://www.theguardian.com/world/2014/jan/20/evidence-industrial-scale-killing-syria-war-crimes

Blacks Academy. (n.d.). *Theories of poverty: The culture of poverty.* Retrieved 13/12/2007, from http://www.blacksacademy.net/content/3253.html

Blackwell, J. C., Smith, M. E. G., & Sorenson, J. S. (Eds.). (2003). *Culture of prejudice: Arguments in critical social science.* Peterborough, ON: Broadview Press.

Blackwood, E. (2009). Trans identities and contingent masculinities: Being tombois in everyday practice. *Feminist Studies, 35*(3), 454–480.

Blank, R. M., Card, D., Levy, F., & Medoff, J. L. (1993). Poverty, income distribution, and growth: Are they still connected? *Brookings Papers on Economic Activity, 1993*(2), 285–339.

Blauner, R. (1972). *Racial oppression in America.* New York: Harper & Row.

Blee, K., & Currier, A. (2011). Ethics beyond the IRB: An introductory essay. *Qualitative Sociology, 34,* 401–413.

Block, J. L. (2008). Issues for DSM-V: Internet addiction. *American Journal of Psychiatry, 165*(3), 306–307. doi:10.1176/appi.ajp.2007.07101556

Bloomquist, E. (2000). *Responsible non-monogamy: A brief introduction to polyamory.* Retrieved 10/07/2008, from http://www.biresource.org/pamphlets/nonmonogamy.html

Blumer, H. (1969). Collective behavior. In A. M. Lee (Ed.), *Principles of sociology* (3rd ed., pp. 65–121). New York: Barnes & Noble.

Boe, R. (2002). Future deomographic trends may help Canada's Aboriginal youth. *Forum on Corrections Research, 14*(3), 13–16.

Boeri, M. W., Sterk, C. E., & Elifson, K. W. (2004). Rolling beyond raves: Ecstasy use outside the rave setting. *Journal of Drug Issues, 34*(4), 831–859. Retrieved from http://library.mtroyal.ca:2048/login?url=http://search.ebscohost.com/login.aspx?direct=true&AuthType=ip,url,cookie,uid&db=a9h&AN=15559027&site=ehost-live

Boero, N. (2007). All the news that's fat to print: The American "obesity epidemic" and the media. *Qualitative Sociology, 30*(1), 41–60. doi:10.1007/s11133-006-9010-4

Bogardus, E. (1925). Measuring social distance. *Journal of Applied Sociology, 9,* 299–308.

Bogardus, E. (1967). *A forty year racial distance study*. Los Angeles: University of Southern California Press.

Boin, A., & McConnell, A. (2007). Preparing for critical infrastructure breakdowns: The limits of crisis management and the need for resilience. *Journal of Contingencies & Crisis Management, 15*(1), 50–59. doi:10.1111/j.1468-5973.2007.00504.x

Bolender, J. (2003). The genealogy of the moral modules. *Minds & Machines, 13*(2), 233–255.

Bond, C. D. (2010). Laws of Race/Laws of representation: The construction of race and law in contemporary American film. *Texas Review of Entertainment & Sports Law, 11*(2), 219–265. Retrieved from http://library.mtroyal.ca:2057/login.aspx?direct=true&AuthType=ip,url,cookie,uid&db=a9h&AN=51229488&site=ehost-live

Bonilla-Silva, E. (2013). *Racism without racists: Color-blind racism and the persistence of racial inequality in America* Lanham, MD: Rowman & Littlefield Publishers.

Bonner, K. (1998). Reflexivity, sociology and the rural-urban distinction in marx, tonnies and weber. *Canadian Journal of Sociology & Anthropology, 35*(2), 165–189.

Booker, K. C. (2007). Perceptions of classroom belongingness among African American college students. *College Student Journal, 41*(1), 178–186.

Bordo, S. (1993). *Unbearable weight: Feminism, western culture and the body*. Berkeley: University of California Press.

Bornschier, S. (2009). Cleavage politics in old and new democracies. *Living Reviews in Democracy, 1*, 1–13. Retrieved from http://search.ebscohost.com/login.aspx?direct=true&AuthType=ip,url,cookie,uid&db=a9h&AN=48617731&site=ehost-live

Borowik, I. (2011). The changing meanings of religion. Sociological theories of religion in the perspective of the last 100 years. *International Review of Sociology, 21*(1), 175–189. doi:10.1080/03906701.2011.544196

Bottomore, T. B., Harris, L., & Miliband, R. (Eds.). (1991). *A dictionary of Marxist thought* (2nd ed.). Malden, MA: Blackwell Publishing Limited.

Bouchard, B., & Zhao, J. (2000). University education: Recent trends in participation, accessibility and returns. *Education Quarterly Review, 6*(4), 24–32.

Bouma, G., Ling, R., & Wilkinson, L. (2009). *The research process*. Don Mills: Oxford University Press.

Bourdieu, P. (1973). Cultural reproduction and social reproduction. In R. Brown (Ed.), *Knowledge, education and cultural change* (pp. 71–112). London: Tavistock.

Bourdieu, P. (1991). *Language and symbolic power*. Cambridge: Polity Press.

Bourgeault, R. (1983). The Indian, the Metis and the fur trade: Class, sexism and racism in the transition from "communism" to capitalism. *Studies in Political Economy, 12*, 45–80.

Bower, B. (2010). *Evolution's bad girl*. Retrieved 17/03/2010, from http://www.sciencenews.org/view/feature/id/52228/title/Evolutions_Bad_Girl

Bowie, A. (1990). *Aesthetics and subjectivity: From Kant to Nietzsche*. Manchester, UK: Manchester University Press.

Bowles, S., & Gintis, H. (1976). *Schooling in capitalist america: Educational reform and the contradictions of economic life*. New York: Basic Books.

Boxer, M. J. (2007). Rethinking the socialist construction and international career of the concept "bourgeois feminism." *American Historical Review, 112*(1), 131–158.

Boyd, D. (2007). *Viewing American class divisions through Facebook and MySpace*. Retrieved 11/05/2008, from http://www.danah.org/papers/essays/ClassDivisions.html

Boyd, M., & Myles, J. (1991). Gender, power and postindustrialism. *Canadian Review of Sociology & Anthropology, 28*(4), 407–436.

Bradfield, O. M., Parker, C., & Goodwin, L. (2009). Sustaining performance: Learning from buyers' experience of Viagra. *Journal of Medical Marketing, 9*(4), 343–353.

Bradford, N. (2007). Placing social policy? Reflections on Canada's new deal for cities and communities. *Canadian Journal of Urban Research, 16*(2), 1–26. Retrieved from http://library.mtroyal.ca:2048/login?url=http://search.ebscohost.com/login.aspx?direct=true&AuthType=ip,url,cookie,uid&db=a9h&AN=31934353&site=ehost-live

Bradshaw, T. K. (2007). Theories of poverty and anti-poverty programs in community development. *Community Development, 38*(1), 7–25.

Bradshaw, Y. W. (1988). Reassessing economic dependency and uneven development: The Kenyan experience. *American Sociological Review, 53*(5), 693–708.

Brain, J. (2004). Asexuality. In J. Eadie (Ed.), *Sexuality* (pp. 9–9). London: Arnold.

Brancato, J. (2007). Domesticating politics: The representation of wives and mothers in american reality television. *Film & History, 37*(2), 49–56.

Brannigan, A. (2000). Notes on the discipline/Notes sociologiques: A personal take on some engaging books from the past decade. *Canadian Journal of Sociology, 25*(3), 383–389.

Bratton, J., Denham, D., & Deutschmann, L. (2009). *Capitalism and classical sociological theory*. Toronto, ON: University of Toronto Press.

Brecher, J., & Costello, T. (2006). Globalization and the race to the bottom. In J. M. Charon, & L. G. Vigilant (Eds.), *Social problems: Readings with four questions* (pp. 127–135). Belmont, CA: Thomson Wadsworth.

Brennan, S. (2012). Police-reported crime statistics in Canada, 2011. *Juristat*. Statistics Canada Catalogue no. 85-002-x. Accessed 08/01/2013, from www.statcan.gc.ca/pub/85-002-x/2012001/article/11692-eng.htm#a4

Brest, P., & Vandenberg, A. (1987). Politics, feminism, and the constitution: The anti-pornography movement in minneapolis. *Stanford Law Review, 39*(3), 607–661.

Breti, D. (1998). *Internment camps in British Columbia and Canada*. Retrieved 22/01/2008, from http://www.britishcolumbia.com/general/details.asp?id=44

Breton, R. (2005). *Ethnic relations in Canada: Institutional dynamics* [Jeffrey G. Reitz (Ed.)]. Montreal: McGill-Queen's University Press.

Brey, P. (2008). The technological construction of social power. *Social Epistemology, 22*(1), 71–95. doi:10.1080/02691720701773551

Brickell, C. (2006). A symbolic interactionist history of sexuality? *Rethinking History, 10*(3), 415–432.

Brien, S., Lewith, G., & Bryant, T. (2003). Ultramolevular homeopathy has no observable clinical effects. A randomized, double-blind, placebo-controlled proving trial of Belladonna 30C. *British Journal of Clinical Pharmacology, 56*(5), 562–568.

Brink, P., Smith, T. F., & Kitson, M. (2008). Determinants of do-not-resuscitate orders in palliative home care. *Journal of Palliative Medicine, 11*(2), 226–232.

Brint, S. (2001). Gemeinschaft revisited: A critique and reconstruction of the community concept. *Sociological Theory, 19*(1), 1.

British Museum. (n.d.). *The rosetta stone*. Retrieved 01/05/2008, from http://www.britishmuseum.org/explore/highlights/highlight_objects/aes/t/the_rosetta_stone.aspx

Brito, J., & Castillo, A. (2013). *BITCOIN: A primer for policymakers*. Fairfax County, Virginia: Mercatus Center, George Mason University.

Britt, B. M. (2010). Curses left and right: Hate speech and biblical tradition. *Journal of the American Academy of Religion, 78*(3), 633–661. Retrieved from http://www.jstor.org/stable/27919231

Britt, B. (2003). Manufactured consent or purloined dissent? *Radical Society: Review of Culture & Politics, 30*(1), 47–60. doi:10.1080/1476085032000125529

Brizendine, L. (2006). *The female brain*. New York: Broadway Books.

Broadcaster. (2010). *Internet usage exceeds TV viewing*. Retrieved 23/05/2010, from http://www.broadcastermagazine.com/issues/story.aspx?aid=1000364782&link_source=aypr_BM&link_targ=DailyNews

Broadway, M. (2007). Meatpacking and the transformation of rural communities: A comparison of Brooks, Alberta and Garden City, Kansas. *Rural Sociology, 72*(4), 560–582. Retrieved from http://library.mtroyal.ca:2048/login?url=http://search.ebscohost.com/login.aspx?direct=true&AuthType=ip,url,cookie,uid&db=a9h&AN=28097521&site=ehost-live

Brock University. (2008). *Sociology department*. Retrieved 07/08/2008, from http://www.brocku.ca/sociology/facultylist.php#anaisla

Bromley, P. (2011). Multiculturalism and human rights in civic education: The case of British Columbia, Canada. *Educational Research, 53*(2), 151–164.

Bronfen, E. (2006). Reality check: Image affects and cultural memory. *Differences: A Journal of Feminist Cultural Studies, 17*(1), 20–46. doi:10.1215/10407391-2005-003

Brown, A. (2007). Perestroika and the end of the cold war. *Cold War History, 7*(1), 1–17. doi:10.1080/14682740701197631

Brown, G. R., & Richerson, P. J. (2013). Applying evolutionary theory to human behaviour: Past differences and current debates. *Journal of Bioeconomics,* (Sep 2013). doi:10.1007/s10818-013-9166-4.

Brown, K., & Cullen, C. (2006). Maslow's hierarchy of needs used to measure motivation for religious behaviour. *Mental Health, Religion & Culture, 9*(1), 99–108.

Brown, S. K., & Bean, F. D. (2006). *New migrants, new models of assimilation.* Retrieved 23/01/2008, from http://www.cri.uci.edu/pdf/NewImmigrantsNewModelsOfAssimilation_082306.pdf

Browne, K., & Nash, C. (2010). Queer methods and methodologies: An introduction in Kath Browne and Catherine Nash (eds.), *Queer Methods and Methodologies.* Surrey: Ashgate.

Browning, S., & Erickson, P. (2012). Neighbourhood variation in the link between alcohol use and violence among Canadian adolescents. *Canadian Journal of Criminology and Criminal Justice, 54*(1), 170–201.

Brownridge, B. (2006). Violence against women post-separation. *Aggression and Violent Behavior, 11,* 514–530.

Bruce, S., & Voas, D. (2007). Religious toleration and organisational typologies. *Journal of Contemporary Religion, 22*(1), 1–17. doi:10.1080/13537900601114388

Bruns, A., Highfield, T., & Burgess, J. (2013). The Arab spring and social media audiences English and Arabic Twitter users and their networks. *American Behavioral Scientist, 57*(7), 871–898.

Brym, R., & Saint-Pierre, C. (1997). Canadian sociology. *Contemporary Sociology, 26*(5), 543–546.

Bryman, A., Teevan, J., & Bell, E. (2009). *Social research methods* (2nd Canadian ed.). Don Mills: Oxford University Press.

Brzozowski, J. (2004). *Family violence in Canada: A statistical profile 2004.* (No. 85-224-XIE). Ottawa: Statistics Canada.

Buch-Hansen, M., Oksen, P., & Prabudhanitisarn, S. (2006). Rethinking natural resource habitat in Thailand. *Journal of Political Ecology, 13,* 48–59.

Budgeon, S., & Roseneil, S. (2004). Editors' introduction: Beyond the conventional family. *Current Sociology, 52*(2), 127–134.

Budilova, E. A. (2003). Social-psychological problems in Russian science in the second half of the nineteenth century and early twentieth century. *Journal of Russian & East European Psychology, 41*(1), 5. Retrieved from http://library.mtroyal.ca:2048/login?url=http://search.ebscohost.com/login.aspx?direct=true&AuthType=ip,url,cookie,uid&db=a9h&AN=10457527&site=ehost-live

Buechler, S. M. (1993). Beyond resource mobilization? Emerging trends in social movement theory. *Sociological Quarterly, 34*(2), 217–235.

Bullard, R. D. (1990). *Dumping in Dixie: Race, class, and environmental quality.* Boulder, CO: Westview Press.

Bumb, J. *Annie Marion MacLean.* Retrieved 03/01/2010, from http://www.webster.edu/~woolflm/anniemaclean.html

Burchard, M. (2009). *Feminist jurisprudence.* Retrieved 31/10/2010, from http://www.iep.utm.edu/jurisfem

Burke, B. (2005). Antonio Gramsci, schooling and education. *The encyclopedia of informal education,* from http://www.infed.org/thinkers/et-gram.htm

Burtch, B. (2003). *The sociology of law: Critical approaches to social control* (2nd ed.). Toronto: Harcourt Brace.

BusinessETC.com. (2014). 50 billion instant messages expected to be sent each day in 2014. Accessed 05/05/2014, from http://businessetc.thejournal.ie/sms-messaging-falls-1262017-Jan2014/

BusinessWire. (2013). *The huffington post announces record year in audience growth, video, native advertising, and international expansion.* Retrieved 07/23/2014, from http://www.businesswire.com/news/home/20131216005482/en/HuffingtonPostAnnouncesRecordYearAudienceGrowth#.U8_esbGTFnE

Buss, D. M. (2008). *Evolutionary psychology: The new science of the mind.* Boston, MA: Pearson Education.

Butler, J. (1990). *Gender trouble.* New York: Routledge.

Butler, J. (1997). *Excitable speech: A politics of the performative.* New York: Routledge.

Buunk, A. P., Zurriaga, R., & González, P. (2006). Social comparison, coping and depression in people with spinal cord injury. *Psychology & Health, 21*(6), 791–807. doi:10.1080/14768320500444117

Byrd, M. Y., Martinez, J., & Scott, C. L. (2014). Social class and diversity in the workforce. In *Diversity in the Workforce: Current Issues and Emerging Trends,* edited by Marilyn Y. Byrd, Jose Martinez, and Chaunda L. Scott (pp. 181–182). New York, NY: Routledge.

Cabezas, A. L. (2006). The eroticization of labor in Cuba's all-inclusive resorts: Performing race, class and gender in the new tourist economy. *Social Identities, 12*(5), 507–521. Retrieved from http://library.mtroyal.ca:2048/login?url=http://search.ebscohost.com/login.aspx?direct=true&AuthType=ip,url,cookie,uid&db=a9h&AN=22373124&site=ehost-live

Caduff, Carlo. (2011). Anthropology's ethics: Moral positionism, cultural relativism, and critical analysis. *Anthropological Theory, 11*(4), 468–472.

Cady Stanton, E. (1895). *The Woman's Bible.* New York: European Publishing Company.

CAEFS. (2004). *CAEFS' fact sheets: Human and fiscal costs of prison.* Retrieved 13/09/2008, from http://dawn.thot.net/election2004/issues32.htm

CAEFS. (2008). *Criminalized and imprisoned women.* Retrieved 13/09/2008, from http://www.elizabethfry.ca/eweek08/pdf/crmwomen.pdf

Cagetti, M., & De Nardi, M. (2006). Entrepreneurship, frictions, and wealth. *Journal of Political Economy, 114*(5), 835–870.

Calasanti, T., Slevin, K. F., & King, N. (2006). Ageism and feminism: From "et cetera" to center. *NWSA Journal, 18*(1), 13–30. Retrieved from http://library.mtroyal.ca:2048/login?url=http://search.ebscohost.com/login.aspx?direct=true&AuthType=ip,url,cookie,uid&db=a9h&AN=20712362&site=ehost-live

Calhoun, C., Gerteis, J., Moody, J., Pfaff, S., & Virk, I., eds. (2012). *Classical Sociological Theory.* 3rd ed. West Sussex, UK: John Wiley & Sons.

Calixte, S., Johnson, J., & Motpanyane, J.M. (2010). Liberal, socialist, and radical feminism: An introduction to three theories about women's oppression and social change. In N. Mandell (Ed.), *Feminist issues: Race, class, and sexuality* (5th ed., pp. 1–39). Toronto: Pearson.

Camiscioli, E. (2001). Producing citizens, reproducing the "French race": Immigration, demography, and pronatalism in early twentieth-century France. *Gender and History, 13*(3), 593–621.

Campanella, R. (2007). An ethnic geography of New Orleans. *The Journal of American History, December,* 704–715.

Campbell, A. (2005). Keeping the "lady" safe: The regulation of femininity through crime prevention literature. *Critical Criminology, 13*(2), 119–140.

Campbell, S. (2008). Nursing the planet. *Primary Health Care, 18*(3), 41–48. Retrieved from http://library.mtroyal.ca:2048/login?url=http://search.ebscohost.com/login.aspx?direct=true&AuthType=ip,url,cookie,uid&db=a9h&AN=31697372&site=ehost-live

Canadian Centre for Justice Statistics. (2003). *Crime statistics in Canada.* Ottawa: Statistics Canada.

Canadian Centre for Justice Statistics. (2006). *Crime statis in Canada* No. Cat. No. 85-002-XIE Vol 27, (no. 5). Ottawa: Statistics Canada.

Canadian Council of Human Resources Associations. (n.d.). *HR profession defined.* Retrieved 28/03/2008, from http://www.cchra.ca/Web/profession/content.aspx?f=29754

Canadian Council on Learning. (2007). *Lessons in learning: Canada slow to overcome limits for disabled learners*. Retrieved 27/06/2008, from http://www.ccl-cca.ca/CCL/Reports/LessonsInLearning/LinL20070222_Slow_overcome_limits_disabled_learners.htm

Canadian Council on Social Development. (2006). *The progress of Canada's children and youth*. Retrieved from http://www.ccsd.ca/pccy/2006/index.htm

Canadian Feminist Alliance for International Action (CFAIA)/Canadian Labour Congress (CLC). (2010). *Reality check: Women in Canada and the Beijing declaration and platform for action fifteen years on*. CFAIA; CLC.

Canadian Heritage. (1998). *Visible minority workers are at greater economic risk*. Retrieved 11/12/2007 from http://publications.gc.ca/site/eng/78639/publication.html

Canadian Heritage. (2004a). *Canadians and their government: A resource guide*. Vol. 2 (July). Retrieved 04/04/2008, from http://www.canadianheritage.gc.ca/special/gouv-gov/section2/infobox1_e.cfm

Canadian Heritage. (2004b). *Multiculturalism - Canadian diversity: Respecting our differences*. Retrieved 05/06/2008, from http://www.pch.gc.ca/progs/multi/respect_e.cfm

Canadian Heritage. (2004c). *The top jobs*. Retrieved 04/04/2008, from http://www.canadianheritage.gc.ca/special/gouv-gov/section2/infobox2_e.cfm

Canadian Heritage. (2007a). *Canadian multiculturalism: An inclusive citizenship*. Retrieved 25/01/2008, from http://www.pch.gc.ca/progs/multi/inclusive_e.cfm

Canadian Heritage. (2007b). *Canadian television fund*. Retrieved 02/06/2008, from http://www.canadianheritage.gc.ca/progs/ac-ca/progs/fct-ctf/index_e.cfm

Canadian Heritage. (2007c). *Guide to the Canadian charter of rights and freedoms*. Retrieved 06/27/2008, from http://www.pch.gc.ca/progs/pdp-hrp/canada/guide/equality_e.cfm

Canadian Human Rights Commission. (n.d.). Denying minorities the right to vote. Accessed 08/05/2014, from http://www.chrc-ccdp.ca/en/timePortals/milestones/2mile.asp

Canadian Institute for Health Information. (2010a). *Heart attacks more likely among lower-income groups, but quality of care about the same for all Canadians*. Retrieved 10/07/2010, from http://www.icis.ca/cihiweb/dispPage.jsp?cw_page=media_20100527_e

Canadian Institute for Health Information. (2010b). *Injury hospitalizations and socio-economic status*. Retrieved 10/07/2010, from http://secure.cihi.ca/cihiweb/products/Injury_aib_vE4CCF_v3_en.pdf

Canadian Institutes of Health Research. (2010). *Gender and sex-based analysis in health research: A guide for CIHR researchers and reviewers*. Retrieved 12/07/2010, from http://www.cihr-irsc.gc.ca/e/32019.html

Canadian Institute for Health Information. (2013). *National health expenditure trends, 1975–2013*. 978-1-77109-232-6. Ottatwa, ON: Canadian Institute for Health Information.

Canadian Internet Registration Authority. (2014). *The Canadian internet*. Retrieved 07/21/2014, from http://cira.ca/factbook/2014/thecanadianinternet.html

Canadian Labour Congress. (n.d.). *History of labour*. Retrieved 29/03/2008, from http://canadianlabour.ca/index.php/history_of_labour

Canadian Lawyers for International Human Rights. (n.d.). *Residential schools truth commission*. Retrieved 01/06/2010, from http://www.claihr.ca/projects/residentialSchoolsTruthCommission.html

Canadian Nurses Association (CNA). (2011). RN and baccalaureate education table. Accessed 16/10/ 2013, from http://www.cna-aiic.ca/en/becoming-an-rn/education/rn-baccalaureate-education-table/

Canadiana. (2010). *Canada in the making: The deportation of the Acadians, 1755-1762*. Retrieved 18/06/2010, from http://library.mtroyal.ca:3811/citm/specifique/deportation_e.html#deportation

Cantril, H. (1940). *The invasion from Mars: A study in the psychology of panic*. Princeton, NJ: Princeton University Press.

Cardoso, F. H., & Faletto, E. (1979). *Dependency and development in Latin America* (M. M. Urquidi Trans.). Berkeley, CA: University of California Press.

Carey, J. W. (1967). Harold Adams Innis and Marshall McLuhan. *The Antioch Review, 27*(1), 5–39.

Carlson, R., Boyd, K, & Webb, D. (2004). The revision of the declaration of Helsinki: Past, present and future. *British Journal of Clinical Pharmacology, 57*(6), 695–713.

Carneiro, R. L., & Perrin, R. G. (2002). Herbert Spencer's principles of sociology: A centennial retrospective & appraisal. *Annals of Science, 59*(3), 221–261. doi:10.1080/00033790110050768

Carolan, M. S. (2004). Ecological modernization theory: What about consumption? *Society & Natural Resources, 17*(3), 247–260. Retrieved from http://library.mtroyal.ca:2048/login?url=http://search.ebscohost.com/login.aspx?direct=true&AuthType=ip,url,cookie,uid&db=a9h&AN=12255240&site=ehost-live

CARP. (2005). *CARP's fight against scams & frauds: Report & recommendations*. Retrieved 26/06/2008, from http://www.carp.ca/article_display.cfm?documentID=1467&CabinetID=256&LibraryID=70&cityID=0

Carpay, J. (2006). *Health care laws challenged in Alberta courts*. Retrieved 30/06/2008, from http://www.fcpp.org/main/publication_detail.php?PubID=1526

Carrington, P. (2013). Trends in the seriousness of youth crime in Canada, 1984–2011. *Canadian Journal of Criminology and Criminal Justice 55*(2), 293–314.

Carroll, T. (2007). Curious conceptions: Learning to be old. *Studies in Continuing Education, 29*(1), 71–84. doi:10.1080/01580370601146338

Carroll, W. K., & Ratner, R. S. (2007). Ambivalent allies: Social democratic regimes and social movements. *BC Studies*, (154), 41–66. Retrieved from http://library.mtroyal.ca:2048/login?url=http://library.mtroyal.ca:2924/login.aspx?direct=true&AuthType=ip,url,cookie,uid&db=a9h&AN=27232715&site=ehost-live

Carruthers, B. G., & Babb, S. (2000). *Economy/Society: Markets, meanings, and social structure*. London, UK: Pine Forge Press.

Carstensen, L. L. (1995). Evidence for a life-span theory of socioemotional selectivity. *Current Directions in Psychological Science, 4*(5), 151–156. doi:10.1111/1467-8721.ep11512261

Carter, G. W. (2003). *J.K. Lasser's taxes made easy for your home-based business: The ultimate tax handbook for the self-employed* (5th ed.). Hoboken, NJ: John Wiley & Sons Inc.

Carty, V. (2010). New information communication technologies and grassroots mobilization. *Information, Communication & Society, 13*(2), 155–173. doi:10.1080/13691180902915658

Cassano, G. (2008). The acquisitive machine: Max Weber, Thorstein Veblen, and the culture of consumptive individualism. In D. J. Charlcraft, F. Howell, M. L. Menendez & V. Hector (Eds.), *Max Weber matters: Interweaving past and present* (pp. 177–189). Surrey, UK: Ashgate Publishing Co.

Cassem, N. (1988). The person confronting death. In A. Nicholi (Ed.), *The new harvard guide to psychiatry* (pp. 728–758). Cambridge, MA: Belknap.

Castañeto, M. V., & Willemsen, E. W. (2006). Social perception of the personality of the disabled. *Social Behavior & Personality: An International Journal, 34*(10), 1217–1231. Retrieved from http://library.mtroyal.ca:2048/login?url=http://search.ebscohost.com/login.aspx?direct=true&AuthType=ip,url,cookie,uid&db=a9h&AN=23218520&site=ehost-live

Catton Jr., W. R., & Dunlap, R. E. (1978). Environmental sociology: A new paradigm. *American Sociologist, 13*(1), 41–49. Retrieved from http://library.mtroyal.ca:2048/login?url=http://search.ebscohost.com/login.aspx?direct=true&AuthType=ip,url,cookie,uid&db=a9h&AN=4945426&site=ehost-live

Causa, O., & Johansson, A. (2010). Intergenerational social mobility in OECD countries. *OECD Journal, Economic Studies 2010*, 1–44.

CAUT (Canadian Association of University Teachers). (2001a). Academic freedom in jeopardy at Toronto. *CAUT Bulletin Online, 48*(5) Retrieved from http://www.caut.ca/en/bulletin/issues/2001_may/default.asp

CAUT. (2001b). *Law suit launched against U of T and CAMH in Dr. David Healy controversy.* CAUT.

CAUT. (2005). *Policy statement on academic freedom.* CAUT.

CAUT. (2006). *Statement on the controversy over Professor Shiraz Dossa.* CAUT.

CAUT. (2007a). *Issues and campaigns: David Healy.* CAUT.

CAUT. (2007b). *Issues and campaigns: Dr. Nancy Olivieri.* CAUT.

CAUT. (2007c). *CAUT almanac of post-secondary education.*

CAUT. (2010). *CAUT almanac of post-secondary education in Canada 2010/2011.* Ottawa: CAUT.

CAUT. (2013). CAUT almanac of post-secondary education in Canada, 2013–2014.

CAUT. (2014). Judge upholds researchers' right to protect research confidentiality. *CAUT news release.* Retrieved 30/01/2014, from http://www.caut.ca/news/2014/01/22/judge-upholds-researchers-right-to-protect-research-confidentiality?utm_source=CAUT+NewsWire+EN&utm_medium=newsletter&utm_campaign=January+2014

CBC News in Review. (1999). *Chinese boat people: Human cargo.* Retrieved 28/01/2008, from http://www.cbc.ca/newsinreview/oct 99/Boat People/Chi-Can.html

CBC News: The Fifth Estate - Failing Jeffery Baldwin. (2007). Retrieved 31/10/2007, from http://www.cbc.ca/fifth/failingjeffrey/

CBC News. (2004a). *Indepth: Marijuana.* Retrieved 12/10/2007, from http://www.cbc.ca/news/background/marijuana/statistics.html

CBC News. (2004b). *SPANKING spanking in Canada: A timeline.* Retrieved 29/05/2010, from http://www.canadiancrc.com/Newspaper_Articles/CBC_Spanking_indepth_Timeline_Canada_28JAN04.aspx

CBC News. (2008a). *Cosmetic surgery: Balancing risk.* Retrieved 09/07/2010, from http://www.cbc.ca/news/background/health/cosmetic-surgery.html

CBC News. (2008b). *Retiring mandatory retirement.* Retrieved 25/06/2008, from http://www.cbc.ca/news/background/retirement/mandatory_retirement.html

CBC News. (2008c). *Rise in female, Aboriginal inmates alters prison population: Stats Can.* Retrieved 31/10/2010, from http://www.cbc.ca/canada/story/2008/12/15/statscan-prisons.html#ixzz12BtYqkeR

CBC News. (2011a). Canada pulls out of Kyoto Protocol. Accessed 08/05/2014, from http://www.cbc.ca/news/politics/canada-pulls-out-of-kyoto-protocol-1.999072

CBC News. (2011b). Timeline: Alleged 'honour killings' in Canada. Accessed 10/05/2014, from http://www.cbc.ca/news/world/alleged-honour-killings-in-canada-1.1008451

CBC Radio Canada. (n.d.). *History - 1901–1939.* Retrieved 04/05/2008, from http://www.cbc.radio-canada.ca/history/1901-1939.shtml

CBC. (1989). *The Montreal massacre.* http://archives.cbc.ca/society/crime_justice/topics/398/

CBC. (2010). Col. Russell Williams pleads guilty to all 88 Charges. http://www.cbc.ca/canada/stroty/2010/10/18/col-williams-court-1018.html

CBS. (n.d.). *CBS 6 Albany : WRGB history.* Retrieved 05/05/2008, from http://www.cbs6albany.com/sections/wrgb/history/

Cech, R., & Marks, M. B. (2007). Pedagogical tools for teaching supply and demand using lessons from transitional economies. *Social Studies, 98*(1), 3–7. Retrieved from http://library.mtroyal.ca:2048/login?url=http://search.ebscohost.com/login.aspx?direct=true&AuthType=ip,url,cookie,uid&db=a9h&AN=24660560&site=ehost-live

Cella III, P. J. (2010). The financial crisis and the scientific mindset. *Current,* (522), 16–19. Retrieved from http://library.mtroyal.ca:2057/login.aspx?direct=true&AuthType=ip,url,cookie,uid&db=a9h&AN=51433472&site=ehost-live

Centre for Marine Biodiversity. (n.d.). *What is marine biodiversity?* Retrieved 29/07/2008, from http://www.marinebiodiversity.ca/cmb/what-is-marine-biodiversity

Cernohous, S. (2007). Wikis: Open source information communities for educators and students. *Athletic Therapy Today, 12*(3), 2–5. Retrieved from http://library.mtroyal.ca:2048/login?url=http://search.ebscohost.com/login.aspx?direct=true&AuthType=ip,url,cookie,uid&db=a9h&AN=24993180&site=ehost-live

Chaudhari, D. M. (2013). Socialization of the society: The ground reality. *International Journal for Research in Education, 2*(2).

Chagnon, N. (1983). In Chagnon N. (Ed.), *Yanomamö: The fierce people* (3rd ed.). New York: Holt, Rinehart and Winston.

Chagnon, N. (1997). *Yanomamo* (5th ed.). Fort Worth, TX: Harcourt Brace.

Chan, C. S. (2013). Doing ideology amid a crisis collective actions and discourses of the Chinese Falun Gong movement. *Social Psychology Quarterly, 76* (1), 1–24.

Chan, K., & McNeal, J. (2004). Chinese children's attitudes towards television advertising: Truthfulness and liking. *International Journal of Advertising, 23,* 337–359.

Chan, W., & Rigakos, G. (2002). Risk, crime and gender. *British Journal of Criminology, 42*(4), 743–761.

Chappell, N., McDonald, L., & Stones, M. (2008). *Aging in contemporary Canada* (2nd ed.). Toronto, ON: Pearson Education Canada.

Charmaz, K., & Rosenfeld, D. (2006). Reflections of the body, images of self: Visibility and invisibility in chronic illness and disability. In D. Waskul, & P. Vannini (Eds.), *Body/Embodiment: Symbolic interaction and the sociology of the body* (pp. 35–49). Burlington, VT: Ashgate Publishing Co.

Cheal, D. (2002). *Sociology of family life.* New York: Palgrave.

Chen, J. C., Owusu-Ofori, S., Pai, D., Toca-McDowell, E., Wang, S. & Waters, C. K. (2003). *A study of female academic performance in mechanical engineering.* Retrieved January 15, 2008, from http://fie.engrng.pitt.edu/fie96/papers/276.pdf

Cheng, C. (2009). New media and event: A case study on the power of the internet. *Knowledge, Technology & Policy, 22*(2), 145–153. doi:10.1007/s12130-009-9078-8

Chesnay, C., Bellot, C., & Sylvestre, M.-E. (2013). Taming disorderly people one ticket at a time: The penalization of homelessness in Ontario and British Columbia. *Canadian Journal of Criminology and Criminal Justice, 55*(2), 161–185.

Chilana, R. S., & Zabel, D. (2005). *Sikhism* American Library Association. Retrieved from http://library.mtroyal.ca:2048/login?url=http://search.ebscohost.com/login.aspx?direct=true&AuthType=ip,url,cookie,uid&db=a9h&AN=20290979&site=ehost-live

Childe, V. G. (1951). *Social evolution.* London, UK: Watts.

Chilly Collective (Ed.). (1995). *Breaking anonymity: The chilly climate for women faculty.* Waterloo: Wilfrid Laurier University Press.

Chinese Canadian National Council. (2006). *Chinese Canadians remember veterans' contributions, urge inclusive redress.* Retrieved 22/06/2010, from http://www.ccnc.ca/content/pr.php?entry=89

Chirot, D., & McCauley, C. (2006). *Why not kill them all?: The logic and prevention of mass political murder.* Princeton, NJ: Princeton University Press.

Chrisjohn, R., & Young, S. (1997). *The circle game: Shadow and substance in the residential school experience in Canada.* Penticton, BC: Theytus Books Ltd.

Christensen Hughes, J. M., & McCabe, D. L. (2006). Academic misconduct within higher education in Canada. *Canadian Journal of Higher Education, 36*(2), 1–21.

Christian, J., & Abrams, D. (2004). A tale of two cities: Predicting homeless. People's uptake of outreach programs in London and New York. *Basic and Applied Social Psychology, 26*(2 & 3), 169–182.

Chui, T., Tran, K. & Maheux, H. (2007). *Immigration in Canada: A portrait of the foreign-born population, 2006 census.* Retrieved 22/07/2011, from http://www12.statcan.ca/census-recensement/2006/as-sa/97-557/pdf/97-557-XIE2006001.pdf

Chunn, D., & Gavigan, S. (2006). Welfare law, welfare fraud, and the moral regulation of the "never deserving" poor. In A. Glasbeek (Ed.), *Moral regulation and governance in Canada: History, context, and critical issues* (pp. 327–356). Toronto: Canadian Scholars' Press.

CIDA. (2007). *Women and men working together for rural development in Rwanda.* Retrieved 15/07/2008, from http://acdi-cida.gc.ca/CIDAWEB/acdicida.nsf/En/NAT-711113816-LCG

CIDA. (2009). *CIDA in brief.* Retrieved 23/07/2010, from http://www.acdi-cida.gc.ca/acdi-cida/ACDI-CIDA.nsf/eng/JUD-829101441-JQC

Cipriani, R. (2011). About religion in contemporary societies. *International Review of Sociology, 21*(1), 103–105. doi:10.1080/03906701.2011.544187

Clark, W. (2003). *Pockets of belief: Religious attendance patterns in Canada* No. Canadian Social Trends (Spring) catalogue (No. 11-008). Ottawa, ON: Statistics Canada.

Clarke, P. B. (Ed.). (2008). *Encyclopedia of new religious movements.* London, UK: Routledge, Taylor & Francis Group.

Clarke, S. (2006). *From enlightenment to risk: Social theory and contemporary society.* Basingstoke: Palgrave Macmillan.

Clement, W. (2001). Canadian political economy's legacy for sociology. *Canadian Journal of Sociology, 26*(3), 405–420.

Clifton, J. A. (Ed.). (1968). *Introduction to cultural anthropology - essays in the scope and methods of the science of man.* Boston, MA: Houghton Mifflin Co.

Clow, B., Pederson, A., Haworth-Brockman, M., & Bernier, J. (Eds.). (2009). *Rising to the challenge: Sex-and gender-based analysis for health planning, policy and research in Canada.* Halifax, NS: Atlantic Centre of Excellence for Women's Health. Retrieved from http://www.acewh.dal.ca/pdf/Rising_to_the_challenge.pdf

Cloward, R., & Ohlin, L. (1960). *Delinquency and opportunity: A theory of delinquent gangs.* Glencoe, IL: Free Press.

CMAJ. (2003). *Reasonable control: Gun registration in canada.* Canadian Medical Association. Retrieved from http://library.mtroyal.ca:2048/login?url=http://library.mtroyal.ca:2924/login.aspx?direct=true&AuthType=ip,url,cookie,uid&db=a9h&AN=9057470&site=ehost-live

CNN. (2004). Transsexual athletes OK for Athens. Retrieved 18/05/2004, from http://cnn.allpolitics.printthis.clickability.com/pt/cpt?expire=&title=CNN.com+-+Transsexual+athletes+OK+for+Athens+-+May+18%2C+2004&urlID=10284627&action=cpt&partnerID=2001&fb=Y&url=http%3A%2F%2Fedition.cnn.com%2F2004%2FSPORT%2F05%2F17%2Folympics.transsexual%2F February 4, 2014

CNRS (Centre National de la Recherche Scientifique). (2008). *Evolution of greenhouse gases over the last 800,000 years.* Retrieved 23/07/2008, from http://www2.cnrs.fr/en/1201.htm

Coad, D. (2008). *The metrosexual: Gender, sexuality and sport.* Albany: SUNY Press.

Codjoe, H. (2001). Fighting a "Public enemy" of black academic achievement – the persistence of racism and the schooling experiences of black students in Canada. *Race Ethnicity and Education, 4*(4), 343–375.

Cohen, J. J. (2006). Professionalism in medical education, an American perspective: From evidence to accountability. *Medical Education, 40*(7), 607–617. Retrieved from http://library.mtroyal.ca:2048/login?url=http://search.ebscohost.com/login.aspx?direct=true&AuthType=ip,url,cookie,uid&db=a9h&AN=21326051&site=ehost-live

Colleoni, E., Rozza, A., & Arvidsson, A. (2014). Echo chamber or public sphere? Predicting political orientation and measuring political homophily in Twitter using big data. *Journal of Communication, 64*(2), 317–332.

Collin, C., & Jensen, H. (2009). *A statistical profile of poverty in Canada.* (No. PRB 09-17E). Library of Parliament-Parliamentary Information and Research Services.

Collins, E., Freeman, J., & Chamarro-Premuzic, T. (2012). Personality traits associated with problematic and non-problematic massively multiplayer online role playing game use. *Personality and Individual Differences, 52,*(2), 133–138.

Collins, R. (1979). *The credential society.* New York: Academic Press.

Comack, E., & Brickey, S. (2007). Constituting the violence of criminalized women. *Canadian Journal of Crime and Criminal Justice, 49*(1), 1–36.

Comfort, D., Johnson, K., & Wallace, D. (2003). *Part-time work and family-friendly practices in Canadian workplaces.* (No.71-584-M1E, no.6). Statistics Canada.

Comor, E. (2003). Harold innis. In C. May (Ed.), *Key thinkers for the information society: Vol 1* (pp. 85–108). London, UK: Routledge, Taylor & Francis Group.

Conklin, B. (2008). *Revenge and reproduction: The biopolitics of caring and killing in native Amazonia.* In *Revenge in the Cultures of Lowland South America,* edited by Stephen Beckerman and Paul Valentine (pp. 10–21). Gainesville, FL: University of Florida Press.

Connell, C., & Elliott, S. (2009). Beyond the birds and the bees: Learning inequality through sexuality education. *American Journal of Sexuality Education, 4,* 83–102.

Connell, R. (2002). Hegemonic masculinity. In S. Jackson, & S. Scott (Eds.), *Gender: A sociological reader* (pp. 60–62). New York: Routledge.

Connell, R. W. (1987). *Gender and power.* Stanford: Stanford University Press.

Connor, S. (2011). Structure and agency: A debate for community development? *Community Development Journal, 46,* ii97–ii110. Retrieved from http://search.ebscohost.com/login.aspx?direct=true&AuthType=ip,url,cookie,uid&db=a9h&AN=59688405&site=ehost-live

Conrick, M. (2006). The challenges of linguistic duality for francophone Canada: Contact, conflict and continuity. *International Journal of Francophone Studies, 9*(3), 311–328. doi:10.1386/ijfs.9.3.311_1

Contoyannis, P., & Dooley, M. (2010). The role of child health and economic status in educational, health, and labour market outcomes in young adulthood. *Canadian Journal of Economics, 43*(1), 323–346.

Cook, N. (2001). *Introduction to postcolonial studies.* Unpublished manuscript.

Cook, N. (2006). Bazaar stories of gender, sexuality and imperial spaces in gilgit, northern Pakistan. *ACME: An International E-Journal for Critical Geographies, 5*(2), 230–257.

Cook, N. (Ed.). (2007). *Gender relations in global perspective: Essential readings.* Toronto: Canadian Scholars' Press Inc.

Cooke, H., & Philpin, S. (2008). *Sociology in nursing and healthcare.* Philadelphia, PA: Elsevier Health Sciences.

Cooke, R. (1999). History of ancient Indian conquest told in modern genes, experts say. *San Francisco Chronical,* C-2. Retrieved from http://www.sfgate.com/cgi-bin/article.cgi?f=/c/a/1999/05/26/MN84858.DTL

Cooley, C. H. (1902). *Human nature and the social order.* New York: C. Scribner's sons.

Coontz, S. (1992). *The way we never were: American families and the nostalgia trap.* New York: Basic Books, Harper Collins.

COP. (2008). *Colour of poverty fact sheet #7 understanding the racialization of poverty in Ontario in justice and policing in 2007.* Retrieved 31/10/2010, from www.colourofpoverty.ca

Corak, M., & Heisz, A. H. (1999). The intergenerational earnings and income mobility of Canadian men: Evidence from longitudinal income tax data. *The Journal of Human Resources, 34*(3). Retrieved from http://www.jstor.org/stable/146378

Corbett, J. B. (2006). *Communicating nature: How we create and understand environmental messages.* Washington, DC: Island Press.

Coreno, T. (2002). Fundamentalism as a class culture. *Sociology of Religion, 63*(3), 335–360. Retrieved from http://library.mtroyal.ca:2048/login?url=http://search.ebscohost.com/login.aspx?direct=true&AuthType=ip,url,cookie,uid&db=a9h&AN=7451598&site=ehost-live

Corman, M. K. (2009). The positives of caregiving: Mothers' experiences caregiving for a child with autism. *Families in Society, 90*(4), 439–445. doi:10.1606/1 044-3894.3923

Cornock, M. (2005). Deathly definitions. *Nursing Standard, 19*(41), 34–34. Retrieved from http://library.mtroyal.ca:2048/login?url=http://search.

ebscohost.com/login.aspx?direct=true&AuthType=ip,url,cookie,uid&db=a9h&AN=17480907&site=ehost-live

Coser, L. (1956). *The functions of social conflict*. New York: Free Press.

Coser, R. (Ed.). (1964). *The family: Its structures and functions*. New York: St. Martin's Press.

Cotgrove, S. (1976). Environmentalism and utopia. *Sociological Review, 24*(1), 23–42. doi:10.1111/1467-954X.ep5463422

Cotgrove, S., & Duff, A. (1980). Environmentalism, middle-class radicalism and politics. *Sociological Review, 28*(2), 333–351. doi:10.1111/1467-954X.ep5467932

Cotgrove, S., & Duff, A. (1981). Environmentalism, values, and social change. *British Journal of Sociology, 32*(1), 92–110. Retrieved from http://library.mtroyal.ca:2048/login?url=http://search.ebscohost.com/login.aspx?direct=true&AuthType=ip,url,cookie,uid&db=a9h&AN=5295847&site=ehost-live

Couch, C. J. (1996). *Information technologies and social orders*. New Brunswick (USA): AldineTransaction.

Couldry, N. (2004). Theorising media as practice. *Social Semiotics, 14*(2), 115–132. doi:10.1080/1035033042000238295

Council of Canadians with Disabilities. (1998). *Publications: Latimer watch*. Retrieved 28/06/2008, from http://www.ccdonline.ca/publications/latimer-watch/1098e.htm

Council of Ministers of Education Canada (CMEC). (2010). *Education indicators in Canada: An international perpsective*. Ottawa: Canadian Education Statistics Council.

Couric, K. (2010). Ask CBS news: *How long will oil hurt gulf?* Retrieved 18/07/2010, from http://www.cbsnews.com/stories/2010/07/16/eveningnews/main6685746.shtml

Courtenay, W. (2000). Constructions of masculinity and their influence on men's well being: A theory of gender and health. *Social Science and Medicine, 50*, 1385–1401.

Cowan, J. (2008). *Environmentalists take ottawa to court over Kyoto*. Retrieved 09/08/2008, from http://www.canada.com/topics/news/national/story.html?id=fbcb81d2-a9ab-4ebe-bd11-a26fdff802a3

Cox, O. C. (1948). *Caste, class, and race: A study in social dynamics*. Garden City, NY: Doubleday.

Cram, F., & Jackson, S. (2003). Disrupting the sexual double standard: Young women's talk about heterosexuality. *British Journal of Social Psychology, 42*, 113–127.

Crawford, A. (2011). Prison watchdog probes spike in number of black inmates. *CBC News*. http://www.cbc.ca/news/politics/prison-watchdog-probes-spike-in-number-of-black-inmates-1.1039210

Creatore, M. I., Moineddin, R., Booth, G., Manuel, D. H., DesMeules, M., McDermott, S., et al. (2010). Age- and sex-related prevalence of diabetes mellitus among immigrants to Ontario, Canada. *CMAJ: Canadian Medical Association Journal, 182*(8), 781–789. doi:10.1503/cmaj.091551

Creese, G., & Wiebe, B. (2012). 'Survival employment': Gender and deskilling among African immigrants in Canada. *International Migration, 50*(5), 56–76.

Creswell, J. (2003). *Research design: Qualitative, quantitative, and mixed methods approaches* (2nd ed.). Thousand Oaks: Sage Publications.

Cristi, M. (2001). *From civil to political religion*. Waterloo, ON: Wilfred Laurier Press.

Cronk, G. (2005). *George Herbert Mead [internet encyclopedia of philosophy]*. Retrieved 17/09/2007, from http://www.iep.utm.edu/m/mead.htm#SH3c

Croteau, D., & Hoynes, W. (2003). *Media society: Industries, images, and audiences* (3rd ed.). Thousand Oaks, CA: Sage Publications, Ltd.

Crothers, C. (2004). Merton as a general theorist: Structures, choices, mechanisms, and consequences. *American Sociologist, 35*(3), 23–36. Retrieved from http://search.ebscohost.com/login.aspx?direct=true&AuthType=ip,url,cookie,uid&db=a9h&AN=17395140&site=ehost-live

Crouch, M., & McKenzie, H. (2006). The logic of small samples in interview-based qualitative research. *Social Science Information, 45*(4), 483–499.

Crowley, B. J., Hayslip Jr., B., & Hobdy, J. (2003). Psychological hardiness and adjustment to life events in adulthood. *Journal of Adult Development, 10*(4), 237.

CRTC. (2001). *The MAPL system*. Retrieved 02/06/2008, from http://www.crtc.gc.ca/eng/INFO_SHT/R1.HTM

CRTC. (2004). *Canadian content for radio and television*. Retrieved 02/06/2008, from http://www.crtc.gc.ca/public/old_pubs_e/G11.htm

CRTC. (2007). *Mandate*. Retrieved 02/06/2008, from http://www.crtc.gc.ca/eng/cancon/mandate.htm

CRTC. (2009). *The MAPL system defining a Canadian song*. Retrieved 07/21/2014, from http://www.crtc.gc.ca/eng/info_sht/r1.htm

CTV News. (2008). Canada must protect its water from the U.S.: Report. Accessed 08/05/2014, from http://www.ctvnews.ca/canada-must-protect-its-water-from-u-s-report-1.287077

Cumming, E., & Henry, W. E. (1961). *Growing old: The process of disengagement*. New York: Basic Books.

Currie, J., & Newson, J. (Eds.). (1998). *Universities and globalization: Critical perspectives*. Thousand Oaks, California: Sage.

Curtis, G. (2006). *Jesus camp shuts down due to negative response (Christian today)*. Retrieved 28/02/2008, from http://www.christiantoday.com/article/jesus.camp.shuts.down.due.to.negative.response/8539.htm

Curtis, J., Grabb, E., & Guppy, G. (Eds.). (2004). *Social inequality in Canada: Patterns, problems and policies* (Fourth ed.). Toronto: Pearson Prentice Hall.

Curtis, L. J., & MacMinn, W. J. (2008). Health care utilization in Canada: Twenty-five years of evidence. *Canadian Public Policy, 34*(1), 65–87.

Curtis, N. (2010). 'Customer' isn't always right: Market model could head to disaster. *CAUT Bulletin*, A2, A7.

Cutler, M. (2006). Negotiating Jewish identity in a southern Christian context. *Journal of Contemporary Ethnography, 35*(6), 696–728.

D'Emilio, J. (2005). Capitalism and gay identity. In T. L. Steele (Ed.), *Sex, self, and society: The social context of sexuality*. California: Wadsworth.

Dafnos, T. (2007). What does being gay have to do with it? A feminist analysis of the Jubran case. *Canadian Journal of Criminology & Criminal Justice, 49*(5), 561–585. Retrieved from http://search.ebscohost.com/login.aspx?direct=true&AuthType=ip,url,cookie,uid&db=a9h&AN=31494592&site=ehost-live

Dagenais, D. (2013). Multilingualism in Canada: Policy and education in applied linguistics research. *Annual Review of Applied Linguistics, 33*, 286–301.

Dahrouge, S., Hogg, W., Tuna, M., Russell, G., Devlin, R. A., Tugwell, P., et al. (2010). An evaluation of gender equity in different models of primary care practices in Ontario. *BMC Public Health, 10*, 151–162. Retrieved from http://library.mtroyal.ca:2057/login.aspx?direct=true&AuthType=ip,url,cookie,uid&db=a9h&AN=50258056&site=ehost-live

Dalal, F. (2002). *Race, colour and the processes of racialization: New perspectives from group analysis, psychoanalysis and sociology*. New York, NY: Brunner-Routledge.

Dalit Freedom Network Canada. (n.d.). *Dalit freedom network Ccanada*. Retrieved 05/06/2010, from http://www.dalitfreedom.net/

Daly, K. (2000). *It keeps getting faster: Changing patterns of time in families*. Ottawa: Vanier Institute of the Family.

Dam, K. (2009). The subprime crisis and financial regulation:An international perspective. *MPI Studies on Intellectual Property, Competition and Tax Law, 10*(4), 1–12.

Danielewicz, I. (2005). *Show us yer tits!* Retrieved 06/07/2008, from http://gauntlet.ucalgary.ca/story/5201

Danzon, P. M. (1992 (Spring)). Hidden overhead costs: Is Canada's system really less expensive? *Health Affairs*, 21–43.

David Suzuki Foundation. (2007). *Climate change: Kyoto: Canada's emissions*. Retrieved 23/07/2008, from http://www.davidsuzuki.org/Climate_Change/Kyoto/Canadian_Emissions.asp

David Suzuki Foundation. (2009). The air we breathe. Accessed 08/05/2014, from http://www.davidsuzuki.org/issues/health/science/air-quality/the-air-we-breathe/

Davidson, I., & McGrew, W. C. (2005). Stone tools and the uniqueness of human culture. *Journal of the Royal Anthropological Institute, 11*(4), 793–817.

Davies, I. R. L., Sowden, P. T., Jerrett, D. T., Jerrett, T. i., & Corbett, G. G. (1998). A cross-cultural study of English and Setswana speakers on a colour triads task: A test of the Sapir-Whorf hypothesis. *The British Journal of Psychology, 89,* 1–15. Retrieved from http://library.mtroyal.ca:2083/pqdweb?did=27463825&Fmt=7&clientId=65345&RQT=309&VName=PQD

Davies, S., & Guppy, N. (2006). *The schooled society: An introduction to the sociology of education.* Don Mills: Oxford University Press.

Davis-Delano, L., Pollock, A., & Vose, J. E. (2009). Apologetic behavior among female athletes. *International Review for the Sociology of Sport, 44*(2–3), 131–150.

Davis, D. M. (2007). The Los Angeles riots revisited: The changing face of the Los Angeles unified school district and the challenge for educators. *Educational Studies, 42*(3), 213–229. doi:10.1080/00131940701632613

Davis, K. (1937). The sociology of prostitution. *American Sociological Review, 2*(5), 744–755.

Davis, K. (1947). Final note on a case of extreme isolation. *American Journal of Sociology, 52,* 432–437.

Davis, K., & Moore, W. E. (1945). Some principles of stratification. *American Sociological Review, 10,* 242–249.

Dawkins, M. A. (2010). Close to the edge: The representational tactics of Eminem. *Journal of Popular Culture, 43*(3), 463–485. doi:10.1111/j.1540-5931.2010.00753.x

Dawley, A., & Faler, P. (1976). Working-class culture and politics in the industrial revolution: Sources of loyalism and rebellion. *Journal of Social History, 9*(4), 466.

DAWN. (2003). *The feminist principle of equality and inclusion.* Retrieved 25/07/2008, from http://dawn.thot.net/feminism8.html

Dawson, L. L. (2006). *Comprehending cults: The sociology of new religious movements* (2nd ed.). Oxford: Oxford University Press.

Dawson, L., & Kass, N. (2005). Views of US researchers about informed consent in international collaborative research. *Social Science and Medicine, 61,* 1211–1222.

Dawson, M., Bunge, V. P., & Balde, T. (2009). National trends in intimate homicides: Explaining declines in Canada 1976–2001. *Violence Against Women, 15*(3), 276–306.

Day, S. (2007). Book review of Sandra Harding (2006) science and social inequality: Feminist and postcolonial issues. urbana and Chicago, Ill: University of illinois press. *Canadian Journal of Sociology Online, 2007* (March).

de la Luz Inclán, M. (2008). From the Ya Basta! to the Caracoles: Zapatista mobilization under transitional conditions. *American Journal of Sociology, 113*(5), 1316–1350. Retrieved from http://www.jstor.org/stable/10.1086/525508

de Leeuw, S. (2009). 'If anything is to be done with the indian, we must catch him very young': Colonial constructions of aboriginal children and the geographies of Indian residential schooling in British Columbia. *Children's Geographies, 7*(2), 123–140.

de Vries, M. (2006). An enduring bond? Jews in the Netherlands and their ties with Judaism. *Journal of Ethnic & Migration Studies, 32*(1), 69–88. Retrieved from http://library.mtroyal.ca:2048/login?url=http://search.ebscohost.com/login.aspx?direct=true&AuthType=ip,url,cookie,uid&db=a9h&AN=18807113&site=ehost-live

Dean, S. (2013). *World's oldest newspaper goes digital.* Retrieved 10/07/2014, from http://mashable.com/2013/09/28/lloyds-list-going-digital/

Deffeyes, K. S. (2008). *Hubbert's peak: The impending world oil shortage.* Princeton, NJ: Princeton University Press.

Dei, G. J. S., & Calliste, A. (2000). Mapping the terrain: Power, knowledge and anti-racism education. In G. J. S. Dei, & A. Calliste (Eds.), *Power, knowledge and anti-racism education: A critical reader* (pp. 11–22). Halifax: Fernwood Publishing.

Dei, G. S. (1997). Race and the production of identity in the schooling experiences of African-Canadian youth. *Discourse: Studies in the Cultural Politics of Education, 18*(2), 241–257.

Dei, G. S. (2003). Challenges for anti-racist educators in Ontario today. *Orbit, 33*(3), 2–5.

Dei, G. S. (2008). Schooling as community: Race, schooling, and the education of African youth. *Journal of Black Studies, 38*(3), 346–366.

DeKeseredy, W. (2001). Patterns of family violence. In M. Baker (Ed.), *Families: Changing trends in Canada* (4th ed., pp. 238–266). Toronto: McGraw-Hill.

Delamotte, Y., & Walker, K. F. (1976). Humanization of work and the quality of working life - trends and issues. *International Journal of Sociology, 6*(1), 8–40.

Delaney, T. (2004). *Classical social theory: Investigation and application.* Upper Saddle River, NJ: Prentice-Hall, Inc.

Delgado, R., & Stefanic, J. (2001). *Critical race theory: An introduction.* New York: New York University Press.

Deliovsky, K., & Kitossa, T. (2013). Beyond black and white when going beyond may take us out of bounds. *Journal of Black Studies, 44*(2), 158–181.

Della Porta, D. (1995). Power in movement. social movements, collective actions and politics (book). *Acta Sociologica (Taylor & Francis Ltd), 38*(3), 275–278. Retrieved from http://library.mtroyal.ca:2048/login?url=http://search.ebscohost.com/login.aspx?direct=true&AuthType=ip,url,cookie,uid&db=a9h&AN=9510290767&site=ehost-live

Dellbrügge, K. (2010). *The critical period hypothesis: Support and challenge form encounters with feral children.* Munich, Germany: GRIN Verlag.

deMarrais, K., & LeCompte, M. (1999). *The way schools work: A sociological analysis of education* (3rd ed.). New York: Longman.

Denney, D., Ellis, T., & Barn, R. (2006). Race diversity and criminal justice in Canada: A view from the UK. *Internet Journal of Criminology*, Retrieved from http://www.internetjournalofcriminology.com

Denzin, N. (2007). Katrina and the collapse of civil society in New Orleans. *Cultural Studies Critical Methodologies, 7*(2), 145–153.

Denzin, N. K. (1992). *Symbolic interactionism and cultural studies: The politics of interpretation.* Cambridge, MA: Blackwell.

DePalma, A. (1999). *Tough rules stand guard over Canadian culture.* Retrieved 5/15/2008, from http://www.globalpolicy.org/globaliz/cultural/canadian.htm

Derenne, J. L., & Beresin, E. V. (2006). Body image, media, and eating disorders. *Academic Psychiatry, 30*(June), 257–261.

Desfor Edles, L., & Appelrouth, S. (2010). *Sociological theory in the classical era: Text and readings.* 2nd ed. Thousand Oaks, CA: Pine Forge Press.

Desyllas, M. C. (2007). A critique of the global trafficking discourse and U.S. policy. *Journal of Sociology & Social Welfare, 34*(4), 57–79.

Devadoss, V. A., & Ismail, M. S. (2013). A study on religious practices in Islam towards sustainable development using neutrosophic relational maps. *International Journal of Computing Algorithm, 2,* 211–213.

Developmental Disabilities Association. (2010). 1 Retrieved 27/12/2010, from http://www.develop.bc.ca/about/development-disabilities.html

Devor, H. (2005). More than manly woman: How female transsexuals reject lesbian identities. In T. L. Steele (Ed.), *Sex, self and society: The social context of sexuality.* California: Wadsworth.

Dhanda, M. (2009). Punjabi dalit youth: Social dynamics of transitions in identity. *Contemporary South Asia, 17*(1), 47–64. doi:10.1080/09584930802624661

Dhruvarajan, V., & Vickers, J. (2002). *Gender, race and nation: A global perspective.* Toronto, ON: University of Toronto Press.

Diamond, L. (2010). Liberation technology. *Journal of Democracy, 21*(3), 69–83.

Diaz, J., & Nuñez, N. (1993). *Mapuche of Chile demand self-determination.* Retrieved 1/27/2008, from http://www.greenleft.org.au/1993/90/4514

Dickens, B. M., Boyle, J. M., & Ganzini, L. (2008). Euthansia and assisted suicide. In P. A. Singer, & A. M. Viens (Eds.), *The Cambridge textbook of bioethics* (pp. 72–77). Cambridge, UK: Cambridge University Press.

Dicum, G. (2006a). *Environmental justice and environmental racism.* Retrieved 26/07/2008, from http://environment.about.com/od/activismvolunteering/a/robert_bullard.htm

Dicum, G. (2006b). *Meet Robert Bullard, the father of environmental justice.* Retrieved 02/08/2008, from http://www.grist.org/news/maindish/2006/03/14/dicum/

Diehm, C. (2007). Identification with nature: What it is and why it matters. *Ethics & the Environment, 12*(2), 1–22. Retrieved from http://library.mtroyal.ca:2048/login?url=http://search.ebscohost.com/login.aspx?direct=true&AuthType=ip,url,cookie,uid&db=a9h&AN=29363016&site=ehost-live

Diem, C., & Pizarro, J. (2010). Social structures and family homicides. *Journal of Family Violence, 25*(5), 521–532.

DiGiorgio, C. (2009). Application of bourdieuian theory to the inclusion of students with learning/physical challenges in multicultural school settings. *International Journal of Inclusive Education, 13*(2), 179–194. doi:10.1080/13603110701350622

Ding, Q. J., & Hesketh, T. (2006). Family size, fertility preferences, and sex ration in China in the era of the one child policy. *British Medical Journal, 333,* 371–373.

Dirks, N. B. (2001). *Castes of mind: Colonialism and the making of modern India.* Princeton, NJ: Princeton University Press.

Disapearing languages. (2014). Accessed 01/20/2014, from http://travel.nationalgeographic.com/travel/enduring-voices/

Dixon, S. M., & Quirke, L. (2014). Looking for work: The coverage of work in Canadian introductory sociology textbooks. *Teaching Sociology*: April 19, 2014. doi:10.1177/0092055X14528718.

Dixon, R. (2014). Rwanda makes great progress 20 years after genocide. Accessed 05/09/2014, from http://www.latimes.com/world/africa/la-fg-rwanda-genocide-20140407-story.html#page=1

Doane, A. W., Jr. (1997). Dominant group ethnic identity in the United States: The role of "hidden" ethnicity in intergroup relations. *Sociological Quarterly, 38*(3), 375. Retrieved from http://proquest.umi.com/pqdweb?did=14478129&Fmt=7&clientId=65345&RQT=309&VName=PQD

Dockery, T. M., & Bedeian, A. G. (1989). "Attitudes versus actions": LaPiere's (1934) classic study revisted. *Social Behavior and Personality, 17*(1), 9–16.

Dodd, N. (1999). *Social theory and modernity* [Nigel Dodd, 1999 Polity Press]. Cambridge, UK: Polity Press.

Dodds, L., & Hopwood, B. (2006). BAN waste, environmental justice and citizen participation in policy setting. *Local Environment, 11*(3), 269–286. doi:10.1080/13549830600558762

Doherty, B. (2002). *Ideas and action in the green movement.* London, UK: Routledge.

Dohnt, H., & Tiggemann, M. (2006). The contribution of peer and media influences to the development of body satisfaction and self-esteem in young girls: A prospective study. *Developmental Psychology, 42*(5), 929–936.

Dolezal, J. A. (2008). Literary activism, social justice, and the future of bioregionalism. *Ethics & the Environment, 13*(1), 1–22. Retrieved from http://library.mtroyal.ca:2048/login?url=http://search.ebscohost.com/login.aspx?direct=true&AuthType=ip,url,cookie,uid&db=a9h&AN=32132413&site=ehost-live

Dollard, J., Doob, L. W., Miller, N. E., Mowrer, O. W., & Sears, R. R. (1939). *Frustration and aggression.* New Haven, Connecticut: Yale University Press.

Domínguez, S., & Arford, T. (2010). It is all about who you know: Social capital and health in low-income communities. *Health Sociology Review, 19*(1), 114–129. doi:10.5172/hesr.2010.19.1.114

Donnelly, M. K. (2013). Drinking with the Derby girls: Exploring the hidden ethnography in research of women's flat track roller derby. *International Review for the Sociology of Sport*: Jan 30, 2014. doi:10.1177/1012690213515664.

Donnelly, P. G., & Kimble, C. E. (2006). An evaluation of the effects of neighborhood mobilization on community problems. *Journal of Prevention & Intervention in the Community, 32*(1), 61–80. doi:10.1300/J005v32n0105

Donovan, P. (2007). How idle is idle talk? One hundred years of rumor research. *Diogenes, 54*(1), 59–82.

Doolin, E. (2010). Bridging the gap for lesbian youth: Making our community their community. *Journal of Lesbian Studies, 14,* 93–103.

Doucet, A. (2004). Fathers and the responsibility for children: A puzzle and a tension. *Atlantis: A Women's Studies Journal, 28*(2), 103–114.

Doucet, A. (2007). Stay-at-home fathering. *Community, Work & Family, 10*(4), 455–473.

Doucet, C. (2000). *Notes from exile: On being Acadian.* Toronto, ON: McClelland & Stewart.

Douglas, D. (2008). Racism in Canada: The evidence of things not seen. *The Ardent Review, 1*(1), 41–44. Retrieved from http://www.arts.ualberta.ca/~aadr/Documents/Delia%20Douglas.pdf

Dowler, K. (2006). Sex, lies, and videotape: The presentation of sex crime in local television news. *Journal of Criminal Science, 34,* 383–392.

Dowsett Johnston, A., & Dwyer, M. (2004). Ranking Canadian universities: Ann Dowsett Johnston and Mary Dwyer explain the methodology behind the annual Maclean's survey. *Macleans,* 38–39.

Doyle, S. (2008, April 7). Lobbyists make final preparations for high-stakes CRTC hearings. *The Hill Times,* Retrieved from http://www.thehilltimes.ca/html/index.php?display=story&full_path=2008/april/7/lobbying/&c=2

Drakich, J., & Stewart, P. (2007). Years later, how are university women doing? *Academic Matters, February,* 6–9.

Drakich, J., Grant, K., & Stewart, P. (2002). The academy in the 21st century: Editors' introduction. *The Canadian Review of Sociology and Anthropology, 39*(3), 249–260.

Dresselhaus, M. S., Dresselhaus, G., & Avouris, P.,eds. (2001). *Carbon Nanotubes: Synthesis, Structure, Properties, and Applications.* Berlin: Springer-Verlag.

Drexhage, J., & Murphy, D. (2010). *Climate change and foreign policy in Canada: Intersection and influence* (No. Energy Report No.2). Toronto, ON: Canadian International Council. Retrieved from http://www.onlinecic.org/research/research_areas/energy

Duay, D., & Bryan, V. (2006). Senior adults' perceptions of successful aging. *Educational Gerontology, 32*(6), 423–445. doi:10.1080/03601270600685636

Dube, S. C. (1988). *Modernization and development: The search for alternative paradigms.* Tokyo: The United Nations University.

Dubuc, N., & Thompson, M. (Producers), & Ewing, H. and Grady, R. (Directors). (2006). *Jesus camp.* [Video/DVD] Magnolia Home Entertainment.

Duck, W. (2009). Black male sexual politics: Avoidance of HIV/AIDS testing as a masculine health practice. *Journal of African American Studies, 13,* 283–306.

Duffy, A., & Momirov, J. (2005). Family violence: A twenty-first century issue. In N. Mandell, & A. Duffy (Eds.), *Canadian families* (3rd ed., pp. 144–175). Toronto: Thomson Nelson.

Dumme, T. J. B. (2008). Health geography: Supporting public health policy and planning. *CMAJ: Canadian Medical Association Journal, 178*(9), 1177–1180. doi:10.1503/cmaj.071783

Dunlap, R. E. (2000). The evolution of environmental sociology: A brief history and assessment of the American experience. In M. Redclift, &

G. Woodgate (Eds.), *The international handbook of environmental sociology* (pp. 21–39). Cheltenham, UK: Edward Elgar Publishing Ltd.

Dunlap, R. E. (2002). Paradigms, theories and environmental sociology. In R. E. Dunlap, F. H. Buttel, P. Dickens & A. Gijswijt (Eds.), *Sociological theory and the environment: Classical foundations, contemporary insights* (pp. 329–350). Lanham, MD: Rowman and Littlefield Publishers, Inc.

duPreez, P. (1994). *Genocide: The psychology of mass murder.* New York: Marion Boyers.

Durkheim, É. (1897). *Le suicide.* Paris: Felix Alcan.

Dyck, E. (2005). Flashback: Psychiatric experimentation with LSD in historical perspective. *Canadian Journal of Psychiatry, 50*(7), 381–388.

Dyck, N. (1997). Tutelage, resistance and co-optation in Canadian Indian administration. *The Canadian Review of Sociology and Anthropology, 34*(3), 333–348.

Dyer, C. (2010). Lancet retracts Wakefield's MMR paper. *British Medical Journal* (BMJ), *340*, c696).

Dyer, K. (2009). Raising our heads above the parapet? societal attitudes to assisted suicide and consideration of the need for law reform in England and Wales. *Denning Law Journal, 21,* 27–48. Retrieved from http://search.ebscohost.com/login.aspx?direct=true&AuthType=ip, url,cookie,uid&db=a9h&AN=47574149&site=ehost-live

Dyer, R. (1997). *White.* London: Routledge.

Dyer, R. (2002). *Only entertainment* (2nd ed.). New York: Routledge, Inc.

Easton, D., & Liszt, C. A. (1997). *The ethical slut.* California: Greenery Press.

Edwards, B. H. (Ed.). (2007). *The souls of black folk.* Oxford, UK: Oxford University Press.

Egan, D. (2006). Resistance under the black light: Exploring the use of music in two exotic dance clubs. *Journal of Contemporary Ethnography, 35*(2), 201–219.

Eichler, M. (1988). *Families in Canada today* (2nd ed.). Toronto: Gage Educational Publishing.

Eichler, M. (1991). *Non-sexist research methods: A practical guide.* New York: Routledge.

Eichler, M. (2001). Women pioneers in Canadian sociology: The effects of a politics of gender and a politics of knowledge. *Canadian Journal of Sociology, 26*(3), 375–403.

Eichler, M. (2008). *Marriage and divorce.* The Canadian Encyclopedia. Historica Foundation.

Eisenkraft, H., & Berkowitz, P. (February, 2007). Critics call for more data but universities say they already issue more reports than ever and are accountable to the public. *University Affairs,* 29–30.

Eisenstadt, E. N. (Ed.). (1968). *Max Weber: On charisma and institution building.* Chicago: University of Chicago Press.

Eisenstadt, S. N. (1966). *Modernization: Protest and change.* Englewood Cliffs, NJ: Prentice-Hall, Inc.

Eisenstein, E., L. (1979). *The printing press as an agent of change: Communications and cultural transformations in early-modern Europe.* Cambridge, UK: Cambridge University Press.

Elbers, C., Lanjouw, P. F., Mistiaen, J. A., Özler, B., & Simler, K. (2004). On the unequal inequality of poor communities. *The World Bank Economic Review, 18*(3), 401. Retrieved from http://proquest.umi.com/pqdweb?did=800025471&Fmt=7&clientId=65345&RQT=309&VName=PQD

Elections Canada. (2008a). *40th general election.* Retrieved 25/10/2008, from http://enr.elections.ca/National_e.aspx

Elections Canada. (2008b). *Estimation of voter turnout by age group at the 2008 federal general election.* Retrieved 16/08/2011, from http://www.elections.ca/res/rec/part/estim/estimation40_e.pdf

Elections Canada. (2008c). *Final election expenses limits for registered political parties.* Retrieved 08/07/2010, from http://www.elections.ca/content.asp?section=pas&document=index&dir=40ge/limpol&lang=e&textonly=false

Elections Canada. (2008d). *The electoral system of Canada.* Retrieved 05/04/2008, from http://www.elections.ca/content.asp?section=gen&document=part1&dir=ces&lang=e&anchor=2&textonly=false#2

Elections Canada. (2010a). *Financial reports: Candidate's electoral campaign return.* Retrieved 08/07/2010, from http://www.elections.ca/scripts/webpep/fin2/summary_report.aspx

Elections Canada. (2010b). *There are limits to what you can give.* Retrieved 08/07/2010, from http://www.elections.ca/content.asp?section=fin&document=index&dir=lim&lang=e&textonly=false

Elections Canada. (2010c). *Voter turnout at federal elections and referendums, 1867–2008.* Retrieved 16/08/2011, from http://www.elections.ca/content.aspx?section=ele&dir=turn&document=index&lang=e

Elections Canada. (2011). *General election.* Retrieved 15/08/2011, from http://enr.elections.ca/National_e.aspx

Elkington, J. (1997). *Cannibals with forks: The triple bottom line of 21st century business.* Oxford: Capstone Publishing Ltd.

Elliott, A. (2009). Drastic plastic and the global electronic economy. *Society, 46*(4), 357–362. doi:10.1007/s12115-009-9226-5

Elliott, K. (2013). *Subsidizing farmers and biofuels in rich countries: An incoherent agenda for food security.* Retrieved 07/23/2014, from http://www.cgdev.org/publication/subsidizingfarmersandbiofuelsrichcountriesincoherentagendafoodsecurity

Ellis, S. (2009). Diversity and inclusivity at university: A survey of the experiences of lesbian, gay, bisexual and trans (LGBT) students in the UK. *Higher Education, 57,* 723–739.

Ellwood, W. (2003). *The no-nonsense guide to globalization.* Oxford OX4 1BW, UK: New Internationalist Publications Ltd.

Elvin, J. (2010). The continuing use of problematic sexual stereotypes in judicial decision-making. *Feminist Legal Studies, 18*(3), 275–297.

eMarketer. (2014). *Smartphone users worldwide will total 1.75 billion in 2014 smartphone users worldwide will total 1.75 billion in 2014.* Retrieved 07/21/2014, from http://www.emarketer.com/Article/SmartphoneUsersWorldwideWillTotal175Billion2014/1010536

Employment and Social Development Canada. (2014). Health - Life expectancy at birth. Accessed 04/08/2014, from http://www4.hrsdc.gc.ca/.3ndic.1t.4r@-eng.jsp?iid=3

Environment Canada. (2007a). *Clean air online - CEPA 1999 section 71.* Retrieved 8/7/2008, from http://library.mtroyal.ca:2137/cleanair-airpur/Turning_the_Corner/CEPA_1999,_Sec._71-WS074B0A75-1_En.htm

Environment Canada. (2007b). *The green lane: Climate change.* Retrieved 22/07/2008, from http://www.ec.gc.ca/climate/overview_science-e.html

Environment Canada. (2007c). *Water.* Retrieved 24/07/2008, from http://www.ec.gc.ca/default.asp?lang=en&n=76d556b9-1

Environment Canada. (2012). National pollutant release inventory - 2012 data and trends. Accessed 08/05/2014, from http://www.ec.gc.ca/inrp-npri/default.asp?lang=En&n=C0B6019F-1.

Environment Canada. (2014). Greenhouse gas emissions data. Accessed 05/14/2014, from https://www.ec.gc.ca/indicateurs-indicators/default.asp?lang=en&n=BFB1B398-1#ghg4

Environmental Protection Agency. (2007). *Ecosystems and biodiversity.* Retrieved 21/07/2008, from http://www.epa.gov/climatechange/effects/eco.html

Erikson, K. T. (1998). Trauma at Buffalo Creek. *Society, 35*(2), 153–161. Retrieved from http://library.mtroyal.ca:2048/login?url=http://search.ebscohost.com/login.aspx?direct=true&AuthType=ip,url,cookie,uid&db=a9h&AN=34411&site=ehost-live

Ernst, E. (2002). A systematic review of systematic reviews of homeopathy. *British Journal of Clinical Pharmacology, 54,* 577–582.

Eryilmaz, D., & Darn, S. (2005). *BBC British council teaching English - methodology - non-verbal communication.* Retrieved 01/10/2007, from http://www.teachingenglish.org.uk/think/methodology/nonverbal.shtml

Esmail, N. (2007). *Complementary and alternative medicine in Canada: Trends in use and public attitudes, 1997–2006.* Retrieved 30/08/2008, from http://www.fraserinstitute.org/commerce.web/product_files/Altmedicine.pdf

Etzkowitz, H. (1992). Inventions. In E. Borgatta, & M. L. Borgatta (Eds.), *Encyclopedia of sociology* (pp. 1001–1005). New York: Macmillan.

Evans-Pritchard, E. E. (1966). *Theories of primitive religion* (2nd ed.). London, UK: Oxford (Clarendon Press).

Evans, D. (1993). *Sexual citizenship: The material construction of sexualities*. London: Routledge.

Evans, M. (2006). Memories, monuments, histories: The re-thinking of the second world war since 1989. This article is based on a keynote address given to the 'War and memory conference,' university of sydney, 4 august 2006. *National Identities, 8*(4), 317–348.

Evans, P. (1995). *Embedded autonomy: States and industrial transformation*. Princeton, NJ: Princeton University Press.

Evans, P., & Swift, K. (2000). Single mothers and the press: Rising tides, moral panic and restructuring discourses. In S. Neysmith (Ed.), *Restructuring caring labour: Discourse, state practice and everyday life* (pp. 93–115). Toronto: Oxford University Press.

Facebook. (2008). *World wide pillow fight club 3.0*. Retrieved 07/07/2008, from http://www.facebook.com/event.php?eid=2411934188

Fagan, A. (2004). *Environment and democracy in the czech republic: The environmental movement in the transition Process*. Cheltenham, UK: Edward Elgar Publishing Inc.

Fahs, B. (2010). Radical refusals: On the anarchist politics of women choosing asexuality. *Sexualities, 13*(4), 445–461.

Fairness & Accuracy in Reporting. (2014). *Interlocking directorates*. Retrieved from http://www.fair.org/index.php

Falls, J. (2008). *Social classes and social networking*. Retrieved 11/05/2008, from http://www.socialmediaexplorer.com/2008/01/23/social-classes-and-social-networking/

Farganis, J. (Ed.). (2000). *Readings in social theory: The classical tradition to post-modernism*. (3rd. ed.). Boston, MA: McGraw-Hill Higher Education.

Farron, S. (2000). Prejudice is free but discrimination has costs. *Journal of Libertarian Studies, 14*(2), 179–245.

Fausto-Sterling, A. (2009). Dualing dualisms. In A. Ferber, K. Holcomb & T. Wentling (Eds.), *Sex, gender, and sexuality: The new basics* (pp. 6–20). New York: Oxford University Press.

Fay, B. (1987). *Critical social science: Liberation and its limits*. Ithaca, NY: Cornell University Press.

Feagin, J. R., & Feagin, C. B. (2008). *Racial and ethnic relations* (8th ed.). New York: Prentice-Hall, Inc.

Federal Communications Commission. (2005). *Internet: Something to share*. Retrieved 07/05/2008, from http://www.fcc.gov/omd/history/internet/something2share.html

Federman, M. (2004). *What is the meaning of the medium is the message?* Retrieved 01/06/2008, from http://individual.utoronto.ca/markfederman/article_mediumisthemessage.htm

Feffer, J. (2002). Challenging globalization: An introduction. In J. Feffer (Ed.), *Living in hope: People challenging globalization* (pp. 1–22). New York: Zed Books.

Feinstein, D. (2008). *The distraction of offshore drilling*. Retrieved 29/07/2008, from http://www.latimes.com/news/opinion/commentary/la-oe-feinstein18-2008jul18,0,4078387.story

Fellegi, I. P. (1997). *On poverty and low income*. Retrieved 09/12/2007, from http://www.statcan.ca/english/research/13F0027XIE/13F0027XIE.htm

Fendler, L., & Tuckey, S. F. (2006). Whose literacy? Discursive constructions of life and objectivity. *Educational Philosophy & Theory, 38*(5), 589–606.

Ferguson, H. (1986). Double-blind challenge studies of behavioral and cognitive effects of sucrose-aspartame ingestion in normal children. *Nutrition Reviews, 44*(Supplement), 144–150.

Ferrante, J. (2006). Global inequality and the challenges of reducing extreme poverty. (cover story). *Sociological Viewpoints, 22,* 5–19.

Retrieved from http://library.mtroyal.ca:2048/login?url=http://search.ebscohost.com/login.aspx?direct=true&AuthType=ip,url,cookie,uid&db=a9h&AN=21435791&site=ehost-live

Ferrao, V. 2010. *Paid work*. Ottawa: Statistics Canada. Retrieved from http://www.statcan.gc.ca/pub/89-503-x/2010001/article/11387-eng.pdf February 7, 2014

Ferreira, F. H. G., & Ravallion, M. (2008). *Global poverty and inequality: A review of the evidence* (No. WPS4623). Washington, DC: The World Bank.

Fielder, D. (2003). *Mid-life crisis FAQs | MaleHealth*. Retrieved 28/05/2010, from http://www.malehealth.co.uk/node/18837

Finch, J. (1989). *Family obligations and social change*. London: Polity.

Fine, M., & Torre, M. (2006). Intimate details: Participatory action research in prison. *Action Research, 4*(3), 253–269.

Fine, S. (2014). B.C. women's case reopens supreme court's assisted-suicide debate. Accessed 04/09/2014, from http://www.theglobeandmail.com/news/politics/supreme-court-to-revisit-assisted-suicide/article16383462/

Finger, J., & Flanagan, N. (2006). *The management bible*. Cape Town, SA: Zebra Press.

Finlay, B. (Ed.). (2007). *Before the second wave: Gender in the sociological -tradition* (2nd ed.). Upper Saddle River, New Jersey: Pearson Education Inc.

Fischer, M. J. (2007). Settling into campus life: Differences by Race/Ethnicity in college involvement and outcomes. *Journal of Higher Education, 78*(2), 125–161.

Fish, J. M. (2011). *The Myth of Race*. New York: Springer.

Fitzgerald, R. (2008). *Fear of crime and the neighbourhood context in Canadian cities* (No. 85-561-M NO 013). Ottawa: Minister of Industry.

Fitzgerald, R., & Carrington, P. (2011). Disproportionate minority contact in Canada: Police and visible minority youth. *Canadian Journal of Criminology and Criminal Justice, 53*(4), 449–486.

Fitzpatrick, M., & Nguyen, L. (2008). *Residential schools 'a sad chapter in our history,' Harper tells first nations*. Retrieved 22/06/2010, from http://www.nationalpost.com/story.html?id=580506

Fleras, A. (2009). *Unequal relations: An introduction to race, ethnic and aboriginal dynamics in Canada* (6th ed.). Toronto: Pearson.

Fleras, A., & Elliot, J. (2006). *Unequal relations: An introduction to race, ethnic and aboriginal dynamics in Canada* (5th ed.). Toronto: Pearson.

Foley, C., Holzman, C., & Wearing, S. (2007). Moving beyond conspicuous leisure consumption: Adolescent women, mobile phones and public space. *Leisure Studies, 26*(2), 179–192. doi:10.1080/02614360500418555

Fontaine, K. R., & Allison, D. B. (2002). Obesity and the internet. In C. G. Fairburn, & K. D. Brownell (Eds.), *Eating disorders and obesity: A comprehensive handbook* (2nd ed., pp. 609–612). New York: The Guilford Press.

Food Banks Canada. (2013). *Hunger count 2013*. Mississauga, ON: Food Banks Canada.

Foote, L., Krogman, N., & Spence, J. (2009). Should academics advocate on environmental issues? *Society and Natural Resources,22*(6), 579–589.

Forbes.com. (2014). The world's billionaires: #21 Mark Zuckerberg. Accessed 05/05/2014, from http://www.forbes.com/profile/mark-zuckerberg/

Ford-Jones, P. (2009). Physician brain drain: Exercising human rights or exploitation of the south? Understanding the multidimensional problem. *Undercurrent, 6*(3), 6–13. Retrieved from http://search.ebscohost.com/login.aspx?direct=true&AuthType=ip,url,cookie,uid&db=a9h&AN=48636165&site=ehost-live

Foreign Affairs, Trade and Development Canada. (2013). Statistical report on international assistance 2011–2012. Accessed 04/30/2014, from http://www.acdi-cida.gc.ca/acdi-cida/acdi-cida.nsf/eng/ANN-325135628-P2U

Forero, O. A., & Redclift, M. R. (2007). The production and marketing of sustainable forest products: Chewing gum in mexico. *Development in Practice, 17*(2), 196–207. doi:10.1080/09614520701195907

Fortin, I., Guay, S., Lavoie, V., Boisvert, J-M., & Beaudry, M. (2012). Intimate partner violence and psychological distress among young couples: Analysis of the moderating effect of social support. *Journal of Family Violence, 27*, 63–73.

Foster, J. B. (2007). *The imperialist world system.* Retrieved 17/06/2008, from http://www.monthlyreview.org/0507jbf.htm

Fotopoulos, T. (1999). Mass media, culture, and democracy. *Democracy & Nature: The International Journal of Inclusive Democracy, 5*(1), 33. Retrieved from http://library.mtroyal.ca:2048/login?url=http://search.ebscohost.com/login.aspx?direct=true&AuthType=ip,url,cookie,uid&db=a9h&AN=6651944&site=ehost-live

Foucault, M. (1975). *Discipline and punish: The birth of the prison* (A. Sheridan Trans.). New York, New York: Vintage Books.

Foucault, M. (1977). *Discipline and punish: The birth of the prison.* New York: Vintage.

Foucault, M. (1978). *The history of sexuality: An introduction volume I.* New York: Vintage.

Foucault, M. (1980). *Power/Knowledge.* New York: Pantheon Books.

Fowler, L., & Moore, A. R. (2012). Breast implants for graduation: A sociological examination of daughter and mother narratives. *Sociology Mind, 2*(1).

Fox, C., J., & Miller, H. T. (2005). Postmodern philosophy, postmodernity, and public organization theory. In T. D. Lynch, & P. L. Cruise (Eds.), *Handbook of organization theory and management: The philosophical approach* (2nd ed., pp. 631–661). London, UK: CRC Press.

Francis, B. (2006). The nature of gender. In C. Skelton, B. Francis & L. Smulyan (Eds.), *Handbook on gender and education* (pp. 7–17). London: Sage.

Francis, B. (2010). Gender, toys, and learning. *Oxford Review of Education, 36*(3), 325–344.

Frank, A. G. (1969). The development of underdevelopment. *Latin America: Underdevelopment or revolution.* (pp. 3–17). London and New York: Monthly Review Press.

Frank, A. G. (1972). *Lupenbourgeoisie: Lumpendevelopment: Dependence, class, and politics in Latin America.* New York and London: Monthly Review Press.

Frank, A. G. (1998). *Reorient: Global economy in the Asian age.* Berkeley, CA: University of California Press.

Frankenberg, R. (1993). *The social construction of whiteness: White women, race matters.* London: Routledge.

Frankfort-Nachmias, C., & Leon-Guerrero, A. (2011). *Social statistics for a diverse society* (6th ed.). Los Angeles: Sage Publications Pine Forge.

Frazer, E. (2008). Mary wollstonecraft on politics and friendship. *Political Studies, 56*(1), 237–256. doi:10.1111/j.1467-9248.2007.00670.x

Frediani, A. A. (2007). Amartya sen, the world bank, and the redress of urban poverty: A Brazilian case study. *Journal of Human Development, 8*(1), 133–152. doi:10.1080/14649880601101473

Free The Children. (2014). Results and impacts. Accessed 01/30/2014, from http://www.freethechildren.com/about-us/our-model/results-and-impacts/

Frei, M. (2011). *Is this the Twitter revolution?* Retrieved 4/27/2011, from http://www.bbc.co.uk/blogs/thereporters/mattfrei/2011/01/where_is_wikileaks_when_you_ne.html

Frempong, G., Ma X., & Mensah, J. (2012). Access to postsecondary education: Can schools compensate for socioeconomic disadvantage? *Higher Education, 63*, 19–32.

French Embassy. (n. d.). *Political party funding in france.* Retrieved 08/07/2010, from http://www.ambafrance-uk.org/Politics-Political-party-funding.html

Freudenburg, W. R. (2006). Environmental degradation, disproportionality, and the double diversion: Reaching out, reaching ahead, and reaching beyond. *Rural Sociology, 71*(1), 3–32. Retrieved from http://library.mtroyal.ca:2048/login?url=http://search.ebscohost.com/login.aspx?direct=true&AuthType=ip,url,cookie,uid&db=a9h&AN=19780047&site=ehost-live

Freudenburg, W. R., Gramling, R., Laska, S., & Erikson, K. T. (2009). Disproportionality and disaster: Hurricane Katrina and the Mississippi River-gulf outlet. *Social Science Quarterly (Blackwell Publishing Limited), 90*(3), 497–515. doi:10.1111/j.1540-6237.2009.00628.x

Frey, R. S., Dietz, T., & Kalof, L. (1992). Characteristics of successful American protest groups. *American Journal of Sociology, 98*(2), 368–387.

Frideres, J. S. (1996). The royal commission on Aboriginal peoples: The route to self-government. *The Canadian Journal of Native Studies, 16*(22), 247–266.

Frideres, J. S. (2002). Overcoming hurdles: Health care and Aboriginal people. In B. S. Bolaria, & H. D. Dickinson (Eds.), *Health, illness, and health care in Canada* (3rd ed.,). Scarborough, ON: Nelson Canada.

Friends of Canadian Broadcasting. (2005). *Controversy over Canadian content by Mindelle Jacobs.* Retrieved 5/15/2008, from http://www.friends.ca/News/Friends_News/archives/articles06280503.asp

Fries, C. J. (2008a). Classification of complementary and alternative medical practices: Family physicians' ratings of effectiveness. *Canadian Family Physician, 54*, 1–7.

Fries, C. J. (2008b). Governing the health of the hybrid self: Integrative medicine, neoliberalism, and the shifting biopolitics of subjectivity. *Health Sociology Review, 17*(4), 353–367. Retrieved from http://search.ebscohost.com/login.aspx?direct=true&AuthType=ip,url,cookie,uid&db=a9h&AN=35886702&site=ehost-live

Fries, C. J. (2010). In Bruce Ravelli (Ed.), *Personal communication*

Frosdick, S., & Newton, R. (2006). The nature and extent of football hooliganism in England and Wales. *Soccer & Society, 7*(4), 403–422. Retrieved from http://library.mtroyal.ca:2048/login?url=http://search.ebscohost.com/login.aspx?direct=true&AuthType=ip,url,cookie,uid&db=a9h&AN=22564308&site=ehost-live

Fuchs, L. H. (2000). *Beyond patriarchy: Jewish fathers and families.* Hanover, MA: University Press of New England.

Fujiwara, S. (2007). Problems of teaching about religion in Japan: Another textbook controversy against peace? *British Journal of Religious Education, 29*(1), 45–61.

Gaetz, S., Donaldson, J., Richter, T., & Gulliver, T. (2013). *The State of Homelessness in Canada. Canadian Homelessness.* Toronto, ON: Research Network Press.

Gagné, M., Tourigny, M., Joly, J., & Pouliot-Lapointe, J. (2007). Predictors of adult attitudes toward corporal punishment of children. *Journal of Interpersonal Violence, 22*(10), 1285–1304.

Gaille, B. (2014). How many blogs are on the internet? Accessed 08/05/2014, from http://www.wpvirtuoso.com/how-many-blogs-are-on-the-internet/

Gale Encyclopedia of Childhood and Adolescence. (1998). *Feral children.* Retrieved 11/1/2007, from http://findarticles.com/p/articles/mi_g2602/is_0002/ai_2602000247

Galison, P. L. (1999). Buildings and the subject of science. In P. L. Galison, & E. Thompson (Eds.), *The architecture of science.* Cambridge, MA: The MIT Press.

Gallupe, O., Boyce, W., & Fergus, S. (2009). Non-use of condoms at last intercourse among Canadian youth: Influence of sexual partners and social expectations. *The Canadian Journal of Human Sexuality, 18*(1-2), 27–34.

Galt, V. (2008, May 23). Older workers a drain? not a chance, study finds. *Globe and Mail,* B5.

Gamson, J. (2007). Publicity traps: Television talk shows and lesbian, gay, bisexual and transgender visibility. In N. Cook (Ed.), *Gender relations in global perspective: Essential readings* (pp. 253–264). Toronto: CSPI inc.

Gamson, W. A. (1990). *The strategy of social protest* (2nd ed.). Belmont, CA: Wadsworth.

Gangestad, S. W., & Scheyd, G. J. (2005). The evolution of human physical attractiveness. *Annual Review of Anthropology, 34*(1), 523–548.

Gannon, S. (2002). "Who am I?" an application of Foucault's social construction of identity to the caste system in India. *The Western Journal of Graduate Research, 11*(1), 1–14.

Gans, H. J. (2004). Journalism, journalism education, and democracy. *Journalism & Mass Communication Educator, 59*(1), 10–16. Retrieved from http://search.ebscohost.com/login.aspx?direct=true&AuthType= ip,url,cookie,uid&db=a9h&AN=13858276&site=ehost-live

Gans, H., J. (1995). *The war against the poor: The underclass and antipoverty policy*. New York: BasicBooks.

Gantsho, M. S., & Karani, P. (2007). Entrepreneurship and innovation in development finance institutions for promoting the clean development mechanism in Africa. *Development Southern Africa, 24*(2), 335–344. doi:10.1080/03768350701327269

Gardner, D. (2000). *When racial categories make no sense*. Retrieved 10/01/2008, from http://www.sinc.sunysb.edu/Stu/lmarfogl/project/ race_gerdner.htm

Garland-Thomson, R. (1997). Feminist theory, the body, and the disabled figure. In L. J. Davis (Ed.), *The disabilities studies reader* (pp. 279–294). New York: Routledge, Inc.

Garland, D. (1996). The limits of the sovereign state: Strategies of crime control in contemporary society. *British Journal of Criminology, 36*(4), 445–471.

Garner, R. (Ed.). (2000). *Social theory: Continuity and confrontation: A reader*. Peterborough, ON: Broadview Press.

Garner, R. (Ed.). (2007). *Social theory: Continuity and confrontation A reader* (2nd ed.). Peterborough: Broadview Press.

Garner, R., Carrière, G. & Sanmartin, C. (2010). *The health of Inuit, Métis and First Nations adults living off-reserve in canada: The impact of socio-economic status on inequalities in health*. Retrieved 24/12/2010, from http://www.statcan.gc.ca/pub/82-622-x/82-622- x2010004-eng.htm

Gartner, R., Dawson, M., & Crawford, M. (1998). Woman killing: Intimate femicide in Ontario, 1974–1994. *Resources for Feminist Research, 26*(3/4), 151–173.

Gaskell, J., McLaren, A., & Novogrodsky, M. (1989). *Claiming an education: Feminism and Canadian schools*. Toronto: Our Schools Our Selves.

Gaston, K. J. (2008). Biodiversity and extinction: The importance of being common. *Progress in Physical Geography, 32*(1), 73–79. doi:10.1177/0309133308089499

Gastwirth, J., Modarres, R., & Bura, E. (2005). The use of the lorenz curve, gini index and related measures of relative inequality and uniformity in securities law. *METRON - International Journal of Statistics, 3*, 451–469.

Gauthier, M. (2004). Incentives and accountability: The Canadian context. *Higher Education Management and Policy, 16*(2), 95–108.

Gazso, A. (2004). Women's inequality in the workplace as framed in news discourse: Refracting from gender ideology. *The Canadian Review of Sociology and Anthropology, 41*(4), 449–473. Retrieved from http:// library.mtroyal.ca:2083/pqdweb?did=778900691&Fmt=7&clientId= 65345&RQT=309&VName=PQD

Geertzen, J., Van Wilgen, C., Schrier, E., & Dijkstra, P. (2006). Chronic pain in rehabilitation medicine. *Disability & Rehabilitation, 28*(6), 363–367. doi:10.1080/09638280500287437

Gellman, B. (2010). *Runner-up: Julian Assange - person of the year 2010*. Retrieved 28/04/2011, from http://www.time.com/time/specials/ packages/article/0,28804,2036683_2037118_2037146,00.html

Gentleman, J., & Park, E. (1997). Divorce in the 1990s. *Health Reports, 9*(2), 53–58.

George, J., & Wilcox, L. M. (1996). *American extremists: Militias, supremacists, klansmen, communists & others*. Amherst, NY: Prometheus Books.

George, S. (2008). *Globalization and war*. Retrieved 23/07/2010, from http://www.tni.org/detail_page.phtml?act_id=18042

Gerald, G. (2007). The "down low": New jargon, sensationalism, or agent of change? In G. Herdt, & C. Howe (Eds.), *21st century sexualities:*

Contemporary issues in health, education, and rights (pp. 44–46). New York: Routledge.

Gerhardt, U. (2001). Parsons's analysis of the societal community. In J. A. Trevino, & N. J. Smelser (Eds.), *Talcott parsons today: His theory and legacy in contemporary sociology* (pp. 177–222). Lanham, MD: Rowman and Littlefield Publishers, Inc.

Gerlach, C. (2006). Extremely violent societies: An alternative to the concept of genocide. *Journal of Genocide Research, 8*(4), 455–471.

Germain, A., & Kidwell, J. (2007). Not separate, still unequal: The Beijing agreement and the feminization of HIV/AIDS. *21st century sexualities: Contemporary issues in health, education, and rights* (pp. 121–123). New York: Routledge.

Gershon, R. A. (2005). The transnationals: Media corporations, international TV trade and entertainment flows. In A. Cooper-Chen (Ed.), *Global entertainment media: Content, audiences, issues* (pp. 17–38). Mahwah, NJ: Lawrence Erlbaum Associates.

Gibson, J. L., & Howard, M. M. (2007). Russian anti-semitism and the scapegoating of Jews. *British Journal of Political Science, 37*, 193–223.

Giddens, A. (1990). The consequences of modernity. London: Polity.

Giddens, A. (1997). *Sociology* (3rd ed.). London: Polity Press.

Giddens, A. (1998). *The third way: The renewal of social democracy*. Cambridge: Polity.

Giddens, A. (2003). *Runaway world: How globalization is reshaping our lives*. New York: Routledge.

Gilbert, D., & Kahl, J. A. (1993). *The American class structure: A new synthesis* (4th ed.). Belmont, CA: Wadsworth.

Gilder, G. (1986). *Men and marriage*. New York: Pelican.

Gill, C. (2007). 'Cuz the black chick always gets it first. In N. Cook (Ed.), *Gender relations in global perspective: Essential readings* (pp. 243–252). Toronto: CSPI.

Gillis, A. (2007, November, 15). Cheating themselves. *University Affairs,*

Ginsberg, P., & Gekonge, M. (2004). MTV, technology, the secular trend, and HIV/AIDS: Why Kenyan parents need to learn about adolescent development. *Dialectical Anthropology, 28*(3), 353–364. doi:10.1007/ s10624-004-3587-3

Ginsburg, J. A., Doherty, R. B., Ralston Jr, F., & Senkeeto, N. (2008). Achieving a high-performance health care system with universal access: What the United states can learn from other countries. *Annals of Internal Medicine, 148*(1), 55–75. Retrieved from http:// library.mtroyal.ca:2048/login?url=http://library.mtroyal.ca:2924/ login.aspx?direct=true&AuthType=ip,url,cookie,uid&db=a9h&AN =28331372&site=ehost-live

Gintis, H. (2006). Moral sense and material interests. *Social Research, 73*(2), 377–404.

Gitelson, A., Dudley, R., & Dubnick, M. (2012). *American Government*. Boston, MA: Wadsworth.

Gladwell, M. (2000). *The tipping point: How little things can make a big difference*. New York: Little, Brown and Company.

Glasbeek, A. (2005). *Family violence*. Unpublished manuscript.

Glasbeek, A. (2006a). "My wife has endured a torrent of abuse": Gender, safety and anti-squeegee discourses in Toronto, 1998–2000. *Windsor Yearbook of Access to Justice, 24*(1), 55–76.

Glasbeek, A. (2006b). *Moral regulation and governance in Canada: History, context and critical issues*. Toronto: Canadian Scholars' Press.

Glasser, R. (1976). Leisure policy, identity and work. In J. Haworth, & M. A. Smith (Eds.), *Work and leisure* (pp. 36–52). Princeton, NJ: Princeton Book Co.

Global Campaign for Education. (2004). *Undervaluing teachers: IMF policies squeeze Zambia's education system*. Retrieved 17/08/2011, from http://www.oxfam.org.uk/resources/policy/education/downloads/ gce_zambia_imf.pdf

Global Initiative to End All Corporal Punishment of Children. (2007). *End all corporal punishment of children*. Retrieved 11/12/2007, from http:// www.endcorporalpunishment.org/

Glover, K. (2009). *Racial profiling: Research, racism and resistance*. Lanham: Rowman and Littlefield.

Göçmen, D. (2006). *[Marxism-thaxis] false consciousness*. Retrieved 11/09/2007, from http://www.mail-archive.com/marxism-thaxis@lists.econ.utah.edu/msg03424.html

Godelier, M. (1999). *The enigma of the gift* (Nora Scott Trans.). Chicago: University of Chicago Press.

Godley, J., & McLaren, L. (2010). Socioeconomic status and body mass index in Canada: Exploring measures and mechanisms SES and BMI in Canada. *Canadian Review of Sociology, 47*(4), 381–403. doi:10.1111/j.1755-618X.2010.01244.x

Goff, C. (2011). *Criminal justice in Canada* (5th ed.). Scarborough: Nelson.

Goffman, E. (1959). *The presentation of self in everyday life*. New York: Anchor.

Goffman, E. (1961). *Asylums: Essays on the social situation of mental patients and other inmates*. New York: Anchor Books.

Goffman, E. (1977). The arrangement between the sexes. *Theory and Society, 4*(3), 301–331.

Goldenberg, S. (2010). *World bank's $3.75bn coal plant loan defies environment criticism*. Retrieved 07/23/2014, from http://www.theguardian.com/business/2010/apr/09/worldbankcriticisedoverpowerstation

Goldie, T. (2008). *Queersexlife*. Vancouver: Arsenal Pulp Press.

Goldstein, J. (2004). *International relations* (5th ed.). New York: Pearson Longman.

Goode, E. (2010). *Deviant behaviour* (9th ed. ed.). Toronto: Prentice Hall.

Goodman, E. (2003). *Nature's terror rides man-made wings*. Retrieved 9/4/2008, from http://community.seattletimes.nwsource.com/archive/?date=20030425&slug=goodman25

Goodrich, P. (1993). Oedipus lex: Slips in interpretation and law. *Legal Studies, 13*(3), 381–395.

Goodwin, J., & Jasper, J. M., eds. (2009). *The Social Movements Reader: Cases and Concepts*. Second ed. Oxford, UK: Blackwell Publishing.

Gordon, J. A. (2006). From liberation to human rights: Challenges for teachers of the burakumin in Japan. *Race, Ethnicity & Education, 9*(2), 183–202.

Gordon, J., & Blum, I. (2004). Shifting programs or undercutting equity? A preliminary study using three university academic calendars. In M. Reimer (Ed.), *Inside corporate U: Women in the academy speak out* (pp. 103–117). Toronto: Sumach Press.

Gordon, L. (1984). Paul willis-education, cultural production, and social reproduction. *British Journal of Sociology of Education, 5*(2), 105–115.

Gordon, L., Deaning Sharpley-Whiting, T., & T. White, R. (Eds.). (1996). *Fanon: A critical reader*. Oxford: Blackwell Publishers Ltd.

Gorlick, C. (2005). Divorce: Options available, constraints forced, pathways taken. In N. Mandell, & A. Duffy (Eds.), *Canadian families: Diversity, conflict and change* (3rd ed., pp. 210–238). Toronto: Thomson Nelson.

Gorman-Murray, A. (2007). Contesting domestic ideals: Queering the Australian home. *Australian Geographer, 38*(2), 195–213.

GourmetSpot.com. (n.d.). *How many people can one farmer feed?* Retrieved 27/03/2008, from http://www.gourmetspot.com/know/farmerfeeds.htm

Government of Canada. (2003). *The Canada health act: Overview and options (94-4E)*. Retrieved 29/06/2008, from http://www.parl.gc.ca/information/library/prbpubs/944-e.htm#chistoricaltxt

Government of Canada. (2007a). *Canadian environmental sustainability indicators 2007*. Retrieved 23/07/2008, from http://www.ec.gc.ca/environmentandresources/CESIHL2007/CESIHL2007_e.cfm#s4

Government of Canada. (2007b). *Chinese head tax and historical recognition initiatives*. Retrieved 1/8/2008, from http://www.pch.gc.ca/progs/multi/redress-redressement/index_e.cfm

Government of Canada. (2014). *Members of parliament*. Retrieved 29/06/2010, from http://webinfo.parl.gc.ca/MembersOfParliament/MainMPsCompleteList.aspx?TimePeriod=Current&Language=E

Govinda, R. (2008). Re-inventing dalit women's identity? Dynamics of social activism and electoral politics in rural north india. *Contemporary South Asia, 16*(4), 427–440. doi:10.1080/09584930802472772

Goyder, J., & Frank, K. (2007). A scale of occupational prestige in Canada, based on NOC major groups. *Canadian Journal of Sociology, 32*(1), 63–83.

Goyder, J., Guppy, N., & Thompson, M. (2003). The allocation of male and female occupational prestige in an Ontario urban area: A quarter-century replication. *The Canadian Review of Sociology & Anthropology, 40*(4), 417–439. Retrieved from http://library.mtroyal.ca:2083/pqdweb?did=665951271&Fmt=7&clientId=65345&RQT=309&VName=PQD

Grabb, E. G. (1990). *Theories of social inequality: Classical and contemporary perspectives* (2nd ed.). Toronto, ON: Holt, Rinehart and Winston.

Gracey, H. L. (1977). Learning the student role: Kindergarten as academic boot camp. In H. Gracey, & D. Wrong (Eds.), *Readings in introductory sociology* (3rd ed.). Boston, MA: Allyn and Bacon.

Graefe, E. A. (2010). The conflicting obligations of museums possessing Nazi-looted art. *Boston College Law Review, 51*(2), 473–515. Retrieved from http://search.ebscohost.com/login.aspx?direct=true&AuthType=ip,url,cookie,uid&db=a9h&AN=51641677&site=ehost-live

Graham, M., & Bruce, E. (2006). "Seen and not heard" sociological approaches to childhood: Black children, agency and implications for child welfare. Journal of Sociology & Social Welfare, 33(4), 51–67.

Granatstein, J. L., & Johnson, G. A. (2008). The evacuation of the Japanese Canadians, 1942: A realist critique of the received version. In B. Walker (Ed.), *The history of immigration and racism in Canada: Essential readings* (pp. 221–236). Toronto, ON: Canadian Scholars Press.

Grant, K. R. (2002). A conversation on th eFuture of the academy with James Turk, PhD, executive director, Canadian association of university teachers. *Canadian Review of Sociology & Anthropology, 39*(3), 261–274.

Gravlee, C. C. (2009). How race becomes biology: Embodiment of social inequality. *American Journal of Physical Anthropology, 139*(1), 47–57. doi:10.1002/ajpa.20983

Gray, J. (n.d.). *The pros and cons of text messages*. Retrieved 07/05/2008, from http://www.helium.com/items/633125-nothing-embodies-modern-living

Gray, J. (2009). Review of *The Viagra Ad Venture: Masculinity, Media, and the Performance of Sexual Health*. *Journal of Health Communication, 14*, 96–98.

Graycar, R. (2008). Gender, race, bias and perspective: Or, how otherness colours your judgment. *International Journal of the Legal Profession, 15*(1-2), 7386.

Greeley, A. M. (1972). *The denominational society: A sociological approach to religion in America*. Glenview, IL: Scott, Foresman.

Green, A. (2010). Remembering Foucault: Queer theory and disciplinary power. *Sexualities, 13*(3), 316–337.

Green, A. I. (2007). Queer theory and sociology: Locating the subject and the self in sexuality studies. *Sociological Theory, 25*(1), 26–45.

Greenberg, E. S., & Page, B. I. (2007). *The struggle for democracy* (8th ed.). New York: Pearson Longman.

Greenemeier, L. (2009, Caster Semenya and the issue of gender ambiguity. *Scientific American, August 21* Retrieved from http://www.scientificamerican.com/blog/60-second-science/post.cfm?id=runner-semenyas–case-highlights-the-2009-08-21

Greer, G. (2011). *Julian assange*. Retrieved 28/04/2011, from http://www.time.com/time/specials/packages/article/0,28804,2066367_2066369_2066107,00.html

Greist, J. (2010). The internet: Every good thing has a dark side. *World Psychiatry, 9*(2), 95–96.

Grelland, H. H. (2006). The Sapir-Whorf hypothesis and the meaning of quantum mechanics. *AIP Conference Proceedings, 810*(1), 325–329.

Griffin, F. J. (2003 [1903]). *The souls of black folks (introduction)* Barnes & Nobles Classics.

Grimshaw, D., Beynon, H., Rubery, J., & Ward, K. (2002). The restructuring of career paths in large service sector organizations: 'delayering', upskilling and polarisation. *Sociological Review, 50*(1), 89–116. Retrieved from http://library.mtroyal.ca:2048/login?url=http://search.ebscohost.com/login.aspx?direct=true&AuthType=ip,url,cookie,uid&db=a9h&AN=6412541&site=ehost-live

Grindstaff, L., & West, E. (2006). Cheerleading and the gendered politics of sport. *Social Problems, 53*(4), 500–518.

Griswold, D. T. (2006). Globalization promotes democracy. In L. I. Gerdes (Ed.), *Globalization opposing viewpoints* (pp. 49–57). New York: Thompson/Gale.

Gronow, J. (1988). The element of irrationality: Max Weber's diagnosis of modern culture. *Acta Sociologica, 31*(4), 319–331.

Gross, R. M. (1996). *Feminism and religion: An introduction.* Boston, MA: Beacon Press.

Gross, T. M. (2009). If races don't exist, then why am I white?": The race concept within contemporary forensic anthropology. Retrieved 18/06/2010, from http://www.focusanthro.org/archive/2008-2009/Gross_0809.pdf

Grubler, A. (1996). Time for a change: On the patterns of diffusion of innovation. *Daedalus, 125*(3), 19–43.

Guibernau, M. (2006). National identity, devolution and secession in Canada, Britain and Spain. *Nations & Nationalism, 12*(1), 51–76. doi:10.1111/j.1469-8129.2005.00230.x

Gupta, S., & Ross, N. A. (2010). *Under the microscope: Health disparities within Canadian cities.* Retrieved 10/07/2010, from http://www.hc-sc.gc.ca/sr-sr/pubs/hpr-rpms/bull/2007-people-place-gens-lieux/dispartities-disparites-eng.php#f3d

Gupta, P., & Chan, E. (2012). Apple, Foxconn set new standard for Chinese workers. Accessed 08/05/2014, from http://www.reuters.com/article/2012/03/30/us-apple-foxconn-idUSBRE82S19720120330

Hagan, J., & McCarthy, B. (1992). Mean streets: The theoretical significance of situational delinquency among homeless youths. *American Journal of Sociology, 98*(3), 597–627.

Hagan, J., & McCarthy, B. (1998). *Mean streets: Youth crime and homelessness.* Cambridge, UK: Cambrige University Press.

Hagan, J., & Hansford-Bowles, S. (2005). From resistance to activism: The emergence and persistence of activism among American Vietnam war resisters in Canada. *Social Movement Studies, 4*(3), 231–259.

Haggerty, K. (2004). Ethics creep: Governing Social science research in the name of ethics. *Qualitative Sociology, 27*(4), 391–414.

Haigh, R. A. (1999). Reconstructing paradise: Canada's health care system, alternative medicine and the *charter of rights. Health Law Journal, 7*(141), 191.

Hale, S. (1990). *Controversies in sociology.* Toronto: Copp Clark Pitman.

Haley, E. (2004). The 'captive scientist': Corporate influences over scientific research. In M. Reimer (Ed.), *Inside corporate U: Women in the academy speak out* (pp. 87–99). Toronto: Sumach Press.

Hall, J. D. (2005). 'The mind that burns in each body': Women, rape, and racial violence. In T. Steele (Ed.), *Sex, self, and society: The social context of sexuality* (pp. 363–375). Belmont: Thomson.

Hall, R., & Sandler, B. (1982). *The classroom climate: A chilly one for women.* Washington: Project on the Status and Education of Women.

Hall, S., Held, D., Hubert, D., & Thompson, K. (Eds.). (1996). *Modernity: An introduction to modern societies.* Oxford, UK: Blackwell Publishing Limited.

Hallgrimsdottir, H. K., & Benoit, C. (2007). From wage slaves to wage workers: Cultural opportunity structures and the evolution of the wage demands of the knights of labor and the American federation of labor, 1880–1900. *Social Forces, 85*(3), 1393–1411. http://www.jstor.org/stable/4494978

Hallgrimsdottir, H. K., Benoit, C., & Phillips, R. (2013). The mother-citizen and the working girl: First-wave feminist citizenship claims in Canada and discursive opportunities for twenty-first century childcare policy. *Canadian Review of sociology/revue Canadienne De Sociologie, 50*(1), 27–51.

Hamdad, M. (2003). *Valuing households' unpaid work in Canada, 1992 and 1998: Trends and sources of change.* Ottawa: Statistics Canada.

Hamilton, M. (2001). *The sociology of religion: Theoretical and comparative perspectives* (2nd ed.). New York, New York: Routledge.

Hammond, I. (2005). Lessons from Ivan Illich. *Canadian Association of Radiologists Journal, 56*(1), 13–14.

Hampton, R. (2010). Black learners in Canada. *Race & Class, 52*(1), 103–110.

Haney, T. J. (2011). In Bruce Ravelli (Ed.), *Personal correspondence*

Haney, T. J., Elliott, J. R., & Fussell, E. (2007). Families and Huhricane response: Evacuation, separation, and the emotional toll of hurricane Katrina. *The Sociology of Katrina: Perspectives on a Modern Catastrophe, 8*, 71. Lanham, MA: Rowman & Littlefield.

Hannigan, J. (2006). *Environmental sociology* (2nd ed.). New York: Routledge, Taylor & Francis Group.

Hansen, X. (2004). Back to the future: The origins and return of sociology as the scientific study of societal development. *American Sociological Association, 2004 Annual Meeting,* San Francisco, CA. 1–22.

Harding, S. (2005). "Science and democracy": Replayed or redesigned? *Social Epistemology, 19*(1 (January-March)), 5–18.

Harding, S. (2006). *Science and social inequality: Feminist and postcolonial issues.* Chicago, ILL: University of Illinois Press.

Harkin, J. (2003). *Mobilisation: The growing public interest in mobile technology.* London, UK: Demos.

Harman, L. (2005). Family poverty and economic struggles. In N. Mandell, & A. Duffy (Eds.), *Canadian families: Diversity, conflict and change* (pp. 241–275). Toronto: Thomson Nelson.

Harmes, A. (2011). The limits of carbon disclosure: Theorizing the business case for investor environmentalism. *Global Environmental Politics, 11*(2), 98–119.

Harnois, C. E. (2005). Different paths to different feminisms? Bridging multiracial feminist theory and quantitative sociological gender research. *Gender & Society, 19*(6), 809–828.

Harper, C. L. (2008). *Environment and society: Human perspectives on environmental issues* (4th ed.). Upper Saddle River, New Jersey: Pearson Prentice Hall.

Harris, R., Ellicott, A., & Holmes, D. (1986). The timing of psychosocial transitions and changes in women's lives: An examination of women aged 45 to 60. *Journal of Personality and Social Psychology, 51,* 409–416.

Harrison, K. D. (2007). *When languages die: The extinction of the world's languages and the erosion of human knowledge.* New York, NY: Oxford University Press.

Harrison, K. D. (2010). *The last speakers: The quest to save the world's most endangered languages.* Washington, DC: National Geographic Books.

Hartl, R. F., Novak, A. J., Rao, A. G., & Sethi, S. P. (2003). Optimal pricing of a product diffusing in rich and poor populations. *Journal of Optimization Theory and Applications, 117*(2), 349. Retrieved from http://proquest.umi.com/pqdweb?did=983551831&Fmt=7&clientId=65345&RQT=309&VName=PQD

Hartman, C., & Squires, G. (2006). *There is no such thing as a natural disaster: Race, class, and hurricane Katrina.* New York: Routledge.

Harvey, D. L., & Reed, M. H. (1996). The culture of poverty: An ideological analysis. *Sociological Perspectives, 39*(4), 465. Retrieved from http://proquest.umi.com/pqdweb?did=10976631&Fmt=7&clientId=65345&RQT=309&VName=PQD

Hastings, P. D., McShane, K. E., Parker, R., & Ladha, F. (2007). Ready to make nice: Parental socialization of young sons' and daughters' prosocial behaviors with peers. *Journal of Genetic Psychology, 168*(2), 177–200.

Hawthorne, S. (2007). Land, bodies, and knowledge: Biocolonialism of plants, indigenous peoples, women, and people with disabilities. *Signs: Journal of Women in Culture & Society, 32*(2), 314–323. Retrieved from http://library.mtroyal.ca:2048/login?url=http://search.ebscohost.com/login.aspx?direct=true&AuthType=ip,url,cookie,uid&db=a9h&AN=23730418&site=ehost-live

Hay, D. (2009). *Poverty reduction policies and programs.* Canadian Council on Social Development.

Hayden, C. (2005). Bioprospecting's representational dilemma. *Science as Culture, 14*(2), 185–200. doi:10.1080/09505430500110994

Hayes, M. (2013). Tim Bosma murder: Men accused of slaying say they want to tell their story, but can't. *Toronto Star.* Accessed 23/09/2013, from http://www.thestar.com/news/gta/2013/09/12/tim_bosma_murder_men_accused_of_slaying_say_they_want_to_tell_their_story_but_cant.html

Head, J. W. (2005). *The future of global economic organizations: An evaluation of criticisms leveled at the IMF, the multilateral development banks, and the WTO.* New York, NY: Transnational Publishers.

Health Canada. (2004). *Home & continuing care.* Retrieved 26/06/2008, from http://www.hc-sc.gc.ca/hcs-sss/home-domicile/index-eng.php

Health Canada. (2005). *Statistical profile on the health of First Nations in Canada.* Retrieved 28/01/2008, from http://www.hc-sc.gc.ca/fnih-spni/pubs/gen/stats_profil_e.html

Health Canada. (2006a). *2003 first ministers' accord on health care renewal.* Retrieved 29/06/2008, from http://www.hc-sc.gc.ca/hcs-sss/delivery-prestation/fptcollab/2003accord/index-eng.php

Health Canada. (2006b). *Healthy Canadians: A federal report on comparable health indicators 2006.* Retrieved 30/06/2008, from http://www.hc-sc.gc.ca/hcs-sss/pubs/system-regime/2006-fed-comp-indicat/2006-fed-comp-indicat-3-eng.php

Health Council of Canada. (2008). *Rekindling reform: Health care renewal in Canada, 2003–2008.* Toronto, ON: Health Council.

Health, Poverty, Action. (2014). *Debt and global health.* Retrieved 07/23/2014, from http://www.healthpovertyaction.org/policyandresources/debtandglobalhealth/

Healy, J. P. (2011). Involvement in a new religious movement: From discovery to disenchantment. *Journal of Spirituality in Mental Health, 13*(1), 2–21. doi:10.1080/19349637.2011.547125

Heard, A. (2008). *Historical voter turnout in Canadian federal elections - 1867–2008.* Retrieved 30/06/2010, from http://www.sfu.ca/~aheard/elections/historical-turnout.html

Heclo, H. (2007). Is America a christian nation? *Political Science Quarterly, 122*(1), 59–87.

Hedley, R. A. (2002). *Running out of control: Dilemmas of globalization.* Bloomfield, CT: Kumarian Press, Inc.

Heidensohn, F. (2010). The deviance of women: A critique and an enquiry. *The British Journal of Sociology, 61*(Supplement 1), 111–126.

Heilman, S. C. (2000). *Defenders of the faith: Inside ultra-orthodox jewry.* Berkeley, CA: University of California Press.

Heit, E., & Rotello, C. M. (2010). Relations between inductive reasoning and deductive reasoning. *Journal of Experimental Psychology / Learning, Memory & Cognition, 36*(3), 805–812. doi:10.1037/a0018784

Helleiner, J. (1997). "Women of the itinerant class": Gender and anti-traveller racism in Ireland. *Women's Studies International Forum, 20*(2), 275–287.

Helleiner, J. (2000). *Irish travellers: Racism and the politics of culture.* Toronto: University of Toronto Press.

Helly, D. (2004). Are Muslims discriminated against in Canada since September 2001? *Canadian Ethnic Studies, 36*(1), 24–47.

Helsper, E. J. (2010). Gendered internet use across generations and life stages. *Communication Research, 37*(3), 352–374.

Hemphill, H., & Haines, R. (1997). *Discrimination, harassment, and the failure of diversity training: What to do now?.* Westport, Connecticut: Quorum Books.

Henry, F., & Tator, C. (Eds.). (2009). *Racism in the Canadian university.* Toronto: University of Toronto Press.

Henry, F., & Tator, C. (1994). The ideology of racism—'democratic racism'. *Canadian Ethnic Studies, 26*(2), 1–14.

Henry, S. (2009). School violence beyond Columbine: A complex problem in need of an interdisciplinary analysis. *American Behavioral Scientist, 52*(9), 1246–1265. Retrieved from http://search.ebscohost.com/login.aspx?direct=true&AuthType=ip,url,cookie,uid&db=a9h&AN=37615354&site=ehost-live

Heo, U., & Hahm, S. D. (2007). The political economy of U.S. direct investment in east Asian NICs, 1966–2000. *International Interactions, 33*(2), 119–133. doi:10.1080/03050620701277723

Herbert Emery, J. C., & Matheson, J. (2008). *Public pensions and elderly mortality in Canada: Comparing means tested and universal eligibility, 1921–1966.* Retrieved 28/05/2010, from http://qed.econ.queensu.ca/CNEH/papers/EmeryMatheson.pdf

Herdt, G., & Howe, C. (2007). Sexual health, wellness, and medical models. In G. Herdt, & C. Howe (Eds.), *21st century sexualities: Contemporary issues in health, education, and rights* (pp. 89–91). New York: Routledge.

Herman, E. S. (1999 (Winter)). The threat of globalization. *New Politics, 7*(22), 13/06/2008. Retrieved from http://www.globalpolicy.org/globaliz/define/hermantk.htm

Herman, E. S. (2003). The propaganda model: A retrospective. *Against all Reason, 1,* 1–14.

Herman, E. S., & Chomsky, N. (1988). *Manufacturing consent: The political economy of the mass media.* New York: Pantheon Books.

Herriot, P. (2009). *Religious fundamentalism: Global, local, and personal.* New York, New York: Routledge.

Herzog, H. (2005). On home turf: Interview location and its social meaning. *Qualitative Sociology, 28*(1), 25–47.

Hetherington, E., & Baltes, P. (1988). Child psychology and life-span development. In E. Hetherington, R. Lerner & M. Perlmutter (Eds.), *Child development in life-span perspective.* Hillsdale, NJ: Erlbaum.

Heyes, C. (2007). Cosmetic surgery and the televisual makeover: A Foucauldian feminist reading. *Feminist Media Studies, 7*(1), 17–32.

Heyes, C. J. (2009). Diagnosing culture: Body dysmorphic disorder and cosmetic surgery. *Body & Society, 15*(4), 73–93.

Hietalahti1, J., & Linden, M. (2006). Socio-economic impacts of microfinance and repayment performance: A case study of the small enterprise foundation, South Africa. *Progress in Development Studies, 6*(3), 201–210. doi:10.1191/1464993406ps138oa

Hill Collins, P. (2005). The sexual politics of black womanhood. In T. L. Steele (Ed.), *Sex, self and society: The social context of sexuality.* California: Wadsworth.

Hill Lindley, S. (2003). *"You have stept out of your place": A history of women and religion in America.* Lousiville, KY: Westminster John Knox Press.

Hiller, H. (2001). Legacy for a new millennium: Canadian sociology in the twentieth century as seen through its publications. *Canadian Journal of Sociology, 26*(3), 257–263.

Hiller, H. (1996). *Canadian society: A macro analysis* (3rd ed.). Scarborough: Prentice Hall.

Hiller, H. H., & Di Luzio, L. (2001). Text and context: Another 'chapter' in the evolution of sociology in Canada. *Canadian Journal of Sociology, 26*(3), 487–512.

Hilsdon, A. (2007). Transnationalism and agency in east Malaysia: Filipina migrants in the nightlife industries. *Australian Journal of Anthropology, 18*(2), 172–193. Retrieved from http://search.ebscohost.com/login.aspx?direct=true&AuthType=ip,url,cookie,uid&db=a9h&AN=25857458&site=ehost-live

Hilton, I. (2008). The reality of global warming. *World Policy Journal, 25*(1), 1–8. Retrieved from http://library.mtroyal.ca:2048/login?url=http://search.ebscohost.com/login.aspx?direct=true&AuthType=ip,url,cookie,uid&db=a9h&AN=32695579&site=ehost-live

Hilton, M. (2007). Social activism in an age of consumption: The organized consumer movement. *Social History, 32*(2), 121–143. doi:10.1080/03071020701245751

Hinderliter, R. (2007). *The history of YouTube*. Retrieved 10/05/2008, 2008, from http://mediatedcultures.net/ksudigg/?p=108

Hine, C. (2005). Internet research and the sociology of cyber-social-scientific knowledge. *The Information Society, 21,* 239-248.

Hines, S. (2004). Transgender. In J. Eadie (Ed.), *Sexuality* (pp. 231–232). London: Arnold.

Hinton, S. E. (1967). *The outsiders*. New York: Puffin Books.

Hird, M. (2004). Pansexual. In J. Eadie (Ed.), *Sexuality: The essential glossary* (pp. 150). London: Arnold.

History News Network. (2006). *What is the difference between Sunni and Shiite Muslims—and why does it matter?* Retrieved 09/03/2008, from http://hnn.us/articles/934.html

Hlynka, D. (2004). *CM magazine: McLuhan's wake*. Retrieved 5/5/2008, from http://library.mtroyal.ca:2521/cm/vol11/no5/mcluhanswake.html

Hochschild, A. (1989). *The second shift: Working parents and the revolution at home*. New York: Viking/Penguin.

Hochschild, A. (2001). *The time bind: When work becomes home and home becomes work* (2nd ed.). New York: Holt.

Hochschild, A. (2003). *The commercialization of intimate life: Notes from home and work*. Berkeley: University of California Press.

Hodson, J., & Vannini, P. (2007). Island time: The media logic and ritual of ferry commuting on Gabriola Island, BC. *Canadian Journal of Communication, 32*(2), 261–275. Retrieved from http://library. ca:2048/login?url=http://library.mtroyal.ca:2924/login.aspx?direct=true& AuthType=ip,url,cookie,uid&db=a9h&AN=25930269&site=ehost-live

Hoff Sommers, C. (1994). *Who stole feminism?* New York: Simon & Schuster.

Hoffman, D. (2000). Mothers in the motherland: Stalinist pronatalism in its pan-European context. *Journal of Social History, 34*(1), 35–54.

Hogan, R., Perucci, C., & Behringer, A. (2005). Enduring inequality: Gender and employment income in late career. *Sociological Spectrum, 25*(1), 53–77.

Höhn, C. (1987). Population policies in advanced societies: Pronatalist and migration strategies. *European Journal of Population, 3*(3/4), 459–481.

Holford, J. (1995). Why social movements matter: Adult education theory, cognitive practice, and the creation of knowledge. *Adult Education Quarterly, 45*(2), 95–111.

Holland, J., Ramazanoglu, C., Sharpe, S., & Thomson, R. (1996). Reputations: Journeying into gendered power relations. In J. Weeks (Ed.), *Sexual cultures, communities, values and intimacy* (pp. 239–260). London: Macmillan.

Holland, K. M. (2007). A history of Chinese immigration in the United States and Canada. *American Review of Canadian Studies, 37*(2), 150–160. Retrieved from http://search.ebscohost.com/login.aspx? direct=true&AuthType=ip,url,cookie,uid&db=a9h&AN= 27331589&site=ehost-live

Hollinger, R. (1982). Introduction. *Qualitative Sociology, 5*(2), 75.

Holmes, D. (2005). *Communication theory: Media, technology and society*. Thousand Oaks, CA: Sage Publications, Ltd.

Holmes, B. J. (2009). Media coverage of Canada's obesity epidemic: Illustrating the subtleties of surveillance medicine. *Critical Public Health, 19*(2), 223–233. doi:10.1080/09581590802478048

Holstein, M. B. (2005). A normative defense of universal age-based public policy. In R. B. Hudson (Ed.), *The new politics of old age policy* (pp. 23–41). Baltimore, Maryland: Johns Hopkins University Press.

Holt, M. (2009). 'Just take Viagra': Erectile insurance, prophylactic certainty and deficit correction in gay men's accounts of sexuopharmaceutical use. *Sexualities, 12,* 746–764.

Holton, G. (2004). Robert K. Merton. *Proceedings of the American Philosophical Society, 148*(4), 506–517.

Honour Based Violence Awareness Network. (2014). Statistics and data. Accessed 10/05/2014, from http://hbv-awareness.com/statistics-data/

Hooker, R. (1996). *The industrial revolution of the eighteenth century*. Retrieved 17/05/2007, from http://www.wsu.edu/~dee/ENLIGHT/ INDUSTRY.HTM

hooks, b. (1981). *Ain't i a woman: Black women and feminism*. Boston: South End Press.

hooks, b. (1990). *Yearning: Race, gender and cultural politics*. Boston: South End Press.

Hooks, G., & Smith, C. L. (2004). The treadmill of destruction: National sacrifice areas and Native Americans. *American Sociological Review, 69*(4), 558–575. Retrieved from http://library.mtroyal.ca:2048/ login?url=http://search.ebscohost.com/login.aspx?direct=true&AuthTy pe=ip,url,cookie,uid&db=a9h&AN=14774023&site=ehost-live

Hooper, M. K. (2001). Civil disorder and policing. In M. A. Dupont-Morales, M. K. Hooper & J. H. Schmidt (Eds.), *Handbook of criminal justice administration* (pp. 159–166). New York: Marcel Dekker, Inc.

Hopcroft, R. L. (2009). The evolved actor in sociology. *Sociological Theory, 27*(4), 390–406. doi:10.1111/j.1467-9558.2009.01354.x

Hopen, D. (2010). The changing role and practices of successful leaders. *Journal for Quality & Participation, 33*(1), 4–9. Retrieved from http:// search.ebscohost.com/login.aspx?direct=true&AuthType=ip,url,cookie, uid&db=a9h&AN=51197863&site=ehost-live

Hopkins, N., Greenwood, R. M., & Birchall, M. (2007). Minority understandings of the dynamics to intergroup contact encounters: British Muslims' (sometimes ambivalent) experiences of representing their group to others. *South African Journal of Psychology, 37*(4), 679–701. Retrieved from http://library.mtroyal.ca:2048/login?url=http://search. ebscohost.com/login.aspx?direct=true&AuthType=ip,url,cookie,uid&d b=a9h&AN=27615752&site=ehost-live

Hornosty, J. (2004). Corporate challenges to academic freedom and gender equity. In M. Reimer (Ed.), *Inside corporate U: Women in the academy speak out* (pp. 43–66). Toronto: Sumach Press.

Horton, S., Baker, J., & Deakin, J. M. (2007). Stereotypes of aging: Their effects on the health of seniors in North American society. *Educational Gerontology, 33*(12), 1021–1035. doi:10.1080/03601270701700235

Hou, F., & Coulombe, S. (2010). Earnings gaps for Canadian-born visible minorities in the public and private sectors. *Canadian Public Policy, 36*(1), 29–43.

Houmanfar, R., & Johnson, R. (2003). Organizational implications of gossip and rumor. *Journal of Organizational Behavior Management, 23*(2), 117–138. doi:10.1300/J075v23n02_07

Howard, L. (2006). Untouchable citizens: Dalit movements and democratization in Tamil Nadu. *Contemporary Sociology, 35*(5), 521. Retrieved from http://library.mtroyal.ca:2083/pqdweb?did=1151118821&Fmt= 7&clientId=65345&RQT=309&VName=PQD

HRSDC. (2007). *Looking-ahead: A 10-year outlook for the Canadian labour market (2006–2015)*. Retrieved 25/07/2008, from http://www.hrsdc. gc.ca/en/publications_resources/research/categories/labour_market_e/ sp_615_10_06/page05.shtml

HRSDC. (2010). *Canadians in context - households and families HRSDC*. Retrieved from http://www4.hrsdc.gc.ca/.3ndic/1t/4r@-eng.jsp?id=37

Huber, J., & Form, W. H. (1973). *Income & ideology*. New York: Free Press.

Huber, M., & Hennessy, P. (2005). *Long-Term care for older people*. Paris: Organisation for Economic Cooperation and Development.

Huffington Post. (2013). Fortune global 500: Top 10 most profitable companies in the world. Accessed 04/30/2014, from http://www .huffingtonpost.com/2013/07/08/fortune-global-500_n_3561233.html

Huggan, G., & Tiffin, H. (2007). Green postcolonialism. *Interventions: The International Journal of Postcolonial Studies, 9*(1), 1–11. doi:10.1080/ 13698010601173783

Hughes, G., & Roesler, K. (2004). *Angry farmers storm the city of Ottawa*. Retrieved 03/08/2007, from http://www.ruralcouncil.ca/angry_ farmers_040408.htm

Human Resources and Social Development Canada. (2006a). *Advancing inclusion of people with disabilities 2006*. Retrieved 05/01/2008, from http://www.hrsdc.gc.ca/en/hip/odi/documents/advancingInclusion06/chapter3.shtml

Human Resources and Social Development Canada. (2006b). *Canada's retirement income system - simply stated.* Retrieved 25/06/2008, from http://www.hrsdc.gc.ca/en/isp/common/hrsdc/ris/simple.shtml

Human Resources and Social Development Canada. (2007). *Mandatory retirement in Canada.* Retrieved 25/06/2008, from http://www.hrsdc.gc.ca/en/lp/spila/clli/eslc/19Mandatory_Retirement.shtml

Huneault, L., Mathieu, M., & Tremblay, A. (2011). Globalization and modernization: An obesogenic combination. *Obesity Reviews, 12,* e64–e72. doi:10.1111/j.1467-789X.2010.00817.x

Hunt, A. (2003). Risk and moralization in everyday life. In R. Ericson, & A. Doyle (Eds.), *Risk and morality* (pp. 165–192). Toronto: University of Toronto Press.

Hunt, A., & Wickham, G. (1994). *Foucault and law: Towards a sociology of law as governance.* Boulder: Pluto Press.

Hurtado, A. (1996). *The color of privilege: Three blasphemies on race and feminism.* Ann Arbor: University of Michigan Press.

Ietto-Gilles, G. (2003). The role of transnational corporations in the globalisation process. In J. Michie (Ed.), *The handbook of globalisation* (pp. 139–149). Cheltenham, UK: Edward Elgar Publishing Ltd.

Illich, I. (2003). Medical nemesis. *Journal of Epidemiology & Community Health, 57*(12), 919–922. Retrieved from http://search.ebscohost.com/login.aspx?direct=true&AuthType=ip,url,cookie,uid&db=a9h&AN=12926712&site=ehost-live

Indian and Northern Affairs Canada. (1998). *The international decade of the world's indigenous people.* Retrieved 1/27/2008, from http://www.ainc-inac.gc.ca/pr/info/info123_e.html

Indian and Northern Affairs Canada. (2004a). *Backgrounder - the residential school system.* Retrieved 12/10/2007, from http://www.ainc-inac.gc.ca/gs/schl_e.html

Indian and Northern Affairs Canada. (2004b). *First Nations reserves - appendix 3.* Retrieved 23/01/2008, from http://www.ainc-inac.gc.ca/pr/pub/atr/atr21_e.html

Indian and Northern Affairs Canada. (2006). *Government of Canada announces expert panel to advise on regulatory framework to ensure safe drinking water in First Nations communities.* Retrieved 27/07/2008, from http://www.ainc-inac.gc.ca/nr/prs/m-a2006/2-02764_e.html

Indian Claims Commission. (2005). *The facts on claims.* Retrieved 22/04/2008, from http://www.indianclaims.ca/pdf/facts_treaties_2005.pdf

Ingalls, R. (2006). Unmasking the brilliant disguise: Smallness, authority and the irony of a teacher's body. *Review of Education, Pedagogy & Cultural Studies, 28*(3), 239–252.

Inglehart, R., & Baker, W. E. (2000). Modernization, cultural change, and the persistence of traditional values. *American Sociological Review, 65*(1), 19. Retrieved from http://proquest.umi.com/pqdweb?did=51111067&Fmt=7&clientId=65345&RQT=309&VName=PQD

Innis, H. A. (1930/2001). *The fur trade in Canada.* Toronto, ON: University of Toronto Press.

Innis, H. A. (1940[1954]). *The cod fisheries: The history of an international economy.* Toronto, ON: University of Toronto Press.

Innis, H. A. (1951). *The bias of communication.* Toronto, ON: University of Toronto Press.

International Labour Organization. (2013). *Marking progress against child labour: Global estimates and trends 2000–2012.* Geneva, Switzerland: International Labour Organization.

International Labour Organization. (2014). *Global Employment Trends 2014.* Geneva, Switzerland: International Labour Organization.

International Monetary Fund. (2009). *Annual report 2009.* Retrieved 22/07/2010, from http://www.imf.org/external/pubs/ft/ar/2009/eng/pdf/ar09_eng.pdf

International Monetary Fund. (2010). *About the IMF: Overview: Membership.* Retrieved 22/07/2010, from http://www.imf.org/external/about/members.htm

International Monetary Fund. (n. d.). *About the IMF: History: Cooperation and reconstruction* (1944–71). Retrieved 22/07/2010, from http://www.imf.org/external/about/histcoop.htm

International Society of Aesthetic Plastic Surgery. (2012). Retrieved 7/2/2014, from http://www.isaps.org/Media/Default/global-statistics/ISAPS-Results-Procedures-2011.pdf

Internet World Stats. (2013). Canada. Accessed 30/01/2014, from http://www.internetworldstats.com/america.htm

IPC Media. (2006). *The growth of advertising clutter - magazine effectiveness.* Retrieved 02/06/2008, from http://www.magazine-engagement.co.uk/topic4/The_Growth_of_Advertising_Clutter_article_110868.html

Isaak, R. A. (2005). *The globalization gap.* New York: Prentice-Hall, Inc.

Isla, A. (2007). An ecofeminist perspective on biopiracy in Latin America. *Signs: Journal of Women in Culture & Society, 32*(2), 323–332. Retrieved from http://library.mtroyal.ca:2048/login?url=http://search.ebscohost.com/login.aspx?direct=true&AuthType=ip,url,cookie,uid&db=a9h&AN=23730419&site=ehost-live

Iyenda, G. (2007). Researching urban poverty in sub-Saharan Africa. *Development in Practice, 17*(1), 27–38. doi:10.1080/09614520601092683

Jackson, M. (1995). Search for the cause of crime: Biological and psychological perspectives. In M. Jackson, & C. Griffiths (Eds.), *Canadian criminology: Perspectives on crime and criminality* (2nd ed.,). Toronto: Harcourt Brace.

Jackson, J. (2011). Cultivating cosmopolitan, intercultural citizenship through critical reflection and international, experiential learning. *Language & Intercultural Communication, 11*(2), 80–96. doi:10.1080/14708477.2011.556737

Jackson, J. P., & Weidman, N. M. (2006). *Race, racism, and science: Social impact and interaction.* New Brunswick, NJ: Rutgers University Press.

Jacobs, M. (2005). *Canada has four-tiered health care.* Retrieved 30/06/2008, from http://www.edmontonsun.com/News/Columnists/Jacobs_Mindelle/2005/06/11/1081809.html

Jæger, M. M. (2011). A thing of beauty is a joy forever?: Returns to physical attractiveness over the life course. *Social Forces, 89*(3), 983–1003.

Jaffee, D. (1998). *Levels of socio-economic development theory.* Westport, CT: Praeger.

Jain, A. R., & Kripal, J. J. (2009). Quietism and karma. *Common Knowledge, 15*(2), 197–207. doi:10.1215/0961754X-2008-049

Jakobsh, D. R. (2006). Sikhism, interfaith dialogue, and women: Transformation and identity. *Journal of Contemporary Religion, 21*(2), 183–199. Retrieved from http://library.mtroyal.ca:2048/login?url=http://search.ebscohost.com/login.aspx?direct=true&AuthType=ip,url,cookie,uid&db=a9h&AN=20855126&site=ehost-live

Janssen, R. (2010). *Greece and the IMF: Who exactly is being saved?.* Washington, DC: Center for Economic and Policy Research.

Jardine, C. G., Boyd, A. D., & Furgal, C. M. (2009). Gender and place influences on health risk perspectives in northern Canadian Aboriginal communities. *Gender, Place & Culture: A Journal of Feminist Geography, 16*(2), 201–223. doi:10.1080/09663690902795837

Jarvis, D. S. L. (2010). *Theorizing risk: Ulrich Beck, globalization and the rise of the risk society.* Retrieved 31/05/2011, from http://www.risk-and-regulation.com/wp-content/uploads/2010/05/RR3-Beck.pdf

Jarvis, D. S. L. (2005). Multinational enterprises, international relations and international business: Reconstituting intellectual boundaries for the new millennium. *Australian Journal of International Affairs, 59*(2), 201–223. doi:10.1080/10357710500134459

Jasper, J., M. (2011). Emotions and social movements: Twenty years of theory and research. *Annual Review of Sociology, 37,* 285.

Jedwab, J. (2007). *Shared Canadian values: Issues and symbols.* Retrieved 09/27/2007, from http://www.acs-aec.ca/_media/polls/11882311426341.pdf

Jenkins, J. C., & Perrow, C. (1977). Insurgency of the powerless. *American Sociological Review, 42*(2), 249–268.

Jensen, R. (2007). *Media reform should include critique of sexual-exploitation media*. Retrieved 28/05/2008, from http://www.atlanticfreepress.com/content/view/698/81/

Jersild, A. T. (1952). *In search of self*. New York: Teachers College Press.

Jezek, G. (2006). *The history of television*. Retrieved 04/05/2008, from http://www.thehistoryoftelevision.com/

Jiwani, Y., & Young, M. (2006). Missing and murdered women: Reproducing marginality in news discourse. *Canadian Journal of Communication, 31*(4), 895–917.

Johansen, D. (2007). *Bulk water removals: Canadian legislation (PRB 02-13E)*. Retrieved 07/08/2008, from http://www.parl.gc.ca/information/library/PRBpubs/prb0213-e.htm

Johnson, A. (1997). The underrepresentation of minorities in the legal profession: A critical race theorist's perspective. *Michigan Law Review, 95*(4), 1005–1062.

Johnson, A. G. (2000). *The blackwell dictionary of sociology* (2nd ed.). London, UK: Blackwell Publishers.

Johnson, C. (2009). *Cutting through advertising clutter*. Retrieved 17/08/2011, from http://www.cbsnews.com/stories/2006/09/17/sunday/main2015684.shtml?tag=contentMain;contentBody

Johnson, C. (2007, Activists engage in cola war. *The Daily Tar Heel*.

Johnson, H. (1996). *Dangerous domains: Violence against women in Canada*. Toronto: Nelson.

Johnson, H., & Klandermans, B. (Eds.). (1995). *Social movements and culture*. Minneapolis, MN: University of Minnesota Press.

Johnson, E. W. (2008). Social movement size, organizational diversity and the making of federal law. *Social Forces, 86*(3), 967–993. Retrieved from http://library.mtroyal.ca:2048/login?url=http://search.ebscohost.com/login.aspx?direct=true&AuthType=ip,url,cookie,uid&db=a9h&AN=31673135&site=ehost-live

Johnson, S., Abonyi, S., Jeffery, B., Hackett, P., Hampton, M., McIntosh, T., et al. (2008). Recommendations for action on the social determinants of health: A Canadian perspective. *Lancet, 372*(9650), 1690–1693. Retrieved from http://library.mtroyal.ca:2057/login.aspx?direct=true&AuthType=ip,url,cookie,uid&db=a9h&AN=35250619&site=ehost-live

Johnston, H., & Almeida, P. (Eds.). (2006). *Latin American social movements: Globalization, democratization and transnational networks*. Lanham, MD: Rowman and Littlefield Publishers, Inc.

Jones, A. (2006). *Genocide: A comprehensive introduction*. New York: Routledge Taylor and Francis Group.

Jones, K. C. (2008). *'LOL' slips into homework but formal writing still valued*. Retrieved 07/05/2008, from http://www.informationweek.com/news/internet/social_network/showArticle.jhtml?articleID=207402196

Jones, W. T. (1969). *The classical mind: A history of western philosophy*. (Second ed.) Harcourt, Brace & World, Inc.

Jones, C. (2010). Better women: The cultural politics of gendered expertise in Indonesia. *American Anthropologist, 112*(2), 270–282. doi:10.1111/j.1548-1433.2010.01225.x

Joosse, P. (2012). The presentation of the charismatic self in everyday life: Reflections on a Canadian new religious movement. *Sociology of Religion, 73*(2), 174–199. doi:10.1093/socrel/srr045.

Joshi, T. L. (1996). *Critique of hinduism and other religions* (Suman Oak Trans.). Bombay: Popular Prakashan.

Judge, T., & Cable, D. (2004). The effect of physical height on workplace success and income. *Journal of Applied Psychology, 89*(3), 428–441.

Juhasz, A. (2006). Globalization increases poverty in developing nations. In L. I. Gerdes (Ed.), *Globalization opposing viewpoints* (pp. 114–118). New York: Thompson/Gale.

Jung, J., & Peterson, M. (2007). Body dissatisfaction and patterns of media use among preadolescent children. *Family and Consumer Sciences Research Journal, 36*(1), 40–54.

Jurajda, Š., & Harmgart, H. (2007). When do female occupations pay more? *Journal of Comparative Economics, 35*(1), 170–187.

Juristat. (2008). *Prison justice*. http://www.prisonjustice.ca/politics/facts stats.html

Juteau, D. (2002). The citizen makes an entrée: Redefining the national community in quebec. *Citizenship Studies, 6*(4), 441–458.

Kahlenberg, S., & Hein, M. (2010). Progression on Nickelodeon? Gender-role stereotypes in toy commercials. *Sex Roles, 62*, 830–847.

Kain, G. (2000). In Nelson E. S. (Ed.), *Asian American novelists: A bio-bibliographical critical sourcebook*. Westport, CT: Greenwood Publishing Group, Inc.

Kaiser, C., Eccleston, C., & Hagiwara, N., (2008). Post-hurricane Katrina racialized explanations as a system threat: Implications for whites' and blacks' racial attitudes. *Social Justice Research, 21*, 192–203.

Kallaway, P. (2002). In Kallaway P. (Ed.), *The history of education under apartheid, 1948–1994: The doors of learning and culture shall be opened*. Cape Town, SA: Pearson South Africa.

Kamel Boulos, M. N., & Wheeler, S. (2007). The emerging Web 2.0 social software: An enabling suite of sociable technologies in health and health care education. *Health Information & Libraries Journal, 24*(1), 2–23. doi:10.1111/j.1471-1842.2007.00701.x

Kaplan, D. E. (2001). The educational crisis in American reform Judaism. *Journal of Beliefs & Values: Studies in Religion & Education, 22*(2), 183–196. Retrieved from http://library.mtroyal.ca:2048/login?url=http://search.ebscohost.com/login.aspx?direct=true&AuthType=ip,url,cookie,uid&db=a9h&AN=5402311&site=ehost-live

Karaian, L., & Mitchell, A. (2010). Third wave feminisms. In N. Mandell (ed.) *Feminist Issues: Race, Class and Sexuality* (5th ed.) (pp. 63–86). Toronto, ON: Pearson.

Karger, H., Iyiani, C., & Shannon, P. (2007). The challenge of community work in a global economy. *Journal of Sociology & Social Welfare, 34*(2), 69–85. Retrieved from http://library.mtroyal.ca:2048/login?url=http://library.mtroyal.ca:2924/login.aspx?direct=true&AuthType=ip,url,cookie,uid&db=a9h&AN=25301790&site=ehost-live

Karliner, J. (1997). *The corporate planet: Ecology and politics in the age of globalization*. San Francisco, CA: Sierra Club Books.

Kastenbaum, R. (1998). *Death, society, and human experience* (6th ed.). Boston, MA: Allyn & Bacon.

Katz, C. (2008). Bad elements: Katrina and the scoured landscape of social reproduction. *Gender, Place & Culture: A Journal of Feminist Geography, 15*(1), 15–29.

Katz, C., J. (1993). Karl Marx on the transition from feudalism to capitalism. *Theory & Society, 22*(3), 363–389.

Katz, J. N. (2005). The invention of heterosexuality. In T. L. Steele (Ed.), *Sex, self and society: The social context of sexuality*. California: Wadsworth.

Kavka, G. S. (1983). Hobbes's war of all against all. *Ethics, 93*(2), 291–310.

Kaya, Y. (2010). Globalization and industrialization in 64 developing countries, 1980–2003. *Social Forces, 88*(3), 1153–1182. Retrieved from http://search.ebscohost.com/login.aspx?direct=true&AuthType=ip,url,cookie,uid&db=a9h&AN=49094172&site=ehost-live

Keane, C. (1998). Evaluating the influence of fear of crime as an environmental mobility restrictor on women's routine activities. *Environment and Behaviour, 30*(1), 60–74.

Kegley, C. W., & Wittkopf, E. R. (2006). *World politics: Trends and transformation*. Belmont, CA: Thomson Wadsworth.

Keister, L. A. (2007). Average earnings by sex and work pattern. *Social Forces, 85*(3), 1195–1225.

Kellner, D. (1990). *Television and the crisis of democracy*. Boulder, CO: Westview Press.

Kellner, D. (2005). Western Marxism. In A. Harrington (Ed.), *Modern social theory: An introduction* (pp. 154–174). Oxford: Oxford University Press.

Kellner, D. (2007). *Jean Baudrillard 1929–2007*. Retrieved 29/05/2008, from http://www.ubishops.ca/baudrillardstudies/obituaries_dkellner.html

Kelly, D., Pomerantz, S., & Currie, D. (2006). "No boundaries"? Girls' interactive, online learning about femininities. *Youth and Society, 38*(1), 3–28.

Kelly, D., Pomerantz, S., & Currie, D. (2005). Skater girlhood and emphasized femininity: 'You can't land an ollie properly in heels.' *Gender & Education, 17*(3), 229–248. Retrieved from http://library.mtroyal.ca:2048/login?url=http://search.ebscohost.com/login.aspx?direct=true&AuthType=ip,url,cookie,uid&db=a9h&AN=17575613&site=ehost-live

Kelly, M. B. (2012). Divorce cases in civil court, 2010/2011. Retrieved 14/10/2013, from http://www.statcan.gc.ca/pub/85-002-x/2012001/article/11634-eng.pdf

Kendall, D., Lothian Murray, J., & Linden, R. (2007). *Sociology in our times.* Toronto: Thomson Nelson.

Kennedy, M. D. (2004). Evolution and event in history and social change: Gerhard Lenski's critical theory. *Sociological Theory, 22*(2), 315–327. doi:10.1111/j.0735-2751.2004.00220.x

Kenny, M. G. (2004). Racial science in social context. *ISIS: Journal of the History of Science in Society, 95*(3), 394–419.

Keown, J. (2000). Voluntary euthanasia and physician assisted suicide: Beyond control? *Readings in health care ethics* (Boetzkes, Elisabeth; Waluchow, Wilfrid J. ed., pp. 390–394). Peterborough, ON: Broadview Press.

Kessler, S. (1990). The medical construction of gender: Case management of intersexed infants. *Signs, 16*(1), 3–26.

Khan, W. A. (2009). Domestic legitimacy and international conflict. *International Journal on World Peace, 26*(3), 7–38. Retrieved from http://search.ebscohost.com/login.aspx?direct=true&AuthType=ip,url,cookie,uid&db=a9h&AN=45044849&site=ehost-live

Khanna, P. (2008). *The second world: Empires and influence in the new global order.* New York, NY: Random House.

Kiely, R. (1995). *Sociology and development: The impasse and beyond.* Abington, UK: Routledge, Taylor & Francis Group.

Kim, J., Sorsoli, C. L., Collins, K., Zylbergold, B., Schooler, D., & Tolman, D. (2007). From sex to sexuality: Exposing the heterosexual script on primetime network television. *Journal of Sex Research, 44*(2), 145–157.

Kim, M., & Chung, A. (2005). Consuming orientalism: Images of Asian/American women in multicultural advertising. *Qualitative Sociology, 28*(1), 67–91.

Kimble, G. A., & Wertheimer, M. (1998). *Portraits of pioneers in psychology.* Washington, D.C.; Mahwah, NJ: American Psychological Association; Lawrence Erlbaum Associates.

Kimmel, M. (2001). Masculinity as homophobia: Fear, shame, and silence in the construction of gender identity. In T. Cohen (Ed.), Men and masculinity (pp. 29–41). Belmont: Wadsworth.

Kimmel, M. (2004). *The gendered society* (2nd ed.). New York: Oxford University Press.

Kimmel, M. S. (1990). *Revolution, a sociological interpretation.* Philadelphia, PA: Temple University Press.

Kimmel, M. S. (Ed.). (2007). *Classical sociological theory* (2nd ed.). New York, New York: Oxford University Press.

King, M. (2010). Chronic diseases and mortality in Canadian Aboriginal peoples: Learning from the knowledge. *Chronic Diseases in Canada, 31*(1), December 24, 2010. Retrieved from http://www.phac-aspc.gc.ca/publicat/cdic-mcc/31-1/PDF/Vol31n1-Article02-eng.pdf

Kingston, A., & Köhler, N. (2006). *Canada's rich, troubled Thomson family.* Retrieved 14/07/2008, from http://www.thecanadianencyclopedia.com/index.cfm?PgNm=TCE&Params=M1ARTM0012842

Kinser, P. A., & Lewis, J. A. (2005). Understanding gender construction: Creating space for feminist health care practice and research. *Health Care for Women International, 26*(5), 422–429. doi:10.1080/07399330590933953

Kinsman, G. (2004). National security as moral regulation: Making the normal and the deviant in the security campaigns against gay men and lesbians. In M. Webber, & K. Bezanson (Eds.), *Rethinking society* in the 21st century: Critical readings in sociology (pp. 258–274). Toronto: Canadian Scholars Press.

Kinzler, K. D., Shutts, K., & Correll, J. (2010). Priorities in social categories. *European Journal of Social Psychology, 40*(4), 581–592. Retrieved from http://library.mtroyal.ca:2057/login.aspx?direct=true&AuthType=ip,url,cookie,uid&db=a9h&AN=50715218&site=ehost-live

Kivisto, P. (2004). *Key ideas in sociology* (2nd ed.). Thousand Oaks, CA: Pine Forge Press, an imprint of SAGE Publications, Inc.

Klapper, B. S. (2008). *WTO talks break down.* Retrieved 30/07/2008, from http://www.huffingtonpost.com/2008/07/29/wto-talks-break-down_n_115696.html

Klassen, J., & Carroll, W. K. (2011). Transnational class formation? Globalization and the Canadian corporate network. *Journal of World-Systems Research, 17*(2), 379.

Kleg, M., & Yamamoto, K. (1998). As the world turns: Ethno-racial distances after 70 years. *Social Science Journal, 35*(2), 183.

Klein, N. (2007). *The shock doctrine: The rise of disaster capitalism.* Toronto, ON: Knopf Canada.

Klesse, C. (2005). Bisexual women, non-monogamy and differentialist anti-promiscuity discourses. *Sexualities, 8*(4), 445–464.

Klesse, C. (2006). Polyamory and its "others": Contesting the terms of non-monogamy. *Sexualities, 9*(5), 565–583.

Klingemann, H. (Ed.). (2009). *The comparative study of electoral systems.* Oxford, UK: Oxford University Press.

Knöbl, W. (2003). Theories that won't pass away: The never-ending story of modernization theory. In G. Delanty, & E. F. Isin (Eds.), *Handbook of historical sociology* (pp. 96–107). London, UK: Sage Publications, Ltd.

Knowles, E. D. & Lowery, B. S. (2012). Meritocracy, self-concerns, and whites' denial of racial inequity. *Self and Identity, 11*(2), 202–222.

Knox, R. (1988, February 16). Test shows smart people's brains use nutrients better. *Boston Globe,*

Kobali, H. L. (2004). Crossing the threshold: Men's incomes, attitudes toward the provider role, and marriage timing. *Sex Roles, 51*(7), 387–395. Retrieved from http://library.mtroyal.ca:2048/login?url=http://search.ebscohost.com/login.aspx?direct=true&AuthType=ip,url,cookie,uid&db=a9h&AN=15542170&site=ehost-live

Kobayashi, K. M., & Prus, S. G. (2012). Examining the Gender, Ethnicity, and Age Dimensions of the Healthy Immigrant Effect: Implications for Health Care Policy. *International Journal for Equity in Health, 11*(8).

Koerner, E. F. K. (2000). Towards a 'full pedigree' of the 'Sapir-Worf hypothesis' from Locke to Lucy. In *Explorations in Linquistic Relativity,* edited by M. Putz and M. Verspoor, (pp. 11–23). Amsterdam: John Benjamins Publishing Company.

Kohm, S., Waid-Lindberg, C., Weinrath, M., O'Connor, S. T., & Dobbs, R. (2012). The impact of media on fear of crime among university students: A cross-national comparison. *Canadian Journal of Criminology and Criminal Justice, 54*(1), 67–100.

Korgen, K. O. (2010). *Multiracial Americans and social class: The influence of social class on racial identity.* New York, NY: Routledge.

Kornhauser, W. (1959). *The politics of mass society.* New York: Free Press.

Koropov, V. (2006). Models of global culture. In M. Tehranian, & J. B. Lum (Eds.), *Globalization and identity: Cultural diversity, religion and citizenship* (pp. 45–54). New Brunswick (USA): Transaction Publishers.

Kosut, M. (2006). An ironic fad: The commodification and consumption of tattoos. *Journal of Popular Culture, 39*(6), 1035–1048. doi:10.1111/j.1540-5931.2006.00333.x

Kovach, K. A. (1996). *Comparable worth: The Canadian legislation - implementation of pay equity laws in Canada.* Retrieved 14/07/2008, from http://findarticles.com/p/articles/mi_m1038/is_n1_v39/ai_17957857/pg_1

Kovecses, Z. (2006). *Language, Mind, and Culture: A Practical Introduction.* New York, New York: Oxford University Press Inc.

Kramar, K. (2005). *Unwilling mothers, unwanted babies*. Vancouver: UBC Press.

Kramar, K. (2011a). Sociological theories of crime and criminality. In K. Kramar (Ed.), *Criminology: Critical Canadian perspectives* (pp. 93–115). Toronto: Pearson.

Kramar, K. (2011b). Feminist contributions to criminology. In K. Kramar (Ed.), *Criminology: Critical Canadian perspectives* (pp. 117–144). Toronto: Pearson.

Kramer, L. (2005). *The Sociology of Gender: A Brief Introduction*. 2nd ed. Los Angeles, CA: Roxbury.

Kujundzic, P. (2014). China January foreign direct investment rises in sign of confidence. Accessed 07/05/2014, from http://www.reuters.com/article/2014/02/18/us-china-economy-fdi-idUSBREA1H02W20140218

Kumar, N., Larkin, J., & Mitchell, C. (2002). Gender, youth and HIV risk. *Canadian Women's Studies, 21*(2), 35–40.

Kuntsler, J. H. (2006). *The long emergency: Surviving the end of oil, climate change, and other converging catastrophes in the twenty-first century*. New York: Grove Press.

Kuperman, A. J. (2000). Rwanda in retrospect. *Foreign Affairs, 79*(1), 94–118.

Kurzman, C. (2008). Meaning-making in social movements. *Anthropological Quarterly, 81*(1), 5–15. Retrieved from http://library.mtroyal.ca:2048/login?url=http://search.ebscohost.com/login.aspx?direct=true&AuthType=ip,url,cookie,uid&db=a9h&AN=31280285&site=ehost-live

Kuznets, S. (1955). Economic growth and income inequality. *The American Economic Review, 45*, 1–28.

La Prairie, C. (1990). The role of sentencing in the over-representation of Aboriginal people in correctional institutions. *Canadian Journal of Criminology, 32*(3), 429–440.

La Prairie, C. (2002). Aboriginal over-representation in the criminal justice system: A tale of nine cities. *Canadian Journal of Criminology, 44*(2), 181–208.

Labonte, M., & Nagel, J. C. (2013). *Foreign Holdings of Federal Debt: 2013*: Congressional Research Service.

Ladson-Billings, G., & Tate IV, W. F. (1995). Toward a critical race theory of education. In S. J. Ball (Ed.), *Sociology of education: Major themes* (pp. 322–342). New York: Routledge.

Lafontaine, A. Brian Sinclair was profiled to death. Accessed 07/15/2014, from http://www.winnipegfreepress.com/opinion/analysis/brian-sinclair-was-profiled-to-death-248318091.html?device=mobile

Lahiri, R. (2005). *Caste system in Hinduism: A historical and analytical approach*. Retrieved 29/11/2007, from http://www.boloji.com/hinduism/108.htm

Lampard, A. M., Jurkowski, J.M., & Davison, K. K. (2013). The family context of low-income parents who restrict child screen time. *Childhood Obesity, 9*(5), 386–392.

Landman, A., Cortese, D. K., & Glantz, S. (2008). Tobacco industry sociological programs to influence public beliefs about smoking. *Social Science & Medicine, 66*(4), 970–981. doi:10.1016/j.socscimed.2007.11.007

Lang, K, R. (2010). Global warming: Heating by the greenhouse effect. Accessed 08/05/2014, from http://ase.tufts.edu/cosmos/view_chapter.asp?id=21&page=1

Lang, T., Barling, D., & Caraher, M. (Eds.). (2009). *Food policy: Integrating health, environment and society*. Oxford: Oxford University Press.

Lang, T., & Heasman, M. (2004). *Food wars: The battle for mouths, minds and markets*. London, UK: Earthscan.

Langlois, J. H., & Kalakanis, L. (2000). Maxims of myths of beauty? A meta-analytic and theoretical review. *Psychological Bulletin, 126*(3), 390.

Langlois, S. (2000). A productive decade in the tradition of Canadian sociology. *Canadian Journal of Sociology, 25*(3), 391–397.

Lano, K., & Parry, C. (1995). Preface. In K. Lano, & C. Parry (Eds.), *Breaking the barriers to desire* (pp. v–vi). Nottingham: Five Leaves Publications.

LaPierre, R. (1934). Attitudes versus actions. *Social Forces, 13*, 230–237.

Lapierre-Adamcyk, E., Marcil-Gratton, N., & Le Bourdais, C. (2006). A balancing act: Parents' work arrangements and family time. In K. McQuillan, & Z. Ravanera (Eds.), *Canada's changing families: Implications for individuals and society* (pp. 49–75). Toronto: University of Toronto Press.

Lapon, G. (2011). What do we mean by exploitation? Accessed 01/14/2014, from http://socialistworker.org/2011/09/28/what-do-we-mean-exploitation

Lareau, A. (1989). *Home advantage: Social class and parental involvement in elementary education*. London: Falmer Press.

Larkin, J., Andrews, A., & Mitchell, C. (2006). Guy talk: Contesting masculinities in HIV prevention education with Canadian youth. *Sex Education, 6*(3), 207–227.

LaRochelle-Côté, S. (2010). *Self-employment in the downturn*. Retrieved 28/06/2010, from http://www.statcan.gc.ca/pub/75-001-x/2010103/article/11138-eng.htm

LaRochelle-Côté, S., Myles, J., & Picot, G. (2008). *Income security and stability during retirement in Canada* (No. 11F0019M - No.306). Ottawa, ON: Minister of Industry.

Lasch, C. (1977). *Haven in a heartless world*. New York: Basic Books.

Latimer, J., & Foss, L. (2004). *A one day snapshot of Aboriginal youth in custody across Canada. phase II*. Ottawa: Department of Justice Canada.

Latimer, J., & Foss, L. (2005). The sentencing of Aboriginal and non-Aboriginal youth under the YOA: A multivariate analysis. *Canadian Journal of Criminology and Criminal Justice, 47*(3), 481–500.

Latta, P. A. (2007). Citizenship and the politics of nature: The case of Chile's alto bío bío. *Citizenship Studies, 11*(3), 229–246. doi:10.1080/17450100701381805

Lauzen, M., Dozier, D., & Horan, N. (2008). Constructing gender stereotypes through social roles in prime-time television. *Journal of Broadcasting & Electronic Media, 52*(2), 200–214.

Laverack, G. (2004). *Health promotion practice: Power and empowerment*. London, UK: Sage Publications, Ltd.

Lawler, A. (2001). Writing gets a rewrite. *Science, New Series, 292*(5526) Retrieved from http://www.jstor.org/stable/3083953

Lawrence, C., Matsuda, M., Delgado, R., & Crenshaw, K. (1993). Introduction. In M. Matsuda, C. Lawrence, R. Delgado & K. Crenshaw (Eds.), *Words that wound: Critical race theory, assaultive speech and the 1st amendment* (pp. 1–15). Boulder: Westview Press.

Laxer, G. (2004). Democracy and global capitalism. In J. Curtis, E. Grabb & N. Guppy (Eds.), *Social inequality in Canada* (4th ed., pp. 31–37). Toronto, ON: Pearson Prentice Hall.

Lazar, F. (2003). *Governance act - chiefs of Ontario*. Retrieved 23/01/2008, from http://www.chiefs-of-ontario.org/governance/ga_mar21-03-3.html

Le Bon, G. (1895). *The crowd: A study of the popular mind*. London, UK: T. Fisher Unwin.

Le Gates, M. (2001). *In their time: A history of feminism in western society*. New York: Routledge.

Le Goff, P. (2005). *The Canadian and American health care systems: Funding and effectiveness* (No. PRB04-61E). Ottawa, ON: Parliamentary Information and Research Service - Library of Parliament.

Leach, B. (2005). Agency and the gendered imagination: Women's actions and local culture in steelworker families. *Identities: Global Studies of Culture and Power, 12*, 1–22.

Leach, B. (2013). Slutwalk and sovereignty: Transnational protest as emergent global democracy, paper presented at the American Political Science Association Annual Meeting. Retrieved 23/06/2014, from http://papers.ssrn.com/sol3/papers.cfm?abstract_id=2300699

Leach, C. W., Iyer, A., & Pedersen, A. (2007). Angry opposition to government redress: When the structurally advantaged perceive themselves as relatively deprived. *British Journal of Social Psychology, 46*(1), 191–204. doi:10.1348/014466606X99360

Leach Scully, J. (2010). Hidden labor: Disabled/nondisabled encounters, agency, and autonomy. *International Journal of Feminist Approaches to Bioethics,3*(2), 25–42.

Leacock, E. (1992). Women's status in egalitarian society. *Current Anthropology, 33*(1), 225–259. Retrieved from http://library.mtroyal.ca:2048/login?url=http://library.mtroyal.ca:2924/login.aspx?direct=true&AuthType=ip,url,cookie,uid&db=a9h&AN=5668996&site=ehost-live

Leahy, S. (2007). *Canada: Losing water through NAFTA.* Retrieved 7/31/2008, from http://www.globalresearch.ca/index.php?context=va&aid=6859

Lechner, F. J. (1989). Fundamentalism revisited. *Society, 26*(2), 51–59. Retrieved from http://library.mtroyal.ca:2048/login?url=http://search.ebscohost.com/login.aspx?direct=true&AuthType=ip,url,cookie,uid&db=a9h&AN=10979232&site=ehost-live

Lee, M. (2007). *Eroding tax fairness: Tax incidence in Canada, 1990 to 2005.* Toronto, ON: Canadian Centre for Policy Alternatives. Retrieved from http://www.policyalternatives.ca/documents/National_Office_Pubs/2007/Eroding_Tax_Fairness_web.pdf

Lee, R. B., & DeVore, I. (Eds.). (1968). *Man the hunter.* Hawthorne, NY: Aldine De Gruyter.

Lee, E. (2002). Enforcing the borders: Chinese exclusion along the U.S. borders with Canada and Mexico, 1882–1924. *Journal of American History, 89*(1), 54–86. Retrieved from http://search.ebscohost.com/login.aspx?direct=true&AuthType=ip,url,cookie,uid&db=a9h&AN=6882556&site=ehost-live

Legacy of Hope. (2013). http://www.legacyofhope.ca/about-residential-schools/church-government-of-canada-apologies/the-day-of-the-apology. Retrieved 15/10/2013.

Lehti, A. J., Johansson, E., Bengs, C., Danielsson, U., & Hammarstrom, A. (2010). "The western gaze" - an analysis of medical research publications concerning the expressions of depression, focusing on ethnicity and gender. *Health Care for Women International, 31*(2), 100–112.

Leidman, M. B., & Wiggins, B. E. (2010). Developing a paradigm for describing diversity and multiculturalism in modern America. *Journal of Social Sciences (15493652), 6*(1), 55–59. Retrieved from http://search.ebscohost.com/login.aspx?direct=true&AuthType=ip,url,cookie,uid&db=a9h&AN=48924029&site=ehost-live

Leidner, D., E. (2010). Globalization, culture, and information: Towards global knowledge transparency. *The Journal of Strategic Information Systems, 19*(2), 69–77.

Lenski, G. (1966). *Power and privilege: A theory of social stratification.* New York: McGraw-Hill Book Company.

Lenski, G. (1996). Ecological-evolutionary theory and societal transformation in post-communist Europe. *Czech Sociological Review, 4*(2), 149–156.

Lenski, G., Lenski, J., & Nolan, P. (1970). *Human societies: An introduction to macrosociology* (9th (1999) ed.). New York: McGraw- Hill, Inc.

Leong, S. (2006). Who's the fairest of them all? Television ads for skin-whitening cosmetics in Hong Kong. *Asian Ethnicity, 7*(2), 167–181.

Lerner, S. (2005). *Diamond: A struggle for environmental justice in Louisiana's chemical corridor.* Cambridge, MA: MIT Press.

Levelle, M. (2008). *Exxon's profits: Measuring a record windfall.* Retrieved 13/06/2008, from http://www.usnews.com/articles/business/economy/2008/02/01/exxons-profits-measuring-a-record-windfall.html

Levin, J., & Levin, W. (1982). *The functions of discrimination and prejudice* (2nd ed.). New York: Harper & Row.

Levine, M. (2005). Globalization in the MENA and Europe: Culture, economy and the public sphere in a transnational context. *Journal of Muslim Minority Affairs, 25*(2), 145–170. doi:10.1080/13602000500350306

Levine-Rasky, C. (2011). Intersectionality theory applied to whiteness and middle-classness. *Social Identities, 17*(2), 239–253. doi:10.1080/13504630.2011.558377

Lewis, L. (2007). Contesting the dangerous sexuality of black male youth. In G. Herdt, & C. Howe (Eds.), *21st century sexualities: Contemporary issues in health, education, and rights* (pp. 24–28). New York: Routledge.

Lewis, O. (1966). The culture of poverty. *Scientific American, 215*(4), 19–25.

Lewis, O. (1998). The culture of poverty. *Society, 35*(2), 7–9. Retrieved from http://proquest.umi.com/pqdweb?did=25162980&Fmt=7&clientId=65345&RQT=309&VName=PQD

Lewis, J. (2006). "I'll scratch your back if you'll scratch mine": The role of reciprocity, power and autonomy in the strip club. *Canadian Review of Sociology & Anthropology, 43*(3), 297–311. Retrieved from http://library.mtroyal.ca:2048/login?url=http://search.ebscohost.com/login.aspx?direct=true&????AuthType=ip,url,cookie,uid&db=a9h&AN=22062374&site=ehost-live

Li, P. (1992). Race and gender as bases of class fractions and their effects on earnings. *Canadian Review of Sociology and Anthropology, 29*(4), 488–510.

Liberal Party of Canada: Getting Smart on Crime and Cannabis. Accessed 06/05/2014, from http://www.liberal.ca/getting-smart-on-crime-and-cannabis/

Library and Archives Canada. (2007). *Hot and cool - McLuhan - old messengers, new media.* Retrieved 01/06/2008, from http://www.collectionscanada.gc.ca/innis-mcluhan/002033-2050-e.html

Library of Congress. (n.d.). *The history of the Edison cylinder phonograph.* Retrieved 30/08/2008, from http://memory.loc.gov/ammem/edhtml/edcyldr.html

Lichterman, P. (1995). Piecing together multicultural community: Cultural differences in community building among grassroots environmentalists. *Social Problems, 42*(3), 513–534.

Lim, M. (2007). *Subprime mortgage meltdown: Roots of the crisis.* Retrieved 30/07/2008, from http://opinion.inquirer.net/inquireropinion/talkofthetown/view_article.php?article_id=101568

Lincoln, A. E. (2010). The shifting supply of men and women to occupations: Feminization in veterinary education. *Social Forces, 88*(5), 1969–1998.

Linden, R. (2009). *Criminology: A Canadian perspective* (6th ed.). Toronto: Nelson.

Lindsey, L. L., & Beach, S. (2003). *Essentials of sociology.* Upper Saddle River, NJ: Pearson Education, Inc.

Lindsey, L. L., Beach, S., & Ravelli, B. (2009). *Core concepts in sociology.* (2nd. ed.). Toronto, ON: Pearson Education Canada, Inc.

Lips, H. M. (2013). The gender pay gap: Challenging the rationalizations. Perceived equity, discrimination, and the limits of human capital models. *Sex Roles, 68*(3–4), 169–185.

Lipset, S. M. (1986). Historical traditions and national characteristics: A comparative analysis of Canada and the United States. *Canadian Journal of Sociology, 11*(2), 113–155.

Lipset, S. M. (1993). Revolution and counterrevolution: The United States and Canada. In D. Taras, B. Rasporich & E. Mandel (Eds.), *A passion for identity: An introduction to Canadian studies* (pp. 150–161). Scarborough: Nelson.

Lipset, S. M. (1990). *Continental divide: The values and institutions of the United States and Canada.* New York, NY: Routledge, Chapman and Hall, Inc.

Little, M. (1998). *"No car, no radio, no liquor permit": The moral regulation of single mothers in Ontario, 1920–1997.* Toronto: Oxford University Press.

Little, M. (2006). Manhunts and bingo blabs: The moral regulation of ontario single mothers. In A. Glasbeek (Ed.), *Moral regulation and governance in Canada: History, context, and critical issues* (pp. 217–232). Toronto: Canadian Scholars' Press.

Little, M., & Morrison, I. (2001). The pecker detectors are back: Changes to the spousal definition in Ontario welfare policy. *Journal of Canadian Studies, 34*(2), 110–136.

Little, M. (2001). A litmus test for democracy: The impact of Ontario welfare changes on single mothers. *Studies in Political Economy, 66*, 9–36.

Little, M. (2003). The leaner, meaner welfare machine: The Harris government's ideological and material attack on single mothers. In D. Brock (Ed.), *Making normal: Social regulation in Canada* (pp. 235–258). Toronto: Thomson Nelson.

Littlewood, R. (2002). Three into two: The third sex in northern Albania. *Anthropology & Medicine, 9*(1), 37–50.

Living Tongues Institute For Endangered Languages. (2007). *Living tongues institute for endangered languages*. Retrieved 10/4/2007, from http://www.livingtongues.org/index.html

Llewellyn, J. J. (2002a). Dealing with the legacy of Native residential school abuse in Canada: Litigation, ADR, and restorative justice. *University of Toronto Law Journal, 52*(3), 253–300. Retrieved from http://library.mtroyal.ca:2057/login.aspx?direct=true&AuthType=ip,url,cookie,uid&db=a9h&AN=7201166&site=ehost-live

Llewellyn, J. J. (2002b). *Restorative justice and Native residential schools*. Retrieved 01/06/2010, from www.ccc-cce.ca/english/downloads/JenniferLlewellyn2.doc

Llobera, J. R. (2003). *An invitation to anthropology: The structure, evolution and cultural identity of human societies*. New York: Berghahn Books.

Lochhead, C., & Shalla, V. (1996). Delivering the goods: Income distribution and the precarious middle class. *Perception, 20*(1),. Retrieved 08/12/2007, from http://www.ccsd.ca/perception/201/deliver.html

Lofland, J. F. (2004[1981]). Collective behavior: The elementary forms. In M. Rosenberg, & R. H. Turner (Eds.), *Social psychology: Sociological perspectives* (4th printing ed., pp. 411–446). New Brunswick (USA): Transaction Publishers.

Lofland, L. (1973). *A world of strangers*. New York: Basic Books.

Lombardi, E. (2009). Varieities of Transgender/Transsexual lives and their relationship with transphobia. *Journal of Homosexuality, 56*, 977–992.

London 2012 Olympics. (2011). London 2012 Olympics: Caster Semenya sets sights on 1500m at games. *The Telegraph, April 8, 2011*, Retrieved 29/05/2011, from http://www.telegraph.co.uk/sport/othersports/olympics/8438249/London-2012-Olympics-Caster-Semenya-sets-sights-on-1500m-at-Games.html

Long, T. E., & Hadden, J. K. (1983). Religious conversion and the concept of socialization: Integrating the brainwashing and drift models. *Journal for the Scientific Study of Religion, 22*(1), 1.

Longman, J. (2009). South African runner's sex-verification result won't be public. *New York Times*, Retrieved from http://www.nytimes.com/2009/11/20/sports/20runner.html/_r=1&pagewanted=print

Lothane, Z. (2006). Mass psychology of the led and the leaders. An earlier version of this paper was read at the conference "Prejudice and conflict" organized by international association for psychoanalytic studies, Salt Lake City, Utah, December, 2005. *International Forum of Psychoanalysis, 15*(3), 183–192. doi:10.1080/08037060600924983

Loue, S. (2006). *Sexual partnering, sexual practices, and health*. USA: Springer.

Lovas, G. (2005). Gender and patterns of emotional availability in mother-toddler and father-toddler dyads. *Infant Mental Health Journal, 26*(4), 327–353.

Lubey, K. (2006). Spectacular sex: Thought and pleasure in the encounter with pornography. *Differences: A Journal of Feminist Cultural Studies, 17*(2), 113–131. doi:10.1215/10407391-2006-005

Lucas, R. E., & Schimmack, U. (2009). Income and well-being: How big is the gap between the rich and the poor? *Journal of Research in Personality, 43*(1), 75–78. doi:10.1016/j.jrp.2008.09.004

Luckerson, V. (2014). Everything you need to know about the Chinese version of Twitter. Accessed 07/05/2014, from http://time.com/65792/weibo-ipo/

Lueck, M. (2007). Hope for a cause as cause for hope: The need for hope in environmental sociology. *American Sociologist, 38*(3), 250–261. doi:10.1007/s12108-007-9017-7

Luke, T. W. (2003). Global cities vs. "global cities": Rethinking contemporary urbanism as public ecology. *Studies in Political Economy, 70*, 11–33.

Lunau, K. (2009). *Youth survey: Teens lose faith in droves*. Retrieved 28/07/2010, from http://www2.macleans.ca/2009/04/07/teens-lose-faith-in-droves/

Lundell, L. (2005). *Chaoulli v. Quebec (attorney general): The supreme court of Canada sets the stage for fundamental health care reform*. Retrieved 30/06/2008, from http://www.hg.org/articles/article_698.html

Luxton, M. (2001). Conceptualizing 'families': Theoretical frameworks and family research. In M. Baker (Ed.), *Families: Changing trends in Canada* (4th ed., pp. 28–50). Toronto: McGraw-Hill Ryerson.

Luxton, M., & Corman, J. (2005). Families at work: Making a living. In N. Mandell, & A. Duffy (Eds.), *Canadian families: Diversity, conflict and change* (3rd ed., pp. 346–372). Toronto: Thomson Nelson.

Luxton, M., & Corman, J. (2011). Families at work: Individual versus collective strategies for making a living. In N. Mandell, & A. Duffy (Eds.), *Canadian families: Diversity, conflict and change* (4th ed., pp. 211–242). Toronto: Nelson.

Lynch, M., & McConatha, D. (2006). *Hyper-symbolic interactionism: Prelude to a refurbished theory of symbolic interaction or just old wine? Sociological Viewpoints, 22*(1060), 87–96.

Lyons, H. (2007). Genital cutting: The past and present of a polythetic category. *Africa Today, 53*(4), 3–17.

MacAskill, E. (2011). *Wisconsin protests continue against 'union bashing'*. Retrieved 30/05/2011, from http://www.guardian.co.uk/world/2011/feb/18/wisconsin-union-protests

MacDonald, E., & Rang, S. (2007). *Exposing Canada's chemical valley: An investigation of cumulative air pollution emissions in the Sarnia, Ontario area*. Toronto, ON: EcoJustice.ca.

Mace, E. R. (2009). Feminist forerunners and a usable past: A historiography of Elizabeth Cady Stanton's *The Woman's Bible. Journal of Feminist Studies in Religion, 25*(2), 5–23.

Macionis, J. J., & Gerber, L. M. (2011). *Sociology* (7th ed.). Toronto, ON: Pearson Education Canada, Inc.

Mackenzie, H. (2014). *All in a Day's Work? CEO Pay in Canada*. Canadian Centre for Policy Alternatives.

Mackie, M. (1973). Arriving at "truth" by definition: The case of stereotype inaccuracy. *Social Problems, 20*(4 (spring)), 431–447.

Mackie, V., & Stevens, C. S. (2009). Globalisation and body politics. *Asian Studies Review, 33*(3), 257–273. doi:10.1080/10357820903153699

Mackrael, K. (2013). Foreign-aid agency cut, merged with foreign affairs and trade department. Accessed 08/05/2014, from http://www.theglobeandmail.com/news/politics/foreign-aid-agency-cut-merged-with-foreign-affairs-and-trade-department/article10074258/

MacLean, A. M. (1910). *Wage earning women*. New York, New York: The MacMillan Company.

MacLennan, H. (1945). *Two solitudes*. Toronto, ON: Collins.

MacPhail, C., & Campbell, C. (2001). "I think condoms are good, but aai, I hate those things": Condom use among adolescents and young people in a South African township. *Social Science and Medicine, 52*(11), 1613–1627.

Makarenko, J. (2010). *Immigration policy in Canada: History, administration and debates*. Retrieved 22/05/2011, from http://www.mapleleafweb.com/features/immigration-policy-canada-history-administration-and-debates

Makuch, E. (2014). World of Warcraft subscriptions on the rise, ended 2013 at 7.8 million. Accessed 05/05/2014, from http://www.gamespot.com/articles/world-of-warcraft-subscriptions-on-the-rise-ended-2013-at-7-8-million/1100-6417575/

Malley-Morrison, K., & Hines, D. A. (2004). *Family violence in a cultural perspective: Defining, understanding, and combating abuse*. Thousand Oaks, CA: Sage Publications, Ltd.

Malthus, T. (1998/1798). *An essay on the principle of population*. Retrieved 10/07/2007, from http://www.esp.org/books/malthus/population/malthus.pdf

Mancini, T., Fruggeri, L., & Panari, C. (2006). An extention of the school moral atmosphere construct, and its association with aggressive behaviours in secondary school. *European Journal of Psychology of Education - EJPE, 21*(2), 209–228. Retrieved from http://library

.mtroyal.ca:2048/login?url=http://search.ebscohost.com/login .aspx?direct=true&AuthType=ip,url,cookie,uid&db=a9h&AN=21647 376&site=ehost-live

Mandell, N., & Duffy, A. (Eds.). (2005a). *Canadian families: Diversity, conflict and change* (3rd ed.). Toronto: Thomson Nelson.

Mandell, N., & Duffy, A. (2005b). Explaining family lives. In N. Mandell, & A. Duffy (Eds.), *Canadian families: Diversity, conflict and change* (3rd ed., pp. 3–30). Toronto: Thomson Nelson.

Mandell, N., & Momirov, J. (2005). Family histories. In N. Mandell, & A. Duffy (Eds.), *Canadian families* (3rd ed., pp. 31–63). Toronto: Thomson Nelson.

Mann, S., & Huffman, D. (2005). The decentering of second wave feminism and the rise of the third wave. *Science and Society, 69*(1), 56–91.

Manoli, C. C., Johnson, B., & Dunlap, R. E. (2007). Assessing children's environmental worldviews: Modifying and validating the new ecological paradigm scale for use with children. *Journal of Environmental Education, 38*(4), 3–13. Retrieved from http://library.mtroyal.ca:2048/ login?url=http://search.ebscohost.com/login.aspx?direct=true&AuthTy pe=ip,url,cookie,uid&db=a9h&AN=27718370&site=ehost-live

Manseau, H., Blais, M., Engler, K., & Bossé, M. (2007). Integrating the perspective of vulnerable heterosexual male adolescents to prevent premature paternity and sexually transmitted infection. *American Journal of Sexuality Education, 2*(4), 43–66.

Marbley, A. F. (2005). African-American women's feelings on alienation from third-wave feminism: A conversation with my sisters. *Western Journal of Black Studies, 29*(3), 605–614.

Marciniak, K. (2006). Immigrant rage: Alienhood, "hygienic" identities, and the second world. *Differences: A Journal of Feminist Cultural Studies, 17*(2), 33–63. doi:10.1215/ 10407391-2006-002

Marger, M. (1998). *Social inequality: Patterns and processes*. Mountain View, CA: Mayfield.

Margolis, E., & Rowe, J. (n.d.). *Manufacturing assimilation: Photographs of Indian schools in Arizona*. Retrieved 13/11/2007, from http://www .public????.asu.edu/~jeremy/indianschool/paper.htm

Markle, T. (2007). *Coke part 1*. Retrieved 21/10/2007, from http://www .theknoll.ca/php/display.php?article_id=53

Marlow, I. (2011). *Shaw network delayed, but primed for 4G push*. Retrieved 29/04/2011, from http://www.theglobeandmail.com/news/technology/ mobile-technology/shaw-network-delayed-but-primed-for4g-push/ article1868967/

Marotta, T. (2006). What made Stonewall different? *The Gay and Lesbian Review, March April,* 33–35.

Marriott, M. (1997, At home with bell hooks; the eye of the storm. *The New York Times,* Retrieved from http://query.nytimes.com/gst/fullpage. html?res=9F00EFD81F39F930A25752C1A961958260

Marsh, J. H. *The Canadian encyclopedia*. Retrieved 9/10/2007, from http:// www.thecanadianencyclopedia.com/index.cfm?PgNm=ArchivedFeatur es&Params=A2126

Marshall, G. (2008). *Naomi Klein: No logo: Ad nauseum | book reviews | SpikeMagazine.com*. Retrieved 5/11/2008, from http://www .spikemagazine.com/0400nologo.php

Marshall, S. (1984). Keep us on the pedestal: Women against feminism in twentieth-century America. In J. Freeman (Ed.), *Women: A feminist perspective* (3rd ed., pp. 568–581). Palo Alto: Mayfield.

Marshall, G., Rose, D., Vogler, C., & Newby, H. (1985). Class, citizenship, and distributional conflict in modern Britain. *British Journal of Sociology, 36*(2), 259. Retrieved from http://library.mtroyal.ca:2048/ login?url=http://search.ebscohost.com/login.aspx?direct=true&AuthTy pe=ip,url,cookie,uid&db=a9h&AN=5304796&site=ehost-live

Marsman, H. J. (2003). *Women in Ugarit and Israel: Their social and religious position in the context of the ancient Near East*. Leiden: Brill.

Martel, J., Brassard, R., & Jaccoud, M. (2011). When two worlds collide: Aboriginal risk management in Canadian corrections. *British Journal of Criminology. 51*(2), 235–255.

Martell, L. (2010). *The sociology of globalization*. Cambridge, UK: Polity Press.

Martin, E. (2009). The egg and the sperm: How science has constructed a romance based on stereotypical male-female roles. In A. Ferber, K. Holcomb & T. Wentling (Eds.), *Sex, gender, and sexuality: The new basics* (pp. 248–254). University of Chicago Press.

Martin, K., Vieraitis, L., & Britto, S. (2006). Gender equality and women's absolute status. *Violence Against Women, 12*(4), 321—39.

Martin, D. (2005). Secularisation and the future of Christianity. *Journal of Contemporary Religion, 20*(2), 145–160. Retrieved from http:// library.mtroyal.ca:2048/login?url=http://search.ebscohost.com/login. aspx?direct=true&AuthType=ip,url,cookie,uid&db=a9h&AN=170187 93&site=ehost-live

Martinelli, A. (2005). *Global modernization: Rethinking the project of modernity*. London, UK: Sage Publications, Ltd.

Martino, W., & Frank, B. (2006). The tyranny of surveillance: Male teachers and the policing of masculinities in a single sex school. *Gender and Education, 18*(1), 17–33.

Martinson, D. L. (2005). Pornography and deceptive advertising: What is the role of government in a free society? *Social Studies, 96*(1), 30–33. Retrieved from http://library.mtroyal.ca:2048/login?url=http://search. ebscohost.com/login.aspx?direct=true&AuthType=ip,url,cookie,uid&d b=a9h&AN=16429291&site=ehost-live

Marx, K., & Engels, F. (1846). *The German ideology* (1964th ed.). London: Lawrence & Wishart.

Marx, K., & Engels, F. (1964). *On religion*. New York: Schocken Books (Updated Scholars Press Reprint).

Masko, A. L. (2005). "I think about it all the time": A 12-year-old girl's internal crisis with racism and the effects on her mental health. *Urban Review, 37*(4), 329–350.

Mason, M., & Goulden, M. (2004). Do babies matter: Closing the baby gap. *Academe, 90*(6), 3–7.

Mason, C. (2007). Reproducing the souls of white folk. *Hypatia, 22*(2), 98–121.

Matheson, C., & Endicott, L. (1998). Lesbian and bisexual identity: Discourse on difference. *Atlantis, 23*(1), 38–47.

Matheson, V. A., & Baade, R. A. (2004). Race and riots: A note on the economic impact of the Rodney King riots. *Urban Studies, 41*(13), 2691–2696. doi:10.1080/0042098042000294628

Matthews, B., & Beaman, L. (2007). *Exploring gender in Canada: A multidimensional approach*. Toronto: Pearson Prentice Hall.

Matthews, B. J. (2005). The body beautiful: Adolescent girls and images of beauty. In B. Ravelli (Ed.), *Exploring Canadian sociology: A reader* (pp. 39–50). Toronto, ON: Pearson Education Canada, Inc.

Mauss, A. (1975). *Social problems as social movements*. Philadelphia, PA: Lippincott.

Mayer, A. (1960). Russell woods: Change without conflict. A case study of neighborhood transition in detroit. In N. Glazer, & D. McIntire (Eds.), *Studies in housing and minority groups*. Berkeley, CA: University of California Press.

Mayer, S. (1997). *What money can't buy*. Cambridge, MA: Harvard University Press.

Mayo, M. (2005). *Global citizens: Social movements and the challenge of globalization*. London, UK: Zed Books.

Mazur, A. (1993). Signs of status in bridal portraits. *Sociological Forum, 8 (June),* 273–283.

Mazzarella, W. (2004). Culture, globalization, mediation. *Annual Review of Anthropology, 33,* 345. Retrieved from http://proquest.umi.com/pqdw eb?did=749594031&Fmt=7&clientId=65345&RQT=309&VName= PQD

McAdam, D. (1999). *Political process and the development of black insurgency, 1930–1970* (2nd ed.). Chicago, IL: University of Chicago Press.

McAdam, D., & Paulsen, R. (1994). Specifying the relationship between social ties and activism. *American Journal of Sociology, 99*(3), 640–667.

McAndrew, S., & Warne, T. (2010). Coming out to talk about suicide: Gay men and suicidality. *International Journal of Mental Health Nursing, 19,* 92–101.

McCabe, D. (1998). *Listening to the voices for change.* Retrieved 6/29/2008, from http://reporter-archive.mcgill.ca/Rep/r3017/staggenborg.html

McCarney, J. (2005). *Ideology and false consciousness.* Retrieved 11/09/2007, from http://marxmyths.org/joseph-mccarney/article.htm

McCarthy, B., & Casey, T. (2008). Love, sex, and crime: Adolescent romantic relationships and offending. *American Sociological Review,* 73(6), 944–969. Retrieved from http://library.mtroyal.ca:2057/login.aspx?direct=true&AuthType=ip,url,cookie,uid&db=a9h&AN=35623883&site=ehost-live

McCarthy, J. D., & Zald, M. N. (1977). Resource mobilization & social movements: A partial theory. *American Journal of Sociology, 82*(6), 1212–1241.

McCarthy, S. (2014). Emissions will soar after 2020 without oil-sector regulation, federal report says. Accessed 05/02/2014, from http://www.theglobeandmail.com/news/politics/emissions-will-soar-after-2020-without-oil-sands-regulation-federal-report-says/article16250220/

McCarthy, W. (2007). *What's love got to do with it?: Adolescent romantic relationships and crime* Monsebraaten.

McCarty, T. L., Romero, M. E., & Zepeda, O. (2006). Reclaiming the gift: Indigenous youth counter-narratives on native language loss and revitalization. *American Indian Quarterly, 30*(1), 28–48.

McChesney, R. W. (1999). The new global media. *The Nation, 269*(18), 11–15.

McClintock, E. A. (2010). When does race matter? Race, sex, and dating at an elite university. *Journal of Marriage & Family, 72*(1), 45–72. doi:10.1111/j.1741-3737.2009.00683.x

McDaniel, S., & Tepperman, L. (2002). *Close relations: An introduction to the sociology of families* (Brief edition ed.). Toronto: Prentice Hall.

McDaniel, S., & Tepperman, L. (2011). *Close relations: An introduction to the sociology of families* (4th ed.). Toronto: Pearson.

McDermott, E. (2004). Telling lesbian stories: Interviewing and the class dynamics of "talk". *Women's Studies International Forum, 27,* 177–187.

McGee, J. D. (1977). The contribution of A. A. Campbell Swinton, F.R.S., to television. *Notes and Records of the Royal Society of London, 32*(1), 91–105.

McGill University. (2008). *Suzanne Staggenborg.* Retrieved 6/29/2008, from http://www.mcgill.ca/sociology/faculty/staggenborg/

McGrath, A. (2005). *Introduction to queer theory.* Unpublished manuscript.

McGruder, K. (2009). Black sexuality in the U.S.: Presentations as non-normative. *Journal of African American Studies, 13,* 251–262.

McGuigan, B. (1997). Issues in Canadian culture. In M. Kanwar, & D. Swenson (Eds.), *Issues in Canadian sociology* (2nd ed., pp. 35–60). Dubuque, IA: Kendall/Hunt.

McHugh, N. A. (2007). *Feminist philosophies A-Z.* Edinburgh: Edinburgh University Press.

McIntire, C. T. (2006). Transcending dichotomies in history and religion. *History & Theory, 45*(4), 80–92. Retrieved from http://library.mtroyal.ca:2048/login?url=http://library.mtroyal.ca:2924/login.aspx?direct=true&AuthType=ip,url,cookie,uid&db=a9h&AN=22930670&site=ehost-live

McIntosh, P. (1990). White privilege: Unpacking the invisible knapsack. *Independent School, Winter,* 31–36.

McIntyre, L. J. (2006). *The practical skeptic : Core concepts in sociology* (3rd ed.). Montreal, QC; Boston, MA: McGraw-Hill Higher Education.

McKay, A. (2004a). Sexual health education in the schools: Questions and answers. *The Canadian Journal of Human Sexuality, 13*(3–4), 129–141.

McKay, A. (2004b). Oral sex among teenagers: Research, discourse and eduation. *The Canadian Journal of Human Sexuality, 13*(3-4), 201–203.

McKay, I. (1998). Changing the subject(s) of the 'history of Canadian sociology': The case of Colin McKay and Spencerian Marxism, 1890–1940. *Canadian Journal of Sociology, 23*(4), 389–426.

McKenzie, C. (2004). Transphobia. In J. Eadie (Ed.), *Sexuality: The essential glossary* (pp. 232–233). London: Arnold.

McKinney, D. W. (1973). *The authoritarian personality studies.* The Hague, Netherlands: Mouton.

McKinney, S. J. (2004). *Jewish education and formation in Glasgow: A case study.* Routledge. Retrieved from http://library.mtroyal.ca:2048/login?url=http://search.ebscohost.com/login.aspx?direct=true&AuthType=ip,url,cookie,uid&db=a9h&AN=13310130&site=ehost-live

McKown, C., & Weinstein, R. (2002). Modeling the role of child ethnicity and gender in children's differential response to teacher expectations. *Journal of Applied Social Psychology, 32,* 159–184.

McKown, C., & Weinstein, R. (2003). The development and consequences of stereotype consciousness in middle childhood. *Child Development, 7,* 498–515.

McLaren, P., & Farahmandpur, R. (2000). Reconsidering Marx in post-Marxist times: A requiem for postmodernism? *Educational Researcher, 29*(3 (April)), 25–33.

McLeod, K. (1992). Multiculturalism and multicultural education in Canada: Human right and human rights education. In K. Moodley (Ed.), *Beyond multicultural education: International perspectives* (pp. 215–242). Calgary: Detselig Enterprises.

McLuhan, E. (n.d.). FAQS - Marshall McLuhan. Retrieved 07/06/2007, from http://www.marshallmcluhan.com/faqs.html

McLuhan, M. (1962). *The Gutenberg galaxy: The making of typographic man.* Toronto: University of Toronto Press.

McLuhan, M. (1964). *Understanding media: The extensions of man.* Toronto; New York: McGraw-Hill Book Co.

McMahon, M. (2011). Standard fare or fairer standards: Feminist reflections on agri-food governance. *Agriculture and Human Values, 28*(3), 401–412.

McMahon, M., & Johra, F. (2012). Gender and Food Security. *Women and Environments, 88*(89), 2.

McMaster. (2007). *WWW virtual library: Sociology - departments - Canada.* Retrieved 11/01/2010, from http://socserv2.mcmaster.ca/w3virtsoclib/cansoc.htm

McMillan, J., & Coveney, J. (2010). What took you so long? Sociology's recent foray into food. *Health Sociology Review, 19*(3), 282–284.

McMullan, J., & Miller, D. (2009). Wins, winning and winners: The commercial advertising of lottery gambling. *Journal of Gambling Studies, 25*(3), 273–295.

McMullen, K., Gilmore, J. & Le Petit, C. (2010). *Women in non-traditional occupations and fields of study.* Retrieved 18/09/2010, from http://www.statcan.gc.ca/pub/81-004-x/2010001/article/11151-eng.htm

McPhail, C. (1991). *The myth of the madding crowd.* New York: Aldine deGruyter.

McPhail, C., & Wohlstein, R. T. (1983). Individual and collective behaviors within gatherings, demonstrations and riots. *Annual Review of Sociology, 9,* 579–600.

McQueen, C. (2005). *Humanitarian intervention and safety zones: Iraq, Bosnia and Rwanda.* New York, NY: Palgrave MacMillan.

McWhorter, J. H. (2003). *Double consciousness in black America.* Retrieved 28/05/2010, from http://www.cato.org/pubs/policy_report/v25n2/mcwhorter.pdf

Mead, G. H. (1934). *Mind, self and society from the standpoint of a social behaviorist.* Chicago: University of Chicago Press.

Meaghan, D. (2004). College 'equity' centres and women's studies faculty: Regulation of feminism? In M. Reimer (Ed.), *Inside corporate U: Women in the academy speak out* (pp. 177–197). Toronto: Sumach Press.

Measor, L. (2006). Condom use: A culture of resistance. *Sex Education, 6*(4), 393–402.

Media Awareness Network. (2010). *Beauty and body image in the media.* Retrieved 21/03/2010 from http://www.media-awareness.ca/english/issues/stereotyping/women_and_girls/women_beauty.cfm

Meier, W. A. (2002). Media ownership - does it matter? *Learning and Training, VI*(4), 298–302.

Melendez, R. (2007). No place to call home: Transgender persons, discrimination, and HIV. *21st century sexualities: Contemporary issues in health, education, and rights* (pp. 10–109). New York: Routledge.

Mellow, M. (2005). The work of rural professionals: Doing the gemeinschaft-gesellschaft gavotte. *Rural Sociology, 70*(1), 50–69.

Merton, R. K. (1938). Social structure and anomie. *American Sociological Review, 3,* 672–682.

Merton, R. K. (1968). *Social theory & social structure* (2nd. ed.). New York: Free Press.

Messner, M., & Montez de Oca, J. (2005). The male consumer as loser: Beer and liquor ads in mega sports media events. *Signs, 30*(3), 1879–1909.

Messner, S., & Rosenfeld, R. (2007). *Crime and the American dream* (4th ed.). Belmont, CA: Wadsworth Publishing.

Metzger, P. (2007). *CBC news in depth: Technology.* Retrieved 04/05/2008, from http://www.cbc.ca/news/background/tech/hd-video.html

Microcredit Summit. (n.d.). *The microcredit summit campaign.* Retrieved 14/07/2008, from http://www.microcreditsummit.org/Aboutmicrocredit.htm

Microsoft. (2008). *People make the difference.* Retrieved 26/03/2008, from http://www.microsoft.com/business/peopleready/overview/default.mspx?WT.svl=1

Mielo, G. (2004). Why Mcluhan's still hot and cool. *Et Cetera, 61*(2), 215. Retrieved from http://proquest.umi.com/pqdweb?did=678673211&Fmt=7&clientId=65345&RQT=309&VName=PQD

Milanovic, B. (2006). *Global income inequality: What it is and why it matters* (No. 3865). Washington, DC: World Bank.

Miles, R., & Brown, M. (2003). *Racism* (2nd ed.). London: Routledge.

Millar, W. J. (2001). Patterns of use: Alternative health care providers. [Catalogue No. 82-003] *Health Reports (December), 13*(1), June 30, 2008.

Millard, J., & Grant, P. (2006). The stereotypes of black and white women in fashion magazine photographs: The pose of the model and the impression she creates. *Sex Roles, 54*(9), 659–673.

Miller, D. (1985). *Introduction to collective behavior.* Belmont, CA: Wadsworth.

Miller, H. V. (2010). If your friends jumped off a bridge, would you do it too? Delinquent peers and susceptibility to peer influence. *Justice Quarterly, 27*(4), 473–491.

Miller-Bernal, L., & Poulson, S. L. (Eds.). (2007). *Challenged by coeducation women's colleges since the 1960s.* Nashville, TN: Vanderbilt University Press.

Milloy, J. (1999). *A national crime: The Canadian government and the residential school system – 1879 to 1986.* Winnipeg: University of Manitoba Press.

Mills, C. W. (1959[2000]). *The sociological imagination* (Fortieth Anniversary Edition ed.). New York: Oxford University Press.

Mills, S. (2008). *Language and sexism.* Cambridge: Cambridge University Press.

Mishra, S. (2011). *MySpace users number starts declining from last month.* Retrieved 4/28/2011, from http://www.buzzom.com/2011/03/myspace-users-number-started-decling-from-last-month/

Miss G. Project. (2011). *The Miss G. project.* Retrieved 03/07, from http://www.themissgproject.org/about/wgs.html

Mitchell, B. A. (2010). Midlife marital happiness and ethnic culture: A life course perspective. *Journal of Comparative Family Studies, 41*(1), 167–183. Retrieved from http://library.mtroyal.ca:2057/login.aspx?direct=true&Auth????Type=ip,url,cookie,uid&db=a9h&AN=48095747&site=ehost-live

Mitchell, B. A., & Lovegreen, L. D. (2009). The empty nest syndrome in midlife families. *Journal of Family Issues, 30*(12), 1650–1670.

Miyake, K. (2007). How young Japanese express their emotions visually in mobile phone messages: A sociolinguistic analysis. *Japanese Studies, 27*(1), 53–72. doi:10.1080/10371390701268646

Mol, A. P. J., & Spaargaren, G. (2004). Ecological modernization and consumption: A reply. *Society & Natural Resources, 17*(3), 261–265. Retrieved from http://library.mtroyal.ca:2048/login?url=http://search.ebscohost.com/login.aspx?direct=true&AuthType=ip,url,cookie,uid&db=a9h&AN=12255245&site=ehost-live

Molnar, A. (2006). The commercial transformation of public education. *Journal of Education Policy, 21*(5), 621–640. doi:10.1080/02680930600866231

Mondello, B. (2005). *100th anniversary of first-ever U.S. movie theater: NPR.* Retrieved 03/05/2008, from http://www.npr.org/templates/story/story.php?storyId=4707873

Monsebraaten, L. (2009). Fighting for dignity on the job. *The Toronto Star,* Retrieved from http://www.thestar.com/news/gta/2009/07/11/fighting_for_dignity_on_the_job.html

Montgomery, K. (2005). Imagining the anti-racist state:Representations of racism in Canadian history textbooks. *Discourse: Studies in the Cultural Politics of Education, 26*(4), 427–442.

Moody, H. R. (2006). *Aging: Concepts and controversies* (5th ed.). Thousand Oaks, CA: Pine Forge Press.

Moore, B. J. (1966). *Social origins of dictatorship and democracy.* Boston, MA: Beacon Press.

Moore, D. S. (2013). Current thinking about nature and nurture. In *The Philosophy of Biology: A Companion for Educators,* edited by Kostas Kampourakis. Vol. 1, (pp. 629–652).

Moore, E., & Peniston, B., E. (2004). *Wage inequality in Oregon – still growing?* Retrieved 12/12/2007, from http://www.olmis.org/olmisj/ArticleReader?itemid=00003899&segmentid=0003&tour=0&p_date=1

Moore, E. E. (2010). Braveheart, sacred heart: Exploring resistance to patriarchal discourses in mainstream media and faith in the American spiritual marketplace. *WSQ: Women's Studies Quarterly, 38*(3), 94-115.

Moran, E. F. (1981). Human adaptation to arctic zones. *Annual Review of Anthropology, 10,* 1–25. Retrieved from http://library.mtroyal.ca:2048/login?url=http://search.ebscohost.com/login.aspx?direct=true&AuthType=ip,url,cookie,uid&db=a9h&AN=11238159&site=ehost-live

Morck, R. K., Stangeland, D. A., & Yeung, B. (1998). *Inherited wealth, corporate control and economic growth: The Canadian disease?* Retrieved 12/7/2007, from http://www.business.ualberta.ca/rmorck/Research%20Papers/NBER%20CCO%20Inherited%20Wealth.pdf

Morgan, K. P. (2011). Foucault, ugly ducklings, and technoswans: Analyzing fat hatred, weight-loss surgery, and compulsory biomedicalized aesthetics in America. *International Journal of Feminist Approaches to Bioethics, 4*(1), 188–220.

Morgan-Knapp, C. (2010). Materialism and economics. *Ethics, Place & Environment, 13*(1), 27–30. doi:10.1080/13668790903554121

Morgensen, S. L. (2011). The biopolitics of settler colonialism: Right here, right now. *Settler Colonial Studies, 1*(1), 52–76.

Morris, D. B. (1998). *Illness and culture in the postmodern age.* Berkeley, CA: University of California Press.

Morris, E. (2007). "Ladies" or "loudies"? Perceptions and experiences of black girls in classrooms. *Youth and Society, 38*(4), 490–515.

Morris, J. (2008). Out of New Orleans: Race, class, and researching the Katrina diaspora. *Urban Education, 43*(4), 463–487.

Morrison, D. E. (1971). Some notes toward theory on relative deprivation, social movements and social change. *American Behavioral Scientist, 14*(5), 675–690.

Morrison, I. (1998). Ontario works: A preliminary assessment. *Journal of Law and Social Policy, 13,* 1–46.

Morrow, A. (2013).Majority of Canadians approve of assisted suicide: Poll. Accessed 04/09/2014, from http://www.theglobeandmail.com/news/national/majority-of-canadians-approve-of-assisted-suicide-poll/article14819642/

Morrow-Howell, N., Hinterlong, J., & Sherraden, M. (Eds.). (2001). *Productive aging: Concepts and challenges*. Baltimore, Maryland: Johns Hopkins University Press.

Morton, H., Klein, C., & Gorzalka, B. (2012). Attitudes, beliefs, and knowledge of prostitution and the law in Canada. *Canadian Journal of Criminology and Criminal Justice, 54*(2), 229–244.

Moser, S. C. (2007). In the long shadows of inaction: The quiet building of a climate protection movement in the United States. *Global Environmental Politics, 7*(2), 124–144. Retrieved from http://library. mtroyal.ca:2048/login?url=http://search.ebscohost.com/login. aspx?direct=true&AuthType=ip,url,cookie,uid&db=a9h&AN=248931 46&site=ehost-live

Mosher, C., & Hagan, J. (1994). Constituting class and crime in Upper Canada: The sentencing of narcotics offenders, circa 1908–1953. *Social Forces, 72*(3), 613–641.

Mosher, J. (2000). Managing the disentitlement of women: Glorified markets, the idealized family and the undeserving other discourses. In S. Neysmith (Ed.), *Restructuring caring labour: Discourse, state practice and everyday life* (pp. 30–51). Toronto: Oxford University Press.

Mourougane, A. (2008). *Achieving sustainability in the energy sector in Canada* (No. Economics Department Working Paper No. 618). Paris: OECD. Retrieved from http://www.olis.oecd.org/olis/2008doc.nsf/ LinkTo/NT00003436/$FILE/JT03248408.PDF

Mukherjee, R. (2006). The ghetto fabulous aesthetic in contemporary black culture. *Cultural Studies, 20*(6), 599–629.

Mulder, M. B. (1999). On pastoralism and inequality. *Current Anthropology, 40*(3), 366–367. Retrieved from http://library.mtroyal.ca:2048/ login?url=http://library.mtroyal.ca:2924/login.aspx?direct=true&AuthT ype=ip,url,cookie,uid&db=a9h&AN=2194267&site=ehost-live

Mulyadi, S. (2006). Max Weber's remarks on Islam: The protestant ethic among Muslim puritans. *Islam & Christian-Muslim Relations, 17*(2), 195–205.

Murdoch, G. (1949). *Social structure*. New York: Macmillan.

Murphy, S. (2009). "Compassionate" strategies of managing homelessness: Post-revanchist geographies in San Francisco. *Antipode, 41*(2), 305–325. doi:10.1111/j.1467-8330.2009.00674.x

Murray, R. T. (2003). Can money undue the past: A Canadian example. *Comparative Education, 39*(3), 331–343.

Myhill, D., & Jones, S. (2006). 'She doesn't shout at no girls': Pupils' perceptions of gender equity in the classroom. *Cambridge Journal of Education, 36*(1), 99–113.

Myles, J. (2003). Where have all the sociologists gone? Explaining economic inequality. *Canadian Journal of Sociology, 28*(4), 551–559.

Nack, A. (2005). Identity and stigma of women and STDs. In T. L. Steele (Ed.), *Sex, self and Society: The social context of sexuality* (California Trans.). Wadsworth:

Naess, A. (1988). Deep ecology and ultimate premises. *The Ecologist, 18*(4/5), 128–131.

Nagel, J. (1994). Constructing ethnicity. *Social Problems, 41*(1), 152–176.

Nakashima, R. (2008). *MySpace to allow users to share data with yahoo, others*. Retrieved 11/05/2008, from http://www.foxnews.com/wires/2008 May08/0,4670,MySpaceDataSharing,00.html

Nakhaie, R. M. (1997). Vertical mosaic among the elites: The new imagery revisited. *Canadian Review of Sociology and Anthropology, 34*(1), 1–24.

Nakhaie, R., Lin, X., & Guan, J. (2009). Social capital and the myth of minority self-employment: Evidence from Canada. *Journal of Ethnic & Migration Studies, 35*(4), 625–644. doi:10.1080/13691830902765244

Namaste, V. (2005). *Sex change, social change: Reflections on identity, institutions, and imperialism*. Toronto: Women's Press.

Nangia, P. (2013). Discrimination Experienced by Landed Immigrants in Canada. www.ryerson.ca/content/.../RCIS_WP_Parveen_Nangia_ No_2013_7.pdf

Napier, J. L., Mandisodza, A. N., Andersen, S. M., & Jost, J. T. (2006). System justification in responding to the poor and displaced in the aftermath of hurricane Katrina. *Analyses of Social Issues & Public Policy, 6*(1), 57–73. doi:10.1111/j.1530-2415.2006.00102.x

Nash, C. (2008). *Material entanglements: Queer geographies and trans experiences*. Unpublished manuscript.

National Climatic Data Center, National Oceanographic and Atmospheric Administration. (2013). Billion-Dollar Weather/Climate Disasters. Accessed 06/05/2014, from http://www.ncdc.noaa.gov/billions/

National Council of Welfare. (2009). *Poverty profile 2007*. Retrieved 15/06/2010, from http://www.ncwcnbes.net/en/research/povertyprofile2007/bulletin2.html

National Post. (2005). *The Canadian values study: A joint project of innovative research group, the dominion institute and the National Post*. Retrieved from http://www.innovativeresearch.ca/Canadian%20Values%20 Study_Factum%20280905.pdf

Native Women's Association of Canada. (n.d.). *The Native women's association of Canada releases action plan for Aboriginal women*. Retrieved 26/09/2010, from http://www.nationtalk.ca/modules/news/article .php?storyid=34097

Naugler, D. (2010). Wearing pink as a stand against bullying: Why we need to say more. *Journal of Homosexuality, 57*(3), 347–363. doi:10.1080/00918360903542958

Nayebi, H., & Abdollahyan, H. (2006). Social stratification and its indices: A critique. *Critique: Critical Middle Eastern Studies, 15*(3), 249–263.

Nederveen Pieterse, J. (2009). *Globalization and culture: Global mélange* (2nd ed.). Plymouth, UK: Rowman & Littlefield Publishers, Inc.

Neegan, E. (2005). Excuse me: Who are the first peoples of Canada? A historical analysis of Aboriginal education in Canada then and now. *International Journal of Inclusive Education, 9*(1), 3–15.

Nell, V. (1998). Why young men drive dangerously: An evolutionary perspective. *The Safety and Health Practitioner, 16*(10), 19–23.

Nelson, A. (2004). *Gender in Canada* (2nd ed.). Toronto: Pearson.

Nelson, A. (2006). *Gender in Canada* (3rd ed.). Toronto: Pearson.

Nelson, A. (2009). *Gender in Canada* (4th ed.). Toronto: Pearson.

Neugarten, B. L., Havighurst, R. J., & Tobin, S. (1968). Personality and patterns of aging. In B. L. Neugarten (Ed.), *Middle age and aging*. Chicago, IL: Chicago University Press.

Newbold, D. (2005). Foundation trusts: Economics in the '-postmodern hospital'. *Journal of Nursing Management, 13*(5), 439–447. doi:10.1111/j.1365-2834.2005.00587.x

NewHealthGuide. (2013). Where is euthanasia legal? Accessed 04/09/2014, from http://www.newhealthguide.org/Where-Is-Euthanasia-Legal.html

Newman, D. M. (2006). *Sociology: Exploring the architecture of everyday life* (6th ed.). Thousand Oaks, CA: Pine Forge Press, an imprint of SAGE Publications, Inc.

Newman, D., & Smith, R. (1999). *Newman study site huber*. Retrieved 07/12/2007, from http://www.pineforge.com/newman4study/ resources/huber1.htm

Newman, P. C. (1998). *Titans: How the new Canadian establishment seized power*. Toronto, ON: McClelland and Stewart.

Ng, K. H. (2007). Political context, policy networks and policy change: The complexity of transition in Hong Kong. *Pacific Review, 20*(1), 101–126. doi:10.1080/09512740601133245

Ng, G. (2013). Canadians sent 24 billion text messages in Q1 2013. Accessed 04/21/2014, from http://www.iphoneincanada.ca/carriers/ canadians-sent-24-billion-text-messages-in-q1-2013/

Nielsen, T. (2008). In Ravelli B. (Ed.), *Personal correspondence*.

Nkansah-Amankra, S., Agbanu, S. K., & Miller, R.J. (2013). Disparities in health, poverty, incarceration, and social justice among racial groups in the United States: A critical review of evidence of close links with neoliberalism. *International Journal of Health Services, 43*(2), 217–240.

Nishimura, Y. (2010). Civic engagement and community development among Japan's burakumin. In H. Vinken, Y. Nishimura, B. L. J. White & M. Deguchi (Eds.), *Civic engagement in contemporary Japan:*

Established and emerging repertoires (pp. 119–138). New York, New York: Springer.

Noble, B. (2006). *Sons of the movement: FtMs risking incoherence on a postqueer cultural landscape*. Toronto: Women's Press.

Nolan, M. (2001). *CTV, the network that means business*. Edmonton, AB: University of Alberta.

Nolan, P., & Lenski, G. (2006). *Human societies: An introduction to MacroSociology* (10th ed.). Boulder, CO: Paradigm Publishers.

Novak, M., & Campbell, L. (2006). *Aging and society: A Canadian perspective* (5th ed.). Toronto, ON: Thomson/Nelson.

Noymer, A. (2001). The transmission and persistence of 'urban legends': Sociological application of age-structured epidemic models. *Journal of Mathematical Sociology, 25*(3), 299. Retrieved from http://library.mtroyal.ca:2048/login?url=http://search.ebscohost.com/login.aspx?direct=true&????AuthType=ip,url,cookie,uid&db=a9h&AN=5512689&site=ehost-live

Nuri Yurdusev, A. (2006). Thomas Hobbes and international relations: From realism to rationalism. *Australian Journal of International Affairs, 60*(2), 305–321.

Nuyen, A. T. (2003). Confucianism, globalisation and the idea of universalism. *Asian Philosophy, 13*(2), 75–86. Retrieved from http://library.mtroyal.ca:2048/login?url=http://search.ebscohost.com/login.aspx?direct=true&AuthType=ip,url,cookie,uid&db=a9h&AN=11762884&site=ehost-live

O'Dea, T. F. (1966). *The sociology of religion*. Englewood Cliffs, NJ: Prentice-Hall, Inc.

O'Hara, B. (2012). How did Nate Silver predict the U.S. election? Accessed 05/05/2014, from http://www.theguardian.com/science/grrlscientist/2012/nov/08/nate-sliver-predict-us-election

Oates, T., & Durham, M. (2004). The mismeasure of masculinity: The male body, "race", and power in the enumerative discourses of the NFL draft. *Patterns of Prejudice, 38*(3), 301–320.

Obach, B. K. (2007). Theoretical interpretations of the growth in organic agriculture: Agricultural modernization or an organic treadmill? *Society & Natural Resources, 20*(3), 229–244. doi:10.1080/08941920601117322

Oberg, K. (1960). Culture shock: Adjustments to new cultural environments. *Practical Anthropology, 7,* 177–182.

O'Brien, R. (2005). *Bodies in revolt: Gender, disability, and a workplace ethic of care*. London, UK: Routledge, Taylor & Francis Group.

O'Connell, A. (2010). An exploration of redneck whiteness in multicultural Canada. *Social Politics: International Studies in Gender, State and Society, 17*(4), 536–563.

O'Connell, A. M. B. (2005). *Poverty and race: Colonial governmentality and the circuits of empire*. Unpublished Ph.D., University of Toronto, Toronto, ON. (NR07841)

Odd, A. W. (2005). *The global cold war: Third world interventions and the making of our times*. Cambridge, UK: Cambridge University Press.

OECD. (2001). *OECD economic outlook* (No. 70 (December)). Paris: OECD.

OECD. (2008). *Factbook 2008- municipal waste*. Retrieved 24/07/2008, from http://oberon.sourceoecd.org/vl=4895345/cl=20/nw=1/rpsv/factbook/080202.htm

OECD. (2010a). *Agricultural policies in OECD countries*. Retrieved 22/07/2010, from http://www.oecd.org/dataoecd/17/0/45539870.pdf

OECD. (2010b). *Long-term care expenditures*. Retrieved 27/12/2010, from http://www.oecd.org/dataoecd/31/8/46458681.xls

OECD. (2010c). *Net offical development assistance in 2009*. Retrieved 23/07/2010, from http://www.oecd.org/dataoecd/17/9/44981892.pdf

OECD. (2012). Environment: Act now or face costly consequences, warns OECD. Accessed 05/02/2014, from http://www.oecd.org/newsroom/environmentactnoworfacecostlyconsequenceswarnsoecd.htm

OECD. (2013). Support to agriculture rising after hitting historic lows, OECD says. Accessed 04/30/2014, from http://www.oecd.org/newsroom/support-to-agriculture-rising-after-hitting-historic-lows-oecd-says.htm

OECD Observer. (2003). *News brief - July 2003 edition*. Retrieved 05/09/2008, from http://www.oecdobserver.org/news/fullstory.php/aid/1020/News_brief_-_July_2003_edition.html

Ogden, R. (1997). An insult to free inquiry. *Simon Fraser News*. Retrieved 04/09/2010, from http://www.sfu.ca/sfunews/sfnews/1997/Oct30/opinion.html

Ogburn, W. F. (1957). *Cultural Lag as Theory*. Indianapolis: Bobbs-Merrill.

Ogden, R. D., Hamilton, W. K., & Whitcher, C. (2010). Assisted suicide by oxygen deprivation with helium at a Swiss right-to-die organisation. *Journal of Medical Ethics, 36*(3), 174–179.

Ogden, L. A. (2008). 'Race' in post-universalist perspective. *Cultural Geographies, 15*(2), 155–171. Retrieved from http://library.mtroyal.ca:2048/login?url=http://search.ebscohost.com/login.aspx?direct=true&AuthType=ip,url,cookie,uid&db=a9h&AN=31626321&site=ehost-live

Ogrodnik, I. (2010). *Murder or mercy?* Retrieved 27/12/2010, from http://www.globalnews.ca/story.html?id=3905582

O'Hara, P. (2002). The contemporary relevance of Thorstein Veblen's institutional-evolutionary political economy. *History of Economics Review, 35,* 78–103.

Oliver, E. J. (2006). *Fat politics: The real story behing America's obesity epidemic*. New York, New York: Oxford University Presss.

Olzak, S. (2006). *The global dynamics of racial and ethnic mobilization*. Palo Alto, CA: Stanford University Press.

O'Malley, A. L. (2010). Canada's colonialism. Message posted to http://www.themarknews.com/articles/842-canadas-colonialism

Omi, M., & Winant, H. (2008). *Racial formation in the new millennium*. New York: Routledge.

O'Neil, D. (2006). *Patterns of subsistence: Foraging*. Retrieved 18/05/2007, from http://anthro.palomar.edu/subsistence/sub_2.htm

O'Neil, D. (2007). *Patterns of subsistence: Pastoralism*. Retrieved 25/03/2008, from http://anthro.palomar.edu/subsistence/sub_3.htm

Ontario Health Quality Council. (2008). *Annual report summary (2008)*. Toronto, ON: Ontario Health Quality Council.

Ontario Ministry of Education. (1987). *The development of a policy on race and ethnocultural equity* (Provincial Advisory Committee on Race Relations' Report (Ontario Ministry of Education). Toronto: Queen's Printer.

Ontario Ministry of Education. (2009). *Realizing the promise of diversity*. Retrieved 08/11/2014, from www.edu.gov.on.ca/eng/policyfunding/equity.pdf

Oringderff, J. (2004). "My way": Piloting an online focus group. *International Journal of Qualitative Methods, 3*(3), http://www.ualberta/~ijqm/backissues/3_3/html/oringderff.html

Ornstein, M. (2011). Cohort and period perspectives on gender, education, and earnings in Canada. *Canadian Public Policy, 37,* S95–S113.

Orum, A. R., Johnston, J. W. C., & Riger, S. (1999). *Changing societies: Essential sociology for our times*. Lanham, MD: Rowman and Littlefield Publishers, Inc.

Osberg, L. (2008). *A quarter century of economic inequality in Canada: 1981–2006*. Retrieved 27/05/2011, from http://www.policyalternatives.ca/sites/default/files/uploads/publications/National_Office_Pubs/2008/Quarter_Century_of_Inequality.pdf

Osberg, L., & Sharpe, A. (2009). *New estimates of the index of economic well-being for Canada and the provinces, 1981–2008* (No. 2009-10). Ottawa, ON: Centre for the Study of Living Standards.

Osborne, K. (2000). Public schooling and citizenship education in Canada. *Canadian Ethnic Studies, 32*(1), 8–37.

Ostrander, S. A. (1984). *Women of the upper class*. Philadelphia, PA: Temple University Press.

Ottawa Citizen. (2008). *Government extends gun-registration amnesty*. Retrieved 15/08/2011, from http://www.canada.com/ottawacitizen/news/story.html?id=80f74558-04f9-469f-8dd1-5a7cf4b8ce7e

Owen Sound's Black History. (2004). *The underground rail road*. Retrieved 28/01/2008, from http://www.osblackhistory.com/underground.php

Owens, I. (2000). Maintaining diversity in information agencies: Accountability, professionalism, job performance, policies and standards. *Bulletin, 26* (April/May)(4), 14/01/2008. Retrieved from http://www.asis.org/Bulletin/May-00/owens.html

Oxfam Canada. (2013). The Cost of Inequality: How Wealth and Income Extremes Hurt Us all. Accessed 01/01/2014, from www.oxfam.ca/sites/default/files/cost-of-inequality-briefing-note.pdf

Oxley, H. (2009). *Policies for healthy ageing: An overview* (No. 2010). Paris, France: OECD. Retrieved from http://www.oecd.org/official documents/displaydocumentpdf/?cote=DELSA/HEA/WD/HWP(2009)1&doclanguage=en

Paasonen, S. (2010). Online pornography: Ubiquitous and effaced. In R. Burnett, M. Consalvo & C. Ess (Eds.), *The handbook of internet studies* (1st ed., pp. 424–439). Malden, MA: Blackwell Publishing Ltd.

Pagnan, C., Lero, D., & MacDermid Wadsworth, S. (2011). It doesn't always Add up: Examining dual-earner couples' decision to off-shift. *Community, Work & Family, 14*(3), 297–316.

Palamarek, M. (2008). *Personal communication*.

Palmore, E. B. (2004). Research note: Ageism in Canada and the United States. *Journal of Cross-Cultural Gerontology, 19*(1), 41–46. Retrieved from http://library.mtroyal.ca:2048/login?url=http://search.ebscohost.com/login.aspx?direct=true&AuthType=ip,url,cookie,uid&db=a9h&AN=12233298????&site=ehost-live

Parent & Bruckert v Queen & Magnotta. (2014). DR. COLETTE PARENT, DR. CHRISTINE BRUCKERT, Petitioners v. HER MAJESTY THE QUEEN, Respondent and LUKA ROCCO MAGNOTTA, Mis en cause [2014] Q.J. No. 65 2014 QCCS 132 No.: 500-36-006329-125 Quebec Superior Court District of Montreal The Honourable Sophie Bourque, J.S.C. Heard: April 3, 4, 2013. Judgment: January 21, 2014. (217 paras.)

Parenti, M. (2001). *Monopoly media manipulation*. Retrieved 12/05/2008, from http://www.michaelparenti.org/MonopolyMedia.html

Parenti, M. (2007). *Contrary notions: The Michael Parenti reader*. San Francisco, CA: City Lights Books.

Parenti, M. (1993). *Inventing Reality: The politics of news media* (2nd ed.). New York: St. Martin's Press.

Park, H. (2010). The stranger that is welcomed: Female foreign students from Asia, the English language industry, and the ambivalence of 'Asia rising' in British Columbia, Canada. *Gender, Place and Culture, 17*(3), 337–355.

Park, S. (1996). Research, teaching and service: Why shouldn't women's work count? *The Journal of Higher Education, 67*(1), 46–67.

Park, S. (2006). Adoptive maternal bodies: A queer paradigm for rethinking mothering? *Hypatia, 21*(1), 201–226.

Park, M. A. (2004). *Biological anthropology* (4th ed.). Montreal, QC; Boston, MA: McGraw-Hill.

Parker Oliver, D., Porock, D., & Oliver, D. (2006). Managing the secrets of dying backstage: The voices of nursing home staff. *Omega, 53*(3), 193–207.

Parkinson, G., & Drislane, R. (2007). *Thomson Nelson Canadian dictionary for the social sciences*. Toronto, ON: Nelson.

Parks, C. (2005). *Ancestors of science: Papyrus paper technology*. Retrieved 05/01/2008, from http://nextwave.sciencemag.org/career_development/previous_issues/articles/3430/ancestors_of_science_papyrus_paper_technology/(parent)/158

Parrillo, V. N., & Donoghue, C. (2005). Updating the bogardus social distance studies: A new national survey. *The Social Science Journal, 42*(2), 257–251.

Parsons, T., & Bales, R. (1955). *Family, socialization and interaction process*. New York: Free Press.

Parsons, T., Bales, R., & and Shils, E. (1962). *Working papers on the theory of action*. London: Collier-Macmillan.

Parsons, T. (Ed.). (1947). *Max Weber: The theory of economic and social organization*. New York: The Free Press.

Parsons, T. (1951). *The social system*. Glencoe, IL: Free Press.

Parsons, T. (1955). The American family: Its relation to personality and to social structure. In T. Parsons, & R. Bales (Eds.), *Family, socialization and interaction process* (pp. 3–33). New York: The Free Press.

Parsons, T. (1959). The social class as a social system: Some of its functions in American society. *Harvard Educational Review, 29,* 291–318.

Pascali, L. (2006). Two stoves, two refrigerators, due cucine: The italian immigrant home with two kitchens. *Gender, Place & Culture: A Journal of Feminist Geography, 13*(6), 685–695. doi:10.1080/09663690601019935

Pastore, R. T. (1997). *Aboriginal peoples: The Beothuks: Newfoundland and Labrador heritage*. Retrieved 22/01/2008, from http://www.heritage.nf.ca/aboriginal/beothuk.html

Patterson, C., Sutfin, E., & Fulcher, M. (2004). Division of labor among lesbian and heterosexual parenting couples: Correlates of specialized versus shared patterns. *Journal of Adult Development, 11*(3), 179–189.

Paul, L. J. (2004). The untenured female academic in the corporate university. In M. Reimer (Ed.), *Inside corporate U: Women in the academy speak out* (pp. 226–244). Toronto: Sumach Press.

Paul, A. M. (2011). The 'other' looks back: Racial distancing and racial alignment in migrant domestic workers' stereotypes about white and Chinese employers. *Ethnic & Racial Studies, 34*(6), 1068–1087. doi:10.1080/01419870.2010.528783

Paulson, J. (2007). No logo. *Science & Society, 71*(3), 361–363.

Peat, D. (2008). *3 patients die waiting for a bed: EMS*. Retrieved 30/06/2008, from http://chealth.canoe.ca/channel_health_news_details.asp?channel_id=41&relation_id=1826&news_channel_id=41&news_id=24297

Pechlaner, G. (2010). The sociology of agriculture in transition: The political economy of agriculture after biotechnology. *Canadian Journal of Sociology, 35*(2), 243–269. Retrieved from http://library.mtroyal.ca:2057/login.aspx?direct=true&AuthType=ip,url,cookie,uid&db=sih&AN=55274660&site=ehost-live

Pedwell, T. (2008). *Morgentaler to get order of Canada*. Retrieved 10/07/2008, from http://cnews.canoe.ca/CNEWS/Politics/2008/07/01/6036816-cp.html

Pellow, D. N. (2007). *Resisting global toxics: Transnational movements for environmental justice*. Cambridge, MA: MIT Press.

Pelz, H., Rost, S., Hunerberg, M., Fregin, A., Heiberg, A., Baert, K., et al. (2005). The genetic basis of resistance to anticoagulants in rodents. *Genetics, 170*(4), 1839–1847.

Pereira, J. (2003). From Canada. *Palliative Medicine, 17*(2), 167–168. doi:10.1191/0269216303pm722op

Périer, P. (1998). Le play and his followers: Over a century of achievement. *International Social Science Journal, 50*(157), 343.

Perkins, J. (2004). *Confessions of an economic hit man*. New York, NY: Plume.

Peron, J. (2006). Globalization reduces poverty in developing nations. In L. I. Gerdes (Ed.), *Globalization opposing viewpoints* (pp. 113–119). New York: Thompson/Gale.

Persaud, C. (2008). The smart-phone - what's in a name? *Marketnews, 33* (March), 44–45.

Perse, E. M. (2001). *Media effects and Society*. Mahwah, New Jersey: Lawrence Erlbaum Associates.

Pertusati, L. (1997). *In defense of Mohawk land: Ethnopolitical conflict in native North America*. Albany, NY: State University of New York Press.

Pesce, A. (2011). *Fear-mongering masquerading as reform: The debate on age-sensitive spending by governments*. Retrieved 25/05/2011, from http://www.pesceassociates.com/pdfs/13b Age-Sensitive Spending by Governments.pdf

Petch, J. (2002). *Luddites*. Retrieved 03/07/2008, from http://web.uvic.ca/philosophy/department_files/sophia/issues/sophia2002/jpetch.htm

Peters, J. (1999). Redefining western families. *Marriage and Family Review, 28*(3/4), 55–66.

Peters, M. (2013). Managerialism and the neoliberal university: Prospects for new forms of "open management" in higher education. *Contemporary Readings in Law and Social Justice, 5*(1), 11–26.

Peterson, V. S. (2003). *A Critical Rewriting of Global Political Economy: Integrating Reproductive, Productive, and Virtual Economies.* New York, NY: Routledge.

Pettett, C. (2007). Homophobia and harassment in school-age populations. In G. Herdt, & C. Howe (Eds.), *21st century sexualities: Contemporary issues in health, education, and rights* (pp. 29–31). New York: Routledge.

Philipps, L. (2004). Measuring the effects of feminist legal research: Looking critically at "failure" and success". *Osgoode Hall Law Journal, 42*(4), 603–614.

Phillips, P. C., & Phillips, E. (2000). *Women and work: Inequality in the Canadian labour market.* Toronto, ON: Lorimer. Retrieved from http://isbndb.com/d/book/women_and_work_a28

Phillips, D. J. (2013). Pfizer's expiring Viagra patent adversely affects other drugmakers too. *Forbes,* 12/20/2013.

Phillips, S. (2007). *A brief history of facebook.* Retrieved 10/05/2008, from http://www.guardian.co.uk/technology/2007/jul/25/media.newmedia

Phipps, S., & Lethbridge, L. (2006). *Income and the outcomes of children.* Retrieved 09/07/2011, from http://dsp-psd.pwgsc.gc.ca/Collection/Statcan/11F0019MIE/11F0019MIE2006281.pdf

Pidgeon, A. & Harker, R. A. (2013). Body-focused anxiety in women: Associations with internalization of the thin-ideal, dieting frequency, body mass index and media effects. *Open Journal of Medical Psychology, 2*(4B), 17–24.

Piirimäe, P. (2006). The explanation of conflict in Hobbes's Leviathan. *TRAMES: A Journal of the Humanities & Social Sciences, 10*(1), 3–21.

Pinch, T. (2010). The invisible technologies of Goffman's sociology from the merry-go-round to the internet. *Technology and Culture, 51*(2), 409–424.

Pinterics, N. (2001). Riding the feminist waves: In with the third? *Canadian Woman Studies, 20/21*(4/1), 15–21.

Pintor, R. L., Gratschew, M., & Sullivan, K. (2002). *Voter turnout rates from a comparative perspective.* Stockholm, Sweden: IDEA. Retrieved from http://www.idea.int/publications/vt/upload/Voter%20turnout.pdf

Pitt, C. (2011). U.S. patriot act and racial profiling: Are there consequences of discrimination? *Michigan Sociological Review, 25,* 53–69. http://www.jstor.org/stable/41289191

Pitts-Taylor, V. (2007). *Surgery junkies: Wellness and pathology in cosmetic culture.* Piscataway, NJ: Rutgers University Press.

Pitts-Taylor, V. (2009). Becoming/Being a cosmetic surgery patient: Semantic instability and the intersubjective self. *Studies in Gender and Sexuality, 10*(3), 119–128.

Piven, F. F., & Cloward, R. A. (1977). *Poor people's movements: Why they succeed, how they fail.* New York: Random House.

Plummer, K. (2010). A round up of some recent books on prostitution and sex work. *Sexualities, 13*(3), 394–400.

Pollak, O. (1961). The Criminality of Women. Philadelphia, PA: University of Pennsylvania Press.

Polster, C. (2004). Intellectual property, higher education and women's inequality. In M. Reimer (Ed.), *Inside corporate U: Women in the academy speak out* (pp. 138–152). Toronto: Sumach Press.

Pope, W. (1976). *Durkheim's "suicide": A classic analyzed.* Chicago: Chicago University Press.

Porter, J. (1965). *The vertical mosaic: An analysis of social class and power in Canada.* Toronto, ON: University of Toronto Press.

Possamaï, A., & Lee, M. (2004). New religious movements and the fear of crime. *Journal of Contemporary Religion, 19*(3), 337–352. doi:10.1080/1353790042000266354

Postner, H. H. (1992). Book review of: *If women counted: A new feminist economics* by Mailyn Waring. *Review of Income and Wealth, 38*(2), 237–243. Retrieved from http://www.roiw.org/1992/237.pdf

Potts, M. (2006). China's one child policy. *British Medical Journal, 333,* 361–362.

Poulin, D., & Boame, A. K. (2009). *Mad cow disease and beef trade.* Retrieved 03/05/2011, from http://www.statcan.gc.ca/pub/11-621-m/11-621-m2003005-eng.htm

Powell, C. (2014). Defending Giordano Bruno: A response from the co-writer of "Cosmos". Accessed 05/06/2014, from http://blogs.discovermagazine.com/outthere/2014/03/13/cosmos-giordano-bruno-response-steven-soter/#.UypFa_ldV8E

Pratt, A., & Thompson, S. (2008). Chivalry, 'race' and discretion at the Canadian border. *British Journal of Criminology, 48,* 620–640.

Preckel, F., Holling, H., & Vock, M. (2006). Academic underachievement: Relationship with cognitive motivation, achievement motivation, and conscientiousness. *Psychology in the Schools, 43*(3), 401–411.

Preibisch, K., & Binford, L. (2007). Interrogating racialized global labour supply: An exploration of the racial/national replacement of foreign agricultural workers in Canada. *The Canadian Review of Sociology and Anthropology, 44*(1), 5. Retrieved from http://library.mtroyal.ca:2083/pqdweb?did=1366162351&Fmt=7&clientId=65345&RQT=309&VName=PQD

Prendergast, C. (2008). The unexceptional schizophrenic: A postmodern introduction. *Journal of Literary Disability, 2*(1), 55–62.

Prensky, M. (2001). Digital natives, digital immigrants. *On the Horizon, 9*(5), 1–5.

Prentice, A. (1977). *The school promoters: Education and social class in mid-nineteenth century Upper Canada.* Toronto: McClelland & Stewart.

Price, M. E., Kang, J., Dunn, J., & Hopkins, S. (2011). Muscularity and attractiveness as predictors of human egalitarianism. *Personality & Individual Differences, 50*(5), 636–640. doi:10.1016/j.paid.2010.12.009

Price, T. D., & Feinman, G. M. (2010). Social Inequality and the Evolution of Human Social Organization. In *Pathways to Power* (pp. 1–14). New York: Springer.

Prince, M. J. (2010). What about a disability rights act for Canada? Practices and lessons from America, Australia, and the United Kingdom. *Canadian Public Policy, 36*(2), 199–214. Retrieved from http://search.ebscohost.com/login.aspx?direct=true&AuthType=ip,url,cookie,uid&db=a9h&AN=52339675&site=ehost-live

Prohaska, A., & Gailey, J. (2010). Achieving masculinity through sexual predation: The case of hogging. *Journal of Gender Studies, 19*(1), 13–25.

Proulx, C., & Helms, H. (2008). Mothers' and fathers' perceptions of change and continuity in their relationships with young adult sons and daughters. *Journal of Family Issues, 29*(2), 234–261.

Province of Nova Scotia. (2003). *Halifax Gazette - Canada's first newspaper.* Retrieved 03/05/2008, from http://www.gov.ns.ca/nsarm/virtual/gazette/

Prügl, E. (2002). Toward a feminist political economics. *International Feminist Journal of Politics, 4*(1), 31–36. Retrieved from http://library.mtroyal.ca:2048/login?url=http://search.ebscohost.com/login.aspx?direct=true&????AuthType=ip,url,cookie,uid&db=a9h&AN=6774876&site=ehost-live

Prüss-Üstün, A., Bos, R., Gore, F., & Bartram, J. (2008). *Safer water, better health: Costs, benefits and sustainability of interventions to protect and promote health.* Geneva: World Health Organization.

Public Health Agency of Canada (PHAC). (2009a). *HIV and AIDS in Canada.* Retrieved 22/11/2010, from http://www.phac-aspc.gc.ca/aids-sida/publication/survreport/2008/dec/pdf/surrepdec08.pdf

Public Health Agency of Canada (PHAC). (2009b). *Sexually transmitted infections data tables.* Retrieved 22/11/2010, from http://www.phac-aspc.gc.ca/std-mts/sti-its_tab/index-eng.php

Public Health Agency of Canada (PHAC). (2008). *Canadian guidelines on sexually transmitted infections.* Ottawa: Public Health Agency of Canada.

Public Health Agency of Canada. (2011). Summary: Estimates of HIV Prevalence and Incidence in Canada, 2011. Accessed 28/02/2014, from http://www.phac-aspc.gc.ca/aids-sida/publication/survreport/estimat2011-eng.php#tphp

Public Health Agency of Canada. (2012). Sexual and Reproductive Health Day. Accessed 28/02/2014, from www.phac-aspc.gc.ca/cpho-acsp/statements/20120213-eng.php

Public Health Agency of Canada. (2013). What makes Canadians healthy or unhealthy? Accessed 07/15/2014, from http://www.phac-aspc.gc.ca/ph-sp/determinants/determinants-eng.php#income

Public Health Service. (1969). Public health service reports on smoking. *Congressional Digest, 48*(6/7), 166–167.

Public Safety Canada. (2007). *Backgrounder: The long-gun registry*. Retrieved 16/06/2008, from http://www.publicsafety.gc.ca/media/nr/2007/nr20071116-2-eng.aspx

Quan-Haase, A. (2007). University students' local and distant social ties: Using and integrating modes of communication on campus. *Information, Communication & Society, 10*(5), 671–693.

Quiet PC. (2008). *The official site of Marshall McLuhan*. Retrieved 5/5/2008, from http://www.marshallmcluhan.com/

Quinion, M. (1999). *World wide words: Rule of thumb*. Retrieved 14/11/2007, from http://www.worldwidewords.org/qa/qa-rul1.htm

Rahimi, R., & Liston, D. (2009). What does she expect when she dresses like that? Teacher interpretation of emerging adolescent female sexuality. *Educational Studies, 45,* 512–533.

Rahman, A. S. (2009). *An exceptionally simple theory of industrialization* (No. WORKING PAPER 2010-27). Annapolis, Maryland: United States Naval Academy, Department of Economics.

Räikkä, J. (2004). The self-fulfilling prophecies and global inequality. *Philosophy & Geography, 7*(2), 193–200.

Rajiva, M. (2006). Brown girls, white worlds: Adolescence and the making of racialized selves. *Canadian Review of Sociology & Anthropology, 43*(2), 165–183. Retrieved from http://library.mtroyal.ca:2048/login?url=http://search.ebscohost.com/login.aspx?direct=true&AuthType=ip,url,cookie,uid&db=a9h&AN=21214089&site=ehost-live

Ramage-Morin, P. L. (2008). *Chronic pain in Canadian seniors*. Retrieved 24/06/2008, from http://www.statcan.ca/english/freepub/82-003-XIE/2008001/article/10514/findings-en.htm

Raman, S. M. (1999). Caste in stone. *Harvard International Review, 21*(4), 30. Retrieved from http://library.mtroyal.ca:2083/pqdweb?did=47034960&Fmt=7&clientId=65345&RQT=309&VName=PQD

Randeria, S. (2007). Global designs and local lifeworlds. *Interventions: The International Journal of Postcolonial Studies, 9*(1), 12–30. doi:10.1080/13698010601173791

Rasberry, C. N. (2008). Battling body image: Confessions of a health educator. *Journal of American College Health, 56*(4), 423–426. Retrieved from http://library.mtroyal.ca:2048/login?url=http://library.mtroyal.ca:2924/login.aspx?direct=true&AuthType=ip,url,cookie,uid&db=a9h&AN=31161528&site=ehost-live

Rashed, M. A., & El Azzazi, I. (2011). The Egyptian revolution: A participant's account from Tahrir Square, January and February 2011. *Anthropology Today, 27*(2), 22–27. doi:10.1111/j.1467-8322.2011.00798.x

Ravallion, M., Chen, S., & Sangraula, P. (2008). *Dollar a day revisited* (No. WPS4620). Washington, DC: The World Bank.

Ravanera, Z., & McQuillan, K. (2006). Introduction. In K. McQuillan, & Z. Ravanera (Eds.), *Canada's changing families: Implications for individuals and society* (pp. 3–11). Toronto: University of Toronto Press.

Ravelli, B. (1994). Health care in the United States and Canada. In R. Luhman (Ed.), *The sociological outlook: A text with readings* (4th ed., pp. 467–468). San Diego: Collegiate Press.

Ravelli, B. (2000). Culture. In M. Kanwar, & D. Swenson (Eds.), *Canadian sociology* (3rd ed., pp. 39–61). Dubuque, IA: Kendall/Hunt.

Ravelli, B., Webber, M., & Patterson, J. (2011). *Sociology for Everyone*. Toronto, ON: Pearson Education Canada.

Ray, J. J. (1988). Why the F scale predicts racism: A critical review. *Political Psychology, 9*(4), 671–679.

Rea, M. C. (2006). Polytheism and Christian belief. *Journal of Theological Studies, 57*(1), 133. Retrieved from http://proquest.umi.com/pqdweb?did=1008676081&Fmt=7&clientId=65345&RQT=309&VName=PQD

Reay, D. (2013). Social mobility, a panacea for austere times: Tales of emperors, frogs, and tadpoles. *British Journal of Sociology of Education, 34*(5–6), 660–677.

Reddy, S. (2009). Hindu concepts of time. In L. G. Fiorini, & J. Canestri (Eds.), *The experience of time: Psychoanalytic perspectives* (pp. 175–194). London, UK: Karnac Books, Ltd.

Redhead, S. (2007). This sporting life: The realism of the football factory. *Soccer & Society, 8*(1), 90–108. Retrieved from http://library.mtroyal.ca:2048/login?url=http://search.ebscohost.com/login.aspx?direct=true&AuthType=ip,url,cookie,uid&db=a9h&AN=23368982&site=ehost-live

Reid, L. W., Adelman, R. M., & Jaret, C. (2007). Women, race, and ethnicity: Exploring earnings differentials in metropolitan America. *City & Community, 6*(2), 137. Retrieved from http://proquest.umi.com/pqdweb?did=1274477011&Fmt=7&clientId=65345&RQT=309&VName=PQD

Reimer, M. (2004). Will women's studies prgorams survive the corporate university? In M. Reimer (Ed.), *Inside corporate U: Women in the academy speak out* (pp. 118–137). Toronto: Sumach Press.

ReligionFacts. (2008a). *Church of scientology*. Retrieved 09/03/2008, from http://www.religionfacts.com/scientology/index.htm

ReligionFacts. (2008b). *Jehovah's witnesses*. Retrieved 11/03/2008, from http://religionfacts.com/jehovahs_witnesses/index.htm

ReligionFacts. (2008c). *Overview of Judaism*. Retrieved 10/03/2008, from http://www.religionfacts.com/judaism/fastfacts/overview.htm

Renold, E. (2006). 'They won't let us play...unless you're going out with one of them': Girls, boys and butler's 'heterosexual matrix' in the primary years. *British Journal of Sociology of Education, 27*(4), 489–509.

Renton, D. (2007). *C. L. R. James: The enigma of cricket's philosopher*. London, England: Haus Publishers Ltd.

Renzetti, C., & Curran, D. (1999). *Women, men and society* (4th ed.). Boston: Allyn and Bacon.

Research Institute. (2012). Global wealth report 2012. Zurich, Switzerland: Research Institute.

Research Machines. (2007). *Reign of terror*. Retrieved 26/06/2007, from http://www.tiscali.co.uk/reference/encyclopaedia/hutchinson/m0011716.html

Reuters. (2009). *Every G20 nation wants to be Canada, insists PM*. Retrieved 22/06/2010, from http://www.reuters.com/article/idUSTRE58P05Z20090926

Reutter, L., Veenstra, G., Stewart, M., Raphael, D., Love, R., Makwarimba, E., et al. (2006). Public attribution for poverty in Canada. *Canadian Review of Sociology and Anthropology, 43*(1), 1–22.

Reynolds, P. (2004). Queer theory. In J. Eadie (Ed.), *Sexuality: The essential glossary* (pp. 178–179). London: Arnold.

Reznick, O. I. (2006). *The secrets of medical decision making: How to avoid becoming a victim of the health care machine*. Ann Arbor, MI: Loving Healing Press.

Rhoads, J. K. (1991). *Critical issues in social theory*. University Park, PA: Penn State Press.

Rhodes, R. (2005). Rethinking research ethics. *The American Journal of Bioethics, 5*(1), 7–28.

Ricciardelli, R., & Moir, M. (2013). Stigmatized among the stigmatized: Sex offenders in Canadian penitentiaries. *Canadian Journal of Criminology and Criminal Justice, 55*(3), 353–385.

Ricciardelli, R., Clow, K., & White, P. (2010). Investigating hegemonic masculinity: Portrayals of masculinity in men's lifestyle magazines. *Sex Roles, 63,* 64–78.

Richards, J. G., Vining, A. R., & Weimer, D. L. (2010). Aboriginal performance on standardized tests: Evidence and analysis from provincial schools in British Columbia. *Policy Studies Journal, 38*(1), 47–67. doi:10.1111/j.1541-0072.2009.00344.x

Richardson, J. T., Best, J., & Bromley, D. G. (1991). Satanism as a social problem. In J. T. Richardson, J. Best & D. G. Bromley (Eds.), *The satanism scare* (pp. 3–17). New York: Aldine De Gruyter.

Richey, C. (Producer), & Richey, C. (Director). (1993). *In the gutter and other good places.* [Video/DVD] Ladder to the Moon Productions.

Richman, M. H. (2002). *Sacred revolutions: Durkheim and the college of sociology.* Minneapolis, MN: University of Minnesota Press.

Ringen, S. (2005). The freedom of liberty. *Society, 42*(4), 42–48. Retrieved ????from http://search.ebscohost.com/login.aspx?direct=true&AuthType= ????ip,url,cookie,uid&db=a9h&AN=16553133&site=ehost-live

Ringen, S. (2006). *Citizens, families & reform.* New Brunswick (USA): Transaction Publishers.

Ringrose, J., & Renold, E. (2012). Slut-shaming, girl power and 'sexualisation': thinking through the politics of the international SlutWalks with teen girls. *Gender and Education, 24*(3), 333–343.

Rist, R. (1970). Student social class and teacher expectations: The self-fulfilling prophecy in ghetto education. *Harvard Educational Review, 40*(3), 411–451.

Ritchie, A., & Barker, M. (2006). There aren't words for what we do or how we feel so, we have to make them up: Constructing polyamorous languages in a culture of compulsory monogamy. *Sexualities, 9*(5), 584–601.

Ritzer, G. (1998). *The McDonaldization thesis: Explorations and extensions.* London & Thousand Oaks, CA: Sage.

Ritzer, G. (2000). *Sociological theory* (5th ed.). New York: McGraw-Hill.

Ritzer, G. (2002). Enchanting McUniversity: Toward a spectacularly irrational university quotidian. In D. Hayes, & R. Wynyard (Eds.), *The McDonaldization of higher education* (pp. 19–32). Westport: Bergin & Garvey.

Ritzer, G. (2004). *The McDonaldization of society* (Revised New Century Edition ed.). Thousand Oaks, CA: Sage Publications, Ltd.

Ritzer, G. (2008a). *Modern sociological theory* (7th ed.). New York: McGraw-Hill.

Ritzer, G. (2008b). *Sociological theory* (7th ed.). New York, New York: McGraw-Hill Higher Education.

Roach, M. (1998). Why men kill. *Discover, 19*(12), 100.

Robards, B. (2012). Leaving MySpace, joining Facebook: 'Growing up' on social network sites. *Continuum: Journal of Media & Cultural Studies, 26*(3), 385–398.

Roberts, A. (n.d.). *Extracts from Erving Goffman.* Retrieved 13/11/2007, from http://www.mdx.ac.uk/WWW/STUDY/xgof.htm

Roberts, F. (2013). *2012's Carbon Emissions in Five Graphs.* Accessed 05/01/2014, from http://www.carbonbrief.org/blog/2013/11/2012s-carbon-emissions-in-five-graphs/

Roberts, J. (2001). *Public fear of crime and perceptions of the criminal justice system.* Ottawa: Solicitor General of Canada.

Roberts, L. W., Kampen, K., & Peter, T. (2009). *The Methods Coach: Learning Through Practice.* Oxford: Oxford University Press.

Roberts, J., & Doob, A. (1997). Race, ethnicity and criminal justice in Canada. *Crime and Justice, 21,* 469–522.

Robertson, I. (2009, Doors open to Africentric school. *Toronto Sun,*

Robertson, R. (2002). *Women in management: Analysis of current population survey data* (No. GAO-02-156). US General Accounting Office.

Rochlin, M. (2009). The heterosexual questionnaire. In A. Ferber, K. Holcomb & T. Wentling (Eds.), *Sex, gender and sexuality: The new basics, an anthology* (pp. 299–300). New York: Oxford University Press.

Rodríquez Rust, P. (Ed.). (2000). *Bisexuality in the United States.* New York: Columbia University Press.

Rokach, A., Lechcier-Kimel, R., & Safarov, A. (2006). Loneliness of people with physical disabilities. *Social Behavior & Personality: An International Journal, 34*(6), 681–699. Retrieved from http://library.mtroyal.ca:2048/login?url=http://search.ebscohost.com/login.aspx?direct=true&AuthType=????ip,url,cookie,uid&db=a9h&AN=21903298&site=ehost-live

Ronen, S. (2010). Grinding on the dance floor: Gendered scripts and sexualized dancing at college parties. *Gender and Society, 24*(3), 355–377.

Rose, D. B. (2008). Love in the time of extinctions. *Australian Journal of Anthropology, 19*(1), 81–84. Retrieved from http://library.mtroyal.ca:2048/login?url=http://search.ebscohost.com/login.aspx?direct=true&AuthType=ip,url,cookie,uid&db=a9h&AN=31341444&site=ehost-live

Rosen, J. (2008, March 27, 2008). Researchers play tune recorded before Edison. *The New York Times,*

Rosenberg, M. (1999). *Conceiving the self.* New York: Basic Books.

Rosenthal, J. L. (1992). *The fruits of revolution: Property rights, litigation, and French agriculture, 1700–1860* Cambridge University Press.

Ross, L. E., Epstein, R., Goldfinger, C., & Yager, C. (2009). Policy and practice regarding lesbian, gay, bisexual, transgender, transsexual and two-spirit adoption in Ontario. *Canadian Public Policy, 35*(4), 451.

Rossides, D. W. (1998). *Social theory: Its origins, history, and contemporary relevance.* Dix Hills, NY: General Hall.

Rostow, W. W. (1960). *Stages of economic growth: A non-communist manifesto.* Cambridge, UK: Cambridge University Press.

Rotermann, M., & McKay, A. (2009). Condom use at last sexual intercourse among unmarried, not living common-law 20- to 34-year old Canadian young adults. *The Canadian Journal of Human Sexuality, 18*(3), 75–87.

Roth, C. F. (2002). Goods, names, and selves: Rethinking the tsimshian potlatch. *American Ethnologist, 29*(1), 123. Retrieved from http://proquest.umi.com/pqdweb?did=128816021&Fmt=7&clientId=65345&RQT=309&VName=PQD

Rovere, M. (2010). *The unsustainable growth of government health care spending.* Retrieved 12/07/2010, from http://www.fraserinstitute.org/WorkArea/DownloadAsset.aspx?id=15807

Royal Commission on the Status of Women in Canada. (2007). *Briefs to the royal commission on the status of women in Canada.* Retrieved 29/05/2007, from http://www.library.utoronto.ca/mediacommons/microtext/collection/pages/carylcos.html

Royal Commission on the Status of Women. (1970). *Report of the royal commission on the status of women.* Hull: Information Canada.

Rubin, L. (1994). *Families on the fault line.* New York: Harper Collins.

Rubin, L. B. (1976). *Worlds of pain: Life in the working class family.* New York: Basic.

Rubin, R. H. (2001). Alternative lifestyles revisited, or whatever happened to swingers, group marriages, and communes? *Journal of Family Issues, 22*(6), 711–726.

Rudel, T. K., & Hooper, L. (2005). Is the pace of social change accelerating? Latecomers, common languages, and rapid historical declines in fertility. *International Journal of Comparative Sociology, 46*(4), 275–296.

Rumbaut, R. G. (2004). Ages, life stages, and generational cohorts: Decomposing the immigrant first and second generations in the United States. *The International Migration Review, 38*(3), 1160. Retrieved from http://proquest.umi.com/pqdweb?did=762568041&Fmt=7&clientId=65345&RQT=309&VName=PQD

Russell, C. L. (2008). How are your person first skills? *Teaching Exceptional Children, 40*(5), 40–43. Retrieved from http://library.mtroyal.ca:2048/login?url=http://search.ebscohost.com/login.aspx?direct=true&AuthType=ip,url,cookie,uid&db=a9h&AN=32197150&site=ehost-live

Russell, J. W. (2009). *Race and Class Formation in North America.* Toronto, ON: University of Toronto Press.

Rust, P. (1995). *Bisexuality and the challenge to lesbian politics: Sex, loyalty and revolution.* New York: New York University Press.

Ruth, D. (2014). Misconceptions of science in religion found in new study. Accessed 03/25/2014, from http://news.rice.edu/2014/02/16/misconceptions-of-science-and-religion-found-in-new-study/

Ryan, W. (1971). *Blaming the victim*. New York: Pantheon.

Saad, O. B., Salmon, D. A., Orenstein, W. A., deHart, M. P., & Halsey, N. (2009). Vaccine refusal, mandatory immunization, and the risks of vaccine-preventable diseases. *N Engl J Med, 360*(19), 1981–1988. doi:10.1056/NEJMsa0806477

Sacco, V., & Kennedy, L. (2008). *The criminal event: An introduction to criminology in Canada* (4th ed.). Toronto: Nelson.

Sachs, J. D. (2005). *The end of poverty: Economic possibilities for our time.* New York: The Penguin Press.

Sachsenmaier, D. (2006). *Global history and critiques of western perspectives.* Routledge. Retrieved from http://library.mtroyal.ca:2048/login?url=http://search.ebscohost.com/login.aspx?direct=true&AuthType=ip,url,cookie,uid&db=a9h&AN=23233532&site=ehost-live

Sadker, M., & Sadker, D. (2009). Missing in interaction. In E. Disch (Ed.), *Reconstructing gender: A multicultural anthology* (5th ed., pp. 362–368). New York: McGraw Hill.

Saettler, P. (2004). *Evolution of American educational technology*. Charlotte, NC: Information Age Publishing.

Sahib, P. R., Koning, R., & van Witteloostuijn, A. (2006). Putting your best cyber identity forward: An analysis of "success stories" from a russian internet MArriage agency. *International Sociology, 21*(1), 61–82.

SAHRDC. (2001). *Caste, ethnicity and nationality: Japan finds plenty of space for discrimination.* Retrieved 30/11/2007, from http://www.hrdc.net/????sahrdc/hrfeatures/HRF39.htm

Said, E. (1978). *Orientalism.* New York: Pantheon Books.

Salaff, J. W., Greve, A. & Ping, L. X. L. (2002). *When ties do not tie in? Can skilled Chinese immigrants find jobs outside Chinatown?* Retrieved 17/01/2008, from http://www.chass.utoronto.ca/~salaff/Salaff-Greve-Xu-labor.pdf

Salari, S., & Zhang, W. (2006). Kin keepers and good providers: Influence of gender socialization on well-being among USA birth cohorts. *Aging & Mental Health, 10*(5), 485–496.

Salerno, R. (2013). *Contemporary Social Theory.* Upper Saddle River, NJ: Pearson.

Sallot, J. (1999, January 11). Latimer sentence too harsh, poll told. *Globe and Mail,* A5.

Salzman, P. C. (2004). *Pastoralists: Equality, hierarchy and the state.* Boulder, CO: Westview Press.

Salzmann, Z. (2007). *Language, culture, and society: An introduction to linguistic anthropology.* Boulder, CO: Westview Press.

Sampson, T. D. (2012). *Virality: Contagion Theory in the Age of Networks.* Minneapolis, MN: University of Minnesota Press.

Sanders, S., Graham, C., Yarber, W., Crosby, R., Dodge, B., & Milhausen, R. (2006). Women who put condoms on male partners: Correlates of condom application. *American Journal of Health Behavior, 30*(5), 460–466.

Sandler, B. R., & Hall, R. (1986). *The campus climate revisited: Chilly climate for women faculty, administrators, and graduate students.* Project on the Status and Education of Women. Washington, DC: Association of American Colleges.

Sanger, T. (2008). Trans governmentality: The production and regulation of gendered subjectivities. *Journal of Gender Studies, 17*(1), 41–53.

Sangster, J. (2007). Making a fur coat: Women, the labouring body, and working-class history. *International Review of Social History, 52,* 241. Retrieved from http://proquest.umi.com/pqdweb?did=1331477351&Fmt=7&clientId=65345&RQT=309&VName=PQD

Saniotis, A. (2009). Technologies of the mind neuroanthropology and memetics. *NeuroQuantology, 7*(2), 318–324.

Santos, C. A., Tainsky, S., Schmidt, K. A., & Shim. C. (2013). Framing the octagon: An analysis of news-media coverage of mixed martial arts. *International Journal of Sport Communication, 6*(1), 66–86.

Sassen, S. (2011). *Cities in a world Economy* (4th ed.). Newbury Park, CA: Pine Forge Press.

Sassoon, A. S. (1994). Hegemony. In W. Outhwaite, & T. Bottomore (Eds.), *The Blackwell dictionary of twentieth-century social thought* (pp. 255–256). Oxford: Blackwell.

Savage, N. (2011). Twitter as medium and message. *Communications of the ACM, 54*(3), 18–20. doi:10.1145/1897852.1897860

Sawchuk, D. (2009). The raging grannies: Defying stereotypes and embracing aging through activism. *Journal of Women & Aging, 21*(3), 171–185. doi:10.1080/08952840903054898

Scanlon, L., Rowling, L., & Weber, Z. (2007). 'You don't have like an identity...you are just lost in a crowd': Forming a student identity in the first-year transition to university. *Journal of Youth Studies, 10*(2), 223–241.

Schaefer, R. T. (2008). *Racial and ethnic groups* (11th ed.). Upper Saddle River, New Jersey: Prentice-Hall, Inc.

Schippert, C. (2007). Can muscles be queer? Reconsidering the transgressive hyper-built body. *Journal of Gender Studies, 16*(2), 155–171.

Schissel, B., & Wotherspoon, T. (2003). *The legacy of school for Aboriginal people.* Don Mills: Oxford University Press.

Schlosberg, D., & Carruthers, D. (2010). Indigenous struggles, environmental justice, and community capabilities. *Global Environmental Politics, 10*(4), 12–35.

Schnaiberg, A. (1980). *The environment: From surplus to scarcity.* New York: Oxford University Press.

Schnaiberg, A., & Gould, K. A. (1994). *Environment and society: The enduring conflict.* New York: St. Martin's Press.

Schneider, B., & Jenness, V. (2005). Social control, civil liberties, and women's sexuality. In T. Steele (Ed.), *Sex, self, and society: The social context of sexuality* (pp. 388–401). Belmont: Thomson.

Schneider, T. (2008). How we know global warming is real. (cover story). *Skeptic, 14*(1), 31–37. Retrieved from http://library.mtroyal.ca:2048/login?url=http://search.ebscohost.com/login.aspx?direct=true&AuthType=ip,url,cookie,uid&db=a9h&AN=31987878&site=ehost-live

Schoenthaler, S. (2000). *Intelligence, academic performance and brain function.* California: California State University Press.

Schweingruber, D., & Wohlstein, R. T. (2005). The madding crowd goes to school: Myths about crowds in introductory sociology textbooks. *Teaching Sociology, 33,* 136–153.

Scott-Joynt, J. (2005). *What MySpace means to Murdoch.* Retrieved 10/05/2008, from http://news.bbc.co.uk/2/hi/business/4697671.stm

Scott, A. J. (2007). Capitalism and urbanization in a new key? The cognitive-cultural dimension. *Social Forces, 85*(4), 1465–1482.

Scott, B., Schwartz, M., & VanderPlaat, M. (2000). *Sociology: Making sense of the social world* (Canadian Edition ed.). Toronto: Pearson.

Scott, D. (2010). What would Veblen say? *Leisure Sciences, 32*(3), 288–294. doi:10.1080/01490401003712713

Scott, H. (2003). Stranger danger: Explaining women's fear of crime. *Western Criminology Review, 4*(3), 203–214.

Scott, J. T., ed. (2012). *The Major Political Writings of Jean-Jacques Rousseau: The Two "Discourses" and the "Social Contract."* Translated by John T. Scott. Chicago: University of Chicago Press.

Segal, A. F. (2002). The Jewish tradition. In W. G. Oxtoby (Ed.), (2nd ed., pp. 33–157). Don Mills, ON: Oxford University Press.

Seidman, S. (1998). Empire and knowledge: More troubles, new opportunities for sociology. In D. Clawson (Ed.), *Required reading: Sociology's most influential books* (pp. 167–172). Amherst: University of Massachusetts Press.

Seidman, S. (2008). *Contested knowledge: Social theory today* (4th ed.). Oxford: Blackwell.

Seidman, S. (2010). *The social construction of sexuality* (2nd ed.). New York: W. W. Norton.

Selfe, P., & Starbuck, M. (1998). *Religion.* London, UK: Hodder & Stoughton.

Sen, A. (2003). Missing women - revisited. *British Medical Journal, 327,* 1297–1298.

Service Canada. (2008). *Occupations.* Retrieved 27/03/2008, from http://www.jobsetc.ca/category_drilldown.jsp?lang=en&category_id=125

Service, E. (1962). *Primitive social organization: An evolutionary perspective.* New York: Random House.

Sethna, C. (2010). Animal sex: Purity education and the naturalization of the abstinence agenda. *Sex Education, 10*(3), 267–279.

Sev'er, A. (2009). More than wife abuse that has gone old: A conceptual model for violence against the aged in Canada and the US. *Journal of Comparative Family Studies, 40*(2), 279–292. Retrieved from http://search.ebscohost.com/login.aspx?direct=true&AuthType=ip,url,cookie,uid&db=a9h&AN=38604077&site=ehost-live

Sex Information and Education Council of Canada (SIECCAN). (2009). Sexual health education in the schools. *The Canadian Journal of Human Sexuality, 18*(1-2), 47–60.

Shaffer, L. S. (2005). Beyond the looking glass self: Cooley's social self and its treatment in introductory textbooks. *Journal of Clinical Psychology, 61*(1), 47–65.

Shah, A. (2007). *Media conglomerates, mergers, concentration of ownership - global issues.* Retrieved 30/08/2008, from http://www.globalissues.org/HumanRights/Media/Corporations/Owners.asp#MediaConglomeratesMegaMergersConcentrationofOwnership

Shah, A. (2009a). *Poverty facts and stats.* Retrieved 18/01/2010, from http://www.globalissues.org/article/26/poverty-facts-and-stats

Shah, A. (2009b). *World military spending - global issues.* Retrieved 03/22/2010, from http://www.globalissues.org/Geopolitics/ArmsTrade/Spending.asp

Shalizi, Z., & Lecocq, F. (2010). To mitigate or to adapt: Is that the question? Observations on an appropriate response to the climate change challenge to development strategies. *World Bank Research Observer (2010), 25*(2), 295–321.

Shalla, V. (2004). Time warped: The flexibilization and maximization of flight attendant working time. *The Canadian Review of Sociology and Anthropology, 41*(3), 345. Retrieved from http://proquest.umi.com/pqdweb?did=724484591&Fmt=7&clientId=65345&RQT=309&VName=PQD

Shanahan, T., & Jones, G. (2007). Shifting roles and approaches: Government coordination of postsecondary education in Canada from 1995–2006. *Higher Education Research and Development, 26*(1), 31–43.

Shankar, I. (2010). In Bruce Ravelli (Ed.), *Personal communication.*

Shanklin, E. (1994). *Anthropology and race.* Belmont, CA: Wadsworth.

Shanklin, E. (2000). Representations of race and racism in American anthropology. *Current Anthropology, 41*(1), 99–103.

Shaou-Whea Dodge, P., & Suter, E. (2008). "It's okay to have a girl": Patronymy and china's one child policy. *Women and Language, 31*(1), 13–22.

Sharkey, P. (2007). Survival and death in New Orleans: An empirical look at the human impact of Katrina. *Journal of Black Studies, 37*(4), 482–501.

Sharma, N. (2005). Anti-trafficking rhetoric and the making of a global apartheid. *NWSA Journal, 17*(3), 88–111.

Shaw, D. J. (2002). *Canada's productivity and standard of living: Past, present and future* No. PRB 02-23E). Ottawa: Parliamentary Research Branch.

Shaw, D. J. (2009). *Productivity: Its increasing influence over Canadians' standard of living and quality of life (PRB-0315E).* Retrieved 28/06/2010, from http://www2.parl.gc.ca/Content/LOP/ResearchPublications/prb0315-e.htm

Sheff, E. (2005). Polyamorous women, subjectivity, and power. *Journal of Contemporary Ethnography, 34*(3), 253–283.

Shelton, P. (2013). The Hidden Costs of US and EU Farm Subsidies. Accessed 08/05/2014, from http://www.ifpri.org/blog/hidden-costs-us-and-eu-farm-subsidies

Sheppard, R. (2006). *CBC news indepth: The 39th parliament - Harper at the helm.* Retrieved 28/01/2008, from http://www.cbc.ca/news/background/parliament39/quebecnation-history.html

Shields, J. A. (2007). Between passion and deliberation: The Christian right and democratic ideals. *Political Science Quarterly, 122*(1), 89–113. Retrieved from http://library.mtroyal.ca:2048/login?url=http://search.

ebscohost.com/login.aspx?direct=true&AuthType=ip,url,cookie,uid&db=a9h&AN=24632322&site=ehost-live

Shiva, V. (2000). *Tomorrow's biodiversity.* London, UK: Thames & Hudson.

Shiva, V. (2007). Comparative perspectives symposium: Bioprospecting/Biopiracy: Bioprospecting as sophisticated biopiracy. *Signs: Journal of Women in Culture & Society, 32*(2), 307–313. Retrieved from http://library.mtroyal.ca:2048/login?url=http://search.ebscohost.com/login.aspx?direct=true&AuthType=ip,url,cookie,uid&db=a9h&AN=23730417&site=ehost-live

Siegal, L., & McCormick, C. (2006). *Criminology in Canada: Theories, patterns, and typologies* (3rd ed.). Toronto: Thomson Nelson.

Siegel, L., & McCormick, C. (2010). *Criminology in Canada: Theories, patterns and typologies* (4th ed.). Toronto: Nelson.

Sigl, M. (2013). The Dark Enlightenment: The Creepy Internet Movement You Better Take Seriously. Accessed 03/03/2014, from http://www.vocativ.com/culture/uncategorized/dark-enlightenment-creepy-internet-movement-youd-better-take-seriously/

Sikhism.com. (2007). *Sikhism introduction.* Retrieved 10/03/2008, from http://www.sikhism.com/

Simmel, G. (1978). *The philosophy of money.* London, UK: Routledge and Kegan Paul.

Simmerling, M., & Schwegler, B. (2005). Beginning anew: Same principles, different direction for research ethics. *The American Journal of Bioethics, 5*(1), 44–46.

Simon, W., & Gagnon, J. (1986). Sexual scripts: Permanence and change. *Archives of Sexual Behavior, 15*(2), 97–122.

Simpson, G. E., & Yinger, M. J. (1985). *Racial and cultural minorities* (5th ed.). New York: Plenum.

Simpson, I. H., Stark, D., & Jackson, R. A. (1988). Class identification processes of married, working men and women. *American Sociological Review, 53*(2), 284–293.

Sinclair, S. (2003). The WTO and its GATS. In J. Michie (Ed.), *The handbook of globalization* (pp. 347–357). Cheltenham, UK: Edward Elgar Publishing.

Sinha, M. (2012). *Family Violence in Canada: A Statistical Profile 2010.* Ottawa: Statistics Canada.

Sivakumar, B. (2011). Global climate change and its impacts on water resources planning and management: Assessment and challenges. *Stochastic Environmental Research & Risk Assessment, 25*(4), 583–600. doi:10.1007/s00477-010-0423-y

Skelton, C. (1997). Women and education. In D. Richardson, & V. Robinson (Eds.), *Introducing women's studies: Feminist theory and practice* (2nd ed.,). London: Palgrave MacMillan.

Skinner, D. (2000). McLuhan's world–and ours. *The Public Interest,* (138), 52. Retrieved from http://proquest.umi.com/pqdweb?did=47771691&Fmt=?????7&clientId=65345&RQT=309&VName=PQD

Slattery, M. (2003). *Key ideas in sociology.* Cheltenham, UK: Nelson Thornes, Ltd.

Slevin, K. F. (2010). "If I had lots of money…I'd have a body makeover:" managing the aging body. *Social Forces, 88*(3), 1003–1020. Retrieved from http://search.ebscohost.com/login.aspx?direct=true&AuthType=ip,url,cookie,uid&db=a9h&AN=49094166&site=ehost-live

Sloan, F., & Chepke, L. (2011). Litigation, settlement, and the public welfare: Lessons from the master settlement agreement. *Widener Law Review, 17*(1), 159–226. Retrieved from http://vnweb.hwwilsonweb.com/hww/jumpstart.jhtml?prod=OMNIS&query=201100108801005+%3Cin%3E+an

Smart, C. (1989). *Feminism and the power of the law.* London: Routledge.

Smedley, A. (2007). *Race in North America: Origin and evolution of a worldview* (3rd ed.). Boulder, CO: Westview Press.

Smith, C. (2008). Future directions in the sociology of religion. *Social Forces, 86*(4), 1561–839. Retrieved from http://vnweb.hwwilsonweb.com/hww/jumpstart.jhtml?prod=OMNIS&query=200815300654011+%3Cin%3E+an

Smith, C. (Ed.). (2003). *The secular religion: Power, interests and conflict in the secularization of American public life.* Berkeley, CA: University of California Press.

Smith, D. (1987). *Everyday world as problematic: A feminist sociology.* Boston, MA: Northeastern University Press.

Smith, D. (1990a). *The conceptual practices of power.* Toronto: University of Toronto Press.

Smith, D. (1990b). *Texts, facts, and femininity: Exploring the relations of ruling.* London: Routledge.

Smith, D. (1992). Whistling women: Reflections on rage and rationality. In W. Carroll, L. Christainsen-Ruffman, R. Currie & D. Harrison (Eds.), *Fragile truths: Twenty-five years of sociology and anthropology in Canada* (pp. 207–226). Ottawa: Carleton University Press.

Smith, D. (1999). *Writing the social: Critique, theory and investigations.* Toronto: University of Toronto Press.

Smith, D. (2000a). Comment on Hekmna's 'truth and method: Feminist standpoint theory revisited'. In C. Allen, & J. Howard (Eds.), *Provoking feminisms* (pp. 59–65). Chicago: The University of Chicago Press.

Smith, D. (2004). Despoiling professional autonomy: A woman's perspective. In M. Reimer (Ed.), *Inside corporate U: Women in the academy speak out* (pp. 31–42). Toronto: Sumach Press.

Smith, J. M. (2007). Time-binding communication: Transmission and decadence of tradition. *Ethics, Place & Environment, 10*(1), 107–119. doi:10.1080/13668790601149984

Smith, M. (1988). Women's fear of violent crime: An exploratory test of a feminist hypothesis. *Journal of Family Violence, 3*(1), 29–38.

Smith, M. (1993). *The Rodriguez case: A review of the supreme court of Canada decision on assisted suicide (BP349e).* Retrieved 26/06/2008, from http://dsp-psd.tpsgc.gc.ca/Collection-R/LoPBdP/BP/bp349-e.htm

Smith, M. (1998). Social movements and equality seeking: The case of gay liberation in Canada. *Canadian Journal of Political Science, 31*(2), 285–309.

Smith, P., & Alexander, J. C. (1996). Review essay: Durkheim's religious revival. *American Journal of Sociology, 102*(2), 585.

Smith, S., Kennard, C., & Granados, A. (2011). *Sexy socialization: Today's media and the next generation of women.* http://communicationleadership.usc.edu/publications/sexy_socialization_todays_media_and_the_next_generation_of_women.html

Smith, S., Pieper, K., Granados, A., & Choueiti, M. (2010). Assessing gender-related portrayals in top-gros sing G-rated films. *Sex Roles, 62,* 774–786.

Smithsonian National Museum of Natural History. (n.d.). *Smithsonian human origins program.* Retrieved 17/03/2010, from http://humanorigins.si.edu/

Smolej, M., & Kivivuori, J. (2006). The relation between crime news and fear of violence. 1(2), 211–227. doi:10.1080/14043850601002429

Snider, L. C. (2007). *The end of poverty by Jeffrey D. Sachs (book review).* Retrieved 15/06/2008, from http://www.cumminghome.com/business/economy/book-review-the-end-of-poverty-by-jeffrey-d-sachs.shtml

Snipp, C. M., & Hirschman, C. (2004). Assimilation in American society: Occupational achievement and earnings for ethnic minorities in the United States, 1970 to 1990. *Research in Social Stratification and Mobility, 22,* 93–117.

Snow, D. A., Soule, S. A., & Cress, D. M. (2005). Identifying the precipitants of homeless protest across 17 U.S. cities, 1980 to 1990. *Social Forces, 83*(3), 1183–1210. Retrieved from http://library.mtroyal.ca:2048/login?url=http://search.ebscohost.com/login.aspx?direct=true&AuthType=ip,url,cookie,uid&db=a9h&AN=16832479&site=ehost-live

Snyder, C. (2008). What is third-wave feminism? A new directions essay, *Signs, 34*(1), 175–196.

Sodikoff, G. (2004). Land and languor: Ethical imaginations of work and forest in northeast Madagascar. *History & Anthropology, 15*(4), 367–398. Retrieved from http://library.mtroyal.ca:2048/login?url=http://search.

ebscohost.com/login.aspx?direct=true&AuthType=ip,url,cookie,uid&db=a9h&AN=15219039&site=ehost-live

Sommerville, C. J. (1998). Secular Society/Religious population: Out tacit rules for using the term "secularization". *Journal for the Scientific Study of Religion, 37*(2), 249.

Soukeroff, W. A. (1959). *The origin of the freedomite movement.* Retrieved 03/10/2007, from http://www.doukhobor.org/Soukeroff.htm

Soules, M. (2007). *Harold Adams Innis: The bias of communications & monopolies of power.* Retrieved 01/06/2008, from http://www.media-studies.ca/articles/innis.htm

Southcott, C. (1999). The study of regional inequality in quebec and english Canada: A comparative analysis of perspectives. *Canadian Journal of Sociology, 24*(4), 457–484.

Sparks, A. (1990). *The mind of South Africa.* New York: Knopf.

Spector, M., & Kitsuse, J. (1977). *Constructing social problems.* Menlo Park, CA: Cummings.

Spisak, S. (2009). The evolution of a cosmopolitan identity: Transforming culture. *Current Issues in Comparative Education, 12*(1), 86–91.

Srivastava, L. (2005). Mobile phones and the evolution of social behaviour. *Behaviour & Information Technology, 24*(2), 111–129. doi:10.1080/0144 9290512331321910

St. Pierre, E. (2011). *International transgender day of remembrance.* Retrieved 23/07/2011, from http://www.transgenderdor.org/?page_id=4

Stack, C. B. (1975). *All our kin: Strategies for survival in a black community.* New York: Harper & Row.

Staggenborg, S. (2005). *Feminism in the university.* Unpublished manuscript.

Stampf, O. (2007). *Global warming: Not the end of the world as we know it.* Retrieved 23/07/2008, from http://www.spiegel.de/international/germany/0,1518,481684,00.html

Stark, R., & Bainbridge, W. S. (1985). *The future of religion: Secularization, revival and cult formation.* Berkeley, CA: University of California Press.

Stark, R., & Bainbridge, W. S. (1996). *Religion, deviance and social control.* New York: Routledge, Inc.

Stastna, K. (2006). *The golden age of the silver screen.* Retrieved 03/05/2008, from http://www.canada.com/montrealgazette/news/montreal/story.html?id=22268330-0af4-4443-bf95-fd0883f81775&k=47902

Statham, A. (2000). Environmental awareness and feminist progress. *NWSA Journal, 12*(2), 89. Retrieved from http://library.mtroyal.ca:2083/pqdweb?did=58675096&Fmt=7&clientId=65345&RQT=309&VName=PQD

Statistic Brain. (2014). *Facebook statistics.* Retrieved 05/05/2014, from http://www.statisticbrain.com/facebookstatistics/

Statistics Canada. (2003a). *Canadian community health survey: Mental health and well-being.* Retrieved 27/06/2008, from http://www.statcan.ca/Daily/English/030903/d030903a.htm

Statistics Canada. (2003b). *Earnings of Canadians: Making a living in a new economy.* http://www12.statscan.ca/English.census01/Products/Analytic/companion/ear/contents.Cfm

Statistics Canada. (2003c). Ethnic diversity study: Portrait of a multicultural society. *Catalogue no. 89-593-XIE*

Statistics Canada. (2005a). *Canadian community health survey: Obesity among children and adults.* Retrieved 28/06/2008, from http://www.statcan.ca/Daily/English/050706/d050706a.htm

Statistics Canada. (2005b). *Human activity and the environment: Solid waste.* Retrieved 24/07/2008, from http://www.statcan.ca/Daily/English/051202/d051202b.htm

Statistics Canada. (2005c). *Population projections for Canada, provinces and territories, 2005–2031.* Retrieved 28/05/2010, from http://www.statcan.gc.ca/pub/91-520-x/91-520-x2005001-eng.pdf

Statistics Canada. (2005d). *Report of the pan-Canadian education initiators program 2005 - highlights.* Ottawa, ON: Statistics Canada. Retrieved from http://www.statcan.ca/english/freepub/81-582-XIE/2006001/highlights.htm#D

Statistics Canada. (2005e). *Study: Diverging trends in unionization. the daily, friday, april 22, 2005.* Retrieved 28/03/2008, from http://www.statcan.ca/Daily/English/050422/d050422c.htm

Statistics Canada. (2005f). *Use of alternative health care.* Retrieved 30/06/2008, from http://www.statcan.ca/Daily/English/050315/d050315b.htm

Statistics Canada. (2006a). *Access to health care services.* Retrieved 30/08/2008, from http://www.statcan.ca/Daily/English/060711/d060711c.htm

Statistics Canada. (2006b). *Census of canada: National occupational classification for statistics 2006.* Ottawa, Ontario.

Statistics Canada. (2006c). *Census of canada: Topic-based tabulations* Ottawa, Ontario.

Statistics Canada. (2006d). *Divorces by province and territory.* http://www40.statcan.ca/l01/cst01/famil02.htm

Statistics Canada. (2006e). *Education matters: Insights on education, learning and training in Canada.* Retrieved 10/12/2007, from http://www.statcan.ca/english/freepub/81-004-XIE/2006003/backto.htm#p

Statistics Canada. (2006f). *Television viewing, by age and sex, by province.* Retrieved 09/11/2007, from http://www40.statcan.ca/l01/cst01/arts23.htm

Statistics Canada. (2006g). *The daily, friday, march 31, 2006. television viewing.* Retrieved 09/11/2007, from http://library.mtroyal.ca:2069/Daily/English/060331/d060331b.htm

Statistics Canada. (2006h). *The daily, friday, march 31, 2006. television viewing.* Retrieved 07/05/2008, from http://www.statcan.ca/Daily/English/060331/d060331b.htm

Statistics Canada. (2006i). *The daily, thursday, october 26, 2006. Canada's population by age and sex.* Retrieved 13/11/2007, from http://www.statcan.ca/Daily/English/061026/d061026b.htm

Statistics Canada. (2006j). *The daily, tuesday, august 15, 2006. Canadian internet use survey.* Retrieved 09/11/2007, from http://library.mtroyal.ca:2069/Daily/English/060815/d060815b.htm

Statistics Canada. (2006k). *The daily, tuesday, november 7, 2006. University enrolment.* Retrieved 28/05/2007, from http://library.mtroyal.ca:2069/Daily/English/061107/d061107a.htm

Statistics Canada. (2006l). *The daily, wednesday, december 13, 2006. Study: Inequality in wealth.* Retrieved 06/12/2007, from http://www.statcan.ca/Daily/English/061213/d061213c.htm

Statistics Canada. (2006m). *Women in Canada: A gender-based statistical report* (No. 89-503-XPE). Ottawa, ON: Minister of Industry. Retrieved from http://www.statcan.ca/english/freepub/89-503-XIE/0010589-503-XIE.pdf

Statistics Canada. (2007a). *A portrait of seniors in Canada.* Retrieved 13/11/2007, from http://library.mtroyal.ca:2069/english/freepub/89-519-XIE/2006001/demographic.htm

Statistics Canada. (2007b). *Family portrait: Continuity and change in Canadian families and households in 2006.* Retrieved 10/11/2007, from http://www12.statcan.ca/english/census06/analysis/famhouse/ind1.cfm

Statistics Canada. (2007c). *Family violence in Canada: A statistical profile 2007* (No. 85-224 XIE). Ottawa, ON: Minister of Industry.

Statistics Canada. (2007d). *Immigration in Canada: A portrait of the foreign-born population, 2006 census.* Retrieved 26/01/2008, from http://www12.statcan.ca/english/census06/analysis/immcit/highlights.cfm

Statistics Canada. (2007e). *Labour force survey.* Retrieved 29/03/2008, from http://www.statcan.ca/Daily/English/070706/d070706a.htm

Statistics Canada. (2007f). *Lower income and declines in self-rated health.* Retrieved 29/06/2008, from http://www.statcan.ca/Daily/English/070605/d070605a.htm

Statistics Canada. (2007g). *Participation and activity limitation survey.* Retrieved 27/06/2008, from http://www.statcan.ca/Daily/English/071203/d071203a.htm

Statistics Canada. (2007h). *Population by mother tongue and age groups, 2006 counts, for Canada, provinces and territories – 20% sample data.* Retrieved 25/04/2008, from http://www12.statcan.ca/english/census06/data/highlights/language/Table401.cfm?Lang=E&T=401&GH=4&SC=1&S=99&O=A

Statistics Canada. (2007i). *Registered retirement savings plan contributions.* Retrieved 24/06/2008, from http://www.statcan.ca/Daily/English/071108/d071108d.htm

Statistics Canada. (2007j). *Seniors as victims of crime.* Retrieved 26/06/2008, from http://www.statcan.ca/Daily/English/070306/d070306b.htm

Statistics Canada. (2007k). *The daily, monday, september 24, 2007. study: High-income Canadians.* Retrieved 07/12/2007, from http://www.statcan.ca/Daily/English/070924/d070924a.htm

Statistics Canada. (2007l). *The daily, thursday, may 3, 2007. Income of Canadians.* Retrieved 09/12/2007, from http://www.statcan.ca/Daily/English/070503/d070503a.htm

Statistics Canada. (2007m). *The daily, tuesday, february 27, 2007. A portrait of seniors.* Retrieved 16/06/2008, from http://www.statcan.ca/Daily/English/070227/d070227b.htm

Statistics Canada. (2007n). *The daily, tuesday, june 26, 2007. Radio listening.* Retrieved 06/05/2008, from http://www.statcan.ca/Daily/English/070626/d070626b.htm

Statistics Canada. (2007o). *The evolving linguistic portrait, 2006 census: The proportion of francophones and of French continue to decline.* Retrieved 22/06/2010, from http://library.mtroyal.ca:2512/english/census06/analysis/language/continue_decline.cfm

Statistics Canada. (2008a). *2006 census: Labour market activities, industry, occupation, education, language of work, place of work and mode of transportation.* Retrieved 01/07/2008, from http://library.mtroyal.ca:2069/Daily/English/080304/d080304a.htm

Statistics Canada. (2008b). *Canada at a glance 2008 - households.* Retrieved 07/05/2008, from http://www45.statcan.gc.ca/2008/cgco_2008_006-eng.htm

Statistics Canada. (2008c). *Canadian community health survey.* Retrieved 28/06/2008, from http://www.statcan.ca/Daily/English/080618/d080618a.htm

Statistics Canada. (2008d). *Canadian internet use survey.* Retrieved 19/06/2008, from http://www.statcan.ca/Daily/English/080612/d080612b.htm

Statistics Canada. (2008e). *Composting organic waste.* Retrieved 24/07/2008, from http://www.statcan.ca/Daily/English/080327/d080327c.htm

Statistics Canada. (2008f). *Earnings and incomes of Canadians over the past quarter century, 2006 census: Incomes of families.* Retrieved 24/06/2008, from http://www12.statcan.ca/english/census06/analysis/income/eicopqc30.cfm

Statistics Canada. (2008g). *Educational portrait of Canada, 2006 census: National picture.* Retrieved 25/06/2008, from http://www12.statcan.ca/english/census06/analysis/education/historical.cfm

Statistics Canada. (2008h). *Employment by industry.* Retrieved 27/03/2008, from http://www40.statcan.ca/l01/cst01/econ40.htm

Statistics Canada. (2008i). *Hourly wages, by occupation and sex.* Retrieved 09/06/2010, from http://www.statcan.gc.ca/pub/71-222-x/2008001/sectionj/j-hourly-horaire-eng.htm

Statistics Canada. (2008j). *Labour force and participation rates by sex and age group, 2003–2007* Statistics Canada.

Statistics Canada. (2008k). *Latest release from the labour force survey.* Retrieved 29/03/2008, from http://www.statcan.ca/english/Subjects/Labour/LFS/lfs-en.htm

Statistics Canada. (2008l). *Low income cut-offs for 2007 and low income measures for 2006.* Ottawa: Minister of Industry.

Statistics Canada. (2008m). *Participation and activity limitation survey 2006: A profile of assistive technology for people with disabilities.* Retrieved 27/06/2008, from http://www.statcan.ca/english/freepub/89-628-XIE/89-628-XIE2008005.htm

Statistics Canada. (2008n). *Preliminary results of the pension satellite account, 1990 to 2007.* Retrieved 25/06/2008, from http://www.statcan.ca/english/freepub/13-605-XIE/13-605-XIE2008002.htm

Statistics Canada. (2008o). *Selected dwelling characteristics and household equipment.* Retrieved 09/11/2007, from http://library.mtroyal.ca:2567/l01/cst01/famil09c.htm

Statistics Canada. (2008p). *Study: Impact of neighbourhood income on child obesity.* Retrieved 11/07/2010, from http://www.statcan.gc.ca/daily-quotidien/080218/dq080218a-eng.htm

Statistics Canada. (2008q). *The daily, friday, january 25, 2008. study: Immigrants in the hinterlands.* Retrieved 25/01/2008, from http://www.statcan.ca/Daily/English/080125/d080125d.htm

Statistics Canada. (2008r). *The daily, tuesday, january 15, 2008. Aboriginal peoples in Canada in 2006: Inuit, Métis and First Nations, 2006 census.* Retrieved 23/01/2008, from http://www.statcan.ca/Daily/English/080115/d080115a.htm

Statistics Canada. (2009a). *Canada's population estimates: Age and sex: Table 1 population estimates, age distribution and median age as of July 1, 2009.* Retrieved 28/05/2010, from http://www.statcan.gc.ca/daily-quotidien/091127/t091127b1-eng.htm

Statistics Canada. (2009b). *Income in Canada* (No. Cat 75-202-X). Ottawa: Statistics Canada.

Statistics Canada. (2009c). *Population of French mother tongue, Canada, provinces, territories and Canada less Quebec, 1996 to 2006.* Retrieved 22/06/2010, from http://library.mtroyal.ca:2512/census-recensement/2006/as-sa/97-555/table/A5-eng.cfm

Statistics Canada. (2009d). *The daily, wednesday, april 22, 2009. National graduates survey.* Retrieved 11/06/2010, from http://www.statcan.gc.ca/daily-quotidien/090422/dq090422a-eng.htm

Statistics Canada. (2009e). *Transitions to the labour market* (No. 81-599-X — Issue no. 002). Toronto, ON: Canadian Education Statistics Council.

Statistics Canada. (2009f). *University enrollments by program level and instructional program.* Retrieved 1/18/2010, from http://www40.statcan.gc.ca/l01/cst01/educ54a-eng.htm

Statistics Canada. (2010a). *After-tax income unchanged in 2008 after four years of growth.* Retrieved 16/05/2011, from http://www.statcan.gc.ca/pub/75-202-x/2008000/analysis-analyses-eng.htm

Statistics Canada. (2010b). *Canadian internet use survey.* Retrieved 4/27/2011, from http://www.statcan.gc.ca/daily-quotidien/100510/dq100510a-eng.htm

Statistics Canada. (2010c). *Criminal victimization in Canada, 2009* (No. 85-002-x). Ottawa: Statistics Canada.

Statistics Canada. (2010d). *Income in Canada.* Retrieved 07/02/2014, from http://www.statcan.gc.ca/pub/75-202-x/2010000/hl-fs-eng.htm

Statistics Canada. (2010d). *Life expectancy at birth, by sex, by province.* Retrieved 11/07/2010, from http://www40.statcan.gc.ca/l01/cst01/health26-eng.htm

Statistics Canada. (2010e). *Low income cut-offs.* Retrieved 18/09/2010, from http://www.statcan.gc.ca/pub/75f0002m/2010005/lico-sfr-eng.htm

Statistics Canada. (2010f). *Marriages by province and territory.* Retrieved 23/05/2010, from http://www40.statcan.gc.ca/l01/cst01/famil04-eng.htm

Statistics Canada. (2010g). *Persons in low income before tax.* Retrieved 13/01/2010, from http://www40.statcan.gc.ca/l01/cst01/famil41a-eng.htm

Statistics Canada. (2010h). *Police-reported crime statistics in Canada, 2009* (No. 85-002-x). Ottawa: Statistics Canada.

Statistics Canada. (2010i). *Recycling by Canadian households, 2007.* Retrieved 06/05/2011, from http://www.statcan.gc.ca/pub/16-001-m/2010013/part-partie1-eng.htm

Statistics Canada. (2010i). Projected Life Expectancy at Birth by Sex, by Aboriginal Identity, 2017. Accessed 04/08/2014, from http://www.statcan.gc.ca/pub/89-645-x/2010001/c-g/c-g013-eng.htm

Statistics Canada. (2010j). *Religious attendance rates, by sex, 1985 to 2008.* Retrieved 27/07/2010, from http://www.statcan.gc.ca/pub/11-008-x/2010001/c-g/11132/c-g001-eng.htm

Statistics Canada. (2010k). *Unemployment rates of population aged 15 and over, by educational attainment, Canada, 1990 to 2009.* Retrieved 28/06/2010, from http://www.statcan.gc.ca/pub/81-582-x/2010003/tbl/tble3.1-eng.htm

Statistics Canada. (2010l). *Waste disposal by source, province and territory.* Retrieved 07/05/2011, from http://www40.statcan.ca/l01/cst01/envir25a-eng.htm

Statistics Canada. (2010m). *Waste management industry: Business and government sectors.* Retrieved 06/05/2011, from http://www.statcan.gc.ca/daily-quotidien/101222/dq101222b-eng.htm

Statistics Canada. (2011). *Family violence in Canada: A statistical profile* (No. 85-224-X).

Statistics Canada. (2011a). Aboriginal Peoples in Canada: First Nations People, Métis and Inuit. Accessed 03/06/2014, from http://www12.statcan.gc.ca/nhs-enm/2011/as-sa/99-011-x/99-011-x2011001-eng.cfm

Statistics Canada. (2011b). Focus on Geography Series, 2011 Census. Accessed 05/04/2014, from http://www12.statcan.gc.ca/census-recensement/2011/as-sa/fogs-spg/Facts-pr-eng.cfm?Lang=Eng&GC=59

Statistics Canada. (2011c). Income of Canadians, 2011. Accessed 12/02/2014, from http://www.statcan.gc.ca/daily-quotidien/130627/dq130627c-eng.htm

Statistics Canada. (2011d). Portrait of Canada's Labour Force. Accessed 05/05/2014, from http://www12.statcan.gc.ca/nhs-enm/2011/as-sa/99-012-x/99-012-x2011002-eng.cfm

Statistics Canada. (2011e). *Women in Canada: A Gender-Based Statistical Report.* Retrieved 07/02/2014, from http://www.statcan.gc.ca/pub/89-503-x/89-503-x2010001-eng.htm

Statistics Canada. (2012a). Canadian Internet use Survey, Internet use, by Age Group, Internet Activity, Sex, Level of Education and Household Income. Accessed 05/05/2014, from http://www5.statcan.gc.ca/cansim/pick-choisir?lang=eng&id=03580153&p2=33

Statistics Canada. (2012a). Fifty Years of Families in Canada: 1961–2011. Retrieved 14/10/2013, from http://www12.statcan.gc.ca/census-recensement/2011/as-sa/98-312-x/2011003/fig/fig3_1-1-eng.cfm

Statistics Canada. (2012b). Immigration and Ethnocultural Diversity in Canada. Accessed 05/05/2014, from https://www12.statcan.gc.ca/nhs-enm/2011/as-sa/99-010-x/99-010-x2011001-eng.cfm

Statistics Canada. (2012c). Life Expectancy at Birth and at Age 65, by Sex and by Province and Territory. Accessed 01/04/2014, from http://www.statcan.gc.ca/tables-tableaux/sum-som/l01/cst01/health72a-eng.htm

Statistics Canada. (2013). Canadian Survey on Disability, 2012. Accessed 04/09/2014, from http://www.statcan.gc.ca/daily-quotidien/131203/dq131203a-eng.htm

Statistics Canada. (2013a). Canadian Internet use Survey. Accessed 30/01/2014, from http://www.statcan.gc.ca/daily-quotidien/100510/dq100510a-eng.htm

Statistics Canada. (2013b). Labour Force Characteristics by Sex and Age Group. Retrieved 14/10/2013, from http://www.statcan.gc.ca/tables-tableaux/sum-som/l01/cst01/labor05-eng.htm

Statistics Canada. (2013c). Measuring Violence Against Women: Statistical Trends: Highlights. Accessed 10/05/2014, from http://www.statcan.gc.ca/pub/85-002-x/2013001/article/11766/hl-fs-eng.htm

Statistics Canada. (2013e). Unemployment Rates of Population Aged 15 and Over, by Educational Attainment, Canada, 1990 to 2012. Accessed 05/05/2014, from http://www.statcan.gc.ca/pub/81-582-x/2013001/tbl/tble3.1-eng.htm

Statistics Canada. (2014). French and the *Francophonie* in Canada. Accessed 05/05/2014, from http://www12.statcan.gc.ca/census-recensement/2011/as-sa/98-314-x/98-314-x2011003_1-eng.cfm

Statistics Canada. (n.d.). *Religions in Canada.* Retrieved 31/07/2011, from http://www12.statcan.ca/english/census01/Products/Analytic/companion/rel/canada.cfm

Statistics Norway. (2013). Foreign Aid Expenditure in OECD Countries, 2012. Accessed 04/30/2014, from http://www.ssb.no/en/offentlig-sektor/statistikker/uhjelpoecd

Stearns, P. N. (1998). *The industrial revolution in world history* (2nd ed.). Boulder, CO: Westview Press.

Steele, T. L. (2005a). 'Doing it': The social construction of S-E-X. In T. L. Steele (Ed.), *Sex, self and society: The social context of sexuality*. California: Wadsworth.

Steele, T. (Ed.). (2005b). *Sex, self, and society*. Belmont: Thompson.

Steffen, W., Crutzen, P. J., & McNeill, J. R. (2007). The anthropocene: Are humans now overwhelming the great forces of nature? *AMBIO - A Journal of the Human Environment, 36*(8), 614–621. Retrieved from http://library.mtroyal.ca:2048/login?url=http://search.ebscohost.com/login.aspx?direct=true&AuthType=ip,url,cookie,uid&db=a9h&AN=28601278&site=ehost-live

Steger, M. B. (2002). *Globalism: The new market ideology*. Lanham, MD: Rowman and Littlefield Publishers, Inc.

Stephens, P. (1998). *Think sociologically*. Cheltenham, UK: Nelson Thornes Ltd.

Stephens, W. (1963). *The family in cross-cultural perspective*. New York: Holt Rinehart & Winston.

Stevenson, B., & Wolfers, J. (2008). *Economic growth and subjective well-being: Reassessing the easterlin paradox*. Retrieved April 23, 2008, from http://bpp.wharton.upenn.edu/jwolfers/Papers/EasterlinParadox.pdf

Stieger, S., & Burger, C. (2010). Implicit and explicit self-esteem in the context of internet addiction. *CyberPsychology, Behavior & Social Networking, 13*(6), 681–688. doi:10.1089/cyber.2009.0426

Stier, H., & Mandel, H. (2009). Inequality in the family: The institutional aspects of women's earning contribution. *Social Science Research, 38*, 594–608.

Stiglitz, J. (2003). *Globalization and its discontent*. New York: W.W. Norton.

Stoddart, M. C. (2008). *Anthropocentrism and environmental sociology: Re-evaluating the HEP-NEP dichotomy*. Retrieved 07/18/2008, from http://www.allacademic.com/meta/p93848_index.html

Stoddart, M. C. J., & Tindall, D. B. (2011). Ecofeminism, hegemonic masculinity, and environmental movement participation in British Columbia, Canada, 1998–2007: 'Women always clean up the mess'. *Sociological Spectrum, 31*(3), 342–368. doi:10.1080/02732173.2011.557065

Stoett, P. (2006). *Canada, Kyoto, and the conservatives: Thinking/Moving ahead*. Retrieved 06/09/2008, from http://www.wilsoncenter.org/events/docs/paperstoett1.pdf

Stott, C., & Pearson, G. (2006). Football banning orders, proportionality, and public order policing. *Howard Journal of Criminal Justice, 45*(3), 241–254. doi:10.1111/j.1468-2311.2006.00419.x

Stotzer, R. (2009). Violence against transgender people: A review of United States data. *Aggression and Violent Behavior, 14*, 170–179.

Streeten, P. P. (1995). *Thinking about development*. Cambridge, UK: Cambridge University Press.

Strinati, D. (1993). The big nothing? Contemporary culture and the emergence of postmodernism. *Innovation in Social Sciences Research, 6*(3), 359–374. Retrieved from http://library.mtroyal.ca:2048/login?url=http://search.ebscohost.com/login.aspx?direct=true&AuthType=ip,url,cookie,uid&db=a9h&AN=9707202883&site=ehost-live

Strinati, D. (2004). *An introduction to the theories of popular culture* (2nd ed.). London, UK: Routledge.

Struthers, J. (2007). *Great depression*. Retrieved 12/19/2007, from http://www.thecanadianencyclopedia.com/index.cfm?PgNm=TCE&Params=A1ARTA0003425

Stubblefield, A. (2007). *"Beyond the pale": Tainted whiteness, cognitive disability, and eugenic sterilization*. Indiana University Press. Retrieved from http://library.mtroyal.ca:2048/login?url=http://search.ebscohost.com/login.aspx?direct=true&AuthType=ip,url,cookie,uid&db=a9h&AN=24127104&site=ehost-live

Sukidi. (2006). Max Weber's remarks on Islam: The Protestant ethic among Muslim puritans. *Islam & Christian-Muslim Relations, 17* (April)(2), 195–205.

Sulkowski, L. (2012). Neoevolutionism - the new paradigm of the social sciences? *Journal of Intercultural Management, 4*(2), 5.

Sullivan, P. (2008). *CMA pegs air pollution's annual national toll at 21,000 deaths - and growing*. Retrieved 24/08/2008, from http://www.cma.ca/index.cfm/ci_id/10042903/la_id/1.htm

Sulloway, F. J. (2009)Why Darwin rejected intelligent design. *Journal of Biosciences, 34*(2), 173–183.

Sullum, J. (2007). Thank Deng Xiaoping for little girls. *Reason, 39*(7), 40–48.

Sumner, W. G. (1906/1960). *Folkways*. New York: New American Library.

Suter, E., Daas, K., & Bergen, K. M. (2008). Negotiating lesbian family identity via symbols and rituals. *Journal of Family Issues, 22*(1), 26–47.

Sutherland, E. (1939). *Principles of criminology* (1st ed.). Philadelphia: J.B. Lippincott.

Sutherland, E., & Cressey, D. (1960). *Principles of criminology* (6th ed.). Philadelphia: J.B. Lippincott.

Sutton, P. W. (2007). *The environment: A sociological introduction*. Cambridge, UK: Polity Press.

Swatos, W. H., Jr. (1998). *Encyclopedia of religion and society*. Walnut Creek, CA: AltaMira Presee.

Swauger, M. (2011). Afterword: The ethics of risk, power and representation. *Qualitative Sociology, 34*, 497–502.

Swenson, D. (1999). *Society, spirituality, and the sacred*. Peterborough, ON: Broadview Press.

Swenson, D. (2008). *Society, spirituality, and the sacred* (2nd ed.). Peterborough, ON: Broadview Press.

Swift, K., & Birmingham, M. (2000). Location, location, location: Restructuring and the everyday lives of "welfare moms." In S. Neysmith (Ed.), *Restructuring caring labour: Discourse, state practice and everyday life* (pp. 93–115). Toronto: Oxford University Press.

Swift, R. (1991). Among the believers. *Utne Reader, 45 (May/June)*, 99–104.

Symes v. Canada. (1993). *4. S.C.R. 695*. http://www.hrcr.org/safrica/equality/symes_canada.html

Symonds, P. (1995). *Frederick Engels 1820–1895: 100 years since the death of the co-founder of scientific socialism*. Retrieved 08/09/2007, from http://www.wsws.org/history/1995/aug1995/engels.shtml

Tait, S. (2007). Television and the domestication of cosmetic surgery. *Feminist Media Studies, 7*(2), 119–135.

Tanenbaum, L. (2005). Slut! Growing up female with a bad reputation. In T. L. Steele (Ed.), *Sex, self and society: The social context of sexuality*. California: Wadsworth.

Tartaro, C., & Lester, D. (2005). An application of Durkheim's theory of suicide to prison suicide rates in the United States. *Death Studies, 29*(5), 413–422.

Tattersall, I. (2008). An evolutionary framework for the acquisition of symbolic cognition by homo sapiens. *Comparative Cognition & Behavior Reviews, 3*, 99–114. doi:10.3819/ccbr.2008.30006

Tatum, H., Schwartz, B., Schimmoeller, P., & Perry, N. (2013). Classroom participation and student-faculty interactions: Does gender matter? *The Journal of Higher Education, V84*(N6), 745–768.

Tauli-Corpuz, V. (2007). Is biopiracy an issue for feminists in the Philippines? *Signs: Journal of Women in Culture & Society, 32*(2), 332–337. Retrieved from http://library.mtroyal.ca:2048/login?url=http://search.ebscohost.com/login.aspx?direct=true&AuthType=ip,url,cookie,uid&db=a9h&AN=23730420&site=ehost-live

Taylor, D., & Offner, C. (1975). In Anderson N. (Ed.), *The world's religions*. Grand Rapids: InterVarsity.

Taylor, V. A., Rupp, L. J., & Whittier, N. (2006). *Feminist frontiers* (7th ed.). Boston, MA: McGraw-Hill.

Television Bureau of Canada. (2013). *Tvbasics 2013–2014*.

Terrier, J. (2006). The idea of a republican tradition: Reflections on the debate concerning the intellectual foundations of the French third Republic. *Journal of Political Ideologies, 11*(3), 289–308. doi:10.1080/13569310600923865

The Alberta Pioneer Railway Association. (2007). *History of the telegraph*. Retrieved 03/05/2008, from http://www.railwaymuseum.ab.ca/?q=node/44

The Centre for Spatial Economics. (2008). *The economic cost of wait times in Canada*. Ottawa, ON: Canadian Medical Association.

The Economist. (2009). Idea: *Triple bottom line*. Retrieved 02/05/2011, from http://www.economist.com/node/14301663?story_id=14301663

The White House. (2001). *Text of a letter from the president*. Retrieved 06/09/2008, from http://www.whitehouse.gov/news/releases/2001/03/20010314.html

The World Bank. *India - water*. Retrieved 05/10/2007, from http://www.worldbank.org.in/WBSITE/EXTERNAL/COUNTRIES/SOUTHASIAEXT/INDIAEXTN/0,,contentMDK:20668501~pagePK:141137~piPK:141127~theSitePK:295584,00.html

Thibos, M., Lavin-Loucks, D., & Martin, M. (2007). *The feminization of poverty*. Dallas, TX: The J. Mcdonald Williams Institute. Retrieved from http://www.thewilliamsinstitute.org/Portals/10/Poverty_Disparity/Feminization%20of%20Poverty.pdf

Thiem, A. (2007). Foucault and the unfaithful body – an anti-catechism. *Religion & Theology, 14*(3), 330–346. doi:10.1163/157430107X241348

Thomas, J. E., & Kukulan, A. (2004). Why don't I know about these women?: The integration of early women sociologists with classical theory courses. *Teaching Sociology, 32*(3), 252–263.

Thomas, W. I., & Thomas, D. S. (1928). *The child in America*. New York: Knopf.

Thompson Jr., E. H. (2006). Images of old men's masculinity: Still a man? *Sex Roles, 55*(9), 633–648.

Thompson, J., Baird, P., & Downie, J. (2005). The Olivieri case: Context and significance. *Ecclectica, December,* http://www.ecclectica.ca/issues/2005/3/index.asp?Article=2.

Thompson, L., & Cupples, J. (2008). Seen and not heard? Text messaging and digital sociality. *Social & Cultural Geography, 9*(1), 95–108. doi:10.1080/14649360701789634

Thomson, A. (2010). *The Making of Social Theory* (2nd ed.). Toronto: Oxford University Press.

Thomson, I. (2005). The theory that won't die: From mass society to the decline of social capital. *Sociological Forum, 20*(3), 421–448. doi:10.1007/s11206-005-6596-3

Thorne, B. (1982). *Feminist rethinking of the family: An overview*. New York: Longman.

Thornham, S. (2000). Second wave feminism. In S. Gamble (Ed.), *The routledge critical dictionary of feminism and postfeminism* (pp. 29–42). New York: Routledge.

Tibbetts, J. (2008). *Students look overseas for cheaper tutors*. Retrieved 17/06/2008, from http://www.canada.com/calgaryherald/news/story.html?id=a1df434e-9af5-493a-9de4-34b6d33d0e6b

Tiefer, L. (2006). The Viagra phenomenon. *Sexualities, 9*(3), 315–332.

Tieffer, L. (2005). In pursuit of the perfect penis. In T. L. Steele (Ed.), *Sex, self and society: The social context of sexuality*. California: Wadsworth.

Tigawalana, D. (2010). *Why African women are more vulnerable to HIV/AIDS*. Retrieved 22/11/2010, from http://www.rnanews.com/health/4206-why-african-women-are-more-vulnerable-to-hivaids

Tomasik, M. J. & Silbereisen, R. K. (2009). Demands of social change as a function of the political context, institutional filters, and psychosocial resources. *Social Indicators Research, 94*(1), 13–28. http://www.jstor.org/stable/27734946

Tominaga, K. (1993). Early sociology and the modernization of Japan. *Sociology in Europe: In search of identity* (Nedelman, Birgitta; Sztompka, Piotr ed., pp. 191–212). Berlin: Walter de Gruyter.

Tomlinson, J. (2006). Women's work-life balance trajectories in the UK: Reformulating choice and constraint in transitions through part-time work across the life-course. *British Journal of Guidance & Counselling, 34*(3), 365–382.

Tonkiss, F. (2006). *Contemporary economic sociology: Globalization, production, inequality*. London and New York: Routledge.

Torjman, S. (1997 (November)). *Welfare warfare*. Retrieved 12/12/2007, from www.caledoninst.org/Publications/PDF/welfare.pdf

Toronto District School Board. (2008). *Minutes January 29, 2008*. Unpublished manuscript.

Townsend, S. S. M., Markus, H. R., & Bergsieker, H. B. (2009). My choice, your categories: The denial of multiracial identities. *Journal of Social Issues, 65*(1), 185–204.

Tran, J. (2007). Sold into slavery. *Christian Century, 124*(24), 22–26.

Traxler, J. (2009). Mobile subcultures. In S. Wheeler (Ed.), *Connected minds, emerging cultures: Cybercultures in online learning* (pp. 17–28). Charlotte, NC: IAP- Information Age Publishing, Inc.

Tredoux, C., & Finchilescu, G. (2007). The contact hypothesis and intergroup relations 50 years on: Introduction to the special issue. *South African Journal of Psychology, 37*(4), 667–678.

Treiman, D. J. (1970). Industrialization and social stratification. *Sociological Inquiry, 40*(2), 207–234. Retrieved from http://search.ebscohost.com/login.aspx?direct=true&AuthType=ip,url,cookie,uid&db=a9h&AN=13744598&site=ehost-live

Tremblay, T. (1999). Internet censorship as 'Cybriety': Freud, McLuhan, and media pleasures. *Mosaic: A Journal for the Interdisciplinary Study of Literature, 32*(1), 167–182.

Trevino, J. A., & Smelser, N. J. (Eds.). (2001). *Talcott Parsons today: His theory and legacy in contemporary sociology* (M. Lanham Trans.). Rowman and Littlefield Publishers, Inc.

Trochim, W. M. K. (2006). *Two research fallacies*. Retrieved 14/01/2008, from http://www.socialresearchmethods.net/kb/fallacy.php

Trounstine, P. J., & Christensen, T. (1982). *Movers and shakers: The study of community power*. New York: St. Martin's Press.

Trovato, F. (2004). Population and society. In L. Tepperman, & J. Curtis (Eds.), *Sociology* (pp. 458–485). Toronto: Oxford University Press.

Trussell, D. (2011). *Mobs and democracy: The Facebook-Twitter-YouTube revolution*. Retrieved 29/04/2011, from http://www.politicsdaily.com/2011/02/01/mobs-and-democracy-the-facebook-twitter-youtube-revolution/

Tsfato, Y., Elfassi, D. M., & Waismel-Manor, I. (2010). Exploring the association between Israeli legislators' physical attractiveness and their television news coverage. *The International Journal of Press/Politics, 15*(2), 175–192.

Tuchman, G. (1978). Introduction: The symbolic annihilation of women. In A. Kaplan Daniels, & J. Benet (Eds.), *Hearth & home: Images of women in the mass media* (pp. 3–38). New York: Oxford University Press.

Tudiver, N. (1999). *Universities for sale: Resisting corporate control over Canadian higher education*. Toronto: Lorimer.

Tullberg, J. (2012). Triple Bottom Line - a Vaulting Ambition? *Business Ethics: A European Review, 21*(3), 310–324. doi:10.1111/j.1467-8608.2012.01656.x

Tumin, M. M. (1953). Some principles of stratification: A critical analysis. *American Sociological Review, 18*, 387–393.

Turcotte, M., & Schellenberg, G. (2007). *A portrait of seniors in Canada*. Retrieved 24/06/2008, from http://www.statcan.ca/english/freepub/89-519-XIE/89-519-XIE2006001.htm

Turkle, S. (2012). Connected, but Alone? Accessed 05/07/2014, from http://www.ted.com/talks/sherry_turkle_alone_together#t-367950

Turner, B. (1986). *Equality*. London: Tavistock.

Turner, B. S. (1998). *Max Weber: Classic monographs (volume VII: Weber and Islam)*. London, UK: Routledge.

Turner, J. H., Beeghley, L., & Powers, C. H. (2002). *The emergence of sociological theory* (5th. ed.). Belmont, CA: Wadsworth.

Turner, L. (2004). Cosmetic surgery: The new face of reality TV. *British Medical Journal, 328*(7449), 1208.

Turner, R. H., & Killian, L. M. (1993). *Collective behavior* (4th ed.). Upper Saddle River, NJ: Prentice-Hall, Inc.

Turner, W. (2000). *A Genealogy of Queer Theory*. Philadelphia: Temple University Press.

Turney, L., & Pocknee, C. (2005). Virtual focus groups: New frontiers in research. *International Journal of Qualitative Methods, 4*(2), http://www.ualberta.ca/~ijqm/backissues/4_2/pdf/turney.pdf.

Twine, F. W., & Gallagher, C. (2008). The future of whiteness: A map of the 'third wave.' *Ethnic & Racial Studies, 31*(1), 4–24. doi:10.1080/01419870701538836

Twitter Blog. (2014). *Numbers*. Retrieved 4/28/2014, from http://blog.twitter.com/2011/03/numbers.html

Twitter. (2011). Retrieved 4/27/2011, from http://twitter.com/about

Tylor, E. B. (1883). *Primitive culture: Researches into the development of mythology, philosophy, religion, language, art and custom*. New York: Henry Holt and Company.

U.S. Census Bureau. (2010). *United states - school enrollment*. Retrieved 11/01/2010, from http://factfinder.census.gov/servlet/STTable?_bm=y&-geo_id=01000US&-qr_name=ACS_2008_3YR_G00_S1401&-ds_name=ACS_2008_3YR_G00_&-redoLog=false

Udefi, A. (2009). Metaphysics and the challenge of logical positivism: An interrogation. *Journal of Social Science, 21*(1), 7–11.

Uhl-Bien, M., & Pillai, R. (2007). The romance of leadership and the social construction of followership. In B. Shamir, R. Pillai, M. C. Bligh & M. Uhl-Bien (Eds.), *Follower-centered perspectives on leadership* (pp. 187–210). Greenwich, CN: Information Age Publishing.

Heo, U., & Hahm, S. D. (2007). The political economy of U.S. direct investment in east Asian NICs, 1966–2000. *International Interactions, 33*(2), 119–133. doi:10.1080/03050620701277723

UNAIDS. (2000). *AIDS epidemic update: December 2000*. Geneva: UNAIDS.

United Nations Framework Convention on Climate Change. (2008a). *Emissions trading*. Retrieved 06/09/2008, from http://unfccc.int/kyoto_protocol/mechanisms/emissions_trading/items/2731.php

United Nations Framework Convention on Climate Change. (2008b). *Status of ratification*. Retrieved 06/09/2008, from http://unfccc.int/kyoto_protocol/status_of_ratification/items/2613.php

United Nations Office on Drugs and Crime (UNODC). (2006). *Trafficking in persons: Global patterns* United Nations. www.unodc.org/documents/human-trafficking/HT-globalpatterns-en.pdf

United Nations Office on Drugs and Crime. (2010). *World drug report 2010* UNODC.

United Nations Permanent Forum on Indigenous Issues. (2007). *International day of the world's indigenous people*. Retrieved 1/27/2008, from http://157.150.195.10/esa/socdev/unpfii/en/news_internationalday2006.html

United Nations. (1987). *Report of the world commission on environment and development: Our common future* (No. A/42/427). Geneva: United Nations.

United Nations. (1999). *Report of the independent inquiry into the actions of the United Nations during the 1994 genocide in Rwanda*.

United Nations. (2003). *World youth report*. Vienna: United Nations.

United Nations. (2006). *The world's women 2005: Progress in statistics* (No. ST/ESA/STAT/SER.K/17). New York: United Nations.

United Nations. (2009). State of the world's indigenous peoples. Accessed 03/06/2014, from http://www.un.org/esa/socdev/unpfii/documents/SOWIP_web.pdf

United Nations. (2012). *World urbanization prospects: The 2011 revision*. New York, NY: United Nations: Department of Economic and Social Affairs.

United Nations. (2013a). Human Development Reports. Accessed 04/19/2014, from http://hdr.undp.org/en/countries/profiles/CAN

United Nations. (2013b). UN Secretary-General Warns: "Economic Losses from Natural Disasters are Out of Control". Accessed 06/05/2014, from http://www.unisdr.org/archive/33003

United Nations. (2014). Refugees: The Numbers. Accessed 03/06/2014, from http://www.un.org/en/globalissues/briefingpapers/refugees/index.shtml

United States Department of State. (2007). *Definitions*. Retrieved 12/13/2007, from http://www.state.gov/g/tip/c16507.htm

United Way. (2011). *Revisiting Family Security in Insecure Times: 2011 Report Card on Child and Family Poverty in Canada*. Toronto, ON: United Way.

University of Colorado. *Charles H. Cooley*. Retrieved 17/09/2007, from http://socsci.colorado.edu/SOC/SI/si-cooley.htm

University of Regensburg. (2007). *Beautycheck - beautiful figure*. Retrieved 05/06/2008, from http://www.uni-regensburg.de/Fakultaeten/phil_Fak_II/Psychologie/Psy_II/beautycheck/english/figur/figur.htm

US Food and Drug Administration. (2013). Risks of Breast Implants. Accessed 01/01/2014, from http://www.fda.gov/MedicalDevices/ProductsandMedicalProcedures/ImplantsandProsthetics/Breastimplants/ucm064106.htm

Vafaei, A., Rosenberg, M. W., & Pickett, W. (2010). Relationships between income inequality and health: A study on rural and urban regions of Canada. *Rural and Remote Health, 1430 (online)*

Vago, S. (2009). *Law and society* (9th ed. ed.). Upper Saddle River, NJ: Prentice Hall.

Vago, S., & Nelson, A. (2010). *Law and society* (3rd Canadian edition ed.). Toronto: Pearson.

Valentine, C. (2006). Academic constructions of bereavement. *Mortality, 11*(1), 57–78. doi:10.1080/13576270500439274

Valverde, M. (2006). Introduction to the age of light, soap and water. In A. Glasbeek (Ed.), *Moral regulation and governance in Canada: History, context, and critical issues* (pp. 117–142). Toronto: Canadian Scholars Press.

van den Bos, K., & Maas, M. (2009). On the psychology of the belief in a just world: Exploring experiential and rationalistic paths to victim blaming. *Personality and Social Psychology Bulletin, 35*(12), 1567–1578.

van den Hoonaard, W. (2001). Is research-ethics review a moral panic? *Canadian Review of Sociology and Anthropology, 38*(1), 19–36.

Van Der Veen, R. J., & Van Parijs, P. (1986). A capitalist road to communism. *Theory & Society, 15*(5), 635–655. Retrieved from http://library.mtroyal.ca:2048/login?url=http://search.ebscohost.com/login.aspx?direct=true&AuthType=ip,url,cookie,uid&db=a9h&AN=10747579&site=ehost-live

Van Dyke, N., Dixon, M., & Carlon, H. (2007). Manufacturing dissent: Labor revitalization, union summer and student protest. *Social Forces, 86*(1), 193–214. Retrieved from http://library.mtroyal.ca:2048/login?url=http://search.ebscohost.com/login.aspx?direct=true&AuthType=ip,url,cookie,uid&db=a9h&AN=26297700&site=ehost-live

Vandegriend, B. (2006). *Why blogs are popular*. Retrieved 08/05/2008, from http://www.basilv.com/psd/blog/2006/why-blogs-are-popular

Vandenbosch, L. & Eggermont, S. (2012). Understanding sexual objectification: A comprehensive approach toward media exposure and girls' internalization of beauty ideals, self-objectification, and body surveillance. *Journal of Communication, 62*(5), 869–887.

Vanlaar, W., Robertson, R. Marcoux, K., Mayhew, D., Brown, S., & Boase, P. (2012). Trends in alcohol-impaired driving in Canada. *Accident Analysis & Prevention, 48*, 297–302.

Vares, T., & Braun, V. (2006). Spreading the word, but what word is that? Viagra and male sexuality in popular culture. *Sexualities, 9*(3), 315–332.

Varnhagen, C., Gushta, M., Daniels, J., Peters, T., Parmar, N., Law, D., et al. (2005). How informed is online informed consent? *Ethics & Behavior, 15*(1), 37–48.

Veblen, T. (2004 [1919]). *The vested interests and the common man*. Whitefish, MT: Kessinger Publishing.

Veenstra, G. (2006). Neo-marxist class position and socioeconomic status: Distinct or complementary determinants of health? *Critical Public Health, 16*(2), 111–129.

Venturini, B., Castelli, L., & Tomelleri, S. (2006). Not all jobs are suitable for fat people: Experimental evidence of a link between being fat and "out-of-sight" jobs. *Social Behavior & Personality: An International Journal, 34*(4), 389–398. Retrieved from http://library.mtroyal.ca:2048/

login?url=http://library.mtroyal.ca:2924/login.aspx?direct=true&Auth
Type=ip,url,cookie,uid&db=a9h&AN=21148944&site=ehost-live

Verheyen, R. (2005). *Climate change damage and international law: Prevention duties and state responsibility.* The Netherlands: Koninklijke Brill NV.

Villaroman, N. G. (2009). The loss of sovereignty: How international debt relief mechanisms undermine economic self-determination. *Journal of Politics and Law, 2*(4), 3–16.

Vineburgh, N. T., Ursano, R. J., & Fullerton, C. S. (2005). Workplace preparedness and resiliency: An integrated response to terrorism. In V. Bowie, B. S. Fisher & C. L. Cooper (Eds.), *Workplace violence: Issues, trends, strategies* (pp. 207–216). Portland, OR: Willan Publishing.

Viruell-Fuentes, E. A. (2006). "My heart is always there": The transnational practices of first-generation Mexican immigrant and second-generation Mexican American women. *Identities, 13*(3), 335–362.

Vision Critical. (2011). *Social networks transforming how Canadians get the news.* Retrieved 01/05/2011, from http://www.visioncritical.com/newsroom/social-networks-transforming-how-canadians-get-the-news/

Vivian, J., & Maurin, P. J. (2009). *The media of mass communication* (5th Canadian ed.). Toronto, ON: Pearson Education Canada, Inc.

Volti, R. (2005). *Society and technological change* (5th ed.). New York: Worth Publishers.

Waddington, D., & King, M. (2005). The disorderly crowd: From classical psychological reductionism to socio-contextual theory – the impact on public order policing strategies. *Howard Journal of Criminal Justice, 44*(5), 490–503. doi:10.1111/j.1468-2311.2005.00393.x

Waddle, R. (2006). *Reality TV: Guilty pleasure or window to our souls?* http:www.archives.umc.org/interior.asp?ptid=1&mid=1284

Wade, D. T. (2007). *Social roles and long-term illness: Is it time to rehabilitate convalescence?* Sage Publications, Ltd. Retrieved from http://library.mtroyal.ca:2048/login?url=http://search.ebscohost.com/login.aspx?direct=true&AuthType=ip,url,cookie,uid&db=a9h&AN=25553584&site=ehost-live

Wade, L. (2013). Wrinkle-washed: Female faces in film marketing. *The Society Pages.* Retrieved 04/02/2014, from http://thesocietypages.org/socimages/tag/media/

Wagner, J. (2009). Coming home: The evolutionary roots of utopia. *Utopian Studies, 20*(2), 299–320. Retrieved from http://library.mtroyal.ca:2057/login.aspx?direct=true&AuthType=ip,url,cookie,uid&db=a9h&AN=47903312&site=ehost-live

Wagner, K. (2010). In Bruce Ravelli (Ed.), *E-mail correspondence July 15, 2010.*

Waldrep, B. D. (2007). Lewis Sperry Chafer and the roots of nondenominational fundamentalism in the south. *Journal of Southern History, 73*(4), 807–836. Retrieved from http://library.mtroyal.ca:2048/login?url=http://search.ebscohost.com/login.aspx?direct=true&Auth Type=ip,url,cookie,uid&db=a9h&AN=27375328&site=ehost-live

Waldron, J. (2000). What is cosmopolitan? *Journal of Political Philosophy, 8*(2), 227–244.

Walker, G. (2007). Climate change 2007: A world melting from the top down. *Nature, 446*(7137), 218–221. doi:10.1038/446718a

Walker, G. J. (2010). The effects of personal, contextual, and situational factors on the facilitation of intrinsic motivation: The case of Chinese/Canadians. *Journal of Leisure Research, 42*(1), 43–66. Retrieved from http://search.ebscohost.com/login.aspx?direct=true&AuthType=ip,url,cookie,uid&db=a9h&AN=49387350&site=ehost-live

Walker, I., & Smith, H. J. (Eds.). (2002). *Relative deprivation: Specification, development, and integration.* Cambridge, UK: Cambridge University Press.

Walker, R. C. (2006). Interweaving Aboriginal/Indigenous rights with urban citizenship: A view from the Winnipeg low-cost housing sector, Canada. *Citizenship Studies, 10*(4), 391–411.

Walks, R. A., & Bourne, L. S. (2006). Ghettos in Canada's cities? Racial segregation, ethnic enclaves and poverty concentration in Canadian urban areas. *Canadian Geographer, 50*(3), 273–297. Retrieved from

http://library.mtroyal.ca:2083/pqdweb?did=1162629781&Fmt=7&clientId=65345&RQT=309&VName=PQD

Wall, G. (2013). 'Putting family first': Shifting discourses of motherhood and childhood in representations of mothers' employment and child care. *Women's Studies International Forum, 40,* 162–171.

Wallace, P. (2014). Internet addiction disorder and youth: There are growing concerns about compulsive online activity and that this could impede students' performance and social lives. *EMBO Reports, 15*(1), 12–16. doi:10.1002/embr.201338222; 10.1002/embr.201338222.

Wallace, R. A., & Wolf, A. (2006). *Contemporary sociological theory: Expanding the classical tradition.* (6th. ed.). Upper Saddle River, NJ: Prentice-Hall, Inc.

Waller, H. M. (1990). Book review of continental divide: The values and institutions of the United States and Canada by S.M. Lipset. *Canadian Journal of Political Science, 23,* 380–381.

Wallerstein, I. (1976). *The modern world-system.* New York: Academic Press, Inc.

Wallerstein, I. (2004). *World-systems analysis: An introduction.* Durham, NC: Duke University Press.

Walsh, Y. (2001). Deconstructing 'brainwashing' within cults as an aid to counselling psychologists. *Counselling Psychology Quarterly, 14*(2), 119–128.

Walter, P. (2007). Adult learning in new social movements: Environmental protest and the struggle for the Clayoquot Sound rainforest. *Adult Education Quarterly, 57*(3), 248–263. Retrieved from http://library.mtroyal.ca:2048/login?url=http://search.ebscohost.com/login.aspx?direct=true&AuthType=ip,url,cookie,uid&db=a9h&AN=24957352&site=ehost-live

Walters, D., Phythian, K., & Anisef, P. (2007). The acculturation of Canadian immigrants: Determinants of ethnic identification with the host society. *The Canadian Review of Sociology and Anthropology, 44*(1), 37. Retrieved from http://library.mtroyal.ca:2083/pqdweb?did=1366162361&Fmt=7&clientId=65345&RQT=309&VName=PQD

Wang, E. Q. (2010). Globalization, global history and local identity in 'greater China.' *History Compass, 8*(4), 320–329.

Wang, E. S., Chen, L. S., Lin, J. Y., & Wang, M. C. (2008). The relationship between leisure satisfaction and life satisfaction of adolescents concerning online games. *Adolescence, 43*(169), 177–184. Retrieved from http://library.mtroyal.ca:2048/login?url=http://library.mtroyal.ca:2924/login.aspx?direct=true&AuthType=ip,url,cookie,uid&db=a9h&AN=31526226&site=ehost-live

Wanless, D., Mitchell, B. A., & Wister, A. V. (2010). Social determinants of health for older women in Canada: Does rural–urban residency matter? *Canadian Journal on Aging / La Revue Canadienne Du Vieillissement, 29*(2), 233–247.

Ward, A. (n.d.). *Feral children.* Retrieved 02/11/2007, from http://www.feralchildren.com/en/index.php

Ward, D. A. (1980). Toward a normative explanation of "old fashioned revivals". *Qualitative Sociology, 3*(1), 3–22. Retrieved from http://library.mtroyal.ca:2048/login?url=http://search.ebscohost.com/login.aspx?direct=true&AuthType=ip,url,cookie,uid&db=a9h&AN=16371292&site=ehost-live

Ward, J. (2008). Dude-sex: White masculinities and "authentic" heterosexuality among dudes who have sex with dudes. *Sexualities, 11*(4), 413–444.

Waring, M. (1990). *If women counted: A new feminist economics.* San Francisco: HarperCollins.

Warnica, R. (2013). Cashing in on the UFC mania: Who makes money on MMA in Canada? *Canadian Business* (April 8), Jan 20, 2014.

Warren, J. R. (2009). Socioeconomic status and health across the life course: A test of the social causation and health selection hypotheses. *Social Forces, 87*(4), 2125–2153.

Watchtower. (2006). *Jehovah's witnesses–who are they? What do they believe?* Retrieved 11/03/2008, from http://www.watchtower.org/e/jt/index.htm?article=article_03.htm

Watkins, R. N. (2008). The southern roots of ida B. wells-barnett's revolutionary activism. (pp. 108–126) University of Southern Mississippi. Retrieved from http://search.ebscohost.com/login.aspx?direct=true&AuthType=ip,url,cookie,uid&db=a9h&AN=33662809&site=ehost-live

Watkinson, A. M. (2006). Supreme court of Canada stands behind corporal punishment - sort of... *International Social Work, 49*(4), 531–536.

Watson, J. K. (2007). Imperial mimicry, modernisation theory and the contradictions of postcolonial South Korea. *Postcolonial Studies, 10*(2), 171–190. doi:10.1080/13688790701348565

Watson, S. (2008). *Howstuffworks "how podcasting works."* Retrieved 09/05/2008, from http://computer.howstuffworks.com/podcasting.htm/printable

Watson, T. J. (2003). *Sociology, work and industry* (4th ed.). London, UK: Routledge, Taylor & Francis Group.

Wayland, S. V. (1997). Immigration, multiculturalism and national identity in Canada. *International Journal of Minority and Group Rights, 5*(1), 33–58.

Weatherley, D. (1988). Error without trial: Psychological research on antisemitism. In W. Bergmann, & H. A. Strauss (Eds.), (pp. 87–97). Berlin: de Gruyter. Retrieved 1/15/2010, from http://intraspec.ca/web_2008_Count_Executive_Summary_FINAL_Sept_15.pdf

Webb, J. (2001). *Marconi: Newfoundland and Labrador heritage.* Retrieved 04/05/2008, from http://www.heritage.nf.ca/society/marconi.html

Webber, M. (2005). "Don't be so feminist": Exploring student resistance to feminist approaches in a Canadian university. *Women's Studies International Forum, 28,* 181–194.

Webber, M. (2009). *Women navigating academia in the early career years.* Paper Presented at 6th European Conference on Gender Equality in Higher Education, University of Stockholm, Stockholm, Sweden.

Webber, M. (2010a). *Early career academic women navigating contemporary Canadian universities.* Paper presented at the International Teaching and Learning Conference, Las Vegas, Nevada.

Webber, M. (2010b). Women and education. In N. Mandell (Ed.), *Feminist issues: Race, class and sexuality* (5th ed ed., pp. 247–271). Toronto: Pearson.

Weber, M. (1946[1906]). Protestant sects and the spirit of capitalism. In H. Garth, & C. W. Mills (Eds.), *From Max Weber* (pp. 302–322). New York: Oxford University Press.

Weber, M. (1968). *Economy and society: An outline of interpretive sociology.* New York: Bedminster Press.

Weeks, J. (2005). *Inequality trends in some developed OECD countries.* Retrieved 11/30/2007, from http://www.un.org/esa/desa/papers/2005/wp6_2005.pdf

Weeks, J. (2009). *Sexuality* (3rd ed.). London: Taylor and Francis.

Weiner, B., Osborne, D., & Rudolph, U. (2011). An attributional analysis of reactions to poverty: The political ideology of the giver and the perceived morality of the receiver. *Personality and Social Psychology Review, 15*(2), 199–213.

Weiss, J. (2004). Trans studies. In J. Eadie (Ed.), *Sexuality* (pp. 230–230). London: Arnold.

Weldon, R. A. (2001). An 'urban legend' of global proportion: An analysis of nonfiction accounts of the ebola virus. *Journal of Health Communication, 6*(3), 281. Retrieved from http://library.mtroyal.ca:2048/login?url=http://search.ebscohost.com/login.aspx?direct=true&AuthType=ip,url,cookie,uid&db=a9h&AN=5762721&site=ehost-live

Wells, E. (2006). Recent trends in theorizing prehispanic mesoamerican economies. *Journal of Archaeological Research, 14*(4), 265–312. doi:10.1007/s10814-006-9006-3

Welshman, J. (2006). *Underclass: A history of the excluded, 1880–2000.* London, UK: Hambledon Continuum.

Wessel, T. (2009). Does diversity in urban space enhance intergroup contact and tolerance? *Geografiska Annaler Series B: Human Geography, 91*(1), 5–17. doi:10.1111/j.1468-0467.2009.00303.x

West, C., & Fenstermaker, S. (2002). Doing difference. In S. Fenstermaker, & C. West (Eds.), *Doing gender, doing difference: Inequality, power and institutional change* (pp. 55–80). New York: Routledge.

West, C., & Zimmerman, D. (1991). Doing gender. In J. Lorber, & S. Farrell (Eds.), *The social construction of gender* (pp. 13–37). London: Sage.

West, C., & Zimmerman, D. (2002). Doing gender. In S. Fenstermaker, & C. West (Eds.), *Doing gender, doing difference: Inequality, power and institutional change* (pp. 3–24). New York: Routledge.

Westby, D. L. (1991). *The growth of sociological theory: Human nature, knowledge, and social change.* Englewood Cliffs, NJ: Prentice-Hall, Inc.

Western, M., & Wright, E. O. (1994). The permeability of class boundaries to intergenerational mobility among men in the United States, Canada, Norway and Sweden. *American Sociological Review, 59*(4), 606. Retrieved from http://proquest.umi.com/pqdweb?did=1528774&Fmt=7&clientId=65345&RQT=309&VName=PQD

Westheimer, J. (2010). Higher education or education for hire? Corporatization and the threat to democratic thinking. *Academic Matters, 8.*

Westra, L. (1999). *Environmental racism and the First Nations of Canada: Terrorism at Oka.* Wiley-Blackwell. Retrieved from http://search.ebscohost.com/login.aspx?direct=true&AuthType=ip,url,cookie,uid&db=a9h&AN=4370841&site=ehost-live

Westra, L., & Lawson, B. E. (Eds.). (2001). *Faces of environmental racism: Confronting issues of global justice* (2nd ed.). Lanham, MD: Rowman and Littlefield Publishers, Inc.

Weststrate, N., & McLean, K. (2010). The rise and fall of gay: A cultural-historical approach to gay identity development. *Memory, 18*(2), 225–240.

Wherrett, J. (1999). *Aboriginal self-government.* Retrieved 22/04/2008, from http://www.parl.gc.ca/information/library/PRBpubs/962-e.htm

White, J. (1999). Work-family stage and satisfaction with work-family balance. *Journal of Comparative Family Studies, 30*(2), 163–175.

White, J., & Klein, D. (2008). *Family theories* (3rd ed.). Los Angeles: SAGE.

White, R., & Haines, F. (2009). *Crime and criminology* (4th ed. ed.). Sydney: Oxford University Press.

Whitlock, J., Lader, W., & Conterio, K. (2007). The internet and self-injury: What psychotherapists should know. *Journal of Clinical Psychology, 63*(11), 1135–1143. doi:10.1002/jclp.20420

Whitney, C. (2007). Culture, human nature, and the democratic republic of Congo, triangulated from the mid-Pacific and Iraqi Kurdistan. *Review of Human Factor Studies, 13*(1), 41–73.

Whitt, L. A. (1998). Biocolonialism and the commodification of knowledge. *Science as Culture, 7*(1), 33. Retrieved from http://library.mtroyal.ca:2048/login?url=http://search.ebscohost.com/login.aspx?direct=true&AuthType=ip,url,cookie,uid&db=a9h&AN=6870325&site=ehost-live

Wicks, A. (2006). Older women's "ways of doing": Strategies for successful ageing. *Ageing International, 31*(4), 263–275. Retrieved from http://library.mtroyal.ca:2048/login?url=http://search.ebscohost.com/login.aspx?direct=true&AuthType=ip,url,cookie,uid&db=a9h&AN=25640364&site=ehost-live

WikiLeaks. (2011). *About.* Retrieved 17/08/2011, from http://wikileaks.org/About.html

WikiLeaks.org. (2014). *About.* Retrieved 07/23/2014, from https://wikileaks.org/About.html

Wilkes, R. (2006). The protest actions of Indigenous peoples: A Canadian-U.S. comparison of social movement emergence. *The American Behavioral Scientist, 50*(4), 510–525.

Williams, C. (2000). Income and expenditures. *Canadian Social Trends, Winter* (59), 7–12.

Williams, C. (2005). The sandwich generation. *Canadian Social Trends, Summer,* 16–21.

Williams, J., & Keating, F. (2005). Social inequalities and mental health — an integrative approach. In A. Bell, & P. Lindley (Eds.), *Beyond the water towers: The unfinished revolution in mental health services 1985–2005* (pp. 113–125). London, UK: The Sainsbury Centre for Mental Health.

Williams, P. A., Deber, R., Braneck, P., & Gildiner, A. (2001). From medicare to home care: Globalization, state retrenchment, and the profitization of Canada's health care system. In P. Armstrong, H. Armstrong & D. Coburn (Eds.), *Unhealthy times: Political economy perspectives on heath and care* (pp. 7–30). Don Mills, ON: Oxford University Press.

Williams, S. C., & Mackey, M. C. (1999). Women's experiences of preterm labor: A feminist critique. *Health Care for Women International, 20*(1), 29–48. doi:10.1080/073993399245944

Willis, P. (1977). *Learning to labour: How working class kids get working class jobs*. Farborough: Saxon House.

Willmott, W. E. (1970). Approaches to the study of the Chinese in British Columbia. *BC Studies, 4*(Spring), 38–52.

Wilson, B. (2009). *Sick and tired: The compromised health of social assistance recipients and the working poor in Ontario*. Toronto, ON: Wellesley Institute. Retrieved from http://wellesleyinstitute.com/files/sickandtiredfinal.pdf

Wilson, G. (2009). *Correctional services Canada working together enhancing the role of Aboriginal communities in federal corrections*. http://www.csc-scc.gc.ca/aboriginal/index-eng.shtml

Wilson, M., & Daly, M. (1994). *Spousal homicide*. Ottawa: Canadian Centre for Justice Statistics.

Wimmer, R. D., & Dominick, J., R. (2006). *Mass media research: An introduction*. Belmont, CA: Thomson Wadsworth.

Wingfield, M., & Karaman, B. (1995). *Arab stereotypes and American educators*. Retrieved 05/09/2008, from http://www.adc.org/index.php?id=283

Winichakul, T. (2008). Toppling democracy. *Journal of Contemporary Asia, 38*(1), 11–37. Retrieved from http://library.mtroyal.ca:2048/login?url=http://search.ebscohost.com/login.aspx?direct=true&AuthType=ip,url,cookie,uid&db=a9h&AN=29741092&site=ehost-live

Winston, B. (1998). *Media technology and society: A history: From the telegraph to the internet*. London, UK: Routledge, Inc.

Winterdyke, J. (2006). *Canadian criminology*. Toronto: Pearson.

Winterich, J. (2007). Aging, femininity, and the body: What appearance changes mean to women with age. *Gender Issues, 24*(3), 51–69. doi:10.1007/s12147-007-9045-1

Wolf-Wendel, L., & Ward, K. (2003). Negotiating work and family: Parenting and dual-career dilemmas. In B. Ropers-Huilman (Ed.), *Gendered futures in higher education: Critical perspectives for change* (pp. 111–134). Albany: State University of New York.

Wolf, N. (1991). *The beauty myth: How images of beauty are used against women*. New York: William Morrow.

Wolff, A. (1994). *Strategies for working families*. Toronto: Ontario Coalition for Better Child Care.

Wolloch, N. (2011). The civilizing process, nature, and stadial theory. *Eighteenth-Century Studies, 44*(2), 245–259.

Wollstonecraft, M. (1792). *A vindication of the rights of women*. London, England: Joseph Johnson.

Wolosky, S. (2009). Foucault and Jewish feminism: The MeHitzah as dividing practice. *Nashim: A Journal of Jewish Women's Studies & Gender Issues, (17)*, 9–32. Retrieved from http://search.ebscohost.com/login.aspx?direct=true&AuthType=ip,url,cookie,uid&db=a9h&AN=43090022&site=ehost-live

Women's Health Bureau. (2000). *Female genital mutilation and health care*. Health Canada.

Women's Legal Education and Action Fund (LEAF). (1997). *News release: Supreme court of Canada decides black judge is not guilty of bias*. Retrieved 26/09/2010, from http://www.leaf.ca/media/releases/RDS Media Release September 26 1997.pdf#target

Wood, L., Giles-Corti, B., & Bulsara, M. (2005). The pet connection: Pets as a conduit for social capital? *Social Science and Medicine, 61*, 1159–1173.

Woodcock, K., Rohan, M., & Campbell, L. (2007). Equitable representation of deaf people in mainstream academia: Why not? *Higher Education, 53*(3), 359–379. doi:10.1007/s10734-005-2428-x

Woodward, J. (2007). B.C.'s native languages rapidly dying: Linguists. *The Vancouver Sun*, September 19, 2007. Retrieved from http://www.canada.com/vancouversun/news/story.html?id=2acdcf66-acf0-470a-b029-74d096de7c23

World Association of Newspapers. (2007). *World digital media trends, 2007: Executive summary*. Retrieved 05/01/2008, from http://www.wan-press.org/IMG/doc/Executive_Summary_wdmt.doc

World Bank Group. (2010). *Development*. Retrieved 11/01/2010, from http://youthink.worldbank.org/issues/development/

World Bank. (2007a). *Atlas of global development*. Washington, DC: World Bank.

World Bank. (2007b). *World development indicators 2007*. Retrieved 05/09/2008, from http://siteresources.worldbank.org/DATASTATISTICS/Resources/WDI07section4-intro.pdf

World Bank. (2010). *About us*. Retrieved 22/07/2010, from http://web.worldbank.org/WBSITE/EXTERNAL/EXTABOUTUS/0,,pagePK:50004410~piPK:36602~theSitePK:29708,00.html

World Bank. (2012). *Global Development Finance: External Debt of Developing Countries*. Washington, DC: World Bank.

World Commission on Environment and Development. (1987). *Our common future: The world commission on environment and development*. Oxford: Oxford University Press.

World Economic Forum. (2007). *The global gender gap report 2007*. Geneva: World Economic Forum.

World Economic Forum. (2009). *The global gender gap report*. Geneva: World Economic Forum.

World Economic Forum. (2012). *The Global Gender Gap Report*. Geneva: Switzerland. Retrieved 08/04/2013 from http://www3.weforum.org/docs/WEF_GenderGap_Report_2012.pdf

World Health Organization. (2006). *Obesity in Europe*. Retrieved 28/06/2008, from http://www.euro.who.int/obesity/import/20060220_1

World Health Organization. (2008). *Governance of WHO*. Retrieved 29/06/2008, from http://www.who.int/about/governance/en/

World Health Organization. (2010a). *Global strategy to stop health-care providers from performing female genital mutilation*. Geneva: WHO. Retrieved from http://whqlibdoc.who.int/hq/2010/WHO_RHR_10.9_eng.pdf

World Health Organization. (2010b). *Social determinants of health*. Retrieved 10/07/2010, from http://www.who.int/social_determinants/en/

World Health Organization. (2013a). Female Genital Mutilation. Retrieved 04/02/2014, from http://www.who.int/mediacentre/factsheets/fs241/en/#

World Health Organization. (2013b). HIV/AIDS. Accessed 28/02/2014, from www.who.int/mediacentre/factsheets/fs360/en

World Health Organization. (2014). WHO Definition of Health. Accessed 01/04/2014, from http://www.who.int/about/definition/en/print.html.

World Resources Institute. (n.d.). *Losses of biodiversity and their causes*. Retrieved 23/07/2008, from http://www.wri.org/publication/content/8184

World Trade Organization. (2010). *Trade to expand by 9.5% in 2010 after a dismal 2009, WTO reports - Press/598*. Retrieved 22/07/2010, from http://www.wto.org/english/news_e/pres10_e/pr598_e.htm

World Trade Organization. (2013).Trade to remain subdued in 2013 after sluggish growth in 2012 as European economies continue to struggle. Accessed 09/05/2014, from http://www.wto.org/english/news_e/pres13_e/pr688_e.htm

World Trade Organization. (n.d.). *Understanding the WTO - the GATT years: From Havana to Marrakesh*. Retrieved 12/06/2008, from http://www.wto.org/english/thewto_e/whatis_e/tif_e/fact4_e.htm

Worstall, T. (2014). *Fun number; Apple has twice as much cash as the US Government*. Retrieved 07/23/2014, from http://www.forbes.com/sites/timworstall/2014/04/13/funnumberapplehastwiceasmuchcashastheus government/

Wortley, S. (1999). Northern taboo: Research on race, crime and criminal justice in Canada. *Canadian Journal of Criminology, 41*(2), 261–274.

Wortley, S., & Owusu-Bempah, A. (2011). The usual suspects: Police stop and search practices in Canada. *Policing and Society, 21*(4), 395–407.

Wotherspoon, T. (2004). *The sociology of education in Canada: Critical perspectives* (2nd ed.). Toronto: Oxford University Press.

Wotherspoon, T. (2008). Education. In L. Tepperman, J. Curtis & P. Albanese (Eds.), *Sociology: A Canadian perspective* (2nd ed., pp. 244–275). Don Mills: Oxford University Press.

Wright, E. O. (1996). *Class counts: Comparative study in class analysis*. Cambridge, UK: Cambridge University Press.

Wrong, D. H. (1959). The functional theory of stratification: Some neglected considerations. *American Sociological Review, 24*, 772–782.

Wu, Z., & Li, N. (2003). Immigration and the dependency ratio of a host population. *Mathematical Population Studies, 10*(1), 21. Retrieved from http://library.mtroyal.ca:2048/login?url=http://search.ebscohost.com/login.aspx?direct=true&AuthType=ip,url,cookie,uid&db=a9h&AN=9036992&site=ehost-live

Yan, W., Wu, Q., Liang, J., Chen, Y., & Fu, X. (2013). How fast are the leaked facial expressions: The duration of micro-expressions. *Journal of Nonverbal Behavior, 37*(4), 217–230.

Yao, P. (2002). The status of pleasure courtesan and literati connections in T'ang China (618 - 907). *Journal of Women's History, 14*(2), 1. Retrieved from http://library.mtroyal.ca:2048/login?url=http://library.mtroyal.ca:2924/login.aspx?direct=true&AuthType=ip,url,cookie,uid&db=a9h&AN=6969489&site=ehost-live

Yates, R., Yates, R., & Bain, P. (2000). *Introduction to law in Canada* (2nd ed.). Scarborough: Prentice Hall.

Young, C. (2003). Tax policy, theoretical explorations, and social realities. *Canadian Tax Journal, 51*(5), 1922–1930.

Young, M. (2010). Gender differences in precarious work settings. *Relations Industielles/Industrial Relations, 65*(1), 74–97.

Young, N., & Dugas, E. (2011). Representations of climate change in Canadian national print media: The banalization of global warming. *Canadian Review of Sociology, 48*(1), 1. doi:10.1111/j.1755-618X.2011.01247.x

YouTube. (2014). Statistics. Accessed 05/05/2014, from http://www.youtube.com/yt/press/statistics.html

Yuan, X. (2004). The impact of the one child family on China. *Innovation, 5*(1), 58–59.

Zahoor, A. (1996). *Ibn Khaldun*. Retrieved 22/04/2008, from http://www.unhas.ac.id/~rhiza/saintis/khaldun.html

Zarifa, D. (2012). Persistent inequality or liberation from social origins? Determining who attends graduate and professional schools in Canada's expanded postsecondary system. *Canadian Review of Sociology, 49*(2), 109–137.

Zeitlin, I. (1994). *Ideology and the development of sociological theory*. (Fifth. ed.). Englewood Cliffs, NJ: Prentice-Hall, Inc.

Zimbardo, P. (2008). *The Stanford prison experiment*. Retrieved 13/07/2008, from http://www.prisonexp.org

Zimmerman, A. L., McDermott, M. J., & Gould, C. (2009). The local is global: Third wave feminism, peace and social justice. *Contemporary Justice Review, 12*(1), 77–90.

Zinn, H. (2012). *The Historic Unfulfilled Promise*. San Francisco, CA: City Light Books.

Zohrabian, A. (2005). The long-term effects and economic consequences of treatments for obesity: Work in progress. *Lancet, 365*(9454), 104–105. Retrieved from http://library.mtroyal.ca:2048/login?url=http://search.ebscohost.com/login.aspx?direct=true&AuthType=ip,url,cookie,uid&db=a9h&AN=15591034&site=ehost-live

Zottarelli, L. (2008). Post-hurricane Katrina employment recovery: The interaction of race and place. *Social Science Quarterly, 89*(3), 592–607.

Zukeran, P. (2002). *Buddhism*. Retrieved 09/03/2008, from http://www.leaderu.com/orgs/probe/docs/buddhism.html

Zweigenhaft, R. L., & Domhoff, W. G. (1998). *Diversity in the power elite: Have women and minorities reached the top?* New Haven, CT: Yale University Press.

Name Index

Subject Index